INTERMEDIATE MICROECONOMICS

AND ITS APPLICATION Fifth Edition

INTERMEDIATE MICROECONOMICS

AND ITS APPLICATION Fifth Edition

Walter Nicholson
Amherst College

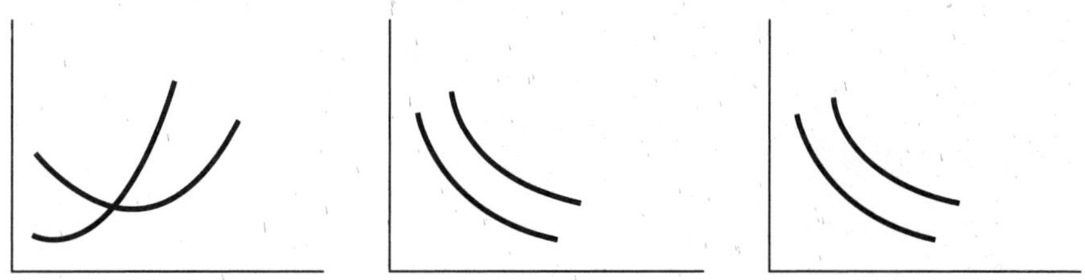

THE DRYDEN PRESS
Chicago Fort Worth San Francisco Philadelphia
Montreal Toronto London Sydney Tokyo

Acquisitions Editor: Rebecca Ryan
Project Editor: Teresa Chartos
Production Manager: Barb Bahnsen
Director of Editing, Design, and Production: Jane Perkins

Text and Cover Designer: Jeanne Calabrese
Copy Editor: Patricia Lewis
Indexer: Leoni McVey
Compositor: Beacon Graphics Corporation
Text Type: 10/12 Sabon

Library of Congress Cataloging-in-Publication Data

Nicholson, Walter.
Intermediate microeconomics and its application / Walter Nicholson.—5th ed.
p. cm.
Includes bibliographical references.
ISBN 0-03-031392-9
1. Microeconomics. I. Title.
HB172.N48 1990
338.5—dc20 89-16896
CIP

Printed in the United States of America
901-032-987654321

Address orders:
The Dryden Press
Orlando, FL 32887

Address editorial correspondence:
The Dryden Press
908 N. Elm Street
Hinsdale, IL 60521

The Dryden Press
Holt, Rinehart and Winston
Saunders College Publishing

Cover Source: Barbara Kasten/John Weber Gallery.

To Susan

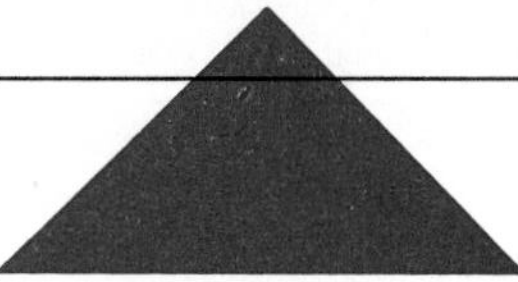

THE DRYDEN PRESS SERIES IN ECONOMICS

Aronson
The Electronic Scorecard

Asch and Seneca
Government and the Marketplace,
Second Edition

Breit and Elzinga
The Antitrust Casebook: Milestones in Economic Regulation,
Second Edition

Breit and Ransom
The Academic Scribblers,
Second Edition

Campbell, Campbell, and Dolan
Money, Banking, and Monetary Policy

Dolan and Lindsey
Economics,
Fifth Edition

Dolan and Lindsey
Macroeconomics,
Fifth Edition

Dolan and Lindsey
Microeconomics,
Fifth Edition

Eckert and Leftwich
The Price System and Resource Allocation,
Tenth Edition

Fort and Lowinger
Applications and Exercises in Intermediate Microeconomics

Gardner
Comparative Economic Systems

Hyman
Public Finance: A Contemporary Application of Theory to Policy,
Third Edition

Johnson and Roberts
Money and Banking: A Market-Oriented Approach,
Third Edition

Kaufman
The Economics of Labor Markets and Labor Relations,
Second Edition

Kidwell and Peterson
Financial Institutions, Markets, and Money,
Third Edition

Landsburg
Price Theory and Applications

Link, Miller, and Bergman
EconoGraph II: Interactive Software for Principles of Economics

Nicholson
Intermediate Microeconomics and Its Application,
Fifth Edition

Nicholson
Microeconomic Theory: Basic Principles and Extensions,
Fourth Edition

Pappas and Hirschey
Fundamentals of Managerial Economics,
Third Edition

Pappas and Hirschey
Managerial Economics,
Sixth Edition

Puth
American Economic History,
Second Edition

Rukstad
Macroeconomic Decision Making in the World Economy: Text and Cases,
Second Edition

Thomas
Economics: Principles and Applications

Thomas
Macroeconomics: Principles and Applications

Thomas
Microeconomics: Principles and Applications

Welch and Welch
Economics: Theory and Practice,
Third Edition

Yarbrough and Yarbrough
The World Economy: Trade and Finance

Preface

As in the previous editions of *Intermediate Microeconomics and Its Application,* the goal of this fifth edition is to provide a clear, concise introduction to microeconomic reasoning. The book is intended to give students the tools they will need if they are to delve deeper into economics and to make the subject interesting enough that they will want to do so. All of the topics presented are developed in nontechnical, intuitive ways, so the requirements for using the book are quite modest—a course in introductory economics and a bit of elementary algebra (which is reviewed in Chapter 2) should suffice. Most of the theoretical concepts encountered in the text are illustrated with real-world applications. I hope readers will find these both instructive and, at times, amusing.

New to the Fifth Edition

The most important change incorporated into this fifth edition is a major reorganization of the later chapters in the book. Following the development of the economic theory of individual choice and the theory of the firm, the book now provides a complete exposition of the perfectly competitive model including the concepts of multimarket equilibrium and economic efficiency. This analysis is then followed by descriptions of monopoly models and models of imperfect competition. I believe this reorganization offers a number of advantages over the organization used previously for this book (and by several other leading texts) in which various types of markets are discussed in a partial equilibrium context before turning to general equilibrium notions.

First, by providing a detailed definition of economic efficiency earlier, the reorganization permits a much clearer answer to the question "What's wrong with monopoly?" Similarly, by introducing general equilibrium ideas earlier, it becomes possible to provide a more comprehensive picture of what is happening in other markets throughout the discussion in the remainder of the book. Finally, the fifth edition's new organization follows what I believe is becoming an increasingly standard way of teaching intermediate microeconomics. As a result instructors can use this edition without needing to skip around.

In addition to this organizational change, this edition also includes a number of new topics. To reflect economists' increasing interest in problems of uncertainty and information, the book has three new chapters:

- A chapter on individual behavior under uncertainty that focuses on risk aversion and the steps people take to reduce risks (Chapter 7);
- A chapter on information and competitive equilibrium that illustrates some of the issues that arise when market participants are not fully informed (Chapter 14);
- A chapter on strategy and game theory in imperfectly competitive markets (Chapter 17).

New Topics

In addition, this edition incorporates a significant amount of new material on such topics as consumer demand theory, the organizational theory of the firm, models of imperfect competition, and the theory of environmental regulation. Much of the coverage of "standard" theoretical topics has been streamlined, so the net increase in pages represented by these new topics is rather small.

New Applications

A primary goal of this edition has been to develop a set of thoroughly revised and updated applications. Overall, the book now contains 110 (mainly full-page) applications, about one-third of which are new to this edition. In these new applications I have tried to illustrate how economic analysis can help to explain such widely divergent recent issues as the wave of leveraged buyouts, problems in the breakup of AT&T, and environmental concerns about acid rain and the "greenhouse effect." Many of the applications that appeared in the fourth edition have been updated or given a new twist that captures recent policy concerns. Previous applications that seemed just fine have been left alone, whereas those that showed signs of wear have been dropped. Overall, I hope that the attention to both the content and formatting of the applications in this edition will help to ensure that the book remains an interesting and enjoyable one to read.

New Learning Aids

All of the many learning aids that were incorporated into the fourth edition of *Intermediate Microeconomics and Its Application* have been retained in this edition as well. The primary addition is the inclusion of end-of-chapter "Review Questions" that test students' understanding of the material covered in the chapter. Although all of these questions should be relatively easy for students to answer, I hope they prove a bit more thought provoking (and thereby a better aid to learning) than the usual "repeat the definition" review questions that appear in many texts. Many new problems have also been added to this edition, and the solutions provided at the end of the text have been thoroughly revised and expanded.

The companion workbook and study guide—*Problems and Exercises for Intermediate Microeconomics* by Frank Westhoff—has been significantly improved and expanded for this edition. Frank's computer wizardry shows through even more in this version, which incorporates all of the latest that desktop publishing can offer. Students seemed to find the study guide for the fourth edition quite helpful, and I believe the benefits from using the guide will become even more apparent for this edition.

To the Instructor

Although adopting a new organization for a reasonably successful text is always somewhat of a gamble, I hope most instructors will appreciate the reasons for the change in this edition. By moving the discussion of the full perfectly competitive model to an earlier place in the text, I believe that the discussion of general equilibrium, economic efficiency, and market organization has been made much clearer than was previously the case. Instructors who prefer to follow the previous organization should have no difficulty, however, if they take up the chapters on market organization (Chapters 15–17) directly after covering the perfectly competitive model (Chapter 12). Under this approach, the material on general equilibrium and economic efficiency (Chapters 13 and 14) can then be covered later in the course. Because the notion of consumer surplus and its relationship to economic efficiency is now covered earlier in the text (in Chapter 6), it is relatively easy to develop a discussion of the allocational harm from imperfect competition using partial equilibrium tools.

The fifth edition of *Intermediate Microeconomics and Its Application* is a bit longer than the fourth, primarily because of the three new chapters that have been added. All of these focus on issues of uncertainty and information and therefore provide students with access to some of the most important current developments in microeconomic theory. These chapters (numbers 7, 14, and 17) come at the ends of the major parts of the text, however, so it is a relatively simple matter to skip them if time is tight. The material developed in these chapters is used only infrequently in the other chapters of the text.

Another reason for the expanded size of this edition is the addition of review questions for students at the end of each chapter. In developing these I have attempted to provide relatively thoughtful questions about all the major topics in the chapter. Instructors may therefore wish to use the questions, perhaps in conjunction with the chapter summaries, in devising their approaches to the material in class. Some of the review questions can also be used as the basis of discussion sections. The "To Think About" queries at the end of each application could also serve that role.

The *Instructor's Manual and Test Bank* that accompanies this edition also offers a number of suggestions about how the material might be presented in class. In addition, the *Manual* includes detailed solutions to all the problems in the book (solutions to the odd-numbered problems are also in the text itself) and an extensive set of multiple-choice and essay-type questions. I hope instructors will find this material helpful.

My decision to change the organization of the latter portion of this text came from a number of informal discussions I have had with instructors currently teaching intermediate microeconomics. Although I believe I have made the right decision, I would be happy to hear contrary points of view. If you have any thoughts on that matter, or on any other aspects of this edition, I would be most happy to have your input. Even after nearly twenty years, I am sure there is a lot more to learn about how a text of this type should be put together.

To the Student

Throughout the various editions of this book I have constantly tried to improve its usefulness as a learning aid for students. You, of course, are the ultimate judge of how successful I have been on that score. In this edition I have improved many of the graphs, rewritten some of what were previously rather dense portions of the text, and added a large number of review questions that are intended to help you avoid the usual traps laid by your wily instructors. I hope you will let me know how well I have done. Many of the changes in this book have come from the thoughtful suggestions of previous student users. If you are so inclined, let me know what you think.

Acknowledgments

As for the previous editions of this book, I owe major debts to many friends and colleagues for most of the good ideas that appear in this fifth edition. People have been remarkably candid and helpful in telling me what they think of the book, and I have tried to learn from what they say. Detailed and careful reviews for this new edition were developed by

- Sam Alapati, *Rutgers University*
- Cheryl Asher, *Villanova University*
- Douglas Brown, *Georgetown University*
- Lynne Conrad, *University of New Mexico*
- William Frazer, *University of Florida*
- John Helmuth, *Rochester Institute of Technology*
- Gabriel Lozada, *Texas A&M University*
- Peter Nickerson, *Seattle University*

- Bojan Popovic, *University of Illinois*
- Mary Jean Rivers, *Seattle University*
- Paul Segerstrom, *Michigan State University*

These reviewers pinpointed several places where the book needed improvement and often suggested better ways to proceed. Although I have not always adopted their advice, I appreciate the efforts of these economists to force me to think things through more completely. So many other users of the book also made helpful suggestions for this new edition that if I were to try to list them, I would run the danger of missing someone. I hope it is sufficient to offer a blanket "thank you" and to encourage all users to continue to offer any ideas that occur to them. My customary disclaimer for what passes for humor in some of the problems in this book applies to this edition as well. All of these were developed by Amherst students (Mark Bruni, Adrian Dillon, David Macoy, Katie Merrell, and Jeff Rodman), and I take none of the blame. My contributions to the problems consisted only of the most mundane matters of economic logic—contributions that I hope do not destroy the fun.

After contributing a great deal to several editions of my books, Liz Widdicombe has moved ever higher into the publishing empire of which Dryden is only a small part. I wish her all the best. For this edition, Becky Ryan did a fine job of ensuring that things proceeded apace and even made some helpful contractual suggestions in the process. Production of the book was coordinated by Teresa Chartos. Although she may never wish to hear my voice on the phone again, certainly one more call is needed to thank her for the fine job she did. My turgid prose benefited greatly from the copyediting suggestions of Pat Lewis who always seems to have a better way of saying something. As for many previous editions, the artwork here owes a great deal to the careful attention provided by Jeanne Calabrese. Joanne McNamara's design work helped to ensure an attractive format for the book. Once again, then, the Dryden team did a fine, professional job, and I truly appreciate all the help I received.

Happi Cramer produced this new edition in record time on her ever more sophisticated word processing system. I have now given up all hope of keeping up with her and only hope I am not too badly embarrassed by my sloth. Without Happi's fine efforts and her good-natured prodding, I doubt this edition would have been completed during the 1980s, if at all.

As readers of my prefaces know, my children (Kate, David, Tory, and Paul) love to see their names in print. Even though this may not be so true as it once was (especially for the older ones), they will have to suffer some embarrassment to entertain my whim. Perhaps a bit less whimsical is my dedication of this edition to my wife. After Susan's 20 years as an unindicted coconspirator, it's about time that I confess to the crucial role she has played in providing much needed support throughout the many editions of my texts.

Walter Nicholson
Amherst, Massachusetts
November 1989

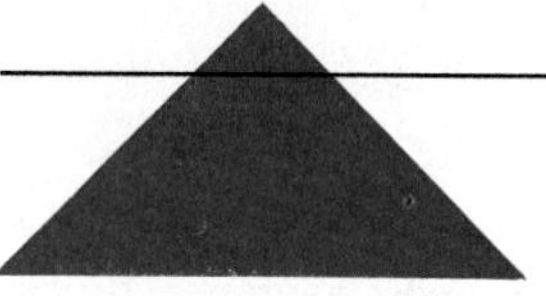

ABOUT THE AUTHOR

Walter Nicholson is Professor of Economics at Amherst College. He received a B.A. degree in mathematics from Williams College and a Ph.D. in economics from the Massachusetts Institute of Technology. Professor Nicholson's primary research interest is in the econometric analysis of labor market policy. He has published papers on such topics as unemployment insurance, welfare policy, and the domestic labor market impact of international trade. He is also the author of *Microeconomic Theory: Basic Principles and Extensions,* fourth edition (The Dryden Press, 1989). He and his wife Susan live in Amherst, Massachusetts, where they are just beginning to worry about college and how to pay tuition for their children, Kate, David, Tory, and Paul.

CONTENTS

PART 1 INTRODUCTION 3

CHAPTER 1
Economic Models 5

Defining Economics 6
Application 1.1 Scarcity in the Natural World 7
Why Economists Use Theoretical Models 8
Supply and Demand: The Development of an Economic Model 8
Early Economists 8
Adam Smith and the Invisible Hand 9
David Ricardo and Diminishing Returns 10
Marginalism and Marshall's Model of Supply and Demand 12
Market Equilibrium 12
Change in Market Equilibrium 13
Models of Many Markets 14
Application 1.2 Politics and Economics of the U.S.–Soviet Wheat Trade 15
The Production Possibility Frontier 16
Opportunity Cost 16
How Economists Verify Theoretical Models 18
The Direct Approach 18
The Indirect Approach 18
Using Empirical Examples 19
Positive versus Normative Economics 19
Application 1.3 Poor Models That Forgot about Prices 20
An Overview of the Book 21
Three Recurring Themes 22
Using the Optimization Assumption to Explain Behavior 22
Describing a Market Equilibrium 23
The Benefits of Free Exchange 23
Summary 23
Review Questions 24

CHAPTER 2
Mathematical Tools Used in Economics 27

Functions of One Variable 27
Graphing Functions of One Variable 29
Linear Functions: Intercepts and Slopes 30
Slope and Units of Measurement 31
Changes in Slope 32
Changes in Intercept 32
Nonlinear Functions 34
Application 2.1 Property Tax Assessment 36
Functions of Two or More Variables 37
Application 2.2 The Changing U.S. Income Tax Structure 38
A Simple Example 40
Graphing Functions of Two Variables 40
Simultaneous Equations 42
Application 2.3 Oil Pipelines 43
Changing Solutions for Simultaneous Equations 44
Graphing Simultaneous Equations 44
Special Features of Mathematics in Economics 45
Summary 46
Review Questions 47
Problems 48

PART 2 CHOICE AND DEMAND 53

CHAPTER 3
Utility Maximization: How People Make Economic Choices 55

Definition of Utility 55
Ceteris Paribus Assumption 56
Utility from Consuming Two Goods 56
Measurability of Utility 57
Application 3.1 The Pursuit of Happiness 58
Assumptions about Utility 59
Basic Properties of Preferences 59
Application 3.2 Transitivity in Sports, Marriage Partners, and Consumption 60
More is Better: Defining an Economic "Good" 61
Voluntary Trades and Indifference Curves 62
Indifference Curves 62
Indifference Curves and the Marginal Rate of Substitution 63
Diminishing Marginal Rate of Substitution 64
Balance in Consumption and the Assumption of a Diminishing Marginal Rate of Substitution 64
Indifference Curve Maps 65

Illustrating Particular Preferences 67
Utility-Maximization Hypothesis: An Initial Survey 69
Choices Are Constrained 69
The Basic Result 69
Application 3.3 Irrational Behavior 70
Graphic Analysis of Utility Maximization 71
The Budget Constraint 71
An Algebraic Approach 72
Utility Maximization 73
Importance of the Diminishing Marginal Rate of Substitution 75
Application 3.4 Rationing in War and Peace 76
A Numerical Example of Utility Maximization 76
Using the Model of Choice 79
Generalizations 82
Summary 83
Review Questions 84
Problems 85

CHAPTER 4
How Changes in Income and Prices Affect Choices 89

Demand Functions 90
Homogeneity 90
Changes in Income 91
Normal Goods 91
Inferior Goods 92
Changes in a Good's Price 92
Application 4.1 Engel's Law 93
Substitution and Income Effects from a Fall in Price 94
Application 4.2 Are Children Inferior? 96
Substitution and Income Effects from an Increase in Price 97
Summary of Substitution and Income Effects 99
Substitution and Income for an Inferior Good 99
Application 4.3 The Lump-Sum Principle 100
Giffen's Paradox 102
Changes in the Price of Another Good 104
Substitutes and Complements 105
Construction of Individual Demand Curves 106
Shape of the Demand Curve 108
Shifts in an Individual's Demand Curve 109
Application 4.4 Religious Practices and Fish Consumption 110
Be Careful in Using Terminology 111
Summary 111
Review Questions 112
Problems 113

CHAPTER 5
Market Demand and Elasticity 117

Market Demand Curves 117
Construction of the Market Demand Curve 118
Shifts in the Market Demand Curve 118
Application 5.1 Consumption and Income Taxes 120
A Word on Notation and Terms 121
Elasticity 121
Price Elasticity of Demand 122
Values of the Price Elasticity of Demand 122
Price Elasticity and the Shape of the Demand Curve 123
Price Elasticity and the Substitution Effect 123
Price Elasticity and Time 124
Price Elasticity and Total Expenditures 124
Application 5.2 Rising Gasoline Prices and Substitution Effects among Automobiles 125
Is the Price Elasticity of Demand Constant? 126
Application 5.3 The Paradox of Agriculture 127
Application 5.4 The States' Take at the Track 128
Linear Demand Curves and Price Elasticity 129
Income Elasticity of Demand 131
Cross-Price Elasticity of Demand 132
Empirical Studies of Demand 132
Estimating Demand Curves 132
Some Income and Price Elasticity Estimates 134
Some Cross-Price Elasticity Estimates 135
Application 5.5 National Health Insurance 136
Summary 137
Review Questions 138
Problems 139

CHAPTER 6
Further Applications of the Theory of Choice 143

Compensated Demand Curves 144
Welfare Effects of Price Changes 145
Application 6.1 The Excess Burden of a Tax 147
Consumer Surplus 148
Index Numbers 148
The Consumer Price Index 148
The CPI and True Inflation 149
Application 6.2 Substitution Biases and Revising the Consumer Price Index 151
Other Problems with the CPI 152
Index Number Problems 152

Application 6.3 International Comparisons of Real Income 153
Gains from Voluntary Trade 154
A Simple Exchange Situation 154
Distribution of the Gains from Trade 156
Edgeworth Box Diagram 156
Mutually Beneficial Trades 157
Efficiency in Exchange 158
Application 6.4 The Gains from Trading among Nations 160
Contract Curve 161
Summary 161
Review Questions 162
Problems 163

CHAPTER 7
Uncertainty and Information 167

Probability and Expected Value 167
Risk Aversion 168
Application 7.1 Blackjack Systems 169
Diminishing Marginal Utility 171
Graphic Analysis of Risk Aversion 171
Methods for Reducing Risk 172
Insurance 172
Diversification 175
Application 7.2 Provisions of Group Health Insurance Policies 176
The Economics of Information 178
Balancing the Gains and Costs of Acquiring Information 178
Application 7.3 Mutual Funds 179
Application 7.4 The Value of Accurate Weather Forecasts to Raisin Growers 180
Asymmetry of Information 181
Special Properties of Information 181
Application 7.5 Prices and Information 182
Summary 183
Review Questions 184
Problems 185

PART 3 FIRMS, PRODUCTION, AND SUPPLY 189

CHAPTER 8
Production 191

Production Functions 191
A Simplification 192
Marginal Physical Productivity 193
Diminishing Marginal Physical Productivity 193
Marginal Physical Productivity Curve 195

Average Physical Productivity 195

Application 8.1 Average Productivity in Steel Production 196

Physical Productivity Curves and the *Ceteris Paribus* Assumption 197

Isoquant Maps 198

Application 8.2 Sources of the Japanese Advantage in Automobile Production 199

Rate of Technical Substitution 200
The RTS and Marginal Productivities 201
Diminishing RTS 201

Returns to Scale 202

Adam Smith on Returns to Scale 202
A Precise Definition 203
Graphic Illustrations 203

Input Substitution 203

Application 8.3 Ocean Shipping 205

Fixed-Proportions Production Function 206
The Relevance of Input Substitutability 207
A Numerical Example 208
Input Substitution in Less Developed Countries 208

Application 8.4 Energy and Capital 209

Changes in Technology 210

Application 8.5 The Worldwide Productivity Decline 211

Technical Progress versus Input Substitution 212

Summary 212

Review Questions 213

Problems 214

CHAPTER 9
Costs 217

Basic Concepts of Costs 217

Labor Costs 218
Capital Costs 218
Entrepreneurial Costs 219
Using Economic Costs 219

Application 9.1 Economic Costs of Homeowning 220

Two Simplifying Assumptions 221
Economic Profits and Cost Minimization 221

Cost-Minimizing Input Choice 222

Graphic Presentation 222
Derived Demand for Inputs 223

The Firm's Expansion Path 224

Inferior Inputs 225

Cost Curves 226

Average and Marginal Costs 227
Marginal Cost Curves 228
Average Cost Curves 230

Distinction between the Short Run and the Long Run 231

Short-Run Production Function 231

Application 9.2 Findings on Long-Run Costs 232

Application 9.3 A Detailed Look at Costs 233

A Note on Input Flexibility 234
Short-Run Total Costs 234
Short-Run Fixed and Variable Cost Curves 235
Short-Run Total Cost Curve 236
Input Inflexibility and Cost Minimization 237
The Relationship between Short-Run and Long-Run Total Costs 238

Per-Unit Short-Run Cost Curves 239

Short-Run Average Variable Costs 240
Relationship between Short-Run and Long-Run Per-Unit Cost Curves 241

Shifts in Cost Curves 242

Changes in Input Prices 242

Application 9.4 Congestion Costs 243

Application 9.5 Two Examples of Dramatic Declines in Cost 244

Technological Innovation 245

Summary 245

Review Questions 246

Problems 247

APPENDIX TO CHAPTER 9
Numerical Example of a Production Function and Its Cost Curves 250

The Production Function 250

Marginal and Average Productivities 250
The Isoquant Map 251
Constant Returns and the RTS 253

Cost Minimization 254

A Graphic Proof 255
The Expansion Path 256
Long-Run Cost Curves 257

Short-Run Cost Curves 257

Short-Run Average and Marginal Costs 259
Relationship of Long-Run and Short-Run Cost Curves 261

Summary 262

CHAPTER 10
Profit Maximization and Supply 263

Nature of Firms 263

Firms' Goals 264

Profit Maximization 264

Application 10.1 What Does the U.S. Corporate Profits Tax Actually Tax? 265

Marginalism 266
The Output Decision 266
The Marginal Revenue/Marginal Cost Rule 267
Marginalism in Input Choices 268

Marginal Revenue 269

Marginal Revenue for a Downward-Sloping Demand Curve 269
A Numerical Example 269
Marginal Revenue and Price Elasticity 271

Marginal Revenue Curve 273

Shifts in Demand and Marginal Revenue 273

Controversy over the Profit-Maximization Hypothesis 274

Application 10.2 Profit Maximization and Airline Deregulation 275

Evidence on Profit Maximization 276
Survivorship Principle and the Market for Firms 276

Alternatives to Profit Maximization 277

Revenue Maximization 277
Markup Pricing 278

Application 10.3 Textbook Royalties 279

Short-Run Supply by a Price-Taking Firm 280

Profit-Maximizing Decision 280

Application 10.4 Actual Markup Pricing Behavior 281

The Firm's Supply Curve 283
The Shutdown Decision 283

Application 10.5 The Demise of OPEC and Drilling for Oil in the United States 284

Summary 285

Review Questions 286

Problems 287

CHAPTER 11
Further Applications of the Theory of the Firm 291

Why Do Firms Exist? 291

Advantages of the Market 292
Advantages of Integration 293
Size and Scope of the Firm 293

Contracts within Firms 294

Contracts with Workers 294

Job-Specific Skills and Long-Term Contracts 295
Effects on Employment Decisions 295

Application 11.1 Short-Time Compensation and Layoffs 297

Other Effects of Implicit Contracts 298

Contracts with Managers 298

Application 11.2 Wage Bonuses in Japan 299

Conflicts in the Agent Relationship 299

Application 11.3 Principals and Agents in Franchising and Medicine 302
Reactions of Owners and the Development of Management Contracts 303
The Market for Firms 303
Application 11.4 Stock Ownership and Manager Behavior 304
Profit Opportunities in the Market for Firms 305
Application 11.5 Corporate Raiders 306
Summary 307
Review Questions 308
Problems 309

PART 4 THE PERFECTLY COMPETITIVE MODEL 313

CHAPTER 12
Pricing in a Perfectly Competitive Market 315

Timing of a Supply Response 315
Pricing in the Very Short Run 316
Shifts in Demand: Price as a Rationing Device 316
Applicability of the Very Short-Run Model 317
Application 12.1 Auctions for Fish and Flowers 318
Short-Run Supply 319
Construction of a Short-Run Supply Curve 319
Slope of the Supply Curve 319
Short-Run Price Determination 320
Functions of the Equilibrium Price 321
Effect of an Increase in Market Demand 322
Shifts in Supply and Demand Curves 322
Short-Run Supply Elasticity 322
Shifts in Supply Curves and the Importance of the Shape of the Demand Curve 323
Shifts in Demand Curves and the Importance of the Shape of the Supply Curve 324
Application 12.2 Dairy Price Supports 326
A Numerical Illustration 327
The Long Run 329
Equilibrium Conditions 329
Profit Maximization 329
Entry 329
Long-Run Equilibrium 330
Long-Run Supply: Constant Cost Case 330
Market Equilibrium 331
A Shift in Demand 332
Long-Run Supply Curve 332
An Illustration Using the Model: Tax Incidence Theory 332
Application 12.3 Cigarette Taxes 334
Shape of the Long-Run Supply Curve 335
The Increasing Cost Industry 335
Price Controls and Shortages 336

Long-Run Supply Elasticity 337
Application 12.4 Rent Controls 338
The Decreasing Cost Industry 339
Infant Industries 339
Application 12.5 Long-Run Supply Elasticities 340
Summary 342
Review Questions 343
Problems 344

CHAPTER 13
General Equilibrium and Economic Efficiency 349

Perfectly Competitive Price System 349
An Illustration of General Equilibrium 350
Application 13.1 Modeling the Impact of Taxes with a Computer 353
A Simple Demonstration of Efficiency 354
Application 13.2 Missing Markets 356
Efficiency in Production 357
Definition of Technical Efficiency 357
Efficient Input Use and the Edgeworth Production Box 357
Efficient Allocations 359
Production Possibility Frontier 360
Rate of Product Transformation 361
Shape of the Production Possibility Frontier 362
Rate of Product Transformation Is the Ratio of Marginal Costs 362
Increasing Marginal Costs and the Shape of the Production Possibility Frontier 363
Production Possibility Frontier and Opportunity Cost 363
An Efficient Mix of Outputs 363
Application 13.3 Production Possibilities for "Guns and Butter" 364
A Graphic Demonstration 365
Efficiency of Perfect Competition 365
Efficiency in Input Use 365
Efficiency in Output Mix 367
A Graphic Demonstration 367
Prices, Efficiency, and Laissez-Faire Economics 369
Why Markets Fail to Achieve Economic Efficiency 369
Application 13.4 Gains from Free Trade and Political Obstacles to Achieving Them 370
Imperfect Competition 372
Externalities 372
Public Goods 373
Imperfect Information 374
What to Do about These Problems 374

Efficiency and Equity 375
Defining and Achieving Equity 375
Equity and Voluntary Exchange 375
Equity, Efficiency, and Perfect Competition 377
Money in the Perfectly Competitive Model 377
Nature and Function of Money 377
Money as the Accounting Standard 378
Commodity Money 379
Fiat Money and the Monetary Veil 379
Application 13.5 Exchange and Money in a POW Camp 380
Summary 381
Review Questions 382
Problems 383

APPENDIX TO CHAPTER 13
Linear Programming, Pricing of Inputs, and Duality 388

The Problem 388
A Graphic Demonstration 388
A Linear Programming Statement of the Problem 390
Production Functions for Cars and Trucks 390
Resource Constraints 390
Construction of the Production Possibility Frontier 391
Linear Programming Solution of the Problem 392
Duality and the Pricing of Inputs 394
Solution to the Dual Problem 395
Further Observations on Duality 396
Summary 397

CHAPTER 14
Information and Competitive Equilibrium 399

Establishing Competitive Equilibrium Prices 399
The Impartial Auctioneer and Recontracting 400
Walrasian Price Adjustment 400
Marshallian Quantity Adjustment 401
Market Adjustments and Transactions Costs 402
Models of Disequilibrium Pricing 403
Application 14.1 Experimenting with Equilibrium 404
Cobweb Model 405
Stability of Equilibrium 405
Rational Expectations 406
Application 14.2 Speculation 407
Information and Economic Efficiency 408
Asymmetric Information and the “Lemons” Problem 409
Adverse Selection 409

Application 14.3 Unemployment 410
Acquisition and Provision of Information 410
Information and Equilibrium 411
Application 14.4 The Winner's Curse in Common Value Auctions 412
Application 14.5 Looking for Lemons 413
Equilibrium and Pareto Efficiency 414
Summary 414
Review Questions 415
Problems 416

PART 5 IMPERFECT COMPETITION 419

CHAPTER 15 Pricing in Monopoly Markets 421

Causes of Monopoly 421
Technical Barriers to Entry 422
Legal Barriers to Entry 422
Profit Maximization 423
Application 15.1 Entry Restriction by Licensing: Dry Cleaning and Liquor Stores 424
Monopoly Supply Curve 426
Monopoly Profits 426
Application 15.2 Deregulation and the Value of Stock Exchange Seats 427
What's Wrong with Monopoly? 428
Profitability 428
Distortion of Resource Allocation 428
Measuring Monopolistic Distortions 430
Distributional Effects 432
Monopolists' Costs 432
A Numerical Illustration of Deadweight Loss 433
Application 15.3 Social Costs of Monopoly in the United States 434
Market Separation and Price Discrimination 435
A Graphic Analysis 435
Conditions for Successful Price Discrimination 436
Regulation of Monopolies 437
Marginal Cost Pricing and the Natural Monopoly Dilemma 437
Application 15.4 Pricing at Disneyland 438
Two-Tier Pricing Systems 439
Application 15.5 The Breakup of AT&T 441
Rate of Return Regulation 442

Benefits of Monopoly 442
Monopoly Profits and Economic Growth 442
Monopoly and Cost Saving 443
Summary 443
Review Questions 444
Problems 445

CHAPTER 16
Pricing in Imperfectly Competitive Markets 449

Pricing of Homogeneous Goods 450
Quasi-competitive Model 450
Cartel Model 451
Other Pricing Possibilities 452
Kinked Demand Curve Model 452
Price Leadership Model 454
Product Differentiation 455
Application 16.1 OPEC Pricing Strategy 456
Market Definition 457
Firms' Choices 457
Market Equilibrium 457
Advertising 458
Allocation of Resources to Advertising 458
Application 16.2 Brand Proliferation in Breakfast Cereals 459
Advertising as Information 460
Application 16.3 Cigarette Advertising 461
Entry by New Firms 462
Zero-Profit Equilibrium 462
Contestable Markets and Market Equilibrium 462
Determination of Industry Structure 464
Barriers to Entry 464
Application 16.4 Airline Deregulation, Revisited 465
Application 16.5 Standard Oil and Predatory Pricing 467
Industrial Organization Theory 468
Market Structure 468
Application 16.6 The IBM Case 470
Firm Conduct 471
Industry Performance 472
Summary 473
Review Questions 474
Problems 474

CHAPTER 17
Strategy and Game Theory 479

A Simple Model of Duopoly 479
The Cournot Model 481
Strategic Equilibrium 482
Stackelberg Leadership Model 483
Application 17.1 The Great Electrical Equipment Conspiracy 484
Price Leadership 485
Application 17.2 Price Leadership in Steel 486
Comparison of the Models: Approaching the Competitive Solution 487
The Theory of Games: Basic Concepts 488
A Game 488
Players 488
Strategies 489
Payoffs 489
Strategic Equilibrium 489
Zero-Sum Games 490
A Nash Equilibrium 491
A Nonequilibrium Game 492
A Non-Zero-Sum Game 492
Application 17.3 Nash Equilibrium Tariff Policy 493
The Prisoner's Dilemma 494
The Duopoly Model as a Non-Zero-Sum Game 495
Application 17.4 The Game of Chicken 496
Games against Nature and Bayesian Decision Making 497
Bayesian Decision Rules 497
Application 17.5 Terrorism 499
Bayesian Decisions and Information Theory 500
Summary 500
Review Questions 501
Problems 502

PART 6 PRICING OF FACTORS OF PRODUCTION 507

CHAPTER 18
The Demand for Factors of Production 509

Assumptions about Supply 509
Derived Demand 510
Economic Rent 511
Economic Rent and Opportunity Cost 512
Land Rent 513
Ricardian Rent 514
Graphic Presentation of Ricardo's Analysis 514
Generalizations of Ricardo's Analysis 516

Marginal Productivity Theory of Factor Demand 516
Profit-Maximizing Behavior and the Hiring of Inputs 516
Application 18.1 Rent Capitalization of Commuting Costs in Washington, D.C. 517
Price-Taking Behavior 518
Marginal Revenue Product 518
A Special Case — Marginal Value Product 519
Application 18.2 Input Demand by Nonprofit Firms 520
A Graphic Demonstration 521
Responses to Changes in Input Prices 522
Single-Input Case 522
A Numerical Example 523
Two-Input Case 524
Substitution Effect 524
Output Effect 525
Summary of a Firm's Demand for Labor 526
Responsiveness of Input Demand to Price Changes 526
Ease of Substitution 527
Costs and the Output Effect 527
Monopsony 528
Marginal Expense 528
A Numerical Illustration 528
Application 18.3 The Minimum Wage 529
Monopsonist's Input Choice 530
A Graphic Demonstration 531
Monopsonistic Exploitation 532
Causes of Monopsony 533
Geography 533
Specialized Employment 533
Monopsonistic Cartels 534
Discrimination in Hiring 534
A Graphic Analysis 534
Application 18.4 Monopsony in the Market for Baseball Players 535
Limits to Discrimination 536
Application 18.5 Sex Discrimination 537
Summary 538
Review Questions 538
Problems 539

CHAPTER 19
Pricing of Labor 545

Allocation of Time 545
A Simple Model of Time Use 546
The Opportunity Cost of Leisure 546
Utility Maximization 547
Application 19.1 The Opportunity Cost of Time 548
Flexibility of Work 549

Income and Substitution Effects of a Change in the Real Wage Rate 550
A Graphic Analysis 550
Individual Supply Curve for Labor 552
Market Supply Curve for Labor 553
Application 19.2 The Volunteer Army and the Draft 554
Occupational Choice and Compensating Wage Differentials 555
Application 19.3 Changing Labor Force Participation for Married Women and Older Males 556
A Graphic Demonstration 557
Labor Unions 558
Unions' Goals and the Monopoly Supply Decision 558
Application 19.4 Compensating Wage Differentials 559
Application 19.5 Unionization of Fire Fighters 561
Other Union Goals: Job Security and Fringe Benefits 562
Summary 562
Review Questions 563
Problems 564

CHAPTER 20
Pricing of Capital 567

Definition of Capital 567
Rate of Return 568
Determination of the Rate of Return 569
A Supply-Demand Analysis 569
Equilibrium Price of Future Goods 570
The Equilibrium Rate of Return 571
Application 20.1 The Rate of Return to Storing Wine 572
Rental Rate on Machines and the Theory of Investment 573
Determinants of Market Rental Rates 573
A Nondepreciating Machine 574
Ownership of Equipment 574
Theory of Investment 575
Tax Policy and Investment 576
A Graphic Demonstration 576
Present Discounted Value and Investment 577
Present Discounted Value 577
Application 20.2 Effects of Tax Policies on Investment 578
Present Discounted Value Approach to Investment Decisions 581
Present Discounted Value and the Rental Rate 582
Application 20.3 The Economist and the Car Dealer 583
Human Capital 584
Calculating the Yield on an Investment 584

Application 20.4 Yields on Investments in Schooling and On-the-Job Training **585**

Special Features of Human Capital **586**

Pricing of Exhaustible Natural Resources **586**

Scarcity Costs **586**

Scarcity Costs and Resource Prices **588**

The Time Pattern of Resource Prices **588**

Application 20.5 What Should the Price of Oil Be? **589**

Summary **590**

Review Questions **590**

Problems **591**

APPENDIX TO CHAPTER 20
Compound Interest **593**

Interest **593**

Compound Interest **593**

Interest for One Year **594**

Interest for Two Years **594**

Interest for Three Years **595**

A General Formula **595**

Compounding with Any Dollar Amount **596**

Present Discounted Value **596**

Application 20A.1 Compound Interest Gone Berserk **597**

An Algebraic Definition **597**

General PDV Formulas **598**

Discounting Payment Streams **599**

Application 20A.2 Zero-Coupon Bonds **600**

An Algebraic Presentation **600**

Perpetual Payments **601**

Varying Payment Streams **603**

Frequency of Compounding **603**

Application 20A.3 Mortgage Market Innovations **604**

Calculating Yields **605**

More Complex Cases **606**

Summary **607**

PART 7 LIMITS OF THE MARKET **609**

CHAPTER 21
Externalities and Property Rights **611**

Defining Externalities **611**

Examples of Externalities **612**

Externalities between Firms **612**

Externalities between Firms and People **613**

Externalities between People **613**

Reciprocal Nature of Externalities 613

Application 21.1 Reciprocal Effects of Externalities, Past and Present 614

Externalities, Markets, and Allocational Efficiency 615

A Graphic Demonstration 615

Traditional Solutions to the Externality Problem 617

Taxation 617

Application 21.2 Power Plant Emissions and Acid Rain 618

Merger and Internalization 618

Bargaining 620

Property Rights, Bargaining, and the Coase Theorem 621

Costless Bargaining and the Free Market 621

Ownership by the Polluting Firm 621

Ownership by the Injured Firm 622

The Coase Theorem 622

Distributional Effects 623

The Role of Bargaining Costs 623

Application 21.3 Bargains in the Orchard—Bees and Apples 624

Bargaining Costs, Environmental Externalities, and Environmental Regulation 625

Bargaining Costs and Allocation 625

Environmental Regulation 626

Fees, Benefits, and Direct Controls 627

Application 21.4 The Phosphate Ban and Clean Clothes 628

Uncertainty in Environmental Regulation 629

The Evolution of Property Rights—Economics and the Law 629

Application 21.5 The Greenhouse Effect and What to Do about It 630

The Common Property Problem 631

Ocean Fisheries and Common Property 631

Application 21.6 Land Contracts in the California Gold Rush 632

Application 21.7 Applying Economics to Oysters and Lobsters 634

Private Property and Internalization 635

Summary 635

Review Questions 636

Problems 636

CHAPTER 22
Public Goods and Public Choice 641

Public Goods 641

Attributes of Public Goods 642

Nonexclusivity 642

Nonrivalry 643

Categories of Public Goods 643

Public Goods and Market Failure 644
An Example of Public Goods Externalities 644
A Graphic Demonstration 645
Voluntary Solutions to the Problem 646
Application 22.1 Are Lighthouses Public Goods? 647
The Lindahl Equilibrium 648
Discovering the Demand for Public Goods: The Free Rider Problem 649
Compulsory Taxation 650
Local Public Goods 650
Direct Voting and Resource Allocation 650
Application 22.2 Searching for Free Riders 651
Majority Rule 652
The Paradox of Voting 652
Single-Peaked Preferences and the Median Voter Theorem 653
Intensity of Preferences, Logrolling, and Efficient Resource Allocation 654
Application 22.3 Voting for School Budgets 655
Analysis of Representative Government 656
The Majority Principle 657
Pluralism 657
Interest Groups and Rent-Seeking Behavior 658
Application 22.4 Rent Seeking through Agricultural Marketing Orders 659
Reelection constraint 659
Application 22.5 Economics and the Tax Revolt 660
Bureaucracies 661
Summary 661
Review Questions 662
Problems 663

Solutions to Odd-Numbered Problems 665

Glossary 692

Name Index 697

Subject Index 699

PART 1

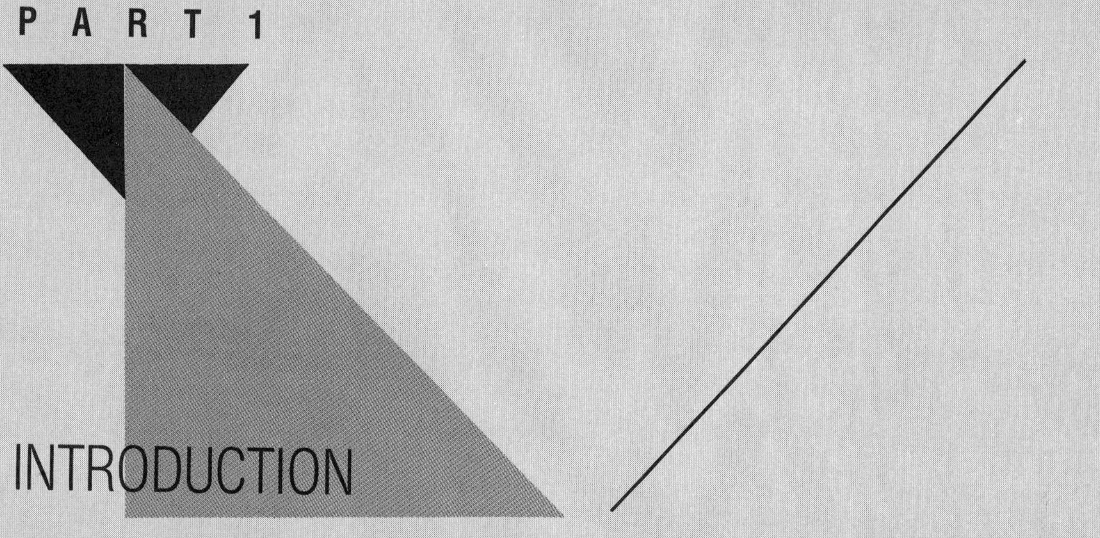

INTRODUCTION

Part 1 provides some background for your study of microeconomics. Chapter 1 examines a few definitions of "economics" and shows how economic tools help us understand how real-world economies work. The chapter also briefly reviews some basic principles of supply and demand, which should look familiar from your introductory economics course. This review is especially important because supply and demand models serve as a starting point for much of the deeper theory covered later in this book. Chapter 1 ends with a short outline of the text that shows how several important themes are repeated throughout.

Mathematical tools are now widely used in practically all areas of economics. Although the math used in this book is not especially difficult, Chapter 2 provides a brief summary of what you will need to know. These basic principles are usually covered in an elementary algebra course. Most important for our purposes are the relationships between algebraic functions and the representation of these functions in graphs. Because we will be using graphs heavily throughout the book (and because they are widely used in the field of economics as a whole), it is important to be sure you understand this basic material before proceeding. ▲

CHAPTER 1

Economic Models

In 1789 the British political philosopher Edmund Burke observed, "The Age of Chivalry is gone: that of sophisters, economists, and calculators has succeeded."[1] What was true in eighteenth-century England is even truer today—chivalry is long gone, and the age of economists (and certainly calculators if not sophisters) is upon us. Not a day goes by when the economy is not front-page news. Oil or food prices, imports of all sorts of goods, skyrocketing real estate values, and new and complex environmental concerns, such as acid rain, increasingly affect our lives. Just because economic issues have become such an important part of our lives, however, does not mean they are well understood. There is probably no field in which uninformed opinions can be both so prevalent and so wrong as in economics. Hopefully, after studying the analysis presented in this book, you should be better able to tell good economic arguments from bad ones and to develop more informed judgments about today's pressing economic questions.

This book introduces you to how economists think about the world. We will examine how economic decisions are made and how the economic decisions of one group affect those of another. A step-by-step, commonsense study of these relationships is what economics is all about.

[1]Edmund Burke, in *Reflections on the French Revolution*, F. G. Selby, ed. (London: The MacMillan Co., 1902), p. 84.

This first chapter introduces the philosophy behind the study of economics. It first defines the subject and then looks at some simple theoretical models that economists use for making sense out of the economy. The chapter ends with an overview of the remainder of the book.

Defining Economics

Several definitions of economics are in use today. The most widely quoted definition describes economics as the "study of the allocation of scarce resources among alternative end uses." This definition introduces two important aspects of society that concern economists: *scarce resources* and *alternative end uses*.

Resources are scarce—there are simply not enough resources available to satisfy all human wants and desires. The amount of land, labor, and capital that is available and the technology that exists for using them limit what society can produce. These scarce resources can be devoted to many alternative end uses. For example, a society may choose to have television sets or automobiles or clean air or beautiful cities. In fact, a society is likely to choose some combination of all of those desirable "end uses" for its resources. Economists are particularly interested in studying how those choices are made. Of course, as Application 1.1: Scarcity in the Natural World shows, the problem of scarcity is a universal one. Economic tools can help us understand the choices that necessarily arise in the face of such scarcity.

A second definition, building on these ideas, describes economics as the "study of the ways in which choices are made." Not only does society as a whole, through governmental decisions, choose how its resources are used, but, more importantly, the people in that society also make a wide variety of decisions on their own. They choose what to buy with their incomes, how to spend their leisure time, for whom to vote, how many (if any) children to have, and so on. Beyond these personal decisions, people also make choices in their jobs. A manager of a firm, for example, must decide which techniques to use and which resources to obtain (both labor and raw materials) to make the firm's products. An employee must decide whether working conditions in his or her job are acceptable or whether it is time to look for work elsewhere. As we will see, **microeconomics** studies all of these kinds of individual choices.

Microeconomics
The study of the economic choices individuals and firms make and how those choices create markets.

A final, not entirely serious, definition of economics describes it as "what economists do." This definition shows how difficult it is to describe all the questions that interest economists. Economists ask the "big" questions, such as whether capitalism or socialism is better or what the proper role of government in a free market economy is. They also study "minor" questions, such as why farmers choose to plant hybrid seeds to grow corn or what rates an electric utility company should charge its customers. Even though these questions are very different, all economic studies use similar methods to focus general economic principles on a particular issue. This book is about those general principles.

APPLICATION 1.1

Scarcity in the Natural World

Scarcity is as important in the nonhuman biological world as it is in the human world. Of course, the choices of even the most social and intelligent animals do not reflect the complexity, sophistication, and free will that characterize human choices. Biological societies usually evolve slowly through time in response to various environmental pressures. But these pressures are in many ways similar to the forces that shape the evolution of human societies. So it is no accident that Charles Darwin, in his theories of evolution, drew from the writings of nineteenth-century economists on scarcity.

Foraging for Food

All animals must expend time and energy in their daily search for food. In many ways, this poses an "economic" problem for them in deciding how to use these resources most effectively. Biologists' models suggest that animals may be quite sophisticated in the ways in which they choose to conserve time and energy and that they react to the scarcity of these resources in much the same way that humans do.[1]

Two examples from biology may help illustrate this "economic" approach to foraging. First, in studying birds of prey (eagles, hawks, and so forth), biologists have found that the length of time a bird will hunt in a particular area is determined both by the prevalence of food in that area and by the flight time to another location. These hunters recognize a clear trade-off between spending time and energy looking in one area and using those same resources to go somewhere else.

A second, related observation about foraging behavior is that no animal will stay in a given area until all of the possible food there is exhausted. For example, once a certain fraction of the prey in a particular area has been found, a hawk will go elsewhere. Similarly, studies of honeybees have found that they generally do not gather all of the nectar in a particular flower before moving on. Collecting the last drop of nectar is not worth the time and energy the bee must expend to get it. Such a weighing of incremental benefits and costs is precisely what an economist would predict in the presence of scarcity.

[1]See, for example, David W. Stephens and John R. Krebs, *Foraging Theory* (Princeton, N.J.: Princeton University Press, 1986).

Social Organization

The impact of scarcity is also visible in the behavior of "social" insects such as ants or termites. These insects face scarcity in the availability of their food supply and in the amount of work each individual insect is able to do. In order to ensure their survival (which is based on the survival of their queens), an elaborate system of castes has evolved. Different members of the species perform different specialized tasks to promote the overall welfare of the hive.

A number of biological researchers have applied economic logic to these activities and have concluded that social insects operate very efficiently.[2] In particular, the degree of specialization in various species of termites and ants is based on the number of problems the hive may face. Social insects in tropical climates tend to have a greater number of castes than do those in temperate climates because tropical problems (such as floods and droughts) don't occur elsewhere. Similarly, those castes that must deal with the most frequently recurring problems have more insects. Later chapters show how the economic logic of the problem of scarcity predicts exactly these results—specialization and the allocation of resources among members of society with specialized skills is a principal reaction to resource scarcity.

To Think About

1. Does it make sense to argue that animals or insects "choose" an optimal strategy for dealing with the scarcity of resources? Since it seems unlikely that ants or even hawks could make very complex calculations, how do you explain the findings that they tend to behave "rationally"?
2. Living creatures can be viewed as a collection of cells whose activities are regulated by genetic material. How can behavior be explained as being motivated by incentives facing genes rather than by incentives facing the organism as a whole? How would such a distinction help to explain altruistic behavior by some organisms?

[2]See E. O. Wilson, "The Ergonomics of Caste in the Social Insects," *American Economic Review* (December 1978): 25–35.

Why Economists Use Theoretical Models

The most striking feature of any developed economy is its overall complexity. Thousands of firms produce millions or even billions of different products and services. Millions of people work in all kinds of jobs and buy a bewildering variety of products, ranging from yoyos to gaudy yachts. These actions must somehow work together. Wheat, for example, must be harvested at the right time; the farmer must ship it to a miller, who grinds it and ships it to a baker, who bakes it into bread. Enough bread must be sent to the grocery store for people to buy. To describe every action of an economy in complete detail would be impossible—lengthy books on every product and job could be written! Instead, economists develop simple **models** to capture the "essentials" of how the economy works. Just as a road map does not need to show every house to be useful, economic models are useful in understanding the real world even though they do not record every feature of the economy. This book covers the most widely used economic models.

Models
Simple theoretical descriptions that capture the essentials of how the economy works.

The use of models is widespread both in the sciences (including economics) and in everyday life. In physics, for example, scientists use the abstractions of a "perfect" vacuum to study the force of gravity in a simplified setting. Chemistry uses the atom or the molecule as a very simplified model of the structure of matter. In more everyday life, architects use scale models to plan buildings. Television repairers use wiring diagrams in their work, and dressmakers use patterns and plans.

In much the same way economists use models to understand the infinitely complex real world. These models show how people make decisions, how firms make decisions, and how these two types of decisions are coordinated in the marketplace. As an illustration we will briefly review the development of one such model, a model that you have undoubtedly encountered before.

Supply and Demand: The Development of an Economic Model

"Even your parrot can become an economist—just teach it to say 'supply and demand.'" Like many catchy slogans, this one reflects a basic truth—economists use notions of supply and demand practically all the time in order to explain economic events. The **supply-demand model of price determination** is such a familiar staple of introductory economics courses that it is hard to imagine what the subject would be like without it. In fact, however, this model is a relatively recent one, having been developed in the latter part of the nineteenth century. Showing how that model was developed illustrates why the process of economic theorizing is greatly aided by using models and also provides a chance for a brief review.

Supply-demand model
A model describing how a good's price is determined by the behavior of the individuals who buy the good and the firms that sell it.

Early Economists

Commodities have had prices throughout human history. Money has been used as a way of making transactions for at least three thousand years, and even before the invention of money, early peoples engaged in widespread barter transactions. Even though prices were a familiar feature of virtually all societies, however, few people tried to develop any general explanation for these prices.[2] Instead, most economic theorizing was done by traders who hoped to make a profit by buying goods where they were "cheap" and selling them where they were "dear." A crafty merchant who could become wealthy by buying and selling (say, salt or spices) had little need to delve more deeply into the general determinants of prices. Not until the latter part of the eighteenth century did writers begin to display an interest in developing a general theory of price determination.

Adam Smith and the Invisible Hand

The Scottish philosopher Adam Smith (1723–1790) is generally credited with being the first true "economist." In *The Wealth of Nations* (published in the year 1776) Smith examined a large number of the pressing economic issues of his day and tried to develop economic tools for understanding them. Smith's most important insight was his recognition that the system of market-determined prices that he observed was not as chaotic and undisciplined as most other writers had assumed. Rather, Smith saw the prices that arose from the market system as providing a powerful "invisible hand" that directed resources into activities where they would be most valuable. Prices play the crucial role of telling both consumers and firms what resources are "worth" and thereby prompt these economic actors to make efficient decisions about how to use them. To Smith it was this ability to use resources efficiently that provided the ultimate explanation for a nation's "wealth." At many points later in this book we will return to this fundamental insight about the role of market prices to see whether recent thinking tends to support or to contradict Smith's conjectures.

Because Adam Smith placed great importance on the role of prices in directing how a nation's resources are used, he needed to develop some theories about how those prices are determined. He offered a very simple and, as we will see, only partly correct explanation—the prices of goods are determined by what it costs to produce them. Since, in Smith's day (and, to some extent, even today), the primary costs of producing goods were costs associated with the labor that went into a good, it was only a short step for him to embrace a labor-based theory of prices. For example, to paraphrase an illustration from

[2]Perhaps the most important early writer on economics was Aristotle, who introduced a distinction between the "value in exchange" (price) of a good and its "value in use." Although most economists do not make such a distinction today, the notion that some goods might be "worth" more or less than their market price played an important role in economic discussions of "just prices" in the Middle Ages and continues to influence some modern Marxist economists. See, for example, J. A. Schumpeter *History of Economic Analysis* (New York: Oxford University Press, 1954), Chapters 1 and 2.

The Wealth of Nations, if it takes twice as long for a hunter to catch a deer as to catch a beaver, one deer should trade for two beavers. The relative price of a deer is high because of the extra labor costs involved in catching one. Of course, producing many kinds of economic goods is not as simple a process as catching a deer or a beaver, but Smith believed that most differences in relative prices could ultimately be traced back to differences in underlying labor costs.

Smith's explanation for the price of a good is illustrated in Panel a of Figure 1.1. The horizontal line at P* shows that any number of deer can be produced without affecting the relative cost of doing so. That relative cost sets the price of deer (P*), which might be measured in beavers (a deer costs two beavers), in dollars (a deer costs $200 whereas a beaver costs $100), or in any other units that this society uses to indicate exchange value. This value will change only when the technology for producing deer changes. If, for example, this society developed better running shoes (which would aid in catching deer, but be of little use in capturing beavers), the relative labor costs associated with hunting deer might fall. Now a deer would trade for, say, 1.5 beavers, and the supply curve illustrated in the figure would shift downward. In the absence of such technical changes, however, the relative price of deer would remain constant, reflecting relative costs of production.

David Ricardo and Diminishing Returns

The early nineteenth century was a period of considerable controversy in economics, especially in England. The two most pressing issues of the day were the effects that expanding international trade was having on the economy and the effects that industrial growth was having on the availability of good farmland and other natural resources. It is testimony to the timelessness of economic questions that these are some of the same issues that dominate political discussions in the United States (and elsewhere) today. Much of the rhetoric in today's discussions is virtually identical to that which was heard in London streets more than a century and a half ago. One of the most influential contributors to the earlier debates was the British financier and pamphleteer David Ricardo (1772–1823). Throughout this book we will encounter Ricardo's many contributions to economics. Here we will examine only one of them—the concept of diminishing returns.

Although Ricardo generally accepted Adam Smith's views about the power of market prices to influence the allocation of resources and of the importance of labor costs in determining prices, he argued that Smith's view of price determination was incomplete. Ricardo believed that labor (and other) costs would tend to rise as the level of production of a particular good expanded. He drew this insight primarily from his consideration of the way in which cultivation of farmland was expanding in England at the time. As new and less fertile land was brought into use, it would naturally take more labor (say, to pick out the rocks in addition to planting crops) to produce an extra bushel of grain. Hence, the relative price of grain would rise. Similarly, as

Figure 1.1
Early Views of Price Determination

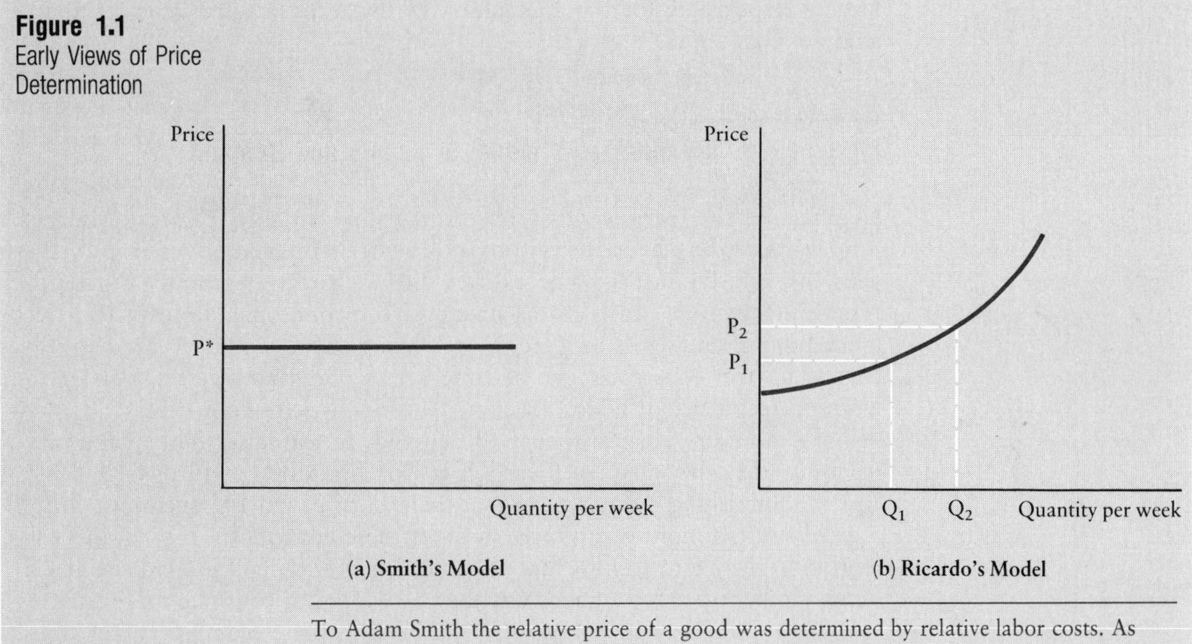

(a) Smith's Model

(b) Ricardo's Model

To Adam Smith the relative price of a good was determined by relative labor costs. As shown in the left-hand panel, relative price would be P* unless something altered such costs. Ricardo added the concept of diminishing returns to this explanation. In the right-hand panel, relative price rises as quantity produced rises from Q_1 to Q_2.

deer hunters exhaust the stock of deer in a given area, they must spend more time locating their prey so the relative price of deer would also rise. Ricardo believed that the phenomenon of increasing costs was quite general, and today we refer to his discovery as the **law of diminishing returns.** This generalization of Smith's notion of supply is reflected in Panel b of Figure 1.1 in which the supply curve slopes upward as quantity produced expands.

Law of diminishing returns
Hypothesis that the cost associated with producing one more unit of a good rises as more of that good is produced.

The problem with Ricardo's explanation was that it really didn't explain how prices are determined. Although the notion of diminishing returns undoubtedly made Smith's model more realistic, it did so by showing that relative price was not determined by production technology alone. Instead, according to Ricardo, the relative price of a good can be practically any level depending on how much of it is produced and the extent to which diminishing returns are encountered.

To complete his explanation, Ricardo tended to rely on a subsistence argument. If, for example, the current population of a country needs Q_1 units of output to survive, Panel b of Figure 1.1 shows that the relative price would be P_1. With a growing population, these subsistence needs might expand to Q_2, and the relative price of this necessity would rise to P_2. Ricardo's suggestion that the relative prices of goods necessary for survival would rise in response to diminishing returns provided the basis for much of the concern about population growth in England during the 1830s and 1840s. It was largely responsible for the application of the term "dismal science" to the study of economics.

Marginalism and Marshall's Model of Supply and Demand

Contrary to the fears of many observers (most notably, Thomas Malthus, whose name has become synonymous with concerns over population growth), relative prices of necessities did not rise significantly during the nineteenth century. Instead, as productive technologies improved, prices tended to fall and levels of material well-being improved rather dramatically. As the notion of subsistence became a less plausible explanation of the amounts of particular goods consumed, economists found it necessary to develop some more general theory of demand. In the latter half of the nineteenth century they adapted Ricardo's law of diminishing returns to this task. Just as diminishing returns mean that the cost of producing one more unit of a good rises as more is produced, so too, these economists argued, the willingness of people to pay for that last unit declines. Only if individuals are offered a lower price for a good, will they be willing to consume more of it. By focusing on the last, or "marginal," unit bought, these economists had at last developed a comprehensive theory of price determination.

The clearest statement of these ideas was presented by the English economist Alfred Marshall (1842–1924) in his *Principles of Economics,* published in 1890. In it Marshall showed how the forces of demand and supply *simultaneously* determine price. Marshall's analysis is illustrated by the familiar cross diagram shown in Figure 1.2.

As before the amount of a good purchased per period (say, each week) is shown on the horizontal axis, and the price of the good appears on the vertical axis. The curve labeled "Demand" shows the amount of the good demanded at each price. The negative slope of this curve reflects the marginalist principle: because people are willing to pay less and less for the last unit purchased, they will buy more only at a lower price. The curve labeled "Supply" shows the increasing cost of making one more unit of the good as the total amount produced increases. In other words, the upward slope of the supply curve reflects *increasing* marginal costs, just as the downward slope of the demand curve reflects *decreasing* marginal usefulness.

Market Equilibrium

Equilibrium price The price at which the quantity demanded by buyers of a good is equal to the quantity supplied of the good by sellers.

The two curves intersect at P*, Q*. Here P* is an **equilibrium price**—both buyers and sellers are content with the amount of goods being traded and the price at which they are traded. If the good is sold at a price above P*, people will want to buy *less* than the amount being produced. Too much of this good is being supplied. On the other hand, if the good is sold at a price below

Figure 1.2
The Marshall
Supply-Demand Cross

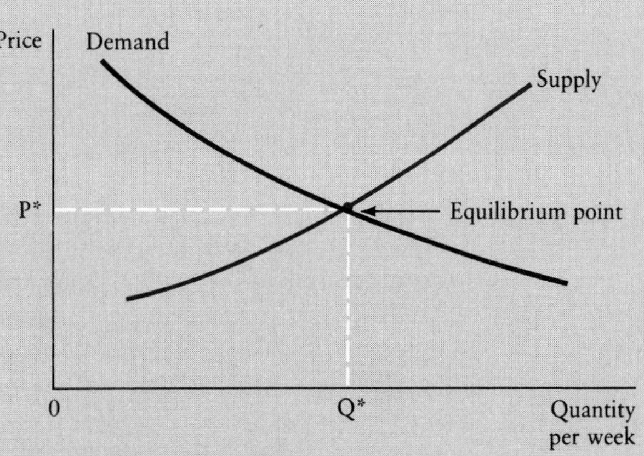

Marshall believed that demand and supply together determine the equilibrium price (P*) and quantity (Q*) of a good. The positive slope of the supply curve reflects diminishing returns (increasing marginal cost) whereas the negative slope of the demand curve reflects diminishing marginal usefulness.

P*, people will want to buy more of the good than is being produced—demand will exceed supply. Only at the equilibrium price of P* does the quantity demanded by buyers and the quantity supplied by sellers agree. Hence, the forces of both supply and demand determine price. Marshall used the analogy of a pair of scissors to illustrate this point—just as both blades of the scissors work together to cut cloth, so too both the forces of supply and demand work together to establish prices.

Change in Market Equilibrium

If either the demand or supply curve should shift, however, the equilibrium price would also change. In Figure 1.3, people's demand for the good increases. In this case the demand curve moves outward (from curve D to curve D′). At each price people now want to buy more of the good. The equilibrium price increases (from P* to P**). This higher price both tells firms to supply more goods and restrains individuals' demand for the good. At the new equilibrium price of P** supply and demand again balance—at this higher price the amount of goods demanded is exactly equal to the amount supplied. In Chapter 2 we will illustrate how the extent of this price rise might be predicted if algebraic expressions for the supply and demand curves were known.

Marshall's model of supply and demand should be quite familiar to you since it provides the principal focus of most courses in introductory economics. Indeed, the concepts of marginal cost, marginal value, and market equi-

Figure 1.3
An Increase in Demand Alters Equilibrium Price and Quantity

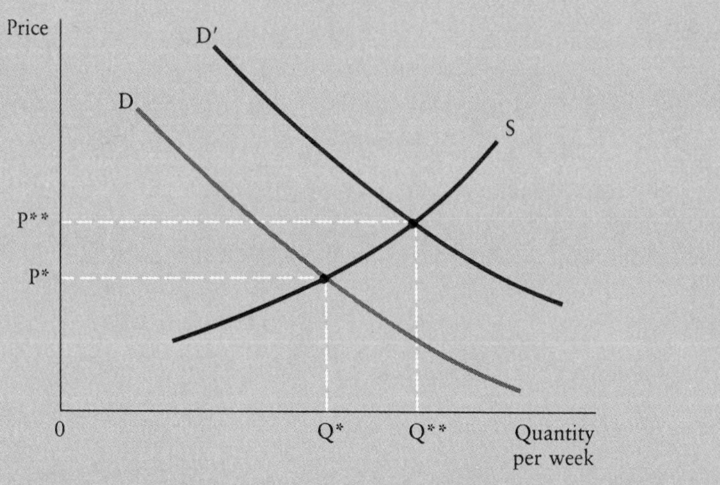

If the demand curve shifts outward to D′ because there is more desire for the product, P*, Q* will no longer be an equilibrium. Instead, equilibrium occurs at P**, Q**, where D′ and S intersect.

librium encountered in this model provide the starting place for most of the economic models you will learn about in this book. Although today we tend to regard Marshall's model as a fairly obvious application of a few simple ideas, our brief sketch of the history of the development of the model shows that was not always the case. Notice how earlier economists constantly refined their models of price determination in the light of real-world observations and experiences. As we shall see in later chapters, this process continues to this day as economists seek to explain a constantly expanding set of economic issues. The simple Marshallian model can be a very good way to start investigating many questions, however, as Application 1.2: Politics and Economics of the U.S.-Soviet Wheat Trade clearly illustrates.

Models of Many Markets

Partial equilibrium model
An economic model of a single market.

Probably the most important shortcoming of Marshall's model of supply and demand is that it does not show how different markets work together in an economy. The basic model pictured in Figures 1.2 and 1.3 is a **partial equilibrium model** of a single market. It does not show how results in one market affect those in another. For example, Figure 1.3 shows how an increase in demand for a good causes its price to rise, but not how that price increase might affect other markets.

If we were examining the market for imported French wine, say, we know that an increase in demand would result in a rise in its price. But it also seems likely that this price rise would have effects on the market for California wine where demand would increase as people shifted from French to California

APPLICATION 1.2

Politics and Economics of the U.S.-Soviet Wheat Trade

The historical inefficiency of Soviet agriculture combined with highly variable weather in Russian wheat-growing areas has resulted in a frequent need for the Russians to buy wheat from other countries—most notably from the United States. Not surprisingly, this trade has had political as well as economic dimensions as recent history clearly illustrates.

The 1972 Wheat Deal

On July 8, 1972, the Soviet Union announced it would purchase 400 million bushels of wheat from the United States—nearly one-fourth of total annual U.S. wheat production. The size of the proposed sale caught both wheat farmers and middlemen in the wheat market by surprise. As might have been predicted, such a large increase in demand resulted in a rapid escalation in prices. At the end of June, the price of hard winter wheat (which figured predominantly in the sale) was about $1.60 per bushel. By mid-September the price had risen to $2.25 per bushel—more than a 40 percent increase over only slightly more than two months. This dramatic price rise brought forth a variety of charges of profiteering by grain traders and improprieties by officials who may have known about the sale beforehand.

The Grain Purchase Agreement

The Russian wheat deal of 1972 had important consequences for the longer run as well. As a result of the sharp run-up in wheat prices, farmers increased their planting of wheat significantly. Acres harvested rose by nearly 50 percent from 43 million acres in the 1970–1971 growing season to over 65 million acres in the 1974–1975 growing season. This shift in supply is precisely the kind of response to increasing price that might have been expected in the long run. The 1972–1973 experience also resulted in a long-term wheat-purchasing agreement between the United States and the Soviet Union signed in 1975. A stated purpose of the agreement was to regularize grain trade between the two countries and thereby lead to "fewer surprises" in the future.[1]

[1]For a discussion, see C.B. Luttrell, "Grain Export Agreements—No Gains, No Losses," *Federal Reserve Bank of St. Louis Review* (August/September 1981) 23–29.

The 1980 Grain Embargo

The next surprise in the United States-Soviet wheat trade came in response to the Soviets' invasion of Afghanistan in the spring of 1980. In response to this action, President Carter announced that the United States would not honor the wheat trade agreement and would instead embargo shipments to the Soviets. This move seemed to have little effect on the Russians' ability to get wheat since the Canadians, Australians, and Argentinians were more than willing to provide what the United States didn't. But the embargo did result in a shift inward in the demand for U.S. wheat, and prices fell by about 15–20 percent.[2]

Grain Policy and U.S. Elections

These lessons of the grain embargo have had a significant influence on U.S. presidential elections in wheat-growing states. In the 1980 election, for example, candidate Ronald Reagan attacked Carter's grain embargo and made major political gains by doing so. Lingering problems in the wheat market re-emerged in the 1988 election debates when candidate George Bush attacked Michael Dukakis over the Carter embargo—even though Dukakis disavowed any thought of pursuing such a program in the future (he did cause a stir, however, by suggesting that wheat farmers should consider growing Belgian endive instead).

To Think About

1. Suppose the Soviets had decided to buy their wheat from Canada or Australia only. Would U.S. prices have been affected as much as they actually were? Is the wheat market a national or a world market?
2. One purpose of the long-term wheat deal with the Soviets was to "regularize" grain trade. Would farmers be better-off (with higher revenues) under such a system or under one in which the same total quantity is bought, but at erratic and unexpected intervals?

[2]See U.S. Council of Economic Advisors, *Economic Report of the President, 1984* (Washington, D.C.: U.S. Government Printing Office, 1989), Chapter 4.

products. Indeed, the effects could be far more widespread than this, including repercussions in the market for fine cheeses (to consume with wine), for wine glasses and corkscrews, and possibly even affecting the wages of California grape harvesters. And, to complicate the story, some of these effects may have repercussions on the original market with which we started our discussion (the market for French wine). Suppose, for example, that California grape harvesters just happen to like French wine. Then a rise in their wages might cause them to buy more of this product, and that would disturb the initial equilibrium. To show all the effects of a change in one market on other markets, we need a **general equilibrium model,** which includes workings of all markets together. Later sections of this book look closely at some of these multimarket models.

General equilibrium model
An economic model of a complete system of markets.

The Production Possibility Frontier

Production possibility frontier
A graph showing all possible combinations of goods that can be produced with a fixed amount of resources.

Here these models are introduced using another graph you should remember from introductory economics—the **production possibility frontier.** This graph shows the various amounts of two goods that an economy can produce during some period (again, say, one week). Because the production possibility frontier shows two goods, rather than the single good in Marshall's model, it is used as a basic building block for general equilibrium models.

Figure 1.4 shows the production possibility frontier for two goods, food and clothing. The graph looks at the supply of these goods by showing the combinations that can be produced with this economy's resources. For example, 10 pounds of food and 3 units of clothing could be made, or 4 pounds of food and 12 units of clothing. Many other combinations of food and clothing could also be produced. The production possibility frontier shows all of them. Combinations of food and clothing outside the frontier cannot be made because not enough resources are available. The production possibility frontier is a reminder of the basic economic fact that resources are scarce—there are not enough resources available to produce all we might want of every good.

Opportunity Cost

Opportunity cost
The cost of a good or service as measured by the alternative uses that are forgone by producing the good or service.

This scarcity means that we must choose how much of each good to produce. Figure 1.4 makes clear that each choice has its costs. For example, if this economy produces 10 pounds of food and 3 units of clothing at point A, producing 1 more unit of clothing would "cost" $\frac{1}{2}$ pound of food—to increase the output of clothing by 1 unit means the production of food would have to decrease by $\frac{1}{2}$ pound. Economists would say that the **opportunity cost** of 1 unit of clothing at point A is $\frac{1}{2}$ pound of food. On the other hand, if the economy initially makes 4 pounds of food and 12 units of clothing at point B, it would cost 2 pounds of food to make 1 more unit of clothing. The opportu-

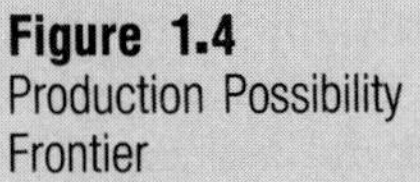
Figure 1.4
Production Possibility Frontier

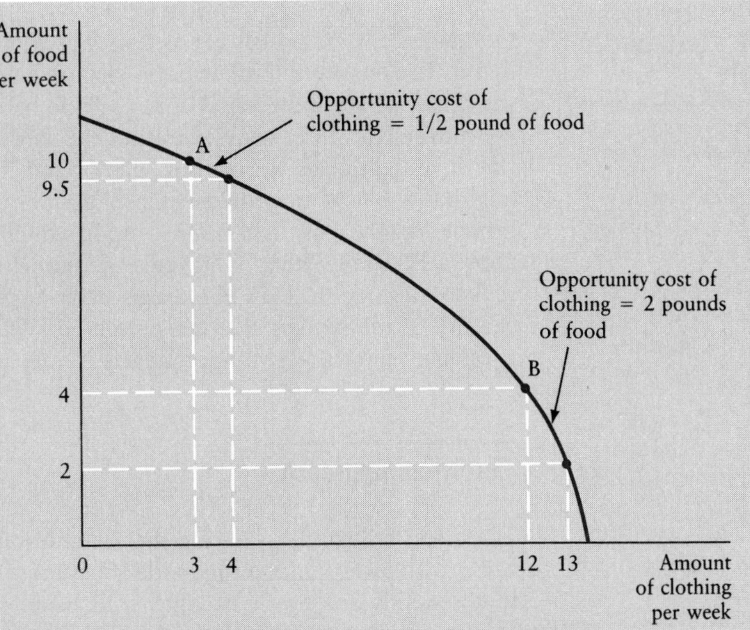

The production possibility frontier shows the different combinations of two goods that can be produced from a certain amount of scarce resources. It also shows the opportunity cost of producing more of one good as how much of the other good then cannot be produced. The opportunity cost at two different levels of production of a good can be seen by comparing points A and B.

nity cost of 1 more unit of clothing at point B has increased to 2 pounds of food. Because more units of clothing are produced at point B than at point A, both Ricardo's and Marshall's ideas of increasing marginal costs suggest that the opportunity cost of an additional unit of clothing will be higher at point B than at point A. This effect is just what Figure 1.4 shows.

The production possibility frontier in Figure 1.4 provides two general equilibrium results that are not clear in Marshall's supply and demand model of a single market. The first of these is that producing more of one good means producing less of another good because resources are scarce. Economists often (perhaps too often!) use the expression "there is no such thing as a free lunch" to explain that every economic action involves opportunity costs. An important part of economic analysis is to discover those costs. A second result shown by the production possibility frontier is that the extent of these opportunity costs depend on how much of each good is produced. The frontier is like a supply curve for two goods—it shows the opportunity cost of producing more of one good as the decrease in the amount of a second good. The production possibility frontier is therefore a particularly useful tool for studying the way in which diminishing returns affect several markets at the same time.

How Economists Verify Theoretical Models

Direct approach A method of verifying economic models that examines the validity of the assumptions on which the model is based.

Indirect approach A method of verifying economic models that asks if the model can accurately predict real-world events.

Of course, not all models are as useful as Marshall's model of supply and demand. For example, Ptolemy's theory of planetary motion put the earth as the center of the universe; it could not be believed when it could not explain the movement of the planets around the sun. An important purpose of scientific investigation is to sort out such "bad" models from "good" ones. Two methods are used to provide such a test of economic models. The **direct approach** looks at the assumptions upon which a model is based; the **indirect approach,** on the other hand, uses the model to see if it can correctly predict real-world events. This book uses both approaches to try to illustrate the validity of the models that are presented. We now look briefly at the differences between these two approaches.

The Direct Approach

The direct approach to testing the assumptions of an economic model might begin with intuition. Do the model's assumptions seem "reasonable"? Unfortunately, this question is fraught with problems, since what appears reasonable to one person may seem preposterous to someone else (try arguing with a noneconomics student about whether people usually behave "rationally," for example).

Assumptions can also be tested with empirical evidence. For example, economists usually assume that firms are in business to "maximize profits"—in fact, much of our discussion in this book is based on that assumption. Using the direct approach to test this assumption with real-world data, you might send questionnaires to managers asking them how they make decisions and whether they really do try to maximize profits. This approach has been used many times but the results are often difficult to interpret and do not shed much light on the profit-maximization assumption. Like many opinion polls, surveys of business managers do not provide evidence that economists find very convincing.

The Indirect Approach

Many economists, such as Milton Friedman, do not believe that a theory can be tested by looking only at its assumptions.[3] They argue that all theories are based on unrealistic assumptions; the very nature of theorizing demands that

[3]Milton Friedman, *Essays in Positive Economics* (Chicago: University of Chicago Press, 1953), Chapter 1. Another view stressing the importance of realistic assumptions can be found in H. A. Simon, "Rational Decision Making in Business Organizations," *American Economic Review* (September 1979): 493–513.

we make what may appear to be unrealistic assumptions. Such economists believe that in order to decide if a theory is valid, we must see if it is capable of explaining and predicting real-world events. The real test of any economic model is whether it is consistent with events from the economy itself.

Friedman gives a good example of this idea by asking what theory explains the shots an expert pool player will make. He argues that the laws of velocity, momentum, and angles from classical physics make a suitable theoretical model, because the pool player certainly shoots *as if* he or she followed these laws. If we asked the players whether they understood these physical principles, they would undoubtedly answer that they did not. That does not matter, Friedman argues, because the physical laws give very accurate predictions of the shots made and are therefore useful as theoretical models.

Going back to the question of whether firms try to maximize profits, the indirect approach would try to predict the firms' behavior by assuming that they do act *as if* they were maximizing profits. If we find that we can predict firms' behavior, then we can believe the profit-maximization hypothesis. Even if these firms said on questionnaires that they don't really try to maximize profits, the theory will still be valid, much as the pool player's disclaiming knowledge of the laws of physics does not make these laws untrue. The ultimate test in both cases is the theory's ability to predict real-world events.

Using Empirical Examples

This book is about economic theories. Because our real objective is to learn about the real world, we must be able to decide whether those theories are acceptable. This book uses both the direct and indirect methods to test the models presented. Occasionally, we will follow the direct approach by pointing out that a model is based on "reasonable" assumptions. More often, however, we will look at examples from the real world in which behavior can be predicted using economic theory. These real-world examples are included not only because they are interesting applications of economics in their own right, but also because they are used as empirical support for the theories presented here. They are especially important to understanding economic model building. Application 1.3: Poor Models That Forgot about Prices looks at some inaccurate predictions based on rather poor economic models and shows why we might reject those models.

Positive versus Normative Economics

So far we have been talking about **positive economic analysis,** which uses the real world as an object to be studied—it seeks to explain real economic events. Positive economics tries to determine how resources actually are used

APPLICATION 1.3

Some Poor Models That Forgot about Prices

Adam Smith's "invisible hand" image was intended to suggest that prices play a major role in determining the allocation of resources. Consequently, the price mechanism is central to most models of the economy. Sometimes, however, model builders tend to forget Smith's lesson, and frequently this results in the construction of unreliable models. Here we look at two examples.

The Limits to Growth Models

In the early 1970s many books and reports predicted dire consequences for the future of humanity. *World Dynamics* by Jay W. Forrester and *The Limits to Growth* by Donnella H. Meadows et al. (based largely on the Forrester book) were very influential.[1] Using complex computer models, these books suggested strongly that by the mid-1980s and on into the twenty-first century the world would experience major economic disruptions, with per capita availability of food and other necessities falling at a disturbingly rapid rate. Since the models were first published, their assumptions have been looked at closely. Not only do these assumptions seem faulty, but there is increasing evidence that the predictions may be wrong as well.

Economists criticized these books because they did not consider how people might change their behavior in response to changing market prices. For example, the models assumed that a certain amount of natural resources was needed for each unit of goods produced by the economy. This assumption ignores how the price of resources works to make producers use these resources more efficiently. One of the most dramatic recent examples is the case of energy, particularly oil. During the 1970s the real price of oil to users increased more than sixfold, mostly because the Organization of Petroleum Exporting Countries (the infamous OPEC cartel) was formed to control oil production early in the decade. The world economy responded to these energy price increases by cutting back on the use of energy in many ways, such as developing more efficient, smaller cars and more efficient industrial machines. In the United States, for example, real energy prices rose about 60 percent between 1973 and 1980, but energy use per dollar of real gross national product declined by nearly 20 percent. The models used in the *Limits* book did not, however, allow for such possibilities. They therefore vastly exaggerated the economic problems that economic growth causes.

Models for Predicting Electricity Demand

During the late 1960s and early 1970s electricity sales grew very rapidly in the United States. Electric power companies generally used these historical growth rates to predict how much they would need to produce in the 1980s and beyond. Overall, they planned for a 6–7 percent annual growth rate in kilowatt sales and consequently started construction of many new power plants.

Simply extrapolating growth rates for the 1960s into the 1970s and 1980s disregarded one important fact—real electricity prices had been falling during the 1960s at the rate of about 2 percent per year as new, more efficient generating units were brought on stream. This price decline added a strong impetus to demand. By the mid-1970s, however, electricity prices were rising—real prices rose by about 4 percent per year during the period 1975–1980. This price rise severely constrained kilowatt sales, which rose very little during the late 1970s. Electric power companies found themselves with large numbers of new generating plants but little demand for their power. The result was major financial problems for some power companies. For example, the default of the Washington Water Power System in 1987 was the largest municipal bankruptcy in history. Using demand models that paid inadequate attention to prices proved to be a very costly mistake.

To Think About

1. Hasn't the world been running out of resources since Adam and Eve? Does the market price of a resource tell whether it is scarce, or should other factors be considered too?
2. Can you think of other examples (such as electricity demand) where the failure to consider reactions to price changes has resulted in wildly erroneous predictions? Did rising gasoline prices in the 1970s, for example, cause problems for automobile companies?

[1] J. W. Forrester, *World Dynamics* (Cambridge, Mass.: Wright Allen Press, 1971), and Donnella H. Meadows et al., *The Limits to Growth* (New York: Universe Books, 1972).

Positive economic analysis
Theories that explain how resources actually are used in an economy.

Normative analysis
Theories that make judgments about how the economy's resources should be used.

in an economy. A somewhat different use of economic theory is **normative analysis.** In this type of economic theory, economists seek to say something about how an economy's resources *should* be used. For example, an economist engaged in positive analysis might explain health care prices in terms of the behavior of doctors, patients, hospitals, insurance companies, and so forth. The economist might also measure the costs and benefits of devoting more resources to health care. But if the economist argues that more resources *should* be allocated to health care, he or she has moved into normative analysis. By suggesting what policies should be undertaken, the economist is making judgments that go beyond basic analytical questions about how prices and quantities of health care are determined and has moved into the role of an advocate for some specific policy.

Some economists believe that only positive analysis is proper. They argue that economics should be as "scientific" as the physical sciences and should only describe and possibly predict real-world events. Moralistic positions and pleading for special interests are improper for an economist. According to this view, the choice of a particular health care policy should be left to the political process, not to the economist who should have no more influence than any other citizen in choosing a policy.

This book takes a positive economic approach by seeking to explain actual economic behavior. At the same time we consider several normative questions. For example, our discussion of monopoly shows how monopolistic firms may misallocate resources. Our analysis of incomplete property rights shows how these can cause goods to be misallocated as well. Each of these conclusions may suggest a change in policy (such as regulation of monopoly or full legal specification of property rights), but by pointing out the problems we are not necessarily recommending specific corrections. Our goal is to show the consequences of undertaking any particular policy that might be proposed.

An Overview of the Book

This book is divided into six parts. Each part explains a broad area of economic analysis in several closely related chapters.

Part I introduces the topics that follow later. Chapter 1 discusses some of the methodological issues arising in economic analysis. This chapter also reviews the basic model of supply and demand developed by economists to explain how prices are determined, which is the framework for most of the analysis in this book. Chapter 2 reviews basic concepts of algebra, especially algebraic functions and graphs. These concepts are widely used in economics and are essential to this book.

Parts II and III examine the two important participants in the economic process. Part II develops in detail the economic theory of *individual behavior*. It explains how economists treat individuals' preferences and how these preferences affect decisions. Ultimately, this analysis leads to the concept of demand. Part III is concerned with *firms' behavior*. It focuses primarily on firms' costs and how firms' decisions affect costs; this leads to the concept of supply.

Part IV describes how prices are determined in perfectly competitive markets. These markets have so many buyers and sellers that not one of them has any influence on prices. Because of this, it is possible to analyze these markets rather completely. Not only does Part IV provide such a complete description, but it also develops the notion of economic efficiency as a way of evaluating whether markets are operating properly. The models developed in this part therefore provide a convenient benchmark against which to measure other economic situations.

In Part V we examine situations in which firms have some power to influence the market price of their products. The simplest case of this is when a monopoly firm is the sole supplier to a market and therefore can choose any price that it wishes. Our analysis will show why this circumstance is economically inefficient. We then proceed to examine more complex cases involving only a few producers and show that these also raise important questions about the markets' operating efficiency.

Many of the issues that arise when we study the way that prices of goods are determined also arise when we study the way in which prices paid to factors of production (wages of labor, rent on capital and land, and so forth) are determined. Part VI shows how the models developed previously can be adapted to the study of factor pricing. Because people get their incomes from renting out the labor and capital they possess, a study of these markets is a necessary part of the study of any economic system.

Finally, Part VII looks at a few problems that tend to extend beyond interactions between suppliers and demanders. Such problems as environmental pollution or the need to provide for a common defense may not be solvable through market mechanisms, and some sort of government action may be required. Our analysis in Part VII focuses on the reasons for such needs and on some of the difficulties that can arise in attempting to meet them.

Three Recurring Themes

Although we will describe many different economic models in this book, most of them are based on the same common elements, three of which are particularly important.

Using the Optimization Assumption to Explain Behavior

In order to develop economic models of behavior, we need to make some assumption about why individuals and firms do what they do. Usually we will assume that these economic actors are working toward some goal and that they will choose to undertake actions that best achieve that goal. You have already seen one example of this approach—the profit maximization assumption. By adopting this assumption, it is possible to develop many implications about how firms will behave and to test those implications with data from the real world. Throughout this book we will be making similar assumptions about the motives of the economic actors we are looking at. We will see that such assumptions can provide many insights about how resources are ultimately allocated by these actors.

Describing a Market Equilibrium

Since Marshall's model of supply and demand is at the heart of many of the models we will examine in this book, it is not surprising that his concept of a market equilibrium is a crucial one. Because the establishment of equilibrium prices results in a situation in which buyers and sellers are both satisfied with what is happening, such a situation will tend to persist until something changes it. And, as we saw in our application on U.S.-Soviet grain dealings, frequently it is possible to predict what a new equilibrium will be when something does change. Our goal in many of the economic models we will be describing will be to be able to make such predictions.

The Benefits of Free Exchange

Adam Smith's ideas about the beneficial effects of the "invisible hand" of market forces are alive and well today. Many recent governmental initiatives such as the deregulation of airlines in the United States or the selling-off of nationalized firms in the United Kingdom have been importantly motivated by just such ideas. Throughout this book we will be encountering examples that further illustrate what Smith had in mind. Of course, as we will also illustrate, in some cases free exchange may lead to undesirable results—unregulated disposal of toxic wastes and the production of acid rain are results of some free market activities that could hardly be claimed to be beneficial. Our models will attempt to explain such undesirable results as well.

These three themes are basic to practically all of microeconomics. Since they apply to a broad range of economic questions, you will be encountering them in many different forms throughout this book. In many respects these themes summarize the fundamental ways in which economists think about the world.

Summary

This chapter provides you with the background to begin your study of microeconomics. Much of this material should be familiar to you from your introductory economics course, but that should come as no surprise. In many respects the study of economics repeatedly investigates the same questions with an increasingly sophisticated set of tools. This course gives you some more of these tools. In establishing the basis for that investigation, this chapter reminds you of several important ideas:

- Economics is the study of allocating scarce resources among possible uses. Because resources are scarce, choices have to be made on how they will be used. Economists develop theoretical models to explain these choices.
- The most commonly used model of the allocation of resources is the model of supply and demand developed by Alfred Marshall in the latter part of the nineteenth century. That model shows how prices are determined as an equilibrium between the amount people want to buy and the amount firms are willing to produce. If supply and demand curves shift, new prices are established to restore equilibrium to the market.
- Marshall's model of supply and demand is a "partial equilibrium" model because it looks at only one market. Models of many markets are complicated by the number of relationships among the various markets.
- The production possibility frontier provides a simple illustration of the supply conditions in two markets. The curve clearly shows the limits imposed on any economy because resources are scarce. Producing more of one good means that less of something else must be produced. This reduction in output elsewhere is a measure of the opportunity cost involved in such additional production. Its size depends on how much of the various goods are being produced.
- Proving the validity of economic models is difficult and sometimes controversial. Occasionally the validity of a model can be determined by whether it is based on reasonable assumptions. More often, however, models are judged by how well they explain actual economic events.

Review Questions

1. We define economics as the "study of the allocation of scarce resources among alternative end uses." Give some examples of this definition as applied to natural resources. How do you know these resources are scarce? What are some of the alternative end uses to which these might be put? Can you think of any resources that are not scarce? Do issues arise in choosing how to use nonscarce resources?
2. In many economic problems time is treated as a scarce resource. Describe how problems in using time meet our definition of "economics." Can you think of any ways in which using time differs from using physical resources?
3. In Application 1.1 we described some biological research on foraging behavior. For the case of hawks, say, describe which scarce resources are being allocated by the hawk's decisions, and illustrate some of the alternative uses that might be made of those resources. Provide a similar analysis for some other foraging animal (a deer, a squirrel, or a whale, for example).
4. Provide a formal economic analysis of why honeybees find it in their interest to leave some nectar in each flower they visit. Can you think of any human activities that produce a similar outcome?

5. Classical economists struggled with the "water-diamond paradox," which seeks an explanation for why water, which is very useful, has a low price, whereas diamonds, which are not particularly important to life, have a high price. How would Smith explain the relative prices of water and diamonds? Would Ricardo's concept of diminishing returns pose some problem for this explanation? Can you resolve matters by using Marshall's model of supply and demand? Is water "very useful" to the demanders in Marshall's model?
6. In Figure 1.3 we examined the implications of a shift outward in the demand curve for a product and showed why this would cause the equilibrium price to rise. What kind of a shift in the supply curve would result in a similar price rise? How could you tell from market data whether a price rise were caused by a shift in the demand curve or by a shift in the supply curve?
7. Use the information from Application 1.2 to construct a simple supply-demand graph of the U.S. wheat market during the period described. Show how shifts in the demand curve for U.S. wheat can be used to explain the major price moves described in the application. What additional information would you need to decide whether this model is really adequate for explaining the wheat market during the period? Discuss some of the complications in the market that would not be accounted for by a simple supply-demand model.
8. Because Friedman's model of a pool player is based on clearly simplistic assumptions (most players do not explicitly know the laws of physics that apply to the game), it must be verified by empirical observations. How would you go about devising such a test of his model? What kind of evidence might refute the model?
9. Much of the "limits to growth" debate summarized in Application 1.3 is based on the notion that we are "running out" of resources. What does it mean to say we are "running out" of, say, oil? Since crude oil deposits were created many millions of years ago, haven't we been "running out" of it ever since prehistoric times? Can you make any economic sense of the possibility that the finiteness of oil supplies is "more important" today than it used to be? How would you know whether this was the case?
10. In the following conversation four economists are discussing whether the minimum wage should be increased:

    Economist A: "Increasing the minimum wage would reduce employment of minority teenagers."

    Economist B: "Increasing the minimum wage would be an unwarranted interference in the private relations between workers and their employers."

    Economist C: "Increasing the minimum wage would raise the incomes of some unskilled workers."

    Economist D: "Increasing the minimum wage would benefit higher wage workers and would probably be supported by organized labor."

    Which of these economists is using positive analysis and which is using normative analysis in arriving at his or her conclusions? Which of these predictions might be tested with empirical data? How might such tests be conducted?

CHAPTER 2

Mathematical Tools Used in Economics

Mathematics began to be widely used in economics near the end of the nineteenth century. For example, Marshall's *Principles of Economics,* published in 1890, included a lengthy mathematical appendix that developed his arguments more systematically than the book itself. Today, mathematics is indispensable for economists. They use it not to hide behind symbols or to make their arguments hard to understand, but to show their results precisely. Just as the physical sciences use mathematics, economists use it to move logically from the basic assumptions of a model to deriving the results of those assumptions. Without mathematics, this process would be both more cumbersome and less accurate.

The models we discuss in this book are based on mathematical arguments. Sometimes these arguments are presented step by step, and in other cases they are discussed in a less rigorous, more literary way. Although the mathematics we use here is no more complex than basic algebra, some of the theories themselves are based on more advanced mathematics. That level of mathematics may be presented in footnotes, but more often you will be told to go to more advanced works.

This chapter reviews some of the basic concepts of algebra. We then discuss a few issues that arise in applying those concepts to the study of economics. We use the tools introduced here throughout the rest of the book.

Functions of One Variable

The basic elements of algebra are called **variables.** These are usually called X and Y and may be given any numerical value. Sometimes the values of one

Variables
The basic elements of algebra, usually called X, Y, and so on, that may be given any numerical value in an equation.

Functional notation
A way of denoting the fact that the value taken on by one variable (Y) depends on the value taken on by some other variable (X) or set of variables.

Independent variable
In an algebraic equation, a variable that is unaffected by the action of another variable and may be assigned any value.

Dependent variable
In algebra, a variable whose value is determined by another variable or set of variables.

variable (Y) may be related to those of another variable (X) according to a specific functional relationship. This relationship is denoted by the **functional notation:**

$$Y = f(X). \tag{2.1}$$

This is read as saying, "Y is a function of X," meaning that the value of Y depends on the value given to X. For example, if we make X calories eaten per day and Y body weight, then Equation 2.1 shows the relationship between the amount of food intake and an individual's weight. The form of Equation 2.1 also shows causality. X is an **independent variable** and may be given any value. On the other hand, the value Y takes on is completely determined by X; Y is a **dependent variable.** The functional notation in Equation 2.1 shows that "X causes Y."

The exact functional relationship between X and Y may take on a wide variety of forms. The two most common ones are the following:

1. Y is a *linear function* of X. In this case

$$Y = a + bX, \tag{2.2}$$

where a and b are constants that may be given any numerical value. For example, if a = 3 and b = 2, Equation 2.2 would be written as

$$Y = 3 + 2X. \tag{2.3}$$

We could give Equation 2.3 an economic interpretation. For example, if we make Y the labor costs of a firm and X the number of labor hours hired, then the form of Equation 2.3 could record the relationship between costs and workers hired. In this case there is a fixed cost of $3 (when X = 0, Y = $3), and the wage rate is $2 per hour. A firm that hired 6 labor hours, for example, would incur total labor costs of $15 [= 3 + 2(6) = 3 + 12]. Table 2.1 illustrates some other values for this function for various values of X.

2. Y is a *quadratic function* of X. In this case

$$Y = a + bX + cX^2, \tag{2.4}$$

where a, b, and c are constants that may be given any numerical value. One specific example of a quadratic function would make a = −5, b = 6, and c = −1; Equation 2.4 would then be written as

$$Y = -5 + 6X - X^2. \tag{2.5}$$

We could also give an economic interpretation to Equation 2.5. Suppose we make Y the output of corn on an acre of land and X the amount of

Table 2.1
Values of X and Y for Linear and Quadratic Functions

Linear Function		Quadratic Function	
X	$Y = f(X)$ $= 3 + 2X$	X	$Y = f(X)$ $= -5 + 6X - X^2$
−3	−3	−3	−32
−2	−1	−2	−21
−1	1	−1	−12
0	3	0	−5
1	5	1	0
2	7	2	3
3	9	3	4
4	11	4	3
5	13	5	0
6	15	6	−5

fertilizer applied to that land. In this case, the ability of fertilizer to increase corn output declines as more fertilizer is added. This decline can be easily seen later when we illustrate the graph of this equation in Figure 2.4.

Sometimes it may be useful to look at the relationship between X and Y for several different values of X. Table 2.1 lists the values for Y for the integral values of X between −3 and +6 for both the linear and quadratic functions. Of course, many more values of X (including fractional values) could have been included in this table, and you should be able to compute the value for Y for any preassigned value of X.

Graphing Functions of One Variable

When we write down the functional relationship between X and Y, we are summarizing all there is to know about that relationship. In principle, this book, or any book that uses mathematics, could be written using only these equations. Graphs of some of these functions, however, are very helpful. Graphs not only make it easier for us to understand certain arguments, they also can take the place of a lot of the mathematical notation that must be developed. For these reasons, this book relies heavily on graphs to develop its basic economic models. Here we will look at a few simple graphing techniques.

A graph is simply one way to show the relationship between two variables. Usually the values of the dependent variable (Y) are shown on the vertical axis, and the values of the independent variable (X) are shown on the hori-

Figure 2.1
Graph of the Linear Function Y = 3 + 2X

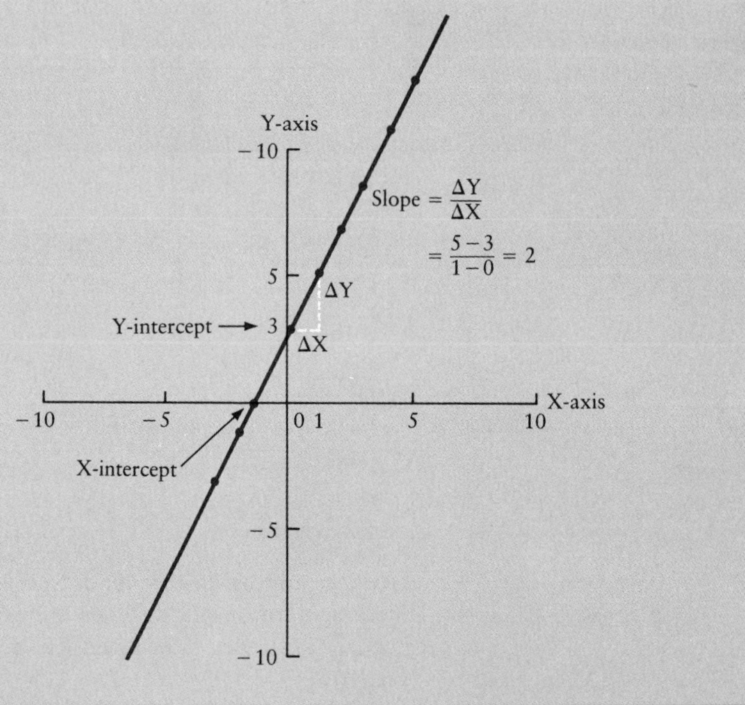

The Y-intercept is 3, when X = 0, Y = 3. The slope of the line is 2: an increase by 1 in X will increase Y by 2.

zontal axis.[1] Figure 2.1 uses this form to graph Equation 2.3. Although we use heavy dots to show only the points of this function that are listed in Table 2.1, the graph applies to the function of every possible value of X. The graph of Equation 2.3 is a straight line, which is why this is called a **linear function.** In Figure 2.1, X and Y can take on both positive and negative values. The variables used in economics generally take on only positive values, and therefore we only have to use the upper right-hand (positive) quadrant of the axes.

Linear function
An equation that is represented by a straight-line graph.

Linear Functions: Intercepts and Slopes

Slope
The direction of a line on a graph. Shows the change in Y that results from a unit change in X.

Intercept
The value of Y when X equals zero.

Two important features of the graph in Figure 2.1 are its **slope** and its **intercept** on the Y-axis. The Y-intercept is the value of Y when X is equal to 0.

[1]In economics this convention is not always followed. Sometimes a dependent variable is shown on the horizontal axis as, for example, in the case of demand and supply curves. In that case the independent variable (price) is shown on the vertical axis and the dependent variable (quantity) on the horizontal axis.

For example, as we can see in Figure 2.1, when X = 0, Y = 3; this means that 3 is the Y-intercept.[2] In the general linear form of Equation 2.2,

$$Y = a + bX,$$

the Y-intercept will be Y = a, since this is the value of Y when X = 0.

We define the slope of any straight line to be the ratio of the change in Y to the change in X for a movement along the line. The slope can be defined mathematically as

$$\text{Slope} = \frac{\text{Change in Y}}{\text{Change in X}} = \frac{\Delta Y}{\Delta X},$$

where the Δ ("delta") notation simply means "change in." For the particular function shown in Figure 2.1, the slope is equal to 2. We can clearly see from the dashed lines, representing changes in X and Y, that a given change in X is met by a change of twice that amount in Y. Table 2.1 shows the same result—for example, as X increases from 0 to 1, Y increases from 3 to 5. Consequently

$$\text{Slope} = \frac{\Delta Y}{\Delta X} = \frac{5-3}{1-0} = 2.$$

It should be obvious that this is true for all the other points in Table 2.1. Everywhere along the straight line, the slope is the same. Generally, for any linear function, the slope is given by b in Equation 2.2.[3] The slope of a straight line may be positive (as it is in Figure 2.1) or it may be negative, in which case the line would run from upper left to lower right.

A straight line may also have a slope of 0, which is a horizontal line. In this case the value of Y is constant; changes in X will not affect Y. The function would be Y = a + 0X, or Y = a. This equation is represented by a horizontal line (parallel to the X-axis) through point a on the Y-axis.

Slope and Units of Measurement

The slope of a function depends on the units in which X and Y are measured. For example, a study of a family's consumption of oranges might discover

[2]One can also speak of the X-intercept of a function, which is defined to be that value of X for which Y = 0. For Equation 2.3 it is easy to see that Y = 0 when $X = -\frac{3}{2}$, which is then the X-intercept. The X-intercept for the general linear function in Equation 2.2 is given by X = −a/b, as may be seen by substituting that value into the equation.

[3]In calculus, mathematicians call the slope of a function at a particular point "the derivative" and denote this concept by dY/dX where the d means the change in Y brought about by a very small change in X. For the general linear Equation 2.2, dY/dX = b.

that the number of oranges (Y) purchased in a week is equal to 3 + 2X, where X is the family's income measured in hundreds of dollars per week. Consequently, $\Delta Y/\Delta X = 2$: that is, a \$100 increase in income one week causes 2 more oranges to be purchased. If income (X) is measured in single dollars, the relationship is $Y = 3 + .02X$ and $\Delta Y/\Delta X = .02$. In this case, although the interpretation of this slope is the same (a \$100 increase in income still increases orange purchases by 2 per week), the numerical value of the slope is very different. Similarly, if Y were measured in dozens of oranges per week and X in hundreds of dollars, the relationship would be $Y = \frac{1}{4} + \frac{1}{6}X$. An increase in family income of \$100 still increases orange purchases by 2 ($\frac{1}{6}$ of a dozen), but now the slope is different again. Clearly, one must be very careful when discussing "the" slope of a function to know how the variables are measured. In later chapters we look at some methods that help solve this "units" problem.

Changes in Slope

Quite often in this text we are interested in changing the parameters (that is, a and b) of a linear function. We can do this in two ways; we can change the Y-intercept, or we can change the slope. Figure 2.2 shows the graph of the function

$$Y = -X + 10. \quad [2.6]$$

This linear function has a slope of -1 and a Y-intercept of $Y = 10$. Figure 2.2 also shows the function

$$Y = -2X + 10. \quad [2.7]$$

We have doubled the slope of Equation 2.6 from -1 to -2 and kept the Y-intercept at $Y = 10$. This causes the graph of the function to become steeper and to rotate about the Y-intercept. In general, a change in the slope of a function will cause this kind of rotation without changing the value of its Y-intercept. Since a linear function takes on the value of its Y-intercept when $X = 0$, changing the slope will not change the value of the function at this point.

Changes in Intercept

Figure 2.3 also shows a graph of the function $Y = -X + 10$. It shows the effect of changes in the constant term, that is, the Y-intercept only, while the slope stays at -1. Figure 2.3 shows the graphs of

$$Y = -X + 12 \quad [2.8]$$

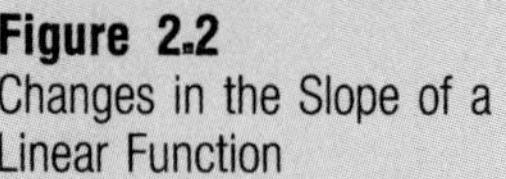

Figure 2.2
Changes in the Slope of a Linear Function

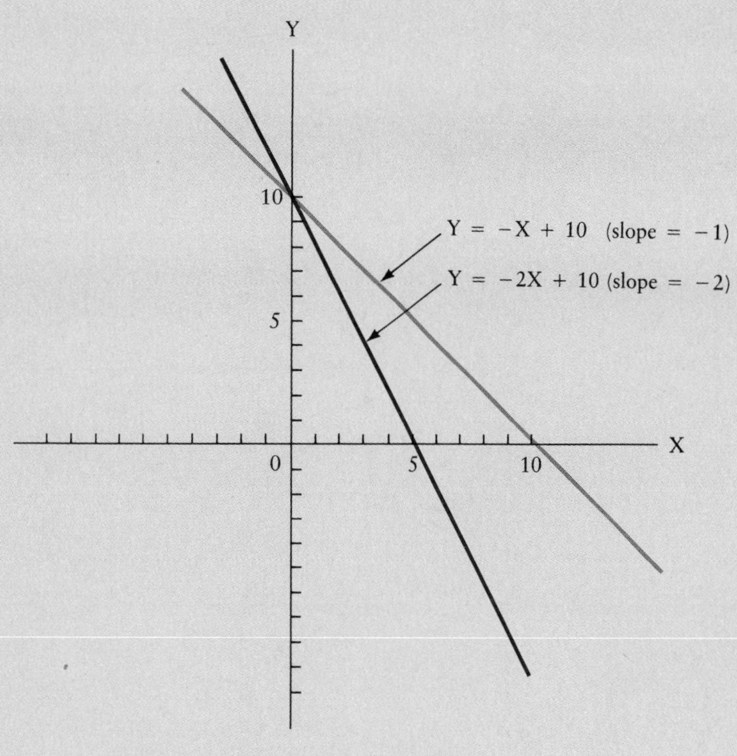

When the slope of a linear function is changed but the Y-intercept remains fixed, the graph of the function rotates about the Y-intercept.

and

$$Y = -X + 5. \quad [2.9]$$

All three lines are parallel; they have the same slope. Changing the Y-intercept only makes the line shift up and down; its slope does not change. Of course, changes in the Y-intercepts also cause the X-intercepts to change, and you can see these new intercepts.

You should also be able to see that the graphs of any two linear functions are different only in their slopes and Y-intercepts. In this book we usually discuss changes in slopes and changes in Y-intercepts separately. Although the economic context will vary, the mathematical form of these changes will be of the general type shown in Figures 2.2 and 2.3. These graphs are quite helpful for showing the effects of changes in economic circumstances. Applica-

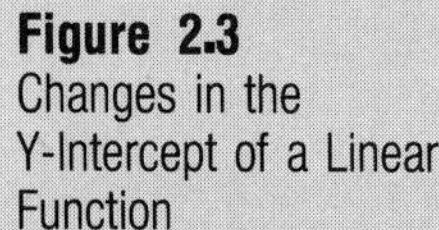

Figure 2.3
Changes in the Y-Intercept of a Linear Function

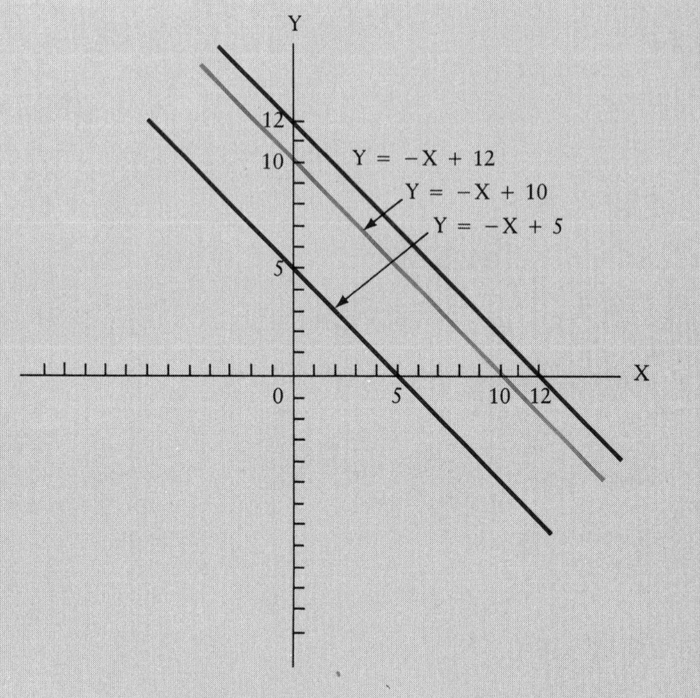

When the Y-intercept of a function is changed, the graph of the function shifts up or down and is parallel to the other graphs.

tion 2.1: Property Tax Assessment uses these linear concepts to illustrate one such application that may be depressingly familiar to homeowners.

Nonlinear Functions

Quadratic function
An equation that includes terms in X^2 and (possibly) X.

Nonlinear functions of one variable are also simple to graph. Figure 2.4 shows the graph of the **quadratic function** in Equation 2.5:

$$Y = -5 + 6X - X^2. \quad [2.10]$$

Heavy dots again show the points listed in Table 2.1, although the function could also, with a bit of effort, be computed for fractional values of X as well as for the integral values shown in the table. The Y-intercept is the constant

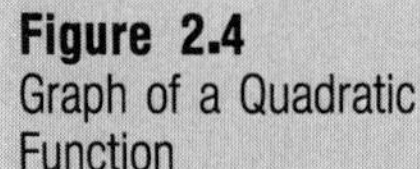

Figure 2.4
Graph of a Quadratic Function

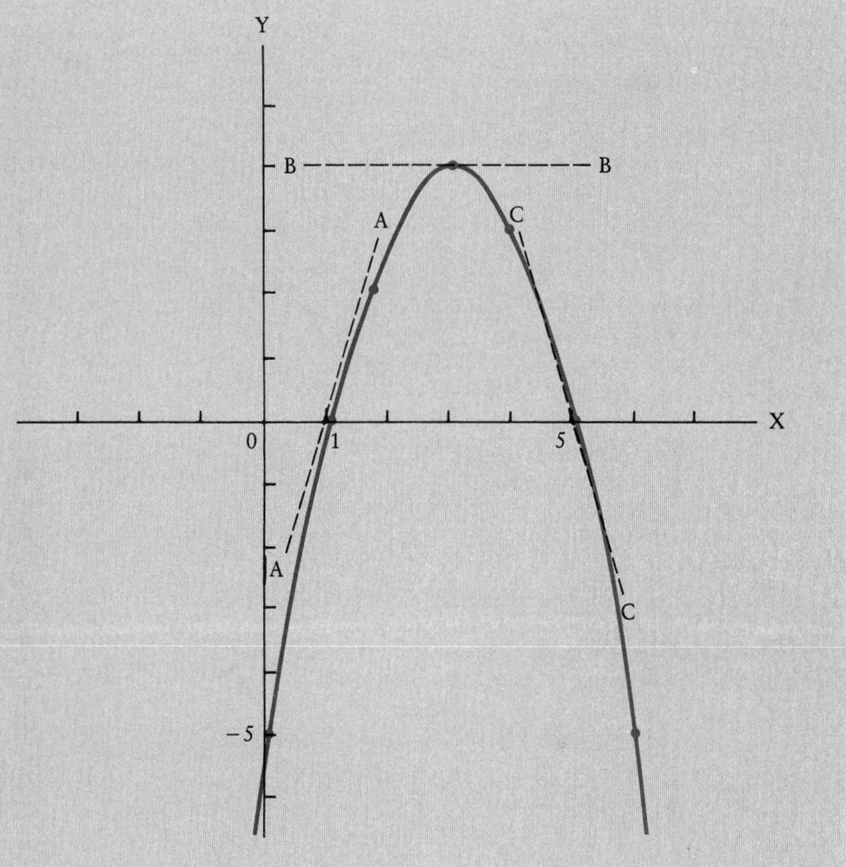

The slope of a nonlinear curve at any point is the slope of a line tangent to the curve at that point. For example, at the point X = 3, Y = 4, the slope of the diagrammed function is 0. This is the slope of the line BB.

term (−5) in Equation 2.5.[4] In general, unlike linear functions, the slope of a nonlinear function is not the same everywhere.

---

[4]The X-intercepts (the values of X for which Y = 0) are called the "roots" of the quadratic function. They may be found by using the quadratic formula, which states that if $Y = a + bX + cX^2$, the roots are given by

$$X = \frac{-b \pm \sqrt{b^2 - 4ac}}{2c}.$$

You should be able to show that this formula provides the roots X = 1 and X = 5 for the example shown in the text.

APPLICATION 2.1

Property Tax Assessment

Property taxes are the most important source of local revenues in the United States. In most communities they pay for schools, local police forces, the fire department, and so forth. Conceptually, figuring what a property owner owes in taxes is a simple matter—the town assessors multiply the tax rate by the market value of the property. A major problem with this procedure is that precise current market values for most properties are not known since properties only rarely change hands. To come up with accurate market values, localities increasingly have turned toward sophisticated computer methods to assess properties.

A Simple Linear Model

Consider the case of houses. Local property assessors begin by collecting information on all houses that were recently sold. With these data they can estimate a relationship between sales price (Y) and some relevant characteristic of the house, say, its square footage (X). Such a relationship might be stated as

$$Y = \$10{,}000 + \$50X. \quad [1]$$

This equation means that a house with zero square footage (X = 0) should sell for $10,000 (because of the value of its land), and each square foot of living space adds $50 to the value of the house. Using the square footage of a house, the assessor can "predict" its current value by using Equation 1. This procedure is shown in Figure 1. According to the figure, a house with 2,000 square feet of living space would have a market value of $110,000, and one with 3,000 square feet would be worth $160,000.

Valuing Other Features of Homes

Of course, the procedures used in actual property assessment are considerably more complicated than this. For example, assessors must take into account far more features of houses than square footage. One way to do that is to use current sales information to value other factors, such as a nice view. Suppose current sales suggest that a view is worth $30,000 in the current housing market. The values for houses with views can be computed by

$$Y = \$30{,}000 + \$10{,}000 + \$50X = \$40{,}000 + \$50X. \quad [2]$$

Figure 1
Relationship between the Floor Area of a House and Its Market Value

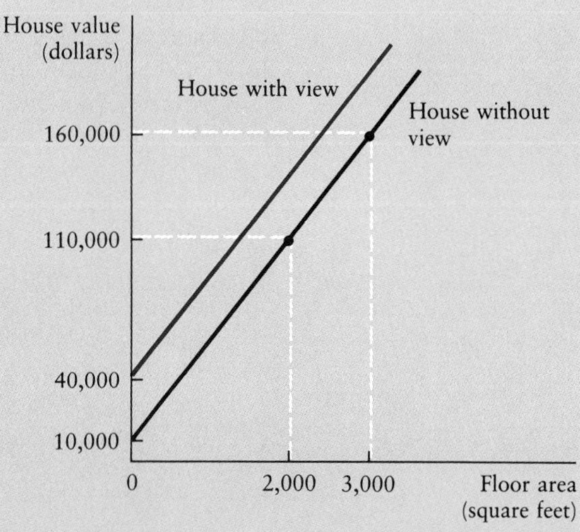

Using data on recent house sales, real estate appraisers can calculate a relationship between floor area (X—measured in square feet) and market value (Y). The entire relationship shifts upward by $30,000 if a house has a nice view.

That is, having a view shifts the relationship between living space and value up by a constant $30,000. This relationship is also shown in Figure 1. You can now use this figure to predict that 2,000 and 3,000 square foot houses with views are worth $140,000 and $190,000, respectively. Using similar procedures allows the assessor to evaluate all possible types of houses.

To Think About

1. Suppose spectacular views are more valuable in large houses than in small ones because large houses have more space for picture windows. How would this effect be represented with algebra and in a graph for property tax assessment?
2. Do you think that using these mathematical methods for assessment ends people's disputes over their tax bills? How would you argue with an assessor who tried to use the equations in this example to calculate your taxes?

We define the slope of a nonlinear function at some particular point as the slope of the straight line that is tangent to the function at that point. For example, the slope of the function in Figure 2.4 at the point X = 1, Y = 0 is given by the slope of the line AA. The slope at the point X = 3, Y = 4 is given by the slope of the line BB; at the point X = 5, Y = 0, the slope is given by the line CC. When the function reaches its highest point (at X = 3, Y = 4), the slope of the function is 0. To the left of this highest point the graph has a positive slope, and to the right of it the slope is negative. We can define the slopes of much more complex curves in the same way by looking at the slope of the straight line tangent to the curves.[5]

Whenever a function reaches its maximum value, the slope of the function generally will be 0 at that point. To use a mountain as an illustration, the slope of the ground at the mountaintop must be 0. Otherwise you would not be on the top, since walking in the appropriate direction will put you higher. Only if the slope is 0 will you be unable to go higher. Since throughout this book we are interested in maximum (that is highest) points, this mountain example is very helpful to keep in mind.

The fact that the slope of a function (or of its graph) must be 0 at a maximum point is very important in economics. The marginalist ideas in Chapter 1 grew directly out of this mathematical law. As long as the slope of a function is positive, increasing X will increase Y also. If Y is crop yield and X is fertilizer, adding fertilizer will increase yields if the slope of the graph is positive. The law of diminishing returns, however, implies that this slope will decline as fertilizer use (X) increases. If the slope becomes zero, adding X will not raise crop yields at all—the marginal value of fertilizer is zero. Application 2.2: The Changing U.S. Income Tax Structure illustrates these marginal ideas in the context of recent tax "reform" initiatives.

Functions of Two or More Variables

Economists are usually concerned with functions of more than just one variable, since there is almost always more than a single cause of an economic outcome. To see the effects of many causes, economists must work with functions of several variables. A two-variable function might be written in functional notation as

$$Y = f(X, Z). \qquad [2.11]$$

This equation shows that Y's values depend on the values of two independent variables, X and Z. For example, an individual's weight (Y) depends not only on calories eaten (X), but also on how much the individual exercises (Z). In-

[5]In elementary calculus it is shown that the slope of Y = f(X) at some point is given by the value of the derivative of this function at that point. For Equation 2.5, $dY/dX = -2X + 6$. At X = 1 the slope is +4, at X = 3 it is 0, and at X = 5 the slope is −4. The function reaches its maximum value when the derivative (and the slope) is equal to 0.

APPLICATION 2.2

The Changing U.S. Income Tax Structure

The mathematical concept of slope and the economic idea of marginalism are clearly related since both refer to a change in one variable brought about by a small change in some other variable. We can see this relationship in the determination of income taxes.

Progressive Income Taxation

Many governments use income taxes as their principal source of revenue, and most of the rate schedules for those taxes are "progressive"; that is, the proportion of income paid in taxes is greater for people with high incomes than for people with low incomes. Marginal tax rates (that is, the rate of tax on the last dollar earned) increase with increasing income levels, and it is this feature that leads to progressivity.

The top half of Table 1 shows federal income taxes owed by taxpayers at various income levels under rates that prevailed for married couples in 1980. Marginal tax rates, which are shown in the second column of the table, were steeply progressive rising from 21 percent for a couple with a taxable income of $10,000 to 59 percent for someone earning $100,000. The top marginal tax rate in 1980 was 70 percent for couples with incomes over $215,000. The third and fourth columns of Table 1 show the effects of these rates on taxes owed. Because some income is excluded from taxes for all taxpayers and because marginal tax rates apply only to the last dollar earned, average tax rates always fall below marginal tax rates. Still, judged by the percentage of taxable income paid in taxes, the federal income tax was quite progressive in 1980.

These features of the U.S. tax structure are shown graphically in Figure 1. In this figure, the curve 0T shows the relationship between taxable income and tax liabilities under the 1980 rate schedules. Increasing marginal tax rates are reflected by the increasing slope of the 0T curve. Average tax rates, on the other hand, can be calculated from the curve as the slope of a ray through the origin to the appropriate point on 0T. The slope of the ray 0A, for example, shows that the average tax rate for a couple with a taxable income of $50,000 is 32.9 percent (= $16,444/$50,000). If we drew rays similar to 0A for higher income levels, these would be steeper than 0A thereby showing how aver-

Figure 1

Graphic Representation of the Relationship between Taxable Income and Tax Liability

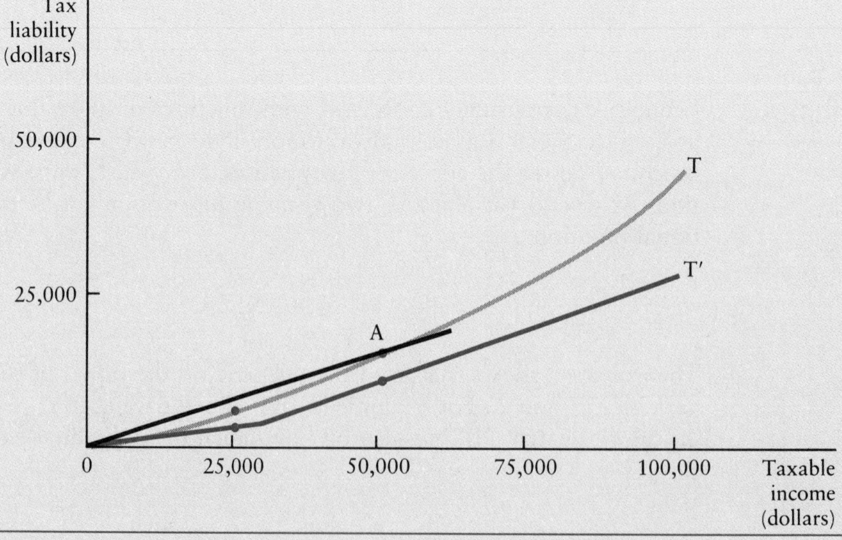

The curve 0T shows the relationship between taxable income and federal income taxes owed that prevailed in 1980. Increasing marginal tax rates are reflected by the increasing slope of 0T whereas increasing average tax rates are shown by the increasing slopes of rays (such as 0A) through the origin to 0T. The Tax Reform Act of 1986 lowered both marginal and average rates of income taxation, shifting the curve to 0T′.

Table 1
Federal Income Tax Liabilities in 1980 and 1986

Taxable Annual Income	Marginal Tax Rate (Percent)	Taxes Owed	Average Tax Rate (Percent)
	Liabilities under 1980 Schedule		
$ 10,000	21	$ 1,719	17.2
25,000	32	5,721	22.8
50,000	49	16,444	32.9
100,000	59	44,004	44.0
	Liabilities under 1986 Schedule		
$ 10,000	15	$ 1,500	15.0
25,000	15	3,750	15.0
50,000	33	11,100	22.2
100,000	33	27,600	27.6

Note: Figures apply to a married couple taking the standard deduction. Tax liabilities apply to taxable income, not gross income, which is larger.

Source: Author's tax forms, courtesy the Internal Revenue Service.

age tax rates increase. Similarly, for incomes les than $50,000, rays through the origin would be flatter than 0A showing that lower income couples paid lower average tax rates. Elsewhere in this book we will frequently use this method to illustrate the relationship between marginal magnitudes (as reflected by the slope of a curve) and average magnitudes (as reflected by the slopes of rays through the origin).

The Reagan Tax Reforms

High marginal tax rates that prevailed as of 1980 were one of the principal targets of tax policy under the Reagan administration. It was argued that such high rates harmed individuals' incentives to work and to save and that the rates only encouraged tax avoidance and evasion. Starting with the Economic Recovery Act of 1981, Congress and the president agreed on a phased-in program of reductions in marginal (and average) tax rates in the hope of improving U.S. economic performance. The final installment of the Reagan tax reductions was implemented as the Tax Reform Act of 1986. When fully implemented (by 1989), this act specified a very simple tax schedule with much lower marginal rates: Incomes between 0 and $30,000 were to be taxed at 15 percent whereas income over $30,000 was to be taxed at 33 percent. For example, a couple with an income of $50,000 would pay $11,100 in tax—$4,500 on the first $30,000 and $6,600 on the next $20,000. Hence, both the marginal tax rate (33 percent) and the average tax rate (22.2 percent = $11,100/$50,000) were much lower for such a couple than they had been in 1980.[1]

The final effects of these reductions are illustrated in the bottom half of Table 1 and by the curve 0T′ in Figure 1. Notice especially how the simple two-bracket form for the schedule specified in 1986 resulted in the tax curve 0T′ having two linear segments. The kink in the curve at $30,000 reflects the change in marginal tax rates at that income level. Of course, considerable controversy remains over whether these reductions really did prompt people to work and save more. And the effects of the reductions seem to have helped cause the budget deficits encountered in the late 1980s. At many spots in this book, therefore, we will return to examine additional issues involved in studying the effects of taxation on economic behavior.

To Think About

1. Income tax "progressivity" is usually judged by the ratio of tax liability to income for various income levels. Does an income tax need to have increasing marginal rates to be "progressive" under this definition? Is the post-1989 income tax schedule much less progressive than the one that prevailed in the early 1980s? Can you develop a geometric analysis of the relationship between a progressive income tax and a set of increasing marginal rates?
2. The income tax schedules in this example are applied to "taxable income," but the definition of this concept has also changed over time. How would adoption of an increasingly broad definition of taxable income affect the tax schedules illustrated? How would such a change affect conclusions about the progressivity of the tax system?

[1]In an attempt to ameliorate revenue losses from these tax reductions, the 33 percent rate includes an extra 5 percent surtax imposed for incomes between $30,000 and $108,000. For incomes over $108,000, the marginal tax rate declines to 28 percent. We have not shown this in Figure 1.

creases in X increase Y but increases in Z decrease Y. The functional notation in Equation 2.11 hints at the possibility that there might be trade-offs between eating and exercise. In Chapter 3 we will start to explore such trade-offs.

A Simple Example

In general, we could have Y depend on the values of more than two variables, but a simple two-variable function can be used to explain most of the relevant facts about how multiple variable functions work. Suppose the relationship between Y, X, and Z is given by

$$Y = X \cdot Z. \qquad [2.12]$$

The form of this particular function is widely used in economics. Later chapters use a closely related form to show the utility (Y) that an individual receives from using two goods (X and Z) and also to show the production relationship between an output (Y) and two inputs (say, labor, X, and capital, Z). Here, however, we are interested mainly in this function's mathematical properties.

Some values for the function in Equation 2.12 are recorded in Table 2.2. Two important facts are shown by this table. First, even if one of the variables is held constant (say, at $X = 2$), changes in the other independent variable (Z) will cause the value of the dependent variable (Y) to change. The value of Y increases from 4 to 6 as Z rises from 2 to 3, even though X is held constant. In economic terms, this illustrates the "marginal" influence of variable Z. Second, several different combinations of X and Z will result in the same value of Y. For example, $Y = 4$ if $X = 2, Z = 2$ or if $X = 1, Z = 4$ (or, indeed, for an infinite number of other X, Z combinations if fractions are used). Using this equality of values of Y for a number of X, Z combinations, functions of two variables can be graphed rather simply.

Graphing Functions of Two Variables

We would need to use three dimensions to graph a function of two variables completely: one axis for X, one for Z, and one for Y. Drawing three-dimensional graphs in a two-dimensional book is very difficult. Not only must an artist be good enough to be able to show depth in only two dimensions, but the reader must have enough imagination to read the graph as a three-dimensional model. Since economists are not necessarily good artists (and some would argue because economists lack imagination), they graph these functions another way that is much like the techniques mapmakers use.

Contour lines
Lines in two dimensions that show the sets of values of the independent variables that yield the same value for the dependent variable.

Mapmakers are also confined to working with two-dimensional drawings. They use **contour lines** to show the third dimension. These are lines of equal altitude that outline the physical features of the territory being mapped. For example, a contour line labeled "1,000 feet" on a map shows all those points

Table 2.2
Values of X, Z, and Y That Satisfy the Relationship $Y = X \cdot Z$

X	Z	Y
1	1	1
1	2	2
1	3	3
1	4	4
2	1	2
2	2	4
2	3	6
2	4	8
3	1	3
3	2	6
3	3	9
3	4	12
4	1	4
4	2	8
4	3	12
4	4	16

of land that are 1,000 feet above sea level. By using a number of contour lines, mapmakers can show the heights and steepness of mountains and the depths of valleys and ocean trenches. In this way they add the third dimension to a two-dimensional map.

Economists also use contour lines; that is, lines of equal "altitude." Equation 2.12 can be graphed in two dimensions (one dimension for the values of X and another dimension for values of Z), with contour lines to show the values of Y, the third dimension. This equation is graphed in Figure 2.5, with three contour lines: one each for $Y = 1$, $Y = 4$, and $Y = 9$.

Each of the contour lines in Figure 2.5 is a rectangular hyperbola. The contour line labeled "$Y = 1$" is a graph of

$$Y = 1 = X \cdot Z, \qquad [2.13]$$

"$Y = 4$" is a graph of

$$Y = 4 = X \cdot Z, \qquad [2.14]$$

and the line labeled "$Y = 9$" is a graph of

$$Y = 9 = X \cdot Z. \qquad [2.15]$$

Some of the values along these contour lines are shown in Table 2.2. It would be easy to compute other points on the curves. Other contour lines for the function could also be drawn by making Y equal to the desired level and graphing the resulting relationship between X and Z. Since we can give Y any value we want, an infinite number of contour lines can be drawn. In this way

Figure 2.5
Contour Lines for
$Y = X \cdot Z$

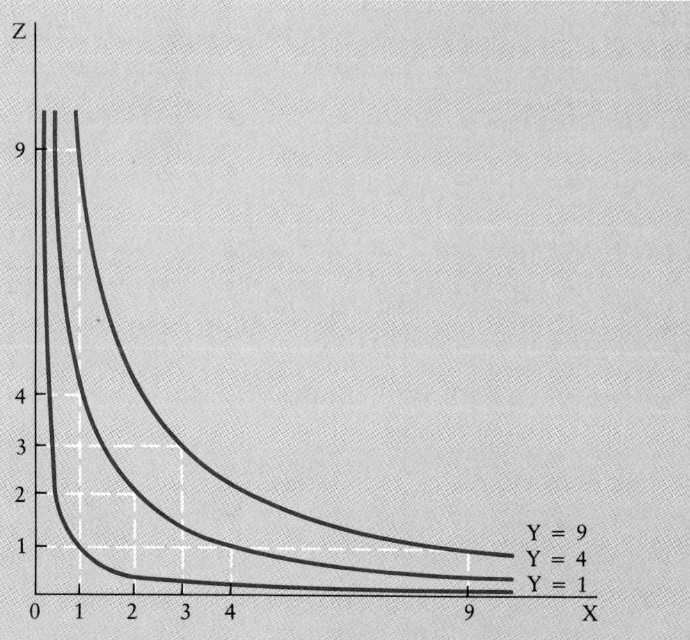

Contour lines for the function $Y = X \cdot Z$ are rectangular hyperbolas. They can be represented by making Y equal to various supplied values (here $Y = 1$, $Y = 4$, and $Y = 9$), and then graphing the relationship between the independent variables X and Z.

we can show the original function in Equation 2.12 as accurately as we want without even resorting to three dimensions. One practical application of this type of graph is discussed in Application 2.3: Oil Pipelines.

Simultaneous Equations

Simultaneous equations A set of equations with more than one variable that must be solved together for a particular solution.

Another mathematical concept that is often used in economics is **simultaneous equations.** When two variables (say, X and Y) are related by two different equations, it is sometimes, though not always, possible to solve these equations together for a single set of values for X and Y that satisfies both of the equations. For example, it is easy to see that the two equations

$$\begin{aligned} X + Y &= 3 \\ X - Y &= 1 \end{aligned} \tag{2.16}$$

have a unique solution of

$$\begin{aligned} X &= 2 \\ Y &= 1. \end{aligned} \tag{2.17}$$

APPLICATION 2.3

Oil Pipelines

The amount of crude oil that can be put through a pipeline depends on the diameter of the pipe and the force with which the oil is pumped. Although a number of other engineering issues are involved, a simple mathematical model of pipeline throughput closely resembles the algebraic example discussed in the previous section. Specifically, if we make Y the amount of oil pumped (measured in thousands of barrels per day), X the pumping force applied (in thousands of horsepower), and Z the pipe diameter (in inches), the approximate relationship is[1]

$$Y = 4\sqrt{X \cdot Z}. \qquad [1]$$

This equation makes clear that there are many ways to obtain a throughput of, say, 50,000 barrels per day. A 12-inch pipeline requires about 13,000 horsepower to pump this amount. A 16-inch pipeline needs only 10,000 horsepower to pump the same amount. These combinations are illustrated in Figure 1, which shows a portion of the Y = 50 contour line for Equation 1. This contour line is a graph of the equation

$$Y^2 = 2{,}500 = 16X \cdot Z$$
$$156.25 = X \cdot Z. \qquad [2]$$

Other contour lines for higher and lower levels of oil pipeline throughout can be calculated in the same manner.

The importance of this kind of information to pipeline planners should be obvious. Knowing that they can achieve pipeline throughput a number of different ways, they can figure out how to do so in the least costly way by taking account of the prices of pipe and pumps, for example. In Chapter 9 we examine the general issue of input choices and how they are affected by input prices in considerable detail. Contour lines similar to the one shown in Figure 1 will play an important role in our analysis since they illustrate the options open to a firm.

Figure 1
Alternative Combinations of Pumping Force and Pipeline Diameter That Allow a Throughput of 50,000 Barrels per Day

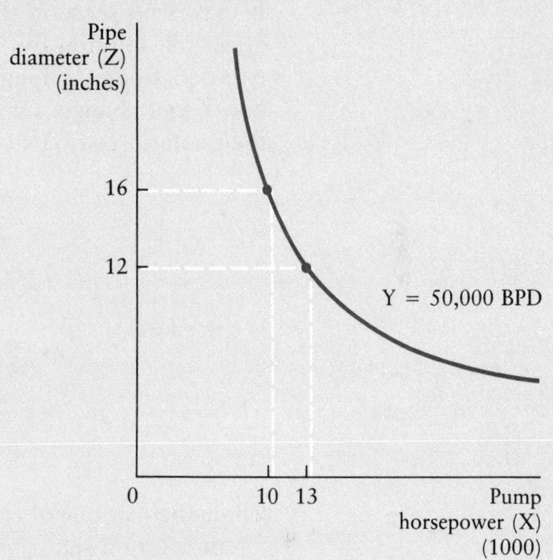

Using the relationship between output (Y), pumping force (X), and pipeline diameter (Z), we can draw a contour line for Y = 50 (thousand barrels per day). This curve shows that there are a number of ways to achieve this same level of throughput.

To Think About

1. Suppose a pipeline firm wished to move 50,000 barrels of crude oil per day as cheaply as possible. What would this firm need to know in order to decide what size pipeline to build? Can you illustrate this choice in Figure 1?
2. Suppose pipeline throughput depends not only on pipe diameter and horsepower, but also on the nature of the terrain (whether the pipeline goes uphill or downhill). How might this be reflected in Equation 2? How would it alter Figure 1?

[1]This relationship is adapted from L. Cookenboo, *Crude Oil Pipelines and Competition in the Petroleum Industry* (Cambridge, Mass.: Harvard University Press, 1955).

These equations operate "simultaneously" to determine the solutions for X and Y. One of the equations alone cannot determine each variable—the solution depends on both of the equations.

Changing Solutions for Simultaneous Equations

It makes no sense in these equations to ask how a change in, say, X would affect the solution for Y. There is only one solution for X and Y from these two equations. As long as both equations must hold, the values of neither X nor Y can change. Of course, if the equations themselves are changed, then their solution will also change. For example, the equation system

$$X + Y = 5$$
$$X - Y = 1 \qquad [2.18]$$

is solved as

$$X = 3$$
$$Y = 2. \qquad [2.19]$$

Changing just one of the parameters in Equation 2.16 gives us an entirely different solution set.

Graphing Simultaneous Equations

These results are illustrated in Figure 2.6. The two equations in the set in Equation 2.16 are straight lines that intersect at the point (2, 1). This point is the solution to the two equations since it is the only one that lies on both lines. Changing the constant in the first equation of this system gives us a different intersection for Equation 2.18. In that case the lines intersect at point (3, 2), and that is the new solution. Even though only one of the lines shifted, both X and Y take on new solutions.

The similarity between the algebraic graph in Figure 2.6 and the supply and demand graphs in Figures 1.2 and 1.3 is striking. The point of intersection of two curves is called a "solution" in algebra and an "equilibrium" in economics, but in both cases we are finding the point that satisfies both relationships. The shift of the demand curve in Figure 1.3 clearly resembles the change in the simultaneous equation set in Figure 2.6. In both cases the shift in one of the curves results in new solutions for both of the variables. Marshall's analogy of the blades of the supply and demand "scissors" determining market price and quantity can be seen in the algebraic notion of simultaneous systems and their solutions. Throughout this book we will be using such supply-demand intersections to show how markets arrive at

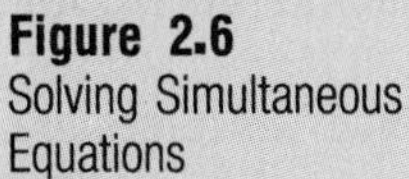

Figure 2.6
Solving Simultaneous Equations

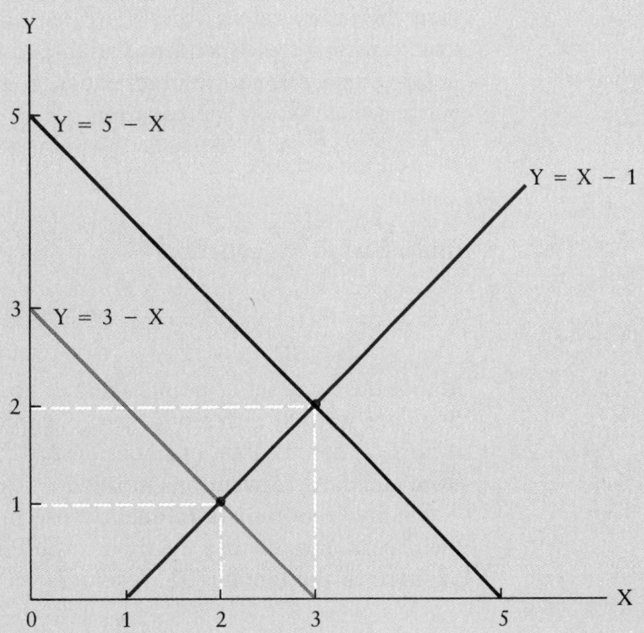

The linear equations X + Y = 3 (Y = 3 − X) and X − Y = 1 (Y = X − 1) can be solved simultaneously to find X = 2, Y = 1. This solution is shown by the point of intersection of the graphs of the two equations. If the first equation is changed (to X + Y = 5, or Y = 5 − X), the solution will also change (to X = 3, Y = 2).

equilibrium outcomes that satisfy both supply and demand relationships simultaneously.

Special Features of Mathematics in Economics

A few peculiarities arise when the mathematical tools described in this chapter are applied to economic problems. First, as we mentioned before, practically all the variables used in economic analysis can take on only positive values. Economists talk about prices, quantities of output, and quantities of factors of production. In most situations these variables are either positive or zero; a negative price or quantity would have no meaning. Most graphs in this book show only the positive quadrant and its axes, where both of the variables are always nonnegative.

A second peculiarity is the economist's tendency to "reverse" the axes in a graph by putting the dependent variable on the horizontal axis. The supply and demand graphs in Figures 1.2 and 1.3 show this arrangement. Economists usually assume that price is the independent variable in a supply and demand situation and that individuals and firms react to this price by choosing the quantities they will demand and the quantities they will produce, respectively. As we show later in Part 4, economists use the vertical axis to record the independent variable (price) in these relations and the horizontal axis to record the dependent variable (quantity).

Of course, the nature of an equation is not affected by which variables are put on which axes. The equation

$$Y = 2 + 2X \tag{2.20}$$

is identical to the equation

$$X = \tfrac{1}{2}Y - 1 \tag{2.21}$$

in that the same set of points satisfies both equations. Nevertheless, the equations are written differently (for example, the slope of Equation 2.21 is the reciprocal of the slope of Equation 2.20), and we should keep this departure from standard conventions in mind.

Subscripts
Small numbers used at the bottom of variables to identify them as separate variables.

Finally, economists frequently use more than two or three variables in their work and identify them with **subscripts**. Instead of using more letters in addition to the familiar X, Y, and Z, economists identify variables as

$$X_1, X_2, X_3, \ldots, X_n,$$

where each X_i is a separate variable. In this way many variables can be used with a very compact notation.

Summary

This chapter reviews material that should be familiar to you from prior math classes. What we have done here is to go over some basic algebra and show how simple functions can be graphed. Some of the results presented here that will be used throughout the rest of this book are:

- Linear equations have graphs that are straight lines. These lines are described by their slopes and by their intercepts with the Y-axis.
- Changes in the slope cause the graph of a linear equation to rotate about its Y-intercept. Changes in the Y-intercept cause the graph to shift in a parallel way.
- Nonlinear equations have graphs that have curved shapes. The most common such shapes are parabolas and hyperbolas.
- Economists often use functions of two or more variables because economic outcomes have many causes. These functions can sometimes be graphed in two dimensions by using contour lines.
- Simultaneous equations determine solutions for two (or more) variables that satisfy all of the equations. An important use of such equations is to show how supply and demand curves determine equilibrium prices. For that reason, such equations are widely encountered in economics.

Review Questions

1. Using mathematics presents a number of advantages for economists in their construction of models of the economy. What are some of those advantages? In what ways does the use of mathematical models help avoid "mistakes" in model construction? Can you think of disadvantages in using mathematics? Are certain mistakes more likely in mathematical models than would be the case with less formal ways of constructing economic theories?
2. When we use the functional notation $Y = f(X)$, we mean that for each possible value of X there is precisely one value of Y. What does this imply about the graphs of functions? Can you think of graphs that cannot be represented by simple functions (how about a circle, for example)? Can you think of any economic situations in which a functional representation might not be appropriate—that is, can you think of economic activities where a single value for X might be consistent with several different values for Y?
3. If a graph of a linear function has a positive slope, what does this imply about the qualitative relationship between X and Y—do increases in X increase or decrease Y? Which of the following linear relationships have positive slopes?

   a. $Y = 3 + 5X$.
   b. $Y = 3 - 5X$.
   c. $Y + 5X = 3$.
   d. $Y - 5X = 3$.
   e. $-Y + 5X = 3$.
   f. $-Y - 5X = 3$.

   Answer this question also for the case of negatively sloped linear functions. Describe the qualitative relationship between two variables whose graph is a negatively sloped line, and indicate which of the listed functions have negative slopes.
4. Application 2.1 shows how a property tax assessment formula based on square footage might be generalized to take account of a good view. How might that formula be generalized further to take account of other factors such as a landscaped yard or a swimming pool? Would a graphical description of the effects of such factors resemble the graph shown in Figure 1 in the application?
5. Following on question 4, how might property tax assessment formulas be adjusted for "interactions" between the values of characteristics of houses? Suppose, for example, that each square foot of a house were more valuable if the house had a good view than if it did not. How would you reflect this fact algebraically and in a graph?
6. Explain why the economic notion of a "marginal" effect is reflected by the algebraic concept of slope. Write down a functional representation that summarizes each of the following economic relationships, indicate what a graph of the relationship might look like, and suggest how the slope of that relationship might be interpreted in marginal terms:

Dependent Variable	Independent Variable
a. Quantity produced	Labor hired
b. Total cost	Units of output
c. Revenue received	Units of output
d. Happiness (utility)	Ice cream eaten
e. Taxes paid	Income
f. Fish caught	Fishing lines used

7. A logical extension of the Tax Reform Act of 1986 (see Application 2.2) would be to adopt a single marginal tax rate (say, 40 percent) together with the

exclusion of a certain minimal income (say, the first $10,000) from taxation. How would you graph such a tax schedule? Suppose the government desired that someone with a $50,000 taxable income would pay the same amount of tax under such a simplified tax schedule as under the 1986 act. If the income exemption were kept at $10,000, what would the marginal tax rate have to be to collect these revenues?

8. Suppose we tried to write down a functional representation of a contour map. This might be done by specifying

$$Y = \text{Altitude} = f(\text{latitude, longitude}) = f(X, Z).$$

Hence, given the coordinates of any location (in terms of latitude and longitude), we could use f to calculate the altitude of this place. Interpret the following algebraic ideas for the function f in terms of physical movements over the actual contour map:

   a. An increase in X holding Z constant.
   b. An increase in Z holding X constant.
   c. The increase in Y that results from increasing X (or Z) alone.
   d. The increase in Y that results from increasing X and Z by the same amounts.
   e. The implication of discovering that any small changes in X or Z always reduce Y. In physical terms, what kind of a place is this on the map and in the real world the map represents?
   f. The implication of discovering that any small changes in X or Z always increase Y. What kind of a place is this?
   g. Finding a particular set of changes in X and Z that always keep Y constant. Would these map coordinates provide a good route for a railroad through this territory?

9. Explain why the following statement is nonsense: "In a pair of simultaneous equations the relationship between X and Y can be found by finding two solutions and then joining them with a straight line. For example, the two solutions found in the text, (2, 1) and (3, 2) show that whenever X is increased by 1, Y will also increase by 1."

10. "In supply and demand graphs it is not possible to predict how much equilibrium price will rise when the demand curve shifts up just by knowing the vertical shift in the curve. If demanders decided they were willing to pay $1 per bushel more for any given quantity of wheat, the demand curve would shift uniformly upward by $1. But the equilibrium price of wheat would probably rise by less than $1." Explain why this is so intuitively and illustrate your intuition with a suitable graph. Demonstrate cases in which price would rise by $1, by $.50, and in which price would not rise at all.

Problems

2.1 Consider the equation

$$Y = 15 + 3X.$$

   a. If $X = 0$, what is the value of Y?
   b. If $Y = 0$, what is the value of X?
   c. Calculate Y for $X = 3$ and for $X = 4$. What do you conclude about the relationship between changes in Y and changes in X?
   d. Graph the equation.

e. Graph the equation for

$$Y = 20 + 3X$$

and answer parts a through c for this equation.

f. Graph the equation

$$Y = 15 + 5X$$

and answer parts a through c for that equation.

g. Briefly describe why your answers to parts a through c differ for these three examples.

2.2 Consider the equation

$$Y = X^2 - 6X + 8 .$$

a. If $X = 0$, what is the value of Y?
b. For what values of X does $Y = 0$?
c. If $X = 3$, what does Y equal? Can Y ever be less than this amount?
d. Graph the equation.
e. Using calculus it can be shown that the slope of the equation at any point is given by

$$\text{Slope} = 2X - 6 .$$

Show that this slope is negative for $X < 3$ and positive for $X > 3$.

f. Explain intuitively why Y takes on its minimum value at $X = 3$ and why the slope of the equation is zero there.

2.3 The demand for potatoes is given by

$$Q_D = 40 - 2P + .001I ,$$

where Q_D = Quantity of potatoes in millions of pounds
P = Price of potatoes in cents per pound
I = Average income in dollars.

a. If $I = 10{,}000$, graph the demand curve for potatoes. How many potatoes are demanded at a price of 0? How many are demanded at a price of 10 cents per pound? At what price does $Q_D = 0$?
b. Suppose now $I = 20{,}000$. How would your answers to part a change? Graph your results.
c. Suppose the government imposes an excise tax of 10 cents per pound on potatoes. Now

$$P = P_P + 10 ,$$

where P is the price paid by potato consumers and P_P is the price received by producers. If producers charge 10 cents per pound and I = \$10,000, how many potatoes will be demanded? If producers charge 0, how many will be demanded? At what producer price will potato demand go to zero? Graph the new demand curve and compare it to your results from part a.

2.4 The supply curve for flounder is given by

$$Q_S = -100 + 5P \text{ (for } Q_S > 0) ,$$

where Q_S is the quantity of flounder supplied in tons and P is the wholesale price of flounder received by producers in cents per pound.

a. Graph the flounder supply curve. At what price will producers actually start supplying flounder to the market?
b. Suppose the government imposes a 25 percent tax on flounder production. Hence

$$P_M = 1.25P,$$

where P_M is the market price of flounder. What will be the market supply curve for flounder (with Q_S as a function of P_M)? At what market price will any flounder be produced? Graph your results and compare them to your graph for part a.

2.5 This problem involves solving demand and supply equations together to determine price and quantity.

a. Consider a demand curve of the form

$$Q_D = -2P + 20,$$

where Q_D is the quantity demanded of a good and P is the price of the good. Graph this demand curve. Also draw a graph of the supply curve

$$Q_S = 2P - 4,$$

where Q_S is the quantity supplied. Be sure to put P on the vertical axis and Q on the horizontal axis. Assume that all the Q's and P's are nonnegative for parts a, b, and c. At what values of P and Q do these curves intersect—that is, where does $Q_D = Q_S$?
b. Now suppose that individuals demand four more units of output at each price—that the demand curve shifts to

$$Q_{D'} = -2P + 24.$$

Graph this new demand curve. At what values of P and Q does the new demand curve intersect the old supply curve—that is, where does $Q_{D'} = Q_S$?
c. Now, finally, suppose the supply curve shifts to

$$Q_S' = 2P - 8.$$

Graph this new supply curve. At what values of P and Q does $Q_D' = Q_S'$? You may wish to refer back to this simple problem when we discuss shifting supply and demand curves in later sections of this book.

2.6 a. Graph the demand curve

$$Q_D = -4P + 32.$$

At what value of P does $Q_D = 0$? At $P = 0$ what is Q_D?
b. Now graph the demand curve

$$Q_D' = -2P + 16.$$

Again, at what value of P does $Q_D' = 0$; what is Q_D' when $P = 0$? Call this value Q^*.

c. Referring back to the demand curve Q_D, what are demanders willing to pay for Q^*? Call this price P^*. What is the product P^* times Q^*? Can you give an economic interpretation to this figure?

d. Now consider all possible products of P times Q where both P and Q lie on the demand curve Q_D. Show that P^* times Q^* is the largest value of these products.

We consider an example similar to this one in Chapter 8 when we discuss the concept of marginal revenue.

2.7 Taxes in Oz are calculated according to the formula

$$T = .01I^2,$$

where T represents thousands of dollars of tax liability and I represents income measured in thousands of dollars. Using this formula, answer the following questions:

a. How much in taxes is paid by individuals with incomes of \$10,000, \$30,000, and \$50,000? What are the average tax rates for these income levels? At what income level does tax liability equal total income?

b. Graph the tax schedule for Oz. Use your graph to estimate marginal tax rates for the income levels specified in part a. Also show the average tax rates for these income levels on your graph.

c. Marginal tax rates in Oz can be estimated more precisely by calculating tax owed if persons with the incomes in part a get one more dollar. Make this computation for these three income levels. Compare your results to those obtained from the calculus-based result that for the Oz tax function its slope = .02I.

2.8 Consider the function

$$Y = \sqrt{X \cdot Z}$$

where $X > 0$, $Z > 0$. Draw the contour lines (in the positive quadrant) for this function for $Y = 4$, $Y = 5$, and $Y = 10$. What do we call the shape of these contour lines? Where does the line $20X + 10Z = 200$ intersect the contour line $Y = 50$? (Hint: As in Application 2.3, it may be easier to graph the contour lines for Y^2 here.)

*2.9 Using the function $Y = \sqrt{X \cdot Z}$ from the previous problem, find that combination of X and Z for which Y is as large as possible and which also satisfies the following linear equations. Graph your results using contour lines for Y. (Hint: For this problem the slope of Y contour lines is given by $-Z/X$.)

a. $2X + Z = 20$.
b. $X + Z = 20$.
c. $X + 2Z = 40$.
d. $X + 5Z = 100$.
e. $2X + Z = 40$.
f. $X + Z = 40$

---

* Denotes a problem that is rather difficult. Answers to all odd-numbered problems appear at the end of the book.

P A R T 2

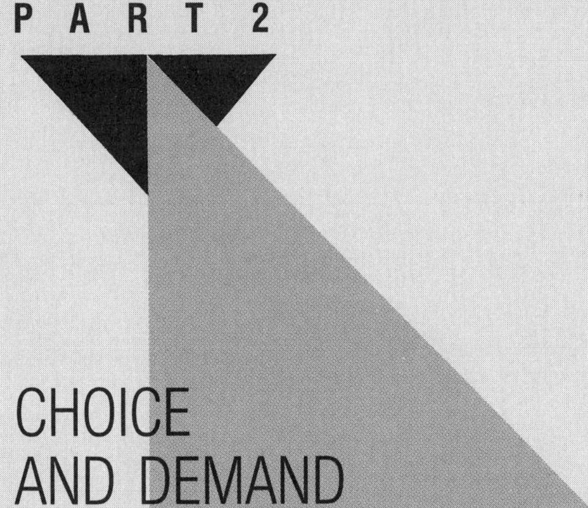

CHOICE AND DEMAND

Part 2 examines how economists look at people's demand for the goods they buy. Our main goal in this part is to develop Marshall's demand curve for a product and to show why this demand curve is likely to be downward sloping. You will see how economists treat the way people make choices and also how the choices of many individuals can be summarized by a market demand curve. The economic theory of the way people make choices has many other applications that are discussed here and elsewhere in this book.

Economists explain consumer demand as the interaction of two forces: (1) consumers have preferences or desires for goods, but (2) they have limited incomes to purchase these commodities. How the consumer resolves these conflicting forces determines which commodities he or she will purchase. For example, the first force may tell the consumer to buy a car (since a car provides desirable services), but the second warns not to (since there are many other uses for the income). Only when the right balance in expenditures is reached will the individual consumer obtain as much satisfaction as the available income allows. Part 2 shows how this balance is reached and how changes in preferences, income, or prices affect the consumer's choices.

Chapter 3 describes how economists treat the consumer's decision problem. We first define the concept of utility, which represents a consumer's preferences. Since not everyone likes the same thing, economists work with models that can deal with these differences. The first half of Chapter 3 develops the idea of a person's tastes. These tastes are the first force that influences demand decisions. The second half of the chapter discusses how people decide to spend their incomes on different goods to get the greatest satisfaction possible—that is, to "maximize" their utility. Because this is the first example of the optimization hypothesis you encounter in this book, it is covered in detail.

Chapter 4 investigates how people change their choices when their income changes or as prices change. This is the first example in the book of "comparative statics" analysis. In this analysis we compare two situations to see how the choices in these situations differ. Most economic analysis is comparative. The results of such comparisons can be very interesting. For example, they can show how people react to changes in the price of a commodity. The analysis can then be used to draw an individual demand curve for the commodity since we now know how the person reacts to price changes.

Chapter 5 shows how these individual demand curves can be "added up" to make market demand curves. These curves are basic to the price determination process. By constructing market demand curves from the decisions that individual consumers make, we are in a good position to see how changing influences on people may affect the market curve. Chapter 5 also discusses how market demand is measured in the real world.

Chapter 6 applies the theory of individual choice developed in Chapters 3 through 5 to three additional economic topics. First, the model of utility maximization is used to show how welfare improvements can be measured. The concept of "consumer surplus" introduced here is widely used in other sections of this book and in many real-world economic applications. Second, the utility-maximization model is used to analyze price indices, such as the gross national product (GNP) price deflator and the Consumer Price Index (CPI). Since these indices are widely used in economics, showing how they are arrived at is an especially important application of microeconomic theory. Finally, the utility-maximization model is used to look at trading between individuals. Since the mutually beneficial nature of trade gives rise to organized markets, trading between individuals can be used as the foundation for supply and demand analysis.

In the last chapter of Part 2, Chapter 7, we look at how people act in uncertain or risky situations. In this application of the utility-maximization model we show why people dislike risk and are usually willing to "pay" something to avoid it. "Risk aversion" is especially important to some economic decisions, such as buying insurance and investing in risky assets, that cannot be understood without considering the uncertainties involved in them. In Chapter 7 we also examine how such riskiness may affect equilibrium prices actually observed in a market. ▲

CHAPTER 3

Utility Maximization: How People Make Economic Choices

An economic system is nothing more than a collection of people and a set of institutions (such as firms or government agencies) that these people operate. Economists therefore place the study of individuals' behavior at the center of their models. People's desires are assumed to have a strong effect in determining what goods are demanded and ultimately produced by the economy; people, to a large extent, decide what levels of productive services (labor and capital) they will supply; and, through their political activities, people influence the government's goals, including its economic goals.

These roles cannot be separated from one another. Any decision a person makes as a consumer, say, to buy a new car, will affect his or her decisions as a provider of resources (to save less or to work harder to pay for the car) and also his or her decisions as a voter (he or she may now favor government spending for new or better highways on which to drive the new car). Economic texts used to refer to "economic man" (*homo economicus*) and considered only the individual's role as a consumer. Even though most authors recognized the individual's other roles, they were never explicitly discussed. Modern microeconomics does consider the mixture of the individual's roles and has developed tools to help understand the interrelationships among them.

Definition of Utility

Economists have developed a useful model to simplify their analysis of an individual's decision problems. This model formalizes the concepts of preferences and income and lets us describe how these two forces determine the choices that are made. More than anything else, this conceptual apparatus underlies the economists' thinking about people's decisions—it is the fundamental economic **theory of choice.**

Theory of choice
The interaction of preferences and income that causes people to make the choices they do.

People's preferences can be formalized with the concept of **utility**, which is defined as the satisfaction that a person receives from his or her activities. This concept is very broad, and in the next few sections we define it more precisely. We use the simple case of a single consumer who receives utility from just two commodities. We will eventually analyze how that person chooses to allocate income between these two goods, but first we need to develop a better understanding of utility itself.

Utility
The pleasure, satisfaction, or need fulfillment that people get from their economic activity.

Ceteris Paribus Assumption

To identify all the factors affecting a person's feelings of satisfaction would be a lifelong task for an imaginative psychologist; to measure these factors precisely would probably be impossible. Economists focus on basic, quantifiable economic factors and look at how people choose among them. Economists clearly recognize that nonmeasurable factors (aesthetics, love, security, envy, and so forth) affect behavior, but they develop models in which these kinds of factors are held constant and are not specifically analyzed.

Much economic analysis is based on this ***ceteris paribus*** (other things being equal) **assumption.** We can simplify the analysis of a person's consumption decisions by assuming that satisfaction is affected only by choices made among the options being considered and that other effects on satisfaction remain constant. In this way we can isolate the economic factors that affect consumption behavior. This narrow focus is not intended to imply that other things that affect utility are "unimportant"; we are conceptually holding these other factors constant so that we may study consumption choices in a simplified setting.

***Ceteris paribus* assumption**
In economic analysis, holding all other factors constant so that only the factor being studied is allowed to change.

Utility from Consuming Two Goods

This chapter concentrates on an individual's problem of choosing the quantities of two goods (which for most purposes we will call simply "X" and "Y") to consume. We assume that the person receives utility from these goods and that we can show this utility in functional notation (see Chapter 2) by

$$\text{Utility} = U(X, Y; \text{other things}). \qquad [3.1]$$

This notation indicates that the utility an individual receives from consuming X and Y over some period of time depends on the quantities of X and Y consumed and on "other things." These other things might include easily quantifiable items such as the amounts of other kinds of goods consumed, the number of hours worked, or the amount of time spent sleeping. They might also include such unquantifiable items as love, security, and feelings of self-worth. These other things appear after the semicolon in Equation 3.1 because we assume that they are held constant while we examine the individual's choice between X and Y. If one of the other things should change, the utility from some particular amounts of X and Y might be very different than it was before.

For example, several times in this chapter we consider the case of a person choosing how many hamburgers (Y) and soft drinks (X) to consume during one week. Although our example uses seemingly trivial commodities, the analysis is quite general and will apply to any two goods. In analyzing the hamburger–soft drink choices, we assume that all other factors affecting utility are held constant. The weather, the person's preferences for hamburgers and soft drinks, the person's exercise pattern, and everything else are assumed not to change during the analysis. If the weather, for instance, were to become warmer, we might expect soft drinks to become relatively more desirable, and we wish to eliminate such effects from our analysis, at least for the moment. We usually write the utility function in Equation 3.1 as

$$\text{Utility} = U(X, Y) \tag{3.2}$$

with the understanding that many other things are being held constant. All economic analyses impose some form of *ceteris paribus* assumption so that the relationship between a selected few variables can be studied. You should try to identify the "important" things that are being held constant in this book as we explore various simplified models of choice.

Measurability of Utility

The first economists to deal with the concept of utility thought that it might be measurable. Some early psychological experiments on people's responses to electrical stimuli gave rise to the mistaken belief that all individual reactions were not only quantifiable but also of the same general type. If utility were measurable, many economic questions could be easily answered. Firms could understand and predict individual consumer behavior and thereby experience less uncertainty in their business, or the government could, if it wished, produce a "fair" distribution of goods (and utility) among people. Perhaps it is for the best that such accurate measures of preferences have proved impossible to obtain.

The obstacles to measuring utility have proved to be of two major types. The first concerns what to use for a unit of measurement. We have no very good psychological idea of what a *util* (that is, a unit of utility) might be. There is also no way of determining how one person's utils compare to another's. When asked, "On a scale of 1 to 10, how happy are you?" for example, people respond in very different ways. Application 3.1: The Pursuit of

APPLICATION 3.1

The Pursuit of Happiness

Even though the problems in measuring utility seem formidable, imaginative social scientists have not been shy about attempting to do so anyway. The nineteenth-century psychologists Weber and Fechner, for example, conducted numerous experiments in which subjects were given mild electrical shocks. They found that an increase of five volts was clearly discernable at low levels of voltage, but at higher levels the increase was barely noticeable. Although, thankfully, such experiments seem to be frowned on today, Weber and Fechner's observation of what appeared to be diminishing retuns in the application of electric current continues to influence thinking about utility. For example, whether a dollar of extra income is worth less (in terms of utility) to a rich person than to a poor one has been one major focus of this research.

Does Money Buy Happiness?

One approach to studying the relationship between income and utility relies on survey questions that ask people how happy they are. Sometimes respondents are asked whether they are "very happy," "fairly happy," or "not very happy" whereas in other cases they are asked to indicate their happiness on a scale of 1 to 10. Although many economists regard such questions as hopelessly vague, the survey responses do, nevertheless, show certain regularities.[1] The clearest finding is that people with higher incomes, not surprisingly, report that they are happier than do those with lower incomes. There is also some evidence that the fraction who report that they are "very happy" tends to level off at about 60 percent; after some point increasing amounts of income do not seem to add very much to reported happiness. That happiness may also be, to some extent, a relative concept is suggested by the fact that there are no major differences in reported happiness between middle income people in high- and low-income countries even though such people in high-income countries have much higher incomes in absolute terms. Similarly, people on average do not seem to have become a lot happier in the United States during the past 30 years even though average incomes have risen substantially. Hence, although there is a sense in which money seems to "buy" happiness, the exact relationship is not a simple one.

The Pursuit of Poverty

The relationship between an individual's purchasing power and his or her feelings of well-being is also reflected in attempts to measure what it means to say that someone is "poor." For example, since the 1960s, the U.S. government has published an official count of the number of families living in "poverty" in the United States using a definition that calculates the income required to purchase a specific set of necessities. Numerous disputes have arisen over defining exactly what such a set of necessities should include. A more subjective approach has been taken by several European researchers who base their definition of "poverty" on survey responses to the question "What do you think is the minimum income needed to 'get along'?" These researchers have found that there is some consensus in various specific European countries about what it takes to "get along," but that respondents' answers tend to be importantly affected by their own incomes.[2] People with higher incomes think it takes more income to "get along" than do low-income people. And, for some reason, people in France tend to believe it requires a much higher income to "get along" than do people in Germany.

To Think About

1. Why worry about the relationship between income and utility? Since higher income makes it possible for a person to consume bundles of goods that were previously unaffordable, isn't he or she necessarily better-off? Isn't that all we need to know?
2. Sometimes people are said to be poor if they "have to" spend more than, say, 25 percent of their income on food or if they spend more than 35 percent on housing. Do such definitions make sense? Even if there were no differences among people's preferences for food or housing, what does such an approach implicitly assume about the relationship between income and purchases of these goods?

---

[1]For a summary of some of this evidence, see Richard A. Easterlin, "Does Economic Growth Improve the Human Lot?" in *Nations and Households in Economic Growth,* Paul A. David and Melvin W. Reder, eds. (New York: Academic Press, 1974), pp. 89–126.

[2]See A. J. M. Hagenaars, *The Perception of Poverty* (Amsterdam: North Holland Publishing Company, 1986).

Happiness illustrates some of the problems that researchers have had in making such measurements.

A second difficulty that arises in measuring utility in the study of individuals' choices concerns the *ceteris paribus* assumption. In simple psychological experiments it may be possible to hold everything except the stimulus under question constant (that is, to provide an adequate experimental "control"). In economics, however, the myriad factors that affect a person's economic choices are impossible to list and quantify. To hold some of them constant in order to measure the utility people get from various choices is out of the question.

Consequently, we must expect much less than measurability from a utility theory. All that can be assumed is that people rank the options open to them in some consistent way. If we were talking about consumption behavior, for example, we would assume that the individual can rank all possible combinations of goods that he or she might consider. To say that the utility of one set of goods, A, is greater than that of another set, B, only means that A is preferred to B. We cannot say how much A is preferred to B, since a hard-and-fast measure of utility is beyond our grasp. For example, we may be able to assert that a person prefers a roast beef dinner to a fried chicken dinner, but we cannot say that he or she is "5 percent happier" with the roast beef or that the chicken provides "7 fewer utils." There are many things we can say about individual choices despite this problem, however. Most observable economic behavior can be explained without having to measure utility.

Assumptions about Utility

What do we mean by saying that people's preferences are "consistent"? How do we describe the trades people are willing to make? Can these preferences (utility) be shown graphically? In this section we will explore these questions as we begin our study of economists' model of choice.

Basic Properties of Preferences

Although we cannot expect to be able to measure utility, we might expect people to express their preferences in a reasonably consistent manner. Between two consumption bundles, A and B, we might expect a person to be able to state clearly either "I prefer A to B," or "I prefer B to A," or "A and B are equally attractive to me." We do not expect the individual to be paralyzed by indecision, but rather to be able to say precisely how he or she feels about any potential consumption possibilities. This rules out such situations as the mythical jackass, who, finding himself midway between a pile of hay and a bag of oats, starved to death because he was unable to decide which way to go. Formally, we are assuming preferences are **complete**—that people can always make a choice between any two options presented to them.

Complete preferences
The assumption that an individual is able to state which of any two options is preferred.

In addition to expecting people to be able to state preferences clearly and completely, we might also expect people's preferences not to be self-contradictory. We do not expect a person to make statements about his or her preferences that conflict with each other. In other words, we assume that

APPLICATION 3.2 

Transitivity in Sports, Marriage Partners, and Consumption

Whether or not people obey the assumption of transitivity and thereby make consistent decisions has been the subject of some controversy among economists and psychologists. Many examples have been proposed that purport to show the assumption is widely violated in the real world. One popular example is scoring at sporting events. By invoking (incorrectly) the assumption of transitivity, it is often possible to draw absurd conclusions about how potential matchups might turn out. Consider the following question: Can Amherst College (a major football power of the Connecticut Valley) beat the University of Oklahoma? Using the assumption of transitivity, the answer is a definite yes. In a recent season, for example, Amherst beat Bowdoin, Bowdoin beat Bates, Bates beat C. W. Post, and (to make a very long story short) C. W. Post beat a team that beat a team that beat a team that beat Pitt. Since Pitt beat Kansas and (in that year) Kansas beat Oklahoma, the result is proved.[1] An Amherst-Oklahoma matchup would be no contest since the law of transitivity assures that Amherst would win in a walkaway.

The absurdity of the above conclusion stems from the fact that athletic contests do not necessarily obey the assumption of transitivity. Of greater interest to economists is whether individuals' choices obey or violate the transitivity assumption.

Marriage Partners

In a 1958 study, J. M. Davis asked a group of undergraduate male students to express their marital preferences from among a set of written descriptions of nine women.[2] A set of choices was judged intransitive if a subject reported, for example, that he preferred woman 1 to woman 3, that he preferred woman 3 to woman 7, and that he preferred woman 7 to woman 1. In all, Davis examined nearly 4,000 such triples and found that only about 1 out of 8 of them showed intransitivity. Davis concluded that the vast majority of preferences were transitive and that the intransitivities that were observed could probably be explained as random choices among women judged to be equally desirable by the subjects.

Consumption Experiments

A similar approach to the study of transitivity was taken by A. A. Weinstein in a 1968 experiment that examined how individuals ranked consumption items.[3] Overall, 10 items were used ranging from $3 in cash, to three Beatles records, or a 15-inch pizza. Among adults, Weinstein found few (less than 7 percent) such intransitivities. The author did find, however, that younger people (notably children ages 9 through 12) exhibited considerably more intransitivities (about 20 percent of the choices made). This led him to conclude that consistency may to some extent be an acquired skill.

Actual Consumption Patterns

Actual consumption data are also broadly consistent with the notion of transitivity. In a detailed study of families' food purchases over a four-year period in Michigan, for example, relatively few intransitive choices were found.[4] Those that did occur seemed to be related to family circumstances. Families where both spouses were employed tended to have relatively larger numbers of intransitivities whereas families with many children (and large food demands) tended to have fewer. Such observations suggest that the rationality required to exhibit consistent, transitive preferences may to some extent be costly to families.

To Think About

1. Do people have to learn to behave "rationally"? Don't young children, even babies, seem to know exactly what they want? If that is so, how do you explain the fact that children seem to make a fairly large number of inconsistent choices?
2. Are sporting matches between individuals (say, tennis or boxing) transitive? Do the people who usually lose to you at some game also lose to the people who can beat you?

[1]This example was developed by Frank Westhoff, an economist and die-hard football fan.

[2]J. M. Davis, "Transitivity of Preferences," *Behavioral Science* (Fall 1958): 26–33.

[3]A. A. Weinstein, "Transitivity of Preferences," *Journal of Political Economy* (March/April 1968): 307–311.

[4]A. Y. C. Koo and Georg Haverkamp, "Structure of Revealed Preference: Some Preliminary Evidence," *Journal of Political Economy* (July/August 1972): 724–744.

Figure 3.1
More of a Good Is Preferred to Less

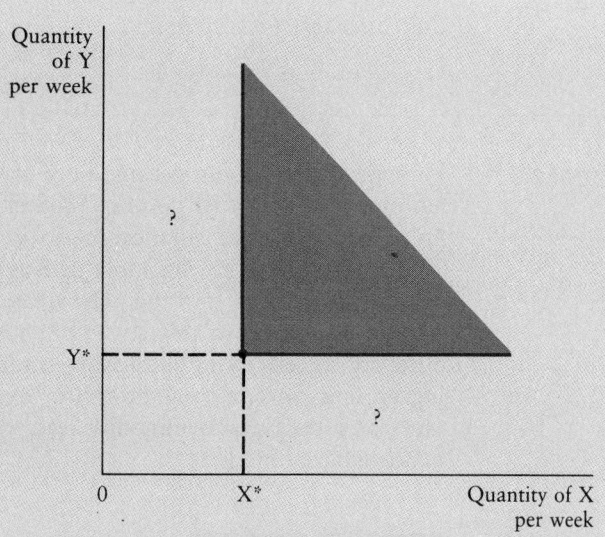

The blue-shaded area represents those combinations of X and Y that are unambiguously preferred to the combination X*, Y*. This is why goods are called "goods"; individuals prefer having more of any good rather than less. Combinations of X and Y in the white area are inferior to the combination X*,Y* whereas those in the gray area may or may not be superior to X*,Y*.

Transitivity of preferences
The property that if A is preferred to B, and B is preferred to C, then A must be preferred to C.

preferences are **transitive.** If a person says, "I prefer A to B," and "I prefer B to C," then he or she can be expected to say, "I prefer A to C." A person who instead states the contrary (that is, "I prefer C to A") would appear to be hopelessly inconsistent. We wish to rule out such inconsistency from our analysis. In Application 3.2: Transitivity in Sports, Marriage Partners, and Consumption, we discuss some of the ways in which economists have tried to investigate whether people's choices really are transitive.

More Is Better: Defining an Economic "Good"

A third assumption we make about individual preferences is that a person prefers more of a good to less. In Figure 3.1 all points in the blue-shaded area are preferred to the amounts X* of good X and Y* of good Y. Movement from point X*, Y* to any point in the shaded area is an unambiguous improvement, since in this area the individual can obtain more of one good without taking less of another. This idea of preferences is implicit in our definition of an "economic good" as an item that yields positive benefits to people.[1] That is, more of a good is, by definition, better. Combinations of

[1]Later in this chapter, we briefly describe a theory of "bads"—items for which less is preferred to more. Such items might include toxic wastes, mosquitoes, or, for this author, lima beans.

goods in the white area of Figure 3.1 are definitely inferior to X*, Y* since they offer less of *both* goods.

Voluntary Trades and Indifference Curves

How people feel about getting more of some good when they must give up an amount of some other good is another important aspect of preferences. The areas identified with question marks in Figure 3.1 are difficult to compare to X*, Y* since they involve more of one good and less of the other. Whether a move from X*, Y* into the gray areas would increase utility is not clear. To be able to look into this situation, we need some additional terminology. Studying the effects of ambiguous trades is very common in economics. Giving up units of one commodity (for example, money) to get back additional units of some other commodity (say, candy bars) is what gives rise to trade and organized markets.

Indifference Curves

Indifference curve
All the combinations of goods or services that provide the same level of utility.

To study voluntary trades we will introduce the concept of an **indifference curve.** Such a curve shows all those combinations of two goods that provide the same utility to an individual; that is, the individual is "indifferent" about which particular combination on the curve he or she actually has. For example, Figure 3.2 records the quantity of soft drinks consumed by an individual in one period (again, say, one week) on the horizontal axis and the quantity of hamburgers consumed on the vertical axis. The curve U_1 in Figure 3.2 includes all those combinations of hamburgers and soft drinks with which the individual is equally happy. For example, the curve shows that the individual would be just as happy with six hamburgers and two soft drinks per week (point A) as with four hamburgers and three soft drinks (point B) or with three hamburgers and four soft drinks (point C). The points on U_1 all provide the same level of utility to the individual, and therefore he or she does not have any particular reason for preferring any point on U_1 to any other point.

The indifference curve U_1 is similar to a contour line on a map (discussed in Chapter 2) in that it shows those combinations of hamburgers and soft drinks that provide an identical "altitude" (that is, amount) of utility. Points to the northeast of U_1 promise a higher level of satisfaction and are preferred to points on U_1. Point E (five soft drinks and four hamburgers) is preferred to point C because it provides more of both goods. As in Figure 3.1, our definition of goods assures that combination E is preferred to combination C. Similarly, our assumption of transitivity assures that combination E is also preferred to combinations A, B, and D and to all other combinations on U_1.

Combinations of hamburgers and soft drinks that lie below U_1, on the other hand, are less desirable to the individual since they offer less satisfaction. Point F offers less of both goods than does point C. The fact that the in-

Figure 3.2
Indifference Curve

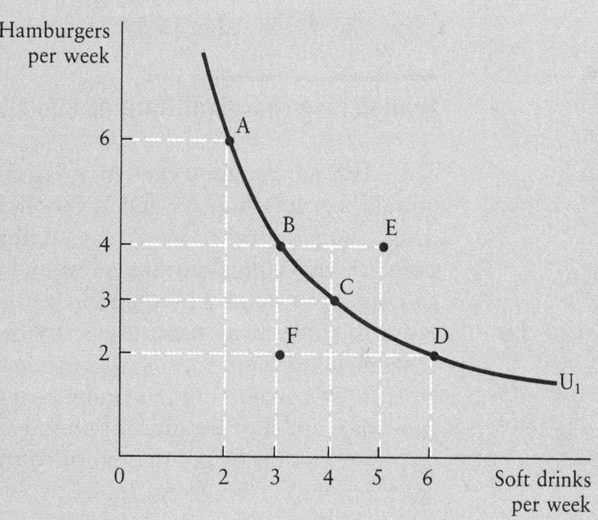

The curve U_1 shows the combinations of hamburgers and soft drinks that provide the same level of utility to an individual. The slope of the curve shows the trades an individual will freely make. For example, in moving from point A to point B, the individual will give two hamburgers to get one additional soft drink. In other words, the marginal rate of substitution is approximately 2 in this range. Points below U_1 (such as F) provide less utility than points on U_1. Points above U_1 (such as E) provide more utility than U_1.

difference curve U_1 has a negative slope (that is, the curve runs from the upper left portion of the figure to the lower right portion) indicates that if an individual is forced to give up some hamburgers, he or she must receive additional soft drinks to remain equally well-off. This type of movement along U_1 represents those trades that a person might freely make. Knowledge of U_1 therefore eliminates the ambiguity associated with the gray areas we showed in Figure 3.1.

Indifference Curves and the Marginal Rate of Substitution

Marginal rate of substitution (MRS) The rate at which an individual is willing to reduce consumption on one good when he or she gets one more unit of another good while remaining equally well off. The negative of the slope of an indifference curve.

What happens when an individual moves from point A (six hamburgers and two soft drinks) to point B (four hamburgers and three soft drinks)? The individual remains equally well off since the two commodity bundles lie on the same indifference curve. The individual will voluntarily give up two of the hamburgers that were being consumed at point A in exchange for one additional soft drink. The slope of the curve U_1 between A and B is therefore approximately $-\frac{2}{1} = -2$. That is, Y (hamburgers) declines two units in response to a one-unit increase in X (soft drinks). We call the absolute value of this slope the **marginal rate of substitution** (MRS). Hence, we would say that the

MRS (of soft drinks for hamburgers) between points A and B is 2: the individual is willing to give up two hamburgers in order to get one more soft drink.

Diminishing Marginal Rate of Substitution

The MRS varies along the curve U_1. For points such as A the individual has quite a few hamburgers and is relatively willing to trade them away for soft drinks. On the other hand, for combinations such as those represented by point D, the individual has an abundance of soft drinks and is reluctant to give up any more hamburgers to get more soft drinks. The increasing reluctance to trade away hamburgers follows the notion that the consumption of any one good (here soft drinks) can be pushed too far. This characteristic can be seen by considering the trades that take place in moving from point A to B, from point B to C, and from point C to D. In the first trade two hamburgers are given up to get one more soft drink—the MRS is 2 (as we have already shown). The second trade involves giving up one hamburger to get one additional soft drink. In this trade, the MRS has declined to 1, reflecting the individual's increased reluctance to give up hamburgers to get more soft drinks. Finally, for the third trade (from point C to D), the individual is willing to give up a hamburger only if two soft drinks are received in return. In this final trade, the MRS is ½ (the individual is willing to give up one-half of a hamburger to get one more soft drink), which is a further decline from the MRS of the previous trades.

Balance in Consumption and the Assumption of a Diminishing Marginal Rate of Substitution

Our conclusion of a diminishing MRS is based on the idea that people prefer balanced consumption bundles to unbalanced ones.[2] This assumption is illus-

[2]If we assume utility is measurable, we can provide an alternative analysis of a diminishing MRS. To do so we introduce the concept of the marginal utility of a good X (denoted by MU_X). Marginal utility is defined as the extra utility obtained by consuming one more unit of good X. The concept is meaningful only if utility can be measured and is not as useful as the MRS. If the individual is asked to give up some Y (ΔY) to get some additional X(ΔX), the change in utility is given by

$$\text{Change in utility} = MU_Y \cdot \Delta Y + MU_X \cdot \Delta X. \qquad \text{[i]}$$

It is equal to the utility gained from the additional X less the utility lost from the reduction in Y. Since utility does not change along an indifference curve, we can use Equation (i) to derive

$$\frac{-\Delta Y}{\Delta X} = \frac{MU_X}{MU_Y}. \qquad \text{[ii]}$$

Along an indifference curve, the negative of its slope is given by MU_X/MU_Y. That slope is, by definition, the MRS. Hence we have

$$MRS = MU_X/MU_Y. \qquad \text{[iii]}$$

For example, if an extra hamburger yields two utils ($MU_Y = 2$) and an extra soft drink yields four utils ($MU_X = 4$), MRS = 2 since the individual will be willing to trade away two hamburgers to get an additional soft drink. If it is assumed that MU_X falls and MU_Y increases as X is substituted for Y, Equation (iii) shows that MRS will fall as we move counterclockwise along U_1.

Figure 3.3
Balance in Consumption Is Desirable

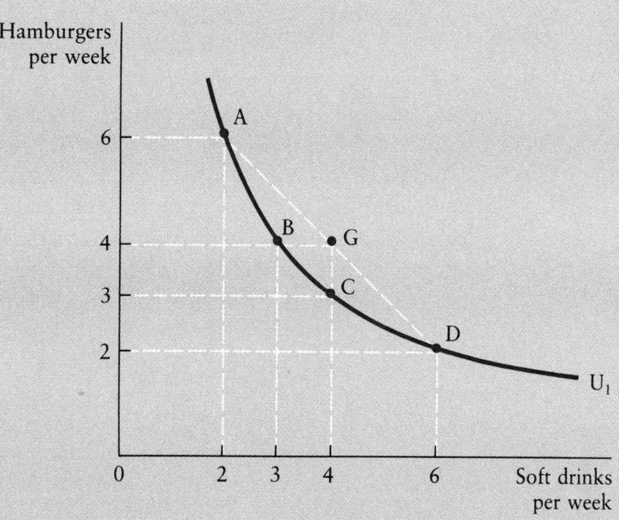

The consumption bundle G (four hamburgers, four soft drinks) is preferred to either of the extreme bundles A and D. This is a result of the assumption of a diminishing MRS. Because individuals become progressively less willing to give up hamburgers as they move in a southeasterly direction along U_1, the curve U_1 will have a convex shape. Consequently all points on a straight line joining two points such as A and D will lie above U_1. Points such as G will be preferred to any of those on U_1.

trated precisely in Figure 3.3, where the indifference curve U_1 from Figure 3.2 is redrawn. Our discussion here concerns the two extreme consumption options A and D. In consuming A the individual receives six hamburgers and two soft drinks; the same satisfaction could be received by consuming D (two hamburgers and six soft drinks). Now consider a bundle of commodities (say, G) "between" these extremes. With G (four hamburgers and four soft drinks) the individual obtains a higher level of satisfaction (point G is northeast of the indifference curve U_1) than with either of the extreme bundles A or D.

The reason for this increased satisfaction should be geometrically obvious. All of the points on the straight line joining A and D lie above U_1. Point G is one of these points (as the figure shows, there are many others). As long as the indifference curve obeys the assumption of a diminishing MRS, it will be convex; any bundle that represents an "average" between two equally attractive extremes will be preferred to those extremes. The assumption of a diminishing MRS is consistent with the notion that people prefer some variety in consumption.

Indifference Curve Maps

Although Figures 3.2 and 3.3 each show only one indifference curve, the positive quadrant contains many such curves, each one corresponding to a different level of utility. Since every combination of hamburgers and soft

Figure 3.4
Indifference Curve Map for Hamburgers and Soft Drinks

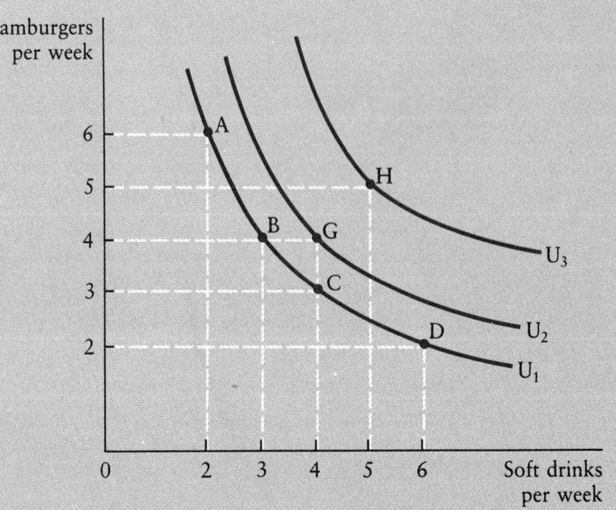

The positive quadrant is full of indifference curves, each of which reflects a different level of utility. Three such curves are illustrated. Combinations of goods on U_3 are preferred to those on U_2, which in turn are preferred to those on U_1. This is simply a reflection of the assumption that more of a good is preferred to less, as may be seen by comparing points C, G, and H.

drinks must yield some level of utility, every point must have one (and only one) indifference curve passing through it. These curves are, as we said earlier, similar to the contour lines that appear on topographical maps in that they each represent a different "altitude" of utility. In Figure 3.4 three of these curves have been drawn and are labeled U_1, U_2, and U_3. These are only three of the infinite number of curves that characterize an individual's entire **indifference curve map.** Just as a map may have many contour lines (say, one for each inch of altitude), so too the gradations in utility may be very fine, as would be shown by very closely spaced indifference curves. For graphic convenience, our analysis generally deals with only a few indifference curves that are relatively widely spaced.

Indifference curve map
A contour map that shows the utility an individual obtains from all possible consumption options.

The labeling of the indifference curves in Figure 3.4 has no special meaning except to indicate that utility increases as we move from combinations of goods on U_1 to those on U_2 and then to those on U_3. As we have repeatedly pointed out, there is no precise way to measure the level of utility associated with, say, U_2. Similarly, we have no way of measuring the amount of extra utility an individual receives from consuming bundles on U_3 instead of U_2. All we can assume is that utility increases as the individual moves to higher indifference curves. That is, the individual would prefer to be on a higher curve rather than on a lower one.

Illustrating Particular Preferences

An indifference curve map tells us all we need to know about this person's preferences for these two goods. To illustrate some of the ways in which indifference curve maps might be used to reflect preferences, Figure 3.5 shows four special cases.

A Useless Good. Panel a of Figure 3.5 shows an individual's indifference curve map for food (on the horizontal axis) and smoke grinders (on the vertical axis). Since smoke grinders are totally useless, increasing purchases of them does not increase utility. Only by getting additional food does this person enjoy a higher level of utility. The vertical indifference curve U_2, for example, shows that utility will be U_2 as long as this person has 10 units of food no matter how many smoke grinders he or she has.

Economic Bads. The situation illustrated in Panel a of Figure 3.5 implicitly assumes that useless goods cause no harm—having more smoke grinders causes no problem since one can always throw them away. In some cases, however, such free disposal is not possible, and additional units of a good can cause actual harm. For example, Panel b of Figure 3.5 shows an indifference curve map for food and houseflies. Holding food consumption constant at 10, utility declines as the number of houseflies increases. Because additional houseflies reduce utility, an individual might even be willing to give up some food (and buy flypaper instead, for example) in exchange for fewer houseflies.

Perfect Substitutes. Our illustrations of convex indifference curves in Figures 3.2 through 3.4 reflected the assumption that diversity in consumption is desirable. If, however, the two goods we were examining were essentially the same (or at least served identical functions), we could not make this argument. In Panel c of Figure 3.5, for example, we show an individual's indifference curve map for Exxon and Mobil gasoline. Since this individual is unconvinced by television advertisements, he or she has adopted the sensible proposition that all gallons of gasoline are virtually identical. Hence, he or she is always willing to trade one gallon of Exxon for a gallon of Mobil—the MRS all along any indifference curve is 1.0. The straight-line indifference curve map in Panel c of Figure 3.5 reflects the perfect substitutability between these two goods.

Perfect Complements. In Panel d of Figure 3.5, on the other hand, we illustrate a situation in which two goods go together. This individual prefers to

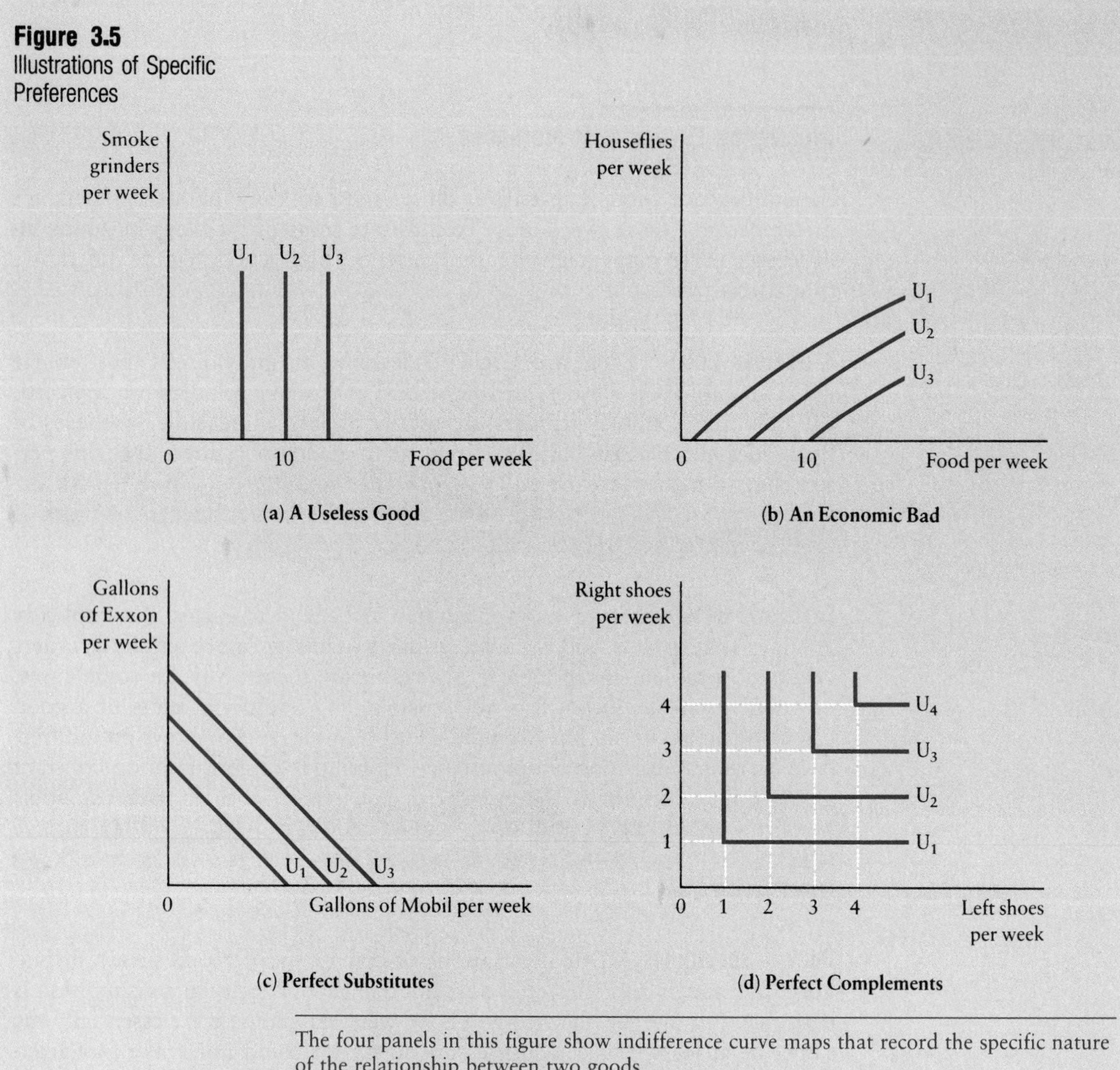

Figure 3.5
Illustrations of Specific Preferences

The four panels in this figure show indifference curve maps that record the specific nature of the relationship between two goods.

consume left shoes (on the horizontal axis) and right shoes (on the vertical axis) in pairs. If, for example, he or she currently has three pairs of shoes, additional right shoes provide no more utility (compare this to the situation in Panel a). Similarly, additional left shoes alone provide no additional utility. An extra pair of shoes, on the other hand, does increase utility (from U_3 to U_4) since this individual likes to consume these two goods together. Any situation in which two goods have such a strong complementary relationship to one another would be described by a similar map of L-shaped indifference curves.

Of course, these simple examples only hint at the variety in types of preferences that can be illustrated by indifference curve maps. Later in this chapter we will be encountering other examples that help to explain observed economic behavior. Because indifference curve maps reflect people's basic preferences about the goods they might select, such maps provide an important first building block for developing a theory of economic choice.

Utility-Maximization Hypothesis: An Initial Survey

Economists assume that when a person is faced with a choice from among a number of possible options, he or she will choose the one that yields the highest utility. As Adam Smith remarked more than two centuries ago, "We are not ready to suspect any person of being defective in selfishness."[3] In other words, economists assume that people know their own minds and make choices consistent with their preferences. This section surveys in general terms how such choices might be made.

Choices Are Constrained

The most interesting feature of the utility-maximization problem is that people are constrained in what they can buy by the size of their incomes. Of those combinations of goods that an individual can afford, he or she will choose the one that is most preferred. This most preferred bundle of goods may not provide complete bliss; it may even leave this person in misery. It will, however, reflect the best use of limited income. All other combinations of goods that can be bought with that limited income would leave him or her even worse off. It is the limitation of income that makes the individual's problem of choice an economic one of allocating a scarce resource (the limited income) among alternative end uses. Application 3.3: Irrational Behavior illustrates how general the economist's notion of making the best of one's situation is.

The Basic Result

Consider the following trivial problem: How should an individual choose to allocate a net income among two goods (hamburgers and soft drinks) if he or

[3]Adam Smith, *The Theory of Moral Sentiments* (1759; reprint, New Rochelle, N.Y.: Arlington House, 1969), p. 446.

APPLICATION 3.3

Irrational Behavior

The assumption that people seek to maximize their utility is essentially an assumption that individuals act in a "rational" way to achieve certain ends. To many noneconomists such an assumption seems preposterous. Instead, they argue that people are "irrational" in that they make unsystematic decisions dominated as much by whim and ignorance as by any sort of rational thought process. Here we examine two examples of allegedly irrational behavior in order to show how economists explain them using the utility-maximizing model. Of course, much purportedly irrational behavior represents differences in tastes between the observer and the person being observed. Some people claim it is "irrational" for people to eat at McDonald's or to watch soap operas, but such statements really amount to assertions that the speakers' preferences are "superior" to those being observed; economists wish to make no such value judgments. Here instead we are interested in the type of behavior that at first glance seems to suggest that people make decisions that are not in their own best interest.

Self-Imposed Constraints

One type of behavior that might be termed "irrational" occurs when individuals impose additional constraints on their own actions. People participate in compulsory savings plans (such as Christmas Clubs) that pay very low rates of interest; they pay to join stop smoking clinics to break the cigarette habit; and they hide the key to the freezer to make sure they stay on a diet. These types of behavior seem irrational because people are voluntarily subjecting themselves to unnecessary constraints. Recent examinations of the notion of "self-control" have shown why such behavior is indeed rational.[1] Introducing constraints for a specific purpose allows individuals to attain long-term goals (saving for a specific goal, stopping smoking, or losing weight) while maintaining considerable discretion in day-to-day decision making. Self-imposed constraints are therefore just one way in which individuals rationally pursue long-term goals.

Criminal Behavior

Most people regard criminal behavior as "deviant." Economists would not deny that many criminals exhibit antisocial characteristics or that some crimes are particularly bizarre. However, economists differ from many other social scientists in viewing much criminal behavior (particularly property crimes such as burglary, robbery, and auto theft) as fundamentally rational. Rather than viewing criminals as psychotic, economists treat them as utility maximizers who are responding to the incentives they face. For example, in one study of how various factors affect crime rates, Isaac Ehrlich found that each 1 percent increase in the likelihood that someone committing a property crime will be caught was associated with a reduction in such crimes of 0.8 percent. Ehrlich also found that each 1 percent increase in the severity of the penalty imposed on a convicted felon reduced the rate of property crime by nearly 1 percent.[2] Similar results were found for specific categories of property crimes such as burglary or auto theft. Even for the types of crimes that seem least subject to rational economic calculation (such as aggravated assault), there was some evidence that the incentives faced by criminals had an impact on observed crime rates.

To Think About

1. How might you explain the following types of "irrational behavior" as being completely in accord with the notion of utility maximization: (a) never shopping for bargains; (b) refusing to use a seat belt; (c) living in an "unsafe" neighborhood; (d) smoking; (e) drinking "too much" alcohol?
2. What types of "irrational" behavior do you engage in (if in doubt, ask your parents or roommate)? How do you explain your behavior in such situations? Does it represent utility maximization on your part or not?

[1] See, for example, R.H. Thaler and H.M. Shefrin, "An Economic Theory of Self-Control," *Journal of Political Economy* (April 1981): 392–406.

[2] Isaac Ehrlich, "Participation in Illegitimate Activities: A Theoretical and Empirical Investigation," *Journal of Political Economy* (May/June 1973): 550.

she is to obtain the highest level of utility possible? Answering this question provides fundamental insights into all of microeconomics. The basic result can easily be stated at the outset. In order to maximize utility given a fixed amount of income to spend on two goods, an individual will spend the entire income and will choose a combination of goods for which the marginal rate of substitution between the two goods is equal to the ratio of those goods' market prices.

The reasoning behind the first part of this proposition is straightforward. Because we assume that "more is better," an individual will spend the entire amount budgeted for the two items. The only alternative here is throwing the money away, which is obviously less desirable than buying something.

The reasoning behind the second part of the proposition can be seen with our hamburger–soft drink example. Suppose that an individual is currently consuming some combination of hamburgers and soft drinks for which the MRS is equal to 1; he or she is willing to do without one hamburger in order to get an additional soft drink. Assume, on the other hand, that the price of hamburgers is $1.00 and that of soft drinks is $.50. The ratio of their prices is $.50/$1.00 = ½. The individual is able to obtain an extra soft drink in the market by giving up only one-half of a hamburger. In this situation the individual's MRS is not equal to the ratio of the goods' market prices, and we can show that some other combination of goods provides more utility.

Suppose this person consumes one less hamburger. This frees $1.00 in purchasing power. He or she can now buy one more soft drink (at a price of $.50) and is now as well-off as before since the MRS was assumed to be 1. However, $.50 (= $1.00 − $.50) is still unspent that can now be spent on either soft drinks or hamburgers (or some combination of the two). Such additional consumption clearly makes the individual better-off than in the initial situation.

Our numbers here were purely arbitrary. Whenever the individual selects a combination of goods for which the MRS differs from the price ratio, a similar beneficial change in spending patterns can be made. This reallocation will continue until the MRS is brought into line with the price ratio, at which time maximum utility is attained. We now turn to presenting a more formal proof of this.

Graphic Analysis of Utility Maximization

To develop a graphic demonstration of the process of utility maximization, we will begin by showing how to illustrate an individual's **budget constraint.** This constraint shows which combinations of goods are affordable. It is from among these that the individual can choose the bundle that provides the most utility.

Budget constraint
The limit that income places on the combinations of goods and services that an individual can buy.

The Budget Constraint

Figure 3.6 shows the combinations of two goods (which we will call simply X and Y) that an individual with a fixed amount of money to spend can afford.

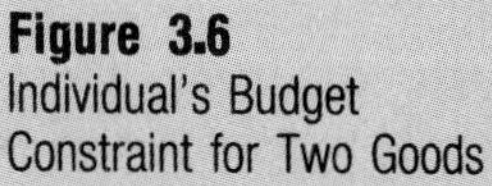

Figure 3.6
Individual's Budget Constraint for Two Goods

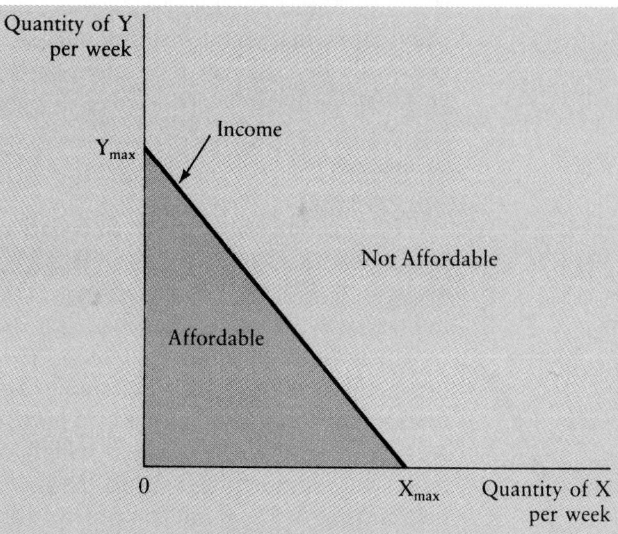

Those combinations of X and Y that the individual can afford are shown in the shaded triangle. If, as we usually assume, the individual prefers more than less of every good, the outer boundary of this triangle is the relevant constraint where all of the available funds are spent on either X or Y. The slope of this straight boundary is given by $-P_X/P_Y$.

If all available income is spent on good X, the number of units that can be purchased is recorded as X_{max} in the figure. If all available income is spent on Y, Y_{max} is the amount that can be bought. The line joining X_{max} to Y_{max} represents the various mixed bundles of goods X and Y that can be purchased using all the available funds. Points in the shaded area below the budget line are also affordable, but these leave some portion of funds unspent, so these points would usually not be chosen.

The downward slope of the budget line shows that the individual can afford more X only if Y purchases are cut back. The precise slope of this relationship depends on the unit prices of the two goods. If Y is expensive and X is cheap, the line will be relatively flat since choosing to consume one less Y will permit the purchasing of many units of X (an individual who decides not to purchase a new designer suit can instead choose to purchase many pairs of socks). Alternately, if Y is relatively cheap per unit and X is expensive, the budget line will be steep. Reducing Y consumption does not permit very much more of good X to be bought. All of these relationships can be made clearer by using a bit of algebra.

An Algebraic Approach

Suppose that the individual has I dollars to spend on either good X or good Y. Suppose also that P_X represents the price of good X and P_Y the price of good Y. The total amount spent on X is given by the price of X times the amount purchased ($P_X \cdot X$). Similarly, $P_Y \cdot Y$ represents total spending on good Y. Since the available income must be spent on either X or Y we have

$$\text{Amount spent on X} + \text{Amount spent on Y} = I$$

or

$$P_X \cdot X + P_Y \cdot Y = I. \quad [3.3]$$

Equation 3.3 is an algebraic statement of the budget line shown in Figure 3.6. To make the relationship clearer we can solve this equation for Y so that the budget line has the standard form for a linear equation ($Y = a + bX$) discussed in Chapter 2. This solution of Equation 3.3 gives

$$Y = -\left(\frac{P_X}{P_Y}\right)X + \frac{I}{P_Y}. \quad [3.4]$$

Although the two representations of the budget constraint say exactly the same thing, the relationship between Equation 3.4 and Figure 3.6 should be somewhat clearer. It is obvious from that equation that if the individual chooses to spend all available funds on Y (that is, if $X = 0$), he or she can buy I/P_Y units. If hamburgers cost $1.00 each and this person has decided to spend his or her $10.00 income only on hamburgers, it is clear that 10 can be bought. That point is the Y-intercept in the figure, which we previously called Y_{max}. Similarly, a slight manipulation of the budget equation shows that if $Y = 0$, all income will be devoted to X purchases, and the X-intercept will be I/P_X. If $10.00 is spent only on soft drinks, 20 (= $10.00 ÷ $.50) can be bought. Again, this point is labeled X_{max} in the figure. Finally, the slope of the budget constraint is given by the ratio of the goods' prices, $-P_X/P_Y$. This shows the ratio at which Y can be given up to get more X in the market. In the hamburger–soft drink case, the slope would be −½ (= −$.50 ÷ $1.00) showing that the opportunity cost of one soft drink is half a burger. More generally, as we noted before, if P_X is low and P_Y is high, the slope will be small and the budget line will be flat. On the other hand, a high P_X and a low P_Y will make the budget line steep. As for any linear relationship, the budget constraint can be shifted to a new position by changes in its Y-intercept or by changes in its slope. In Chapter 4 we will use this fact to examine how changes in income or in the prices of goods affect an individual's choices.

Utility Maximization

The individual can afford all bundles of X and Y that fall within the shaded triangle in Figure 3.6. From among these, this person will choose the one that offers the greatest utility. The budget constraint can be used together with the

Figure 3.7
Graphic Demonstration of Utility Maximization

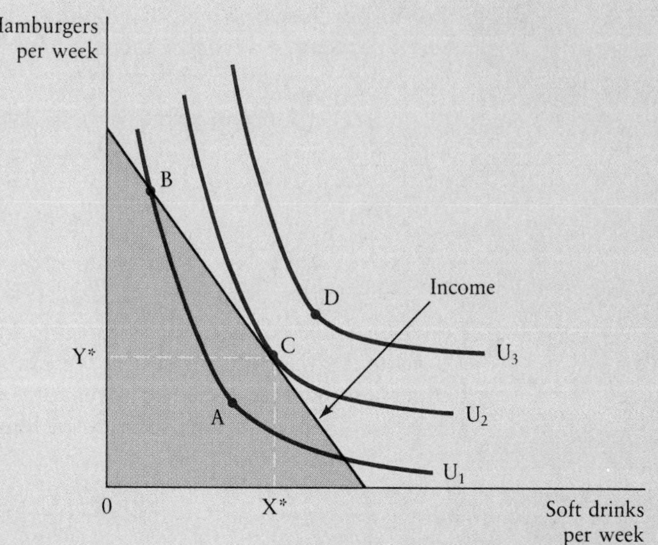

Point C represents the highest utility that can be reached by this individual, given the budget constraint. The combination X*, Y* is therefore the rational way for this person to use the available purchasing power. Only for this combination of goods will two conditions hold: all available funds will be spent; and the individual's psychic rate of trade-off (MRS) will be equal to the rate at which the goods can be traded in the market (P_X/P_Y).

individual's indifference curve map to show this utility-maximization process. Figure 3.7 illustrates the procedure. The individual would be irrational to choose a point such as A—he or she can get to a higher utility level just by spending some of the unspent portion of his or her income. Similarly, by reallocating expenditures the individual can do better than point B. This is the case in which the MRS and the price ratio differ, and the individual can move to a higher indifference curve by choosing to consume less Y and more X. Point D is out of the question because income is not large enough to permit the purchase of that combination of goods. It is clear that the position of maximum utility will be at point C where the combination X*, Y* is chosen. This is the only point on indifference curve U_2 that can be bought with I dollars, and no higher utility level can be bought. C is a point of tangency between the budget constraint and the indifference curve. Therefore all funds are spent and

$$\text{Slope of budget constraint} = \text{Slope of indifference curve} \qquad [3.5]$$

or (neglecting the fact that both slopes are negative)

$$\frac{P_X}{P_Y} = \text{MRS}. \quad [3.6]$$

The result is proved—for a utility maximum the MRS should equal the ratio of the prices of the goods. The diagram shows that if this condition is not fulfilled, this person could be made better off by reallocating expenditures.[4] You may wish to try several other combinations of X and Y that the individual can afford in order to show that they provide a lower utility level than does combination C. In Application 3.4: Rationing in War and Peace, we examine a case in which people may not have such complete freedom in how they spend their incomes. We will show why this results in a lower level of utility than when they do have this freedom.

Importance of the Diminishing Marginal Rate of Substitution

If the individual is to maximize utility subject to a budget constraint, he or she must choose consumption bundles that exhaust income and whose MRS is equal to P_X/P_Y. Points of maximum satisfaction are characterized by a tangency between an individual's indifference curve map and the budget constraint. Not every such point of tangency must provide maximum satisfaction, however, as Figure 3.8 illustrates. Here a point of tangency (C) is inferior to a point of nontangency (B). The true maximum is, as it must be, at another point of tangency (A). The failure of the tangency condition to produce an unambiguous maximum can be attributed to the peculiar shape of the indifference curves in Figure 3.8. If the indifference curves are shaped like those in Figure 3.7 and elsewhere, no such problem can arise: if the MRS is assumed always to be diminishing, the condition of tangency assures a true

[4]If we use the results of note 2 on the assumption that utility is measurable, Equation 3.6 can be given an alternative interpretation. Since

$$P_X/P_Y = \text{MRS} = MU_X/MU_Y \quad [i]$$

for a utility maximum, we have

$$\frac{MU_X}{P_X} = \frac{MU_Y}{P_Y}. \quad [ii]$$

The ratio of the extra utility from consuming one more unit of a good to its price should be the same for each good. Each good should provide the same extra utility per dollar spent. If that were not true, total utility could be raised by reallocating funds from a good that provided a relatively low level of marginal utility per dollar to one that provided a high level. For example, suppose that consuming an extra hamburger would yield 5 utils (units of utility) whereas an extra soft drink would yield 2 utils. Then each util costs $.20 (= $1.00 ÷ 5) if hamburgers are bought and $.25 (= $.50 ÷ 2) if soft drinks are bought. Clearly hamburgers are a cheaper way to buy utility. So this individual should buy more hamburgers and fewer soft drinks until each is an equally costly way to get utility.

APPLICATION 3.4

Rationing in War and Peace

Because economic goods do not exist in quantities sufficient to satisfy all human wants, such goods must always be allocated among individuals in some way. The most common method of allocation is through the price system. The study of that process is the central focus of this book. At times, however, goods may be allocated by nonmarket means.

Figure 1
The Effect of Rationing Is to Reduce Utility

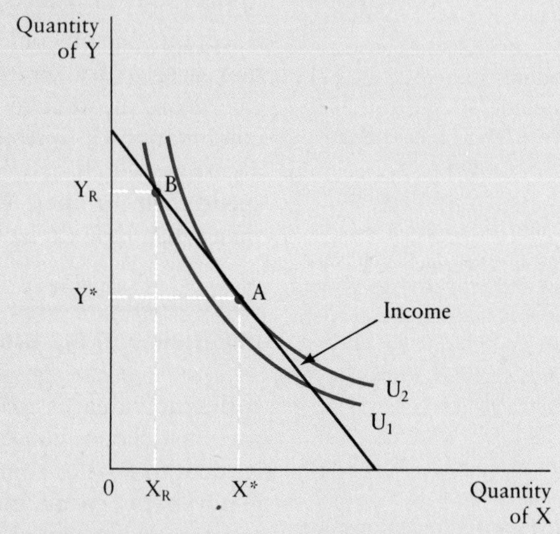

Rationing that allows an individual to purchase only X_R reduces utility (if $X_R < X^*$) from U_2 to U_1. Rationing is more likely to affect the choices of high-income consumers than of low-income consumers.

Wartime Rationing

Government rationing is one of the most common of these methods. Either because a society may not wish to allocate goods by price for ideological or humanitarian reasons (as with rice allotments in China) or because temporary shortages arise that, it is believed, should be shared by all (as was the case in many countries during World War II), governments may choose to ration existing stocks of goods equally (or nearly equally) among everyone.

Figure 1 illustrates such a situation. Given market prices and income, the individual wishes to consume the combination X^*, Y^*. If rationing limits the quantity of X available to any individual to an amount X_R (which must still be purchased at the prevailing price), that preferred point will be unattainable. Rather, the effective budget constraint then becomes only that portion of the original constraint that is to the left of B. Hence, some other utility-maximizing point must be chosen. From the figure it is clear that point B provides the maximum utility, given this additional constraint.

Rationing of X has reduced the individual's utility from U_2 to U_1 by forcing the purchase of less X (and more Y) than is desired. For example, rationing of consumer

maximum. Without this assumption, we would have to be very careful in applying the tangency rule.

A Numerical Example of Utility Maximization

We can give a numerical example of utility maximization if we assume for the moment that utility is measurable. Again suppose that an individual is choosing between hamburgers (Y) and soft drinks (X) and that the prices of these goods are $P_Y = \$1.00$, $P_X = \$.50$. Assume also that the individual has \$10.00 to spend. Finally, suppose that the utility from consuming X and Y is

goods in the United States during World War II caused the personal saving rate to triple (from around 7 to 8 percent of disposable income to nearly 25 percent). Because of the constrained consumption choices, individuals turned to the only other beneficial use for their incomes—additional savings. In fact, these savings were later used to finance the postwar boom in durable goods purchases.

Two aspects of the solution pictured in Figure 1 might be highlighted. First, rationing has an effect on the individual's choices only if $X_R < X^*$. If $X_R > X^*$, the individual is permitted to purchase more of good X than would be freely chosen, and rationing is, for this person, ineffective. Since, as we show in the next chapter, it is likely that X^* will be greater the higher an individual's income, the probability that rationing will effectively limit choices is greater for high-income persons than for low-income persons. For example, rations of meat in England during World War II provided only half the amount usually eaten by high-income families, but virtually all of peacetime consumption for low-income families.

Black Markets

A second feature of this problem concerns the stability of the rationed solution. Since the unrationed optimal choice (A) provides more utility than does the rationed choice (B), there is an incentive for the individual to find some way of moving from B to A. The appearance of black markets in rationed commodities attests to the strength of this incentive. Such markets were relatively uncommon during World War II because social pressures against them were strong. But in peacetime situations such markets have flourished. Widespread "scalping" of World Series or rock concert tickets, for example, arises because the tickets are usually rationed by nonmarket means (first come, first served). Figure 1 suggests that high-income individuals would be more likely to make such black market purchases because they would have more to gain by doing so. When a low-income person sells his or her World Series tickets to a high-income person at an inflated price, both people gain.

To Think About

1. Are the black markets that almost always arise in situations of rationing undesirable? Why should anyone object to people trading away their rations if they choose to? Should the government discourage black markets in some kinds of goods and encourage them in other kinds of goods?
2. Suppose the government required people to buy more of some good than they would freely choose to purchase. Would this result in a lower utility than in the absence of such a requirement? Can you think of any examples for which such an analysis would be appropriate (that is, what kinds of things does the government require you to buy that you would not freely choose)?

given by

$$\text{Utility} = U(X, Y) = \sqrt{XY}. \quad [3.7]$$

We are assuming not only that utility can be measured but also that its value is given by the square root (denoted by $\sqrt{\ }$) of the product of X times Y. This particular utility function is suitable for our purposes because its indifference curves (contour lines) have the familiar convex shape (see, for example, the pipeline application in Chapter 2).

Table 3.1 lists several possible ways in which this person might spend \$10.00 and calculates the utility associated with each choice. For example, if the individual buys six hamburgers and eight soft drinks (totally exhausting

Figure 3.8
Example of an Indifference Curve Map for Which the Tangency Condition Does Not Ensure a Maximum

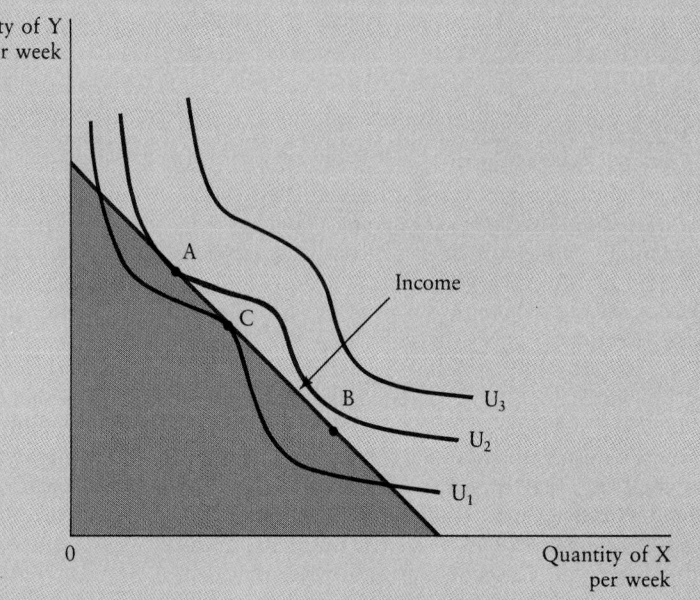

If indifference curves do not obey the assumption of a diminishing MRS, not all points of tangency (points for which MRS = P_X/P_Y) may truly be points of maximum utility. In this example, tangency point C is inferior to many other points that can also be purchased with the available funds.

Table 3.1
Alternative Combinations of Hamburgers (Y) and Soft Drinks (X) That Can Be Bought with \$10.00 (When P_Y = \$1.00, P_X = \$.50) and the Utility of Each Combination

Hamburgers Y	Soft Drinks X	$U(X, Y) = \sqrt{XY}$
0	20	$\sqrt{0} = 0$
1	18	$\sqrt{18} = 4.2$
2	16	$\sqrt{32} = 5.7$
3	14	$\sqrt{42} = 6.5$
4	12	$\sqrt{48} = 6.9$
5	10	$\sqrt{50} = 7.1$
6	8	$\sqrt{48} = 6.9$
7	6	$\sqrt{42} = 6.5$
8	4	$\sqrt{32} = 5.7$
9	2	$\sqrt{18} = 4.2$
10	0	$\sqrt{0} = 0$

the \$10.00), utility will be 6.9 (= $\sqrt{48}$). The other entries in the table all cost \$10.00, but they yield very different levels of utility. Of those combinations listed, the bundle Y = 5, X = 10 yields the most utility, and that would seem to be how this fast-food gourmet should spend the \$10.00.

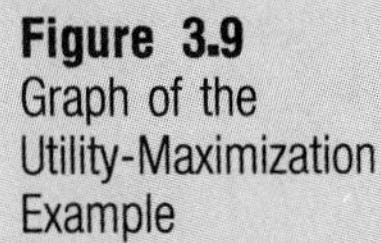

Figure 3.9
Graph of the Utility-Maximization Example

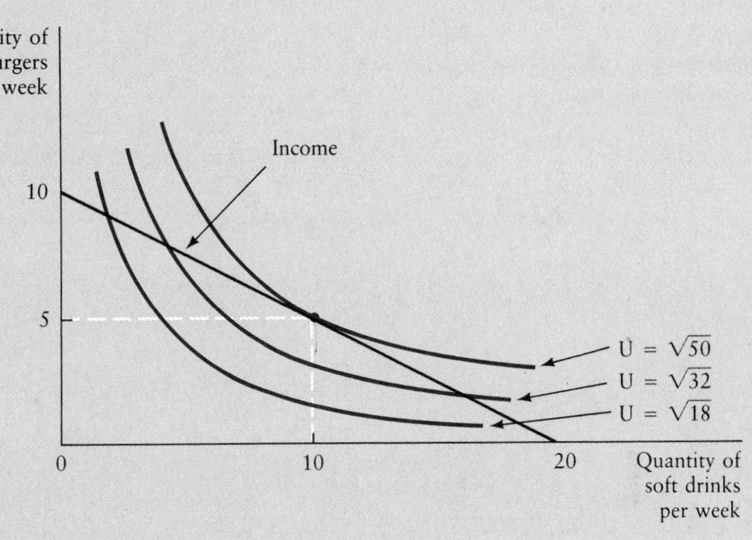

If $P_X = \$.50$, $P_Y = \$1.00$, and $I = \$10.00$, then the utility-maximizing choice for X and Y is $X^* = 10$, $Y^* = 5$. At this point, the budget constraint is just tangent to the indifference curve $U = \sqrt{XY} = \sqrt{50}$ (or $X \cdot Y = 50$), and this is the highest utility level obtainable.

Figure 3.9 confirms this view. Since the budget constraint is

$$\$.50X + \$1.00Y = \$10.00, \qquad [3.8]$$

the Y-intercept is 10 (= \$10.00 ÷ \$1.00), and the X-intercept is 20 (= \$10.00 ÷ \$.50). The slope of this line ($-\frac{1}{2}$) again shows that the opportunity cost of one soft drink is ½ of a hamburger. As shown in Figure 3.9, the individual with this budget constraint can just reach the indifference curve $U = \sqrt{50}$ at the single point $Y = 5$, $X = 10$. Any other choices that cost \$10.00 or less yield a lower utility. At the point $Y = 5$, $X = 10$ the budget constraint is just tangent to the indifference curve;[5] the MRS is equal to the ratio of the goods' prices.

Using the Model of Choice

This simple model of utility maximization can be used to explain a number of common observations. Figure 3.10, for example, provides an illustration of why people with the same purchasing power choose to spend this in different

[5] This indifference curve is a graph of $XY = 50$. Hence it is similar to the contour lines graphed in Chapter 2.

Figure 3.10
Differences in Preferences Result in Differing Choices

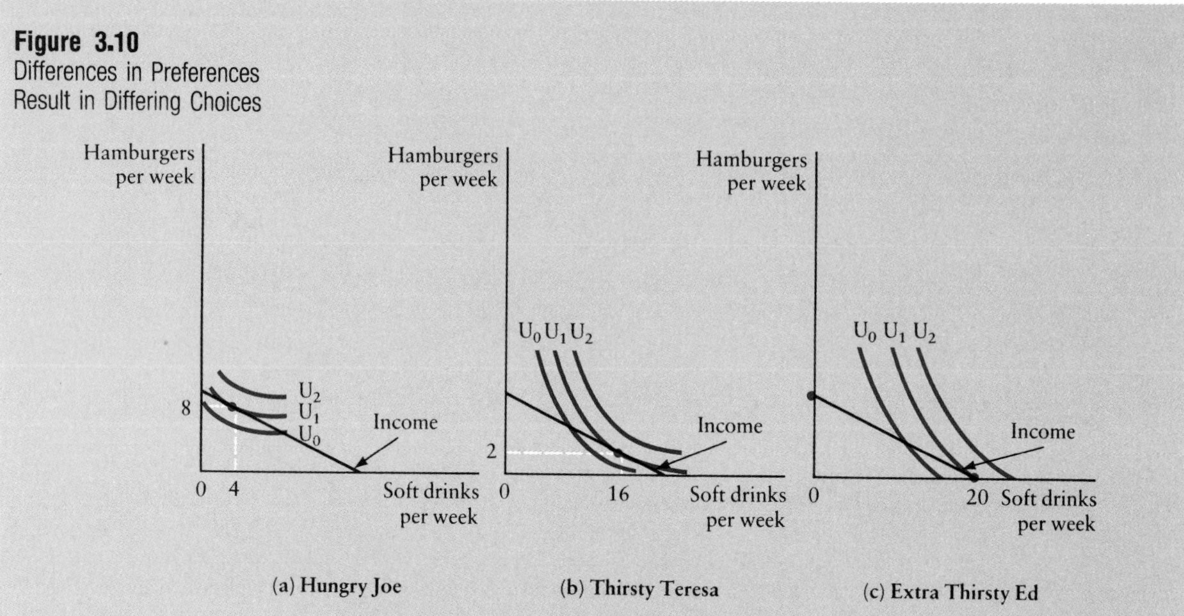

The three individuals illustrated here all have the same budget constraint. They choose very different consumption bundles because they have differing preferences for the two goods.

ways. In all three panels of Figure 3.10 the budget constraints facing each individual are the same. However, Hungry Joe in Panel a of the figure has a clear preference for hamburgers. He chooses to spend his \$10 almost exclusively on burgers. Thirsty Teresa, on the other hand, chooses to spend most of her \$10 on soft drinks. She does buy two hamburgers, however, because she feels some need for solid food. Extra thirsty Ed, whose situation is shown in Panel c of Figure 3.10, wants a totally liquid diet. He gets the most utility from spending his entire \$10 on soft drinks. Even though he would in some circumstances buy hamburgers, in the current case he is so thirsty that the opportunity cost of giving up a soft drink to do so is just too high.[6]

Figure 3.11 presents again the four specific indifference curve maps that were introduced earlier in this chapter. Now we have superimposed a budget constraint on each one and indicated the utility-maximizing choice by E. Some obvious implications can be drawn from these illustrations. Panel a

[6]For example, suppose that with Y = 0, X = 20 the marginal utility of one more hamburger is 5 utils whereas for one more soft drink it is 3 utils. Then even when Ed is consuming only soft drinks, an extra util costs \$.20 if he buys hamburgers, but only \$.17 (= \$.50 ÷ 3) if he buys soft drinks. Soft drinks are still the best buy for this thirsty person.

Figure 3.11
Utility-Maximizing Choices for Special Types of Goods

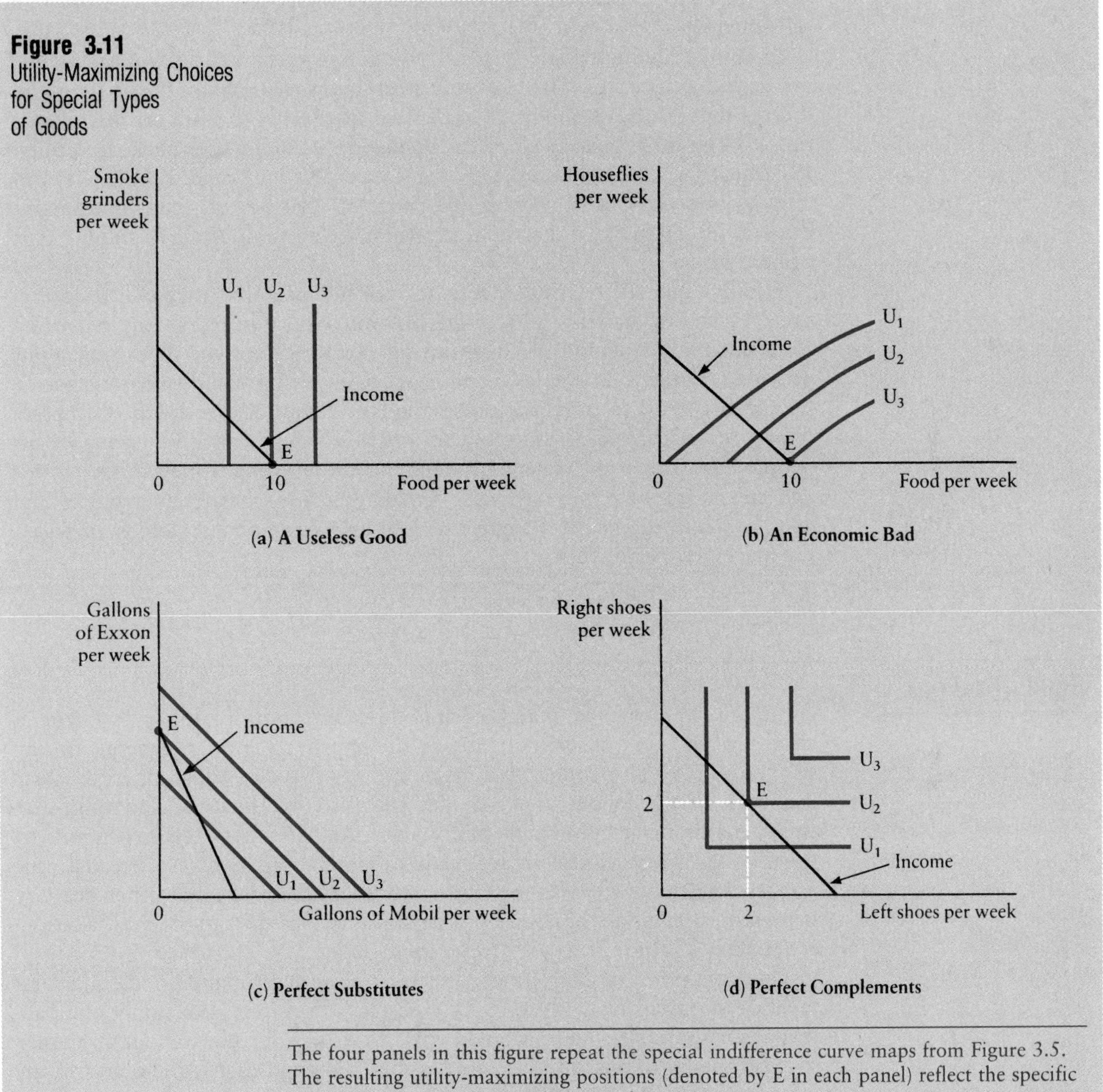

The four panels in this figure repeat the special indifference curve maps from Figure 3.5. The resulting utility-maximizing positions (denoted by E in each panel) reflect the specific relationships among the goods pictured.

makes clear that a utility-maximizing individual will never buy a useless good. Utility is as large as possible by consuming only food. There is no reason for this person to incur the opportunity cost involved in consuming any smoke grinders. A similar result holds for Panel b—there is no reason for this person to spend anything on houseflies (assuming there is a store that sells them).

In Panel c the individual buys only Exxon even though Exxon and Mobil are perfect substitutes. The relatively steep budget constraint in the figure indicates that Mobil is the more expensive of the two brands so this person opts to buy only Exxon. Since the goods are virtually identical, the utility-maximizing decision is to buy only the least expensive brand. People who buy only generic versions of prescription drugs or who buy all their brand name household staples at a discount supermarket are exhibiting a similar type of behavior.

Finally, the utility-maximizing situation illustrated in Panel d of Figure 3.11 shows that this person will only buy shoes in pairs. Any departure from this pattern would result in buying extra left or right shoes that alone provide no utility. In similar circumstances involving complementary goods, people also tend to purchase those goods together. Other items of apparel (gloves, earrings, socks, and so forth) are also bought mainly in pairs. Most people have preferred ways of concocting the beverages they drink (coffee and cream, gin and vermouth) or of making sandwiches (peanut butter and jelly, ham and cheese). And people seldom buy automobiles, stereos, or washing machines by the part.

Generalizations

Although the previous examples studied only the individual's problem in choosing between two specific goods, the approach is quite general. In any situation in which people must make choices that are constrained by their economic circumstances, a very similar analysis could be used. The result that utility-maximizing individuals will equate the MRS between two goods to those goods' prices carries over directly to more complex cases.[7] Because economics is in many respects the study of how choices are made when scarcity is present, this model of choice lies behind many of the approaches taken by economists to study real-world questions.

One common graphing procedure for dealing with many goods might be mentioned. Often we wish to study a person's decisions about only one particular good and are not concerned with his or her decisions about any other specific goods. In this case we could record the good that is the object of attention on the horizontal (X) axis and treat all other goods as one single com-

---

[7]To examine such many-good cases requires the use of advanced mathematics since graphical techniques cannot be easily adapted to many dimensions. A relatively simple treatment of these mathematical derivations can be found in Walter Nicholson, *Microeconomic Theory: Basic Principles and Extensions,* 4th ed. (Hinsdale, Ill.: Dryden Press, 1989), pp. 109–112. For a more complex discussion, see Paul A. Samuelson, *Foundations of Economic Analysis* (Cambridge, Mass.: Harvard University Press, 1947), Chapter 5.

Composite good
Combining expenditures on several different goods whose relative prices do not change into a single good for convenience in analysis.

modity shown on the vertical (Y) axis. That is, good Y is treated as a **composite good** that includes spending on everything except the good being explicitly examined. In this way, the standard two-dimensional analysis of choice is more general than might first appear to be the case.[8] In Chapter 4 we use this technique on several occasions.

Summary

This chapter covers a lot of ground. In it we have seen how economists explain the kinds of choices people make and the ways in which those choices are constrained by economic circumstances. The chapter has been rather tough going in places. The theory of choice is one of the most difficult parts of any study of microeconomics, and it is unfortunate that it usually comes at the very start of the course. But that placement clearly shows why the topic is so important—practically every model of economic behavior we will study starts with the building blocks introduced in this chapter.

Our principal conclusions in this chapter are:

- Economists use the term "utility" to refer to the satisfaction that people derive from their economic activities. Usually only a few of the things that affect utility are examined in any particular analysis. All other factors are assumed to be held constant so that a person's choices can be studied in a simplified setting.
- Utility can be represented by an indifference curve map. Each indifference curve shows those bundles of goods that the individual considers to be equally attractive. Higher levels of utility are represented by higher indifference curve "contour" lines.
- The slope of indifference curves shows how individuals are willing to trade one good for another while remaining equally well-off. The negative of this slope is called the "marginal ate of substitution" (MRS), since it shows the degree to which an individual is willing to substitute one good for another in his or her consumption choices.
- People are limited in what they can buy. Economists refer to such limits as "budget constraints." When a person is choosing between two goods, his or her budget constraint is usually a straight line. The negative of the slope of this line represents the price ratio of the two goods—it shows what one of the goods is worth in terms of the other in the marketplace.
- If individuals are to obtain the maximum possible utility from their limited incomes, they should spend all the available funds and should

[8]To make this convention rigorously correct requires that we assume that the relative prices of all the goods that constitute "everything else" are not changing during the analysis. Then it is possible to view the individual's choice problem as one of deciding how much income to devote to the purchase of X and how much to devote to everything else. For a discussion, see Nicholson, *Microeconomic Theory,* pp. 168–170.

choose a bundle of goods for which the MRS is equal to the price ratio of the two goods. Such a utility maximum is shown graphically by a tangency between the individual's budget constraint and the highest indifference curve that his or her income can afford.

Review Questions

1. Our notion of utility is an "ordinal" one for which it is assumed that people can rank combinations of goods as to their desirability, but that they cannot assign a unique numerical ("cardinal") categorization of the goods that identifies by "how much" one combination is preferred to another. For each of the following ranking systems, describe whether an ordinal or cardinal ranking is being used: (a) military or academic ranks; (b) prices of vintage wines; (c) rankings of vintage wines by the French Wine Society; (d) press rankings of the "Top Ten" football teams; (e) results of the current U.S. Open Golf Championships (which are contested using stroke play); (f) results of early U.S. Open Golf Championships (which were conducted using match play).
2. Our discussion of actual food consumption patterns in Application 3.2 suggests that some particularly harried individuals may exhibit intransitivities in their choices. Under what conditions might people find it in their interest to demonstrate some irrationality in their choices of food items? Would these situations necessarily violate the assumption of utility maximization?
3. What kind of behavior would an economist consider truly "irrational"? Can you think of choices that people make that are not truly in their best interest, broadly conceived?
4. Explain why using the concept of the marginal rate of substitution (MRS) to describe voluntary trades does not require us to adopt any specific way to measure utility. Why is the MRS that an individual exhibits measured independently of how his or her utility is measured?
5. Show that no two of an individual's indifference curves can intersect. What assumptions about behavior would be violated if two such curves did intersect? (*Hint:* Why can't two different contour lines [e.g., one for "100 feet" and one for "150 feet"] intersect on a topographic map?)
6. Sometimes an individual who has chosen a utility-maximizing combination of goods is said to have achieved an "equilibrium" in his or her decision problem. Why is this described as an equilibrium? What forces are being balanced in the individual's mind? In what sense will the equilibrium tend to persist until something changes?
7. Using the marginal utility interpretation of the utility-maximization process that is described in footnotes 2, 4, and 6 of this chapter, explain why the individual's decision problem can be described as "deciding how to get the biggest bang for his or her bucks." Use this to explain what it means to say that something "costs too much."
8. How might you draw an indifference curve map that illustrates the following ideas?

   a. Margarine is just as good as the high-priced spread.
   b. Things go better with Coke.
   c. A day without wine is like a day without sunshine.
   d. Popcorn is addictive—the more you eat, the more you want.
   e. If he doesn't wear English Leather, he wears nothing at all.
   f. It takes two to tango.

9. Application 3.4 illustrates how rationing of a commodity may reduce utility. Develop a similar graphic analysis to show why requiring the purchase of some particular amount of an item would have the same effect.
10. Suppose an individual consumes three items: steak, lettuce, and tomatoes. If we were interested only in examining this person's steak purchases, we might group lettuce and tomatoes into a single composite good called "salad." How would you define this good? What would this person's budget constraint for steak and salad be? What would it mean to say that "the relative price of salad has risen"?

Problems

3.1 Suppose a person has \$8.00 to spend only on apples and oranges. Suppose apples cost \$.40 each and oranges cost \$.10 each.

a. If this person buys *only* apples, how many can be bought?
b. If the person buys *only* oranges, how many can be bought?
c. If the person were to buy 10 apples, how many oranges could be bought with the funds left over?
d. If the person consumes one less apple (that is, nine), how many more oranges could be bought? Is this rate of trade-off the same no matter how many apples are relinquished?
e. Write down the algebraic equation for this person's budget constraint, and graph it showing the points mentioned in parts a through d (using graph paper would improve the accuracy of your work).

3.2 Suppose the person faced with the budget constraint described in problem 3.1 has preferences for apples (A) and oranges (O) given by

$$\text{Utility} = \sqrt{A \cdot O}.$$

a. If A = 5 and O = 80, what will utility be?
b. If A = 10, what value for O will provide the same utility as in part a?
c. If A = 20, what value for O will provide the same utility as in parts a and b?
d. Graph the indifference curve implied by parts a through c.
e. Given the budget constraint from problem 3.1, which of the points identified in parts a through c can be bought by this person?
f. Show through some examples that every other way of allocating income provides less utility than does the point identified in part e. Graph this utility-maximizing situation.

3.3 Oliver D. Dancefloor gets his utility by going to discos or rock concerts. His utility function is $U = \sqrt{D \cdot C}$, where D = the number of discos and C = the number of concerts he attends in a month. Draw the contour lines (in the positive quadrant) for this function for utility levels of 4, 5, and 10 (that is, for U = 4, U = 5, and U = 10). What do we call the shape of these contour lines? (Hint: Here it may be easier to graph U^2 rather than U.)
3.4 Assume Oliver D. Dancefloor has the utility function described in problem 3.3. If concert tickets are \$4, the cover charge at the disco is \$2, and Oliver's monthly entertainment budget is \$64, what is his budget constraint? Where

does this line intersect the indifference curve for $U = \sqrt{128}$? Does this seem to be the highest utility possible given the budget constraint?

3.5 Ms. Caffeine enjoys coffee (C) and tea (T) according to the function $U(C, T) = 3C + 4T$. What does her utility function say about her MRS of coffee for tea? What do her indifference curves look like? If coffee and tea cost $3 each and Ms. Caffeine has $12 to spend on these products, how much coffee and tea should she buy to maximize her utility? Draw the graph of her indifference curve map and her budget constraint, and show that the utility-maximizing point occurs only on the T-axis where no coffee is bought. Would she buy any coffee if she had more money to spend? How would her consumption change if the price of coffee fell to $2?

3.6 Mr. A derives utility from martinis in proportion to the number he drinks, $U(M) = M$. Mr. A is very particular about his martinis, however: he only enjoys them made in the exact proportion of two parts gin (G) to one part vermouth (V). Graph Mr. A's indifference curve in terms of G and V for various levels of martini consumption. (Hint: Does Mr. A have an MRS of G for V?) Show that regardless of the prices of the two ingredients, Mr. A will never alter the way he mixes martinis. Graph this result.

3.7 Assume consumers are choosing between housing services (H) measured in square feet and consumption of all other goods (C) measured in dollars.

a. Show the equilibrium position in a diagram.
b. Now suppose the government agrees to subsidize consumers by paying 50 percent of their housing cost. How will their budget line change? Show the new equilibrium.
c. Show in a diagram the minimum amount of income supplement the government would have to give individuals instead of a housing subsidy to make them as well-off as they were in part b.

*3.8 Suppose low-income people have preferences for nonfood consumption (NF) and for food consumption (F). In the absence of any income transfer programs, a person's budget constraint is given by

$$NF + P_F F = I,$$

where P_F is the price of food relative to nonfood items and NF and I are measured in terms of nonfood prices (that is, dollars).

a. Graph the initial utility-maximizing situation for this low-income person.
b. Suppose now that a food stamp program is introduced that requires low-income people to pay C (measured in terms of nonfood prices) in order to receive food stamps sufficient to buy F* units of food (presumably $P_F F^* > C$). Show this person's budget constraint if he or she participates in the food stamp program.
c. Show graphically the factors that will determine whether the person chooses to participate in the program.
d. Show graphically what it will cost the government to finance benefits for the typical food stamp recipient. Show also that this person could reach a higher utility level if this amount were simply given with no strings attached.

---

*Denotes a problem that is rather difficult.

*3.9 Suppose individuals derive utility from two goods, housing (H) and all other consumption (C). Show that if the government requires individuals to buy more housing than they would freely choose (say, by setting minimum housing "standards"), such a policy may reduce utility. Which group would you expect to suffer the greatest losses of utility from such a policy? (Hint: Use the analysis from Application 3.4.)

---

*Denotes a problem that is rather difficult.

CHAPTER 4

How Changes in Income and Prices Affect Choices

This chapter studies how people change their choices when conditions change. In particular, we will study how changes in income or changes in the price of a good affect the amount that people choose to consume. We will compare the new choices with those that were made before conditions changed. This kind of investigation is sometimes called **comparative statics** analysis because it compares two utility-maximizing choices. One result of this approach will be to construct the individual's demand curve for a good since such a curve shows how the individual responds to changes in the good's price.

Comparative statics
The investigation of new choices people make when conditions change, as compared to the choices they made under the former conditions.

You need to be careful about two aspects of this kind of approach. First, the *ceteris paribus* assumption is important here. We are changing only one thing that affects choices at a time; everything else is being held constant. In particular, we are assuming that people's preferences do not change. In graphic terms, we will be keeping the individual's indifference curve map unchanged and studying the effects of shifting the budget constraint to alternative positions.

Second, you should understand that the general notion of "changing conditions" is only a beginning for our investigation. Ideally, we would like to explain why economic conditions change. Instead of supposing that, say, the price of potatoes has risen, we will eventually be more interested in finding out *why* the price of potatoes has risen. This chapter is only the first step in answering this larger question, which we will not discuss in detail until Part 4.

Demand Functions

Demand function
A representation of how quantity demanded depends on prices, income, and preferences.

Chapter 3 showed that the quantities of X and Y that an individual chooses depend on the person's preferences (that is, on the shape of the indifference curve map) and on the budget constraint. If we knew a person's preferences and all of the economic forces that affect the choices, we could predict how much of each good would be chosen. We can summarize this conclusion using the **demand function** for some particular good, say, X:

$$\text{Quantity of X demanded} = d_X(P_X, P_Y, I; \text{preferences}) . \quad [4.1]$$

This functional notation contains the three elements that determine what the individual can buy—the prices of X and Y and the person's income (I)—as well as a reminder that choices are also affected by preferences for the goods. These preferences appear to the right of the semicolon in Equation 4.1 because for most of our analysis we assume that preferences do not change. People's basic likes and dislikes are assumed to be developed through a lifetime of experience. They are unlikely to change as we examine their reactions to relatively short-term changes in their economic circumstances caused by changes in commodity prices or incomes.

The quantity demanded of good Y depends on these same general influences and can be summarized by

$$\text{Quantity of Y demanded} = d_Y(P_X, P_Y, I; \text{preferences}) . \quad [4.2]$$

Preferences again appear to the right of the semicolon in Equation 4.2 because we assume that the person's taste for good Y will not change during our analysis. Here we are interested only in examining how choices change when economic conditions change.

Homogeneity

One important result that follows directly from Chapter 3 is that if the prices of X and Y and income (I) were all to double (or to change by any identical percentage), the same quantities of X and Y would be demanded. The budget constraint

$$P_XX + P_YY = I \quad [4.3]$$

is identical to the budget constraint

$$2P_XX + 2P_YY = 2I . \quad [4.4]$$

Graphically, Equations 4.3 and 4.4 are exactly the same lines. Consequently, both budget constraints are tangent to the individual's indifference curve map at precisely the same point. The quantities of X and Y the individual chooses when faced with the constraint in Equation 4.3 are exactly the same as when the individual is faced by the constraint in Equation 4.4.

Homogeneous demand function
Demand does not change when prices and income increase in the same proportion.

Hence, we have shown an important result: the quantities an individual demands depend only on the relative prices of goods X and Y and on the "real" value of income. Proportional changes in the prices of X and Y and in income change only the units we count in (such as dollars instead of cents). They do not affect the quantities demanded. Individual demands are said to be **homogeneous** for identical proportional changes in all prices and income.[1] People are not hurt by general inflation of prices if their incomes increase in the same proportion. They will be on exactly the same indifference curve both before and after the inflation. Only if inflation increases some incomes faster or slower than prices change does it have an effect on budget constraints, on the quantities of goods demanded, and on people's well-being.

Changes in Income

As a person's total income rises, assuming prices don't change, we might expect the quantity purchased of each good also to increase. This situation is illustrated in Figure 4.1. As income increases from I_1 to I_2 to I_3, the quantity of X demanded increases from X_1 to X_2 to X_3, and the quantity of Y demanded increases from Y_1 to Y_2 to Y_3. Budget lines I_1, I_2, and I_3 are all parallel because we are changing only income, not the relative prices of X and Y. Remember the slope of the budget constraint is given by the ratio of the two goods' prices, and these prices are not changing in this analysis. Increases in income do, however, make it possible for this person to consume more; and such increased purchasing power is reflected by the outward shift in the budget constraint and an increase in overall utility.

Normal Goods

Normal good
A good that is bought in greater quantities as income increases.

In Figure 4.1 both good X and good Y increase as income increases. Goods that follow this tendency are called **normal goods.** Most goods seem to be normal goods—as their incomes increase, people tend to buy more of practically everything. Of course, as Figure 4.1 shows, the demand for some "luxury" goods (such as Y) may increase rapidly when income rises, but the demand for "necessities" (such as X) may grow less rapidly. The relationship between income and the amounts of various goods purchased has been extensively examined by economists as Application 4.1: Engel's Law shows.

[1]Technically, a function $f(X, Y)$ is said to be homogeneous of degree zero in X and Y if $f(tX, tY) = f(X, Y)$ for any $t > 0$. Doubling X and Y for a function homogeneous of degree zero leaves the value of f unchanged. This is precisely the case for demand functions.

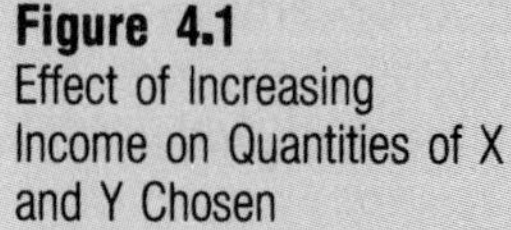

Figure 4.1
Effect of Increasing Income on Quantities of X and Y Chosen

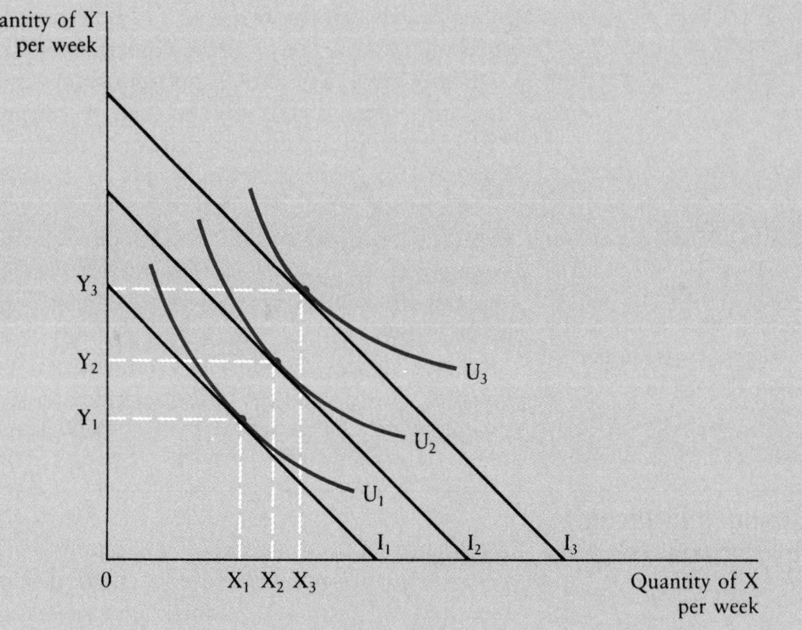

As income increases from I_1 to I_2 to I_3, the optimal (utility-maximizing) choices of X and Y are shown by the successively higher points of tangency. The budget constraint shifts in a parallel way because its slope (given by the ratio of the goods' prices) does not change.

Inferior Goods

Inferior good
A good that is bought in smaller quantities as income increases.

The demand for certain goods probably decreases as a person's income increases. Some examples of these goods are "rotgut" whiskey, potatoes, and secondhand clothing. This kind of good is called an **inferior good.** How the demand for an inferior good responds to rising income is shown in Figure 4.2. The good Z is inferior because the individual chooses less of it as his or her income increases. Although the curves in Figure 4.3 continue to obey the assumption of a diminishing MRS, they exhibit inferiority. Good Z is inferior only because of the way it relates to the other goods available (good Y here), not because of its own qualities. Purchases of rotgut whiskey decline as income increases, for example, because an individual is able to afford more expensive goods (such as Jack Daniel's). Inferior goods are probably quite rare. Application 4.2: Are Children Inferior? exhibits a common pitfall that makes some goods appear to be inferior when they really are not.

Changes in a Good's Price

Examining how a price change affects the quantity demanded of a good is more complex than looking at the effect of a change in income. Changing the

APPLICATION 4.1

Engel's Law

The relationship between income and the consumption of certain goods has been studied by economists since the eighteenth century.

Engel's Studies

Probably the most famous sample data are those used by the Prussian economist Ernst Engel (1821–1896) in his original studies of household behavior. An abbreviated set of these data is shown in Table 1. They show the spending patterns of 153 Belgian families in 1853. Engel drew one major conclusion from these data: the proportion of income spent on food declines as income rises. This hypothesis has come to be known as Engel's law. It has been verified in hundreds of studies. Cross-country comparisons also show that, on average, people in less-developed countries spend more of their incomes on food than people in richer industrial countries and over time the percentage of income spent on food also tends to decline as incomes rise. For example, in nineteenth-century America people spent nearly 50 percent of their incomes on food. Today, that figure has fallen to below 20 percent.

Engel was cautious about drawing conclusions from the other data in his table. Even today no other laws of consumption are believed to hold as true as Engel's law of food consumption. For example, according to the data, shelter expenses seem to be a constant fraction of income. Whether housing spending is really proportional to income has been hotly debated for many years, particularly in regard to how property taxes affect various income groups.

Table 1
Percentage of Total Expenditures on Various Items by Belgian Families in 1853

	Annual Income		
Expenditure Item	$225–$300	$450–$600	$750–$1,000
Food	62.0%	55.0%	50.0%
Clothing	16.0	18.0	18.0
Lodging, light, and fuel	17.0	17.0	17.0
Services (education, legal, health)	4.0	7.5	11.5
Comfort and recreation	1.0	2.5	3.5
Total	100.0	100.0	100.0

Source: Reproduced in A. Marshall, *Principles of Economics,* 8th ed. (London: Macmillan & Co., Ltd., 1920), p. 97. Some items have been aggregated.

Table 2
Percentage of Total Expenditures on Various Items by U.S. Families in 1984

	Annual Income		
Expenditure Item	$10,000–$12,000	$18,000–$20,000	$40,000+
Food	18.8%	16.4%	13.1%
Clothing	5.4	5.2	6.1
Lodging, light, and fuel	34.5	30.9	28.3
Other expenditures	41.3	47.5	52.5
Total	100.0	100.0	100.0

Source: Statistical Abstract of the United States, 1987, Table 718.

Recent Data

Table 2 updates Engel's work with data for the United States in 1984. Although there have been vast changes since 1853 in the types of goods that people consume (which means the categories in the two tables are not directly comparable), some of Engel's conclusions remain valid. Most importantly, Engel's law continues to hold. Higher income people still spend less of their income on food than people with lower incomes do. The growth in income since the nineteenth century is reflected in the huge increase in spending devoted to "other goods." The necessities of life now occupy a less important portion of the individual's budget than they did in the previous century.

To Think About

1. In Application 3.1 we described how budget share data might be used to define whether a person or family is "poor." What does this discussion of Engel's law suggest about using food expenditures for such a purpose? How about using expenditures on housing?
2. In recent years the percentage of income devoted to food eaten away from home has been rising. Does this trend contradict Engel's law? What do people who eat at restaurants actually "consume"?

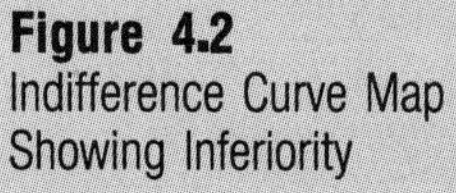

Figure 4.2
Indifference Curve Map Showing Inferiority

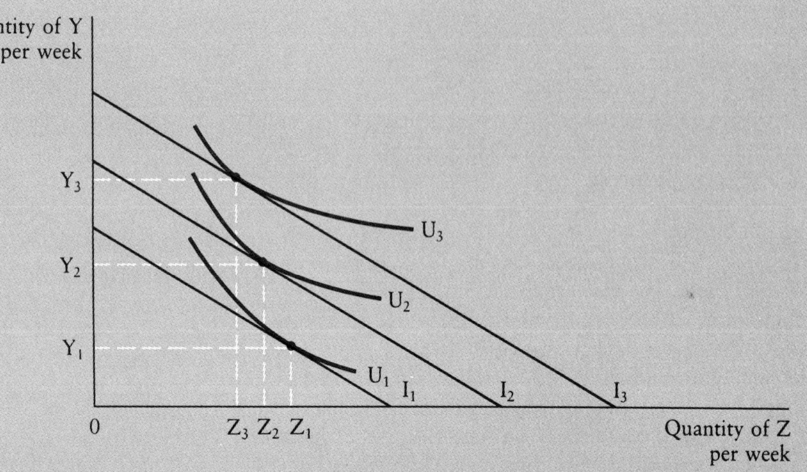

Good Z is inferior because the quantity purchased declines as income increases. Y is a normal good (as it must be if only two goods are available), and purchases of it increase as total expenditures increase.

price geometrically involves not only changing the intercept of the budget constraint but also changing its slope. Moving to the new utility-maximizing choice means moving to another indifference curve and also changing the MRS.

When a price changes, it has two different effects on people's choices. With the **substitution effect,** even if the individual stays on the same indifference curve, consumption has to be changed to equate MRS to the new price ratio of the two goods. With the **income effect,** because the price change also changes "real" purchasing power, people will move to a new indifference curve that is consistent with their new purchasing power. We now look at these two effects of price changes in several different situations.

Substitution effect
The part of the change in quantity demanded of a good whose price has changed that is caused by substitution of the good that is now relatively cheaper for the other that is now relatively more costly. A movement along an indifference curve.

Income effect
The part of the change in quantity demanded of a good whose price has changed that is caused by the change in real income that results from the price change.

Substitution and Income Effects from a Fall in Price

Let's look first at how the quantity consumed of good X changes in response to a fall in its price. This situation is illustrated in Figure 4.3. Initially the individual maximizes utility by choosing the combination X*, Y*. Suppose that the price of X falls. The budget line now shifts outward to the new budget constraint as shown in the figure. Remember that the budget constraint meets the Y-axis at the point where all available income is spent on good Y. But, since neither the person's income nor the price of good Y has changed here, this Y-intercept is the same for both constraints. The new X-intercept is to the right of the old one because the lower price of X means that, with

Figure 4.3
Income and Substitution Effects of a Fall in Price

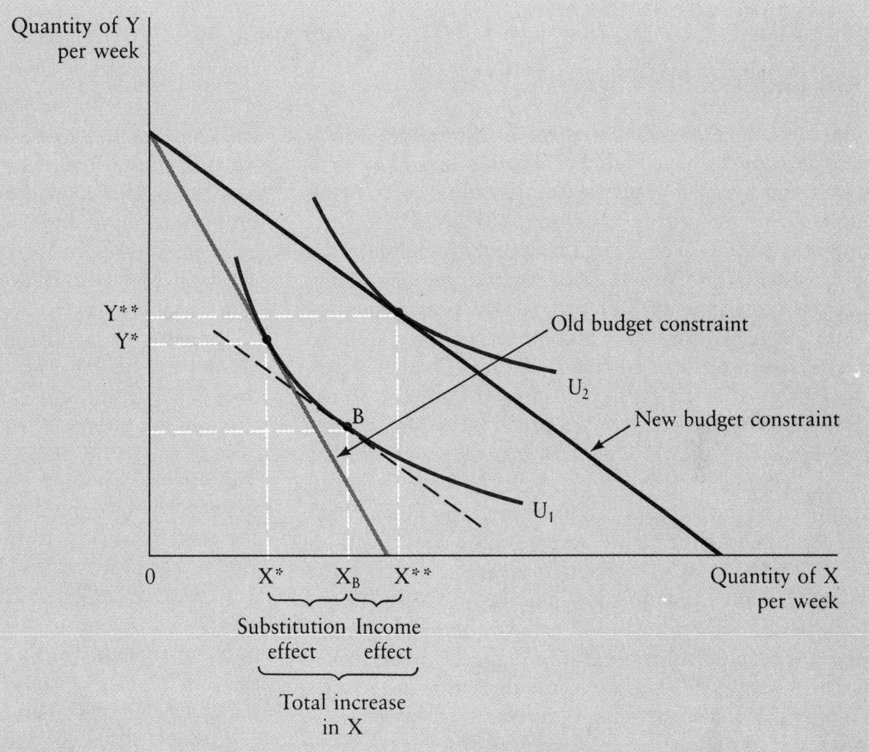

When the price of X falls, the utility-maximizing choice shifts from X*, Y* to X**, Y**. This movement can be broken down into two effects: first, a movement along the initial indifference curve to point B where the MRS is equal to the new price ratio (the substitution effect); second, a movement to a higher level of utility, since real income has increased (the income effect). Both the substitution and income effects cause more X to be bought when its price declines. The Y-intercept is the same for both budget constraints because both P_Y and I are held constant.

the lower price, more of it can now be bought. The flatter slope of the budget constraint shows us that the relative price of X to Y (that is, P_X/P_Y) has fallen.

With this change in the budget constraint, the new position of maximum utility is at X**, Y**. There the new budget line is tangent to the indifference curve U_2. The movement to this new set of choices is the result of two different effects. First, the change in the slope of the budget constraint would have motivated the individual to move to point B even if the person had stayed on the original indifference curve U_1. The dashed line in Figure 4.3 has the same slope as the new budget constraint, but it is tangent to U_1 because we are holding "real" income (that is, utility) constant. A relatively lower price for X causes the individual to move from X*, Y* to B if he or she is not better-off as a result of the lower price. This movement is a graphic demonstration of

APPLICATION 4.2

Are Children Inferior?

One decision that seems to involve an inferior good is the decision to have children. Table 1 lists U.S. birth rates and average annual earnings (adjusted to 1980 dollars) for the census years from 1890 to 1980. During that period, except for a temporary increase in the years after World War II, birth rates fell rather sharply. At the same time average real income nearly quadrupled. As Americans have become richer, they seem to have chosen to demand fewer children. Does this pattern mean that children are "inferior" goods? Somehow the notion that people's preferences for children are similar to their preferences for rotgut whiskey or used clothing is a bit hard to believe. People seem to enjoy parenthood too much and spend too much effort on their children for us to accept such a conclusion.

Economists are reluctant to accept at face value these data that seem to show inferiority. They look for other explanations for the observed pattern. Most commonly, economists argue in this case that many other factors besides the decline in the birth rate are associated with rising income levels. Interpreting the relationship of income and birth rates is more difficult than it at first appears since it is not a *ceteris paribus* relationship.

Quality versus Quantity

Economist Gary Becker was one of the first to point out that a couple's decision to have children really has two dimensions: a decision about how many to have (quantity) and a series of decisions about how much money to spend on their upbringing (quality).[1] As people earn more money, it seems likely that they will be more interested in the quality dimension of their children (by buying braces, violin lessons, college educations, and so forth). They may choose to have fewer children but to spend much more in total on the quality of their upbringing. Hence, the data on number of children may be entirely consistent with the notion that children are "normal" goods.

Table 1

U.S. Birth Rates and Earnings since 1890

Year	Birth Rate per 1,000 Population	Average Annual Earnings in 1980 Dollars
1890	33.7	$ 4,210
1900	32.3	4,515
1910	30.1	4,905
1920	27.7	5,370
1930	21.3	6,275
1940	19.4	7,104
1950	24.1	9,580
1960	23.7	12,694
1970	18.4	15,239
1980	15.3	15,475

Source: Computed from various series in *U.S. Historical Statistics from Colonial Times to 1970* and *U.S. Statistical Abstract, 1980.*

The Price of Children

Another view of the data on birth rates considers how the cost of having children changes with increasing levels of affluence. This view argues that costs rise rapidly primarily because of the opportunity cost of the wages that are no longer earned by parents who stay home to provide child care. In the United States during the past hundred years, for example, it is argued that rising wages for women have sharply increased the opportunity cost of childbearing, and that is one reason why birth rates have fallen. Once this cost is taken into account, many authors find that the direction of the relationship between income and birth rate is reversed.[2]

To Think About

1. How would the analysis provided in this application explain the rapid population growth rates of many less-developed countries, and what would it suggest about the likely success of birth control programs? Would economic growth be a successful way to limit population growth?
2. How do high income tax rates affect couples' decisions to have children? Might such taxes have different effects depending on which family member we examine? Should tax rates be varied to take family responsibilities into account?

[1]Gary S. Becker, "An Economic Analysis of Fertility," in *Demographic and Economic Change in Developed Countries,* National Bureau Conference Series 11 (Princeton, N.J.: Princeton University Press, 1960).

[2]A great deal of this evidence is reviewed in T. W. Schultz, ed., "New Economic Approaches to Fertility," *Journal of Political Economy* (March/April 1973).

the substitution effect. Even though the individual is no better-off, the change in price still causes a change in consumption choices.

The further move from B to the final consumption choice X**, Y** is identical to the kind of movement we described in Figure 4.1 for changes in income. Because the price of X has fallen, but nominal income (I) has stayed the same, the individual has a greater "real" income and can afford a higher utility level (U_2). If X is a normal good, the individual will now demand more of it. This is the income effect that arises from a decline in the price of X. As is clear from the figure, both the substitution effect and the income effect cause the individual to choose more X when the price of X declines.

People do not actually move from X*, Y* to point B and then to X**, Y** when the price of good X falls. We never observe the point B; only the two actual choices of X*, Y* and X**, Y** are reflected in this person's behavior. But the analysis of income and substitution effects is still valuable because it shows that a price change affects the quantity demanded of a good in two conceptually different ways.

We can use the hamburger–soft drink example from Chapter 3 to show these effects at work. Suppose that the price of soft drinks falls to $.25 from the earlier price of $.50. This price change will increase the individual's purchasing power. Whereas earlier 20 soft drinks could be bought with an income of $10.00, now 40 of them can be bought. The price decrease shifts the budget constraint outward and increases utility. The individual now will choose some different combination of hamburgers and soft drinks than before, if only because the previous choice of five hamburgers and 10 soft drinks (under the old budget constraint) now costs only $7.50—there is $2.50 left unspent, and this person will choose to do something with it.

In making the new choices, the individual is influenced by two different effects. First, even if we hold constant the individual's utility by somehow compensating for the positive effect the price change has on utility, the individual will still act so that the MRS is brought into line with the new price ratio (now one hamburger to four soft drinks). This compensated response is the substitution effect. Even with a constant real income the individual will still choose more soft drinks and fewer hamburgers since the opportunity cost of eating a burger is now higher than before.

In actuality, real income has also increased; in order to assess the total effect of the price change on the demand for soft drinks, we must also investigate the effect of the change in purchasing power. Because the individual's real income has increased, this (assuming soft drinks are normal goods) would be another reason to expect soft drink purchases to increase.

Substitution and Income Effects from an Increase in Price

We can use a similar analysis to see what happens if the price of good X increases. The budget line in Figure 4.4 shifts inward because of an increase in the price of X. The Y-intercept for the budget constraint again does not change since neither income nor P_Y has changed. The slope of the budget constraint is now steeper, however, because X costs more than it did before.

Figure 4.4
Income and Substitution Effects of an Increase in Price

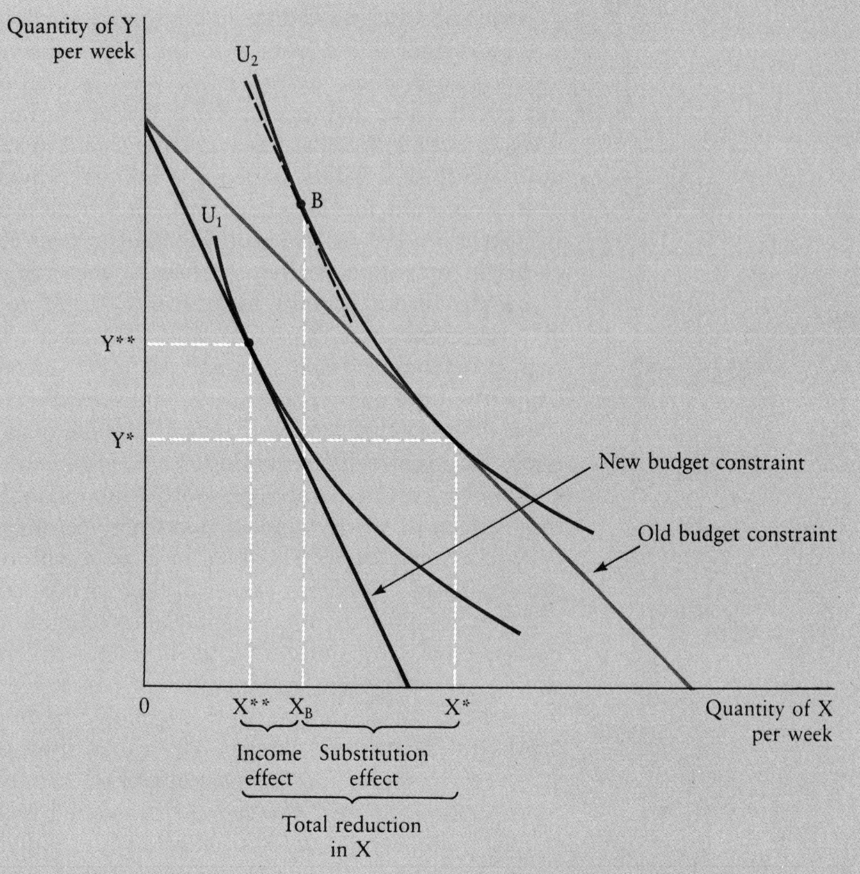

When the price of good X increases, the budget constraint shifts inward. The movement from the initial utility-maximizing point (X*, Y*) to the new point (X**, Y**) can be analyzed as two separate effects. The substitution effect causes a movement to point B on the initial indifference curve (U_2). The price increase would also create a loss of purchasing power. This income effect causes a consequent movement to a lower indifference curve. The income and substitution effects together cause the quantity demanded of X to fall as a result of the increase in its price. Again, the Y-intercept of the budget constraint is not affected by the change in the price of X.

The movement from the initial point of utility maximization (X*, Y*) to the new point X**, Y** is again caused by two forces. First, even if the individual stayed on the initial indifference curve (U_2), he or she would substitute Y for X and move along U_2 to point B. At this point the dashed line (with the same slope as the new budget constraint) is just tangent to the indifference curve U_2. The movement from X*, Y* to B along U_2 is the substitution effect. However, because purchasing power is reduced by the increase in the price of X (the amount of income remains constant, but now X costs more), the person must move to a lower level of utility, which is the income effect of the higher price. In Figure 4.4 both the income and substitution effects work in the same direction and cause the quantity demanded of X to fall in response to an increase in its price.

Summary of Substitution and Income Effects

In conclusion, then, how does the quantity demanded of X change graphically in response to changes in its price (P_X)? Because of the substitution effect, the quantity demanded of X always moves in a direction opposite to the direction of the price change. A decrease in P_X lowers the price ratio (P_X/P_Y). To reestablish the tangency condition for utility maximization, the MRS must also fall. In order to reduce the MRS, the person will choose more X and less Y by moving in a southeasterly direction along the indifference curve. Consequently, the quantity of X increases as a result of the substitution effect. This result is a direct consequence of the assumption (introduced in Chapter 3) of a diminishing MRS. Similarly, an increase in the price of X raises the price ratio (P_X/P_Y). The individual moves to a point on the indifference curve with a higher MRS. This means choosing more Y and less X; the quantity demanded of X decreases.

Substitution effects are only part of the story. To determine the total effect of a change in P_X on the quantity demanded of X, we must also consider income effects. Now the analysis may become somewhat more complex. A change in the price of good X affects an individual's real income, and we must analyze how this income change affects quantity demanded. When X is a normal good (that is, the quantity demanded of X increases as income increases), income effects reinforce substitution effects: again, price and quantity move in opposite directions. For example, a decrease in P_X causes real income to rise, and the person will choose to consume more X (since X is a normal good). The substitution effect is reinforced by the income effect. Similarly, when P_X increases, real income falls, and the quantity of X demanded falls; this also reinforces the substitution effect. For normal goods, then, income and substitution effects reinforce each other. Both cause the price of X and the quantity demanded of X to move in opposite directions. That was the case in both Figures 4.3 and 4.4. Our analysis of substitution and income effects is therefore consistent with the idea a person will buy more of a good whose price has fallen. This will provide the basis for our development of demand curves later in this chapter. Using substitution and income effects also clarifies some important issues about the effects of tax-induced price changes on individual welfare, as Application 4.3: The Lump-Sum Principle shows.

Substitution and Income Effects for an Inferior Good

We cannot predict exactly the effect of a price change on consumption of an inferior good. The income and substitution effects of a change in such a

APPLICATION 4.3

The Lump-Sum Principle

Notions of income and substitution effects can also be used to demonstrate that taxes on general purchasing power are more efficient than taxes on a single item. Here the term "more efficient" means that if the two taxes yield equal governmental revenues, the general purchasing power tax can be shown to reduce utility less (and, therefore, have a smaller "burden") than does the tax on a single commodity. Hence consumers should favor lump-sum taxes.

Theoretical Discussion

A theoretical proof is shown in Figure 1. Initially, the individual has I to spend and chooses to consume X* and Y*. This combination yields utility level U_3. A tax on good X alone would raise its price, and the budget constraint would become steeper. With that budget constraint (shown as line I′ in the figure) this person would be forced to accept a lower utility level (U_1) and would choose to consume the combination X_1, Y_1.

Suppose now that the government decided to institute a general income (purchasing power) tax that raised the same revenue as this sales tax. This would shift the individual's budget constraint to I″. The fact that I″ passes through X_1, Y_1 shows that both taxes have reduced the individual's purchasing power by the same amount.[1]

However, with budget constraint I″, this person will choose to consume X_2, Y_2 (rather than X_1, Y_1). Even though the individual pays the same tax bill in both instances, the combination chosen under the purchasing power tax yields a higher utility (U_2) than does the tax on a single commodity.

An intuitive explanation of this result is based on the recognition that a single commodity tax affects people's well-being in two ways: it reduces general purchasing power (an income effect), and it directs

Figure 1
The Efficiency of Lump-Sum Taxes

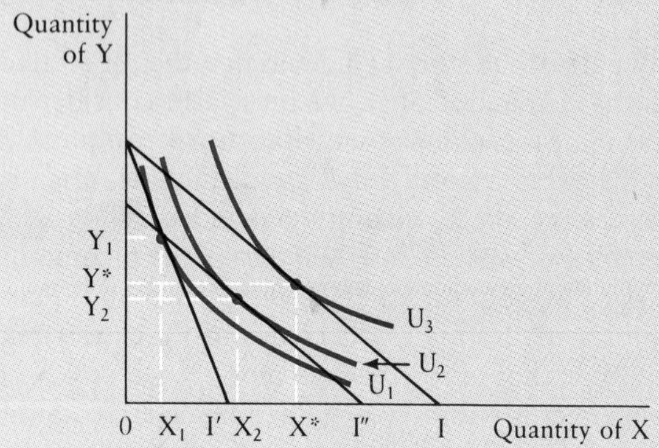

A per-unit tax on good X causes the utility-maximizing point to shift to X_1, Y_1 and utility to fall from U_3 to U_1. A lump-sum tax that collects the same revenue would shift the budget constraint to I″ and would only reduce utility to U_2. The lump-sum tax may therefore be preferred on efficiency grounds.

[1]Some algebra may clarify this. Total taxes collected under the sales tax are given by $T = tX_1$ (where t is the tax rate). An income tax of T dollars would leave after-tax income of

$$I'' = I - T = I - tX_1.$$

But the budget constraint with a sales tax is

$$I = (P_X + t)X_1 + P_Y Y_1,$$

so

$$I'' = P_X X_1 + P_Y Y_1,$$

which shows that I″ passes through X_1, Y_1 also.

good's price have opposite effects on the quantity demanded. Because inferior goods are relatively rare, we will only look briefly at this case.

Figure 4.5 shows the income and substitution effects from an increase in P_X when X is an inferior good. As the price of X rises, the substitution effect causes the individual to choose less X. This substitution effect is represented by a movement from the initial point X*, Y* to point B in the initial indiffer-

consumption away from the taxed commodity (a substitution effect). A purchasing power tax incorporates only the first effect, and, with equal tax revenues raised, individuals are better off under it.

Tax Policy Applications

This analysis provides a formal rationale for the belief that lump-sum taxes (those that reduce purchasing power on an across-the-board basis) are superior to excise or sales taxes on individual items. One must be careful not to apply that argument uncritically, however. The most commonly proposed real-world approximation to a lump-sum tax is a general tax on income. Because such a tax affects a person's after-tax wage, however, it is not really a lump-sum reduction in purchasing power. For example, in an important 1981 study, J. Hausman found that the average taxpayer loses about 22 percent more utility under the existing U.S. progressive income tax than would be lost from paying lump-sum taxes of an equal magnitude.[2]

Transfer Policy Applications

The argument presented here for positive taxes applies to negative taxes (that is, income subsidies) as well. A general income subsidy is a more efficient way of raising utility than the provision of some good at below market prices would be. For example, in a 1977 report on the antipoverty effects of various transfer programs, T. Smeeding shows that \$1 of existing subsidies for food, housing, and medical care was worth considerably less than \$1 in cash to the individuals who received the subsidies.[3] Specifically, the author found that food subsidies were worth about 88 percent, housing subsidies about 56 percent, and medical care subsidies about 68 percent of their actual cash values. The author therefore concluded that the ability of such programs to increase the overall well-being of poor people was considerably lessened by providing subsidies for specific goods rather than cash.

To Think About

1. What kinds of taxes seem to come closest to the lump-sum principle? That is, which actual taxes seem to have the least distorting effect on the economic choices people make? Should we make more use of such taxes? Or, are there good reasons to have some taxes (for example, taxes on cigarettes) that do distort people's choices?
2. If direct income grants are more effective in raising people's utility than subsidies on particular goods, why does the government operate so many subsidy programs (in food, housing, medical care, legal services, and education, to name just a few)? Couldn't these all be "cashed out" to provide a great deal more utility to the low-income people for whom they are intended? Or, are there good reasons to retain subsidies on specific goods?

[2] Jerry A. Hausman, "Labor Supply," in *How Taxes Affect Economic Behavior*, Henry J. Aaron and Joseph H. Pechman, eds. (Washington, D.C.: Brookings Institution, 1981), p. 54.

[3] Timothy M. Smeeding, "The Antipoverty Effectiveness of In-Kind Transfers," *Journal of Human Resources* 12, no. 3 (Summer 1977): 365.

ence curve, U_2. This movement is exactly the same as in Figure 4.4 for a normal good. Because P_X has increased, however, the individual now has a lower real income and must move to a lower indifference curve, U_1. The individual will choose X^{**}, Y^{**}. At X^{**} more X is chosen than at point B. This happens because good X is an inferior good: as real income falls, the quantity demanded of X increases rather than declines as it would for a normal good. In Figure 4.5, however, X^{**} is less than X^*; less X is ultimately demanded in

Figure 4.5
Income and Substitution Effects for an Inferior Good

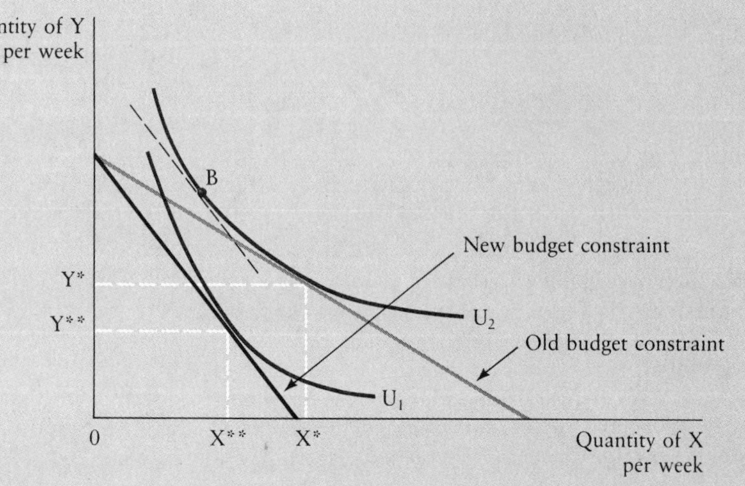

When the price of X increases, the substitution effect causes less X to be demanded (as shown by a movement to point B on the indifference curve U_2). However, because good X is inferior, the lower real income brought about by its price increase causes the quantity demanded of X to increase from B to X**. In this particular example, the substitution effect outweighs the income effect and X** < X*.

response to the rise in its price. In our example here the substitution effect is strong enough to outweigh the "perverse" income effect of an inferior good's price change. The next section shows a different result using a famous, though partially incorrect, example.

Giffen's Paradox

If the income effect of a price change is strong enough, the change in P_X and the resulting change in the quantity demanded of X actually could move in the same direction. Legend has it that the English economist Robert Giffen observed this paradox in nineteenth-century Ireland—when the price of potatoes rose, people reportedly consumed more of them. This peculiar result can be explained by looking at the size of the income effect of a change in the price of potatoes. Potatoes were not only inferior goods but also used up a large portion of the Irish people's income. An increase in the price of potatoes therefore reduced real income substantially. The Irish were forced to cut back on other luxury food consumption in order to buy more potatoes. Even though this rendering of events is historically implausible, the possibility of

Figure 4-6
Giffen's Paradox

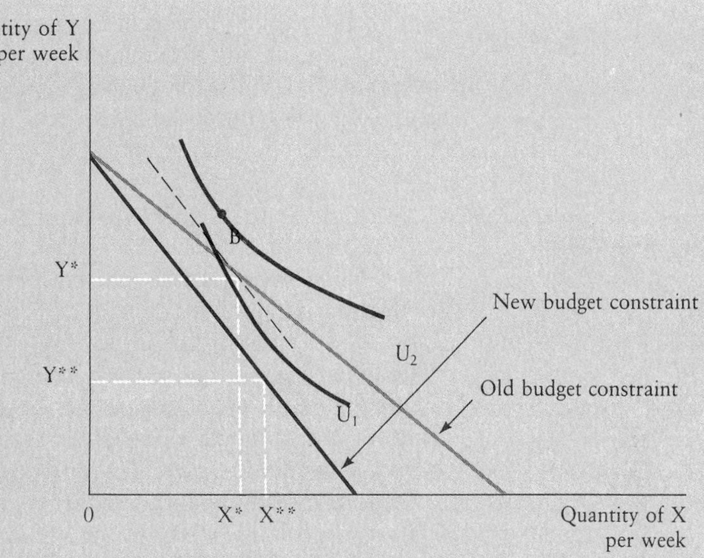

An increase in the price of X (potatoes, in this case) increases the quantity demanded of X. The substitution effect (the movement from X*, Y* to point B) is outweighed by the strong positive income effect from the inferiority of good X (compare this to Figure 4.2). Not every inferior good would exhibit Giffen's paradox.

Giffen's paradox
A situation in which the increase in a good's price leads people to consume more of the good.

an increase in the quantity demanded in response to the price increase of a good has come to be known as **Giffen's paradox.**[2]

The paradox is illustrated graphically in Figure 4.6, which shows potato consumption on the X-axis and all other goods on the Y-axis. The graph shows that in response to the increase in the price of potatoes, more are demanded. Even though the substitution effect reduces consumption, the "perverse" income effect is strong enough to make the total effect of the price increase positive. Real income falls and, since potatoes are inferior goods, the demand for them increases.

This paradox is probably quite rare in the real world—not only must the good be inferior, but the positive income effect must be strong enough to outweigh the negative substitution effect. A strong income effect will not usually

[2]A major problem with this explanation is that it disregards Marshall's observation that both supply and demand factors must be taken into account when analyzing price changes. If potato prices increased because of a decline in supply due to the potato blight, how could *more* potatoes possibly have been consumed? Also, since many Irish people were potato farmers, the potato price increase should have increased real income for them. For a detailed discussion of these and other fascinating bits of potato lore, see G. P. Dwyer and C. M. Lindsey, "Robert Giffen and the Irish Potato," *American Economic Review* (March 1984): 188–192.

exist unless the good makes up a large part of the individual's expenditures (as with potatoes in nineteenth-century Ireland). We can therefore conclude that price and quantity demanded of a good will usually move in opposite directions, even when the good is inferior. That is, Giffen's paradox will not occur except in unusual circumstances.

Changes in the Price of Another Good

Figures 4.3, 4.4, and 4.5 show that a change in the price of X will also have an effect on the quantity demanded of the other good (Y). In Figure 4.3, for example, a decrease in the price of X causes not only the quantity demanded of X to increase, but the quantity demanded of Y to increase as well. We can explain this result by looking at the substitution and income effects on the demand for Y associated with the decrease in the price of X.

First, as we see in Figure 4.3, the substitution effect caused less Y to be demanded. In moving along the indifference curve U_1 from X*, Y* to point B, X is substituted for Y because the lower ratio of P_X/P_Y required an adjustment in the MRS. In this figure the income effect of the decline in the price of good X is strong enough to reverse this result. Since Y is a normal good, and since real income has increased, more Y is demanded: the individual moves from point B to X**, Y**. Here Y** exceeds Y*, and the total effect of the price change is to increase the demand for Y.

A slightly different set of indifference curves (that is, different preferences) could have shown different results. Figure 4.7 shows a relatively flat set of indifference curves where the substitution effect from a decline in the price of X is very large. In moving from X*, Y* to point B, a large amount of X is substituted for Y. The income effect on Y is not strong enough to reverse this large substitution effect. In this case the quantity of Y finally chosen (Y**) is smaller than the original amount. The effect a change in the price of one good has on the quantity demanded of some other good is ambiguous—it all depends on what the person's preferences, as reflected by his or her indifference curve map, look like. We have to examine carefully income and substitution effects that (at least in the case of only two goods) work in opposite directions.

Using our hamburger–soft drink example, we have already discussed the substitution and income effects that a fall in the price of soft drinks (from $.50 to $.25) will have on the number of soft drinks bought. What happens to the number of hamburgers chosen? The substitution effect predicts that fewer hamburgers will be purchased. Since hamburgers are now relatively more expensive than they were before soft drink prices fell, the initial level of utility can be achieved at lower cost by drinking more soft drinks and eating fewer hamburgers.

The total effect of the soft drink price decrease on hamburger purchases also depends on the income effect of the price change, however. As a result of the decrease in the price of soft drinks, the person has a higher real income and may buy more soft drinks and more hamburgers. The total effect of the

Figure 4.7
Effect on the Demand for Good Y of a Decrease in the Price of Good X

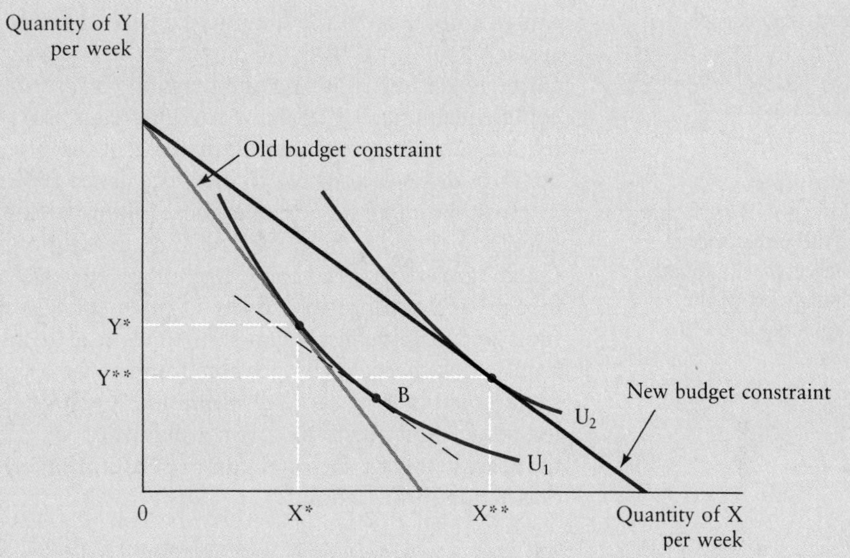

In contrast to Figure 4.3, the quantity demanded of Y now declines (from Y* to Y**) in response to a decrease in the price of X. The relatively flat indifference curves cause the substitution effect to be very large. Moving from X*, Y* to point B means giving up a substantial quantity of Y for additional X. This effect more than outweighs the positive income effect (from B to X**, Y**), and the quantity demanded of Y declines. So, purchases of Y may either rise or fall when the price of X falls.

price change on hamburger purchases is therefore ambiguous. This substitution effect works to decrease hamburger purchases, whereas the income effect works to increase such purchases. The final result depends on how the individual feels about the two goods.

Substitutes and Complements

Economists use the terms substitutes and complements to describe the way people may see these relationships between goods. Complements are goods that go together in the sense that people will increase their use of both goods simultaneously. Examples of complements might be coffee and cream, fish and chips, peanut butter and jelly, or brandy and cigars. Substitutes, on the other hand, are goods that replace one another. Tea and coffee, hamburgers and hot dogs, or wheat and corn are some goods that are substitutes for each other.

Whether two goods are substitutes or complements of each other is primarily a question of the shape of people's indifference curves. The market behavior of individuals in their purchases of goods helps define these

Complements
Two goods such that when the price of one increases, the quantity demanded of the other falls.

Substitutes
Two goods such that if the price of one increases, the quantity demanded of the other rises.

relationships. Two goods are **complements** if an increase in the price of one causes a decrease in the quantity consumed of the other. For example, an increase in the price of coffee might cause not only the quantity demanded of coffee to decline, but also the demand for cream to decrease because of the complementary relationship between cream and coffee. Similarly, coffee and tea are **substitutes** because an increase in the price of coffee might cause the quantity demanded of tea to increase, as tea replaces coffee in use.

How the demand for one good relates to the price increase of another good is a result of both income and substitution effects. It is only the combined "gross" result of these two effects that we can observe. Including both income and substitution effects of price changes in our definitions of substitutes and complements can sometimes lead to problems, however. For example, it is theoretically possible for X to be a complement for Y and at the same time for Y to be a substitute for X. This perplexing state of affairs has led some economists to favor a definition of substitutes and complements that looks only at the direction of substitution effects. We do not make that distinction in this book.[3]

Construction of Individual Demand Curves

We have now completed our discussion of how the individual's demand for good X is affected by various changes in economic circumstances. We started by writing the demand function for good X as

$$\text{Quantity of X demanded} = d_X(P_X, P_Y, I; \text{preferences}). \quad [4.1]$$

And then we examined how changes in each of the economic factors P_X, P_Y, and I might affect an individual's decision to purchase good X. The principal purpose of this examination has been to permit us to derive individual demand curves and to analyze those factors that might cause a demand curve to shift its position. This section shows how a demand curve can be constructed. The next section analyzes why this curve might shift.

Individual demand curve
A graphic representation of the relationship between the price of a good and the quantity of it demanded by a person, holding all other factors constant.

An **individual demand curve** shows the *ceteris paribus* relationship between the quantity demanded of a good (say, X) and its price (P_X). Not only are preferences held constant under the *ceteris paribus* assumption (as they have been throughout our discussion in this chapter), but the other economic factors in the demand function (that is, the price of good Y and income) are also held constant. In demand curves we are limiting our study to only the relationship between the quantity of a good chosen and changes in its own price.

[3]For a slightly more extended treatment of this subject, see Walter Nicholson, *Microeconomic Theory: Basic Principles and Extensions,* 4th ed. (Hinsdale, Ill.: Dryden Press, 1989), pp. 163–168. For a complete treatment, see J. R. Hicks, *Value and Capital* (London: Cambridge University Press, 1939), Chapter 3 and the mathematical appendix.

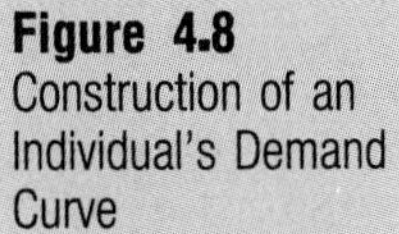

Figure 4.8
Construction of an Individual's Demand Curve

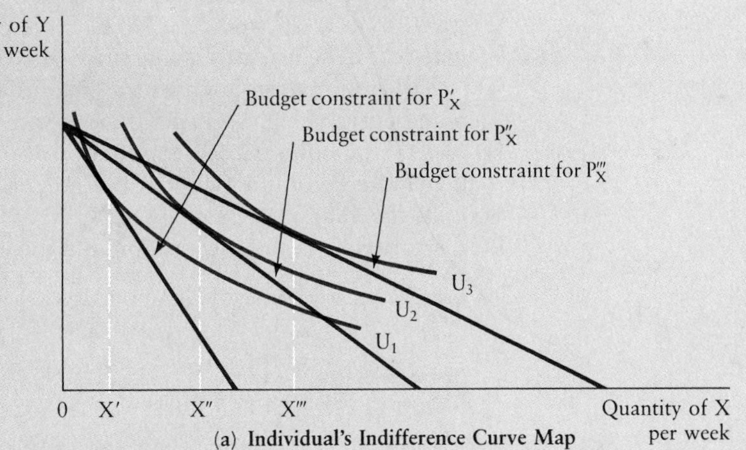

(a) **Individual's Indifference Curve Map**

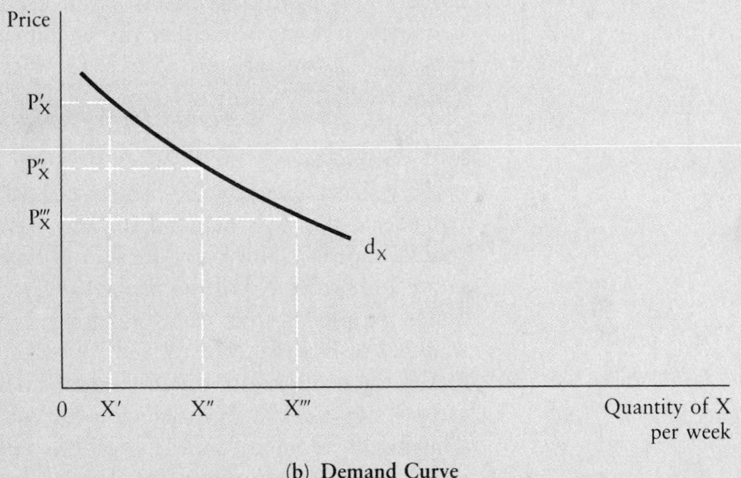

(b) **Demand Curve**

In Panel a the individual's utility-maximizing choices of X and Y are shown for three successively lower prices of X. In Panel b this relationship between P_X and X is used to construct the demand curve for X. The demand curve is drawn on the assumption that the price of Y and money income remain constant as the price of X varies.

Figure 4.8 shows how we can construct a person's demand curve for good X. In Panel a the individual's indifference curve map is drawn using three different budget constraints in which the price of X decreases. These decreasing prices are P'_X, P''_X, and P'''_X. The other economic factors that affect the position of the budget constraint (the price of good Y and income) do not change. In graphic terms, all three constraints have the same Y-intercept. The successively lower prices of X rotate this constraint outward. Given the three separate budget constraints, the individual's utility-maximizing choices of X are given by X′, X″, and X‴. These three choices show that the quantity demanded of X increases as the price of X falls.

The information in Panel a in Figure 4.8 can be used to construct the demand curve shown in Panel b. The price of X is shown on the vertical axis, and the quantity chosen continues to be shown on the horizontal axis. The demand curve (d_X) is downward sloping, showing that when the price of X falls, the quantity demanded of X increases. As we have shown, this increase represents both the substitution and income effects of the price decline.

Shape of the Demand Curve

The precise shape and slope of the demand curve are determined by the income and substitution effects when the price of X changes. An individual's demand curve may be either rather flat or quite steeply sloped, depending on the nature of his or her indifference curve map. If X has many close substitutes, the indifference curves will be nearly straight lines (such as those shown in Figure 4.7), and the substitution effect from a price change will be very large. The quantity of X chosen may fall substantially in response to a rise in its price; consequently the demand curve will be relatively flat. For example, consider a person's demand for one particular brand of cereal (say, the famous Brand X). Since any one brand has many close substitutes, the demand curve for Brand X will be relatively flat. A rise in the price of Brand X will cause people to shift easily to other kinds of cereal, and the quantity demanded of Brand X will be reduced significantly.

On the other hand, the individual's demand curve for some goods may be steeply sloped. That is, price changes will not affect consumption very much. This might be the case if the good has no close substitutes. For example, consider a person's demand for water. Because water satisfies many unique needs, it is unlikely that it would have any substitutes when the price of water rose, and the substitution effect would be very small. However, since water does not use up a large portion of a person's total income, the income effect of the increase in the price of water would also not be large. The quantity demanded of water probably would not respond greatly to changes in its price; that is, the demand curve would be nearly vertical.

As a third possibility, consider the case of food. Because food as a whole has no substitutes (although individual food items obviously do), an increase in the price of food will not induce important substitution effects. In this sense, food is similar to our water example. However, food is a major item in a person's total expenditures, and an increase in its price will have a significant effect on purchasing power. It is possible, therefore, that the quantity demanded of food may be reduced substantially in response to a rise in food prices because of this income effect. The demand curve for food might be

Figure 4.9
Shifts in an Individual's Demand Curve

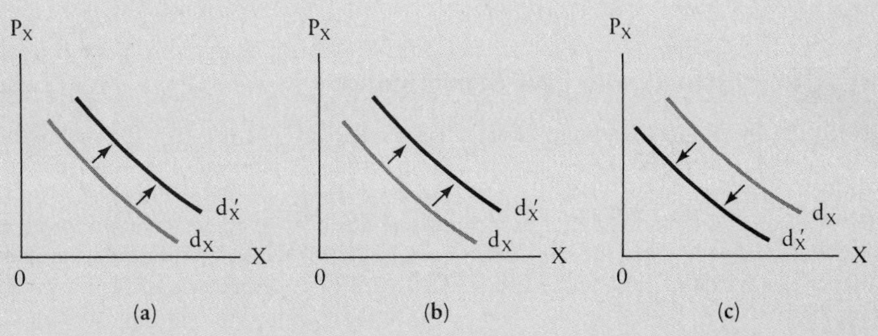

In Panel a the demand curve shifts outward because the individual's income has increased. More X is now demanded at each price. In Panel b the demand curve shifts outward because the price of Y has increased, and X and Y are substitutes for the individual. In Panel c the demand curve shifts inward because of the increase in the price of Y—X and Y are complements.

flatter (that is, demand reacts more to price) than we might expect if we thought of food only as a "necessity" with few, if any, substitutes.[4]

Shifts in an Individual's Demand Curve

The individual's demand curve summarizes the *ceteris paribus* relationship between the price of X and the quantity demanded of X. The income and substitution effects of changes in that price cause the person to move along his or her demand curve. If one of the factors (the price of Y, income, or preferences) that we have so far been holding constant were to change, the entire curve would shift. The demand curve remains fixed only while the *ceteris paribus* assumption is in effect. Figure 4.9 shows the kinds of shifts that might take place. In Panel a the effect on good X of an increase in income is shown. Assuming that good X is a normal good, an increase in income causes more X to be demanded at each price. This is the kind of effect we described early in this chapter (Figure 4.1). When income increases, people buy more X even if its price has not changed, and the demand curve shifts outward. Panels b and c in Figure 4.9 record two possible effects that an increase in the price of Y might have on the demand curve for good X. In Panel b, X and Y

[4]For this reason sometimes it is convenient to talk about demand curves that reflect only substitution effects. These compensated demand curves are constructed on the assumption that any effect of a price change on the individual's purchasing power is automatically compensated for. Hence, real income rather than nominal income is being held constant. In Chapter 6 we will briefly examine this concept.

APPLICATION 4.4

Religious Practices and Fish Consumption

Historically the Roman Catholic Church has required its members to abstain from eating meat during certain periods of the year. Because fish is considered a substitute for meat, this abstinence increases the demand for fish during those periods. We can use the results of a statistical study of the demand for fish by F. W. Bell to show the effects of these shifts in demand.[1] Table 1 reports the estimated shifts in the demand curves for four species of fish in the New England states.

The effects of abstinence from eating meat during Lent and the end of the "meatless Friday" practice in December 1966 are shown here. For both cases the shifts in demand curves have been measured in a horizontal direction; that is, the figures report the total change in quantity of fish consumed, holding price constant.

Seasonal Effects during Lent

As the table shows, the increase in demand for fish during Lent is substantial. During this period people substitute fish for meat, thereby shifting their demand curves for various species of fish to the right. This type of seasonal influence on demand is quite common. For example, demand for ice cream and air conditioning increases during the summer months, demand for turkeys increases at Thanksgiving, and demand for wedding cakes increases in June. Since these shifts are reasonably predictable, firms can take them into account in planning their production and inventory holdings.

Table 1
Effects of Religious Practices on Fish Consumption in the New England States (in Thousands of Pounds per Month)

Species	Increase in Demand during Lent	Reduction in Demand after December 1966
Yellowtail flounder	+17.8	−4.4
Large haddock	+25.3	−7.1
Small haddock (scrod)	+13.3	−0.6
Cod	+29.0	−4.5

Source: F. W. Bell. "The Pope and the Price of Fish," *American Economic Review* (December 1968): 1346–1350.

Long-Run Effects of Meat on Friday

In December 1966, Roman Catholic bishops in the United States ended mandatory meatless Fridays. As Table 1 shows, the demand for some kinds of fish decreased as people changed their purchases back to meat. Similar reductions in demand for other goods in recent years have been related to health concerns (cranberries, swordfish, and artificially sweetened beverages have all been subject to "cancer scares"), political motivations (boycotting table grapes or certain textile manufacturers), or development of superior substitutes (slide rules and mechanical calculators being replaced by electronic calculators). Some of these shifts were relatively permanent (rather than seasonal) and may have imposed hardships on some producers. In the case of fish, that hardship is ironic since one reason for the original papal decree for meatless Fridays was to aid the troubled fishing industry in Naples more than one thousand years ago.

To Think About

1. In this chapter we have identified three factors that shift a demand curve: changes in income, changes in the price of some other good, and changes in preferences. Which of these explanations best fits the case described in this example? Might it be possible to use two of the explanations?
2. Why do fish prices change so sharply in response to such a readily predictable event as Lent? Can't a speculator make a lot of money by buying fish when they are cheap prior to Lent and selling them when they are in high demand?

[1] F. W. Bell, "The Pope and the Price of Fish," *American Economic Review* (December 1968): 1346–1350. The original Bell study reported shifts in the vertical (price) direction. We have recalculated them here to show quantity changes.

are assumed to be substitutes—for example, coffee (X) and tea (Y). An increase in the price of tea causes the individual to substitute coffee for tea. More coffee (that is, good X) is demanded at each price than was previously the case. Consequently, the demand curve shifts outward.

On the other hand, suppose X and Y are complements—for example, coffee (X) and cream (Y). An increase in the price of cream causes the demand curve for coffee to shift inward. Because coffee and cream "go together," less coffee (that is, good X) will now be demanded at each price. This shift in the demand curve is shown in Panel c.

Changes in preferences might also cause the demand curve to shift. For example, a sudden warm spell would undoubtedly shift the entire demand curve for soft drinks outward. More drinks would be demanded at each price because now the individual's desire for them has increased. Similarly, the fashion for longer hairstyles for men in the 1960s shifted many men's demand curves for haircuts toward the origin. At each price a man would buy fewer haircuts per year than he would have in the past. Application 4.4: Religious Practices and Fish Consumption shows another historical situation that caused the position of an entire demand curve to shift rather abruptly.

Be Careful in Using Terminology

Increase or decrease in quantity demanded
The increase or decrease in quantity demanded caused by a change in the good's price. Graphically represented by the movement along a demand curve.

Increase or decrease in demand
The change in demand for a good caused by changes in the price of another good, income, or preferences. Graphically represented by a shift of the entire demand curve.

It is important that we keep the distinction between the shift in a demand curve and movement along a stationary demand curve clearly in mind. Changes in the price of X lead to movements along the demand curve for good X. Changes in other economic factors (such as a change in income or a change in another good's price) cause the entire demand curve for X to shift. If we wished to see how a change in the price of steak would affect a person's steak purchases, we would use a single demand curve and study movements along it. On the other hand, if we wanted to know how a change in income would affect the quantity of steak purchased, we would have to study the shift in the position of the entire demand curve.

To keep these matters straight, economists must speak carefully. The movement downward along a stationary demand curve in response to a fall in price is called an **increase in quantity demanded.** A shift outward in the entire curve is an **increase in demand.** A rise in the price of a good causes a **decrease in quantity demanded** (a move along the demand curve), whereas a change in some other factor may cause a **decrease in demand** (a shift of the entire curve to the left). It is important to be precise in using those terms; they are not interchangeable.

Summary

This chapter uses the model of individual choice to examine how people react to changes in income or prices. We have come to five major conclusions about the factors that affect the demand for a good:

- Proportionate changes in all prices and income will not affect choices since such changes do not shift the budget constraint.
- When income alone increases, the demand for a good will increase unless that good is inferior.
- A change in the price of a good has substitution and income effects that together cause changes in consumption choices. Except in the unlikely case of Giffen's paradox, a reduction in a good's price will cause more of it to be demanded. An increase in price will cause less of the good to be demanded.
- A change in the price of one good will usually affect the demand for other goods. If two goods are complements, an increase in the price of one will reduce the demand for the other. If the goods are substitutes, an increase in the price of one will increase the demand for the other.
- The demand for a good is also affected by preferences. Preferences are usually held constant under the *ceteris paribus* assumption in theoretical analysis.

Probably the most important tool developed in this chapter is the individual's demand curve, which shows the relationship between the quantity demanded of a product and its price (when all other influences are held constant). Demand curves are usually drawn downward sloping. They shift if one of the factors held constant (income, other prices, preferences) changes. In Chapter 5 we show how individual demand curves can be combined to come up with the market demand curve, which helps to determine market prices.

Review Questions

1. Explain why the homogeneity of demand functions requires that the demand for a good remain unchanged if all prices *and* income were to double. What would happen to the budget constraint if all prices doubled but income did not? Suppose income doubled but prices remained unchanged?
2. Suppose an individual consumes only two goods, X and Y, and that the prices of these goods are fixed. How would the set of utility-maximizing points traced out by successively higher incomes look if

   a. the individual always split his or her income equally between X and Y?
   b. X were a luxury, Y a necessity?
   c. Y were a luxury, X a necessity?
   d. a constant amount of X were bought as income expanded above some minimal amount?
   e. X were an inferior good? (Can Y be inferior here too?)

3. Suppose an individual always spends half his or her income on food. How will changes in the price of food affect the quantity of food consumed? How will changes in the price of food affect total spending on food? How large an increase in income would be needed to offset the effect of a 10 percent increase in the price of food?
4. An individual always buys left and right shoes in pairs. Explain why a sale on right shoes will have an income effect, but no substitution effect on his or her left and right shoe purchases.

5. Suppose an individual doesn't care what brand of toothpaste he or she buys. Show graphically why he or she will always buy the cheapest brand.
6. Is the following statement true or false? Explain.
"Every Giffen good must be inferior, but not every inferior good exhibits the Giffen paradox."
7. Suppose that an individual never changes the quantity of water he or she consumes when the price of water changes. How would you illustrate this situation with a graph? Does this imply water is an inferior good? How do income and substitution effects work in this case?
8. When coffee prices rise, an individual buys more tea but fewer coffee mugs. Explain the substitution and income effects of the price change on these two goods.
9. Does the theory of consumer choice require that an individual's demand curve for a good be downward sloping? In what case would a demand curve be vertical? When might it be positively sloped?
10. Explain whether the following events would result in a move along an individual's demand curve for popcorn or in a shift of the curve. If the curve would shift, in what direction?

    a. An increase in the individual's income.
    b. A decline in popcorn prices.
    c. An increase in prices for pretzels.
    d. A reduction in the amount of butter included in a box of popcorn.
    e. The presence of long waiting lines to buy popcorn.
    f. A sales tax on all popcorn purchases.

Problems

4.1 Ms. Boring maximizes her utility by spending her entire income on goods A, B, and C (whose prices stay constant in this problem). Ms. Boring makes $300 per week and purchases 10 units of good A, 10 units of good B, and 10 units of good C. When Ms. Boring's income rises to $400 per week, she buys 9 units of good A, 17 units of good B, and 14 units of good C. Finally, Ms. Boring gets another pay increase to $500 per week and purchases 8 units of good A, 26 units of good B, and 16 units of good C.

a. Using the above information, graph the relationship between income and purchases of goods A, B, and C.
b. Explain the nature of each good: is it normal or inferior? A "luxury" or "necessity"?

4.2 Elizabeth M. Suburbs makes $200 a week at her summer job and spends her entire weekly income on new sweaters and designer jeans since these are the only two items that provide utility to her. Furthermore, Elizabeth insists that for every sweater she buys, she must also buy a pair of jeans (without the jeans, the new sweater is worthless). Therefore, she buys the same number of sweaters and jeans in any given week.

a. If jeans cost $20 and sweaters cost $20, how many will Elizabeth buy of each?
b. Suppose that the price of jeans rises to $30 a pair. How many sweaters and jeans will she buy?
c. Show your results by graphing the budget constraints from parts a and b. Also draw Elizabeth's indifference curves. Why do these "curves" look different from those you have seen before? (Hint: Elizabeth insists on

buying in a fixed proportion of one sweater to one pair of jeans. Buying one more sweater without purchasing jeans does *not* increase her utility.)

d. To what effect (income or substitution) do you attribute the change in utility levels between parts a and b?

4.3 Mr. Wright, a clothing salesman, is forced by his employer to spend at least $50 of his weekly income of $200 on clothing. Show that his utility level is lower than if he could freely allocate his income between clothing and other goods.

4.4 Pete Moss buys 100 units of fertilizer and 80 units of grass seed along with quantities of other goods. The price of fertilizer rises by $.40 per unit, and the price of grass seed drops by $.50 per unit; other prices and Pete's income remain unchanged. Will Pete buy more, less, or the same amount of fertilizer? Explain.

4.5 If a person consumes only two goods, potatoes and automobiles, and potatoes exhibit Giffen's paradox, how does an increase in the price of potatoes affect the quantity of automobiles purchased? What happens to total spending on the two goods?

4.6 Show that if there are only two goods (X and Y) to choose from, whether they are substitutes or complements will depend on whether the substitution or income effect is larger. Illustrate each case with a carefully drawn graph.

*4.7 David N. gets $3 per month as an allowance to spend any way he pleases. Since he only likes peanut butter and jelly sandwiches, he spends the entire amount on peanut butter (at $.05 per ounce) and jelly (at $.10 per ounce). Bread is provided free of charge by a concerned neighbor. David is a particular eater and makes his sandwiches with exactly 1 oz. of jelly and 2 oz. of peanut butter. He is set in his ways and will never change these proportions.

a. How much peanut butter and jelly will David buy with his $3 allowance in a week?

b. Suppose the price of jelly were to rise to $.15 per ounce. How much of each commodity would be bought?

c. By how much should David's allowance be increased to compensate for the rise in the price of jelly in part b?

d. Graph your results of parts a through c.

e. In what sense does this problem only involve a single commodity, peanut butter and jelly sandwiches? Graph the demand curve for this single commodity.

f. Discuss the results of this problem in terms of the income and substitution effects involved in the demand for jelly.

4.8 Suppose the government imposes an excise tax on gasoline and rebates all proceeds to taxpayers.

a. Show that the size of the average tax rebate will generally not be large enough to permit the average consumer to return to his or her pretax utility level.

b. Show that if gasoline and other goods must be used in fixed proportion (that is, that there are no substitutes for gasoline), the tax rebate is just sufficient to return to the original equilibrium.

c. What can you conclude about the relationship between substitution effects and the inefficiency of various taxation schemes?

---

* Denotes a problem that is rather difficult.

*4.9 Each year Sam Mellow grows 200 units of wheat and 100 units of sunflower seeds for his own consumption and for sale to the outside world. Wheat and sunflower seeds are the only two items that provide utility to Sam. They are also his only source of income. Sam cannot save his proceeds from year to year.

a. If the price of wheat is $2 per unit and sunflower seeds sell for $10 per unit, Sam chooses to sell 20 units of the sunflower seeds he produces while retaining 80 units for his own use. Show Sam's utility-maximizing situation and indicate both his initial production levels and the amount of additional wheat he will buy with the proceeds from his sunflower seed sales.
b. Suppose sunflower seed prices fall to $6 per unit while wheat prices remain unchanged. Will Sam be made better- or worse-off by this price decline? Or is the situation ambiguous? Explain carefully using a graphic analysis. Show that if Sam is to be made better-off by the price decline, he must become a seller of wheat and a buyer of sunflower seeds.
c. Explain using the terms "income effect" and "substitution effect" why the analysis in part b differs from the usual case in which a price decline always increases an individual's utility level.

Hint: To start this problem show that Sam's budget constraint always passes through the point

$$\text{Wheat} = 200, \qquad \text{sunflower seeds} = 100.$$

4.10 The Jones family spends all its income on food and shelter. It derives maximum utility when it spends 2/3 of its income on shelter and 1/3 on food.

a. Use this information to calculate the demand functions for shelter and food. Show that there are homogeneous in all prices and incomes.
b. Graph the demand curves for shelter and food for the Jones family if their family income is $12,000.
c. Show how the demand curves for shelter and food would shift if income rose to $15,000.

* Denotes a problem that is rather difficult.

CHAPTER 5

Market Demand and Elasticity

Chapter 4 demonstrated how an individual's demand curve for a good can be constructed using his or her indifference curve map. This demand curve generally will be downward sloping, and the curve will shift when factors such as income and other prices change. Now Chapter 5 describes how individual demand curves are "added up" to create the market demand curve for a good. Market demand curves reflect the actions of many people and show how these actions are affected by market price.

We also will define a few ways of measuring market demand curves. We introduce the concept of elasticity and show how we can use it to record the extent to which the quantity demanded of a good changes in response to changes in income and prices. The final section of the chapter reviews some empirical evidence relating to real-world demand curves. We show how this evidence can be used to predict changes in people's consumption patterns.

Market Demand Curves

The **market demand** for a good is the total quantity of the good demanded by all potential buyers. The **market demand curve** shows the relationship between this total quantity demanded and the market price of the good, when all other factors are held constant. The market demand curve's shape and position are determined by the shape of individuals' demand curves for the product in question. Market demand is nothing more than the combined effect of many people's economic choices.

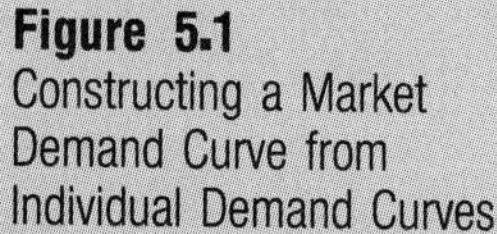

Figure 5.1
Constructing a Market Demand Curve from Individual Demand Curves

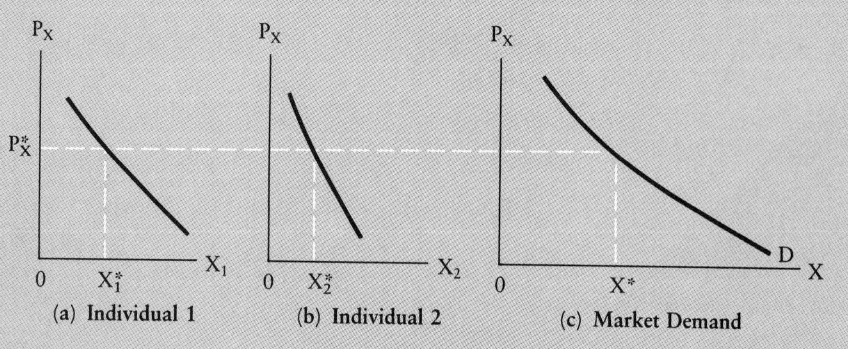

A market demand curve is the horizontal sum of individual demand curves. At each price the quantity demanded in the market is the sum of the amounts each person demands. For example, at P_X^* the demand in the market is $X_1^* + X_2^* = X^*$.

Construction of the Market Demand Curve

Market demand
The total quantity of a good or service demanded by all potential buyers.

Market demand curve
The relationship between the total quantity demanded of a good or service and its price, holding all other factors constant.

Figure 5.1 shows the construction of the market demand curve for good X when there are only two buyers. For each price, the point on the market demand curve is found by summing the quantities demanded by each individual. For example, at a price of P_X^*, individual 1 demands X_1^*, and individual 2 demands X_2^*. The total quantity demanded at the market at P_X^* is therefore the sum of these two amounts: $X^* = X_1^* + X_2^*$. Consequently the point X^*, P_X^* is one point on the market demand curve D. The other points on the curve are plotted in the same way. The market curve is simply the horizontal "sum" of each individual's demand curve. At every possible price, we ask how much is demanded by each person, and then we sum up these amounts to arrive at the quantity demanded by the whole market. The demand curve summarizes the *ceteris paribus* relationship between the quantity demanded of X and its price. If other factors do not change, the position of the curve will remain fixed and will reflect how people as a group respond to price changes.

Shifts in the Market Demand Curve

Why would a market demand curve shift? We already know why individual demand curves shift. To discover how some event might shift a market demand curve, we must first find out how this event causes individual demand curves to shift and then compare the sum of these new demand curves with the old market demand. In some cases the direction of a shift in the market demand curve is reasonably predictable. For example, using our two-buyer case, if both of their incomes increase and both regard X as a normal good,

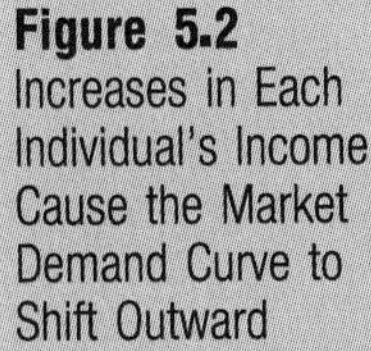

Figure 5.2
Increases in Each Individual's Income Cause the Market Demand Curve to Shift Outward

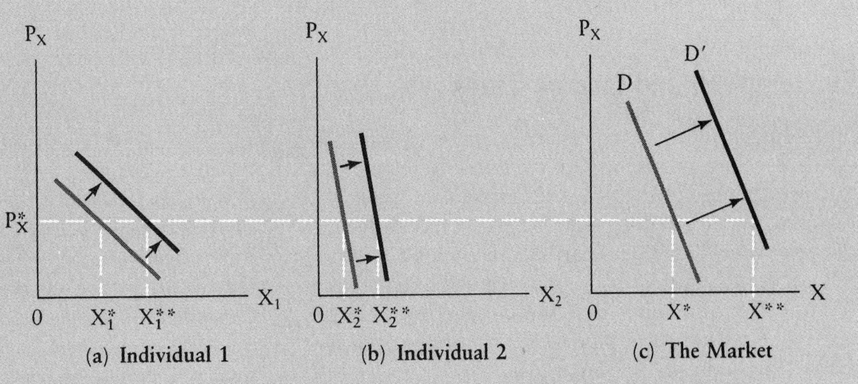

An increase in income for each individual causes the individual demand curve for X to shift out (assuming X is a normal good). For example, at P_X^*, individual 1 now demands X_1^{**} instead of X_1^*. The market demand curve shifts out to D′. X^* was demanded at P_X^* before the income increase. Now X^{**} $(= X_1^{**} + X_2^{**})$ is demanded.

then each person's demand curve would shift outward. Hence, the market demand curve would also shift outward. At each price more would be demanded in the market because each person wants to buy more. This situation in which a general rise in income increases market demand is illustrated in Figure 5.2. Application 5.1: Consumption and Income Taxes shows how this notion can be used to study the effects of tax cuts although, as is often the case in economics, the story is not quite as simple as it appears to be.

In some cases the direction that a market demand curve shifts may be ambiguous. For example, suppose that one person's income increases but a second person's income decreases. The location of the new market demand curve now depends on the relative shifts in the individual demand curves that these income changes cause. Figure 5.3 shows the market demand curve shifting to a different position because of different income changes for our two buyers. Individual 2's demand curve shifts inward more than individual 1's shifts outward. The net result of these shifts is to shift the market demand curve inward to D′.

What holds true for our simple two-person example also applies to much larger groups of demanders—perhaps even to the entire economy. In this case, the market demand summarizes the behavior of all possible consumers. If personal income in the United States as a whole were to rise, the effect on the market demand curve for pizza would depend greatly on whether the income gains went to people who love pizza or to people who never touch it. If the gains went to pizza lovers, the U.S. market demand for pizza would shift outward significantly. It would be little changed if the income gains went to pizza haters.

A change in the price of some other good (Y) will also affect the market demand for X. If the price of Y rises, for example, the market demand curve

APPLICATION 5.1

Consumption and Income Taxes

Individuals' ability to use their incomes to purchase goods is obviously affected by the taxes they must pay. Because changes in income taxes cause changes in this purchasing power, it might be expected that such changes will affect individuals' demands for a wide variety of goods. In this application we will examine that relationship and show that the connection between taxes and consumption may be a bit more complicated than at first appears to be the case.

The Permanent Income Hypothesis

In the 1950s Milton Friedman was one of the first economists to recognize that a person's consumption decisions are not based simply on his or her current income.[1] Rather, Friedman argued, such decisions are based on a longer term view of what a person's purchasing power is. Temporary increases or decreases in income will have little effect on consumer spending since this is determined by only slowly changing habits. Instead, temporary income fluctuations will be reflected in increases or decreases in savings. Friedman's notion then is that the individual's demand (and therefore the market demand) for goods is based on a long-term, "permanent" concept of income.

Effects of Temporary Tax Changes

One implication of the permanent income hypothesis is that changes in taxes that are only temporary (say, for only one year) will have little or no effect on the demand for consumption goods. The available data tend to support this presumption. For example, a temporary income tax surcharge was imposed by the Nixon administration in 1968–1969, but most researchers have found that the tax had practically no effect on actual consumer spending. Similarly, in mid-1975 during the Ford administration a temporary rebate of 1974 taxes was enacted, but this rebate also seems to have had no effect on purchases of goods and services.

The Reagan Tax Cuts

President Reagan entered office with the expressed intention of cutting income taxes, and by August 1981 one of the largest tax reductions in history became law. These tax cuts were to be "permanent"; that is, income tax rates were reduced, and both the president and Congress expressed the desire to keep them at their new lower levels. But the Reagan tax cuts were phased-in over a three-year period and were not to become fully effective until 1984. Hence, the precise effect of the tax reduction on consumer demand was difficult to predict.

Some economists have argued that the Reagan tax program should be regarded as a permanent cut in income taxes in 1981, which was accompanied by a series of temporary tax surcharges in 1981, 1982, and 1983. In this view, then, Friedman's permanent income hypothesis would predict a big increase in consumer spending in 1981 and later years since people would only respond to the permanent reductions the Reagan plan promised. The fact that the program was phased-in should be irrelevant to consumption decisions.

Unfortunately for economic theory, things don't seem to have worked out that way. Several statistical studies of the Reagan tax cuts have concluded that the "permanent" cuts had virtually no effect until they were fully implemented in 1984.[2] It seems that people were skeptical about whether the rate reductions would really come into effect, or whether the president and the Congress would reverse themselves before the cuts were fully phased-in. Only when they actually had an increased net pay in their pockets did individuals increase their demands for consumer goods.

To Think About

1. If consumers' spending decisions are based on a long-term notion of permanent income, how do they cope with short-term fluctuations in their incomes? Aren't they constrained by their actual incomes in what they can spend? What does the permanent income idea assume about access to savings or credit?
2. What types of spending decisions do you think are based on long-term income prospects? Which types probably respond to short-term income fluctuations? Are your own spending patterns consistent with Friedman's permanent income notion?

---

[1]Milton Friedman, *A Theory of the Consumption Function* (Princeton, N.J.: Princeton University Press, 1957).

[2]See, for example, A. S. Blinder and A. Deaton "The Time Series Consumption Function Revisited," *Brookings Papers on Economic Activity,* no. 2, (1985) pp. 465–511.

Figure 5.3
Effect of Income Changes on Market Demand Depends on How These Changes Are Distributed

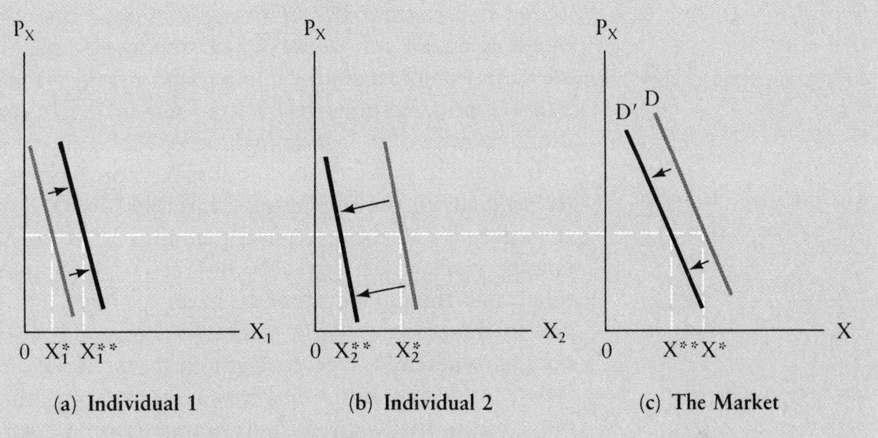

Individual 1's income has increased, but individual 2's has decreased. The net result of these changes is to shift the market demand curve inward to D′.

for X will shift outward if most buyers regard X and Y as substitutes. On the other hand, an increase in the price of Y will cause the market demand curve for X to shift inward if most people regard the two goods as complements.

A Word on Notation and Terms

Often in this book we will be looking at only one market. In order to simplify the notation, we use the letter Q for the quantity of a good demanded (per week) in this market, and we use P for its price. When we draw a demand curve in the Q, P plane, we will assume that all other factors affecting demand are held constant. That is, income, the price of other goods, and preferences are assumed not to change. If one of these factors should change, the demand curve would probably shift. As was the case for individual demand curves, the term "change in quantity demanded" is used for a movement along a given market demand curve, and the term "change in demand" is used for a shift in the entire curve.

Elasticity

Economists frequently need to show how changes in one variable, say, A, affect some other variable, say, B. They ask, for example, how much does a change in the price of electricity affect the quantity of it demanded, or how does a change in income affect total expenditures on automobiles? One problem in determining these kinds of effects is that economic goods are measured in different units. For example, steak is typically sold per pound, whereas oranges are sold per dozen. A $.10 per pound rise in the price of steak might cause consumption of it to fall by two pounds per week, and a $.10 per dozen rise in the price of oranges might cause orange purchases to fall by one-half dozen per week. When two goods are measured in different units, we cannot make a simple comparison between them to determine which item is more price responsive (that is, which item's quantity demanded changes more because of a change in price).

Elasticity
The measure of the percentage change in one variable brought about by a 1 percent change in some other variable.

In order to make these comparisons, economists use the concept of **elasticity.** In general, the elasticity of variable B with respect to changes in variable A is defined as the percentage change in B brought about by a 1 percent change in A. Elasticity is "unit-free"—it compares one percentage to another, and the units disappear. In our oranges and steak example, a 1 percent rise in the price of steak might lead to a 2 percent decline in the quantity bought, whereas a 1 percent rise in the price of oranges might lead to only a 1 percent decline in the quantity bought. Steak purchases in this example are more responsive to price than orange purchases are. The fact that steak and oranges are measured in different units is no longer a problem because we can use percentage changes, which do not depend on how units of the good are measured.

Price Elasticity of Demand

Price elasticity of demand
The percentage change in the quantity demanded of a good in response to a 1 percent change in its price.

Although there are many different applications of elasticity in this book, probably the most important is the **price elasticity of demand.** Changes in P (the price of a good) will lead to changes in Q (the quantity of it purchased), and the price elasticity of demand measures this relationship. Specifically, the price elasticity of demand ($e_{Q,P}$) is defined as the percentage change in quantity in response to a 1 percent change in price. In mathematical terms:

$$\text{Price elasticity of demand} = e_{Q,P} = \frac{\text{Percentage change in Q}}{\text{Percentage change in P}}. \quad [5.1]$$

This elasticity records how Q changes in percentage terms in response to a percentage change in P. Since P and Q move in opposite directions (except in the rare case of Giffen's paradox), $e_{Q,P}$ will be negative.[1] For example, a value of $e_{Q,P}$ of -1 means that a 1 percent rise in price leads to a 1 percent decline in quantity, whereas a value of $e_{Q,P}$ of -2 shows that a 1 percent rise in price causes quantity to decline by 2 percent.

Values of the Price Elasticity of Demand

A distinction is often made among values of $e_{Q,P}$ that are less than, equal to, or greater than -1. Table 5.1 lists the terms used for each value. For an elas-

[1]Sometimes the price elasticity of demand is defined as the absolute value of the definition in Equation 5.1. Using this definition, elasticity is never negative; curves are classified as elastic, unit elastic, or inelastic depending on whether $e_{Q,P}$ is greater than, equal to, or less than 1. You need to recognize this distinction since there is no consistent use in economic literature.

Table 5.1
Terminology for the Ranges of $e_{Q,P}$

Value of $e_{Q,P}$ at a Point on Demand Curve	Terminology for Curve at This Point
$e_{Q,P} < -1$	Elastic
$e_{Q,P} = -1$	Unit elastic
$e_{Q,P} > -1$	Inelastic

tic curve ($e_{Q,P}$ is less than -1), a price increase causes a more than proportional quantity decrease. If $e_{Q,P} = -3$, for example, each 1 percent rise in price causes quantity to fall by 3 percent. For a unit elastic curve ($e_{Q,P}$ is equal to -1), a price increase causes a decrease in quantity of the same proportion. For an inelastic curve ($e_{Q,P}$ is greater than -1), price increases proportionally more than quantity decreases. If $e_{Q,P} = -½$, a 1 percent rise in price causes quantity to fall by only ½ of 1 percent. In general then, if a curve is elastic, its price affects quantity "a lot"; if the curve is inelastic, price does not have much of an effect on quantity demanded.

Price Elasticity and the Shape of the Demand Curve

We often classify the market demand for goods by their price elasticities of demand. For example, the quantity of medical services demanded is undoubtedly very inelastic. The market demand curve here may be almost vertical, showing that the quantity demanded is not responsive to price changes. On the other hand, price changes will have a greater effect on the quantity demanded of a particular kind of candy bar (the demand is elastic). Here the market demand curve would be relatively flat. If market price were to change even slightly, the quantity demanded would change significantly because people would buy other kinds of candy bars.

Price Elasticity and the Substitution Effect

Hence, the price elasticity of demand is a convenient way to compare the responsiveness of the quantity demanded of a good to changes in its price. The discussion of income and substitution effects in Chapter 4 gives us some theoretical basis for judging what the size of the price elasticity for particular goods might be. Goods with many close substitutes (brands of breakfast cereal, small cars, brands of electronic calculators, and so on) are subject to large substitution effects from a price change. For these kinds of goods we can presume that demand will be relatively elastic ($e_{Q,P} < -1$). On the other hand, goods with few close substitutes (water, insulin, and salt, for example) have small substitution effects when their price changes. Demand for such goods will probably be inelastic with respect to price changes ($e_{Q,P} > -1$; that is, $e_{Q,P}$ is between 0 and -1). Of course, as we mentioned previously, price changes also create income effects on the quantity demanded of a good, which we must consider to completely assess the likely size of overall price elasticities. Still, because the price changes for most goods have only a small effect on individuals' real incomes, the existence (or nonexistence) of substitutes is probably the principal determinant of price elasticity.

Price Elasticity and Time

Making substitutions in consumption choices may take time. To change from one brand of cereal to another may only take a week (to finish eating the first box), but to change from one type of home heating fuel to another may take years since a new heating system must be installed. Similarly, Application 5.2: Rising Gasoline Prices and Substitution Effects among Automobiles shows how trends in gasoline prices may have little short-term impact because people already own their cars and have relatively fixed travel needs. Over the longer term, however, there is clear evidence that people will change the kinds of cars they drive (and hence the amount of gasoline used) depending on gasoline prices. In general then, it might be expected that substitution effects and price elasticities would be larger the longer the time period that people have to change their behavior. In some situations, therefore, it is important to make a distinction between short-term and long-term price elasticities of demand, since the long-term concept may show much greater responses to price change.

Price Elasticity and Total Expenditures

The price elasticity of demand can be used to evaluate how total expenditures on a good change in response to a price change. Total expenditures on a good are found by multiplying the good's price (P) times the quantity purchased (Q). If demand is elastic, a price increase will cause total expenditures to fall. When demand is elastic, a given percentage increase in price is more than counterbalanced in its effect on total spending by the resulting large decrease in quantity demanded. For example, suppose people are currently buying 1 million automobiles at $10,000 each. Total expenditures on automobiles amount to $10 billion. Suppose also that the price elasticity of demand for automobiles is −2. Now, if the price increases to $11,000 (a 10 percent increase), the quantity purchased would fall to 800,000 cars (a 20 percent fall). Total expenditures are now $8.8 billion. Because demand is elastic, the price increase causes total expenditures to fall. This example can be easily reversed to show that if demand is elastic, a price fall will cause total expenditures to increase. The extra sales generated by the price decline more than compensate for the reduced price in this case.

If demand is unit elastic ($e_{Q,P} = -1$), total expenditures stay the same when prices change. A movement of P in one direction causes an exactly opposite proportional movement in Q, and the total price-times-quantity stays fixed. Even if prices fluctuate substantially, total spending on a good with unit elastic demand never changes.

APPLICATION 5.2

Rising Gasoline Prices and Substitution Effects among Automobiles

People's reactions to the rapidly rising gasoline prices during the 1970s provide a good example of the larger size of substitution effects and price elasticities over the long run. Over the short term, gasoline purchases are relatively difficult to alter. People own particular types of cars they must drive to work and for other necessary reasons. Everyone will complain about the higher gasoline prices, but in the short run there is little they can do about it.

If prices stay high for a long time, however, a number of adjustments can be made. People may change their commuting patterns by joining car poools, they may take fewer spur-of-the-moment trips to the store or to visit friends, and, eventually, they may buy more fuel-efficient automobiles. Even though people would take a while to adapt to higher gasoline prices, the changes resulting from the higher prices could be substantial.

Empirical Estimates

Some of these changes are presented in Table 1, which shows estimated responses to a 50 percent increase in the price of gasoline in the United States. This is approximately the level of increase in both 1973–1974 and 1979–1980. It is estimated that this increase causes a decrease in gasoline consumption of about 15 percent over the short term. Roughly half of that adjustment is caused by a reduction in the number of miles driven. The other half comes from an increase in the number of miles per gallon experienced by the total fleet of cars in the United States. Since this stock of cars does not change much in the short run, the small mileage improvement probably results from better automobile maintenance and lower highway speeds.

Table 1

Estimated Reaction of U.S. Consumers to a 50 Percent Rise in the Retail Price of Gasoline

Time Period	Reduction in Miles Driven	Increase in Miles per Gallon	Total Change in Consumption
Short term	−7%	+8%	−15%
Long term	−4	+24	−28

Source: Calculated from figures given in Carol A. Dahl, "Consumer Adjustment to a Gasoline Tax," *Review of Economics and Statistics* (August 1979): 427–431.

In the long run, older, low-mileage cars may be traded in for more fuel-efficient models, and then the mileage effect becomes substantial. Table 1 indicates that a 50 percent increase in gasoline price would cause a 24 percent increase in miles per gallon (say, from an average of 14 miles per gallon to over 17 miles per gallon) in the long term, and that effect provides the bulk of the overall long-term response to the price change. The lesson in the gasoline price increase is that it may take time for people to react and adjust to price changes. That is especially true when major changes in behavior (such as buying a new car) must be made before long-term adjustments are completed and their effect calculated.

Evidence from the Automobile Market

Evidence on actual car sales provides clear support for these suggestions. In 1970 only about 18 percent of total U.S. automobile sales were of small (compact or subcompact) cars. By 1980 this figure had increased to more than 50 percent, mainly in response to the fourfold increase in gasoline prices during the period. If rapidly rising imports of Japanese automobiles are included, the shift toward small cars becomes even more dramatic. After 1980, however, gasoline prices tended to stabilize and even fall a bit in real terms. This had the effect of curtailing small car sales as U.S. buyers shifted back toward full-size automobiles. By the late 1980s small cars had fallen to about 40 percent of all U.S. car sales. Even Toyota and Nissan were sending large, luxury cars to eager American buyers.

To Think About

1. During the 1970s, the federal government implemented "fuel economy standards" that U.S. auto makers were required to meet by 1985. Can you think of any reasons why the government should require people to buy more fuel-efficient cars than they would choose to buy on their own? Should the standards be different depending on whether gasoline prices are high or low?
2. Higher energy prices during the 1970s caused people to economize on many other kinds of energy use in addition to automobiles. What were some of these other types of energy consumption? Do you think these markets adjusted more or less quickly to rising energy prices than did the auto market?

Table 5.2
Relationship between Price Changes and Changes in Total Expenditure

If Demand Is	In Response to an Increase in Price, PQ Will	In Response to a Decrease in Price, PQ Will
Elastic	Fall	Rise
Unit elastic	Not change	Not change
Inelastic	Rise	Fall

Finally, when demand is inelastic, a price rise will cause total expenditures to rise. A price rise in an inelastic situation does not cause a very large reduction in quantity demanded, and total expenditures will increase. For example, suppose people buy 100 million bushels of wheat per year at a price of $3 per bushel. Total expenditures on wheat are $300 million. Suppose also that the price elasticity of demand for wheat is −0.5 (demand is inelastic). If the price of wheat rises to $3.60 per bushel (a 20 percent increase), quantity demanded will fall by 10 percent (to 90 million bushels). The net result of these actions is to increase total expenditures on wheat to $324 million. Because the quantity of wheat demanded is not very responsive to changes in price, total revenues are increased by a price rise. This same example could also be reversed to show that, in the inelastic case, total revenues are reduced by a fall in price.

These relationships between price elasticity and total expenditures are summarized in Table 5.2. You should think through the logic of each entry in the table to obtain a working knowledge of the elasticity concept. These relationships are used many times in later chapters. Application 5.3: The Paradox of Agriculture shows the importance of an inelastic demand for most agricultural goods. The alternative case of an elastic demand is illustrated in Application 5.4: The States' Take at the Track.

Is the Price Elasticity of Demand Constant?

So far in this section we have treated the price elasticity of demand as if it had the same value at every point on a demand curve. In Application 5.3, when we report that the demand for agricultural products is inelastic, we assume that demand would be inelastic no matter what the market price is. In the racetrack wagering application we assert that demand for betting is elastic, implying that it is elastic at all possible prices. Although this rather loose use of the terms elastic and inelastic is quite common, it is important to point out that it is not strictly correct. Nothing in economic theory requires that the elasticity of demand be the same everywhere along a demand curve. We would be more correct to say that *at current prices* the demand for agricultural products is inelastic, or that *at current prices* pari-mutuel wagering has an elastic demand. We need to leave open the possibility that elasticities could differ at different price levels.

This distinction may not be very important when only relatively small price changes are considered. When large changes in price are being consid-

APPLICATION 5.3

The Paradox of Agriculture

Demand for most agricultural products is relatively inelastic; even sharp changes in price do not have much effect on the quantity of food that people demand. This inelasticity of demand implies that even small changes in agricultural output can have a major impact on market prices, since these prices will have to change substantially in order to restore market equilibrium. This result gives rise to what is sometimes called the "paradox of agriculture." During periods of drought, crops are reduced and farm prices (and farmers' incomes) rise substantially. What is bad weather for the crops sometimes ends up being good for farmers. Similarly, good weather results in bumper crops and much lower agricultural prices, which may ultimately be a disaster for farmers' incomes.

The Paradox in Prior Years

Table 1 shows this paradox clearly with data on farm output and prices for a few periods. Prior to the 1980s these data show that when agricultural output expanded rather rapidly (in 1951–1954, 1966–1967, and 1975–1977), prices tended to fall more than proportionally. When output fell (in 1972–1974), prices rose significantly. Real farm income followed the trends in farm prices, falling when prices fell and rising when prices rose.

The data in the table do not identify all of the factors that affected farm prices during these periods. For example, the explosion in agricultural prices during 1972–1974 was probably caused more by an unusually large sale of grain to the Soviet Union (see Application 1.2) than by the rather slight fall in U.S. output.

Table 1
The Paradox of Agriculture during Four Recent Periods

	Percentage Change in		
Period	Farm Output	Farm Prices	Real Farm Income
1951–1954	+5.3%	−19.0%	−24.9%
1966–1967	+5.3	− 5.7	−14.6
1972–1974	−3.6	+53.6	+39.6
1975–1977	+4.4	− 4.5	−35.5

Source: Calculated from *Economic Report of the President, 1981,* Tables B-92, 94, and 95.

Still, the data clearly show the importance of the relatively inelastic nature of agricultural demand.

The Paradox during the 1980s

Two factors have tended to obscure the paradox of agriculture during the 1980s. First, many farm products have increasingly come to be traded on a worldwide basis. Simply looking at data from the United States will not reveal important influences from supply and demand patterns in foreign markets. Second, during the 1980s government payments to farmers have grown rapidly. In 1986, for example, agricultural subsidies represented more than one-third of the total value of farm output in the United States. In such a situation it is very difficult to determine patterns of supply and demand from actual data.

Despite these problems, agricultural markets continue to display some paradoxical results deriving from the inelasticity of demand. Consider the drought of 1988, one of the most severe on record. During the early summer of 1988 television reporters made repeated trips to the U.S. Midwest to film crops withering on the ground from lack of rainfall. But these reporters missed half the story. Because of the drought, grain prices exploded. Corn prices, for example, rose from \$2.35 per bushel in April to nearly \$3.60 in mid-June. By the end of the year, once initial scares about the severity of the drought had subsided, corn prices still stood nearly 50 percent higher than they had a year earlier. Although some farmers were clearly devastated by the drought and a much larger number suffered reduced crop yields, overall farm receipts and total net farm income proved to be quite healthy.

To Think About

1. This example suggests that farmers as a whole benefit from poor weather because they receive higher prices for their crops. How does that notion square with the more commonsense idea that farmers are impoverished by droughts? How are the income gains from poor weather distributed among farmers?
2. Would farmers be better-off if the prices of their crops did not fluctuate so much? Would farmers take in more revenue if, say, the price of a bushel of wheat was fixed at \$3 rather than constantly fluctuating between \$2.50 and \$3.50?

APPLICATION 5.4

The States' Take at the Track

A good example of an elastic demand is the case of legal and illegal gambling on horse races. Betting on horses is big business in the United States, and many states obtain substantial revenues by taxing pari-mutuel wagering. New York and other states also operate offtrack betting (OTB) parlors, where betting is also taxed. Since these taxes raise the "price" that bettors must pay for gambling, states pay close attention to how increases in taxes affect the total amount bet. If the demand for pari-mutuel wagering is very elastic with respect to the states' take, too high a tax rate will divert many would-be bettors to illegal bookmakers who do not collect such taxes.

Some Elasticity Estimates

A 1979 article by D. B. Suits provides some evidence of this elasticity.[1] One case that Suits examined concerned a major reduction in federal taxes on Nevada bookmakers in 1974. Following the reduction, bets placed with bookmakers on horse races nearly doubled. Increases in betting on sporting events were even larger. From these experiences and from other information about wagering at the track in many states, Suits concluded that the demand for gambling was price elastic—at least −1.6 and perhaps as large as −2.

States' Experiences with This Elastic Demand

The findings that the demand for gambling is quite sensitive to the price (in terms of taxes and other costs) that people have to pay have been reflected in states' experiences in taxing horse racing. In one study of wagering in southern California, for example, W. D. Morgan and J. D. Vasche found that the state take-out rate of nearly 16 percent in 1978 was not optimal from the state government's point of view.[2] They argued that a lower rate (of about 12 percent) would have generated enough additional attendance and wagering at thoroughbred racing to raise state revenues. As for any elastic demand curve, a reduction in price would have increased total revenues. Similar suggestions have been made for the New York OTB operation. In particular, several observers have noted that a special 5 percent surcharge placed on OTB bets in 1974 actually resulted in a loss in total state revenues from OTB since average bets per parlor fell dramatically. It appears that the main beneficiaries of this surcharge were the illegal bookmakers (who provide the major substitute to OTB) rather than the state treasury.

To Think About

1. Do people really recognize that states tax their betting at the track? Isn't racetrack betting by its very nature an irrational, emotional activity not really subject to very careful economic calculations? Is this just one more example of carrying economic analysis too far?
2. The relatively elastic demand for betting at the track reported here implies that there must be close substitutes for such activities. What are these substitutes? How will the demand for them respond to the state's tax policies? Are these effects desirable? How would this case compare to other state taxes on specific commodities for which there are no close substitutes (for example, cigarettes and liquor)?

[1]D. B. Suits, "The Elasticity of Demand for Gambling," *Quarterly Journal of Economics* (February1979): 155–162.

[2]W. D. Morgan and J. D. Vasche, "Horseracing Demand, Pari-mutuel Taxation and State Revenue Potential," *National Tax Journal* (June 1979): 185–194.

ered, however, the possibility that the elasticity may change must be taken into account. This distinction is also true for all of the other elasticity concepts developed in this book. Even though we usually treat the elasticities as being unchanged throughout the ranges of the demand and supply curves we are examining for convenience in teaching, you still must remember that

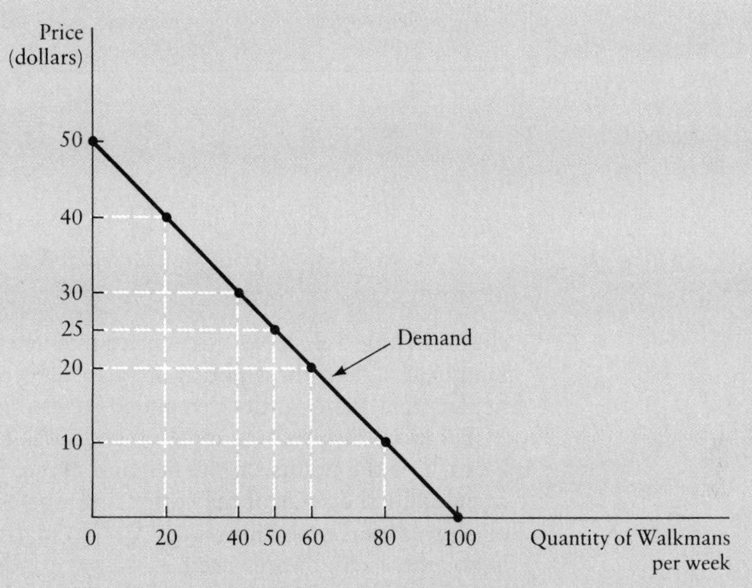

Figure 5.4
Elasticity of Demand Varies along a Straight-Line Demand Curve

A straight-line demand curve is elastic in its upper portion, inelastic in its lower portion. This relationship is illustrated by considering how total expenditures change for different points on the demand curve.

the elasticities can change in response to relatively large variations of price or quantity.

Linear Demand Curves and Price Elasticity

Probably the most important illustration of this warning about elasticities occurs in the case of a linear (straight-line) demand curve. As one moves along such a curve, the price elasticity of demand is always changing in value. At high price levels, demand is elastic; that is, a fall in price increases quantity purchased more than proportionally. At low prices, on the other hand, demand is inelastic; a further decline in price has relatively little proportional effect on quantity.

This result can be most easily proved with a numerical example. Figure 5.4 illustrates a straight-line (linear) demand curve for, say, Walkman cassette tape players. In looking at the changing elasticity of demand along this curve, we will assume it has the specific algebraic form

$$Q = 100 - 2P, \tag{5.2}$$

where Q is the quantity of players demanded per week and P is their price. The demonstration would be the same for any other linear equation we might

Table 5.3
Price, Quantity, and Total Expenditures on Walkmans for the Demand Function Q = 100 − 2P

Price (P)	Quantity (Q)	Total Expenditures (P · Q)
$50	0	$ 0
40	20	800
30	40	1,200
25	50	1,250
20	60	1,200
10	80	800
0	100	0

choose. Table 5.3 shows a few price-quantity combinations that lie on the demand curve, and these points are also reflected in Figure 5.4. Notice, in particular, that the quantity demanded is zero for prices of $50 or greater.

Table 5.3 also records total expenditures on Walkmans (P · Q) represented by each of the points on the demand curve. These expenditures are also represented by the areas of the various rectangles in Figure 5.4. For prices of $50 or above, total expenditures are $0. No matter how high the price, if nothing is bought, expenditures are $0. As price falls below $50, total expenditures increase. At P = $40, total expenditures are $800 ($40 · 20), and for P = $30 the figure rises to $1,200 ($30 · 40).

For relatively high prices, the demand curve in Figure 5.4 is elastic—a fall in price causes enough additional sales to increase total expenditures. This increase in total expenditures begins to slow as price drops still further. In fact, total expenditures reach a maximum at a price of $25. When P = $25, Q = 50 and total expenditures on tape players are $1,250. For prices below $25, reductions in price cause total expenditures to fall. At P = $20, expenditures are $1,200 ($20 · 60), whereas at P = $10, they are only $800 ($10 · 80). At these lower prices the increase in quantity demanded brought about by a further fall in price is simply not large enough to compensate for the price decline itself, and total expenditures fall.

This relationship is quite general. At relatively high prices on a linear demand curve, demand is elastic ($e_{Q,P} < -1$). Demand is unit elastic ($e_{Q,P} = -1$) at a price halfway between $0 and the price at which demand drops to nothing (given by P = $50 in the prior example). Hence, demand is unit elastic at a price of P = $25. Below that price demand is inelastic. Further reductions in price actually reduce total revenues.

Because of this property of linear demand curves, it is particularly important when using them to note clearly the point at which price elasticity is to be measured.[2] When looking at economic data from such a demand curve, if

---

[2]In some empirical work, demand curves are assumed to be linear in the logarithms of Q and P, that is, it is assumed that

$$\log Q = a + b \log P,$$

where a and b are constants. In this case calculus can be used to show that the price elasticity of demand is given by b (which will be negative) and is the same at every point on the demand curve.

the price being examined has not changed very much over the period being analyzed, the distinction may be relatively unimportant. But, if the analysis is being conducted over a period of substantial price change, the possibility that elasticity may have changed should be considered.[3]

Income Elasticity of Demand

Income elasticity of demand
The percentage change in the quantity demanded of a good in response to a 1 percent change in income.

Another type of elasticity is the **income elasticity of demand** ($e_{Q,I}$). This concept records the relationship between income changes and change in quantity demanded:

$$\text{Income elasticity of demand} = e_{Q,I} = \frac{\text{Percentage change in Q}}{\text{Percentage change in I}}. \qquad [5.3]$$

For a normal good, $e_{Q,I}$ is positive since increases in income lead to increases in purchases of the good. For the unlikely case of an inferior good, on the other hand, $e_{Q,I}$ would be negative, implying that increases in income lead to decreases in quantity purchased.

Among normal goods, whether $e_{Q,I}$ is greater than or less than 1 is a matter of considerable interest. Goods for which $e_{Q,I} > 1$ might be called luxury goods, in that purchases of these goods increase more rapidly than income. For example, if the income elasticity of demand for automobiles is 2, then a 10 percent increase in income will lead to a 20 percent increase in automobile purchases. On the other hand, as Engel's law suggests, food probably has an income elasticity of much less than 1. If the income elasticity of the demand for food were 0.5, for example, then a 10 percent rise in income would result in only a 5 percent increase in food purchases.[4] Considerable research has been done to determine the actual values of income elasticities for various items, and we discuss the results of some of these studies in the final section of this chapter.

[3]A commonly used formula for the elasticity of demand at some point (P^*, Q^*) on a linear demand curve (given by $Q = a + bP$) can be derived directly from the definition. If

$$e_{Q,P} = \frac{\text{Percentage change in Q}}{\text{Percentage change in P}} = \frac{\Delta Q/Q}{\Delta P/P} = \frac{\Delta Q}{\Delta P} \cdot \frac{P}{Q}$$

and, at P^*, Q^*

$$e_{Q,P} = \frac{\Delta Q}{\Delta P} \cdot \frac{P^*}{Q^*} = b \cdot \frac{P^*}{Q^*}.$$

This formula also shows that the greater the ratio P/Q, the greater will be the absolute value of the point elasticity.

[4]It seems obvious that not every good can have an income elasticity greater than 1. People cannot, in total, increase all of their expenditures proportionally more than their income increases since they are bound by budget constraints. In general, it can be shown that goods for which $e_{Q,I} > 1$ must be roughly balanced by those for which $e_{Q,I} < 1$.

Cross-Price Elasticity of Demand

Cross-price elasticity of demand
The percentage change in the quantity demanded of a good in response to a 1 percent change in the price of another good.

In Chapter 4 we showed that a change in the price of one good will affect the quantity demanded of most other goods. To measure such effects, economists use the **cross-price elasticity of demand.** This concept records the percentage change in quantity demanded (Q) that results from a 1 percentage point change in the price of some other good (call this other price P′). That is,

$$\text{Cross-price elasticity of demand} = e_{Q,P'} = \frac{\text{Percentage change in Q}}{\text{Percentage change in P}'}. \quad [5.4]$$

If these two goods are substitutes, the cross-price elasticity of demand will be positive since the price of one good and the quantity demanded of the other good will move in the same direction. For example, the cross-price elasticity for changes in the price of tea on coffee demand might be 0.2. Each 1 percentage point increase in the price of tea results in a 0.2 percentage point rise in the demand for coffee since coffee and tea are substitutes in people's consumption choices. A fall in the price of tea would cause the demand for coffee to fall also since people would choose to drink tea rather than coffee.

If two goods are complements, the cross-price elasticity will be negative showing that the price of one good and the quantity of the other good move in opposite directions. The cross-price elasticity of doughnut prices on coffee demand might be, say, −1.0. This would imply that a 1 percent increase in the price of doughnuts would cause the demand for coffee to fall by 1 percent. When doughnuts are more expensive, it becomes less attractive to drink coffee since many people like to have a doughnut with their morning coffee. A fall in the price of doughnuts would raise coffee demand since, in that case, people will choose to consume more of both complementary products. As for the other elasticities we have examined, considerable empirical research has been conducted to try to measure actual cross-price elasticities of demand.

Empirical Studies of Demand

Economists have for many years studied the demand for all sorts of goods. Some of the earliest studies generalized from the expenditure patterns of a small sample of families.[5] More recent studies have examined a wide variety of goods to estimate both income and price elasticities. Although it is not possible for us to discuss in detail here the statistical techniques used in such studies, we can show in a general way how these economists proceeded.

Estimating Demand Curves

The first important problem faced in any empirical investigation is how to implement the *ceteris paribus* assumption. In studying the relationship be-

[5]For an interesting survey of some of the early empirical work in demand analysis, see George J. Stigler, "The Early History of Empirical Studies of Consumer Behavior," *Journal of Political Economy* (April 1954): 95–113.

Figure 5.5
Fitting a Demand Curve to Empirical Observations

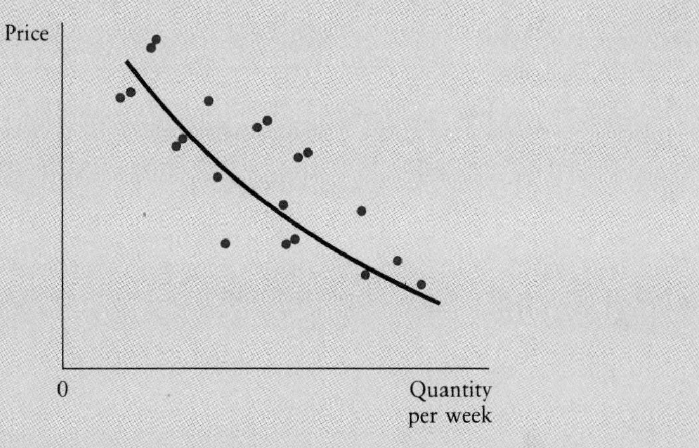

The points show various combinations of P and Q. It is important that these points be observed while holding constant the other factors that affect the demand for Q. Otherwise they will not lie on a single demand curve.

tween the price of a good and the quantity demanded, for example, our theory requires that we hold income, other prices, and preferences constant. Otherwise, if income and other prices are not held constant, observed combinations of P and Q will lie on many different demand curves rather than on the single curve we are trying to measure. Ideally we would find several people to study who are identical in every respect except that each faces a different price for the good in question. We could then plot the price and quantity chosen on a graph such as that shown in Figure 5.5. If we were sure that our individuals were, in fact, identical, the points in Figure 5.5 would indeed reflect the *ceteris paribus* influence of price on quantity.

Of course, in practice it is impossible for us to impose the *ceteris paribus* assumption in this way. Finding a group of identical people is probably impossible, and in most cases, there is little variation in the prices people pay for the things they buy. It may be possible in the experimental sciences (such as biology) to isolate a single factor, but economists usually rely on the real world for their data. They must then use statistical techniques to impose the *ceteris paribus* assumption. The most widely used technique is "multiple regression analysis."[6] Although we will not examine this technique here, it was used to estimate all of the elasticities we will discuss below.

[6]Multiple regression analysis, instead of looking at only the simple relationship $Q = a + bP$, attempts to estimate a relationship of the form $Q = a + bP + cI + dP' +$ other terms. Once this relationship is estimated, all the terms other than P can be held constant while the partial relationship between Q and P is examined. This is precisely what is required by the *ceteris paribus* assumption.

Table 5.4
Representative Income and Price Elasticities

Item	Income Elasticity	Price Elasticity
Food	0.28	−0.21
Medical services	0.22	−0.20
Automobiles	3.00	−1.20
Housing		
Rental	1.00	−0.18
Owner occupied	1.20	−1.20
Gasoline	1.06	−0.54
Electricity	0.61	−1.14
Coffee	0.51	−0.16
Beer	0.93	−1.13
Marijuana	0.00	−1.50
Gambling	1.00	−1.60

Source: Food: H. Wold and L. Jureen, *Demand Analysis* (New York: John Wiley & Sons, Inc., 1953), p. 203. Medical Services: income elasticity from R. Andersen and L. Benham, "Factors Affecting the Relationship between Family Income and Medical Care Consumption"; price elasticity from G. Rosenthal, "Price Elasticity of Demand for Short-Term General Hospital Services"; both in *Empirical Studies in Health Economics,* Herbert Klarman, ed. (Baltimore: Johns Hopkins Press, 1970). Automobiles: Gregory C. Chow, *Demand for Automobiles in the United States* (Amsterdam: North Holland Publishing Company, 1957). Housing: income elasticities from F. deLeeuw, "The Demand for Housing," *Review of Economics and Statistics* (February 1971); price elasticities from H. S. Houthakker and L. D. Taylor, *Consumer Demand in the United States* (Cambridge, Mass.: Harvard University Press, 1970), pp. 166–167. Gasoline: Data Resources, Inc., "A Study of the Quarterly Demand for Gasoline," a study prepared for the Council on Environmental Quality, December 1973. Electricity: R. F. Halvorsen, "Residential Demand for Electricity," unpublished PH.D. dissertation, Harvard University, December 1972. Coffee: J. Huang, J. J. Siegfried, and F. Zardoshty "The Demand for Coffee in the United States, 1963–77," *Quarterly Journal of Business and Economics* (Summer 1980): 36–50. Beer: T. F. Hogarty and K. G. Elsinger, "The Demand for Beer," *Review of Economics and Statistics* (May 1972): 195–198. Marijuana: T. C. Misket and F. Vakil, "Some Estimates of Price and Expenditure Elasticities among UCLA Students," *Review of Economics and Statistics* (November 1972): 474–475. Gambling: D. B. Suits, "The Elasticity of Demand for Gambling," *Quarterly Journal of Economics* (February 1979): 155–162.

Once the problem of the *ceteris paribus* assumption has been resolved, how do we decide which curve to use to fit the data points? Since a large number of possible curves could represent the points in Figure 5.5, we must develop some criteria for choosing which of them is the "best." Again, this is a statistical problem that we cannot investigate in detail here. Usually the decision depends on which curve comes closest to the observed points and which curve seems most intuitively plausible.

Some Income and Price Elasticity Estimates

Table 5.4 lists a few income and price elasticities of demand that economists have estimated. Although these estimates come from many sources, they do have certain similarities. The income elasticities for necessities (food and medical services) are considerably below those for luxuries (automobiles), as we might expect from the way purchases of these types of goods respond to

Table 5.5
Representative Cross-Price Elasticities of Demand

Demand for	Effect of Price of	Elasticity Estimate
Butter	Margarine	1.53
Electricity	Natural gas	.50
Coffee	Tea	.15

Source: Butter: Dale M. Heien, "The Structure of Food Demand: Interrelatedness and Duality," *American Journal of Agricultural Economics* (May 1982): 213–221. Electricity: G. R. Lakshmanan and W. Anderson, "Residential Energy Demand in the United States," *Regional Science and Urban Economics* (August 1980): 371–386. Coffee: J. Huang, J. J. Siegfried, and F. Zardoshty "The Demand for Coffee in the United States, 1963–77," *Quarterly Journal of Business and Economics* (Summer 1980): 36–50.

income changes. A second observation is that most of the price elasticities are fairly low (although, as we expected, they are all negative). Price changes do not induce substantial proportional changes in quantities demanded.

A few of the elasticities in Table 5.4 are worth looking at more closely. For example, the table suggests that the demand for electricity is price elastic. As we saw in Application 1.3, one result of sharply increasing energy prices in the 1970s was a significant decrease in the demand for electric power. This decrease in demand caused a number of utility companies to cancel large power plant projects as they discovered that historical patterns significantly overstated the actual growth in electricity demand.

For housing, the finding that income elasticity of demand equals or exceeds 1 has interesting implications for the fairness of property taxation. If spending on housing increases more rapidly than income, a proportional tax on housing values will actually be relatively progressive since people with higher incomes will pay proportionally more in taxes than low-income people. The "commonsense notion" that property taxes are regressive because housing is a necessity is erroneous once one looks at the actual data.

Finally, the relatively high price elasticities for beer and marijuana might be noted. These imply that taxes or (what amounts to the same thing) legal restrictions on the sale of such items will reduce consumption significantly. Of course, as we will see in Chapter 13, the imposition of taxes on elastically demanded items will create a significantly larger burden on consumers than will a similar tax on an inelastically demanded item. But, in these cases the desire to tax may be related to concerns that extend beyond economics. In Application 5.5: National Health Insurance, we pursue the subject of price elasticities of demand a bit further by showing how they have played a major role in the debate about an important question of public policy.

Some Cross-Price Elasticity Estimates

Table 5.5 shows a few cross-price elasticity estimates that economists have derived. All of the pairs of goods illustrated are probably substitutes, and the

APPLICATION 5.5

National Health Insurance

Most developed countries have some form of a national health insurance plan. In the United States, the elderly are covered under the Medicare program, and many of the poor receive Medicaid. In recent years a number of more comprehensive plans have been proposed. These plans vary greatly in cost, with a price tag of more than $200 billion per year for some of the more generous of them. A principal determinant of a plan's cost is the precise mix of services that it covers. Very basic plans cover only hospital stays and physicians' costs for major illnesses, whereas more extensive plans may cover a wide variety of additional services such as family counseling or dental care. An important question in choosing among such plans is how their adoption will affect the demand for specific medical services. Because insurance lowers the out-of-pocket cost to patients (who don't have to pay for services as they use them), there is certain to be some increase in demand. The empirical question is how large that increase might be.

Low Elasticities for Hospitals and Doctors' Visits

The estimated price elasticity of demand for medical services given in Table 5.4 is −.20. This figure might be a starting point in predicting the effect of insurance on demand for medical services. This value indicates that, as might be expected, the demand for most medical services is quite inelastic. There would probably still be some expansion in demand as effective prices fall because of insurance coverage, but this increase would be fairly small. For example, in a study of patients' responses to actual out-of-pocket costs for medical services, J. P. Newhouse and C. E. Phelps found very low (between 0 and −.10) price elasticities of demand for the lengths of stays in hospitals and for office visits to physicians.[1] These services then would show relatively little increase in demand if they were included in national health insurance plans.

Some Elastically Demanded Services

On the other hand, several authors have found much larger price elasticities for services such as dental care, ophthalmological care, and psychiatric counseling. These services may have a somewhat greater discretionary element to their consumption. For these items a substantial increase in demand as a result of insurance coverage might be expected. Suggestions for ways of limiting this increase in demand have ranged from outright exclusion of such services from national health insurance plans to cost sharing by patients using the services.

Consider, for example, the case of dental care. Existing research on such care concludes that it is rather price responsive. For some elective services such as dental examinations or regular teeth cleanings, the price elasticity of demand may be as large as −1 or larger.[2] For this reason many private dental insurance plans exclude such services from coverage or require that patients incur some minimum "deductible" before part of their costs are covered. Similar exclusions and copayment provisions occur in the Medicare and Medicaid programs and in dental coverage in other countries' health insurance plans. Although proposing such limits to coverage can sometimes be political suicide, it seems likely that those interested in the further development of national health insurance in the United States will find it necessary to take people's reactions to such coverage into account.

To Think About

1. Does the relatively high price elasticity of demand for some medical services imply that these services are not really "necessary"? Should health care planners use such elasticity estimates as a guide for the kinds of services people really need, or are there important drawbacks to basing such a judgment on people's responses to prices? How would you judge what medical services are really necessary for a person's well-being?
2. Isn't the use of demand concepts in the health care field inappropriate since a great deal of medical demand is determined by physicians, not by the patient? Is there any reason for physicians to take the price of a service into account when deciding what to prescribe? Does the model of a utility-maximizing consumer have any validity in this case?

[1]J. P. Newhouse and C. E. Phelps, "Price and Income Elasticities for Medical Care Services," in *The Economics of Health and Medical Care*, M. Perlman, ed. (New York: John Wiley & Sons, 1974), pp. 139–161.

[2]See W. G. Manning and C. E. Phelps, "The Demand for Dental Care," *The Bell Journal of Economics* (Autumn 1979): 503–525.

positive estimated values for the elasticities confirm that view. The figure for the relationship between butter and margarine is the largest in Table 5.5. Even in the absence of health issues, the competition between these two spreads on the basis of price is clearly very intense. Natural gas prices have an important effect on electricity sales since they help to determine how people will heat their homes. The elasticity presented in the table was derived in ways that permitted such long-run responses to be captured. The final entry in the table suggests that coffee and tea are not particularly close substitutes. Although economics teachers (including your author) persist in using these commodities as examples of substitutes, apparently relative prices play only a minor role in determining which of them people choose to drink.

Summary

In this chapter we have constructed a market demand curve by adding up the demands of many consumers. This curve shows the relationship between the market price of a good and the amount that people choose to purchase of that good, assuming all the other factors that affect demand do not change. The market demand curve is a basic building block for the theory of price determination. We will be using the concept frequently throughout the remainder of this book. You should therefore keep in mind the following points about this concept:

- The market demand curve represents the summation of the demands of a given number of potential consumers of a particular good. The curve shows the *ceteris paribus* relationship between the market price of the good and the amount demanded by all consumers.
- Factors that shift individual demand curves also shift the market demand curve to a new position. Such factors include changes in incomes, changes in the prices of other goods, and changes in people's preferences.
- The price elasticity of demand provides a convenient way of measuring the extent to which market demand responds to price changes. Specifically, the price elasticity of demand shows the percentage change in quantity demanded in response to a 1 percent change in market price. Demand is said to be "elastic" if a 1 percent change in price leads to a greater than 1 percent change in quantity demanded. Demand is "inelastic" if a 1 percent change in price leads to a smaller than 1 percent change in quantity.
- There is a close relationship between the price elasticity of demand and total expenditures on a good. If demand is elastic, a rise in price will reduce total expenditures. If demand is inelastic, a rise in price will increase total expenditures.
- Other elasticities of demand are defined in a way similar to that used for the price elasticity. For example, the income elasticity of demand measures the percentage change in quantity demanded in response to a 1 percent change in income.

- Economists have estimated elasticities of demand for many different goods based on real-world data A major problem in making such estimates is to devise ways of holding constant all other factors that affect demand so that the points being used lie on a single demand curve.

Review Questions

1. In the construction of the market demand curve shown in Figure 5.1, why is a horizontal line drawn at the prevailing price, P_X^*? What does this assume about the price facing each person? How are people assumed to react to this price?
2. Explain how the following events might affect the market demand curve for prime filet mignon:

   a. A fall in the price of filet mignon because of a decline in cattle prices.
   b. A general rise in consumers' incomes.
   c. A rise in the price of lobster.
   d. Increased health concerns about cholesterol.
   e. An income tax increase for high income people used to increase welfare benefits.
   f. A cut in income taxes and welfare benefits.

3. Why is the price elasticity of demand negative for a normal good? If the price elasticity of demand for automobiles is less than the price elasticity of demand for medical care, which demand is "more" elastic? Give a numerical example.
4. "Gaining extra revenue is easy for any producer—all it has to do is raise the price of its product." Do you agree? Explain when this would be true, when it might not be true.
5. Develop an intuitive proof of why the price elasticity of demand varies along a linear demand curve. What would the elasticity be near the price intercept (where Q = 0)? What would it be near the quantity intercept (where P = 0)?
6. Explain the relationship between the income elasticity of demand for an item and the fraction of income spent on that item. How can the income elasticity of demand be used to predict what will happen to the fraction of income spent on a good as income rises?
7. J. Trueblue always spends one-third of his income on American flags. What is the income elasticity of his demand for such flags? What is the price elasticity of his demand for flags?
8. Table 5.4 reports an estimated price elasticity of demand for electricity of −1.14. Explain what this means with a numerical example. Does this number seem "large"? Do you think this is a short- or long-term elasticity estimate? How might this estimate be important for owners of electric utilities or for bodies that regulate them?
9. Table 5.5 reports that the cross-price elasticity of demand for electricity with respect to the price of natural gas is 0.50. Explain what this means with a numerical example. What does the fact that the number is positive imply about the relationship between electricity and natural gas use? Do you think that the cross-price elasticity of the demand for natural gas with respect to electricity prices would be about the same? Or, are there situations where the elasticities would not be symmetric?
10. What are some of the influences on the demand for housing that should be controlled for if you were trying to estimate a demand curve for housing? What would happen if you didn't control for these? How might shifts in the supply curve for housing interfere with your ability to identify a single demand curve? Illustrate your discussion with the appropriate graphs.

Problems

5.1 Suppose the demand curve for flyswatters is given by

$$Q = 500 - 50P$$

where Q is the number of flyswatters demanded per week and P is the price in dollars.

a. How many flyswatters are demanded at a price of \$2? How about a price of \$3? \$4? Suppose flyswatters were free; how many would be bought?
b. Graph the flyswatter demand curve—remember to put P on the vertical axis and Q on the horizontal axis. To do so, you may wish to solve for P as a function of Q.
c. Suppose during July the flyswatter demand curve shifts to

$$Q = 1{,}000 - 50P.$$

Answer parts a and b for this new demand curve.

5.2 The market demand for potatoes is given by:

$$Q = 1{,}000 + 0.3I - 300P + 200P'$$

where

Q = Annual demand in pounds

I = Average income in dollars per year

P = Price of potatoes in cents per pound

P′ = Price of rice in cents per pound.

a. Suppose I = \$10,000 and P′ = \$.25; what would be the market demand for potatoes? At what price would Q = 0? Graph this demand curve.
b. Suppose I rose to \$20,000 with P′ staying at \$.25. Now what would the demand for potatoes be? At what price would Q = 0? Graph this demand curve. Explain why more potatoes are demanded at every price in this case than in part a.
c. If I returns to \$10,000 but P′ falls to \$.10, what would the demand for potatoes be? At what price would Q = 0? Graph this demand curve. Explain why fewer potatoes are demanded at every price in this case than in part a.

5.3 Tom, Dick, and Harry constitute the entire market for scrod. Tom's demand curve is given by

$$Q_1 = 100 - 2P$$

for $P \leq 50$. For $P > 50$, $Q_1 = 0$. Dick's demand curve is given by

$$Q_2 = 160 - 4P$$

for $P \leq 40$. For $P > 40$, $Q_2 = 0$. Harry's demand curve is given by

$$Q_3 = 150 - 5P$$

for $P \leq 30$. For $P > 30$, $Q_3 = 0$. Using this information, answer the following:

a. How much scrod is demanded by each person at P = 50? At P = 35? At P = 25? At P = 10? And at P = 0?

b. What is the total market demand for scrod at each of the prices specified in part a?
c. Graph each individual's demand curve.
d. Use the individual demand curves and the results of part b to construct the total market demand for scrod.

5.4 Suppose the quantity of good X demanded by individual 1 is given by

$$X_1 = 10 - 2P_X + 0.01I_1 + 0.4P_Y,$$

and the quantity of X demanded by individual 2 is

$$X_2 = 5 - P_X + 0.02I_2 + 0.2P_Y.$$

a. What is the market demand function for total X ($= X_1 + X_2$) as a function of P_X, I_1, I_2, and P_Y?
b. Graph the two individual demand curves (with X on the horizontal axis, P_X on the vertical axis) for the case $I_1 = 1{,}000$, $I_2 = 1{,}000$, and $P_Y = 10$.
c. Using these individual demand curves, construct the market demand curve for total X. What is the algebraic equation for this curve?
d. Now suppose I_1 increases to 1,100 and I_2 decreases to 900. How would the market demand curve shift? How would the individual demand curves shift? Graph these new curves.
e. Finally, suppose P_Y rises to 15. Graph the new individual and market demand curves that would result.

5.5 Assume that $e_{X,PX} = -2$, $e_{X,PY} = .5$, and $e_{X,I} = .8$.

a. If originally $P_X = \$10$, $P_Y = \$10$, average I = \$20,000, and total consumption of good X is 1,000 units, how much of good X will be consumed when P_X rises to \$10.10?
b. If P_Y rises to \$10.10 instead and P_X stays at \$10, how will consumption of good X be affected?
c. Now assume that P_X and P_Y stay constant at \$10 but average I rises by \$200. How will consumption of good X be affected?

5.6 The market demand for cashmere socks is given by

$$Q_c = 1{,}000 = .5I - 400P_c + 200P_w$$

where

Q_c = Annual demand in number of pairs

I = Average income in dollars per year

P_c = Price of one pair of cashmere socks

P_w = Price of one pair of wool socks

Given that I = \$20,000, $P_c = \$10$, and $P_w = \$5$, determine $e_{Qc,Pc}$ $e_{Qc,Pw}$ and $e_{Qc,I}$ at this point.

5.7 Suppose ham and cheese are pure complements—they are always used in the ratio of one slice of ham to one slice of cheese to make a sandwich. Suppose also that ham and cheese sandwiches are the only goods that consumers can buy and that bread is free.

a. Show that if the price of a slice of ham equals the price of a slice of cheese, the price elasticity of demand for ham is $-1/2$.

b. Show that if the price of a slice of ham equals the price of a slice of cheese, the cross-price elasticity of a change in the price of cheese on ham consumption is also $-1/2$.

c. How would your answers to parts a and b change if a slice of ham cost twice as much as a slice of cheese?

5.8 A luxury is defined as a good for which the income elasticity of demand is greater than 1. Show that for a two-good economy, both goods cannot be luxuries. (Hint: What happens if both goods are luxuries and income is increased by 10 percent?)

5.9 If $e_{X,P} = -.6$ and $e_{X,P} = -.8$ in a two-good economy, what is $e_{X,I}$? (Hint: A 10 percent increase in income can be seen as a 10 percent drop in all prices.)

5.10 For the linear demand curve shown in Figure A show that the price elasticity of demand at any given point (say, point E) is given by minus the ratio of distance X to distance Y in the figure. (Hint: Use footnote 3 of this chapter.)

Figure A

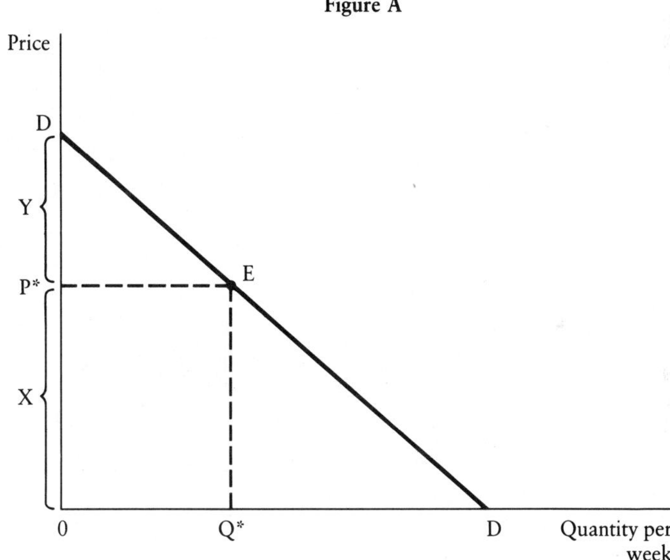

CHAPTER 6

Further Applications of the Theory of Choice

In Chapters 4 and 5 we used the utility-maximization model of people's consumption choices to develop the market demand curve. Although this is probably the model's most important application, it is by no means the only one. Because the notion of utility maximization is a very general theory of how choices are made, it can be applied to a wide variety of economic issues. This chapter looks at a few of these additional applications. All of these involve using our previous model to examine whether certain economic events make people better-off or worse-off.

We begin with the development of a different type of demand curve than the one we derived in Chapter 4. This new curve illustrates only the substitution effects that arise from price changes—any effects of price changes on a person's real purchasing power are "compensated" for by the way the curve is constructed. We use this curve to show how the effects of price changes on people's welfare can actually be measured.

Our second, related application concerns the properties of "index numbers." Such numbers are frequently encountered in economics—measuring "real" (inflation-adjusted) gross national product (GNP) and defining the Consumer Price Index (CPI) are the two most important examples. This section shows how the consumer choice model can be used to investigate the accuracy of these measurements using the case of the CPI.

Finally, this chapter concludes with a discussion of the "gains from trade." We use the utility-maximization model to show how voluntary trading between two people can make both of them better-off. Although our demonstration is quite simple, voluntary trade is the basis of many economic

Figure 6.1
Construction of a Compensated Demand Curve

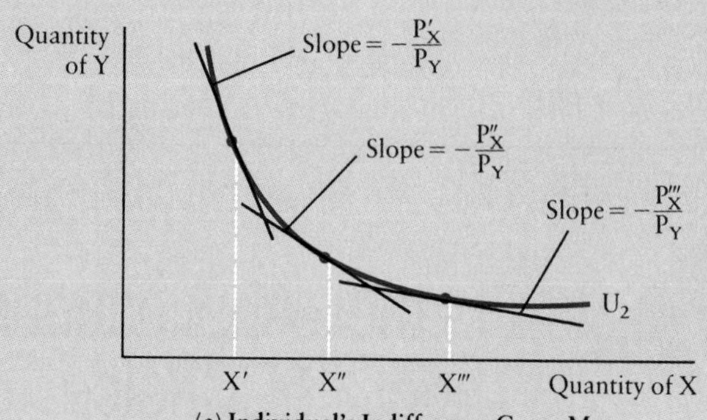

(a) Individual's Indifference Curve Map

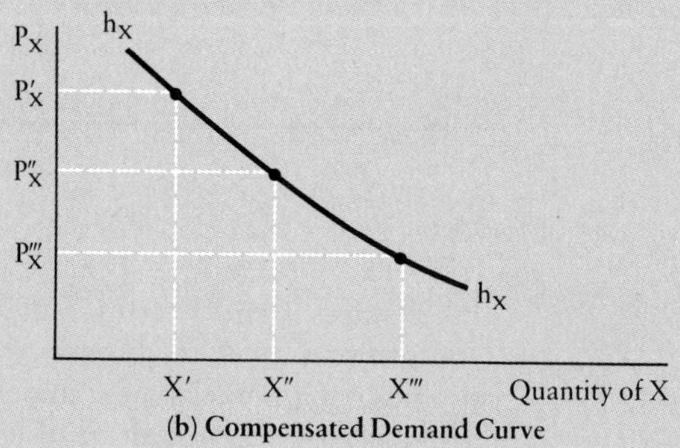

(b) Compensated Demand Curve

The curve h_X shows how the quantity of X demanded changes when P_X changes, holding P_Y and *utility* constant. That is, the individual's income is "compensated" so as to keep utility constant. Hence h_X reflects only the substitution effects of changing prices.

activities, including the law of contracts between individuals and, on a much larger scale, the benefits of international trade between nations. Some of these applications are examined here and at many places later in this book.

Compensated Demand Curves

In our prior development of the individual demand curve (Figure 4.8), utility changes as we move along the curve. As P_X falls, the individual is made increasingly better-off as shown by the increase in utility from U_1 to U_2 to U_3. The reason this happens is that the demand curve is drawn on the assumption that nominal income and other prices are held constant; hence a decline in P_X makes the individual better-off by increasing his or her real purchasing power. Although this is the most common way to impose the *ceteris paribus* assumption in developing a demand curve, it is not the only way. An alternative approach holds the individual's utility constant while examining reactions to changes in P_X. The derivation is illustrated in Figure 6.1. There we hold utility constant (at U_2) while successively reducing P_X. As P_X falls, the

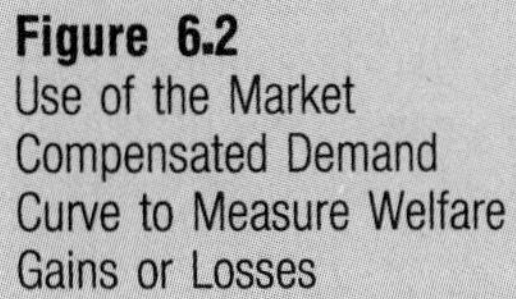

Figure 6.2
Use of the Market Compensated Demand Curve to Measure Welfare Gains or Losses

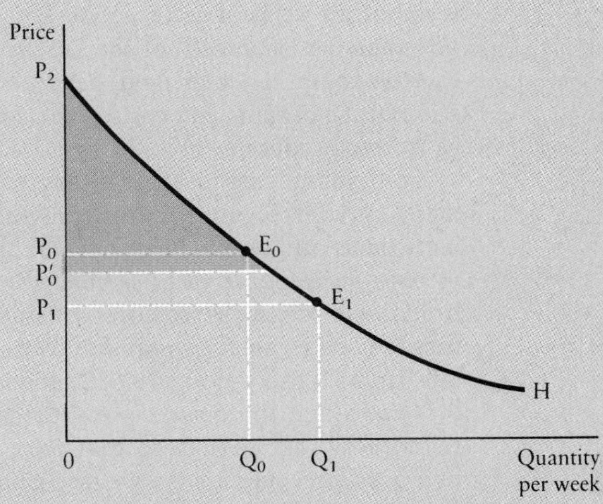

When the price of computer games falls from P_0 to P_1 the area $P_0E_0E_1P_1$ provides an estimate of the real income that people gain. The area $P_2E_0P_0$ provides an estimate of how much people would spend for the right to purchase Q_0 computer games at a price of P_0 rather than doing without the games. This represents the consumer surplus available from people's current expenditure plans.

individual's nominal income is reduced to prevent any increase in utility from occurring. In other words, the effects of the price change on purchasing power are "compensated" so as to constrain the individual to remain on U_2. If we were to examine increases in P_X instead, such compensation would be positive. The individual's income would have to be increased to permit him or her to stay on U_2. The resulting **compensated demand curve,** therefore, shows this individual's reactions to price changes of a good on the assumption that all other prices and utility are held constant. Compensated demand curves for individuals can be added up in much the same way we did in the previous chapter to get market demand curves. For our discussion we will use only compensated demand curves for the market as a whole.

Compensated demand curve
A demand curve drawn on the assumption that other prices and utility are held constant. Income effects of price changes are compensated for along the curve, and it reflects only substitution effects.

Welfare Effects of Price Changes

Although the compensated demand curve is probably not used as widely in economics as is the ordinary ("Marshallian") demand curve, it still has a number of important applications. Most of these involve using the curve to measure the dollar costs or benefits to people of various price changes. To see how this is done, consider the compensated demand curve for, say, video games illustrated in Figure 6.2. Suppose that initially the price of games is P_0 and people choose to consume a quantity of Q_0. If the price of games were to fall (because of the invention of better electronic chips) to P_1 , we know, from our discussion in Chapter 4, that people would be better-off. But can we attach a dollar value to this increase in welfare? In a variety of applications it is important to be able to do so. For example, it is sometimes claimed that one valuable "spin-off" of the U.S. space program was the development of cheaper computer chips (and, hence, cheaper electronic games). A full evaluation of the benefits and costs of the space program should take these welfare gains into account.

To develop such a dollar estimate, remember how the compensated demand curve in Figure 6.1 was constructed. For movements along the curve, individuals' utility was held constant by making suitable adjustments to their incomes in response to price changes. Hence a measure of the welfare gain from lower priced electronics is provided by the size of the income compensation that takes place in response to the decline in price. That is, when price falls from P_0 to P_1 in Figure 6.2, individuals would normally be made better-off, but along the compensated demand curve their purchasing power is reduced by just enough so that they gain nothing from the price fall. To find a dollar value for the welfare gain, therefore, we must measure this income compensation.

Suppose the price of computer games had fallen by just a very small amount, say, to P_0'. If this change were small enough, we could treat Q as remaining unchanged at Q_0. People would therefore save $(P_0 - P_0') \cdot Q_0$ in their game purchases—an amount that can be measured by the top shaded rectangle in Figure 6.2. This is the amount of income that people could spend on something else and represents the amount of compensation required to keep them from being made better-off by the price decline.

By continuing to drop the price of computer games in small increments, the additional compensation rectangles shown in Figure 6.2 could be computed. Adding these up provides our measure of the total income adjustment required to compensate for the total price decline. If we used very small rectangles, it is clear that this total area would be given by $P_0E_0E_1P_1$. This then is our measure of the welfare gain from the fall in price.

This result is quite general: changes in welfare that are caused by changes in prices can be given an approximate[1] dollar value by finding the area under the compensated demand curve that is bounded by the extent of the price change. In Application 6.1: The Excess Burden of a Tax, for example, we show how this measure can be used to appraise the true burden of a tax on a consumer good. The concept has a number of other applications that we will encounter at several places later in the book.

---

[1]The word "approximate" is used here for two reasons. First, the compensated demand curve concept for an individual involves some ambiguity about exactly what level of utility should be used to construct the curve—the location of the compensated demand curve depends on the utility level assumed in its construction. Second, the use of a market compensated demand curve assumes away many important problems about how compensation should be made to specific individuals when prices change. For a discussion of these issues, see Walter Nicholson, *Microeconomic Theory: Basic Principles and Extensions,* 4th ed. (Hinsdale, Ill.: Dryden Press, 1989), pp. 143–146.

APPLICATION 6.1

The Excess Burden of a Tax

In Application 4.3 we showed that most commodity taxes will affect people's welfare not only because they reduce individuals' purchasing power but also because they provide incentives to change behavior. Such taxes, therefore, impose an "excess burden" relative to lump-sum taxes that affect only purchasing power. By using the compensated demand curve, we can show this result in a very simple way.

A Graphic Analysis

Figure 1 again shows the compensated demand curve for video games. With a current price of P_0 individuals choose to consume quantity Q_0. If the government were to institute a tax of t per computer game (as a way of saving players from a wasted life), the price of the game would rise[1] to $P_0 + t$ and consumption would be reduced to Q_2. The total welfare loss to consumers of this price rise would be given by area $AE_2E_0P_0$. Tax receipts, which are given by area AE_2BP_0, constitute a portion of this loss—consumers of computer games pay the tax by suffering a loss in utility. But the total value of the loss exceeds tax revenues by the size of the triangular area E_2E_0B. That area then represents the excess burden of the tax; it is a loss of consumer welfare that is not captured by the tax collector nor by anyone else.

Figure 1
Excess Burden of a Tax

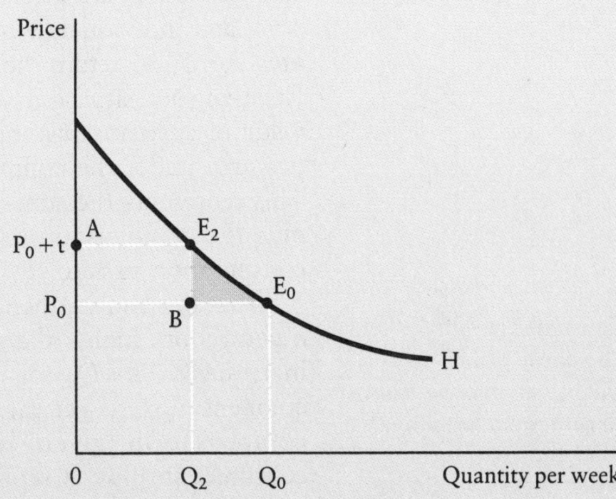

Imposition of a tax on video games raises their price to $P_0 + t$ and reduces quantity bought to Q_2. The welfare loss from this price change is given by the area $AE_2E_0P_0$ under the compensated demand curve, H. This amount exceeds total tax collections, which are given by area AE_2BP_0. The triangular area E_2E_0B represents the excess burden of the tax.

Measuring Excess Burden

If the shape of the compensated demand curve is known, measuring the excess burden associated with a particular tax is a simple matter. Information on the size of the price change brought about by the tax and on the reduction in demand the price change causes (this can be computed if the price elasticity of the compensated demand curve is known) can be used to evaluate the size of the triangular area in Figure 1.

Unfortunately, providing an exact measure can run into many pitfalls in correctly defining the compensated demand curve for a good. Still, economists have not been shy about putting forth estimates. In one recent set of articles about the excess burden involved in taxing wages, for example, various authors calculated that the excess burden associated with raising income taxes in the United States could constitute between 15 and 50 percent of the amount of tax revenues collected.[2] Hence, although these estimates do not pin down the size of the excess burden of such taxes very precisely, they do suggest that the excess burden issue is an important one.

To Think About

1. Cigarettes and alcohol taxes are frequently supported because they will (a) reduce consumption of these "sinful" items; and (b) because they may involve relatively little excess burden. Are these two rationales for such taxes consistent with each other?
2. Some authors differentiate between the "average" excess burden of a tax (total excess burden as a percentage of taxes collected) and the "marginal" excess burden (the extra excess burden from raising a tax as a percentage of extra taxes collected). Explain why the marginal excess burden of a tax will usually exceed the average excess burden.

[1] In Chapter 12 we will want to amend this analysis a bit by allowing for supply effects in the video games market.

[2] For a summary, see E. K. Browning, "On the Marginal Welfare Cost of Taxation," *American Economic Review* (March 1987): 11–23.

Consumer Surplus

Using these observations also provides a way to estimate how much a particular good is "worth" to people. In the video game illustration in Figure 6.2, for example, we know that people are currently spending $P_0 \cdot Q_0$ for such games. If the price of games were to rise to P_2, demand would fall to zero, and individuals would require an income compensation represented by area $P_2E_0P_0$ to retain the same utility level they enjoyed before the price rise. Relative to a situation where they consume no video games, therefore, the value of current consumption is given by area $P_2E_0Q_00$—that is, by the entire area under the compensated demand curve up to consumption level Q_0. This represents the sum of what people currently spend on games ($P_0E_0Q_00$) plus the compensation they would demand in order to voluntarily reduce consumption to zero ($P_2E_0P_0$).

Consumer surplus
The extra value individuals receive from consuming a good over what they pay for it. What people would be willing to pay for the right to consume a good at its current price.

What this shows, then, is that individuals tend to value the consumption of a good more highly than simply what they spend on it. Although they willingly spend $P_0 \cdot Q_0$ for computer games, they would need some additional compensation to get them to do without the games completely. This extra compensation (given by area $P_2E_0P_0$ in Figure 6.2) is sometimes called **consumer surplus.** It represents the extra value people get from being able to consume a good that is in excess of what they actually pay for it. In later chapters we will show how the consequences of many economic activities for people's welfare can often be judged by whether the activities cause consumer surplus to increase or decrease.

Index Numbers

Index number
An average of many different trends into one number.

Consumer Price Index (CPI)
The current value of the market basket of goods and services purchased by a typical household compared to a base year value of the same market basket.

Economists frequently need to average many different trends into a single number. In measuring "the" rate of inflation, for example, some method must be found for averaging the different price trends of a wide variety of commodities. Calculating changes in the real quantity of production (that is, changes in real gross national product) means finding some way to add up changes in the quantities produced of a number of different goods. Although these kinds of constructions are often viewed as tedious exercises in "number crunching," the development of **index numbers** raises a number of interesting conceptual issues. As a second application of the model of utility maximization, we examine a few of these issues. We focus mainly on the problems that arise in constructing the Consumer Price Index as a measure of inflation since these are representative of the issues involved in all index number constructions.

The Consumer Price Index

One of the principal measures of inflation in the United States is provided by the **Consumer Price Index (CPI),** which is published monthly by the U.S. Department of Labor. To construct the CPI, the Bureau of Labor Statistics first defines a typical market basket of commodities purchased by consumers in some base year (1982 is the year currently used). Then data are collected every month about how much this market basket of commodities currently costs the consumer. The ratio of the current cost to the bundle's original cost (in 1982) is then published as the current value of the CPI. The rate of change in this index between two periods is reported to be the rate of inflation.

This construction can be clarified with a simple two-good example. Suppose that in 1982 the typical market basket contained X^{82} of good X and Y^{82} of good Y. The prices of these goods are given by P_X^{82} and P_Y^{82}. The cost of this bundle in the 1982 base year would be written as

$$\text{Cost of bundle in 1982} = B^{82} = P_X^{82} \cdot X^{82} + P_Y^{82} \cdot Y^{82}. \quad [6.1]$$

To compute the cost of the same bundle of goods in, say, 1990, we must first collect information on the goods' prices in that year (P_X^{90}, P_Y^{90}) and then compute

$$\text{Cost of bundle in 1990} = B^{90} = P_X^{90} \cdot X^{82} + P_Y^{90} \cdot Y^{82}. \quad [6.2]$$

Notice that now, the quantities purchased in 1982 are being valued at 1990 prices. The CPI is defined as the ratio of the costs of these two market baskets:

$$\text{CPI (for 1990)} = \frac{B^{90}}{B^{82}}. \quad [6.3]$$

The rate of inflation can be computed from this index. For example, if a market basket of items that cost \$100 in 1982 costs \$140 in 1990, the value of the CPI would be 1.40, and we would say there had been a 40 percent increase in prices over this eight-year period.[2] It might be said that people would need a 40 percent increase in 1982 income to enjoy the same standard of living in 1990 that they had in 1982. Cost-of-living adjustments in Social Security benefits and in many job agreements are calculated in precisely this way.

The CPI and True Inflation

The problem with the above calculation of inflation should be obvious from the material presented in the previous three chapters. This calculation assumes that people who are faced with 1990 prices will continue to demand

[2]Frequently, index numbers are multiplied by 100 to avoid computation to several decimal places. Instead of reporting the CPI as 1.40, a value of 140 would be reported. Each figure shows a 40 percent gain in the index over the base period.

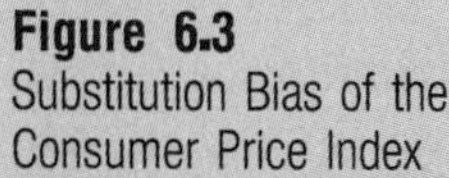

Figure 6.3
Substitution Bias of the Consumer Price Index

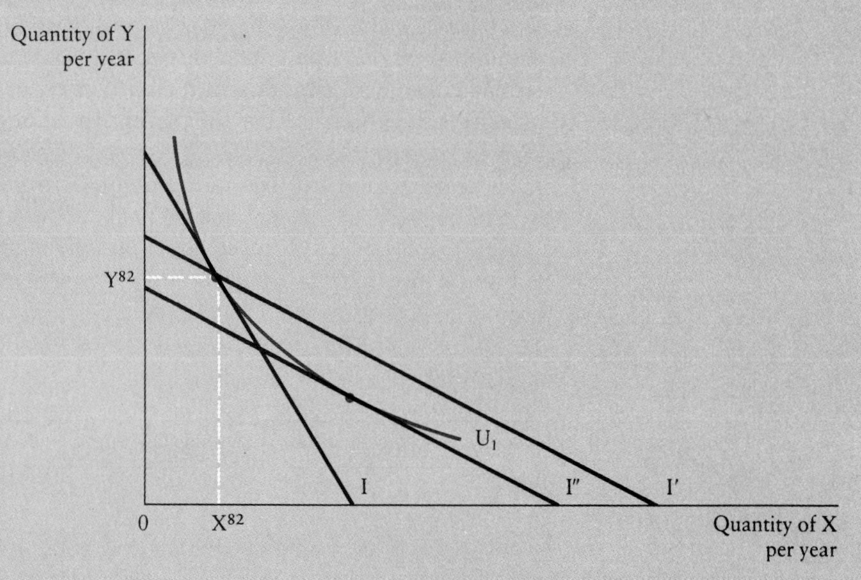

In 1982 with income I the typical consumer chose X^{82}, Y^{82}. If this market basket is used to construct a price index when different relative prices prevail, the basket's cost will be given by I′. This cost exceeds what is actually required to permit the consumer to reach the original level of utility, I″.

the same basket of commodities that they consumed in 1982. The analysis makes no allowance for substitutions among commodities in response to changing prices. The calculation may overstate the decline in purchasing power that inflation has caused, since it takes no account of how people will seek to get the most utility for their dollars when prices change.

In Figure 6.3, for example, a typical individual initially is consuming X^{82}, Y^{82}. Presumably this choice provides maximum utility (U_1), given his or her budget constraint in 1982 (which we call I). Suppose that by 1990 relative prices have changed in such a way that P_X/P_Y falls—that is, assume that good X becomes relatively less expensive. Using these new prices, the CPI calculates what X^{82}, Y^{82} would cost. This cost would be reflected by the budget constraint I′, which is flatter than I (to reflect the changed prices) and passes through the 1982 consumption point. As the figure makes clear, the erosion in purchasing power that has occurred is overstated. With I′ our typical individual could now reach a higher utility level than could have been attained in 1982.

A true measure of inflation would be provided by evaluating an income level, say, I″, which reflects the new prices but just permits the individual to remain on U_1. By failing to take account of the substitutions in consumption that people might make in response to changed prices (they would consume more X and less Y in moving along U_1), the CPI has exaggerated the true decline in purchasing power that people have experienced. In Application 6.2:

APPLICATION 6.2

Substitution Biases and Revising the Consumer Price Index

Several economists have tried to estimate the extent to which a fixed market basket-type price index overstates the true rate of price increase by failing to consider the types of substitutions individuals make in response to changing relative prices. Table 1 reports the results of one such study by S. D. Braithwait. In this study the author compared the actual performance of the U.S. Consumer Price Index over the period 1958–1973 to the performance of an estimated true cost-of-living index that takes account of substitutions in consumption. As the table shows, the actual CPI rose 47.5 percent during the 15-year interval being examined (from 100 to 147.5) whereas the true index rose only 46.0 percent. Hence, over the entire period the CPI tended to overstate inflation by about 1.5 percent by failing to consider substitution among items in the market basket.

Inflation in Particular Items

For major consumption categories within the CPI, rather different patterns emerged. In the case of food and clothing, little substitution tended to occur among specific items within each category in response to changing relative prices (and, indeed, relative prices within the categories changed only slightly), so the bias was quite small—less than 1 percent over the entire period. In the recreation category, on the other hand, relative prices changed more significantly, and substitution was more prevalent. Hence, the bias was larger, amounting to nearly one-half a percentage point per year. By failing to account for individuals' shifting demands among such items as televisions, spectator events, and use of hotels and motels, the CPI tended to exaggerate the general inflation rate for the goods in this category.

Table 1
Estimated Substitution Bias in the Consumer Price Index, 1958–1973

Category	Actual CPI (1958 = 100)	True Cost-of-Living Index (1958 = 100)
Food	156.1	155.4
Clothing	149.3	148.5
Shelter	136.8	135.8
Transportation	134.0	132.5
Personal services	172.6	168.1
Recreation	146.9	139.9
Total consumption	147.5	146.0

Source: S. D. Braithwait, "The Substitution Bias of the Laspeyres Price Index: An Analysis Using Estimated Cost of Living Indices," *American Economic Review* (March 1980): 80.

Revising the CPI

One question that the data in Table 1 shed some light on is how often CPI weights should be revised. Since gathering new data with which to develop weights is quite costly (the most recent revisions in 1982 cost about $250 million), there is a natural desire to delay. From the table, it appears that the 15-year period between revisions did not seriously bias the index, at least during the years 1958–1973. Of course, the judgment that 15 years is about the right length of time for a CPI revision depends on whether the 1958–1973 period was a normal period and whether more recent experience suggests a need for more frequent revisions. In the 1982 revisions, for example, housing expenditures as a percentage of the total increased by nearly five percentage points over what they had been previously. Similarly, during a period when many new goods are coming on the market (such as the number of home electronic products in the early 1980s), more frequent revisions may also be called for.

To Think About

1. This example shows that the bias of the CPI during the period 1958–1973 was fairly small. Do you think this result would hold up for the period after 1973? How would the probability that the CPI is a biased measure of inflation affect your view of cost-of-living adjustments in wages or Social Security benefits?
2. How should new or improved goods be handled in constructing the CPI? What would be the consequences of disregarding quality improvements in some goods when computing the CPI? What would be the consequences of completely excluding newly invented goods?

Substitution Biases and Revising the Consumer Price Index, we show how large this error might be.

This problem of determining a more precise measure of inflation is not an easy one to solve. Without knowing an individual's actual preferences, there is no precise way to know how much real purchasing power has been eroded through price changes. An individual's actual spending patterns may not provide sufficient information. For example, using the 1990 market basket to calculate the CPI leads to the same sort of problems that are illustrated in Figure 6.3. Economists have experimented with a variety of more sophisticated indices of price change, but none of these has proven to be completely satisfactory.[3] Some care must always be taken in interpreting the CPI (and other index number) statistics.

Other Problems with the CPI

Two additional problems with this type of price index construction are related to the need to choose a base year "market basket." The first problem concerns what specific commodities should be included in the basket. Both everyday observations and more sophisticated studies (as shown in our earlier discussion of Engel's law) suggest that people's consumption choices may vary greatly depending on their circumstances. It has been proposed that a separate index be constructed for poor people to reflect the kinds of goods they can afford, and that people living in colder climates also need a separate index to reflect costs of goods such as heating and ear muffs. The choice of a market basket has important implications for the performance of the index and for the calculation of cost-of-living adjustments. Seemingly "objective" questions about how to measure inflation have become highly politicized in recent years.

The development of new or improved goods presents a second problem in the construction of the CPI. Some products that are currently sold (such as compact disc players, cellular phones, and Nintendo's Super Mario Brothers game) were not even available in 1982. Modern personal computers are much more reliable and long-lasting than those from the early 1980s. Deciding how these new or improved products should be included in the CPI market basket (if at all) brings up many issues that have not been completely resolved.

Index Number Problems

The difficulties in constructing the CPI are fairly typical of a broad class of problems in developing any index numbers that average together various economic magnitudes. Whenever trends in two or more different commodities

---

[3]For a detailed treatment of index numbers and their associated problems, see R. G. D. Allen, *Index Numbers in Theory and Practice* (London: Macmillan Co., 1975).

APPLICATION 6.3

International Comparisons of Real Income

A problem similar to the substitution bias in the CPI arises in comparing real income (or GNP) between two countries. Ideally data are available on the quantities of various goods produced in each country, but the problem is choosing what prices to use in adding up these quantities into a real income measure. Two solutions might be adopted. First, we could use the prices that actually prevail in each country: for example, to compare U.S. and Colombian real GNP, we could use U.S. prices to compute U.S. GNP and Colombian prices to compute Colombian GNP. To do this we would need some method to convert Colombian pesos into U.S. dollars (or vice versa) so that our comparison will be meaningful. Changes in this exchange rate could then have a major effect on how countries rank. For example, the rapid increase in the value of the Japanese yen in the late 1980s caused per capita GNP in Japan to approximate or even exceed that in the United States although most observers believed Japanese standards of living were actually quite a bit lower.

A second solution is to use only one nation's prices to evaluate GNP in both countries. For example, both U.S. and Colombian GNP could be computed using U.S. prices for the quantities of goods. This approach, raises another problem of its own. We can assume that Colombian consumers buy relatively little of goods that are especially expensive in Colombia (household appliances, for example) and that U.S. consumers have similarly economized on items that are expensive in the United States (coffee, for example). If different goods are expensive in each country (as with household appliances and coffee), this method may produce biases since some high U.S. prices (for coffee, say) will be applied to goods that Colombians consume in large amounts, whereas low U.S. prices will be applied to goods on which Colombians economize (appliances). Real Colombian income will be overstated.

Table 1 shows 1973 data on various countries' per capita GNPs (actually per capita gross domestic products—GDPs) as a percentage of the per capita GDP in the United States. The table compares GDPs in two ways: in terms of each country's own prices and in terms of only U.S. prices. As you can see, which prices are used can make a big difference in the comparison. In the case of India, the lowest income country compared, per capita GDP is less than 4 percent of that in the United States when India's GDP is evaluated using India's own prices, but nearly 8 percent of the U.S. GDP when India's GDP is evaluated using U.S. prices. Colombia is another country whose position relative to the U.S. level is more than doubled by using U.S. rather than local prices (from 11.9 percent to 26.1 percent). As the table seems to indicate, large differences occur primarily for low-income countries, whereas they are less dramatic for high-income countries, such as Japan or Germany. Higher income countries' expenditure patterns are probably more like those in the United States than low-income countries' are, so the effect of using different prices should be less noticeable. Nevertheless, the problem of which country's prices to use in comparing international GNPs has no completely satisfactory solution.

Table 1
International Comparisons of Gross Domestic Product per Capita as a Percentage of the U.S. Level of GDP

	Own Domestic Prices	U.S. Prices
India	3.8%	7.9%
South Korea	8.2	15.3
Colombia	11.9	26.1
Hungary	36.0	51.7
Japan	54.5	66.0
United Kingdom	54.7	66.4
West Germany	65.0	79.8
United States	100.0	100.0

Source: I. B. Kravis et al., *International Comparisons of Real Product and Purchasing Power* (Baltimore: Johns Hopkins University Press, 1978), p. 219.

To Think About

1. Comparisons of real gross national product among countries usually include only those goods that are traded in organized markets. Nonmarket transactions (such as trading among farmers or the revenue from illegal activities) are not included in the calculations. Would the poor nations look relatively poorer or relatively richer if such transactions were included in GNP?
2. Would problems similar to those that arise in comparing GNP among countries arise in comparing the real incomes of people living in different parts of the United States? Can you think of reasons why such comparisons might be easier to make than comparisons among countries?

must be averaged to form a single index, some sort of weighting scheme is always necessary. In the case of the CPI, the 1982 market basket is used to average together the prices for goods X and Y in various years. Calculating real inflation-adjusted gross national product figures reverses this process with a set of base prices to value the physical quantities of commodities produced in successive years in different countries. Application 6.3: International Comparisons of Real Income contains some examples of the pitfalls involved in this sort of calculation. In all such computations, the precise weights that are chosen can have a major impact on the final averages obtained. But, that choice (as in the case of the CPI) will always be arbitrary to some extent. To study the properties of such calculations requires the development of an economic model of the concepts being measured to help establish standards of accuracy. The study of index numbers is therefore another major area in economics in which issues of measurement are closely linked to the underlying theory of choice.

Gains from Voluntary Trade

Our final application of the theory of choice is to show that two people can be made better-off through voluntary trading with each other. Two-person trades need not have a "winner" and a "loser," but can be mutually beneficial. For example, everyone participates in voluntary trading when he or she gives up some amount of money to buy something (say, a candy bar) that is valued more highly than the cash—as it must be or it would not be bought. The seller also benefits from this transaction—the seller values the cash more highly than the candy bar since he or she is willing to make the sale. Although we begin by studying mutually beneficial transactions in a very simple setting, the results of our examination are quite general and reappear in various forms throughout this book. People's desires to make mutually beneficial transactions is in many ways what the study of economics is all about.

A Simple Exchange Situation

We can begin by assuming that only two goods, our old favorites, hamburgers (which again we will call Y) and soft drinks (which we will call X) are available. Assume also that there are fixed total amounts of X = 15 and Y = 15. Person 1 starts out with X = 5 and Y = 10, and person 2 starts out with X = 10 and Y = 5. These initial quantities appear in the first columns of Table 6.1.

To look at voluntary trades away from this initial position, we need to know these people's preferences to determine what trades would make each of them better-off. Figure 6.4 presents indifference curve maps for our two traders, including the initial allocations of X and Y. At X = 5, Y = 10, person 1 has a marginal rate of substitution (MRS) of 2—because she has an abundance of hamburgers, she is willing to give up two of them to get one

Figure 6.4
Both Individuals Gain from a Trade

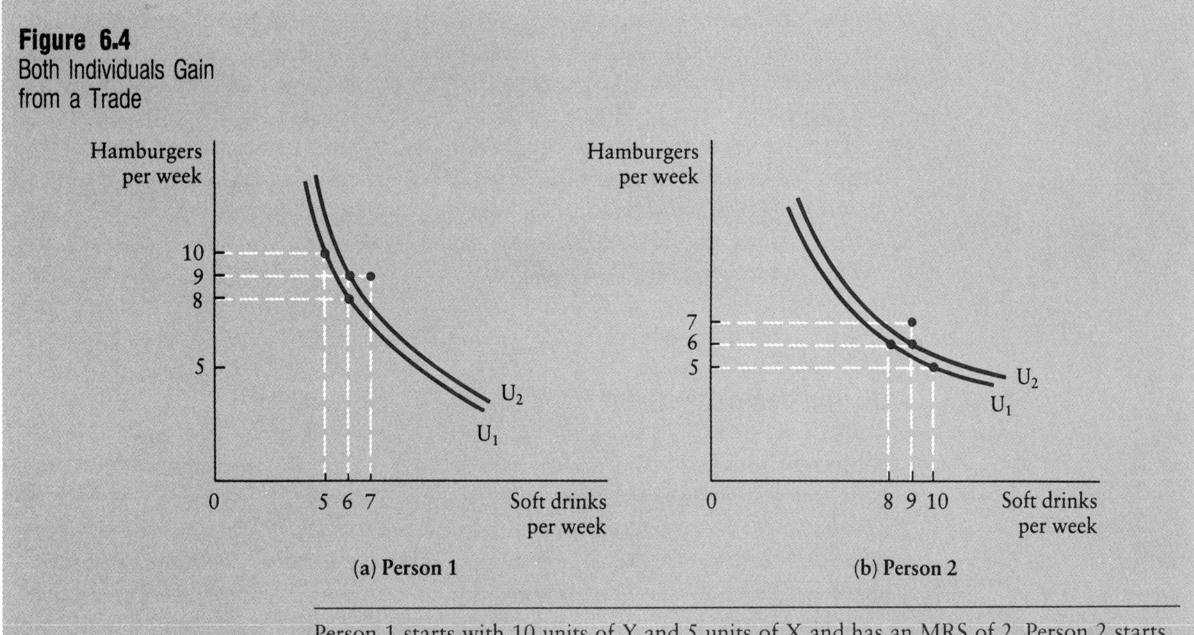

Person 1 starts with 10 units of Y and 5 units of X and has an MRS of 2. Person 2 starts with 10 units of X and 5 units of Y and has an MRS of $\frac{1}{2}$. If person 1 trades one Y to person 2 for one X, each person will be on a higher indifference curve than in their initial situation. In other examples the actual distribution of the trading gains depends on the terms of trade that are established.

Table 6.1
A Trade in Which Both Parties Gain

	Initial Quantity		Quantity Traded		Final Quantity	
	X	Y	X	Y	X	Y
Person 1	5	10	+1	−1	6	9
Person 2	10	5	−1	+1	9	6

more soft drink. For person 2, on the other hand, the MRS is ½—because she has quite a lot of soft drinks already, she is rather unwilling to give up hamburgers to get even more of them.

Suppose now that these two people reach an agreement under which person 1 trades one Y to person 2 for one X. Results of this trade are recorded in Table 6.1 and shown graphically in Figure 6.4. The striking fact of the trade is that it makes both people better-off. Person 1 now has X = 6 and Y = 9. Since she would have been as well-off as in her initial situation if the trade resulted in X = 6, Y = 8 (because her MRS is assumed to be 2), the posttrade allocation is clearly better—she still gets the same amount of X and more Y. Person 2 now has X = 9, Y = 6, which improves her utility. She would have been willing to accept X = 8, Y = 6 (with her assumed MRS of ½), but the proposed trade leaves her with one more X over what would have been acceptable. The proposed voluntary trade would make both people better-off.

A similar demonstration could be made anytime two people have combinations of goods that result in their having different marginal rates of substitution (if MRSs were the same, there would be no gains to trade). If they agree to trade goods in some ratio that lies between these two MRSs, both will be made better-off.

Distribution of the Gains from Trade

Although both individuals may gain from a voluntary trading situation, the gains may sometimes be unevenly divided. We would not expect people to agree to a trade that actually resulted in lower utility (people might be forced into such trades, however—a gun is an effective form of coercion for a mugger!). But, even in voluntary trades, one person may get the bulk of the gains. Two such situations are illustrated in Table 6.2. In case 1, our two people have decided to exchange Y for X in the ratio of two Y for one X. This trade leaves person 1 (with X = 6, Y = 8) precisely as well-off as before the trade. As shown in Figure 6.4, both the initial combination of goods and this new posttrade combination lie on the same indifference curve, U_1. Although person 1 doesn't lose from the trade, she doesn't gain anything either.

In this new trade, person 2 is the big winner. She now has X = 9, Y = 7, which, as Figure 6.4 shows, is not only preferred to her initial position, but also makes her better-off than in our first trading example.

Case 2 of Table 6.2 shows a trade in which person 1 gets the better deal. Now the two individuals have agreed to trade at a ratio of one Y for two X. After this trade person 2 is still on her initial indifference curve. Person 1 with X = 7, Y = 9 is now better-off than in any of the previous cases. With these "terms of trade," person 1 is the primary gainer from trading. In general, then, as this example suggests, most of the gains from trade accrue to the person whose MRS differs most from the terms of trade that are decided upon.

Edgeworth Box Diagram

Obviously, the numbers in this example were purely arbitrary. Any allocation in which the MRSs of two individuals differ and in which the individuals consume both goods can be shown to be "inefficient" in that these goods can be reallocated in an unambiguously better way; that is, a "better" allocation can be found. There may be many such allocations, however, and we can most easily demonstrate them by using a graphic device known as the *Edge-*

Table 6.2
Distribution of the Gains from Trade Depends on the Terms of Trade

Case 1: 1 X trades for 2 Y—only person 2 gains.

	Initial Quantity		Quantity Traded		Final Quantity	
	X	Y	X	Y	X	Y
Person 1	5	10	+1	−2	6	8
Person 2	10	5	−1	+2	9	7

Case 2: 2 X trade for 1 Y—only person 1 gains.

	Initial Quantity		Quantity Traded		Final Quantity	
	X	Y	X	Y	X	Y
Person 1	5	10	+2	−1	7	9
Person 2	10	5	−2	+1	8	6

worth box,[4] the construction of which is shown in Figure 6.5. The Edgeworth box has dimensions given by the total (fixed) quantities of the two goods (call these goods simply X and Y). The horizontal dimension of the box represents the total quantity of X available, whereas the vertical height of the box is the total quantity of Y. The point O_S is considered to be the origin for person 1 (call her Smith). Quantities of X are measured along the horizontal axis rightward from O_S; quantities of Y, along the vertical axis upward from O_S. Any point in the box can be regarded as some allocation of X and Y to Smith. For example, at point A, Smith gets X_S^A and Y_S^A. The useful property of the Edgeworth box is that the quantities received by person 2 (say Jones) are also recorded by point A. Jones simply gets that part of the total quantity that is "left over." In fact, we can regard Jones's quantities as being measured from the origin O_J. Point A therefore also corresponds to the quantities X_J^A and Y_J^A for Jones. Notice that the quantities assigned to Smith and Jones in this manner exactly exhaust the total quantities of X and Y available.

Mutually Beneficial Trades

Any point in the Edgeworth box represents an allocation of the available goods between Smith and Jones, and all possible allocations are contained somewhere within the box. To discover which of the allocations offer mutu-

[4]Named for F.Y. Edgeworth (1854–1926), who in 1881 derived the concept of a contract curve in his *Mathematical Psychics: An Essay on the Application of Mathematics to the Moral Sciences* (New York: August M. Kelley, 1953).

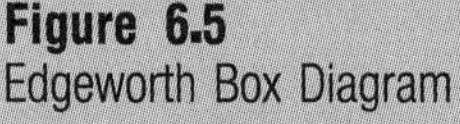

Figure 6.5
Edgeworth Box Diagram

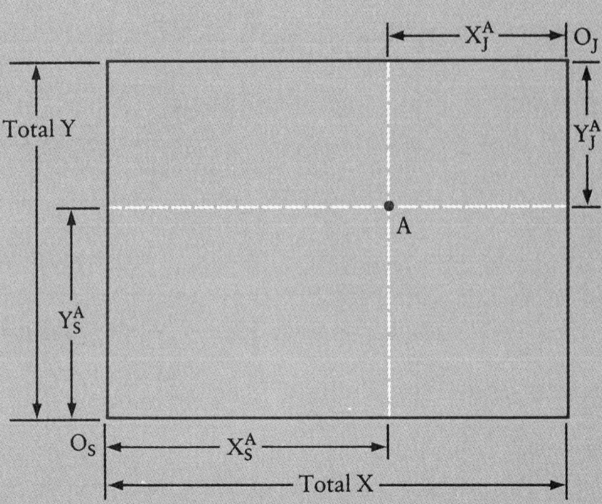

The Edgeworth box diagram permits all possible allocations of two goods (X and Y) to be visualized. If we consider the corner O_S to be Smith's (person 1) "origin" and O_J to be Jones's (person 2), then the allocation represented by point A would have Smith getting X_S^A and Y_S^A, and Jones would receive what is left over (X_J^A, Y_J^A). The purpose of this diagram is to discover which of the possible locations within the box are efficient.

ally beneficial trades, we must introduce preferences. In Figure 6.6 Smith's indifference curve map is drawn with origin O_S. Movements in a northeasterly direction represent higher levels of utility to Smith. In the same figure, Jones's indifference curve map is drawn with the corner O_J as an origin. We have taken Jones's indifference curve map, rotated it 180°, and fit it into the northeast corner of the Edgeworth box. Movements in a southwesterly direction represent increases in Jones's utility level.

Using these superimposed indifference curve maps, we can identify the allocations from which some mutually beneficial trades might be made. Any point for which the MRS for Smith is unequal to that for Jones represents such an opportunity. Consider an arbitrary initial allocation such as point A in Figure 6.6. This point lies on the point of intersection of Smith's indifference curve U_S^1 and Jones's indifference curve U_J^3. Obviously, the marginal rates of substitution (the slopes of the indifference curves) are not equal at A. Any allocation in the oval-shaped shaded area in Figure 6.6 represents a mutually beneficial trade for these two people—they can both move to a higher level of utility by adopting a trade that moves them into this area.

Efficiency in Exchange

When the marginal rates of substitution of Smith and Jones are equal, however, such mutually beneficial trades are not available. The points, M_1, M_2,

Figure 6.6
Edgeworth Box Diagram of Pareto Efficiency in Exchange

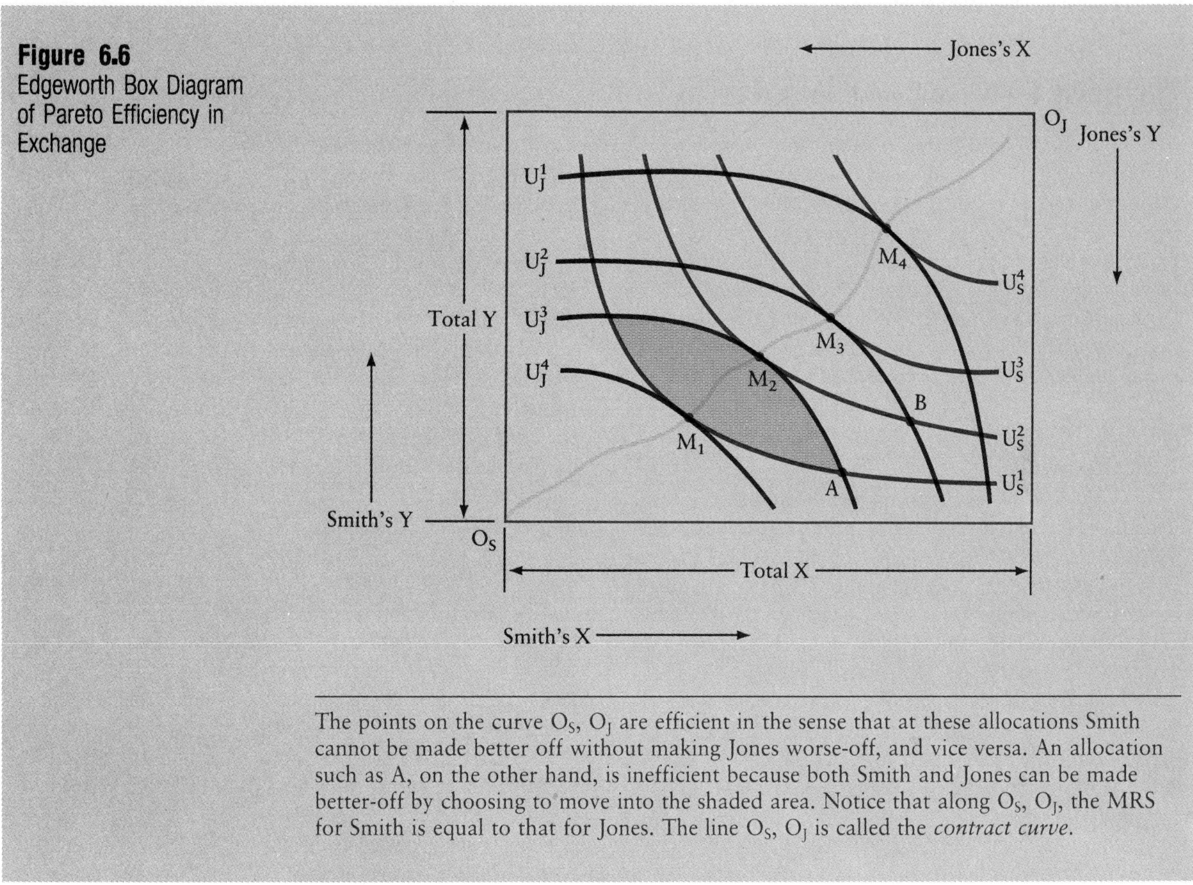

The points on the curve O_S, O_J are efficient in the sense that at these allocations Smith cannot be made better off without making Jones worse-off, and vice versa. An allocation such as A, on the other hand, is inefficient because both Smith and Jones can be made better-off by choosing to move into the shaded area. Notice that along O_S, O_J, the MRS for Smith is equal to that for Jones. The line O_S, O_J is called the *contract curve*.

Pareto efficient allocation
An allocation of available resources in which no mutually beneficial trading opportunities are unexploited. That is, an allocation in which no one person can be made better-off without someone else being made worse-off.

M_3, and M_4 in Figure 6.6 indicate tangencies of these individuals' indifference curves, and movement away from such points must make at least one of the people worse-off. A move from M_2 to A, for example, reduces Smith's utility from U_S^2 to U_S^1 even though Jones is made no worse-off by the move. Alternatively, a move from M_2 to B makes Jones worse-off, but keeps the utility level of Smith constant. In general, then, these points of tangency do not offer the promise of additional mutually beneficial trading. Such points are called **Pareto efficient allocations** of resources after the Italian scientist Vilfredo Pareto (1878–1923) who pioneered in the development of the formal theory of exchange. Notice that the Pareto definition of efficiency does not require any interpersonal comparisons of utility—we never have to compare Jones's gains to Smith's losses or vice versa. Rather, individuals decide for themselves whether particular trades improve utility. For efficient allocations there are no such additional trades to which both parties would agree.

APPLICATION 6.4

The Gains from Trading among Nations

The analysis of the gains from trading between two individuals applies to far more complex trading situations as well. Consider, for example, the case of trading among nations. In this situation all parties may gain from voluntary trade. A principal source of much of those gains derives from production considerations (as we discuss in Chapter 13), but some gains also arise because of the wider options that trade offers to consumers in the countries involved.

Trade Restrictions

Most countries restrict international trade through tariffs, quotas, and various nonquantitative measures such as product "safety" laws. During the late 1970s, for example, tariff rates averaged about 11 percent in the major industrialized countries. Table 1 shows a series of estimates of how much trade would be created (and welfare improved) by elimination of such barriers, based on the Tokyo round of tariff negotiations in the late 1970s. For example, the complete elimination of tariffs would have resulted in a nearly $17 billion (in 1974 dollars) expansion in the annual level of trade among countries, and it is estimated that real income in those countries would have increased by about $2 billion. The estimated welfare gains reported in the table probably substantially underestimate the true gains. They take no account of the side benefits of freer trade (a more efficient economy, greater technical advancement, better relations among nations, and so forth), nor of the fact that the gains are expected to occur each year into the future. Some authors have estimated that the overall true gains from reductions in trade restrictions may be about one hundred times those listed in the table, or actually $200 billion if tariffs and other barriers were completely eliminated.

The effects of tariff reduction formulas proposed by the United States, Japan, and the European Economic Community (EEC), respectively, are also reported in Table 1. Although the welfare gains under these proposals are not as large as those for complete tariff elimination, they are nevertheless quite substantial. The different reduction formulas probably relate to the different countries' domestic political situations, since free trade can be very controversial if some workers' jobs are threatened by eliminating tariffs. Differences in the formulas also relate to how specific goods would be treated under each proposal and how the countries feel about expanding trade in those items. For example, the United States has generally advocated freer trade in agricultural products, whereas the EEC and Japan have tried to protect their own farmers. The United States has tended to restrict trade in steel and automobiles, whereas Japan (and to a much lesser extent the EEC) has sought to expand such trade. Analysis developed later in this book will help to explain such political preferences.

Table 1

Estimated Trade and Welfare Gains for Industrial Countries from the Tokyo Round of Tariff Reductions

Plan	Average Reduction	Additional Trade per Year ($ Billions)	Basic Welfare Gain per Year ($ Billions)
Complete elimination	100%	$16.9	$2.0
United States	65	11.0	1.7
Japanese	46	8.0	1.6
European Economic Community	33	5.7	1.4

Source: W. R. Cline, N. Kawanaabe, T. O. M. Kronsjo, and T. Williams, *Trade Negotiations in the Tokyo Round* (Washington, D.C.: Brookings Institute, 1978).

To Think About

1. Does "everyone" gain from trade among nations? Who might lose in such trading? Are these people "voluntary" participants in the trading?
2. Some authors claim that less-developed countries do not gain very much from trade since prices for internationally traded goods are mainly determined by markets in the industrialized countries. How does this notion relate to our simple example of who gains from voluntary trade?

Contract Curve

Contract curve
The set of all efficient allocations of the existing goods in an exchange situation. Points off that curve are necessarily inefficient, since individuals can be made unambiguously better-off by moving to the curve.

The set of all the efficient allocations in an Edgeworth box diagram is called the **contract curve.** In Figure 6.6 this set of points is represented by the line running from O_S to O_J and includes the tangencies M_1, M_2, M_3, and M_4 (and many other such tangencies). Points off the contract curve (such as A or B) are inefficient, and mutually beneficial trades are possible. But, as its name implies, moving onto the contract curve exhausts all such mutually beneficial trading opportunities. A move along the contract curve (say, from M_1 to M_2) does not represent a mutually beneficial trade since there will always be a winner (Smith) and a loser (Jones).

In the case where the contract curve is interior to the Edgeworth box (as in Figure 6.6), individuals' MRSs will be equal along the contract curve. If preferences are such that for some efficient allocations some individuals choose not to consume all goods, corner solutions will arise in which rates of substitution are not necessarily equalized (for a simple case, see problem 6.6). Whatever their quantitative nature, all such efficient allocations are depicted on the contract curve. Some additional examples are illustrated in the problems in this chapter. Application 6.4: The Gains from Trading among Nations shows how voluntary trading among nations produces efficiency gains from international trade.

Summary

This chapter looks at three different applications of the notion that people make economic choices in a utility-maximizing way. Each of these applications shows how economists have tried to study a particular problem in the theory of choice, and each has important implications for a number of economic subjects. The principal conclusions that can be drawn from these applications are:

- The individual's compensated demand curve shows the quantity that would be demanded at various prices if utility were held constant by compensating for the effects of price changes on real income. The curve summarizes only the substitution effects of price changes.
- Dollar values for the welfare effects of price changes can be approximated by areas under the compensated demand curve for the market as a whole. One application of this is the notion of consumer surplus, which represents the total amount individuals would be willing to pay to continue with their current consumption plans rather than being forced to consume none of a good.
- Construction of economic index numbers is a complex process that involves selecting weights to be used in adding up different magnitudes. A primary reason that the construction of some index numbers is particularly difficult is that they seek to approximate individuals' preferences, which are essentially unmeasurable.

- Voluntary trade can make both of the parties involved better-off. The possibility for such mutually beneficial transactions occurs whenever two people's current consumption choices result in their having unequal marginal rates of substitution (MRS).
- The gains from trade may be unequally shared in any particular transaction. Generally, the closer the terms of trading are to an individual's MRS, the smaller that person's gains from trading will be.
- All efficient trading outcomes in a simple exchange situation can be illustrated using an Edgeworth box diagram. The set of such Pareto efficient allocations is called the contract curve. For points on the contract curve, one person can be made better-off only by making someone else worse-off.

Review Questions

1. Explain why the principal difference between the Marshallian (uncompensated) demand curve and the compensated demand curve arises from the definition of income being held constant in their derivation. For uncompensated demand curves, nominal income is held constant whereas for compensated demand curves, real income is held constant.
2. Why do compensated and uncompensated demand curves intersect at an individual's current utility-maximizing choice? Explain why, for a normal good, the uncompensated demand curve is more elastic at this point.
3. Consumer surplus shows the amount that people would be willing to pay to maintain their current consumption of a good rather than doing without it. How might you illustrate this idea with the individual's indifference curve map?
4. Explain why a market basket-type price index (such as the CPI) yields an overestimate of "true" inflation because it disregards substitution effects. If people consumed items in fixed proportions, would such a price index be biased?
5. Suppose that the CPI were developed by defining a current market basket of goods and asking what this basket would have cost in *prior* years. Would this type of calculation also encounter a substitution bias? Can you think of any advantages or disadvantages to this approach?
6. Explain why the per capita GNP comparisons in Application 6.3 are subject to the same types of substitution biases as the CPI.
7. Could mutually beneficial trade occur if two individuals had exactly the same preferences? Could such trade occur if the individuals had the same preferences *and* the same initial holdings of the available goods?
8. Suppose David and Goliath decide to engage in voluntary exchange. Goliath, being much the larger of the two, demands that trade be conducted at his pre-trade MRS. Who gains the most from this demand? What advice might you give Goliath?
9. Can you think of a case where the contract "curve" in a two-good Edgeworth box diagram would be a single point? How about a case where the contract "curve" would consist of all points in the box?
10. Explain why, if traders start out with particular initial holdings of the goods in an Edgeworth box, not all points on the contract curve may be attainable through voluntary transactions. How will the final utility levels attained through such transactions tend to reflect the utility levels associated with the initial holdings?

Problems

6.1 Irene consumes only pizza and chianti. She consumes these goods in fixed proportions—2 slices of pizza for each bottle of chianti. Her current income is $100 per week.

a. If pizza costs $1 per slice and chianti is $3 per bottle, how much of each good will Irene consume?
b. If pizza costs $.50 per slice, how much of each good will Irene consume?
c. Graph Irene's (uncompensated) demand curve for pizza. Why does this curve have a negative slope?
d. Graph Irene's compensated demand curve for pizza for the utility level described in part a. Explain why the curve has the shape it has.
e. Graph Irene's compensated demand curve for pizza for the utility level described in part b. How has this curve shifted from the position described in part d?
f. Combine the graphs from parts c, d, and e. What do you conclude about the relationship between the compensated and uncompensated demand curves for a good? Explain why the curves intersect where they do.

6.2 Irving consumes only pizza and chianti, but, unlike Irene in problem 6.1, he is willing to substitute one of these goods for the other. Irving has a weekly income of $100. If pizza costs $1 per slice and chianti costs $3 per bottle, he chooses to consume 40 pizza slices and 20 bottles of chianti each week.

a. Graph Irving's budget co straint and show his utility-maximizing point.
b. Explain why both Irving's uncompensated demand curve for pizza and his compensated demand curve for pizza must pass through the point

$$\text{Price} = \$1, \qquad \text{pizza} = 40.$$

c. If pizza prices fall to $.50 per slice but nothing else changes, Irving chooses to consume 68 slices per week. How many bottles of chianti will he consume?
d. Graph Irving's new budget constraint and his new utility-maximizing choices of pizza and chianti. Explain why Irving's utility has increased as a result of the fall in the price of pizza.
e. Does the point

$$\text{Price} = \$.50, \qquad \text{pizza} = 68$$

lie on the uncompensated demand curve for pizza described in part b?
f. How might you use the demand curves described in parts b and e to illustrate Irving's utility gain from the reduction in pizza price?

6.3 Assume that martini drinkers always use a ratio of 10 units of gin to 1 unit of vermouth when mixing their cocktails. Assuming they spend all their income on martinis, show that real income calculations for martini drinkers will be the same regardless of whether base year or current year price indices are used.

6.4 Suppose oil prices, natural gas prices, and coal prices always move together, with the price of a gallon of fuel oil being exactly equal to the price of 1,000 cubic feet of natural gas and 50 pounds of coal. Show that in this situation an index of fossil fuel (that is, oil, natural gas, and coal) prices will give the same estimate of inflation regardless of whether base year or current year quantities are used as weights.

6.5 The residents of Uurp consume only pork chops (X) and Coca-Cola (Y). The utility function for the typical resident of Uurp is given by

$$\text{Utility} = U(X, Y) = \sqrt{X \cdot Y}.$$

In 1986 the price of pork chops in Uurp was \$1 each and Cokes were also \$1 each. The typical resident consumed 40 pork chops and 40 Cokes (saving is impossible in Uurp). In 1987 swine fever hit Uurp, and pork chop prices rose to \$4 with the Coke price remaining unchanged. At these new prices the typical Uurp resident consumed 20 pork chops and 80 Cokes.

a. Show that utility for the typical Uurp resident was unchanged between the two years.
b. Show that using 1986 prices would indicate an increase in real income between 1986 and 1987.
c. Show that using 1987 prices would indicate a decrease in real income between 1986 and 1987.
d. What do you conclude about the ability of these indices to measure changes in real income?

6.6 The nation of Oskago is a rocky island whose inhabitants are particularly hardworking and adept fishermen. They are able to catch eight tons of fish per year, yet they can gather only four tons of coconuts per year. The going price for one coconut on the island is two fish. Nearby is the island paradise of Silveto whose lazy inhabitants catch only four tons of fish per year but gather eight tons of coconuts every year from the lush forests. On Silveto, the price of one fish is two coconuts. With the advent of lightweight boats, the possibility of virtually cost-free trade now exists. Should the two island nations trade products? Why or why not? Graph your results.

6.7 Backyard Jack has a yard full of trees and firewood, but cannot grow very much corn due to poor sunlight. Sunshine Steve, on the other hand, has wide open cornfields but little firewood to keep him warm. Jack starts out with 20 cords of firewood and only 5 bushels of corn and has a MRS (of firewood for corn) of 1/3. Steve begins with 25 bushels of corn and only 10 cords of firewood and has a MRS of 2. How can both men be made better-off through trade? Illustrate this situation with a graph.

6.8 Smith and Jones are stranded on a desert island. Each has in his possession some slices of ham (H) and cheese (C). Smith is a very choosy eater and will eat ham and cheese only in the fixed proportions of 2 slices of cheese to 1 slice of ham. Jones is more flexible in his dietary tastes and has a utility function given by $U_J = 4H + 3C$. Total endowments are 100 slices of ham and 200 slices of cheese.

a. Draw the Edgeworth box diagram that represents the possibilities for exchange in this situation. What is the only exchange ratio that can prevail in any equilibrium?
b. Suppose that Smith initially had 40H and 80C. What would the equilibrium position be?
c. Suppose that Smith initially had 60H and 80C. What would the equilibrium position be?
d. Suppose that Smith (much the stronger of the two) decides not to play by the rules of the game. Then what could the final equilibrium position be?

6.9 Suppose, as in problem 6.8, that there are only two individuals (Smith and Jones) and two goods (ham and cheese) in an exchange economy. As before,

Smith chooses to consume ham and cheese in fixed proportions of 2C to 1H and Jones has flexible preferences and utility given by $U_J = 4H + 3C$. Initial endowments for Smith are H = 60, C = 80 and for Jones H = 40, C = 120.

a. Graph the Edgeworth box diagram for this exchange economy and indicate all the mutually beneficial trades that might be made.
b. Explain why trades that result in Smith having H and C in other than fixed proportions are inefficient.
c. What is the contract curve for this economy? What portion of the curve might be attainable through voluntary trading?

CHAPTER 7

Uncertainty and Information

So far in this book we have assumed that people's choices do not involve any degree of uncertainty: once they decide how to spend their income, they get what they have chosen. That is not always the way things work in many real-world situations, however. When you buy a lottery ticket, invest in shares of common stock, or play poker, what you get back is subject to chance. Many of the choices that people must make involve incomplete information (such as which used car is a lemon and which isn't), and these choices must be made somewhat "in the dark." In this chapter we will look at two questions raised by such economic problems involving uncertainty: (1) why do people generally dislike risky situations, and (2) what can they do to avoid or reduce risks?

Probability and Expected Value

Central to both questions are some simple mathematical ideas. The study of individual behavior under uncertainty and the mathematical study of probability and statistics have a common historical origin in games of chance. Gamblers who try to devise ways of winning at blackjack and casinos trying to keep the game profitable for them instead are a modern example of this popular pastime. Two statistical concepts that originated from studying games of chance, "probability" and "expected value," will be very important to our study of economic choices in uncertain situations.

Probability
The relative frequency with which an event occurs.

The **probability** of an event happening is, roughly speaking, the relative frequency with which it will occur. For example, to say that the probability of a head coming up on the flip of a fair coin is ½ means that if a coin is flipped a large number of times, we can expect a head to come up in approximately one-half of the flips. Similarly, the probability of rolling a "2" on a single die is 1/6. In approximately one out of every six rolls, a "2" should come up. Of course, before a coin is flipped or a die is rolled, we have no idea what will come up, so each flip or roll has an uncertain outcome as reflected by these probabilities.

Expected value
The average outcome from an uncertain gamble.

The **expected value** of a game with a number of uncertain outcomes (or prizes) is the size of the prize that the player will win on average. Suppose Jones and Smith agree to flip a coin once. If a head comes up, Jones will pay Smith $1; if a tail comes up, Smith will pay Jones $1. From Smith's point of view there are two prizes, or outcomes, (X_1 and X_2) in this game: if the coin is a head, $X_1 = +\$1$; if a tail comes up, $X_2 = -\$1$ (the minus sign indicates that Smith must pay). From Jones's point of view the game is exactly the same, except that the signs of the outcomes are reversed. The expected value of the game is then

$$1/2X_1 + 1/2X_2 = 1/2(\$1) + 1/2(-\$1) = 0. \qquad [7.1]$$

The expected value of this game is zero. If the game were played a large number of times, it is not likely that either player would come out very far ahead.

Now suppose the prizes of the game were changed slightly so that, from Smith's point of view, $X_1 = \$10$, and $X_2 = -\$1$. Smith will win $10 if a head comes up, but will lose only $1 if a tail comes up. The expected value of this game is $4.50:

$$1/2X_1 + 1/2X_2 = 1/2(\$10) + 1/2(-\$1) = \$5 - \$.50 = \$4.50. \qquad [7.2]$$

If this game is played many times, Smith will certainly end up the big winner. In fact, Smith might be willing to pay Jones something for the privilege of playing the game. Smith might even be willing to pay as much as $4.50, the expected value, for a chance to play. Games such as the one in Equation 7.1 with an expected value of zero and games such as the one in Equation 7.2 that cost their expected values for the right to play (here $4.50) are called actuarially **fair games.** If fair games are played many times, the monetary losses or gains are expected to be rather small. Application 7.1: Blackjack Systems shows the importance of the expected value concept in the game of blackjack, a game in which players and casinos struggle endlessly to gain an advantage.

Fair games
Games that cost their expected value.

Risk Aversion

Why would people refuse to bet in fair games? Economists have found that when people are faced with a risky but fair situation, they will usually choose

APPLICATION 7.1 

Blackjack Systems

The game of blackjack (or twenty-one) provides an interesting illustration of the expected value notion and its relevance to people's behavior in uncertain situations. This game is a very simple one. Each player is dealt two cards (with the dealer coming last). The dealer asks each player if he or she wishes another card. The player getting a hand that totals closest to 21, without going over 21, is the winner. If receipt of a card puts a player over 21, he or she automatically loses. Played in this way, blackjack offers a number of advantages to the dealer. Most important, the dealer, who plays last, is in a somewhat more favorable position since other players can go over 21 (and therefore lose) before the dealer plays. Under the usual rules, the dealer has the additional advantage of winning ties. These two advantages give the dealer a margin of winning of about 6 percent on average. Players can expect to win 47 percent of all hands played, whereas the dealer will win 53 percent of the time.

Betting Systems

Because the rules of blackjack make it relatively unfair to the players, casinos have gradually liberalized them to entice more players. At Las Vegas casinos, for example, dealers must play under fixed rules that allow no discretion depending on the individual game situation, and dealers must return bets to the players in the case of ties rather than winning them. These rules change the fairness of the game quite a bit. By some estimates, Las Vegas casinos enjoy an advantage in blackjack of as little as 0.1 percent, if that. Indeed, in recent years some players have claimed that they have developed systems that result in a net advantage for the player.[1] These systems involve card counting, systematic varying of bets, and numerous other strategies for special situations that arise in the game. Computer simulations of literally billions of potential blackjack hands have shown that careful adherence to a correct strategy can result in an advantage to the player of as much as 1 or 2 percent.

Casinos' Responses

It should come as no surprise that Las Vegas does not particularly welcome players who use these blackjack systems. The casinos made several rule changes (such as using multiple card decks to make card counting more difficult) to reduce system players' advantages. They also started to refuse admission to known system players. Recent books on blackjack systems have long sections on how to avoid detection.

All of this turmoil shows the importance of small changes in expected values for a game such as blackjack that involves many repetitions. The strategy systems pay relatively little attention to the variability of outcomes on a single hand. Instead they focus on improving the average outcome after many hours at the card table.

To Think About

1. If blackjack systems increase people's expected winnings, why doesn't everyone use them? Who would you expect to be most likely to learn how to use the systems? Who would be least likely?
2. Casinos make money by gearing their games of chance to have a positive expected value for them. They are therefore assured of making a profit with many players. Explain why the house wins, on average, in slot machines, craps, roulette, and stud poker.

[1]For an amusing although slightly outdated introduction, see E. O. Thorpe, *Beat the Dealer,* new ed. (New York: Vintage Press, 1966).

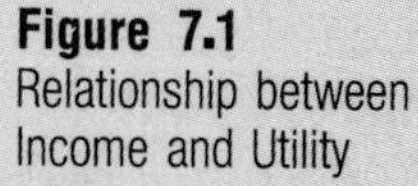

Figure 7.1
Relationship between Income and Utility

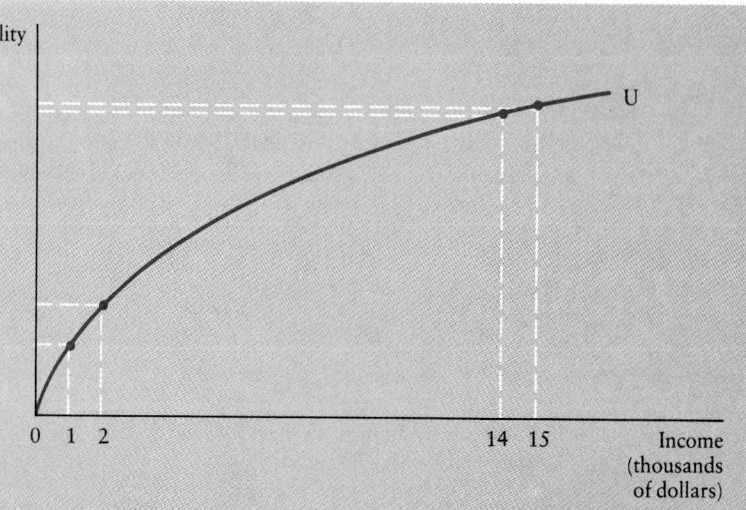

The curve U shows the utility of different levels of income (or prizes) from a game. On the assumption that the additional utility provided by an extra dollar of income declines as income increases, the curve will have the concave shape shown in the figure. This can be seen by comparing the utility gain associated with going from \$1,000 to \$2,000 to the gain associated with going from \$14,000 to \$15,000.

Risk aversion
The tendency of people to refuse to accept fair games.

not to participate.[1] A major reason for this **risk aversion** was first identified by the Swiss mathematician Daniel Bernoulli in the eighteenth century.[2] In his early study of behavior under uncertainty, Bernoulli theorized that it is not the strictly monetary payoff of a game that matters to people. Rather, it is the expected utility (what Bernoulli called the "moral value") associated with the game's prizes that is important for people's decisions. If the game's money prizes do not completely reflect utility, people may find that games that are fair in dollar terms are in fact unfair in terms of utility. Specifically, Bernoulli (and most later economists) assumed that the utility associated with the payoffs in a risky situation increases less rapidly than the dollar value of these payoffs. That is, the extra (or marginal) utility that winning an extra dollar in prize money provides is assumed to decline as more dollars are won.

[1]The games we discuss here are assumed to yield no utility in their play other than the prizes. The observation that many people gamble at "unfair" odds (for instance, in the game of roulette there are 38 possible outcomes, but the house pays only 36 to 1 for a winning number) is not necessarily a refutation of risk aversion. These people can reasonably be assumed to derive some utility from the circumstances associated with the play of the game (perhaps playing the game makes them feel like James Bond). We try to differentiate the consumption aspect of gambling from the pure risk aspect.

[2]Bernoulli's original article is well worth reading in Daniel Bernoulli, "Exposition of a New Theory on the Measurement of Risk," *Econometrica* (January 1954): 23–36.

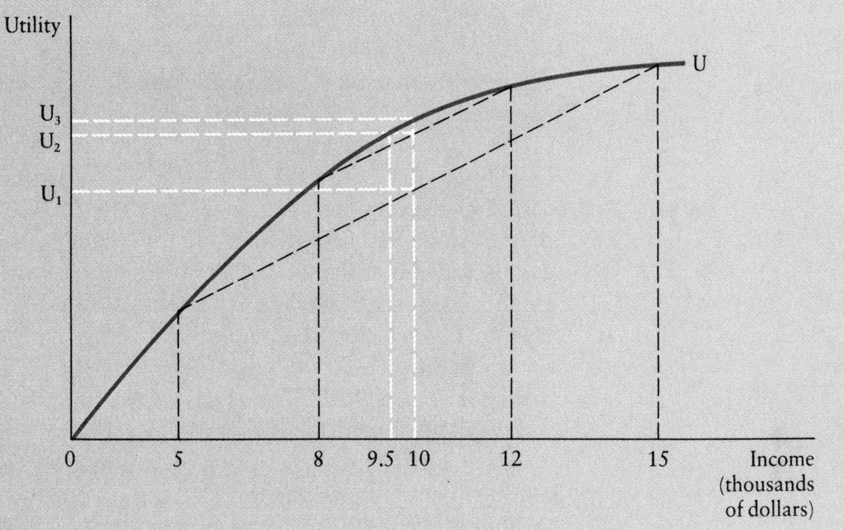

Figure 7.2
Risk Aversion

An individual characterized by the utility of income curve U will obtain a higher utility (U_3) from a risk-free income of \$10,000 than from a 50–50 chance of winning or losing \$2,000 (U_2). He or she will be willing to pay up to \$500 to avoid having to take this bet. A fair bet of \$5,000 provides even less utility (U_1) than the \$2,000 bet.

Diminishing Marginal Utility

This assumption is illustrated in Figure 7.1, which shows the utility associated with possible prizes (or incomes) from \$0 to \$15,000. The concave shape of the curve reflects the assumed diminishing marginal utility of these prizes. Although additional income always raises utility, the increase in utility resulting from an increase in income from \$1,000 to \$2,000 is much greater than the increase in utility that results from an increase in income from \$14,000 to \$15,000. It is this assumed diminishing marginal utility of income (which is in some ways similar to the assumption of a diminishing MRS introduced in Chapter 3) that gives rise to risk aversion. For example, a fair game that promises a gain of \$1,000 when you win and a loss of \$1,000 when you lose is not "fair" in utility terms. The \$1,000 loss brings more pain than the \$1,000 gain brings pleasure. Consequently, most people will refuse to play the game. People are more averse to playing fair games with big prizes than to playing fair games with small prizes for the same reason.

Graphic Analysis of Risk Aversion

Figure 7.2 illustrates risk aversion. The figure repeats the utility of income curve from Figure 7.1 and assumes that three options are open to this person.

He or she may (1) retain the current level of income ($10,000) without taking any risk; (2) take a fair bet with a 50–50 chance of winning or losing $2,000; or (3) take a fair bet with a 50–50 chance of winning or losing $5,000. To examine the person's preferences among these options, we must compute the expected utility available from each.

The utility received by staying at the current $10,000 income is given by U_3. The U curve shows directly how the individual feels about this current income. The utility level obtained from the $2,000 bet is simply the average of the utility of $12,000 (which the individual will end up with by winning the game) and the utility of $8,000 (which he or she will end up with when the game is lost). This average utility is given by U_2.[3] Because it falls short of U_3, we can assume that the person will refuse to make the $2,000 bet. Finally, the utility of the $5,000 bet is the average of the utility from $15,000 and the utility from $5,000. This is given by U_1, which falls below U_2. In other words, the person dislikes the risky $5,000 bet even more than the $2,000 bet.

Diminished marginal utility of income, as Figure 7.2 documents, means that people will be averse to risk. Among options with the same expected dollar values ($10,000 in all of our examples), people will prefer risk-free incomes to risky options. In fact, a person would be willing to give up some amount of certain income to avoid taking a risk. In Figure 7.2, for example, a risk-free income of $9,500 provides the same utility as the $2,000 gamble ($U_2$). The individual is willing to pay up to $500 to avoid taking that risk. There are a number of ways this person might spend these funds to reduce the risk or avoid it completely. In the next section we will look at a few of them.

Methods for Reducing Risk

In many situations taking risks is unavoidable. Even though driving a car or eating a meal at a restaurant subjects an individual to some uncertainty about what will actually happen, short of becoming a hermit, there is no way all such risks can be avoided. Our analysis in the previous section suggests, however, that people will generally be willing to pay something to reduce these risks. In this section we examine two methods for doing so—insurance and diversification. In the final section of this chapter, we look at more general issues involved in acquiring information to reduce risks.

Insurance

Each year people in the United States spend nearly half a trillion dollars on insurance of all types. Most commonly, they buy coverage for their own life,

[3]Through simple geometry this average utility can be found by drawing the chord joining U($12,000) and U($8,000) and finding the midpoint of that chord. Since the vertical line at $10,000 is midway between $12,000 and $8,000, it will also bisect the chord.

Figure 7.3
Insurance Reduces Risk

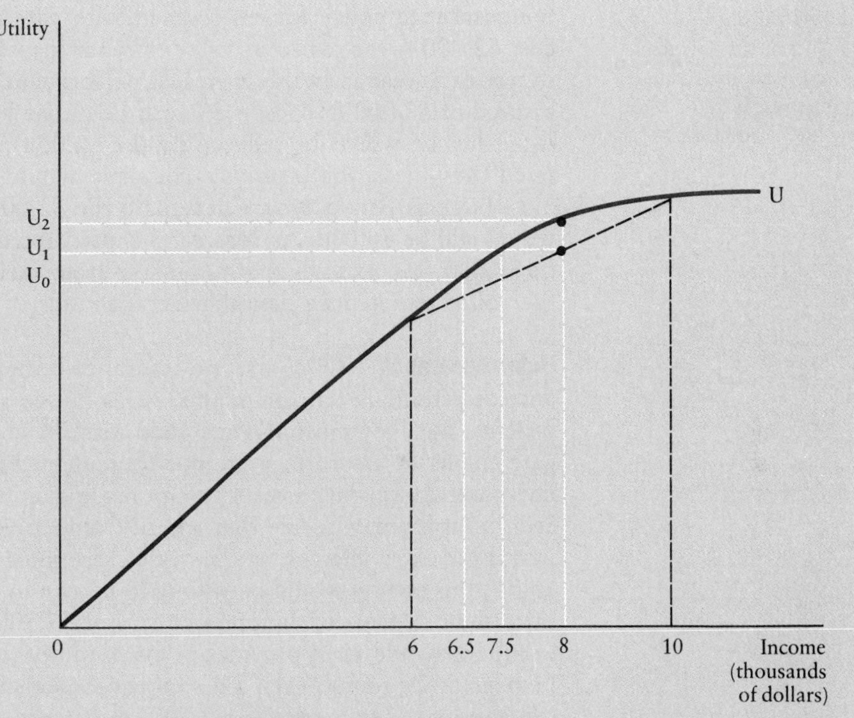

A person with \$10,000 in income who faced a 50–50 chance of \$4,000 in medical bills would have an expected utility of U_1. With fair insurance (which costs \$2,000) utility would be U_2. Even unfair insurance costing \$2,500 would still yield the same utility (U_1) as facing the world uninsured. But a premium of \$3,500, which provides a utility of only U_0, would be too costly.

for their home and automobiles, and for their health care costs. But, insurance can be bought (perhaps at a very high price) for practically any risk imaginable. Many people in California buy earthquake insurance, outdoor swimming pool owners can buy special coverage for injuries to falling parachutists, and surgeons or basketball players can insure their hands. In all of these cases, individuals are willing to pay a premium to an insurance company in order to be assured of compensation if something goes wrong.

The underlying motive for insurance purchases is illustrated in Figure 7.3. Here we have repeated the utility of income curve from Figure 7.2, but now we assume that during the next year this person with a \$10,000 current income (and consumption) faces a 50 percent chance of having \$4,000 in unexpected medical bills, which would reduce his or her consumption to \$6,000. Without insurance this person's utility could be U_1—the average of the utility from \$10,000 and the utility from \$6,000.

Fair Insurance. This person would clearly be better-off with an actuarially **fair insurance** policy for his or her health care needs. Such a policy would cost \$2,000—the expected value of what insurance companies would have to pay each year in health claims. A person who bought the policy would be assured of \$8,000 in consumption. If he or she bought the policy and stayed well, income would be reduced by the \$2,000 premium. If this person suffered the illness, the insurance company would pay the \$4,000 in medical bills, but this person would have paid the \$2,000 premium so consumption would still be \$8,000. As Figure 7.3 shows, the utility from a certain income of \$8,000 (U_2) exceeds that attainable from facing the world uninsured, so the policy represents a desirable use for funds.

Fair insurance
Insurance for which the premium is equal to the expected value of the loss.

Unfair Insurance. Of course, no insurance company can afford to sell insurance at actuarially fair premiums. Not only do such companies have to pay benefits, but they must also maintain records, collect premiums, and investigate claims to assure they are not fraudulent. Hence, a would-be insurance purchaser can always expect to pay more than an actuarially fair premium. Still, a buyer may decide that the risk reduction that insurance provides is worth the extra charges. In the health care illustration in Figure 7.3, for example, this person would be willing to pay up to \$2,500 for health insurance since the risk-free consumption stream of \$7,500 that buying such "unfair" insurance would yield provides as much utility (U_1) as does facing the world uninsured. Of course, even a desirable product such as insurance can become too expensive. At a price of \$3,500, the utility provided with full insurance (U_0) falls short of what would be obtained from facing the world uninsured. In this case, this person is better-off taking the risk of paying his or her own medical bills than accepting such an actuarially unfair insurance premium.

Uninsurable Risks. The preceding discussion shows that risk-averse individuals will always buy insurance against risky outcomes unless insurance premiums exceed the expected value of a loss by too much. Three types of factors may result in such high premiums and thereby cause some risks to become uninsurable. First, some risks may be so unique or difficult to evaluate that an insurer may have no idea how to set the premium level. Determining an actuarially fair premium requires that a given risky situation must occur frequently enough so that the insurer can both estimate the expected value of the loss and rely on being able to cover expected payouts with premiums from individuals who do not suffer losses. For rare or very unpredictable events such as wars, nuclear power plant mishaps, or invasions from Mars, would-be insurers may have no basis for establishing insurance premiums and therefore will refrain from offering any coverage.

Two other reasons for absence of insurance coverage relate to the behavior of the individuals who want to buy insurance. In some cases these individuals may know more about the likelihood they will suffer a loss than will an insurer. Those who expect large losses will buy insurance whereas those who expect small ones will not. This **adverse selection** will result in the insurer paying out more in losses than expected unless the insurer finds a way to con-

Adverse selection
When buyers and sellers have different information, market outcomes may exhibit adverse selection—the quality of goods or services traded will be biased toward market participants with better information.

trol who buys the policies offered. The insurer will therefore either raise the premiums to a very unfair level or, as we illustrate in Application 7.2: Provisions of Group Health Insurance Policies, put major restrictions on the sales of this type of policy

The behavior of individuals once they are insured may also affect the possibility for insurance coverage. If having insurance makes people more likely to incur losses, insurers' premium calculations will be incorrect, and again they may be forced to charge premiums that are too unfair in an actuarial sense. For example, if people who have insurance on the cash they carry in their pockets are far more likely to lose it through carelessness than those who do not have insurance, insurance premiums to cover such losses may have to be very high. Insurance against accidental losses of cash will not be available on any reasonable terms. Application 7.2 also presents some other illustrations of this problem of **moral hazard** since it is quite pervasive in insurance situations.

Moral hazard
The effect that having insurance has on the behavior of the insured.

Diversification

A second way for risk-averse individuals to reduce risk is by diversifying. This is the economic principle underlying the adage, "Don't put all your eggs in one basket." By suitably spreading risk "around," it may be possible to raise utility above that provided by following a single course of action. This possibility is illustrated in Figure 7.4, which shows the utility of income for an individual with a current income of $10,000 who must invest $4,000 of that income in risky assets.

For simplicity, assume there are only two such assets, shares of stock in company A or company B. One share of stock in either company costs $1, and the investor believes that the stock will rise to $2 if the company does well during the next year; if the company does poorly, however, the stock will be worthless. Each company has a 50–50 chance of doing well. How should this individual invest the $4,000? At first it would seem that it doesn't matter since the two companies' prospects are identical. But, if we assume the company's prospects are unrelated to one another, it is possible to show that holding both stocks will reduce this person's risks.

Suppose the individual decides to plunge into the market by investing only in 4,000 shares of company A. Then he or she has a 50 percent chance of having $14,000 at the end of the year and a 50 percent chance of having $6,000. This undiversified investment strategy will therefore yield a utility of U_1.

Let's consider a diversified strategy in which the investor buys 2,000 shares of each stock. There are now four possible outcomes depending on how each company does. These are illustrated in Table 7.1 together with the individual's income in each of these eventualities. Each of these outcomes is equally likely. Notice that the diversified strategy only achieves very good or very bad results when both companies do well or poorly, respectively. In half the cases illustrated, the gains in one company's shares balance the losses in

APPLICATION 7.2

Provisions of Group Health Insurance Policies

Health insurance is one of the most important fringe benefits that most workers get on their jobs. In many cases the value of this benefit may exceed 10 or even 15 percent of a person's total wages, and firms' health insurance costs have been escalating rapidly in recent years. Although much of this increasing cost can be attributed to general inflation in the price of medical care, some of it may be attributable to features of the health insurance policies themselves. Here we will examine some of the provisions that are included in many group health insurance policies in order to control costs. As a specific example, consider the plan that is provided to your author by Blue Cross/Blue Shield (BC/BS) of Massachusetts.

Provisions to Control Adverse Selection

People are in a position to know more about their own health than is an insurance company. Individuals usually cannot buy regular health insurance on their own without an extensive physical examination. Even with an exam, undetected "preexisting" health problems are often not covered by a policy. With group health insurance (such as that offered by BC/BS) adverse selection problems are mitigated since one must belong to the defined "group" (e.g., employees of a certain small college) before being eligible for coverage. Even with group health insurance, however, BC/BS finds it must control adverse selection by (1) limiting entry into the program to a single date each year (otherwise people would not join until they needed coverage) and (2) excluding coverage for some preexisting conditions that are common and quite costly (pregnancy care and childbirth, for example). Only by instituting such provisions can BC/BS be reasonably sure that the rates it sets for group coverage will not prove inadequate because only certain high-cost individuals choose to participate in the plan.

Provisions to Control Moral Hazard

As we discussed in Application 5.5, one effect of insurance coverage may be to increase the demand for covered services. This effect reflects the moral hazard[1] problem in the health insurance context. Your author's BC/BS policy attempts to control such responses in three ways. First, some types of services are completely excluded from coverage. These include such things as cosmetic dentistry or surgery, which are believed to experience relatively significant utilization in response to insurance coverage. Similarly, for some services (such as psychiatric services) the BC/BS policy imposes a fixed dollar ceiling ($500 per year). Finally (and most importantly), costs of practically all medical services other than in-patient hospital care are subject to deductible and coinsurance provisions. Specifically, the policyholder must pay the first $25 of any such expenditure per calendar quarter and then pay 20 percent of all additional costs. The purpose of the first of these provisions is to prevent the insurance system from being clogged by numerous small claims. The second provision is intended to raise a degree of cost-consciousness among consumers who have larger medical care costs. Extensive paperwork and documentation requirements from BC/BS increase the costs associated with claiming benefits even further.

To Think About

1. Adverse selection can also wreak havoc with the pricing of other types of insurance such as automobile or life insurance. How might this problem occur in offerings of "safe driver" policies or in the move to "unisex" pricing of life insurance?
2. Many economists point to the problems experienced by banks and savings and loan institutions in the late 1980s as an example of the moral hazard created by government deposit insurance. What is the reasoning behind this statement? Would banking be more efficient without such deposit insurance?

[1]Unfortunately the term "moral hazard" carries the implication that people who respond to insurance coverage behave "immorally." Although such responses may create problems for the allocation of resources, few economists would call them "immoral." For a discussion, see M. Pauly, "The Economics of Moral Hazard," *American Economic Review* (June 1968): 531–537.

Figure 7.4
Diversification Reduces Risk

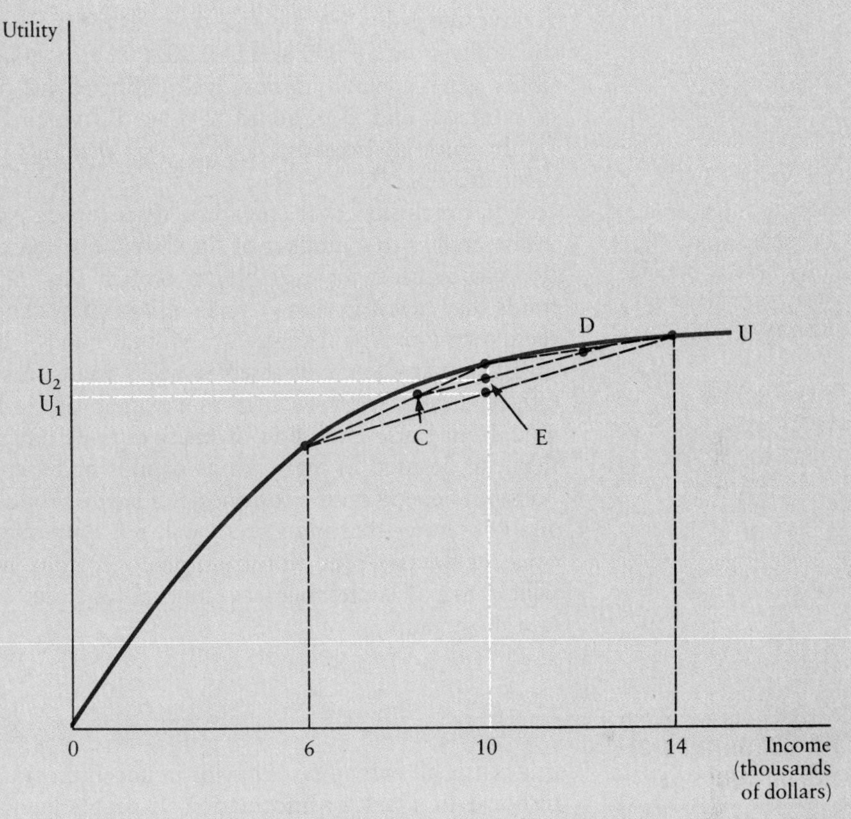

Here an investor must invest \$4,000 in risky stocks. If he or she invests in only one stock, utility will be U_1. Although two unrelated stocks may promise identical returns, investing in both of them can, on average, reduce risk and raise utility to U_2.

Table 7.1
Possible Outcomes from Investing in Two Companies

		Company B's Performance	
		Poor	Good
Company A's Performance	Poor	\$ 6,000	\$10,000
	Good	10,000	14,000

the other's, and the individual ends up with the original \$10,000. The diversified strategy, although it has the same expected value (\$10,000) as the single stock strategy, is less risky.

Illustrating the utility gain from this reduction in risk requires a bit of ingenuity since we must average the utilities from the four outcomes shown in

Table 7.1. We do so in a two-step process. Point C in Figure 7.4 represents the average utility for the case where company B does poorly (the average of the utility from $6,000 and $10,000) whereas point D represents the average utility when company B does well ($10,000 and $14,000). The final average of points C and D is found at point E, which represents a utility level of U_2. Because U_2 exceeds U_1, it is clear that this individual has gained from diversification.

Diversification
The spreading of risk among several options rather than choosing only one.

The conclusion that spreading risks through **diversification** can increase utility applies to a number of situations. The reasoning in our simple illustration can be used, for example, to explain why individuals opt to buy mutual funds that invest in many stocks rather than choosing only a few stocks on their own (see Application 7.3: Mutual Funds). It also explains why people invest in many kinds of assets (stocks, bonds, cash, precious metals, real estate, and durable goods such as automobiles) rather than in only one. Individuals may also choose to diversify their earnings stream by obtaining skills that can be used in many kinds of jobs or by choosing jobs whose success does not depend on the fortunes of a single product. In all of these cases, our analysis shows that individuals will not only obtain higher utility levels because of the risk reduction from diversification, but that they might even be willing to pay something (say, mutual fund fees or educational costs) to obtain these gains.

The Economics of Information

In a sense, all individual behavior in uncertain situations can be regarded as a response to a lack of information. If people knew that a coin were going to come up a head, or knew how their investments would fare next year, they would be better-off. They may even be willing to pay for additional information to reduce uncertainty, and probably will do so as long as the expected gains from this information exceed its cost. For example, someone trying to decide whether to buy a used car may pay an impartial mechanic to evaluate the car's condition before buying it; someone wishing to buy a color television may check around to find the best price. They may also consult *Consumer Reports* magazine, which gives its subscribers detailed information on various consumer goods. Similarly, farmers may use information about the weather to make decisions about what to grow and when to harvest their crops. As Application 7.4: The Value of Accurate Weather Forecasts to Raisin Growers shows, such information can be quite valuable in making these decisions.

Balancing the Gains and Costs of Acquiring Information

These examples make clear that acquiring information is like any other economic activity in some ways. The individual receives utility from having information because it helps him or her to make better decisions. But many

APPLICATION 7.3

Mutual Funds

One of the most convenient ways for individuals to invest in common stocks is by purchasing mutual fund shares. These funds pool the money from many investors and use it to buy shares in many different companies. For this service, individuals pay an annual management fee of about 1 to 2 percent of the value of the money they have invested.

Diversification and Riskiness of Funds

Although mutual fund managers usually sell their services on the basis of their supposed superiority in picking stocks, the diversification that funds offer probably provides a better explanation of why individuals choose them. Any single investor who tried to purchase shares in, say, one hundred different companies would find that most of his or her funds would be used for brokerage commissions with little left over to buy the shares themselves. Because mutual funds deal in large volume, brokerage commissions are lower on a percentage basis. It then becomes feasible for an individual to own a proportionate share in many companies' stocks. For the reasons illustrated in Figure 7.4, this diversification reduces risk.

Still, investing in stocks generally is a risky enterprise, so mutual fund managers offer products that allow investors to choose the amount of risk they are willing to tolerate. "Money market" and short-term bond funds tend to offer little risk, "balanced" funds (which hold some common stock and some bonds) are a bit riskier, and "growth" funds offer the greatest risk. As might be expected, on average the riskier funds have tended to yield a somewhat higher return to investors. For example, one well-known study of mutual fund performance during the 1960s found that each 10 percent increase in riskiness resulted in an increase in average total yield from the funds of about one percentage point.[1] Funds did seem to offer investors a wide array of choices among varying degrees of risk.

[1]M. Jensen, "Risk, the Pricing of Capital Assets, and the Evaluation of Investment Performance," *Journal of Business* (April 1969).

Individual Investment Choices

Investors may be able to reduce their risks further by making suitable choices among the investment options available. Our numerical illustration of the benefits of diversification assumed that the returns on the shares of the two companies were independent of each other. That situation is clearly superior in terms of risk reduction to a situation in which the returns moved together—if the fortunes of the two companies were always the same, there would be no reason to buy shares in both of them. But if an individual can find investments whose returns tend to move in opposite directions (that is, when one does well, the other does not and vice versa), he or she can reduce risks even more by holding both of these assets. For example, investors in common stock often hold some of their funds in gold (or other precious metals) since gold prices tend to rise when stock prices fall. More generally, investors may even be able to develop complex strategies involving short sales or stock options that allow them to hedge their returns from a given investment even further. The rapid growth in financial innovations such as standardized put and call options, stock index options, and specialized mutual funds illustrates the demand for such risk reduction vehicles.

To Think About

1. Most studies of mutual fund performance conclude that managers cannot consistently exceed the average return in the stock market as a whole. What does this imply about investors' motives in buying mutual funds? Why might a believer in the "efficient markets hypothesis" (discussed later in this chapter) expect this result?
2. Some mutual funds are managed by computer so as to have a performance that precisely duplicates the performance of a particular stock market average (e.g., the Standard & Poor's 500 Stock Average). Why would an investor want to buy such a fund? Alternatively, given that such index funds tend to have low management costs, why would an investor buy any other kind of fund?

APPLICATION 7.4

The Value of Accurate Weather Forecasts to Raisin Growers

Accurate weather forecasts are crucial to many situations in which decisions depend on the weather. People must make decisions about where to spend their vacations or whether to go to a baseball game; commuters must decide how they will get to work in bad weather; builders must schedule their outside work to take advantage of good weather; and ski slope operators must decide whether to turn on their artificial snow machines. One of the most important examples of the impact of the weather on production is agriculture, where anticipated rainfall affects a number of decisions, such as which crop to plant, when to harvest, and whether to use the sun or indoor facilities for crop drying.

The Raisin Industry

These calculations are particularly important in the raisin industry of the San Joaquin Valley in California. Raisins are produced by sun-drying grapes in the early fall. If conditions for drying are expected to be unfavorable, the grapes can be crushed instead to produce wine, although this may be somewhat less profitable. A farmer who opts for drying raisins takes a considerable gamble because rain could virtually destroy the raisin crop (leaving the grapes with only a scrap value if sold to a winery). Weather forecasting therefore plays a major role in growers' decisions: a fall forecast of rain could prompt many to sell their grapes for wine, whereas a sunny forecast would cause many farmers to try to make it through the required 21-day drying period for raisins.

The Value of Information

In an important 1963 study, Lester Lave estimated the value that more accurate weather forecasts would have for raisin growers.[1] He first carefully outlined all of the relevant decisions that growers make as the fall harvest approaches and calculated how each decision depends on the expected weather. He then compared the expected profits under average (but uncertain) weather patterns with the profits that might be expected if the likelihood of rain could be accurately forecast over a three-week period. Using this procedure, Lave estimated that improved forecasting accuracy would increase raisin growers' profits by about $91 per acre. Applied to all acres planted in 1960, this figure yielded an estimate of over $20 million for the value of better weather information to the industry as a whole.[2] Even for this relatively small segment of the economy, the value of information can be substantial.

To Think About

1. How can better weather forecasts make raisin growing more profitable? After all, better forecasts don't bring better weather, so why should it matter if growers know what the weather will be? How can better forecasts have any economic value at all?
2. Most weather forecasting in the United States is done by the U.S. Weather Service, a government agency. If weather forecasts are so valuable, why don't private firms buy their own forecasts just as they buy other productive services? What kinds of weather forecasts do you think would be most likely to be provided through private markets? Which kinds through the government?

---

[1]Lester B. Lave, "The Value of Better Weather Information to the Raisin Industry," *Econometrica* (January/April 1963): 151–164.

[2]Lave also pointed out that this kind of aggregate estimate may be an overestimate for the industry as a whole because the increased raisin production brought about through better information may cause raisin prices to fall. Lower prices would benefit consumers, however, so Lave's estimates may understate the social value of better forecasts.

kinds of information are costly to obtain, so we would expect that people would stop short of being "fully" informed. It may not make sense to a person to hire an auto mechanic or to subscribe to *Consumer Reports* if he or she doubts that the information obtained will lead to greatly improved decisions. For example, one might assume that all of the color television sets in a certain price range at Crazy Eddie's are about the same and just choose the most convenient model. Although there may be slight performance differences among the sets, the costs of finding out what they are probably exceed the benefits to be obtained. In such a case the utility-maximizing model suggests that some ignorance is best.

Asymmetry of Information

The principal implication of this discussion is that the level of information that an individual acquires will depend on how much the information costs. Unlike the market prices for most goods (which are usually assumed to be the same for everyone), there are many reasons to believe that information costs may differ significantly among individuals. Some people may possess specific skills relevant to information acquisition (they may be trained mechanics, for example) whereas others may not possess such skills. Some individuals may have other types of experience that yields valuable information whereas others may lack that experience. For example, the seller of a product will usually know more about its limitations than will a buyer since the seller will know precisely how the good was made and where possible problems might arise. Similarly, large-scale repeat buyers of a good may have greater access to information about it than do first-time buyers. Finally, some individuals may have invested in some types of information services (for example, by having a computer link to a brokerage firm or by subscribing to *Consumer Reports*) that make the cost of obtaining additional information lower than for someone without such an investment.

All of these factors suggest that the level of information may differ among the participants in market transactions. Of course, in many instances, information costs may be low, and such differences will be minor. Most people can appraise the quality of fresh vegetables fairly well just by looking at them, for example. But when information costs are high and variable across individuals, we would expect them to find it advantageous to acquire different amounts of information. Some of the implications of that possibility are described in later sections of this book.

Special Properties of Information

Acquiring information and using it in making market transactions are activities that differ in many ways from most other types of economic transactions. Although we cannot pursue all of these differences here, a brief discussion

APPLICATION 7.5

Prices and Information

It should come as no surprise to anyone who has ever searched for bargains that it is important to know the prices being quoted by various sellers. Obtaining such information is undoubtedly subject to economic calculations. If one were buying a major item (say, a color television), it would probably make sense to call around to find the best price available. When buying a tube of toothpaste, however, such an effort may be unwarranted.

Gasoline Prices

An illustration of this sort of situation was provided in a 1976 study of gasoline prices by H. Marvel.[1] In that study the author examined the dispersion of prices for regular-grade gasoline in 20 U.S. cities. He found that the average observed price range within the cities was nearly 5 cents per gallon and that, in some instances, ranges as wide as 20 cents per gallon seemed to persist for long periods.

Perhaps more interesting, Marvel found that the degree of price dispersion in particular cities seemed to be associated with the costs and benefits of price information to consumers. For example, cities in which gasoline use was relatively greater tended to have less price dispersion possibly because drivers in such cities had greater incentives to seek out low prices. Similarly, cities that required gas stations to post prices that were readable from the highway tended to have smaller price dispersions. Again, this probably occurred because of the efficiency with which such posting provided price information to passing motorists.

Price Advertising

Advertising of prices can also have the effect of reducing the average amount consumers pay for goods by making it more difficult for high-price sellers to take advantage of consumer ignorance. An early study of such effects found that prices for eyeglasses in states that permitted price advertising were about half as much as in states that did not.[2] Similar results of the effects of price advertising have been found for electronics, prescription drugs, and children's toys.

The beneficial effects of price advertising have been recognized in a number of legal cases, particularly those that have struck down bans on price advertising in certain professions. For example, a 1977 Supreme Court decision that struck down barriers imposed by the Arizona Bar Association against price advertising of legal services led to the elimination of such restrictions in many other states. Prices of routine legal services (such as writing wills or conducting closings on house sales) seem to have declined as a result. Legal suits against advertising restrictions by real estate agents, tax preparers, dentists, and some medical specialists have also been brought, though in many of these cases it is too early to appraise the results. Clearly, however, the courts have come to recognize that the information provided by price advertising is valuable to consumers.

To Think About

1. Some states require price posting for goods other than gasoline. Can you think of other products for which the availability of easily readable price information would be important to consumers? Are there cases where such price posting would be undesirable?
2. Some professional groups argue that permitting price advertising is sure to attract charlatans and quacks and lead to a decline in the quality of services provided. Does this seem a reasonable concern? Would active price advertising make consumers' problems in appraising quality more difficult?

[1]H. Marvel, "The Economics of Information and Retail Gasoline Price Behavior," *Journal of Political Economy* 84 (October 1976): 1033–1059.

[2]L. Benham "The Effect of Advertising on the Price of Eyeglasses," *Journal of Law and Economics* (October 1972): 337–352.

can indicate some of the issues that arise. Most important of the special properties of information is that it may not be a purely private good for the individual who acquires it. It may have some characteristics of a public good (see Chapter 22) in that many individuals may benefit from it. The principal example of this is scientific inventions. Once a scientific discovery is made, the information from it is relatively available to anyone. It is very hard for an inventor to keep an important new technology a secret, especially if it is used to produce products to be sold openly in the market. In order to preserve the incentive to acquire scientific information, most countries offer some degree of patent protection to inventors to permit them to garner most of the gains from the invention. In this way, scientific information that would normally be public in nature can be privatized. Patent laws are usually designed to seek a balance between preserving the incentive to innovate and providing scientific information for everyone in a timely manner.

Many other information-acquisition activities yield side benefits to third parties. The information from government and private product testing, for example, is widely disseminated. Perhaps the most important way in which privately acquired information is spread, however, is through its effects on market prices. If people discover that one brand of television receiver is superior to other brands, the price of the better brand may rise because more people will want to buy it. Similarly, when people learn that a particular product is unsafe, its price may fall.

Efficient markets hypothesis
The hypothesis that all information is reflected in prevailing market prices.

In financial markets it is generally assumed that new information is rapidly disseminated through changes in prices of stocks or foreign exchange. A stringent form of the assumption that financial information is disseminated quickly is the **efficient markets hypothesis,** which asserts that prevailing market prices accurately reflect all currently available information. This hypothesis is widely used in economic literature on financial topics, and we shall encounter it in several places in this book. One implication of the efficient markets hypothesis is that the private return to information acquisition may be rather low since in efficient markets, prices will already reflect all there is to know. In Application 7.5: Prices and Information we show how prices can sometimes be used to discover something about the nature of information in a market.

Summary

In this chapter we have briefly surveyed the economic analysis of individual behavior in uncertain situations. From that survey we reached several conclusions that have relevance throughout the study of microeconomics.

- In uncertain situations individuals are concerned with the expected utility associated with various outcomes. If individuals have a diminishing marginal utility for income, they will be risk averse. That is, they will generally refuse bets that are actuarially fair in dollar terms but result in an expected loss of utility.

- Risk-averse individuals will purchase insurance that allows them to avoid participating in fair bets. Even if the premium is somewhat unfair (in an actuarial sense), they will still buy insurance in order to minimize the risk.
- Diversification among several uncertain options may reduce risk. Such risk spreading may sometimes be costly, however.
- New information is valuable because it permits individuals to make better choices that increase expected utility.
- Individuals may face differing costs of obtaining information and may therefore acquire different amounts of it. Information may also have some characteristics of a public good (it may sometimes be available to everyone at zero cost). In particular, information may sometimes be reflected in the market prices of goods.

Review Questions

1. What does it mean to say we "expect" a fair coin to come up heads about half the time? Would you expect the fraction of heads to get closer to exactly 0.5 as more coins are flipped? Explain how this "law of large numbers" applies to the risks faced by casinos or insurance companies.
2. Explain why the assumption of diminishing marginal utility of income implies risk aversion. Can you think of other assumptions that would result in risk-averse behavior but would not require the difficult-to-verify notion of diminishing marginal utility?
3. Why does the purchase of fair insurance provide a certain, nonrandom income to the buyer? Why must all insurance premiums be somewhat unfair in a statistical sense? What determines whether a person will purchase insurance at an unfair premium?
4. Explain why the presence of imperfect information in insurance markets can result in adverse selection. Why does adverse selection pose a problem for insurance companies in their rate setting?
5. "The term 'moral hazard' is entirely inappropriate since it maligns individuals' reactions to economic incentives provided by insurance that in other circumstances are regarded as perfectly normal." Do you agree? Explain.
6. The diversification example illustrated in Table 7.1 and Figure 7.4 requires that returns on the two stocks be independent. Explain what "independent" means in this context and why independence of returns provides opportunities for diversification. Why would such opportunities be limited if the returns on the stocks in the example moved together?
7. Do you think firms exhibit risk-averse choices? If the owners of firms can hold a diversified selection of stocks, would they want to enforce risk-averse behavior on managers? Would managers choose risk-averse strategies on their own? (For further observations on firms, owners, and managers, see Chapter 11.)
8. What benefits do individuals derive from obtaining additional information? Explain why the marginal value to additional information declines as a person becomes more fully informed.
9. Explain why the marginal cost of acquiring additional information increases. Can you think of a personal example that illustrates this situation?
10. Why do the observations in questions 8 and 9 suggest that individuals have a utility-maximizing amount of information? Why is some ignorance optimal? Would this optimum differ among people? Can you develop a graph that illustrates these points?

Problems

7.1 Suppose a person must accept one of three bets.

- Bet 1: Win $100 with probability 1/2; lose $100 with probability 1/2.
- Bet 2: Win $100 with probability 3/4; lose $300 with probability 1/4.
- Bet 3: Win $100 with probability 9/10 ; lose $900 with probability 1/10.

a. Show that all of these are fair bets.
b. Graph each bet on a utility of income curve similar to Figure 7.2.
c. Explain carefully which bet will be preferred and why.

7.2 Two fast food restaurants are located next to each other and offer different procedures for ordering food. The first offers five lines leading to a server, whereas the second has a single line leading to five servers, with the next person in the line going to the first available server. Use the assumption that most individuals are risk averse to discuss which restaurant will be preferred.

7.3 Show that if an individual's utility of income function is convex (rather than concave as shown in Figure 7.1), he or she will prefer fair gambles to income certainty and may even be willing to accept somewhat unfair gambles. Do you believe this sort of risk-taking behavior is common? What factors might tend to limit its occurrence?

7.4 A person purchases a dozen eggs and must take them home. Although making trips home is costless, there is a 50 percent chance that all of the eggs carried on one trip will be broken during the trip.
This person considers two strategies:

- Strategy 1: Take all 12 eggs in one trip.
- Strategy 2: Make two trips, taking 6 eggs in each trip.

a. List the possible outcomes of each strategy and the probabilities of these outcomes. Show that, on average, 6 eggs make it home under either strategy.
b. Develop a graph to show the utility obtainable under each strategy.
c. Could utility be improved further by taking more than two trips? How would the desirability of this possibility be affected if additional trips were costly?

7.5 Jimmy the Greek is seen to place an even money $100,000 bet on the Lakers to win their NBA Championship final with the Pistons. If Jimmy has a logarithmic utility of wealth function and if his current wealth is $1,000,000, what must he believe the minimum probability that the Lakers will win is?

7.6 Suppose there is a 50–50 chance that a risk-averse individual with a current wealth of $20,000 will contract a debilitating disease and suffer a loss of $10,000.

a. Calculate the cost of actuarially fair insurance in this situation and use a utility of wealth graph (such as shown in Figure 7.1) to show that the individual will prefer fair insurance against this loss to accepting the gamble uninsured.
b. Suppose two types of insurance policies were available:

    1. A fair policy covering the complete loss.
    2. A fair policy covering only half of any loss incurred.

    Calculate the cost of the second type of policy and show that the individual will generally regard it as inferior to the first.

c. Suppose individuals who purchase cost-sharing policies of the second type take better care of their health, thereby reducing the loss suffered when ill to only \$7,000. In this situation, what will be the cost of a cost-sharing policy? Show that some individuals may now prefer this type of policy. (This is an example of the "moral hazard" problem in insurance theory.)

*7.7 It is known that parking in an illegal space in downtown Podunk leads to a 50 percent chance of getting a \$10 parking ticket.

a. Graph the individual's decision to park in this space. Show that, unless the space provides substantial convenience, the individual will not choose to park there.
b. Podunk is considering increasing its parking fine to \$20. Show that this would reduce the utility of parking in the illegal space further.
c. The police chief of Podunk argues that increasing patrols to ensure that any violator is caught (that is, to ensure that there is a 100 percent likelihood of getting a \$10 ticket if one parks in the illegal space) would be more effective at deterring illegal parking than increasing the fine. Would you agree? Graph your results.

*7.8 Ms. Fogg is planning an around-the-world trip. The utility from the trip is a function of how much she spends on it (Y) given by

$$U(Y) = \log Y.$$

Ms. Fogg has \$10,000 to spend on the trip. If she spends all of it, her utility will be

$$U(10{,}000) = \log 10{,}000 = 4.$$

(In this problem we are using logarithms to the base 10 for ease of computation.)

a. If there is a 25 percent probability that Ms. Fogg will lose \$1,000 of her cash on the trip, what is the trip's expected utility?
b. Suppose that Ms. Fogg can buy insurance against losing the \$1,000 (say, by purchasing traveler's checks) at an "actuarially fair" premium of \$250. Show that her utility is higher if she purchases this insurance than if she faces the chance of losing the \$1,000 without insurance.
c. What is the maximum amount that Ms. Fogg would be willing to pay to insure her \$1,000?
d. Suppose that people who buy insurance tend to become more careless with their cash than those who don't, and assume that the probability of their losing \$1,000 is 30 percent. What will be the actuarially fair insurance premium? Will Ms. Fogg buy insurance in this situation?

7.9 Blue-eyed people are more likely to lose their expensive watches than are brown-eyed people. Specifically, there is an 80 percent probability that blue-eyed people will lose a \$1,000 watch during a year, but only a 20 percent probability that a brown-eyed person will. Blue-eyed and brown-eyed people are equally represented in the population.

a. If an insurance company assumes blue-eyed and brown-eyed people are equally likely to buy watch loss insurance, what will the actuarially fair insurance premium be?

---

*Denotes a problem that is rather difficult.

b. If blue-eyed and brown-eyed people have logarithmic utility of wealth functions and current wealths of $10,000 each, will these individuals buy watch insurance at the actuarially fair premium?
c. Given your results from part b, will the insurance premium be correctly computed? What should the premium be? What will utility for each type of person be?
d. Suppose that an insurance company charged different premiums for blue-eyed and brown-eyed people. How would these individuals' maximum utilities compare to those computed in parts b and c? (This problem is an example of adverse selection in insurance.)

PART 3

FIRMS, PRODUCTION, AND SUPPLY

Part 3 considers the production and supply of economic goods. The institutions that are engaged in this process are called "firms." They may be large, complex organizations, such as IBM or the U.S. Defense Department, or they may be quite small, such as "mom and pop" stores or self-employed farmers. The organizations may also have different goals—IBM may pursue maximum profits, while the U.S. Defense Department may be interested in the "protection" it can provide with the overall size of its budget. Whatever goals they pursue, all firms must make choices about what inputs they will use and the level of output they will supply. Part 4 looks at these choices.

To be able to produce any output firms must hire many inputs (labor, capital, natural resources, and so forth). Because these inputs are scarce, they have costs associated with their use. Our goal in Chapters 8 and 9 is to develop cost curves that relate these input costs to the level of the firm's output. In Chapter 8 we introduce the firm's production function, which shows the relationship between inputs used and the level of output that results. Once the relationship between inputs and outputs is known, the costs of various input levels can be determined for corresponding levels of output, as shown in Chapter 9. By developing cost relationships from the underlying notion of production functions, we can more clearly see why cost curves might shift or how short-run and long-run costs might differ. An appendix to Chapter 9 uses a numerical example to show these results.

Chapter 10 then uses the cost curves developed in Chapter 9 to discuss firms' supply decisions. The primary model presented in the chapter is of a firm that seeks maximum profits given the markets it faces. Several controversial issues that arise in connection with this assumption of profit maximization are briefly discussed. The chapter concludes with a detailed analysis of the supply decisions of profit-maximizing firms that will be used, with our analysis of demand from the previous part, to discuss price determination in Part 4.

The final chapter in Part 3, Chapter 11, looks at a few additional applications of the theory of the firm. The chapter is specifically concerned with the types of agreements (that is, "contracts") that exist between firms and their employees and managers. The study of such agreements has become a major area of interest to economists in recent years, and a general purpose of the chapter is to introduce you to some of this recent work. ▲

CHAPTER 8

Production

Chapters 8 and 9 develop the relationship between the level of production in a firm and the input costs associated with that level. This description of costs provides the basis for our analysis of firms' supply decisions—the principal topic of Part 3. Chapter 8 begins this process with an analysis of the physical aspects of production. We show how economists conceptualize the relationship between the inputs a firm uses and the output it thereby obtains.

Production Functions

Firm
Any organization that turns inputs into outputs.

Production function
The mathematical relationship between inputs and outputs.

The purpose of any **firm** is to turn inputs into outputs: General Motors combines steel, glass, workers' time, and hours of assembly line operation to produce automobiles; farmers combine their labor with seed, soil, rain, fertilizer, and machinery to produce crops; and colleges combine professors' time with books and (perhaps) hours of student study to produce (perhaps) educated students. Because economists are interested in the choices that firms make to accomplish their goals, and because they wish to avoid many of the intricacies involved in actual production decisions, they have developed a rather abstract model of production. In this model the relationship between inputs and outputs is formalized by a **production function** of the form

$$Q = f(K, L, M \ldots), \quad [8.1]$$

where Q represents the output of a particular good[1] during a period, K represents the machine (that is, capital) use during the period, L represents hours of labor input, and M represents raw materials used. The form of the notation indicates the possibility of other variables affecting the production process. The production function, therefore, summarizes what the firm knows about mixing various inputs to yield output.

For example, this production function might represent a farmer's output of wheat during one year as being dependent on the quantity of machinery employed, the amount of labor used on the farm, the amount of land under cultivation, the amount of fertilizer and seeds used, and so forth. The function also shows that, say, 100 bushels of wheat could be produced in many different ways. The farmer could use a very labor-intensive technique that would require only a small amount of mechanical equipment (as tends to be the case in China). The 100 bushels could also be produced using large amounts of equipment and fertilizer with very little labor (as in the United States). A great deal of land might be used to produce the 100 bushels of wheat with less of the other inputs (as in Brazil or Australia); or relatively little land could be used with great amounts of labor, equipment, and fertilizer (as in British or Japanese agriculture). All of these combinations are represented by the general production function in Equation 8.1. For any possible combination of land, equipment, labor, and other inputs, the function records the maximum wheat output that can be produced from those given inputs. The important question about the production function from an economic point of view is how the firm chooses the individual levels of Q, K, L, and M. We take this question up in detail in the next several chapters.

A Simplification

We simplify the production function here by assuming that the firm's production depends on only two inputs: capital (K) and labor (L). Hence, our simplified production function is now

$$Q = f(K, L). \qquad [8.2]$$

Our decision to focus on capital and labor is arbitrary. Most of our analysis here will hold true for any two inputs that might be investigated. For example, if we wished to examine the effects of rainfall and fertilizer on crop production, we could use those two inputs in the production function while holding other inputs (quantity of land, hours of labor input, and so on) constant. In the production function that characterizes a school system, we could

[1]Sometimes the output for a firm is defined to include only its "value added"; that is, the value of intermediate inputs used by the firm is subtracted to arrive at a net value of output for the firm.

examine the relationship between the "output" of the system (say, academic achievement) and the inputs used to produce this output (such as teachers, buildings, and learning aids). The two general inputs of capital and labor are used here for convenience, and we will frequently show these inputs on a two-dimensional graph.

Marginal Physical Productivity

Marginal physical productivity
The additional output that can be produced by one more unit of a particular input while holding all other inputs constant.

A first question we might ask about the relationship between inputs and outputs is how much extra output can be produced by adding one more unit of an input to the production process. The **marginal physical productivity** of an input is defined as the quantity of extra output provided by employing one additional unit of that input while holding all other inputs constant. For our two principal inputs of capital and labor, the marginal physical product of labor (MP_L) is the extra output obtained by employing one more worker while holding the level of capital equipment constant. Similarly, the marginal physical productivity of capital (MP_K) is the extra output obtained by using one more machine while holding the number of workers constant.

As an application of these definitions, consider the case of a farmer hiring one more person to harvest a crop while holding all other inputs constant. The extra output produced by this person is the marginal physical productivity of labor input. The concept is measured in physical quantities such as bushels of wheat, crates of oranges, or heads of lettuce. We might, for example, observe that 25 workers on a farm are able to produce 10,000 bushels of wheat per year, whereas 26 workers (with the same land and equipment) can produce 10,200 bushels. The marginal physical product of the 26th worker is 200 bushels per year.

Diminishing Marginal Physical Productivity

We might expect the marginal physical productivity of an input to depend on how much of that input is used. Workers, for example, cannot be added indefinitely to the harvesting of a given field (while keeping the amount of equipment, fertilizer, and so forth fixed) without the marginal productivity eventually deteriorating. This possibility is illustrated in Figure 8.1. The relationship between the quantity of a particular input (labor) and total output is recorded in Panel a of Figure 8.1. At low levels of labor usage, output increases rapidly as additional labor is added. However, because *other inputs are held constant,* the ability of additional labor to generate additional output eventually begins to deteriorate. Finally, at L^{***} output reaches its maximum level. Any labor added beyond this point actually decreases output. Beyond L^{***} additional laborers get in each other's way to such an extent that total output begins to decline.

The total output curve in Panel a of Figure 8.1 shows graphically the assumption that labor's marginal physical productivity eventually declines as

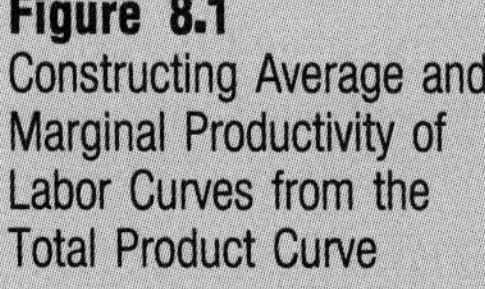

Figure 8.1
Constructing Average and Marginal Productivity of Labor Curves from the Total Product Curve

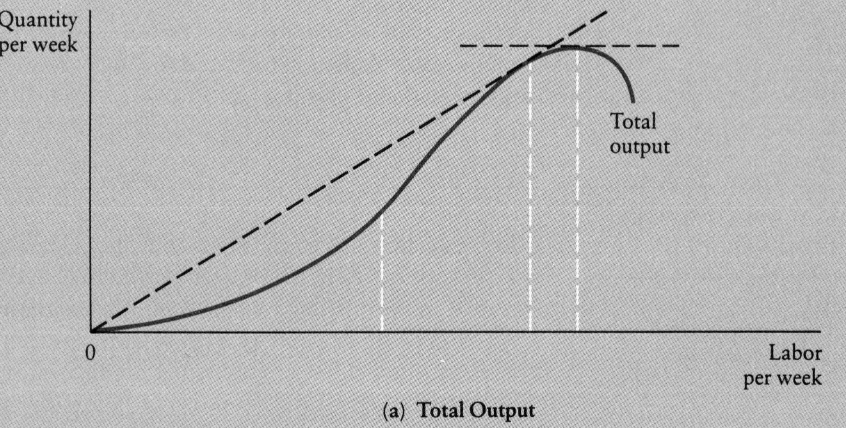

(a) **Total Output**

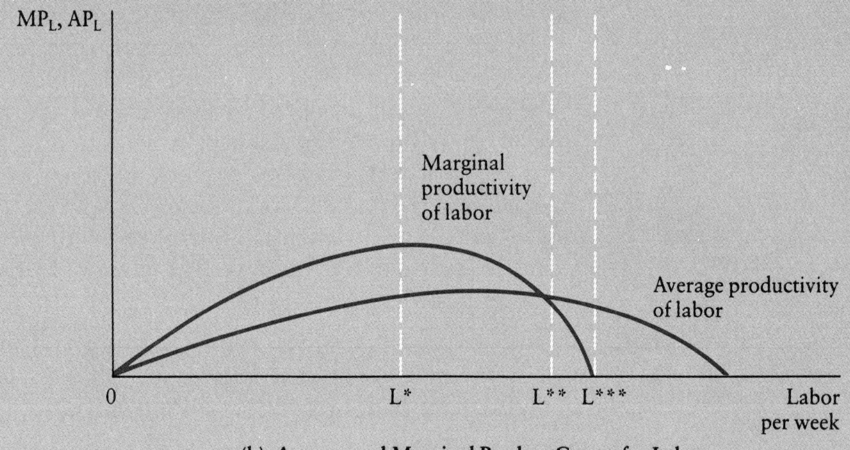

(b) **Average and Marginal Product Curves for Labor**

These curves show how the average and marginal productivity of labor curves can be derived from the total output curve. The total output (TP_L) curve in Panel a represents the relationship between labor input and output, on the assumption that all other inputs are held constant. In Panel b, the slope of this curve shows the marginal productivity of labor (MP_L), and the slope of a chord joining the origin to a point on the TP_L curve gives the average productivity of labor (AP_L).

more labor is added to the production process while other inputs are held constant. This assumption is extremely important in economic analysis. If a firm continues to add workers, it must eventually run into diminishing returns. The inputs that are being held fixed (such as machinery or land) will eventually become "overutilized," and a decline in marginal productivity will set in.

The nineteenth century philosopher Thomas Malthus used these ideas to argue that if additional labor is constantly added to a fixed supply of land, the productivity of labor in food production eventually must diminish.[2] Since the quantity of land is absolutely fixed in the long run, Malthus predicted that population growth would outpace the growth in food production (with not enough food for everyone). This led to economics being called the "dismal science." Most modern economists believe that Malthus did not adequately recognize the possibilities for added capital equipment and technical advances that would prevent the decline of labor's productivity in agriculture. Nevertheless, the basic observation that the marginal productivity of labor (or any other factor) declines when *all other inputs and technology* are held constant is still recognized as an empirically valid proposition.

Marginal Physical Productivity Curve

From the total labor productivity curve in Panel a of Figure 8.1, several other productivity curves can be constructed. The marginal physical product of labor is simply the slope of the total output curve, since this slope shows how output expands as additional labor is added. In Panel b in Figure 8.1, the marginal product curve (MP_L) is drawn. This curve reaches a maximum at L^* and declines as labor input is added beyond this point. This movement is a reflection of the assumption of a diminishing marginal product of labor. MP_L is equal to 0 at the point L^{***} at which total output reaches a maximum. Beyond L^{***} further additions of labor input actually reduce output. In other words, MP_L is negative in this range. Production will not take place beyond L^{***} since using more labor (which is presumably costly) will result in less output for the firm.

Average Physical Productivity

"Labor productivity" usually means average productivity. When it is said that a certain industry has experienced productivity increases, this is taken to mean that output per unit of labor input has increased. In Application 8.1: Average Productivity in Steel Production, for example, we use this measure to look at some issues involving the production of steel. Because average productivity is easily measured (say, as so many tons of steel per hour of labor input), it is often used as a measure of efficiency.

[2]A somewhat facetious "proof" of the diminishing marginal productivity of labor input argues that if it were not true, the entire world food supply could be grown in a single flowerpot if a sufficient quantity of labor were applied to the pot. Since this situation is obviously absurd, the marginal productivity of labor must diminish after some point.

APPLICATION 8.1

Average Productivity in Steel Production

Table 1 reports data on the average productivity of labor in steel production during a tumultuous period for the steel industry, 1970 through 1976. The data came from three producing areas: the United States, Japan, and the European Coal and Steel Community (ECSC). Entries in the table represent the output of steel (measured in metric tons) per 100 hours of labor input.

Cross-Country Comparisons

We can draw a number of interesting conclusions from the table. First, there is clear evidence of an upward trend in average productivity. Increasing amounts of capital used in steel production and improved steel-making technology (such as wider adoption of the basic oxygen process) probably accounted for this trend. During this period, labor productivity rose much more rapidly in Japan than in the United States or in the ECSC, and that development may also be related to Japan's more rapid adoption of new technologies.

One result of these trends was the emergence of Japan as the world's low-cost steel producer. Between 1967 and 1977, Japanese steel exports tripled, and this brought increased demands for protection by European and American producers. In response, both European and American governments instituted "fair" price standards with the intent of stemming Japanese imports.

Table 1

Average Physical Productivity in Steel Production, 1970–1976, in Metric Tons of Finished Steel per 100 Labor-Hours

Year	United States	Japan	European Coal and Steel Community
1970	7.4	5.7	5.2
1971	7.9	5.6	5.2
1972	8.2	6.4	5.8
1973	9.3	8.0	6.4
1974	9.4	8.1	6.9
1975	8.1	7.5	6.7
1976	8.6	8.1	6.5

Source: Calculated from Council on Wage and Price Stability, *Report to the President on Prices and Costs in the United States Steel Industry* (Washington, D.C., October 1977), Appendix Table No. 20.

Gradually these evolved into "Voluntary Restraint Agreements" with Japan and other low-cost producers that were intended to give European and U.S. producers some "breathing room" within which to adopt better methods of production. Although such restrictions continued to exist throughout the 1980s, it is unclear whether they succeeded in prompting producers to take adequate steps to raise productivity.

Productivity and the Business Cycle

A second fact illustrated by Table 1 concerns the behavior of labor productivity over the business cycle. Each of the producers saw its average productivity of labor in steel production fall during 1975—a year of worldwide recession. This pattern can better be explained as the reaction of steel firms to a downturn in demand than as a shift in the underlying productivity relationships. When orders for steel fall off (as they do in a recession), firms are reluctant to lay off workers immediately. Adopting a quick layoff policy would impose current costs on firms (such as having to make severance payments to laid-off workers) and might make it hard for the firms to hire their skilled workers back when demand conditions improve. Consequently, firms may "hoard" labor during temporary recessions (see Chapter 11). Since output (Q) falls and the work force (L) stays relatively constant, average productivity (Q/L) falls during such periods. In judging overall productivity trends in an industry (or in the entire economy), we must be careful not to put too much importance on short-term, cyclical movements.

To Think About

1. Some authors argue that Japan had an "advantage" in adopting new techniques for making steel because most of its older facilities were destroyed during World War II. Does this argument make sense? Are there reasons why a firm with older facilities might delay in scrapping them to adopt the best available technology?
2. How can labor productivity vary over the business cycle if the production function purports to show the relationship between inputs used and output obtained? Is the cyclical variation caused by changes in some other input? If so, which input?

Average productivity The ratio of total output produced to the quantity of a particular input employed.

It is a simple matter to derive average productivity relationships from the total product curve. This is also done in Figure 8.1. By definition the **average productivity** of any input (say, labor) is the ratio of total output produced to the quantity of the input employed. That is

$$\text{Average productivity of labor} = AP_L = Q/L. \quad [8.3]$$

Geometrically, the value of the average productivity of labor for any quantity of labor input is the slope of the chord drawn from the origin in Panel a in Figure 8.1 to the relevant point on the total output curve. This is true since the slope of such a chord is simply Q/L. By drawing a series of chords through the origin to various points on the total output curve, the average product of labor curve (AP_L) can be constructed. This curve is shown in Panel b in Figure 8.1. It can be seen that the average and marginal productivities of labor are equal at L**. For this level of labor input, the chord through the origin in Panel A in Figure 8.1 is just tangent to the total output curve. The average and marginal productivities of labor are equal.

Also at L** the average productivity of labor is at its maximum value. This feature of the curve can be demonstrated as follows: for levels of labor input less than L**, the marginal productivity of labor (MP_L) exceeds its average productivity (AP_L). Consequently, adding one more worker will raise the average production of all workers since the increased output from hiring this additional worker exceeds that produced by the average worker previously. A good example of this is a baseball team with a team batting average of .260. If the team acquires a .300 hitter, the team average will rise. For labor input greater than L**, the average productivity of labor falls. Beyond L**, labor's average productivity exceeds its marginal productivity, so AP_L is falling. Adding a worker to the production process causes output to rise by less than the average that previously prevailed. Consequently, the average productivity of labor will fall. In our baseball analogy, adding a .200 hitter to the team will indeed cause the team average to fall.

We have shown that to the left of L** the AP_L curve is rising; to the right of L** it is falling. Therefore, the average productivity of labor reaches its maximum value at L**. Labor added beyond this point will cause the average productivity of labor to fall.

Physical Productivity Curves and the *Ceteris Paribus* Assumption

Figure 8.1 records all the available information about the way in which varying labor input (or any other input) affects output. It is important to remember the assumption that lies behind the construction of these curves: all possible inputs, other than labor, are being held constant at some specified levels. The marginal productivity curve records the *ceteris paribus* productivity of additional units of labor input, and the average productivity curve similarly records the *ceteris paribus* average productivity of various levels of labor input. If the firm were to hire more of some other input (say, more ma-

Figure 8.2
Isoquant Map

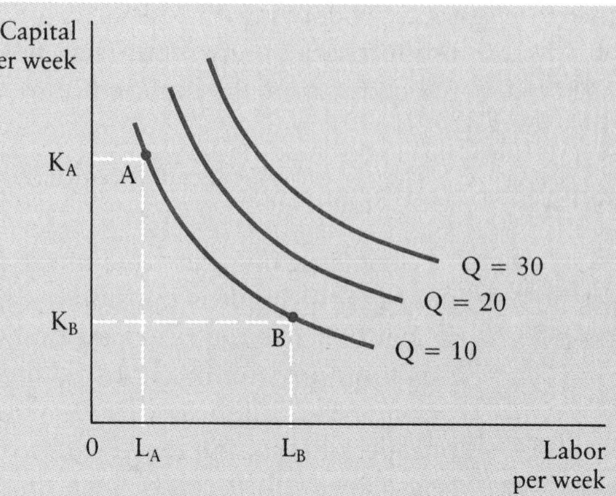

Isoquants record the alternative combinations of inputs that can be used to produce a given level of output. The slope of these curves shows the rate at which L can be substituted for K while keeping output constant. The negative of this slope is called the (marginal) rate of technical substitution (RTS). In the figure, the RTS is positive, and it is diminishing for increasing inputs of labor.

chines), all of the curves pictured in Figure 8.1 would move to new positions. For example, if a farmer were to double the land under cultivation and the use of machinery to work that land, we would expect both the marginal and the average productivity curves for labor to shift upward and to the right. With increased levels of complementary inputs, more labor can be used before diminishing returns begin to appear.

The *ceteris paribus* assumption limits the application of the curves in Figure 8.1 to real-world production processes. Most firms change the levels of both labor *and* machines in response to changes in economic circumstances. We will therefore never observe a neat tracing of a single total productivity of labor curve, but rather a series of Q, L points that lie on a number of different curves. Because of these differences, it may sometimes be difficult to interpret data on average productivity as Application 8.2: Sources of the Japanese Advantage in Automobile Production illustrates for the case of international comparisons of productivity in automobile production.

Isoquant Maps

Isoquant map
A contour map of a firm's production function.

One way to picture an entire production function in two dimensions is to look at its **isoquant map.** We can again use a production function of the form $Q = f(K, L)$, using capital and labor as convenient examples of any two inputs that might happen to be of interest. To show the various combinations of capital and labor that can be employed to produce a particular output

APPLICATION 8.2

Sources of the Japanese Advantage in Automobile Production

In 1979 Japan overtook the United States as the world's largest producer of automobiles. Imports of Japanese cars have topped 2 million per year since 1983. A glance at practically any parking lot in the United States will reveal numerous Japanese models. Driving one provides convincing evidence of their competitiveness with domestic brands.

By most estimates, the Japanese enjoy a considerable productivity advantage in making cars. In terms of average labor productivity, for example, it is estimated that it takes about 20 labor hours to produce a vehicle in Japan versus 25–30 hours in the United States. Similar differentials have been found for differences in total production costs.[1] Unlike the steel case (Application 8.1), however, it is not possible to trace these differentials to any specific differences in capital equipment. Automobiles are far more complex products than steel, and explanations for productivity differences are likely to be equally complex.

Differences in Production Methods

Still, some of the productivity differences between U.S. and Japanese producers may be related to differing production methods. Because most Japanese cars and pickup trucks are about the same size, many types of vehicles can be produced on the assembly line. U.S. producers tend to use many more assembly lines to accommodate their greater variability in vehicle size. Automating production (through the use of robots, for example) is therefore somewhat easier in Japan.

There are also differences in the way auto production is organized in the United States and Japan. Although firms in both countries tend to buy many components of cars from independent suppliers, in Japan the suppliers are better integrated with the assembly firms. Information and engineering staffs are more widely shared so that redesigning is needed less frequently. Higher levels of quality control are also made possible by this relationship.

Differences in Industrial Relations

In addition to these technical differences, some observers have also suggested that Japanese industrial relations practices may aid productivity. Because many Japanese workers effectively cannot be fired, usually belong to a company union, and obtain a large portion of their pay in year-end bonuses (see Application 11.2), they may feel a greater attachment to their firm than in the United States where relations between workers and employers are more adversarial. Some evidence that Japanese practices may make a difference is provided by the experiences of Japanese-run automobile plants (for example, the Toyota–General Motors plant in Fremont, California) in the United States. In these, labor productivity appears to be only slightly lower than for the same firms in Japan. There is no general agreement about the causes of such productivity differences, however.

To Think About

1. Why would auto producers in Japan and in the United States use different methods to make cars? Since no great secret is involved in auto production (U.S. and Japanese engineers visit each others' factories all the time), why wouldn't firms everywhere adopt the same production function?
2. If Japanese industrial relations practices really do make workers more productive, how would you represent this with a production function? Is "good labor relations" a separate input? If so, why don't all firms use some of it?

---

[1]For further discussion, see C. Winston and Associates, *Blind Intersection? Policy and the Automobile Industry* (Washington, D.C.: Brookings Institute, 1987) and H. C. Katz, T. A. Kochan, and J. H. Keefe, "Industrial Relations and Productivity in the U.S. Automobile Industry," *Brookings Paper in Economic Activity*, no. 3, (1987): 685–727.

Isoquant
A curve that shows the various combinations of inputs that will produce the same amount of output.

level, we use an **isoquant** (from the Greek *iso,* meaning equal). For example, all those combinations of K and L that fall on the curve labeled "Q = 10" in Figure 8.2 are capable of producing 10 units of output per period. This single isoquant records the many alternative ways of producing 10 units of output. One combination is represented by point A. A firm could use L_A and K_A to produce 10 units of output. Alternatively, the firm might prefer to use relatively less capital and more labor, and would therefore choose a point such as B. The isoquant clearly demonstrates that a firm can produce 10 units of output in many different ways just as the indifference curves in Part II showed that many different bundles of goods yield the same utility.

There are infinitely many isoquants in the K–L plane. Each isoquant represents a different level of output. The isoquants record successively higher levels of output as we move in a northeasterly direction since using more of each of the inputs will permit output to increase. Two other isoquants (for Q = 20 and Q = 30) are also shown in Figure 8.2. They record those combinations of inputs that can produce the specified level of output. You may notice the similarity between an isoquant map and the individual's indifference curve map discussed in Part 2. Both are "contour" maps. For isoquants, however, the labeling of the curves is measurable (an output of 10 units has a quantifiable meaning), and we are more interested in the shape of these curves than we were in the exact shape of indifference curves.

Rate of Technical Substitution

Marginal rate of technical substitution (RTS)
This shows the amount by which one input can be reduced while holding output constant when one more unit of another input is added. The negative of the slope of an isoquant.

The slope of an isoquant shows how one input can be traded for another while holding the output constant. Examining the slope gives some information about the technical possibilities for substituting labor for capital. Because of this, the slope of an isoquant (or, more properly, its negative) is called the **marginal rate of technical substitution (RTS)** of labor for capital. More precisely, the RTS is defined as the amount by which capital input can be reduced while holding quantity produced constant when one more unit of labor input is used. Mathematically,

$$\begin{aligned}\begin{array}{c}\text{Rate of technical substitution}\\ \text{(of labor for capital)}\end{array} &= \text{RTS} \quad \text{(of L for K)}\\ &= -(\text{Slope of isoquant})\\ &= -\frac{\text{Change in capital input}}{\begin{array}{c}\text{Change in labor input}\\ \text{(holding Q constant)}\end{array}}. \end{aligned} \qquad [8.4]$$

The particular value of this trade-off rate will depend not only on the level of output but also on the quantities of capital and labor being used. Its value depends on the point on the isoquant map at which the slope is to be measured. At a point such as A in Figure 8.2, relatively large amounts of capital can be given up if one or more units of labor are employed—at point A, the RTS is a high positive number. On the other hand, at point B the availability of an additional unit of labor does not permit a very large reduction in capital input, and the RTS is relatively small.

The RTS and Marginal Productivities

We can use the RTS concept to discuss the likely shape of a firm's isoquant map. Most obviously, it seems clear that the RTS should be positive; that is, each isoquant should have a negative slope. If the quantity of labor employed by the firm increases, the firm should be able to reduce capital input and still keep output constant. Since labor presumably has a positive marginal productivity, the firm should be able to get by with less capital input when more labor is used. If increasing labor actually required the firm to use more capital, it would imply that the marginal productivity of labor (or of capital[3]) is negative, and no firm would be willing to hire an input with a negative marginal physical productivity. All isoquants that are actually observed should therefore be negatively sloped, showing that there is a trade-off between capital and labor input use.

Diminishing RTS

The isoquants in Figure 8.2 are drawn not only with a negative slope (as they should be) but also as convex curves. Along any one of the curves the RTS is *diminishing*. For a high ratio of K to L, the RTS is a large positive number indicating that a great deal of capital can be given up if one more unit of labor is employed. On the other hand, when a lot of labor is already being used, the RTS is low, signifying that only a small amount of capital can be traded for an additional unit of labor if output is to be held constant. This shape seems intuitively reasonable: the more labor (relative to capital) that is used, the less labor can substitute for capital. The diminishing RTS shows that a particular input can be pushed too far. Firms will not want to use

[3]This result can be shown formally by recognizing that the RTS is equal to the ratio of the marginal productivity of labor to the marginal productivity of capital. That is,

$$\text{RTS (of L for K)} = MP_L/MP_K,$$

since this value of marginal productivities shows how L can be traded for K while holding Q constant. For example, if $MP_L = 2$ and $MP_K = 1$, the RTS will be 2, since the extra output produced by hiring one more unit of labor input can replace the production of two units of capital. Given this result, it is clear that if the RTS is negative (that is, if an isoquant has a positive slope), either MP_L or MP_K must be negative.

"only labor" or "only machines" to produce a given level of output.[4] They will choose a more balanced input mix that uses at least some of each input. In Chapter 9 we will see exactly how an optimal (that is, minimum cost) mix of inputs might be chosen.

Returns to Scale

Because production functions represent tangible, measurable productive processes, economists pay considerable attention to the form of these functions. The shape and properties of a firm's production function are important for a variety of reasons. Using such information, a firm may decide how its research funds might best be spent on developing technical improvements. Or, public policymakers might study the form of production functions to argue that laws prohibiting very large-scale firms would harm economic efficiency. In this section we develop some terminology to aid in examining such issues.

Adam Smith on Returns to Scale

Returns to scale
The rate at which output increases in response to proportional increases in all inputs.

The first important question we might ask about production functions is, how does the quantity of output respond to increases in all inputs together? For example, suppose all inputs were doubled. Would output also double, or is the relationship not quite so simple? Here we are asking about the **returns to scale** exhibited by a production function, a concept that has been of interest to economists ever since Adam Smith intensively studied (of all things) the production of pins in the eighteenth century. Smith identified two forces that come into play when all inputs are doubled (for a doubling of scale). First, a doubling of scale permits a greater "division of labor." Smith was intrigued by the skill of people who made only pin heads, or who sharpened pin shafts, or who stuck the two together. He suggested that efficiency might increase—production might more than double—as greater specialization of this type becomes possible.

Smith did not envision that these benefits to large-scale operations would always be available, however. He recognized that large firms may encounter inefficiencies in managerial direction and control if scale is dramatically increased. Coordination of production plans for more inputs may become more difficult when there are many layers of management and many specialized workers involved in the production process.

[4]An incorrect, but possibly instructive, argument (based on footnote 3 of this chapter) might proceed as follows. In moving along an isoquant, more labor and less capital are being used. Assuming that each factor exhibits a diminishing marginal productivity, it might be argued that MP_L would decrease (since the quantity of labor has increased) and that MP_K would increase (since the quantity of capital has decreased). Consequently, the RTS ($= MP_L/MP_K$) should decrease. The fallacy in this argument is that *both* factors are changing together. It is not possible to make such simple determinations about changes in marginal productivities when two inputs are changing, since the marginal productivity concept requires that all other inputs be held constant.

A Precise Definition

Which of these two effects of scale is more important is an empirical question. To investigate this question, economists need a precise definition of returns to scale. A production function is said to exhibit *constant returns to scale* if a doubling of all inputs results in a precise doubling of output. If a doubling of all inputs yields less than a doubling of output, the production function is said to exhibit *decreasing returns to scale.* If a doubling of all inputs results in more than a doubling of output, the production function exhibits *increasing returns to scale.*

Graphic Illustrations

These possibilities are illustrated in the three graphs of Figure 8.3. In each case production isoquants for Q = 10, 20, 30, and 40 are shown, together with a ray (labeled 0A) showing a uniform expansion of both capital and labor inputs. Panel a illustrates constant returns to scale. There, as both capital and labor inputs are successively increased from 1 to 2, then 2 to 3, and then 3 to 4, output expands proportionally. That is, output and inputs move in unison. In Panel b, by comparison, the isoquants get further apart as output expands. This is a case of decreasing returns to scale—an expansion in inputs does not result in a proportionate rise in output. For example, the doubling of both capital and labor inputs from 1 to 2 units is not sufficient to increase output from 10 to 20. That increase in output would require more than a doubling of inputs. Finally, Panel c illustrates increasing returns to scale. In this case the isoquants get closer together as input expands—a doubling of inputs is more than sufficient to double output. Large-scale operation would in this case appear to be quite efficient.

The types of scale economies experienced in the real world may, of course, be rather complex combinations of these simple examples. A production function may exhibit increasing returns to scale over some output ranges and decreasing returns to scale over other ranges. Or, some aspects of a good's production may illustrate scale economies, whereas other aspects may not. For example, the production of computer chips exhibits significant scale economies since the process of making chips can be highly automated. But the assembly of chips into electronic components is more difficult to automate and may exhibit few such scale economies. Application 8.3: Ocean Shipping illustrates similar complex possibilities for the case of oceangoing ships.

Input Substitution

Another important characteristic of a production function is how "easily" capital can be substituted for labor, or, more generally, how any one input can be substituted for another. This characteristic depends more on the shape

Figure 8.3
Isoquant Maps Showing Constant, Decreasing, and Increasing Returns to Scale

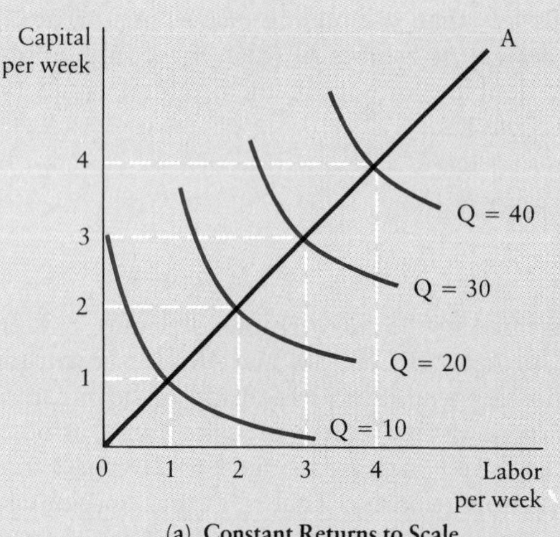

(a) Constant Returns to Scale

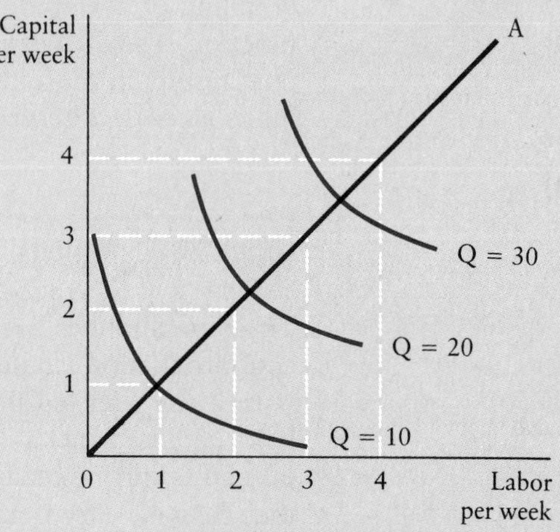

(b) Decreasing Returns to Scale

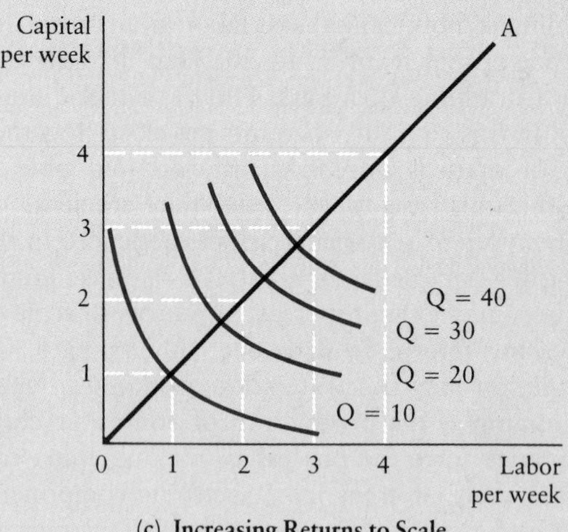

(c) Increasing Returns to Scale

In Panel a an expansion in both inputs leads to a similar, proportionate expansion in output. This is constant returns to scale. In Panel b an expansion in inputs yields a less than proportionate expansion in output, illustrating decreasing returns to scale. Panel c shows increasing returns to scale—output expands proportionately faster than inputs.

APPLICATION 8.3

Ocean Shipping

Oceangoing ships are a good illustration of the importance of the returns to scale concept for practical decision making as well as the complications that can arise when this concept is examined closely. We can see why ships might exhibit increasing returns to scale using a geometric example. Picture a ship as an empty cube. If the lengths of the four sides and top and bottom of the cube are doubled, its overall surface area will increase fourfold. The volume of the cube, on the other hand, will increase eightfold. A doubling of inputs (here the size of the ship's hull) will more than double its carrying capacity. Because other ship features such as power plants, staff, and control devices also probably exhibit increasing returns to scale, the cube analogy may not be very far from the truth.

Cargo Ships

A closer examination of specific types of ships reveals substantial problems with increases in size. Loading and unloading cargo from very large ships can be a difficult and costly process: larger cranes are needed, interior handling equipment must be used in the large holds, and goods must sometimes be moved substantial distances just to get them off the ship. The geometric allure of large ships must be tempered somewhat by the logistical problems of cargo handling.

In a 1978 study J. O. Jansson and D. Shneerson illustrated these considerations quite clearly.[1] They showed that a 50 percent increase in the carrying capacity of a cargo ship on average increases the ship's capital cost by only about 25 percent. Ships' operating costs are increased even less (for example, a ship needs only one captain, no matter how large the ship is). On the other hand, the authors found that a 50 percent increase in carrying capacity tends to increase capital costs associated with cargo handling by nearly 90 percent, with similar cost increases in the operating of the handling equipment. Shipping firms must make very careful calculations in deciding how to trade off these advantages and disadvantages of very large-sized vessels.

Bulk Carriers

Factors limiting the size of ships are somewhat less important for bulk carriers than for cargo ships. Vessels that carry crude oil or grain can usually be unloaded with high-speed pumps so cargo accessibility is not such a problem. Similarly, automation has made it possible for these carriers to be managed by crews as small as 12 to 15 persons, far fewer than are needed on most cargo ships. The geometric analogy promising economies of scale appears to play a major role in shippers' decisions about bulk carriers, and some as large as 500,000 tons have been built in recent years. About the only limits to further increases in size are those posed by engineering considerations related to hull strength and by the size of existing port facilities.

To Think About

1. Why might the optimal size of a ship change over time as economic conditions change? For example, what factors might have led oil companies to opt to start building very large crude oil carriers (VLCCs) in the early 1970s whereas before they had used smaller vessels?
2. How would some of the issues discussed in connection with economies of scale in ships apply to other methods of transportation such as railroads, trucking, or air cargo carriers? Can you think of examples where large-size carriers would be appropriate? How about applications where small sizes would be more efficient?

[1] J. O. Jansson and D. Shneerson, "Economies of Scale of General Cargo Ships," *Review of Economics and Statistics* (May 1978): 291–296.

of a single isoquant than on the whole isoquant map. So far we have assumed that a given output level can be produced with a variety of different input mixes—that is, we assumed firms could substitute labor for capital while keeping output constant. How easily that substitution can be accomplished may, of course, vary. In some cases the substitution can be made easily and quickly in response to changing economic circumstances. Mine owners found it relatively easy to automate in response to rising wages for miners, for example. In other cases firms may have little choice about the input combination they must use. Producers of operas have little chance to substitute capital (scenery) for labor (singers). Economists can measure this degree of substitution very technically, but for us to do so here would take us too far afield.[5] We can look at one special case in which input substitution is impossible, which will show us the kinds of problems in substitution that economists have noted.

Fixed-Proportions Production Function

Figure 8.4 demonstrates a case where no substitution is possible. This case is rather different from the ones we have looked at so far. Here the isoquants are L-shaped, indicating that machines and labor must be used in absolutely fixed proportions. Every machine has a fixed complement of workers that cannot be varied. For example, if K_1 machines are in use, L_1 workers are required to produce output level Q_1. Employing more workers than L_1 will not increase output with K_1 machines, since the Q_1 isoquant is horizontal beyond the point K_1, L_1. In other words, the marginal productivity of labor is zero beyond L_1. On the other hand, using fewer workers would result in excess machines. If only L_0 workers were hired, for instance, only Q_0 units could be produced, but these units could be produced with only K_0 machines. When L_0 workers are hired, there is an excess of machines of an amount given by $K_1 - K_0$.

Fixed-proportions production function
A production function in which the inputs must be used in a fixed ratio to one another.

The production function whose isoquant map is shown in Figure 8.4 is called a **fixed-proportions production function.** Both inputs will be fully employed only if a combination of K and L that lies along the ray 0A which passes through the vertices of the isoquants, is chosen. Otherwise one input will be excessive in the sense that it could be cut back without restricting output. If a firm with such a production function wishes to expand, it must increase all inputs simultaneously so that none of the inputs are excessive.

The fixed-proportions production function has a wide variety of applications to real-world production techniques. Many machines do require a fixed complement of workers; more than these would be excessive. For example,

[5]Formally, the ease of input substitution is measured by the *elasticity of substitution,* which is defined as the ratio of the percentage change in K/L to the percentage change in the RTS along an isoquant. See K. J. Arrow et al., "Capital-Labor Substitution and Economic Efficiency," *Review of Economics and Statistics* (August 1961): 225–250.

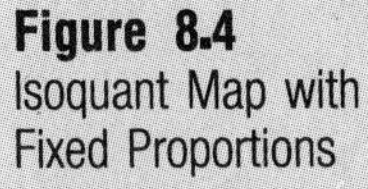

Figure 8.4
Isoquant Map with Fixed Proportions

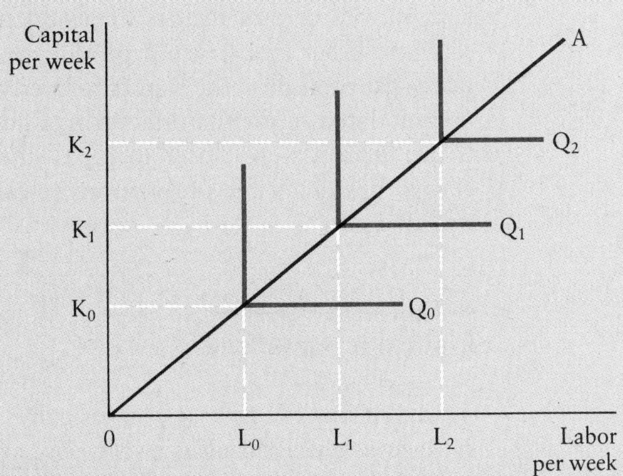

The isoquant map shown here has no substitution possibilities. Capital and labor must be used in fixed proportions if neither is to be redundant. For example, if K_1 machines are available, L_1 units of labor should be used. If L_2 units of labor are used, there will be excess labor since no more than Q_1 can be produced from the given machines. Alternatively, if L_0 laborers were hired, machines would be in excess to the extent $K_1 - K_0$.

consider the combination of capital and labor required to mow a lawn. The lawn mower needs one person for its operation, and a worker needs one lawn mower in order to produce any output. Output can be expanded (that is, more grass can be mowed at the same time) only by adding capital and labor to the productive process in fixed proportions. Many production functions may be of this type, and the fixed-proportions model is in many ways appropriate for production planning.[6]

The Relevance of Input Substitutability

The ease with which one input can be substituted for another is of considerable interest to economists. They can use the shape of an isoquant map to see the relative ease with which different industries can adapt to the changing availability of productive inputs. For example, over the past hundred years the output of the American economy has shifted markedly away from agri-

[6]The lawn mower example points up another possibility. Presumably there is some leeway in choosing what size and type of lawn mower to buy. Any device, from a pair of clippers to a gang mower, might be chosen. Prior to the actual purchase, the capital-labor ratio in lawn mowing can be considered variable. Once the mower is purchased, however, the capital-labor ratio becomes fixed.

cultural production and toward manufacturing and service industries. This shift moved certain factors of production, (notably labor) out of agriculture and into other industries. If production were relatively flexible in terms of input substitutability, the inputs formerly used in agriculture could be easily accommodated in the manufacturing and service industries. On the other hand, if production were closer to fixed proportions, the inputs might not be absorbed in exactly the proportions released by agriculture, and unemployment might result.

A Numerical Example

To make this example (unrealistically) simple, suppose that the capital-labor ratio in manufacturing is two to one; that is, it takes two machines to equip one worker. Suppose, on the other hand, that the capital-labor ratio in agriculture is one to one. If demand shifts so that agricultural production must be reduced and manufacturing output increased, problems will arise. The reduction in agricultural output will release capital and labor in the ratio of one to one. However, manufacturing can absorb capital and labor only in the ratio of two to one. It needs two machines from the agricultural sector in order to be able to employ one more worker. Half of the workers released by the agricultural sector will be unemployed. On the other hand, the released labor might easily have been absorbed if the capital-labor ratio in manufacturing could be changed. To assess the effects on inputs of a shift in demand, we need to know how flexible production techniques are.

Input Substitution in Less-Developed Countries

Some authors suggest that inflexibility in input substitution is a major concern for underdeveloped countries.[7] Since small, less-developed countries are subject to rather sudden changes in the demand for the products they export, and since these countries are experiencing a movement of their labor forces from rural to urban areas, this lack of flexibility can cause serious problems. For example, the substantial unemployment in the urban areas of many less-developed countries may be a direct result of an inability to substitute labor for capital in these countries' industries. Because less-developed countries often must use capital equipment produced in the industrialized countries, this equipment may not be suited for the abundant labor supplies they have. Application 8.4: Energy and Capital looks at the substitutability between two

[7]This problem was first explored in detail by R. S. Eckaus in "The Factor-Proportions Problem in Underdeveloped Areas," *American Economic Review* (September 1955): 539–565.

APPLICATION 8.4

Energy and Capital

One issue that has been of considerable recent interest to economists is the relationship between energy and capital in production. That interest was particularly sparked by the rapid increase in energy prices during the 1970s, which aroused concerns about firms' flexibility to respond to those increases. If energy and capital had a high degree of substitutability, firms could adapt rather quickly to rising energy prices by adopting more and better capital equipment that used less energy. On the other hand, if such substitutions were difficult, firms would have problems adapting to the increase in energy prices.

Energy-Capital Complementarity

Studies of the relationship between capital and energy inputs during the 1970s suggested a third and even more damaging possibility: capital and energy may be complements in production. Some authors suggested that more sophisticated capital equipment would need more energy to operate, and that the only way firms could cope with increases in energy prices was to cut back on both capital and energy. A 1975 study by E. R. Berndt and D. O. Wood indicated this possibility was indeed true for many industries, and several later investigations reached similar conclusions.[1] The commonsense idea that energy and capital equipment are used jointly in production seems to be supported by these studies.

As an example of complementarity between capital and energy, consider the case of jet aircraft. Rapid increases in the price of jet fuel during the late 1970s had a substantial influence on airlines' costs, making them think carefully about which planes to fly. Daily hours of use for fuel-inefficient versions of such planes as the 707, the DC8, and the DC9 were shortened or cancelled altogether. The airlines' use of capital was, at least over the short term, reduced significantly. Over the longer term, airlines have demanded more fuel-efficient planes such as the Boeing 757 and 767 models, and these have increasingly made earlier models obsolete.

Effects on Labor Productivity

The idea that capital and energy are complements may also help to explain the decline in labor productivity in the United States during the 1970s. Prior to 1973, average output per worker in the United States grew at about 2 to 2.5 percent per year. After 1973 (the year of the Arab oil embargo and the consequent rise in energy prices), productivity grew at less than 1 percent per year. A possible reason for this slower growth is that (as in the airline case) higher energy prices made use of some existing capital equipment uneconomical and also reduced the demand for new machinery. Both of these influences sharply reduced the amount of equipment that the typical employee had to work with, and thereby reduced his or her productivity. (Application 8.5 discusses some other reasons for this decline in productivity growth.)

To Think About

1. Can you think of recent technical improvements in which capital and energy seem to substitute for each other? How about innovations in which capital and energy use seem to go together? How would changing energy prices affect the desirability of these different types of innovations?
2. How would you judge whether two inputs are substitutes or complements in production? What would be the problems in trying to develop a definition similar to those for substitute and complementary goods introduced in Chapter 4?

---

[1]E. R. Berndt and D. O. Wood, "Technology, Prices, and the Derived Demand for Energy," *Review of Economics and Statistics* (August 1975): 259–268.

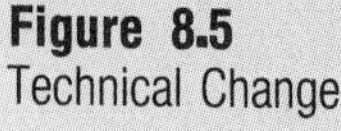

Figure 8.5
Technical Change

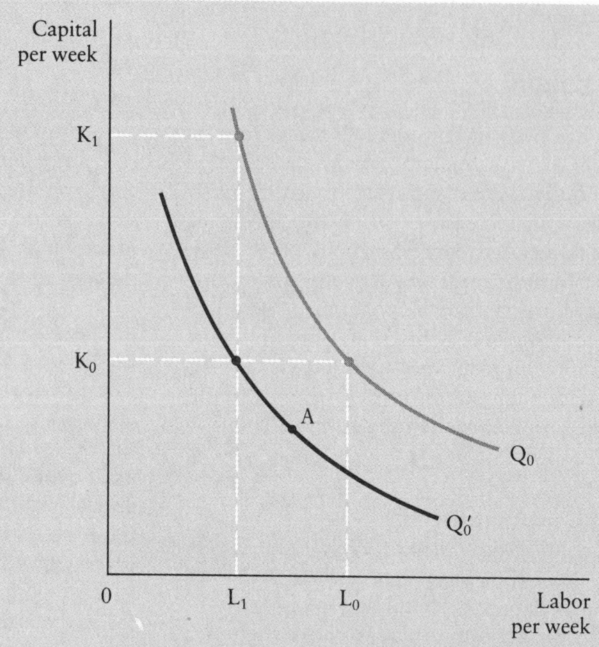

Technical progress shifts the Q_0 isoquant inward to Q_0'. Whereas previously it required K_0, L_0 to produce Q_0, now, with the same amount of capital, only L_1 units of labor are required. This result can be contrasted to capital-labor substitution in which the required labor input for Q_0 also declines to L_1 as more capital (K_1) is used.

important inputs and examines how that substitutability affected the performance in some sectors of the U.S. economy following the energy price shocks of the 1970s.

Changes in Technology

A production function reflects firms' technical knowledge about how to use inputs to produce outputs. When firms improve their production techniques, the production function changes. This kind of technical advancement occurs constantly as older, outmoded machines are replaced by more efficient ones that embody state-of-the-art techniques. Workers too are part of this technical progress as they become better educated and learn special skills for doing their jobs. Today, for example, steel is made far more efficiently than in the nineteenth century both because blast furnaces and rolling mills are better and because workers are better trained to use these facilities.

The production function concept and its related isoquant map are important tools for understanding the effect of technical change. Formally, technical progress represents a shift in the production function, such as that illustrated in Figure 8.5. In this figure the isoquant Q_0 summarizes the initial

APPLICATION 8.5

The Worldwide Productivity Decline

Since the early 1970s rates of productivity growth seem to have declined in most industrialized countries. One simple measure of this decline is provided by the data on growth rates in *per capita* GNP in Table 1. In all of the countries listed, growth rates during the 1973–1986 period were only about half what they were in the earlier period. More detailed studies of productivity growth reach a similar conclusion. In the United States, for example, growth in "total factor productivity" (a measure that controls for growth rates in all inputs, not just labor alone) averaged about 1.5 percent per year prior to 1973 and only about 0.5 percent after.

Explanations of the Decline

Many explanations have been made for the worldwide productivity decline depicted in Table 1. One author lists at least 10 proposed explanations.[1] These range from fairly straightforward suggestions about lagging research and development spending and possible declines in opportunities for major new technical advances to more conjectural possibilities such as the notion that workers "don't want to work hard any more."

Four specific explanations have particularly interested economists. First is the question of whether the high rates of inflation during the 1970s and early 1980s contributed to poor productivity by making it more difficult for business managers to plan their production activities. A second related explanation focuses on changing energy prices after 1973 and how they affected firms' use of capital (this explanation is discussed in Application 8.4). Third, a number of authors have pointed to increasing government regulation of the economy (particularly in the environmental and health areas) as a possible cause of lagging productivity growth. In this view, much investment currently produces output (e.g., clean air) that is not included in GNP statistics. Finally, some authors have suggested that the shift in output toward services in most industrialized economies may have caused productivity growth to decline since service jobs cannot easily be automated. Despite voluminous research, there is no general agreement about the importance of each of these explanations.

Table 1
Annual Growth Rates in per Capita GNP for Selected Countries (Percent)

	1955–1973	1973–1986
United States	2.0	1.3
Canada	3.0	2.0
France	4.6	1.9
Germany	4.2	2.0
Italy	4.9	2.0
Japan	8.8	3.1
United Kingdom	2.5	0.9

Source: International Financial Statistics (Washington, D.C.: International Monetary Fund, 1988).

Productivity Policy

Similarly, there is no agreement about what kinds of policies might reverse the productivity decline. In the United States, for example, much interest has focused on improving schools (George Bush billed himself as the "education president") and on encouraging investment in research. Whether such actions will have any important economic effect remains to be seen, however.

To Think About

1. Explain why figures for growth in "total factor productivity" are smaller than the figures for growth in labor productivity. Which of the measures do you think is more appropriate for judging improvements in technology? Which is better for judging how much workers should be paid?
2. How would you judge whether environmental and safety regulation played some role in the recent productivity decline? How would you evaluate the disadvantages of such a decline if it were possible to measure it? Shouldn't you include the benefits of the regulations (if any) in an overall assessment? How would you do that?

[1] M. N. Baily, "What Has Happened to Productivity Growth," *Science* (October 24, 1986): 443–451.

state of technical knowledge. That level of output can be produced using K_0, L_0, or any of a number of input combinations. With the discovery of new production techniques, the Q_0 isoquant shifts toward the origin—the same output level can now be produced using smaller quantities of inputs. If, for example, the Q_0 isoquant shifts inward to Q_0', it is now possible to produce Q_0 with the same amount of capital as before (K_0) but with much less labor (L_1). It is even possible to produce Q_0 using both less capital and less labor than previously by choosing a point such as A. **Technical progress** represents a real savings on inputs and (as we shall see in the next chapter) a reduction in the costs of production.

Technical progress
A shift in the production function that allows a given output level to be produced using less inputs.

Technical Progress versus Input Substitution

We can use Figure 8.5 to show an important distinction between true technical advancement and simple capital-labor substitution. With technical progress, the firm can continue to use K_0, but it produces Q_0 with less labor (L_1). The average productivity of labor rises from Q_0/L_0 to Q_0/L_1. Even in the absence of technical improvements the firm could increase the average productivity of labor by choosing to use K_1 units of capital. This substitution of capital for labor would also have caused the average productivity of labor to rise from Q_0/L_0 to Q_0/L_1. This rise would not mean any real improvement in the way goods are made, however. In studying productivity data, especially data on output per worker, we must be careful that the changes being observed represent technical improvements rather than capital-labor substitution. Application 8.5: The Worldwide Productivity Decline illustrates this distinction.

Summary

Chapter 8 shows how economists conceptualize the process of production. We introduced the concept of a production function, which records the relationship between input use and output, and we showed how this function can be illustrated with an isoquant map. Several features of the production function are explicitly discussed in the chapter:

- The marginal productivity of any input is the extra output that can be produced by adding one more unit of that input while holding all other inputs constant. The marginal productivity of an input declines as more of that input is used.
- The possible input combinations that a firm might use to produce a given level of output are shown on an isoquant. The slope of the isoquant is called the rate of technical substitution (RTS)—it shows how one input can be substituted for another while holding output constant.
- "Returns to scale" refers to the way in which a firm's output responds to proportionate increases in all inputs. If a doubling of all inputs

causes output to more than double, there are increasing returns to scale. If such a doubling of inputs causes output to less than double, returns to scale are decreasing. The middle case, when output exactly doubles, is constant returns to scale.

- In some cases it may not be possible for the firm to substitute one input for another. In these cases, the inputs must be used in fixed proportions. Such production functions will have L-shaped isoquants.
- Technical progress will shift the firm's entire isoquant map. A given output level can be produced with fewer inputs.

Review Questions

1. Provide a brief description of the production function for each of the following firms. What is the firm's output? What inputs does it use? Can you think of any special features of the way production takes place in the firm?

   a. An Iowa wheat farm
   b. An Arizona vegetable farm
   c. U.S. Steel Corporation
   d. A local arc welding firm
   e. Sears
   f. Joe's Hot Dog Stand
   g. The Metropolitan Opera
   h. The Metropolitan Museum of Art
   i. The National Institute of Health
   j. Dr. Smith's private practice
   k. Paul's lemonade stand.

2. Why are firms' isoquant maps and individuals' indifference curve maps basically the same idea? What are the most important ways in which these concepts differ?
3. On a firm's isoquant map, what is held constant along a single isoquant? What does the slope of an isoquant show? Why would you never expect a firm to operate in a region of its isoquant map where the slope of the isoquants is positive?
4. Much discussion of productivity focuses on "output per worker." Is this an average or a marginal productivity notion? Which of these concepts do you think is most relevant to a firm's hiring decisions?
5. Contrast the notions of diminishing marginal productivity and diminishing returns to scale. Why do economists believe production usually exhibits diminishing marginal productivity for inputs but not necessarily diminishing returns to scale? Could a production function exhibit diminishing marginal productivities for *every* input and still exhibit either constant or increasing returns to scale?
6. Answer question 5 for two specific production functions:

   a. A fixed-proportions production function;
   b. A Cobb-Douglas Production Function of the form

$$Q = \sqrt{K \cdot L}$$

(see problems 8.4, 8.7 and 8.8 for a discussion of this case).

7. "Most purported cases of diminishing returns to scale actually arise because one input is held constant. These therefore represent a misuse of the notion of returns to scale and should instead be viewed as an illustration of diminishing marginal productivities." Do you agree? Explain the theoretical notion of "returns to scale" and describe some of the problems in using the precise definition of the term in real-world situations.
8. Explain why a firm with a fixed-proportions production function would not be able to substitute one input for another while holding output constant. By analogy to consumer theory, what would an isoquant map that illustrated very easy substitution look like?
9. Could a fixed-proportions production function exhibit increasing or decreasing returns to scale? What would its isoquant map look like in these cases?
10. Explain why it is difficult to differentiate between technical progress and capital-labor substitution as a cause of changes in the average productivity of labor. How might a measure of "total factor productivity" ameliorate this problem?

Problems

8.1 Imagine that the production function for beer cans is given by

$$Q = 6K + 4L$$

where

Q = Output of beer cans per hour

K = Capital input per hour

L = Labor input per hour.

a. Assuming capital is fixed at $K = 6$, how much L is required to produce 60 beer cans per hour? To produce 100 per hour?
b. Now assume that capital input is fixed at $K = 8$; what L is required to produce 60 beer cans per hour? To produce 100 per hour?
c. Graph the $Q = 60$ and $Q = 100$ isoquants. Indicate the points found in parts a and b. What is the RTS along the isoquants?

8.2 Frisbees are produced according to the production function

$$Q = 2K + L$$

where

Q = Output of frisbees per hour

K = Capital input per hour

L = Labor input per hour.

a. If $K = 10$, how much L is needed to produce 100 frisbees per hour?
b. If $K = 25$, how much L is needed to produce 100 frisbees per hour?
c. Graph the $Q = 100$ isoquant. Indicate the points on that isoquant defined in parts a and b. What is the RTS along this isoquant? Explain why the RTS is the same at every point on the isoquant.
d. Graph the $Q = 50$ and $Q = 200$ isoquants for this production function also. Describe the shape of the entire isoquant map.

e. Suppose technical progress resulted in the production function for frisbees becoming

$$Q = 3K + 1.5L.$$

Answer parts a through d for this new production function and discuss how it compares to the previous case.

8.3 Digging clams by hand in Sunset Bay requires only labor input. The total number of clams obtained per hour (Q) is given by

$$Q = 100\sqrt{L}$$

where L is labor input per hour.

a. Graph the relationship between Q and L.
b. What is the average productivity of labor in Sunset Bay? Graph this relationship and show that AP_L diminishes for increases in labor input.
c. It can be shown that the marginal productivity of labor in Sunset Bay is given by

$$MP_L = 50/\sqrt{L}.$$

Graph this relationship and show that $MP_L < AP_L$ for all values of L. Explain why this is so.

*8.4 The production of barstools (Q) is characterized by a production function of the form

$$Q = K^{1/2} \cdot L^{1/2} = \sqrt{K \cdot L}.$$

a. What is the average productivity of labor and capital for barstool production (AP_L will depend on K, and AP_K will depend on L)?
b. Graph the AP_L curve for $K = 100$.
c. For this particular function it can be shown that $MP_L = 1/2\ AP_L$, and $MP_K = 1/2\ AP_K$. Using that information, add a graph of the MPL function to the graph calculated in part b (again for $K = 100$). What is unusual about this curve?
d. Sketch the $Q = 10$ isoquant for this production function.
e. Using the results from part c together with footnote 3 of this chapter, what is the RTS on the $Q = 10$ isoquant at the points: $K = L = 10$; $K = 25$, $L = 4$; and $K = 4$, $L = 25$? Does this function exhibit a diminishing RTS?

*8.5 Suppose the production function for widgets is given by

$$Q = KL - .8K^2 - .2L^2$$

where Q represents the annual quantity of widgets produced, K represents annual capital input, and L represents annual labor input.

a. Supposing $K = 10$, graph the total and average productivity of labor curves. At what level of labor input does this average productivity reach a maximum? How many widgets are produced at that point?
b. Again assuming that $K = 10$ and using the information that the MP_L curve is a straight line with an intercept of 10 (for $L = 0$), graph this curve. At what level of labor input does $MP_L = 0$?

---

*Denotes a problem that is rather difficult

c. Suppose capital inputs were increased to K = 20. How would your answers to parts a and b change?

8.6 Power Goat Lawn Company uses two sizes of mowers to cut lawns. The smaller mowers have a 24-inch blade and are used on lawns with many trees and obstacles. The larger mowers are exactly twice as big as the smaller mowers and are used on open lawns where maneuverability is not so difficult. The two production functions available to Power Goat are:

	Output per Hour (Square Feet)	Capital Input (No. of 24″ Mowers)	Labor Input
Large mowers	8,000	2	1
Small mowers	5,000	1	1

a. Graph the Q = 40,000 square feet isoquant for the first production function. How much K and L would be used if these factors were combined without waste?
b. Answer part a for the second function.
c. How much K and L would be used without waste if half of the 40,000 square foot lawn were cut by the method of the first production function and half by the method of the second? How much K and L would be used if three-fourths of the lawn were cut by the first method and one-fourth by the second? What does it mean to speak of fractions of K and L?
d. On the basis of your observations in part c, draw a Q = 40,000 isoquant for the combined production functions.

8.7 The production function

$$Q = K^a L^b$$

where $0 \leq a, b \leq 1$ is called a Cobb-Douglas production function. This function is widely used in economic research. Using the function, show that

a. The barstool production function in problem 8.4 is a special case of the Cobb-Douglas.
b. If $a + b = 1$, a doubling of K and L will double Q.
c. If $a + b < 1$, a doubling of K and L will less than double Q.
d. If $a + b > 1$, a doubling of K and L will more than double Q.
e. Using the results from parts b – d, what can you say about the returns to scale exhibited by the Cobb-Douglas function?

8.8 For the Cobb-Douglas production function in problem 8.7, it can be shown (using calculus) that

$$MP_K = aK^{a-1}L^b$$

$$MP_L = bK^a L^{b-1}$$

If the Cobb-Douglas exhibits constant returns to scale $(a + b = 1)$, show that

a. Both marginal prouctivities are diminishing;
b. The RTS for this function is given by

$$RTS = \frac{bK}{aL}$$

c. The function exhibits a diminishing RTS.

CHAPTER 9

Costs

Now that we have developed concepts to describe the technical aspects of production, we can calculate the costs associated with productive activities. This chapter answers two basic questions about costs. First, how should the firm choose its inputs to produce any given level of output as cheaply as possible? Second, how does this process of cost minimization differ between the short run when the firm has rather limited flexibility and the long run when responses can be much more flexible? We are still not considering the crucial issue of how a firm chooses the level of output it will supply. That topic will be studied in Chapter 10.

Basic Concepts of Costs

Opportunity cost
The cost of a good or service as measured by the alternative uses that are forgone by producing the good or service.

At least three different concepts of costs can be distinguished: opportunity cost, accounting cost, and economic cost. For economists the most general of these is **opportunity cost** (sometimes called *social cost*). Because resources are limited, any decision to produce more of one good means doing without some other good. When an automobile is produced, for example, an implicit decision has been made to do without 15 bicycles, say, that could have been produced using the labor, chrome, and glass that goes into the automobile. The opportunity cost of one automobile is 15 bicycles.

Since it is often inconvenient to express opportunity costs in terms of physical goods, we sometimes choose monetary units instead. The price of a car may often be a good reflection of the costs of the goods that were given up to produce it. We could then say the opportunity cost of an automobile is

$10,000 worth of other goods. This may not always be the case, however. If something were produced with resources that could not be usefully employed elsewhere, the true opportunity cost of this good's production would be close to 0, even though the resources may have been paid something.

Although the concept of opportunity cost is fundamental to all economic analysis, it may be too theoretical to be of practical use to firms. Our two other concepts of cost are directly related to the firm's choices. **Accounting cost** stresses out-of-pocket expenses, historical costs of machines and depreciation related to them, and other bookkeeping entries. **Economic cost** (which draws, in obvious ways, on the idea of opportunity cost), on the other hand, is defined as the payment required to keep a resource in its present employment, or the remuneration that the resource would receive in its next best alternative use.

Accounting cost
The concept that goods or services cost what was paid for them.

Economic cost
The cost concept that goods or services cost the amount required to keep them in their present use: the amount that they would be worth in their next best alternative use.

To look at how the economic definition of cost might be applied in practice and how it differs from accounting ideas, we now consider the economic costs of three specific inputs: labor, capital, and the services of entrepreneurs.

Labor Costs

Economists and accountants view labor costs in much the same way. To the accountant, expenditures on wages and salaries are current expenses and therefore are costs of production. Economists regard such payments as an *explicit cost:* labor services (worker-hours) are purchased at some hourly **wage rate** (which we will denote by w), and it is assumed that this rate is the amount that workers would earn in their next best alternative employment. If a firm hires a worker at, say, $10 per hour, we usually assume that this figure represents about what the worker could earn elsewhere.

Wage rate (w)
The cost of hiring one worker for one hour.

Capital Costs

In the case of capital services (machine-hours), accounting and economic definitions of costs differ greatly. Accountants, in calculating capital costs, use the historical price of a particular machine and apply some (more or less) arbitrary depreciation rule to determine how much of that machine's original price to charge to current costs. For example, a machine purchased for $1,000 and expected to last 10 years might be said to "cost" $100 per year, in the accountant's view. Economists, on the other hand, regard the historical price of a machine as a "sunk cost." They focus instead on the *implicit cost* of a machine as being what someone else would be willing to pay for its use. Thus, the cost of one machine hour is the **rental rate** for that machine in the best alternative use. By continuing to use the machine, the firm is implicitly forgoing the rental rate someone else would be willing to pay for its use. We will use v to denote this rental rate for one machine-hour. This is the rate that the firm must pay for the use of the machine for one hour regardless of

Rental rate (v)
The cost of hiring one machine for one hour.

whether the firm owns the machine (in which case it is an implicit cost) or rents the machine from someone else (in which case it is an explicit cost).

Entrepreneurial Costs

The owner of a firm is entitled to whatever is left from the firm's revenues after all costs have been paid. To an accountant all of this excess would be called "profits" (or "losses" if costs exceed revenues). Economists, however, ask whether owners (or "entrepreneurs") also encounter opportunity costs by being engaged in a particular business. If so, their entrepreneurial services should be considered an input to the firm, and some cost should be imputed to that input. For example, suppose a highly skilled computer programmer starts a software firm with the idea of keeping any (accounting) profits that might be generated. Then the programmer's time is clearly an input to the firm, and a cost should be imputed for it. Perhaps the wage that the programmer might command if he or she worked for someone else could be used for that purpose. Hence, some part of the accounting profits generated by the firm would be categorized as entrepreneurial costs by economists. Residual economic profits would be smaller than accounting profits. They might even be negative if the programmer's opportunity costs exceeded the accounting profits being earned by the business. Application 9.1: Economic Costs of Home Owning looks at these ideas as they relate to home ownership—a subject for which differences in economists' and accountants' cost definitions matter quite a lot.

Using Economic Costs

In this book, not surprisingly, we shall use economists' definition of cost for all inputs that the firm uses. Use of this definition is not meant to imply that accountants' concepts are irrelevant to economic behavior. Indeed, bookkeeping methods are integrally important to any manager's decision-making process because they can greatly affect the rate of taxation to be applied against profits. They also have the desirable property of being readily available sources of data. Since the "economic costs" of General Motors are seldom calculated, it is usually necessary to use some accounting concepts for empirical work. Economists' definitions, however, do have the desirable features of being broadly applicable to all firms and of forming a conceptually consistent system.[1]

[1]In fact, in recent years accountants have moved toward economists' definitions. For example, the conceptual model of economic costs has been applied to several topics in depreciation accounting.

APPLICATION 9.1

Economic Costs of Home Owning

To examine some differences between accounting and economic notions of cost, consider the following claim: "Rent is just money down a rat hole: it will never be seen again. The same money spent on mortgage payments will build an investment. Once your mortgage is paid off, housing costs will be much cheaper." Although this claim is frequently made by prudent parents to their spendthrift children, it is simply wrong. It confuses the notion of the out-of-pocket costs of home ownership with the true economic costs of that ownership. Once a mortgage is paid off, out-of-pocket expenses are reduced. But someone who has a substantial investment in a house incurs an opportunity cost in terms of the interest these funds could have earned on some other investment. Even though this opportunity cost is implicit rather than explicit, it will still influence home-owning behavior.

Table 1
Alternative Views of the Profitability of Owning Rental Housing

Accounting View		Economic View	
Rental income	$24,000	Rental Income	$24,000
Less:		Less:	
Costs (maintenance and depreciation)	15,000	Explicit costs (maintenance and depreciation)	15,000
Accounting profit	$ 9,000	Implicit costs (forgone interest)	16,000
		Loss before capital gain	−7,000
		Capital gain	10,000
		Economic profit	$ 3,000

Profitability Calculation

Consider the relationship between owning and renting homes in southern California in the late 1980s. At that time a $200,000 home could be rented for about $2,000 per month, or $24,000 per year. The owner of this home might have incurred maintenance, taxes, and other expenses of $15,000 per year, so in terms of explicit costs, renting to someone else looks like a profitable enterprise. From this accounting point of view, renting the home out provides a profit of $9,000 per year to the owner (see Table 1). But had the owner been able to invest the $200,000 value of the house at the prevailing bank interest rate of about 8 percent, this sum would have earned $16,000 per year in interest. This forgone interest is an opportunity cost of home owning. Economic profits are therefore −$7,000. From an economic perspective, renting a home to another person might more properly be viewed as a losing proposition for the owner. Indeed, since people who live in their own homes can be regarded as renting from themselves, such ownership appears to be more costly than renting.

Effects of Inflation

Why should property owners in southern California be willing to rent homes to someone else (or even to themselves) at a loss? The answer is that they expect the value of their homes to increase. Even a rather small annual rate of appreciation in house prices (say, 5 percent—much less than the 15-plus percent increase often encountered in rapidly growing areas) would have turned owning rental property into a profitable activity. The $10,000 capital gain on a house (5 percent of $200,000) would result in net economic profits of $3,000. Hence, owners are willing to rent "at a loss" in the belief that the returns on their housing investments will result in a true overall profit. People who live in their own homes expect similar gains. If such possibilities for gains were reduced, we would expect both explicit and implicit rents to more closely approximate economic costs.

To Think About

1. "Burning the mortgage papers" is a popular custom once the mortgage on a house has been paid off. Does paying off a mortgage have any economic significance? Should people try to get their mortgage paid off as quickly as possible? Is it better to live in a "debt-free" house?
2. Sometimes older people are said to be "house poor," meaning that too large a portion of their total assets is tied up in their house. What problems does being house poor pose for older people? Is there a cure for this problem?

Two Simplifying Assumptions

We will make two simplifying assumptions about the inputs a firm uses. First, we will assume, as before, that there are only two inputs: homogeneous labor (L, measured in labor-hours) and homogeneous capital (K, measured in machine-hours). Entrepreneurial services will be assumed to be included in capital input. That is, it will be assumed that the primary opportunity costs faced by a firm's owner are those associated with the capital the owner provides.

A second assumption will be that the inputs to the firm are hired in perfectly competitive markets. Firms can buy (or sell) all the labor or capital services they want at the prevailing rental rates (w and v). In graphic terms the supply curve for these resources that the firm faces is horizontal at the prevailing factor prices.

Economic Profits and Cost Minimization

Given these simplifying assumptions, total costs for the firm during a period can be represented by

$$\text{Total costs} = TC = wL + vK, \quad [9.1]$$

where, as before, L and K represent input usage during the period. Assuming the firm produces only one output, its total revenues are given by the price of its product (P) times its total output [$Q = f(K, L)$, where $f(K, L)$ is the firm's production function]. **Economic profits** (π) are then the difference between total revenues and total economic costs:

Economic profits
The difference between a firm's total revenues and its total economic costs.

$$\begin{aligned} \pi &= \text{Total revenues} - \text{Total costs} = PQ - wL - vK \\ &= Pf(K, L) - wL - vK. \end{aligned} \quad [9.2]$$

In general, then, Equation 9.2 shows that the economic profits obtained by a firm are simply a function of the amount of capital and labor employed. If, as we will assume in many places in this book, the firm seeks maximum profits, we might study its behavior by examining how it chooses K and L so as to do so. This would, in turn, lead to a theory of the "derived demand" for capital and labor inputs—a topic we take up explicitly in Chapter 18.

Here, however, we wish to develop a theory of costs that is somewhat more general and might apply to firms that are necessarily profit maximizers. Hence we begin our study of costs by finessing a discussion of output choice for the moment. That is, we assume that for some reason the firm has decided to produce a particular output level (say, Q_1). The firm's revenues are therefore fixed at PQ_1. Now we wish to examine how the firm might choose to produce Q_1 at minimal costs. The precise connection between such a cost-minimizing choice and the assumption of profit maximization will be illustrated in Chapter 10.

Cost-Minimizing Input Choice

In order to minimize the cost of producing Q_1, a firm should choose that point on the Q_1 isoquant for which the marginal rate of technical substitution (RTS) of L for K is equal to the ratio of the inputs' costs, w/v. It should operate where the rate at which K can be substituted for L in the productive process is equal to the rate at which they can be traded in the marketplace. To see why this is so intuitively, let's ask what would happen if a firm chose an input combination for which this was not true. Suppose the firm is producing output level Q_1 using $K = 10$, $L = 10$, and the RTS is 2 at this point. Assume also that $w = \$1$, $v = \$1$, and hence that $w/v = 1$, which is unequal to the RTS of 2. At this input combination the cost of producing Q_1 is \$20, which is not the minimal input cost. Q_1 can also be produced using $K = 8$ and $L = 11$; the firm can give up two units of K and keep output constant at Q_1 by adding one unit of L. At this input combination the cost of producing Q_1 is only \$19. A proof similar to this one can be demonstrated any time the RTS and the ratio of the input costs differ. Therefore, we have shown that to minimize total cost the firm should produce where the RTS is equal to the ratio of the prices of the two inputs.

Graphic Presentation

This cost-minimization principle is demonstrated graphically in Figure 9.1. The isoquant Q_1 shows all the combinations of K and L that are required to produce Q_1. We wish to find the least costly point on this isoquant. Using Equation 9.1 we can see that those combinations of K and L that keep total costs constant lie along a straight line with slope $-w/v$.[2] Consequently, all lines of equal total cost can be shown in Figure 9.1 as a series of parallel straight lines with slopes $-w/v$. Three lines of equal total cost are shown in Figure 9.1: $TC_1 < TC_2 < TC_3$. It is clear from the figure that the minimum total cost for producing Q_1 is given by TC_1 where the total cost curve is just tangent to the isoquant. The cost-minimizing input combination is L^*, K^*.

We have therefore shown that for a cost minimum the slope of the isoquant should equal $-w/v$. At that point of tangency the rate at which the

[2]For example, if $TC = \$100$, Equation 9.1 would read $100 = -wL + vK$. Solving for K gives $K = -w/vL + 100/v$. Hence, the slope of this total cost line is $-w/v$, and the intercept is $100/v$ (which is the amount of capital that can be purchased with \$100).

Figure 9.1
Minimizing the Costs of Producing Q_1

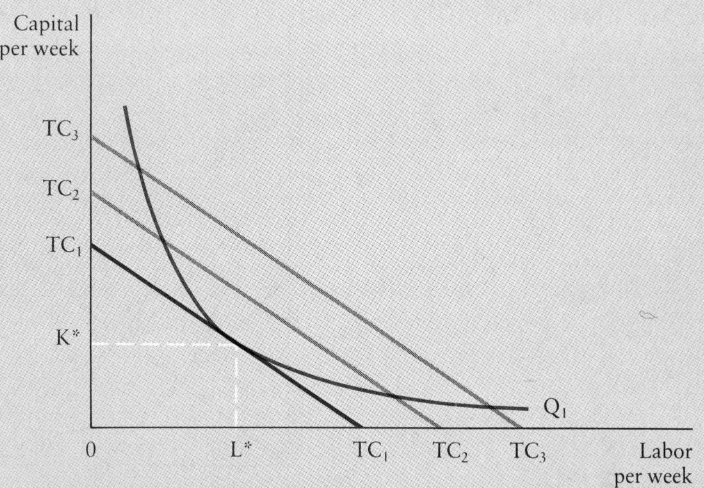

A firm is assumed to choose capital (K) and labor (L) to minimize total costs. The condition for this minimization is that the rate at which L can be substituted for K (while keeping $Q = Q_1$) should be equal to the rate at which these inputs can be traded in the market. In other words, the RTS (of L for K) should be set equal to the price ratio w/v. This tangency is shown here in that costs are minimized at TC_1 by choosing inputs K* and L*.

firm is technically able to trade L for K (the RTS) is equal to the rate at which the firm can trade L for K in the market.[3]

Derived Demand for Inputs

Figure 9.1 shows the formal similarity between the firm's cost-minimization problem and the individual's utility-maximization problem. In both cases we

[3]An alternative interpretation can be made using the result from note 3 of Chapter 8 that

$$\text{RTS (of L for K)} = \frac{MP_L}{MP_K}.$$

Hence, cost minimization requires

$$\text{RTS} = \frac{MP_L}{MP_K} = \frac{w}{v},$$

or, using the final two equations

$$\frac{MP_L}{w} = \frac{MP_K}{v}.$$

To minimize cost the firm should choose K and L so that the marginal productivity per dollar spent is the same for all inputs used. If the firm were to spend an extra dollar on inputs, it could get the same amount of extra output regardless of which input it hired.

Figure 9.2
Firm's Expansion Path

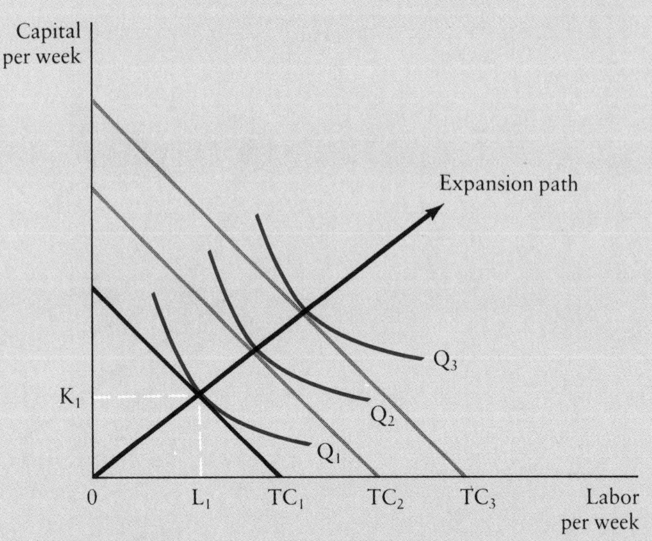

The firm's expansion path is the locus of cost-minimizing tangencies. On the assumption of fixed input prices, the curve shows how input use increases as output increases.

took prices as fixed and derived the tangency conditions. In Chapter 4 we analyzed how the utility-maximizing choice of goods would change if a price were to change and used this idea to construct the familiar downward-sloping demand curve. Can we do the same for the firm's demand for an input—could we change some input price (change the slope of the TC curves) and then trace out the effects of this price change on the quantity of the factor demanded?

The analogy to the individual's utility-maximization process can be misleading at this point. In order to analyze what happens to K^* as v changes, say, we also have to know what happens to output. The demand for K is a *derived demand* based on the demand for the firm's output. We cannot answer questions about K^* without looking at the market for the good being produced. This means that although the analogy to the theory of individual behavior is useful in pointing out basic similarities, it is not an exact analogy—the derivation of a firm's demand for an input is considerably more complex, and we will not discuss it in detail until Part 6.

The Firm's Expansion Path

We can perform an analysis such as the one we just performed for any level of output by a firm. For each Q we would find that input combination that minimizes the cost of producing Q. If input costs (w and v) remain constant for all amounts the firm chooses to use, we can easily trace out this locus of cost-minimizing choices, as shown in Figure 9.2. This ray records the cost-

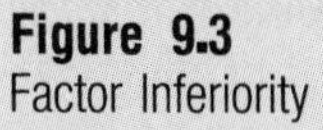

Figure 9.3
Factor Inferiority

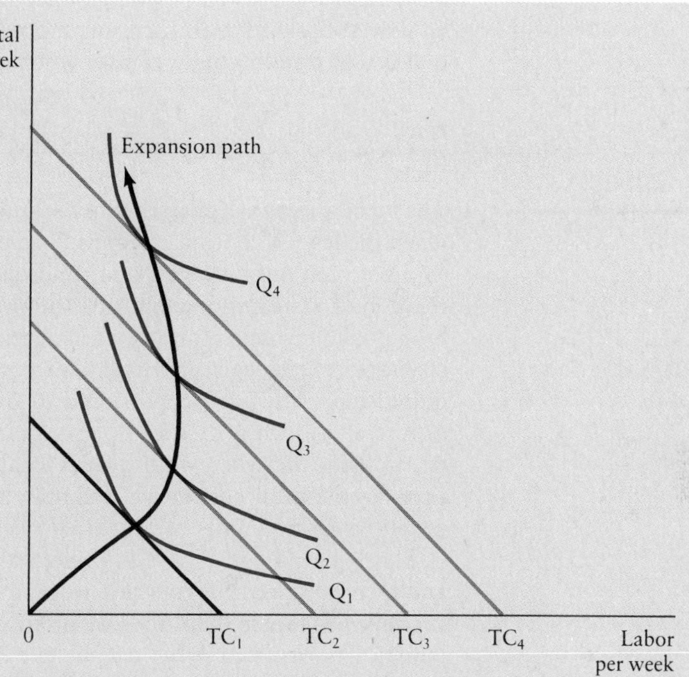

With this particular set of isoquants, labor is an inferior input since less L is chosen as output expands beyond Q_2. Such input inferiority is rare, however.

minimizing tangencies for successively higher levels of Q. For example, the minimum cost for producing output level Q_1 is given by TC_1, and inputs K_1 and L_1 are used. Other tangencies in the figure can be interpreted in a similar way. The locus of these tangencies is called the firm's **expansion path** because it records how input use expands as output expands while holding the prices of the inputs constant. As shown later in Figure 9.3, the expansion path need not necessarily be a straight line. The use of some inputs may increase faster than others as output expands. Which inputs expand more rapidly will depend on the shape of the production isoquants.

Expansion path
The locus of cost-minimizing input combinations a firm will choose to produce various levels of output (when the prices of inputs are held constant).

Inferior Inputs

It would seem reasonable to assume that the expansion path will be positively sloped—that successively higher output levels will require more of both inputs. This assumption may not always be true, however, as Figure 9.3 illustrates. Increases of output beyond Q_2 actually cause the quantity of labor used to decrease. In this range labor would be said to be an *inferior input*—less is used as output expands. Inferior inputs are a theoretical possibility that may occur even when isoquants have their usual convex shape. We will not be very concerned with them here, however. Instead, we will usually assume that use of both inputs increases when a firm expands its level of production.

Cost Curves

The firm's expansion path shows how minimum-cost input use increases when the level of output expands. The path allows us to develop the relationship between output levels and total input costs. Cost curves that reflect this relationship are fundamental to the theory of supply. Figure 9.4 illustrates four possible shapes for this cost relationship. Panel a reflects a situation of constant returns to scale. In this case, as Figure 9.3 showed, output and required input use are proportional to one another. A doubling of output requires a doubling of inputs. Assuming input prices do not change, the relationship between output and total input costs is also directly proportional—the total cost curve is simply a straight line that passes through the origin (since no inputs are required if $Q = 0$).[4]

Panels b and c in Figure 9.4 reflect the cases of decreasing returns to scale and increasing returns to scale, respectively. With decreasing returns to scale, successively larger quantities of inputs are required to increase output, and input costs rise rapidly as output expands. This possibility is shown by the convex total cost curve in Panel b. With increasing returns to scale, on the other hand, successive input requirements decline as output expands. In that case the total cost curve is concave, as shown in Panel c. In this case considerable cost advantages result from large-scale operations.

Finally, Panel d in Figure 9.4 demonstrates a situation in which the firm experiences ranges of both increasing and decreasing returns to scale. Such a situation might arise if the firm's production process required a certain "optimal" level of internal coordination and control by its managers. For low levels of output this control structure is underutilized, and expansion in output is easily accomplished. At these levels the firm would experience increasing returns to scale—the total cost curve is concave in its initial section. As output expands, however, the firm must add additional workers and capital equipment, which perhaps need entirely separate buildings or other production facilities. The coordination and control of this larger scale organization may be successively more difficult, and diminishing returns to scale may set in. The convex section of the total cost curve in Panel d reflects that possibility.

The four possibilities in Figure 9.4 illustrate most of the types of relationships between a firm's output and its input costs that arise from the desire to

---

[4]A technical property of constant returns to scale production functions is that the RTS depends only on the ratio of K to L, not on the scale of production. For given input prices, the expansion path is a straight line, and cost-minimizing inputs expand proportionally along with output. For an illustration, see the appendix to this chapter.

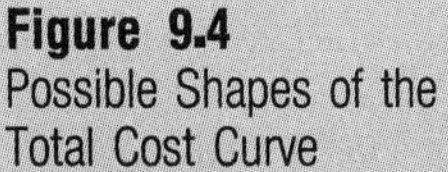

Figure 9.4
Possible Shapes of the Total Cost Curve

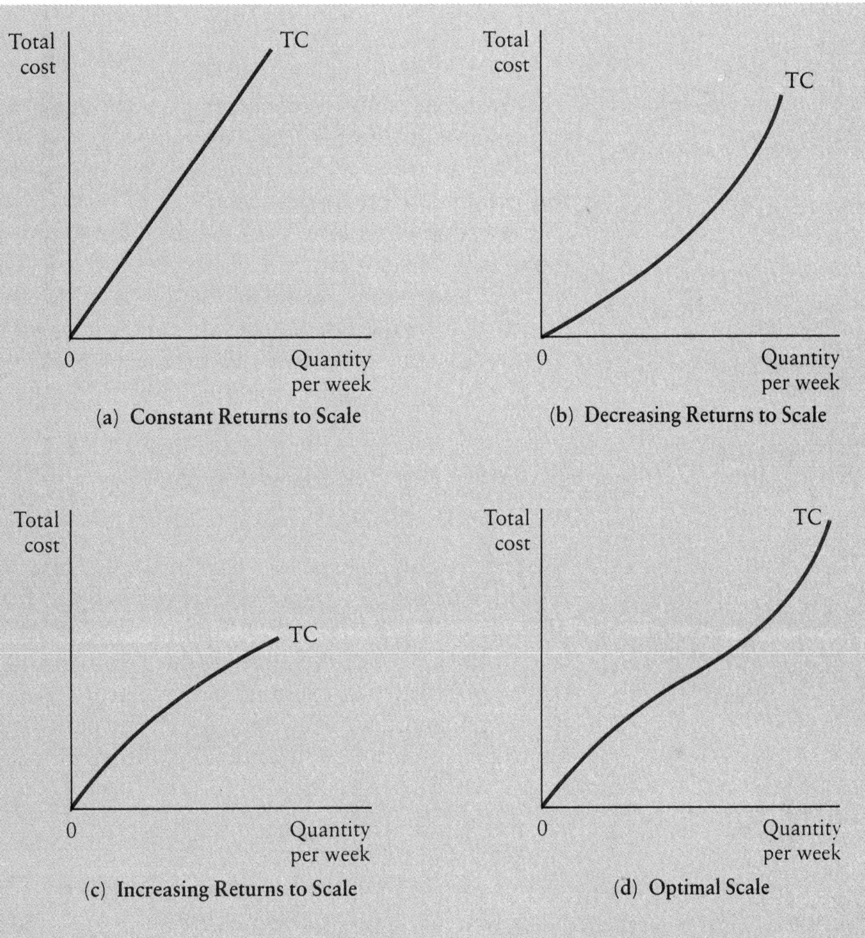

The shape of the total cost curve depends on the nature of the production function. Panel a represents constant returns to scale: as output expands, input costs expand proportionately. Panels b and c show decreasing returns to scale and increasing returns to scale, respectively. Panel d represents costs where the firm has an "optimal scale" of operations.

minimize costs. The cost information shown in Figure 9.4 can also be depicted on a per-unit-of-output basis. Although this depiction adds no new details to the information implicit in the total cost curves, it will be quite useful when we analyze the supply decision in Chapter 10.

Average and Marginal Costs

Average cost
Total costs divided by output: a common measure of cost per unit.

Two per-unit-of-output cost concepts are average and marginal costs. **Average cost** (AC) measures total costs per unit. Mathematically,

$$\text{Average cost} = \text{AC} = \frac{\text{TC}}{\text{Q}}. \quad [9.3]$$

This is the per-unit-of-cost concept with which people are most familiar. If, for example, a firm has total costs of $100 in producing 25 units of output, it is quite natural to consider the cost per unit to be $4. Equation 9.3 reflects this common averaging process.

For economists, however, average cost is not necessarily the most meaningful cost-per-unit figure. In Chapter 1, we introduced Marshall's analysis of demand and supply. In his model of price determination, Marshall focused on the cost of the last unit produced since it is that cost that influences the supply decision. To reflect this notion of incremental cost, economists have developed the concept of **marginal cost** (MC). By definition then,

Marginal cost
The additional cost of producing one more unit of output.

$$\text{Marginal cost} = \text{MC} = \frac{\text{Change in TC}}{\text{Change in Q}}. \quad [9.4]$$

That is, as output expands, total costs increase, and the marginal cost concept measures this increase only *at the margin*. For example, if producing 24 units costs the firm $98, but producing 25 units costs it $100, the marginal cost of the 25th unit is $2: to produce that unit the firm incurs an increase in cost of only $2. This example shows that the average cost of a good ($4) and its marginal cost ($2) may be quite different. This possibility has a number of important implications for pricing and overall resource allocation.

Marginal Cost Curves

Now that we have defined costs on a per-unit basis, we can show them graphically. Figure 9.5 compares average and marginal costs for the four total cost relationships shown in Figure 9.4. As our definition makes clear, marginal costs are reflected by the slope of the total cost curve since (as we discussed in Chapter 2) the slope of any curve shows how the variable on the vertical axis (here total cost) changes for a unit change in the variable on the horizontal axis (here quantity). In Panel a of Figure 9.4 the total cost curve is linear—it has the same slope throughout. In this case, marginal cost (MC) is constant. No matter how much is produced, it will always cost the same to produce *one more unit*. The horizontal MC curve in Panel a of Figure 9.5 reflects this fact.

In the case of a convex total cost curve (Panel b in Figures 9.4 and 9.5), marginal costs are increasing. The total cost curve becomes steeper as output expands, so at the margin, the cost of one more unit is becoming greater. The MC curve in Panel b in Figure 9.5 is positively sloped reflecting these increasing marginal costs.

For the case of a concave total cost curve (Panel c in Figures 9.4 and 9.5), this situation is reversed. Since the total cost curve becomes flatter as output

Figure 9.5
Average and Marginal Cost Curves

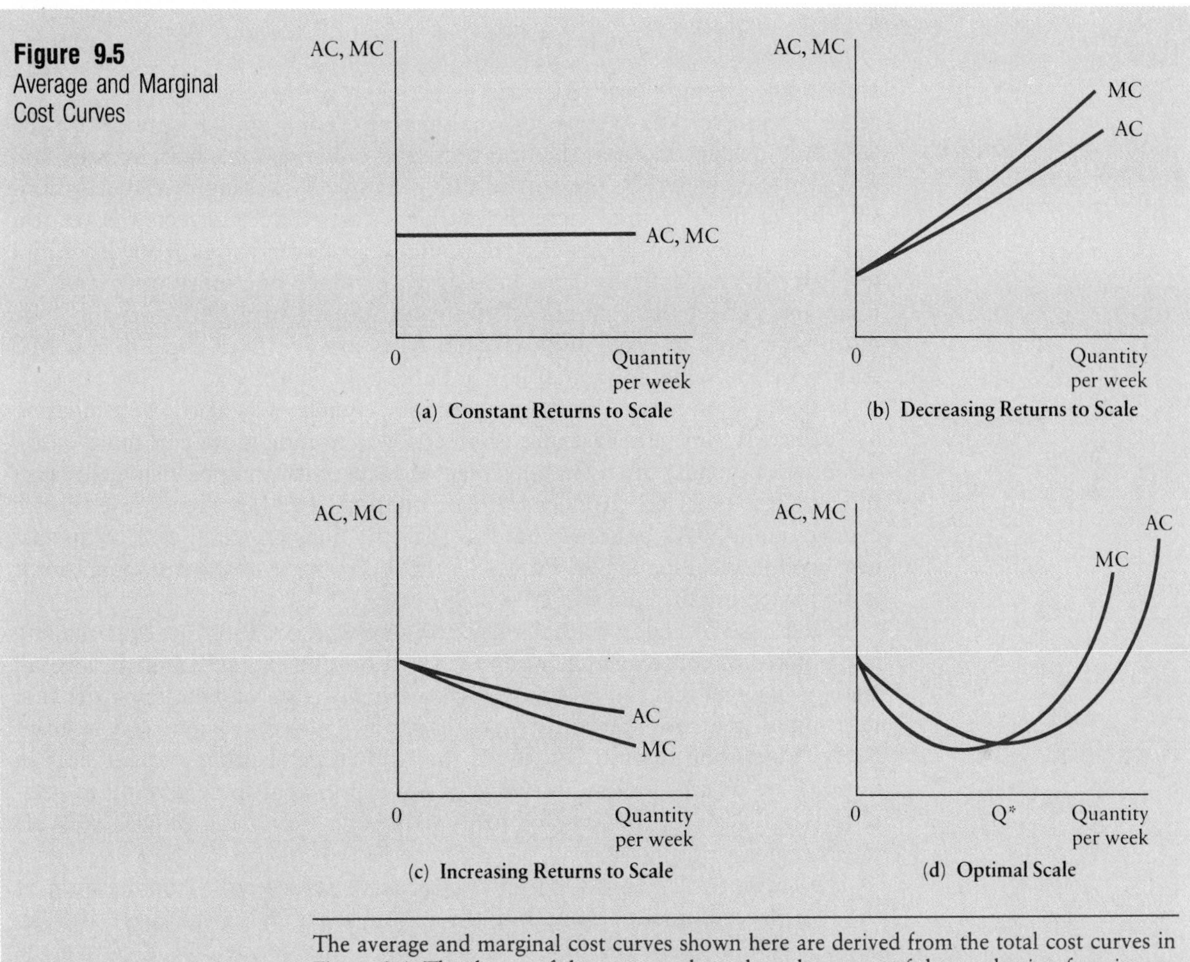

(a) Constant Returns to Scale

(b) Decreasing Returns to Scale

(c) Increasing Returns to Scale

(d) Optimal Scale

The average and marginal cost curves shown here are derived from the total cost curves in Figure 9.4. The shapes of these curves depend on the nature of the production function.

expands, marginal costs fall. The marginal cost curve in Panel c in Figure 9.5 has a negative slope.

Finally, the case of first concave, then convex total costs (Panel d in Figures 9.4 and 9.5) yields a U-shaped marginal cost curve. Initially marginal costs fall because the coordination and control mechanism of the firm is being utilized more efficiently. Diminishing returns eventually appear, however, and the marginal cost curve turns upward. The MC curve in Panel d in Figure 9.5 reflects the general idea that there is some optimal level of operation for the firm—if production is pushed too far, very high marginal costs will be the result. We will make this idea of optimal scale more precise as we study average costs.

Average Cost Curves

Developing average cost (AC) curves for each of the cases in Figure 9.5 is relatively simple. The average and marginal cost concepts are identical for the very first unit produced. If the firm produced only one unit, both average and marginal cost would be the cost of that one unit. Graphing the AC relationship begins at the point where the marginal cost curve intersects the vertical axis. For Panel a in Figure 9.5, marginal cost never varies from its initial level. It always costs the same amount to produce one more unit, and AC must also reflect this amount. If it always costs a firm $4 to produce one more unit, both average and marginal costs are $4. Both the AC and MC curves are the same horizontal line in Panel a in Figure 9.5.

In the case of convex total costs, rising marginal costs also result in rising average costs. Since the last unit produced is becoming more and more costly as output expands, the overall average of such costs must be rising. Because the first few units are produced at low marginal costs, however, the overall average will always be somewhat less than the high marginal cost of the last unit produced. In Panel b in Figure 9.5 the AC curve is upward sloping, but it is always below the MC curve.

In the case of concave total costs, the opposite situation prevails. Falling marginal costs cause average costs to fall as output expands, but the overall average also reflects the relatively high marginal costs of producing the first few units. As a consequence, the AC curve in Panel c in Figure 9.5 is negatively sloped and always lies above the MC curve. Falling average cost in this case is, as we shall see in Chapter 13, a principal force leading to relatively large-scale operations for firms with such increasing returns to scale technologies.

The case of a U-shaped marginal cost curve represents a combination of the two preceding situations. Initially falling marginal costs cause average costs to decline also. For low levels of output, the configuration of average and marginal cost curves in Panel d in Figure 9.5 resembles that in Panel c. Once the marginal costs turn up, however, the situation begins to change. As long as marginal cost is below average cost, average cost will continue to decline since the last good produced is still less expensive than the prior average. When MC < AC, producing one more unit pulls AC down. Once the rising segment of the marginal cost curve cuts the average cost curve from below, however, average costs begin to rise. Beyond point Q* in Panel d in Figure 9.5, MC exceeds AC. The situation now resembles that in Panel b and AC must rise.[5] Average costs are being pulled up by the high cost of producing one more unit. Since AC is falling to the left of Q* and rising to the right

[5]An analogy may help here. If, on your most recent quiz (that is, your "marginal" quiz) you received a lower grade than your previous average, that average must be falling. On the other hand, if your most recent quiz score exceeded your previous average, the average must be rising. When the marginal and average grades are identical, your average will not change.

of Q^*, average costs of production are lowest at Q^*. In a sense Q^* represents an "optimal scale" for a firm whose costs are represented in Panel d in Figure 9.5. Later chapters show that this output level plays an important role in the theory of price determination. Application 9.2: Findings on Long-Run Costs looks at how average cost curves can be used to determine which industries might find large-scale firms more appropriate. Application 9.3: A Detailed Look at Costs then looks more closely at the average costs of two particular industries and describes how these are affected by different methods of organization.

Distinction between the Short Run and the Long Run

Short run
The period of time in which a firm must consider some inputs absolutely fixed in making its decisions.

Long run
The period of time in which a firm may consider all of its inputs to be variable in making its decisions.

It has been traditional in economics to distinguish between the **short run** and the **long run** for firms. These terms denote the length of time over which a firm may make decisions. As we will see, this distinction is quite useful for studying market responses to changed conditions. For example, if only the short run is considered, the firm may need to treat some of its inputs as fixed, because it may be technically impossible to change those inputs on short notice. If a time interval of only one week is involved, the size of a firm's factory would have to be treated as absolutely fixed. Similarly, an entrepreneur who is committed to a particular business in the short run would find it impossible (or extremely costly) to change jobs—in the short run, the entrepreneur's input to the production process is essentially fixed. Over the long run, however, neither of those inputs needs to be considered fixed, since a firm's plant size can be altered and an entrepreneur can indeed quit the business.

Short-Run Production Function

Probably the easiest method to introduce the distinction between the short run and the long run into our analysis of a firm's costs is to assume that one of the inputs is held constant in the short run. Specifically, we will assume that capital input is held constant at a level of K_1 and that (in the short run) the firm is free to vary only its labor input. The short-run production function now can be written as

$$Q = f(K_1, L). \quad [9.5]$$

This notation explicitly shows that capital input may not vary. The firm still can change the level of Q only by altering its use of labor. We have already studied this possibility in Chapter 8, when we examined the marginal productivity of labor. Here we are interested in analyzing how changes in a firm's output level in the short run are related to changes in total costs. We can then contrast this relationship to the cost relationships studied earlier, in which both inputs could be changed.

APPLICATION 9.2

Findings on Long-Run Costs

Economists have investigated long-run cost curves for many industries. Most studies of long-run cost curves have found that average costs decrease up to some particular output level and then remain relatively constant. These average cost curves have a modified L-shape, such as that shown in Figure 1.

Some Evidence

Table 1 reports the results of representative studies of long-run average cost curves for six industries: aluminum smelting, banking, electric power, hospitals, life insurance, and trucking. Entries in the table represent the long-run average cost for a firm of a particular size (small, medium, or large) as a percentage of the minimal average cost firm in the industry. For example, the data for hospitals indicate that small hospitals have average costs that are about 29.6 percent greater than average costs for large ones. Hospitals, therefore, are one industry for which there do appear to be some cost advantages to larger scale operations.

Table 1
Long-Run Average Cost Estimates for Six Industries (Average Cost as a Percentage of Minimal Average Cost)

	Firm Size		
Industry	**Small**	**Medium**	**Large**
Aluminum smelting	166.6%	131.3%	100.0%
Commercial banking			
Demand deposits	116.1	104.7	100.0
Installment loans	102.4	101.5	100.0
Electric power generation	113.2	101.0	101.5
Hospitals	129.6	111.1	100.0
Life insurance (Canada)	113.6	104.5	100.0
Trucking	100.0	102.1	105.6

Sources: Aluminum: J. C. Clark and M. C. Fleming, "Advanced Materials and the Economy," *Scientific American* (October 1986): 51–56. Banking: F. W. Bell and N. B. Murphy, *Costs in Commercial Banking* (Boston: Federal Reserve Bank of Boston Research Report No. 41, 1968). Electric power: L. H. Christensen and W. H. Greene, "Economies of Scale in U.S. Power Generation," *Journal of Political Economy* (August 1976): 655–676. Hospitals: H. A. Cohen, "Hospital Cost Curves," in *Empirical Studies in Health Economics*, H. F. Klarman, ed. (Baltimore: Johns Hopkins Press, 1970), pp. 279–293. Life insurance: R. Geehan, "Returns to Scale in the Life Insurance Industry," *The Bell Journal of Economics* (Autumn 1977): 497–516. Trucking: R. Koenka, "Optimal Scale and the Size Distribution of American Trucking Firms," *Journal of Transport Economics and Policy* (January 1977): 54–67.

Figure 1
Long-Run Average Cost Curve Found in Many Empirical Studies

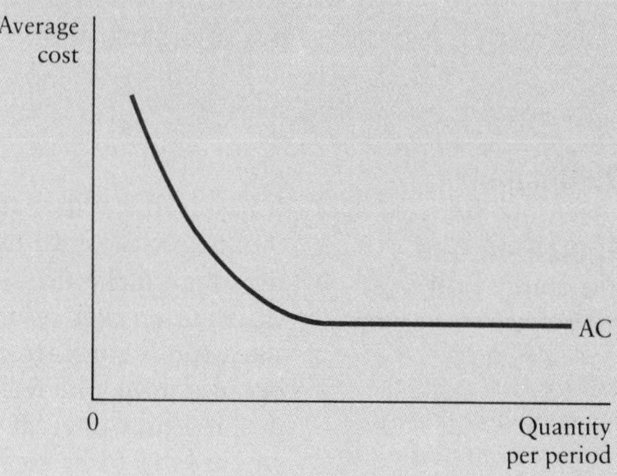

In most empirical studies the AC curve has been found to have this modified L-shape.

Most other industries seem to be similar to that illustrated in Figure 1. Average costs are lower for medium and large firms than for smaller ones; that is, there appears to be a "minimum efficient scale" (termed, appropriately, MES in the field of industrial organization). Except for aluminum, these advantages are not great, however. And for at least one case (trucking), smaller firms seem to operate with lower average costs.

To Think About

1. Many of the industries listed in Table 1 seem to exhibit modest cost economies of large-scale operation. For one of these, explain what you think the source of these economies is. Why don't you think this seems to apply to trucking?
2. The average cost estimates in Table 1 typically refer to costs for an entire firm. But, large firms may sometimes operate many individual plants. How might that possibility explain why Adam Smith's hypothesis of increasing average costs does not occur?

APPLICATION 9.3

A Detailed Look at Costs

Economists have examined the cost structures of some industries in considerable detail. Here we briefly review their findings for two industries: railroads and refuse collection.

Railroad Costs

An early but important study by George Borts looked at the long-run costs of 61 *class I* (large) American railway firms.[1] He found that railways in the West exhibited slightly decreasing long-run average costs, but those in the East exhibited increasing average costs. Borts attributed this difference to the higher traffic density of the Eastern railroads, which led to higher costs of switching and yard operations.

More recently, possible "excess capacity" of some railroads has been examined. Because government agencies require railroads to retain little-used lines, they may not be minimizing long-run average costs—these railroads may be operating with too much capital, given prevailing output levels. T. E. Keeler estimated a series of short-run cost curves for American railroads and used those cost curves to calculate a long-run cost curve.[2] He concluded that railroads possess an enormous amount of excess capacity (over 200,000 miles of track) and that a more appropriately sized rail network might save over $2.5 billion in annual operating costs.

If railroads were allowed to abandon the excess track and if smaller lines were allowed to merge, average costs might fall not only because of reduced capital costs but also because the remaining, larger railroads would exhibit some economies of scale. A 1981 paper found that the increase in haul lengths made possible by rail mergers in the 1960s and early 1970s provided substantial cost savings.[3]

[1]G. Borts, "The Estimation of Rail Cost Functions," *Econometrica* (January 1960): 108–131.

[2]T. E Keeler, "Railroad Costs, Returns to Scale and Excess Capacity," *Review of Economics and Statistics* (May 1974): 201–209.

[3]D. W. Caves, L. R. Christensen, and J. A. Swanson, "Productivity Growth, Scale Economies and Capacity Utilization in U.S. Railroads, 1955–74," *American Economic Review* (December 1981): 994–1002.

Refuse Collection Costs

Refuse collection is a major municipal service carried out by both private and public enterprises. The question of scale economies plays an important role in deciding exactly how this service should be organized to achieve minimal costs. Two types of scale economies might be distinguished. First, operating a large number of trucks may provide some reductions in average costs if it would reduce costs of maintenance facilities and allow purchasing of specialized equipment. A number of studies have found that these scale economies are relatively insignificant, however.

A second, more important source of economies in refuse collection stems from customer density. As density increases, multiple pickups from a single stop become possible, and collection times (and costs) fall dramatically. One study finds that each 10 percent increase in density of collection tonnage results in a 5 percent reduction in costs.[4]

These research findings on refuse collection costs have two implications for how the service might be organized. First, the absence of scale economies provides little support for the notion that collection should be done on a citywide basis. Contracting with several different firms instead would not result in increased costs. Second, offering exclusive contracts to service entire areas because of density economies (rather than permitting a totally free market with overlapping collection routes) should minimize overall average costs of refuse collection.

To Think About

1. How would you interpret the notion that railroads (or any other industry) have "excess capacity"? What would the average and marginal cost curves for such a railroad look like?
2. How is trash collected in your town? If it is done by the government, do there seem to be any cost advantages in doing so? If by private firms, do they have overlapping routes despite the obvious inefficiencies involved?

[4]Peter Kemper and J. M. Quigley, *The Economics of Refuse Collection* (Cambridge, Mass.: Ballinger Publishing Company, 1976), p. 53.

A Note on Input Flexibility

Any firm obviously uses far more than two inputs in its production process. The level of some of these inputs may be changed on rather short notice. Firms may ask workers to work overtime, hire part-time replacements from an employment agency, or rent equipment (such as power tools or automobiles) from some other firm. Other types of inputs may take somewhat longer to be adjusted; for example, to hire new, full-time workers is a relatively time-consuming (and costly) process, and ordering new machines designed to unique specifications may involve a considerable time lag. At the most lengthy extreme, entirely new factories can be built, new managers may be recruited and trained, and new raw material supplies can be developed. It would be impossible to cover all such variations of input types in any detail. Our analysis continues using only our two-input model holding the level of capital input fixed. This treatment should not be taken to imply that labor is a more flexible input than capital. We are considering only the distinction between fixed and variable inputs, and this approach enables us to do so. You could substitute any other inputs for capital and labor in the discussion that follows.

Short-Run Total Costs

Total cost for the firm continues to be given by

$$TC = vK + wL \qquad [9.6]$$

for our short-run analysis, but now capital input is fixed at K_1. To denote this fact, we will write

$$STC(K_1) = vK_1 + wL. \qquad [9.7]$$

Fixed costs
Costs associated with inputs that are fixed in the short run.

Variable costs
Costs associated with inputs that can be varied in the short run.

The addition of the S to our notation makes it clear that we are analyzing short-run costs, and the notation also records the level of capital that is being held constant. The two types of input costs in Equation 9.7 are given special names. The term vK_1 is referred to as (short-run) **fixed costs;** since K_1 is constant, these costs will not change in the short run. If the firm has 20 machines each of which rents for \$500 per week, short-run fixed costs are \$10,000 per week and cannot be varied. The term wL is referred to as (short-run) **variable costs,** since labor input can indeed be varied in the short run. Using the terms $SFC(K_1)$ for short-run fixed costs and $SVC(K_1)$ for short-run variable costs, we have

$$\begin{aligned} SFC(K_1) &= vK_1 \\ SVC(K_1) &= wL \end{aligned} \qquad [9.8]$$

Figure 9.6
Fixed and Variable Costs in the Short Run

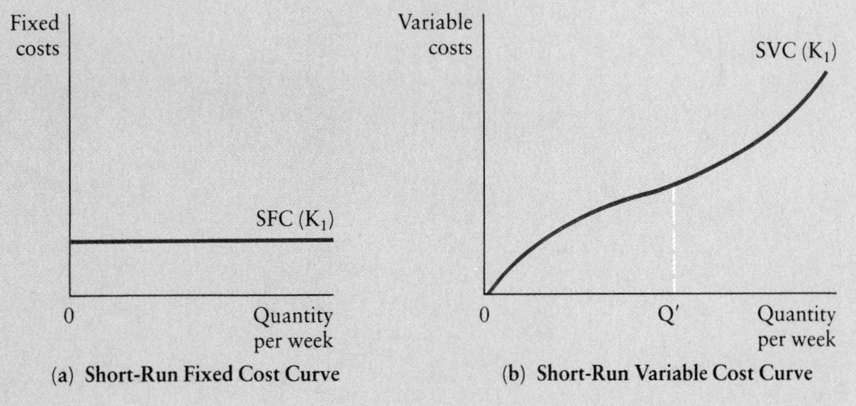

(a) Short-Run Fixed Cost Curve

(b) Short-Run Variable Cost Curve

The curve SFC(K_1) in Panel a shows that fixed costs do not vary in the short run. They are determined by the fixed input of capital (here K_1) being used. Variable costs do change as the output increases. The shape shown in Panel b assumes that initially labor exhibits an increasing marginal productivity but that, after some point, the marginal productivity of labor diminishes, causing short-run costs to rise rapidly.

and therefore

$$STC(K_1) = SFC(K_1) + SVC(K_1). \quad [9.9]$$

Short-run total costs are now classified as being either fixed or variable. How do these short-run costs change as the firm's output changes?

Short-Run Fixed and Variable Cost Curves

In the short run, fixed costs are obviously fixed. They do not change as the level of output changes. This relationship is shown in Panel a in Figure 9.6. The SFC(K_1) curve is a horizontal line representing the cost of the fixed amount of capital being employed.

Panel b in Figure 9.6 records one possible relationship between short-run variable costs and output. Initially the marginal productivity of labor is assumed to rise as labor is added to the production process. The fixed input of capital is initially "underutilized," and labor's marginal productivity rises as the amount of labor available to work with this fixed amount of capital increases. Because the marginal product of labor is increasing, short-run variable costs rise less rapidly than output expands—in its initial section, the SVC(K_1) curve is concave. Beyond some output level, say, Q', however, the marginal product of labor will begin to decline. Because capital input is constant at K_1, the ability of labor to generate extra output will diminish; since the per-unit cost of labor is assumed to be constant, costs of production will

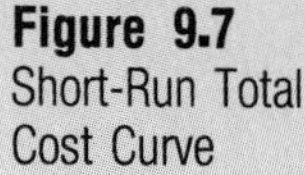

Figure 9.7
Short-Run Total Cost Curve

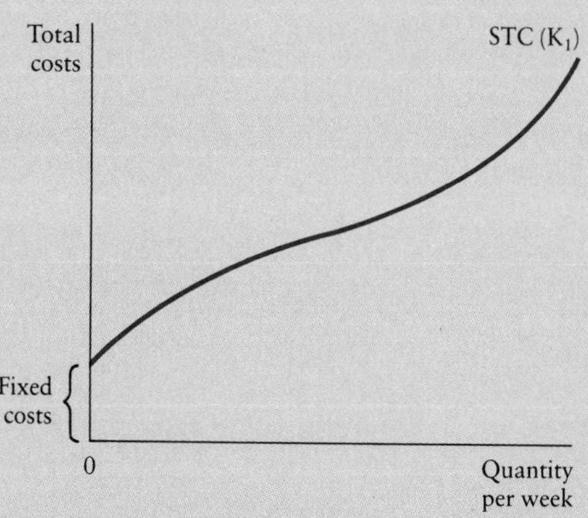

This curve summarizes the two curves shown in Figure 9.6. Short-run fixed costs determine the zero-output intercept for the curve, whereas the short-run variable cost curve determines the short-run total cost curve's shape.

begin to rise rapidly. Beyond Q′ the SVC(K_1) curve becomes convex to reflect this diminishing marginal productivity of labor. For output levels to the right of Q′, existing capital inputs are now being "overutilized." The shape of the SVC(K_1) curve in Panel b in Figure 9.6 is in general agreement with our hypotheses about the marginal productivity of labor in Figure 8.1. It is also quite similar to the case of U-shaped (long-run) marginal costs we discussed in the previous section.

Short-Run Total Cost Curve

We can now construct the short-run total cost curve by summing the two cost components in Figure 9.6. This total cost curve is shown in Figure 9.7, which has two important features. First, when output is 0, total costs are given by fixed costs, SFC(K_1). Since capital input is fixed, it must be paid its rental rate even if no production takes place. The firm cannot avoid these fixed costs in the short run. Contrary to the long-run case, therefore, the STC curve does not pass through the origin. The firm can, of course, avoid all variable costs simply by hiring no labor. A second important feature of Figure 9.7 is that the shape of the curve is determined solely by the shape of the short-run variable cost curve. The way that changes in output affect costs determines the shape of the curve. Since fixed costs are constant, they play no role in determining the shape of the STC(K_1) curve other than determining its zero-output intercept.

Figure 9.8
"Nonoptimal" Input Choices Must Be Made in the Short Run

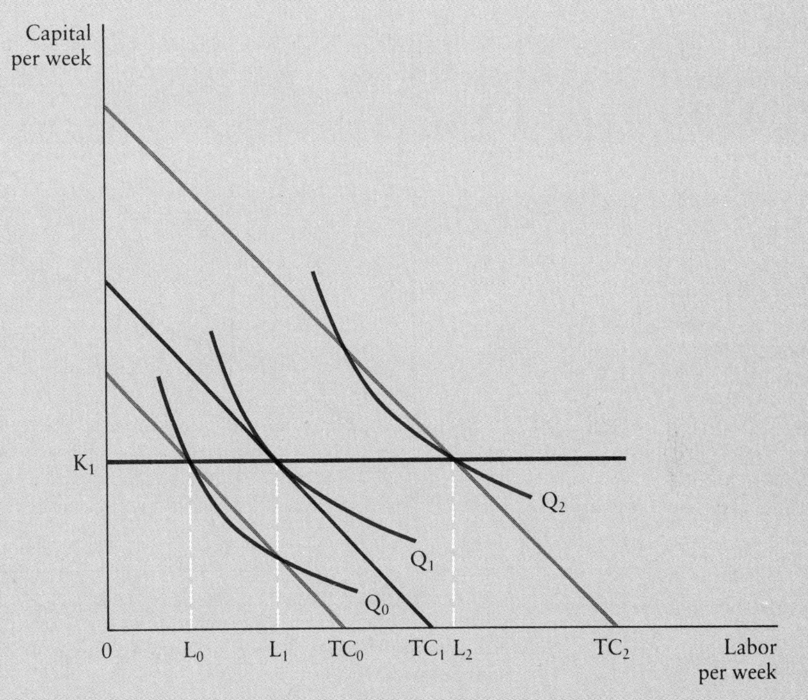

Because capital input is fixed at K_1 in the short run, the firm cannot bring its RTS into equality with the ratio of input prices. Given the input prices, Q_0 should be produced with more labor and less capital than it will be in the short run, whereas Q_2 should be produced with more capital and less labor than it will be.

Input Inflexibility and Cost Minimization

The total costs shown in Figure 9.7 are not the minimal costs for producing the various output levels shown. Because we are holding capital fixed in the short run, the firm does not have the flexibility in input choice that was assumed when we discussed cost minimization and the related long-run cost curves earlier in this chapter. Rather, to vary its output level in the short run, the firm will be forced to use "nonoptimal" input combinations: the RTS will not be equal to the ratio of the input prices.

This is shown in Figure 9.8. In the short run, the firm can use only K_1 units of capital. To produce output level Q_0, it must use L_0 units of labor, L_1 units of labor to produce Q_1, and L_2 units to produce Q_2. The total costs of these input combinations are given by TC_0, TC_1, and TC_2, respectively. Only for the input combination K_1, L_1 is output being produced at minimal cost.

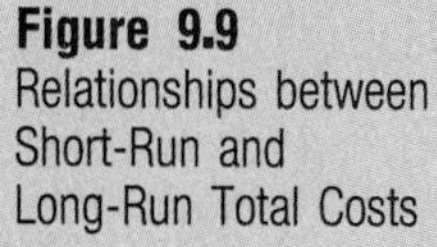

Figure 9.9
Relationships between Short-Run and Long-Run Total Costs

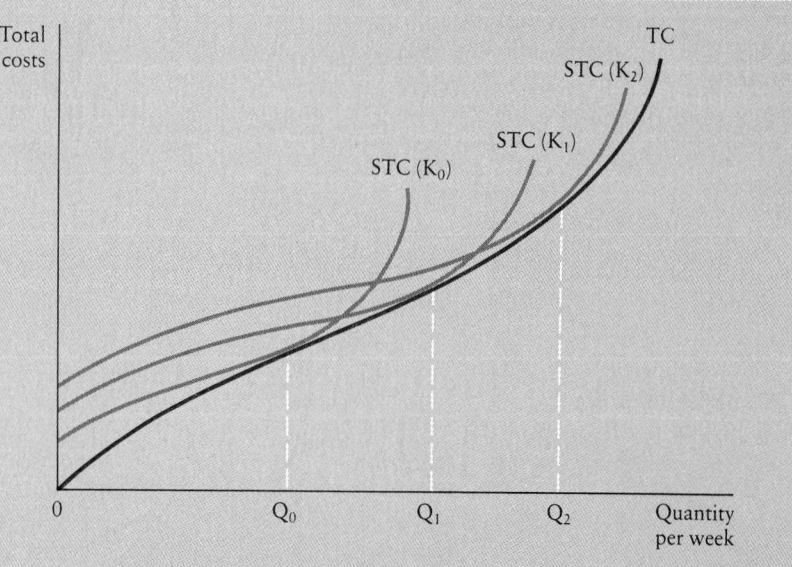

The firm's long-run total cost curve (TC) represents the lower profile (or "envelope") of its short-run total cost curves. Only when the capital stock is that which produces a given output at minimal cost will the short-run and long-run total costs be the same. Only at Q_1 is TC equal to STC(K_1).

Only at that point is the RTS equal to the ratio of the input prices. From Figure 9.8 it is clear that Q_0 is being produced with "too much" capital in this short-run situation. Cost minimization should suggest a southeasterly movement along the Q_0 isoquant, indicating a substitution of labor for capital in production. On the other hand, Q_2 is being produced with "too little" capital, and costs could be reduced by substituting capital for labor. Neither of these substitutions is possible in the short run. However, over the long run the firm will be able to change its level of capital input and will adjust its input usage to the cost-minimizing combinations. This flexible case was discussed earlier in this chapter when we assumed that both labor and capital could be varied.

The Relationship between Short-Run and Long-Run Total Costs

The high-cost nature of the short-run cost-minimization process can also be illustrated using total cost curves. Figure 9.9 shows the long-run total cost curve (TC) corresponding to the fourth case of optimal scale in Panel d in Figure 9.4. To this graph we have added the short-run total cost curve associated with K_1 units of capital input—STC(K_1)—and two other short-run total cost curves, one for a somewhat smaller amount of capital, STC(K_0), and one for a somewhat larger amount of capital, STC(K_1).

The configuration of the curves in Figure 9.9 reflects many of the principles of cost minimization we have been discussing. The zero-output intercept for the STC curves is higher for larger amounts of capital. Fixed costs are obviously greater when there is more capital for which rent must continue to be paid in the short run. The curves also reflect the cost penalties suffered by the firm in the short run. Each of the short-run cost curves lies above the long-run curve at every output level but one.[6] Only for that level of output for which the available capital input is optimal (that is, output Q_1 when K_1 units of capital are employed—see Figure 9.8) do short-run and long-run costs agree. Elsewhere short-run costs are higher. A firm that wished to produce output level Q_2 in the long run, for example, would have to pay much higher costs if it tried to do so with K_1 units of capital than if it adjusted its capital stock to the optimal level K_2. The kind of information in Figure 9.9 gives firms another route to minimizing costs in the long run.

Per-Unit Short-Run Cost Curves

Using the short-run total cost curve already derived, we can easily derive the per-unit short-run cost curves related to it. As for the long run, we define

$$\text{Short-run average cost} = \text{SAC} = \frac{\text{STC}(K_1)}{Q} \qquad [9.10]$$

and

$$\text{Short-run marginal cost} = \text{SMC} = \frac{\text{Change in STC}(K_1)}{\text{Change in } Q}. \qquad [9.11]$$

These short-run concepts are similar to those defined earlier for the long run in Equations 9.3 and 9.4 except that now they are based on total costs incurred with the level of capital input fixed at K_1. Because having capital fixed in the short run yields a total cost curve that has both concave and convex sections, the resulting short-run average and marginal cost relationships will also be U-shaped. These are illustrated in Figure 9.10.

As before, the curves not only are U-shaped, but the marginal cost curve (SMC) passes through the lowest point in the average cost curve (SAC) for exactly the same reason as in long-run curves. When SMC $<$ SAC, average cost is falling since the last produced goods were relatively low in cost and lowered the average. Once SMC $>$ SAC, however, the higher costs associated with successive increments of production pull up the average.

[6]The long-run total cost curve is technically termed an "envelope" of the various short-run total cost curves.

Figure 9.10
Per-Unit Short-Run Cost Curves

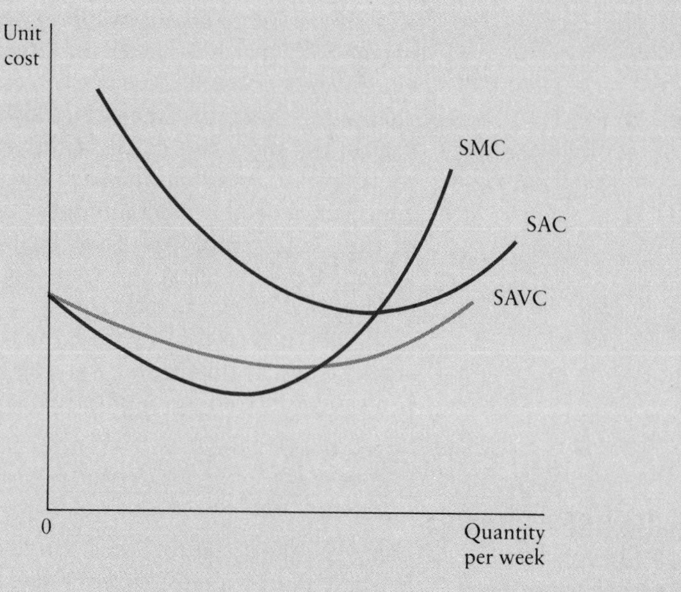

Short-run average and marginal cost curves are U-shaped because one input is held fixed in the short run. The figure illustrates short-run average variable costs (SAVC), which are also relevant to short-run production decisions.

Short-Run Average Variable Costs

Although the SAC and SMC curves will be used frequently in our discussions of supply and price determination, one other short-run cost concept will be needed occasionally. Recall from Equation 9.9 that short-run costs are categorized as being either "fixed" or "variable." That is,

$$\text{STC} = \text{SFC} + \text{SVC}. \qquad [9.12]$$

For simplicity we have omitted the notation of the level of capital being used in the short run. Using these two categories of short-run costs, we can break down short-run average cost into fixed and variable components by dividing Equation 9.12 by Q. That is,

$$\frac{\text{STC}}{\text{Q}} = \text{SAC} = \frac{\text{SFC}}{\text{Q}} + \frac{\text{SVC}}{\text{Q}} \qquad [9.13]$$

$$= \text{Short-run average fixed cost} + \text{Short-run average variable cost}$$

$$= \text{SAFC} + \text{SAVC}.$$

Although the concept of average fixed cost is of little economic usefulness (since fixed costs never change), short-run average variable cost (SAVC) does enter the analysis on a few occasions. SAVC indicates the average "avoidable" costs that firms must incur to produce anything—unlike fixed costs, these costs are avoidable if the firm produces no output. In Chapter 10 we will show that avoidable costs clearly can affect firms' short-run production decisions. As shown in Figure 9.10, the SAVC curve looks very much like the SAC curve. SAVC always lies below SAC (the vertical difference being average fixed costs), but the two curves approach each other at high levels of output for which average fixed costs are quite small.[7]

Relationship between Short-Run and Long-Run Per-Unit Cost Curves

Implicit in the relationship between short-run and long-run total costs illustrated in Figure 9.9 is also a complex set of relations among the per-unit cost curves. Long-run average and marginal cost curves represent cost-minimizing solutions to an entire family of equivalent short-run curves (one for each possible level of capital input). Although it is possible to illustrate the precise relationship among all these curves, a detailed presentation is not essential here.[8] For firms with U-shaped long-run average and marginal cost curves, one particular set of relationships is useful to us, however.

Figure 9.11 shows all of these cost relationships for such a firm. For this firm, long-run average costs reach a minimum at output level Q^*, and as we have noted in several places, at this output level MC = AC. Also associated with Q^* is a certain level of capital usage, K^*. What we wish to do now is to examine the short-run average and marginal cost curves based on this level of capital input. We now look at the costs of a firm whose level of capital input is consistent with its minimum long-run average cost to see how costs vary in the short run as Q departs from its optimal level of Q^*.

Our discussion about the total cost curves in Figure 9.9 shows that when the firm's level of capital input yields minimum costs for the output it wishes to produce, short-run and long-run total costs are equal. Average costs then are equal also. At Q^*, AC is equal to SAC(K^*). Figure 9.9 also shows that the short-run and long-run total cost curves are just tangent to each other at Q^*. This means that at Q^*, MC and SMC(K^*) are also equal, since each represents the slope of the respective total cost curve. At Q^* in Figure 9.11, the following equality holds:

$$AC = MC = SAC(K^*) = SMC(K^*). \qquad [9.14]$$

[7]The SMC and SAVC curves in Figure 9.10 have the same zero-output intercept. The marginal cost and the average variable costs of the first unit produced in the short run are equal. The zero-output intercept for short-run average total cost is undefined since for Q = 0 this represents positive fixed costs divided by zero.

[8]Some of these relationships are illustrated by the numerical example in the appendix to this chapter.

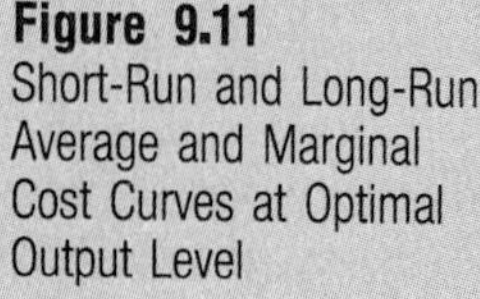

Figure 9.11
Short-Run and Long-Run Average and Marginal Cost Curves at Optimal Output Level

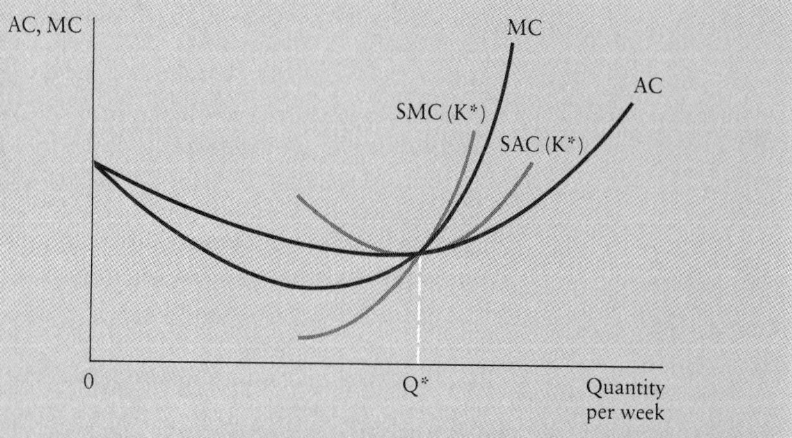

When long-run average cost is U-shaped and reaches a minimum at Q*, SAC and SMC will also pass through this point. For departures from Q* short-run costs are higher than long-run costs.

For increases in Q above Q*, short-run costs are higher than long-run costs. These higher per-unit costs reflect the inflexibility in the short run because some inputs are fixed. This inflexibility has important consequences for firms' short-run supply responses and for price changes in the short run. In Application 9.4: Congestion Costs we look at some cases where short-run costs rise rapidly as the traffic using roads and airports increases. As we show, devising pricing schemes to reflect these escalating costs may be quite difficult, however.

Shifts in Cost Curves

We have shown how the cost curves for a firm's output are derived from its cost-minimizing expansion path. Any change in economic conditions that affects this expansion path will also affect the shape and position of the cost curves. Two kinds of economic changes are likely to have such effects: changes in input prices and technological innovations.

Changes in Input Prices

A change in the price of an input will tilt the firm's total cost lines and alter its expansion path. A rise in wage rates will, for example, cause firms to produce any output level using relatively more capital and relatively less labor. To the extent that a substitution of capital for labor is possible (remember substitution possibilities depend on the shape of the isoquant map), the entire

APPLICATION 9.4

Congestion Costs

One obvious case of the phenomenon of increasing short-run costs is traffic congestion. The demand placed on transportation facilities (for example, expressways) during peak travel hours can be viewed as an increase in output (vehicle miles) in the short run. Because some inputs (the size of the roadway) are held fixed when this output increases, we would expect that costs will rise. The primary increased cost will be increased time delays for travelers, although other costs (such as the costs of road maintenance) may increase as well. Anyone who has driven on a busy urban expressway at 8:00 A.M. or tried to land at a major airport at 4:00 P.M. knows that these costs can be substantial.

Some evidence on rising costs as a result of congestion is presented in Table 1. This table reports the marginal costs of automobile travel on San Francisco Bay area expressways and of landing at LaGuardia Airport in New York City. Both sets of figures are for the marginal costs incurred by producing one more "unit of output": one more vehicle mile or one more arriving flight, respectively. As the table shows, these costs increase markedly during the hours of peak travel demand. For both facilities, peak hour marginal costs are more than four times those incurred during off-peak hours. These data show that people who choose to travel during peak hours impose considerable costs (primarily in terms of time delays) on each other. Suggestions that users should pay these costs (say, in terms of tolls or landing fees) are often met with stiff opposition, however.

To Think About

1. Can you think of other examples of congestion costs? That is, are there other circumstances where a temporary need to expand output causes costs to rise rapidly? How about the opposite case of a temporary increase in output leading to lower costs? In your examples, do prices change temporarily to meet these temporary changes in costs? Can you explain the price movements you do see?
2. Economists have had a rather difficult time measuring increasing short-run marginal costs for many production processes. Suppose you wanted to make such a measurement. How would you proceed? How would you define "short-run increases in output"? How would you try to hold one or several inputs constant for the firm you were studying?

Table 1
Increasing Marginal Time Costs during Peak Travel Hours

	San Francisco Expressways		LaGuardia Airport	
Time Period	Marginal Costs per Vehicle Mile	Time of Day	Marginal Costs per Arriving Flight	Time of Day
Peak hours	38.1¢	7–8 A.M., 5–6 P.M.	$1,025	3–5 P.M.
Near-peak hours	8.9	6–7, 8–9 A.M., 4–5, 6–7 P.M.	670	1–3, 5–7 P.M.
Off-peak hours	7.7	Other times	0–200	Other times

Sources: Expressways: T. E. Keeler and K. A. Small, "Optimal Peak-Load Pricing, Investment, and Service Levels on Urban Expressways," *Journal of Political Economy* (February 1977): 1–26; figures are calculated from equation 16 and from Table 5, p. 18. LaGuardia Airport: A. Carlin and R. F. Park, "Marginal Cost Pricing of Airport Runway Capacity," *American Economic Review* (June 1970): 310–319; figures are averaged from Table 2, p. 314.

APPLICATION 9.5

Two Examples of Dramatic Declines in Cost

Technical progress can sometimes cause large declines in costs (and price). Here we look at two examples that occurred more than 150 years apart.

Textile Costs

One of the most dramatic economic events in the history of the United States was the adoption of the power loom by the New England textile industry following the War of 1812. First developed by Francis Cabot Lowell in Boston in 1814, the designs for these looms were based on looms operating in Lancashire, England. As experience with the new technology expanded and the looms were adapted to American conditions, costs of textile production fell rapidly. Between 1815 and 1823 it is estimated that average total costs of cotton textile production were halved. These declines continued into the 1830s and 1840s with average costs falling by another 30 to 50 percent as firms adapted more completely to the new technology.[1] Prices of textiles fell along with these cost declines, and the quantity of cloth produced expanded greatly. Between 1815 and 1826 output of the New England cotton industry expanded by a factor of 40. This growth was in large measure responsible for the early economic growth of the new nation. By 1870 the economy of New England had been largely transformed from an agricultural one to one based on manufacturing, and the industrial revolution in the New World was under way.

[1]These figures are taken from R.B. Zevin, "The Growth of Cotton Textile Production after 1815," in *The Reinterpretation of American Economic History*, R.W. Fogel and S.L. Engerman, eds. (New York: Harper and Row, 1971).

Calculator Costs

Perhaps even more dramatic were the declines in costs of producing small electronic calculators during the 1970s as the result of the invention of lower cost components. In 1971 a simple four-function pocket calculator cost nearly $200 to produce. More than half of this cost came from the complex internal electronics required. With the development of integrated circuits and computer chips, however, these costs declined dramatically. By the early 1980s the internal mechanism for a simple calculator cost only a few dollars. Advances in the technology of batteries and electronic displays also helped to reduce costs. By the mid-1980s even relatively sophisticated pocket calculators cost only $10 to $15 to produce, and simple versions were often given away free as promotions at supermarkets and banks.

To Think About

1. For many years the British tried to keep their textile production techniques a secret so that they could enjoy cost advantages over other producers. Were they successful in this? What would have prevented the British from obtaining significant advantages from their technology? What forces would be at work tending to spread the information to other countries? Do you remember from your high school history course how the British technology came to the United States?
2. By some estimates, the cost of "computing power" has been halved every two or three years since the 1970s. What implications has this dramatic fall in costs had for input choices by firms? What has determined the extent to which various industries can take advantage of this trend?

expansion path of the firm will rotate toward the capital axis. This movement in turn implies a new set of cost curves for the firm. A rise in the price of labor input has caused the entire relationship between output levels and costs to change. Presumably all cost curves would be shifted upward, and the extent of the shift would depend both on how "important" labor is in production and on how successful the firm is in substituting other inputs for labor.

If labor is relatively unimportant or if the firm can readily shift to more mechanized methods of production, increases in costs resulting from a rise in wages may be rather small. On the other hand, if labor is a very important part of a firm's costs and input substitution is difficult (remember the case of singers and operas), production costs may rise significantly.

Technological Innovation

New technologies can also have important effects on cost curves. Since technical advances alter a firm's production function (as discussed in Chapter 8), isoquant maps as well as the firm's expansion path will shift when technology changes. For example, an advance in knowledge might simply shift all isoquants toward the origin, with the result that any output level could then be produced with a lower level of input and a lower cost. Alternatively, technical change might be "biased" in that it might save only on the use of one input—if workers become more skilled, for instance, this would save only on labor input. Again the end result would be to alter isoquant maps, shift expansion paths, and finally affect the shape and location of a firm's cost curves. In Application 9.5: Two Examples of Dramatic Declines in Cost we look at two important historical cases where technical improvements have had such an effect.

Summary

This chapter shows how to construct the firm's cost curves. These curves show the relationship between the amount that a firm produces and the costs of the inputs required for that production. In later chapters we will see how these curves are important building blocks for developing the theory of supply. The primary results of this chapter are:

- To minimize the cost of producing any particular level of output, the firm should choose a point on the isoquant for which the rate of technical substitution (RTS) is equal to the ratio of the inputs' market prices.
- By repeating this cost-minimization process for every possible level of output, the firm's expansion path can be constructed. This shows the minimum cost way of producing any level of output. The firm's total cost curve can be calculated directly from the expansion path.
- The two most important unit cost concepts are average cost (that is, cost per unit of output) and marginal cost (that is, the incremental cost of the last unit produced). Average and marginal cost curves can be constructed directly from the total cost curve. The shape of these curves depends on the shape of the total cost curve.
- Short-run cost curves are constructed by holding one of the firm's inputs constant in the short run. These short-run costs will not generally be the lowest cost the firm could achieve if all inputs could be adjusted.

Short-run costs also increase rapidly as output expands because the inputs that can be increased experience diminishing marginal productivities.

- Cost curves will shift to a new position whenever the prices of inputs change. Improvements in production techniques will also shift cost curves since the same output can then be produced with fewer inputs.

Review Questions

1. Trump Airlines is thinking of buying a new plane for its shuttle service. Why does the economist's notion of cost suggest that Trump should consider the plane's price in deciding whether it is a profitable investment, but that once bought, the plane's price is not directly relevant to Trump's profit-maximizing decisions? In such a case of "sunk costs," what cost should be assigned in deciding how to use the plane? (See Chapter 20 for further details on capital costs.)
2. Farmer McDonald was heard to complain, "Although my farm is still profitable, I just can't afford to stay in this business any longer. I'm going to sell out and start a fast-food business." In what sense is McDonald using the word "profitable" here? Explain why his statement might be correct if he means profits in the accountant's sense, but would be dubious if he is referring to economic profits.
3. Explain why the assumption of cost minimization implies that the total cost curve must have a positive slope. An increase in output will always increase *total* cost.
4. Suppose a firm had a production function with linear isoquants, implying that its two inputs were perfect substitutes for each other. What would determine the firm's expansion path in this case? For the opposite case of a fixed-proportions production function, what would the firm's expansion path be?
5. Consider two possible definitions of marginal cost:

   a. The extra cost involved in producing one more unit of output.
   b. The cost of the last unit produced.

   Are these definitions identical? If not, which is more correct? Why might the other be misleading?
6. Explain why the average cost associated with any level of output can be depicted graphically as the slope of a chord joining the appropriate point on the TC curve to the origin. Use this fact to show why average and marginal costs are equal at the point of minimum average cost.
7. Late Bloomer is taking a course in microeconomics. Grading in the course is based on 10 weekly quizzes, each with a 100 point maximum. On the first quiz Late Bloomer receives a 10. In each succeeding week he raises his score by 10 points, scoring a 100 on the final quiz of the year.

   a. Calculate Late Bloomer's quiz average for each week of the semester. Why, after the first week, is his average always lower than his current week's quiz?
   b. To help Late Bloomer, his kindly professor has decided to add 40 points to the total of his quiz scores before computing the average. Recompute Late Bloomer's weekly averages given this professorial gift.
   c. Explain why Late Bloomer's quiz averages now have a U-shape. What is his lowest average during the term?

d. Explain the relevance of this problem to the construction of cost curves. Why does the presence of a "fixed cost" of 40 points result in a U-shaped curve? Are Late Bloomer's average and marginal test scores equal at his minimum average?

8. Why does the assumption of cost minimization imply that short-run costs for any level of production must be at least as high as long-run costs? If long-run costs are lower, why can't the firm use the input mix required for these lower costs in the short run?
9. Why does the result of question 8 necessarily imply that short-run *average* costs must be at least as great as long-run *average* costs? Can the SAC curve ever be below the AC curve?
10. Do the observations about total and average costs in questions 8 and 9 apply also to the distinction between short-run and long-run *marginal* costs? Explain why the distinction in this case draws more directly on the assumption of diminishing marginal productivities for variable inputs. Why do we expect SMC to exceed MC for increases in output above minimum AC? How are the SMC and MC curves related for levels of output below minimum AC?

Problems

9.1 A widget manufacturer has an infinitely substitutable production function of the form

$$Q = 2K + L.$$

a. Graph the isoquant maps for Q = 20, Q = 40, and Q = 60. What is the RTS along these isoquants?
b. If the wage rate (w) is \$1 and the rental rate on capital (v) is \$1, what cost-minimizing combination of K and L will the manufacturer employ for the three different production levels in part a? What is the manufacturer's expansion path?
c. How would your answer to part b change if v rose to \$3 with w remaining at \$1?

9.2 A stuffed wombat manufacturer determined that the lowest average production costs were achieved when eight wombats were produced at an average cost of \$1,000 each. If the marginal cost curve is a straight line intersecting the origin, what is the marginal cost for producing the ninth wombat?

9.3 The long-run total cost function for a firm producing skateboards is

$$TC = Q^3 - 40Q^2 + 430Q$$

where Q is the number of skateboards per week.

a. What is the general shape of this total cost function?
b. Calculate the average cost function for skateboards. What shape does the graph of this function have? At what level of skateboard output does average cost reach a minimum? What is average cost at this level of output?
c. The marginal cost function for skateboards is given by

$$MC = 3Q^2 - 80Q + 430.$$

Show that this marginal cost curve intersects average cost at its minimum value
d. Graph the average and marginal cost curves for skateboard production.

9.4 Trapper Joe, the fur trader, has found that his production function in acquiring pelts is given by

$$Q = 2\sqrt{H}$$

where Q = the number of pelts acquired in a day and H = the number of hours Joe's employees spend hunting and trapping in one day. Joe pays his employees \$8 an hour.

a. Calculate Joe's total and average cost curves (as a function of Q).
b. What is Joe's total cost for the day if he acquires four pelts? Six pelts? Eight pelts? What is Joe's average cost per pelt for the day if he acquires four pelts? Six pelts? Eight pelts?
c. Graph the cost curves from part a and indicate the points from part b.

9.5 A firm producing hockey sticks has a production function given by

$$Q = 2\sqrt{K \cdot L}.$$

In the short run, the firm's amount of capital equipment is fixed at K = 100. The rental rate for K is v = \$1, and the wage rate for L is w = \$4.

a. Calculate the firm's short-run total cost curve. Calculate the short-run average cost curve.
b. The firm's short-run marginal cost curve is given by SMC = Q/50. What are the STC, SATC, and SMC for the firm if it produces 25 hockey sticks? Fifty hockey sticks? One hundred hockey sticks? Two hundred hockey sticks?
c. Graph the SATC and the SMC curves for the firm. Indicate the points found in part b.
d. Where does the SMC curve intersect the SATC curve? Explain why the SMC curve will always intersect the SATC at its lowest point.

*9.6 Professor Smith and Professor Jones are going to produce a new introductory textbook. As true scientists they have laid out the production function for the book as

$$Q = S^{1/2}J^{1/2}$$

where Q = the number of pages in the finished book, S = the number of working hours spent by Smith, and J = the number of hours spent working by Jones.

Smith values his labor at \$3 per working hour. He has spent 900 hours preparing the first draft. Jones, whose labor is valued at \$12 per working hour, will revise Smith's draft to complete the book.

a. How many hours will Jones have to spend to produce a finished book of 150 pages? Of 300 pages? Of 450 pages?
b. What is the marginal cost of the 150th page of the finished book? Of the 300th page? Of the 450th page?

---

*Denotes a problem that is rather difficult.

*9.7 An enterprising entrepreneur purchases two firms to produce widgets. Each firm produces identical products and each has a production function given by

$$Q_i = \sqrt{K_i \cdot L_i}$$
$$i = 1, 2.$$

The firms differ, however, in the amount of capital equipment each has. In particular, firm 1 has $K_1 = 25$, whereas firm 2 has $K_2 = 100$. The marginal product of labor is $MP_L = 5/(2\sqrt{L})$ for firm 1, and $MP_L = 5/\sqrt{L}$ for firm 2. Rental rates for K and L are given by $w = v = \$1$.

a. If the entrepreneur wishes to minimize short-run total costs of widget production, how should output be allocated between the two firms?
b. Given that output is optimally allocated between the two firms, calculate the short-run and total average cost curves. What is the marginal cost of the 100th widget? The 125th widget? The 200th widget?
c. How should the entrepreneur allocate widget production between the two firms in the long run? Calculate the long-run total and average cost curves for widget production.
d. How would your answer to part c change if both firms exhibited diminishing returns to scale?

9.8 Suppose a firm's constant returns to scale production function requires it to use capital and labor in a fixed ratio of two workers per machine to produce 10 units and that the rental rates for capital and labor are given by $v = 1$, $w = 3$.

a. Calculate the firm's long-run total and average cost curves.
b. Suppose K is fixed at 10 in the short run. Calculate the firm's short-run total and average cost curves. What is the marginal cost of the 10th unit? The 25th unit? The 50th unit? The 100th unit?

*9.9 In a famous article by Jacob Viner, "Cost Curves and Supply Curves," *Zeitschrift fur Nationalokonomie,* September 1931, pp. 23–46, Viner criticized his draftsman because he could not draw a family of short-run average cost curves whose points of tangency with the long-run average cost curve were also the minimum points on each SAC curve. The draftsman protested that such a drawing was impossible to construct. Use Figure 9.9 to describe how such a family of SAC curves might be constructed for differing levels of capital input. Using this graph, decide whom you would support in this debate. Are there cases in which either might be correct?

---

*Denotes a problem that is rather difficult.

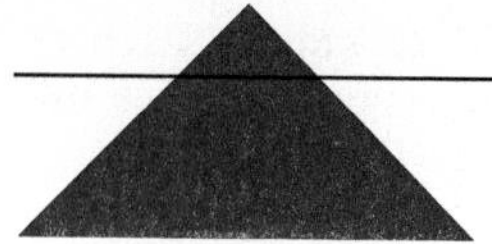

APPENDIX TO CHAPTER 9
NUMERICAL EXAMPLE OF A PRODUCTION FUNCTION AND ITS COST CURVES

This appendix looks at a simple numerical example of a production function and its associated cost curves. The example illustrates in detail the precise way in which cost curves are derived from production functions. The appendix may help you understand how the two concepts are related. The example we have chosen is not necessarily a realistic one, but it does reflect features found in many actual situations.

The Production Function

For our simple example we assume that the firm Hamburger Heaven is in the business of producing exquisite hamburgers using grills (that is, capital, K) and hours of workers' time (L). We assume that the production function for burgers is given explicitly by

$$\text{Burgers per hour} = Q = 10\sqrt{K \cdot L}. \qquad [9A.1]$$

Table 9A.1 shows that this production function exhibits constant returns to scale.[1] As grills and workers are increased proportionately, hourly hamburger output also increases in the same proportion.

Marginal and Average Productivities

Tables 9A.2 and 9A.3 show the total productivity of labor, the marginal productivity of labor, and the average productivity of labor for two possible grill configurations Hamburger Heaven might use—four grills and nine grills. Two features of those tables are immediately clear. First, the marginal productivity and average productivity of labor both decline in each table as the quantity of labor hired increases. This is a reflection of the fact that the number of grills (that is, capital) is held constant in the tables. Although the production function exhibits constant returns to scale when both factors are

[1]This production function can also be written as $Q = 10K^{1/2}L^{1/2}$. That particular form is one example of what is called a Cobb-Douglas production function (after its discoverers). Such a function will exhibit constant returns to scale whenever the exponents of K and L sum to 1. See problem 8.7.

Table 9A.1
Production of Hamburgers Exhibits Constant Returns to Scale

Grills	Workers	Hamburgers per Hour
1	1	10
2	2	20
3	3	30
4	4	40
5	5	50
6	6	60
7	7	70
8	8	80
9	9	90
10	10	100

Table 9A.2
Total Output and Marginal and Average Productivity for Workers with Four Grills

Workers	Grills	Hamburgers per Hour	MP_L	AP_L
1	4	20.0		20.0
2	4	28.3	8.3	14.2
3	4	34.6	6.3	11.5
4	4	40.0	5.4	10.0
5	4	44.7	4.7	8.9
6	4	49.0	4.3	8.2
7	4	52.9	3.9	7.6
8	4	56.6	3.7	7.1
9	4	60.0	3.4	6.7
10	4	63.2	3.2	6.3

increased together, holding grills constant causes workers to exhibit a diminishing marginal productivity. Because the marginal productivity is falling, the average is falling also. Since an extra worker produces fewer hamburgers than the average number of hamburgers per worker output that previously prevailed, hiring this extra worker causes the overall average to fall.

A second feature to note about the tables is that the marginal and average productivities of labor are all higher in Table 9A.3 than they are in Table 9A.2. This simply shows that the workers in the latter table have a larger number of grills to work with than do those in the former. Even though the marginal productivity of labor declines in both cases, labor is more productive in Table 9A.3 because it has more capital input with which to make hamburgers—there is less crowding around the grills in Table 9A.3 than in Table 9A.2.

The Isoquant Map

As a final example of using this simple production function, we shall construct its isoquant map. Of course, there are infinitely many isoquants that

Table 9A.3
Total Output and Marginal and Average Productivity for Workers with Nine Grills

Workers	Grills	Hamburgers per Hour	MP_L	AP_L
1	9	30.0		30.0
2	9	42.4	12.4	21.2
3	9	52.0	9.6	17.3
4	9	60.0	8.0	15.0
5	9	67.1	7.1	13.4
6	9	73.5	6.4	12.3
7	9	79.4	5.9	11.3
8	9	84.8	5.4	10.6
9	9	90.0	5.2	10.0
10	9	94.9	4.9	9.5

might be drawn (one for each conceivable output level), but we will consider only two—for 40 hamburgers per hour and for 100 hamburgers per hour.

For the 40-hamburger isoquant, we are interested in those combinations of K and L for which

$$40 = 10\sqrt{K \cdot L}. \qquad [9A.2]$$

Manipulating this expression, we get

$$16 = K \cdot L \qquad [9A.3]$$

or

$$K = \frac{16}{L}. \qquad [9A.4]$$

Holding hamburger output constant implies a relationship that shows potential trade-offs between grills and workers. We can graph that relationship. In Table 9A.4 we have calculated the number of grills that combine with integral values of L (from 1 to 10) to produce 40 hamburgers (of course, it makes no sense to speak of fractions of grills, but then again, this example is far-fetched anyway). For each of these input combinations we have also calculated the RTS as the ratio of the change in capital input to the change in labor input. From this information, the 40-hamburger isoquant can be constructed in Figure 9A.1. This isoquant clearly shows those combinations of grills and workers that produce 40 hamburgers. As demonstrated by Table 9A.5, the isoquant exhibits a diminishing RTS (of L for K) and resembles those drawn in Chapters 8 and 9.

Table 9A.5 for the 100-hamburger-per-hour isoquant is constructed in an identical manner. By an algebraic manipulation similar to that shown pre-

Figure 9A.1
Graph of the 40- and 100-Hamburger-per-Hour Isoquants for Hamburger Heaven

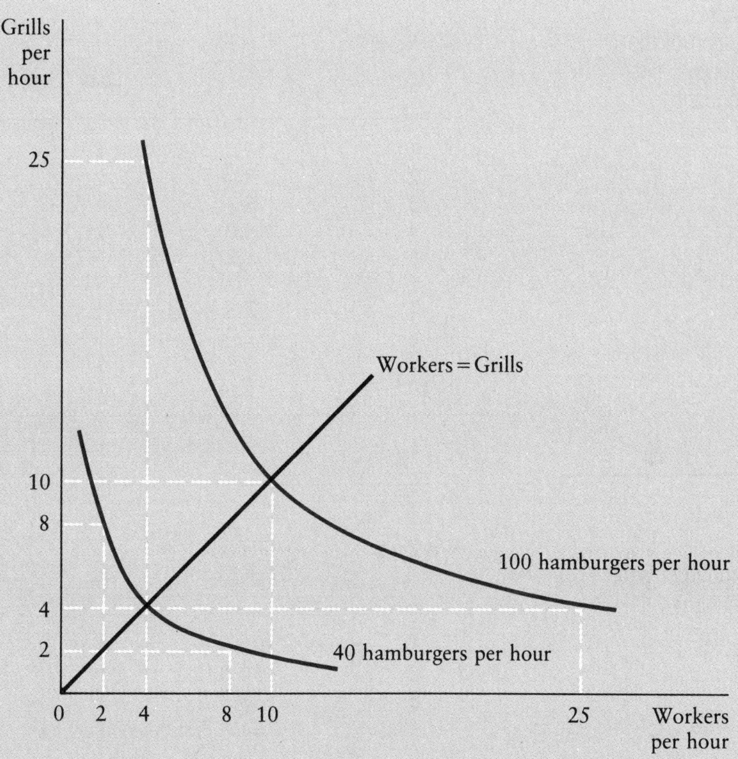

These isoquants are taken directly from Tables 9A.4 and 9A.5. They show those combinations of grills and workers that can produce 40 and 100 hamburgers per hour, respectively. The isoquants clearly display a diminishing RTS.

viously, it is an easy matter to calculate that those combinations of K and L that can produce 100 hamburgers per hour satisfy the relation

$$K = \frac{100}{L}. \qquad [9A.5]$$

Some of those combinations are also shown in Figure 9A.1. Again the isoquant exhibits a diminishing RTS.

Constant Returns and the RTS

One useful fact illustrated by these two isoquants is that the RTS depends only on the ratio of K to L, not on the scale of production. This is true for any constant returns to scale production function. For example, with the four

Table 9A.4
Construction of the 40-Hamburger-per-Hour Isoquant

Workers (L)	Grills (K)	ΔL	$-\Delta K$	$RTS = \frac{-\Delta K}{\Delta L}$
1	16.0	1		
2	8.0	1	8.0	8.0
3	5.3	1	2.7	2.7
4	4.0	1	1.3	1.3
5	3.2	1	0.8	0.8
6	2.7	1	0.5	0.5
7	2.3	1	0.4	0.4
8	2.0	1	0.3	0.3
9	1.8	1	0.2	0.2
10	1.6	1	0.2	0.2

Table 9A.5
Construction of the 100-Hamburger-per-Hour Isoquant

Workers (L)	Grills (K)	ΔL	$-\Delta K$	$RTS = \frac{-\Delta K}{\Delta L}$
1	100.0	1		
2	50.0	1	50.0	50.0
3	33.3	1	16.7	16.7
4	25.0	1	8.3	8.3
5	20.0	1	5.0	5.0
6	16.7	1	3.3	3.3
7	14.3	1	2.4	2.4
8	12.5	1	1.8	1.8
9	11.1	1	1.4	1.4
10	10.0	1	1.1	1.1

grills on the 40-hamburger isoquant, four workers are employed per hour and the RTS is approximately 1. Similarly, on the 100-hamburger-per-hour isoquant, with 10 grills, 10 workers are required, and the RTS is also approximately 1. This example shows that for a constant returns to scale production function the isoquants are simply radial blowups of one another—the RTS depends only on the ratio of grills (K) to workers (L). The RTSs do not agree exactly in the tables, but this results from the fact that we are studying "large" changes in K and L rather than the very small changes that are actually required by the definition of the RTS. If we had calculated such minute changes, the RTSs would agree exactly.

Cost Minimization

In order to discuss Hamburger Heaven's cost-minimizing input choices, we must know the costs of capital and labor. Suppose that the firm rents its grills from a grill-leasing firm at $1 per hour. Suppose also, to make things simple,

Table 9A.6
Costs of Producing 40 Hamburgers per Hour Using Various Combinations of Inputs

Workers	Grills	Total Cost
1	16.0	$17.00
2	8.0	10.00
3	5.3	8.30
4	4.0	8.00
5	3.2	8.20
6	2.7	8.70
7	2.3	9.30
8	2.0	10.00
9	1.8	10.80
10	1.6	11.60

that workers are hired at $1 per hour (Hamburger Heaven pays little attention to the minimum wage law). Total costs are given by

$$TC = \$1 \cdot K + \$1 \cdot L. \qquad [9A.6]$$

Suppose the firm wants to minimize the total costs of producing 40 hamburgers per hour. There are many possible ways of producing 40 hamburgers, and all of those possible combinations lie on the isoquant shown in Figure 9A.1. The first two columns of Table 9A.6 repeat some of the information about grills and workers that can produce 40 hamburgers per hour that appears in Table 9A.5. In the third column of Table 9A.6, we have computed the total costs of each of those input combinations. As Table 9A.6 makes clear, the cost-minimizing way to produce 40 hamburgers per hour is by using four grills and four workers. These will cost $8, and this is the lowest cost attainable. That this is the cost-minimizing input combination should have been obvious from our previous discussion in which we showed that the RTS on the 40-hamburger-per-hour isoquant is 1 for this input combination. This is exactly the ratio of the wage rate (w) to the rental rate of capital (v). At this point the RTS is equal to the ratio of the inputs' prices, and this is what must be true for cost minimization.

A Graphic Proof

In Figure 9A.2 we have redrawn the 40-hamburger-per-hour isoquant together with the TC = $8 line. For four grills and four workers, total costs are indeed $8, and all other input combinations capable of producing 40 hamburgers per hour cost more than $9. It should also be clear from the figure that had the ratio of labor to capital costs been other than 1, some other capital-labor combination would have been chosen. For example, if the wage had been $2 per hour instead of $1, the ratio w/v would be 2; Hamburger Heaven would have used more grills and fewer workers to produce 40 hamburgers per hour. This new input price ratio would cause the firm to use

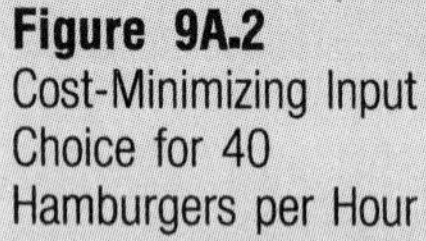
Figure 9A.2
Cost-Minimizing Input Choice for 40 Hamburgers per Hour

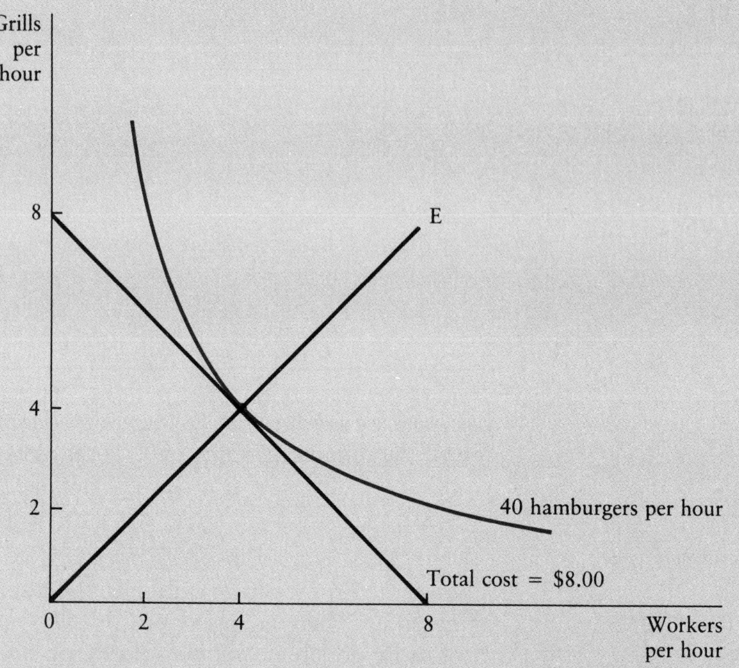

Using four grills and four workers is the minimal cost combination of inputs that can be used to produce 40 hamburgers per hour. For this input choice, the RTS is equal to the factor price ratio w/v. In other words, the slope of the 40-hamburger-per-hour isoquant with four grills and four workers is −1.

about 2.8 worker hours and 5.6 grills to produce 40 hamburgers per hour most cheaply. Total costs would then be \$11.20 [= \$2 · (2.8) + \$1 · (5.6)], which is the lowest level of costs attainable given the new input prices.

The Expansion Path

If wage rates and grill rental rates do not change, it is easy to construct Hamburger Heaven's expansion path. We have already shown that if w = \$1 and v = \$1, then the cost-minimizing input choice is four grills and four workers, because at this point the RTS is equal to the input price ratio. We also know that for a constant returns to scale production function (such as the one we are using) the RTS depends only on the ratio of the two inputs, not on the scale of production. Consequently the RTS will always be 1 when equal numbers of grills and workers are used. Since w/v is also always equal to 1, the desire to minimize costs will result in the firm always using grills and workers in a ratio of 1:1. The firm's expansion path is then just the ray through the origin along which grills and workers are used in equal amounts. This ray is

Table 9A.7
Expansion Path for Hamburger Heaven

Hamburgers per Hour	Workers	Grills	Total Cost
10	1	1	$ 2.00
20	2	2	4.00
30	3	3	6.00
40	4	4	8.00
50	5	5	10.00
60	6	6	12.00
70	7	7	14.00
80	8	8	16.00
90	9	9	18.00
100	10	10	20.00

labeled 0E in Figure 9A.2. Table 9A.7 calculates this expansion path for output levels ranging from 10 to 100 hamburgers per hour. It also computes the (minimum) total cost for producing each of these output levels. The table clearly reflects the constant returns to scale nature of the production function—total costs are exactly proportional to hamburger output. Along the expansion path, hamburgers always cost exactly $.20 each.

Long-Run Cost Curves

Given the information in Table 9A.7, it is a simple matter to graph Hamburger Heaven's long-run total cost curve. As Panel a in Figure 9A.3 shows, this total cost curve is a straight line that passes through the origin. This is another reflection of the constant returns to scale in this example. The slope of the total cost curve is 0.20, indicating that marginal (and average) costs are always $.20 per hamburger. Hence, as Panel b in Figure 9A.3 shows, the long-run average and marginal cost curves are the same horizontal line. No matter how much is produced, if Hamburger Heaven has complete flexibility in choosing the mix of grills and workers it uses, the firm can produce all the hamburgers it wants at $.20 each.

Short-Run Cost Curves

To analyze short-run costs, assume that Hamburger Heaven's cooking facilities are fixed at four grills. Short-run fixed costs are $4 per hour—$1 rental for each grill used. Variable costs are $w \cdot L$—the total cost of paying the number of workers hired. The short-run relationship between Q and L is

$$Q = 10\sqrt{4 \cdot L} = 20\sqrt{L}$$

Figure 9A.3
Total, Average, and Marginal Cost Curves

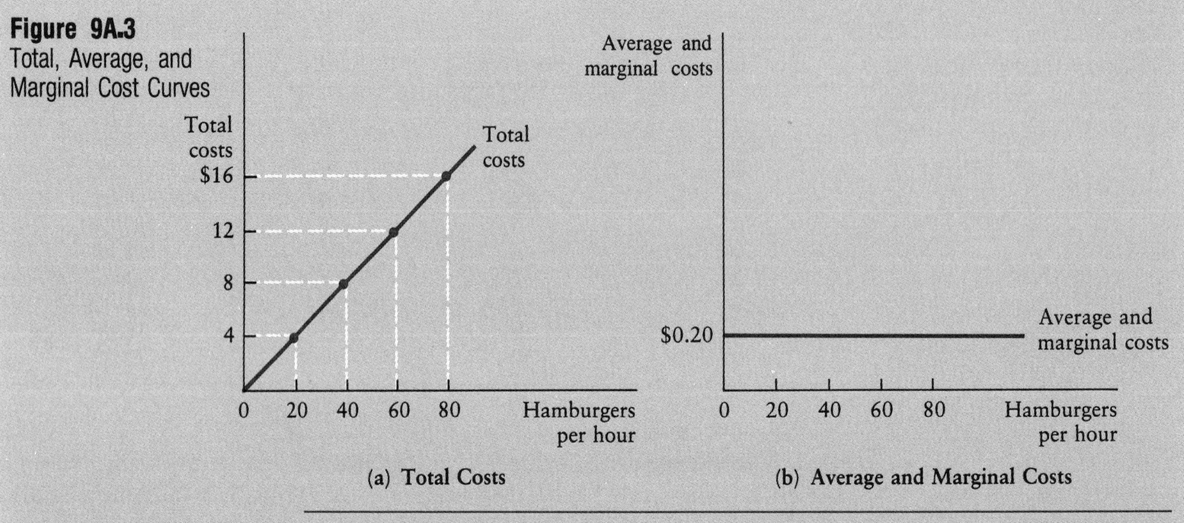

The total cost curve is simply a straight line through the origin reflecting constant returns to scale. Long-run average and marginal costs are constant at $.20 per hamburger.

or

$$L = \frac{Q^2}{400}. \quad [9A.7]$$

In the short run Hamburger Heaven's total costs are given by

$$TC = 4 + wL = 4 + \frac{Q^2}{400}, \quad [9A.8]$$

which shows the relationship between Q and total costs when cooking facilities are limited to four grills.

In Table 9A.8 we have calculated short-run total costs for output levels ranging from 10 to 100 hamburgers. It is important to notice two features of Table 9A.8. First, total costs increase rapidly as more hamburgers are grilled. This is a reflection of the diminishing marginal productivity of cookers when they are increasingly crowded around the four available grills. A second, related observation is that all but one of the entries in the table exceed those for long-run costs in Table 9A.7. The fact that grills are fixed at four causes all the input combinations except $K = 4$, $L = 4$ to be more costly than if both inputs can be adjusted. Only when the "correct" amount of labor (here four workers per hour) is being used with the available facilities to produce 40 hamburgers per hour will costs truly be minimized. A comparison of the tables indicates the kinds of adjustments that a firm would like to make in the long run when all inputs become variable.

Table 9A.8
Short-Run Total Costs for Hamburger Heaven with Four Grills

Hamburgers per Hour	Grills	Workers	Short-Run Total Cost
10	4	0.25	$ 4.25
20	4	1.00	5.00
30	4	2.25	6.25
40	4	4.00	8.00
50	4	6.25	10.25
60	4	9.00	13.00
70	4	12.25	16.25
80	4	16.00	20.00
90	4	20.25	24.25
100	4	25.00	29.00

Table 9A.9
Short-Run Average and Marginal Costs for Hamburger Heaven with Four Grills

Hamburgers per Hour	Short-Run Total Cost	Short-Run Average Cost	Short-Run Marginal Cost
10	$ 4.25	$0.425	
20	5.00	0.250	$0.075
30	6.25	0.208	0.125
40	8.00	0.200	0.175
50	10.25	0.205	0.225
60	13.00	0.217	0.275
70	16.25	0.232	0.325
80	20.00	0.250	0.375
90	24.25	0.269	0.425
100	29.00	0.290	0.475

Short-Run Average and Marginal Costs

Table 9A.9 uses the total cost information from Table 9A.8 to calculate short-run average and marginal costs. As long as marginal costs are below average costs, average costs decline. Average costs decline from $.425 per hamburger to $.20 each as output expands from 10 to 40 burgers per hour.[2] For expansions beyond 40 per hour, however, marginal costs exceed average costs; therefore average costs rise. At output levels of 100 or more hamburg-

[2]Again, here the marginal cost figures do not reflect small changes as they should. Rather, for pedagogic purposes, marginal costs have been recorded for rather large changes in output (10 hamburgers per hour). For this reason, marginal and average costs are not equal at the minimum point of the SATC curve (that is, at 40 hamburgers per hour). Had the figures been computed for small changes, SATC and SMC would be identical ($.20) at 40 hamburgers per hour. This is shown in Figure 9A.3.

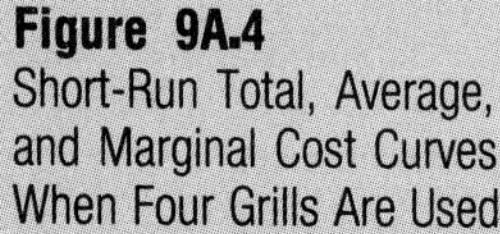

Figure 9A.4
Short-Run Total, Average, and Marginal Cost Curves When Four Grills Are Used

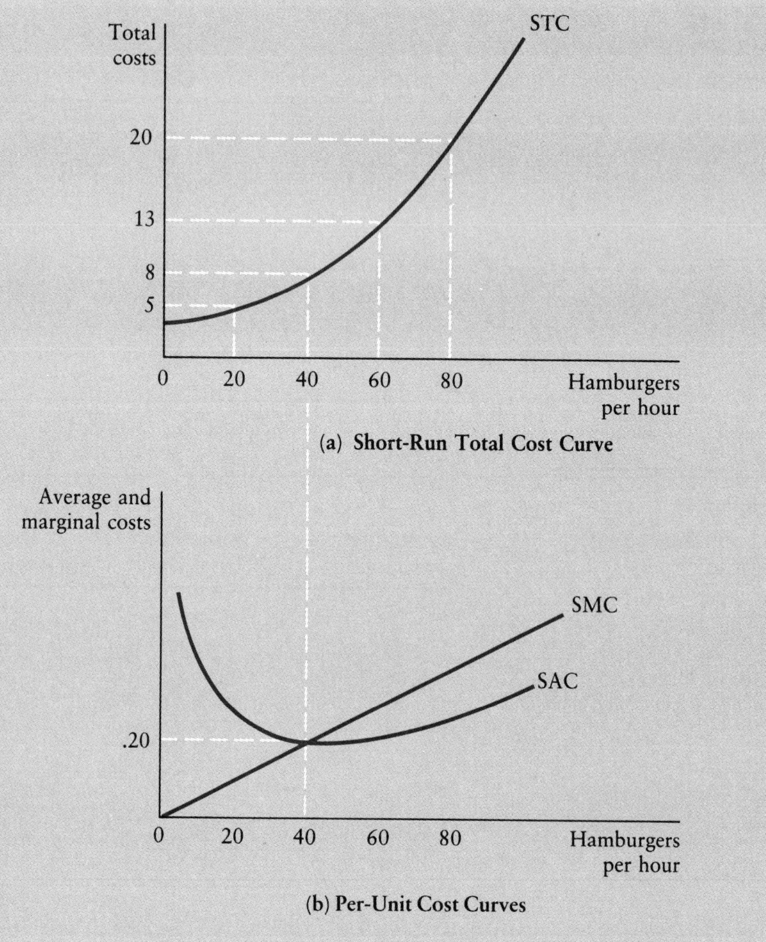

These curves are derived from Tables 9A.8 and 9A.9. They show that for our example the total, average, and marginal cost curves more or less resemble those we drew in Chapter 9.

ers per hour, average and marginal costs are rising quite rapidly. During the lunchtime rush, Hamburger Heaven gets so crowded and the workers get so harried that the spoilage and other costs rise rapidly.

Graphs of the costs recorded in Tables 9A.8 and 9A.9 are presented in Figure 9A.4. The total cost curve is a rapidly increasing function of Q with an intercept of $4 (this reflects the fixed cost of the four grills).[3] The average cost curve in the figure has the familiar U-shape and reaches a minimum at 40 hamburgers per hour. The marginal cost curve passes through this mini-

[3]Technically, the cost function is a quadratic equation since it involves terms in Q^2.

Figure 9A.5
Short-Run and Long-Run Total Cost Curves for Hamburger Heaven

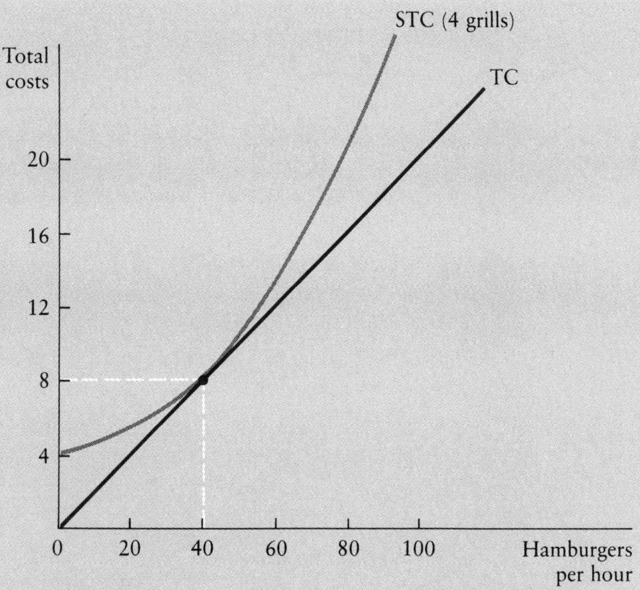

The short-run total cost curve when four grills are used lies above the long-run total cost curve except at an output level of 40 hamburgers per hour. At that output level, the constant number of grills (four) is also appropriate for long-run cost minimization. Hence at that output level, the short-run and long-run total cost curves are tangent.

mum and, in this example, is simply a straight line. All of the curves in Figure 9A.4 clearly show the effect that holding cooking facilities fixed in the short run has on costs. Since producing extra hamburgers can only be accomplished by hiring more workers, this process runs into diminishing marginal productivities, and costs rise rapidly.

Relationship of Long-Run and Short-Run Cost Curves

Figure 9A.5 is a combined graph of the information on short-run and long-run total costs. As in Figure 9A.3, the TC curve is a straight line. The STC curve for four grills is tangent to the TC curve at an output of 40 hamburgers per hour since that is an appropriate level of output when Hamburger Heaven opts for four grills. The vertical axis intercept of the STC curve reflects fixed costs of $4. In the long run, there are no fixed costs; the TC curve passes through the origin.

Finally, Figure 9A.6 depicts the short-run and long-run average and marginal cost curves for Hamburger Heaven. This configuration of curves resembles that which was shown in Chapter 9 for the general theoretical case. Again, the curves show that per-unit costs may rise rapidly as output expands

Figure 9A.6
Short-Run and Long-Run Average and Marginal Cost Curves for Hamburger Heaven

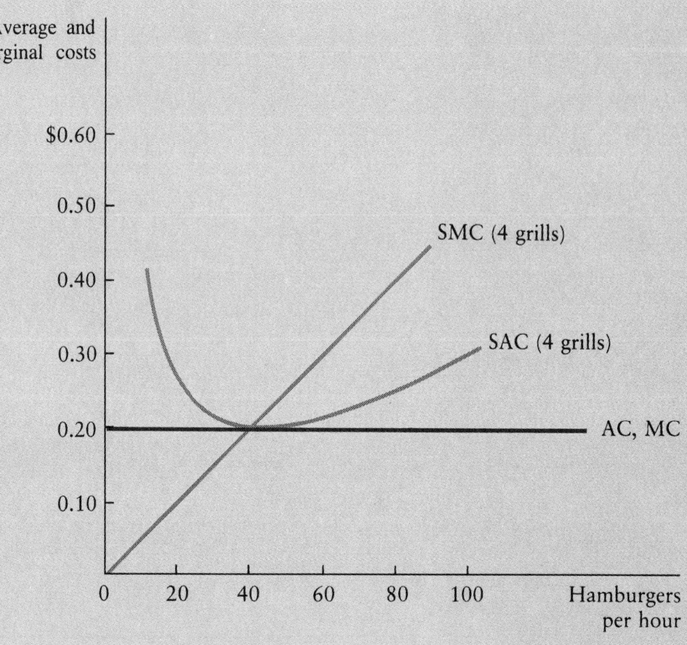

For this constant returns to scale production function AC and MC are constant over all ranges of output. Since w = v = $1, this constant average cost is $.20 per unit. The short-run average cost curve does, however, have a general U-shape since the number of grills is held constant. The SAC curve is tangent to the AC curve at an output of 40 hamburgers per hour.

in the short run even though the long-run marginal cost curve is horizontal. Only at the appropriate output levels are short-run and long-run average costs equal.

Summary

This analysis of our trivial hamburger example shows how, once input costs are known, all of Hamburger Heaven's cost curves can be derived directly from its production function. Because of the cost-minimization assumption, it is always possible to obtain information about a firm's cost curves from its production function and vice versa. Of course, the mathematics associated with such a process may not always be as simple as in the example presented here, but the approach used would be identical. In empirical studies of production this relationship between the two concepts is frequently used to derive important conclusions about the nature of production in various industries.

CHAPTER 10

Profit Maximization and Supply

Chapter 9 looked at how firms minimize costs for any level of output. This chapter now focuses on how firms determine what level of output they will produce. Before we investigate that decision, we discuss briefly the nature of firms themselves and how their output choices might be analyzed.

Nature of Firms

As we pointed out in Chapter 8, a firm is a collection of people who turn inputs into outputs. Different individuals supply different types of inputs, such as workers' skills and types of capital equipment, to the output process, and they expect to receive some type of reward for doing so. The relationships among these providers of inputs in a firm may be quite complicated. Each provider agrees to devote his or her input to production activities under a set of understandings about how the input is to be used and what benefit the provider will receive. In some cases these relationships are explicitly set down in contracts. Workers often negotiate contracts that specify in considerable detail what hours are to be worked, what rules of work are to be followed, and what rate of pay is to be received. Similarly, capital owners invest in a firm under a set of explicit legal principles about how the capital will be used and the compensation the owners will receive. In addition to these formal arrangements, there are many more implicit relationships among the people in a firm. For example, managers and workers follow certain procedures in making production decisions, and there are many implicit understandings about who has the authority to do what. Capital owners often delegate considerable authority to managers and workers to make decisions on their behalf. General Motors shareholders, for example, are never involved in the decision of how assembly line equipment will be used, though technically they own it. All of these explicit and implicit relationships among providers change through time in response to experiences and to events external to the firm. Much as a basketball team will try out new plays and defensive strategies, so too firms will alter the nature of their internal organizations in order to achieve better long-run results.[1]

Firms' Goals

These complicated relationships among the providers of inputs in a firm pose some problems for economists who wish to develop theoretical generalizations about how firms behave. In our study of demand theory, it made some sense to talk about choices by a rational consumer because we were examining decisions by only a single person. But for firms, many people may be involved in decisions, and any detailed study of such decisions may quickly become deeply mired in questions of psychology, sociology, and group dynamics.

Although some economists have adopted an "organizational behavior" approach to studying firms' decisions, that approach can be too cumbersome for general purposes. Instead, most economists treat the firm as a single decision-making unit, an approach that sweeps away all the complicated behavioral issues about relationships among employees and capital owners. This approach often assumes that firms' decisions are made by a single dictatorial manager who rationally pursues some goal, usually the maximization of the firm's economic profits. This is the approach we will take in this chapter to develop the theory of a firm's supply behavior.

Profit Maximization

If firms pursue the goal of achieving the largest economic profits possible, by definition they seek to make the difference between total revenues and total economic costs as big as possible. Here we are using economic concepts of costs and profits. Accounting notions of profits may be relevant to questions about how the firm is taxed (Application 10.1: What Does the U.S. Corporate Profits Tax Actually Tax? looks at this relationship), but, as we will show, maximizing economic profits is assumed to be the fundamental goal motivating actual behavior.

[1]All of these points are examined in more detail in Chapter 11.

APPLICATION 10.1

What Does the U.S. Corporate Profits Tax Actually Tax?

A corporate income (or profits) tax was first imposed in the United States in 1909—about four years before the personal income tax was put into effect. In 1988 corporate income tax revenues amounted to more than $105 billion, or approximately 11 percent of total federal tax collections. Many people view this tax as a natural complement to the personal income tax. Since under U.S. law, corporations enjoy many of the same rights as individuals, it might seem only reasonable that corporations should be taxed in a similar way. Some economists, however, believe that the corporate profits tax seriously distorts the allocation of resources, both because the tax law fails to use an economic concept of profits and because a substantial portion of corporate income is taxed twice.

Definition of Profits

A large portion of what are defined as corporate profits under the tax laws are in fact a normal return to shareholders for the equity funds they have invested in corporations. These shareholders might expect such a return from any other investment they might have made, such as depositing their funds in a bank. This portion of corporate profits should be considered an economic cost of business since it reflects what owners have forgone by making an equity investment. If this cost were added to other corporate costs, the correctly defined economic profits would be reduced substantially.

Effects of the Double Tax

The corporate profits tax is less a tax on profits than a tax on the equity investments of corporate shareowners. Such taxation may have two consequences. First, corporations will find it more attractive to finance new capital investments through loans and bond offerings (whose interest payments are a deductible cost) than through new stock issues (whose implicit costs are not deductible under the tax law). A second effect arises because a part of corporate income is taxed twice—first when it is earned by the corporation and then later when it is paid out to owners in the form of dividends. Hence, the total rate of tax applied to corporate equity investments is much higher than that applied to other investments. As a consequence, investors will be less willing to invest in corporate businesses than in other assets that are not subject to the corporate profits tax. A number of economists have found that such distortionary effects are rather large and have suggested ways in which the corporate profits tax might be changed so as to reduce them.[1]

The Leveraged Buyout Wave

Some observers have suggested that these peculiarities of the corporate income tax are partly responsible for the wave of leveraged buyouts (LBOs) that swept financial markets in the late 1980s. The basic principle of an LBO is to use borrowed funds to acquire most of the outstanding stock of a corporation. Essentially those involved in such a buyout are responding to the opportunity to substitute a less highly taxed source of capital (debt) for a more highly taxed form (equity). Such huge deals as the $25 billion buyout of RJR Nabisco by the Kohlberg Kravis Roberts Company may derive in part from fundamental differences in the way accounting and economic profits are defined.

To Think About

1. Would the defects of the corporate profits tax be cured by taxing only economic profits? How could this be achieved in practice? Is it possible to redefine accounting concepts of costs to reflect economic concepts?

2. A popular slogan of some tax reformers is "Corporations don't pay taxes, people do." Do you agree? If so, why do we have a separate corporate tax? Which "people" end up paying the tax?

[1]See C. E. McClure, *Must Corporate Income Be Taxed Twice?* (Washington, D.C.: Brookings Institution, 1979).

Marginalism

If firms are strict profit maximizers, they will make decisions in a marginal way. The manager-owner will adjust the things that may be controlled until it is impossible to increase profits further. The manager looks, for example, at the incremental (or marginal) profit from producing one more unit of output, or the additional profit from hiring one more laborer. As long as this incremental profit is positive, the manager will decide to produce the extra output or hire the extra laborer. When the incremental profit of an activity becomes zero, the manager has pushed the activity far enough—it would not be profitable to go farther.

The Output Decision

We can show this relationship between profit maximization and marginalism most directly by looking at the output level that a firm will choose to produce. A firm sells some level of output, Q, and from these sales the firm receives its revenues, R(Q). The amount of revenues received obviously depends on how much output is sold and on what price it is sold for. Similarly, in producing Q certain economic costs are incurred, TC(Q), and these also will depend on how much is produced. As in Chapter 9, economic profits (π) are therefore defined as

$$\pi = R(Q) - TC(Q). \quad [10.1]$$

In deciding how much output to produce, the firm will choose the amount for which economic profits are as large as possible. This process is illustrated in Figure 10.1. There the curve TC(Q) is drawn with the same general shape as the total cost curves we introduced in Chapter 9. The curve R(Q), which represents total revenue, is drawn so that selling more output leads to greater revenues.[2] We can calculate profits by looking at the vertical distance between the R(Q) and TC(Q) curves, and profits are shown explicitly in the bottom panel of the figure. It is clear that profits reach a maximum at Q^*. For outputs either larger or smaller than Q^*, profits are lower than they are at Q^*. We wish to examine those conditions that must hold at Q^* for maximum profits.

[2]We will examine the exact shape of the R(Q) curve when we reintroduce demand curves. For the moment, the curve R(Q) is drawn so that increasing output leads to increasing revenues. In the case where the firm's decisions do not affect price, the R(Q) curve would be the straight-line $R(Q) = P \cdot Q$, where P is the market price of the firm's output. Later in this chapter we will make a distinction between output by a single firm (q) and in the market as a whole (Q), but we do not do so here.

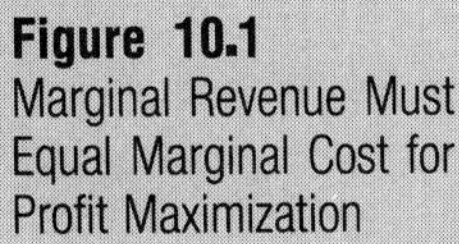

Figure 10.1
Marginal Revenue Must Equal Marginal Cost for Profit Maximization

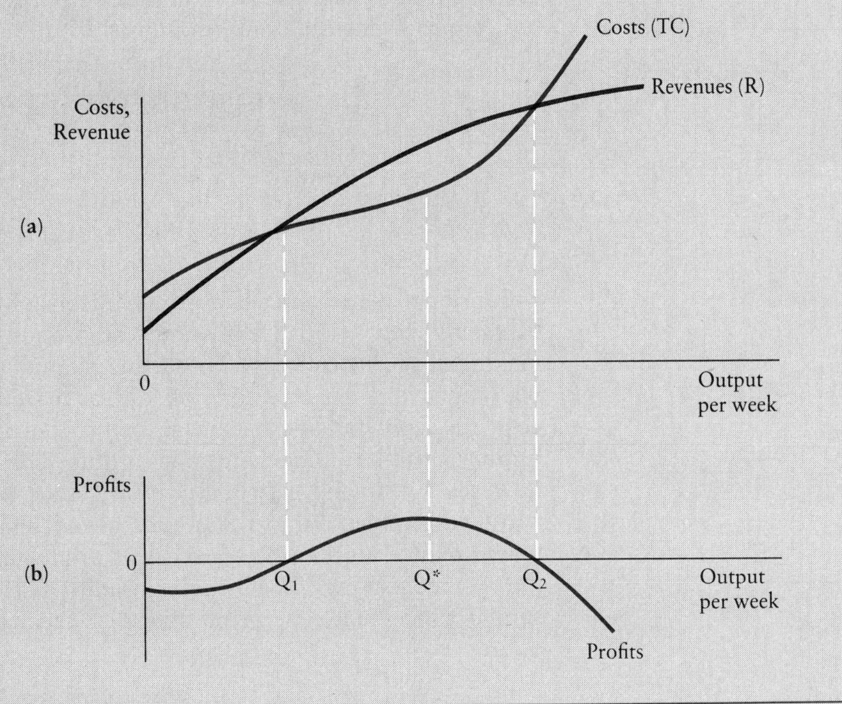

Since economic profits are defined as total revenues minus total economic costs, profits reach a maximum when the slope of the revenue function (marginal revenue) is equal to the slope of the cost function (marginal cost). In the figure this occurs at Q^*. Profits are zero at both Q_1 and Q_2.

The Marginal Revenue/Marginal Cost Rule

Marginal revenue The extra revenue a firm receives when it sells one more unit of output.

For output levels below Q^*, an increase in output brings in more additional revenue than producing this additional output costs. A firm interested in maximizing profits would never stop short of Q^*. If a firm decided to increase its output level beyond Q^*, it would reduce its profits. The additional revenues from increasing Q fall short of the additional costs incurred in expanding output. Consequently, at Q^* the additional costs of producing an infinitesimal amount more are exactly equal to the additional revenues that this extra output will bring in. Economists would say that at Q^*, *marginal cost* (we have already met this concept in Chapter 9) is equal to **marginal revenue** (the extra revenue provided by the sale of one more unit). In order to maximize profits, a firm should produce that output level for which the marginal revenue from selling one more unit of output is exactly equal to the marginal cost of producing that unit of output.[3] More succinctly,

$$\text{Marginal revenue} = \text{Marginal cost} \tag{10.2}$$

or

$$MR = MC. \tag{10.3}$$

This principle is so important for the theory of the firm (and for the analysis of supply) that it deserves further elaboration. A firm might determine its maximum profits conceptually starting at an output level of zero and increasing output one unit at a time. As long as marginal revenue exceeds marginal cost, the firm should continue to increase output—each additional unit it produces will add something to its profits. The firm can push things too far, however. Eventually marginal costs will start to rise. As soon as they equal marginal revenue, the firm has gone far enough. Further increases in output would reduce profits since the cost of producing more output would exceed the revenue it brings in. Whenever conditions change, the firm can conduct a similar conceptual experiment and thus decide on a new profit-maximizing output level.

Marginalism in Input Choices

So far we have developed a firm's marginal decision rules as they relate to output choices; we can make a similar argument for input choices as well. Hiring additional labor, for example, entails some increase in costs, and a profit-maximizing firm should balance the additional costs against the extra revenue brought in by selling the output produced by the extra labor. A similar analysis holds for the firm's decision on the number of machines to rent. Additional machines should be hired only as long as their marginal contributions to profits are positive. As the marginal productivity of machines begins to decline, the ability of machines to yield additional revenue also declines. The firm will eventually reach a point at which the marginal contribution of an additional machine to profits is exactly zero—the extra sales generated precisely match the costs of the extra machines. The firm should not expand the rental of machines beyond this point. In Chapter 18 we will see how this application of marginalism leads to a theory of input demand. For the moment, our attention is centered on a firm's output choice and on the profit-

[3]Geometry provides another way of visualizing this result. The distance between any two curves is greatest when the slopes of the curves are equal—if the slopes aren't equal, you can get farther apart by moving one way or the other. For the R(Q) and TC(Q) curves, this geometric fact again proves that profits are maximized when marginal revenue equals marginal cost.

maximizing condition: Marginal revenue equals marginal cost. Since we have already discussed the concept of marginal cost in detail, we now analyze the notion of marginal revenue.

Marginal Revenue

Price taker
A firm or individual whose decisions regarding buying or selling have no effect on the prevailing market price of a good or service.

It is the revenue from selling one more unit of output that is relevant to the profit-maximizing firm. If a firm can sell all it wishes without affecting market price (that is, if the firm is a **price taker**), the market price will indeed be the extra revenue obtained from selling one more unit. Phrased in another way, if a firm's output decisions will not affect market price, marginal revenue is equal to price. We can easily demonstrate this result. Suppose a firm were selling 50 widgets at $1 each. Then total revenues would be $50. If selling one more widget does not affect price, that additional widget will also bring in $1, and total revenue will rise to $51. Marginal revenue from the 51st widget will be $1 (= $51 − $50). For a firm that does not affect market price, we therefore have

$$MR = P. \quad [10.4]$$

Marginal Revenue for a Downward-Sloping Demand Curve

A firm may not always be able to sell all it wants at the prevailing market price. If it faces a downward-sloping demand curve for its product, it can sell more only by reducing its selling price. In this case marginal revenue will be less than market price. To see why, assume in our prior example that to sell the 51st widget the firm must reduce its price to $.99. Total revenues are now $50.49 (= $.99 × 51), and the marginal revenue from the 51st widget is only $.49 (= $50.49 − $50.00). Even though the 51st widget sells for $.99, the extra revenue obtained from selling the widget is a net gain of only $.49 (a $.99 gain on the 51st widget less a $.50 reduction in revenue from the first 50). When selling one more unit causes market price to decline, marginal revenue is less than market price:

$$MR < P. \quad [10.5]$$

Firms that must reduce their prices to sell more of their products (that is, firms facing a downward-sloping demand curve for their products) must take this fact into account in deciding how to obtain maximum profits.

A Numerical Example

The result that marginal revenue is less than price for a downward-sloping demand curve is illustrated with a numerical example in Table 10.1. There

Table 10.1
Total and Marginal Revenue for Cassette Tapes (Q = 10 − P)

Price (P)	Quantity (Q)	Total Revenue (P · Q)	Marginal Revenue (MR)
$10	0	$ 0	
9	1	9	$ 9
8	2	16	7
7	3	21	5
6	4	24	3
5	5	25	1
4	6	24	−1
3	7	21	−3
2	8	16	−5
1	9	9	−7
0	10	0	−9

we have recorded the quantity of, say, tape cassettes demanded per week (Q), their price (P), total revenues from cassette sales (P · Q), and marginal revenue (MR) for a simple linear demand curve of the form

$$Q = 10 - P. \tag{10.6}$$

Total revenue from tape sales reaches a maximum at Q = 5, P = 5. For Q > 5, total revenues decline. Increasing tape sales beyond 5 per week actually causes marginal revenue to be negative.

In Figure 10.2 we have drawn this hypothetical demand curve and can use the figure to illustrate the marginal revenue concept. Consider, for example, the extra revenue obtained if the firm sells four tapes instead of three. When output is three, the market price per tape is $7 and total revenues (P · Q) are $21. These revenues are shown by the area of the rectangle P*AQ*0. If the firm produces four tapes per week instead, price must be reduced to $6 to sell this increased output level. Now total revenue is $24, illustrated by the area of the rectangle P**BQ**0. A comparison of the two revenue rectangles shows why the marginal revenue obtained by producing the fourth tape is less than its price. The sale of this tape does indeed increase revenue by the price at which it sells ($6). Revenue increases by the area of the light gray rectangle in Figure 10.2. But to sell the fourth tape, the firm must reduce its selling price from $7 to $6 on the first three tapes sold per week. That price reduction causes a fall in revenue of $3, shown as the area of the dark gray rectangle in Figure 10.2.

The net result is an increase in revenue of $3 ($6 − $3) rather than the gain of $6 that would be assumed if only the sale of the fourth tape is considered in isolation. The marginal revenue for other points in this hypothetical demand curve could also be illustrated. In particular, if you draw the case of a firm producing eight tapes instead of seven, you will see that marginal revenue at that level of output is negative.

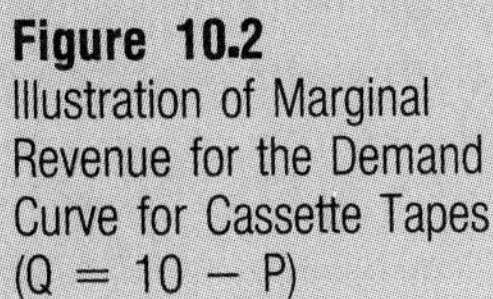

Figure 10.2
Illustration of Marginal Revenue for the Demand Curve for Cassette Tapes ($Q = 10 - P$)

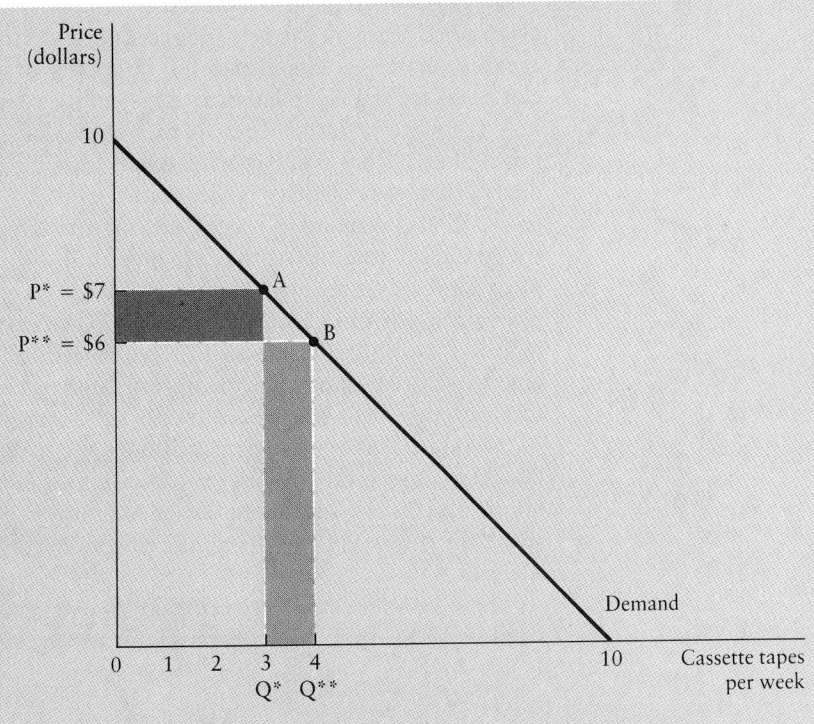

For this hypothetical demand curve, marginal revenue can be calculated as the extra revenue from selling one more tape. If the firm sells four tapes instead of three, for example, revenue will be $24 rather than $21. Marginal revenue from the sale of the fourth tape is therefore $3. This represents the gain of $6 from the sale of the fourth tape *less* the decline in revenue of $3 as a result of the fall in price for the first three tapes from $7 to $6.

Marginal Revenue and Price Elasticity

In Chapter 5 we introduced the concept of the price elasticity of demand ($e_{Q,P}$), which we defined as

$$e_{Q,P} = \frac{\text{Percentage change in Q}}{\text{Percentage change in P}}. \qquad [10.7]$$

We also showed that the price elasticity of demand provides some information about how total expenditures ($P \cdot Q$) change when price changes. A fall in price will increase total expenditures if demand is elastic ($e_{Q,P} < -1$), but such a fall will decrease total expenditures if demand is inelastic ($e_{Q,P} > -1$).

Marginal revenue is concerned with changes in quantity, not price. However, since for a negatively sloped demand curve increases in Q imply decreases in P, it is clear that the concepts of marginal revenue and price elasticity are closely related. In particular, attempting to sell one more unit may require a firm to reduce its price (if it doesn't, MR = P and the firm is a price taker). What will happen to total revenues (that is, to the product P · Q) depends on the elasticity of demand. From our previous discussion it is easy to see that if demand is elastic, selling one more unit will increase revenues: the marginal revenue of the last unit sold will be positive. Since demand is price responsive, selling one more unit will necessitate only a "small" fall in price; consequently total revenues will increase. On the other hand, if demand is inelastic, the firm will have to reduce the price substantially to be able to sell one more unit of output. This price decline will be so large that total revenues will be reduced by the sale: marginal revenue now is negative.[4] As an intermediate case, demand might be of unitary elasticity ($e_{Q,P} = -1$), in which case total revenues are constant. Selling one more unit will bring about a price decline of the exact magnitude necessary to keep P · Q constant. In that case the marginal revenue from the sale of one more unit is zero.

These relationships between marginal revenue and elasticity are summarized in Table 10.2. More generally, it can be shown that

$$MR = P\left(1 + \frac{1}{e_{Q,P}}\right), \qquad [10.8]$$

and all of the relationships in Table 10.2 can be derived from this basic equation.[5] For example, if demand is elastic ($e_{Q,P} < -1$), Equation 10.8 shows that MR is positive. Indeed, if demand is infinitely elastic ($e_{Q,P} = -\infty$), MR will equal price since, as we showed before, the firm is a price taker and cannot affect the price it receives.

As another use of Equation 10.8, suppose that a firm knew that the elasticity of demand for its product was −2. It might derive this figure from historical data that show that each 10 percent decline in its price has usually led to an increase in sales of about 20 percent. Now assume that the price of the firm's output is $10 per unit and the firm wishes to know how much additional revenue the sale of one more unit of output would yield. The additional unit of output will not yield $10 since the firm faces a downward-sloping demand curve: to sell the unit requires a reduction in its overall selling price. The firm can, however, use Equation 10.8 to calculate that the

---

[4]As long as marginal costs are positive, a profit-maximizing firm will not produce at a point on the demand curve for its products where demand is inelastic. In such a case, marginal revenue (negative) could not be equated to marginal cost (positive). In Chapters 15 and 16 we use this observation to show how the elasticity of demand may reflect something about market structure.

[5]The proof requires calculus. See Walter Nicholson, *Microeconomic Theory: Basic Principles and Extensions,* 4th ed. (Hinsdale, Ill.: Dryden Press, 1989), p. 357.

Table 10.2
Relationship between Marginal Revenue and Elasticity

Demand Curve	Marginal Revenue
Elastic ($e_{Q,P} < -1$)	MR > 0
Unit elastic ($e_{Q,P} = -1$)	MR = 0
Inelastic ($e_{Q,P} > -1$)	MR < 0

additional revenue yielded by the sale will be \$5 [= \$10 · (1 + 1/−2) = \$10 · ½]. The firm will produce this extra unit if marginal costs are less than \$5; that is, if MC < \$5, profits will be increased by the sale of one more unit of output. Although firms in the real world may use more complex means to decide on the profitability of increasing sales (or of lowering prices), our discussion here illustrates the logic these firms must use. They must recognize how changes in quantity sold affect price (or vice versa) and how these price changes affect total revenues.

Marginal Revenue Curve

Any demand curve has a marginal revenue curve associated with it. It is sometimes convenient to think of a demand curve as an *average revenue curve* in that it shows the revenue per unit (in other words, the price) yielded by alternative output choices. The marginal revenue curve, on the other hand, shows the extra revenue provided by the last unit sold. In the usual case of a downward-sloping curve, the marginal revenue curve will lie below the demand curve since at any level of output, marginal revenue is less than price.[6] In Figure 10.3 we have drawn such a curve together with the demand curve from which it was derived. For output levels greater than Q_1, marginal revenue is negative. As Q increases from 0 to Q_1, total revenues (P · Q) increase. However, at Q_1 total revenues ($P_1 \cdot Q_1$) are as large as possible; beyond this output level, price falls proportionately faster than output rises.[7]

Shifts in Demand and Marginal Revenue

In Chapter 5 we talked in detail about the possibility of a demand curve's shifting because of changes in factors such as income, other prices, or preferences. Whenever a demand curve shifts, its associated marginal revenue curve

[6] If demand is infinitely elastic (that is, if the demand curve is a horizontal line at some price), the average and marginal revenue curves coincide. Selling one more unit has no effect on price; therefore marginal and average revenue are equal.

[7] Another way of saying this is that beyond Q_1 demand is inelastic. See our discussion of elasticity along a linear demand curve in Chapter 5.

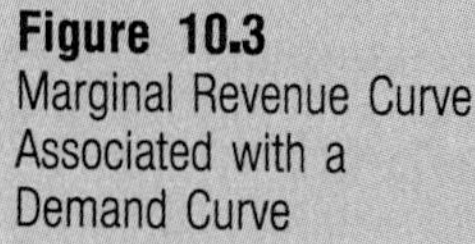

Figure 10.3
Marginal Revenue Curve Associated with a Demand Curve

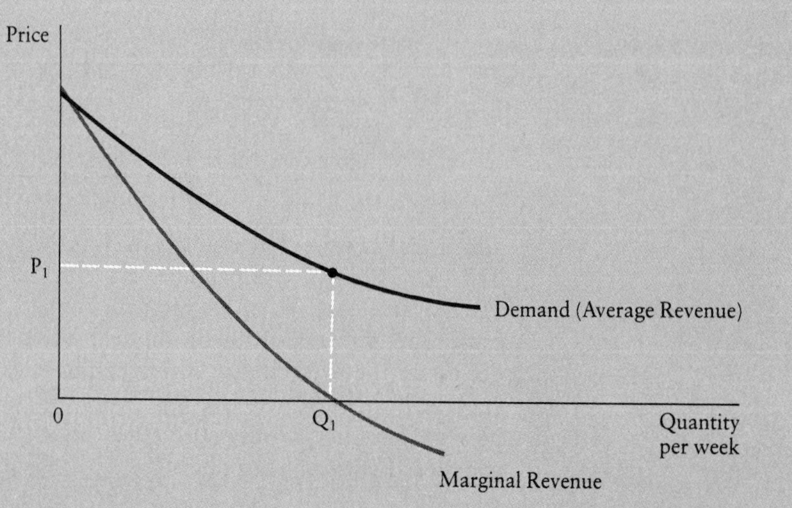

Since the demand curve is negatively sloped, the marginal curve will fall below the demand ("average revenue") curve. For output levels beyond Q_1, marginal revenue is negative. At Q_1 total revenue ($P_1 \cdot Q_1$) is a maximum; beyond this point additional increases in Q actually cause total revenues to fall because of the related declines in price.

shifts with it. This should be obvious since the marginal revenue curve is always calculated by referring to a specific demand curve. In later analysis we will have to keep in mind the kinds of shifts that marginal revenue curves might make when we talk about changes in demand.

Some economists doubt that firms are able to make calculations about marginal revenue or marginal cost with any degree of accuracy. For this and other reasons, there is considerable controversy over the precise meaning of the profit-maximization hypothesis. Before examining that controversy, Application 10.2: Profit Maximization and Airline Deregulation shows the importance of marginal decisions to the behavior of the airline industry following deregulation.

Controversy over the Profit-Maximization Hypothesis

The marginalist, profit-maximizing approach to firm behavior has been criticized on two general grounds: (1) that real-world firms do not have suitable information to be able to maximize profits, nor would they particularly want to maximize profits if they had such information and (2) that there exist alternative, equally simple hypotheses that can better explain what firms do. The second of these criticisms is dealt with later in this chapter, where some other simple motives that have been proposed as substitutes for profit maxi-

APPLICATION 10.2

Profit Maximization and Airline Deregulation

Under the Airline Deregulation Act of 1978, a variety of legal restrictions on the operations of U.S. airlines were to be gradually phased out. Regulation of airline fares was reduced or eliminated entirely, and rules governing the assignment of airline routes were relaxed significantly. These dramatic changes in the legal environment under which airlines operated provided economists with an ideal opportunity to observe how firms respond to altered circumstances. In general, these responses were quite consistent with the profit-maximization hypothesis.

Marginal Revenue

A clear example of the airlines' attention to marginal revenue was their development of new fare structures following deregulation. Prices for standard coach fares dropped relatively little since these fares are usually utilized by people traveling on business who have relatively inelastic demands. Little, if any, extra revenue would have been brought in by trying to lure additional coach fare passengers into flying. For special discount fares, it was an entirely different story, however. These fares were generally targeted at people with highly elastic travel demands (tourists, families traveling together, and so forth). In this case, large price reductions increased passenger demand significantly, thereby improving the passenger levels on many flights. Overall the increased use of discount fares resulted in a 17 percent decline in the average price per passenger-mile flown.[1] The structure of the price declines ensured that they generated far more additional revenue for the airlines than would an across-the-board fare cut of a similar magnitude. Whether airlines can continue such price discrimination in the new, more competitive environment is open to question, however.

Marginal Cost

The airlines' attention to marginal cost in response to deregulation also reflected what might have been expected on the basis of the profit-maximization hypothesis. Their fleets of aircraft could not be changed significantly in the short run, so airlines altered their route structures to coincide with the aircraft they already had. As Alfred Kahn has observed, from an economic point of view their planes represented "marginal costs with wings" that could easily be moved around once deregulation came.

Effects of such reallocations by airlines were readily apparent. Service in many small communities (previously required under Civil Aeronautics Board regulation) was curtailed. Flight lengths were generally brought into greater correspondence with the optimal operating characteristics of the aircraft. Many airlines adopted a "hub-and-spoke" system for connecting flights. Finally, slackening in the growth of air traffic in 1979–1980 left many airlines with excess capacity in their "wide-bodied" aircraft (747s, DC-10s, and L1011s). Since marginal costs of carrying additional passengers on such flights were quite low, fare discounting was aimed particularly at these flights. At times during the 1980s it was cheaper to fly coast-to-coast than to fly from New York to Cleveland.

To Think About

1. Some critics of airline deregulation have charged that it has led to an airline industry of uncertain financial health and has caused airlines to skimp on safety-related maintenance to keep costs down. Does this really reflect profit maximization? How would a determined advocate of deregulation respond to these charges?
2. How do you think airline employees (pilots, cabin attendants, luggage handlers, and so forth) feel about deregulation? Might employees of United Airlines or American Airlines feel differently than Eastern Airlines' employees?

[1]This figure and much of the analysis in this example are based on J. R. Meyer et al., *Airline Deregulation—The Early Experience* (Boston: Auburn House, 1981). See also S. Morrison and C. Winston, *Economic Effects of Airline Deregulation* (Washington, D.C.: Brookings Institution, 1986).

mization are mentioned. This section summarizes the arguments of the first type.[8]

Evidence on Profit Maximization

The empirical evidence on whether firms maximize profits is ambiguous. As we mentioned in Chapter 1, when firms answer questionnaires, they seldom rank profits as their only goal. Similarly they often say they lack sufficient information about their revenues or costs to make precise marginal choices. On the other hand, economists have found the profit-maximization hypothesis to be accurate in predicting certain aspects of firms' behavior. For example, many firms seem eager to enter into the most profitable industries, and large, stagnant firms often seek to diversify to increase profitability. Many firms have also adopted a "profit center" form of organization in which managers are judged by the profits their divisions earn.

Some of the attempts to reconcile this ambiguous evidence about profit maximization center on the question of the role of assumptions in economics. Many economists argue that one cannot judge the assumption of profit maximization either by *a priori* logic or by asking firms what they do. They feel the ultimate test is the predictive ability of the hypothesis. Remember Milton Friedman's analogy of the expert pool player who has no knowledge of the rules of physics that determine the movements of the balls on the table. Friedman argued that this ignorance on the part of the player does not prevent an observer from accurately predicting the player's behavior by applying physical principles.[9] Just as Molière's Monsieur Jourdain spoke prose all his life without knowing it, firms may in fact maximize profits despite the fuzziness of their responses to questions about their motives.

Survivorship Principle and the Market for Firms

A second set of reasons why economists tend to favor profit maximization as an explanation of firm behavior concerns competitive pressures. Profits represent a return to the owners of a firm. If the firm does not make the largest profits possible, owners may take their assets elsewhere. Indeed, in Chapter 12 we will see that competition itself can force all firms in an industry to operate with, at most, zero economic profits. If a firm opts not to follow the marginal rules, it will have negative profits. In that event, the owner will be even more likely to close down. Those firms that survive in such an environ-

[8]Further details on the material discussed here can be found in a series of debates between R. A. Lester and Fritz Machlup in the *American Economic Review* during the years 1946 and 1947.

[9]See Milton Friedman, "The Methodology of Positive Economics," in *Essays in Positive Economics* (Chicago: University of Chicago Press, 1953).

Survivorship principle The idea that in competitive markets only profit-maximizing firms are likely to survive.

ment will be those that do maximize profits. The **survivorship principle** states that we are likely to find only profit-maximizing firms in competitive markets.

Related to this principle is the fact that firms themselves can be bought and sold. Any firm that is not making maximum profits with its existing assets is a tempting target for an investor who believes he or she can do better. Like any economic goods, firms will gravitate toward those buyers who can do the most with them. This "market for corporate control" provides another force that encourages profit-maximizing behavior. The study of this market is one of the major new areas of research in the economics of business behavior, and we examine it in a bit more detail in the next chapter.

Alternatives to Profit Maximization

The debate over whether firms have enough information actually to maximize profits has caused economists to examine a number of other possible goals that may not be so hard for firms to achieve. Two of these are *revenue maximization* and *markup pricing*.

Revenue Maximization

Revenue maximization A goal for firms in which they work to maximize their total revenue rather than profits.

One alternative to profit maximization for firms is **revenue maximization.** This goal was first proposed by William J. Baumol who observed that most managerial incentives are tied to increases in sales revenues rather than to profits.[10] For example, higher salaries are paid to the managers of the largest corporations (with the highest dollar volume of sales) rather than to the managers of the most profitable ones. Other pieces of evidence also suggested to Baumol that revenue maximization might be the most important goal for firms. Often a firm's success is judged by the share of the market it commands. Firms that dominate the market may have a number of advantages over other firms, such as better credit with banks or greater consumer recognition of products.[11]

Figure 10.4 shows that a strictly revenue-maximizing firm would produce that quantity of output for which marginal revenue equals zero—the quantity Q^{**}. Output will be expanded as long as any additional revenue is obtainable. Baumol suggests that a firm may not go this far in pursuing sales volume to the exclusion of any consideration of cost, however. Instead, the firm's owners may require that some minimum amount of profits be earned. Baumol's firm would probably produce some quantity between that which a

[10] A clear statement of this hypothesis is found in Chapter 6 of William J. Baumol, *Business Behavior, Value and Growth*, rev. ed. (New York: Harcourt, Brace & World, 1967).

[11] It has also been suggested that maintaining market share is a reasonable long-run profit-maximizing strategy in an uncertain market environment.

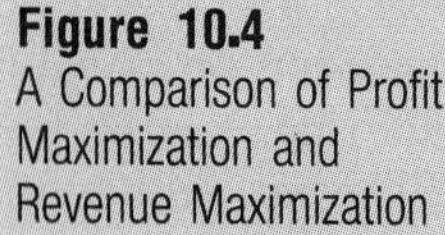

Figure 10.4
A Comparison of Profit Maximization and Revenue Maximization

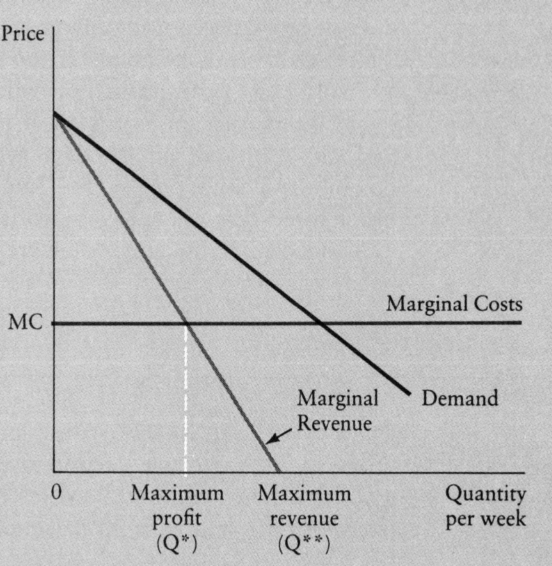

For simplicity we assume that each unit of output can always be produced at a cost of MC. A profit-maximizing firm will therefore produce output level Q*, for which MR = MC. If the firm pursues the goal of revenue maximization, however, it would proceed to output level Q**, since at this level of output marginal revenue is zero.

profit maximizer would produce (Q* in Figure 10.4) and that which a revenue maximizer would produce (Q** in Figure 10.4). Some of the issues involved in the conflict between profit maximization and sales maximization are reflected in Application 10.3: Textbook Royalties, which focuses on textbook pricing.

Markup Pricing

Even when they do profess to seek profits, many firms use very different methods than those described in our analysis. The most common such management technique for seeking profits is **markup pricing.** This section compares this technique to the profit-maximization model we have developed.

Markup pricing
Determining the selling price of a good by adding a percentage to the average cost of producing it.

The markup pricing technique works as follows. Management first computes the average total cost of producing some normal level of output. To this cost it then adds a profit "markup" to arrive at the good's selling price. Usually the profit markup is a fixed percentage of average costs, which means that the selling price is some multiple of average cost. With a markup of 50 percent, for example, firms would price their goods at 1.5 times average total cost. Unlike a revenue-maximizing firm, the firm that uses a markup pricing strategy is obviously paying some attention to costs. But is this firm actually maximizing profits?

APPLICATION 10.3

Textbook Royalties

Most authors (including the author of this textbook) receive royalties based on total book sales. Royalty rates usually range between 10 and 20 percent of the sales price of a book, although some particularly popular authors may be able to negotiate a higher rate. Once a contract is signed, royalties are a fixed fraction of the total value of sales, so authors would like their publishers to price their books in such a way as to maximize total sales revenue. That is, the authors would prefer the price to be set so that the quantity demanded will be that quantity for which marginal revenue is zero.

Potential Conflict

Publishers, on the other hand, may not agree with their authors. They may wish to price their books so that the quantity demanded is the quantity for which marginal revenue is equal to marginal cost. As Figure 10.4 illustrates, this will usually result in a higher price for the book and a lower quantity sold than revenue-maximizing authors would prefer.

The potential conflict between authors and publishers may also arise in their wishes about inputs. Authors may prefer publishers to invest additional resources to sell books as long as those resources yield any new sales, regardless of what these resources cost the publishers. Authors prefer elaborate sales efforts, large customer service departments, and special book features (such as elaborate graphics). Publishers, on the other hand, will want to use these devices only if the additional revenues they generate will exceed the cost of the devices. Conflicts about the marketing of a text may therefore be expected to arise frequently.

Textbook Contracts

This view of the author-publisher conflict may be too simplistic, however. The prevalence of royalty contracts for textbook publishing suggests that these provide benefits to both parties relative to other ways in which authors might be paid. In part this occurs because there may be little difference between revenue maximization and profit maximization in the case of textbooks. Since the marginal cost of a book is very low once the type has been set, the difference between MR = 0 and MR = MC may be trivial.

More generally, the royalty rate specified in a contract is open to negotiation. Therefore, it may be in both the author's and the publisher's interest to adopt sales strategies that make total profits as large as possible. Then they can choose a royalty rate that gives the author a "fair" share of these profits. Royalty contracts, especially those with rates that rise as a book's sales increase, also offer incentives to authors to produce a good product. As is often the case in economics, a deeper examination of the terms of an author's contract may suggest that it is more efficient than it first appears.

To Think About

1. Most textbook contracts also include an "advance" on the royalties that are expected to be earned. How do such advances reduce the risks for authors? Why are publishers willing to make such payments?
2. Many textbook "ancillaries" (workbooks, test banks, instructor's manuals, and so forth) have fixed fee contracts—that is, the author is simply paid a fixed amount for the product. Why might authors and publishers adopt such contracts? What are the likely consequences of these procedures?

A first distinction between profit maximization and markup pricing is that the former requires firms to use marginal cost in their calculations whereas the latter requires them to use average total cost. As we showed in Chapter 9, if a firm is producing at the low point of its average total cost curve, average and marginal costs are equal. Markup pricing and profit maximization, at least with regard to the cost side of the calculation, may not be very different in this case, especially if firms have long-run average total cost curves that are horizontal over a broad range of output levels.

A second principal difference between profit-maximizing behavior and markup pricing is that markup pricing seems to take no account of demand. A profit maximizer must, as we have shown, consider the marginal revenue from selling one more unit of output. A firm using a markup over average cost would appear to make no such consideration. Only if firms' markup were in some way influenced by demand would this not be the case.

Several observations suggest that firms do indeed consider demand in deciding on a markup. For example, convenience stores have much higher markups on specialty or emergency items, such as deli foods or cold remedies, than on everyday items such as milk or soft drinks that can be bought anywhere. Hot dogs sold at ball games or amusement parks usually have a higher price than hot dogs sold by street vendors, which probably reflects the greater choices available to consumers of the street vendors' hot dogs. If firms using a markup pricing strategy are profit maximizers, the markup would be higher for goods that are inelastically demanded.[12] Application 10.4: Actual Markup Pricing Behavior shows that there is some evidence to support this possibility.

Short-Run Supply by a Price-Taking Firm

Short-run supply decisions by a price-taking firm are our final and most important illustration of the profit-maximizing assumption. Our analysis here leads directly into the study of market supply and price determination that we take up in the next part. Here we focus only on the profit-maximizing decisions of a single firm.

Profit-Maximizing Decision

By definition, a price-taking firm has no effect on the price it receives for its product. In this case, as we showed earlier in this chapter, market price is also the marginal revenue from selling one more unit. No matter how much the firm sells, its decisions have no effect on this price. Under these assumptions the firm's desire to maximize profits then dictates that it should produce

[12]A precise analysis of this result would use Equation 10.8 together with the MR = MC rule:

$$MC = MR = P\left(1 + \frac{1}{e}\right),$$

where e is the price elasticity of demand. If AC = MC, we have,

$$\text{Markup} = \frac{P}{AC} = \frac{P}{MC} = \frac{e}{1 + e}.$$

If $e > -1$, demand is inelastic, and MR cannot be equal to MC; we need only examine elastic cases where $e < -1$. If demand is infinitely elastic ($e = -\infty$), then P/MC = 1 and there is no markup. As e gets closer to -1, the markup increases. If, for example, $e = -2$, the profit-maximizing markup is 2.0—price should be set at twice average and marginal cost.

APPLICATION 10.4

Actual Markup Pricing Behavior

Most available evidence indicates that major corporations take demand into account in their pricing policies. Markups are broadly consistent with the notion of profit maximization.

Evidence for Major Corporations

In their study of the pricing policies of U.S. Steel Corporation, Kaplan, Dirlam, and Lanzillotti found that the markup on steel products varied inversely with the elasticity of demand for these products. Margins were high on steel rails, for example, since this was a product line in which U.S. Steel faced little competition. On the other hand, margins were low on stainless steel and tin plate, since these products faced strong competition from aluminum and lumber producers. The authors found similar results for many major corporations, including E. I. du Pont de Nemours, Standard Oil Company of New Jersey, and Aluminum Company of America.[1] In all of them, target profit margins seemed to be related to the elasticity of demand, just as profit maximization requires. In a study of large Danish firms, B. Fog also found that target profit margins vary with demand conditions. He reports that many companies respond to questions about how profit margins are set by noting they will "charge what the traffic will bear" or that "market conditions determine the price."[2] In other words, markups are determined in a profit-maximizing way.

Evidence from Retailing

In their study of retailing, R. M. Cyert and J. G. March spent considerable effort analyzing the feedback from the market for the pricing of a product. Even though the firm may set prices and profit margins without considering demand, the subsequent reaction of the market (which provides information on the true demand situation) causes the firm to adjust its prices accordingly. Cyert and March applied their model to a department store's markdown policy and concluded that the prices of items are adjusted over time to meet demand conditions.[3] Any experienced bargain hunter knows that retailers adjust the prices of unpopular items downward much more rapidly than they reduce the prices of "hot" items. Price changing such as this is consistent with the notion that markups are set with profit-maximization goals in mind.

Evidence over the Business Cycle

Markups also seem to vary over the business cycle, and this is also consistent with profit maximization. During recessions, demand is weak and buyers may readily shift their purchases among firms. When business conditions are strong, firms may have somewhat increased market power. Profit maximization would therefore suggest that markups should vary systematically with overall business conditions; empirical evidence for the U.S. economy tends to support this supposition. Not only do markups seem to vary with general business conditions, but they also seem to be affected by other events that may affect overall product demand such as military purchases by the government or even what political party is in power.[4]

To Think About

1. Profit markups are much higher in the prescription drug industry than in the fast food industry. Is this consistent with profit-maximizing behavior?
2. Are price markups a good measure of the overall profitability of an industry? Is a high ratio of price to average cost an indication that an industry would represent a desirable investment?

[1] A. D. H. Kaplan, J. B. Dirlam, and R. F. Lanzillotti, *Pricing in Big Business: A Case Approach* (Washington, D.C.: Brookings Institution, 1958), pp. 172–174.

[2] B. Fog, *Industrial Pricing Policies* (Amsterdam: North-Holland Publishing Company, 1960), p. 104. See especially Chapter 6.

[3] R. M Cyert and J. G. March, *A Behavioral Theory of the Firm* (Englewood Cliffs, N.J.: Prentice-Hall, 1963), Chapter 7.

[4] See R. E. Hall, "The Relation between Price and Marginal Cost in U.S. Industry," *Journal of Political Economy* (October 1988): 921–947.

Figure 10.5
Short-Run Supply Curve for a Price-Taking Firm

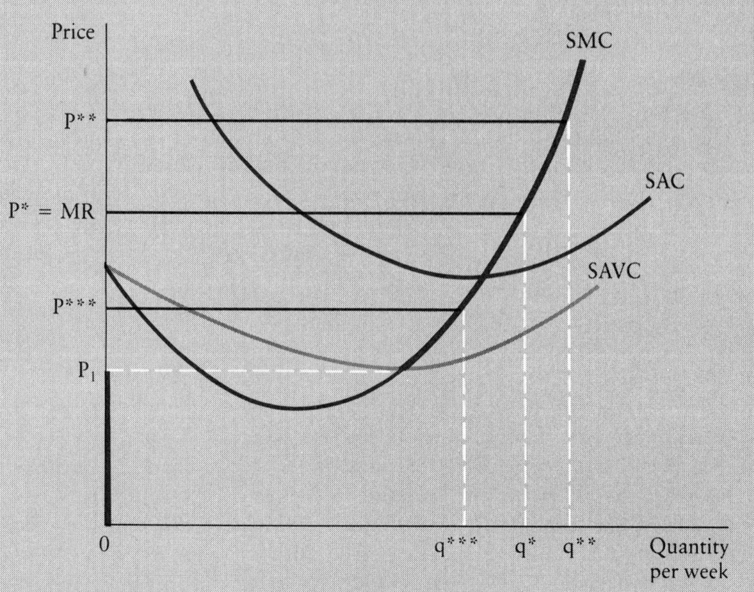

In the short run a price-taking firm will produce the level of output for which SMC = P. At P*, for example, the firm will produce q*. The SMC curve also shows what will be produced at other prices. For prices below SAVC, however, the firm will choose to produce no output. The heavy blue lines in the figure represent the firm's short-run supply curve.

that quantity for which marginal cost equals price. The short-run marginal cost curve is relevant to this decision in the short run.

Figure 10.5 shows the individual firm's short-run decision. The market price is given by P*. The demand curve facing the firm is therefore a horizontal line through P*. This line is labeled P* = MR as a reminder that this price-taking firm can always sell an extra unit without affecting the price. Output level q* provides maximum profits, since at q* price is equal to short-run marginal cost.[13] The fact that profits are positive can be seen by noting that at q* price exceeds average costs. The firm earns a profit on each unit sold. If price were below average cost (as is the case at q***), the firm would have a loss on each unit sold. If price and average cost were equal, profits would be zero.

[13]Here we use a lowercase q to denote the firm's output. In Chapter 12, the uppercase Q is used to denote the output of the industry as a whole. Here, and throughout Parts 4–6, firms' supply will be shown in color in the graphs.

A geometric proof that profits are at a maximum at q^* would proceed as follows. For output levels slightly less than q^*, price (P^*) exceeds short-run marginal cost. Reducing output below q^* would cut back more on revenues than on costs, and profits would fall. For output levels greater than q^*, marginal costs exceed P^*. Producing more than q^* would now cause costs to rise more rapidly than revenues, and again profits would fall. This means that if a firm produces either more or less than q^*, its profits will be lowered. Only at q^* are profits at a maximum.

Notice that at q^* the marginal cost curve has a positive slope. This is required if profits are to be a true maximum. If P = MC on a negatively sloped section of the marginal cost curve, this is not a point of maximum profits, since increasing output would yield more in revenues (price times the amount produced) than this production would cost (marginal cost would decline if the MC curve had a negative slope). Consequently, profit maximization requires both that P = MC and that at this point marginal cost is increasing.

The Firm's Supply Curve

The positively sloped portion of the short-run marginal cost curve is the short-run supply curve for this price-taking firm, since the curve shows how much the firm will produce for every possible market price. At a higher price of P^{**}, for example, the firm will produce q^{**} since it will find it in its interest to incur the higher marginal costs q^{**} entails. With a price of P^{***}, on the other hand, the firm opts to produce less (q^{***}) since only a lower output level will result in lower marginal costs to meet this lower price. By considering all possible prices that the firm might face, we can see by the marginal cost curve how much output the firm should supply at each price.

The Shutdown Decision

For very low prices we have to be careful about this conclusion. Should market price fall below P_1, the profit-maximizing decision would be to produce nothing. Prices less than P_1 do not cover variable costs. There will be a loss on each unit produced in addition to the loss of all fixed costs. By shutting down production, the firm still must pay fixed costs, but it avoids the losses incurred on each unit produced. Since, in the short run, the firm cannot close down and avoid all costs, its best decision is to produce no output. On the other hand, a price only slightly above P_1 means the firm should produce some output. Even though profits may be negative (which they will be if price falls below short-run average total costs—the case at P^{***}), as long as variable costs are covered, the profit-maximizing decision is to continue produc-

APPLICATION 10.5

The Demise of OPEC and Drilling for Oil in the United States

Beginning in the early 1970s the Organization of Petroleum Exporting Countries (OPEC) came to exercise a dramatic effect on the world pricing of crude oil. Between 1971 and 1980 world oil prices increased more than 800 percent. In real, inflation-adjusted terms the increase was somewhat less spectacular, but still amounted to a threefold increase in the relative price of crude oil. For oil well drillers throughout the world this price increase provided a clear signal to produce more. In the United States, for example, as Table 1 shows, the number of wells drilled more than tripled between 1971 and 1980. Increasingly these additional wells were drilled in high-cost locations (for example, in deep water offshore or in difficult environments such as Alaska). The data in Table 1 also show that the wells were drilled to a somewhat greater average depth, further illustrating the willingness of firms to incur higher marginal costs to produce crude oil.

Price Decline and Supply Behavior

The steep recession of 1982 and 1983, combined with vast new supplies of crude oil becoming available (in the North Sea and Mexico, for example), put considerable pressure on the OPEC pricing structure. By 1984 nominal crude oil prices had declined by about 25 percent from their highest levels. In real terms the decline was even sharper. U.S. drillers were quick to respond to these changed circumstances. As Table 1 shows, 58 percent fewer wells were drilled in 1984 than in 1981, and those wells that were drilled were not quite as deep as had previously been the case.

Table 1

World Oil Prices and Oil Well Drilling Activity in the United States

	World Price per Barrel	Real Price per Barrel[a]	Number of Wells Drilled	Average Depth (ft)
1973	3.89	3.04	9,705	3,946
1981	31.77	11.78	38,725	4,183
1984	24.59	8.44	16,276	3,918

Source: Statistical Abstract of the United States, 1985.
[a]World price divided by the Producer Price Index (1967 = 100).

The decline in oil prices also prompted oil well operators to shut down some marginal operations. Many "stripper wells" (wells producing less than 10 barrels of oil per day) have relatively high operating costs so the decline in oil prices caused many to cease operation. In some cases it would be a simple matter to reopen these wells if prices rise, but in other cases the shutdown may be permanent since water may seep into the depleted oil reservoirs.

Consequences of the Decline in Drilling

The decline in drilling and oil production activity after 1983 posed significant problems for suppliers to the oil drilling industry. For example, producers of high-strength oil pipe in Texas and Louisiana suffered huge financial losses as they were not able to sell enough pipe to keep their factories fully utilized. Similarly, firms in the business of supplying oil drilling teams with everything from food and clothing to candy and VCR movies found that there was little work to be had. Many cities in Louisiana and Texas experienced sharp economic downturns as the effects of the drilling cutback spread. By 1988 the federal government had adopted special programs to aid workers affected by the cutback, and fears were being increasingly expressed in Congress about the long-term health of the industry.[1]

To Think About

1. Are U.S. producers of crude oil accurately described as price takers? How many companies are there in this industry? Is a firm such as Exxon too large to be a price taker? Perhaps you'll need to look up some data on the oil industry to resolve these issues.
2. This example shows that there are many kinds of margins to consider in connection with marginal cost (for example, location and depth of drilling). What are some of the other factors that may influence the marginal cost of drilling for oil?

[1]For a thorough discussion of drilling costs in the oil industry, see U.S. Congress, Office of Technology Assessment, *U.S. Oil Production: The Effect of Low Prices* (Washington, D.C.: U.S. Government Printing Office, 1987).

tion. Fixed costs must be paid in any case, and any price that covers variable costs will provide some revenue as a partial offset to these fixed costs.[14]

Shutdown price
The price below which the firm will choose to produce no output in the short run. Equal to minimum average variable cost.

For prices above P_1 the firm's short-run marginal cost curve shows how much output will be supplied. The price P_1 represents a **shutdown price,** however. If price falls below that level, nothing will be produced. The colored segment of the vertical axis up to P_1 reflects these zero-output decisions. Our later analysis of competitive markets makes considerable use of this short-run supply curve for price-taking firms. Application 10.5: The Demise of OPEC and Drilling for Oil in the United States illustrates the kinds of effects that changing prices can have on firms' willingness to incur various levels of marginal cost.

Summary

In this chapter we examine the assumption that firms seek to achieve maximum profits in making their decisions. Although some questions have been raised about whether firms have all of the information that would be required to make such decisions, we show that much available evidence supports the profit-maximizing approach to analyzing firm behavior. We also describe how a variety of market pressures may enforce profit maximization by firms. The profit-maximization assumption seems to provide a good foundation for our study of firm behavior. A number of conclusions follow from this assumption:

- In making output decisions a firm should produce the output level for which marginal revenue equals marginal cost. Only at this level of production is the cost of extra output, at the margin, exactly balanced by the revenue it yields.
- Similar marginal rules apply to the hiring of inputs by profit-maximizing firms. These are examined in Part 6.
- For a firm facing a downward-sloping demand curve, marginal revenue will be less than price. In this case the marginal revenue curve will lie below the market demand curve.
- The techniques of analyzing profit-maximizing firms can also be used to study firms that use other strategies, such as revenue maximization or

[14]Some algebra may clarify matters. Since we know total costs equal the sum of fixed and variable costs,

$$TC = FC + VC,$$

profits are given by

$$\pi = TR - TC = P \cdot q - FC - VC.$$

If $q = 0$, variable costs are zero, so

$$\pi = -FC,$$

so the firm will only produce if $\pi > -FC$. But that means that

$$P \cdot q > VC \quad \text{or} \quad P > VC/q = AVC.$$

markup pricing. In some cases, pursuit of such other strategies may be consistent with profit maximization.

- A firm whose decisions have no effect on the price of its product (a price taker) will maximize profits where price equals marginal cost. The marginal cost curve will be the supply curve for such a firm. If price falls below short-run average variable costs, however, the firm will choose to shut down and produce no output.

Review Questions

1. Why do economists assume firms seek maximum economic profits? Since accounting rules determine what the dollar value of profits actually is, why should firms be concerned with the economists' concept of cost? Which notion of profits do you believe is most important to entrepreneurs who are considering starting a business?
2. For its owners a firm represents an asset that they own. Why would the pursuit of profit maximization by the firm make this asset as valuable as possible?
3. Explain whether each of the following actions would affect the firm's profit-maximizing decision by describing how it would affect the firm's marginal revenue function or its marginal cost function. Or, would the action have no effect on the firm's profit-maximizing decision?

    a. An increase in the cost of a variable input such as labor.
    b. A decline in the market price for a price-taking firm.
    c. Institution of a small fixed fee to be paid to the government for the right of doing business.
    d. Institution of a 50 percent tax on the firm's profits.
    e. Institution of a per-unit tax on each unit the firm produces.
    f. Receipt of a no-strings-attached grant from the government.
    g. Receipt of a subsidy per unit of output from the government.
    h. Receipt of a subsidy per worker hired from the government.

4. Why is the assumption of profit maximization sometimes referred to as the assumption of "marginal behavior"? Explain how such behavior might be reflected in a firm's choice of output. How would it be reflected in its hiring of inputs? How might it be reflected in decisions such as whether to package its product in a fancy box or whether to invest more in an advertising campaign?
5. What kind of demand curve does a price-taking firm face? For such a curve, what is the relationship between price and marginal revenue? Explain why an individual firm can be a price taker even though the entire market demand for its product may be downward sloping. Why would a firm believe that its output decisions have no effect on market prices?
6. Under what conditions would a firm face a downward-sloping demand curve for its own output? Explain why marginal revenue is less than price in such a situation. Is it possible that a firm can produce one more unit and sell that unit at a positive price, but still find that its total revenue has fallen?
7. If a firm faces a negatively sloped linear demand curve, at what output level does its marginal revenue reach zero? Why would a revenue-maximizing firm choose to produce such a level of output? Would this output level be greater or smaller than what would be produced by a profit-maximizing firm? Are there any situations in which the two output choices would be relatively close to each other?
8. Why might a firm choose to use markup pricing even if it were interested in profit maximization? Explain how a firm interested in maximum profits should choose its markup.

9. Why do economists believe short-run marginal cost curves have positive slopes? Why does this belief lead to the notion that short-run supply curves have positive slopes? What kind of signal does a higher price send to a firm with increasing marginal costs? Would a reduction in output ever be the profit-maximizing response to an increase in price for a price-taking firm?
10. Why might short-run variable costs also be called "avoidable" costs? How can such costs be avoided? Why is it impossible to avoid short-run fixed costs? Why are avoidable costs relevant to the short-run shutdown decision, but fixed costs are not? Would fixed costs be relevant to a firm's decision to stay in business over the long run?

Problems

10.1 John's Lawn Mowing Service is a small business that acts as a price taker (MR = P). The prevailing market price of lawn mowing is \$20 per acre. Although John can use the family mower for free (but see problem 10.2), he has other costs given by

$$\text{Total cost} = .1q^2 + 10q + 50$$

$$\text{Marginal cost} = .2q + 10$$

where q = the number of acres John chooses to mow in a week.

a. How many acres should John choose to mow in order to maximize profit?
b. Calculate John's maximum weekly profit.
c. Graph these results and label John's supply curve.

10.2 Consider again the profit-maximizing decision of John's Lawn Mowing Service from problem 10.1. Suppose John's greedy father decides to charge John for the use of the family lawn mower.

a. If the lawn mower charge is set at \$100 per week, how will this affect the acres of lawns John chooses to mow? What will his profits be?
b. Suppose instead that John's father requires John to pay 50 percent of his weekly profits as a mower charge. How will this affect John's profit-maximizing decision?
c. If John's greedy father imposes a charge of \$2 per acre for use of the family mower, how will this affect John's marginal cost function? How will it affect his profit-maximizing decision? What will his profits be now? How much will John's greedy father get?
d. Suppose finally that John's father collects his \$2 per acre by collecting 10 percent of the revenues from each acre John mows. How will this affect John's profit-maximizing decision? Explain why you get the same result here as for part c.

10.3 Suppose a farmer can sell all the corn that he or she can produce at a price of P. Show the total revenue curve for the farmer and demonstrate geometrically (using a graph similar to Figure 10.1) that in this case the profit-maximizing output level occurs where marginal cost is equal to P.
10.4 Widgets International faces a demand curve given by

$$q = 10 - P$$

and has a constant marginal and average cost of \$3 per widget produced. Complete the following table for the various production levels.

q	P	TR (= P · q)	MR	MC	AC	π	D = TR − TC
1							
2							
3							
4							
5							
6							
7							
8							
9							
10							

How many widgets will the firm produce in order to maximize profits? Explain briefly why this is so.

10.5 Suppose that a firm faces a demand curve that has a constant elasticity of −2. This demand curve is given by

$$q = 256/P^2.$$

Suppose also that the firm has a marginal cost curve of the form

$$MC = .001q.$$

a. Graph these demand and marginal cost curves.
b. Calculate the marginal revenue curve associated with the demand curve; graph this curve. (Hint: Use Equation 10.8 for this part of the problem.)
c. At what output level does marginal revenue equal marginal cost?

10.6 Suppose a firm faces the following demand curve:

$$q = 60 - 2P.$$

a. Calculate the total revenue curve for the firm (in terms of q).
b. Using a tabular revenue proof, show that the firm's MR curve is given by $MR = 30 - q$.
c. Assume also that the firm has a MC curve given by $MC = .2q$. What output level should the firm produce to maximize profits?
d. Graph the demand, MC, and MR curves and the point of profit maximization.

10.7 A firm faces a demand curve given by

$$q = 100 - 2P.$$

Marginal and average costs for the firm are constant at $10 per unit.

a. Use a graphic or tabular proof to show that, for this demand curve, $MR = 50 - q$.
b. What output level should the firm produce to maximize profits? What are profits at that output level?
c. What output level should the firm produce to maximize revenues? What are profits at that output level?
d. Suppose the firm wishes to maximize revenues subject to the constraint that it earn $12 in profits for each of the 64 machines it employs. What level of output should it produce?
e. Graph your results.

*10.8 Universal Widget produces high-quality widgets at its plant in Gulch, Nevada, for sale throughout the world. The cost function for total widget production (q) is given by

$$\text{Total costs} = .25q^2.$$
$$\text{Marginal costs} = .50q.$$

Widgets are demanded only in Australia (where the demand curve is given by $q = 100 - 2P$ and $MR = 50 - q$) and Lapland (where the demand curve is given by $q = 100 - 4P$ and $MR = 25 - 2q$). If Universal Widget can control the quantities supplied to each market, how many should it sell in each location in order to maximize total profits?

*Denotes a problem that is rather difficult.

CHAPTER 11

Further Applications of the Theory of the Firm

Our analysis of the firm and its decisions in Chapter 10 was based on a very simple model in which the manager chooses levels of inputs and outputs with the sole goal of obtaining maximum profits. In this chapter we move beyond this simple model by looking more closely at the internal operations of firms. We focus on the nature of firms and on the kinds of contracts that exist between firms and their workers and between firms' owners and hired managers. By so doing we hope to provide a somewhat more detailed picture of how firms operate. The topics in this chapter represent some of the most important areas of current research in economics. Many economists believe that in order to understand such diverse topics as persistent unemployment, worker productivity, and corporate takeovers, a necessary first step is to develop a better understanding of the firm itself. A major purpose of this chapter, then, is to introduce some of the recent work related to these topics.

Why Do Firms Exist?

The wide variety of existing firms has prompted economists to speculate about the kinds of factors that might influence their organization. Ronald Coase laid out the basic principles of these investigations in a famous 1937 article.[1] To Coase, firms were an alternative to the marketplace as a way of

[1]R. H. Coase, "The Nature of the Firm," *Economica* (November 1937): 386–405. For a more recent survey see O. E. Williamson, "The Modern Corporation: Origins, Evolution, Attributes," *Journal of Economic Literature* (December 1981): 1537–1568.

organizing production. At one extreme, think of a situation in which all production is carried out by individuals. A person who wanted to, say, produce an automobile would buy the parts from thousands of independent suppliers, assemble these parts, and then turn the car over to someone else to sell. All transactions in such a situation would be among individuals who would each be very specialized producers. At the alternative extreme, all production in an economy might take place inside a single vast firm. This firm would coordinate the production of all automobiles, all automobile parts, and everything else through nonmarket, command and control directives. In such a world there would be no need for any market transactions involving intermediate goods.

To Coase, the location of an actual organization of production along this spectrum of possibilities was largely determined by cost considerations. Specifically, he argued that a firm's size and complexity would expand up to the point at which the costs involved in making additional transactions internally were exactly balanced by the costs involved in making the transactions through the market. In order to understand the size and scope of a firm's activities, we must therefore examine the relative significance of these various costs.

Advantages of the Market

Purchasing intermediate products in the marketplace offers a number of potential cost advantages to a firm. Because many firms buy from a single supplier, that supplier may be able to achieve economies of scale in production that would not be attainable if the firm tried to produce the input internally. For example, producers of personal computers (especially IBM "clones") purchase all of the principal internal electronics from one or two suppliers. Since electronic chip manufacturing involves substantial economies of scale whereas computer assembly does not, many computer producers are not integrated backward into the product of chips.

Uncertainties in the demand for a firm's product may also provide a good reason for the firm to purchase its inputs in the market. Since the input supplier can sell to many firms, it may be able to maintain a fairly smooth flow of production even though sales to any one user may be quite erratic. Small convenience stores, for example, depend on outside firms to supply them with a wide range of items they sell only occasionally ("peg-board" items such as scissors, labels, or playing cards) whereas they may develop their own supply of regularly demanded items such as milk or deli sandwiches.

Finally, reliance on markets for inputs may permit the firm to utilize the pressures of competition to restrain costs. It may have the option of taking its business elsewhere if a particular supplier becomes too costly. An integrated firm must instead try to keep its production costs down through various types of internal control mechanisms. Indeed, in some very large firms, competition between divisions may be initiated purposely to keep production costs in line. In many situations reliance on the marketplace serves this function automatically.

Advantages of Integration

Using the marketplace to acquire intermediate inputs for the firm also has many undesirable features, however. Purchasing inputs from someone else requires that the firm undertake some type of transaction, which may have costs associated with it. Thus the firm must find a suitable provider, negotiate contract terms, and arrange for the goods to be delivered. All of these costs may be reduced (or entirely eliminated) if the firm decides to produce the input internally. Of course, internal production requires that the firm spend something for monitoring and controlling the production process. An independent provider would incur similar costs, however, and with internal production a firm may be more certain that production quality standards are met. Overall then, integration of the production process might be expected to enable the firm to obtain significant savings in transactions costs.

The need for specialized equipment provides a second possible rationale for expanding the types of functions carried on within the firm. If a firm must utilize a machine that is useful only to it (perhaps because the equipment must fit into a unique location or use a particular type of fuel), then it is probably less costly for the firm to buy than to try to locate another firm willing to make the investment. Only in relatively rare instances will a supplier firm invest in equipment that is only useful to one buyer since that puts the supplier in a very risky position. In such a case, the supplier can be viewed as a "hostage" of the purchasing firm and may have to make contract concessions to it during the equipment's lifetime. Therefore, in general, suppliers will not invest in such specialized equipment, and firms will usually make such purchases for themselves.

A final, related way in which a firm may enlarge the scope of its activities in order to minimize transactions costs concerns the hiring of workers with specialized skills. If workers must learn special skills that are uniquely valuable to one firm (for example, computer programmers who know the machine language for a particular line of computers), it may be more beneficial for the firm to develop long-term contractual relationships with these workers than to purchase their services from some other firm. In that way, as we shall see in the next section, the firm can structure employment contracts that give the workers an incentive to stay with the firm. If the workers were employed by an outside supplier, they might have fewer incentives to continue to use their specialized skills for the benefit of the final producer.

Size and Scope of the Firm

These considerations suggest that the size and scope of a firm's activities are an important subject for economic analysis. Although it made sense to start our study of demand by defining the basic unit of analysis as the individual (or perhaps the family), defining the basic unit of analysis for supply decisions must necessarily involve some ambiguity. Ultimately, the definition of "the firm" is a fuzzy one that is determined by a constantly changing economic environment. Only a careful consideration of all the costs involved can provide an understanding of why the size of a firm changes over time. Still, at a given time, the firm is a legal entity with a fairly well-defined structure. Now we turn to examine some of the forces that shape the contractual nature of that structure.

Contracts within Firms

Once the basic nature of a firm is decided upon, the activities of workers, managers, and suppliers of capital must be coordinated and controlled. This is accomplished through a series of contracts among these parties. In some cases the contracts may be explicitly written down—for example, the contract between the United Automobile Workers and General Motors runs for hundreds of pages. In many other instances, however, contracts may be in the form of implicit understandings about what the terms of employment are. Even though such contracts are not on paper, they may be very effective in assuring that the rights and responsibilities of the various parties are followed.

The modern study of the theory of the firm is primarily a study of these various contracts. The firm itself is the legal entity (in the United States, legally firms are treated as individuals) that usually represents one side of the contract, and workers, managers, and capital suppliers represent the other side. These parties face the problem of developing contracts that are desirable to everyone concerned. For example, contracts with workers must be desirable from the workers' point of view in terms of the wages paid and the working conditions provided, and desirable from the firm's point of view in terms of providing incentives for the workers to perform in a productive way. Creating such contracts may be a costly and tedious process even when nothing has to be explicitly written down. And the final solutions adopted may, at first glance, seem unusual or even counterproductive. But the contracting process is necessary for any firm, and there will usually be good reasons for the provisions that are chosen.

Contracts with Workers

Fewer than 20 percent of American workers are represented by unions with collective bargaining agreements. The fraction of workers covered by such formal arrangements is somewhat higher in other Western countries, but even in these other countries most workers are not covered by this sort of explicit contract. Still, virtually all employees have clear understandings with their employers about what their duties are and how they will be paid. In Chapters 18 and 19 we will examine the theory of how wage levels are determined. Here we are not interested in the wage itself, but rather will focus on explicit and implicit employment contracts and show how they may affect the firm's costs and its supply decisions.

Job-Specific Skills and Long-Term Contracts

As workers hold a job longer, they learn to do it better. Anyone who has ever started a new job knows the feeling of being confused and perplexed when trying to fit into a new employment situation. A new worker's productivity may be negative for the first few weeks because he or she asks so many questions and makes so many mistakes that total firm output may actually decline for a while. Even after the chaos of orientation has ended, new workers may not be very productive until they learn what the job entails and how they can work most effectively with those around them. In economic terms, any new worker must learn a set of **job-specific skills,** and that learning process will be time-consuming and costly.

Job-specific skills Skills learned on a job that enable a worker to do that specific job better.

Firms wish to reduce these costs as much as possible. The most direct way to do that is to adopt policies that encourage workers to stay with the firm. In Chapters 8 through 10 we were not concerned with this issue. Nothing in those chapters would have prevented a firm from hiring a different set of workers every hour as long as they all could be hired at the prevailing wage rate. In fact, however, such employee turnover would be very costly for firms both because of the expenses involved in hiring new employees (such as the paperwork) and because of the low productivity of new employees. Instead, firms will try to develop a longer-term relationship with their employees.

Effects on Employment Decisions

One consequence of such a long-term employment policy is that firms will be reluctant to vary the number of workers they hire in response to temporary fluctuations in the demand for their products. They may make short-run decisions that are not exactly the same as those we examined in Chapters 9 and 10. Figure 11.1 illustrates such a situation. Panel a of this figure shows a price-taking firm's isoquant map, and Panel b shows its short-run supply (and marginal cost) curve. Initially, the firm faces a market price of P_2 for its output and opts to produce at a level of q_2 per week as shown in Panel b. Assuming the firm has been producing q_2 for some time, it will have adjusted both its capital and labor inputs to their cost-minimizing levels K_2, L_2. These are shown in Panel a.

Suppose now that the market price of this firm's product falls temporarily to P_0—perhaps because a recession temporarily reduces the demand for most goods. How will the firm respond to this decline? According to our discussion in Chapter 10, the firm would reduce output to q_0 and reduce its hiring of labor to L_0 since capital is fixed at K_2 in the short run. Under our previous assumptions, this temporary cutback in hiring could be accomplished by the firm with no special problems.

If workers have unique job-specific skills, however, reducing employment in this way may be costly for the firm. Once a worker is laid off, he or she may seek another job. Job-specific skills already acquired would be lost to the

Figure 11.1
With Implicit Contracts, Output and Hiring Decisions May Be Less Flexible

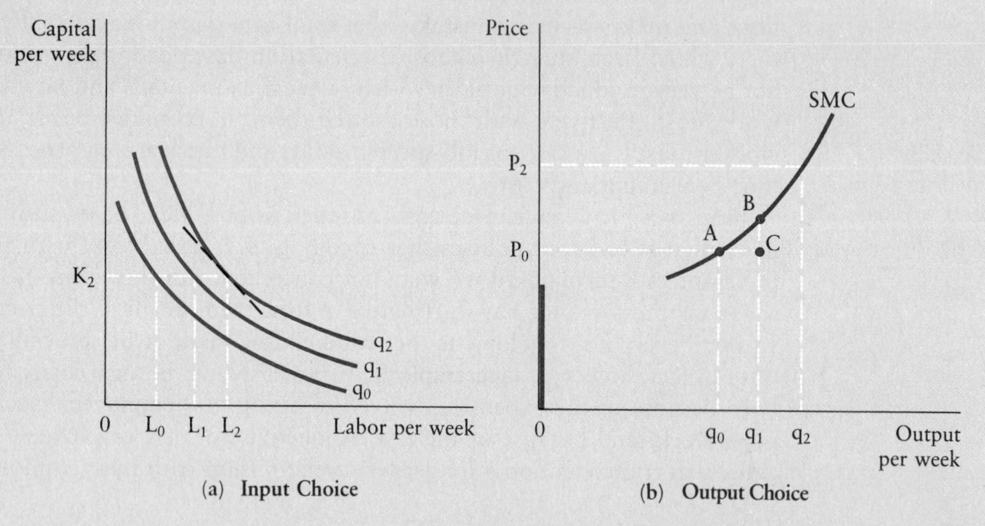

With no costs associated with changing labor input, a firm faced with a decline in price from P_2 to P_0 would reduce output from q_2 to q_0 and reduce labor input from L_2 to L_0. If there were an implicit contract between the workers and the firm, hiring might only fall to L_1, and output to q_1. This would still be the most profitable output level since costs associated with reducing labor input to L_0 would exceed profits lost at q_1 (area ABC).

firm making the layoff. Even if the worker ultimately is hired back by this firm once the price returns to P_2, he or she may still need to readjust to the work process. For these reasons, the firm may hesitate to reduce employment immediately in response to temporary declines in demand. It may, instead, reassign workers to nonproduction activities (for example, cleaning up the stockroom or doing preventive maintenance on machines), or it may continue to produce and add the surplus goods to inventory. The firm might also change work schedules, as discussed in Application 11.1: Short-Time Compensation and Layoffs.

In all of these cases the nature of the explicit or implicit contracts between workers and firms makes employment decisions far more complicated than our previous models assumed. Since a reduction of labor input to L_0 in Figure 11.1 may therefore be very costly, a more modest step might be taken. The firm could, for example, reduce hiring to L_1 and produce output level q_1. Such an output level would not provide maximum profits under our previous analysis of supply (see Panel b of Figure 11.1), but it may be more profitable

APPLICATION 11.1

Short-Time Compensation and Layoffs

When firms need to reduce the labor they employ, they have two options: they can reduce the number of hours each employee works, or they can lay off some employees completely. During recessions firms use both of these methods to adjust their labor input. Firms in the United States seem more willing to use layoffs than do firms in other countries such as West Germany or Japan where hours reductions are much more common.

Disadvantages of Layoffs

This "layoff-prone" nature of the U.S. economy has been a concern to many economists both because of the problems that unemployment poses for laid-off workers and because of the inefficiencies that layoffs may cause. When employees are laid off, they may seek other jobs and, if the layoff lasts for a while, may lose some of their job skills. Rehiring workers after layoffs can be a costly process for the firm. Many of these inefficiencies could be avoided if firms reduced hours of work during recessions, which would keep the employment relationship largely intact.

Encouraging Hours Reductions

One policy that has been suggested to encourage employees and employers to choose hours reductions instead of layoffs is for workers on short time to receive unemployment benefits for the hours they do not work. Under the rules that prevail in most states, unemployment benefits can be collected only if the worker is completely laid off. Some economists believe this policy encourages layoffs rather than hour reductions. As evidence they point to European countries where workers generally are able to collect benefits for hours reductions and where layoffs are much less prevalent. During the economic downturns of the mid-1970s and the early 1980s, for example, over 80 percent of labor force time lost in the United States resulted from layoffs whereas only about 40 percent came from layoffs in Western European economies. If these differences are caused by differences in unemployment insurance laws, some policymakers have argued, perhaps the United States should consider adopting European practices.

Adoption of Short-Time Compensation by the States

In 1977 California became the first state to adopt a short-time compensation provision in its unemployment insurance law. Since that time, about a dozen other states have followed. One study of the 1982–1983 recession found that firms that used short-time benefits reduced their layoffs by about 15 percent over what they would have been without the program.[1] For the relatively few firms that used it, the program did seem to be effective in preserving the long-term employment relationship for some workers. As the program becomes more widely understood, its use in future recessions may be even more substantial.

To Think About

1. Why should firms care whether or not their employees receive unemployment insurance benefits? Can't they make decisions on how to reduce their work forces without thinking about the workers' well-being? What does this example suggest about the relationship between employers and employees?
2. Unemployment insurance is financed by a tax on employers. In some cases tax rates are adjusted to reflect a firm's unemployment history. Would the way in which such rates are calculated have an effect on how firms react to a decline in their labor requirements?

[1]For a summary, see Stuart Kerachsky, Walter Nicholson, Edward Cavin, and Alan Hershey, "Work Sharing Programs: An Evaluation of Their Use," *Monthly Labor Review* (May 1986): 31–33.

than q_0 once all the costs associated with changing labor input are taken into account—that is, if the costs of reducing labor further exceed the profits lost when the output level is q_1 rather than q_0 (area ABC). Consequently, the firm's short-run supply (and hiring) decisions may be less responsive to temporary price changes than our simple models in Chapter 10 suggested.

Other Effects of Implicit Contracts

Long-term implicit contracts may affect other aspects of the worker-firm relationship. Both parties may find it attractive to adopt incentive schemes that encourage workers to stay with a firm rather than to switch jobs in response to other opportunities. Seniority-based wage systems are probably the most important example of the way in which workers are rewarded for staying with a firm. The widespread use of such systems, instead of systems in which compensation is based exclusively on an individual worker's productivity, illustrates how implicit contracts serve to tie workers and firms together as a team in order to develop an efficient overall organization of production.

Special types of nonwage compensation are also used to achieve this result. Pension benefits are usually based on length of service and often depend on the financial success of the firm as well. Some firms use bonus payments as a way of supplementing wages. This practice is quite common in Japan, as Application 11.2: Wage Bonuses in Japan explains. Some authors argue that such bonuses give workers a more direct stake in the success of their firms. Employee stock ownership plans (ESOPs) may also encourage workers to be more productive in their current jobs by giving them a stake in the financial success of the firm.

These possible outcomes of the implicit contract between workers and the firm suggest that, at least in some cases, long-term employees will be paid more than it would cost the firm to hire replacements for them. In the interest of maintaining a long-term productive arrangement, the firm will pay an **efficient wage** higher than the prevailing market wage, w.[2] By itself, such an action would tend to raise costs, but if it succeeds in developing a more efficient enterprise, it may in fact reduce costs. The effect on the marginal cost curve illustrated in Figure 11.1 is therefore indeterminate.

Efficient wage
A wage above the market wage paid to encourage a worker to remain with a firm.

Contracts with Managers

In Chapter 10 we tended to treat the owner of a firm (that is, the owner of the firm's capital) and the manager of that firm as if they were the same person. This treatment makes the assumption of profit-maximizing behavior believable—a person who maximizes the profits in a firm that he or she owns will succeed in making as much income as possible from this ownership. The process of profit maximization is consistent with the process of utility maximization we studied in Part 2.

For many firms, however, managers do not actually own the firm for which they work. Rather, there is a separation between the ownership of the firm and the control of its behavior by hired managers. In this case, a man-

[2]One of the first economists to propose this efficient wage hypothesis was Joseph Stiglitz in "Wage Determination and Unemployment in L.D.C.'s: The Labor Turnover Model," *Quarterly Journal of Economics* (May 1974): 194–227.

APPLICATION 11.2

Wage Bonuses in Japan

Employment relations in Japan have several unique features that clearly reflect the long-term nature of labor contracts. Under the *Nenko* system some workers are assured of more or less permanent employment together with promotions and wage increases based almost exclusively on years of service with the firm. Such an arrangement cements the relationship between employees and employers and gives each an interest in the other's well-being. To increase those incentives further, Japanese workers under the *Nenko* system are often paid semiannual bonuses based on their firm's performance. These bonuses can be quite large, sometimes amounting to one-fourth or more of the total annual earnings.

An Efficient Labor Contract?

Although some authors view the *Nenko* system as a reflection of Japanese cultural traditions, the more common view among economists is that the system arose during rapid industrialization in Japan and reflects an efficient implicit contract between employees and employers. Payment of bonuses is consistent with this latter view. The bonuses can be regarded as a method by which workers and employers share in the firm's success. With such bonuses workers are given strong incentives to accumulate the kinds of job-specific skills that will be most useful to the firm.

Empirical Findings

An important empirical study of the Japanese bonus system found substantial evidence to support this interpretation.[1] Examining information from 647 different industries, the author concluded that bonuses tended to be higher in precisely those industries for which job-specific skills seemed to be most important. Bonuses also tended to be higher in industries (such as machinery production) that are very sensitive to the business cycle. This finding is consistent with the importance of job-specific skills since the productivity of highly skilled workers may be more volatile in such industries. What appears to be a cultural aspect of the Japanese economy may be a response to the universal problem of developing efficient labor contracts.

To Think About

1. How are the three components of the *Nenko* system (lifetime employment, seniority-based wages, and annual bonuses) connected? Why might all these features be required to assure an efficient overall contract? How would omission of one of the components affect the joint behavior of workers and firms?
2. Many college professors (perhaps yours) have tenure, which assures them lifetime employment at their institution. In what ways is this an efficient labor contract? Do both professors and the university gain from it? How does academic tenure differ from the Japanese *Nenko* system? Can you think of reasons for such differences?

[1]Masanori Hashimoto, "Bonus Payments, On-the-Job Training, and Lifetime Employment in Japan," *Journal of Political Economy* (October 1979): 1086–1104.

Agent
The role of making economic decisions for another party, e.g., the manager of a firm being hired to act for the owner.

ager acts as an **agent** for the owner. Do agents perform in the ways that owners want—that is, do they maximize profits?

Conflicts in the Agent Relationship

Adam Smith understood the basic conflict between owners and managers. In *The Wealth of Nations* he observed that "the directors of . . . companies, being the managers of other people's money than of their own, it cannot well be expected that they should watch over it with the same anxious vigilance with which [owners] watch over their own."[3] From this observation Smith went on to look at the behavior of such famous British institutions as the Royal African Company, the Hudson's Bay Company, and the East India Company, which he used to illustrate some of the consequences of management by nonowners. His observations provide an important starting point for the study of modern firms.

The major issue raised by the use of manager-agents is illustrated in Figure 11.2. This figure shows the indifference curve map of a manager's preferences between the firm's profits (which are of primary interest to the owners) and various benefits (such as a fancy office or travel in the corporate jet or helicopter) that accrue mainly to the manager.[4] This indifference curve map has the same shape as those in Part 2 on the presumption that both profits and benefits provide utility to the manager.

To construct the budget constraint that the manager faces in seeking to maximize his or her utility, assume first that the manager is also the owner of this firm. If the manager chooses to have no special benefits from the job, profits will be π_{max}. Each dollar of benefits received by the manager reduces these profits by one dollar. The budget constraint will have a slope of -1, and profits will reach zero when benefits total π_{max}.

Given this budget constraint, the owner-manager maximizes utility by opting for profits of π^* and benefits of B^*. Profits of π^*, while less than π_{max}, still represent profit maximization in this situation since any other owner-manager would also wish to receive B^* in benefits. That is, B^* represents a true cost of doing business, and given these costs, the firm's manager really does maximize profits.

Now suppose that the manager is not the only owner of this firm. Instead, assume that, say, one-third of the capital of the firm is owned by the manager and the other two-thirds are owned by outside investors who play no role in operating the firm. In this case the manager will act as if he or she no longer faces a budget constraint that requires sacrificing one dollar of the profits for each dollar of benefits. Now a dollar of benefits costs the manager only \$.33 in profits, since the other \$.67 is effectively paid by the other owners in terms of reduced profits on their investment. Although the new budget constraint continues to include the point B^*, π^* (since the manager could still make the same decision a sole owner could), for benefits greater than B^* the slope of the budget constraint to the manager appears to be only $-\frac{1}{3}$—profits on the manager's portion of the business decline by only \$.33 for each dollar in benefits received. Given this apparent budget constraint, the manager would choose point B^{**}, π^{**} to maximize his or her utility. Being only a partial

[3]Adam Smith, *The Wealth of Nations,* 1776 Cannan Edition (New York: Modern Library, 1937), p. 700.

[4]Figure 11.2 is based on one presented in Michael C. Jensen and William H. Meckling, "Theory of the Firm: Managerial Behavior, Agency Costs and Ownership Structure," *Journal of Financial Economics* (January 1976): 78–133.

Figure 11.2
Incentives for a Manager Acting as an Agent for a Firm's Owners

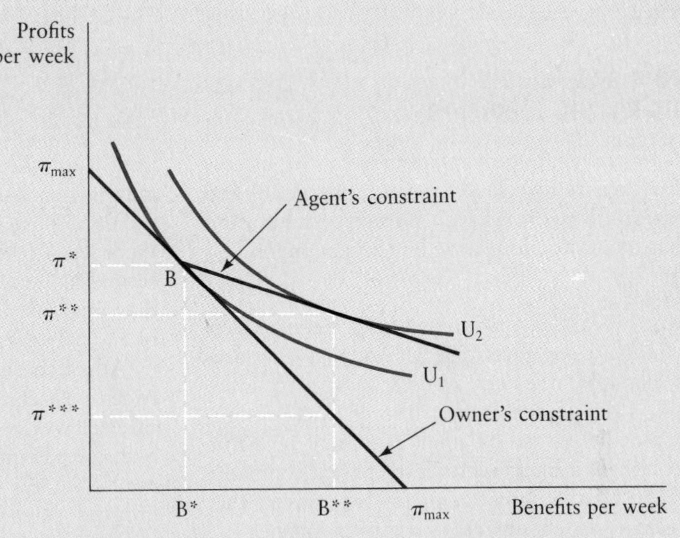

If a manager were the sole owner of a firm, π^*, B* would be chosen since this combination of profits and benefits provides maximum utility. If the manager only owns one-third of the firm, however, the perceived budget constraint will be flatter and B**, π^{**} will be chosen.

owner of the firm causes the manager to choose a lower level of profits and a higher level of benefits than would be chosen by a sole owner.

Point B**, π^{**} is not really attainable by this firm. Although the cost of one dollar of benefits appears to be only $.33 in profits for the manager, in reality, of course, the benefits cost one dollar to all the owners. When the manager opts for B** in benefits, profits are π^{***}. The firm's owners are harmed by having to rely on an agency relationship with the firm's manager. It appears that the smaller the fraction of the firm that is owned by the manager, the greater the extent of the distortions that will be induced by this relationship.

The situation illustrated in Figure 11.2 is representative of a variety of principal-agent problems that arise in economics. Whenever one person (the principal) relies on another person (the agent) to make decisions, the motivation of this agent must be taken into account since the agent may make different decisions than the principal would. Examples of this relationship occur not only in the management of firms, but also in such diverse applications as hiring investment advisors (do they really put their clients' interests first?); relying on an automobile mechanic's assessment in ordering repairs; and buying clothes for a relative. In Application 11.3: Principals and Agents in Franchising and Medicine, we briefly examine two specific examples of the agency relationship.

APPLICATION 11.3

Principals and Agents in Franchising and Medicine

Problems in principal-agent relationships arise in economic situations as diverse as fast-food operations and the provision of medical care. A closer examination shows that these situations have much in common.

Franchising

Many large businesses operate their local retail outlets through franchise contracts. The McDonald's Corporation, for example, does not actually own every place that displays the golden arches. Instead, local restaurants are usually owned by small groups of investors who have bought a franchise from the parent company. The problem for the parent company is to ensure that their franchisee agents operate in a proper manner.

Various provisions of franchise contracts help to ensure this result. McDonald's franchisees, for example, must meet certain food quality and service standards, and they must often buy most of their inputs (hamburgers, frozen fries, buns, napkins and so forth) from the parent company. In return the franchisee gets some management assistance and enjoys the reputation of the McDonald's trademark (together with its national advertising). More important, the franchisee gets to keep a large share of the profits generated by the local restaurant, thereby providing significant incentives to operate it efficiently. The existence of these incentives probably explains why McDonald's and other firms in fields such as electronic retailing, automobile sales, and gasoline service stations have opted for franchising rather than direct ownership—this form of contract is better suited for controlling the principal-agent problems that arise in these industries.[1]

Doctors and Patients

A similar set of problems occurs between physicians and their patients. When people are sick, they often have very little idea of what is wrong or what the most promising treatment is. They place themselves under a physician's care in the belief that the physician is better qualified to make decisions about the proper course of action. The physician then acts as an agent for the patient. But, there are several reasons why a physician may not choose exactly what a fully informed patient would choose. The physician generally pays none of the bills—to the physician the price of anything prescribed is essentially zero. Indeed, since the physician may in many instances also be the provider of care, he or she may even benefit from the services prescribed.

All of these aspects of the agent relationship between physicians and patients suggest that more medical care will be chosen by physicians for their patients than the patients would choose for themselves. A number of studies have gathered evidence on physician-induced demand, and most have reported relatively small but significant effects. For example, a 1978 study of surgery by Victor Fuchs found that the more surgeons there were in a given geographic area, other things being equal, the more surgical operations were performed.[2]

Still, as for the franchise case, there are a number of elements in the physician-patient relationship that serve to bring the interests of the parties into line. Patients can choose not to follow a doctor's advice or to seek second opinions. Physicians must look out for their reputations and may sometimes be accountable to peer review boards. The implicit contract between physicians and patients may therefore be as effective as the explicit franchise contract in controlling the outcomes of the principal-agent relationship.

To Think About

1. Many states have enacted laws that "protect" franchisees from their larger parent firms. In automobile dealerships, for example, many states license dealers and do not allow the same parent to establish new dealerships if they would be "unfair" to existing dealers. How would such restrictions affect the efficiency of franchise contracts?
2. Can you think of other explanations for Fuchs' finding of a correlation between surgeons' locations and the number of operations performed? How would you devise a clear test for physician-induced demand?

[1] For a more complete discussion, see P. H. Rubin, "The Theory of the Firm and the Structure of the Franchise Contract," *Journal of Law and Economics* (April 1978): 223–233.

[2] Victor Fuchs, "The Supply of Surgeons and the Demand for Operations," *Journal of Human Resources,* vol. 13 supplement (1978): 35–56.

Reactions of Owners and the Development of Management Contracts

The firm's owners would be unlikely to take the kind of behavior illustrated in Figure 11.2 lying down. They are being forced to accept lower profits than might be earned on their investments in exchange for manager-oriented benefits that provide no value to them personally. What can they do? Most obviously, they can refuse to invest in the firm if they know the manager will behave in this manner. In that event the manager would have two options. First, he or she could go it alone, financing the company completely with his or her own funds. The firm would then return to the owner-manager situation in which B^*, π^* is the preferred choice of benefits and profits. Alternatively, the manager may obtain outside financing to operate the firm if the operation is too expensive to finance alone. In this case the manager has to work out some sort of contractual arrangement with would-be owners to get them to invest.

Writing a contract under which managers pay completely for benefits out of their share of the profits is probably impossible for owners to do. Enforcing the provisions of such a contract would require constant supervision of the manager's activities—something the owners would prefer not to do since that would force them into a managerial role. Instead, they may try to develop less strict contracts that give managers an incentive to economize on benefits and thereby pursue goals closer to pure profit maximization. By offering such contract options as profit-sharing bonuses, stock option plans, and company-financed pensions, the owner may be able to give managers an incentive to be careful about the benefits they choose to take. As with labor contracts, the development of management contracts requires considerable give-and-take between the parties (owners and managers). The final agreement will be a compromise between owners' desires to incorporate incentives to encourage profit-maximizing behavior and the costs involved in writing the contract and monitoring that behavior. Real-world management contracts may be quite complex and may raise difficult legal questions. In Application 11.4: Stock Ownership and Manager Behavior, we look at some issues related to contracts that encourage managers to own stock in their companies.

The Market for Firms

So far we have discussed labor and management contracts as evolving from bargaining between the parties involved with the firm. Now we take a somewhat broader view by considering the outside market pressures that affect these settlements. Specifically, we focus on the market for firms themselves—what has come to be called "the market for corporate control" in recent economic discussions. Our general goal is to show how the workings of this market help to weed out inefficient, high-cost contractual arrangements and thereby impose some discipline on the contracting process.

Two other types of market pressures on firms should be mentioned. First, any firm must be attentive to the markets for the inputs it hires. Labor con-

APPLICATION 11.4

Stock Ownership and Manager Behavior

An obvious way for a firm's owners to encourage managers to seek maximum profits is to give the managers a financial stake in the success of the business. For public corporations that amounts to encouraging managers to own common stock. Many corporations have rather elaborate stock ownership incentives, especially for their top managers who are most involved in decision making. Some of these plans, such as stock options, offer personal tax benefits to the manager—they are a lower cost way of paying the manager (as opposed to taxable wages) whether they provide any incentive to maximize the firm's profits or not. Other plans, such as those under which managers can buy shares at, say, 85 percent of market price with borrowed funds and no brokerage commissions, offer few direct tax advantages but do directly encourage profit maximization.

Evidence on Stock Purchase Plans

A 1985 study of 130 stock purchase plans provides some evidence of these plans' effects.[1] On average, these plans offered about 8 percent of the corporation's stock to its managers at a discount of 12 to 15 percent from market price. Practically all of the plans allowed the shares to be bought with borrowed funds, usually with the managers paying very low interest rates. Judging by the stock market's reaction, these plans were quite successful in encouraging managers' performance. Following announcement of the plans, the value of the firms' shares tended to rise by about 3 percent over the general market trend. Stock purchase plans for top managers were more effective in prompting such a price rise than were more broadly based plans—perhaps because investors believed that it was more important to have top managers own a portion of the company.

Insider Trading

A particularly controversial question about managers' ownership of stock is whether they should be able to profit from transactions based on "insider" information they may have about their company. To many people the answer appears obvious—insider trading gives an unfair advantage to those doing it, and the practice should be illegal. A variety of infamous insider trading cases have been based on this commonsense idea.

To some economists, however, the case against insider trading is not so clear cut. They argue that permitting insiders to gain from what they know may be a good way to provide incentives to managers to maximize profits—that is, insider trading may act to control the principal-agent problem.[2] In addition, allowing insider trading would provide managers with an incentive to divulge new information quickly and that might help financial markets to operate more efficiently. So far, however, such "perverse" thoughts by economists have had little effect on the actual development of securities laws in the United States.

To Think About

1. If direct stock ownership by managers is desirable, why not require it as a condition of employment? What would be the effects of such a requirement? Would such a requirement necessarily be best for the firm in terms of overall efficiency of operations?
2. How would you define "insider trading"? Doesn't every stock trader know (or think he or she knows) something special? How, if at all, is the practice defined in U.S. law? Do other countries have similar laws?

---

[1]Sanjai Bhagat, James A. Brickley, and Ronald C. Lease, "Incentive Effects of Stock Purchase Plans," *Journal of Financial Economics* (June 1985): 195–215.

[2]See, for example, F. H. Easterbrook, "Insider Trading as an Agency Problem" in *Principals and Agents: The Structure of Business* J. W. Pratt and R. J. Zeckhauser, eds. (Boston: Harvard Business School Press, 1985), pp. 81–100.

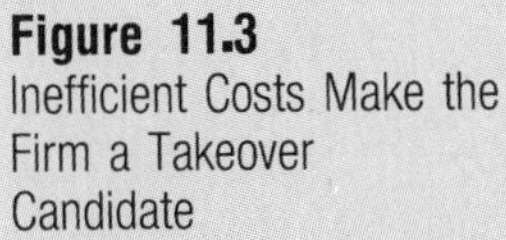

Figure 11.3
Inefficient Costs Make the Firm a Takeover Candidate

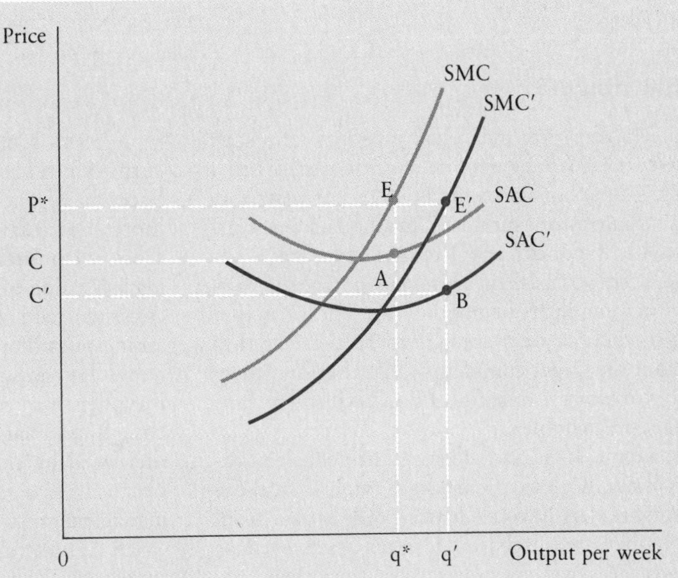

If the firm's costs (SMC, SAC) exceed those that a would-be buyer could achieve (SMC′, SAC′), the firm may be acquired provided the increase in profits exceeds the costs of the acquisition.

tracts that are distinctly inferior to those offered elsewhere will make it impossible for the firm to attract workers. Similarly, inferior management contracts will severely restrict the firm's ability to attract the managers it wishes to hire. The economic operations of these markets is a topic we take up in Part 6. Second, firms must be attentive to the market for their product. If the firm's costs are too high, it may not be able to compete effectively with other producers. Competition in the product market provides a powerful regulator of firms' behavior, and we study that topic extensively in Part 4.

Profit Opportunities in the Market for Firms

The possible attractions of a firm to a would-be buyer are illustrated in Figure 11.3. The firm's short-run average and marginal cost curves are given by SAC and SMC.[5] With a market price of P* this firm will produce q* and, since price exceeds average cost, earn a modest profit.

[5]Figure 11.3 uses short-run curves because, as our discussion in Chapter 12 will show, cost inefficiencies are substantially eliminated over the longer term by competition in the market for goods.

APPLICATION 11.5

Corporate Raiders

"Corporate raiders" are individual investors who seek to take over the management of specific target firms primarily by using borrowed funds. In recent years formerly obscure investors such as T. Boone Pickens, Carl Icahn, David Murdock, and Victor Posner have become widely known as their aggressive pursuit of various firms has made front-page news. The principal objection to these raiders appears to be the fear that they will loot the target company—that they are solely interested in making a quick profit and will then leave the company in shambles.

Both economic logic and the actual evidence contradict this villainous view of corporate raiders. In theoretical terms, raiders have no reason to destroy a firm. Presumably they are purchasing a firm's assets because they believe the assets are worth more than their current value in the market. If the raider were really set on destroying the firm, some other potential buyer would step in to prevent this from happening.

An alternative view is that corporate raiders are performing a useful function by identifying poorly managed firms and promoting new management practices. For example, some observers argue that the persistent raids of T. Boone Pickens on various major oil companies had the effect of making these firms think of themselves as two different businesses—owners of oil-producing properties and refiners of crude oil. By recognizing that many oil companies were poorly managing their crude oil reserves, Pickens was able to find a route to profitable acquisitions.[1]

[1]For a discussion of this case and several other issues related to the market for corporate control, see U.S. Council of Economic Advisors to the President, "The Market for Corporate Control," Chapter 6 in *Economic Report of the President, 1985* (Washington, D.C.: U.S. Government Printing Office, 1985), pp. 187–216.

A 1985 study of the activities of six infamous corporate raiders by Clifford Holderness and Dennis Sheehan reaches a similar conclusion.[2] Here the authors show that announcement of stock purchases by these six influential investors significantly raised the market value of the target firms' shares, a finding inconsistent with the raider notion. The authors then examine possible reasons for this market reaction and conclude that a major portion can be attributed to the investors' ultimate involvement in managing the company. That is, the value of the corporation was increased by the raider's activities in some measure because the raider represented the promise of better management.

Once raiders acquire a firm, they aren't just passive investors. They often move into the new firm and "clean house" by firing unproductive managers and selling unprofitable assets. It is no wonder that managers adopt all kinds of strategies to ward off such changes.

To Think About

1. Why do takeovers by corporate raiders seem to be more controversial than takeovers by other firms (that is, mergers)? Do the raiders have different motives? Would raiders who don't know the business be less successful managers than firms that do? Couldn't the raiders just hire better managers for the firms they acquire?
2. Should the government seek to control takeover activity more closely? What would be the gains from such closer scrutiny? What would be the economic losses from prohibiting certain takeovers?

[2]Clifford G. Holderness and Dennis P. Sheehan, "Raiders or Saviors? The Evidence on Six Controversial Investors," *Journal of Financial Economics* (December 1985): 555–579.

Assume now that a would-be buyer believes that this firm is currently rather inefficient and could be operated at lower cost by a new management team. Specifically, assume this buyer believes that the firm could be operated with costs given by SAC′ and SMC′ if it were under new management. With these new costs, profits would be given by area P*E′BC′ instead of P*EAC.

Such larger profits offer a major incentive for the potential buyer to proceed with plans to purchase the firm. If the firm is privately owned, an offer may be made directly to these owners. If ownership of the firm is spread widely over a large number of shareholders, however, the buyer may make a public offer to these shareholders. In Application 11.5: Corporate Raiders we take a brief look at some of the more spectacular recent examples of such takeover efforts.

Buying an entire firm is a more complex transaction than, say, buying a loaf of bread. Often considerable capital may be required to make the transaction, necessitating complex borrowing arrangements with banks and the accompanying legal formalities. Takeovers may also involve some explicit short-term costs, such as the relocation of a firm's headquarters or the departure of highly skilled employees because they oppose the change. Existing management may make the purchase of their firm difficult by adopting various defensive ploys such as rigging the voting by shareholders or enlisting the government's assistance in opposing the takeover. As a result of these costs, it might be expected that only purchases that are quite profitable would proceed. Situations in which potential buyers would obtain only minor cost improvements over existing management would not produce sufficiently higher short-run profits to warrant incurring these costs. Instead, the normal workings of the marketplace (as we take up in the next part) will ensure that such inefficiencies are reduced over the long run.

Evidence from merger and takeover activity in the 1980s is consistent with this view. One extensive review of the research on this topic finds that shareholders of firms that were acquired in this way experienced a significant increase in the value of their investments.[6] Unsuccessful takeover attempts, on the other hand, actually resulted in a small loss for existing shareholders, perhaps because managers spent real resources fighting off the takeover.

It is possible that some of these gains from successful takeovers represent factors other than the lower operating costs illustrated in Figure 11.3. For example, as we discuss in Chapter 15, some of these gains may reflect monopoly profits that are garnered by the larger firms that result from a merger. But such monopoly gains probably occur in only a few cases, and these mergers are extensively regulated by antitrust law. It seems likely that a substantial portion of shareholders' profits do reflect some type of improved management efficiencies.

Summary

This chapter surveys some recent topics in the theory of the firm. The main purpose of this survey is to show how the traditional theory can be applied to

[6] G. A. Jarrell, J. A. Brickley, and J. M. Netter, "The Market for Corporate Control: The Empirical Evidence since 1980," *Journal of Economic Perspectives* (Winter 1988): 49–68.

a number of new and exciting topics. The principal conclusions from this examination were:

- Firms can be regarded as comprising a set of contracts among workers, capital owners, and managers. The scope of a firm's activities will be affected by the relative costs of market versus internal transactions.
- Contracts with workers will reflect the firm-specific skills that are developed on the job. They promote long-term relationships and deter extensive short-term turnover of employees.
- Managers must act as agents for the firm's owners. In their decisions as managers they may pursue some goals that reduce the firm's profits and are therefore costly to the owners.
- Management contracts will be structured to control these agency problems. Such contracts may be costly for owners to develop and enforce.
- The market for firms will operate to ensure that the firm's contracts are relatively efficient. High-cost, inefficient firms may be acquired by another owner if the profits from such an acquisition exceed the costs involved in making the acquisition.

Review Questions

1. What is Coase trying to explain with his theory of the firm? Why do economists need such a theory? Why not just take the structure of firms as given by historical accident and analyze how they react to changes in prices of their inputs or outputs?
2. Usually we have been treating labor as "homogeneous." What does that term mean? When skills can be learned on the job, is the assumption realistic? How should labor of different skill levels be handled in the production function?
3. Do the comments about labor homogeneity in question 2 apply also to capital? Why might a firm's capital stock exhibit differing productivity depending on when it was acquired?
4. What are job-specific skills? Why should a firm pay higher wages to retain workers with such skills? If a firm does pay higher than the wage that workers could earn in their next best alternative employment, how should labor costs be defined?
5. Why might a firm opt to retain workers in response to a temporary decline in demand? If a firm behaves in this way during recessions, how will its average labor productivity react over the business cycle?
6. Explain how the slope and location of the manager's budget constraint were derived in Figure 11.2. What would the constraint look like if the manager did not own any of the firm? How would he or she choose benefits in this case? Does this solution seem likely?
7. How might managerial contracts be structured to take owners' interests into account? How will the market for managerial talent reflect owners' interests? According to economic theory, which managers should earn the highest wages?
8. Consider another agent relationship such as that between physicians and patients or between advisers and investors. Explain the motives of each party in these relationships. How do the motives suggest divergent behavior? What contractual devices are used to align the parties' interests more closely?
9. Explain why an active market for corporate control can enforce profit-maximizing behavior on firms. If a "raider" threatens to buy a firm, what

precisely does he or she buy? Should the market for corporate control be considered one aspect of the overall market for capital investment?

10. "If the extra profits obtained by a company takeover come from reductions in costs, that is good for the economy. If they come from the ability to raise price and increase revenues, that is bad." Do you agree? Explain why a takeover might have either, both, or none of these effects.

Problems

11.1 How do costs associated with hiring new employees affect the marginal revenue—marginal cost rule for profit maximization? Explain carefully why this effect might depend on whether short-run or long-run marginal costs are used. Why might a firm respond differently to temporary and permanent changes in the price of its product?

11.2 One way of modeling the way firms adjust their work forces is to use a "stock-adjustment model" that assumes the change in labor hired between week t − 1 and week t ($L_t - L_{t-1}$) is a fraction of the difference between what the firm wants to hire (L_t^*) and what it hired last week (L_{t-1}). That is

$$L_t - L_{t-1} = k(L_t^* - L_{t-1})$$

where k is some fraction less than one.

Suppose that a taxidermy shop has a short-run production function given by

$$q = \sqrt{L}$$

where q is the number of animals stuffed per week and L is hours of labor hired per week. Assume that the wage rate is \$1 per hour and that short-run total costs are given by

$$STC = 200 + 10q^2.$$

Short-run marginal costs are given by

$$SMC = 20q.$$

a. If the market price of q is \$200 each, how many will be produced and how many workers will the firm wish to hire each week?
b. Suppose the firm starts in week 0 with 50 hours of workers' time used per week. If k = 1/2, how many workers will be hired in week 1? How many animals will be stuffed?
c. Answer part b for week 2.
d. Graph the firm's output and labor hiring decisions for weeks 0 to 5.
e. How many weeks will it take for the firm to get within one hour of the desired labor input?

11.3 Suppose the production function for high-quality brandy is given by

$$q = \sqrt{K \cdot L}$$

where q is the output of brandy per week and L is labor hours per week. In the short run, K is fixed at 100, so the short-run production function is

$$q = 10\sqrt{L}.$$

a. If capital rents for 10 each and wages are \$5 per hour, show that short-run total costs are

$$STC = 1000 + .05q^2.$$

b. Given the short-run total cost curve in part a, short-run marginal costs are given by

$$SMC = .1q.$$

With this short-run marginal cost curve, how much will the firm produce at a price of \$20 per bottle of brandy? How many labor hours will be hired per week?

c. Suppose that during recessions, the price of brandy falls to \$15 per bottle. With this price, how much would the firm choose to produce and how many labor hours would be hired?

d. Suppose that the firm believes that the fall in the price of brandy will last for only one week, after which it will wish to return to the level of production in part a. Assume also that for each hour that the firm reduces its work force below that described in part a, it incurs a cost of \$1. If it proceeds as in part c, will it earn a profit or a loss? Explain.

e. Is there some level of hiring other than that described in part c that will yield more profits for the firm during the temporary recession?

11.4 United Airbags (A) and United Balloons (B) are two firms in the lighter-than-air parcel post business. For each the number of delivered packages per hour (q) is a simple function of the number of workers hired each hour (L):

$$q = 10L - L^2.$$

Wages of balloon pilots are determined by their opportunity costs of \$40 per hour. Marginal costs are given by

$$MC = \frac{20}{\sqrt{25 - q}}.$$

Initially the competitive cost price of a delivered package is \$10.

a. If firm A is a profit maximizer, how many packages will it deliver and how many pilots will it hire?

b. If firm B wishes to adopt a revenue-sharing formula that also yields \$40 per hour to pilots and results in the same level of employment as for firm A, what share of revenues should it pay to its pilots?

c. Suppose the price of delivered packages falls to \$5, what will happen to hiring at firm A?

d. If the price of delivered packages falls to \$5 and firm B maintains the revenue-sharing formula and employment levels calculated in part b, what will happen to pilots' wages? How might you expect firm B to adjust its contract to the lower price of delivered packages?

11.5 Suppose that Mr. Entrepreneur is the only decision maker in his firm. The profits of this firm depend solely on the amount of time Mr. Entrepreneur spends on the job:

$$\pi = f(H),$$

where H is the number of hours on the job. However, Mr. E, who is a harsh boss, gets on everyone's nerves if he is around too long. Hence π reaches a maximum long before H reaches 24 hours per day.

a. Graph this relationship between π and H.
b. Suppose also that Mr. E has a utility function for profits and leisure ($L = 24 - H$) of the form $U = U(\pi, L)$; graph the indifference curve map for this function.
c. In this situation, will the number of hours of work corresponding to profit maximization be the same number that maximizes Mr. E's utility? What special condition must hold for this to be true? Is this condition "reasonable"?

11.6 Managers often receive liberal severance pay provisions in their contracts (these are sometimes called "golden parachutes"). Why would owners opt for such provisions? Once a manager is fired, he or she no longer can affect profits, so why should owners pay managers anything in such a situation?

*11.7 United Frisbee produces high-quality, jeweled frisbees. The firm's short-run total costs are given by

$$STC = .01q^2 + 10{,}000$$

where q is the quantity of frisbees produced per week. Marginal costs are given by

$$SMC = .02q.$$

a. Suppose United can sell its frisbees at \$30 each. How many will be produced and what will weekly profits be?
b. Suppose Ted Turnover, a famous corporate raider, can operate United at three-fourths the costs of the current management. What would the costs of the firm be in this situation? If frisbee prices remain at \$30, how many would be produced and what would profits be?
c. How much more would Ted be willing to pay for United than would another buyer who could not achieve these cost efficiencies?

11.8 Suppose the managers of a firm could prevent a takeover by lobbying for a law to make such a takeover illegal. Under what conditions would managers choose to do this? Would such an expenditure be in the interest of the original owner of the firm? Are there conditions under which laws banning takeovers might make existing owners better off?

*Denotes a problem that is rather difficult.

PART 4

THE PERFECTLY COMPETITIVE MODEL

The three chapters in this part draw together our analyses of individual and firm behavior to describe how prices are determined. We do so using a particularly simple model of perfect competition. In this model we assume there are large numbers of both buyers and sellers who act as price takers; that is, economic actors on both sides of the market believe they cannot affect market prices, but can only respond to the signals these prices provide. Although, as we will see in Part 5, this assumption may not be reasonable in many situations, here it provides a good starting place for developing some basic principles of how markets work.

Chapter 12, the first chapter in this part, describes the way prices are determined in a single competitive market. It examines how changes in the market price bring about an equilibrium between supply and demand in such a market and how that equilibrium price changes when conditions change. A major portion of the chapter is concerned with the role of economic profits in motivating firms' supply decisions and in encouraging firms to enter or leave the market.

The analysis in Chapter 12 examines only a single market at a time. In Chapter 13 we expand the competitive model a bit to show how many markets operate simultaneously. The purpose of the chapter is to describe a general equilibrium situation involving many competitive markets. We show both how such a market system allocates resources and why, under certain conditions, this resulting allocation will have desirable economic properties. The connection between competitive prices and resource allocation is explored a bit further in a brief appendix to Chapter 13 on linear programming. As we shall see, the model of competitive equilibrium provides a general benchmark against which we will be able to evaluate the ways in which other forms of market organization allocate resources.

Finally, Chapter 14 completes our study of competitive markets by looking again at some of the problems caused by imperfect information in these markets. We will see that, even if most of the assumptions of the competitive model (e.g., price-taking behavior) hold, the absence of full information may make it impossible for markets to reach an equilibrium. Even when equilibrium prices can be found, the resulting allocation of resources may not be very desirable when information is imperfect. For these reasons the material in Chapter 14 should be viewed as offering some caution about the generally positive view of competitive markets taken in Chapters 12 and 13. ▲

CHAPTER 12

Pricing in a Perfectly Competitive Market

This chapter discusses perfectly competitive price determination in a single market. The theory we develop here is an elaboration of Marshall's supply and demand analysis that we introduced in Chapter 1. We show how equilibrium prices are established and describe some of the factors that may tend to change such prices. In its final and complete form the competitive model we develop here is the most basic model of pricing used by economists. It provides a standard against which actual market performance can often be measured.

Timing of a Supply Response

Supply response
The change in quantity of output in response to a change in demand conditions.

In the analysis of pricing it is important to decide the length of time that is to be allowed for a **supply response** to changing demand conditions. The establishment of equilibrium prices will be different if we are talking about a very short period of time during which supply is essentially fixed and unchanging or if we are envisioning a very long-run process in which it is possible for entirely new firms to enter a market. For this reason, it has been traditional in economics to discuss pricing in three different time periods: (1) the very short run, (2) the short run, and (3) the long run. Although it is not possible to give these terms an exact time length, the essential distinction among them concerns the nature of the supply response that is assumed to be possible. In the *very short run* there can be no supply response—quantity supplied is absolutely fixed. In the *short run*, existing firms may change the quantity they are supplying, but no new firms can enter the market. In the *long run*, firms can further change the quantity supplied, and completely new firms may enter an industry; this produces a very flexible supply response. This chapter discusses each of these different types of responses.

Pricing in the Very Short Run

Market period
A short period of time during which quantity supplied is fixed.

In the very short run or **market period,** there is no supply response. The goods are already "in" the marketplace and must be sold for whatever the market will bear. In this situation price acts to ration demand. The price will adjust to clear the market of the quantity that must be sold. Although the market price may act as a signal to producers in future periods, it does not perform such a function in the very short run since current period output cannot be changed.

Figure 12.1 pictures this situation. Market demand is represented by the curve D. Supply is fixed at Q^*, and the price that clears the market is P_1. At P_1 people are willing to take all that is offered in the market. Sellers want to dispose of Q^* without regard to price (for example, the good in question may be perishable and will be worthless if not sold immediately). The price P_1 balances the desires of demanders with the desires of suppliers. For this reason it is called an **equilibrium price.** In Figure 12.1, a price in excess of P_1 would not be an equilibrium price since people would demand less than Q^* (remember firms are always willing to supply Q^* no matter what the price). Similarly, a price below P_1 would not be an equilibrium price since people would then demand more than Q^*. P_1 is the only equilibrium price possible when demand conditions are those represented by the curve D.

Equilibrium price
The price at which the quantity demanded by buyers of a good is equal to the quantity supplied of the good by sellers.

Shifts in Demand: Price as a Rationing Device

If the demand curve in Figure 12.1 shifted outward to D′ (perhaps because incomes increased, or because the price of some substitute increased), P_1 would no longer be an equilibrium price. With the demand curve D′, far more than Q^* is demanded at the price P_1. Some people who wish to make purchases at a price of P_1 would find that not enough of the good is now available to meet the increase in demand. In order to ration the available quantity among all demanders, the price would have to rise to P_2. At that new price, demand would again be reduced to Q^* (by a movement along D′ in a northwesterly direction as the price rises). Hence the price rise would restore equilibrium to the market. The curve labeled S (for "supply") in Figure 12.1 shows all the equilibrium prices for Q^* for any conceivable shift in demand. The price must always adjust to ration demand to exactly what supply is available. In Application 12.1: Auctions for Fish and Flowers, we look at auctions for two perishable items and show how this price-setting mechanism works in practice.

Figure 12.1
Pricing in the Very Short Run

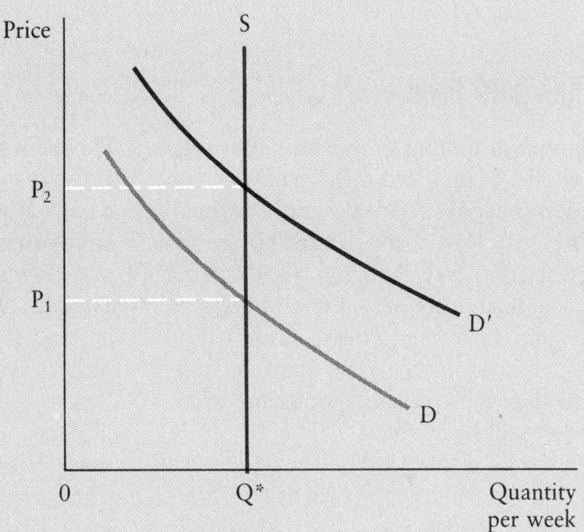

When quantity is absolutely fixed in the very short run, price acts only as a device to ration demand. With quantity fixed at Q*, price P_1 will prevail in the marketplace if D is the market demand curve. At this price, individuals are willing to consume exactly that quantity available. If demand should shift upward to D′, the equilibrium price would rise to P_2.

Applicability of the Very Short-Run Model

The model of the very short run is not particularly useful for most markets. Although the theory may adequately apply to some situations where goods are perishable, the far more common situation involves some degree of supply response to changing demand. It is usually presumed that a rise in price will prompt producers to bring additional quantity into the market. The next section looks at why firms would increase their output levels in the short run in response to a price increase.

Before beginning that analysis, we should understand that increases in quantity supplied need not come only from increased production. In a world in which some goods are durable (that is, last longer than a single market period), current owners of these goods may supply them in increasing amounts to the market as price rises. For example, even though the supply of Rembrandts is absolutely fixed, we would not draw the market supply curve for these paintings as a vertical line, such as that shown in Figure 12.1. As the price of Rembrandts rises, people (and museums) become increasingly willing to part with them. From a market point of view, the supply curve for Rembrandts will have an upward slope even though no new production takes place. A similar analysis would follow for many types of durable goods, such

APPLICATION 12.1 

Auctions for Fish and Flowers

An important example of pricing in the very short run is provided by auctions. In most cases the goods put up for bid at an auction must all be sold. Supply is fixed, and price acts only to allocate the available goods among auction participants. When the goods being auctioned are perishable, market period analysis is even more directly relevant, since auctioneers cannot hold back goods that do not attain what they consider suitable prices. Instead they must sell the goods for whatever price the market will bear.

Fish Auctions

Auctions for freshly caught fish are conducted in practically every major fishing city in the world. Although the particular customs of these auctions differ among nations, the procedures are very similar. First, the auctions are conducted quickly. Since fish must be sold to the final users rapidly to remain fresh, there is no time for middlemen to engage in lengthy haggling about prices. Highly organized, sometimes frantic auction methods have been developed. Second, although a variety of these auction methods are in use, all arrive at equilibrium prices rather accurately. For example, the three most widely used bidding systems (the English ascending bid system, the Dutch descending bid system, and the Japanese simultaneous bid system) all seem to attain equilibrium prices rather quickly.

A final similarity among fish (and other) auctions throughout the world is the importance of market participants knowing the total quantity being sold. Since fish demand is relatively inelastic, rather small differences in quantity supplied can result in great differences in the final prices agreed upon. Hence, market participants must know what the true supply situation is if they are to avoid serious mistakes. For example, in Manila and other Far East fish markets fishermen often unload only part of their day's catch at first so that the supply will appear to be small. By so doing, they hope that higher prices will be bid. Of course, buyers are generally aware of this strategy and may employ elaborate networks of spies to examine fishing boats to find out the true situation.

Flower Auctions

Fresh flowers are also often sold through auctions. Many of the flowers found in American supermarkets were originally sold at auction in London or Amsterdam and flown to their final destination immediately after the sale. As in the case of fish, the perishability of flowers means that they must be sold quickly and that the price fluctuates rapidly in response to supply availability. One way in which flower sellers attempt to influence buyers' perceptions of supply is by setting "reservation" prices for their initial offerings of flowers. If these prices are not reached, the flowers are withdrawn from sale, thereby putting pressure on buyers to raise their bids for the next lot or face the prospect of going home empty-handed. This ploy is intended only to influence the price on future lots since the flowers withdrawn usually have no alternative value and are often destroyed. Success of the strategy depends on sellers being able to take advantage of their superior knowledge of the true supply situation.[1]

To Think About

1. Why do auctions succeed in arriving at equilibrium prices? If price starts well below equilibrium, as in the American bidding system, why does the supply and demand model predict that price must rise to its equilibrium level before bidding stops?
2. This example illustrates two ways in which sellers may use their superior information to try to influence the outcomes of auctions. Can you think of other types of ploys they might use? What kinds of strategies might buyers use to get lower prices? How is the likely success of various strategies dependent on how informed the parties are?

---

[1]For a further discussion of these and other issues, see R. P. McAfee and J. McMillan, "Auctions and Bidding," *Journal of Economic Literature* (June 1987): 699–738.

as antiques, used cars, back issues of the *National Geographic,* or corporate shares, all of which are in nominally fixed supply. Here we are more interested in examining how demand and production are related, however, so we will not look at these other cases in detail.

Short-Run Supply

In analysis of the short run the number of firms in an industry is fixed. It is assumed that firms are not flexible enough either to enter or to leave a given market. However, the firms currently operating in the market are able to adjust the quantity they are producing in response to changing prices. Because there are a large number of firms producing a homogeneous good, each firm will act as a price taker. The model of short-run supply by a price-taking firm in Chapter 10 is therefore an appropriate one to use here. That is, each firm's short-run supply curve is simply the positively sloped section of its short-run marginal cost curve above minimum average variable cost. Using this model to record individual firms' supply decisions, we can add up all of these decisions into a single market supply curve.

Construction of a Short-Run Supply Curve

The quantity of a good that is supplied to the market during some period is the sum of the quantities supplied by each firm. Since each firm considers the market price in deciding how much to produce, the total supplied to the market will also depend on price. This relationship between market price and quantity supplied is called a **short-run supply curve.**

Short-run supply curve
The relationship between market price and quantity supplied of a good in the short run.

Figure 12.2 illustrates the construction of the curve. For simplicity we assume there are only two firms, A and B. The short-run supply (that is, marginal cost) curves for firms A and B are shown in Panels a and b. The market supply curve shown in Panel c is the horizontal sum of these two curves. For example, at a price of P_1, firm A is willing to supply q_1^A, and firm B is willing to supply q_1^B. At this price the total supply in the market is given by Q_1, which is equal to $q_1^A + q_1^B$. The other points on the curve are constructed in an identical way. Because each firm's supply curve slopes upward, the market supply curve will also slope upward. This upward slope reflects the fact that short-run marginal costs increase as firms attempt to increase their outputs. They will be willing to incur these higher marginal costs only at higher market prices.

Slope of the Supply Curve

Although the construction in Figure 12.2 uses only two firms, actual market supply curves represent the summation of many firms' supply curves. Again the market supply curve will have a positive slope because of the positive slope in each firm's underlying marginal cost curve. This market supply curve

Figure 12.2
Short-Run Market Supply Curve

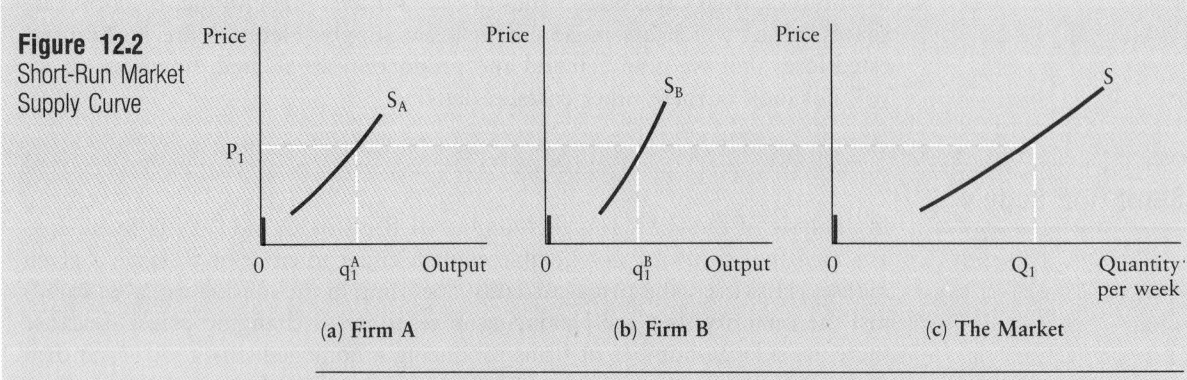

The supply (marginal cost) curves of two firms are shown in Panels a and b. The market supply curve in Panel c is the horizontal sum of these curves. For example, at P_1, firm A supplies q_1^A, firm B supplies q_1^B, and total market supply is given by $Q_1 = q_1^A + q_1^B$.

summarizes the short-run diminishing returns experienced by all firms, the prices of the inputs they use, and the profit-maximizing decisions that each firm makes.

There is a second reason why the short-run supply curve may have a positive slope. Although each firm takes input prices as given in making its decisions, those prices may not remain constant as output for the industry as a whole expands. It is possible that increases in industry output will increase the demand for scarce inputs, thereby bidding up the prices of those inputs. For example, expansion of the professional sports leagues in the 1960s had the effect of bidding up players' salaries, and that raised teams' costs. Similarly, major increases in oil well drilling in the late 1970s (as discussed in Application 10.5: The Demise of OPEC and Drilling for Oil in the United States) resulted in substantially increased demand for steel pipe and well testing equipment, whose prices then rose significantly. Marginal costs of drilling also rose accordingly. These types of effects are called **external price effects**—they arise when expanding output raises input costs and therefore raises all firms' marginal costs. When these effects are present, the short-run market supply curve may be more steeply sloped than a simple summation of firms' marginal cost curves would suggest. Expansion in output raises firms' marginal costs both because of diminishing marginal productivity and because rising input prices may increase overall costs. The short-run supply curve summarizes both effects, and, as we show in the next section, using that curve lets us see how these factors interact with market demand to determine price.

External price effects
Effects that changes in the level of production of an industry have on the prices of inputs to that industry.

Short-Run Price Determination

We can now combine demand and supply curves to demonstrate how equilibrium prices are established in the short run. Figure 12.3 shows this process. In Panel b, the market demand curve D and the short-run supply curve S in-

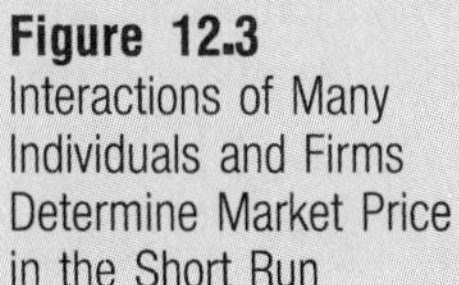

Figure 12.3
Interactions of Many Individuals and Firms Determine Market Price in the Short Run

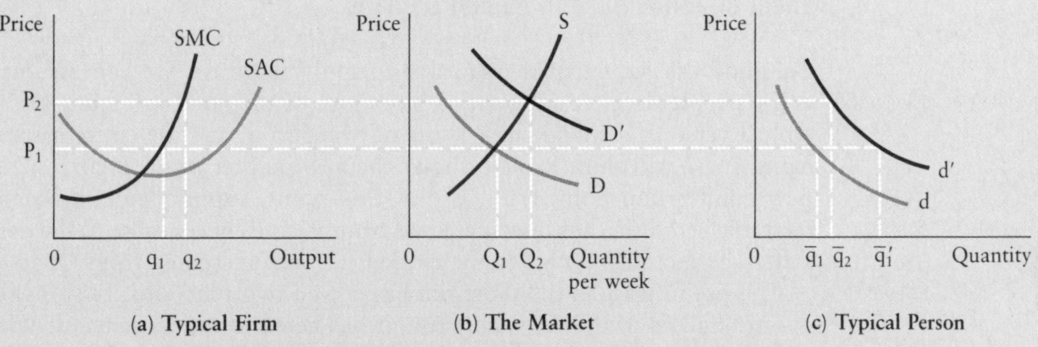

Market demand curves and market supply curves are each the horizontal sum of numerous components. These market curves are shown in Panel b. Once price is determined in the market, each firm and each individual treat this price as fixed in their decisions. If the typical person's demand curve shifts to d′, market demand will shift to D′ in the short run, and price will rise to P_2.

tersect at a price of P_1 and a quantity of Q_1. This price-quantity combination represents an equilibrium between the demands of individuals and the supply decisions of firms—the forces of supply and demand are precisely balanced. What firms supply at a price of P_1 is exactly what people want to buy at that price. This equilibrium will tend to persist from one period to the next unless one of the factors underlying the supply and demand curves should change.

Functions of the Equilibrium Price

Here the equilibrium price P_1 serves two important functions. First, this price acts as a signal to producers about how much should be produced. In order to maximize profits, firms will produce that output level for which marginal costs are equal to P_1. In the aggregate, then, production will be Q_1. A second function of the price is to ration demand. Given the market price of P_1, utility-maximizing individuals will decide how much of their limited incomes to spend on that particular good. At a price of P_1, total quantity demanded will be Q_1, which is precisely the amount that will be produced. This is what economists mean by an equilibrium price. No other price brings about such a balancing of supply and demand.

The implications of the equilibrium price (P_1) for a typical firm and for a typical person are shown in Panels a and c of Figure 12.3, respectively. For the typical firm, the price P_1 will cause an output level of q_1 to be produced. The firm earns a small profit at this particular price because price exceeds short-run average total cost. The initial demand curve d for a typical person is shown in Panel c. At a price of P_1, this person demands $\overline{q}_1$. Adding up the quantities that each person demands at P_1 and the quantities that each firm supplies shows that the market is in equilibrium. The market supply and demand curves are a convenient way of doing that addition.

Effect of an Increase in Market Demand

To study the nature of the short-run supply response, we can assume that many people decide they want to buy more of the good in Figure 12.3. The typical person's demand curve shifts outward to d′ and the entire market demand curve will shift. Panel b shows the new market demand curve, D′. The new equilibrium point is P_2, Q_2: at this point, supply-demand balance is reestablished. Price has now increased from P_1 to P_2 in response to the demand shift. The quantity traded in the market has also increased from Q_1 to Q_2.

The rise in price in the short run has served two functions. First, as shown in our analysis of the very short run, it has acted to ration demand. Whereas at P_1 a typical individual demanded $\overline{q}_1'$, now at P_2 only $\overline{q}_2$ is demanded.

The rise in price has also acted as a signal to the typical firm to increase production. In Panel a the typical firm's profit-maximizing output level has increased from q_1 to q_2 in response to the price rise. That is what economists mean by a short-run supply response: an increase in market price acts as an inducement to increase production. Firms are willing to increase production (and to incur higher marginal costs) because price has risen. If market price had not been permitted to rise (suppose, for example, government price controls were in effect), firms would not have increased their outputs. At P_1 there would have been an excess (unfilled) demand for the good in question. If market price is allowed to rise, a supply-demand equilibrium can be reestablished so that what firms produce is again equal to what people demand at the prevailing market price. At the new price P_2, the typical firm has also increased its profits. This increased profitability in response to rising prices is important to our discussion of long-run pricing later in this chapter.

Shifts in Supply and Demand Curves

In previous chapters we analyzed many of the reasons why either demand or supply curves might shift. Some of these reasons are summarized in Table 12.1. You may wish to review the material in Chapter 5, "Market Demand," and Chapter 9, "Costs," to see why these changes shift the various curves. These types of shifts in demand and supply occur frequently in real-world markets. When either a supply curve or a demand curve does shift, equilibrium price and quantity will change. This section looks briefly at such changes and how the outcome depends on the shapes of the curves.

Short-Run Supply Elasticity

Some terms used by economists to describe the shapes of demand and supply curves need to be understood before we can discuss the effects of these shifts.

Table 12.1
Reasons for a Shift in a Demand or Supply Curve

Demand	Supply
Shifts outward (→) because: ▪ Income increases ▪ Price of substitute rises ▪ Price of complement falls ▪ Preferences for good increase	Shifts outward (→) because: ▪ Input prices fall ▪ Technology improves
Shifts inward (←) because ▪ Income falls ▪ Price of substitute falls ▪ Price of complement rises ▪ Preferences for good diminish	Shifts inward (←) because ▪ Input prices rise

We have already introduced the terminology for demand curves in Chapter 5. There we developed the concept of the price elasticity of demand, which shows how the quantity demanded responds to changes in price. When demand is elastic, changes in price have a major impact on quantity demanded. In the case of inelastic demand, however, a price change does not have very much effect on what people choose to buy. Firms' short-run supply responses can be described along the same lines. If an increase in price causes firms to supply significantly more output, we say that the supply curve is "elastic" (at least in the range currently being observed). Alternatively, if the price increase has only a minor effect on the quantity firms choose to produce, supply is said to be inelastic. More formally:

$$\text{Short-run supply elasticity} = \frac{\text{Percentage change in quantity supplied in short run}}{\text{Percentage change in price}}. \qquad [12.1]$$

For example, if the short-run supply elasticity is 2.0, each 1 percent increase in price results in a 2 percent increase in quantity supplied. Over this range, the short-run supply curve is fairly elastic. If, on the other hand, a 1 percent increase in price leads only to a 0.5 percent increase in quantity supplied, the **short-run elasticity of supply** is 0.5, and we would say that supply is inelastic. As we will see, whether short-run supply is elastic or inelastic can have a significant effect on market performance.

Short-run elasticity of supply
The percentage change in quantity supplied in the short run in response to a 1 percent change in price.

Shifts in Supply Curves and the Importance of the Shape of the Demand Curve

A shift inward in the short-run supply curve for a good might result, for example, from an increase in the prices of the inputs used by firms to produce the good. Whatever the cause of the shift, its effect on the equilibrium levels of P and Q will depend on the shape of the demand curve for the product. Figure 12.4 illustrates two possible situations. The demand curve in Panel a is

Figure 12.4
Effect of a Shift in the Short-Run Supply Curve Depends on the Shape of the Demand Curve

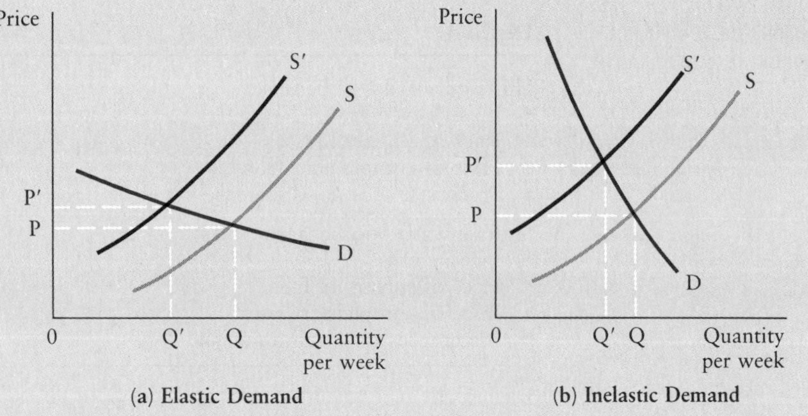

In Panel a the shift inward in the supply curve causes price to increase only slightly, whereas quantity contracts sharply. This results from the elastic shape of the demand curve. In Panel b the demand curve is inelastic; price increases substantially with only a slight decrease in quantity.

relatively price elastic; that is, a change in price substantially affects the quantity demanded. For this case, a shift in the supply curve from S to S′ will cause equilibrium prices to rise only moderately (from P to P′), whereas quantity is reduced sharply (from Q to Q′). Rather than being "passed on" in higher prices, the increase in the firms' input costs is met primarily by a decrease in quantity (a movement down each firm's marginal cost curve) with only a slight increase in price.[1]

This situation is reversed when the market demand curve is inelastic. In Panel b in Figure 12.4, a shift in the supply curve causes equilibrium price to rise substantially but quantity is little changed, because people do not reduce their demands very much if prices rise. Consequently, the shift upward in the supply curve is passed on to demanders almost completely in the form of higher prices.

Shifts in Demand Curves and the Importance of the Shape of the Supply Curve

We can also show that a given shift in a market demand curve will have different implications for P and Q depending on the shape of the short-run sup-

[1]Notice, for example, that on the supply curve S′, the marginal cost of producing output level Q is considerably higher than the marginal cost of producing Q′.

Figure 12.5
Effect of a Shift in the Demand Curve Depends on the Shape of the Short-Run Supply Curve

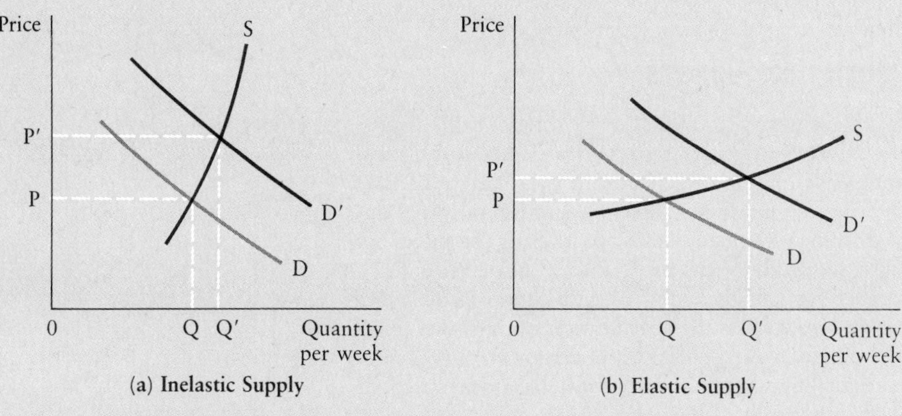

In Panel a supply is inelastic; a shift in demand causes price to increase greatly with only a small increase in quantity. In Panel b, on the other hand, supply is elastic; price rises only slightly in response to a demand shift.

ply curve. Two illustrations are shown in Figure 12.5. In Panel a the supply curve for the good in question is relatively inelastic. As quantity expands, firms' marginal costs rise rapidly, giving the supply curve its steep slope. In this situation, a shift outward in the market demand curve (caused, for example, by an increase in income) will cause prices to increase substantially. On the other hand, the quantity increases only slightly. The increase in demand (and in Q) has caused firms to move up their steeply sloped marginal cost curves. The accompanying large increase in price serves to ration demand. There is little response in terms of quantity supplied.

Panel b in Figure 12.5 shows a relatively elastic short-run supply curve. This kind of curve would occur for an industry in which marginal costs do not rise steeply in response to output increases. For this case an increase in demand produces a substantial increase in Q. However, because of the nature of the supply curve, this increase is not met by great cost increases. Consequently, price rises only moderately.

These examples again demonstrate Marshall's observation that demand and supply together determine price and quantity. In Chapter 1 we quoted his analogy—just as it is impossible to say which blade of a scissors does the cutting, so too it is impossible to attribute price solely to demand or to supply characteristics. Rather, the effect that shifts in either a demand curve or a supply curve will have depends on the shapes of both of the curves. In predicting the effects of shifting supply or demand conditions on market price and quantity in the real world, this simultaneous relationship must be considered. Application 12.2: Dairy Price Supports illustrates how this short-run model might be used to examine some of the problems with government price support schemes.

APPLICATION 12.2

Dairy Price Supports

There are nearly 200,000 dairy farmers in the United States. These farmers represent a powerful political force encouraging the enactment of a variety of laws favoring the industry. Three specific federal programs (not to mention many state programs) raise prices for these goods above the levels that would exist under a competitive equilibrium: (1) classification of milk into various grades and the specification of minimum prices for some of these grades; (2) government purchase of "surplus" butter and cheese; and (3) major restrictions on the importing of dairy products.

A Graphic Analysis

The implication of these actions can be illustrated by the simple short-run supply-demand diagram in Figure 1. In the absence of government programs, the market for dairy products would have an equilibrium price of P* with quantity Q* being bought. The web of protective programs for the industry results in price being raised to P_R. At this higher price, consumers purchase Q_1, farmers produce Q_2, and there is a surplus of $Q_2 - Q_1$. These surplus products are bought through various government programs as a way of supporting the price P_R.

During the 1980s the government regularly bought about 10 percent of total dairy production at annual costs of $2–4 billion.

Some Consequences of the Programs

Government involvement in the dairy industry has had a number of bizarre, even humorous, consequences. In 1983, for example, the U.S. Department of Agriculture sponsored a vast "cheese giveaway" program under which virtually anyone near the delivery truck could get 10 pounds of cheese free. Because of problems in controlling the crowds, the program was quietly canceled. To get rid of butter, a complex deal was worked out in 1985 to sell a large quantity to the Soviet Union. To avoid the political embarrassment of selling to the Russians at the world price (which was about one-half of what American consumers were paying), the United States instead gave the butter to New Zealand (a country with little interest in having surplus U.S. butter). The New Zealanders then made a nice profit on the sale to the Soviets.

Government efforts to support dairy prices have also extended to trying to restrict supply. Cartels of dairy farmers, though not usually very successful, are exempt from antitrust prosecution. At times the government has paid farmers not to produce milk (as it has also done on a larger scale for grain crops). The Agriculture Department even experimented with a "whole herd buyout" program under which dairy farmers could sell all their cows to the government. Unfortunately, it proved very hard to determine whether farmers really had ceased dairy operations—both the cows and the farmers kept turning up somewhere else.

Figure 1
Effect of Dairy Price Supports

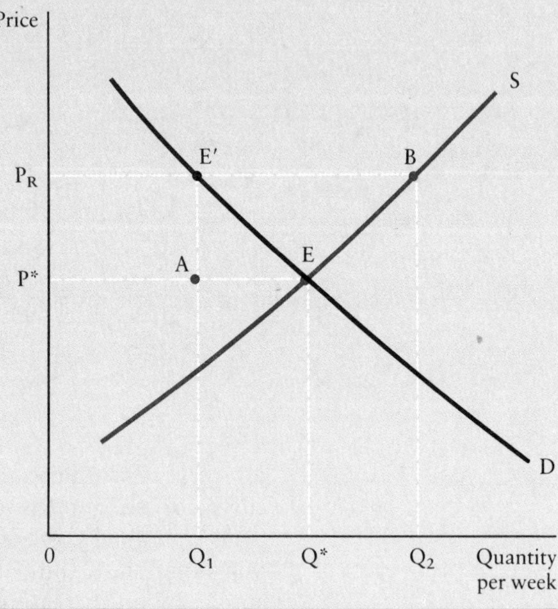

Various measures to help the dairy industry raise prices to P_R. There is a surplus of $Q_2 - Q_1$ which must be bought by the government at a cost of $E'BQ_2Q_1$.

To Think About

1. Proponents of dairy price supports argue that they are needed to prevent "ruinous" competition in the industry and to moderate price fluctuations. How would you evaluate these contentions?
2. Figure 1 represents a short-run analysis. After you finish reading the next section, you may wish to develop a similar analysis of the long-run consequences of dairy price supports.

Figure 12.6
Demand and Supply Curves for Cassette Tapes

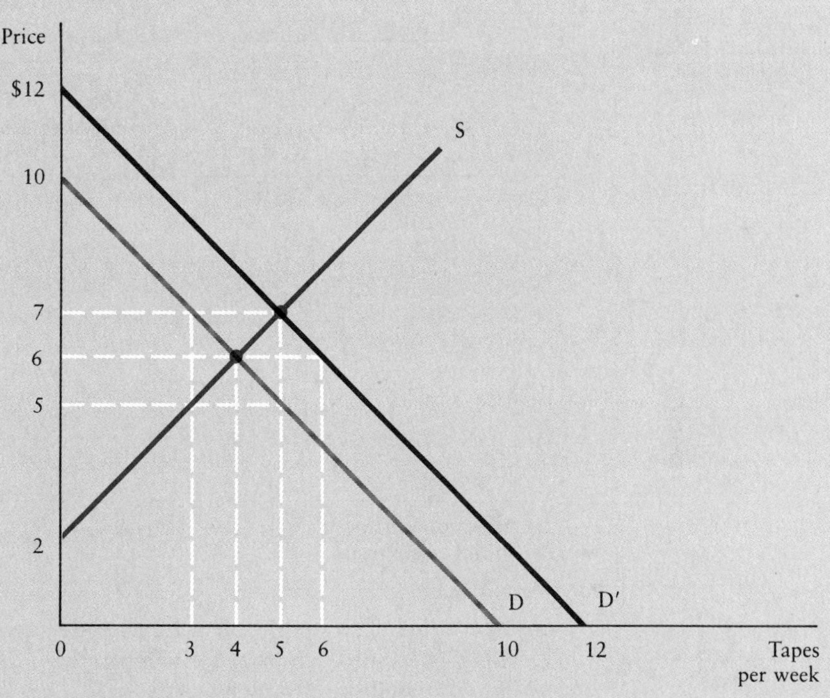

With the curves D and S, equilibrium occurs at a price of $6. At this price people demand four tapes per week, and that is what firms supply. When demand shifts to D′, price will rise to $7 to restore equilibrium.

Numerical Illustration

We can also illustrate changes in market equilibria with a simple numerical example. Suppose, as we did in Chapter 10, that the quantity of cassette tapes demanded per week (Q) depends on the price of tapes (P) according to the simple relation

$$\text{Demand: } Q = 10 - P. \tag{12.2}$$

Suppose also that the short-run supply curve for tapes is given by

$$\text{Supply: } Q = P - 2 \quad \text{or} \quad P = Q + 2. \tag{12.3}$$

Figure 12.6 graphs these equations. As before, the demand curve (labeled D in the figure) intersects the vertical axis at P = $10. At higher prices no tapes

Table 12.2
Supply and Demand Equilibrium in the Market for Cassette Tapes

	Supply	Demand	
		Case 1	Case 2
Price	Q = P − 2 Quantity Supplied (Tapes per Week)	Q = 10 − P Quantity Demanded (Tapes per Week)	Q = 12 − P Quantity Demanded (Tapes per Week)
$10	8	0	2
9	7	1	3
8	6	2	4
7	5	3	5
6	4	4	6
5	3	5	7
4	2	6	8
3	1	7	9
2	0	8	10
1	0	9	11
0	0	10	12

□ New equilibrium.
□ Initial equilibrium.

are demanded. The supply curve (labeled S) intersects the vertical axis at P = 2. This is the shutdown price for firms in the industry—at a price lower than $2 no tapes will be produced. As Figure 12.6 shows, these supply and demand curves intersect at a price of $6 per tape. At that price people demand four tapes per week, and firms are willing to supply four tapes per week. This equilibrium is also illustrated in Table 12.2, which shows the quantity of tapes demanded and supplied at each price. Only when P = $6 do these amounts agree. At a price of $5 per tape, for example, people want to buy five tapes per week, but only three will be supplied: there is an excess demand of two tapes per week. Similarly, at a price of $7 per tape there is an excess supply of two tapes per week.

If the demand curve for tapes were to shift outward, this equilibrium would change. For example, Figure 12.6 also shows the demand curve D′, whose equation is given by

$$Q = 12 - P. \qquad [12.4]$$

With this new demand curve, equilibrium price rises to $7 per tape, and quantity also rises to five tapes per week. This new equilibrium is confirmed by the entries in Table 12.2, which show that this is the only price that clears the market given the new demand curve. For example, at the old price of $6 there is now an excess demand for tapes, since the amount people want (Q = 6) exceeds what firms are willing to supply (Q = 4). The rise in price from $6 to $7 restores equilibrium both by prompting people to buy fewer tapes and by encouraging firms to produce more.

The Long Run

In perfectly competitive markets, supply responses are considerably more flexible in the long run than in the short run for two reasons. First, firms' long-run cost curves reflect the greater input flexibility that firms have in the long run. Second, the long run also allows firms to enter and exit an industry in response to profit opportunities. These actions have important implications for pricing. We begin our analysis of these various effects with a description of the long-run equilibrium for a competitive industry. Then, as we did for the short run, we will show how supply and prices change when conditions change. Later in the chapter we show several illustrations of how our competitive model of long-run supply can be applied.

Equilibrium Conditions

A perfectly competitive market is in equilibrium when no firm has an incentive to change its behavior. Such an equilibrium has two components: firms must be content with their output choices (that is, they must be maximizing profits), and they must be content to stay in (or out of) the market. We discuss each of these components separately.

Profit Maximization

As before, we assume that firms seek maximum profits. Because each firm is a price taker, profit maximization requires that the firm produce where price is equal to (long-run) marginal cost. This first equilibrium condition, $P = MC$, determines both the firm's output choice and its choice of inputs that minimize these costs in the long run.

Entry

A second feature of long-run equilibrium concerns the possibility of the entry of entirely new firms into the industry, or the exit of existing firms from that industry. The perfectly competitive model assumes that such entry and exit entail no special costs.[2] Consequently, new firms will be lured into any market in which (economic) profits are positive. Similarly, firms will leave a market when profits are negative.

If profits are positive, the entry of new firms will cause the short-run industry supply curve to shift outward, since more firms are now producing

[2]In Chapter 15 we discuss some barriers to entry that may make this assumption inappropriate in certain situations.

than were in the industry previously. Such a shift will cause market price (and industry profits) to fall. The process will continue until no firm contemplating entering the industry would be able to earn an economic profit.[3] At that point, entry by new firms will cease, and there will be an equilibrium number of firms in the industry. When the firms in an industry suffer short-run losses, some firms will choose to leave the industry, causing the supply curve to shift to the left. Market price will then rise, eliminating losses for those firms remaining in the industry.

Long-Run Equilibrium

For the purposes of this chapter we assume that all the firms in an industry have identical cost curves; that is, we assume that no single firm controls any special resources or technologies.[4] Because all firms are identical, the equilibrium long-run position requires every firm to earn exactly zero economic profits. In graphic terms, long-run equilibrium price must settle at the low point of each firm's long-run average total cost curve. Only at this point do the two equilibrium conditions hold: P = MC (which is required for profit maximization) and P = AC (which is the required zero-profit condition).

These two equilibrium conditions have rather different origins. Profit maximization is a goal of firms. The P = MC rule reflects our assumptions about firms' behavior and is identical to the output decision rule used in the short run. The zero-profit condition is not a goal for firms. Firms would obviously prefer to have large profits. The long-run operation of the market, however, forces all firms to accept a level of zero economic profits (P = AC) because of the willingness of firms to enter and to leave an industry. Although the firms in a perfectly competitive industry may earn either positive or negative profits in the short run, in the long run only a level of zero profits will prevail.[5]

Long-Run Supply: Constant Cost Case

Before we can discuss long-run pricing in detail, we must make some assumption about how the entry of new firms into an industry affects the costs of inputs. The simplest assumption is that entry has no external price effects.

[3]Remember, we are using the economic definition of profits here. These profits represent the return to the owner of a business in excess of that which is strictly necessary to keep him or her in the business.

[4]The important case of firms having different costs is discussed in Chapter 18. In that chapter we see that very low-cost firms can earn positive, long-run profits. These represent a return to the input that provides the firms' special low cost (e.g., especially fertile land or a low-cost source of raw materials).

[5]These equilibrium conditions also point out what seems to be, somewhat imprecisely, an "efficient" aspect of the long-run equilibrium in perfectly competitive markets. The good under investigation will be produced at minimum average cost. We consider the issue of efficiency in more detail in the next chapter.

Figure 12.7
Long-Run Equilibrium for a Perfectly Competitive Industry: Constant Cost Case

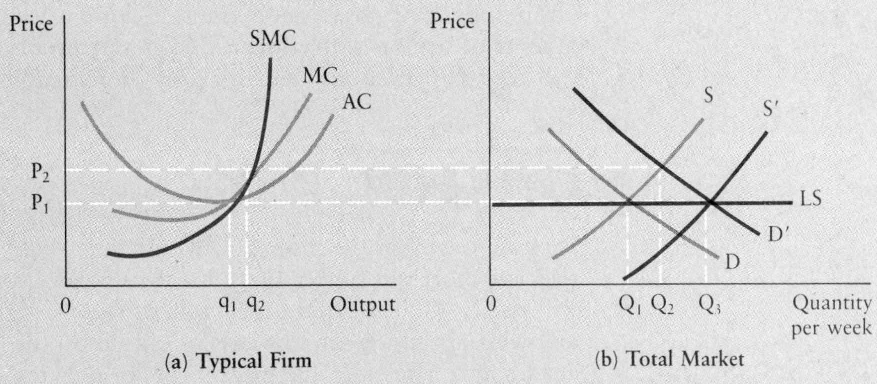

(a) Typical Firm (b) Total Market

An increase in demand from D to D′ will cause price to rise from P_1 to P_2 in the short run. This higher price will create profits in the industry and new firms will be drawn into the market. If the entry of these new firms has no effect on the cost curves of the firms in the industry, new firms will continue to enter until price is pushed back down to P_1. At this price economic profits are zero. The long-run supply curve LS will therefore be a horizontal line at P_1. Along LS, output is increased by increasing the number of firms that each produce q_1.

Hence, the per-unit costs of inputs to firms do not change. Under this assumption, no matter how many firms enter or leave an industry, every firm will retain exactly the same set of cost curves with which it started. There are many important cases for which this constant input cost assumption may not be made; we will analyze these cases later. For the moment, however, we wish to examine the equilibrium conditions for a **constant cost industry.**

Constant cost industry An industry in which the entry or exit of firms has no effect on the cost curves of the firms in the industry.

Market Equilibrium

Figure 12.7 demonstrates long-run equilibrium for a constant cost industry. For the market as a whole, in Panel b, the demand curve is labeled D and the short-run supply curve is labeled S. The short-run equilibrium price is therefore P_1. The typical firm in Panel a will produce output level q_1, since at this level of output price is equal to short-run marginal cost (SMC). In addition, with a market price of P_1, output level q_1 is also a long-run equilibrium position for the firm. The firm is maximizing profits since price is equal to long-run marginal cost (MC). When all possible variations in inputs are considered, q_1 remains the optimal level of output for a profit-maximizing firm. Panel a in Figure 12.7 also shows a second long-run equilibrium property: price is equal to long-run average total costs (AC). Consequently, economic profits are zero, and there is no incentive for firms either to enter or to leave the industry.

The market shown in Figure 12.7 is in both short-run and long-run equilibrium. Each firm is in equilibrium because it is maximizing profits, and the number of firms is stable because economic profits are zero. This equilibrium will tend to persist until either supply or demand conditions change.

A Shift in Demand

Suppose now that the market demand curve shifts outward to D′. If S is the relevant short-run supply curve for the industry, then in the short run, price will rise to P_2. The typical firm will, in the short run, choose to produce q_2, and will earn profits on this level of output. In the long run, these profits will attract new firms into the market. Because of the constant cost assumption, this entry of new firms will have no effect on input costs, and therefore the typical firm's cost curves will not shift. New firms will continue to enter the market until price is forced down to the level at which there are again no pure economic profits. The entry of new firms will therefore shift the short-run supply curve to S′ where the equilibrium price (P_1) is reestablished. At this new long-run equilibrium, the price-quantity combination P_1, Q_3 will prevail in the market. The typical firm will again produce at output level q_1, although now there will be more firms than there were in the initial situation.

Long-Run Supply Curve

By considering many such shifts in demand, we can examine long-run pricing in this industry. Our discussion suggests that no matter how demand shifts, economic forces that cause price always to return to P_1 will come into play. All long-run equilibria will occur along a horizontal line at P_1. Connecting these equilibrium points shows the long-run supply response of this industry. This long-run supply curve is labeled LS in Figure 12.7. For a constant cost industry of identical firms, the long-run supply curve is a horizontal line at the low point of the firms' long-run average total cost curves.

An Illustration Using the Model: Tax Incidence Theory

This model of long-run pricing can be used to examine the important question of who actually bears the burden of various taxes. Consider a *specific tax* of a fixed amount per unit on a firm's production. This is a cost per unit of output that appears to be "paid" by the firm to the government. To show that this view is misleading, we begin by recognizing that such a specific tax merely shifts the demand curve that is relevant to the firms in the industry downward by the amount of the tax. Any quantity that is produced will sell at some market price P, but the after-tax revenue received by firms in the industry will be $P - t$. The after-tax demand curve is labeled D′ in Figure 12.8.

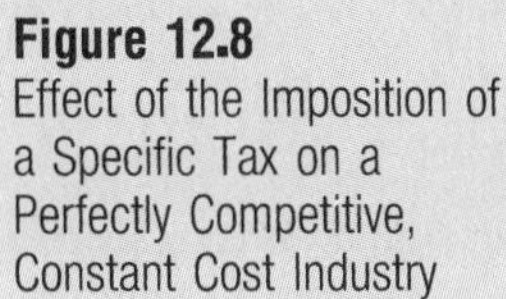

Figure 12.8
Effect of the Imposition of a Specific Tax on a Perfectly Competitive, Constant Cost Industry

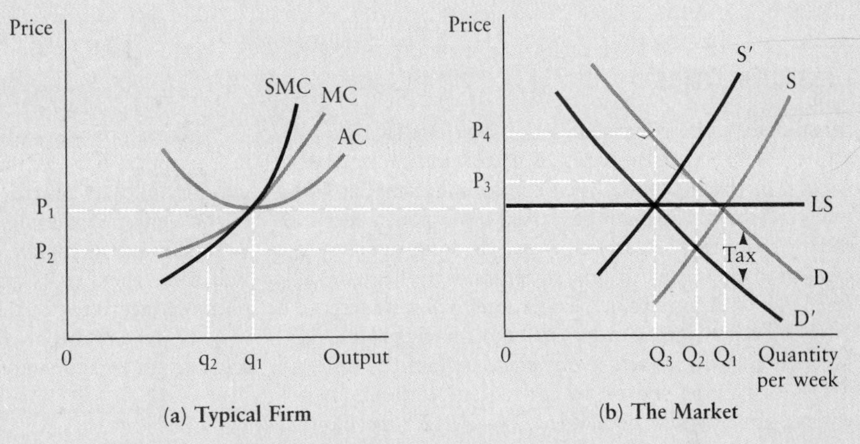

A specific commodity tax of amount t lowers the after-tax demand curve to D′. With this "new" demand curve, Q_2 will be produced in the short run at an after-tax price of P_2. The market price will be P_3. In the long run, firms will leave the industry, and the after-tax price will return to P_1. The entire amount of the tax is shifted onto consumers in the form of a higher market price (P_4).

This is the demand curve on which industry output decisions will be based, although the market price of any output produced will still be determined by the original market demand curve, D.

The initial equilibrium in the market is given by the intersection of the long-run supply curve (LS) and the market demand curve. At this point, market price is P_1, the quantity exchanged in the market is Q_1, and the typical firm will produce output level q_1. With the imposition of the tax, the after-tax demand curve becomes D′. In the short run, industry output will be determined by the intersection of the curve D′ with the industry short-run supply curve S. This intersection occurs at output level Q_2 and price P_2. The after-tax price received by the firm is now P_2, and the typical firm (assuming P_2 exceeds average variable cost) will produce output level q_2. In the market, total output Q_2 will sell for P_3. Notice that $P_3 - P_2 = t$. In the short run, then, the tax is borne partially by consumers of the good (market price has risen from P_1 to P_3) and partially by firms in the industry, which are now operating at a short-term loss because they receive P_2 instead of P_1 for their output.

In the long run, firms will not continue to operate at such a loss. Some firms will leave the industry bemoaning the role of oppressive taxation in bringing about their downfall. The industry short-run supply curve will shift leftward as fewer firms remain in the market. A new long-run equilibrium will be established at Q_3 where the after-tax price received by firms still in the industry enables them to earn exactly zero in economic profits. Those firms remaining in the industry will return to producing output level q_1. The price

APPLICATION 12.3

Cigarette Taxes

Most states impose excise taxes on cigarette sales; usually these are specific taxes of a certain amount per pack. Our discussion of specific taxes suggests that virtually all these taxes will be passed on to consumers in the form of higher cigarette prices. The long-run supply curve for cigarettes in any state is nearly horizontal since increases in sales in a single state will not increase industry costs significantly. Demand for cigarettes, on the other hand, is relatively price inelastic. Higher prices can be passed on to consumers without large changes in quantity demanded. Figure 12.8 probably represents the situation for state cigarette taxes fairly accurately.

Several studies of cigarette pricing have confirmed this theoretical prediction. For example, in 1981 Sumner and Ward found that about 93 percent of any change in a state's tax rate was quickly reflected in cigarette prices.[1] The authors suggested that one reason the amount passed on was less than exactly 100 percent (as predicted by our theory) is that additional consumers may choose to shop across state borders for their cigarettes when state tax rates change (many Massachusetts residents buy their cigarettes in New Hampshire, for example).

[1]M. T. Sumner and R. Ward, "Tax Changes and Cigarette Prices," *Journal of Political Economy* (December 1981): 1261–1265.

Another possible explanation is that under a specific tax, suppliers have an incentive to substitute quality for quantity in their activities, since only quantity is taxed. In the cigarette example, sellers may provide better service or more attractive displays. In the process, they will raise their costs and their prices and sell fewer packs of cigarettes. Such a change in selling techniques may represent the profit-maximizing response for a seller to take to the imposition of the tax.[2]

To Think About

1. Why do governments tax cigarettes so highly? Is it to discourage smoking or because the inelastic demand for cigarettes makes the tax a good revenue raiser? Do these alternative explanations make different implicit assumptions about the price elasticity of demand for cigarettes?
2. Could a local government impose a stiff tax on cigarettes if other local governments did not? Might a modest tax raise more revenues than a large one?

[2]For an example of how this differs from that of a tax on the *value* of sales, see Yoram Barzel, "An Alternative Approach to the Analysis of Taxation," *Journal of Political Economy* (December 1976): 1177–1197.

paid by buyers in the market will now be P_4. In the long run the entire amount of the tax has been shifted into increased prices. Even though the firm ostensibly "pays" the tax, in fact the long-run burden is borne completely by consumers.

Tax incidence theory
The study of the final burden of a tax after considering all market reactions to it.

This analysis is one of the simplest examples of **tax incidence theory.** It shows that in order to determine who ultimately pays a tax, it is necessary to investigate long-run market responses. It would be incorrect to assume that whoever writes a check to the government always bears the burden of the tax. A careful analysis of the supply and demand influences is required. Application 12.3: Cigarette Taxes examines a case that shows this very clearly.

Shape of the Long-Run Supply Curve

In the previous section we pointed out that, contrary to the short-run case, long-run analysis has very little to do with the shape of the marginal cost curve. Rather, the zero-profit condition centers attention on the low point of the long-run average cost curve as the factor most relevant to long-run price determination. In the constant cost case the position of this low point does not change as new firms enter or leave the industry. Consequently, only one price can prevail in the long run regardless of how demand shifts. The long-run supply curve is horizontal at this price.

Once the constant cost assumption is abandoned, this need not be the case. If the entry of new firms causes average costs to rise, the long-run supply curve will have an upward slope. On the other hand, if entry causes average costs to decline, it is even possible for the long-run supply curve to be negatively sloped. We now discuss these possibilities.

The Increasing Cost Industry

The entry of new firms may cause the average cost of all firms to rise for several reasons. New firms may compete for scarce inputs, thus driving up their prices. New firms may impose external costs on existing firms (and on themselves) in the form of air or water pollution. And new firms may place strains on governmental services (police forces, sewage treatment plants, and so forth), and these may show up as increased costs for all firms.

Increasing cost industry An industry in which the entry of firms increases the costs of the firms in the industry.

Figure 12.9 demonstrates market equilibrium in an **increasing cost industry.** The initial equilibrium price is P_1. At this price the typical firm in Panel a produces q_1, and total industry output, shown in Panel c, is Q_1. Suppose that the demand curve for the industry shifts outward to D′. In the short run, price will rise to P_2, which is where D′ and the industry's short-run supply curve (S) intersect. At this price, the typical firm will produce q_2 and will earn a substantial profit. This profit attracts new entrants into the market and shifts the short-run supply curve outward.

Suppose that the entry of new firms causes the cost curves of all firms to rise. The new firms may, for example, compete for scarce inputs and thereby drive the prices of these inputs up. A typical firm's new (higher) set of cost curves is shown in Panel b of Figure 12.9. The new long-run equilibrium price for the industry is P_3 (here P = MC = AC), and at this price Q_3 is demanded. We now have two points (P_1, Q_1, and P_3, Q_3) on the long-run supply curve.[6] All other points on the curve can be found in an analogous way by considering all possible shifts in the demand curve. These shifts would trace out the long-run supply curve LS. Here LS has a positive slope because of the increasing cost nature of the industry. Therefore this positive slope is

[6]Figure 12.9 also shows the short-run supply curve associated with the point P_3, Q_3. This supply curve has shifted to the right because more firms are producing now than initially.

Figure 12.9
An Increasing Cost Industry Has a Positively Sloped Long-Run Supply Curve

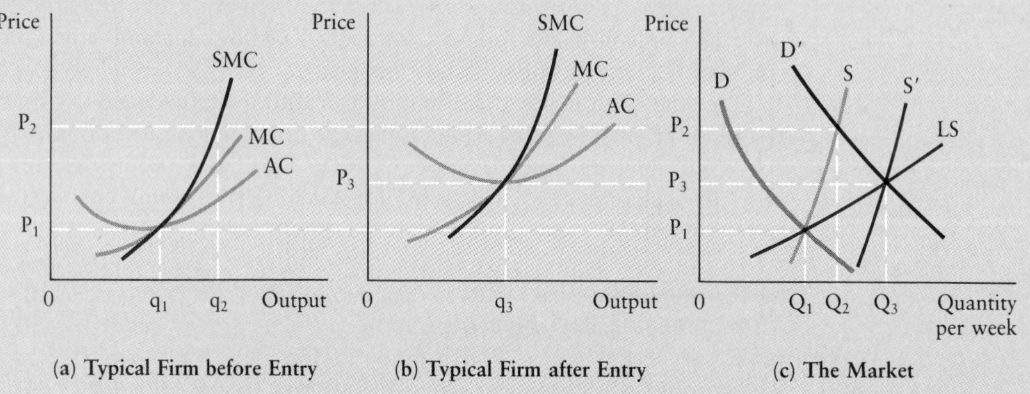

Initially the market is in equilibrium at P_1, Q_1. An increase in demand (to D′) causes price to rise to P_2 in the short run, and the typical firm produces q_2 at a profit. This profit attracts new firms into the industry. The entry of these new firms causes costs to rise to the levels shown in Panel b. With this new set of curves, equilibrium is reestablished in the market at P_3, Q_3. By considering many possible demand shifts and connecting all the resulting equilibrium points, the long-run supply curve LS is traced out.

caused by whatever causes average costs to rise in response to entry. Most commonly, a positively sloped LS curve occurs because entry drives up input costs for all firms. The LS curve is somewhat flatter than the short-run supply curves, which indicates the greater flexibility in supply response that is possible in the long run.

Price Controls and Shortages

In our analysis of competitive pricing in the long run, price increases play the crucial role of providing firms with the incentive to increase production in response to increases in demand. Governmental or other controls over prices may short-circuit this process and deter any long-run supply responses. That possibility is illustrated in Figure 12.10. Initially the market is in equilibrium at the point P_1, Q_1 where the market demand curve D and the long-run supply curve LS intersect. Consider the reaction to a shift in the market demand curve to D′. In the absence of price controls, price would rise to P_2 in the short run, and firms would increase output to Q_2. Supply would increase further to Q_3 in the long run as new firms enter the industry in response to profit possibilities. Imposition of price controls prevents both of these supply responses. If price is not allowed to rise above P_1, firms will continue to produce Q_1 even though demand has increased. At a price of P_1 individuals de-

Figure 12.10
Price Controls Inhibit Supply Responses

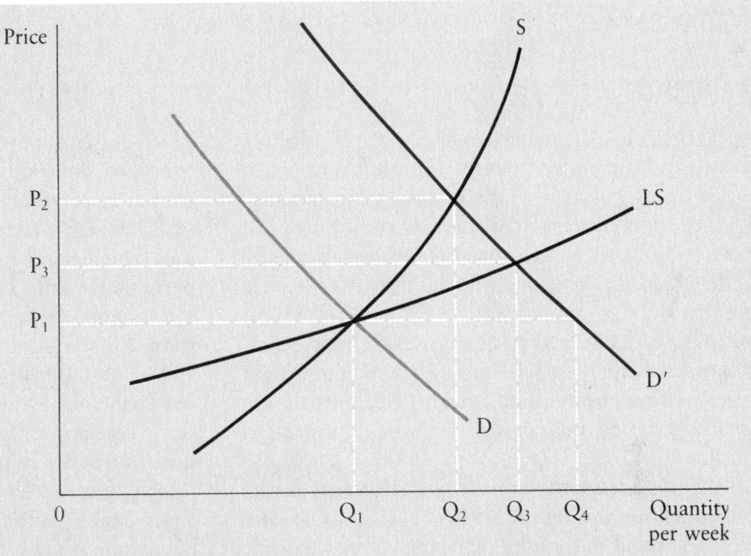

This market is initially in equilibrium at P_1, Q_1. A shift in demand to D′ would cause price to rise to P_2 in the short run and to P_3 in the long run. Quantity would increase to Q_2 and Q_3, respectively. Price controls that hold price at P_1 would inhibit this process since firms would continue to supply Q_1. At P_1 there is a long-run shortage given by $Q_4 - Q_1$.

mand Q_4 (with the demand curve D′), but only Q_1 is produced. There is now a shortage in the market, given by the distance $Q_4 - Q_1$. That shortage will persist as long as price controls retard supply response. The shortage is exacerbated by the fact that more is demanded at the artificially low controlled price (Q_4) than would be demanded at the long-run market clearing price (Q_3).

The model depicted in Figure 12.10 makes two predictions about the impact of price controls: (1) they will cause shortages; and (2) they will result in somewhat lower prices for those who are able to buy the good (for the increasing cost case illustrated in the figure). Application 12.4: Rent Controls looks at the important case of rent control, where these predictions have usually been proved accurate wherever the policy has been tried.

Long-Run Supply Elasticity

Long-run elasticity of supply
The percentage change in quantity supplied in the long run in response to a 1 percent change in price.

As we have just shown, the long-run supply curve for an industry is constructed by considering all possible shifts in the demand curve for the product. In order to predict the effects that such increases in demand will have on market price, it is therefore important to know something about the shape of the supply curve. A convenient measure for summarizing the shape of long-run supply curves is the **long-run elasticity of supply.** This concept records

APPLICATION 12.4

Rent Controls

During World War II, many American cities adopted controls on rent in order to stop rising housing prices that were occurring as a result of increased demand. Many cities (notably New York) and several European countries still maintain such controls. These are usually rationalized on the grounds that landlords (who are assumed to be rich) should not be allowed to exploit tenants (who are assumed to be poor). Without examining the facts behind such assertions, (which are often incorrect), the economic implications of controls are clearly predicted by the competitive model: shortages will result.

Table 1 provides some evidence on shortages in the city of Stockholm during the 1950s. The data indicate the average period in months that families had to wait for an apartment. The data show that this period lengthened greatly during the 1950s as postwar increases in income sharply increased the demand for housing and rent controls retarded long-run supply responses. Existing tenants may have benefited from lower rents, but substantial costs were imposed on families who had to wait more than three years to find a place of their own in which to live.

Rent Control and Housing Conditions

The effects of rent controls may show up in many other ways. In addition to the shortfall in the quantity of housing, the quality of housing may also deteriorate as landlords find it unprofitable to make repairs. For example, one study found that repair expenditures in 1967 on rent-controlled apartments in New York City averaged only about one-half of the expenditures on similar apartments that were not subject to rent controls.[1] Elective repairs (that is, those in excess of minimal requirements for health and safety) were particularly unlikely to be made in the rent-controlled apartments. Sometimes owners simply give up. More than 2,000 rental units are abandoned in New York City each month for this reason. Indeed, the effects of rent control on the condition of housing have caused some economists to equate these effects to the devastation caused by bombing—Vietnamese Foreign Minister Nguyen Co Thach is reported to have said, "The Americans couldn't destroy Hanoi by bombing, but we have done the job by setting low rents."[2]

Rent Control and Tenants

Finally, tenants of rent-controlled apartments may sometimes take advantage of their possession of a good for which there is excess demand. It is a common practice in many cities to require new tenants to pay "key money" to existing tenants for the right to take over their leases. Or sometimes existing tenants will charge new tenants exorbitant prices for the curtain rods or the refrigerator. Rent-controlled apartments are also passed down among family members as if they were valuable heirlooms.

Table 1
Waiting Time in Months for an Apartment in Stockholm

Year	Wait	Year	Wait
1950	9	1955	23
1951	15	1956	30
1952	21	1957	35
1953	24	1958	40
1954	26		

Source: S. Rydenfelt, "Rent Control Thirty Years On" in *Verdict on Rent Control* (London: Institute for Economic Affairs, 1972), p. 65.

To Think About

1. Why do communities vote for rent controls if their effects are so negative? Who gains from the controls? Do losers from rent control have as much political clout as the gainers?
2. Some cities with rent control also provide for "vacancy decontrol"—that is, rents can be raised on vacated apartments. How might existing tenants respond to such provisions? What would you expect to happen to the number of vacancies?

[1]George Sternlieb, *The Urban Housing Dilemma* (New York: Housing and Development Administration, 1972), p. 202.

[2]Quoted in *Fortune*, February 27, 1989, p. 134.

how proportional changes in price affect the quantity supplied, once all long-run adjustments have taken place. More formally:

$$\text{Long-run elasticity of supply} = \frac{\text{Percentage change in quantity supplied in long run}}{\text{Percentage change in price}}. \quad [12.5]$$

An elasticity of 10, for example, would indicate that a 1 percent increase in price would result in a 10 percent increase in the long-run quantity supplied. We would say that long-run supply is very price elastic: the long-run supply curve would be nearly horizontal. A principal implication of such a high price elasticity is that long-run equilibrium prices would not increase very much in response to outward shifts in the market demand curve.

A small supply elasticity would have a quite different implication. If the elasticity were only 0.1, for example, a 1 percent increase in price would increase quantity supplied by only 0.1 percent. In other words, the supply curve would be nearly vertical, and shifts outward in demand would result in rapidly rising prices without significant increases in quantity. Application 12.5: Long-Run Supply Elasticities uses this elasticity concept to describe some evidence about the supply situation in various industries.

The Decreasing Cost Industry

Not all industries must exhibit constant or increasing costs. In some cases entry may reduce costs. The entry of new firms may provide a larger pool of trained labor to draw from than was previously available, which would reduce the costs of hiring new workers. The entry of new firms may also provide a "critical mass" of industrialization that permits the development of more efficient transportation, communications, and financial networks. Whatever the exact nature of the cost reductions, the final result is illustrated in the three panels of Figure 12.11. The initial market equilibrium is shown by the price quantity combination P_1, Q_1 in Panel c. At this price the typical firm in Panel a produces q_1 and earns exactly zero in economic profits. Now suppose market demand shifts outward to D'. In the short run, price will increase to P_2, and the typical firm will produce q_2. At this price level, positive profits are earned. These profits cause new firms to enter the market. If these entries cause costs to decline, a new set of cost curves for the typical firm might resemble those in Panel b. Now the new equilibrium price is P_3. At this price, Q_3 is demanded. By considering all possible shifts in demand, the long-run supply curve LS can be traced out. For this **decreasing cost industry** the long-run supply curve has a negative slope.

Decreasing cost industry
An industry in which the entry of firms decreases the costs of the firms in the industry.

Infant Industries

Industries in underdeveloped countries frequently exhibit high production costs. They must absorb the expense of training workers, contend with an in-

APPLICATION 12.5

Long-Run Supply Elasticities

Table 1 reports a number of long-run supply elasticity estimates that have been gathered from a variety of sources. Many of these concern natural resources, because economists since the time of Thomas Malthus have been interested in the effects of increasing demand for resources on their price. Other estimates are for agricultural crops and for housing.

Agricultural Production

The estimated elasticities for agricultural products are "acreage elasticities." They reflect how acres planted in a particular crop respond to that crop's price. Assuming a constant yield per acre, we can translate them directly into the supply-elasticity concept. All of the reported elasticities are relatively low (less than 1.0). But all are positive, indicating that increases in prices do lead to increases in output. Of course, increases in agricultural output in recent years have come about mainly from improved technology (a shift in the supply curve). The data show that higher prices also lead to more land being planted.

Table 1
Selected Estimates of Long-Run Supply Elasticities

Industry	Elasticity
Agricultural acreage:	
Cotton	0.67
Wheat	0.93
Corn	0.18
Aluminum	Nearly infinite
Chromium	0–3
Coal (eastern reserves)	15–30
Natural gas (U.S. reserves)	0.50
Oil (U.S. reserves)	.75–1.50
Urban housing:	
Density	5.3
Quality	3.8

Sources: Agricultural acreage: M. Nerlove, "Estimates of the Elasticities of Supply of Selected Agricultural Commodities," *Journal of Farm Economics* (May 1956): 496–509. Aluminum and chromium: estimated from *Critical Materials Commodity Action Analysis* (Washington, D.C.: U.S. Department of the Interior, 1975). Coal: estimated from M. B. Zimmerman, "The Supply of Coal in the Long Run: The Case of Eastern Deep Coal" (Cambridge, Mass.: MIT Energy Laboratory Report No. MITEL 75-021, September 1975). Natural gas: J. D. Khazzoom, "The FPC Staff's Econometric Model of Natural Gas Supply in the United States," *The Bell Journal of Economics and Management Science* (Spring 1971). Oil: D. N. Epple, *Petroleum Discoveries and Government Policy* (Cambridge, Mass.: Marc Ballinger Publishing Company, 1984), Chapter 3. Urban housing: B. A. Smith, "The Supply of Urban Housing," *Journal of Political Economy* (August 1976): 389–405.

Natural Resources

Two different types of supply elasticity are reported for natural resources in Table 1. For aluminum and chromium the data refer to the relationship between annual production and market price. They show that the long-run supply of aluminum is nearly infinitely elastic at current market prices. This results from the fact that additional alumina deposits are easy to develop using current technology. The supply elasticity for chromium is considerably lower—primarily because developing new deposits requires incurring much higher average costs than is the case for mining existing deposits.

For coal, natural gas, and oil, supply elasticities refer to the responsiveness of available reserves to price. The data show that coal reserves are far more price responsive than are oil and natural gas reserves. As for aluminum and chromium, that result derives primarily from geology: greater reserves of coal are easily within the reach of current mining methods. For oil and natural gas, most low cost reserves have already been found. New reserves can be developed only at much higher costs.

Housing

The final estimates in Table 1 refer to two aspects of the supply of urban housing. They show that "more housing" can be produced in two ways: by increasing residential density while holding quality constant; and by increasing quality while holding density constant. Both of these output measures seem to be reasonably responsive to price. That is, increases in the demand for housing will not result in sharply increased costs and prices in the long run.

To Think About

1. What does it mean to say some natural resources are "scarcer" than others? Is the formal concept of supply elasticity related to the more commonsense notion of scarcity?
2. The coal and oil supply elasticities in this example refer to finding reserves. How is this activity related to firms' decisions on how much coal or oil to produce from these reserves?

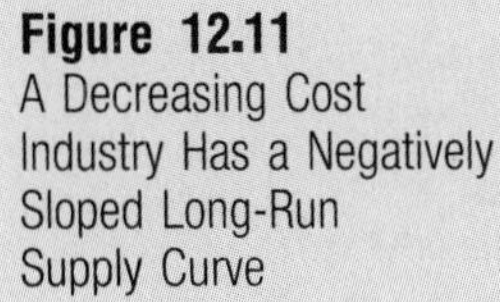

Figure 12.11
A Decreasing Cost Industry Has a Negatively Sloped Long-Run Supply Curve

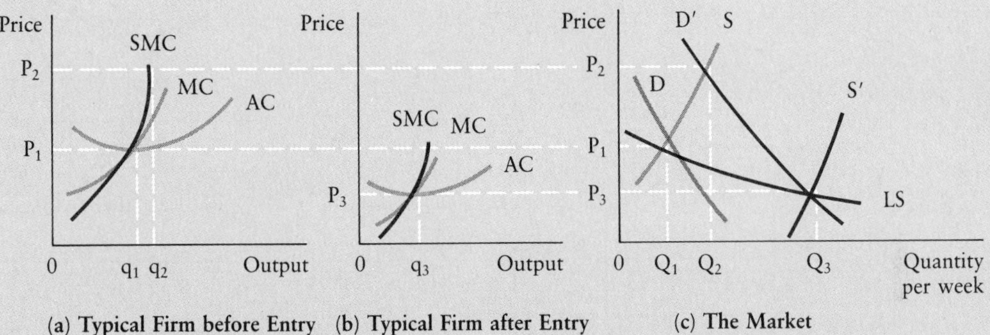

(a) Typical Firm before Entry (b) Typical Firm after Entry (c) The Market

Initially the market is in equilibrium at P_1, Q_1. An increase in demand to D′ causes price to rise to P_2 in the short run, and the typical firm produces q_2 at a profit. This profit attracts new firms to the industry. If the entry of these new firms causes costs to fall, a set of new cost curves might look like those in Panel b. With this new set of curves, market equilibrium is reestablished at P_3, Q_3. By connecting such points of equilibrium, a negatively sloped long-run supply curve LS is traced out.

adequate internal monetary system, and make do with poorly developed transportation facilities and inefficient public utilities. Faced with these costs, such industries frequently cannot compete at prevailing world prices. For example, the cost curves for the firms in an underdeveloped economy might resemble those in Panel a in Figure 12.12. Since the minimum point on the AC curve (P_1) exceeds the world price (P_W), a policy of free trade will cause the good in question to be imported, and a domestic industry will not develop.

In an effort to protect their industries, many underdeveloped countries adopt tariffs that raise the price for imports above P_1. Given the shield of the tariff, the domestic industry can now sell in its home market. If this were the end of the story, many economists would oppose the imposition of the tariff on the grounds that residents of the country are being forced to pay more for the good than would be necessary in a free trade situation. However, it is possible that temporarily protecting the infant industry will permit the country to develop a better-trained labor force and construct more efficient transportation, communication, and utility facilities. If that happens (as it did in the early history of the United States when textile products were protected), cost curves in the industry may be lowered so that firms may eventually compete in world markets. Such a lowering of costs is shown in Panel b in Figure 12.12. Once costs have been reduced, the tariff can be removed, having served its purpose of nurturing the domestic industry. Of course, if costs

Figure 12.12
Infant Industry Argument for Tariff Protection

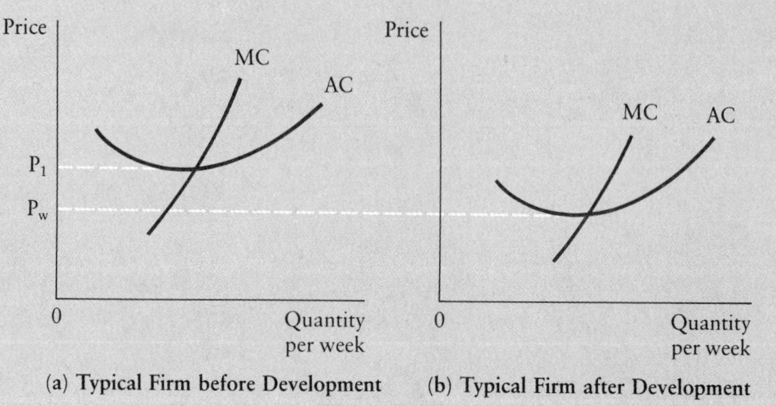

Firms in an underdeveloped country may have high costs, as shown in Panel a. The firms cannot compete at world prices (P_W). A tariff that raises price above P_1 will permit the firms to sell in the domestic market, and their growth may bring about the development of a more efficient economic network. That development may lower firms' costs so that they may now compete at the world price without tariff protection.

never decline, the tariff will only have protected an inefficient domestic industry, so a country should be careful in choosing such a policy.[7]

Summary

The model of pricing in perfectly competitive markets that we present in this chapter is probably the most widely used economic model. Even when markets do not strictly obey all of the assumptions of perfect competition, it is still frequently possible to use that model as a reasonable approximation of how such markets work. Some of the basic features of the perfectly competitive model that are highlighted in this chapter are:

- The short-run supply curve in a perfectly competitive market represents the horizontal sum of the short-run supply curves for many price-taking firms. The upward slope of the short-run supply curve reflects these firms' increasing short-run marginal costs.
- Equilibrium prices are determined in the short run by the interaction of the short-run supply curve with the market demand curve. At the equilibrium price, firms are willing to produce precisely the amount of output that people want to buy.

[7]For a complete theoretical discussion, see H. G. Johnson, "A New View of the Infant Industry Argument," in *Studies in International Economics*, I. A. McDougall and R. M. Snape, eds. (Amsterdam: North Holland Publishing Company, 1979).

- Shifts in either the demand curve or the supply curve will change the equilibrium price. The extent of such a change depends on the particular shape of the two curves.
- Economic profits will attract entrants into a perfectly competitive market in the long run. This entry will continue until economic profits are reduced to zero. At that point, the market price will equal long-run average cost, and each firm will be operating at the low point of its long-run average cost curve.
- Entry of new firms may have an effect on the cost of firms' inputs. In the constant cost case, however, input costs are not affected, so the long-run supply curve is horizontal. If entry raises input costs, the long-run supply curve is upward sloping. If entry reduces such costs, the long-run supply curve is downward sloping.

Review Questions

1. Explain how a market with a fixed supply (such as that shown in Figure 12.1) reaches an equilibrium price. How would market participants know that a nonequilibrium price was too high or too low? How might you use a graph such as this one to explain the way prices are established in an auction?
2. One assumption of a perfectly competitive market is that every firm faces the same, known price. How is this assumption reflected in Figure 12.2? Why do economists believe markets for homogeneous goods may reasonably be assumed to exhibit the "law of one price"?
3. Why is the price for which quantity demanded equals quantity supplied called an "equilibrium price"? Suppose, instead, we viewed a demand curve as showing what price consumers are willing to pay and a supply curve as showing what price firms want to receive. Using this view of demand and supply, how would you define an "equilibrium quantity"?
4. "For markets with inelastic demand and supply curves, most short-run movements will be in prices, not quantity. For markets with elastic demand and supply curves, most movements will be in quantity, not price." Do you agree? Illustrate your answer with a few simple graphs.
5. Why would firms stay in an industry that only promised zero long-run profits? Why would firms ever want to enter such an industry? Wouldn't a firm's owners do better to invest somewhere else?
6. In long-run equilibrium in a perfectly competitive market, each firm operates at minimal average cost. Do firms also operate at minimum long-run average cost when such markets are out of equilibrium in the short run? Wouldn't firms make more in short-run profits if they opted always to produce that output level for which average costs were as small as possible?
7. What do economists assume about the long-run elasticity of supply for the inputs bought by a constant cost industry? How is this assumption changed for the case of an increasing cost industry? Why does the shape of an industry's long-run supply curve ultimately reflect the supply curves for the inputs that the industry employs?
8. Show that for an increasing cost industry the burden of a specific tax in the long run is paid partly by consumers and partly by producers. How can producers "pay" part of the tax if firms in long-run equilibrium in a perfectly competitive industry always earn zero profits? What does the analysis of question 7 suggest about who pays the "producer's share" of a specific tax in the long run?

9. Show that a specific tax on a decreasing cost industry will raise market price by more than the tax. Explain your result intuitively.
10. Is there any connection between the returns to scale (see Chapter 8) exhibited by the firms in a perfectly competitive industry and whether the industry exhibits constant, increasing, or decreasing costs? Explain the relationship between these concepts.

Problems

12.1 Suppose the daily demand curve for flounder at Cape May is given by

$$Q_D = 1{,}600 - 600P$$

where Q_D is demand in pounds per day and P is price per pound.

a. If fishing boats land 1,000 pounds one day, what will the price be?
b. If the catch were to fall to 400 pounds, what would the price be?
c. Suppose the demand for flounder shifts outward to

$$Q_D' = 2{,}200 - 600P.$$

How would your answers to parts a and b change?
d. Graph your results.

12.2 Suppose, as in problem 12.1, the demand for flounder is given by

$$Q_D' = 1{,}600 - 600P,$$

but now assume that Cape May fishermen can, at some cost, choose to sell their catch elsewhere. Specifically, assume that the amount they will sell in Cape May is given by

$$Q_S = -1{,}000 + 2{,}000P \quad \text{for } Q_S \geq 0$$

where Q_S is the quantity supplied in pounds and P is the price per pound.

a. At least what price will flounder have to be if any is to be supplied to the Cape May market?
b. Given the demand curve for flounder, what will the equilibrium price be?
c. Suppose now, as in problem 12.1, demand shifts to

$$Q_D' = 2{,}200 - 600P.$$

What will be the new equilibrium price?
d. Explain intuitively why price will rise by less in part c than it did in problem 12.1.
e. Graph your results.

12.3 A perfectly competitive market has 1,000 firms. In the very short run each of the firms has a fixed supply of 100 units. The market demand is given by

$$Q = 160{,}000 - 10{,}000P.$$

a. Calculate the equilibrium price in the very short run.

b. Calculate the demand schedule facing any one firm in the industry. Do this by calculating what the equilibrium price would be if one of the sellers decided to sell nothing or if one seller decided to sell 200 units. What do you conclude about the effect of any one firm on market price?

12.4 Assuming the same conditions as in problem 12.3, suppose now that in the short run each firm has a supply curve that shows the quantity the firm will supply (q_i) as a function of market price. The specific form of this supply curve is given by

$$q_i = -200 + 50P.$$

Using this short-run supply response, supply new solutions to parts a and b in problem 12.3. Why do you get different solutions in this case?

12.5 Widgets, Inc. is a small firm producing widgets. The widget industry is perfectly competitive; Widgets, Inc. is a price taker. The short-run total cost curve for Widgets, Inc. has the form:

$$STC = 1/3\ q^3 + 10q^2 + 100q + 48$$

and the short-run marginal cost curve is given by

$$SMC = q^2 + 20q + 100.$$

a. Calculate the firm's short-run supply curve with q (the number of widgets produced per day) as a function of market price (P).
b. How many widgets will the firm produce if the market price is P = 121? P = 169? P = 256? (Assume variable costs are covered.)
c. How much profit will Widgets, Inc. make when P = 121? P = 169? P = 256?

12.6 Suppose there are one hundred identical firms in a perfectly competitive notecard industry. Each firm has a short-run total cost curve of the form:

$$STC = 1/300\ q^3 + 0.2q^2 + 4q + 10,$$

and marginal cost is given by

$$SMC = .01q^2 + .4q + 4.$$

a. Calculate the firm's short-run supply curve with q (the number of crates of notecards) as a function of market price (P).
b. On the assumption that there are no interaction effects between costs of the firms in the industry, calculate the industry supply curve.
c. Suppose market demand is given by Q = −200P + 8,000. What will be the short-run equilibrium price-quantity combination?
d. Suppose everyone starts writing more research papers, and the new market demand is given by Q = −200P + 10,000. What is the new short-run price-quantity equilibrium? How much profit does each firm make?

*12.7 Suppose there are 1,000 identical firms producing diamonds and that the total cost curve for each firm is given by:

$$C = q^2 + wq$$

and marginal cost is given by:

$$MC = 2q + w$$

where q is the firm's output level and w is the wage rate of diamond cutters.

a. If w = 10, what will be the firm's (short-run) supply curve? What is the industry's supply curve? How many diamonds will be produced at a price of 20 each? How many more diamonds would be produced at a price of 21?
b. Suppose that the wages of diamond cutters depend on the total quantity of diamonds produced and the form of this relationship is given by

$$w = .002Q$$

where Q represents total industry output, which is 1,000 times the output of the typical firm. In this situation show that the firm's marginal cost (and short-run supply) curve depends on Q. What is the industry supply curve? How much will be produced at a price of 20? How much more will be produced at a price of 21? What do you conclude about the shape of the short-run supply curve?

12.8 Wheat is produced under perfectly competitive conditions. Individual wheat farmers have U-shaped, long-run average cost curves that reach a minimum average cost of $3 per bushel when 1,000 bushels are produced.

a. If the market demand curve for wheat is given by

$$Q_D = 2{,}600{,}000 - 200{,}000P$$

where Q_D is the number of bushels demanded per year and P is the price per bushel, in long-run equilibrium what will be the price of wheat? How much total wheat will be demanded? How many wheat farms will there be?
b. Suppose demand shifts outward to

$$Q_D = 3{,}200{,}000 - 200{,}000P.$$

If farmers cannot adjust their output in the short run (that is, suppose the SMC curve is vertical), what will market price be with this new demand curve? What will the profits of the typical farm be?
c. Given the new demand curve described in part b, what will be the new long-run equilibrium? (That is, calculate market price, quantity of wheat produced, and the new equilibrium number of farms in this new situation.)
d. Graph your results.

*12.9 Gasoline is sold through local gas stations under perfectly competitive conditions. All gas station owners face the same long-run average cost curve given by

$$AC = .01q - 1 + 100/q$$

---

*Denotes a problem that is rather difficult.

and the same long-run marginal cost curve given by

$$MC = .02q - 1$$

where q is the number of gallons sold per day.

a. Assuming the market is in long-run equilibrium, how much gas will each individual owner sell per day? What are the long-run average cost and marginal cost at this output level?
b. The market demand for gasoline is given by

$$Q_D = 2{,}500{,}000 - 500{,}000P$$

where Q_D is the number of gallons demanded per day and P is the price per gallon. Given your answer to part a, what will be the price of gasoline in long-run equilibrium? How much gasoline will be demanded and how many gas stations will there be?
c. Suppose that because of the development of solar-powered cars, the market demand for gasoline shifts inward to

$$Q_D = 2{,}000{,}000 - 1{,}000{,}000P.$$

In long-run equilibrium, what will be the price of gasoline, how much total gasoline will be demanded, and how many gas stations will there be?
d. Graph your results.

*12.10 A perfectly competitive painted necktie industry has a large number of potential entrants. Each firm has an identical cost structure such that long-run average cost is minimized at an output of 20 units ($q_i = 20$). The minimum average cost is $10 per unit. Total market demand is given by

$$Q = 1{,}500 - 50P.$$

a. What is the industry's long-run supply schedule?
b. What is the long-run equilibrium price (P^*)? The total industry output (Q^*)? The output of each firm (q_i^*)? The number of firms? The profits of each firm?
c. The short-run total cost curve associated with each firm's long-run equilibrium output is given by

$$STC = .5q^2 - 10q + 200$$

where $SMC = q - 10$. Calculate the short-run average and marginal cost curves. At what necktie output level does short-run average cost reach a minimum?
d. Calculate the short-run supply curve for each firm and the industry short-run supply curve.
e. Suppose now painted neckties become more fashionable and the market demand function shifts upward to $Q = 2{,}000 - 50P$. Using this new demand curve, answer part b for the very short run when firms cannot change their outputs.
f. In the short run, use the industry short-run supply curve to recalculate the answers to part b.
g. What is the new long-run equilibrium for the industry?

*Denotes a problem that is rather difficult.

CHAPTER 13

General Equilibrium and Economic Efficiency

In Chapter 12 we developed a detailed model of how a single competitive market works. In this chapter we are interested in how a system of many competitive markets operates and whether this operation yields desirable results. Specifically, we will develop a definition of what it means to allocate resources efficiently, and we will then examine whether competitive markets can achieve this goal.

We are examining a question first posed in the eighteenth century by Adam Smith, who saw in market forces an "invisible hand" that guides resources to their best use. Although the vast number of transactions that take place in an economy may seem like utter chaos, Smith viewed them as in fact being quite orderly in moving resources to where they are most valued. A primary purpose of Chapter 13 is to investigate Smith's ideas rigorously and to show that, with some important limitations, his insights were essentially correct.

Perfectly Competitive Price System

Before starting our examination of Smith's invisible hand notion, we must describe the particular model of the economy we will be using. This model is a simple generalization of the supply-demand model of perfectly competitive price determination introduced in the previous chapter. Here we assume that all markets are of this type, and refer to this set of markets as a **perfectly competitive price system.** The assumption is that in this simple economy there is some large number of homogeneous goods. Included in this list of goods

Perfectly competitive price system
An economic model in which individuals maximize utility, firms maximize profits, there is perfect information about prices, and every economic actor is a price taker.

are not only consumption items but also factors of production (whose pricing is described later in Part 5). Each of these goods has an equilibrium price, established by the action of supply and demand.[1] At this set of prices, every market is cleared in the sense that suppliers are willing to supply the exact quantity that is demanded. We also assume that there are no transaction or transportation charges and that both individuals and firms have perfect knowledge of these prices. Both of these assumptions are examined in more detail in the next chapter.

Because we have assumed there are no transactions costs, each good in our model obeys the law of one price: a good trades at the same price no matter who buys it or which firm sells it. If one good were traded at two different prices, people would rush to buy the good where it was cheaper, and firms would try to sell all their output where the good was more expensive. These actions would tend to equalize the price of the good between the markets. This is why we may speak unambiguously of *the* price of a good.

The perfectly competitive model assumes that people and firms react to prices in specific ways:

1. There are assumed to be a large number of people buying any one good. Each person takes all prices as given. Each adjusts his or her behavior to maximize utility, given the prices and his or her budget constraint. People may also be suppliers of productive services (for example, labor), and in such decisions they also regard prices as given.[2]
2. There are assumed to be a large number of firms producing each good, and each firm produces only a small share of the output of any one good. In making input and output choices, firms are assumed to operate to maximize profits. The firm treats all prices as given when making these profit-maximizing decisions. The firm's activities, either as a supplier of goods or as a demander of factor inputs, have no effect on market prices.

These assumptions should be familiar to you since we have usually been making them throughout this book. Our purpose here is to show how an entire economic system operates when all markets work in this way.

An Illustration of General Equilibrium

A major distinction between this model and the perfectly competitive models we have used previously is that now we are interested in studying an entire system of many interconnected markets, not just a single market in isolation.

[1]One aspect of this market interaction should be made clear from the outset. The perfectly competitive market only determines relative (not absolute) prices. For most of this chapter, we speak of relative prices. It makes no difference whether the prices of apples and oranges are $.10 and $.20, respectively, or $10 and $20. The important point in either case is that two apples can be exchanged for one orange in the market. At the end of this chapter we look briefly at how nominal (money) prices are determined.

[2]Since one price represents the wage rate, the relevant budget constraint is in reality a time constraint. This is the way we treat individuals' labor-leisure choices in Chapter 19.

Figure 13.1
The Market for Tomatoes and Several Related Markets

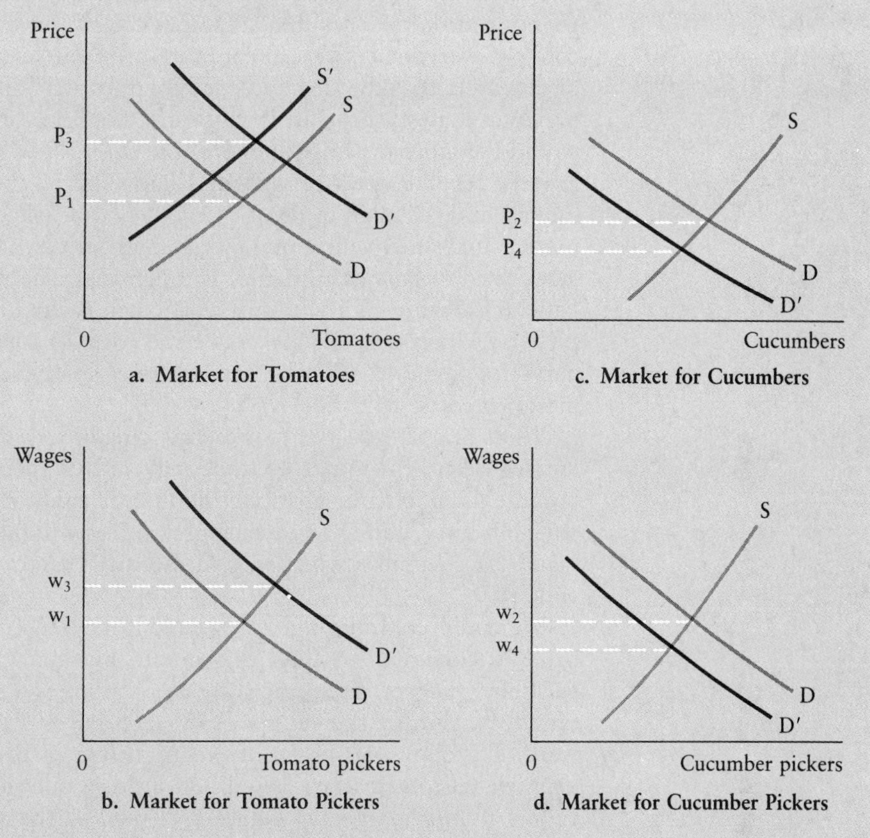

Initially the market for tomatoes is in equilibrium (at P_1) as are the markets for tomato pickers, cucumbers, and cucumber pickers. An increase in demand for tomatoes will disturb these equilibria. Virtually all of the supply and demand curves will shift in the process of establishing a new general equilibrium.

That is, we wish now to take a "general equilibrium" view of the economy rather than the "partial equilibrium" approach used in Chapter 12. To illustrate this approach, Figure 13.1 shows the market for one good, say, tomatoes, and three of the many other markets related to it: (1) the market for tomato pickers; (2) the market for a related product—cucumbers; and (3) the market for cucumber pickers. Suppose that initially all of these markets are in equilibrium as shown by the sets of shaded supply and demand curves in the four panels of Figure 13.1. That is, the equilibrium price of tomatoes is given by P_1, wages of tomato pickers by w_1, the price of cucumbers by P_2, and the wages of cucumber pickers by w_2. Since these prices act to equate the amount supplied and demanded in each of these markets, the general equilibrium shown in Figure 13.1 will persist from week to week until something happens to change it.

Assume now that such a change does occur. Imagine a situation where the government announces that tomatoes have been found to cure the common cold, so everyone decides to eat more of them. An initial consequence of this discovery is that the demand for tomatoes will shift outward to D′. In our previous analysis this shift would cause the price of tomatoes to rise and that would be, more or less, the end of the story. Now, however, we wish to follow the repercussions of what has happened in the tomato market into the other markets shown in Figure 13.1. A first possible reaction would be in the market for tomato pickers. Since tomato prices have risen, the demand for labor used to harvest tomatoes will increase. The demand curve for labor in Panel b in Figure 13.1 will shift to D′. This will tend to raise wages of tomato pickers, which will, in turn, raise the costs of tomato growers. The supply curve for tomatoes (which, under perfect competition, just reflects growers' marginal costs) will shift to S′.

What happens to the market for cucumbers? Since people have an increased desire for tomatoes, they may reduce their demands for cucumbers because these tomato substitutes don't cure colds. The demand for cucumbers will shift inward to D′, and cucumber prices will fall. That will reduce the demand for cucumber workers, and the wage associated with that occupation will fall.

We could continue this story indefinitely. We could ask how the lower price of cucumbers affects the tomato market. Or we could ask whether cucumber pickers, discouraged by their falling wages, might consider picking tomatoes, shifting the supply of labor curve in Panel b in Figure 13.1 outward. To follow this chain of events further or to examine even more markets related to tomatoes would add little to our story. Eventually we would expect all four markets in Figure 13.1 (and all the other markets we have not shown) to reach a new equilibrium, such as that illustrated by the solid supply and demand curves in the figure. Once all the repercussions have been worked out, the final result would be a rise in tomato prices (to P_3), a rise in the wages of tomato pickers (to w_3), a fall in cucumber prices (to P_4), and a fall in the wages of cucumber pickers (to w_4). This is what we mean then by a smoothly working system of perfectly competitive markets. Following any disturbance, all of the markets can eventually reestablish a new set of equilibrium prices at which quantity demanded is equal to quantity supplied in each market.[3] It is this model—or, as in Application 13.1: Modeling the Impact of Taxes with a Computer, a more complex form of this model involving hundreds, perhaps even millions of interconnected markets—that we will use to investigate the question of economic efficiency.

---

[3]Actually, the question of whether many markets can establish a set of prices that brings equilibrium to each of them is a major and difficult theoretical question. For a simple discussion and some references, see Walter Nicholson, *Microeconomic Theory: Basic Principles and Extensions*, 4th ed. (Hinsdale, Ill.: Dryden Press, 1989), pp. 455–463.

APPLICATION 13.1

Modeling the Impact of Taxes with a Computer

In Chapter 12 we illustrated how the competitive model might be used to analyze the impact of taxes on a single market. A primary shortcoming of that approach is that it does not allow a very complete description of the various effects a tax may have. For example, we showed that an excise tax on a good is partly paid by consumers and partly paid by firms, with the respective shares being determined by elasticities of demand and supply. This conclusion tells us very little about who finally bears the burden of the tax. We have no idea how that burden is shared among different consumers of the good, nor do we know who finally pays the firms' share (it could be owners of the firms, workers in the firms, or some combination of the two). Simple models of supply and demand are just not rich enough in detail to answer such questions.

Computers and General Equilibrium Models

The development of large-scale computers and sophisticated programs for modeling the economy has changed this situation dramatically. Now it is possible to use general equilibrium models of the economy to obtain very detailed appraisals of the impact of taxes. Some of these models divide the economy into as many as 50 or more industries and equally many different types of consumers (depending on their incomes or on where they live). A graphic representation of such models might look like Figure 13.1 but with more than 100 different markets represented. Coping with the information necessary to compute equilibrium prices in all of these markets without a computer would be impossible. Using the speed and capacity of modern computers makes it a fairly simple process.

Results of General Equilibrium Models

These large general equilibrium models of the economy have yielded major and sometimes surprising conclusions about the effects of taxes on an economy. Generally, these effects are bigger than have usually been found using partial equilibrium methods.[1] One study of the entire tax system of the United Kingdom, for example, concluded that distortions introduced by that system resulted in an excess burden (see Application 6.1 for a definition of this term) of 6 to 9 percent of total gross national product. The taxes also caused a transfer of nearly one-quarter of all income from high-income to low-income households. The study found that the British tax system imposed particularly heavy costs on its manufacturing industries—perhaps providing an explanation for recent poor industrial performance in that country. Studies of the U.S. tax system tend to reach similar, though perhaps not so dramatic, conclusions. For example, some authors have reported that, at the margin, the U.S. tax system involves large efficiency losses. These studies suggest that moving to simpler tax schemes, such as a flat rate consumption tax, would reduce these losses substantially.

To Think About

1. Suppose the government were to institute a tax on each gallon of gasoline sold. How would you analyze the economic effects of this tax with a partial equilibrium model? What further repercussions of the tax would this simple model miss? How many markets do you think you should study to gain a fairly complete picture of the impact of the tax?
2. In most general equilibrium models of taxation the final results of who pays taxes are reported as how after-tax incomes of various groups of people are affected. There is no notion that firms pay any taxes at all. What do you make of this? How do you reconcile the commonsense (and politically popular) idea that firms do indeed pay taxes with the general equilibrium notion that ultimately only people pay taxes?

[1] For a summary of many of these models, see John B. Shoven and John Walley, "Applied General Equilibrium Models of Taxation and International Trade," *Journal of Economic Literature* (September 1984): 1007–1051.

A Simple Demonstration of Efficiency

Before trying to examine the notion of economic efficiency in many markets, a simple single market example may help to motivate our discussion. Suppose we wished to discover the efficient level of, say, tomato production in an economy. Our first task would be to define what we mean by "efficiency." Although we will be far more precise in our definition later on, here we adopt an intuitive definition based on our discussion of Pareto efficiency in Chapter 6. A particular allocation of resources is "inefficient" if there exist uncompleted transactions that would make some people better-off and no one worse-off. With an "efficient" allocation, all such beneficial transactions have been completed and no further gains are possible.

Consider now the market for tomatoes for which demand and long-run supply curves are illustrated in Figure 13.2. We know from Chapter 4 that points on the tomato demand curve represent buyers' willingness to pay for various amounts of the good. Our analysis of long-run supply in the previous chapter shows that points on the supply curve reflect the marginal costs associated with tomato production and that the positive slope of the curve shows that these costs increase as output expands. If these rising costs can be taken as an accurate indicator of the true opportunity costs to the remainder of the economy of increasing tomato production, we can use Figure 13.2 to illustrate Pareto efficiency.

Consider any level of tomato output, say, Q_1. At Q_1 buyers are willing to pay P_1 for extra tomatoes, and suppliers would incur opportunity costs of P_2 in producing them. The production of additional tomatoes therefore represents a potentially mutually beneficial transaction. Selling some extra tomatoes at any price between P_1 and P_2 would be beneficial to both the buyer (who would get them for less than he or she was willing to pay) and to the seller (who would more than cover opportunity cost). Clearly, therefore, production at Q_1 is inefficient.

A similar argument can be made for any level of tomato output lower than Q^*. Only at Q^* does buyers' willingness to pay equal the opportunity costs involved in additional tomato production. Beyond Q^* the possibilities for mutually beneficial transactions cease since opportunity costs exceed buyers' marginal evaluations of tomatoes. Q^* is therefore the efficient level of tomato output.

Although this simple analysis should not be pushed too far, Figure 13.2 provides a clear indication of why Smith's "invisible hand" conjective may be correct. Under perfect competition, markets will arrive at an equilibrium price of P^*, and at that price Q^* will be produced. Reliance on market forces has therefore resulted in an efficient allocation of resources to tomato production.[4] But this "proof" is not a very complete one since it provides very

[4] A somewhat different proof uses the notions of consumer surplus (see Chapter 6) and "producer surplus" (defined as the extent to which total revenues to producers exceed opportunity costs). With equilibrium at P^*,Q^* in Figure 13.2, total consumer surplus is given by area AEP^* and to-

Figure 13.2
A Simple Demonstration of Efficiency

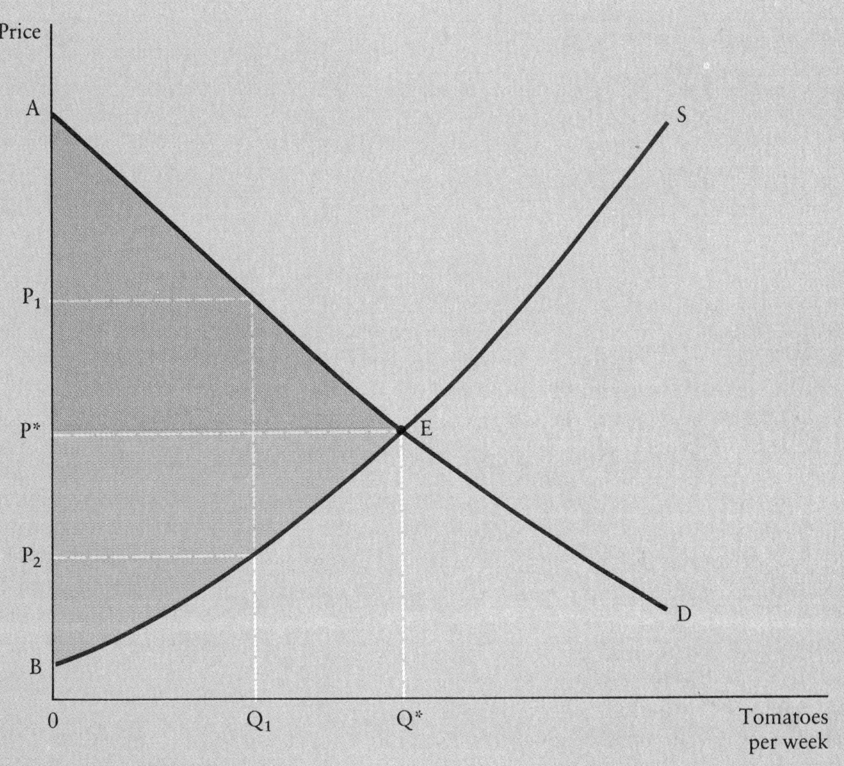

The curve D reflects what people would be willing to pay for additional tomatoes whereas the curve S reflects the opportunity costs of such production. For any output level less than Q^* (say, Q_1) production of more tomatoes is a mutually beneficial transaction for both buyers and sellers. Output level Q_1 is therefore inefficient. At Q^* additional such transactions are not possible, so Q^* is efficient. A competitive equilibrium price of P^* would cause Q^* to be produced.

little indication of what is happening elsewhere in the economy. Whether cucumber production is efficient or whether the markets for inputs to the two industries are operating properly is not readily apparent in Figure 13.2. Consequently, although this type of diagram is sometimes used to describe efficiency in some situations (such as for the case of a "missing market" described in Application 13.2), we need to devise some additional tools to investigate allocational efficiency in more detail.

tal producer surplus is given by P^*EB. The sum of these two magnitudes is as large as possible at Q^*. With output below Q^* there is a loss of consumer and producer surplus and therefore a loss of mutually beneficial transactions. For output greater than Q^*, consumer and producer surplus is reduced below what it is at Q^*, and such transactions would not be mutually beneficial.

APPLICATION 13.2

Missing Markets

Our demonstration of the economic efficiency of voluntary market transactions requires that such markets, in fact, exist. If the costs involved in establishing such a market are high or if establishing such a market is not legally permitted, these trades will not occur, and the resulting allocation of resources may be inefficient.

Transactions Costs

By referring to Figure 1, it is easy to see why high transactions costs may prevent the establishment of a market. The total gain per week from voluntary transactions in the market in Figure 1 is represented by area P_2EP_1. If the cost of conducting transactions (say, the rent on the building where the sales occur or the wages of an auctioneer hired to establish equilibrium prices) exceeds this amount, actors in this market would find it preferable to abstain from trading. None of this good will be produced and exchanged. Although some mutually beneficial transactions will not be made in such a situation, it might not be proper to call this "inefficient." If the inputs that might be used to conduct transactions can be used better somewhere else (as is suggested by the building's positive rent and by the auctioneer's wages), overall economic efficiency requires that no trading be conducted in this good.

Figure 1
Reasons for Missing Markets

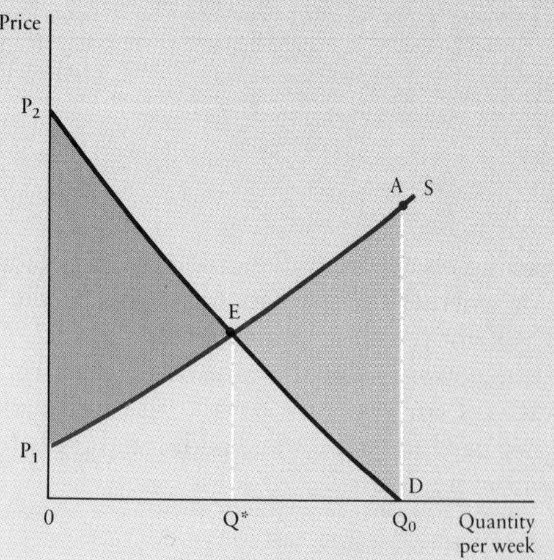

If transactions costs exceed the total gains from voluntary transactions (area P_2EP_1), no goods may be traded in a market. Requiring a zero price in a market will result in consumption of Q_0 and a welfare loss represented by area AQ_0E.

Instances of potentially high transactions costs deterring possible transactions are fairly common. For example, rental markets for such items as television sets, photographic equipment, or business suits are generally not very well developed. The costs involved in operating the rental outlet and assuring the item is returned in good condition probably exceed the potential value of many rental transactions to traders. For other items such as cars or video cassettes, these transactions costs are low relative to the value of potential rental transactions and for these goods, rental markets thrive.

Legal Market Restrictions–the Case of Directory Assistance

Sometimes the development of markets may be restricted by the law. For about two-thirds of the phone systems in the United States, for example, it is illegal to charge for directory assistance even though the provision of this service obviously involves some costs. Contrary to the transactions costs case, this restriction leads to an overuse of directory assistance. Because the price of the service is set at zero, individuals will demand quantity Q_0 in Figure 1. Area AQ_0E provides a measure of the value of inefficient transactions in directory assistance that occur as a result of failing to charge for the service—these are uses of directory assistance for which the value of the services received falls short of the cost of providing them.

A 1980 study of directory assistance usage suggests that these costs may be rather high.[1] Overall, the authors found that in 1978 these costs amounted to \$750 million—more than half of the total cost of providing directory assistance to the jurisdictions that forbid its pricing.

To Think About

1. What is there about the transactions costs involved with television or business suit rentals that sets these goods apart from automobiles and video cassettes? Are rental markets for these items more prevalent in other parts of the world? How do you explain the difference?
2. Our analysis of directory assistance implicitly assumes that there are no costs involved in billing for the service. Might a zero-price regulation make sense if such costs were high? How might changes in telephone technology affect the desirability of charging for directory assistance?

---

[1]A. Daly and T. Mayer, "Estimating the Value of a Missing Market: The Economics of Directory Assistance," *Journal of Law and Economics* (April 1980): 147–166.

Efficiency in Production

We start our detailed analysis of economic efficiency in many markets by describing what it means to say that an economy with fixed amounts of resources has used these resources in a "technically efficient" way. To do this, we use the production possibility frontier concept first introduced in Chapter 1. We show here that an economy that is on its production possibility curve is allocating its resources in a technically efficient way. On the other hand, if production takes place inside the frontier, resources are being poorly allocated and moving them around would improve matters. Before we can show all of this, we first need to define technical efficiency.

Definition of Technical Efficiency

A major problem with defining efficient production is that any economy produces many different goods. For this reason it is impossible to talk about producing "as much total output as possible." There is simply no way to add together apples, oranges, automobiles, and aircraft carriers into something called output.[5] Instead, we adopt what may seem a relatively complicated definition. Under this definition an allocation of resources is said to be **technically efficient** if it is impossible to increase the output of one good without cutting back on the production of something else. Alternatively, resources are said to be allocated inefficiently if it is indeed possible, by moving resources around, to increase output of one good without sacrificing anything.

Technically efficient allocation of resources An allocation of the available resources such that producing more of one good requires producing less of some other good.

For example, suppose an economy produces only two products, wine and cloth. An allocation of resources under which more wine could be produced without having to reduce cloth output would be inefficient—there is no reason why the resources should not be shuffled around to yield more wine output. On the other hand, if increasing wine output meant cutting back on cloth output, the initial allocation would be technically efficient since output cannot be unambiguously increased. By using this definition it is never necessary to compare wine and cloth directly to decide whether or not resources are allocated efficiently. Rather, wine is compared only to wine (to see whether output of it has increased), and cloth is compared only to cloth.

Efficient Input Use and the Edgeworth Production Box

As a starting point in our discussion of technical efficiency in production, we treat the entire economy as a single firm that uses fixed amounts of two inputs, capital (K) and labor (L), to produce two different goods (called X and

[5]Since we do not wish to introduce prices into our discussion of efficiency, it is not possible to add up different goods by valuing them at their market prices. The price system might be used to achieve economic efficiency, but prices cannot be used to define the concept itself.

Figure 13.3
Construction of Edgeworth Box Diagram for Production

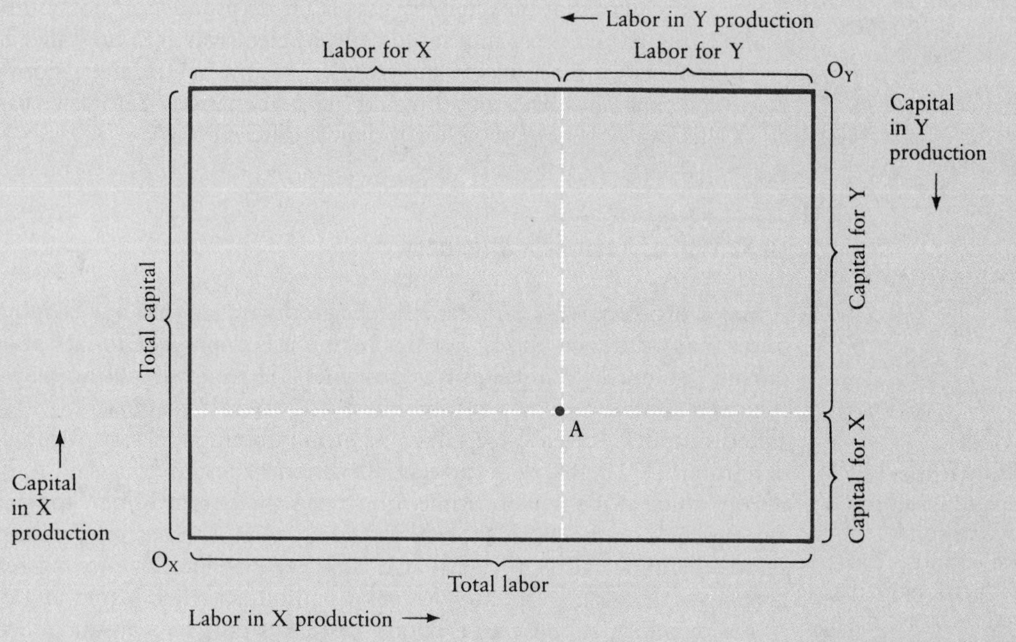

The dimensions of this diagram are given by the total quantities of labor and capital available. Quantities of these resources devoted to X production are measured from origin O_X; quantities devoted to Y are measured from O_Y. Any point in the box represents a fully employed allocation of the available resources to the two goods.

Y). The firm must decide only how to allocate the two inputs between producing X and producing Y. The firm will be operating efficiently if it is not possible for it to reallocate its inputs in such a way that output of X can be increased while keeping Y output constant.

Edgeworth box diagram A graphic device for illustrating all of the possible allocations of two goods (or two inputs) that are in fixed supply.

A particularly useful device for studying this production problem is the **Edgeworth box diagram,** which we first introduced in our discussion of exchange in Chapter 6. The basics for constructing this diagram for the case of production are illustrated in Figure 13.3. Here the length of the box represents total labor hours and the height of the box represents total capital hours that are available in the economy. Now we let the lower left corner of the box represent the "origin" for measuring capital and labor devoted to production of good X. The upper right corner of the box represents the origin for resources devoted to Y. Using these conventions, any point in the box can be regarded as a fully employed allocation of the available resources be-

Figure 13.4
Box Diagram of Efficiency in Production

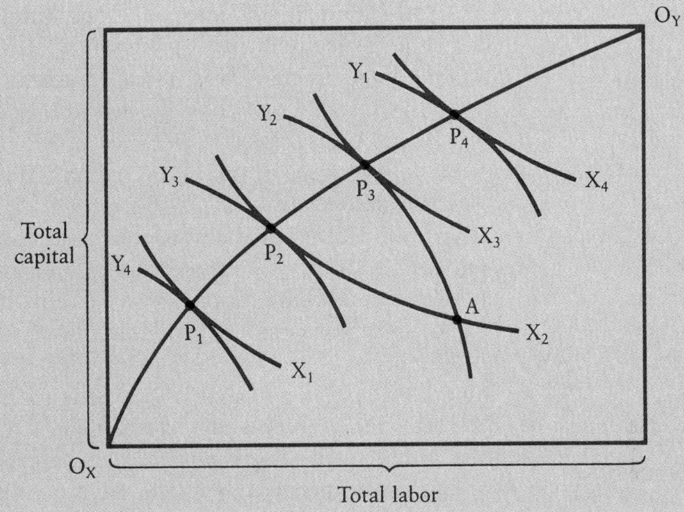

This diagram adds production isoquants for X and Y to Figure 13.3. It then shows technically efficient ways to allocate the fixed amounts of K and L between the production of the two outputs. The line joining O_X and O_Y is the locus of these efficient points. Along this line the RTS (of L for K) in the production of good X is equal to the RTS in the production of Y.

tween goods X and Y. Point A, for example, represents an allocation in which the indicated number of labor hours are devoted to X production together with a specified number of hours of capital. Production of good Y uses whatever labor and capital are left over. At point A, for example, Figure 13.3 shows the exact amount of labor and capital used in the production of good Y. Any point in the box has a similar interpretation. The Edgeworth box shows every possible way the existing capital and labor might be used. Now we wish to discover which of these allocations are efficient.

Efficient Allocations

To discover these efficient allocations we must introduce the isoquant maps (see Chapter 8) for the two goods X and Y, since these show how much can be produced with various levels of capital and labor input. Figure 13.4 contains the isoquant map for good X using O_X as an origin. This isoquant map looks exactly like the ones we used before. For good Y, however, once again the trick of the Edgeworth box diagram is to use O_Y as an origin and rotate the usual diagram 180°. If you turn your book upside down, you will see that the isoquant map for good Y has the usual shape when viewed from that angle. We have been able to put both the isoquant maps on the same diagram, and these will help us identify efficient allocations of labor and capital.

Our arbitrarily chosen point A is clearly not efficient. With capital and labor allocated in this way, Y_2 is produced together with X_2. By moving along the Y_2 isoquant to P_3, we can hold Y output constant and increase X output to X_3. Point A was not an efficient allocation since we were able to increase output of one good (X) without decreasing output of the other good (Y). Point A is inefficient because production of goods X and Y uses the available resources in the wrong combination, not because some of these resources were not used at all. Both point A and point P_3 represent fully employed allocations of the available resources. But, the allocation at point P_3 results in good X using more capital and less labor while Y uses more labor and less capital than at point A (check this for yourself!). This new allocation is a better way to use the available resources.

Which points in Figure 13.4 are the efficient ones? A bit of intuition should suggest to you that only points such as P_1, P_2, P_3, and P_4 are. These represent allocations where the isoquants are tangent to each other. At any other point in the box diagram, the two goods' isoquants will intersect, and we can show inefficiency as we did for point A. At the points of tangency, however, this kind of unambiguous improvement cannot be made. In going from P_2 to P_3, for example, more X is being produced, but at the cost of less Y being produced, so P_3 is not more efficient than P_2—both of the points are efficient. Tangency of the isoquants for good X and good Y implies that their slopes are equal. That is, the RTS of capital for labor is equal in X and Y production. The curve joining O_X and O_Y that includes all of these points of tangency shows all of the efficient allocations of capital and labor. Points off this curve are inefficient in that unambiguous increases in output can be obtained by reshuffling inputs among the two goods. Points on O_X, O_Y are all efficient allocations, however. More X can be produced only by cutting back on Y production.

Production Possibility Frontier

Production possibility frontier
A figure illustrating the technically efficient output possibilities for an economy with fixed amounts of inputs.

We can use the information from Figure 13.4 to construct a **production possibility frontier,** which shows those alternative outputs of X and Y that can be produced with the fixed amounts of capital and labor. In Figure 13.5 the various efficient points from Figure 13.4 have been transferred onto a graph with X and Y outputs on the axes. At O_X, for example, no resources are devoted to X production; consequently Y output is as large as possible using all of the available resources. Similarly, at O_Y, the output of X is as large as possible. The other points on the production possibility frontier (say, P_1, P_2, P_3, and P_4) are derived in an identical way from Figure 13.4.

The production possibility curve clearly exhibits the notion of technical efficiency we have been using. Any point inside the frontier is inefficient because output can be unambiguously increased. The allocation of K and L represented by point A, for example, is inefficient because output levels in the shaded area are both attainable, and preferable, to A. If you look again at

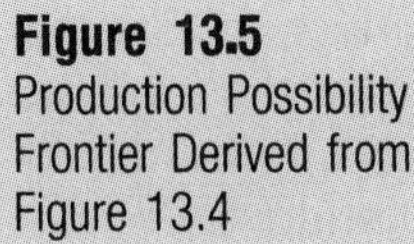

Figure 13.5
Production Possibility Frontier Derived from Figure 13.4

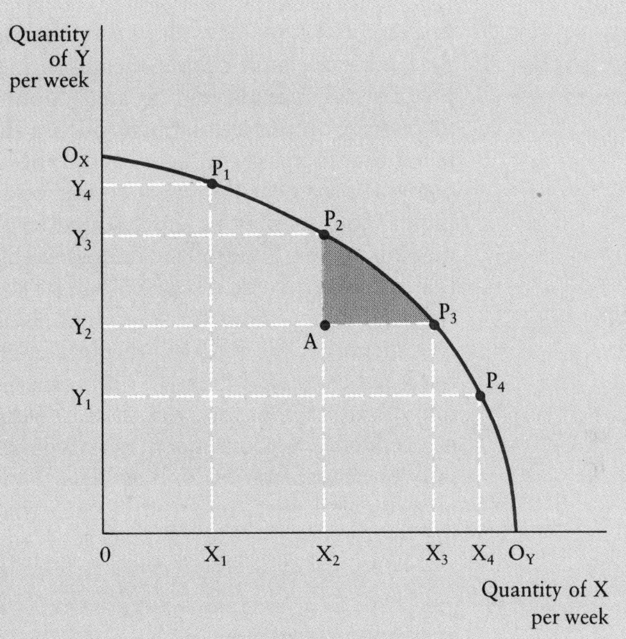

The production possibility frontier shows those alternative combinations of X and Y that can be efficiently produced by a firm with fixed resources. The curve can be derived from Figure 13.4 by varying inputs between the production of X and Y while maintaining the conditions for efficiency. The slope of the production possibility curve is called the rate of product transformation (RPT).

Figure 13.4, you can see how the available resources might be reallocated to obtain those more efficient points.

Rate of Product Transformation

Rate of product transformation
The slope of the production possibility frontier that shows the opportunity costs involved in producing more of one good and less of some other good.

The slope of the production possibility frontier shows how X output can be substituted for Y output when total resources are held constant. For example, for points near O_X on the production possibility frontier, the slope is a small negative number, say, $-\frac{1}{2}$, implying that by reducing Y output by one unit, X output could be increased by two. Near O_Y, on the other hand, the slope is a large negative number, say, -5, implying that Y output must be reduced by five units to permit the production of one more X. The slope of the production possibility frontier shows the possibilities that exist for trading Y and X in production. We call this slope the **rate of product transformation** (RPT) of good X for good Y. This concept indicates the number of units by which Y output must be reduced in order to increase X output by one unit.

Shape of the Production Possibility Frontier

In Figure 13.5 we have drawn the production possibility frontier so that the RPT increases as X output increases. In moving clockwise along the frontier, progressively greater and greater amounts of Y must be given up in order to increase X output by one unit. Such a shape can be justified intuitively by arguing that increases in X (or Y) output encounter increasing costs. For output combinations near O_X, most resources are devoted to Y production. Some of these resources may be more suited to X production than they are to Y production. When X output is increased slightly, it is only reasonable to assume that these particular resources will be shifted into X output first. Such a shift will not reduce Y output very much, but it will increase X significantly. Near O_X, therefore, the RPT will be small. On the other hand, near O_Y, X output has been expanded greatly. To increase X further requires that resources be drawn out of Y production that are very good at producing Y but not good at producing X. Consequently, Y will have to be cut back significantly to get only one more unit of X. Near O_Y, the RPT will be high. An increasing RPT accords well with an intuitive idea that production of X exhibits increasing costs.

Rate of Product Transformation Is the Ratio of Marginal Costs

To show that the shape of the production possibility frontier in Figure 13.5 is rigorously justified, we must make use of the following result: the RPT (of X for Y) is equal to the ratio of the marginal cost of X (MC_X) to the marginal cost of Y (MC_Y). That is,

$$\text{RPT (of X for Y)} = \frac{MC_X}{MC_Y}. \qquad [13.1]$$

Although we will not prove this result mathematically here, we do provide an intuitive proof. Suppose only labor is used in the production of X and Y. Assume that, at some point on the production possibility frontier, the marginal cost of producing more X is 4 (that is, assume that it takes four units of labor input to produce an additional unit of X output). Suppose also that the marginal cost of Y (in terms of the additional labor required to produce one more unit) is 2. In this situation it is clear that, since the total supply of labor is fixed, two units of Y must be given up in order to free enough labor to produce one more unit of X. We would therefore say that the RPT (of X for Y) is 2. But this is simply the ratio of the marginal cost of X to the marginal cost of Y (that is, 4/2); at least for this simple case, Equation 13.1 holds. A more complete analysis would indicate that the equation holds even when many inputs are being used to produce X and Y.

Increasing Marginal Costs and the Shape of the Production Possibility Frontier

We are now in a position to show why the production possibility frontier has a concave shape. Such a shape is based on the presumption that the production of both X and Y exhibits increasing marginal costs. As production of either of these outputs is expanded, marginal costs are assumed to rise. Consider moving along the frontier in a clockwise direction. In so doing, the production of X is being increased, whereas that of Y is being decreased. By the assumption of increasing marginal costs, then, MC_X is rising while MC_Y falls. But, by Equation 13.1, this means that the RPT is rising as X is substituted for Y in production. The concave shape of the production possibility frontier is then justified by the assumption of increasing marginal costs.

Production Possibility Frontier and Opportunity Cost

The reason we have spent so much space in developing the concept of the production possibility frontier is that it is probably the single most important tool for studying technical efficiency in the production and supply of two goods. The curve clearly demonstrates that there are many combinations of goods that are technically efficient. The curve also shows that producing more of one good necessitates cutting back on the production of some other good. As we described in Chapter 1, this is precisely what economists mean by the term *opportunity cost*. The cost of producing more X can be most readily measured by the reduction in Y output that this entails. The opportunity cost of one more unit of X is therefore best measured as the RPT (of X for Y) at the prevailing point on the production possibility frontier. The increasing RPT for clockwise movements along the frontier shows in a general way how the opportunity cost of X increases as more of it is produced. In Application 13.3: Production Possibilities for "Guns and Butter," we show that knowing something about such trade-off possibilities can be very important for public decision making.

An Efficient Mix of Outputs

The goal of an economic system is to satisfy human wants. Being technically efficient in production (that is, being on the production possibility frontier) may not be at all desirable if the "wrong" combination of goods is being produced. It does little good for an economy to be an efficient producer of yo-yos and xylophones if no one wants these goods. Similarly, an economy in which large amounts of resources are devoted to frivolous purposes by the government (say, erecting statues of the ruling leadership) may not be desirable even though production of statues itself uses the available resources in a

APPLICATION 13.3

Production Possibilities for "Guns and Butter"

Traditionally when economics textbooks introduce the production possibility frontier, they label the axes "guns" and "butter" to represent the notion that an economy can produce various combinations of defense ("guns") and nondefense ("butter") items. During wartime the economy reallocates resources toward guns, whereas in more peaceful periods a relatively larger share of resources is devoted to butter. Use of the production possibility frontier concept can be helpful in understanding the kinds of opportunity costs that might be included in such moves.

The 1960s Debate

In the early 1960s there was considerable interest in what the economic dislocations of disarmament might be. At that time, defense spending amounted to about 10 percent of U.S. gross national product, and a number of studies attempted to estimate what the effects of a fairly sharp reduction (say, cutting in half) might be. In many respects the issue was one of deciding how specialized the inputs devoted to defense were. If such inputs had uses that were highly specific to defense, the adjustment costs might be large since these inputs could not be easily employed elsewhere. If, on the other hand, inputs were easily transferable between sectors, opportunity costs of adjustment might be low.

The studies of this issue that were conducted in the early 1960s tended to conclude that for modest reductions in defense spending, these adjustment costs would be relatively small.[1] Many products that are bought by the military can be readily sold to civilians (for example, food), and even for some goods that have solely defense uses (such as military aircraft), problems involved in converting to civilian production may be rather minor. Only for highly specialized industries such as ordinance or defense-related research and development did these authors see substantial dislocations.

Recent Trends

By 1989 the share of U.S. GNP devoted to national defense had fallen to about 6 percent. Because the decline from 10 to 6 percent took place over a relatively long period and because it took place within a growing economy, there were few special costs associated with this decline. However, some people believe that in the 1990s it will be more difficult in economic terms to convert from defense-related production to civilian production than was the case in the 1960s. An increasing array of military goods (for example, nuclear submarines or antimissile defense systems) have no obvious civilian counterparts, and it is generally believed that practically all defense goods have become much more technically sophisticated and specialized in recent years. Although there may be good reasons to adopt policies aimed toward disarmament, the opportunity costs of converting resources to civilian use could be high.

To Think About

1. If defense expenditures were reduced, what industries would be affected? Can you answer that question simply by asking what things the Defense Department would no longer buy? Or should you look further back in the chain of supply?
2. Currently, nearly half of all research and development expenditures in the United States are financed by the Defense Department. How might that affect the long-term growth of the economy? Do research and development in defense result only in improved weapons, or do they spill over into civilian sectors of the economy?

---

[1]For a summary, see Roger E. Bolton, ed., *Defense and Disarmament: The Economics of Transition* (Englewood Cliffs, N.J.: Prentice-Hall, 1966).

Economically efficient allocation of resources A technically efficient allocation of resources in which the output combination also reflects people's preferences.

technically efficient way. In order to assure overall **economic efficiency** in the allocation of resources, we need to tie people's preferences to the economy's productive abilities.

A Graphic Demonstration

Figure 13.6 illustrates the requirements for economic efficiency in the mix of outputs. It assumes that there are only two goods (X and Y) being produced and that there is just one person (or perhaps a number of identical people) in society. Those combinations of X and Y that can be produced in a technically efficient way lie along the production possibility frontier. By superimposing the typical person's indifference curve map on Figure 13.6, we see that only one point on the frontier provides maximum utility. This point of maximum utility is at E, where the frontier is tangent to the typical person's highest indifference curve, U_2. At this point of tangency the person's MRS (of X for Y) is equal to the technical RPT (of X for Y). This is the condition required for economic efficiency in the mix of outputs being produced. Point E is preferred to every other point on the production possibility frontier. In fact, for any other point, such as F, on the frontier, there exist points that are inefficient but that are preferred to F. In Figure 13.6 the technically inefficient point G is preferred to the technically efficient point F. From the typical person's point of view, it would be preferable to produce inefficiently than to consume the "wrong" combination of goods even though these are produced in a technically efficient way.

Figure 13.6 shows, at least for a simple case, how resources might be allocated efficiently in an economy that produces two goods. With this model we are now ready to examine how efficiency might be brought about through the operations of perfectly competitive markets.

Efficiency of Perfect Competition

We illustrate the economic efficiency of perfect competition in two steps. First, we provide a very brief proof of why firms' desires to minimize costs will result in their using an efficient mix of inputs—that is, we show that firms will produce in a technically efficient way on the production possibility frontier. Then, we present a more detailed proof of why competitive markets will result in the "right" final combination of goods being produced.

Efficiency in Input Use

If all inputs are traded in perfectly competitive markets, every firm will act as a price taker in making its decisions about which inputs to use. In this case, as we saw in Chapter 9, a firm will choose an input combination for which the rate of technical substitution (RTS) is equal to the ratio of the inputs'

Figure 13.6
Efficiency of Output Mix

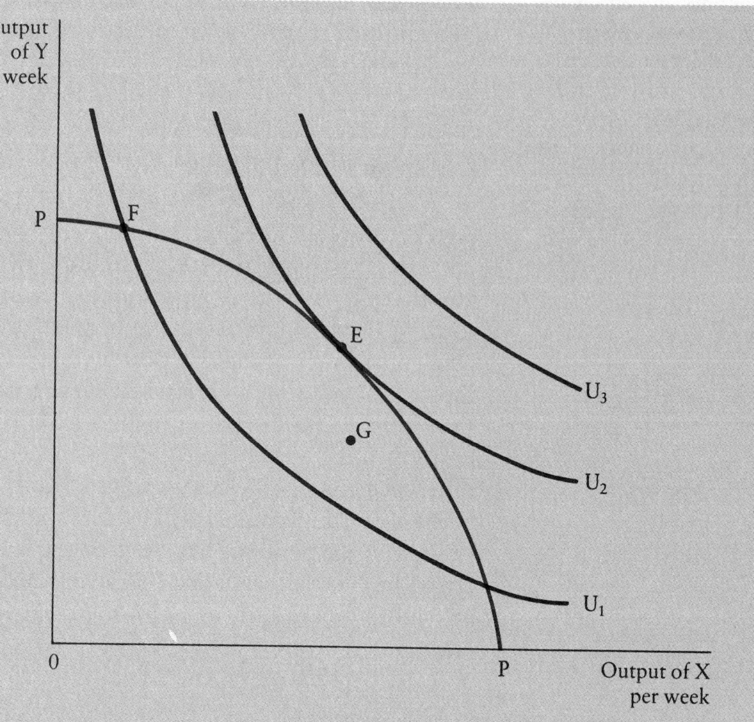

In this economy, the production possibility frontier represents those combinations of X and Y that can be produced. Every point on it is efficient in a technical sense. However, only the output combination at point E is a true utility maximum for the typical person. Only this point represents an economically efficient allocation of resources. At E that person's MRS is equal to the rate at which X can be traded for Y in production (the RPT).

prices (w/v). But, since the producer of each good faces the same equilibrium input prices, w and v, the firms will all be equating their RTS to the same w/v. The desire to minimize costs will lead them to choose the same RTS, just what is required for efficiency. Since w and v are equilibrium prices of labor and capital, respectively, we also know that both inputs will be fully employed. If, in total, firms wished to have fewer workers than were available, the wage would fall to restore equilibrium between the quantity demanded and quantity supplied. Consequently, the workings of competitive markets for inputs ensure that both inputs are fully employed, and firms' desire to minimize costs ensures that they are efficiently employed among various uses. Smith's invisible hand (that is, competitive input markets) leads firms to one of the technically efficient allocations illustrated on the production possibility frontier in Figures 13.5 and 13.6.

Efficiency in Output Mix

A proof that the operations of competitive markets will also lead to an efficient choice of outputs is equally straightforward. Such markets will determine the equilibrium relative price for goods X and Y—we can call this equilibrium relative price P_X^*/P_Y^*. This price ratio is taken as given by both demanders and suppliers. For demanders, utility maximization (as we saw in Chapter 3) will lead each person to equate his or her marginal rate of substitution (MRS) to the equilibrium price ratio (P_X^*/P_Y^*). In maximizing profits, each competitive firm will produce where price equals marginal cost—that is, $P_X^* = MC_X$ and $P_Y^* = MC_Y$. But earlier in this chapter, we showed that the rate of product transformation between two goods (RPT) is given by the ratio of the good's marginal costs:

$$RPT = MC_X/MC_Y. \qquad [13.2]$$

Therefore, profit maximization will result in

$$RPT = MC_X/MC_Y = P_X^*/P_Y^*. \qquad [13.3]$$

Consequently, profit-maximizing firms equate the rate at which they can trade X for Y in production to P_X^*/P_Y^* just as people do in maximizing utility. The RPT of X for Y will equal the MRS and that, combined with the notion that demand must equal supply for each good, meets the requirements for economic efficiency described in Figure 13.6.

A Graphic Demonstration

Figure 13.7 illustrates this result. The figure shows the production possibility frontier for a two-good economy, and the set of indifference curves represents people's preferences for these goods. First, consider any initial price ratio P_X/P_Y. At this price ratio, firms will choose to produce the output combination X_1, Y_1. Only at this point on the production frontier will the ratio of the goods be equal to the ratio of their marginal costs (and equal to the RPT). Hence, only at X_1, Y_1 will competitive firms be maximizing profits. On the other hand, given the budget constraint represented by line C, individuals collectively will demand X_1', Y_1'.[6] Consequently, at this price ratio there is an ex-

[6] It is important to recognize why the budget constraint has this location. Since P_X and P_Y are given, the value of total production is

$$P_X \cdot X_1 + P_Y \cdot Y_1.$$

This is the value of GNP in the simple economy pictured in Figure 13.7. Because of the "value of income = value of output" accounting identity, this is also the total income accruing to people in society. Society's budget constraint passes through X_1, Y_1 and has a slope of $-P_X/P_Y$. This is precisely the line labeled C in the figure.

Figure 13.7
How Perfectly Competitive Prices Bring about Efficiency

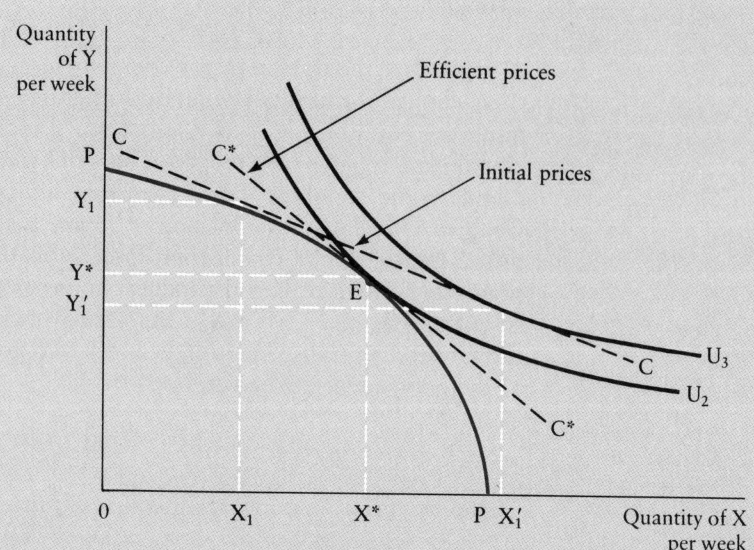

With an arbitrary initial price ratio, firms will produce X_1, Y_1; society's budget constraint will be given by line C. With this budget constraint, individuals demand X_1', Y_1'; that is, there is an excess demand for good X_1 ($X_1' - X_1$) and an excess supply of good Y_1 ($Y_1 - Y_1'$). The workings of the market will move these prices toward their equilibrium levels P_X^*, P_Y^*. At those prices, society's budget constraint will be given by the line C* and supply and demand will be in equilibrium. The combination X^*, Y^* of goods will be chosen, and this allocation is efficient.

cess demand for good X (people want to buy more than is being produced), whereas there is an excess supply of good Y. The workings of the marketplace will cause P_X to rise and P_Y to fall. The price ratio P_X/P_Y will rise; the price line will move clockwise along the production possibility frontier. That is, firms will increase their production of good X and decrease their production of good Y. Similarly, people will respond to the changing prices by substituting Y for X in their consumption choices. The actions of both firms and individuals eliminate the excess demand for X and the excess supply of Y as market prices change.

Equilibrium is reached at X^*, Y^* with an equilibrium price ratio of P_X^*/P_Y^*. With this price ratio, supply and demand are equilibrated for both good X and good Y. Firms, in maximizing their profits, given P_X^* and P_Y^*, will produce X^* and Y^*. Given the income that this level of production provides to people, they will purchase precisely X^* and Y^*. Not only have markets been equilibrated by the operation of the price system, but the resulting equilibrium is also economically efficient. As we showed previously, the equilibrium allocation X^*, Y^* provides the highest level of utility that can be obtained given the existing production possibility frontier. Figure 13.7 provides a simple two-good general equilibrium proof that the results of supply and demand interacting in competitive markets can produce an efficient allocation of resources.

Prices, Efficiency, and Laissez-Faire Economics

We have shown that a perfectly competitive price system, by relying on the self-interest of people and of firms, and by utilizing the information carried by equilibrium prices, can arrive at an economically efficient allocation of resources. In a sense, this finding provides "scientific" support for the *laissez-faire* position taken by many economists. For example, Adam Smith's assertion that:

> The natural effort of every individual to better his own condition, when suffered to exert itself with freedom and security, is so powerful a principle that it is alone, and without any assistance, not only capable of carrying on the society to wealth and prosperity, but of surmounting a hundred impertinent obstructions with which the folly of human laws too often encumbers its operations. . . .[7]

has been shown to have considerable theoretical validity. As Smith noted, it is not the public spirit of the baker that provides bread for people to eat. Rather, bakers (and other producers) operate in their own self-interest in responding to market signals (Smith's invisible hand). In so doing, their actions are coordinated by the market into an efficient, overall pattern. The market system, at least in this simple model, imposes a very strict logic on how resources are used.

That efficiency theorem raises many important questions about the ability of markets to arrive at these perfectly competitive prices and about whether the theorem should act as a guide for government policy (for example, should governments avoid interfering in international markets as suggested by Application 13.4: Gains from Free Trade and Political Obstacles to Achieving Them?). The rest of this chapter makes a start toward answering this question, but this topic will generally occupy us for much of the remainder of this book.

Why Markets Fail to Achieve Economic Efficiency

Showing that perfect competition is economically efficient depends crucially on the assumptions that underlie the competitive model. In this section we examine some of the conditions that may prevent markets from generating such an efficient allocation. We will show that many of these are quite likely to occur, although we generally delay our discussion on what to do about

[7] Adam Smith, *The Wealth of Nations* (1776; New York: Random House, Modern Library ed., 1937), p. 508.

APPLICATION 13.4

Gains from Free Trade and Political Obstacles to Achieving Them

High tariffs on grain imports were imposed by the British government following the Napoleonic Wars. Debate over the effects of these "Corn Laws" dominated the politics of Great Britain during the period 1820–1845. A principal focus of the debate concerned the effect that elimination of tariffs would have on the welfare of British consumers and on the incomes of various groups in society. Here we examine the free trade question in both its historical and more recent forms.

The Corn Laws Debate

The production possibility frontier in Figure 1 shows those combinations of grain (X) and manufactured goods (Y) that could be produced by British factors of production. Assuming (somewhat contrary to fact) that the Corn Laws completely prevented trade, market equilibrium would be at E with the domestic, pretrade price ratio shown in the figure. Removal of the tariffs would reduce this price ratio to the price ratio that prevailed in the rest of the world. Given that new ratio, Britain would produce combination A and consume combination B. Grain imports would amount to $X_B - X_A$ and would be financed by export of manufactured goods equal to $Y_A - Y_B$. Overall utility would be increased by the opening of trade. Figure 1 illustrates that there may be substantial gains from trade because it permits a country's consumers to move beyond the domestic production possibility frontier.

By referring to the Edgeworth production box diagram that lies behind the production possibility frontier (Figure 13.4), it is also possible to analyze the effect of tariff reductions on factor prices. The movement from point E to point A in Figure 1 is similar to a movement from P_3 to P_1 in Figure 13.4. Production of X is decreased and production of Y is increased by such a move, and Figure 13.4 shows the reallocation of capital and labor made necessary by such a move. If we assume that grain production is relatively capital intensive (that is, it uses a lot of land), the movement from P_3 to P_1 causes the ratio of land to labor to rise in both industries. This will, in turn, cause the relative price of capital to fall (since effectively, each acre of land now has fewer workers on it). Figure 13.4 suggests that repeal of the Corn Laws would be harmful to capital owners (that is, landlords) and helpful to laborers. It is not surprising that landed interests fought repeal of these laws.

Figure 1
Analysis of the Corn Laws Debate

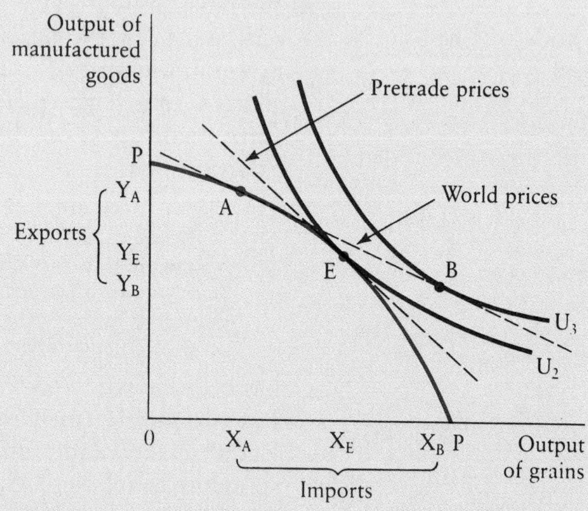

Reduction of tariff barriers on grain would cause production to be reallocated from point E to point A. Consumption would be reallocated from E to B. If grain production were relatively capital intensive, the relative price of capital would fall as a result of these reallocations.

Modern Resistance to Trade

The effect that trade policies may have on the relative incomes of various factors of production continues to exert a major influence on political debates about such policies. In the United States, for example, exports tend to be intensive in their use of skilled labor, whereas imports tend to be intensive in unskilled labor input. By analogy to our discussion of the Corn Laws, it might be expected that further movements toward free trade policies would result in rising relative wages for skilled workers and in falling relative wages for unskilled workers. It is not surprising that unions representing skilled workers (the Machinists, certain segments of the United Auto Workers, and the Petroleum and Atomic Workers) tend to favor free trade, whereas unions of unskilled workers (those in textiles, shoes, and related businesses) tend to oppose it.

Adjustment Costs

A careful study of Figure 1 indicates another reason why workers in firms that produce imported goods may be opposed to moves toward more open world trade. The reallocation of production from point E to point A in the figure requires that factors of production be transferred out of X (import) production into Y (export) production. Making such a reallocation may impose costs on workers. They may have to move to new communities, search for new jobs, or learn new skills. All of these activities are costly to the individuals involved. Even though society as a whole benefits from trade expansion (overall utility increases from U_2 to U_3), individual workers may not be so lucky.

Trade Adjustment Policy

In order to share the costs of adjusting to trade policies, most countries offer some sort of governmental assistance to trade-affected workers. As part of the Trade Expansion Act of 1962, for example, the United States enacted a program of Trade Adjustment Assistance to provide jobless benefits and other services to workers in industries affected by trade expansion. In 1974 all of these benefits were substantially liberalized, primarily by making it easier for workers to establish that they had been harmed by imports. In many respects the adjustment assistance provisions of the 1962 and 1974 trade acts represented "bribes" to entice those workers who would be hurt by increasing imports to refrain from actively opposing such policies. Unfortunately, what in principle seemed a reasonable policy proved in practice quite difficult to administer. In particular, determining which workers were actually injured by trade became largely a political question, and substantial amounts of adjustment assistance went to workers who suffered relatively small import-related costs. In 1981 the program was significantly scaled back and refocused more explicitly on workers suffering major losses from expanded trade.[1]

To Think About

1. This example shows that the typical consumer gains from the opening of trade. Use Figure 1 to discuss under what circumstances these gains would be relatively large. When might they be small or nonexistent? Is it possible that the opening of trade might actually make the typical consumer worse-off?
2. Figure 1 shows that a nation will tend to export goods that have a lower relative price domestically than they do in the international market (in this case, good Y). What factors will determine such differences in relative prices—that is, what factors determine a country's "comparative advantage" in international trade?

---

[1]For a discussion, see Walter Corson and Walter Nicholson, "Trade Adjustment Assistance under the Trade Act of 1974," in R. G. Ehrenberg, ed., *Research in Labor Finance,* vol. 4 (Greenwich, Conn.: JAI Press, 1982).

them until later chapters. The conditions that might interfere with perfect competition can be classed into four general groupings: *imperfect competition, externalities, public goods,* and *imperfect information.* We discuss each separately below.

Imperfect Competition

Imperfect competition
A market situation in which buyers or sellers have some influence on the prices of goods or services.

Imperfect competition in a broad sense includes all those situations in which economic actors (that is, buyers or sellers) exert some market power in determining price. The essential aspect of all such situations is that marginal revenue is different from market price since the firm is no longer a price taker. As we will show in Chapter 15, a profit-maximizing monopoly, by equating marginal revenue with marginal cost, will not produce where price is equal to marginal cost. Because of this behavior, relative prices will no longer accurately reflect relative marginal costs, and the price system no longer carries the information about costs necessary to ensure efficiency. Most of Part 5 in this book is concerned with investigating the consequences of this failure in the market for goods. Similar problems in input markets are briefly examined in Part 6.

Externalities

Externality
The effect of one party's economic activities on another party's well-being that is not taken into account by the price system.

A price system can also fail to allocate resources efficiently when there are relationships among firms or between firms and people that are not adequately represented by market prices. Examples of such occurrences are numerous. Perhaps the most common is the case of a firm that pollutes the air with industrial smoke and other debris. This is called an **externality**. It is an effect of the firm's activities on people's well-being that is not taken directly into account through the normal operation of the price system. The basic problem with externalities is that firms' private costs no longer correctly reflect the social costs of production. In the absence of externalities, the costs a firm incurs accurately measure social costs. The prices of the resources the firm uses represent all the opportunity costs involved in production. When a firm creates externalities, however, there are additional costs—those that arise from the external damage. The fact that pollution from burning coal to produce steel causes diseases and general dirt and grime is as much a cost of production as are the wages paid to the firm's workers. Both types of costs should be considered in a full assessment of the social costs of steel production. However, the firm only responds to private input costs of steel production in deciding how much steel to produce. It disregards the social costs of its pollution. This results in a gap between market price and (social) marginal cost and therefore leads to a misallocation of resources.

This result is illustrated in Figure 13.8. Again, in this figure, point E records an efficient allocation of resources at which the RPT is equal to the

Figure 13.8
Externalities May Cause an Inefficient Allocation of Resources

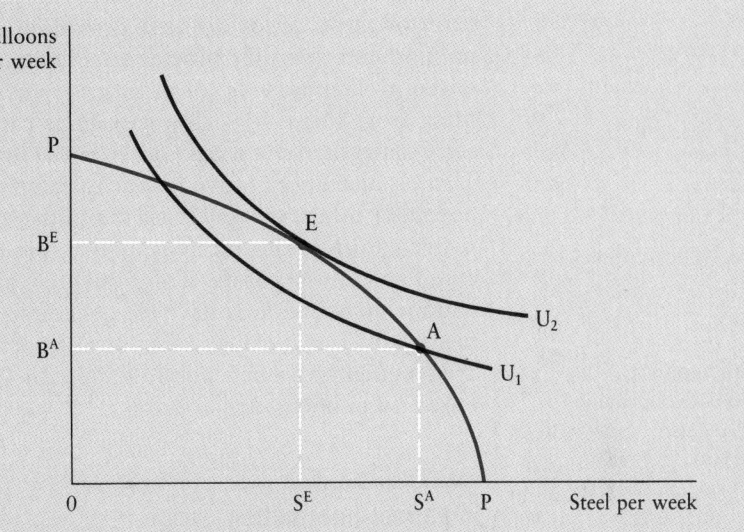

With an externality in steel production, firms choose to produce S^A units of steel and B^A units of balloons. Because of externalities involved in steel production, the market prices at A do not reflect individuals' true marginal rates of substitution. The allocation A is therefore inefficient and results in a lower utility level than does the efficient allocation E.

social MRS. Suppose now there is an externality in the production of good X, say, steel, but none in good Y, say, balloons. In this case, market prices do not lead economic agents to the efficient point E. Rather, firms choose to produce at point A where the RPT is equal to the ratio of equilibrium market prices. Although supply and demand are in equilibrium at these prices, such private decisions consider only the direct consumption values of steel and balloons: the steel-produced pollution is not taken into account. At point A the true MRS is less than the slope of the production possibility frontier, indicating that people are less willing to give up balloons to get more steel than is indicated by the market prices of those goods. The externality causes steel to be overproduced relative to the efficient allocation. Overall utility is reduced from U_2 to U_1 by this misallocation. In Chapter 21 we investigate a number of additional types of externalities and examine several ways in which the allocational problems they cause might be corrected.

Public Goods

A third and somewhat similar possible failure of the price system to yield an efficient allocation of resources stems from the existence of goods that can be provided to users at zero marginal cost and must be provided on a nonexclusive basis to everyone. Such goods include national defense, control of infectious diseases, provision of justice, and pest control. The distinguishing features of these goods are that providing benefits to one more person costs nothing and that they provide benefits to everyone. Once the goods are produced, it is impossible (or at least very costly) to exclude anyone from benefiting from them. In such a case price cannot equal marginal cost (which is zero) since then the fixed cost of providing the good would not be covered. There is also an incentive for each person to refuse to pay for the good in the hope that others will purchase it and thereby provide benefits to all. The pervasive nature of this incentive will ensure that not enough resources are allocated to public goods. To avoid this underallocation, communities (or nations) may decide to have the government produce these goods and finance this production through compulsory taxation. For that reason, such goods are frequently termed **public goods**. In Chapter 22 we treat the problems raised by public goods in detail.

Public goods
Goods that provide nonexclusive benefits to everyone in a group and that can be provided to one more user at zero marginal cost.

Imperfect Information

Throughout our discussion of the connection between perfect competition and economic efficiency, we have been implicitly assuming that the economic actors involved are fully informed. The most important kind of information they are assumed to have is a knowledge of equilibrium market prices. If for some reason markets are unable to establish these prices or if demanders or suppliers do not know what these prices are, the types of "invisible hand" results we developed may not hold. Consider, for example, the problem that any consumer faces in trying to buy a new television receiver. Not only does he or she have to make some kind of judgment about the quality of various brands (to determine what the available "goods" actually are) but this would-be buyer also faces the problem of finding out what various sellers are charging for a particular set. All of these kinds of problems have been assumed away so far by treating goods as being homogeneous and having a universally known market price. As we will see in the next chapter, if such assumptions do not hold, the efficiency of perfectly competitive markets is more problematic.

What to Do about These Problems

Any economic system will undoubtedly have examples of all four of these problems. Can solutions be found that still permit a competitive price system to do its job efficiently? Some solutions do seem possible. In Chapter 15, for example, we discuss several possible solutions to the allocational inefficiencies posed by monopolies. Similarly, in Chapter 21 we discuss solutions to the externality problem. In other cases, however, correcting problems with the competitive price system may be much more difficult. In Chapter 22, for example, we show how devising solutions to the public goods problem is particularly vexing. There seems to be no guarantee that if we leave the production of public goods to the political process (say, to be decided by voting in a democracy), this will result in the efficient amount of public goods being produced. In cases of imperfect information the route to achieving an efficient allocation of resources also may not be clear. Each problem requires a careful examination to see whether it is possible to devise solutions that help to improve allocational efficiency.

Efficiency and Equity

Equity
The fairness of the distribution of goods or utility.

So far in this chapter we have discussed the concept of economic efficiency and whether an efficient allocation of resources can be achieved through reliance on market forces. We have not mentioned questions of **equity** or fairness in the way goods are distributed among people. In this section we briefly take up this question. We show not only that it is very difficult to define what an equitable distribution of resources is, but also that there is no reason to expect that allocations that result from a competitive price system (or from practically any other method of allocating resources, for that matter) will be equitable.

Defining and Achieving Equity

A primary problem with developing an accepted definition of "fair" or "unfair" allocations of resources is that not everyone agrees as to what the concept means. Some people might call any allocation "fair" providing no one breaks any laws in arriving at it—these people would call only acquisition of goods by theft "unfair." Others may base their notions of fairness on a dislike for inequality. Only allocations in which people receive about the same levels of utility (assuming these levels could be measured and compared) would be regarded as fair. On a more practical level, some people think the current distribution of income and wealth in the United States is reasonably fair whereas others regard it as drastically unfair. Welfare economists have devised a number of more specific definitions, but these tend to give conflicting conclusions about which resource allocations are or are not equitable.[8] There is simply no agreement on the issue.

Equity and Voluntary Exchange

Even if everyone agreed on what a fair allocation of resources (and, ultimately, of people's utility) is, there would still be the question of how such a

[8]For a survey of these equity concepts, see Amartya Sen, "Social Choice Theory," in K. J. Arrow and M. D. Intriligator, *Handbook of Mathematical Economics*, vol. 3 (New York: North Holland Publishing Company, 1986), pp. 1106–1127.

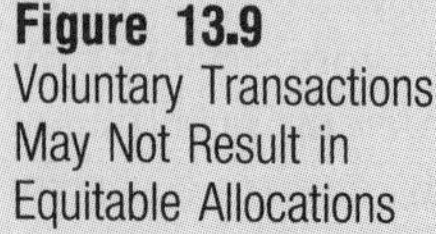

Figure 13.9
Voluntary Transactions May Not Result in Equitable Allocations

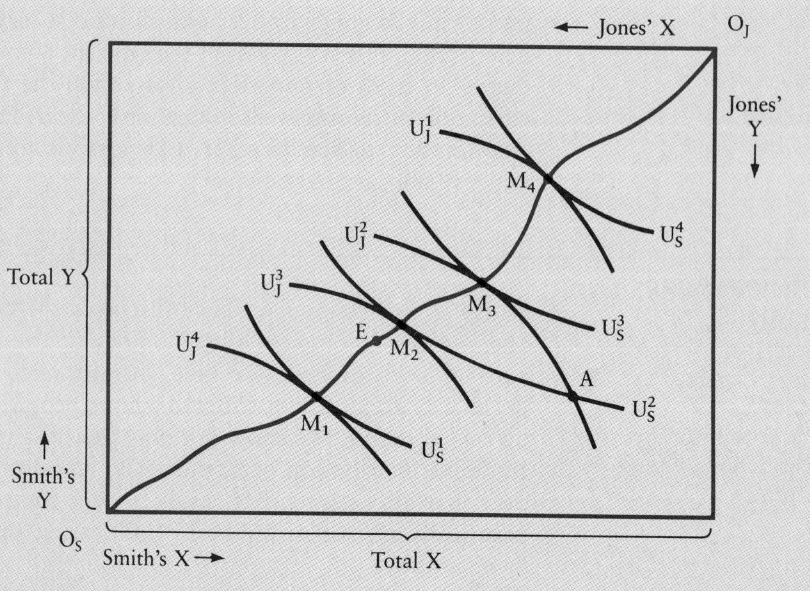

This Edgeworth box diagram for exchange is taken from Figure 6.6. Point E represents a "fair" sharing of the available goods (assuming that can be defined). If individuals' initial endowments are at point A, voluntary transactions cannot be relied on to reach point E since such an allocation makes Smith worse-off than at A.

situation should be achieved. Can we rely on voluntary transactions among people to achieve fairness, or will something more be required? Our discussion of exchange in Chapter 6 shows why voluntary solutions may not always succeed. Suppose, for example, that everyone agreed that the only fair allocation is one of equal utilities. Perhaps everyone remembers his or her childhood experiences in dividing up a cake or candy where equal shares seemed to be the only reasonable solution. This desired allocation might be represented by point E in the Edgeworth exchange box in Figure 13.9 (see Figure 6.6 also). On the other hand, suppose Smith and Jones start out at point A—at which Smith is in a fairly favorable situation. As we described previously, any allocation between M_2 and M_3 is preferable to point A because both people would be better-off by voluntarily making such a move. In this case, however, the point of equal utility (E) does not fall in this range. Smith would not voluntarily agree to a move to point E since that would make him or her worse-off than at point A. Smith would prefer to refrain from any trading rather than accept the "fair" allocation E. In the language of welfare economics, the **initial endowments** (that is, the starting place for trading) of Smith and Jones are so unbalanced that voluntary agreements will not result in the desired equal allocation of utilities. If point E is to be achieved, some coercion must be used to get Smith to accept it.

Initial endowments
The initial holdings of goods from which trading begins.

Equity, Efficiency, and Perfect Competition

Hence, any voluntary system of trading among people (such as occurs under perfect competition) will not necessarily result in an equitable allocation of the available resources. Initial endowments may be too skewed or the concept of equity may itself be too vague to permit such a result. There is no "invisible hand" guiding a competitive system toward equitable solutions. If we insist on equity (however defined), it may be necessary to opt for some governmental coercion (such as taxes to transfer income among people) to get people to agree to allocations they would not voluntarily accept.

Adopting coercive methods to achieve equity may involve problems too. For example, in several places in this book we have shown how taxes may affect people's behavior and result in efficiency losses that arise from this distortion. Using government's power to transfer income may therefore be a costly activity—achieving equity may involve some losses of efficiency. In our simple analysis of exchange, taxing Smith to provide goods for Jones may cause Smith to use some initial endowment to avoid such taxes by bribing the tax collectors. More generally, taxation may affect people's willingness to work and to produce goods, thereby affecting the amounts of goods available. There may consequently be some trade-off between achieving equitable allocations of resources and achieving efficient allocations. Application 13.1: Modeling the Impact of Taxes with a Computer earlier in this chapter suggests that such efficiency costs may be quite high, but the issue is a very broad one that has not been resolved by economists.

Money in the Perfectly Competitive Model

Thus far in this chapter, we have showed how competitive markets can establish a set of relative prices at which all markets are in equilibrium simultaneously. At several places we stressed that such competitive market forces determine only relative, not absolute, prices and that to examine how the absolute price level is determined we must introduce money into our models. Although a complete examination of this topic is more properly studied as part of macroeconomics, here we can briefly explore some questions of the role of money in a competitive economy that relate directly to microeconomics.

Nature and Function of Money

Money serves two primary functions in any economy: (1) it facilitates transactions by providing an accepted medium of exchange; and (2) it acts as a store of value so that economic actors can better allocate their spending decisions over time. Any commodity can serve as "money" provided it is generally accepted for exchange purposes and is durable from period to period. Today most economies tend to use government-created (fiat) money because the costs associated with its production (e.g., printing pieces of paper with portraits of past or present rulers or keeping records on magnetic tape) are very low. In earlier times, however, commodity money was common with the particular good chosen ranging from the familiar (gold and silver) to the obscure and even bizarre (sharks' teeth or, on the island of Yap, large stone wheels). Societies probably choose the particular form that their money will take as a result of a wide variety of economic, historical, and political forces.

Money as the Accounting Standard

One of the most important functions money usually plays is to act as an accounting standard. All prices are then quoted in terms of this standard. In general, relative prices will be unaffected by which good (or possibly basket of goods) is chosen as the accounting standard. For example, if one apple (good 1) exchanges for two plums (good 2):

$$\frac{P_1}{P_2} = \frac{2}{1}, \qquad [13.4]$$

and it makes little difference how those prices are quoted. If, for example, a society chooses clams as a unit of account, an apple might exchange for four clams and a plum for two clams. If we denote clam prices of apples and plums by P_1' and P_2', respectively, we have

$$\frac{P_1'}{P_2} = \frac{4}{2} = \frac{2}{1} = \frac{P_1}{P_2}. \qquad [13.5]$$

We could change from counting in clams to counting in sharks' teeth by knowing that 10 sharks' teeth exchange for one clam. The price of our goods in sharks' teeth would be

$$P_1'' = 4 \cdot 10 = 40 \qquad [13.6]$$

and

$$P_2'' = 2 \cdot 10 = 20.$$

One apple (which costs 40 teeth) would still exchange for two plums which cost 20 teeth each.

Of course, using clams or sharks' teeth is not very common. Instead, societies usually adopt paper money as their accounting standard. An apple might exchange for half a piece of paper picturing George Washington (i.e., \$.50) and a plum for one-fourth of such a piece of paper (\$.25). Thus, with this monetary standard, the relative price remains two for one. Choice of an accounting standard does not, however, necessarily dictate any particular absolute price level. An apple might exchange for four clams or four hundred, but, as long as a plum exchanges for half as many clams, relative prices will be unaffected by the absolute level that prevails. But absolute price levels are obviously important, especially to individuals who wish to use money as a store of value. A person with a large investment in clams obviously cares about how many apples they will buy. Although a complete theoretical treatment of the price level issue is beyond the scope of this book, we do offer some brief comments here.

Commodity Money

In an economy where money is produced in a way similar to any other good (gold is mined, clams are dug, or sharks are caught), the relative price of money is determined like any other relative price—by the forces of demand and supply. Economic forces that affect either the demand or supply of money will also affect these relative prices. For example, Spanish importation of gold from the New World during the fifteenth and sixteenth centuries greatly expanded gold supplies and caused the relative price of gold to fall. That is, the prices of all other goods rose relative to that of gold—there was general inflation in the prices of practically everything in terms of gold. Similar effects would arise from changes in any factor that affected the equilibrium price for the good chosen as money. Application 13.5: Exchange and Money in a POW Camp illustrates how the use of commodity money can arise in even the most trying of circumstances and how increases in this money can cause general inflation.

Fiat Money and the Monetary Veil

For the case of fiat money produced by the government, the analysis can be extended a bit. In this situation the government is the sole supplier of money and can generally choose how much it wishes to produce. What effects will this level of money production have on the real economy? In general, the situation would seem to be identical to that for commodity money. A change in the money supply will disturb the general equilibrium of all relative prices, and, although it seems likely that an expansion in supply will lower the relative price of money (that is, result in an inflation in the money prices of other goods), any more precise prediction would seem to depend on the results of a detailed general equilibrium model of supply and demand in many markets.

Beginning with David Hume, however, classical economists argued that money (especially fiat money) differs from other economic goods and should

APPLICATION 13.5

Exchange and Money in a POW Camp

Prisoner-of-war (POW) camps provide an illustration of ways in which voluntary market-type arrangements may arise even in the most trying of circumstances. The basic goods available to the prisoners in such situations are usually determined by what they are given by their captors and by what goods come through other sources (for example, the Red Cross). Very little actual production takes place. Still, as R. A. Radford shows in a famous article detailing his experiences as a POW during World War II, elaborate arrangements may develop for reallocating the available goods in more efficient ways.[1] Radford shows, for example, that most prisoners were given essentially the same set of basic necessities, but customary barter rates of exchange among these commodities rapidly developed to reflect the prisoners' preferences. Tins of jam typically traded for one-half pound of margarine, whereas tins of diced carrots were worth practically nothing in exchange.

Development of Monetary Institutions

Bartering one good for another involves a potential inefficiency. A person who wants to trade jam for margarine has to find someone willing to make the trade. It is this problem that leads all modern societies to adopt money as a way of facilitating exchange. With a monetary system, one need not find someone willing to trade margarine for jam but can instead trade the jam for money and then use the money to buy margarine. In the POW camps there was no money in the usual sense, but as Radford shows, cigarettes came to play this role. Every commodity had a customary price in terms of cigarettes, and relative cigarette prices reflected relative rates of exchange between commodities. During periods when many Red Cross packages were received, cigarette supplies rose and there was a general inflation of goods' prices in terms of cigarettes. This reflects David Hume's notion that general inflation may simply represent "too much money chasing too few goods." Similarly, Gresham's law (that bad money drives out good) was reflected by the fact that only relatively poor quality cigarettes were used for making transactions—the better ones were smoked instead.

Trade and Specialization

Radford also observed a form of international trade in the POW camps. Since French and British troops were imprisoned in separate areas, different prices developed for goods in these communities. Coffee, for example, was more highly valued in terms of cigarettes among French prisoners than among British prisoners. Risk-taking entrepreneurs who were willing to move between the camps (usually by bribing guards) could get "rich" by buying coffee from the British and selling it to the French.

To Think About

1. Suppose a POW camp's only source of jam was from monthly Red Cross packages. Would you expect sharp declines in jam prices just after the packages arrive? If you, as a prisoner, observed such a regular pattern, what would you do?
2. Some medical officers at the POW camps argued that using cigarettes as money was unfair to smokers, since they might harm their health by selling their food rations for more cigarettes. The medical officers favored "price controls" on some food items. How would you evaluate this argument for price controls? How effective do you think such controls would be?

[1] R. A. Radford, "The Economic Organization of a POW Camp," *Economics* (November 1945): 189–201.

be regarded as being outside the real economic system of demand, supply, and relative price determination. In this view the economy can be dichotomized into a real sector in which relative prices are determined and a monetary sector where the absolute price level (that is, the value of fiat money) is set. Money, therefore, acts only as a "veil" for real economic activity—the quantity of money available has no effect on the real sector.[9]

Whether the classical dichotomy between the real and monetary sectors actually holds in the real world is an empirical question that cannot be resolved on theoretical grounds alone. Although a monetary sector can be incorporated into the standard competitive model of general equilibrium in ways that preserve the dichotomy, many of these are somewhat artificial and rely on rather restrictive assumptions. Discovering whether they still represent a reasonable approximation of the behavior of the economy (especially over the long term) is an important unresolved issue in macroeconomics.

Summary

We began this chapter with a description of a general equilibrium model of a perfectly competitive price system. In that model, relative prices are determined by the forces of supply and demand, and everyone takes these prices as given in their economic decisions. We then arrive at the following conclusions about such a method for allocating resources:

- Profit-maximizing firms will use resources in a technically efficient way to produce goods because each cost-minimizing firm chooses a combination of inputs for which the RTS is equal to the ratio of the inputs' prices. Firms will therefore operate on the production possibility frontier.
- Profit-maximizing firms will also produce an economically efficient mix of outputs. The workings of supply and demand will ensure that the technical rate at which one good can be transformed into another in production (the rate of product transformation—RPT) is equal to the rate at which people are willing to trade one good for another (the MRS). Adam Smith's invisible hand brings considerable coordination into seemingly chaotic market transactions.
- Factors that interfere with the ability of prices to reflect marginal costs under perfect competition will prevent an economically efficient allocation of resources. Such factors include imperfect competition,

[9]This leads directly to the quantity theory of the demand for money, first suggested by Hume:

$$D_M = \frac{1}{V} \cdot P \cdot Q,$$

where D_M is the demand for money, V is the velocity of monetary circulation (the number of times a dollar is used each year), P is the overall price level, and Q is a measure of the quantity of transactions (often approximated by real GNP). If V is fixed and Q is determined by real forces, a doubling of the supply of money will result in a doubling of the equilibrium price level.

externalities, and public goods. Imperfect information about market prices may also interfere with the efficiency of perfect competition.

- Under perfect competition there are no forces to ensure that voluntary transactions will result in equitable final allocations. Achieving equity (if that term can be adequately defined at all) may require some coercion to transfer income. Such interventions may involve costs in terms of economic efficiency.
- A perfectly competitive price system establishes only relative prices. Introduction of money into the competitive model can show how nominal prices are determined. In some cases the amount of money (and the absolute price level) will have no effect on the relative prices established in competitive markets.

Review Questions

1. Why should an economist who is only interested in one market be concerned about general equilibrium relationships? Can't he or she just study shifts in supply or demand in this single market without worrying about what is happening elsewhere? Provide a specific example of how omitting general equilibrium feedback effects might cause an analyst to make mistakes in his or her examination of a single market.
2. The intuitive approach to describing economic efficiency presented in Figure 13.2 shows that a positive gap between the demand curve and the supply curve indicates the possibility for mutually beneficial transactions between buyers and sellers. Explain the nature of such a transaction and why it is mutually beneficial. Are all such possibilities exhausted at the demand-supply intersection? Explain why transactions to the right of the equilibrium quantity might not be mutually beneficial.
3. Why are allocations on the production possibility frontier technically efficient? What is technically inefficient about allocations inside the frontier? Do inefficient allocations necessarily involve any unemployment of factors of production? In the model introduced in this chapter, would unemployment be technically inefficient?
4. Why does the rate of product transformation indicate relative opportunity costs? Why do economists expect the opportunity cost of X to increase as the output of X increases? Suppose the RPT were constant. What would the production possibility curve look like in this case and what would that assume about the marginal costs of X and Y production?
5. Suppose two countries had differing production possibility frontiers and were currently producing with different RPTs. If there were no transportation or other charges associated with international transactions, how might world output be increased by having these firms alter their production plans? Develop a simple numerical example of these gains for the case where both countries have linear production possibility frontiers (with different slopes). Interpret this result in terms of the concept of "comparative advantage" from the theory of international trade.
6. Use a simple two-good model of resource allocation (such as that in Figure 13.6) to explain the difference between technical efficiency and economic (or allocative) efficiency. Would you agree with the statement that "economic efficiency requires technical efficiency, but many technically efficient allocations are not economically efficient"? Explain your reasoning with a graph.
7. How can you read the capital-labor ratio in the production of each good from the Edgeworth box diagram in Figure 13.4? Why does this particular figure

indicate that good X has a higher capital-labor ratio in its production than does good Y? Explain how a reduction in X output and an increase in Y output might affect the demand for capital in this economy. Since the supply of capital is fixed, how might such a shift in demand affect the price of capital? How is this related to the British Corn Laws debate described in Application 13.4?

8. In Chapter 12 we showed how a shift in demand or supply could be analyzed using a model of a single market. How would you illustrate an increase in the demand for good X in the general equilibrium model pictured in Figure 13.7? Why would such a shift in preferences cause the relative price of X to rise? What would happen to the market for good Y in this case? How would you conduct a similar comparative statics analysis of an improvement in the technology for producing good X?
9. Relative prices convey information about both production possibilities and people's preferences. What exactly is that information and how does its availability help attain an efficient allocation of resources? In what ways does the presence of monopoly or externalities result in price information being "inaccurate"?
10. In most of the theoretical examples in this book, prices have been quoted in dollars or cents. Is this choice of currency crucial? Would most examples be the same if prices had been stated in pounds, marks, or yen? Or, would it have mattered if the dollars used were "1900 dollars" or "1990 dollars"? How would you change the endless hamburger–soft drink examples, say, to phrase them in some other currency? Would such changes result in any fundamental differences? Or, do most of the examples in this book seem to display the classical dichotomy between real and nominal magnitudes?

Problems

13.1 Suppose the production possibility frontier for cheeseburgers (C) and milkshakes (M) is given by

$$C + 2M = 600.$$

a. Graph this function.
b. Assuming that people prefer to eat two cheeseburgers with every milkshake, how much of each product will be produced? Indicate this point on your graph.
c. Given that this fast food economy is operating efficiently, what price ratio (P_C/P_M) must prevail?

13.2 Consider an economy with just one technique available for the production of each good, food and cloth:

Good	Food	Cloth
Labor per unit output	1	1
Land per unit output	2	1

a. Supposing land is unlimited but labor equals 100, write and sketch the production possibility frontier.
b. Supposing labor is unlimited but land equals 150, write and sketch the production possibility frontier.
c. Supposing labor equals 100 and land equals 150, write and sketch the production possibility frontier. (Hint: What are the intercepts of the production possibility frontier? When is land fully employed? Labor? Both?)

d. Explain why the production possibility frontier of part c is concave.
e. Sketch the relative price of food as a function of its output in part c.
f. If consumers insist on trading four units of food for five units of cloth, what is the relative price of food? Why?
g. Explain why production is exactly the same at a price ratio of P_F/P_C = 1.1 as at P_F/P_C = 1.9.
h. Suppose that capital is also required for producing food and cloth and that capital requirements per unit of food are 0.8 and per unit of cloth 0.9. There are 100 units of capital available. What is the production possibility curve in this case? Answer part e for this case.

*13.3 Suppose the production possibility frontier for guns (X) and butter (Y) is given by

$$X^2 + 2Y^2 = 900.$$

a. Graph this frontier.
b. If individuals always prefer consumption bundles in which Y = 2X, how much X and Y will be produced?
c. At the point described in part a, what will be the RPT and what price ratio will cause production to take place at that point? This slope should be approximated by considering small changes in X and Y around the optimal point.
d. Show your solution on the figure from part a.

13.4 The country of Extrenum produces only skis (S) and waterskis (W), using capital (K) and labor (L) as inputs. The production functions for both S and W are fixed proportions. It takes two units of labor and one unit of capital to produce a pair of skis. Waterskis, on the other hand, require one unit of labor and one unit of capital. If the total supply of capital is 100 units, construct the production possibility curve for this economy. Are all inputs fully employed at every point on the production possibility curve? How do you explain any unemployment that might exist?

*13.5 Robinson Crusoe obtains utility from the quantity of fish he consumes in one day (F), the quantity of coconuts he consumes that day (C), and the hours of leisure time he has during the day (H) according to the utility function:

$$\text{Utility} = F^{1/4}C^{1/4}H^{1/2}.$$

Robinson's production of fish is given by

$$F = \sqrt{L_F}$$

(where L_F is the hours he spends fishing), and his production of coconuts is determined by

$$C = \sqrt{L_C}$$

(where L_C is the time he spends picking coconuts). Assuming that Robinson decides to work an eight-hour day (that is, H = 16), graph his production possibility curve for fish and coconuts. Show his optimal choices of those goods.

---

*Denotes a problem that is rather difficult.

13.6 Suppose two individuals (Smith and Jones) each have 10 hours of labor to devote to producing either ice cream (X) or chicken soup (Y). Smith's demand for X and Y is given by

$$X_S = .3I_S/P_X$$
$$Y_S = .7I_S/P_Y$$

whereas Jones' demands are given by

$$X_J = .5I_J/P_X$$
$$Y_J = .5I_J/P_Y$$

where I_S and I_J represent Smith's and Jones' incomes, respectively, (which come only from working).

The individuals do not care whether they produce X or Y and the production function for each good is given by

$$X = 2L$$
$$Y = 3L$$

where L is the total labor devoted to production of each good. Using this information, answer the following:

a. What must the price ratio, P_X/P_Y, be?
b. Given this price ratio, how much X and Y will Smith and Jones demand? (Hint: Set the wage equal to 1 here so that each person's income is 10.)
c. How should labor be allocated between X and Y to satisfy the demand calculated in part b?

13.7 In the country of Ruritania there are two regions, A and B. Two goods (X and Y) are produced in both regions. Production functions for region A are given by

$$X_A = \sqrt{L_X}$$
$$Y_A = \sqrt{L_Y}.$$

L_X and L_Y are the quantity of labor devoted to X and Y production, respectively. Total labor available in region A is 100 units. That is,

$$L_X + L_Y = 100.$$

Using a similar notation for region B, production functions are given by

$$X_B = 1/2\sqrt{L_X}$$
$$Y_B = 1/2\sqrt{L_Y}.$$

There are also 100 units of labor available in region B:

$$L_X + L_Y = 100.$$

a. Calculate the production possibility curves for regions A and B.
b. What condition must hold if production in Ruritania is to be allocated efficiently between regions A and B (assuming that labor cannot move from one region to the other)?

c. Calculate the production possibility curve for Ruritania (again assuming that labor is immobile between regions). How much total Y can Ruritania produce if total X output is 12? (Hint: A graphic analysis may be of some help here.)

13.8 There are 200 pounds of food on an island that must be allocated between two marooned sailors. The utility function of the first sailor is given by:

$$\text{Utility} = \sqrt{F_1}$$

where F_1 is the quantity of food consumed by the first sailor. For the second sailor, utility (as a function of food consumption) is given by:

$$\text{Utility} = 1/2\sqrt{F_2}$$

a. If the food is allocated equally between the sailors, how much utility will each receive?
b. How should food be allocated between the sailors to assure equality of utility?
c. Suppose that the second sailor requires a utility level of at least 5 to remain alive. How should food be allocated so as to maximize the sum of utilities subject to the restraint that the second sailor receive that minimum level of utility?
d. What other criteria might you use to allocate the available food between the sailors?

*13.9 Suppose that there are two individuals in an economy. Utilities of those individuals under five possible social states are shown in the following table.

State	Utility 1	Utility 2
A	50	50
B	70	40
C	45	54
D	53	50.5
E	30	84

The individuals do not know which number (1 or 2) they will be assigned when the economy begins operating. They are uncertain about the actual utility they will receive under the alternative social states. Which social state will be preferred if an individual adopts the following strategies in his or her voting behavior to deal with this uncertainty?

a. Choose that state that assures the highest utility to the least well-off person.
b. Assume that there is a 50–50 chance of being either individual and choose that state with the highest expected utility.
c. Assume that, no matter what, the odds are always unfavorable in that there is a 60 percent chance of having the lower utility and a 40 percent chance of higher utility in any social state. Choose the state with the highest expected utility given these probabilities.

*Denotes a problem that is rather difficult.

d. Assume that there is a 50–50 chance of being assigned either number, and that each individual dislikes inequality. Each will choose that state for which:

$$\text{Expected utility} - |U_1 - U_2|$$

is as large as possible (where the |...| notation denotes absolute value).

e. What do you conclude from this problem about the social choices under a veil of ignorance as to an individual's specific identity in society?

13.10 Return to problem 13.6 and now assume that Smith and Jones conduct their exchanges in paper money. The total supply of such money is $60 and each individual wishes to hold a stock of money equal to 1/4 of the value of transactions made per period.

a. What will the money wage rate be in this model? What will the nominal prices of X and Y be?

b. Suppose the money supply increases to $90, how will your answers to part a change? Does this economy exhibit the classical dichotomy between its real and monetary sectors?

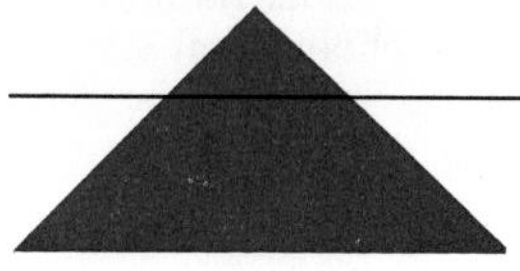

APPENDIX TO CHAPTER 13
LINEAR PROGRAMMING, PRICING OF INPUTS, AND DUALITY

This appendix introduces the mathematical tool of linear programming and uses this tool to demonstrate some additional relationships between the efficient use of resources and the pricing of those resources. Since a detailed treatment of linear programming is beyond the scope of this book, our analysis here is brief.[1]

The Problem

To illustrate some of the basic concepts of linear programming, we will look at one simple example. In this example, an economy is assumed to have fixed amounts of various productive inputs, and a central planner must choose how to allocate these inputs to the production of two goods, cars and pickup trucks. In order to avoid having to study the demand for these goods, we assume that prices of cars and pickups are determined outside of our model and do not change. We assume that the price of each truck (P_T) is \$12,000 and that the price of each car (P_C) is \$15,000. The sole goal of the central planner in our simple economy is to allocate the available resources to car and truck production so that the total value of output is as large as possible. That is, the goal is to choose car output (C) and truck output (T) so that

$$\begin{aligned} \text{Total value} = \text{TV} &= P_T \cdot T + P_C \cdot C \\ &= 12{,}000 \cdot T + 15{,}000 \cdot C \end{aligned} \qquad [13A.1]$$

is as large as possible given available resources.

A Graphic Demonstration

Before we approach the solution to this problem using linear programming, the general kind of answer we will get can be demonstrated very simply. The most direct way to proceed is by using a graphic analysis. In Figure 13A.1 the production possibility frontier is drawn for the economy. The curve PP repre-

[1]For an interesting though fairly difficult survey of linear programming techniques, see Robert Dorfman, P. A. Samuelson, and R. M. Solow, *Linear Programming and Economic Analysis* (New York: McGraw-Hill, 1958).

Figure 13A.1
Value Maximization in a Hypothetical Economy

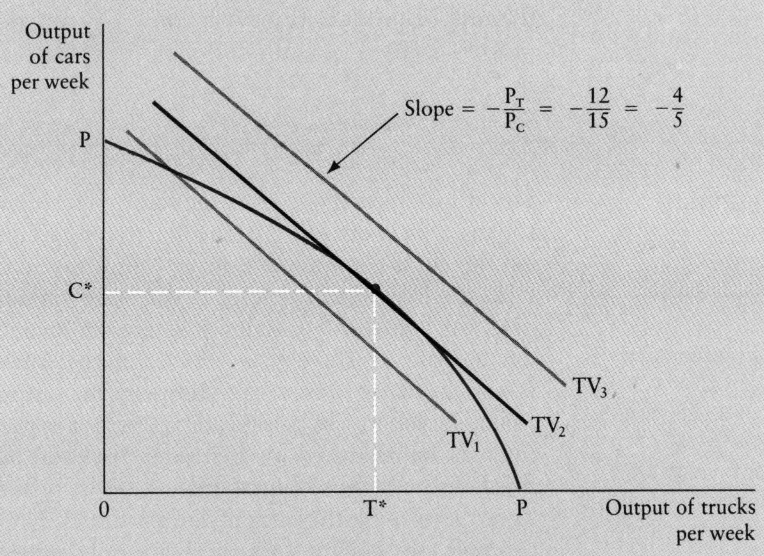

PP represents the feasible combinations of cars and trucks that can be produced with available resources. If a central planner wishes to maximize the total value of production (TV), the combination C*, T* should be produced. At this output combination, the RPT (of trucks for cars) is equal to the ratio of these goods' prices (P_T/P_C).

sents those combinations of cars and pickup trucks that can be produced given the inputs available. Our goal is to choose that point on the PP frontier that provides maximum revenues. This maximization process is shown in the figure. The several parallel straight lines (labeled TV_1, TV_2, TV_3) record those combinations of cars and trucks that provide equal value. The combinations lying along TV_3 provide more in total value than do those on TV_2, which in turn provide more value than do those on TV_1. The slope of these lines is given by

$$-P_T/P_C \quad (= -\$12{,}000/\$15{,}000 = -4/5)$$

since this ratio of prices tells how cars can be traded for trucks in the market while keeping the total value for output constant.

The total value of cars and trucks produced is as large as possible when output combination C*, T* is chosen. This combination produces total revenues of TV_2, and it is the only combination that is capable of providing this amount. All other feasible output combinations on PP provide less total value than does this optimal choice. At C*, T* the production possibility frontier is exactly tangent to the total value line TV_2. This type of result should be familiar to you from Chapter 13. At the optimal point, the rate at which cars can technically be traded for trucks is equal to the rate at which these two goods are willingly traded by buyers in the market. In other words, the rate of product transformation (of trucks for cars) is equal to the price ratio P_T/P_C.

A Linear Programming Statement of the Problem

Linear programming A mathematical technique for finding the maximum (or minimum) value for a linear function whose variables are subject to linear constraints.

Linear programming is a mathematical technique that is particularly suited to solving a problem like the one illustrated in Figure 13A.1. The technique was developed as a systematic way to find the maximum values of linear functions (such as Equation 13A.1) when the variables in these functions—in our case, car and truck production—are constrained in the values they can take on. In order to show how this technique works, we must first examine the factors in the economy that constrain the output choices that are feasible.

As we saw in Chapter 13, there are two types of constraints on the amount that can be produced by any economy: total quantities of various inputs are fixed, and certain technical rules (that is, production functions) must be followed in turning these inputs into outputs. For the purposes of our car-truck example, we assume that there are only three inputs: labor, machines, and steel. The quantities of these inputs that are assumed to be available are shown in the second column of Table 13A.1. No production plan can be implemented that uses more than 720 labor-hours, 900 machine-hours, or 1,800 tons of steel.

Production Functions for Cars and Trucks

Table 13A.1 also indicates the amount of each input required to produce one car or one truck. It takes one labor-hour, three machine-hours, and five tons of steel to build a truck; it takes two labor-hours, one machine-hour, and four tons of steel to build a car. The production techniques shown in Table 13A.1 are fixed proportions (see Chapter 8): no substitution between inputs is possible. This kind of technology is one characteristic of most linear programming problems.

Resource Constraints

We can now examine the constraints that the available amounts of inputs place on the combinations of cars and trucks that can be produced. With C representing the number of cars to be produced and T the number of trucks, the first line of Table 13A.1 shows that all possible choices of T and C must obey the inequality

$$1 \cdot T + 2 \cdot C \leq 720. \qquad [13A.2]$$

Table 13A.1
Resources and Technology in a Hypothetical Economy

Resource	Total Available	Required to Produce 1 Truck	Required to Produce 1 Car
Labor	720 labor-hours	1 labor-hour	2 labor-hours
Machines	900 machine-hours	3 machine-hours	1 machine-hour
Steel	1,800 tons	5 tons	4 tons

That is, the quantity of labor employed in truck production (one labor-hour to build one truck) plus the quantity employed in car production (two labor-hours per car) cannot exceed the 720 labor-hours available. Equation 13A.2 might be called the "labor-hours" constraint in production.

Similar constraints exist for machines and for steel. Again, these can be taken directly from Table 13A.1. The machine-hour constraint is

$$3 \cdot T + 1 \cdot C \leq 900 \tag{13A.3}$$

and the steel constraint is

$$5 \cdot T + 4 \cdot C \leq 1{,}800. \tag{13A.4}$$

These constraints record that no more machines or steel may be used in production than are available.

Given these three resource constraints, our problem is to find values of T and C that satisfy all constraints and to make the total value of output, shown in Equation 13A.1

$$TV = 12{,}000 \cdot T + 15{,}000 \cdot C,$$

as large as possible. That, then, is our linear programming problem.

Construction of the Production Possibility Frontier

One very time-consuming solution to the problem would be to list all the combinations of C and T that satisfy the three constraints, calculate the total value obtained from each combination, and choose the one with the largest value. In practice, however, linear programming problems are usually solved by computer. We can show how such solutions are found by using a simple graphical approach. In Figure 13A.2 we have graphed the three resource constraints. Since any feasible combination of C and T must satisfy *all* three constraints, we are interested only in those points in the diagram that fall on or below all three lines. The heavy line in Figure 13A.2 indicates the outer perimeter of such feasible choices. Combinations of cars and trucks on or

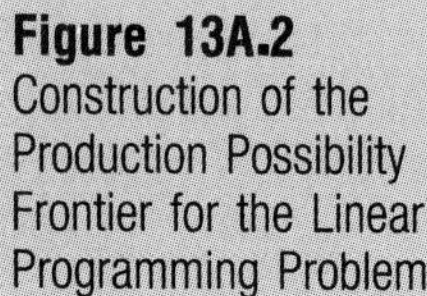

Figure 13A.2
Construction of the Production Possibility Frontier for the Linear Programming Problem

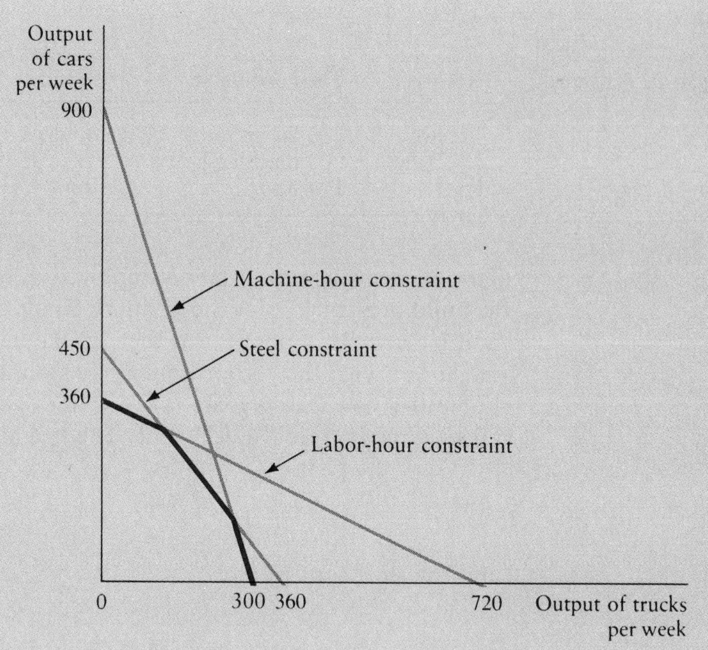

The heavy line in this diagram is the production possibility frontier for cars and trucks applied by the input constraints. It is the perimeter of the set of output combinations that satisfies all the constraints.

Binding constraint
The presence of one or more resources that effectively limits the amount that can be produced. If a particular input is not fully utilized, it does not pose a binding constraint in production.

inside this curve can be produced. Those outside the perimeter cannot be produced because there is not enough of at least one of the resources to do so.

For example, should the central planner in the economy decide to produce only cars, the heavy line indicates that 360 could be produced. In producing only cars, the economy "runs out" of labor-hours first (there is enough steel to produce 450 cars and enough machine-hours to produce 900 cars). For trucks, on the other hand, the **binding constraint** is machine availability. There are only enough machine-hours to build 300 trucks. Other combinations of cars and trucks on or inside the heavy line in Figure 13A.2 similarly satisfy all the constraints. The curve is just the production possibility frontier for the simple economy we have described.

Linear Programming Solution of the Problem

We can use the production possibility frontier derived in Figure 13A.2 to solve our maximum value problem in much the same way that the problem was solved in Figure 13A.1. Figure 13A.3 again shows the production possibility frontier together with several lines of equal revenue. From the figure, we can see that the value-maximizing point is output combination C*, T*,

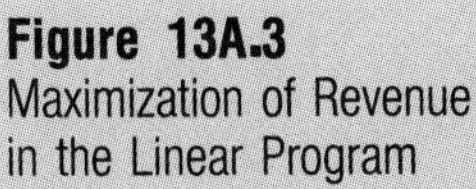

Figure 13A.3
Maximization of Revenue in the Linear Program

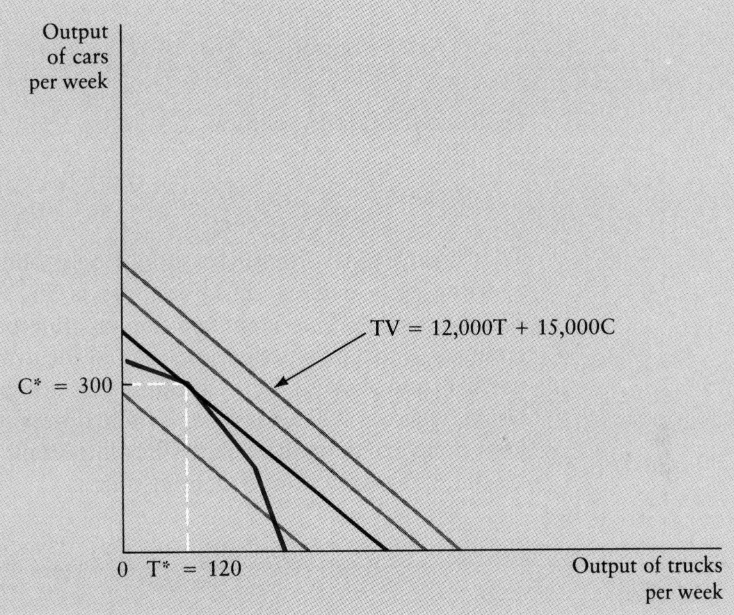

By superimposing several lines of equal revenue on the production possibility frontier, the point of maximum revenue can be found. This point occurs where the labor-hour and steel constraints intersect.

where the labor-hour constraint and the steel constraint intersect.[2] (Refer back to Figure 13A.2 to check that these are indeed the constraints that intersect at C^*, T^*.) Solving the two constraints for C^* and T^* gives

$$1T + 2C = 720 \text{ (labor-hour constraint)}$$
$$5T + 4C = 1{,}800 \text{ (steel constraint)} \quad [13A.5]$$

or, from the labor-hour constraint,

$$T = 720 - 2C. \quad [13A.6]$$

[2]This point, in a sense, satisfies the rule that the RPT should equal the ratio P_T/P_C. The RPT along the labor-hour constraint is $-1/2$; along the steel constraint the RPT is $-5/4$. The vertex at C^*, T^* includes all slopes between $-1/2$ and $-5/4$. But the ratio $-P_T/P_C$ is given by $-4/5$, which lies between these two values. Hence, C^*, T^* is the revenue-maximizing point. In linear programming problems, the optimal solution will usually occur at corners, such as the one illustrated.

Therefore, by substitution into the steel constraint,

$$5(720) - 10C + 4C = 3{,}600 - 6C = 1{,}800. \qquad [13A.7]$$

Hence, our optimal solution is

$$C^* = 300 \qquad T^* = 120. \qquad [13A.8]$$

That means that 120 trucks should be produced along with 300 cars. The revenue provided by these outputs is $5,940,000 (= $12,000 · 120 + $15,000 · 300). This is the maximum value possible given the resource constraints. At this production level not all the available machine-hours are being used. Production of 300 cars and 120 trucks requires only 660 machine hours, whereas 900 are available. The observation that at the optimal output level there are unused machines has important implications for the pricing of machines, as we will now demonstrate.

Duality and the Pricing of Inputs

Dual linear programming problem A minimization problem related to a primal linear programming maximization problem; often involves computation of appropriate resource prices.

So far we have said nothing about the price of inputs in this linear programming problem. The economy had certain amounts of inputs available, and the central planner set about the task of maximizing the value of the economy's output. A linear programming problem related to this *primal* maximization problem is the **dual linear programming problem** of finding the proper input prices associated with the optimal choice of car and pickup truck production. Formally, these dual input prices solve the following linear programming problem.

Minimize

$$M = 720P_L + 900P_K + 1{,}800P_S \qquad [13A.9]$$

subject to

$$\begin{aligned} P_L + 3P_K + 5P_S &\geq 12{,}000 \\ 2P_L + P_K + 4P_S &\geq 15{,}000 \end{aligned} \qquad [13A.10]$$

where P_L, P_K, and P_S are the per-unit prices of labor, capital, and steel.

This dual problem can be given an economic interpretation. We are asked to find prices for the inputs that minimize the total value of all inputs available (that is, minimize total cost). These prices must not be too low (they can't all be zero). The two inequalities in Equation 13A.10 require that neither the production of cars nor trucks earns a pure economic profit. For example, the first inequality says that the costs of producing one pickup (that is, the cost of one labor-hour, three machine-hours, and five tons of steel) should not be less than the price of a truck ($12,000). Similarly, the input costs must be sufficiently high that their cost is not less than the price of a car ($15,000).

Without going into formal detail, it should be clear that the dual problem is related in some way to the original problem. All the constants that appeared in the primal problem also appear in the dual problem, but in different places. In particular, quantities of inputs that appeared in the original constraints now appear as coefficients in the dual objective function (Equation 13A.9) and vice versa. Also the constraints of the primal problem seem to have been "turned on their side" in the dual problem.

Solution to the Dual Problem

A graphic solution to the dual linear programming problem is not presented here because it would require a three-dimensional graph to show all three input prices. It must be taken on faith that the solution to the dual program turns out to be

$$
\begin{aligned}
P_L &= \$4{,}500 \\
P_K &= \$0 \\
P_S &= \$1{,}500. \qquad [13A.11]
\end{aligned}
$$

These are the prices of labor, machines, and steel that minimize Equation 13A.9 and obey the two constraints given by Equation 13A.10. You may wish to check if this is indeed true.

This solution has several important features:

- With these input prices, the inequalities in Equation 13A.10 are exactly satisfied. The cost of a pickup, for example, is $4,500 + 0 + 5 · $1,500, which is precisely $12,000. A similar statement holds for cars. So, neither good is produced at a loss. Hence, both goods can be produced in the economy without needing a subsidy.
- The total value of all the inputs with these input prices is $5,940,000. It is no coincidence that this is identical to the maximum value for the total value of output that we found in the primal problem. Such a relationship holds between the primal and the dual solutions of all linear programs. Here this equality resembles the income-output identity in the *National Income and Product Accounts*. The total value of output is equal to the total value of inputs.
- The input that had some extra amount left over in the primal problem (machine-hours) is given a price of $0 in the dual problem. This result tells economists that adding machines in this economy would have no effect on the value of output. In formal terms, the **shadow price** of machinery in this example is 0 because machinery is not really scarce. On the other hand, since labor and steel are the binding constraints that prevent output from being increased, these inputs are given positive

Shadow prices
Prices for resources in a dual linear programming problem. For resources that represent binding constraints on production, shadow prices will be positive. For resources that do not represent binding constraints, shadow prices are zero.

shadow prices. The values given in Equation 13A.11 for P_L and P_S indicate how much extra value would be provided by one more unit of these inputs. You may wish to show, for example, that an increase in labor-hours by one unit will cause the total output to increase by $4,500 if we allow the economy to produce fractional parts of cars and trucks.[3]

Further Observations on Duality

Our two linear programming problems demonstrate the relationship between the optimal choice of outputs and the correct choice of input prices. The optimal allocation of a fixed amount of inputs to the production of a variety of possible outputs always has associated with it a dual problem that involves the optimal pricing of those inputs available. The solution of one problem is equivalent to the solving of the other.[4] This relationship, which has an obvious similarity to Adam Smith's invisible hand image, has been widely used in practical problems as well.

The computation of input prices from a linear programming model can be very useful for economic planning in less-developed economies. Such shadow prices can provide information about how important certain inputs are, and occasionally such computed prices may differ greatly from the actual prices of the inputs. For example, there are institutional reasons (labor unions, minimum wages, and so forth) why some groups of workers may have high wages even though labor is an overabundant resource in the particular country. On the other hand, linear programming models may suggest that the "real" value of labor is rather low, and planners should adopt production techniques that utilize labor to a greater extent than would seem economically warranted by looking only at market wage rates.

Corporations have used linear programming in a similar way to make more efficient management decisions. One such use arises when a firm wishes to decentralize its decision making. To do so, the firm often divides its operations among several profit centers, which are responsible for all production decisions within a specific area. One problem with which the management of such decentralized firms must contend is how to charge each profit center for the general company inputs (plant and equipment, administrative staff, advertising staff) it uses. Only by correctly choosing the bookkeeping prices of

[3]The firm will produce five-sixths of an additional car in this situation but will cut truck production by two-thirds of a truck. Consequently, total revenue is changed by $5/6 \cdot \$15{,}000 - 2/3 \cdot \$12{,}000$, which is about $4,500.

[4]Linear programming problems may not always have solutions. If a linear programming problem and its associated dual have "feasible" solutions (solutions that satisfy the constraints of the problems), then they each have optimal solutions that have the properties listed above. For an elegant and concise discussion of the relationship between primal and dual linear programming problems with applications to a variety of allocational problems, see David Gale, *The Theory of Linear Economic Models* (New York: McGraw-Hill, 1960).

these inputs can the firm's management be sure that the decisions of the manager of each profit center will produce desirable overall results. Linear programming has been used extensively for calculating the prices of such intracompany resources.

These two examples merely hint at the huge number of applications that linear programming has had. Others include such widely different uses as the planning of natural gas pipelines and railway yards, investigating the optimal portfolio of stocks for a mutual fund to own, and studying the movement of seasonal labor forces in Africa. In many of these applications, a linear program's duality features are utilized.

Summary

This appendix describes the use of the mathematical tool of linear programming as a way to solve economic problems. In addition to illustrating the technique with a simple example, it also discusses the importance of the dual relationship between allocating resources efficiently and the correct pricing of these resources. The specific findings in the appendix are:

- Linear programming can sometimes be used to find the maximum (or minimum) value for a linear function when the values of some of the variables in the function are subject to linear constraints.
- The optimal solution found by linear programming will have many of the characteristics of efficiency illustrated in Chapter 13. Specifically, the marginal rate of product transformation will be approximately equal to the relative prices of the goods being produced.
- Solving the dual to a linear programming problem can provide optimal prices for scarce resources. Resources that are not scarce will be assigned a price of zero in such solutions.

CHAPTER 14

Information and Competitive Equilibrium

Thus far, our model of competitive price determination has assumed that economic actors have complete information. Both demanders and suppliers were assumed to know the prices of all available goods and to use those prices in making their decisions. As we pointed out in Chapter 7, however, such a complete degree of knowledge is unlikely to exist in the real world. Acquiring information about the prices and other characteristics of economic goods is a costly activity. It is also an activity at which some individuals may be better than others—a home builder is in a much better position to judge the true value of an old house than is an uninformed economics professor, for example. We might, therefore, expect actual market information to be both imperfect and unevenly distributed.

In this chapter we will examine some of the consequences of such informational problems. Our coverage parallels the analysis of Chapters 12 and 13. That is, we begin by examining some of the ways in which the existence of imperfect information might affect the ability of markets to establish equilibrium prices. We also discuss some of the ways in which nonequilibrium prices might occur. Finally, we ask whether equilibrium prices that are established in the presence of imperfect information will have the same efficiency properties as those in the simple models of the previous chapter.

Establishing Competitive Equilibrium Prices

One of the most difficult problems faced by any competitive market is how an equilibrium price is discovered. What market signals do suppliers and demanders use to adjust their behavior toward equilibrium? Do they rely on temporary, nonequilibrium prices to make such decisions, or are other mechanisms available? We know from Chapter 12 that for most competitive markets an equilibrium price, P*, exists for which the quantity demanded is equal to the quantity supplied. Now we wish to examine how market price actually gets to P*. We begin with some theoretical answers proposed by economists, then turn to examine briefly some of the problems of information that arise in applying these theoretical suggestions to the real world.

The Impartial Auctioneer and Recontracting

To explain the movement of price to its equilibrium level, some economists have relied on the fictitious notion of an impartial auctioneer. The auctioneer is charged with calling out prices and recording the actions of buyers and sellers. Only when the auctioneer calls a price for which the quantity demanded is identical to that which is supplied will trading be permitted to take place. Presumably, the auctioneer will use information about the market supply and demand curves to guide the pricing decisions, but precise rules for this operation are seldom spelled out.

Although some markets do operate with actual auctioneers (the market for antiques is a good example), in general, no such agents are involved in price determination. Numerous attempts have, therefore, been made to give this fictional concept a behavioral interpretation. One such interpretation is the idea of *recontracting* in which buyers and sellers are assumed to enter into provisional contracts before the exchange of goods actually takes place. Each of these provisional contracts is voided if it is discovered that at the agreed-upon price, the market is not in equilibrium. Only when market-clearing prices for all markets are discovered will exchange take place. Recontracting is then a form of haggling over price, and price determination might be regarded as one aspect of contract theory.

Walrasian Price Adjustment

Excess demand
The extent to which quantity demanded exceeds quantity supplied at a particular price.

A second suggestion, which is similar to recontracting, was proposed by Leon Walras in the nineteenth century. In this scheme, equilibrium prices are a goal toward which the market struggles. Changes in price are motivated by information from the market about the degree of **excess demand** at any particular price.[1] It is assumed price will increase if there is positive excess demand, and decrease if excess demand is negative (that is, if supply exceeds demand).

Figure 14.1 shows the Walrasian process of adjustment schematically. For the supply and demand curves shown in the figure, P* is an equilibrium price. For prices less than P*, there will be an excess demand for this good. At such

[1]Leon Walras, *Elements of Pure Economics,* translated by William Jaffe (Homewood, Ill.: Irwin, 1954).

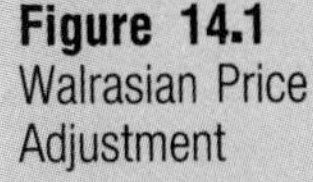

Figure 14.1
Walrasian Price Adjustment

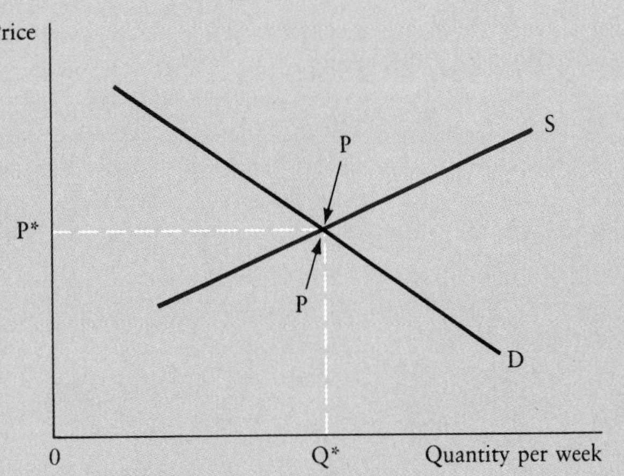

For prices above P*, supply exceeds demand. Such a price may set into motion a chain of events that causes price to fall. For prices less than P*, the quantity demanded exceeds that supplied. In reaction, price may rise.

bargain prices, people will demand more than firms will be willing to supply. Crowds will descend on stores and buy all of this good off the shelves. Walras assumed that this behavior would be translated in the market into an increase in price and that this increase in price will serve to equilibrate supply and demand. In Figure 14.1 the upward-pointing arrow indicates the movement in price in response to excess demand. A similar argument follows for prices above P*. At such prices, the quantity supplied will exceed that which is demanded. Firms will be producing more than individuals demand, and the inventory of the good will begin to accumulate in the firms' warehouses. Eventually, this will lead to a fall in price that will again equilibrate supply and demand. The downward-pointing arrow in the figure indicates that result.

Marshallian Quantity Adjustment

The Walrasian adjustment process views price as the motivating force in the adjustment of markets to equilibrium. Individuals and firms respond to price changes by moving along their respective demand and supply curves until an equilibrium price-quantity combination is reached. A somewhat different picture of the adjustment process was suggested by Alfred Marshall in his classic *Principles of Economics.*[2] Marshall theorized that individuals and firms adjust quantity in response to imbalances in demand and supply, and that price

[2]Alfred Marshall, *Principles of Economics,* 8th ed. (London: Macmillan, 1920), pp. 287–288.

Figure 14.2
Marshallian Quantity Adjustment

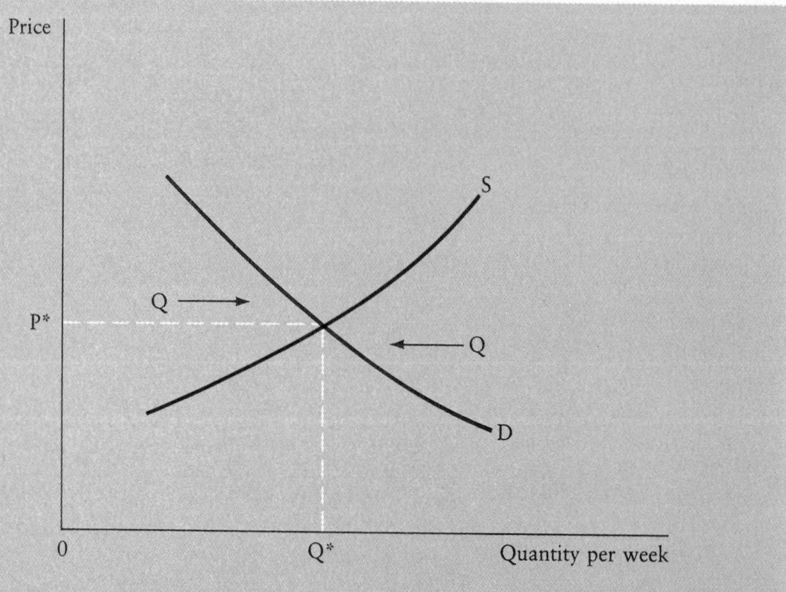

Under Marshallian adjustment, a difference between what demanders are willing to pay and what suppliers require sets up incentives for economic agents to alter output levels. If demand price exceeds supply price, Q will rise. If supply price exceeds demand price, Q will fall. The adjustment mechanism shown in the figure is stable, since Q converges to Q*.

changes follow from these changes in quantity. Movements in quantity toward equilibrium are motivated by discrepancies between the price individuals are willing to pay and the price firms wish to receive. When those two figures coincide, quantity adjustment ceases.

Quantity adjustment is illustrated in Figure 14.2. For quantities below equilibrium (Q*), what individuals are willing to pay exceeds what firms require to cover their marginal costs. Quantity produced and consumed therefore increases. For quantities above equilibrium, marginal costs exceed what demanders are willing to pay, which provides incentives for quantity reduction. As was the case for the price-adjustment mechanism, the Marshallian mechanism pictured in Figure 14.2 implies that the price-quantity equilibrium is a stable one. Starting from any initial position, forces come into play that move economic agents toward equilibrium. The precise mechanism by which the movement comes about, however, differs between the Walrasian and Marshallian models.

Market Adjustments and Transactions Costs

Movement to an equilibrium price-quantity combination will usually involve changes in both price and quantity. The important questions concern the speed with which those variables are adjusted and how buyers and sellers perceive the need to make such adjustments. Although studying this issue in depth would take us beyond the scope of this book, the general approach to be followed is clear. Any theory of the adjustment process must focus on the costs to demanders and suppliers of changing their behavior. Those costs derive both from problems associated with gathering information about the true supply-demand configuration and from difficulties in adapting to this new information once it is acquired. We now turn to examine these costs.

Transactions costs Costs involved in making market transactions and in gathering information with which to make those transactions.

In explaining why markets do not adjust immediately to bring about equilibrium, economists have tended to stress **transactions costs.** Bringing suppliers and demanders together is not as simple a process as the Marshallian diagram suggests. There may be significant costs involved. Such costs include not only the direct costs of finding a place in which to transact business but, more important, the costs to the participants of gaining information about the market. For demanders, all prices are not perfectly known. Rather, they must invest some time in search procedures that permit them to learn market prices.

Suppliers face similar costs in making transactions. The most important of these is the need to find out something about the demand for their product. Since production takes time, the absence of such information can lead to serious mistakes in the quantity a firm chooses to produce. Firms must also consider the random nature of demand over a short period. For example, no retailer knows exactly when he or she will sell shirts of particular sizes. One of the costs incurred in selling shirts is the cost of maintaining an inventory and making adjustments in that inventory.

As this brief discussion suggests, the competitive assumption of zero transactions costs is not likely to be fulfilled in the real world. Although supply and demand analysis provides information about equilibrium prices and about the direction of change in prices, various costs will prevent markets from adjusting promptly. Consequently, in the real word, we should observe examples not only of the systematic influence of supply and demand but also of *disequilibria* caused by transactions costs. In some cases, such as the simple laboratory experiments described in Application 14.1: Experimenting with Equilibrium, these disequilibrium results may be rather short-lived. In other cases, a market disequilibrium may be rather long-lasting, and there is a need to explain price determination in such situations.

Models of Disequilibrium Pricing

One difficulty with describing how markets establish equilibrium prices is that the competitive model pictures supply and demand decisions as being made simultaneously (remember again Marshall's scissors analogy). The model offers no guidance about how markets react when they are out of equilibrium. One way of developing a model in which transactions occur at nonequilibrium prices is to assume that either suppliers or demanders (or both) base their decisions on what they expect prices to be rather than on what market prices actually turn out to be. Under this approach, trading may occur at prices that are not what people expect. Only as market participants

Experimenting with Equilibrium

Because real-world markets are constantly changing, some economists have tried to develop laboratory experiments to study the establishment of equilibrium prices in a simpler, controlled setting. These experiments usually involve students (since they can be hired at a paltry wage) who are asked to assume the roles of various market participants and to conduct hypothetical transactions, usually over a computer network. One difficulty faced by the designers of such experiments is how to get students to behave like economic actors in the real world. Somehow they must be encouraged to maximize utility (for demanders) or profits (for suppliers) if their behavior is to resemble the ways economists believe actual market participants make decisions.

Experimental Design

One solution to this problem that has been adopted for experiments at several universities is to use monetary incentives to induce student subjects to follow the appropriate decisions roles. Table 1, for example, lists the marginal valuation for each of three demanders of a good and marginal costs for each of three suppliers. For each unit traded, demanders are told that they will be paid the difference between their marginal evaluation and the established price. Similarly, each supplier is told that he or she can pocket the difference between price and marginal cost. If, for example, buyer 1 agrees to trade a first unit with seller 2 for $4.25, the buyer will get to keep $.25 ($4.50 − $4.25), and the seller will get $2.25 ($4.25 − $2.00). This pair would not agree to make a second trade at this price (since buyer 1 would lose on such a trade), but seller 2 could still make a mutually beneficial trade with buyer 2 or 3 at this price. Given these incentives, participating students sit at computer terminals and make any trades that can be arranged.

Table 1
Design for a Market Experiment

Number Bought or Sold	Market Value for Buyer Number			Marginal Cost for Seller Number		
	1	2	3	1	2	3
1	$4.50	$5.33	$5.00	$3.00	$2.00	$2.00
2	4.00	4.66	4.00	4.00	4.00	3.00
3	3.50	4.00	3.00	5.00	6.00	4.00
4	3.00	3.33	2.00	6.00	8.00	5.00

Experimental Results

Experiments similar to those illustrated in Table 1 have been replicated literally thousands of times. Usually buyers and sellers are able to focus in on an equilibrium price (approximately $4.00 in the experiment illustrated in the table) at which all mutually beneficial transactions are exhausted. If a given set of players is allowed to repeat a game many times, they are able to get to equilibrium even more quickly.

Market experiments similar to those in Table 1 can be generalized in several ways.[1] More players can be added to the game, different formats for price determination can be used (in some experiments, for example, sellers can set "posted prices" for all buyers to see and change them only as the game proceeds), or the incentives facing a particular player can be varied. In more complex experiments, players may buy or sell two (or even three) goods or perhaps some random elements can be introduced into the trading. In most cases studied, the experimental participants still seem able to reach an equilibrium, but they may take a number of replays to do so. As in the real world that the experiments seek to mimic, the less information that is available to market participants, the more problematic the establishment of market equilibrium becomes.

To Think About

1. In the experiment described in Table 1, no actual good is ever traded—participants get only the monetary value of the consumer surplus or profits that their trades generate. Does this representation of trade as a simple maximization of monetary payoffs seem reasonable? Or, do you think some actual goods would have to be traded to capture what really happens in market situations?
2. Given the experimental design in Table 1, how would you set up a computer network for the six players? How would buyers and sellers "find" each other? How would they set a price? How long would you give them to do all this? Can you think of any actual markets that work in the way your proposed computer system does?

[1]For a more detailed discussion, see V. Smith, "Experimental Methods in the Political Economy of Exchange," *Science* (October 1986): 167–173.

gain information and use this to modify their expected prices will prices move toward equilibrium.

Cobweb Model

Cobweb model A model of price adjustment in which some trading takes place at nonequilibrium prices.

As a simple illustration of this approach, we first look at the **cobweb model** of price determination. In this model demanders base their decisions on actual market prices, but suppliers decide how much to produce based on last period's price (which they assume will continue into this period). This view of the market assumes the following sequence of events: Firms decide how much they will produce by referring to the previous period's price. They produce this output during the current period and sell it in the market for what demanders are willing to pay. Demanders then bid for this output (perhaps in auctions); in so doing they establish the current market price. This price enters into firms' production decisions for the next period. In this way suppliers exhibit a lagged response to the actions of demanders in determining price.

Figure 14.3 illustrates the working of the cobweb model. There P^* is an equilibrium price because the quantity demanded at this price is exactly equal to the quantity supplied. The price P^* can persist from one period to the next since firms, by referring to the previous period's price (which is also P^*), produce Q^*, which is what demanders are willing to buy at P^* in the current period.

We can see why this model is called the "cobweb" by analyzing the sequence of events that follows if price starts from a nonequilibrium position. Suppose that price starts at P_0 in Panel a in Figure 14.3. In period 1, firms will produce output level Q_1 by referring to P_0. For example, P_0 might represent the average price of wheat from the 1989 grain harvest, and farmers use this information to decide the number of acres to be planted in 1990. Once Q_1 is produced, however, it must be sold in the market for whatever it will bring. Since Q_1 represents a relatively large output level, a low price must prevail in the market in period 1 (call this price P_1) to get demanders to buy this amount. In the grain harvest example, the price of wheat will fall substantially in 1990 from its 1989 level because of the overproduction in 1990.

In period 2, firms will base their output decisions on P_1. They will therefore produce a relatively low output level (Q_2). Demanders will bid for this output level and will drive the market price up to P_2. This price will then affect firms' output decision in period 3. As we can see in Panel a of Figure 14.3, this process will proceed until price converges to its equilibrium level at P^*. Over time, price therefore moves from P_0 to P^* because of the way in which supply and demand interact in the market. The price P^* is therefore a **stable equilibrium,** though nonequilibrium prices are observed for a number of periods.

Stable equilibrium A situation in which market forces cause price to move to its equilibrium level.

Stability of Equilibrium

The interaction we have outlined does not necessarily lead to an equilibrium price. Panel b of Figure 14.3 shows a set of supply and demand curves for

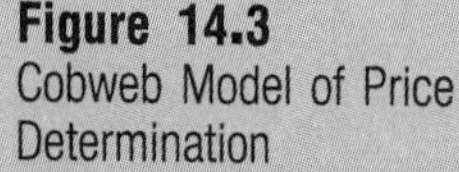

Figure 14.3
Cobweb Model of Price Determination

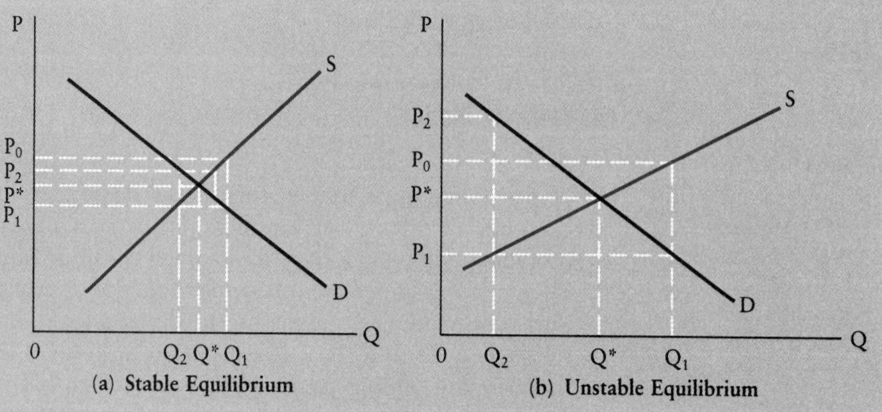

The cobweb model of lagged response to price by firms provides a simple theory of market adjustment. Whether prices will approach an equilibrium level will depend on the relative slopes of the demand and supply curves. In the configuration shown in Panel a, convergence will take place, whereas in Panel b, it will not. A third possibility (not shown) would be for the supply and demand curves to have slopes such that the price perpetually oscillates about P^*.

which the supply curve is somewhat flatter than that in the previous example. By starting at a price of P_0 in Panel b, an argument similar to the one we used for Panel a shows that price will oscillate in wider and wider movements away from P^*. You can follow the sequence of events by which market price moves from P_0 to P_1 to P_2. As Panel b in Figure 14.3 clearly shows, the price P^* is an **unstable equilibrium.** The workings of supply and demand will not suffice to move price to P^* with this particular configuration of supply and demand curves.[3] Since real-world prices probably do not oscillate as wildly as those in Panel b (though Application 14.2: Speculation shows some unusual cases where they have), we must conclude that either most real-world markets have a supply-demand pattern that resembles Panel a or that the real world is characterized by a more complex model than the cobweb model.

Unstable equilibrium
A situation in which market forces cause price to move away from its equilibrium level.

Rational Expectations

The cobweb model is an obvious oversimplification of reality. It would take a peculiar lack of sophistication on the part of buyers and sellers to accept a regularly oscillating price for long, and some kinds of adjustments based on people's expectations of prices are bound to be made. That is, the market

[3]Technically it can be shown that, for the linear demand curves used in this example, stability requires that the supply curve must be more steeply sloped than the demand curve.

APPLICATION 14.2

Speculation

When some people believe there are good reasons for the price of a commodity to move in a particular direction, they may try to profit from such a movement. For example, if speculators believed that the price of a crop were going to move from P_1 to P_2 during the next period in Figure 14.3, they might buy more of the crop this period hoping to make windfall profits out of the price rise. Because speculators will find it profitable to acquire information about true supply-demand conditions in the market, they will maximize profits by taking actions that move the market toward equilibrium. That is, they will sell when price is above its equilibrium level and buy when it is below. Although such speculation will, in the long run, help to stabilize equilibrium market prices, it is possible that in the short run it may lead to wide market gyrations.

Tulipmania

Following the spread of a tulip virus in Holland during the 1630s a wide variety of new bulbs were developed.[1] Because there were no existing markets for these new bulbs, prices fluctuated widely. By 1634, speculating on price movements in bulbs had become a major preoccupation of the Dutch upper class, and tulip trading had started on the stock exchanges in Amsterdam and Rotterdam. Throughout 1635 and 1636, speculators pushed the price of rare bulbs ever higher with the hope of making profits on their purchases. At the height of the trading frenzy, some particularly prized bulbs sold for as much as the equivalent of $50,000. Some economists have pointed to this episode as an example of speculators having a short-run destabilizing effect. Because of the mistaken, though widespread, belief that everyone could make a fortune quickly, bulb prices departed greatly from underlying supply-demand conditions. As might have been expected, the "tulipmania" price bubble was short-lived. In 1637, following a sharp price run-up, the market price of bulbs suddenly fell, and speculators moved rapidly to liquidate their stocks. Although the market for bulbs soon returned to relatively stable conditions, Dutch courts were clogged for many years with lawsuits that resulted from the debacle.

Sugar

A more recent (though less spectacular) example of destabilizing speculation of this type occurred in the market for sugar in 1974. Prices of sugar rose from about 10 cents per pound in late 1973 to over 72 cents per pound in November 1974. Although some part of that movement can probably be explained by shifting supply and demand conditions (crops were poor in some countries and the demand for sugar is relatively price inelastic), a major portion of the increase can be attributed to speculation.[2] At the time of the sugar price increase, there was widespread hoarding of sugar by firms and households in anticipation of further price increases. In addition, the 1973 oil embargo created a shortage mentality that caused some traders to make incautious extrapolations of short-run price movements. Again, it proved impossible for market price to depart forever from its underlying supply-demand equilibrium. By 1977 sugar prices were below their 1973 levels.

To Think About

1. "Buy cheap, sell dear" is a basic principle that should yield speculators long-term profits. Use a simple supply and demand graph to show why this is so. Use the graph also to show why such speculation may help price to adjust to its equilibrium level.
2. To many people, "speculators" are undesirable and almost criminal. For a speculative good such as common stocks or foreign exchange, how would you differentiate between "speculators" and "investors"? Do they have different motives? Do they perform different economic functions?

---

[1] For a discussion of this episode together with some fascinating photographs, see T. Berger, "Tulipomania Was No Dutch Treat to Gambling Burghers," *Smithsonian* (April 1977): 70–77. For a more detailed treatment see P. M. Garber, "Tulipmania," *Journal of Political Economy* (June 1989): 535–560. Garber believes that only common bulbs were subject to speculative price movements. He views the price moves for rare bulbs as being fairly typical of those in the flower industry.

[2] For a discussion, see Council on Wage and Price Stability, "Staff Report on Sugar Prices" (Washington, D.C.: U.S. Government Printing Office, May 1975).

participants may eventually figure out what the equilibrium price is and move to that point without further fluctuations.

A particularly intriguing hypothesis about the formation of price expectations was proposed by Muth in the early 1960s.[4] He suggested that one (and perhaps the only) method of forming expectations that is consistent with general optimizing behavior is to make such expectations on a "rational" basis by incorporating all available information about the market in question. Specifically, a supplier who knew the precise forms of the demand and supply curves in Figure 14.3 could calculate the equilibrium price, P*, as the expected price. If firms use this expected price, supply will be at its equilibrium level, and the market will be free of the fluctuations observed in the cobweb model. In the absence of any other information or transactions costs, equilibrium will be established instantly.

Rational expectations Basing price expectations on complete information about the equilibrium price determined by the interaction of supply and demand in the market.

The information requirements for the **rational expectations** solution are quite severe. Not only must the supplier know the precise values of such magnitudes as the price elasticities of demand and supply, but it must also be assumed that no other random influences affect the supply or demand relationships. Models that relax both of these assumptions have been developed, principally in the field of macroeconomics. As might be expected, the results of the rational expectations approach are not so simple once more realistic assumptions are employed, but the approach has revolutionized economists' thinking about expectations and the attainment of market equilibrium. Application 14.3: Unemployment examines this approach as applied to the study of unemployment.

Information and Economic Efficiency

Existence of imperfect information may not only affect the ability of markets to establish equilibrium prices, but may also call into question the correspondence between competitive prices and economic efficiency. Our proof of the efficiency of competitive prices assumed that these equilibrium prices were known to all economic actors. If some actors are not fully informed about prevailing prices or (what amounts to the same thing) if information about product quality is not freely available, Adam Smith's invisible hand may not be very effective. Incorrect decisions based on faulty information about price or quality can result in an inefficient allocation of resources.

A vast number of economic models seek to explore the consequences of imperfect information about prices. Here we will briefly review some of these models that are based on a competitive framework (that is, models with large numbers of buyers and sellers). In Chapter 16 we will return to the topic of information when we examine product differentiation in markets with relatively few producers.

[4]John Muth, "Rational Expectations and the Theory of Price Movements," *Econometrica* (July 1961): 315–335.

Asymmetric Information and the "Lemons" Problem

Asymmetric information A situation in which buyers and sellers have different amounts of information about a market transaction.

A particularly intriguing problem involving imperfect information occurs when the parties to a transaction possess significantly different (**asymmetric**) amounts of **information.** Since this situation was first examined in detail for the case of used cars by George Akerlof, it is sometimes called the "lemons" problem.[5] Suppose used cars are of two types (good cars and lemons) and only the owner of a car knows for certain into which category that vehicle falls. Since buyers cannot differentiate between good cars and lemons, all used cars of a particular type will sell for the same price—somewhere between the true worth of the two types. The owner of a car will choose to keep his or her car if it is a good one (since a good car is worth more than the prevailing market price), but will sell the car if it is a lemon (since a lemon is worth less than the market price). Consequently, only lemons will be brought to the used-car market, and the quality of cars traded will be less than expected. Of course, this erosion in quality may be retarded by trustworthy used-car dealers, by development of car-buying expertise by the general public, or by sellers providing proof that their cars are trouble-free. But anyone who has ever shopped for a used-car knows the problem of potential lemons is a very real one.

Adverse Selection

Adverse selection When buyers and sellers have different information, market outcomes may exhibit adverse selection—the quality of goods or services traded will be biased toward market participants with better information.

In formal terms, the lemons problem is another example of **adverse selection** in the marketplace (see also Chapter 7). Adverse selection in the used-car market is mirrored in many other markets for used durable goods. Indeed, in some cases (trading between individuals in precious gems, for example) the problem may be so severe as to foreclose practically all exchanges. As we saw earlier, the problem arises in insurance markets when buyers of health or life insurance know more about their own health than do sellers of such insurance. In this case, only high-risk individuals may choose to buy insurance since those who know they are low risk may find insurance too costly. In markets for inputs, adverse selection may be manifested if firms are less able to judge productivity than is the inputs' supplier. Especially productive workers may have no way to illustrate their skills to would-be hirers and may turn down job offers based on employers' perceptions of the average skills of only "typical" workers. In all of these cases, therefore, informational asymmetries may cause competitively determined prices to depart from economic efficiency. Application 14.4: The Winner's Curse in Common Value Auctions looks at how such asymmetries may lead to possibly inefficient outcomes in auctions.

---

[5]G. A. Akerlof, "The Market for 'Lemons': Quality Uncertainty and the Market Mechanism," *Quarterly Journal of Economics* (August 1970): 488–500.

APPLICATION 14.3

Unemployment

A worker is unemployed if he or she is willing to work (at prevailing wages and working conditions) but cannot find a job. Taken at face value, this situation clearly appears to represent a disequilibrium—a potentially mutually beneficial transaction (being hired) between an employer and this worker is not being completed. As is often the case in economics, however, things may not be as simple as they seem. Ever since the 1930s, economists have been debating the causes of unemployment and whether it should be regarded as an equilibrium or a disequilibrium situation. In this application we briefly look at this debate.[1]

An Equilibrium Model

Figure 1 illustrates a very simple model of how the labor market works. In this figure the wage rate[2] (w) influences both firms' willingness to hire workers (as reflected by the demand curve, D) and individuals' willingness to work (as reflected by the supply curve, S). Initially, the equilibrium wage in the labor market is w* with the quantity of labor hired being L*. There may still be some unemployment in this equilibrium situation that arises out of the normal movement of workers from one job to another.

Figure 1
Operation of the Labor Market during Recession

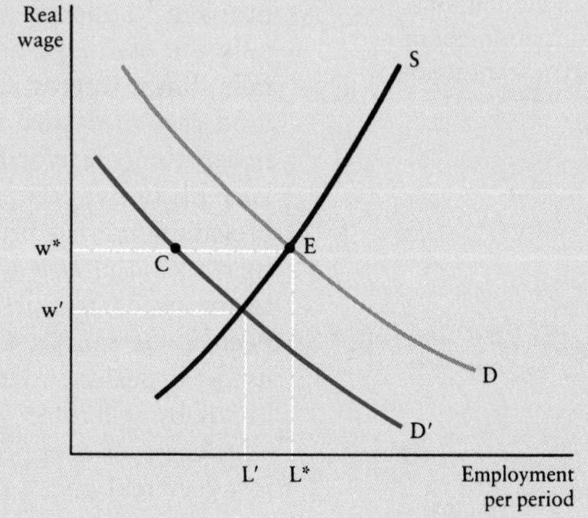

Initially the labor market is in equilibrium with a real wage of w*. If recession reduces the demand for labor to D′, the real wage may not fall to w′. If it remains at w*, unemployment will increase by distance CE.

Suppose now that the demand for labor shifts to D′—perhaps because a recession reduces the demand for the goods that workers produce. The equilibrium labor market model predicts that wages will fall to w′

[1]For a more complete discussion, see R. E. Quandt and H. S. Rosen, *The Conflict between Equilibrium and Disequilibrium Theories: The Case of the U.S. Labor Market* (Kalamazoo, Mich.: Upjohn Institute, 1988).

[2]Here the wage should be interpreted as a "real" wage—that is, a wage rate that is stated relative to the general cost of goods.

Acquisition and Provision of Information

In many situations, however, these conclusions drawn from the lemon model may be premature since they take no account of possible actions by market participants to improve information flows. The inefficiency inherent in the adverse selection outcomes provides a powerful incentive for economic actors to acquire information. It might, therefore, be expected that Smith's invisible hand would also be operating in the market for information. In the used-car case, for example, potential buyers might spend both time and money to appraise used cars they are considering. Sellers might also attempt to provide information by showing maintenance records or by offering limited warranties. That is, they will attempt to "signal" the quality of the car they wish to sell. Of course, such information may not always be accurate. One might, for

and that equilibrium will be reestablished at L′. Again, some normal level of unemployment will exist at L′, but the model in this simple form offers no reason for believing this would be any greater at L′ than at L*.

Cyclical Unemployment

Explaining why unemployment varies over the business cycle, therefore, presents a major challenge to economists who believe in an equilibrium model of the labor market. During the Great Depression of the 1930s, for example, the rate of unemployment exceeded 15 percent for six straight years. In both the 1975–1976 and 1982–1983 recessions, rates of 8 percent or more persisted for some time before they returned to a more usual 4–6 percent range. Such lengthy departures from the normal rate of unemployment are difficult to reconcile with a smoothly functioning equilibrium model.

Disequilibrium

Although some economists have tried to develop elaborate equilibrium models to explain cyclical unemployment,[3] a more common approach has been to assume that the market fails to adjust properly during recessions. If, for example, the wage stays at w* when demand falls to D′, there will be an excess supply of workers given by distance CE. These recession victims will remain unemployed until demand improves. Hence, wage rigidity represents a simple explanation for cyclical unemployment. But why should wages fail to change in response to the decline in the demand for labor? Firms could, after all, hire replacement workers at a wage of w′. Why should they continue to pay w*? Isn't this a violation of the assumption of profit maximization?

Attempting to answer these questions has posed a number of both theoretical and empirical challenges to economists. Most theories attempting to explain wage rigidities have focused on the kinds of implicit contracts (see Chapter 11) that firms have with their workers. Empirical examinations have tried to determine the actual extent of wage movements over the business cycle. Although all of this work has provided various pieces to the puzzle of how the labor market works, there is, as yet, no universally accepted explanation.

[3]One strand of analysis, for example, argues that workers will take the decline in the wage as a sign to consume more leisure currently since the opportunity cost of doing so is temporarily low (see Chapter 19).

To Think About

1. Why does it matter whether cyclical unemployment is an equilibrium or disequilibrium phenomenon? Would different policies to reduce unemployment be appropriate depending on its cause?
2. Economists have also computed a "vacancy rate" for the labor market to measure the percentage of available jobs that remain to be filled. How can vacancies exist together with unemployment? How would you expect the vacancy rate to change over the business cycle?

example, question a ten-year-old car with 45,0000 miles on the odometer. Still, as Application 14.5: Looking for Lemons shows, for the case of pickup trucks, quality deterioration is not a foregone conclusion.

Information and Equilibrium

In general then, the lemons example suggests that information about product quality can be acquired and provided in many different ways and that such information may not always be perfectly accurate. To develop models of how competitive markets operate in such situations is very difficult, and there are no universally accepted results. To illustrate some of the problems in building such models, consider the comparatively simple question of how a market

APPLICATION 14.4

The Winner's Curse in Common Value Auctions

One of the most extensively examined instances of asymmetric information is the behavior of participants in "common value" auctions. In such auctions a particular item is being sold to a group of bidders, each of whom is uncertain as to its true value. When oil companies bid for a tract of land in the Gulf of Mexico or on the North Slope of Alaska, for example, they have only limited information about how much oil the tract will contain. Publishers are in a similar quandary when they make bids for the rights to publish a new novel—they really don't know how well it will sell. Similar informational problems affect the bidding for items as diverse as paintings of undetermined origin, baseball players in the "free agent" draft, or guessing the number of beans in a jar. In all of these cases the item being auctioned has a true value, but the bidders are unsure about what it is.

The Winner's Curse

Faced with these uncertainties, each bidder will make some sort of estimate of what the good being sold is worth and bid accordingly. Because the person making the highest bid will win the item, it seems possible that this bid will be too high. The winner of the auction will be the bidder who has imagined the most inflated value for the item being sold. If we assume that the average bidder's assessment of the item is about right, the high bidder will have paid too much and is sure to be disappointed with the results. This result is sometimes called the "winner's curse."

Of course, a rational bidder will recognize the possibility of overbidding and will adjust his or her strategy accordingly. Even if every bidder at a particular auction follows such a prudent approach, however, deciding how much to bid can be a tricky business, especially for bidders who believe (possibly incorrectly) that the item is quite valuable. Each bidder must take account not only of his or her own valuation, but must also think about how many other bidders there are and what their valuations will be. Only by making such a complete assessment can a bidder with imperfect information guard against overbidding. Needless to say not all auction participants may be able to analyze such a difficult problem completely.

Evidence from Oil Lease Sales

The possibility of a winner's curse being connected with common value auctions was first recognized in connection with bidding for oil leases in the Gulf of Mexico. Several studies of such sales during the 1950s and 1960s have tended to suggest that oil companies typically overbid for the leases they acquired. For example, winning bids often exceeded second place bids by a factor of 3 or more. Clearly the winning bids were based on very optimistic assessments. One 1987 study of over 1,200 leases concludes that firms systematically overbid by nearly 50 percent relative to what would have been (with perfect hindsight) an optimal bidding strategy.[1] They suggest that the winners in these lease sales should not be too pleased with their victories.

To Think About

1. Will the likelihood of a winner's curse be greater in an auction with many participants or one with few participants? How would you feel about winning over 3 or 4 bidders? How about winning over 100 bidders? How should you adapt your bidding strategy to reflect the number of bidders at an auction?
2. If oil companies typically overbid for leases, what can they do about it? Would it make sense for a firm to stay out of such auctions or to reduce its bids unilaterally? Might explicit or implicit collusion improve matters (though it might land the colluders in jail)?

---

[1]K. Hendricks, R. H. Porter and B. Boudreau, "Information, Returns, and Bidding Behavior in OSL Auctions 1954–1969," *Journal of Industrial Economics* (June 1987): 517–542.

equilibrium should be defined. Suppose the quantity demanded of a product can be represented by

$$\text{Quantity demanded} = D(P, \alpha), \tag{14.1}$$

APPLICATION 14.5

Looking for Lemons

The lemons model suggests that asymmetric information will lead to a deterioration in the quality of goods traded in a market. In the used-car case, for example, the model predicts that used cars that are actually traded will be of a lower quality than those that are retained by their original owners. Given this clear prediction, economists have set out to examine a variety of markets to determine whether it is, in fact, borne out or whether various institutions have arisen that help to balance the information needs of buyers and sellers.

Pickup Trucks

Fairly good data exist on maintenance costs for pickup trucks, and these fail to show significant quality deterioration in the market. A 1982 study of pickup purchases during the 1970s found that approximately 60 percent of all such trucks were bought used.[1] After controlling for the mileage that the trucks had traveled, the author found no difference in the repair records for trucks purchased used versus those purchased new. Hence, although it seems likely that the used-truck market does exhibit asymmetric information, this does not appear to result in quality deterioration. Possibly sellers are able to "signal" a truck's true value to would-be buyers by providing repair records. Or possibly, buyers are able to gain some expertise in evaluating pickups by looking at several before they choose which to buy. Unfortunately, the available data do not permit a detailed examination of these various possibilities.

Free Agents in Baseball

After playing in major league baseball for five years, a player can elect to become a "free agent." He is then able to accept contract offers from his own team or from any other team that may be interested. This market in "used" baseball players provides another illustration of asymmetric information since the player's present team will know a great deal more about his physical condition than will any other potential hirer. A team that knows one of its players is injured will let that player go into the free agent market, and the team he moves to may be unpleasantly surprised by his inability to perform.

A 1984 study of player disabilities found that free agents spent almost twice as many days on the disabled list after they were signed than did players whose contracts were renewed by their teams.[2] Such figures tend to suggest that quality deterioration occurs in this market—that many free agents are lemons. Of course, as in the market for pickup trucks, buyers may adapt their behavior to this situation. They may, for example, require physical examinations for players or simply reduce their bids for free agents. Since baseball owners do not want to be saddled with multimillion dollar contracts for "duds," they have a powerful incentive to mitigate the lemons problem.

To Think About

1. Under some versions of the lemons model, quality in a market deteriorates to such an extent that no trading occurs at all. Can you think of any examples of this? Why haven't institutions arisen in these markets to make trading possible by providing a better balance between the informational needs of buyers and sellers?
2. Should the lemons problem be considered an example of inefficiency? Are resources devoted to addressing the problem (e.g., the time spent maintaining repair records for pickup trucks) "wasted"?

[1] E. W. Bond, "A Direct Test of the 'Lemons' Model: The Market for Used Pickup Trucks," *American Economic Review* (September 1982): 836–840.

[2] K. Lehn, "Information Asymmetries in Baseball's Free Agent Market," *Economic Inquiry* (January 1984): 37–44.

where α is the information used by the demander in making his or her decisions. Similarly, supply can be represented by

$$\text{Quantity supplied} = S(P, \beta), \tag{14.2}$$

where β represents the supplier's information. An equilibrium occurs where

$$D(P^*, \alpha) = S(P^*, \beta), \qquad [14.3]$$

where P^* is the equilibrium price for this good given the information α and β. However, as the used car example suggests, this information is chosen as part of demanders' and suppliers' overall decision processes. Furthermore, since the equilibrium price, P^*, reflects this information, rational actors may draw additional information from this price itself. That is, actors may, to some extent, judge quality by price. A rational buyer of expensive cameras, for example, might reason that current prices reflect actual quality differences so he or she need not gain any more information before making a purchase. The fact that other buyers have read *Consumer Reports* can be relied on to ensure that quality differences are already reflected in the market prices. If everyone adopts this position, however, there will not be sufficient pressure on the demand side of the market to assure that such an assumption of efficient pricing is valid.

In these situations, then, the concept of market equilibrium is a complex one—it all depends on how people react to imperfect information. It is possible to develop models in which no such equilibrium exists or in which multiple equilibria exist.[6] Given the current state of information theory, it is not possible to state with any certainty which of these models can be considered to be of general validity.

Equilibrium and Pareto Efficiency

Because of these complexities in defining market equilibria in cases of imperfect information, it is not surprising that there are no fundamental results about the nature of efficient allocations in such situations. It is clear that equilibrium allocations with imperfect information will generally be inferior to allocations with perfect information (as the lemons model suggests). But such a conclusion is not especially interesting. That information is imperfect and costly to acquire is a fact of nature in all economic organizations. The relevant allocational question is which mechanisms produce efficient results from among all those that operate within a given situation. The cost and availability of information pose a series of constraints on any economic system, and efficiency must be defined subject to these constraints. Competitive markets incorporate powerful incentives both to generate and to reveal information. But their efficiency in a variety of imperfect information contexts has not been clearly demonstrated.

Summary

In this chapter we have examined how perfectly competitive markets perform in situations of limited information. The general purpose of this examination

[6]For a discussion, see J. E. Stiglitz "The Causes and Consequences of the Dependence of Quality on Price," *Journal of Economic Literature* (March 1987): 1–48.

was to explore the limits that should be placed on interpretations of the fundamental correspondence between competitive equilibria and economic efficiency. We showed that extending this correspondence to situations involving imperfect information raised many complex questions:

- Information costs may determine how markets adjust to new equilibrium configurations and the time that such adjustments require. For example, whether Walrasian (price) or Marshallian (quantity) adjustment dominates will be importantly influenced by transactions and information costs.
- In some models of market adjustment, disequilibrium prices may occur. The path by which such prices approach equilibrium can be importantly affected by the information available and how expectations are based on that information.
- With asymmetric information, adverse selection may result in economic inefficient allocations, at least in models with no information acquisition possibilities.
- In general, economic actors will wish to acquire and to signal information about market transactions in which they participate. Equilibrium prices (if they exist) will incorporate prevailing information levels and may themselves be sources of information to market participants.

Review Questions

1. What balance of forces does an equilibrium price represent? Why would such forces not be balanced at a nonequilibrium price? How would economic actors know that supply and demand were not in balance?
2. Describe the Walrasian price adjustment mechanism. What types of information motivate price movements? With the usual configuration of supply and demand curves, would price always move toward its equilibrium value if it followed a Walrasian mechanism?
3. Whether markets adjust using the Walrasian or Marshallian mechanism depends mainly on costs. What are some of these costs? The stock market is usually believed to be a market characterized by price adjustment. Explain why this may be so. As Application 14.3 shows, the labor market may be characterized by quantity adjustment. Explain why this may be so and why "sticky wages" pose a problem for macroeconomic stability.
4. Why do "nonequilibrium" prices arise in the cobweb model? What information problems do these reflect? In what sense are the prices in the model really "nonequilibrium"?
5. "The only truly rational expectation about price is its equilibrium value." Do you agree? Doesn't this definition require actors developing such expectations to have too much information? What are some simpler, less costly (though perhaps less accurate) ways in which economic actors might form price expectations?
6. "If speculators follow the simple principle, 'buy cheap, sell dear,' they will both make money and help to equilibrate markets." Explain using a simple supply-demand graph.
7. If, as question 6 suggests, profitable speculation tends to stabilize markets, why are speculators often blamed for causing wild price gyrations? What kinds of price expectations might cause speculators to destabilize a market?
8. What kinds of information do demanders and suppliers need to make "informed" market transactions? Suppose you set out to hire someone to tutor you in microeconomics. Is the price of this transaction all you need to know, or

should more go into your decision? Is the price all the tutor needs to know or might he or she care about other aspects of the transaction?

9. Explain why the "lemons problem" described in this chapter and the problem of adverse selection in insurance described in Chapter 7 are basically the same problem. Show that the definition provided fits both cases.
10. What does "judge quality by price" or "you get what you pay for" mean? Can you name some goods for which this approach to buying seems reasonable? What about the market for these goods suggests such a strategy may be reasonable? Suggest some situations where the strategy might backfire.

Problems

14.1 If the demand curve has a negative slope and the supply curve has a positive slope, the equilibrium price is stable under both Walrasian and Marshallian adjustment. Use a graphic analysis to show that for the case where both demand and supply curves have negative slopes, the equilibrium price will be stable under one method of adjustment, but unstable under the other.

14.2 Suppose that the demand for dog shampoos is given by

$$Q_D = 100 - 5P$$

and the supply by

$$Q_S = 20 + 3P$$

where Q_D and Q_S are the quantity of dog shampoos demanded and supplied each week, respectively.

a. What is the equilibrium price of dog shampoos in this market?
b. Explain why $P = 5$ and $P = 15$ are not equilibrium prices for dog shampoos. How would each of the participants in this market know these were not equilibrium prices?
c. Suppose producers of dog shampoos could lower their price by $1 if they didn't sell out in a week or raise it if they did. Explain the sequence of events by which the price would move from those in part b to its equilibrium value from part a.
d. Graph your results.

14.3 Sometimes economists use the notion of an excess demand function defined as $ED(P) = Q_D(P) - Q_S(P)$. That is, the excess demand for a good at any price is equal to the quantity demanded at that price minus the quantity supplied. Using this notion, show the following:

a. If we graph excess demand on the horizontal axis and price on the vertical axis, this function will usually have a negative slope.
b. An equilibrium price will be one for which $ED(P) = 0$.
c. The equilibrium price will be stable under the Walrasian criterion if the excess demand curve has a negative slope near that price.
d. An excess demand curve may have a negative slope under certain circumstances–what are these circumstances?
e. If the excess demand curve has a negative slope in the neighborhood of an equilibrium price, this price will be unstable under the Walrasian criterion.

14.4 Suppose that the market demand for a particular product is given by

$$Q_D = -2P + 13$$

and the industry supply curve by

$$Q_S = 2P^2 - 12P + 21\,.$$

What are the equilibrium prices for this market? Which of these prices is stable by the Walrasian criterion?

14.5 Suppose that the demand curve for corn at time t is given by

$$Q_t = 100 - 2P_t$$

and that supply in period t is given by

$$Q_t = 70 + E(P_t)$$

where $E(P_t)$ is what suppliers expect the price to be in period t .

a. If in equilibrium $E(P_t) = P_t$, what are the price and quantity of corn in this market?
b. Suppose that suppliers are myopic and use last period's price as their expectation of this year's price (that is, $E(P_t) = P_{t-1}$). If the initial market price of corn is \$8, how long will it take for price to get within \$.25 of the equilibrium price?
c. If farmers have "rational" expectations, how would they choose $E(P_t)$?

14.6 Under the assumptions of part b of problem 14.5, solve explicitly for P_t as a function of the initial price, P_0, and time. Graph this relationship and show that the oscillations about the equilibrium price are damped. Suppose the supply function were instead given by

$$Q_t = 50 + 3P_{t-1}.$$

Would the equilibrium price now be stable?

14.7 The used-car supply in Metropolis consists of 10,000 cars. The values of these cars range from \$5,000 to \$15,000 with exactly one car being worth each dollar amount between these two figures. Used-car owners are always willing to sell their cars for what they are worth. Demanders of used cars in Metropolis have no way of telling the value of a particular car. Their demand depends on the average value of cars in the market ($\overline{P}$) and on the price of the cars themselves (P) according to the equation

$$Q = 1.5\overline{P} - P$$

a. If demanders base their estimate of $\overline{P}$ on the entire used-car market, what will its value be and what will be the equilibrium price of used cars?
b. In the equilibrium described in part a, what will be the average value of used cars actually traded in the market?
c. If demanders revise their estimate of $\overline{P}$ on the basis of the average value of cars actually traded, what will be the new equilibrium price of used cars? What is the average value of cars traded now?
d. Is there a market equilibrium in this situation at which the actual value of $\overline{P}$ is consistent with supply-demand equilibrium at a positive price and quantity?

14.8 A market is "informationally efficient" if *all* available information is instantly and costlessly incorporated into the price of a good.

a. Explain why it is impossible to predict the arrival of new information in such a market.
b. Is it possible to earn private gains from information acquisition in this type of market? What is the optimal information acquisition strategy?
c. In view of your analysis in part b, under what circumstances do you think a market will be informationally efficient?

14.9 The "random walk" hypothesis of the pricing of share prices assumes that these prices move randomly in ways that are totally unpredictable.

a. Explain the relationship between the random walk hypothesis and the concept of informational efficiency defined in problem 14.8.
b. If share prices do follow a random walk, what do stock market advisers do and why are they paid so highly? Do the high salaries of such advisers tend to cast doubt on the random walk hypothesis?

PART 5

IMPERFECT COMPETITION

One of the most important assumptions made throughout Part 4 was that both suppliers and demanders were price takers. All economic actors were assumed to exert no influence on prices, and therefore prices were treated as fixed in their decisions. This behavioral assumption was crucial to most of our analysis, especially that related to the efficiency properties of the competitive price system. In this part we will explore the consequences of dropping the price-taking assumption for suppliers of goods. For most of our presentation, we will continue to assume that demanders are price takers on the presumption that in many important cases there are so many demanders of a good that no one of them has any influence on prices. But, as we shall demonstrate, such an assumption is frequently inappropriate for supplier behavior. Many markets are dominated by only a few sellers. In some cases there may be only one supplier together with major barriers that prevent others from entering the marketplace. Such circumstances raise doubts about the price taker assumption since suppliers will find that their actions do indeed have some influence on market prices. It would, for example, be particularly naive to assume that the managers of General Motors make decisions on the assumption that these decisions cannot affect the market price of automobiles. Instead, models of supplier behavior that assume the firm can influence prices by deciding the types and quantities of cars it will make would seem to provide a better explanation of how the automobile market works. In this part we will examine such models.

We begin our examination of imperfect competition in Chapter 15 with the case of a single supplier of a good. Such a supplier is called a *monopoly*. This supplier faces the entire market demand curve for its product and can choose to operate at any point on that demand curve. That is, the monopoly supplier can choose whatever price-quantity combination on the demand curve it finds most profitable. Its activities are constrained only by the nature of the demand curve for its product, not by the behavior of rival producers. This then is the opposite, polar case from perfect competition in which the existence of many suppliers enforces price-taking behavior on any one firm. In Chapter 15 we will show that it is possible to analyze this case rather completely. We also show in detail why the presence of monopoly results in an allocation of resources that is inefficient. Finally, we illustrate some of the issues that arise in attempting to regulate monopoly in a way that mitigates these inefficiencies.

In Chapter 16 we move from the relatively simple case of monopoly to market structures involving a "few" firms. As we shall see, adding additional suppliers makes matters much more complicated. In such cases any one firm does not face the total market demand curve, but, rather, faces a demand curve for its own output that will have properties determined in part by its rivals' behavior—the demand curve for GM cars depends in part on what Ford and Toyota do. To develop a realistic model, therefore, some assumption must be made about how one firm believes its rivals will behave. Besides exploring some simple models of this type, Chapter 16 also examines situations in which one firm's product is slightly different from that being produced by its rivals. Since many imperfectly competitive markets are characterized by such *differentiated products* (Pontiacs and Toyotas are not identical goods), this type of model has many applications to the real world.

The issues of intrafirm rivalry and product differentiation presented in Chapter 16 can also be approached formally as applications of the economic *theory of games.* In Chapter 17 we provide a brief introduction to some of the tools used in that field. We show how many strategic situations can be interpreted in game-theoretic terms and illustrate how the notion of market equilibrium has analogies in some game-theoretic models. Since concepts drawn from game theory are encountered in many areas of microeconomic theory, Chapter 17 provides important background material for further study. ▲

CHAPTER 15

Pricing in Monopoly Markets

A producer of a good is described as a monopoly if it is the only producer of that good. This single firm faces the entire market demand curve for its output. Using its knowledge of this demand curve, the monopoly makes a decision on how much to produce. Unlike the perfectly competitive firm's output decision (which has no effect on market price), the monopoly output decision will completely determine the good's price. In this sense monopoly markets are the opposite, polar case from perfectly competitive ones. Of course, even though a monopoly has far more market power than a competitive firm, it is not all-powerful. It cannot sell all it wants at whatever price it chooses. The monopoly must still contend with the demand curve for its product and must recognize that it can sell more only by lowering its price. Still, it can choose to operate at any point along the market demand curve that it wishes, so it has considerably more discretion than a price-taking firm.

Causes of Monopoly

The reason monopolies exist is that other firms find it unprofitable or impossible to enter the market. **Barriers to entry** are the source of all monopoly power. If other firms could enter the market, there would, by definition, no longer be a monopoly. There are two general types of barriers to entry: technical barriers and legal barriers.

Barriers to entry
Factors that prevent new firms from entering a market or industry.

Technical Barriers to Entry

A primary technical barrier to entry is that the production of the good in question may exhibit decreasing average cost over a wide range of output levels. That is, relatively large-scale firms are more efficient than small ones. In this situation one firm may find it profitable to drive others out of the industry by price cutting. Similarly, once a monopoly has been established, entry by other firms will be difficult because any new firm must produce at relatively low levels of output and therefore at relatively high average costs. Because this barrier to entry arises naturally as a result of the technology of production, the monopoly created is sometimes called a **natural monopoly.**

Natural monopoly
A firm that exhibits diminishing average cost over a broad range of output levels.

The range of declining average costs for a natural monopoly need only be "large" relative to the market in question. Declining costs on some absolute scale are not necessary. For example, the manufacture of concrete does not exhibit declining average costs over a broad range of output when compared to the total U.S. market. In any particular small town, however, declining average costs may permit a concrete monopoly to be established. The high costs of transporting concrete tend to create local monopolies for this good.

Another technical basis of monopoly is special knowledge of a low-cost method of production. In this case the problem for the monopoly fearing entry by other firms is to keep this technique uniquely to itself. When matters of technology are involved, this may be extremely difficult, unless the technology can be protected by a patent (discussed below). Ownership of unique resources (such as mineral deposits or land locations) or the possession of unique managerial talents may also be a lasting basis for maintaining a monopoly.[1]

Legal Barriers to Entry

Many pure monopolies are created as a matter of law rather than as a matter of economic conditions. One important example of a government-granted monopoly position is the legal protection provided by a patent. Xerox machines and Polaroid cameras are just two notable examples of goods that would-be competitors may be prevented from copying by patent law. Because the basic technology for these products was assigned by the government to only one firm, a monopoly position was established. The rationale of the patent system, originally put forth by Thomas Jefferson, is that it makes innovation more profitable and therefore encourages technical advancement.

[1] "High costs" of entry into a market are sometimes mentioned as a basis for monopoly. Although there are probably cases in which this is correct, it is important to be careful in distinguishing these cases. If there were perfect capital markets, a firm would enter a market as long as the value of future profits exceeded the fixed costs of entry, since it could borrow these costs and repay the loan out of profits.

Whether or not the benefits of such innovative behavior exceed the costs of creating monopolies is an open question.[2]

A second example of a legally created monopoly is the awarding of an exclusive franchise or license to serve a market. These are awarded in cases of public utility (gas and electric) services, communication services, the post office, some airline routes, some television and radio station markets, and a variety of other businesses. The argument usually put forward in favor of creating these monopolies is that having only one firm in the industry is more desirable than open competition.

Several reasons are given for the desirability of such policies. In some cases it is argued that the firm is a natural monopoly. Average cost is diminishing over a broad range of output levels, and minimum average cost can be achieved only by organizing the industry as a monopoly. The public utility and communications industries are representative of these potential natural monopolies. It seems unnecessarily costly to have two or more overlapping local telephone or electricity distribution networks when one will do quite well. Other cases of government franchises (certain airline routes, the post office) do not appear to be natural monopolies, and the reasons for creating monopolies in these cases are less clear.

In some instances it is argued that restrictions on entry into certain industries are needed to assure adequate quality standards (licensing of physicians, for example) or to prevent environmental harm (franchising businesses in the national parks). In many cases there are sound reasons for such entry restrictions, but in some cases, as Application 15.1: Entry Restriction by Licensing shows, the reasons are obscure. The restrictions act mainly to limit the competition faced by existing firms.

Profit Maximization

In order to maximize profits, a monopoly will choose to produce that output level for which marginal revenue is equal to marginal cost. Since the monopoly, in contrast to a perfectly competitive firm, faces a downward-sloping demand curve for its product, marginal revenue will be less than market price. To sell an additional unit, the monopoly must lower its price on all units to be sold in order to generate the extra demand necessary to absorb this marginal unit. In equating marginal revenue to marginal cost, the monopoly will produce an output level for which price exceeds marginal cost. This feature of monopoly pricing is the primary focus of our analysis of the distorting effect of a monopoly on resource allocation later in this chapter.

[2]Some economists have argued that inventors should be rewarded directly by the government and that the invention should then be made available to all firms at no cost. Ideally the prize to inventors would provide the incentive that the patent system currently provides without creating the monopolies that arise under patents. In practice, however, it would be very difficult to decide how much a particular invention is "worth."

APPLICATION 15.1

Entry Restriction by Licensing: Dry Cleaning and Liquor Stores

State governments license many occupations and impose stiff legal penalties on people who practice the business without a license. The principal reason usually stated for such licensing is to assure the safety and quality of the service provided. Using this rationale, states have licensed physicians, dentists, optometrists, and a variety of other occupations. For many of these occupations licensing seems warranted—no one wants to be treated by a quack when he or she is seriously ill. In some cases, however, the urge to license may go too far. In California, for example, it has been estimated that more than 25 percent of the work force is licensed by 52 different regulatory boards. Occupations such as embalmers, guide dog trainers, appliance repairers, and golf course designers are all licensed, though consumer gains in terms of quality or safety from such licensing seem to be unlikely. Here we look in more detail at two specific cases of licensing: dry cleaners and liquor stores.

Entry Restrictions in Dry Cleaning

An alternative explanation for licensing is that existing firms find it in their interest to promote entry restrictions to preserve the market for themselves. A good illustration is provided by dry cleaners in California.[1] In order to enter the business, a would-be cleaner must pass examinations in a variety of specialties (fur cleaning, hat renovating, spot removal, and so forth). In order to take such exams, one must usually attend a dry cleaning "school," and even then, pass rates tend to be very low. Those who try to skirt this process and take in some laundry on the side face stiff fines and even jail sentences for "practicing dry cleaning without a license." Whether Californians have cleaner clothes than the rest of us as a result of all this is unclear. Several studies have found that citizens of that state do pay more for their cleaning and that profits in the industry are higher than in other states. It is no wonder that existing dry cleaning firms are the staunchest defenders of continued regulation by the Board of Fabric Care.

Liquor Stores

Following Prohibition, states adopted a variety of restrictions on the way in which liquor could be sold. Currently, 16 states operate liquor store monopolies—in those states you have to buy liquor from a "State Store" and usually pay extra for the pleasure of doing so. In thirty-four other states liquor stores are licensed and subject to a number of other restrictions on their advertising and pricing policies. The purported rationale for such constraints is to control some of the undesirable side effects of liquor consumption and to ensure that liquor store operators meet certain standards of acceptability. A number of studies of liquor licensing have failed to discern any clear evidence of beneficial effects of such entry restrictions. They have, however, found that liquor prices are higher in states with stringent licensing and other regulations.[2] It is no wonder that existing license owners are among the most vocal opponents to the granting of additional licenses ("This town only needs one liquor store") or to the opening up of competition by allowing grocery stores to sell liquor.

To Think About

1. Can you think of good reasons for regulating entry into the dry cleaning or liquor store business? Is licensing needed to assure quality or other goals? How would you judge whether these goals are met?
2. Why do you think some states have chosen to operate liquor store monopolies whereas others have not? What are the laws in your state? Who are the gainers and losers under the current arrangement relative to a competitive market?

[1]This example is based on David Kirp and Eileen Soffer, "Taking Californians to the Cleaners," *Regulation* (September/October 1985): 24–26. The puns in the article are highly recommended.

[2]For a discussion, see J. K. Smith, "An Analysis of State Regulations Governing Liquor Store Licensees," *Journal of Law and Economics* (October 1982): 301–319.

Figure 15.1
Profit Maximization and Price Determination in a Monopoly Market

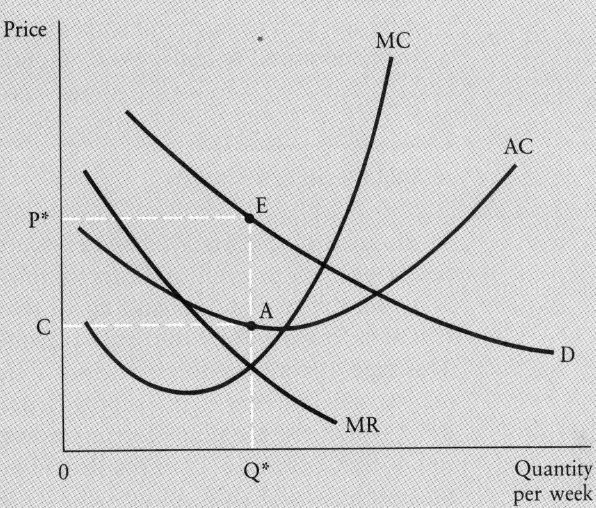

A profit-maximizing monopolist produces that quantity for which marginal revenue is equal to marginal cost. In the diagram this quantity is given by Q*, which will yield a price of P* in the market. Monopoly profits can be read as the rectangle P*EAC.

The profit-maximizing output level for a monopoly is given by Q* in Figure 15.1.[3] For that output, marginal revenue is equal to marginal costs, and profits are maximized. If a firm produced slightly less than Q*, profits would fall, since the revenue lost from this cutback (MR) would exceed the decline in production costs (MC). A decision to produce more than Q* would also lower profits since the additional costs from increased production would exceed the extra revenues from selling the extra output. Consequently, profits are at a maximum at Q*, and a profit-maximizing monopoly will choose this output level.

Given the monopoly's decision to produce Q*, the demand curve D indicates that a market price of P* will prevail. This is the price that demanders as a group are willing to pay for the output of the monopoly. In the market,

[3]In Figure 15.1, and in the other diagrammatic analyses in this chapter, no distinction is made between the behavior of a monopoly in the short run and in the long run. The analysis is the same in both cases, except that different sets of cost curves would be used depending on the possibilities for adjustment that are assumed to be feasible for the firm. Notice though that in the long run, a monopoly will not in general choose that level of capital output for which long-run average cost is a minimum. The only situation in which this would occur would be if MR and MC happened to intersect at the low point of the AC curve. For a multiplant monopoly, however, the firm may vary its number of plants so that production will take place at the minimum average cost of each of them.

an equilibrium price-quantity combination of P*, Q* will be observed.[4] This equilibrium will persist until something happens (such as a shift in demand or a change in costs) to cause the monopoly to alter its output decision.

Monopoly Supply Curve

In the theory of perfectly competitive markets we presented earlier, it was possible to speak of an industry supply curve. We constructed this curve by allowing the market demand curve to shift and observing the supply curve that was traced out by the series of equilibrium price-quantity combinations. This type of construction is not possible for monopoly markets. With a fixed market demand curve, the supply "curve" for a monopoly will be only one point—namely, the point corresponding to the quantity at which MR = MC (point E in Figure 15.1). If the demand curve should shift, the marginal revenue curve would shift along with it, and a new profit-maximizing output would be chosen. However, to connect the resulting series of equilibrium points would have little meaning and would not represent a supply curve. The set of points might have a very strange shape, depending on how the market demand curve's elasticity (and its associated MR curve) changed as the curve was shifted outward. In this sense the monopoly firm has no well-defined supply curve. Instead, each demand curve represents a unique profit-maximizing opportunity for a monopoly, and each has to be studied independently.

Monopoly Profits

Economic profits earned by the monopolist can be read directly from Figure 15.1. These are shown by the rectangle P*EAC and again represent the profit per unit (price minus average cost) times the number of units sold. These profits will be positive when, as in the figure, market price exceeds average total cost. Since no entry is possible into a monopoly market, these monopoly profits can exist even in the long run. For this reason some authors call the profits that a monopoly earns in the long run **monopoly rents.** These profits can be regarded as a return to the factor that forms the basis of the monopoly (such as a patent, a favorable location, or the only liquor license in town). Some other owner might be willing to pay that amount in rent for the right to operate the monopoly and obtain its profits. Application 15.2:

Monopoly rents
The profits that a monopoly earns in the long run.

[4]This combination will be on an elastic section of the demand curve. This will be true because MC is positive so for a profit maximum MR must also be positive. But, if marginal revenue is positive, demand must be elastic, as we showed in Chapter 10 (see especially Equation 10.8). One conclusion to be drawn is that industries that are found to operate along an inelastic portion of the demand curve for their product are not exercising strong monopoly power.

APPLICATION 15.2

Deregulation and the Value of Stock Exchange Seats

The value of a monopoly firm to a would-be buyer depends on the value of the profits the firm is able to generate. The profits depend on the location of the demand curve for the monopolist's product. Shifts in demand can affect potential profits and the market value of the monopoly itself. Table 1 illustrates this for seats on the New York Stock Exchange.

Long-Term Price Patterns

The prices of these seats have fluctuated widely over time. They reached their peak value in 1929 in response to the huge stock trading activity (and brokerage profits) in that year. Prices were relatively low throughout the Depression and during World War II. In the 1960s, trading activity in stocks picked up, which was again reflected in the market value of exchange seats. Although trading volume continued to be high in the 1970s, a number of factors reduced monopoly profits available from New York Stock Exchange membership. The most important was that a growing proportion of stock trades were made off the New York Stock Exchange as improved methods of communication reduced the need for a central marketplace. In a related development, after several years of prodding by the Securities and Exchange Commission, the New York Stock Exchange eliminated fixed commission rates on May 1, 1975. The sales price for exchange memberships reflected these pro-competition developments and by 1977 had fallen to less than one-tenth of the price in 1929.

Table 1
Changing Values of Monopoly Rights: Stock Exchange Seats

Year	Price of an Exchange Seat in Thousands of Dollars
1905	$ 72
1925	99
1929	625
1945	49
1960	135
1970	130
1975	55
1977	42

Source: The New York Stock Exchange Fact Book, 1976 (New York: The New York Stock Exchange, 1976), pp. 58 and 82. 1977 data supplied by the author. All prices are the lowest bid price in a given year.

Deregulation and Brokerage Commission

Results of the "May Day" deregulation of the securities industry were also reflected in brokerage commissions. Table 2 records the trend in brokerage commission rates (in 1975 prices) for the three years following the 1975 decision. For institutional trading, the rates fell dramatically—by 1978 they stood at about 30 percent of their pre–May Day level. For individual rates, some modest declines were also apparent, though in this case the costs of handling individual accounts probably slowed the decline. Prior to deregulation, high institutional brokerage rates tended to shield individuals from some costs of the brokerage services they received (research on stocks, for example), whereas following deregulation, this subsidization no longer existed.

To Think About

1. Prior to "May Day," 1972, many brokers argued that restrictions on entry were necessary to maintain an "orderly central market" for stocks. Would free entry into the brokerage business lead to more unstable stock prices? What have been the results in the years since deregulation?
2. Can you think of other monopoly rights that are traded in the market (for example, what kinds of licenses are bought and sold)? How are such rights created? Who usually gets the proceeds from their sale?

Table 2
Average Stock Commission Rates in Cents per Share (Constant 1975 Dollars)

	Institutional Trades	Individual Trades
1975	27.6¢	32.6¢
1976	18.0	30.3
1977	14.2	28.9
1978	11.5	27.3

Source: Calculated from S. M. Tinic and R. R. West, "The Securities Industry under Negotiated Commissions: Changes in the Structure and Performance of New York Stock Exchange Member Firms," *The Bell Journal of Economics* (Spring 1980): 36.

Deregulation and the Value of Stock Exchange Seats shows that these rights can be quite valuable. This value can also erode immediately if the firm's monopoly profits are threatened.

What's Wrong with Monopoly?

Firms that have a monopoly position in a market are criticized for a variety of reasons. It has been argued that monopolies earn excess profits; give poor, unresponsive service; exploit their employees; stifle technical progress; and distort the allocation of resources. Although each of these complaints may have some truth to it, only two are discussed here: the profitability of monopoly and the effect of monopoly on resource allocation. Some of the other arguments are investigated in other sections of this chapter.

Profitability

Since perfectly competitive firms earn no pure profits in the long run, a firm with a monopoly in a market can earn higher profits than if the market were competitive. This does not imply, however, that monopolies necessarily earn huge profits. Two equally strong monopolies may differ greatly in their profitability. It is the ability of monopolies to raise price above *marginal* cost that reflects their monopoly power. Since profitability reflects the difference between price and *average* cost, profits are not necessarily a sign of monopoly power.

Figure 15.2 exhibits the cost and demand conditions for two firms with essentially the same degree of monopoly power (that is, the divergence between price and marginal cost is the same in both panels). The monopoly in Panel a earns a high level of profits, whereas the one in Panel b actually earns zero in profits since price equals average cost. Hence, excess profitability is not inevitable, even for a strong monopoly.

More than the size of monopoly profits, people are likely to object to the distribution of these profits. If the profits go to relatively wealthy owners at the expense of less well-to-do consumers, there may be valid objections to monopoly profits no matter what their size. Profits from a monopoly may not necessarily always go to the wealthy, however. For example, consider the decision of Navajo blanket makers to form a monopoly to sell their products to tourists at the Grand Canyon. In this situation the monopoly profits make income distribution more equal by transferring income from more wealthy tourists to low-income Navajos.

Distortion of Resource Allocation

Economists (who tend to worry about such matters) raise a second objection to monopolies: that their existence distorts the allocation of resources. Monopolies intentionally restrict their production in order to maximize profits.

Figure 15.2
Monopoly Profits Depend on the Relationship between the Demand and Average Cost Curves

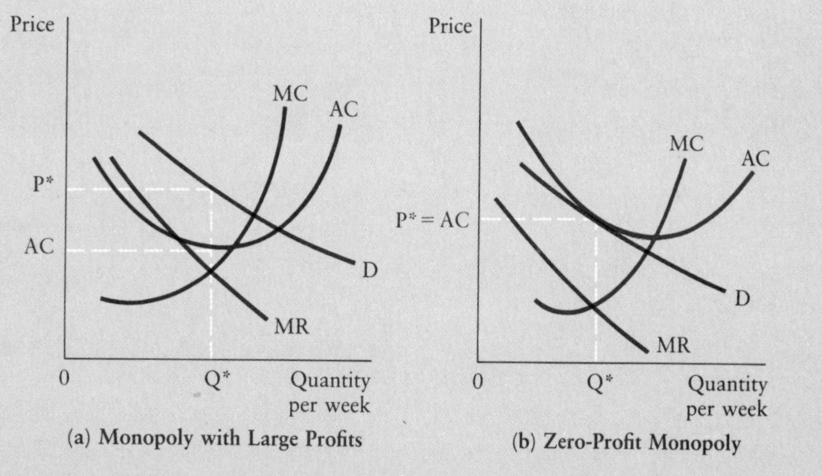

(a) Monopoly with Large Profits

(b) Zero-Profit Monopoly

Both of the monopolies in this figure are equally "strong" in that they have similar divergences between market price and marginal cost. Because of the location of the demand and average cost curves, however, it turns out that the monopoly in Panel a earns high profits, whereas that in Panel b earns no profits. The size of profits is not a measure of the strength of a monopoly.

The discrepancy between price and marginal cost shows that at the monopoly's profit-maximizing output level consumers are willing to pay more for an extra unit of output than it costs to produce that output. From a social point of view, output is too low and some mutually beneficial transactions are being missed.

Figure 15.3 illustrates this observation by comparing the output that will be produced in a market characterized by perfect competition with the output that will be produced in the same market when it contains only one firm. The figure assumes that the monopoly produces under conditions of constant marginal cost and that the competitive industry also exhibits constant costs with the same minimum long-run average cost as the monopolist—an assumption we question in the next section. In this situation a perfectly competitive industry would choose output level Q*, where long-run supply and demand intersect. At this point price is equal to average and marginal cost. A monopoly would choose output level Q**, for which marginal revenue is equal to marginal cost. The restriction in output (Q* − Q**) is then some measure of the allocation harm done by monopoly. Because of the way in which the market is organized, fewer resources are being devoted to the production of the good than the demand curve warrants. People would be willing to pay P** for additional output, which would only cost MC. However, the monopolist's market control and desire to maximize profits prevent the additional resources from being drawn into the industry to fill this demand.

As an admittedly inane example of this distortion, suppose a local hamburger joint has a monopoly in the production of chili dogs because its cook

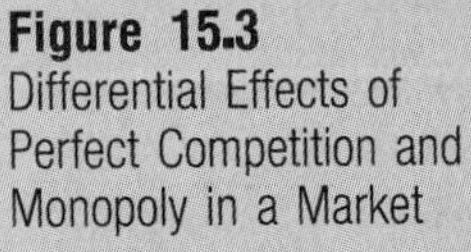

Figure 15.3
Differential Effects of Perfect Competition and Monopoly in a Market

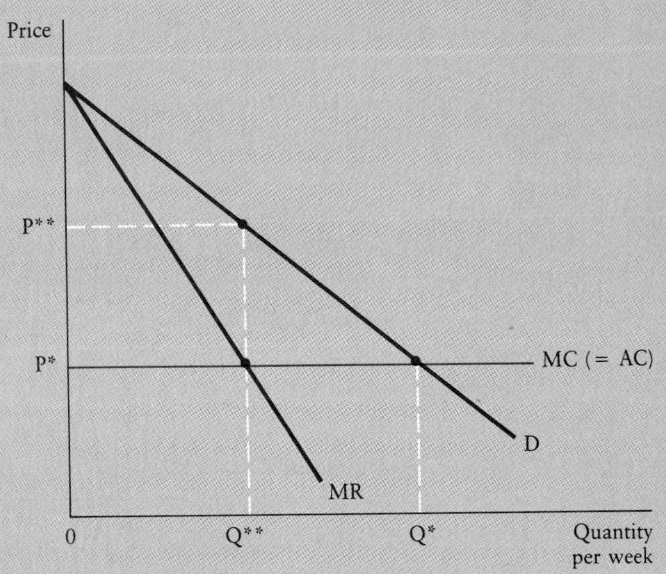

A perfectly competitive industry would produce output level Q* for which price equals marginal (and long-run average) cost. A monopoly, by recognizing the downward slope of the demand curve, would produce Q** where marginal revenue equals marginal cost. This output reduction is a measure of the allocational cost of monopolies. In some cases it may be possible to place a value on this loss in output.

is the only one in town capable of concocting them. To maximize profits the owner of the monopoly restricts chili dog output to a point at which each dog sells for $2.00, but, at the margin, costs only $1.00 in terms of ingredients and the cook's time. Why is this inefficient? Because the well-being of both the cook and chili dog consumers could be improved by further trading. If the cook agreed to sell chili dogs at $1.50 to people who came around to the back door, overall welfare would be improved. Consumers would be better-off (since they would save $.50 per dog), and the cook would be better-off (by effectively getting a higher wage). Of course, the monopoly owner would prevent these illicit sales since they would undercut the profits being made. But the fact that such unexploited mutually beneficial trading opportunities exist is clear evidence that resources (here the cook's time) are not being used efficiently.

Measuring Monopolistic Distortions

Monopolies cause an artificial restriction in output together with an increase in price and thereby distort the allocation of resources. To put a dollar figure on this distortion, economists use the notion of consumer surplus that we introduced in Chapter 6.

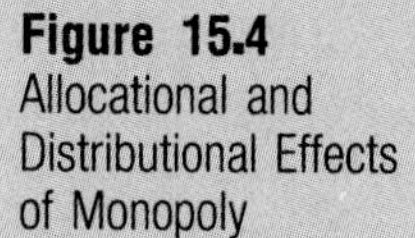

Figure 15.4
Allocational and Distributional Effects of Monopoly

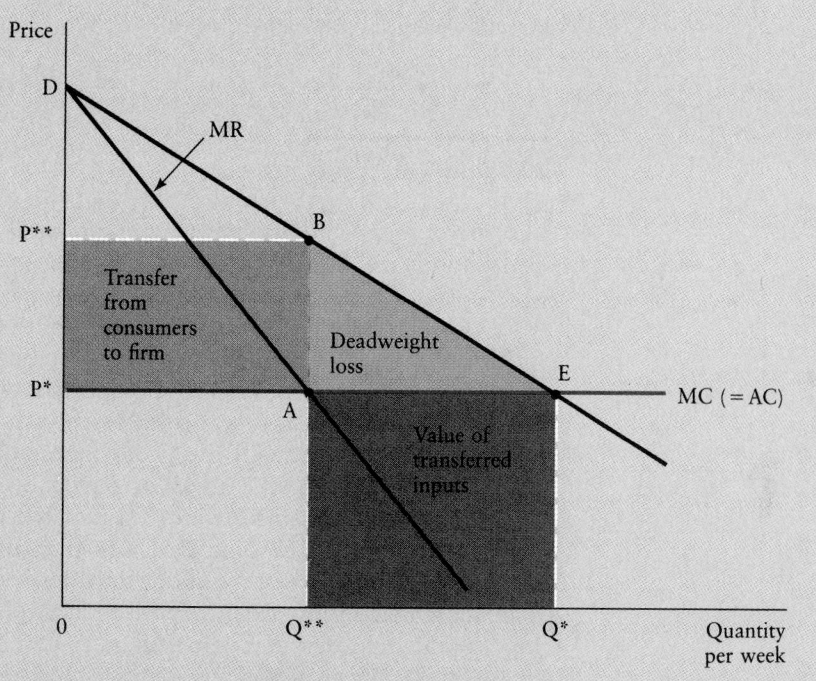

This figure repeats Figure 15.3 to study further the effects of monopolization. Consumer expenditures and productive inputs worth AEQ*Q** are reallocated into the production of other goods. Consumer surplus equal to P**BAP* is transferred into monopoly profits. There is a deadweight loss given by BEA.

Figure 15.4 repeats our previous illustration of the output restriction by a monopoly. When the market is competitively organized, Q* is produced at a price of P*. As we showed in Chapter 6, the total value to consumers of this output level is given by the area under the demand curve (that is, by area DEQ*0), for which they pay P*EQ*0. Total consumer surplus is given by the triangle DEP*.

If this market is monopolized, only Q** is produced, and the price of this output is P**. The restriction in output and consequent price rise has had several effects. The total value of this good that consumers receive has been reduced in Figure 15.4 by the area BEQ*Q**. This reduction is not a total loss, however, since consumers previously had to pay AEQ*Q** for these goods, and they may now spend this money elsewhere. Since the monopoly produces less, it needs to hire fewer inputs. These released inputs will be used to produce those other goods that consumers buy. The loss of consumer surplus given by the area BEA is, however, an unambiguous reduction in welfare as a result of the monopoly. Some authors refer to triangle BEA as the **deadweight loss** from a monopoly. This loss is similar to the excess burden from a

Deadweight loss
A loss of consumer surplus that is not transferred to another economic actor.

tax which we illustrated in Application 6.1. It is the best single measure of the allocational harm caused by monopoly.

Distributional Effects

In addition to the allocational effect of monopolization of a market, there is a distributional effect, which can also be seen in Figure 15.4. At the monopoly's output level of Q^{**}, there exist monopoly profits given by the area $P^{**}BAP^*$. In the case of perfect competition, this area was a part of the consumer's surplus triangle. If the market is a monopoly, that portion of a consumer's surplus is transferred into monopoly profits. The area $P^{**}BAP^*$ in Figure 15.4 does not necessarily represent a loss of social welfare. It does measure the redistributional effects of a monopoly, and these may be undesirable. In order to make such an assessment, however, we would have to introduce an explicit concept of equity so that the welfare of the firm's owners and consumers could be compared. Concepts of equity are not necessary to demonstrate the nature of the allocational loss represented by area BEA. That is an unambiguous loss from the monopolization of the market. If the market were competitive, output would expand to Q^*, and overall welfare would increase by the extent of this area.

Monopolists' Costs

Our analysis in Figures 15.3 and 15.4 assumed that monopolists and competitive firms have essentially the same costs of production. A deeper analysis suggests this may not in fact be the case. Monopoly profits, after all, provide a tantalizing target for firms, and they may spend real resources to achieve those profits. They may, for example, adopt extensive advertising campaigns or invest in ways to erect barriers to entry against other firms and hence obtain monopoly profits. Similarly, firms may seek special favors from the government in the form of tariff protection, restrictions on entry through licensing, or favorable treatment from a regulatory agency. Costs associated with these activities (such as lobbyists' salaries, legal fees, or advertising expenses) may make monopolists' costs exceed those in a competitive industry.

The possibility that costs may be different (and presumably higher) for a monopolist than for a firm in a competitive industry creates some complications for measuring monopolistic distortions to the allocation of resources. In this case, some potential monopoly profits will be dissipated into monopoly-creating costs, and it is possible that some of those costs (advertising, for example) may even shift the demand curve facing the producer. Such effects seriously complicate Figure 15.4, and we will not analyze them in detail

Table 15.1
Effects of Monopolization on the Market for Cassette Tapes

Demand Conditions					Consumer Surplus		
Price	Quantity (Tapes per Week)	Total Revenue	Marginal Revenue	Average and Marginal Cost	Under Perfect Competition	Under Monopoly	Monopoly Profits
$9	1	$ 9	$9	$3	$ 6	$ 3	$ 3
8	2	16	7	3	5	2	3
7	3	21	5	3	4	1	3
6	4	24	3	3	3	0	3
5	5	25	1	3	2	—	—
4	6	24	−1	3	1	—	—
3	7	21	−3	3	0	—	—
2	8	16	−5	3	—	—	—
1	9	9	−7	3	—	—	—
0	10	0	−9	3	—	—	—
				Totals	$21	$6	$12

□ Competitive equilibrium: (P = MC).
□ Monopoly equilibrium: (MR = MC)

here.[5] Application 15.3: Social Costs of Monopoly in the United States shows how the costs induced by monopoly-seeking activities may have a major impact on the estimated degree of the economic harm that monopolies do.

A Numerical Illustration of Deadweight Loss

As a numerical illustration of the types of calculations made by economists in studying the effects of monopoly, consider again the example of cassette tape sales introduced in Chapter 10. Table 15.1 repeats some of the information about this market originally presented in Table 10.1. Assume now that tapes have a marginal cost of $3 per tape. Under a situation of marginal cost pricing, tapes would also sell for $3 each, and as Table 15.1 shows, seven tapes per week would be bought. Consumer surplus can be computed as the amount people were willing to pay for each tape less what they actually pay ($3). For example, someone who was willing to pay $9 for the first tape sold paid only $3. He or she received a consumer surplus of $6. The sixth column of Table 15.1 makes a similar computation for each level of output from one

[5]For a relatively simple treatment, see R. A. Posner, "The Social Costs of Monopoly and Regulation," *Journal of Political Economy* (August 1975): 807–827. Posner also makes the interesting point that social costs of crime (such as robbery) may be, as for the case of monopoly, understated unless the resources invested in crime prevention are also taken into account.

APPLICATION 15.3

Social Costs of Monopoly in the United States

Arnold Harberger was one of the first economists to use the kind of analysis we have been discussing to estimate the allocational losses from monopolization of markets in the U.S. economy.[1] Harberger's method was rather simple. First, he assembled cost and profit data for 73 different industries. For each industry he estimated the percent by which price exceeded average cost. This is equivalent to measuring the distance $P^{**} - P^*$ in Figure 15.4. For example, Harberger found that prices in the cement industry exceeded average costs by 8.4 percent. Next, Harberger calculated the expansion in demand $(Q^* - Q^{**})$ that would occur if prices were lowered to the competitive level. By assuming an elasticity of demand for cement of −1.0, the quantity of cement demanded would be increased by 8.4 percent if competitive prices prevailed. Using those two figures, he then calculated the area of the triangle BEA $[= \frac{1}{2} \times (P^{**} - P^*)(Q^* - Q^{**})]$ as a measure of the welfare loss from monopoly. For the case of cement, this loss amounted to $420,000 for the period under investigation (1924–1928). Making similar calculations for the other 72 industries in his sample, Harberger concluded that the total welfare loss from monopolies was about $150 million. This amounted to about 0.1 percent of gross national product during the period. Most more recent studies have arrived at similar estimates. Although monopoly losses may be relatively large in some industries, in comparison to the overall output of the economy they are rather small.

Monopolist's Costs

Some economists believe these types of calculations substantially understate the social costs of monopoly because they do not take account of possible differences in costs between monopolies and competitive firms. Taking account of such differences, it is claimed, may substantially reverse the notion that the allocational costs of monopoly are small. For example, a 1978 study by K. Cowling and D. C. Mueller estimated the portion of firms' costs that went toward creating monopoly profits.[2] From those estimates the authors calculated that monopolistic distortions may have represented as much as 13 percent of U.S. GNP in 1973. Estimates of such distortions were particularly large for automobile companies (they amounted to more than $1 billion for General Motors) and for household products companies (nearly $500 million each for Unilever and Procter & Gamble). The estimates are controversial because of the necessary arbitrariness in deciding which costs are really directed toward creating a monopoly position. For example, Cowling and Mueller included *all* advertising costs in that category, though they admit that some portion of these expenditures is probably unrelated to monopolistic goals. Despite this arbitrariness, the estimates illustrate the potential importance of the allocational effects of monopolies in situations where they may have significant effects on production costs.

To Think About

1. If the social cost of monopoly is so small (about 0.1 percent of GNP), why does the U.S. government spend so much on antimonopoly regulation through the Federal Trade Commission and the Department of Justice? Is the extent of such efforts misplaced, or does it seek goals (that is, preventing monopoly profits) other than just improving the allocation of resources?
2. The notion that monopolies may make expenditures in order to achieve monopoly profits has applications in other fields as well. Can you think of other ways in which firms may make "rent-seeking" expenditures in order to obtain favorable market positions for themselves?

---

[1]Arnold Harberger, "Monopoly and Resource Allocation," *American Economic Review* (May 1954): 77–87.

[2]K. Cowling and D. C. Mueller, "The Social Cost of Monopoly Power," *Economic Journal* (December 1978): 727–748.

to seven tapes. As the table shows, total consumer surplus is $21 per week when price is equal to marginal cost.

Suppose now that the tape market is monopolized by a single local merchant with a marginal cost of $3. This profit-maximizing firm will supply four tapes per week since at this level of output marginal revenue equals marginal cost. At this level of sales, price will be $6 per tape, profit per tape will be $3, and the firm will have total profits of $15. These profits represent a transfer of what was previously consumer surplus for the first four buyers of tapes. The seventh column of Table 15.1 computes consumer surplus figures for the monopolized situation. With a price of $6, for example, the buyer of the first tape now receives a consumer surplus of only $3 ($9 − $6)—the other $3 he or she enjoyed under marginal cost pricing has been transferred into $3 of profits for the monopoly. As Table 15.1 shows, total consumer surplus under the monopoly amounts to only $6 per week. When combined with the monopolist's profits of $12 per week, it is easy to see that there is now a deadweight loss of $3 per week ($21 − $18). Some part of what was previously consumer surplus has simply vanished with the monopolizing of the market.

Market Separation and Price Discrimination

Price discrimination The practice of charging different prices for a good in different markets.

A firm may have a monopoly position in two different markets for the same good. If these markets are effectively separated so buyers cannot shift their purchasing from one market to the other, the monopolist may be able to increase profits and reduce consumer surplus further by practicing **price discrimination.** The profit-maximizing decision would be to produce that quantity in each market for which marginal revenue equals marginal cost. This may lead to different prices for the same good in the two markets. If the markets can be kept separate by the monopoly, these price differences can persist even though they are unrelated to actual production costs.

A Graphic Analysis

Such a discriminating situation is shown graphically in Figure 15.5. The figure is drawn so that the market demand and marginal revenue curves in the two markets share the same vertical axis, which records the price charged for the good in each market. For simplicity the figure also assumes that marginal cost is constant over all levels of output. The profit-maximizing decision for the monopoly is to produce Q_1^* in the first market and Q_2^* in the second market; these output levels obey the MR = MC rule for each market. The prices in the two markets will then be P_1 and P_2, respectively. It is clear from the figure that the market with the more inelastic demand curve will have the higher

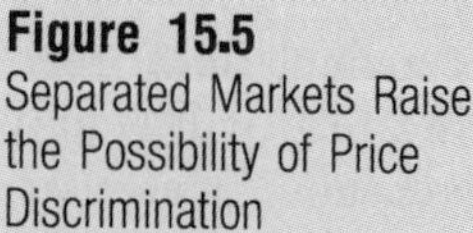

Figure 15.5
Separated Markets Raise the Possibility of Price Discrimination

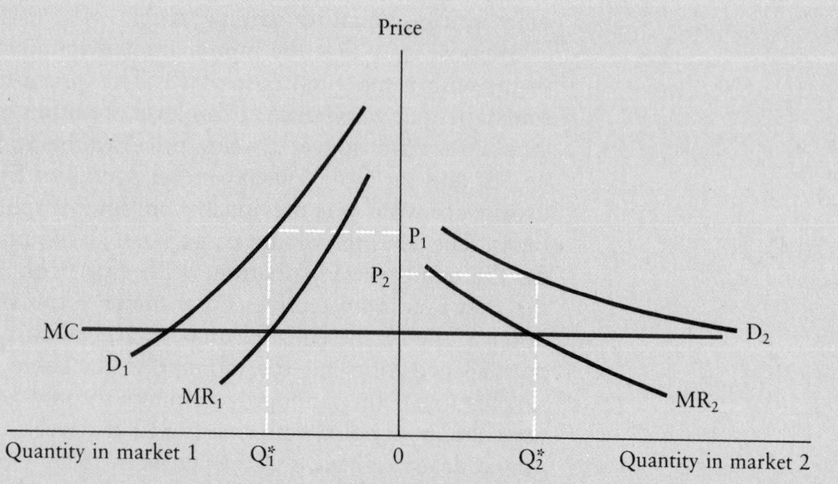

If two markets are separate, a monopolist can maximize profits by selling its product at different prices in the two markets. The firm would choose that output for which MC = MR in each of the markets. The diagram shows that the market that has a less elastic demand curve will be charged the higher price by the price discriminator.

price.[6] The price-discriminating monopolist will charge a higher price in that market in which quantity purchased is less responsive to price changes. Although the analysis in Figure 15.5 assumes that marginal costs are constant, an identical result would hold in the more realistic case of increasing marginal costs. The price discriminator would charge higher prices in the market in which demand is less elastic.

Conditions for Successful Price Discrimination

Whether a monopoly is successful in price discrimination depends critically on its ability to keep the markets separated. In some cases, that separation may be geographic. For example, book publishers tend to charge higher prices in the United States than abroad since foreign markets are more competitive and subject to illegal copying. In this case the oceans enforce market separation since few people would travel abroad simply to buy books. Such a discriminatory policy would not work if transportation costs were low, however. As chain stores that charge different prices in different parts of town have discovered, people will flock to where the bargains are.

[6] *Proof:* Since $MR = P(1 + 1/e)$, $MR_1 = MR_2$ implies $P_1(1 + 1/e_1) = P_2(1 + 1/e_2)$. If $e_1 > e_2$ (if the demand in market 1 is less elastic), then P_1 must exceed P_2 for this equality to hold.

Price discrimination by time of sale may also be possible. For example, tickets to late night or afternoon showings of motion pictures are usually cheaper than for evening shows. Discriminating against those who wish to attend prime-time shows succeeds because the good being purchased cannot be resold later. A firm that tried to sell toasters at two different prices during the day might discover itself to be in competition with savvy customers who bought when the price was low and undercut the firm by selling to other customers during high price periods. If customers themselves can alter when they shop, a discriminatory policy may not work. A firm that offers lower post-Christmas prices may find its pre-Christmas business facing stiff competition from those sales.

Finally, of course, the practice of price discrimination requires monopoly power. Because the discriminator chooses an output level for which price exceeds marginal (and perhaps average) cost, potential competitors may be encouraged to enter the market. Prior to deregulation, for example, airlines practiced a number of discriminatory policies in their pricing. The goal of such policies as advance ticket purchase requirements and minimum stay provisions was to differentiate between business travelers (who had relatively inelastic demands) and discretionary travelers. The large profits made from business travel could not persist in an era of greater competition as new airlines sought to enter this market.

The practice of price discrimination is subject to a number of constraining influences. Still, there are many situations where buyers pay different prices for the same product. Some of these may involve quite intricate pricing strategies, as Application 15.4: Pricing at Disneyland illustrates for the case of the Disney amusement parks.

Regulation of Monopolies

The regulation of monopolies is an important subject in applied economic analysis. The utility, communications, and transportation industries are highly regulated in most countries, and devising regulatory procedures that cause these industries to operate in a desirable way is an important practical problem. Here we look at a few aspects of the regulation of monopolies that relate to pricing policies.

Marginal Cost Pricing and the Natural Monopoly Dilemma

By analogy to the perfectly competitive case, many economists believe that it is important for the prices charged by regulated monopolies to accurately reflect marginal costs of production. In this way the deadweight loss from monopolies is minimized. The principal problem raised by an enforced policy of marginal cost pricing is that it may require natural monopolies to operate at a loss.

APPLICATION 15.4

Pricing at Disneyland

Disneyland and Disney World are unique entertainment attractions. Amusement park aficionados (including this author) agree there are few, if any, substitutes for these products, and therefore the Disney company occupies a strong monopoly position in its pricing decisions. Given this position, it is not surprising that Disney adopts a bewildering array of price policies, all presumably with the purpose of converting available consumer surplus into profits.

The Disneyland Passport

Until recently Disney used a complicated multipart pricing schedule for its rides.[1] Under that schedule, Disneyland patrons had to purchase a "passport" containing a ticket for admission to the park together with coupons for admission to the rides themselves. Contents of a typical passport are summarized in Table 1 as well as the prices of individual tickets for each type of ride. The company enjoyed a great deal of pricing flexibility with this passport arrangement. It could vary the basic price of a passport, it could vary the composition of tickets contained in a passport, it could redefine which ride requires which ticket, and it could alter the prices of extra tickets. In short, the passport pricing method provided the firm with myriad opportunities to increase profits through price discrimination among different types of buyers. For example, the number of "E" ride tickets seems to be carefully chosen both to allow passport purchasers to ride most of the major attractions without permitting second rides, except at additional cost. The lesser attraction tickets in the passport spread patrons around the park. Finally, and perhaps most interesting, the price of extra tickets for rides was quite high (certainly well above marginal cost). This pricing policy is consistent with the low price elasticity of patrons for extra rides once they are already at the park.

Table 1
Structure of a Typical Disneyland Passport

Item	Example	Number of Tickets in Passport	Price of Extra Ticket
Admission	—	1	$4.00
"A" ride	Shooting Gallery	2	.25
"B" ride	Dumbo, Train	3	.50
"C" ride	Peter Pan's Flight	3	.75
"D" ride	Autopia	2	1.00
"E" ride	Space Mountain	5	1.50

Source: Author's 1978 passport. *Note:* As discussed in this application, Disneyland now has a single price admission policy.

Pricing at Disney World

Disney's passport pricing schedule posed problems for the parks. Most importantly, labor costs were substantially higher under such a system (since many ticket collectors and salespersons are needed) than under a single price admission policy, followed at many other amusement parks (Great Adventure and Busch Gardens, for example). Recently, Disney has moved away from individual tickets for rides and toward a single entry fee. This single fee still provides the company with opportunities for price discrimination, such as charging reduced prices for multiday tickets and lower rates for local residents than for tourists. At Disney World (in Florida), Disney uses additional pricing strategies in the way it packages admission tickets to the Magic Kingdom, EPCOT, River Country, the MGM Theme Park, and a number of minor attractions such as the monorails and Discovery Island. Despite many changes in pricing methods, the company still appears to be following the profit motive.

To Think About

1. If you have been to Disneyland or Disney World, can you remember other examples of price discrimination? How is food priced? How about hotel accommodations? Can you explain why the company might adopt seasonal price differentials?
2. The former Disney pricing scheme (in Table 1) is called a two-part pricing schedule. Can you think of other examples of situations where customers are charged a flat fee for basic service and extra fees for additional services?

[1]For an analytical treatment of these points see W. Y. Oi, "A Disneyland Dilemma: Two-Part Tariffs for a Mickey Mouse Monopoly," *Quarterly Journal of Economics* (February 1971): 77–96.

Figure 15.6
Price Regulation for a Natural Monopoly

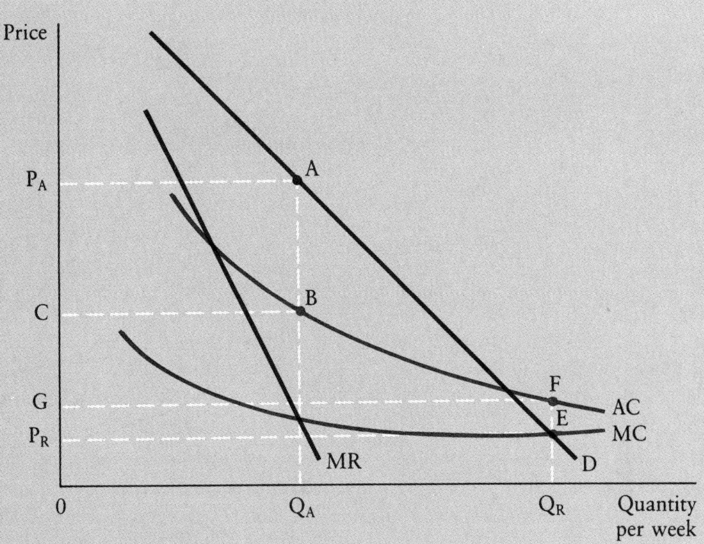

Because natural monopolies exhibit decreasing average cost, marginal costs fall below average cost. Enforcing a policy of marginal cost pricing will entail operating at a loss. A price of P_R, for example, will achieve the goal of marginal cost pricing but will necessitate an operating loss of $GFEP_R$.

Natural monopolies, by definition, exhibit decreasing average costs over a broad range of output levels. The cost curves for such a firm might look like those shown in Figure 15.6. In the absence of regulation the monopoly would produce output level Q_A and receive a price of P_A for its product. Profits in this situation are given by the rectangle P_AABC. A regulatory agency might set a price of P_R for this monopoly. At this price, Q_R is demanded, and the marginal cost of producing this output level is also P_R. Consequently, marginal cost pricing has been achieved. Unfortunately, because of the declining nature of the firm's cost curves, the price P_R (= marginal cost) falls below average costs. With this regulated price the monopoly must operate at a loss of $GFEP_R$. Since no firm can operate indefinitely at a loss, this poses a dilemma for the regulatory agency: either it must abandon its goal of marginal cost pricing, or the government must subsidize the monopoly forever.

Two-Tier Pricing Systems

One way out of the marginal cost pricing dilemma is a two-part pricing system. Under this system the monopoly is permitted to charge some users a high price while maintaining a low price for "marginal" users. In this way

Figure 15.7
Two-Part Pricing Schedule

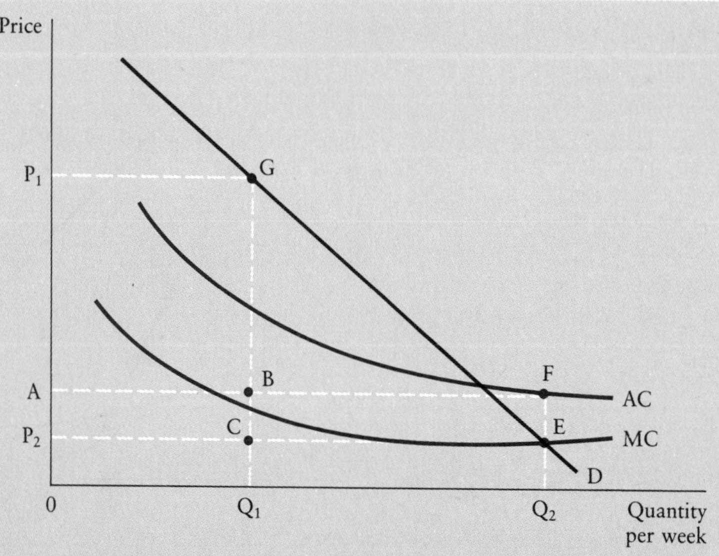

By charging a high price (P_1) to some users and a low price (P_2) to others, it may be possible for a regulatory commission to (1) enforce marginal cost pricing and (2) create a situation where the profits from one class of user (P_1GBA) subsidize the losses of the other class (BFEC).

the demanders paying the high price in effect subsidize the losses of the low-price customers.

Such a pricing scheme is shown in Figure 15.7. Here the regulatory commission has decided that some users will pay a relatively high price, P_1. At this price, Q_1 is demanded. Other users (presumably those who would not buy the good at the P_1 price) are offered a lower price, P_2. This lower price generates additional demand of $Q_2 - Q_1$. Consequently, a total output of Q_2 is produced at an average cost of A. With this two-part pricing system, the profits on the sales to high-price demanders (given by the rectangle P_1GBA) balance the losses incurred on the low-priced sales (BFEC). Furthermore, for the "marginal user," the marginal cost pricing rule is being followed: it is the "intramarginal" user who subsidizes the firm so that it does not operate at a loss.

Although in practice it may not be so simple to establish pricing schemes that maintain marginal cost pricing and cover operating costs, many regulatory commissions do use multipart price schedules that intentionally discriminate against some users to the advantage of others. Application 15.5: The Breakup of AT&T illustrates how this was done for many years in the telephone industry and how this caused major problems in moving to a more competitive situation.

APPLICATION 15.5

The Breakup of AT&T

In 1974 the U.S. Department of Justice filed an antitrust suit against the American Telephone and Telegraph (AT&T) Company charging unlawful monopolization of the telephone equipment and long distance service markets. The filing of an antitrust suit against a regulated natural monopoly was a highly unusual act, and legal wrangling over the suit lasted well into the 1980s. A settlement was finally realized in late 1982 and on January 1, 1984, AT&T formally divested itself of its seven local Bell Operating Companies (Ameritech, Atlantic Bell, Bell South, NYNEX, Pacific Telesis, Southwestern Bell, and U.S. West). AT&T itself retained its manufacturing operations (Western Electric Company) and its long distance operations. The goal of this huge restructuring was to improve the performance and competitiveness of the U.S. telephone industry, but these gains have proven very difficult to obtain.

Subsidization of Local Phone Service

Prior to the breakup, AT&T had been forced by regulators to provide local residential phone service at prices below average cost and to make up these losses by charging above average cost for long distance calls (see Figure 15.7). Over the years immediately prior to the breakup, these subsidies had grown larger as technical improvements (such as satellites) sharply reduced the costs of long distance service, but regulators chose to keep long distance rates high and local rates low. By the early 1980s, residential service was estimated to cost about $26 per month, but the typical charge was only $11 per month. Subsidies from long distance and other sources made up the $15 per month difference.[1] After the breakup, state regulators were faced with the politically unappealing prospect of implementing huge increases in residential telephone rates. Not surprisingly, local regulators opted instead for a continuation of subsidies from AT&T (and, to a lesser extent, from other long distance companies such as MCI or Sprint) to the local operating companies.

Performance of the Long Distance Market

Although the market for telephone equipment has become markedly more competitive since 1984 (mainly through the entry of Japanese producers), the long distance market has not. Long distance rates for AT&T have continued to be regulated at the federal level, and other long distance carriers have found it difficult to gain much of the market despite their cost competitiveness. Both of these results are, at least in part, dictated by the continuing cross-subsidy to local service. Regulation of telephone rates is needed to assure adequate profits are generated to provide the subsidy. Similarly, because local companies get a larger subsidy from AT&T than from other long distance providers, local regulators have been reluctant to proceed to full-scale access for these providers.

Performance of Local Operating Companies

Because of a desire to ensure that operating subsidies are used to keep local rates low, regulators (and the federal judge overseeing the AT&T breakup) have been reluctant to provide very much leeway for the local operating companies to branch out into other fields. Most importantly, they have been forbidden to enter the long distance market (where they would provide formidable competition for AT&T and other firms) and to enter the business of manufacturing telephone equipment for general sale. They have also been prevented from entering a variety of computer and data-transmission markets. What could have been strong competition among the seven operating companies has therefore generally failed to materialize except in relatively small markets such as those for cellular phones.

To Think About

1. Why should local phone service be subsidized? Are there socially desirable benefits from making sure phone service is available to practically everyone? If so, should this service be provided at below cost and who should pay the subsidy?
2. Does the argument that local operating companies should be barred from many businesses because they might use their subsidies to gain an unfair advantage in them make sense? Would a local phone company find it in its interest to do this? How can local phone regulators prevent any such cross-subsidies?

---

[1] P. W. MacAvoy and K. Robinson, "Losing by Judicial Policy Making: The First Year of the AT&T Divestiture," *Yale Journal on Regulation* (January 1985): 225–262.

Rate of Return Regulation

Another approach to setting the price charged by a natural monopoly that is followed in many regulatory situations is to permit the monopoly to charge a price above average cost that will earn a "fair" rate of return on investment. Much analytical effort is then spent on defining the "fair" rate and on developing how it might be measured. From an economic point of view some of the most interesting questions about this procedure concern how the regulatory activity affects the firm's decisions. If, for example, the allowed rate of return exceeds what the firm might earn under competitive circumstances, the firm will have an incentive to use relatively more capital input than needed to truly minimize costs. If regulators typically delay in making rate decisions, firms may be given incentives to minimize costs that would not otherwise exist since they cannot immediately recover their costs through higher rates. Although it is possible to develop a formal analysis of all of these possibilities, we do not do so here.[7]

Benefits of Monopoly

Our analysis in this chapter makes two arguments against monopoly. The first concludes that the allocational effects of monopoly are harmful: too few resources are devoted to the production of a good for which the supply is monopolized. The second argument is somewhat more ambiguous but is probably more important from a policy perspective: monopolies have undesirable distributional effects. Monopolies may make long-run profits, and these profits may accrue to relatively rich owners at the expense of relatively poor consumers. This consideration of the distributional fairness of monopolies reinforces the allocational argument and provides the basis for the notion that monopolies are an unambiguous evil.

This simple conclusion is questioned by some economists. For example, J. A. Schumpeter stressed the beneficial role that monopoly profits can play in the process of economic development.[8] This section briefly reviews some of the possible beneficial aspects of monopoly that have been suggested.

Monopoly Profits and Economic Growth

Authors discussing the possible benefits of monopoly tend to take a dynamic view of the economic process. They emphasize innovation and the ability of particular types of firms to achieve technical advances. In this context, the

[7]For a detailed treatment, see E. E. Bailey, *Economic Theory of Regulatory Constraint* (Lexington, Mass.: D. C. Heath, 1973).

[8]J. A. Schumpeter, *Capitalism, Socialism, and Democracy*, 3d ed. (New York: Harper & Row, 1950), especially Chapter 8.

profits that monopolistic firms earn play an important role. Profits provide the funds to invest in research and development. Whereas perfectly competitive firms must be content with a normal return on invested capital, monopolies have the surplus funds to undertake the risky process of research. More important, perhaps, the possibility of attaining a monopoly position, or the desire to maintain such a position, provides an important incentive to the monopoly to keep one step ahead of potential competitors. Innovations in new products and cost-saving production techniques may be integrally related to the possibility of monopolization. Without a monopoly position, the full benefits of innovation could not be obtained by the innovating firm.

Monopoly and Cost Saving

Schumpeter stresses that the monopolization of a market may make it less costly for a firm to plan its activities. Being the only source of supply for a product eliminates many of the contingencies that a firm in a competitive market must face. For example, a monopoly may not have to spend as much on selling expenses (such as advertising, brand identification, or visiting retailers) as would be the case in a more competitive industry. Similarly, a monopoly may know more about the specific demand curve for its product and may more readily adapt to changing demand conditions.

Of course, whether any of these purported benefits of monopolies outweigh their allocational and distributional disadvantages is an open question. Generally, economists have not been sufficiently convinced about the benefits of monopoly to favor deliberate creation of monopoly power through licensing or other barriers to entry. Instead they tend to regard such barriers as anticompetitive and probably unwise.

Summary

A market in which there is a single seller is called a "monopoly." In a monopoly situation the firm faces the entire market demand curve. Contrary to the case of perfect competition, the monopoly's output decision will completely determine market price. The major conclusions of our investigation of pricing in monopoly markets are:

- The profit-maximizing monopoly will choose an output level for which marginal revenue is equal to marginal cost. Since the firm faces a downward-sloping demand curve, market price will exceed both marginal revenue and marginal cost.
- The divergence between price and marginal cost is a sign that the monopoly causes resources to be allocated inefficiently. Buyers are willing to pay more for one more unit of output than it costs the firm to produce it, but the monopoly prevents this beneficial transaction from occurring.

- Because of barriers to entry, a monopoly may earn positive long-run economic profits. These profits may have undesirable distributional effects.
- A monopoly may adopt a policy of price discrimination among buyers if it can successfully separate those buyers into different markets. Prices will be higher in markets with less elastic demand.
- Governments may choose to regulate the prices charged by monopolies. In the case of a natural monopoly (for which average costs decline over a broad range of output), this poses a dilemma. The regulatory agency can opt for marginal cost pricing (in which case the monopoly will operate at a loss) or for average cost pricing (in which case an inefficient quantity will be produced).

Review Questions

1. In everyday discussions people tend to talk about monopolies "setting high prices," but in this chapter we have talked about the monopoly's profit-maximizing level of output. Are these two approaches saying the same thing? What do both assume about the demand curve facing a monopoly? What kind of rule would a monopoly follow if it wished to choose a profit-maximizing price? Why not charge the highest price possible?
2. Why are barriers to entry crucial to the success of a monopoly firm? Explain why all monopoly profits will show up as returns to the factor or factors that provide the barrier to entry.
3. "At a monopoly's profit-maximizing output, price will exceed marginal cost simply because price exceeds marginal revenue for a downward-sloping demand curve." Explain why this is so and indicate what factors will affect the size of the price-marginal cost gap.
4. The following coversation was overheard during a microeconomics cram session:
   Student A: "In order to maximize profits, a monopoly should obviously produce where the gap between price and *average* cost is the greatest."
   Student B: "No, that will only maximize profit per unit. To maximize total profits, the firm should produce where the gap between price and *marginal* cost is the greatest since that will maximize monopoly power and hence profits."
   Can you make any sense out of this drivel? Do these students still have a lot of studying to do?
5. "Increases in input costs will be passed on to consumers directly by a monopoly, but that would not happen in a competitive market. Hence, monopolies are a major cause of inflation." Do you agree?
6. Figure 15.4 illustrates the "deadweight loss" from the monopolization of a market. What is this a loss of? In the chili dog–cook example, what is the world missing out on?
7. Why must markets be "separated" if a monopoly is to be able to practice price discrimination successfully? What factors can provide such separation? Why don't separated markets obey the "law of one price"?
8. Explain the pricing policy followed by Disney, United Airlines, or any other firm that follows a complex pricing policy. How does this policy take advantage of separated markets? How can the firm ensure that markets remain separated? Does the firm seem to exhibit the relationship between price and the elasticity of demand that is predicted by Figure 15.5?

9. What is a "natural monopoly"? Why does electric power distribution or local telephone service have the characteristics of a natural monopoly? Why might this be less true for electric power generation or long-distance telephone service?
10. Suppose the government wished to regulate the price of the monopoly firms illustrated in Figures 15.1 and 15.3. Would this price regulation pose the same dilemma posed by the natural monopoly in Figure 15.6? Suppose a monopoly owned many plants, each operating at the low point of its long-run average cost curve. Which of these figures would best reflect that situation? Would price regulation or some form of antitrust breakup promise better industry performance in this case?

Problems

15.1 A monopolist can produce at constant average and marginal costs of AC = MC = 5. The firm faces a market demand curve given by Q = 53 − P. The monopolist's marginal revenue curve is given by MR = 53 − 2Q.

a. Calculate the profit-maximizing price-quantity combination for the monopolist. Also calculate the monopolist's profits.
b. What output level would be produced by this industry under perfect competition (where price = marginal cost)?
c. Calculate the consumer surplus obtained by consumers in part b. Show that this exceeds the sum of the monopolist's profits and consumer surplus received in part a. What is the value of the "deadweight loss" from monopolization?

15.2 A monopolist faces a market demand curve given by

$$Q = 70 - P.$$

The monopolist's marginal revenue curve is given by

$$MR = 70 - 2Q.$$

a. If the monopolist can produce at constant average and marginal costs of AC = MC = 6, what output level will the monopolist choose in order to maximize profits? What is the price at this output level? What are the monopolist's profits?
b. Assume instead that the monopolist has a cost structure where total costs are described by

$$TC = .25Q^2 - 5Q + 300$$

and marginal cost is given by

$$MC = .5Q - 5.$$

With the monopolist facing the same market demand and marginal revenue, what price-quantity combination will be chosen now to maximize profits? What will profits be?
c. Assume now that a third cost structure explains the monopolist's position with total costs given by

$$TC = .333Q^3 - 26Q^2 + 695Q - 5{,}800$$

and marginal costs given by

$$MC = Q^2 - 52Q + 695.$$

Again, calculate the monopolist's price-quantity combination that maximizes profits. What will profits be? (Hint: Set MC = MR as usual and use the quadratic formula or simple factoring to solve the equation for Q.)

d. Graph the market demand curve, the MR curve, and the three marginal cost curves from parts a, b, and c. Notice that the monopolist's profit-making ability is constrained by (1) the market demand curve it faces (along with its associated MR curve) and (2) the cost structure underlying production.

15.3 A single firm monopolizes the entire market for Nixon masks and can produce at constant average and marginal costs of

$$AC = MC = 10.$$

Originally, the firm faces a market demand curve given by

$$Q = 60 - P$$

and a marginal revenue curve given by

$$MR = 60 - 2Q.$$

a. Calculate the profit-maximizing price-quantity combination for the firm. What are the firm's profits?

b. Now assume that the market demand curve shifts outward (becoming steeper) and is given by

$$Q = 45 - .5P$$

with the marginal revenue curve given by

$$MR = 90 - 4Q.$$

What is the firm's profit-maximizing price-quantity combination now? What are the firm's profits?

c. Instead of the assumptions of part b, assume that the market demand curve shifts outward (becoming flatter) and is given by

$$Q = 100 - 2P$$

with the marginal revenue curve given by

$$MR = 50 - Q.$$

What is the firm's profit-maximizing price-quantity combination now? What are the firm's profits?

d. Graph the three different situations of parts a, b, and c. Using your results, explain why there is no supply curve for this mask monopoly.

15.4 Suppose that the market for hula hoops is monopolized by a single firm.

a. Draw the initial equilibrium for such a market.

b. Suppose now that the demand for hula hoops shifts outward slightly. Show that, in general (contrary to the competitive case), it will not be possible to predict the effect of this shift in demand on the market price of hula hoops.

c. Consider three possible ways in which the price elasticity of demand might change as the demand curve shifts—it might increase, it might decrease, or it might stay the same. Consider also that marginal costs for the monopolist might be rising, falling, or constant in the range where MR = MC. Consequently there are nine different combinations of types of demand shifts and marginal cost slope configurations. Analyze each of these to determine for which it is possible to make a definite prediction about the effect of the shift in demand on the price of hula hoops.

*15.5 Suppose a company has a monopoly on a game called Monopoly and faces a demand curve given by

$$Q_T = 100 - P$$

and a marginal revenue curve given by

$$MR = 100 - 2Q_T$$

where Q_T equals the combined total number of games produced per hour in the company's two factories ($Q_T = q_1 + q_2$). If factory 1 has a marginal cost curve given by

$$MC_1 = q_2 - 5$$

and factory 2 has a marginal cost curve given by

$$MC_2 = .5q_2 - 5,$$

how much total output will the company choose to produce and how will it distribute this production between its two factories in order to maximize profits?

*15.6 Suppose a textbook monopoly can produce any level of output it wishes at a constant marginal (and average) cost of $5 per unit. Assume that the monopoly sells its books in two different markets that are separated by some distance. The demand curve in the first market is given by

$$Q_1 = 55 - P_1$$

and the curve in the second market is given by

$$Q_2 = 70 - 2P_2.$$

a. If the monopolist can maintain the separation between the two markets, what level of output should be produced in each market and what price will prevail in each market? What are total profits in this situation?

b. How would your answer change if it only cost demanders $5 to mail books between the two markets? What would be the monopolist's new profit level in this situation? How would your answer change if mailing costs were 0? (Hint: Show that for a downward-sloping linear demand curve, profits are maximized when output is set at $Q^*/2$, where Q^* is the output level that would be demanded when P = MC. Use this result to solve the problem.)

---

*Denotes a problem that is rather difficult.

15.7 Suppose a perfectly competitive industry can produce Roman candles at a constant marginal cost of \$10 per unit. Once the industry is monopolized, marginal costs rise to \$12 per unit because \$2 per unit must be paid to lobbyists to ensure that only this firm receives a Roman candle license. Suppose the market demand for Roman candles is given by

$$Q_D = 1{,}000 - 50P$$

and the marginal revenue curve by

$$MR = 20 - Q/25.$$

a. Calculate the perfectly competitive and monopoly outputs and prices.
b. Calculate the total loss of consumer surplus from monopolization of Roman candle production.
c. Graph your results.

15.8 Consider the following possible schemes for taxing a monopoly:

i. A proportional tax on profits
ii. A specific tax on each unit produced
iii. A proportional tax on the gap between price and marginal cost

a. Explain how each of these taxes would affect the monopolist's profit-maximizing output choice. Would the tax increase or decrease the deadweight loss from monopoly?
b. Graph your results for these three cases.

CHAPTER 16

Pricing in Imperfectly Competitive Markets

This chapter discusses the theory of pricing in markets that fall between the polar extremes of perfect competition and monopoly. Although no single model can be used to explain all possible forms of imperfect competition, we look at a few of the basic elements that are common to many of the models in current use. To that end we focus on three specific topics: (1) pricing of homogeneous goods in markets in which there are relatively few firms; (2) product differentiation in these markets; and (3) how entry and exit possibilities affect long-run outcomes in imperfectly competitive markets. A related topic, strategy in the competition between firms, is taken up in Chapter 17.

In a sense, Chapter 16 concerns how the stringent assumptions of the perfectly competitive model can be relaxed and what the results of changing those assumptions are. For this study, the perfectly competitive model provides a useful benchmark, since departures from the competitive norm may involve efficiency losses similar to those described in the previous chapter in connection with monopolistic markets. Two specific criteria we use in this comparison are (1) whether prices under imperfect competition equal marginal costs and (2) whether, in the long run, production occurs at minimum average cost. As we will see, imperfectly competitive markets often lack one or both of these desirable features of perfect competition.

Because the theory of imperfect competition does not yield the precise and well-defined results that the theories of perfect competition and monopoly do, much of the literature on the subject is descriptive and empirical rather than strictly analytical. The field of "industrial organization" provides a number of insights into the behavior of firms in complicated real-world situations. The final sections of this chapter offer a brief glimpse of some of this research.

Pricing of Homogeneous Goods

This section looks at the theory of pricing in markets in which relatively few firms produce a single homogeneous good. As before, we assume that the market is perfectly competitive on the demand side; that is, there are assumed to be many demanders, each of whom is a price taker. We also assume that there are no transactions or informational costs, so that the good in question obeys the law of one price and we may speak unambiguously of *the* price of the good. Later in this chapter we relax this assumption to consider cases where firms sell products that differ slightly from each other and may therefore have different prices. In this section we also assume that there are a fixed small number of identical firms. In Chapter 17 we look at a simple numerical example of a market with exactly two firms, but our analysis here is not restricted to any single number—the main idea is just that the number of firms is small. Later in this chapter we allow the number of firms to vary through entry and exit in response to profitability.

Quasi-competitive Model

The possible outcomes for prices when there are few firms are uncertain—they depend on how the firms react to competitors' activities. At one extreme is what we might call a **quasi-competitive model.** In this case each firm acts as a price taker. For example, a new gas station operator would be a price taker if he or she assumed that opening the station would not affect the local price of gasoline either directly (because opening the station doesn't change the local supply very much) or indirectly (because nearby stations will not change their prices in the face of the new competition). The price taker assumption may not always be valid, especially in volatile, cutthroat markets such as gasoline sales, but this (perhaps naive) assumption is a useful place to start.

Quasi-competitive model
A model of oligopoly pricing in which each firm acts as a price taker.

If a firm acts as a price taker, it will, as before, produce where price equals long-run marginal cost. The market solution in this case will resemble a competitive one even though relatively few firms may be involved. Figure 16.1 shows a particularly simple market solution of this type. The figure assumes that marginal cost (and average cost) is constant for all output levels. Consequently, market price (P_C) must equal this marginal cost. Under this quasi-competitive solution Q_C will be produced and market equilibrium will occur at point C. This equilibrium represents the highest quantity and lowest price that can prevail in the long term with the demand curve D. A price lower than P_C would not cover firms' average cost, so it would not be sustainable in the long run.

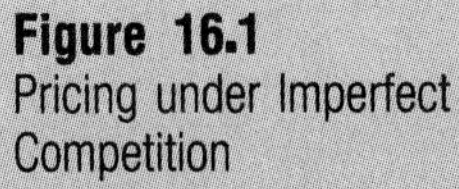

Figure 16.1
Pricing under Imperfect Competition

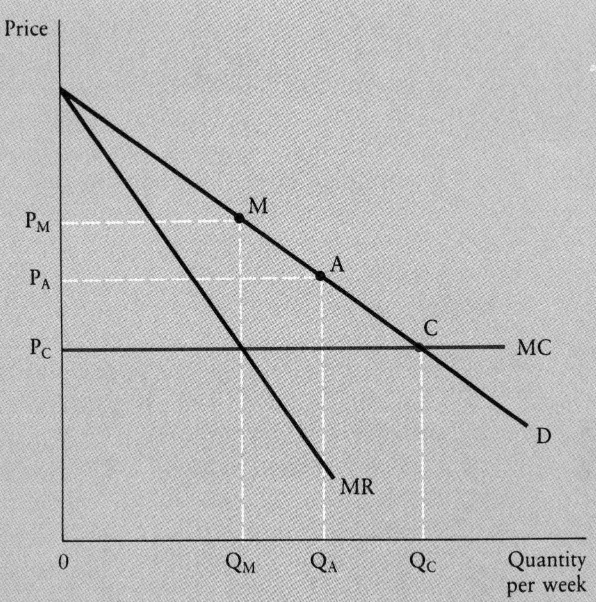

Market equilibrium under imperfect competition can occur at many points on the demand curve. In this figure (which assumes that marginal costs are constant over all output ranges), the quasi-competitive equilibrium occurs at point C and the cartel equilibrium at point M. Many solutions (such as A) may occur between points M and C, depending on the specific assumption made about firms' strategic interrelationships.

Cartel Model

Cartel model
A model of oligopoly pricing in which firms coordinate their decisions to act as a multiplant monopoly.

The assumption of price-taking behavior may be particularly inappropriate in concentrated industries in which each firm's decisions have an effect on price. An alternative assumption here would be that firms as a group recognize that they can affect price and coordinate their decisions to achieve monopoly profits. This case can be described by a **cartel model** in which the cartel acts as a multiplant monopoly and produces in each of its "plants" (that is, in each firm in the cartel) where marginal revenue equals marginal cost. Assuming, as before, that these marginal costs are equal and constant for all firms, the output choice is indicated by point M in Figure 16.1. Because this coordinated plan requires a specific output level for each firm, the plan also dictates how monopoly profits earned by the cartel are to be shared by its members. In the aggregate, these profits will be as large as possible, given the market demand curve and the industry's cost structure.

Maintaining this cartel solution poses three problems for the firms involved. First, cartel formations may be illegal. In the United States, for example, Section I of the Sherman Act of 1890 outlaws "conspiracies in restraint of trade," so would-be cartel members may expect a visit from the FBI. Similar laws exist in many other countries. A second problem with the cartel solution is that it requires that a considerable amount of information be available to the directors of the cartel—specifically, they must know the market demand function and each firm's marginal cost function. This information may be costly to obtain, and some cartel members may be reluctant to provide it. Finally, and most important, the cartel solution may be fundamentally unstable. Since each cartel member will produce an output level for which price exceeds marginal cost, each will have an incentive to expand output to increase its own profits. If the directors of the oligopoly are not able to police such "chiseling," the cartel solution may collapse. The difficulties of the OPEC cartel in dictating output levels to its members during the early 1980s, as we will show, attest to these problems. Ultimately, OPEC's production decisions were widely disobeyed (especially by non-Arab members of the cartel), and by 1984, prices had begun a precipitous decline.

Other Pricing Possibilities

The quasi-competitive and cartel models of pricing tend to determine the outer limits between which actual prices in an imperfectly competitive market will be set (for example, one such intermediate is represented by point A in Figure 16.1). This band of outcomes may be very wide, so economists have tried to develop models to predict where market equilibrium will actually occur within these limits.[1] Developing these models is very difficult. For example, imagine developing a systematic description of how people play poker—complete with betting strategies, bluffing, and each player guessing what the other players are doing. No model can predict such behavior with complete accuracy. The outcomes depend on the skills of the players, the way the cards are running, and even on seemingly irrelevant factors like the time of night or the temperature of the room. Exactly the same types of problems arise in creating a model of pricing in markets with relatively few firms. In this case the outcome depends entirely on how the firms play the game. In Chapter 17 we take up such strategic questions. Here we look at two very simple models that have been widely used.

Kinked Demand Curve Model

Kinked demand curve model
A model in which firms believe that price increases result in a very elastic demand, while price decreases result in an inelastic demand for their products.

The **kinked demand curve model** was first developed by P. M. Sweezy in 1939 to explain why prices in markets with few firms tended to be inflex-

[1]For example, if the elasticity of demand is -2, Equation 10.8 shows that $P = 2 \cdot MR$. Under a quasi-competitive solution $P = MC$; under the cartel solution, price is twice that level ($P = 2MC$). A model that can predict prices only within a 100 percent range is not very useful.

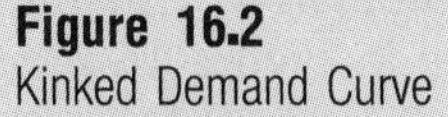

Figure 16.2
Kinked Demand Curve

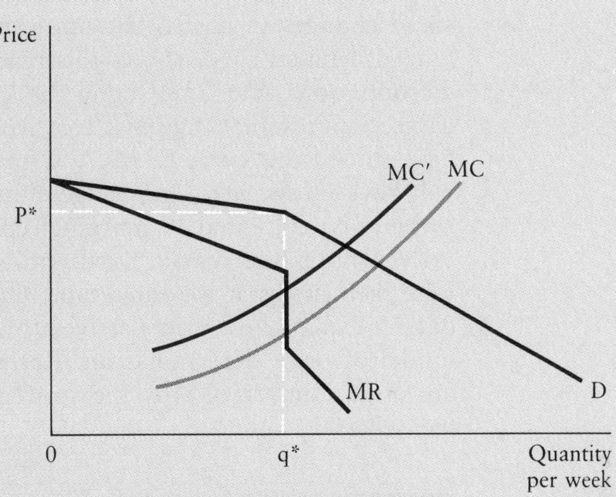

A firm in an oligopoly industry may believe it faces a demand curve (D) with a kink at the prevailing price (P*). If the firm considered raising its price, it may believe others would not follow: demand would appear to be very elastic since customers would shift to its competitors. Conversely, the firm may believe that if it lowered price, all its competitors would do the same. Demand would be relatively inelastic below P*. The kink at P* means that the MR curve will be discontinuous at this point. Therefore, firms may not respond to small shifts in their marginal cost curves.

ible.[2] It asserted that changes in costs were only rarely met by changes in market prices, and that when changes in market price did occur in oligopoly markets, they tended to be of rather large magnitudes. Although whether prices really do behave in this way is debatable, Sweezy tried to explain such price inflexibility by asking about the demand curve faced by a typical firm in an oligopoly market. He hypothesized that firms make their decisions in a cautious and pessimistic way. When contemplating lowering its price, a firm believes all its rivals will follow and, because it cannot gain a lot of extra sales by lowering price, demand is relatively inelastic for price decreases. If a firm were to raise its price alone, Sweezy assumes that the firm believes that others would not follow. For price increases, the firm will find demand very elastic, since its customers will switch to competitors' products whose prices have not been raised. This kinked demand curve possibility is labeled D in Figure 16.2. The prevailing market price is P*, and the firm sells quantity q*. Quantity sold would not increase greatly if the firm lowered its price (since rivals are assumed to follow), but it would be decreased markedly if the firm raised its price.

[2]P. M. Sweezy, "Demand under Conditions of Oligopoly," *Journal of Political Economy* (August 1939): 568–573.

If the firm believes that it faces a kinked demand curve, it may not react to small changes in costs. The marginal revenue curve associated with the kinked demand curve shows this reaction. The MR curve in Figure 16.2 is discontinuous at q^*, reflecting the kinked nature of the assumed demand curve. Suppose that marginal cost were initially MC and that cost increases have shifted this curve to MC′. With this new marginal cost curve the firm will have no incentive to change either price or quantity, because marginal revenue is still equal to marginal costs and profits are being maximized. Prices will tend to remain fixed until some unifying event causes all firms to raise their prices at the same time. One shortcoming of this model is that it doesn't explain how prices arrive at their initial levels, so it is not a complete model of price determination. Rather, it should be viewed as providing an initial glimpse of why the strategy issue is important in markets with few sellers.

Price Leadership Model

Price leadership model A model in which one dominant firm takes reactions of all other firms into account in its output and pricing decisions.

A second model of pricing in markets with few sellers is called the **price leadership model.** It tends to accord with many real-world observations. In some markets one firm or group of firms is looked upon as the leader in pricing, and all firms adjust their prices to what this leader does. Two possible examples of price leadership are the computer industry (where IBM plays the role of a leader) and the commercial banking industry (where the prime rate tends to be determined by the major New York City banks).

Competitive fringe A group of firms that act as price takers in a market dominated by a price leader.

A formal model of pricing in a market dominated by a leading firm is presented in Figure 16.3. The industry is assumed to be composed of a single price-setting leader and a **competitive fringe** of firms who take the leader's price as given in their decisions. The demand curve D represents the total demand curve for the industry's product, and the supply curve SC represents the supply decisions of all the firms in the competitive fringe. Using these two curves, the demand curve (D′) facing the industry leader is derived as follows. For a price of P_1 or above, the leader will sell nothing since the competitive fringe would be willing to supply all that is demanded. For prices below P_2 the leader has the market to itself since the fringe is not willing to supply anything. Between P_2 and P_1 the curve D′ is constructed by subtracting what the fringe will supply from total market demand—that is, the leader gets that portion of demand not taken by the fringe firms.

Given the demand curve D′, the leader can construct its marginal revenue curve (MR′) and then refer to its own marginal cost curve (MC) to determine the profit-maximizing output level, Q_L. Market price will then be P_L. Given that price, the competitive fringe will produce Q_C and total industry output will be Q_T ($= Q_C + Q_L$).

This model does not answer such important questions as how the price leader in an industry is chosen, or what happens when a member of the fringe decides to challenge the leader for its position (and profits). The model does show how elements of both the perfectly competitive and the monopoly theo-

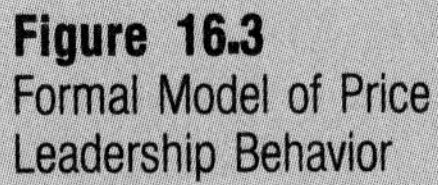

Figure 16.3
Formal Model of Price Leadership Behavior

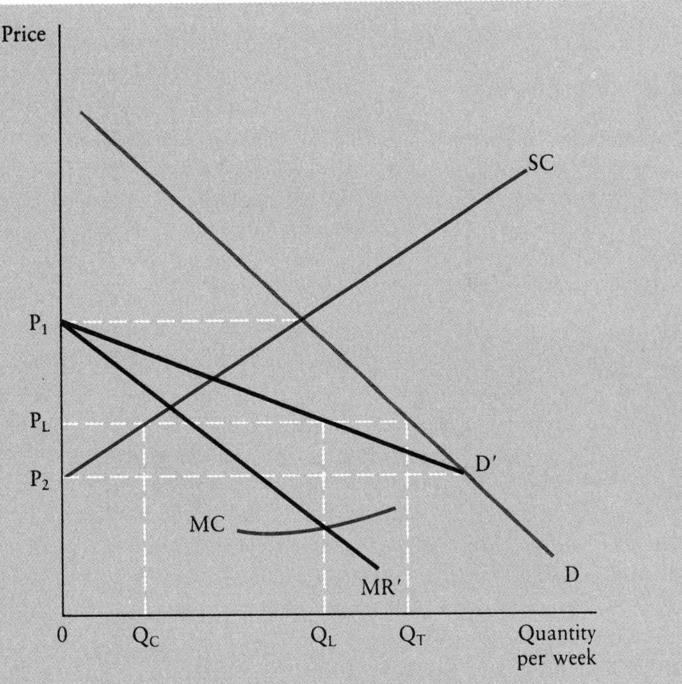

The curve D′ shows the demand curve facing the price leader—it is derived by subtracting what is produced by the competitive fringe of firms (SC) from market demand (D). Given D′, the firm's profit-maximizing output level is Q_L, and a price of P_L will prevail in the market.

ries of price determination can be woven together to produce a model of pricing under imperfectly competitive conditions. Such a model may explain industry behavior in some important situations, as Application 16.1: OPEC Pricing Strategy illustrates.

Product Differentiation

Up to this point we have assumed the good being produced in an imperfectly competitive market is homogeneous. Demanders were assumed to be indifferent about which firm's output they bought, and the law of one price was assumed to hold in the market. These assumptions may not hold in many real-world markets. Firms often devote considerable resources to make their products different from those of their competitors through such devices as quality and style variations, warranties and guarantees, special service features, and product advertising. These activities require firms to employ additional resources, and firms will choose to do so if profits are thereby increased. Product variation also results in a relaxation of the law of one

APPLICATION 16.1

OPEC Pricing Strategy

The Organization of Petroleum Exporting Countries (OPEC) was formed in the early 1960s. Altogether, OPEC members represent about half of total world oil production and perhaps 60 to 70 percent of total crude oil reserves. During its first ten years, OPEC had relatively little influence on world oil prices. But during the 1973 Arab-Israeli war and its associated oil embargo, that situation changed dramatically. In slightly more than one year, oil prices rose nearly fourfold—from about $2.50 to about $12.00 per barrel. After this initial price spurt, oil prices continued to rise (especially in reaction to supply disruptions, such as the Iranian revolution), although at a much slower rate. By 1982, crude oil sold for about $34 per barrel—a 14-fold increase over the span of a decade. Since 1982 prices have fallen to about one-half of this level.

Modeling OPEC Behavior

Economists have developed two types of models to explain OPEC pricing. Both of these attempt to take account of the structure of OPEC membership, particularly the role played by Saudi Arabia and the nearby Persian Gulf states of Kuwait, Qatar, Bahrain, and the United Arab Emirates. These producers constitute more than one-third of total OPEC production and considerably more of its total crude oil reserves. The countries are relatively lightly populated compared to some other OPEC members, such as Indonesia, Nigeria, or Venezuela. They also seem to have substantial excess oil production capability. It is these features that make them crucial to the pricing story.

A Cartel Model

One approach to OPEC pricing treats the organization as a cartel. Under this model, Saudi Arabia is able to hold the cartel together by restricting its own output by the amount necessary to achieve the profit-maximizing level. Saudi Arabia's unique geological position (it has more than 500 billion barrels of crude oil) and its small population make it possible for this cartel to persist much longer than has usually been the case for cartels, since there is no need to enforce major output restrictions on other producers. In exchange for Saudi cooperation, other OPEC members must to some extent bend to that country's wishes. In particular, most observers agree that the Saudis exercise a moderating price influence within OPEC. Their large oil reserves make them more concerned than most other oil producers about possible long-run alternatives (such as nuclear or solar power) to oil-based energy being developed in response to oil's high price.

A Price Leadership Model

Another view of the world oil market assumes a much greater degree of competitiveness than the cartel model. In this view, Saudi Arabia is treated as a price leader with other OPEC nations (and, indeed, all other oil producers) constituting a competitive fringe. Members of the competitive fringe, as shown in Figure 16.3, act as price takers. If this model is correct, the elaborate, regular meetings of the OPEC oil ministers are simply a gaudy ritual with no particular significance for the actual pricing of oil. And Saudi Arabia's much-heralded position as a moderate in oil pricing simply derives from its position as a price leader with low marginal costs of production.

On the whole, the evidence seems to be most consistent with the price leadership model of OPEC behavior. Even during the late 1970s prices seem to have been below those a cartelized monopoly would charge.[1] The sharp declines in 1984 and 1985 probably reflected a major shift in supply by the fringe producers as a result of significant oil discoveries, especially in non-OPEC countries.

To Think About

1. The sharp increase in oil prices between 1973 and 1982 is still a bit of a mystery to economists. Can such a large increase be fully explained by either the cartel or the price leadership model? In the absence of any very large increase in demand, wouldn't both these models predict rather modest price rises?
2. The history of most cartels has been one of failure to last for very long. Most seem to succumb to price chiseling by their members. Is OPEC different? Does it provide a model for what producers of other raw materials (such as copper or tin) should try to do?

[1]By most estimates, the demand for oil is price inelastic at current price levels. Since an inelastic demand implies a negative marginal revenue, current prices are inconsistent with monopoly profit maximization.

price, since now the market will consist of goods that vary from firm to firm and consumers may have preferences about which supplier to patronize.

Market Definition

That possibility introduces a certain fuzziness into what we mean by the "market for a good," since now there are many closely related, but not identical, products. For example, if toothpaste brands vary somewhat from supplier to supplier, should we consider all these products to be in the same market or should we differentiate among fluoridated products, gels, striped toothpaste, smokers' toothpaste, and so forth? Although this question is of great practical importance in industry studies, we do not pursue it here. Instead, we will assume that the market is composed of a few firms, each producing a slightly different product, but that these products can usefully be considered a single **product group.** That is, each firm produces a product that is highly substitutable for that of its rivals. Although this definition has its own ambiguities (arguments about the definition of a product group often dominate antitrust lawsuits, for example), it should suffice for our purposes.

Product group
Set of differentiated products that are highly substitutable for one another.

Firms' Choices

Let us assume that there are a few firms competing within a particular product group. Each firm can choose the amount to spend on differentiating its product from those of its competitors. Again, the profit-maximization model provides some insight about how firms will do this—they will incur additional costs associated with differentiation up to the point at which the additional revenue brought in by such activities equals each activity's marginal cost. With this view, producing differentiated products involves the same types of decisions that firms use in selecting any input.

Market Equilibrium

Although this description of firms' choices seems straightforward, the choices are actually quite complex. Since the demand curve facing any one firm depends on the prices and product differentiation activities of its competitors, that demand curve may shift frequently, and its position at any particular time may only be partly understood. The firm must make some assumptions in order to make decisions. And, whatever one firm decides to do may affect its competitors' actions.

Developing models of markets with differentiated products poses more complex strategic issues than does devising models for the homogeneous good case. Not surprisingly, there are few definite theoretical results about the nature of the market equilibrium that results from the differentiated oligopoly situation. Two very general conclusions might be mentioned, however. First, because of the differentiated nature of goods in the product group, price-taking behavior is unlikely. Each firm will believe that its activities have some effect on the price of its product. Price will exceed marginal revenue and marginal cost, and there may be some allocational inefficiency. Second, because of the uncertain demand facing each firm, information costs may be quite high. Firms may opt for strategies that economize on such costs. For example, they may adopt relatively simple "rules of thumb" in their decisions, such as adopting markup pricing (see Chapter 10) or aiming for a particular share of the market.

As a result of these types of behavior, market equilibria may be somewhat more stable over time than might at first be suggested by the complexities and uncertainties of the problem. Both prices and product types may converge around some median values, so that the homogeneous oligopoly models become appropriate. For example, product attributes may come to approximate those desired by the "typical" consumer, since any firm that departs very far from producing such a good may find itself outflanked by competitors. The tendency of television networks to produce the same types of shows and of political candidates to gravitate to the middle of the road in their positions are probably the most familiar instances of such behavior, but other occurrences come readily to mind. In Application 16.2: Brand Proliferation in Breakfast Cereals, we look at some of the issues of product differentiation that arise in one such market.

Advertising

Because of its economic importance and controversial nature, advertising has been more intensively examined by economists than other aspects of behavior in markets where firms seek to make their products different from those of their competitors. Theoretical studies have covered advertising and resource allocation, empirical studies have been done on the effect of advertising on the demands for specific products, and legal investigations have been made into what should be done about false advertising claims.[3] Here we examine only the allocational issue. Specifically, we look first at arguments that suggest that in an unregulated market, resources may be overallocated to the provision of advertising messages. We conclude with some observations about the value of advertising information to consumers.

Allocation of Resources to Advertising

An analysis of advertising might start with the observation that the market for advertising messages is not separated from the market for the good being

[3]Some of these analyses (together with a wealth of empirical information) are reviewed in Richard Schmalensee, *The Economics of Advertising* (Amsterdam: North Holland Publishing Company, 1972), Chapter 1.

APPLICATION 16.2

Brand Proliferation in Breakfast Cereals

Production of ready-to-eat breakfast cereals in the United States is highly concentrated. The top four firms in the industry (Kellogg's, General Mills, General Foods, and Quaker) supply about 85 percent of total industry output. According to most estimates, the industry is highly profitable with significantly higher rates of return on firms' investments than the average manufacturing company enjoys. Despite these high profits, entry by new firms into the industry has been virtually nonexistent. Although many large food companies could conceivably enter the industry, they have chosen not to do so. Economies of scale in cereal production do not seem to explain this reluctance, since it appears that efficient-size operations can be attained at a fairly small fraction of total industry output of about 2 to 3 percent. There must be some other explanation for the absence of entry.

The FTC Charge

In 1972 the U.S. Federal Trade Commission (FTC) issued a complaint against the four largest cereal producers charging that through proliferating brands and intensive advertising the firms had erected substantial entry barriers, thereby insuring monopoly-type returns to themselves. The brand proliferation argument ran as follows: By creating a huge number of cereal brands (about 80 in 1972), the largest firms had substantially covered all the attributes (sweetness, crunchiness, grain composition, and so forth) that mattered to consumers. There was no room in the market for potential entrants who had no opportunity to differentiate their products successfully. Crucial to this argument were the related issues of intensive advertising and brand identification preventing potential entrants from duplicating the characteristics of an existing cereal at a lower price. That is, it was claimed that consumers would generally be unwilling to purchase a less expensive version of Cheerios, for example.[1]

[1]For a detailed development of this theory see Richard Schmalensee, "Entry Deterrence in the Ready-to-Eat Breakfast Cereal Industry," *The Bell Journal of Economics* (Autumn 1978): 305–327.

Even More Product Differentiation

Although this explanation of entry barriers is intriguing, it is not airtight. The notion that there is no room for new cereal brands implicitly assumes a limit to firms' ingenuity that may not, in fact, exist. For example, the introduction of natural cereals in the 1970s seems to have filled a market niche that had been overlooked by the major companies. Similarly, the belief that look-alike, cheap imitations of major brands will not sell seems to be contradicted by the growing number of house brand cereals offered by supermarkets in the 1980s. New cereals that cater to health concerns (such as those made from oat bran) have also had a period of rapid growth in sales. Cereal companies have, therefore, shown no slackening in their ability to develop new brands, though the gains in consumer welfare from such activities may be open to question.

Demise of the Legal Case

In its complaint, the FTC tried to show that cereal firms had engaged in implicit collusion to proliferate brands with the intent of foreclosing entry. The distinction between such collusion and simple head-to-head competition between major firms proved to be difficult to make. To a large extent the case against the cereal makers remained unproven, and the case was dropped in early 1982. The reasons for brand proliferation in breakfast cereals and whether this has any undesirable economic effects therefore remain unclear.

To Think About

1. Do large cereal producers have advantages that permit them to develop new brands at relatively low cost? Why aren't such techniques available to other firms? Can you think of other products where "brand proliferation" is an important strategy for the firms involved (for example, how about cigarette firms)?
2. Can you think of other ways that producers of differentiated products attempt to prevent the entry of rival producers? How would you explain their decisions to make such expenditures? What would determine their success? Are these strategies subject to other, more favorable interpretations?

Joint products
The inseparable combination of two goods in production or consumption.

advertised. When someone purchases a box of laundry soap, he or she also pays for the advertising messages that the soap maker provides. In other words, a good and its associated advertising are **joint products.** This technical property of the way in which advertising messages are supplied may cause too many messages to be produced. As we have seen, firms will produce additional advertising messages up to the point at which the marginal revenue from the additional demand generated by a message is equal to the message's cost. This additional revenue reflects individuals' willingness to pay both for the goods and for the information provided by the advertising message. Looking at the advertising message alone, individuals value it at less than its production cost (since the good itself must have some value). If the information contained in the advertisement had been marketed separately, its market price would not exceed its production cost. Joint production therefore causes too many advertising messages to be produced.

A second argument that suggests that there may be too much advertising derives from a distinction (first made by Alfred Marshall) between constructive and combative advertising. Constructive advertising conveys useful information to increase the total demand for a product. Combative advertising, on the other hand, reflects the competition among different brands for a share of a fixed market. This kind of advertising is defensive in that any one firm is forced to do it because all the others do. An across-the-board reduction of advertising by all firms would not affect total demand at all, whereas a reduction by any one firm would be harmful to that firm. A reduction in combative advertising would free resources that could be productively employed elsewhere. In Chapter 17 we look at a numerical example of this strategic situation.

Advertising as Information

Although these arguments tend to suggest that many markets will be characterized by "too much" advertising, a number of contrary points have been raised. Advertising provides valuable information to consumers, usually without cost to them. Through advertising consumers can learn about products' prices, about quality differences among products, and about entirely new goods. Because each consumer can use this information without detracting from others' use of it, advertising has some attributes of a "public good" (see Chapter 22), and as we shall show, resources may actually be underallocated to such goods. Advertising may also have beneficial competitive effects on industry structure if the ability to promote a new firm's product reduces barriers to entry created by entrenched brands. For example, the highly successful Volkswagen advertising campaign of the early 1960s may have contributed significantly to opening the U.S. market to imports of small cars.

To the extent there are economies of scale in producing advertising messages, however, these procompetitive effects may be mitigated by cost advantages that will be enjoyed by existing larger firms. There is no general answer to the questions of whether advertising helps or hinders competition and

APPLICATION 16.3

Cigarette Advertising

Prior to 1970, cigarettes were one of the most highly advertised products. Cigarette advertising constituted about 15 percent of all television advertising and a significantly higher fraction of advertising in magazines. Because of this dominance, expenditures on cigarette advertising have been extensively studied. The general conclusion of these studies is that advertising of cigarette brands closely approximates Marshall's notion of combative advertising—that is, it appears that advertising has a major impact on the choice of brand (a favorite example is the hugely successful "Marlboro Man" advertising campaigns of the 1960s), but that such advertising has relatively little effect on the overall level of smoking.

The Advertising Ban

In the late 1960s, cigarette advertising became an extremely controversial subject. As a result of the 1964 Surgeon General's Report linking smoking to lung cancer, Congress passed the Cigarette Labeling and Advertising Act. That act required that all cigarette packs carry a warning label about the possible health hazard of smoking, and that the warning be prominently displayed in advertising. In response to requests from the American Cancer Society and others, the Federal Communications Commission also decided that the "fairness doctrine" required that free television air time be granted for antismoking commercials to combat advertising by cigarette companies. By 1970 antismoking commercials totaled about one-third of cigarette advertising time. In that year, however, Congress, impatient with the continued high level of cigarette sales despite their known health hazards, passed the Public Health Cigarette Smoking Act, which banned cigarette advertising from radio and television. Banning television advertising of cigarettes had the unintended side effect of sharply reducing antismoking commercials since the fairness doctrine no longer applied.

Effects of the Ban

In a 1972 paper, J. L. Hamilton tried to sort out the effects of these changes in the advertising environment on total cigarette sales.[1] He found that cigarette advertising increased average annual cigarette consumption by about 95 cigarettes per year (about 3 percent of average annual consumption). The health scare resulting from the Surgeon General's Report, on the other hand, was estimated to have reduced average sales by 253 cigarettes per year. Even more dramatic results were estimated by Hamilton for the antismoking commercials, which reduced average sales by an average of over 530 cigarettes per year. It appears that scenes of smoke-filled lungs and the appeal of actor Joseph Cotton who was dying of lung cancer left a more vivid impression on viewers than did the Marlboro Man. The failure of cigarette sales to decline very rapidly in the 1980s may also be the result of the reduced level of anti-smoking commercials.

To Think About

1. Did the advertising ban really hurt cigarette sales? Might it actually have helped such sales? Might the ban have helped cigarette companies? How hard do you think they fought the ban?
2. The cigarette example raises the question of how, if at all, the government should regulate advertising. Currently, various rules require that advertisements be "truthful" with respect to claims being made for a product or against a competitor's product. Do these rules seem necessary? Can't consumers decide for themselves whether advertising claims make sense?

[1] J. L. Hamilton, "The Demand for Cigarettes: Advertising the Health Scare, and the Cigarette Advertising Ban," *Review of Economics and Statistics* (November 1972): 401–411.

whether an appropriate level of resources will be devoted to producing advertising messages. A full evaluation will depend on the specific market circumstances. Application 16.3: Cigarette Advertising illustrates some of these complexities for a product for which advertising has been particularly controversial.

Entry by New Firms

The possibility of new firms entering an industry plays an important part in the development of the theory of perfectly competitive price determination. This possibility assures that any long-run profits will be eliminated by new entrants and that firms will produce at the low points of their long-run average cost curves. With relatively few firms, the first of these forces continues to operate. To the extent that entry is possible, long-run profits are constrained. If entry is completely costless, long-run economic profits will be zero (as in the competitive case).

Zero-Profit Equilibrium

Whether or not firms in an imperfectly competitive industry with free entry will be directed to the low point of their average cost curves depends on the nature of the demand curve facing them. If firms are price takers, the analysis given for the competitive case carries over directly. Since P = MR = MC for profit maximization and since P = AC if entry is to result in zero profits, production will take place where MC = AC (that is, at minimum average cost).

Monopolistic competition
Market in which each firm faces a negatively sloped demand curve and there are no barriers to entry.

If firms have some control over the price they receive (perhaps because each produces a slightly differentiated product), each firm will face a downward-sloping demand curve, and the competitive analysis may not hold. Entry still may reduce profits to zero, but now production at minimum average cost is not assured. This situation (which is sometimes termed **monopolistic competition** because it has features of both perfect competition and monopoly) is illustrated in Figure 16.4. Initially, the demand curve facing the typical firm is given by d and economic profits are being earned. New firms will be attracted by these profits, and their entry will shift d inward (because now a larger number of firms are contending with a given market demand curve). Indeed, entry can reduce profits to zero by shifting the demand curve to d′. The level of output that maximizes profits with this demand curve, q′, is not, however, the same as that level at which average costs are minimized, q_m. Rather, the firm will produce less than that "efficient" output level and will exhibit "excess capacity," given by $q_m - q'$. Some economists have hypothesized that this outcome characterizes industries such as service stations, convenience stores, and fast-food franchisers, where product differentiation is prevalent but entry is relatively costless.[4]

Contestable Markets and Market Equilibrium

The conclusion that a zero-profit equilibrium with price above marginal cost (such as that pictured in Figure 16.4) is sustainable in the long run has been

[4]This analysis was originally developed by E. H. Chamberlain, *The Theory of Monopolistic Competition* (Cambridge, Mass.: Harvard University Press, 1950).

Figure 16.4
Entry Reduces Profitability in Oligopoly

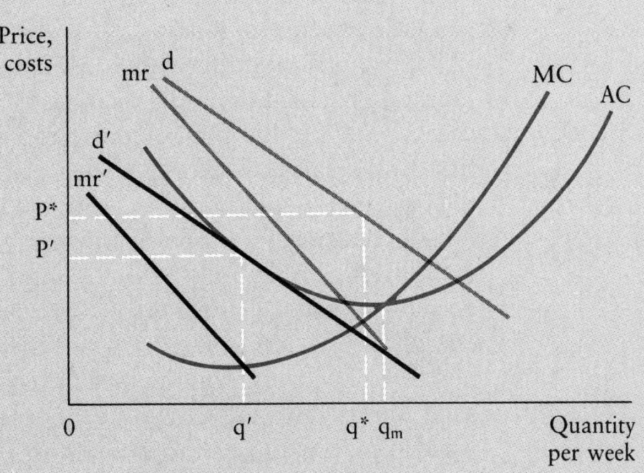

Initially the demand curve facing the firm is d. Marginal revenue is given by mr, and q^* is the profit-maximizing output level. If entry is costless, new firms attracted by the possibility for profits may shift the firm's demand curve inward to d′, where profits are zero. At output level q′, average costs are not a minimum, and the firm exhibits excess capacity given by $q_m - q'$.

challenged recently by several economists.[5] They argue that the model neglects the effects of potential entry on market equilibrium by focusing only on the behavior of actual entrants. This argument introduces the distinction first made by Harold Demetz between competition *in* the market and competition *for* the market by showing that the latter concept provides a more appropriate perspective for analyzing the free entry assumption.[6] Within this broader perspective, the "invisible hand" of competition becomes even more constraining on firms' behavior, and perfect competition results are more likely to emerge.

Contestable market
Market in which entry and exit are costless.

The expanded examination of entry begins by defining a **contestable market** as one in which no potential competitor can enter by cutting price and still make profits (since if profit opportunities existed, potential entrants would take advantage of them). A perfectly contestable market drops the perfectly competitive assumption of price-taking behavior but expands a bit upon the concept of free entry by permitting potential entrants to operate in a hit-and-run manner, snatching up whatever profit opportunities are available. Such an assumption, as we will point out below, is not necessarily accurate in

---

[5]See W. J. Baumol, "Contestable Markets: An Uprising in the Theory of Industry Structure," *American Economic Review* (March 1982): 1–19, and W. J. Baumol, J. C. Panzar, and R. D. Willig, *Contestable Markets and the Theory of Industry Structure* (San Diego, Calif.: Harcourt Brace Jovanovich, 1982).

[6]Harold Demetz, "Why Regulate Utilities?" *Journal of Law and Economics* (April 1968): 55–65.

many market situations, but it does provide a different starting place for a simplified theory of pricing.

The equilibrium illustrated in Figure 16.4 is unsustainable in a contestable market, provided that two or more firms are already in the market. In such a case a potential hit-and-run entrant could turn a quick profit by taking all the first firm's sales by selling q' at a price slightly below P' and making up for the loss this would entail by selling a further increment in output to another firm's customers at a price in excess of average cost. That is, because the equilibrium in Figure 16.4 has a market price that exceeds marginal costs, it permits a would-be entrant to take away one zero-profit firm's market and encroach a bit on other firms' markets where, at the margin, profits are attainable. The only type of market equilibrium that would be impervious to such hit-and-run tactics would be one in which firms earn zero profits and price at marginal costs. As we saw in Chapter 12, this requires that firms produce at the low points of their long-run average cost curves where $P = MC = AC$. Hence, even in the absence of price-taking behavior in markets with relatively few firms, contestability provides an "invisible hand" that guides market equilibrium to a perfectly competitive type of result.

Determination of Industry Structure

This analysis can be taken one step further by showing how industry structure is determined. If, as in Chapter 12, we let q^* represent that output level for which average costs are minimized and Q^* represent the total market for the commodity when price equals marginal (and average) cost, then the number of firms in the industry, n, is given by

$$n = \frac{Q^*}{q^*}. \quad [16.1]$$

Contrary to the perfectly competitive case, this number of firms may be relatively small. In Figure 16.5, for example, exactly four firms fulfill the market demand for Q^*. The contestability assumption will ensure competitive behavior, even though these firms may recognize strategic relationships among themselves. The ability of potential entrants to seize any possible opportunities for profit sharply constrains the types of behavior that are possible and thereby provides a well-defined equilibrium market structure. One of the most important industries that seems to have contestable characteristics is the airline industry and in Application 16.4: Airline Deregulation, Revisited, we look at one aspect of its recent history.

Barriers to Entry

All of the analysis presented so far in this section has assumed free entry and exit. When various barriers prevent such flexibility, these results must be modified. Possible barriers to entry include many of those already discussed

APPLICATION 16.4

Airline Deregulation, Revisited

In Application 10.2 we showed how the passage of the Airline Deregulation Act of 1978 caused major changes in the way airlines operate. Here we look at the market repercussions of these activities. We will be especially interested in whether experiences under deregulation have tended to confirm the predictions of the model of contestable markets.

Airlines' Contestability

In many respects the airline industry represents a perfect illustration of contestability. Because the industry's principal capital assets (planes) are mobile, they can in principle be quickly moved into any market that promises excess profitability. The possibility of such "hit-and-run" entry by potential competitors should keep profits at their competitive levels even in markets with relatively few actual competitors.

The predictions of the contestable model are not, however, ironclad for the case of airlines. A portion of airlines' capital is invested in terminal facilities and is therefore committed to a specific market. Similarly, many flyers tend to prefer to patronize a specific airline (perhaps they belong to its Frequent Flyer Club) so they may not be willing to respond very quickly to differences in price. Finally, some airports (Chicago's O'Hare, Washington, D.C.'s National, and New York's LaGuardia) are operating very close to capacity and have restricted the number of landing slots available to new entrants. All of these factors cause the airline industry to depart from perfect contestability, so empirical analysis is needed to determine whether the industry is still able to obtain relatively competitive results.

Effects of Deregulation

Most studies of airline deregulation have found that fares declined dramatically after 1978. For example, S. Morrison and C. Winston looked at over 800 city-pairs for flights and calculated that by 1983 travelers and airlines had yearly gains of about $8.6 billion from the passage of the Deregulation Act.[1] They note that such estimated gains would be even larger if potential benefits to aircraft manufacturers and to travelers on buses and trains (from lower fares on these modes of transportation) were also taken into account. Still, the authors find that, even after deregulation, the airline industry has some elements of imperfectly competitive behavior. Further annual welfare gains of about $2.5 billion might be obtainable if airline markets more closely approximated the perfectly contestable ideal. Some of these gains might be obtainable by adopting better ways of rationing landing slots at major airports or by making the airline computer reservation system more competitive, but other barriers to competitive behavior may be difficult to crack.

Airline Mergers

One result of airline deregulation was a remarkable shakeup in the structure of the industry. At first, many new firms entered the industry, but in many cases these were quickly consolidated into the larger carriers. In other cases, some major airlines fell on hard times and were sold to other firms. By 1986, for example, the formerly obscure Texas Air, by virtue of its acquisition of Eastern Airlines, had become the largest airline in the United States. Whether all of this turmoil will result in an increased level of airline concentration together with a consequent loss in economic welfare remains unclear, however. Findings from the 1980s suggest some guarded optimism that despite the changing insignia on planes' fuselages, the forces of competition will continue to assure relatively desirable market outcomes.

To Think About

1. How can deregulation of airlines be unambiguously beneficial to both travelers and carriers? Didn't the lower fares brought about by deregulation create some losers? Who were they?
2. Critics of contestability theory argue that the model is, at best, only applicable to two industries—airlines and trucking. Can you think of any other situations where the model might be relevant? Even if hit-and-run entry is impossible, are there other ways in which potential entry constrains market behavior?

[1] S. Morrison and C. Winston, *Economic Effects of Airline Deregulation* (Washington, D.C.: The Brookings Institution, 1986).

Figure 16.5
Contestability and Industry Structure

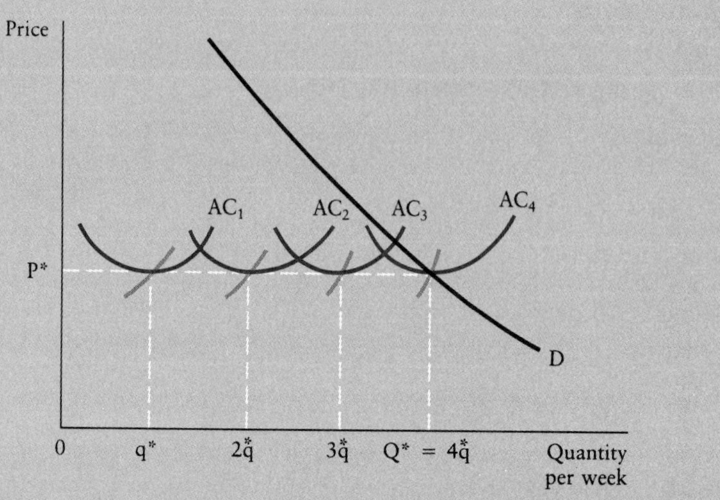

In a contestable market, equilibrium requires that P = MC = AC. The number of firms is determined by market demand (Q*) and by the output level that minimizes average cost (q*).

in connection with monopoly in Chapter 15. They also include those arising specifically out of some features of imperfectly competitive markets. Product differentiation, for example, may raise entry barriers by promoting strong brand loyalty. Or producers may so proliferate their brands that no room remains for would-be entrants to do anything different. In Application 16.2 we showed how this has been alleged to be true in the ready-to-eat breakfast cereal industry. The possibility of strategic pricing decisions may also deter entry if existing firms use them to convince firms wishing to enter that it would be unprofitable to do so. Firms may, for a time, adopt lower, entry-deterring prices in order to accomplish this goal, with the intent of raising prices once potential entrants disappear (assuming they do). A somewhat different version of this theory assumes that large firms may be able to buy up small ones by practicing "predatory pricing." Prices are reduced until the small firms can be bought at a low price, then the large firm can reestablish its high prices. Application 16.5: Standard Oil and Predatory Pricing looks at this possibility both in theory and in its most important historical illustration—the case of the Standard Oil Company.

Finally, the completely flexible type of hit-and-run entry behavior assumed in the theory of contestable markets may be subject to two other types of barriers in the real world. First, some types of capital investments made by firms may not be reversible. A firm cannot build an automobile assembly plant for a week's use and then dismantle it at no loss. In this case there are exit costs that will make recurrent raids on the industry unprofitable. Of course, in other cases, such as the trucking or airline industry, capital may be easily rented for short periods, and exit here poses few costs. So competitive-type

APPLICATION 16.5

Standard Oil and Predatory Pricing

The Standard Oil case of 1911 was one of the landmarks of U.S. antitrust law. In that case Rockefeller's Standard Oil Company was found to have "attempted to monopolize" the production, refining, and distribution of petroleum in the United States and was therefore in violation of the Sherman Act. As a result of this finding, the company was split into several independent companies, many of which still exist today (Exxon, Amoco, Chevron, Mobil, and so forth). One of the ways that Standard Oil was found to have established its monopoly was through the use of "predatory pricing." It was claimed that the company would cut prices dramatically to drive rivals out of a particular market and then raise prices back to monopoly levels after these rivals had left the market or had sold out to the Standard Oil goliath. This view of how Standard Oil operated is one of the more durable legends about nineteenth-century business practices.

Theory of Predatory Pricing

Unfortunately, the notion that Standard Oil practiced such predatory pricing policies in order to discourage entry and encourage exit by its rivals makes little sense in terms of economic theory. If a would-be monopolist wishes to impose such costs on its rivals, it must sell its output below average cost, perhaps below average variable cost. It must also be willing to absorb the extra sales that such lowered prices would bring. The predator must therefore operate with relatively large losses for some time in the hope that the smaller losses this may cause for rivals will eventually cause them to give up. This strategy is inferior to the would-be monopoly simply buying its smaller rivals in the marketplace. Even if such mergers were illegal, it is unclear that the predator has longer staying power than its rivals in sticking to a low-price policy—especially since the rivals know that price must eventually return to providing a normal profit.

Actual Evidence on Standard Oil

These thoughts prompted J. S. McGee to reexamine the historical record of what Standard Oil actually did. In a famous 1958 article McGee concluded that Standard Oil neither tried to use predatory policies nor that its actual price policies had the effect of driving rivals from the oil business.[1] In all, McGee looked at over 100 refineries that were bought by Standard Oil between 1871 and 1900. He could find no evidence that predatory behavior by Standard Oil caused these firms to sell out. Indeed, in many cases Standard paid quite good prices for these refineries, which themselves were reasonably profitable. McGee also looked in detail at the effect that Standard Oil's retailing activities had on the network of jobbers and small retailers who had grown up around the oil and kerosene business in the late nineteenth century. Although it seems clear that Standard's retailing methods were superior to those used previously (and these were quickly adopted by other firms), the company does not seem to have practiced local price cutting. Hence, although Standard Oil did represent a monopoly in oil refining and therefore probably required some attention from policymakers, it does not appear to have attained this position through predatory behavior.

To Think About

1. If the facts do not support the notion of predatory pricing by Standard Oil, why do you think the company is so widely believed to have practiced it? What kinds of marketwide trends were influencing oil pricing during the late nineteenth century? Might these have been mistaken for predatory behavior?
2. A modern version of predatory pricing involves entry deterrence: an existing firm is assumed to deter entry by adopting a price lower than a monopoly would charge. Does this theory make sense? What price would a monopoly have to charge to truly deter entry? Would such a pricing strategy be in the monopoly's long-term interest?

[1] J. S. McGee, "Predatory Price Cutting: The Standard Oil (NJ) Case," *Journal of Law and Economics* (October 1958): 137–169.

results might occur in these industries. Second, the contestable market model requires that quantity demanded respond quickly to price differentials. If, instead, demanders switch slowly to a new product, potential entrants cannot establish themselves in a market rapidly. Hence, their ability to enforce marginal cost pricing in existing firms in the market will be constrained.[7] The importance of all such entry restrictions for market behavior is ultimately an empirical question.

Industrial Organization Theory

So far in this chapter, we have been primarily concerned with a formal analysis of price determination in oligopolistic markets. Although this analysis offered a number of insights into the behavior of such markets, we also saw that it is very difficult to capture in a simple model all of the factors that may affect market outcomes. The field of industrial organization seeks to provide details on those aspects of market behavior that are not easily captured by such models. This concluding section looks at some of this analysis.

It is customary to divide industrial organization theory into three topics: (1) market structure; (2) firm conduct; and (3) economic performance. *Market structure* is concerned with describing the industry. How many firms are there? What types of products are produced? Are there increasing returns to scale? Are there significant barriers to entry? Understanding such facts is necessary to analyzing *firm conduct.* Firm conduct concerns such matters as firms' output and price decisions, product differentiation, advertising, investment decisions, research activities, and so forth — it investigates what firms do. *Economic performance* is concerned with appraising the desirability of particular markets. Criteria used in that appraisal include questions of economic efficiency, distributional equity, and the long-term growth of the industry.

Market Structure

Perhaps the most important types of information on market structure are those that concern the number, size, and general concentration of firms in an industry. A representative selection of these data appears in Table 16.1. Of particular interest to industrial organization economists are the concentration ratios — the percentages of total domestic shipments produced by the 4, 8, 20, and 50 largest firms. The figures indicate, for example, that production of motor vehicles, cigarettes, and organic fibers are all highly concentrated, with 4-firm concentration ratios of around 80 or higher. On the other hand, industries such as commercial printing, bottled soft drinks, and sawmills have a

[7]For some additional criticism of this type, see Michael Spence, "Contestable Markets and the Theory of Industrial Structure," *Journal of Economic Literature* (September 1983): 981–990.

Table 16.1
Representative Data on U.S. Industrial Structure, 1977

Industry	Number of Firms	Total Output[a]	Total Value Added[a]	Percentage of Output Produced by: 4 Largest	8 Largest	20 Largest	50 Largest
Motor vehicles	254	$76,518	$18,724	93%	99%	99+%	99+%
Steel mills	395	41,998	15,332	45	65	84	95
Pharmaceuticals	655	11,459	8,214	24	43	73	91
Aircraft	151	14,834	8,134	59	81	99	99+
Petroleum refining	192	91,689	14,424	30	53	81	94
Photographic equipment	702	9,945	6,732	72	86	90	94
Electronic computers	808	12,924	7,624	44	51	71	85
Commercial printing	10,964	9,360	5,338	6	10	17	26
Tires	121	8,971	4,347	70	88	97	99+
Sawmills	6,966	10,867	4,453	17	23	36	49
Toilet preparations	644	6,557	4,527	40	56	79	90
Cigarettes	8	6,377	3,803	90	100	100	100
Organic fibers	37	6,380	2,804	78	90	99	100
Bottled and canned soft drinks	1,758	10,007	4,085	15	22	36	50

[a]In millions.
Source: Statistical Abstract of the United States, 1981 (Washington, D.C.: U.S. Government Printing Office, 1981), table 1427.

low concentration of production, with less than half of industry output being produced by the 50 largest firms. Thus there appears to be a great variety among the structures of U.S. industries.

The types of data on industry concentration that are illustrated in Table 16.1 suffer from a number of shortcomings. Imports are not reflected in the data, and this may lead to a distorted picture of the degree of competition in industries (such as automobiles) where competition from foreign goods is strong. Similarly, the data presented are quite aggregated, and they may obscure concentration patterns in more narrowly defined markets. For example, the "toilet preparations" industry appears to be relatively unconcentrated on the basis of the data in the table, although some sectors of this market (such as toothpaste production) are very concentrated indeed. Many other problems of interpretation may arise in the data from the specific details of the industry in question. The low concentration in soft drinks, for example, becomes questionable when it is recognized that many of the local bottlers represented in the data operate under exclusive areawide licenses from the Coca-Cola or PepsiCo companies. Or, as Application 16.6: The IBM Case shows for the case of computers, it may sometimes be difficult to define a "market" in an

APPLICATION 16.6

The IBM Case

On the final day of the Johnson administration, an antitrust case was filed by the U.S. Department of Justice against International Business Machines Corporation (IBM). During the ensuing 13 years, the case developed all the elements of a television soap opera. Successive Justice Department officials had considerable difficulty in designing a coherent case, legal careers were made and destroyed at the prestigious firm of Cravath, Swaine and Moore (IBM's attorneys), many economists made tidy consultants' fees on the case, and IBM even sought to have the judge in the case disqualified for being biased. In all, the case generated 66 million pages of documentation and probably cost taxpayers and IBM hundreds of millions of dollars. Despite these vast expenditures of physical and human resources, the federal government ultimately dropped the IBM case on January 8, 1982, on the grounds that it was "flimsy" and "without merit." This long-running and almost farcical saga illustrates several elements of industrial organization theory as it relates to modern antitrust litigation.

Defining the Computer Market

Consider first the question of what market IBM was alleged to have monopolized. In its original complaint, the Justice Department accused IBM of monopolizing the "general purpose computer" market in which, it was asserted, IBM had about a 70 percent share. In its defense, IBM continually sought to expand this market definition (to include all information-processing and retrieval systems, for example) and to show it was really a rather small fish in a big pond (which included, for example, American Telephone and Telegraph Company). At the time the case was dropped, the litigants had, after 13 years of debate, still not reached any agreement on the very basic question of what market IBM monopolized.

IBM's Conduct

Similar ambiguities surrounded the legal arguments of whether IBM had "attempted to monopolize" the computer market. Three of the government's specific charges against IBM's conduct illustrate the dispute. First, the government alleged that IBM introduced "fighting machines" (particularly model 360-70) whose timing was targeted specifically to undermine competitors' efforts to develop new products. Second, it was argued that IBM's practice of selling its maintenance and programming services in a bundle with its machines made it difficult for competitors to gain a foothold in the market since they could not also offer such bundles. Finally, IBM's use of discounts for educational institutions was deemed anticompetitive because they resulted in a generation of students trained only on IBM equipment.

IBM's Defense

IBM, in its defense, attacked each of these conduct charges by asserting they simply reflected aggressive competition and good corporate citizenship. Introduction of new machines was, according to IBM, just normal business practice in the fast-moving computer industry. Similarly, IBM argued it bundled its services and equipment together simply to serve customers better. Other companies were, after all, free to adopt the same practice. Finally, educational discounts were, according to IBM, the natural response of a company seeking to promote general social well-being—to impugn its motives was unfairly cynical.

Most uninvolved observers of the IBM case saw some truths in both the government and IBM briefs. The decision to drop the case probably reflected the sensible judgment that the case had reached a stage where the costs of further litigation outweighed any potential gains from a government victory. In the 13 years since the case was filed, the computer industry had changed greatly, with hundreds of new firms being founded and IBM's share of the market falling rather sharply. It seems that, whatever had happened in the past, the computer industry was functioning rather well in the 1980s, and the social gains from tampering with its structure might be negligible.

To Think About

1. What market was it that IBM may have monopolized in the 1960s? If you were a government attorney, how would you define the relevant market? What if you were an attorney for IBM?
2. In the Alcoa case, Judge Learned Hand ruled that since Alcoa controlled nearly two-thirds of the primary aluminum production capacity in the United States, it was a monopoly. Doesn't the strict definition of monopoly require 100 percent control of the market?

economically meaningful way. Despite all these difficulties, data such as those in Table 16.1 are about all the quantitative information that is available on real-world industrial structure, and such data are widely used.

Several other aspects of market structure have been systematically examined by industrial organization economists. Particular attention has been focused on barriers to entry because this concept plays a key role both in the model of perfectly competitive pricing in the long run and in the theory of contestable markets. Two types of entry barriers have been intensively studied: cost barriers derived from economies of scale and barriers created by firms' strategic decisions. Barriers of the latter type include those derived from firms' pricing decisions and from product differentiation. There is a vast amount of empirical information on all of these topics.[8]

A final structural concern has been the study of mergers. "Horizontal" mergers (that is, two firms producing the same types of goods) raise no particularly novel economic issues—they will clearly increase the concentration in an industry and therefore may create the kinds of allocational inefficiencies outlined previously in this chapter. More difficult to evaluate are "vertical" mergers, in which a firm integrates a given production process within itself rather than relying on a network of sellers of intermediate products. For example, a merger of a computer chip maker and a computer assembler would represent such vertical integration. In this case the effects on the market price of the end product (computers) may be indeterminate. Vertical integration may produce cost efficiencies that tend to reduce prices, but it may also produce some degree of monopolistic control over prices of inputs. Hence, no clear conclusion is possible.

In recent years "conglomerate" mergers have become commonplace among firms in very different industries. Huge firms such as ITT or Textron operate in literally hundreds of markets, and this raises the question of whether those firms' subsidiaries behave in ways similar to independent firms in such markets. As with vertical mergers, a variety of analyses have been proposed, ranging from the notion that conglomerate firms provide "synergistic" cost savings and diversification for their subsidiaries to the hypothesis that conglomerates may aid in monopolization by engaging in cross-subsidization among subsidiaries.

Firm Conduct

The *firm conduct* aspect of industrial organization theory attempts to provide some real-world details that will supplement the various pricing models discussed earlier in this chapter. Because it has proved to be quite difficult to ob-

[8]The classic treatment of the entry issue is presented by J. S. Bain in *Barriers to New Competition* (Cambridge, Mass.: Harvard University Press, 1956). Bain estimates that a new product in a differentiated market may have to sell for 10 to 25 percent less than one already established in the market in order to win customer acceptance.

tain detailed information about firms' strategic motives and assumptions (say, through interviews with managers), the focus of much firm conduct research has been on the narrower question of whether coordination in pricing decisions is possible or likely. Economists have examined the roles of explicit agreements, tacit understandings, price leadership, commonly used rules of thumb, and industrywide price lists as mechanisms for effecting such coordination. All of these have proved to be successful at times. But increasing legal scrutiny of such devices, combined with the instability in cartels created by incentives to chisel on price, have limited the possibility of success of these mechanisms.

Many other aspects of market organization tend to deter interfirm coordination. In particular, dynamic changes in either demand or cost conditions over time may make it very difficult for a would-be cartel to decide precisely how to maximize joint profits. The expected gains from such coordination may appear to be quite small. That judgment may be altered, however, if the cartel can devise some sort of coordinating device or if it can enlist government aid in the pursuit of its goals.

Industry Performance

The final aspect of industrial organization analysis concerns appraising *industry performance*. Traditionally, the primary focus here has been on examining the allocational efficiency of alternative industry structures. Two different types of criteria are employed. The first concerns the "static efficiency" of the industry, which is usually taken to mean how closely behavior in that industry approaches the perfectly competitive ideal. Industries with fairly large numbers of firms, low entry barriers, and prices close to marginal cost are regarded as "effectively" competitive. On the other hand, important departures from these ideals will reverse that assessment, and there may be static losses in social welfare as a result of such failures. A general conclusion of this type of research is that a large portion of the U.S. economy appears to be effectively competitive and that the degree of competition may have increased in recent years. For example, W. G. Shepherd finds that in 1980, 77 percent of U.S. national income was produced in industries that he classifies as effectively competitive, with 2 percent being produced under monopoly, 3 percent in industries with dominant firms, and 18 percent in "tight" oligopolies. He also reports that the share of oligopolies was roughly halved since the 1950s, resulting in a sharply rising incidence of competitive behavior. Shepherd attributes important roles to antitrust enforcement, increasing international trade, and government deregulation efforts in bringing about these results.[9]

[9]W. G. Shepherd, "Causes of Increased Competition in the U.S. Economy," *Review of Economics and Statistics* (November 1982): 613–626.

A second set of allocational criteria concerns "dynamic" efficiency. These criteria focus on industry progress over time. In this case there is no well-defined ideal model to serve as a standard of judgment. Rather, the criteria involve a number of performance measures such as industry growth, productivity improvements, favorable relative price trends, and new product innovation. Much of this research stems from the initial work of Joseph Schumpeter (see Chapter 15) on the importance of entrepreneurial profit-seeking activity to the growth process. Developing and testing specific hypotheses about the effect of market structure on various performance measures have proved rather difficult, however.

In addition to allocational criteria, a number of noneconomic performance measures have also been examined by industrial organization theorists. Questions about the distribution of economic profits among industry participants or the impact of industry structure on relative wage rates have been examined to assess the possibility that departures from a competitive market may be desirable for equity reasons. Similarly, some authors have stressed the ability of various market organizations to generate employment for workers independent of whether such industries do so efficiently. Finally, the political influence of firms has been examined, with the goal of creating market structures (possibly competitive) that minimize that influence. As this partial list of additional criteria makes clear, the field of industrial organization may overlap with many other social science disciplines.

Summary

Many real-world markets resemble neither of the polar cases of perfect competition or monopoly. Rather, such markets are characterized by some degree of concentration, and the individual firms have some effect on market price—they are not price takers—but no single firm exercises complete market control. In these circumstances there is no generally accepted model of market behavior. Aspects of both competitive and monopoly theory must be used, together with particular institutional details of the market in question, in order to develop a realistic picture of how price and output decisions are made. Several specific issues that must be addressed in developing such a model are the following:

- The degree of market concentration and the importance of feedback effects in firms' decision-making processes.
- The importance of nonprice methods of competition, such as product differentiation and advertising.
- Entry conditions in the market and the constraints that potential entry places on attaining monopoly profits.
- The uncertainty faced by individual firms and the strategies they may adopt to cope with it.
- The potential benefits from monopolization of a market and the legal and resource costs associated with maintaining such a position.

Review Questions

1. One way of differentiating among various market structures is by the nature of the demand curve that faces the individual firm. What kind of demand curve faces a firm in a perfectly competitive industry? What demand curve faces a monopolist? In what way is the demand curve facing a firm in an imperfectly competitive industry a mixture of these two extremes?
2. Why is the cartel solution to the oligopoly pricing problem unstable? If one firm in a cartel believes it can increase profits by chiseling on price, what is it implicitly assuming about the pricing behavior of other cartel members?
3. What does each firm in a kinked demand curve model assume about its rivals? Why does the model result in prices that are relatively unresponsive to changes in input prices? What are some of the shortcomings of this model?
4. What does a price leader assume about the behavior of its rivals? If two firms tried to be the price leader, why would both be thwarted? Why would you generally expect the largest firm in an industry to be the price leader?
5. Explain how product differentiation and advertising can be treated as inputs in the firm's decisions. How do these inputs differ from other types of inputs in the way they affect profitability? How would the firm's profit-maximizing decisions about these inputs differ from its decisions about capital or labor input?
6. In Figure 16.4 the demand curve facing a firm in a monopolistically competitive industry is shown as being tangent to its average cost curve at q′. Explain why this is a long-run equilibrium position for this firm. That is, why does marginal revenue equal marginal cost and why are long-run profits zero?
7. Why does the model of a contestable market require that there be no costs of entry or exit? What kinds of costs might a firm incur exiting an industry? Why might such "sunk" costs inhibit entry in the first place?
8. Can firms themselves through their behavior deter entry into a market? What kinds of strategic actions might deter entry? Do firms already "in" a market have advantages over would-be entrants in choosing such strategies?
9. Concentration ratios are one of the most frequently used measures of market structure. Under what conditions would such ratios be fairly good indicators of the kind of pricing behavior that occurs in an industry? When might such measures be particularly inappropriate?
10. Why does the application of U.S. (and most other) antitrust laws require definition of a relevant market? Why will this definitional process usually be somewhat difficult and subject to dispute? How might the concept of the cross-price elasticity of demand help to clarify matters?

Problems

16.1 Suppose there are two firms selling ice cream cones in a small town. The prices charged by the firms are given by P_1 and P_2. Because the firms sell different types of cones, their goods are only partial substitutes for one another. The demand facing firm 1 is given by

$$q_1 = 10 - P_1 + \tfrac{1}{2}P_2$$

and that facing firm 2 is

$$q_2 = 10 - P_2 + \tfrac{1}{2}P_1.$$

Both firms have a constant marginal cost of \$2 per cone.

a. Suppose each firm sets a price equal to marginal cost. How many cones will each sell and what will each firm's profits be?
b. Suppose firm 1 believes firm 2 will have a price of \$2 per cone. How much should this firm charge to maximize profits? (Hint: Price should be halfway between $P = MC$ and the price for which $q_1 = 0$.) What will this firm's profits be if $P_2 = 2$?
c. Suppose firm 2 also follows the strategy described in part b. What price will it charge and what will its profits be if $P_1 = 2$?
d. Are the decisions in parts b and c consistent with each other? How might the firms choose their prices in a consistent way? (See the discussion of Cournot equilibrium in Chapter 17.)
e. Suppose the two firms merged. What pricing policy would maximize their total joint profits? (Hint: Assume they should each charge the same price.)

16.2 Explain the following types of pricing behavior. Why might these represent profit maximization? What, if anything, do these strategies imply about the market power of the firm in these markets?

a. Polaroid Corporation sells instant cameras and film. It prices its cameras relatively cheaply, but prices its film far above marginal cost.
b. IBM sells bundles of computer products (processors, displays, printers, and software) together far more cheaply than the same items bought separately.
c. Pizza Hut charges a high price (\$15) for the first pizza bought, but a low price (\$4) for each additional pizza.
d. Most restaurants have a much higher price markup on wine than on food items.
e. American automobile companies charge high prices for options such as decorative trim, electric windows, and fancy radios. Japanese imports, on the other hand, tend to include many options in their base price.
f. United Way collects for many different charities and determines how a donor's funds will be distributed to these charities.

16.3 Some critics contend that U.S. automobile companies pursue a strategy of planned obsolescence: that is, they produce cars that are intended to become obsolete in a few years. Would that strategy make sense in a monopoly market? How might the production of obsolescence depend on the characteristics of market demand? How would oligopolistic competition affect the profitability of the strategy?

16.4 Suppose advertising expenditures are able to increase a firm's sales. How should a firm decide on the profit-maximizing level of advertising? What marginal rule should it use?

16.5 Under monopolistic competition, each firm sells a product that is slightly different from its competitors. Suppose two firms in this industry merged. Would they continue to produce two different goods? Or should they focus on a single product? Develop an intuitive argument to suggest what the profit-maximizing solution might be.

16.6 In the 1945 Alcoa case, Judge Learned Hand was faced with deciding whether Alcoa had a monopoly in aluminum production. A crucial issue concerned the distribution between "primary" aluminum production (P) and "secondary" (recycled) production (S). Three different market share measures were used to evaluate Alcoa's position:

$$I = P_A/P$$

$$II = P_A/(P + S)$$

$$III = (P_A - F)/(P + S)$$

where P_A = Alcoa's primary production (Alcoa was not significantly engaged in recycling) and F = the amount of Alcoa's primary production that it used for its own fabricated products.

a. Which of these definitions seems to provide the best approximation for the market for aluminum production?
b. How would you answer question a. if you were an Alcoa attorney? How would you answer if you were a government attorney?
c. The figures showed the following results for each of the three market share measures

$$I = .90$$

$$II = .64$$

$$III = .33\,.$$

If you were Judge Hand, how would you rule on the charge that Alcoa had a monopoly? How did the Judge actually rule?

16.7 In the Clorox case, Procter & Gamble was alleged to be a potential entrant into the liquid bleach market and was therefore prevented from buying Clorox. Can you devise a way to use firms' cost curves and the demand curves facing the firms to differentiate among actual entrants? Potential entrants? Nonentrants? Use your analysis to suggest what the court should have looked for in this antitrust case.

*16.8 Suppose that the total market demand for crude oil is given by

$$Q_D = -2{,}000P + 70{,}000$$

where Q is the quantity of oil in thousands of barrels per year and P is the dollar price per barrel. Suppose also that there are 1,000 identical small producers of crude oil, each with marginal costs given by

$$MC = q + 5$$

where q is the output of the typical firm.

a. Assuming that each small oil producer acts as a price taker, calculate the typical firm's supply curve ($q = \ldots.$), the market supply curve ($Q_S = \ldots.$), and the market equilibrium price and quantity (where $Q_D = Q_S$).
b. Suppose a practically infinite supply of crude oil is discovered in New Jersey by a would-be price leader and that this oil can be produced at a constant average and marginal cost of AC = MC = \$15 per barrel. Assume also that the supply behavior of the competitive fringe described in part a is not changed by this discovery. Calculate the demand curve facing the price leader.
c. Assuming that the price leader's marginal revenue curve is given by

$$MR = -Q/1{,}500 + 25\,,$$

how much should the price leader produce in order to maximize profits? What price and quantity will now prevail in the market?

*Denotes a problem that is rather difficult.

d. Graph your result indicating the market demand curve, the supply curve for the competitive fringe, and the price leader's demand, MR, and MC curves.
e. Does consumer surplus increase as a result of the New Jersey oil discovery? How does consumer surplus after the discovery compare to what would exist if the New Jersey oil were supplied competitively?

16.9 Suppose a firm is considering investing in research that would lead to a cost-saving innovation. Assuming the firm can retain this innovation solely for its own use, will the additional profits from the lower (marginal) costs be greater if the firm is a competitive price taker or if the firm is a monopolist? Develop a careful graphical argument. More generally, develop a verbal analysis to suggest how market structure may affect the adoption of cost-saving innovations.

CHAPTER 17

Strategy and Game Theory

Economists have developed several models that attempt to capture the interdependent nature of decisions in markets with relatively few firms. These models range from simple two-firm (*duopoly*) models through complex models that portray an arbitrary number of firms making several different decisions. Although none of the models has won the widespread acceptance that the monopoly and perfectly competitive models have, some of them are useful to demonstrate the nature of interdependence in a simple setting. In this chapter we first look at a simple duopoly model that demonstrates market interdependence. The later sections of the chapter then examine the duopoly problem using game theory, and this offers an opportunity to develop a general survey of that important topic.

A Simple Model of Duopoly

We begin our study of strategy by looking at a simple market situation involving two firms. Suppose the demand function for a good is given by

$$Q = 120 - P, \qquad [17.1]$$

where P is the market price of the good and Q is the quantity sold per week. This curve is shown in Figure 17.1. Assume also that there are no costs of

Figure 17.1
Monopolist's Output Choice

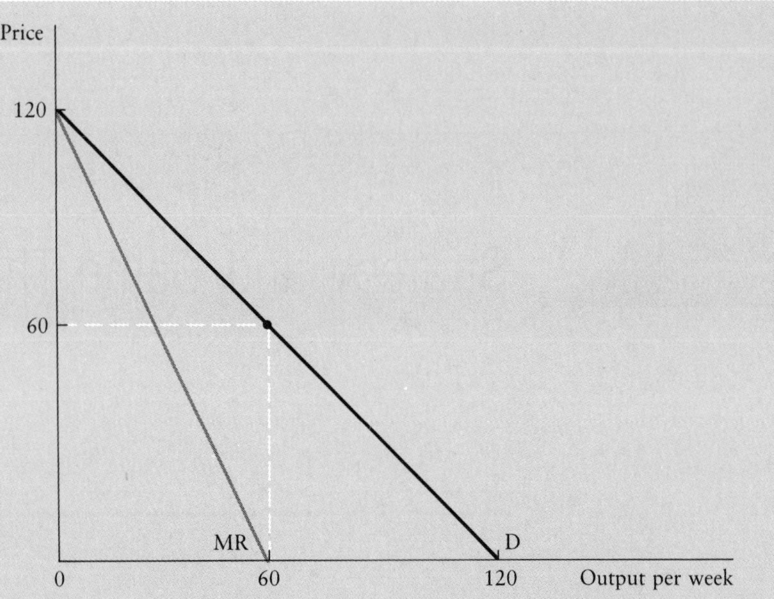

Given the market demand curve $Q = 120 - P$, a zero-cost monopolist would produce that output (60) for which marginal revenue is equal to 0. At this output, a price of \$60 would prevail and profits would be \$3,600. Notice that $MR = 0$ at an output level $= \frac{1}{2}Q_0$ (where Q_0 is the quantity demanded at $P = 0$). This result holds for any linear demand curve.

production.[1] The good may, for example, be water from a spring that is believed to have health benefits. If there were only one firm facing the demand curve in Equation 17.1, or if two firms decide to coordinate their decisions as a cartel, this monopoly will choose to produce 60 units of output. At this output level P will be \$60 and revenues (and profits, since there are no costs) will be \$3,600 (= \$60 × 60). For the future development of a duopoly model, it is important to note how the profit-maximizing output level is chosen. In this case Q is chosen to be one-half of that quantity that would be demanded at a price of zero.[2] Using this conclusion we now turn to an examination of how two independent firms might respond to this market situation.

[1]The assumption of zero costs is for convenience only. The models to be presented can be easily generalized to include any general cost function. To do so would not illustrate anything new about the duopoly problem, however.

[2]It is generally true for a *linear demand* curve that marginal revenue is equal to zero at $Q = \frac{1}{2}Q_0$ (where Q_0 is the quantity demanded at a price of zero). Indeed, if marginal cost is any fixed number, marginal revenue equals marginal cost at $Q = \frac{1}{2}Q_c$ (where Q_c is the quantity demanded when price equals marginal cost). Showing why these results hold is a simple application of our definition of marginal revenue—see Chapter 10.

The Cournot Model

Cournot model
A model of duopoly in which each firm assumes the other firm's output will not change if it changes its own output level.

A French economist, Augustin Cournot, presented the first formal model of duopoly in 1838.[3] In devising this **Cournot model,** the author assumed that each of the two firms in the market took the other firm's activities into account in only a very limited way. In particular, Cournot theorized that firm 1, say, chooses its output level (q_1) on the assumption that the output of firm 2 (q_2) is fixed and will not be adjusted in response to firm 1's actions. Mathematically, total market output is given by

$$Q = q_1 + q_2 = 120 - P. \qquad [17.2]$$

Assuming that q_2 is fixed, the demand curve facing firm 1 is given by

$$q_1 = (120 - q_2) - P. \qquad [17.3]$$

This simply says that some portion of market demand is assumed to be taken by firm 2, and firm 1 makes its choice from what is left. Using the rule discussed in footnote 2, it is obvious that firm 1's profit-maximizing output level would be given by

$$q_1 = \frac{120 - q_2}{2}. \qquad [17.4]$$

Reaction function
In the Cournot model a function or graph that shows how much one firm will produce given what the other firm produces.

That is, firm 1 produces half the output demanded at a price of zero after allowing for firm 2's production. Consequently, the output level actually chosen by firm 1 will depend on the level of output that firm 2 is assumed to produce. For example, if firm 2 chooses to produce 60, firm 1 would choose 30 [= (120 − 60)/2] and market price would be \$30 [= 120 − (q_1 + q_2) = 120 − 90]. Equation 17.4 is called the **reaction function** for firm 1 because it demonstrates how this firm reacts to firm 2's actions. This reaction function is shown graphically in Figure 17.2.

Firm 2 might perform a similar analysis and arrive at a reaction function that expresses q_2 as a function of q_1 of the form

$$q_2 = \frac{120 - q_1}{2}. \qquad [17.5]$$

This reaction function is also shown in Figure 17.2.

---

[3]Augustin Cournot, *Researches into the Mathematical Principles of the Theory of Wealth,* translated by N. T. Bacon (New York: Macmillan, 1897).

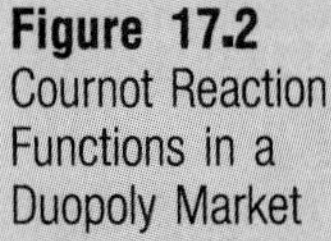

Figure 17.2
Cournot Reaction Functions in a Duopoly Market

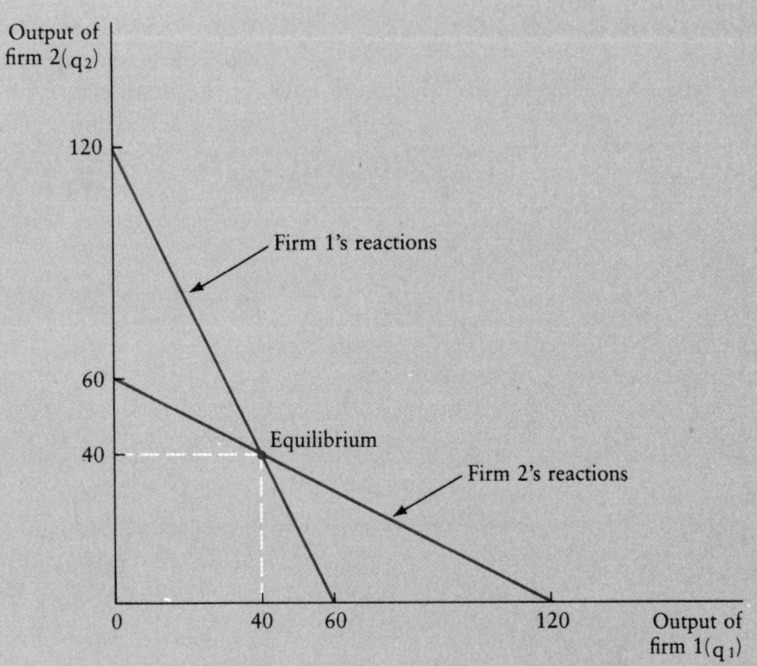

The reaction function for firm 1 shows how that firm will react on the assumption that firm 2's output choice is not affected by the level of q_1 produced. The function for firm 2 shows a similar reaction for firm 2. Only at the point of intersection of the two curves ($q_1 = 40$, $q_2 = 40$) will both of the firms' assumptions be realized. This point of intersection is called the Cournot equilibrium point.

Strategic Equilibrium

So far we know how firm 1 reacts to firm 2's decisions and how firm 2 reacts to firm 1's decisions. These decisions are consistent with each other only at the point where the two lines intersect. At all other points the two firms' output choices are inconsistent because each firm expects the other to be producing at some output level other than what it actually is. The point of intersection is the only **Cournot equilibrium** that can prevail in this two-firm market. It is easy to show that this point of intersection is given by

Cournot equilibrium
A solution to the Cournot model in which each firm makes the correct assumption about what the other firm will produce.

$$q_1 = 40$$
$$q_2 = 40\,. \qquad [17.6]$$

At the Cournot equilibrium both firms will produce 40, total output will be 80, and the market price will be \$40 (= 120 − 80). This Cournot equilibrium solution is stable because each firm has adjusted its output to the actual output level being produced by the other firm. Total industry revenues and profits in this case ($3,200—$1,600 for each firm) are lower than under the monopoly case ($3,600). This is a result of the failure of the firms in the duopoly situation to coordinate their actions perfectly. Only if the firms collude (as in Application 17.1: The Great Electrical Equipment Conspiracy) will they be able to achieve the highest profits possible from the given demand curve. Otherwise, the uncertainties in the market lead to a greater level of production than in the cartel case. It is possible, however, that one of the duopoly firms can still increase its profits (at the expense of the other firm) by recognizing the way in which the other firm reacts.

Stackelberg Leadership Model

Suppose firm 1 recognizes that firm 2 reacts to its output as given by Equation 17.5. If firm 2 always follows such a response, firm 1 can increase its profits by making use of its knowledge of these reactions. Substituting Equation 17.5 into the demand equation (17.3) gives

$$q_1 = 120 - q_2 - P = 120 - \frac{120 - q_1}{2} - P$$

$$= 60 + \frac{q_1}{2} - P \qquad [17.7]$$

or

$$q_1 = 120 - 2P. \qquad [17.8]$$

By knowing firm 2's reaction, we have been able to derive the demand curve facing firm 1 as a function of its output only. Now, using the profit-maximizing rule, firm 1 should produce

$$q_1 = 60 \qquad [17.9]$$

since this is the output level at a price of 0 divided by 2 (= 120/2). Now if firm 1 produces 60 and firm 2 is a faithful follower of its reaction function, it will produce

$$q_2 = \frac{120 - 60}{2} = 30. \qquad [17.10]$$

Consequently, industry output will be 90 and market price will be $30. The profits earned by firm 1 will be

$$\pi_1 = \$30 \times 60 = \$1{,}800 \qquad [17.11]$$

APPLICATION 17.1

The Great Electrical Equipment Conspiracy

Even though an industry may be reasonably profitable, the lure of increased profits provides a considerable incentive to cartelization. This lure is especially strong when there are relatively few firms in an industry and when it is fairly easy for the members of the cartel to police what the others are doing. This was the case for the electrical equipment industry in the early 1950s, which developed an elaborate price-rigging scheme. Unfortunately, the scheme came under both increasing internal friction and external legal scrutiny. By the 1960s the scheme had died, and executives of several major companies were in prison.[1]

The Markets for Generators and Switchgear

Electric turbine generators and high voltage switchgear are sold to electric utilities. Often these are designed to unique specifications and the prices of individual sales can run into many millions of dollars. Because of pent-up demand from the constraints of World War II, the 1950s was a period of rapid growth in the sale of electricity and in the building of new generation facilities. At this time, the electrical equipment industry tended to be dominated by only a few firms: General Electric, Westinghouse, Allis Chalmers, I.T.E. Corp., and Federal Pacific. Although expected growth in the industry promised good prospects for most of these firms, the possibility for cartelization seemed even better.

Bid Rigging Schemes

The principal problem faced by the electrical equipment firms in creating a cartel was that most sales took place through sealed bidding. To avoid open competition, they therefore had to devise a method for coordinating the bids each firm would make. Through a complex strategy that involved dividing up the United States into bidding regions and using the lunar calendar to decide whose turn it was to "win" a bid in a region, the firms were able to overcome the secrecy usually involved in submitting sealed bids. These practices worked quite well until the end of the decade. They probably raised total profits of electrical equipment manufacturers by as much as $50–100 million over the period.

Demise of the Conspiracy

Toward the end of the 1950s the electrical equipment conspiracy came under increasing internal pressure as its leaders (General Electric and Westinghouse) were asked to give a greater share of the business to other firms. New entry by importers and low-cost domestic producers also caused some problems for the cartel. The final blow to the conspiracy came with a series of widely publicized hearings under Senator Kefauver in 1959 and the federal indictment of 52 executives of the leading generator, switchgear, and transformer companies. Although the government recommended jail sentences for 30 of these defendants, only 7 actually served time in jail. Still, the notoriety of the case and the personal disruption it caused to those involved probably had a chilling effect on the future establishment of other cartels of this type.

To Think About

1. Why did the electrical equipment manufacturers opt for a clearly illegal bid-rigging scheme rather than settling for some other form of organized pricing (such as price leadership)? What about the nature of transactions in this business made the price-fixing solution a desirable one?
2. Prosecution of the electrical equipment conspirators was one of the few cases of a successful "cops and robbers" approach to antitrust law. It involved wire tapping, government informers, and so forth. Why are such prosecutions probably easier than those involving monopolistic behavior (such as the IBM case described in Application 16.6)? What lesson do you think would-be conspirators learned from this case?

[1]For a popularized and somewhat sensationalized version of this episode, see J. G. Fuller, *The Gentlemen Conspirators* (New York: Grove Press, 1962).

Table 17.1
Results of the Stackelberg Model (Profits for Each Firm under Various Strategies)

		Firm 2's Strategies	
		Leader	**Follower**
Firm 1's Strategies	**Leader**	1: \$0 2: 0	1: \$1,800 2: 900
	Follower	1: \$ 900 2: 1,800	1: \$1,600 2: 1,600

whereas the profits earned by firm 2 will be

$$\pi_2 = \$30 \times 30 = \$900. \quad [17.12]$$

By using its knowledge of firm 2's reaction function, firm 1 has been able to increase its profits. Of course, the profits of firm 2 have been seriously eroded in the process.

Price Leadership

Stackelberg model
A generalization of the Cournot model in which at least one firm knows the other's reaction function.

This model of a leader-follower relationship was first proposed by the German economist Heinrich von Stackelberg.[4] One ambiguous feature of the **Stackelberg model** is how to decide which firm will be the leader and which the follower. If each firm assumes the other is a follower, each will produce 60 and will be disappointed at the final outcome (with total output of 120, market price will, in the present example, fall to 0). On the other hand, if each acts as a follower, the situation will revert to the Cournot equilibrium we discussed previously. That equilibrium is unstable, however: each firm can perceive the benefits of being a leader and may try to choose its output accordingly. The various outcomes from strategic choices by each firm are shown in Table 17.1. Because of the uncertainty and interdependence inherent in the model, each firm will try to be a leader, and this will have disastrous consequences for the profits of both. An ironclad agreement between the firms with each promising to adopt the follower strategy would lead to larger industry profits than those that are made when one or both of the firms try to adopt the leader strategy.[5] Application 17.2: Price Leadership in

[4]Heinrich von Stackelberg, *The Theory of the Market Economy,* translated by A. T. Peacock (New York: Oxford University Press, 1952), pp. 195–204.

[5]Of course, if we permit ironclad agreements, it is most profitable for the firms to coordinate their strategies and to act as a monopolist.

APPLICATION 17.2

Price Leadership in Steel

The Stackelberg model suggests that pricing decisions in an industry can become quite chaotic when two or more firms seek to take the leadership role. In actual practice, price leadership positions tend to be established over many years, and disruptions are relatively rare. When unexpected factors cause leadership changes, however, past patterns can quickly unravel and competitive-type results can spring up. This was the case in the U.S. steel industry throughout the 1960s and beyond.

U.S. Steel as the Price Leader

In 1901 Andrew Carnegie brought together 12 steel and related companies to form the United States Steel Corporation, the first billion dollar company. For the next fifty years U.S. Steel occupied the undisputed role of leader in determining the price of steel products. At some times, price coordination in the industry resulted from explicit collusion (U.S. Steel chairman Elbert Gary was famous for holding regular "dinners" at which the general "industry situation" was discussed). More often, however, other firms in the industry demurred in allowing the largest firm to act as the price setter.

The Politics of Price Leadership

Public concern about inflation in the early 1960s brought increased scrutiny to this arrangement. U.S. Steel was harshly criticized by President Kennedy in 1962 for an announced price increase and was forced to retract it by the public outcry that followed. With its price leader paralyzed by political vulnerability, the steel industry floundered in search of a new pricing policy. Discounts from list prices became widespread, and several of the leading firms took turns being knocked down as the price leader.[1] One consequence of this turmoil was a sharp decline in the profitability of the industry. By the early 1970s rates of return in the steel industry had dropped far below those in other manufacturing industries.

Enlisting the Government's Help

Steel imports had been growing throughout the 1960s, reaching about 18 percent of total production by the end of the decade. This undoubtedly contributed to the loss of price discipline in steel, but the industry's political position was so weakened from its earlier confrontations with the Kennedy administration that it was unable to press for protection. The situation began to change in the 1970s, especially with the closing of three major steel plants by Youngstown and Bethlehem Steel in 1977. Fearing for the overall health of the U.S. industry, the Carter administration developed a schedule of "reference prices" for steel below which various trade restrictions would be implemented. In the 1980s a similar pricing scheme was adopted by European steel producers. Although these actions did not explicitly reestablish price leadership in steel, they did have the effect of bringing increased coordination in pricing decisions. Although their power was much reduced, the major U.S. producers were able to return to a position of price leaders. The threat of Japanese imports allowed them to enlist government support in what they could not effectively do for themselves.

To Think About

1. Contrary to the discussion of the steel industry, the Stackelberg leadership model that we developed focused on firms' choices of quantities, not prices. Is that an important difference? Or, can the Stackelberg model be easily modified to fit the facts in steel?
2. How can the announcement by the government of "trigger" (minimum) prices for steel imports aid in establishing domestic pricing discipline? How do these prices constrain what domestic leaders can do? Do you think that the industry leaders try to influence what trigger prices the government chooses?

[1] For a description of one particularly dramatic confrontation between U.S. Steel and Bethlehem Steel in 1968, see F. M. Scherer, *Industrial Market Structure and Economic Performance,* 2nd Ed., (Chicago: Rand McNally, 1980), pp. 178–179.

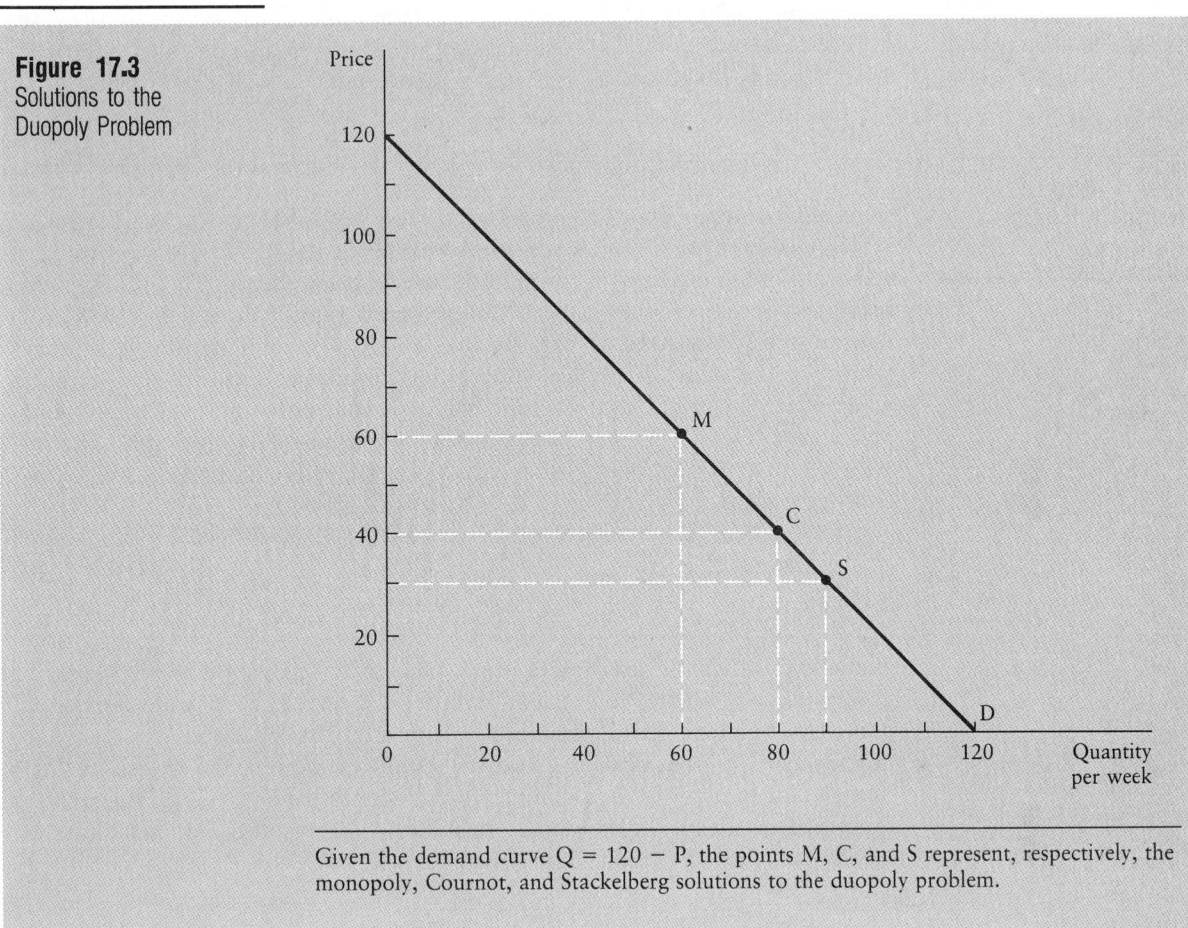

Figure 17.3
Solutions to the Duopoly Problem

Given the demand curve Q = 120 − P, the points M, C, and S represent, respectively, the monopoly, Cournot, and Stackelberg solutions to the duopoly problem.

Steel shows how an industry's pricing decisions can be extremely volatile when leadership roles change.

Comparison of the Models: Approaching the Competitive Solution

We have presented three solutions to our simple duopoly problem: (1) the monopoly solution; (2) the Cournot solution; and (3) the Stackelberg solution. These solutions are shown by the points M, C, and S, respectively on the demand curve in Figure 17.3. These points of market equilibrium approach the competitive solution (where P = MC = 0) as the more sophisticated models of duopoly behavior are examined. Indeed, as we showed in the previous section, if both firms attempt to take Stackelberg leadership roles, the competitive solution will be attained. In a sense, then, the uncertainty about others' reactions in the duopoly model may provide a substitute for competition among many firms. Whether such strategic uncertainty in the real world can provide an adequate substitute for competition, however, remains an open question. It all depends on how each firm views its relationship with other firms.

The Theory of Games: Basic Concepts

Our discussion of duopoly shows that even in simple two-firm situations, strategy is important. One way economists have tried to capture the strategic relationship among firms is through the use of game theory. This subject was originally developed during the 1920s and grew rapidly during World War II in response to the need to develop formal ways of thinking about military strategy.[6] Today the theory has applicability to problems as diverse as the development of optimal strategies for five-card stud poker and the analysis of antimissile defenses. Here we will provide a brief introduction to game theory with a primary focus on its use in explaining behavior in markets with relatively few firms.

A Game

Game theory
The study of the strategies used by the players in a game and the payoffs they receive.

Game theory defines any situation in which individuals must make strategic choices and in which the outcome will depend on what everyone does as a **game.** It is the mutual dependence of any one player's outcomes on what other players do that gives the study of games its interest and generality. Although games differ in their complexity, all games have three basic elements: (1) players, (2) strategies; and (3) payoffs. Some games may also have a fourth element—an equilibrium outcome.

Players

Player
A participant in a game. May be an individual, a firm, or groups of individuals and firms.

Each decision maker in a game is called a **player.** These players may be individuals (as in poker games), firms (as in imperfectly competitive markets), or entire nations (as in military conflicts). All players are characterized as having the ability to choose from among a set of possible actions they might take.[7] Usually the number of players is fixed throughout the "play" of a game, and games are often characterized by the number of players (that is, two-player,

---

[6]Much of the pioneering work in game theory was done by the mathematician John von Neumann. The main reference is J. von Neumann and O. Morgenstern, *The Theory of Games and Economic Behavior* (Princeton, N.J.: Princeton University Press, 1944).

[7]Sometimes one of the players in a game is taken to be "nature." For this player, actions are not "chosen" but rather occur with certain possibilities. For example, the weather may affect the outcomes of a game, but it is not "chosen" by nature. Rather, particular weather outcomes are assumed to occur with various probabilities. Games against nature are discussed briefly later in this chapter.

three-player, or n-player games). In this chapter we will only study two-player games and will denote these players (usually firms) by A and B. One of the important assumptions usually made in game theory is that the specific identity of players is irrelevant. There are no "good guys" or "bad guys" in a game, and players are not assumed to have any special abilities or shortcomings. Each player is simply assumed to choose the course of action that yields the most favorable outcome.

Strategies

Strategies
The various courses of action open to the players of a game.

Each course of action open to a player in a game is called a **strategy**. Depending on the game being examined, a strategy may be a very simple action (take another card in blackjack) or a very complex one (build a laser-based anti-missile defense), but each strategy is assumed to be a well-defined, specific course of action. In our two-player examples we will denote A's strategies by $a_1, a_2 \ldots a_n$ and B's strategies by $b_1, b_2 \ldots b_n$. Usually the number of strategies available to each player will be fairly small, and many aspects of game theory can be illustrated for situations in which each player has only two strategies available.

Payoffs

Payoffs
The outcomes of a game for each player. Payoffs depend on what strategies have been chosen.

The final returns to the players of a game at its conclusion are called **payoffs**. Such payoffs are measured either in money or in levels of utility obtained by the players. In general, it is assumed that players can rank the payoffs of a game from most preferred to least preferred and will seek the highest ranked payoff attainable. In the two-firm case, this simply means that the firms will maximize profits. We will use A_{ij} to represent the payoff to player A of a game in which A plays strategy i and B plays strategy j. Similarly, B_{ij} records the payoff to B when these strategies are used. Table 17.2 shows these payoffs and strategies in matrix form for each player. Sometimes in simple cases we will combine A's and B's payoffs into a single payoff matrix for ease of presentation.

Strategic Equilibrium

In the theory of markets we developed the concept of equilibrium in which both suppliers and demanders were content with the market outcome. Given the equilibrium price and quantity, no market participant has an incentive to change his or her behavior. The question therefore arises whether there are similar equilibrium concepts in game theory models. Are there strategic choices that, once made, provide no incentives for the players to alter this behavior further?

Table 17.2
Payoff Matrices for Two-Player Games

A's Payoff Matrix

		B's Strategies				
		b_1	b_2	b_3	$\cdots$	b_n
A's Strategies	a_1	A_{11}	A_{12}	A_{13}	$\cdots$	A_{1n}
	a_2	A_{21}	A_{22}	A_{23}	$\cdots$	A_{2n}
	a_3	A_{31}	A_{32}	A_{33}	$\cdots$	A_{3n}
	a_n	A_{n1}	A_{n2}	A_{n3}	$\cdots$	A_{nn}

B's Payoff Matrix

		B's Strategies				
		b_1	b_2	b_3	$\cdots$	b_n
A's Strategies	a_1	B_{11}	B_{12}	B_{13}	$\cdots$	B_{1n}
	a_2	B_{21}	B_{22}	B_{23}	$\cdots$	B_{2n}
	a_3	B_{31}	B_{32}	B_{33}	$\cdots$	B_{3n}
	a_n	B_{n1}	B_{n2}	B_{n3}	$\cdots$	B_{nn}

Nash equilibrium
A choice of strategies by the players of a game such that once all the strategies are known, no player has an incentive to choose a different strategy.

Although there are several ways to formalize this equilibrium notion, the most frequently used approach was, as we saw earlier, that proposed by Cournot in the nineteenth century; it was generalized in the early 1950s by J. Nash.[8] Under this procedure a pair of strategies, say, a^*, b^*, is defined to be a **Nash equilibrium** if a^* represents player A's best move when B plays b^* and b^* represents B's best move when A plays a^*. Even if one of the players makes a fixed commitment never to deviate from an equilibrium strategy, the other player cannot benefit from knowing this. For nonequilibrium strategies, as we shall see, this is not the case. If one player knows what the other's strategy will be, he or she can often benefit from that knowledge and, in the process, take actions that reduce the payoff received by the player who has chosen a fixed strategy. In our duopoly model, for example, (see Table 17.1) the Cournot equilibrium was not a Nash equilibrium because each player had an incentive to cheat on it. Indeed, as we shall see, many games do not have a Nash equilibrium. For those that do, however, this outcome seems a natural one to study since once it is reached, no player has an incentive to change his or her behavior.

Our discussion of two-person games involves a specific set of examples of two firms (now we call them A and B) that must choose how much to spend on advertising. Each firm has only two choices: a small advertising budget or a large one. We denote A's strategies by a_1 (a low advertising budget) and a_2 (a high budget). Similarly, B's strategies are denoted by b_1 (a low budget) and b_2 (a high budget). We now look at several different games in which these strategies might be used.

Zero-Sum Games

Zero-sum game
A game in which the amount one player loses the other player wins.

In **zero-sum games** firms A and B are directly competitive. What A "wins," B "loses," and vice versa. This would be the case, for example, if total demand for the output of the two firms were absolutely fixed and consequently adver-

[8]John Nash, "Equilibrium Points in *n*-person Games," *Proceedings of the National Academy of Sciences* 36 (1950): 48–49.

Table 17.3
Payoff Matrix for Equilibrium Zero-Sum Game

		B's Strategies	
		b_1 (Low Budget)	b_2 (High Budget)
A's Strategies	a_1 (Low Budget)	A: + \$5 B: − 5	A: − \$5 B: + 5
	a_2 (High Budget)	A: + \$3 B: − 3	A: \$0 B: 0

□ Nash equilibrium solution

tising would affect only the distribution of sales between the two firms. The payoff matrix for the first zero-sum game we consider here is shown in Table 17.3. In this table A's strategies are shown vertically, and B's strategies are recorded horizontally. The entries in the table record the outcomes (in terms of millions of dollars of profits) that accrue to A and B when the particular strategy choices are made. For example, the upper left corner of the matrix records the fact that when A "plays" a_1 and B "plays" b_1, A receives profits of \$5 and B receives profits of −\$5. Similarly, when both firms have high advertising budgets, profits for each are zero. The other entries in the table should be interpreted in the same way. Total profits for the industry are always zero, indicating that the game is truly "zero sum."

A Nash Equilibrium

Assuming that both A and B fully understand the possible outcomes of the game, we can examine how they might decide on which strategy to pursue. For firm B, strategy b_2 dominates b_1: no matter what A does, B can do best by playing b_2. Against a_1, that strategy promises a gain of \$5, and against a_2 it promises zero profits. Firm A, on the other hand, has no dominant strategy: against b_1, strategy a_1 is preferred, but against b_2, strategy a_2 is preferred. There are numerous ways in which A might choose a strategy in this situation. One method would be for A to adopt the pessimistic assumption that "no matter what I do, B will choose the strategy that harms me the most." Under this assumption, A should choose that strategy for which the worst possible outcome is as good as possible.[9] Here that choice would be a_2. By choosing a_2, A can assure itself zero profits no matter what B does. On the other hand, choosing a_1 runs some risk of getting a profit of −\$5. Consequently A chooses a_2, B chooses b_2, and both end up earning zero profits.

[9]This pessimistic way of choosing a strategy is called a "maximin" (or sometimes "minimax") decision rule.

Table 17.4
Payoff Matrix for Nonequilibrium Zero-Sum Game

		B's Strategies	
		b_1 (Low Budget)	b_2 (High Budget)
A's Strategies	a_1 (Low Budget)	A: \$0 B: 0	A: − \$10 B: + 10
	a_2 (High Budget)	A: − \$5 B: + 5	A: + \$5 B: − 5

The choice of a_2, b_2 is, in this situation, a *Nash equilibrium*. If either A or B knew ahead of time what its competitor were going to do, it would not change its decision: knowing B will choose b_2 does not alter A's determination to choose a_2, and vice versa. Application 17.3: Nash Equilibrium Tariff Policy shows how this equilibrium concept can explain various nations' trading options.

A Nonequilibrium Game

Not all zero-sum games have equilibrium strategies; there are *nonequilibrium* zero-sum games.[10] For example, consider the payoffs shown in Table 17.4, which again sum to zero. By following the pessimistic decision rule, A would choose strategy a_2 since under this choice it can at most suffer a profit loss of −\$5. If B is also pessimistic, it will choose b_1, which assures at least zero profits. The choice a_2, b_1 is not a Nash equilibrium, however. For example, A might reason "I know B will choose b_1, so why should I suffer a loss of −\$5; instead, I'll choose a_1 and end up even." However, B can anticipate this trickery and opt for b_2 thus gaining profits of \$10 for itself and imposing a loss of \$10 on A. Of course, A will see this, and will choose a_2 to avoid the loss. The cycle can continue indefinitely since there is no equilibrium for the game. Each player will keep switching strategies in an effort to keep one step ahead of its competitor.

Non-Zero-Sum Games

Most market situations are not zero sum. It is not usually the case that what one firm gains the other loses but, rather, that a variety of outcomes are pos-

[10]It can be shown, however, that most zero-sum games have equilibrium "mixed strategies" under which players use each of their strategies only a fraction of the time. See R. Duncan Luce and Howard Raiffa, *Games and Decisions* (New York, John Wiley & Sons, 1957), Appendix 2.

APPLICATION 17.3

Nash Equilibrium Tariff Policy

To many economists free trade among nations seems a feasible route to welfare maximization. In national surveys, approximately 90 percent of economists polled tend to take a free trade stance. Still, many economists recognize that in certain situations a country may find it desirable to adopt trade barriers, especially if other countries also do so. In such instances, choices among trade policies can resemble game-theoretic situations—each country must take other countries' reactions into account in choosing what its optimal policy is.

Optimal Tariff Policy

For example, it is well known that implementation of a tariff (that is, a tax on imports) may sometimes raise a country's welfare. Adoption of such a policy can allow a country to behave as a monopolist in its trading relationships with the rest of the world, and this may be able to bring about domestic welfare gains. The difficulty in choosing such an "optimal" tariff policy is, of course, that other countries may retaliate with tariffs of their own. The gains promised from a tariff can quickly evaporate if other nations respond forcefully. One possibility is that the nations involved in a trading situation may be able to discover a Nash equilibrium set of tariff choices—that is, each country's choice is its best, given what the other countries have chosen to do. Whether this equilibrium outcome is also better than free trade is, however, open to question.

A Canada–United States Example

Devising models of the trading relationships among all of the countries in the world is a formidable undertaking. Sometimes economists have tried to simplify matters by looking only at bilateral relationships between two countries, taking the rest of the world's trading decisions as given. This is the approach followed by Markusen and Wigle in an examination of Canadian-U.S. tariff policy.[1] The authors asked how various tariff policies that might be adopted by these countries would affect their overall welfare. Not surprisingly, they found that relative to current tariff rates (an average of 4.6 percent in the United States and 13.2 percent in Canada), both countries would gain from adoption of free trade. But that solution may be unstable in that an ironclad decision by one of the trading partners to adopt free trade offers the other a chance to choose an optimal tariff.

To study the consequences of various tariff policies, the authors compute payoff matrices for Canada and the United States. They show that for Canada tariff reductions from current levels represent a dominant strategy. No matter what the United States does, Canada gains by reducing its tariff rate. For the United States there is no dominant strategy—its optimal tariff depends on what Canada does. Still, the authors show that there is a Nash equilibrium where the United States adopts fairly large increases in its current tariff rates. At this equilibrium the tariff pattern is reversed from what it actually is—equilibrium Canadian rates are only about one third of equilibrium United States rates. Such a result is consistent with the notion that the United States, because of its size in world markets, might gain from higher tariffs (assuming, probably contrary to fact, that other countries do not retaliate!), but that smaller Canada would gain by moving closer to free trade.

[1] J. R. Markusen and R. W. Wigle, "Nash Equilibrium Tariff Rates for the United States and Canada," *Journal of Political Economy* (April 1989): 368–386.

To Think About

1. Payoffs in the tariff "game" analyzed here are measured as total changes in economic welfare. Why might these not provide a very good indication of the tariff policies the countries would actually adopt? Do voters in Canada or the United States care about such aggregate magnitudes?
2. In further analyses the authors also show that Canada might be better-off if it unilaterally cut tariffs and that such gains are more likely if capital can move freely and if Canadian industry experiences increasing returns to scale. Can you provide an intuitive explanation for these results?

Table 17.5
Non-zero-Sum Game

		B's Strategies	
		b_1 (Low Budget)	b_2 (High Budget)
A's Strategies	a_1 (Low Budget)	A: + $7 B: + 7	A: + $ 3 B: + 10
	a_2 (High Budget)	A: + $10 B: + 3	A: + $5 B: + 5

sible depending on the strategies that are chosen. A particularly fascinating non-zero-sum game is shown in Table 17.5. This table is interpreted in exactly the same way as the previous two, except that the outcomes no longer sum to a constant value. In this game, strategy a_2 dominates a_1 for firm A: no matter what B does, A is better off with a_2. Similarly, b_2 dominates b_1 for firm B. Both firms will choose to have high advertising budgets, and both will receive a profit of +$5. An ironclad agreement by both firms to pursue low advertising budgets, however, would result in a profit level of $7 for each. The difficulty with this twin low-budget strategy choice is that it is unstable. If A knows that B will choose b_1, it is to A's advantage to choose a_2 and increase its profits from +$7 to +$10. Similarly, if B knows A will choose a_1, B too has an incentive to cheat. Consequently, both firms, pursuing their own self-interest, will choose their second strategies even though Pareto efficiency would suggest the twin low-budget strategy.

The Prisoner's Dilemma

Prisoner's dilemma
A game in which the players' most desirable joint outcome is unstable because each player has an incentive to cheat in the strategy actually chosen.

The game shown in Table 17.5 is one example of what has come to be known as the **prisoner's dilemma.** The dilemma arises because the best choice of strategies is unstable and provides great incentives to cheat. Faced with the uncertainty inherent in the game, both players end up making a second-best choice. The term *prisoner's dilemma* to describe this situation comes from a game first discussed by A. W. Tucker in the 1940s, in which two people are arrested for a crime. The district attorney has little evidence in the case and is anxious to extract a confession. She separates the suspects and tells each, "If you confess and your companion doesn't, I can promise you a reduced six-month sentence, whereas your companion will, on the basis of your confession, get ten years. If you both confess, you will each get a three-year sentence." Each suspect also knows that if neither of them confesses, the lack of evidence will cause them to be tried for a lesser crime for which they would receive maximum two-year sentences if convicted.

The payoff matrix of this game is presented in Table 17.6. This game closely resembles that shown in Table 17.5, in that the "confess" strategy dominates for both A and B. However, an agreement between the two pris-

Table 17.6
The Prisoner's Dilemma

		Prisoner B	
		Confess	Not Confess
Prisoner A	Confess	A: 3 years B: 3 years	A: 6 months B: 10 years
	Not Confess	A: 10 years B: 6 months	A: 2 years B: 2 years

oners not to confess would reduce their terms from three to a maximum of two years (and possibly less). This efficient solution is not stable, and there is an incentive for either prisoner to cheat on it.

A prisoner's dilemma type of game may occur in many real-world market situations. The example of advertising budgets may actually occur. As we discussed in Chapter 16, some advertising may be merely "defensive" in the sense that a mutual agreement to reduce advertising expenditures would be profitable to both parties. However, such an agreement would be unstable (unless the parties could get the government to endorse it) because one firm could increase its profits even further by cheating on the agreement. Similar situations arise in the tendency for airlines to show in-flight movies (there would be larger profits if all airlines stopped showing movies, but such a solution is unstable); in the instability of farmers' (and other cartel) agreements to restrict milk output since it is just too tempting for the individual farmer to try to sell more milk; or in the banking industry's move to "free" checking accounts (keeping service charges is more profitable, but this is unstable since one bank can greatly increase its deposits by offering free checks). As these examples show, the difficulty of enforcing agreements may be very detrimental to the profits of an industry. Again then, this is a situation where considerations of strategy may lead to competitive-type results.

The Duopoly Model as a Non-Zero-Sum Game

We can tie this discussion of game theory together with our prior examination of duopoly by noting the similarity between the outcomes of the Stackelberg model (in Table 17.1) and the prisoner's dilemma. In both cases the players in the game have a preferred outcome, but that solution is fundamentally unstable because it provides incentives to cheat. As we showed in Chapter 16, this type of outcome is quite common in market situations (such as cartels) in which a gap between price and marginal cost provides participants with an incentive to chisel on price. As in the prisoner's dilemma, although such behavior is rational to each participant, it is collectively irrational to the cartel as a whole. Game theory, therefore, provides one more way of illustrating the ways in which competitive forces may come to dominate various types of markets. Application 17.4: The Game of Chicken shows how some

APPLICATION 17.4

The Game of Chicken

Although the Prisoner's Dilemma is perhaps the most widely used two-person noncooperative game, it is not the only one that reflects commonly occurring strategic situations. Another example is provided by the game of "Chicken" for which a typical payoff matrix is shown in Table 1. In this game each player has two strategies: (1) to "cooperate" or (2) "not to cooperate." Payoffs to the players are recorded in the table with 0 being the least favorable outcome and 3 being the most favorable for each player. This game has two Nash equilibria points—the off-diagonal strategy choices. Both of these solutions are vulnerable to threats, however.

Basic Scenario of the Game

The title "Chicken" for this game derives from a 1950s "game" played by hot-rod gangs (for the true flavor of the game, see the classic James Dean movie, *Rebel without a Cause*). The game's players start at opposite ends of a deserted road with their left wheels on the center line of the road. They then race toward each other with the first one to veer off being branded the "chicken." In this game then "cooperation" consists of veering off the center line whereas "noncooperation" refers to a determined strategy of staying on that line. If both drivers chicken out, they both live, but gain no prestige from their peers. Hence, the twin cooperative strategy is unstable—each driver has an incentive to cheat on it (that is, stick to the center line). If one driver succeeds in cheating in this way, he or she receives considerable prestige (a "3") whereas the chicken loses face (a "1"). A twin strategy of noncooperation is a disaster, however, since the cars crash and both drivers die (a "0"). But each driver has an incentive to threaten to take a noncooperative strategy in the hope that the opponent will be cajoled into taking a cooperative one.

Table 1
The Game of Chicken

		B's Strategies	
		Cooperate	Do Not Cooperate
A's Strategies	Cooperate	2, 2	1, 3
	Do Not Cooperate	3, 1	0, 0

Applications to Oligopoly

Most applications of the game of Chicken focus on explaining why "cooperative" solutions appear to be stable despite the fact that they do not meet the Nash criteria for stability. Consider, for example, the decision of U.S. automakers to refrain from building small cars in the 1950s and early 1960s. Such restraint appeared to many observers to be unstable—a company that built small cars could have made a significant profit by doing so. But the threat that its competitors would quickly enter the market also (thereby seriously eroding profits on both small and large cars) kept any one company from proceeding. Of course, this cooperative solution ultimately failed because the rapid growth of imported small cars forced the U.S. companies to respond. The paralysis induced by the strategic situation of the 1950s placed U.S. makers at a considerable disadvantage because they had not developed the production expertise that they needed in later years.

A related situation concerns the pricing of gasoline on major highways. Although there may be relatively many sellers, all seem to charge about the same price and they change prices together, usually on the same day. Presumably any one seller faces a fairly elastic demand for its gasoline and could gain significant sales by dropping its price a few cents a gallon. But its competitors would probably retaliate, and, since the total demand for gasoline along the highway is relatively inelastic, all firms would be worse-off. Gas "wars" arise because of the periodic breakdown of the cooperative solution, and prices drop dramatically (your author once purchased gasoline for $.12 per gallon in the 1960s). But these price breaks are usually quite short-lived (the $.12 price lasted only about four hours), and discipline quickly returns to the market.

To Think About

1. A threat is "credible" if your opponent believes you will carry it out. Is a threat to be noncooperative in Chicken really credible? Why would anyone pursue a strategy that might make him or her worse-off?
2. Some analysts believe the Chicken game provides a good model for nuclear deterrence between super powers. How would you define the game in this way? Is the twin threat of noncooperation credible?

features of oligopoly markets are reflected in another type of non-zero-sum game.

Games against Nature and Bayesian Decision Making

If the strategic considerations in a game are complex, it may sometimes be appropriate for one of the players to simplify the problem by treating it as a game against nature. Under this approach, the opponent ("nature") is assumed to be neither benevolent nor malevolent—nature does not engage in strategic thinking. Rather, nature chooses strategies on a random basis with no particular thought being given to the consequences of its "choice." Under this approach then, an opponent's choice of strategy is treated much like the weather in a firm's decisions: the strategy nature chooses will affect the payoffs received (weather certainly affects farmers' crops), but the opponent is not considered to be an active player in the game.

To illustrate this approach, consider the advertising game payoffs shown in Table 17.7. In this game neither player has a dominant strategy, so each will choose what to do based on whatever information and intuition he or she has available. One approach would be for, say, firm A to treat this as a game against nature—in this case A would pay no attention to B's decision problem. Instead A would focus only on its own payoff matrix and treat the occurrence of a particular strategy for B as a fact of nature, subject to some random process.[11]

Bayesian Decision Rules

Faced with this situation, there are a variety of ways in which firm A might select a strategy. Application of the type of pessimistic logic we used before, for example, would suggest choosing strategy a_2 since the minimum payoff there (1) exceeds that for a_1 (0). This would not, however, be a very appealing choice if B were known to have a proclivity for high advertising budgets.

An approach to this problem that is consistent with usual economic models of choice in uncertain situations, would be for firm A to assign (subjective) probabilities that reflect the likelihood of strategies b_1 and b_2 occurring. Using these probabilities, A would then choose the strategy that offered the highest expected value (see Chapter 7). If, for example, A believed b_1 and b_2 were equally likely, the expected payoffs associated with each strategy would be

$$\text{Expected payoff of } a_1 = \tfrac{1}{2}(0) + \tfrac{1}{2}(3) = 1\tfrac{1}{2}$$
$$\text{Expected payoff of } a_2 = \tfrac{1}{2}(4) + \tfrac{1}{2}(1) = 2\tfrac{1}{2}, \qquad [17.13]$$

[11]This approach is similar to the one we used to describe choices in uncertain situations in Chapter 7. Much of the theory developed there (about risk aversion, for example) is relevant here as well.

Table 17.7
Payoff Matrix for a Game against Nature

		B's Strategies	
		b_1 (Low Budget)	b_2 (High Budget)
A's Strategies	a_1 (Low Budget)	A: 0 B: 3	A: 3 B: 5
	a_2 (High Budget)	A: 4 B: 2	A: 1 B: 1

and a_2 would be the preferred strategy. On the other hand, if A believed B really did tend to prefer b_2, it might assign a probability of ¾ to that strategy (and ¼ to b_1), in which case expected payoffs would be

$$\text{Expected payoff of } a_1 = \tfrac{1}{4}(0) + \tfrac{3}{4}(3) = 2\tfrac{1}{4}$$
$$\text{Expected payoff of } a_2 = \tfrac{1}{4}(4) + \tfrac{3}{4}(1) = 1\tfrac{3}{4}, \qquad [17.14]$$

and now a_1 would be preferred. At a subjective probability of $\frac{1}{3}$ for b_1, $\frac{2}{3}$ for b_2, firm A would be indifferent about which advertising strategy to choose.

Bayesian decision theory
Definition of subjective probabilities for outcomes of a game and use of those probabilities in making strategic decisions.

This approach to decision making is sometimes called **Bayesian decision theory** after the eighteenth-century English statistician Thomas Bayes who first developed the mathematics associated with the calculation of subjective probabilities. In Bayes's view, the probability of any event occurring is not an objective fact, but rather a subjective parameter derived from the information available to the decision maker. The probability that a coin will come up heads is not, in the view of Bayesians, precisely ½. Rather, the probability of a head is an ever-changing estimate based on individuals' recent experiences. As new information arrives (that, for example, a coin was heads on its last 100 tosses), a rational decision maker would alter his or her subjective probability estimate and make decisions based on these estimates.

Probably, the most desirable property of this decision rule is that it is the only decision procedure that agrees in spirit with the approach to rational choice in uncertain situations that we took in Chapter 7. If a player in a game is an expected utility maximizer, it can be shown that he or she will make decisions in a Bayesian manner when "objective" probabilities are unknown.[12] The Bayesian approach to strategic decisions is therefore widely used in economics and other disciplines.

[12]See Luce and Raiffa, *Games and Decisions,* Chapter 13.

APPLICATION 17.5

Terrorism

Since the late 1960s there has been a substantial increase in the number of terrorist incidents around the world. The media attention given to such events combined with low probabilities of apprehension makes terrorism a relatively profitable activity for those involved. In recent years economists have turned their attention to explaining terrorism and to evaluating various antiterrorist policies. Game theory has been widely used for this purpose.[1]

Detection and Prevention

Consider first the problem of preventing terrorist incidents through direct detection and intervention. The most obvious steps that have been taken involve airport security such as the screening of passengers and luggage with metal detectors. Other methods include the preparation of terrorist profiles for passenger interrogation and the development of informant networks. Although these techniques appear to have had a negative short-term impact on terrorist activity, in the long run terrorists have been able to adjust their strategies accordingly. The 1988 bombing of a Pan American plane in Scotland, for example, seems to have been caused by nonmetallic explosives carried on board by an innocent passenger. In modeling the terrorist game, it is clearly necessary to assume that each side has fairly complete knowledge of the strategies used by the other and that the set of terrorist strategies will change as antiterrorist technologies are improved.

Negotiating with Terrorists

The United States, Israel, and several other nations have announced policies of "never" negotiating with terrorists. The goal of such a policy is to show terrorists that they "can't win" by taking hostages. However, the policy has been violated by each country in a number of important cases. Hence, the probability that a nation will negotiate is subject to some type of calculation by a would-be terrorist. Ideally governments would like to have the reputation of never capitulating. But since terrorists will have information on both past experience and the current circumstances of an incident, developing such a reputation may be difficult. Such actions as "talking tough" will not affect the terrorists' subjective probabilities of being able to draw governments into negotiations.[2]

Retaliation

Because of the difficulties in devising methods to detect terrorists and in coping with hostage taking, some observers have suggested that *ex post* retaliation may be a more effective deterrent. But this approach also poses game-theoretic difficulties. Most obviously, retaliation can only work if the perpetrator of an incident is known. Even if officials assign a high subjective probability to who is to blame, they are often unwilling to act for fear they might be wrong. Several nations have also undercut the retaliation option by offering sanctuary to terrorists. Finally, retaliation has many elements of the free rider problem in the provision of public goods (see Chapter 22)—it may be in the interest of each nation to adopt the stance of letting someone else do it. As might be expected given these difficulties, retaliation is an option that is seldom pursued except in cases (such as Israeli retaliation in Lebanon) where the benefits accrue mainly to one country. For the most part, therefore, terrorists will assign a very low value to the subjective probability of retaliation.

To Think About

1. Game theory assigns a high degree of rationality to the players. Does this seem appropriate for modeling the behavior of terrorists who often claim to be acting out of religious motives and the desire for martyrdom?
2. Terrorism may be a game situation in which the player who chooses whether or not to play has a considerable advantage. Why does the option of deciding where, when, and how to "play" increase the effectiveness of terrorists?

---

[1]See, for example, the papers in "The Political Economy of Terrorism" *American Economic Review Papers and Proceedings* (May 1988): 16–31.

[2]For an attempt at modeling the reputation issue, see H. E. Lapan and T. Sandler, "To Bargain or not to Bargain: That is the Question," *American Economic Review Papers and Proceedings* (May 1988): 16–21.

Bayesian Decisions and Information Theory

Adoption of Bayesian decision theory does involve one major complication over our prior game theory models—the introduction of subjective probabilities. How do individuals develop their views of the probabilities of various events, and how do they gather information with which to revise these probability estimates? In assessing the risks connected with using a consumer product such as a lawn mower, for example, how do buyers decide the relevant risks to attach to the various mowers available? Or, in the oligopoly context, how does firm A decide how likely firm B is to adopt a high-cost advertising budget? Application 17.5: Terrorism on a more political level, looks at how the parties involved form their strategies and how antiterrorist policy might be analyzed.

As these questions suggest, it is in the study of the formulation of subjective probabilities that Bayesian decision theory and formal information theory merge. In Chapters 7 and 14 we discussed some conceptual questions about how utility-maximizing individuals engage in information acquisition, and Bayesian analysis requires an adaptation of these concepts to the question of estimating subjective probabilities. Some experimental research on this topic shows that individuals are able to formulate rather rough probability estimates to use in their decisions, but a number of paradoxical results (such as a prevalent tendency to underestimate small probabilities) have been found.[13] The Bayesian decision model has not, therefore, been widely used in the study of actual firm behavior.

Summary

This chapter is concerned with developing a few simple models to illustrate the strategic relationships among two firms in a simple duopoly market. Our principal observations about such models are:

- Solutions to a duopoly (two-firm) model depend importantly on how the firms treat each other's decisions. If the decisions are fully coordinated, monopoly results will occur.
- In the absence of perfect coordination, a variety of outcomes are possible. Some (such as the Stackelberg model of price leadership) may approach the competitive solution under which price is equal to marginal cost. Other solutions may be closer to the cartel case.

[13]For a survey of some of these paradoxical results, see M. J. Machina, "Choice under Uncertainty: Problems Solved and Unsolved," *Journal of Economic Perspectives* (Summer 1987): 121–154.

- Game theory provides a formal way of analyzing strategic choices made by various players. In zero-sum games (that is, those in which what one player wins the other loses), there will often exist Nash equilibrium strategies that are stable in that no player has an incentive to change his or her choices once the other player's strategy is known.
- An important non-zero-sum game is the prisoner's dilemma. In this game the solution involving each player's preferred strategy is unstable—there is an incentive for each player to cheat. The result of such cheating is to make both players worse-off.
- Sometimes a game can be regarded as a game against nature. In this case a player will assign subjective probabilities to various outcomes and employ Bayesian decision theory to make strategic choices.

Review Questions

1. Some oligopoly pricing models (such as the Cournot and Stackelberg models) are called "conjectural variations" models since one firm makes conjectures about what the other firm will do. Why does the desire to maximize profits require that a firm make such conjectures?
2. In the Cournot model, each firm has a "reaction function." What are these firms reacting to? Under what conditions will their reactions be incorrect? Illustrate a situation of incorrect reactions using Figure 17.2 and then describe why the intersection of the reaction functions represents a Cournot equilibrium.
3. What is a firm that is a Stackelberg leader assumed to know about its rival? What does the Stackelberg model assume about the rival's willingness to change its behavior once it is discovered by the leader?
4. In game theory the identity of players is usually assumed to be irrelevant—relabeling players has no effect on the analysis of the game. Describe the ways in which this assumption is similar to assumptions made about economic actors in competitive markets. Are there important ways in which they differ?
5. Express the notion of a Nash equilibrium as a maximization problem. What does each player maximize? What are the constraints in the problem? What is consistent about these constraints at the Nash equilibrium?
6. Is the Cournot equilibrium described in Figure 17.2 also a Nash equilibrium? How might your answer depend on the way in which we define the players' strategies in this game?
7. Which of the following activities might be represented as a zero-sum game? Which are clearly not zero-sum?

    a. Flipping a coin for $1.
    b. Playing blackjack.
    c. Choosing which candy bar to buy from a vendor.
    d. Reducing taxes through various "creative accounting" methods and seeking to avoid detection by the IRS.
    e. Deciding when to rob a particular house knowing that the residents may adopt various countertheft strategies.

8. A generalization of the zero-sum notion is a "constant-sum" game—the prizes always add to the same amount. Explain why the payoffs of a constant-sum game can always be portrayed in one payoff matrix, whereas for a nonconstant-sum game it will take two matrices to illustrate the possibilities.

9. Why is the Prisoner's dilemma a "dilemma" for the players involved? How might they solve this dilemma through pregame discussions? If the game were repeated many times, can you also think of ways in which the dilemma might be resolved?
10. Why are games against nature in which the player adopts a Bayesian approach similar to the problems in uncertainty that were examined in Chapter 7? Are there any differences in the goals of the individuals involved? In what ways does the use of subjective probabilities in Bayesian analysis represent a generalization of the Chapter 7 material? What additional issues does the use of subjective probabilities raise?

Problems

17.1 Assume that a monopoly owner of the Fountain of Youth has no costs of production and faces a demand curve for Fountain water given by

$$Q = 150 - P.$$

a. Calculate the profit-maximizing price-quantity combination for this monopolist. Also calculate the monopolist's profits.

b. Suppose a second firm discovers a second Fountain of Youth. Let q_1 be the output of the first firm and q_2 the output of the second. Market demand is now given by:

$$q_1 + q_2 = 150 - P.$$

Assuming that this second firm also has no costs of production, use the Cournot model of duopoly to determine the profit-maximizing level of water sales for each firm as well as the market price. Also calculate each firm's profits.

c. How do the results from parts a and b compare to the price and quantity that would prevail in a perfectly competitive water market? Indicate the three different price-quantity combinations on the demand curve.

17.2 A carrot monopolist can produce at constant average (and marginal) costs of AC = MC = 5. The firm faces a weekly market demand curve for carrots given by

$$Q = 53 - P.$$

a. Calculate the profit-maximizing price-quantity combination for this monopolist. Also calculate the monopolist's profits.

b. Suppose that a second firm enters the carrot market. Let q_1 be the output of firm 1 and q_2 the output of firm 2. Market demand now is given by

$$q_1 + q_2 = 53 - P.$$

On the assumption that firm 2 has the same costs as firm 1, calculate the profits of firms 1 and 2 as functions of q_1 and q_2.

c. Suppose (as in the Cournot model) that each of these two firms chooses its level of output so as to maximize profits on the assumption that the other's output is fixed. Calculate each firm's reaction function (which expresses desired output of one firm as a function of the other's output).

d. On the assumption in part c, what is the only level for q_1 and q_2 with which both firms will be satisfied (what q_1, q_2 combination satisfies both reaction curves)?
e. With q_1 and q_2 at the equilibrium level specified in part d, what will be the market price of carrots, the profits for each firm, and the total profits earned?

17.3 Under the conditions of problem 17.2, suppose now that there are n identical carrot producers in the industry. If each firm adopts the Cournot strategy toward all its rivals, what will be the profit-maximizing output level for each firm? What will be the market price? What will be the total profits earned in the industry? (All these will depend on n.) Show that when the number of firms gets very large, the output levels, market price, and profits approach those that would "prevail" in a perfectly competitive carrot market.

17.4 In the game of "Rock, Scissors, Paper," the two players each choose one of these items secretly and then display them simultaneously. Ties do not count, rock defeats scissors, scissors defeats paper, and paper defeats rock. Illustrate the payoff matrix for this game and show that it does not have an equilibrium strategy pair. Explain this result intuitively.

17.5 Smith and Jones are playing a number-matching game. Each chooses either 1, 2, or 3. If the numbers match, Jones pays Smith $3. If they differ, Smith pays Jones $1.

a. Describe the payoff matrix for this game and show that it does not possess an equilibrium strategy pair.
b. Show that with mixed strategies this game does have an equilibrium if each player plays each number with probability 1/3. What is the value of this game?

17.6 An individual is thinking about going on a picnic but is worried about the weather. Utilities from the picnic are

	Rain	No Rain
Picnic	0	20
No Picnic	5	10

a. If this individual follows a maximin (see footnote 9) decision rule, will he or she choose the picnic or no picnic strategy?
b. If this individual believes that the probability of rain is .10 and follows a Bayesian decision rule, which strategy will be chosen? Explain why this choice differs from that in part a.

17.7 An alternative to the maximin criterion for selecting strategies in risky games is the "minimax regret" criterion. This criterion begins by computing the "maximum regret" matrix, which shows for each state of the world the *difference* between the utility obtainable for a given strategy in that state of the world and the highest utility possible with that state of the world. Hence the matrix shows the individual's "regret" at having chosen a particular strategy when a specific state of the world occurs. A final choice is then made by choosing that strategy for which the maximum regret is as small as possible.

a. For the picnic example of problem 17.6, show that the maximum regret matrix is given by

	States of the World	
	Rain	No Rain
Picnic	5	0
No Picnic	0	10

and that the minimax regret criterion results in a different choice (picnic) than does the maximin criterion. Contrast these two criteria.

b. Reformulate the Prisoner's dilemma game in terms of a regret matrix. Does use of the minimax regret criterion change the nature of the solution?

17.8 The entire world's supply of kryptonite is controlled by 20 people with each having 10,000 grams of this potent mineral. The world demand for kryptonite is given by

$$Q = 10{,}000 - 1{,}000P$$

where P is the price per gram.

a. If all owners could conspire to rig the price of kryptonite, what price would they set and how much of their supply would they sell?
b. Why is the price computed in part a an unstable equilibrium?
c. Does a price for kryptonite exist that would be a stable equilibrium in the sense that no firm could gain by altering its output from that required to maintain this market price?

*17.9 Smith and Jones are stranded on a desert island with fixed initial endowments of clams and bread. Instead of seeking mutually beneficial trades directly, they opt for a bidding strategy in which they use their initial clam endowments to bid for bread. The bread is deposited in a safe place, and each person states how many clams he or she will offer for it. When the bids are revealed, the available bread is then split in proportion to each bid, and the net difference in clams bid is paid from one trader to the other. If, for example, Smith bids one clam and Jones bids two clams, Smith gets 1/3 of the bread and Jones gets 2/3. On net, one clam is transferred from Jones to Smith.

a. Sketch an Edgeworth box diagram that shows the initial endowments of Smith and Jones.
b. On your Edgeworth box, show how a final allocation is determined given a particular set of bids by Smith and Jones.

*Denotes a problem that is rather difficult.

c. Use your construction from part b to show Smith's optimal reply to a particular bid by Jones. Develop a similar construction for Jones.
d. How would you define a Nash equilibrium bidding strategy in this situation? Do you believe this Nash equilibrium will be attained?

PART 6

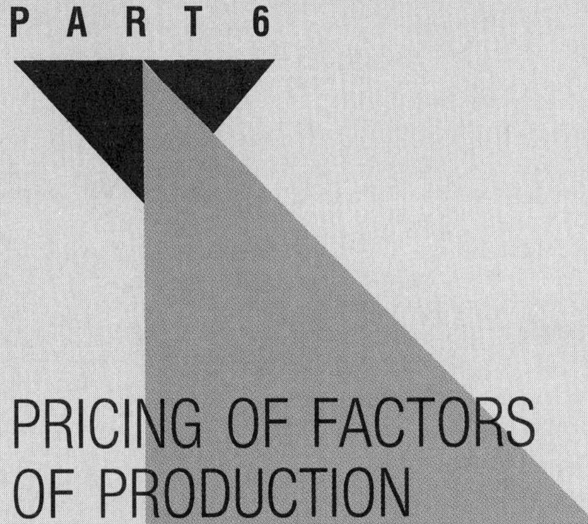

PRICING OF FACTORS OF PRODUCTION

Factors of production also have prices. Labor services are purchased for a wage rate per hour, machines have rental rates, and rent must usually be paid for the use of land. In this part we investigate how those prices are determined. As for the case of goods, we will show that these prices are established by the forces of supply and demand. People supply labor services, and these services are demanded by firms. Owners of capital and land are similarly willing to rent these resources to a firm for a price. In some way, then, prices are determined by the operation of the market.

Chapter 18 discusses the demand for factors of production, which differs in several ways from the demand concepts we have been using so far. Most important, here firms are doing the hiring, and their demand for any factor of production is a *derived demand.* It depends indirectly on the demand for the good that the firm produces. For example, the demand for the services of airline pilots depends on the demand for air travel. If the demand for air travel were to increase, the demand for pilots would also increase. A second important demand concept introduced in Chapter 18 is *economic rent.* Simply defined, any factor of production is said to earn rents when the factor is paid more than the amount necessary to keep the factor in its present employment. The most important example of such economic rent is the rent paid for the use of land. Since, to a first approximation, the supply of land is absolutely fixed, any payment to landowners is an economic rent in the sense that the payment does not induce additional supply—price is solely determined by demand.

Much of the discussion in Chapter 18 assumes that firms hire inputs in perfectly competitive markets. That is, firms are assumed to be price takers—their actions have no effect on the wage rate they must pay for labor or the rental rate they must pay for capital. In the final sections of the chapter, however, we explore the possibility that a firm may have some market power to affect factor prices. Specifically, we examine the situation of a monopsony (single buyer) and show how the market power possessed by the monopsony can lead to the same general kinds of distortions in the allocation of resources that we described earlier for the case of monopoly.

The theory of demand in Chapter 18 is quite general—it applies to any factor of production. In Chapters 19 and 20 we take up several issues specifically related to pricing in the labor and capital markets. In Chapter 19 we discuss three particular aspects of the labor supply. First we analyze the simple labor supply decisions of one person and then construct a market supply of labor curve in much the same way we developed a market demand curve in

Part 2. Next we briefly discuss occupational choice and the concept of compensating wage differentials. Finally, we take note of the fact that important portions of the labor market are characterized by the presence of unions, and we show how they can be incorporated into the general theory of how wages are determined.

In Chapter 20 we look at the market for capital. The central purpose of the chapter is to emphasize the connection between capital and the allocation of resources over time. Any economy's stock of capital equipment represents some output that was produced in the past to be used for production in the future. In Chapter 20 we analyze the choices people make in this process. We are especially interested in illustrating how the theory of capital and investment decisions can be incorporated into the models of firms' behavior from Part 3. The appendix to Chapter 20 presents some mathematical results about interest rates that are widely used in the study of capital and investment.

In *The Principles of Political Economy and Taxation,* David Ricardo wrote:

> The produce of the earth . . . is divided among three classes of the community, namely, the proprietor of the land, the owner of the stock of capital necessary for its cultivation, and the laborers by whose industry it is cultivated. To determine the laws which regulate this distribution is the principal problem in Political Economy.[1]

The purpose of Part 6 is to take up Ricardo's "problem" and show how the prices of factors of production are determined. An understanding of this pricing mechanism not only provides insights into how the market works, but also helps us understand how people get their incomes. The study of factor pricing completes our analysis of the circular flow of goods and payments for those goods throughout an economy. ▲

[1]David Ricardo, *The Principles of Political Economy and Taxation* (1817; reprinted London: J. M. Dent and Son, 1965), p. 1.

CHAPTER 18

The Demand for Factors of Production

A simple way to start a discussion of pricing of factors is to assume that these prices are somehow established by supply and demand. Figure 18.1 depicts this concept. The factor supply curve (S) is drawn positively sloped on the assumption that higher factor rewards, which we will denote by (v), will induce suppliers to offer more factor services (F) in the marketplace. Similarly the demand curve for the factor (D) is drawn with a negative slope on the assumption that demanders (in this case, firms) will hire a smaller quantity of the factor at higher levels of v. The price v* is therefore an equilibrium price at which the total quantity of factor services supplied is exactly equal to the quantity that is demanded. At a price above v* supply would exceed demand, and there would be "unemployment" of this factor; for a price below v* there would be excess demand for the factor.

Assumptions about Supply

The curves in Figure 18.1 were drawn without very much careful thought. As in our examination of pricing in the goods market, the most interesting aspects of the study of factor markets arise when we inquire into the more basic determinants of the shape of these curves. In this chapter we are primarily interested in studying the demand for a factor of production.

We assume here that there are a large number of suppliers of the factor in question. No single supplier can affect the price to be received; he or she will act as a price taker in making decisions. The market supply curve reflects the decisions of all suppliers as a group. This market supply curve can assume a

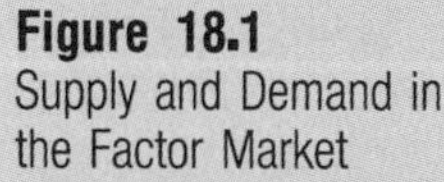

Figure 18.1
Supply and Demand in the Factor Market

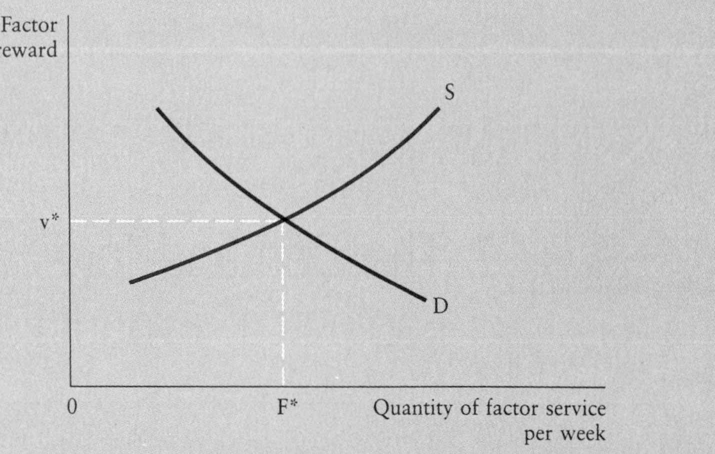

By analogy to the theory of pricing in the goods market, it has been assumed that the quantity of the factor service supplied is an increasing function of the factor payment (v) and that the quantity demanded is a decreasing function of v. The factor reward v* is an equilibrium price, since at this price the quantity supplied is equal to the quantity demanded.

wide variety of possible shapes. For example, the supply curve for land might be assumed to be very inelastic since the amount of land available is more or less fixed. The supply of other factors might be very elastic. For example, it is possible that relatively small increases in the wages of teachers might prompt a lot of people to consider the job. Whatever the shape of the supply curve, we usually assume that its position remains fixed throughout our analysis. In Chapters 19 and 20 we look at a few specific questions about the supply of labor and the supply of capital in detail.

Derived Demand

Derived demand Demand for a factor of production that is determined by the demand for the good it produces.

The demand curve in Figure 18.1 is drawn downward sloping. A lower price for an input is assumed to cause firms to demand more of it. To understand why a firm would hire more of an input in response to a fall in its price, we must recognize that a firm's demand for any factor of production is a **derived demand.** Firms hire labor, capital, and land in order to produce output. The quantities they hire depend on how much output they wish to sell. General Motors' annual demand for production workers, machinery, and land and buildings depends on how many cars it can sell during the year. If the price of an input, say, labor, were to fall, the firm would increase its use of labor for two reasons. First, it would then be able to produce any output level more cheaply by using relatively more labor. Second, if the firm, in response to the fall in the wage, chose to produce more output, it would demand even more labor. For General Motors, for instance, costs of manufacturing cars would fall, and the firm might find it profitable to produce more of them and to hire more labor to do so.

Later in this chapter we analyze this sequence of events in more detail. For the moment, the discussion is sufficiently precise to indicate why a firm's demand curve for an input will be downward sloping. We now look a bit further at the supply-demand equilibrium pictured in Figure 18.1. In particular, we investigate the question of the "rent" earned by factors of production since this concept has many similarities to the notion of consumer surplus we have used in many other chapters.

Economic Rent

Economic rent
The amount by which payments to a factor exceed the minimal amount required to retain it in its present use.

Rent plays an important role in the analysis of factor pricing. Because this term is used in a variety of contexts, it is important to be precise about its economic meaning. We use the term **economic rent** to reflect the extent to which payments to a factor exceed the minimal amount required to retain it in its present use.

One example of economic rent that we have already examined is the long-run profits earned by a monopoly. Since those profits would not be earned if the monopoly's inputs were employed under perfect competition, they are a form of economic rent earned by the factor that provides the basis for the monopoly. Figure 18.2 illustrates a more general case. Since the supply curve records that amount of factor service that would be supplied at each price, the total dollar amount necessary to retain the level F* in this occupation is given by the area AEF*0. If firms could perfectly discriminate among factor suppliers by hiring one unit at a time at an amount necessary to draw *that unit* into this employment, total factor payments would be AEF*0.[1] Competitive markets, however, do not work in this way. Rather, all units of an input are paid the same price, and this price (v*) is determined by what firms have to pay the last unit hired. Because all other units receive a return of v*, but might settle for somewhat less and still remain in their current employment, these "intramarginal" suppliers receive an economic rent. Total factor payments in the competitive case are given by v*EF*0, and total economic rents are given by the shaded area v*EA.

It is easy to see that the flatter the supply curve for a factor is, the smaller will be the area that represents economic rent. If a supply curve were infinitely elastic (a horizontal line at the prevailing price), there would be no economic rent. At the other extreme, all of the return to a factor that is in fixed

[1]Since the factor supply curve S represents the opportunity costs incurred by offering various levels of factor input in the market, area AEF*0 also represents the total opportunity costs involved in supplying F*.

Figure 18.2
Economic Rent

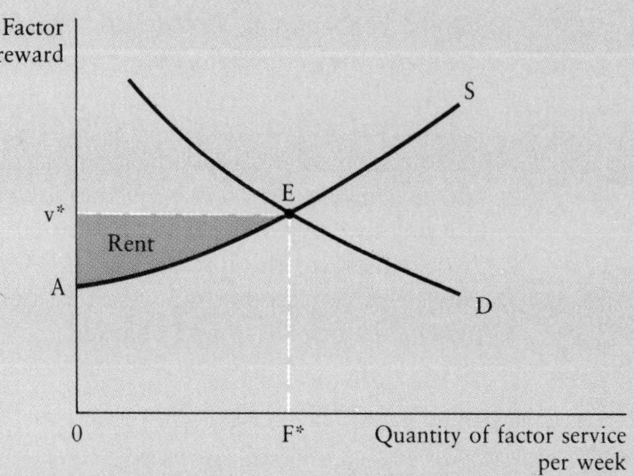

The shaded area represents total factor payments that exceed those necessary to keep F* in its current employment. This quantity is the difference between total factor payments (v*EF*0) and those payments a perfectly discriminating hirer might pay (AEF*0).

supply is in the nature of an economic rent.[2] The factor payments in such a situation are determined solely by demand, and there is no notion of lost opportunities on the part of the supplier of this fixed factor. It will always be supplied no matter what price is offered. Any return that is received is a result of the "accident" of where the demand curve happens to be.

Economic Rent and Opportunity Cost

It is important to recognize the close relationship between the concepts of economic rent and opportunity cost. A factor of production that has many alternative uses will have a very elastic supply curve to any one employment. Since this factor can receive almost as high a price elsewhere, quantity supplied will be reduced sharply if an employer reduces its price offer even slightly. In such a case, economic rents would be small because the factor earns only slightly in excess of what it might earn elsewhere. For example, clerical workers have numerous employment opportunities, all of which offer approximately the same wage. The earnings of a clerical worker in, say, a life insurance firm represent virtually no economic rent, since the worker could earn almost exactly the same amount in employment by some other firm. On

[2]Some authors make a distinction between short-run and long-run rents. In the short run, when supply curves tend to be more inelastic, rent is referred to as quasi rent to indicate that it may disappear when the long-run supply response is permitted. The profits of perfectly competitive firms in the short run are one example of quasi rent.

Figure 18.3
All Returns to a Fixed Supply of Land Are Economic Rent

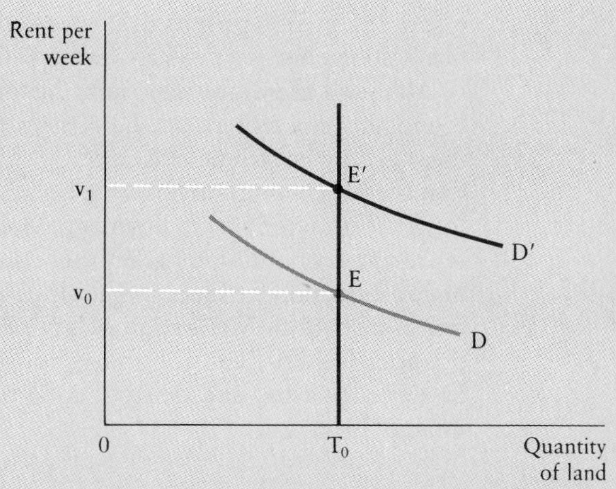

With land in absolutely fixed supply (at T_0), the rental rate will be determined solely by demand conditions. A lump-sum tax on landowners would not affect the quantity of land supplied.

the other hand, some factors of production are uniquely suited to one employment and have a considerably lower value elsewhere. In that case, their supply curve to this employment is inelastic, reflecting the fact that a lower price would not cause a marked reduction in supply. Most of the earnings of such a factor would be called economic rent and would be measured by the difference between the factor's current earnings and earnings in its next best employment. The high wages paid to players in professional baseball or basketball, for example, might be considered, in large part, as economic rent in the sense that the alternative earnings possibilities of these individuals (in occupations outside their sport) may be relatively low.

Land Rent

The most common example of this analysis of economic rent is the case of a fixed land supply. This situation is represented in Figure 18.3 by the vertical supply curve at the existing level of land (T_0). No matter what the level of demand is, this supply will be fixed. If demand were given by curve D, the rent on the land would be v_0, and the total return to the owner of the land is v_0ET_00. If, on the other hand, demand were given by the curve D′, the equilibrium rental rate would be v_1, and total rentals would be $v_1E'T_00$. The increase in price from v_0 to v_1, although it serves to ration the available land among demanders, has no effect on increasing supply. The nineteenth-century American economist Henry George noted this fact and proposed taxing rents going to landowners at a very high level, since this taxation would have no effect on the quantity of land provided.[3] Although there are numerous complications in this proposal, George's idea of a single tax on land still has many adherents, particularly in the British Labour party.

Although there are important historical reasons why the examination of economic rent centers on the returns to owners of land, we have seen that there is little economic reason for such a narrow view. Any factor of production for which alternative uses are slight will have a relatively inelastic supply to its most favorable employment. Most of the total return to this factor will represent economic rent, and this could be taxed away without creating a major reduction in supply. The price paid for rental of a favorably located parcel of land in Manhattan is largely economic rent in the same sense that the price Robert Redford receives for his acting is. In both cases, supply may be quite inelastic, and demand conditions will play the major role in determining price.

Ricardian Rent

In examining the rents earned on different parcels of land, one of the most important observations made by classical economists was that more fertile land tended to command a higher rent. David Ricardo, for example, carefully analyzed the way in which differential rents were related to land's fertility and to the demand for crops grown on the land.[4] Ricardo theorized that additional land of inferior quality would be cultivated up to the point at which the last acre planted earned exactly zero in economic rents. More fertile acres would earn positive rents, however, and these would represent a return based on the land's higher quality. Since the market price of any particular crop is determined by the costs of the marginal producer, and since rents are zero for this marginal producer, Ricardo concluded that economic rent should not be considered a cost element in determining the crop's price. Rather, rent is determined solely by the market demand for crops and by the availabilities of fertile land.

Graphical Presentation of Ricardo's Analysis

Ricardo's argument can easily be demonstrated graphically. Assume many parcels of land are suitable for growing wheat. These parcels range from very fertile (low costs of production) to rather poor and rocky (high cost). The long-run supply curve for wheat can be constructed as follows. At low prices only the best land is used; as price rises, production continues on

[3]Henry George, *Progress and Poverty: An Inquiry into the Cause of Industrial Depression and of Increase of Want with Increase of Wealth* (New York: Henry George, 1881).

[4]See David Ricardo, *The Principles of Political Economy and Taxation* (1817; reprinted London: J. M. Dent and Son, 1965), Chapters 2 and 32.

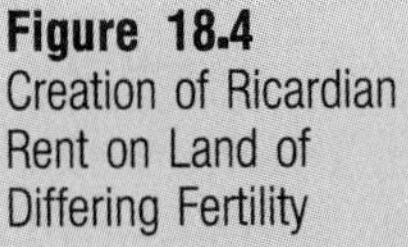
Figure 18.4
Creation of Ricardian Rent on Land of Differing Fertility

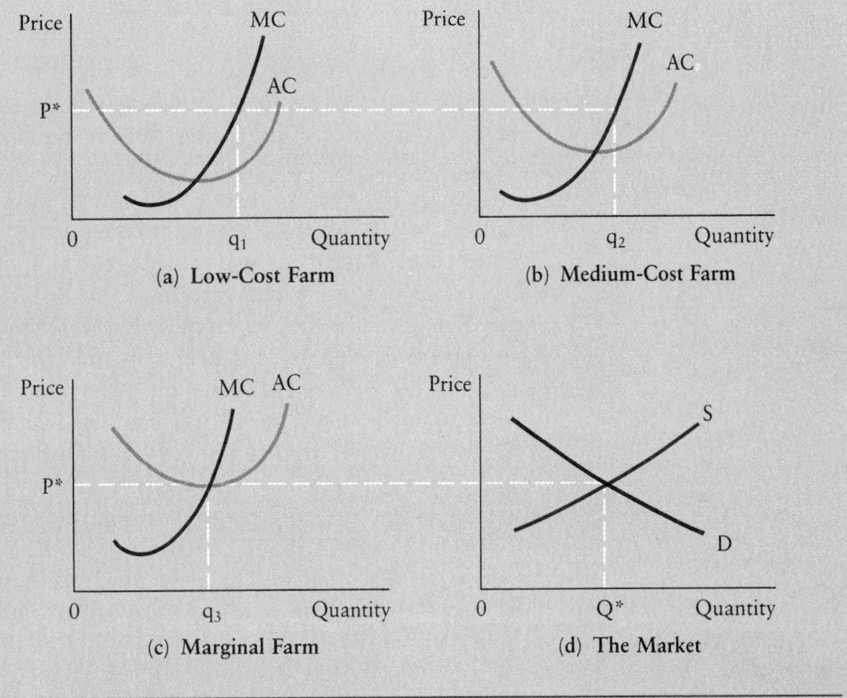

Because land differs in quality, farms with the most fertile land will have lower costs. Since price will be determined by the costs of the marginal supplier, low-cost farms will earn pure economic profits. These profits are called rent and will persist even in the long run since fertile land is in fixed supply.

the fertile land, and additional crops are planted on land of poorer quality. At still higher prices it will be profitable to utilize even lower quality land in production.

The market equilibrium is pictured in Figure 18.4. At the equilibrium price P*, owners of low-cost land parcels earn large economic profits (rent); those less favorably situated earn smaller rents; and the marginal farm earns zero in rents. If it were possible to earn any rents on additional pieces of land, this land would be brought into cultivation. Those acres that are left unplanted must be of lower quality than those of the marginal farm. The equilibrium described in Figure 18.4 is stable in the long run. It is impossible for new entrants to earn a profit even though those farms already in the market, by virtue of controlling the best land, are able to do so.

Notice two things about this analysis. First, it shows how the demand for land is derived from the product market. The location of the market demand curve determines how much land will be cultivated and how much rent will be generated. Notice also that the existence of rent does not affect the price of wheat. Rather, wheat prices only reflect the higher production costs encountered on the "marginal" farm.

Generalizations of Ricardo's Analysis

Ricardo's analysis of rent can be generalized to any situation in which differing productivities of resources result in differing cost curves for the firms that own those resources. Other cases of land rents reflecting cost differences include high rental values of especially favorable locations for retail businesses; higher prices for homes located near transit lines; and the tendency of identical houses to sell for more when they are located in towns with good schools. For the case of natural resource deposits, a similar analysis would hold. Those deposits from which resources can be obtained at low cost will command a rent relative to less accessible deposits. A major controversy over deregulation of natural gas prices in the United States, for example, concerned the distinction between "old" gas (that is, gas produced from older, lower cost wells) and "new" gas produced in more recent and costly locations. It was argued that old gas should continue to be produced under controlled prices so that owners of those low-cost wells would not gain windfall profits (that is, rents) as a result of rising prices that only reflected production costs from new wells. In Application 18.1: Rent Capitalization of Commuting Costs in Washington, D.C., we illustrate how the advantages of a favorable location give rise to rents that are ultimately reflected in the prices of houses.

Marginal Productivity Theory of Factor Demand

Ricardian rent theory was an important start to the development of marginal economics. Ricardo's notion that price is determined by output demand and by the costs of the marginal producer in many ways represents the seed from which modern microeconomics grew. One application of this approach was the development of the "marginal productivity" theory of the demand for factors of production. This section investigates that theory in detail.

Profit-Maximizing Behavior and the Hiring of Inputs

The basic concept of the marginal productivity theory of factor demand has already been stated in Chapter 10 when we discussed profit maximization. There we showed that one implication of the profit-maximization hypothesis is that the firm will make marginal input choices. More precisely, we showed that a profit-maximizing firm will hire additional units of any input up to the point at which the additional revenue from hiring one more unit of the input is exactly equal to the cost of hiring that unit. If we use ME_K and ME_L to denote the marginal expense associated with hiring one more unit of capital and labor, respectively, and let MR_K and MR_L be the extra revenue that hiring

APPLICATION 18.1

Rent Capitalization of Commuting Costs in Washington, D.C.

One of the major ways suburban communities differ in their attractiveness to homebuyers is in their convenience to places of work. Among houses with otherwise similar characteristics (for example, square feet of living space, air conditioning, lot size, and so forth) it would be expected that those in easily accessible locations would command higher prices than those in locations requiring lengthy commuting. In other words, the low commuting costs involved in some locations would be expected to be "capitalized" into the market prices of houses, just as in Ricardo's analysis, land's superior fertility and ability to earn rent would be expected to be reflected in its market value.

Evidence from the Housing Market

The question of how commuting costs are reflected in property values has been examined in a number of studies. One of the most complete studies, by J. P. Nelson, focused on the Washington, D.C., metropolitan area for 1970.[1] By carefully controlling for the many other factors that influence the demand for housing, Nelson estimated that each minute of daily commuting time to major employment areas in Washington reduced house values by about $190. A home that sold for $50,000 in an area that involved commuting time of about half an hour would sell for about $44,300 if it were located in an area involving an hour commute. Housing prices in metropolitan areas throughout the United States suggest that this type of price decline with respect to commuting costs may be quite common. Not only do prices seem to reflect automobile commuting times, but houses located near major railroad lines (say, in New York City suburbs in New Jersey or Connecticut) have higher prices than those located elsewhere.

The Value of Time

One way Nelson was able to check his estimate of the extent to which commuting costs were capitalized in house values was to calculate the implicit value that people were placing on their own time by paying more for favorably located houses. By assuming a certain number of commuting trips per year, he was able to calculate an implicit value of commuting time of around $1.85 per hour (or about one-third of workers' average after-tax wage rates in 1970). That figure was quite consistent with a variety of other studies of how individuals make choices among ways of getting to work that show an implicit time value of between one-third and one-half the market wage.

To Think About

1. Can you think of factors in addition to commuting costs that might be reflected in housing costs? How might proximity to a park or to an environmental hazard affect prices? How might you use house values to estimate the social benefits or costs of these factors?
2. Some stores advertise that they have low prices because they don't have to pay "high downtown rents." Would Ricardo's analysis support this assessment?

[1] J. P. Nelson, "Accessibility and the Value of Time in Commuting," *Southern Economic Journal* (January 1977): 1321–1329.

these units of capital and labor allows the firm to bring in, then profit maximization requires that

$$ME_K = MR_K;$$
$$ME_L = MR_L. \qquad [18.1]$$

Our analysis in the remainder of this chapter applies this marginal concept in various situations.

Price-Taking Behavior

If, as we have been assuming, the firm is a price taker in the capital and labor markets, it is easy to simplify the marginal expense idea. In this case, the firm can always hire an extra hour of capital input at the prevailing rental rate (v) and an extra hour of labor at the wage rate (w). Therefore, Equation 18.1 reduces to

$$v = ME_K = MR_K;$$
$$w = ME_L = MR_L. \qquad [18.2]$$

These equations simply say that a profit-maximizing firm that is a price taker for the inputs it buys should hire these inputs up to the point at which their unit cost is equal to the revenue they generate.

Marginal Revenue Product

To analyze the additional revenue yielded by hiring one more unit of an input is a two-step process. First we must ask how much output the additional input can produce. As we discussed in Chapter 8, this magnitude is given by the input's marginal physical productivity. For example, if a firm hires one more worker for an hour to make shoes, the worker's marginal physical productivity (MP_L) is simply the number of additional pairs of shoes per hour that the firm can make.

Once the additional output has been produced, it must be sold. Assessing the value of that sale is the second step in analyzing the revenue yielded by hiring one more unit of an input. We have looked at this issue quite extensively in previous chapters—the extra revenue obtained from selling an additional unit of output is, by definition, marginal revenue (MR). So, if an extra worker can produce two pairs of shoes per hour and the firm can take in $4 per pair from selling these shoes, then hiring the worker for an hour has increased the firm's revenues by $8. This is the figure the firm will compare to the worker's hourly wage to decide whether he or she should be hired. So now our profit-maximizing rules become

$$v = ME_K = MR_K = MP_K \cdot MR;$$
$$w = ME_L = MR_L = MP_L \cdot MR. \qquad [18.3]$$

Marginal revenue product
The extra revenue obtained from selling the output produced by hiring an extra worker or machine.

The terms on the right side of Equation 18.3 are called the **marginal revenue product** of capital and labor, respectively, since they show how much extra revenue is brought in by hiring one more unit. These are precisely what we need to study the demand for inputs and how the demand might change if wages or rental rates change.

A Special Case—Marginal Value Product

The profit-maximizing rules for input choices can be made even simpler if we assume that the firm we are examining sells its output in a competitive market. In that case, the firm will also be a price taker in the goods market, so the marginal revenue it takes in from selling one more unit of output is the market price (P). Using the result that, for a price taker in the goods market, marginal revenue is equal to price, Equation 18.3 becomes

$$v = MP_K \cdot P;$$
$$w = MP_L \cdot P \quad [18.4]$$

Marginal value product A special case of marginal revenue product in which the firm is a price taker for its output.

as the conditions for a profit maximum.[5] We call the terms on the right-hand side of Equation 18.4 the **marginal value product** (MVP) of capital and labor, respectively, since they do indeed put a value on these inputs' marginal physical productivities. Our final condition for maximum profits in this simple situation is

$$v = MVP_K;$$
$$w = MVP_L. \quad [18.5]$$

To see why these are required for profit maximization, consider again our shoe worker example. Suppose the worker can make two pairs of shoes per hour and that shoes sell for $4. The worker's marginal value product is $8 per hour. If the hourly wage is less than this (say, $5 per hour), the firm can increase profits by $3 by employing the worker for one more hour; profits were not at a maximum. Similarly, if the wage is $10 per hour, profits would rise by $2 if one less hour of labor were used. Only if the wage and labor's marginal value product are equal will profits truly be as large as possible. Of course, as Application 18.2: Input Demand by Nonprofit Firms shows, if a firm has no interest in profits, it will not necessarily follow these rules.

---

[5]Equation 18.4 implies cost minimization. Dividing the two gives

$$\frac{MP_L}{MP_K} = \frac{w}{v},$$

but in Chapter 8 we showed that RTS (of L for K) = MP_L/MP_K. A firm that pursues a marginal productivity approach to input demand will equate

$$\text{RTS (of L for K)} = w/v,$$

and this is what is required for cost minimization.

APPLICATION 18.2

Input Demand by Nonprofit Firms

Studies of nonprofit firms suggest that these firms' input choices may depart in systematic ways from those dictated by profit maximization and that such departures can have important implications for the relative efficiency with which various inputs are used. Here we look at two examples: cultural institutions and hospitals.

Cultural Institutions

Practically all symphonic, theater, opera, and ballet companies operate on a nonprofit basis. Often these firms rely on outside sources of funding (such as gifts or government aid) to cover perennial deficits between costs and revenues. Given this arrangement, it is not surprising that these firms may not employ the various inputs they use (artists, support personnel, and capital) in the same way that profit-maximizing firms would. For example, one study of 154 performing arts companies by J. Gapinski found that these firms typically overemployed artists and underemployed support personnel throughout the 1960s and 1970s.[1] Although profit maximization suggests that an inputs marginal value product should equal its price, Gapinski found that an artist's marginal value product was only about 60 percent of his or her wage in theater and ballet and less than 40 percent of his or her wage in opera and in symphony orchestras. For support personnel such as janitors, ushers, and administrators, on the other hand, the author found that most arts companies operated in a range of increasing marginal productivities—implying that more should be hired by a profit maximizer.

Why should cultural institutions depart in these ways from profit maximization in their input choices? One explanation may be that contributors to the arts have strong preferences favoring the employment of artists. If governments want to subsidize not only the arts but the artists too, or if private donors enjoy postperformance gatherings, administrators will probably respond to these preferences. They may then find it necessary to skimp on support personnel to save on costs.

[1]J. H. Gapinski, "The Production of Culture," *Review of Economics and Statistics* (November 1980): 578-586.

Hospitals

Most hospitals in the United States also operate on a nonprofit basis. They therefore have characteristics that resemble cultural institutions in that their input choices may be different from those that a profit-maximizing firm might make. Indeed, as in our previous example, several studies have found that nonprofit hospitals tend to use more highly skilled labor (physicians, registered nurses) and less low-skilled labor than do proprietary (for profit) hospitals.[2]

Nonprofit hospitals also tend to make more extensive use of high technology surgical and diagnostic equipment than might be warranted by the costs and productivities involved. As for the case of cultural institutions, a possible explanation for this result is that hospital decisions are often made by physicians and other administrators who have preferences favoring use of such inputs. That is, nonprofit hospitals may employ rather elaborate technology such as CAT scanners or intensive care facilities that offer training or other opportunities for their physicians. Profit-making hospitals, on the other hand, may make do with lower cost facilities.

To Think About

1. Does it make sense to talk about an opera, ballet, or orchestra substituting one input for another? After all, it takes a certain size cast to produce *Aida* or *Fidelio* and a full orchestra and chorus to perform Beethoven's *Ninth Symphony*. How could firms economize on artists and use more ancillary personnel?
2. If profit-making hospitals use less elaborate technology than nonprofit hospitals, do they necessarily provide lower quality care? Traditionally, profit-making hospitals have been regarded suspiciously as being more interested in profits than in patients' welfare. How might you judge whether a profit-making hospital's input choices diverged from what the optimal care of patients requires?

[2]See J. P. Newhouse, "Toward a Theory of Non-Profit Institutions: An Economic Model of a Hospital," *American Economic Review* (March 1970): 64–74.

Figure 18.5
Profit-Maximizing Input Choice

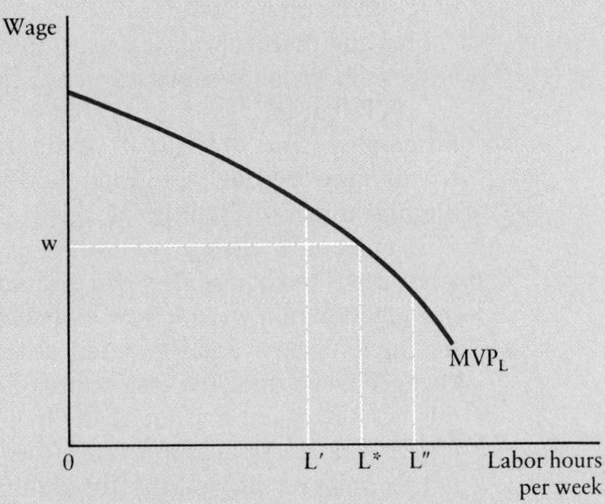

The marginal value product curve for labor (MVP_L) is constructed by multiplying labor's marginal physical productivity times the market price of the firm's output. The curve is downward sloping because of the assumption that labor exhibits a diminishing marginal physical productivity. At a wage of w, profit maximization requires that L* units of labor input be hired.

A Graphical Demonstration

Figure 18.5 shows the profit-maximizing choice of, say, labor input graphically. The horizontal axis in the figure records the hours of labor hired, and the vertical axis shows the MVP for each of these levels.[6] We can construct an MVP curve for labor directly from the marginal physical product of labor curve (MP_L) introduced in Chapter 8 by multiplying MP_L by the market price of the firm's output. The resulting MVP_L curve is shown in Figure 18.5. The downward slope of that curve reflects the assumption of a diminishing marginal physical productivity: the more labor hired, the lower will be labor's marginal physical productivity and the lower also will be its marginal value product.

The profit-maximizing amount of labor to hire can be found by recording labor's hourly wage rate (w) on the vertical axis. At that wage, profit maxi-

[6]Although here we analyze only the case of labor input, an analysis of the demand for capital input would proceed in exactly the same way. Throughout our discussion we assume the firm is a price taker in the output market so that the marginal value product is the correct demand concept.

mization requires hiring L* workers. Only for this level of labor input does $w = MVP_L$. For levels of labor input less than L* (say, L′) labor's MVP will exceed the market wage, and it would be profitable to hire more workers. Quantities of labor input greater than L* (say, L″), on the other hand, have an MVP that falls short of w, and profits would be increased by cutting back on employment. Only at L* is the cost of hiring an extra worker exactly equal to the revenue that hiring the worker provides to the firm: only at L* is the firm maximizing profits.

If w were to change, we would expect the profit-maximizing quantity of labor input to change also. We examine that possibility in the next section. In our investigation we continue to assume that the firm is a price taker for both the inputs it buys and the output it sells. The analysis would be only slightly changed if we studied a case of imperfect competition in the goods market. In this case marginal revenue (MR) would be less than market price (P), but it would be a simple matter to take that into account. The analysis is quite different, however, if we drop the assumption that the firm is a price taker for the inputs it buys—a subject we study in detail later.

Responses to Changes in Input Prices

Suppose the price of labor (w) were to fall. Early in this chapter we indicated why firms might demand more labor in response to such a change. In this section we provide a detailed analysis of this situation.

Single-Input Case

As a simple first case, let us assume that a firm uses only labor to produce its output. The firm's marginal value product curve is shown in Figure 18.6. At a wage of w_1 the firm's profit-maximizing choice of labor input is given by L_1. The firm will persist in hiring L_1 units of labor as long as the conditions it faces do not change.

If the wage rate were to fall to w_2, more labor (L_2) would be demanded. At such a lower wage, more labor can be hired because the firm can "afford" to have a lower marginal physical productivity from the labor it employs. If it continued to hire only L_1, the firm would not be maximizing profits since, at the margin, labor would now be capable of producing more in additional revenue than hiring additional labor would cost. For the single-input case, the assumption of a diminishing marginal productivity of labor ensures that a fall in the price of labor will cause more labor to be hired.[7] The marginal value product curve shows this response.

[7]Since the marginal productivity of labor is positive, hiring more labor also implies that output will increase when w declines.

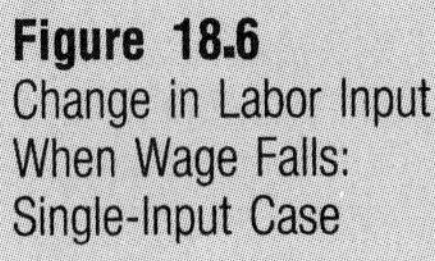

Figure 18.6
Change in Labor Input When Wage Falls: Single-Input Case

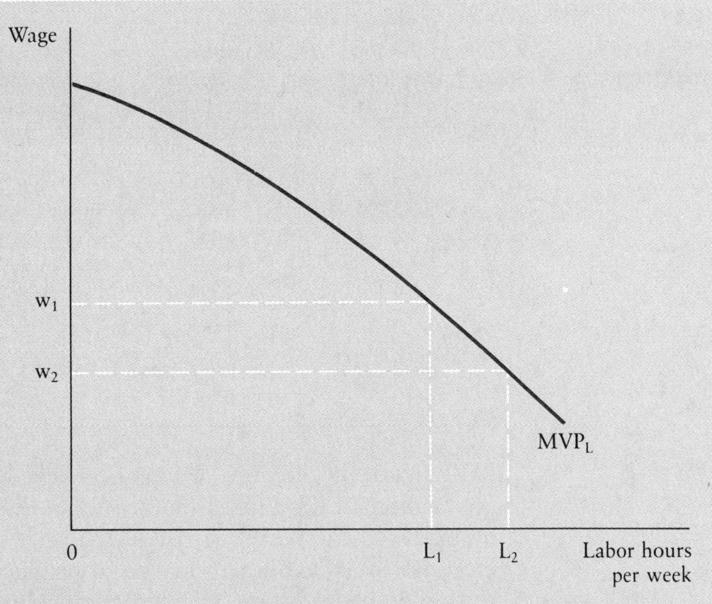

At a wage rate w_1, profit maximization requires that L_1 labor input be hired. If the wage rate falls to w_2, more labor (L_2) will be hired because of the assumed negative slope of the MVP_L curve.

A Numerical Example

As a numerical example of these input choices, let's look again at the hiring decision for Hamburger Heaven first discussed in the appendix to Chapter 9. Table 18.1 repeats the productivity information for the case in which Hamburger Heaven uses four grills (K = 4). As the table shows, the marginal productivity of labor declines as more workers are assigned to use grills each hour—the first worker hired turns out 20 (heavenly) hamburgers per hour, whereas the tenth hired produces only 3.2 hamburgers per hour. To calculate these workers' marginal value products, we simply multiply these physical productivity figures by the price of hamburgers, $.20. These results appear in the final column of Table 18.1. With a market wage of $1.00 per hour, Hamburger Heaven should hire four workers. The marginal value product of each of these workers exceeds $1.00, so the firm earns some incremental profit on each of them. The fifth worker's MVP is only $.94, however, so it does not make sense to add that worker.

The number of workers hired in this example is precisely the number required to minimize average cost with four grills in operation (see the appendix to Chapter 9). Profit maximization and cost minimization yield the same result. If the price of hamburgers had been higher than $.20, however, the

Table 18.1
Hamburger Heaven's Profit-Maximizing Hiring Decision

Labor Input per Hour	Hamburgers Produced per Hour	Marginal Product (Hamburger)	Marginal Value Product ($.20 per Hamburger)
1	20.0	20	$4.00
2	28.3	8.3	1.66
3	34.6	6.3	1.26
4	40.0	5.4	1.08
5	44.7	4.7	0.94
6	49.0	4.3	0.86
7	52.9	3.9	0.78
8	56.6	3.7	0.74
9	60.0	3.4	0.68
10	63.2	3.2	0.64

MVP figures in the final column of Table 18.1 would have been higher, and the firm might have hired more workers (how many would be hired if hamburgers sold for $.25?). A rise in the price of hamburgers would provide an incentive for Hamburger Heaven to produce more burgers and, in the short run, to do so by adding more workers to use its fixed number of grills.

At a wage other than $1.00 per hour, Hamburger Heaven would hire a different number of workers. At $1.25 per hour, for example, only three workers would be hired. With wages of $.75 per hour, on the other hand, seven workers would be employed. The MVP calculation provides complete information about Hamburger Heaven's short-run hiring decisions. Of course, a change in the wages of burger-flippers might also cause the firm to reconsider how many grills it uses—a subject that we now investigate.

Two-Input Case

For the case where the firm can vary two (or more) inputs the story is considerably more complex. The assumption of a diminishing marginal physical product of labor can be misleading here. If w falls, there will be a change not only in labor input but also in capital input as a new cost-minimizing combination of inputs is chosen (see our analysis in Chapter 9). When capital input changes, the entire MP_L function shifts (workers now have a different amount of capital to work with), and our earlier analysis of how wages affect hiring cannot be made. The remainder of this section presents a series of observations that establish that even with many inputs, a fall in w will lead to an increase in the quantity of labor demanded.

Substitution Effect

In some ways analyzing the two-input case is similar to our analysis of the individual's response to a change in the price of a good in Chapter 4. When w

Figure 18.7
Substitution and Output Effects of a Decrease in the Price of Labor

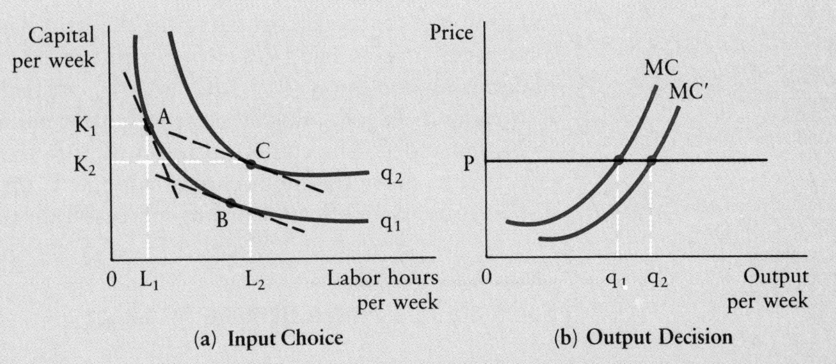

When the price of labor falls, the substitution effect causes more labor to be purchased even if output is held constant. This is shown as a movement from point A to point B in Panel a. The change in w will also shift the firm's expansion path and its marginal cost curve. A normal situation might be for the MC curve to shift downward in response to a decrease in w, as shown in Panel b. With this new curve (MC′) a higher level of output (q_2) will be chosen. The hiring of labor will increase (to L_2) from this output effect.

falls, we can decompose the total effect on the quantity of L hired into two components: a substitution effect and an output effect.

Substitution effect
In the theory of production, the substitution of one input for another while holding output constant in response to a change in the input's price.

To study the **substitution effect,** we hold q constant at q_1. With a fall in w there will be a tendency to substitute labor for capital in the production of q_1. This effect is illustrated in Panel a in Figure 18.7. Since the condition for minimizing the cost of producing q_1 requires that RTS = w/v, a fall in w will necessitate a movement from input combination A to combination B. Because the isoquants have been assumed to exhibit a diminishing RTS, it is clear from the diagram that this substitution effect must cause labor input to rise in response to the fall in w. The firm now decides to produce q_1 in a more labor-intensive way.

Output Effect

Output effect
The effect of an input price change on the amount of the input that the firm hires that results from a change in the firm's output level.

It is, however, not completely correct to hold q output constant when w falls. When the firm changes its level of production—the **output effect**—the analogy to a person's utility-maximization problem breaks down. The reason for this is that consumers have budget constraints, but firms do not. Firms produce as much as profit maximization requires—their need for inputs is derived from these production decisions. In order to investigate what happens to the quantity of output produced, we must therefore investigate the firm's profit-maximizing output decision. A fall in w, because it changes relative factor costs, will shift the firm's expansion path. Consequently, all the firm's cost curves will be shifted, and probably some output level other than q_1 will be chosen.

Panel b in Figure 18.7 illustrates the most common case. As a result of the fall in w, the marginal cost curve for the firm has shifted downward to MC′. The profit-maximizing level of output rises from q_1 to q_2.[8] The profit-maximizing condition (P = MC) is now satisfied at a higher level of output. Returning to Panel a, this increase in output will cause even more labor input to be demanded. The combined result of both the substitution and the output effects is to move the input choice to point C on the firm's isoquant for output level q_2. Both effects work to increase L in response to a decrease in w.[9]

Summary of a Firm's Demand for Labor

We can summarize our findings about a firm's response to a fall in w by concluding that a profit-maximizing firm will increase its hiring of labor for two reasons. First, the firm will substitute the now cheaper labor for other inputs that are now relatively more expensive. This is the substitution effect. Second, the wage decline will reduce the firm's marginal costs, thereby causing it to increase output and to increase the hiring of all inputs including labor. This is the output effect.

This conclusion holds for any input, and it can be reversed to show that an increase in the price of an input will cause the firm to hire less of that input. We have shown that the firm's demand curve for an input will be unambiguously downward sloping: the lower its price, the more of the input will be demanded.[10] The shape of the input demand curve with which we started our discussion (Figure 18.1) is therefore theoretically justified.

Responsiveness of Input Demand to Price Changes

The notions of substitution and output effects help to explain how responsive to price changes the demand for a factor might be. Suppose, to change our already tedious example a bit, the wage rate rose. We already know that less

[8]Price (P) has been assumed to be constant. If all firms in an industry were confronted with a decline in w, all would change their output levels; the industry supply curve would shift outward, and consequently P would fall. As long as the market demand curve for the firm's output is negatively sloped, however, the analysis in this chapter would not be seriously affected by this observation since the lower P will lead to more output being demanded.

[9]No definite statement can be made about how the quantity of capital (or any other input) changes in response to a decline in w. The substitution and output effects work in opposite directions (as can be seen in Figure 18.7), and the precise outcome depends on the relative sizes of these effects.

[10]Actually, a proof of this assertion is not as simple as is implied here. The complicating factor arises when the input in question is "inferior," and it is no longer true that the marginal cost curve shifts downward when the price of such a factor declines. Nevertheless, it can be shown that, as long as the good that is being produced has a downward-sloping demand curve, the firm's demand for the factor will also be negatively sloped. For a mathematical proof, see E. C. Ferguson, *The Neoclassical Theory of Production and Distribution* (Cambridge: Cambridge University Press, 1969), pp. 136–153.

labor will be demanded. Now we wish to investigate whether this decrease in quantity demanded will be large or small.

Ease of Substitution

First, consider the substitution effect. The decrease in the hiring of labor from a rise in w will depend on how easy it is for firms to substitute other factors of production for labor. Some firms may find it relatively simple to substitute machines for workers, and for these firms the quantity of labor demanded will decrease substantially. Other firms may produce with a fixed proportions technology. For them substitution will be impossible. The size of the substitution effect may also depend on the length of time allowed for adjustment. In the short run, a firm may have a stock of machinery that requires a fixed complement of workers. Consequently, the short-run substitution possibilities are slight. Over the long run, however, this firm may be able to adapt its machinery to use less labor per machine; the possibilities of substitution may now be substantial. For example, a rise in the wages of coal miners will have little short-run substitution effect since existing coal-mining equipment requires a certain number of workers to operate it. In the long run, however, there is clear evidence that mining can be made more capital intensive by designing more complex machinery. In the long run, capital can be substituted for labor.

Costs and the Output Effect

An increase in the wage rate will also raise firms' costs. In a competitive market this will cause the price of the good being produced to rise, and people will reduce their purchases of that good. Consequently, firms will lower their levels of production; because less output is being produced, the output effect will cause less labor to be demanded. In this way the output effect reinforces the substitution effect. The size of this output effect will depend on (1) how large the increase in marginal costs brought about by the wage rate increase is, and (2) how much quantity demanded will be reduced by a rising price. The size of the first of these components depends on how "important" labor is in total production costs, whereas the size of the second depends on how price-elastic the demand for the product is.

In industries for which labor costs are a major portion of total costs and for which demand is very elastic, output effects will be large. For example, an increase in wages for restaurant workers is likely to induce a large negative output effect in the demand for such workers, since labor costs are a significant portion of restaurant operating costs and the demand for meals eaten out is relatively price-elastic. An increase in wages will cause a big price rise, and this will cause people to reduce sharply the number of meals they eat out. On the other hand, output effects in the demand for pharmaceutical workers are probably small. Direct labor costs are a small fraction of drug production costs, and the demand for drugs is price-inelastic. Wage increases will have only a small effect on costs, and any increases in price that do result will not cause demand for drugs to be reduced significantly.

Overall, then, the effect of a wage change will be determined by the size of the substitution and income effects it causes. In Application 18.3: The Minimum Wage, we look at how these insights can help to explain the possible effects of increases in the minimum wage.

Monopsony

In many situations, the firm is not a price taker for the inputs it buys. It may frequently be necessary for the firm to offer a wage above that currently prevailing to attract more employees, or the firm may be able to get a better price on some equipment by restricting its purchases. To explore these situations, it is most convenient to examine the polar case of **monopsony** (a single buyer) in a factor market.

Monopsony
A firm that is the only hirer in a particular input market.

Marginal Expense

If there is only one buyer of an input, that firm faces the entire market supply curve for the input. In order to increase its hiring of labor, say, by one or more units, the firm must move to a higher point on this supply curve. This will involve paying not only a higher wage to the last worker hired but also additional wages to those workers already employed. The marginal cost of hiring the extra unit of labor therefore exceeds its wage rate, and the price-taking assumption we made earlier no longer holds. Instead, for a monopsonist facing an upward-sloping supply curve for an input, the **marginal expense** will exceed the market price of the input. For labor input, for example, the marginal expense (ME_L) of hiring one more worker exceeds the market wage (w).

Marginal expense
The cost of hiring one more unit of an input. Will exceed the price of the input if the firm faces an upward-sloping supply curve for the input.

Notice the similarity between the concept of the marginal expense of an input and the marginal revenue for a monopolist. Both concepts are intended to be used when firms possess market power and their choices have an effect on prices. In such situations firms are no longer price takers. Instead, firms will recognize that their actions affect prices and will use this information in making decisions.

A Numerical Illustration

This distinction is easiest to see with a numerical example. Suppose (as is probably the case) that the Yellowstone Park Company is the only hirer of bear wardens. Suppose also that the number of people willing to take this job (L) is a simple positive function of the hourly wage (w) given by

$$L = \tfrac{1}{2}w. \qquad [18.6]$$

APPLICATION 18.3

The Minimum Wage

The Fair Labor Standards Act of 1938 established a national minimum wage of $.25 per hour. Since that time, the minimum wage has been raised several times in response to general inflation and changing social values. Currently the minimum wage is scheduled to rise to $4.55 per hour by the early 1990s.

A Graphic Analysis

Figure 1 illustrates the possible effects of a minimum wage. Panel a shows the supply and demand curves for labor. Given these curves, an equilibrium wage rate, w_1, is established in the market. At this wage, a typical firm hires l_1, and this choice of input is shown on the firm's isoquant map in Panel b. Suppose now that a minimum wage of ($w_2 > w_1$) is imposed by law. This new wage will cause the firm to reduce its demand for labor from l_1 to l_2. At the same time, more labor (L_3) will be supplied at w_2 than was supplied at the lower wage rate. The imposition of the minimum wage will result in an excess of the supply of labor over the demand for labor of $L_3 - L_2$. This excess supply is what we mean by "unemployment."

Minimum Wages and Teenage Unemployment

Teenagers are the labor market participants most likely to be affected by minimum wage laws, since they usually represent the lower end of the spectrum of skills. An increase in minimum wages may cause employers to substitute capital and skilled labor for what has become more expensive, unskilled teenage labor. It may also cause large negative output effects, since the products produced by teenage employees (services, for example) usually have a fairly high price elasticity. In recent years, teenage unemployment has increased rapidly. Particularly hard hit have been teenage minority group members, for whom unemployment rates often exceed 30 percent. Although there are several factors that may account for such statistics (unstable employment opportunities, discrimination in employment, long periods of searching for jobs), many economists assign an important role to statutory changes in the minimum wage. For example, one major study in the 1970s found that each 1 percent increase in the minimum wage resulted in a reduction of 0.3 percent in teenagers' share of total employment.[1]

Figure 1
Effects of a Minimum Wage in a Perfectly Competitive Labor Market

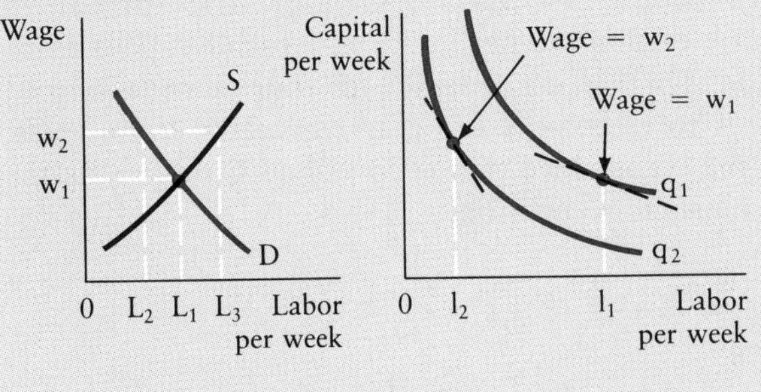

(a) The Market (b) Typical Firm

The imposition of a minimum wage (w_2) causes the firm to reduce labor usage to l_2 because it will both substitute capital (and other inputs) for labor and cut back output.

Minimum Wages and Poverty

Of course, those who keep their jobs when minimum wages increase do earn more. The notion that minimum wages may help the poor is probably the most important reason for the policy's political popularity. But, it is important to be careful about equating minimum wage workers to "the poor" since many people who work in minimum wage jobs live in nonpoor families. Indeed, one study reports that only about 11 percent of the gains from raising the minimum wage go to poor families.[2]

To Think About

1. Does a minimum wage increase or decrease total wages received by workers affected by it? How does your answer depend on the elasticity of demand for labor?
2. How does a minimum wage affect the demand for workers who are paid wages above the minimum wage? Would these workers support legislation raising the minimum wage?

[1]Finis Welch, "Minimum Wage Legislation in the United States," *Economic Inquiry* (September 1974): 285–318.

[2]R. V. Burkhauser and T. A. Finegan, "The Minimum Wage and the Poor: The End of a Relationship," *Journal of Policy Analysis and Management* (Winter 1989): 54–71.

Table 18.2
Labor Costs of Hiring Bear Wardens in Yellowstone Park

Hourly Wage	Workers Supplied per Hour	Total Labor Cost per Hour	Marginal Expense
$ 2	1	$ 2	$ 2
4	2	8	6
6	3	18	10
8	4	32	14
10	5	50	18
12	6	72	22
14	7	98	26

This relationship between the wage and the number of people who offer their services as bear wardens is shown in the first two columns of Table 18.2. Total labor costs ($w \cdot L$) are shown in the third column, and the marginal expense of hiring each warden is shown in the fourth column. The extra expense associated with adding another warden always exceeds the wage rate paid to that person. The reason is clear—not only does a newly hired warden receive the higher wage, but all previously hired wardens also get a higher wage. A monopsonist will take these extra expenses into account in its hiring decisions.

A graph can be used to help to clarify this relationship. Figure 18.8 shows the supply curve (S) for bear wardens. If Yellowstone wishes to hire three wardens, it must pay $6 per hour, and total outlays will be $18 per hour. This situation is reflected by point A on the supply curve. If the firm tries to hire a fourth warden, it must offer $8 per hour to everyone—it must move to point B on the supply curve. Total outlays are now $32 per hour, so the marginal expense of hiring the fourth worker is $14 per hour. By comparing the sizes of the total outlay rectangles, we can see why the marginal expense was higher than the wage paid to the fourth worker. That worker's hourly wage is shown by the gray rectangle—it is $8 per hour. The other three workers, who were previously earning $6 per hour, now earn $8. This extra outlay is shown in light blue. Total labor expenses for four wardens exceed those for three by the area of both the blue and gray rectangles. In this case, marginal expense exceeds the wage since the Yellowstone Company is the sole hirer of people in this unusual occupation.

Monopsonist's Input Choice

As for any profit-maximizing firm, a monopsonist will hire any input up to the point at which the additional revenue and additional cost of hiring one more unit are equal. For the case of labor this requires

$$ME_L = MVP_L. \qquad [18.7]$$

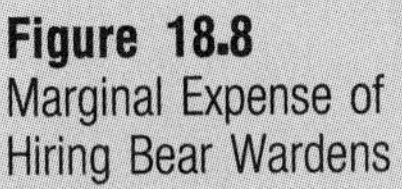

Figure 18.8
Marginal Expense of Hiring Bear Wardens

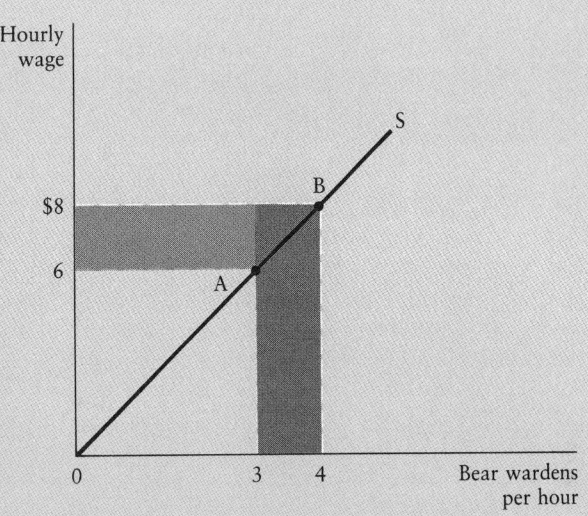

Since Yellowstone Park is (probably) the only hirer of bear wardens, it must raise the hourly wage offered from \$6 to \$8 if it wishes to hire a fourth warden. The marginal expense of hiring that warden is \$14—his or her wage (\$8, shown in gray) plus the extra \$2 per hour that must be paid to the other three wardens (shown in blue).

In the special case of a price taker that faces an infinitely elastic labor supply ($ME_L = w$), Equations 18.5 and 18.7 are identical. However, if the firm faces a positively sloped labor supply curve, Equation 18.7 dictates a different level of input choice, as we now show.

A Graphical Demonstration

The monopsonist's choice of labor input is illustrated in Figure 18.9. The firm's demand curve for labor (D) is drawn initially on the assumption that the firm is a price taker. This curve is negatively sloped, as we have shown it must be. The ME_L curve associated with the labor supply curve (S) is constructed in much the same way that the marginal revenue curve associated with a demand curve can be constructed. Because S is positively sloped, the ME_L curve always lies above S. The profit-maximizing level of labor input for the monopsonist is given by L_1. At this level of input the condition of Equation 18.7 holds marginal expense is equal to marginal value product. At L_1 the wage rate in the market is given by w_1. The quantity of labor demanded falls short of that which would be hired in a perfectly competitive market (L^*). The firm has restricted input demand to take advantage of its monopsonistic position in the labor market.

The formal similarities between this analysis and the monopoly analysis we presented in Chapter 15 should be clear. In particular, the actual "de-

Figure 18.9
Pricing in a Monopsonistic Labor Market

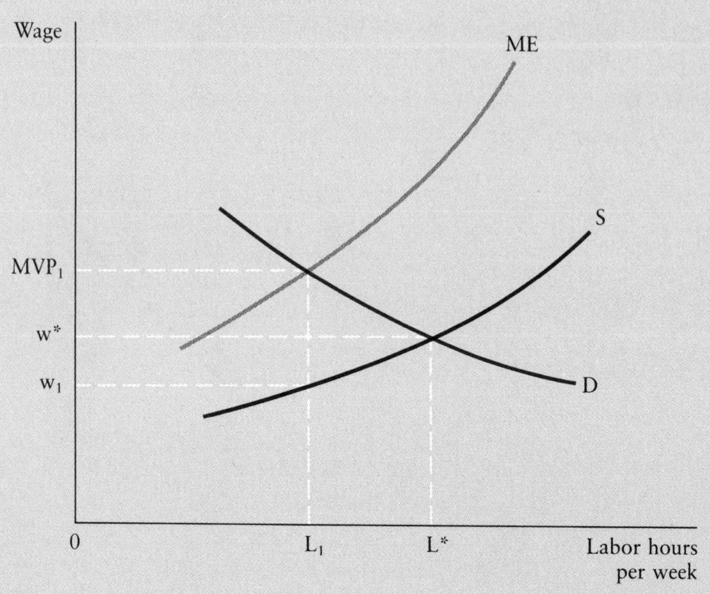

If a firm faces a positively sloped supply curve for labor (S), it will base its decisions on the marginal expense of labor curve (ME_L). Because S is positively sloped, ME_L lies above S. The curve S can be thought of as an average cost of labor curve, and the ME_L curve is marginal to S. At L_1 the equilibrium condition $ME_L = MVP_L$ holds, and this quantity will be hired at a market wage rate w_1.

mand curve" for a monopsonist consists of a single point. In Figure 18.9 this point is given by L_1, w_1. The monopsonist has chosen this point as the most desirable of all those points on the supply curve S. A different point will not be chosen unless some external change (such as a shift in the demand for the firm's output or a change in technology) affects labor's marginal value product.

Monopsonistic Exploitation

In addition to restricting its input demand, the monopsonist pays an input less than its marginal value product. This result is also illustrated in Figure 18.9. At the monopsonist's preferred choice of labor input (L_1), a wage of w_1 prevails in the market. For this level of input demand, the firm is willing to pay an amount equal to MVP_1: this is the amount of extra revenue that hiring another worker would provide to the firm. At L_1 the monopsonist pays workers less than they are "worth" to the firm. In the absence of effective competition, the monopsonist can persist in this behavior. Some authors refer to this gap between an input's MVP and its market price as monopsonistic exploitation. It should be clear from Figure 18.9 that the extent of this exploitation will be greater the more inelastic the supply of labor is to the monopsonist. The less responsive to low wages the labor supply is, the more the monopsonist can take advantage of this situation.

Causes of Monopsony

To practice monopsonistic exploitation a firm must possess considerable power in the market for a particular input. If the market is reasonably competitive, monopsonistic exploitation cannot occur because other firms will recognize the profit potential reflected in the gap between MVPs and input costs. They will therefore bid for these inputs, driving their prices to equality with marginal value products. Under such conditions the supply of labor to any one firm will be nearly infinitely elastic (because of the alternative employment possibilities available), and monopsonistic behavior will be impossible. Our analysis suggests monopsonistic outcomes will be observed in real-world situations in which, for some reason, effective competition for inputs is lacking. We now examine three such causes: geography, specialized employment, and monopsonistic cartels.

Geography

Some firms may occupy a monopsonistic position by being the only source of employment in a small town. Because moving costs for workers are high, alternative employment opportunities for local workers are unattractive, and the firm may be able to exert a strong effect on wages paid. This possibility may, in part, explain the low wage rates that prevailed in the southern United States prior to World War II. Many small southern towns had isolated labor markets that were dominated by one or two firms. The term *company town* originated in this situation and carried a connotation of exploitation that may have been appropriate. A number of factors at work since World War II have tended to undermine these monopsonistic positions. The population has become more willing to relocate in response to wage rate differences. The entry of new firms into southern labor markets (together with improved methods of commuting to work) has further improved workers' alternative earnings possibilities. Finally, noncompetitive forces, such as increasing unionization and the expansion of the minimum wage law, have probably also had an effect on monopsonistic practices.

Specialized Employment

It may sometimes be the case that only one firm hires a particularly specialized type of input. If the alternative earnings prospects for that input are unattractive, its supply to the firm will be inelastic, presenting the firm with the opportunity for monopsonistic behavior. For example, marine engineers with many years of experience in designing nuclear submarines must work for the one or two companies that produce such vessels. Because other jobs would not make use of these workers' specialized training, alternative employment is not particularly attractive. Similarly, experienced telephone circuit designers may find they have to work for the local phone company if they wish to capitalize on their skills without having to move. As a nonlabor example, the McDonald's Corporation for many years bought more than 50 percent of all frozen french fried potatoes produced in the United States; the corporation probably occupied a monopsonistic position in that market.

Monopsonistic Cartels

These examples suggest that monopsonistic hiring of specialized inputs is often associated with a monopoly position in the sale of an output (nuclear submarines, local telephone service, or french fries). A particularly prevalent example of this relationship is in hiring by the federal government. Since the government occupies a monopoly position in the production of a number of goods requiring specialized inputs (space travel, armed forces, and national political offices, to name a few), it would be expected to be in a position to exercise monopsony power. In other cases a group of firms may combine to form a cartel in their hiring decisions (and, perhaps, in their output decisions too). Application 18.4: Monopsony in the Market for Baseball Players illustrates this relationship between a firm's monopoly position and monopsonistic hiring in major league baseball, a situation in which it is possible to obtain direct measures of workers' marginal value.

Discrimination in Hiring

If a monopsony can segregate the supply of a factor into two or more distinct markets, it may be able to increase profits. For example, a monopsony may be able to discriminate in hiring between men and women. Because the firm can readily identify which market a prospective employee belongs to, it will find it profitable to pay different wages in the two markets.

A Graphical Analysis

Such a situation is shown in Figure 18.10. The figure assumes that men and women are equally productive and that the firm has a constant marginal value product of labor no matter how much labor is hired. This curve is shown by the horizontal MVP_L curve. The supply curves for men and women are shown in the figure as sharing the same vertical axis. Given these supply curves the firm will choose that quantity of labor in each market for which the marginal expense (ME) is equal to labor's marginal revenue product. Consequently, the firm will hire L_m from the men's market and L_w from the women's. The wage rate in the two markets will be w_m and w_w, respectively.

APPLICATION 18.4

Monopsony in the Market for Baseball Players

Occasionally powerful cartels of hirers can achieve a successful monopsony. An important example is provided by major league baseball teams during the period in which the reserve clause was in effect. That clause combined with player drafts effectively bound each player to a single team and prevented interteam competition for salaries. Even though there were 18 major league clubs (or firms), their hiring was effectively cartelized—creating the potential for monopsonistic exploitation.

Empirical Estimates

Numerical estimates of the degree of exploitation in major league baseball were constructed by G. W. Scully in a 1974 article.[1] Because baseball players' salaries are more or less a matter of public record, the principal problem Scully faced in measuring the effect of monopsony was to estimate the players' marginal value products. He adopted a two-step procedure. First, he examined the correlation between a team's winning percentage and its attendance figures. Next he analyzed which aspects of individual player performance were most closely related to a team's overall performance. Two significant variables were identified: for hitters, the "slugging average" seemed most important, whereas for pitchers, the ratio of strikeouts to walks proved most relevant. A few of the estimates are presented in Table 1. These data show that most players' MVPs exceeded their salaries by a substantial margin.

Table 1
Monopsonistic Exploitation in Major League Baseball, 1969

Hitters

Slugging Average	Hitters' Net MVP[a]	Estimated Salary
255	$−39,100	$ 9,700
305	103,600	14,100
350	137,800	32,700
375	156,800	39,000
427	296,500	42,200
490	350,400	60,500
525	383,700	68,000

Pitchers

Ratio of Strikeouts to Walks	Pitchers' Net MVP[a]	Estimated Salary
1.50	$−20,800	$ 9,000
2.00	132,000	16,500
2.30	169,200	36,900
2.79	349,600	47,200
3.09	405,300	66,800
3.54	479,700	86,300

[a]Estimated gross MVP less training and related costs. For poor players the net figure is negative.
Source: G. W. Scully, "Pay and Performance in Major League Baseball," *American Economic Review* (December 1974): 928.

Erosion of the Cartel

It was only a matter of time before players came to recognize the cartelizing effect of the reserve clause and took organized action against it. A players' strike in 1972 (coupled with legal action in a suit brought by St. Louis Cardinal outfielder Curt Flood) eventually led to the adoption of a free agent provision in players' contracts as a partial replacement of the reserve clause. Recent spectacular contract settlements for some star players are indicative of the bidding competition that has continued since the breakdown of the cartel. Although the leagues have tried several actions to reestablish their cartel position (such as player drafts and limiting league expansion), they have been unable to return to the powerful position they occupied prior to 1970.

To Think About

1. If players could be freely traded among teams, could monopsonistic exploitation arise? Can you think of reasons other than wage restraint why organized baseball might resist such freedom of movement?
2. How might mergers between two rival leagues (for example, the American and National Football Leagues or the American and National Basketball Associations) affect players' salaries? Would players tend to favor or oppose such mergers?

[1]G. W. Scully, "Pay and Performance in Major League Baseball," *American Economic Review* (December 1974): 915–930.

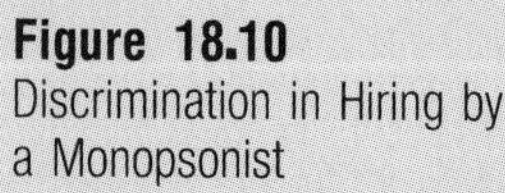

Figure 18.10
Discrimination in Hiring by a Monopsonist

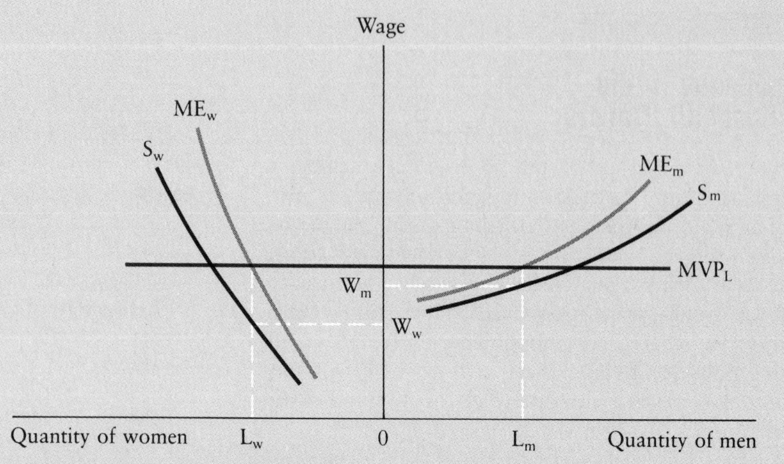

By segregating the labor market, say, between men and women, a monopsonist will minimize labor costs by choosing those quantities of labor such that the marginal revenue product of labor is equal to the marginal expense in each market. In this diagram, the wages of women (w_w) will be below the wages of men (w_m), even though the marginal value product for both types of labor is identical.

The way we have drawn Figure 18.10, men's wages will exceed women's. This happens because women's labor supply is relatively inelastic.[11]

Limits to Discrimination

A similar analysis can be developed for any situation in which a monopsony can segregate the market for its inputs into two separate parts. In order to do so, it must be able to identify workers as belonging to particular markets so that its segmentation strategy will work. It must know how much of each kind of worker it is hiring. For this reason, wage discrimination among geographically distinct labor markets or among individuals with readily identifiable personal characteristics (sex, race, age) would be expected to be the types of discrimination most often encountered. Application 18.5: Sex Discrimination shows that some U.S. data are consistent with this model. But, because it is doubtful that many firms have the kind of monopsony hiring power that such discrimination requires, these data raise more questions about discrimination than they answer.

[11]Women may, for example, have a more inelastic supply curve because they may have relatively few employment alternatives.

APPLICATION 18.5

Sex Discrimination

Table 1 shows median earnings in different occupations for men and women for the year 1983. Overall women's earnings averaged about 60 percent of those of men. Although some part of these male-female differences may be explained by objective characteristics (for example, age, educational differences, or the amount of job experience), a number of statistical studies have found that the gap in earnings continues to persist after controlling for these factors. Such findings are in general accord with the monopsony model of labor market discrimination.

Can the Monopsony Model Explain Wage Differences?
It is hard to believe that monopsony can be an important explanation for the wage differences that are observed in the U.S. labor market. Very few (if any) firms in the United States are the only employer in the labor market from which they draw. If we are to apply the simple monopsony model, it must be assumed that all the firms in a particular labor market are able to collude perfectly in their discriminatory hiring decisions. Since economists generally believe that such collusion is very difficult to achieve, they have instead turned their attention to examining how discrimination might arise in a competitive labor market.

Wage Discrimination in Competitive Markets
An initial observation about discrimination in a competitive market is that it is costly to the discriminator.

Table 1
Median Earnings for Full-Time, Year-Round Workers by Sex and Occupation, 1983

Occupation	Median Earnings for Men	Median Earnings for Women	Ratio Women ÷ Men
Manager and professional	$30,086	$18,886	.63
Technical, sales and administration	22,497	13,522	.60
Service	14,688	9,228	.63
Precision production	21,520	13,245	.62
Operators and laborers	17,819	11,321	.64

Source: Statistical Abstract of the United States, 1986 (Washington, D.C.: U.S. Department of Commerce, 1986), Table 703.

For example, a firm that decides not to hire female workers is raising its labor costs over what they would be if it hired workers solely on the basis of their skills. Nevertheless, discrimination persists, and this fact indicates that firms, workers, and consumers may be willing to pay these costs. The importance of this observation is to demonstrate that discrimination is costly not only to those being discriminated against, but also to those doing the discriminating. Total income of both groups would be higher in the absence of discrimination.[1]

Antidiscrimination Policy
Following from this analysis is the policy question of what should be done about possible discriminatory preferences of employers. In part, these tastes may be based on ignorance. Employers, for example, may discriminate against black or female workers because they incorrectly believe that these workers have lower productivities. A policy of providing information to employers may alter these perceptions. More significantly, governmental equal opportunity and affirmative action programs may lead firms to make hiring decisions they would not freely make; as a result, they may gain more accurate information about true productivities.

To Think About

1. What factors other than wage discrimination might explain the figures in Table 1? Should factors such as education, job skills, or work experience be controlled for when looking at male-female wage differences, or might these too reflect discrimination?
2. How would you explain the economic rationale for affirmative action programs that establish hiring guidelines for minorities and women? Under what conditions might such programs have an effect on the male-female wage differential? When might such policies fail?

[1]One of the first economists to study discrimination in detail was Gary S. Becker. In his book, *The Economics of Discrimination* (Chicago: University of Chicago Press, 1957), he develops a simple model that shows that discrimination harms both the majority and minority groups. This finding is in contrast to other views that discrimination in some way benefits the discriminator.

Summary

In this chapter we examined firms' demands for the inputs they buy. The most fundamental observation was that this demand is necessarily derived from the demand for the output being produced. Firms don't hire workers just to have them around. Rather, a firm's hiring decisions are one aspect of its desire to maximize profits. In analyzing the demand for factors, this connection between factor and goods markets must be kept clearly in mind. Several specific conclusions emerged from our examination of this relationship:

- Factors of production may sometimes earn rents—payments in excess of their next best alternative employment—depending on the demand for their services.
- Firms will hire any input up to the point at which the marginal expense of hiring one more unit is equal to the marginal revenue yielded by selling what that input produces.
- If the firm is a price taker in both the market for its inputs and the market for its output, profit maximization requires that it employ that level of inputs for which the market price of the input (for example, the wage) is equal to the marginal value product of that input (for example, $P \cdot MP_L$).
- If the price of an input rises, the firm will hire less of it for two reasons. First, the higher price will cause the firm to substitute other inputs for the one whose price has risen. Second, the higher price will raise the firm's costs and reduce the amount it is able to sell. This output effect will also cause fewer units of the input to be hired.
- If a firm is the sole hirer of an input (a monopsony), its hiring decisions will affect market prices of inputs. The marginal expense associated with hiring an additional unit of an input will exceed that input's price. Firms will take this into account in their hiring decisions—they will restrict hiring below what it would be under competitive conditions.
- If a firm has a monopsony in two markets, it may increase profits further by practicing input price discrimination.

Review Questions

1. In the supply-demand model of factor pricing, who are the demanders? What type of assumptions would you use to explain their behavior? In this model, who are the suppliers? What types of assumptions would you use to explain their behavior?
2. Explain why factor suppliers earn "rent" if they would be willing to provide their inputs at a price below the prevailing equilibrium. How does this concept compare with the concept of consumer surplus that we examined in Chapter 6?
3. Explain why differences in firms' costs result in Ricardian rent. Who receives this rent? Why is this rent zero for the marginal supplier and is therefore not an element in that firm's marginal costs?
4. Profit maximization implies that firms will make input choices in a marginal way. Explain why the following marginal rules found in this chapter are specific applications of this general idea:

a. $MR_L = ME_L$.
b. $MP_L \cdot MR = ME_L = w$.
c. $MVP_L = ME_L = w$.
d. $MVP_L = w$.
e. $MVP_L = ME_L > w$.

If firms follow these various rules, will they also be producing a profit-maximizing level of output? That is, will they produce when MR = MC? Will they also be minimizing costs if they use these rules?

5. Explain why if a price-taking firm has only one variable input the MVP curve is also its demand curve for that input, but if the firm has two or more variable inputs, its demand curve for one of them reflects a whole family of MVP curves.
6. A fall in the price of an input induces a profit-maximizing firm to experience both substitution and output effects that cause it to hire more of that input. Explain how the profit-maximizing assumption is used in explaining the direction of each of these effects. Did you have to use the assumption that the input is not inferior in your analysis? Do you think a similar statement can be made about inferior inputs?
7. Suppose the price of an input used by firms with fixed proportions production functions were to fall. Why would such a change not cause any substitution effects for these firms' input demand? Would there, however, be output effects? What would determine the size of these effects?
8. Why does the relationship between the firm's marginal expense of hiring an input and the market price of that input depend on the shape of the input supply curve facing the firm? For a price-taking firm, what kind of supply curve faces the firm and what is the relationship between these concepts? What is different about a monopsony? Illustrate the similarity between these ideas and the notion of the output demand curve that faces a firm.
9. How would you measure the strength of a monopsonist in an input market? Would a monopsony necessarily be very profitable? What would you need to add to Figure 18.10 in order to show a monopsonist's profits graphically?
10. To practice input price discrimination, a monopsony must have market power in two separated markets. Why would an inability to separate markets make such discrimination impossible?

Problems

18.1 Suppose the demand for labor is given by

$$L = -50w + 450$$

and the supply is given by

$$L = 100w$$

where L represents the number of people employed and w is the real wage rate per hour.

a. What will be the equilibrium levels for w and L in this market?
b. Suppose the government wishes to raise the equilibrium wage to $4 per hour by offering a subsidy to employers for each person hired. How much will this subsidy have to be? What will the new equilibrium level of employment be? How much total subsidy will be paid?
c. Suppose instead the government declared a minimum wage of $4 per hour. How much labor would be demanded at this price? How much unemployment would there be?

d. Graph your results.

18.2 Assume that the market for rental cars for business purposes is perfectly competitive with the demand for this capital input given by

$$K = 1{,}500 - 25v$$

and the supply given by

$$K = 75v - 500$$

where K represents the number of cars rented by firms and v is the rental rate per day.

a. What will be the equilibrium levels for v and K in this market?
b. Suppose that following an oil embargo gas prices rise dramatically so that now business firms must take account of gas prices in their car rental decisions. Their demand for rental cars is now given by

$$K = 1{,}700 - 25v - 300g$$

where g is the per gallon price of gasoline. What will be the equilibrium levels for v and K if g = \$2? If g = \$3?
c. Graph your results.
d. Since the oil embargo brought about decreased demand for rental cars, what might be the implication for other capital input markets as a result? For example, employees may still need transportation, so how might the demand for mass transit be affected? Since businesspeople also rent cars to attend meetings, what might happen in the market for telephone equipment as employees drive less and use the telephone more? Can you think of any other factor input markets that might be affected?

18.3 A landowner has three farms (A, B, and C) of differing fertility. The levels of output for the three farms with one, two, and three laborers employed are as follows:

	Level of Output		
Number of Laborers	**Farm A**	**Farm B**	**Farm C**
1	10	8	5
2	17	11	7
3	21	13	8

For example, if one laborer were hired for each farm, the total output would be 10 + 8 + 5 = 23. This would represent a poor allocation of labor, since if the farm C laborer were assigned to farm A the total output would be 17 + 8 = 25.

a. If market conditions caused the landowner to hire five laborers, what would be the most productive allocation of that labor? How much would be produced? What is the marginal product of the last worker?
b. If we assume that farm output is sold in a perfectly competitive market with one unit of output priced at \$1, and we assume that labor market equilibrium occurs when five workers are hired, what wage is paid? How much profit does the landowner receive?

18.4 Assume that the quantity of envelopes licked per hour by Sticky Gums, Inc. is $q = 10{,}000\sqrt{L}$ where L is the number of laborers hired per hour by the firm. Assume further that the envelope-licking business is perfectly competitive with a market price of \$.01 per envelope. The marginal product of a worker is given by

$$MP_L = 5{,}000/\sqrt{L}.$$

a. How much labor would be hired at a competitive wage of \$10? \$5? \$2? Use your results to sketch a demand curve for labor.
b. Assume that Sticky Gums hires its labor at an hourly wage of \$10. What quantity of envelopes will be licked when the price of a licked envelope is \$.10? \$.05? \$.02? Use your results to sketch a supply curve for licked envelopes.

*18.5 Suppose there are a fixed number of 1,000 identical firms in the perfectly competitive concrete pipe industry. Each firm produces the same fraction of total market output and each firm's production function for pipe is given by

$$q = \sqrt{KL}$$

and for this production function

$$RTS\ (L \text{ for } K) = K/L.$$

Suppose also that the market demand for concrete pipe is given by

$$Q = 400{,}000 - 100{,}000P$$

where Q is total concrete pipe.

a. If $w = v = \$1$, in what ratio will the typical firm use K and L? What will be the long-run average and marginal cost of pipe?
b. In the long-run equilibrium what will be the market equilibrium price and quantity for concrete pipe? How much will each firm produce? How much labor will be hired by each firm and in the market as a whole?
c. Suppose the market wage, w, rose to \$2 while v remained constant at \$1. How will this change the capital-labor ratio for the typical firm, and how will it affect its marginal costs?
d. Under the conditions of part c, what will the long-run market equilibrium be? How much labor will now be hired by the concrete pipe industry?
e. How much of the change in total labor demand from part b to part d represents the substitution effect resulting from the change in wage and how much represents the output effect?

18.6 Suppose that the supply curve for labor to a firm is given by

$$L = 100w$$

and the marginal expense of labor curve is given by

$$ME_L = L/50$$

*Denotes a problem that is rather difficult.

where w is the market wage. Suppose also that the firm's demand for labor (marginal revenue product) curve is given by

$$L = 1{,}000 - 100MRP_L.$$

a. If the firm acts as a monopsonist, how many workers will it hire in order to maximize profits? What wage will it pay? How will this wage compare to the MRP_L at this employment level?
b. Assume now that the firm must hire its workers in a perfectly competitive labor market, but it still acts as a monopoly when selling its output. How many workers will the firm hire now? What wage will it pay?
c. Graph your results.

18.7 Carl the clothier owns a large garment factory on an isolated island. Carl's factory is the only source of employment for most of the islanders, and thus Carl acts as a monopsonist. The supply curve for garment workers is given by

$$L = 80w$$

and the marginal expense of labor curve is given by

$$ME_L = L/40$$

where L is the number of workers hired and w is their hourly wage. Assume also that Carl's labor demand (marginal value product) curve is given by

$$L = 400 - 40MVP_L.$$

a. How many workers will Carl hire in order to maximize his profits and what wage will he pay?
b. Assume now that the government implements a minimum wage law covering all garment workers. How many workers will Carl now hire and how much unemployment will there be if the minimum wage is set at \$3 per hour? \$3.33 per hour? \$4.00 per hour?
c. Graph your results.
d. How does the imposition of a minimum wage under monopsony differ in results from a minimum wage imposed under perfect competition (assuming the minimum wage is above the market determined wage)?

18.8 Under what conditions would you expect the imposition of a minimum wage to:

a. Have no effect on wages or on the number of workers employed?
b. Increase wages and leave the number of workers unaffected?
c. Increase wages and decrease the number of workers?
d. Increase both wages and the number of workers?

*18.9 The Ajax Coal Company is the only employer in its area. It can hire any number of female workers or male workers it wishes. The supply curve for women is given by

$$L_f = 100w_f$$
$$ME_f = L_f/50$$

---

*Denotes a problem that is rather difficult.

and for men by

$$L_m = 9w_m^2$$
$$ME_m = 1/2\sqrt{L_m}$$

where w_f and w_m are, respectively, the hourly wage rate paid to female and male workers. Assume that Ajax sells its coal in a perfectly competitive market at $5 per ton and that each worker hired (both men and women) can mine two tons per hour. If the firm wishes to maximize profits, how many female and male workers should be hired and what will the wage rates for these two groups be? How much will Ajax earn in profits per hour on its mining machinery? How will that result compare to one in which Ajax was constrained (say, by market forces) to pay all workers the same wage based on the value of their marginal products?

18.10 Assume employers have no "taste for discrimination" against blacks but that the white employees do. A white employee considers the "psychic wage" to be a combination of the money wage and the percentage of blacks in the firm. That is, a white worker demands higher wages in order to work with blacks. Both blacks and whites offer their services in a perfectly competitive market and are equally productive. The wages for whites and blacks are given by

$$w_1 = MVP(1 + \text{percentage of blacks in firm})$$

and

$$w_2 = MVP,$$

respectively. How might you expect a cost-minimizing firm to adjust the racial mix of its employees?

CHAPTER 19

Pricing of Labor

In this chapter we examine some aspects of factor pricing that are particularly related to the labor market. Because we have discussed the demand for labor (or any other factor of production) in some detail previously, in this chapter we are concerned primarily with the supply of labor. The theory of labor supply provides another useful application of the model of individual choice developed in Part 2. With this model it is possible to explain many of the important trends in the U.S. labor market. This chapter also examines labor unions. Because unions are important participants in the labor markets of most Western countries, any treatment of labor supply would be incomplete without such an examination. In addition, the tools used to study union behavior and bargaining can be applied to other situations in which both buyers and sellers exercise some market power.

Allocation of Time

Part 2 analyzed how an individual will choose to allocate a fixed amount of income among a variety of available goods. People must make similar choices in deciding how they will spend their time. The number of hours in a day (or in a year) is absolutely fixed, and time must be used as it passes by. Given this fixed amount of time, any person must decide how many hours to work; how many hours to spend consuming a wide variety of goods, ranging from cars and television sets to operas; how many hours to devote to self-maintenance; and how many hours to sleep. By studying the division of time people choose to make among these activities, economists are able to understand labor supply decisions. Viewing work as only one of a number of choices open to people in the way they spend their time enables us to understand why these decisions may be adjusted in response to changing opportunities.

A Simple Model of Time Use

Leisure
Time spent in any activity other than market work.

We first assume that there are only two uses to which any person may devote his or her time: either engaging in market work at a wage rate of w per hour or not working. We refer to nonwork time as **leisure**, but to economists this word does not mean idleness. Time that is not spent in market work can be used to work in the home, for self-improvement, or for consumption (it takes time to use a television set or a bowling ball).[1] All of these activities contribute to a person's well-being, and time will be allocated to them in a utility-maximizing way.

More specifically, assume that utility depends on consumption of market goods (C) and on the amount of leisure time (H) used. Figure 19.1 presents an indifference curve map for this utility function. The diagram has the familiar shape introduced in Chapter 3, and it shows those combinations of C and H that yield an individual various levels of utility.

To discuss utility maximization we must first describe the budget constraint that faces this person. If the period we are studying is one day, the individual will work (24 − H) hours. That is, he or she will work all of the hours not devoted to leisure. For this work she or he will earn w per hour and will use this to buy consumption goods.

The Opportunity Cost of Leisure

Each extra hour of leisure this person takes reduces his or her income (and consumption) by w dollars. The hourly wage therefore reflects the opportunity cost of leisure. People have to "pay" this cost for each hour they do not work. The wage rate used to make these calculations should be a real wage in that it should reflect the prevailing price level for consumer goods. A nominal wage of $1 per hour provides the same purchasing power when the typical item costs $.25 as does a wage of $100 per hour when that item sells for $25. In either case, the person must work 15 minutes to buy the item. Alternately, in both cases, the opportunity cost of taking one more hour of leisure is to do

[1]For a more theoretical treatment of the allocation of time, see G. S. Becker, "A Theory of the Allocation of Time," *The Economic Journal* (September 1965): 493–517. The author treats the household as both a provider of labor services and a producer of utility, which is made by combining time with goods. The household is seen to be bound by a time constraint and must allocate available time among a number of activities. The implications drawn by Becker are far-reaching and affect most of the traditional theory of individual behavior.

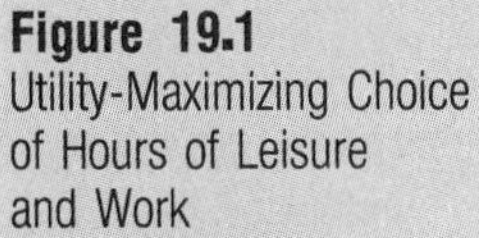

Figure 19.1
Utility-Maximizing Choice of Hours of Leisure and Work

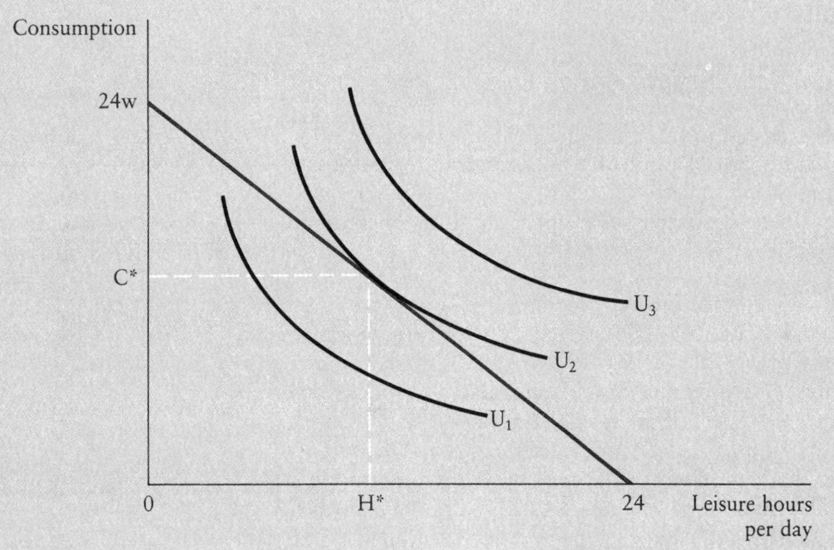

Given his or her budget constraint, this person will maximize utility by choosing H* hours of leisure and consumption of C*. At this point, the rate at which he or she is willing to trade H for C (the MRS) is equal to the rate at which he or she is able to trade these in the market (the real hourly wage—w).

without four consumption items. In Application 19.1: The Opportunity Cost of Time, we look at some cases of competing uses of time and illustrate how the opportunity cost notion can explain the choices people make.

Utility Maximization

To show the utility-maximizing choices of consumption and leisure, we must first graph the relevant budget constraint. This is done in Figure 19.1. If this person doesn't work at all, he or she can enjoy 24 hours of leisure. This is shown as the horizontal intercept of the budget constraint. If, on the other hand, this person works 24 hours per day, he or she will be able to buy $24 \cdot w$ in consumption goods. This establishes the vertical intercept in the figure. The slope of the budget constraint is $-w$. This reflects opportunity costs—each added hour of leisure must be "purchased" by doing without w worth of consumption items.

Given this budget constraint, this person will maximize utility by choosing to take H* hours of leisure and to work the remaining time. With the income earned from this work, he or she will be able to buy C* units of consumption goods. At the utility-maximizing point, the slope of the budget ($-w$) is equal to the slope of indifference curve U_2. In other words, the person's real wage is equal to the marginal rate of substitution of leisure hours for consumption.

APPLICATION 19.1

The Opportunity Cost of Time

Choices that people must make among competing uses of time can usually be analyzed within a utility-maximizing framework, and it is often possible to gain considerable insights by recognizing the opportunity costs involved.

Transportation Choices

In choosing among alternative ways of getting to work, people will take both time and dollar costs into account. Most studies have found that commuters are quite sensitive to time costs, especially those associated with walking to a bus or train station or with waiting for the bus or train to come.[1] By examining people's willingness to pay to avoid such waits, these studies generally conclude that people value travel time at about one-half of their market wage. For example, studies conducted in connection with the Bay Area Rapid Transit System (BART) in San Francisco concluded that fares involved in using the system were less than one-fourth of the total costs people faced. Far more important were the time costs involved in getting to suburban BART stations, waiting for trains, and walking from the downtown BART stations to the final destination. Given the size of these costs, it is not surprising that most commuters in the Bay Area continue to use private cars for their trips.

The Economics of Childbearing

People's decisions to have children are affected by a number of social, religious, and economic factors. Economists have tended to focus primarily on the costs associated with having children and how those costs vary among individuals. One of the most important costs is the forgone wages of parents who choose to care for their children rather than to pursue market employment. Indeed, by some estimates, this cost is far in excess of all other costs of childbearing combined. That type of calculation has led some authors to speculate that increasing real wages for women in the United States since World War II are the principal reason for the decline in the birth rate during that period. Similarly, the lower birth rates in North America and Western Europe as compared to the less-developed world might be attributed to wage rate differences (and hence cost of children differences) between these regions.[2]

Job Search Theory

In seeking new jobs, people are often faced with considerable uncertainty about available openings. Consequently, they must invest some time (and possibly other resources, such as telephone calls or advertising) in finding a suitable job match. To the extent that people must reduce work time to accommodate their job search plans, the hourly cost of searching can be approximated by the market wage. The higher an individual's market wage, the more likely he or she would be to adopt search techniques that economize on time (such as using an employment agency). If, on the other hand, search time is subsidized (say, by unemployment insurance benefits), search time may be prolonged in the hope of finding a better job. By one estimate, a 10 percent increase in weekly unemployment benefits is associated with about one-half week of additional unemployment.[3]

To Think About

1. Why do empirical studies of commuting patterns find that people value their time at about one-half the market wage? Doesn't our theory suggest that the value should be the full wage rate?
2. Studies of people's job search activities indicate that receipt of unemployment insurance benefits causes them to be more choosy about the jobs they take. Isn't that a good thing? Isn't it important that people find the best job for which they are qualified?

---

[1] See, for example, T. A. Domencich and Daniel McFadden, *Urban Travel Demand* (Amsterdam: North Holland Publishing Company, 1975).

[2] For a seminal contribution to the economics of fertility, see G. S. Becker, "An Economic Analysis of Fertility," in *Demographic and Economic Change in Developed Countries* (Princeton, N.J.: Princeton University Press, 1960).

[3] For a summary of some studies of this effect, see Daniel Hamermesch, *Jobless Pay and the Economy* (Baltimore: Johns Hopkins University Press, 1976).

If this were not true, utility would not be as large as possible. For example, suppose a person's MRS were equal to 2, indicating a willingness to give up two units of consumption to get an additional hour of leisure. Suppose also that the real wage is $4. By working one more hour, he or she is able to earn enough to buy four units (that is, $4 worth) of consumption. This is clearly an inefficient situation. By working one hour more, this person can buy four extra units of consumption. But he or she required only two units of consumption to be as well-off as before. By working the extra hour, this person earns two (= 4 − 2) more units of consumption than required. Consequently he or she could not have been maximizing utility in the first place. A similar proof can be constructed for any case in which the MRS differs from the market wage—which proves that the two trade-off rates must be equal for a true utility maximum.

Flexibility of Work

Before we examine how these choices might be affected by a change in the real wage rate, it is important to ask whether this theory of choice has any relevance to the real-world decisions people must make. While we all are relatively free to determine what we will do in our spare time, we may not have complete freedom of choice in selecting our own hours of work. Most jobs require that you work about 40 hours a week, and this figure is not very flexible in response to people's preferences. Nevertheless, the freedom of choice in hours of work that we have been assuming may be justified in several ways. First, the model might apply to a very long period, perhaps a lifetime. Over such a period you have considerable flexibility in the number of hours to be worked since you may choose to work 40 hours during some weeks (or years) and zero hours during others. By moving in and out of the labor market at different stages in their lifetimes, people can adjust their hours of work rather precisely.

A second and similar justification for our model is to regard it as applying to the average person. At any one point in time, some individuals will work 40 hours and others will not work. Consequently, average hours of work will depend on how many people fall into each category. If nearly everyone works, the average person will work about 40 hours, whereas if 50 percent of all people work 40 hours and 50 percent do not work, the average person will be working 20 hours.

A final way to justify the assumption of time flexibility is to note that people do have considerable freedom in choosing the jobs they take. By choosing among the comforts and discomforts of particular jobs, people can be thought of as making a marginal choice, even though actual hours of work are fixed by the employer. For example, someone taking a low-paying job as a surfing instructor can be regarded as choosing an occupation with a significant leisure component, and he or she is thereby adjusting the hours of actual work. We examine some additional questions about occupational choice later in this chapter.

Income and Substitution Effects of a Change in the Real Wage Rate

Substitution effect of a change in w
Movement along an indifference curve in response to a change in the real wage. A rise in w causes an individual to work more.

Income effect of a change in w
Movement to a higher indifference curve in response to a rise in the real wage rate. If leisure is a normal good, a rise in w causes an individual to work less.

A change in the real wage rate can be analyzed the same way we studied a price change in Chapter 4. When w rises, the price of leisure becomes higher—people must give up more in lost wages for each hour of leisure consumed. The **substitution effect** of an increase in w on the hours of leisure will therefore be to reduce them. As leisure becomes more expensive, there is reason to consume less of it. However, the **income effect** of a rise in the wage will tend to increase leisure. Since leisure is a normal good, the higher income resulting from a higher w will increase the demand for it. Hence income and substitution effects work in the opposite direction. It is impossible to predict whether an increase in w will increase or decrease the demand for leisure time. Since leisure and work are mutually exclusive ways to use time, this shows that it is impossible to predict what will happen to the number of hours worked. When the wage rises, the substitution effect tends to increase hours worked. The income effect, because it increases the demand for leisure time, tends to decrease the number of hours worked. Which of these two effects is the stronger is an important empirical question whose answer depends on people's preferences for consumption and leisure.

A Graphical Analysis

Figure 19.2 illustrates two possible reactions to an increase in w. In both graphs the initial wage rate is w_0, and the optimal choices of consumption and leisure are given by C_0 and H_0. When the wage rate increases to w_1, the utility-maximizing combination moves to C_1, H_1. This movement can be divided into two effects. The substitution effect is represented by the movement along the indifference curve U_0 from C_0, H_0 to S. This effect works to reduce the number of hours of leisure in both parts of Figure 19.2. People substitute consumption for leisure since the relative price of leisure has increased.

The movement from S to C_1, H_1 represents the income effect of a higher real wage. Since it is assumed that leisure time is a normal good, increases in income will cause more leisure to be demanded. Consequently, the income and substitution effects induced by the increase in w work in opposite directions. In Panel a in Figure 19.2 the demand for leisure is reduced by the rise in w; that is, the substitution effect outweighs the income effect. On the other hand, in Panel b the income effect is stronger, and the demand for leisure increases in response to an increase in w. This person actually chooses to work fewer hours when w increases. In our analysis of demand we would have considered this result unusual—when the price of leisure rises, this person demands more of it. For the case of normal consumption goods, income and substitution effects work in the same direction, and both cause quantity to decline when price increases. In the case of leisure, however, income and substitution effects work in opposite directions. An increase in w makes a person better-off because he or she is a *supplier* of labor. In the case of a consumption good, an individual is made worse off by a rise in price because he or she

Figure 19.2
Income and Substitution Effects of a Change in the Real Wage Rate

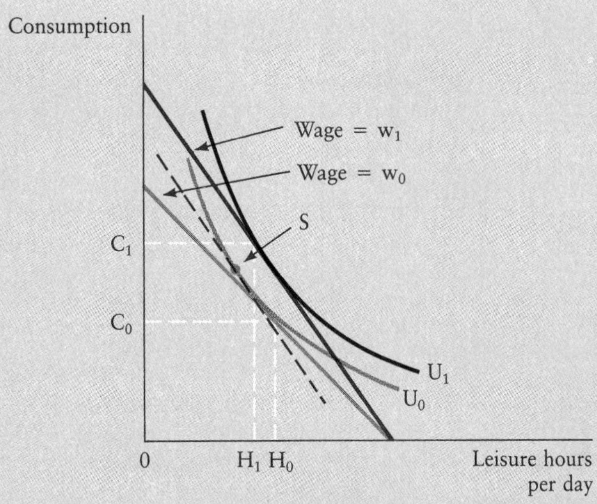

(a) **Rise in Wage Increases Work**

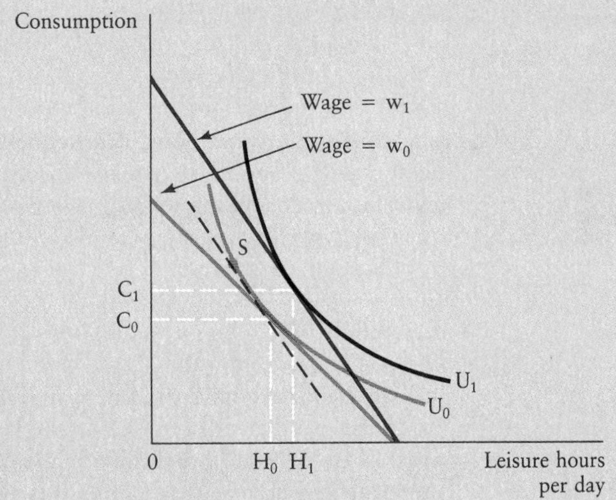

(b) **Rise in Wage Decreases Work**

Since the individual is a supplier of labor, the income and substitution effects of an increase in the real wage rate work in opposite directions in their effect on the hours of leisure demanded (or on hours of work). In Panel a the substitution effect (movement to point S) outweighs the income effect, and a higher wage causes hours of leisure to decline to H_1. Hours of work, therefore, increase. In Panel b the income effect is stronger than the substitution effect, and H increases to H_1. Hours of work in this case fall.

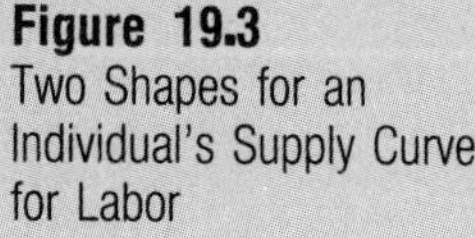

Figure 19.3
Two Shapes for an Individual's Supply Curve for Labor

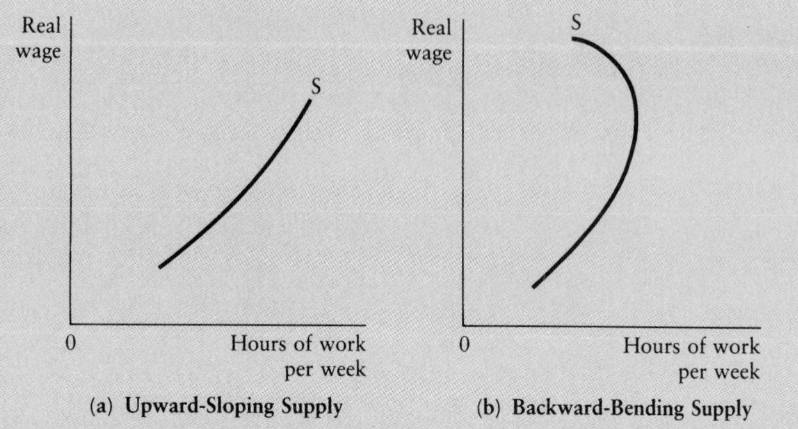

In Panel a a higher real wage induces the individual to supply more labor. The substitution effect of the higher wage outweighs the income effect. In Panel b, on the other hand, the supply curve for labor is backward bending. For relatively high wage rates, the income effect of a higher wage outweighs the substitution effect and causes the individual to demand more leisure.

is a *consumer* of that good. Consequently, it is not possible to predict how a person will respond to a wage increase—he or she may work greater or fewer hours depending on his or her preferences.

Individual Supply Curve for Labor

Backward-bending labor supply curve Labor supply curve in which higher real wages cause less labor to be supplied because the income effect outweighs the substitution effect.

In Figure 19.3 we have drawn an individual's supply of labor curve by calculating the number of hours he or she is willing to work at every possible real wage rate. In Panel a the individual's supply curve is drawn with an upward slope: at higher real wage rates this person chooses to work longer hours. The substitution effect of a higher wage outweighs its income effect. This need not always be the case, however, as Panel b shows. There the supply curve is **backward bending**—once real wages exceed a certain level, even higher wage rates induce this person to work fewer hours. Such a curve is entirely consistent with the theory of labor supply we have developed. At relatively high wage rates, an increase in the wage may cause people to choose to work fewer hours, since the income effect may be stronger than the substitution effect. In this situation a person uses his or her higher real wage rate to "buy" more leisure. High-priced lawyers taking Wednesday afternoons off to play golf is a rational response to their situations—though it does result in the loss of some potential legal fees.

Do people's labor supply curves more nearly resemble that shown in Panel a or Panel b in Figure 19.3? Although there is substantial evidence that short-run labor supply curves have a positive slope (consider, for example, the positive effect on hours of work that offering premium overtime wages has), it appears that over the long run labor supply curves at times may have been backward bending. In 1890 the average workweek in the United States in the manufacturing industry was about 60 hours. Real wages in 1890 were about \$3.40 per hour (in terms of 1989 prices). By 1929 the workweek in manufacturing had dropped to 40 hours, in spite of the fact that real wages had risen to about \$5.85 per hour. American workers chose to take a large part of their increasing incomes in the form of leisure, and this is consistent with the notion of a backward-bending supply curve. Since 1929, real wages in manufacturing have continued to rise (to about \$10 per hour in 1989), but the workweek has not fallen much below 40 hours per week. It appears that in recent years the substitution effect of higher wages has almost exactly balanced the income effect—at least for manufacturing workers. Of course, these numbers only represent average wages for the whole economy. Across occupations and industries relative wages change over time, and this has the effect of causing people to change the kinds of jobs they take. Application 19.2: The Volunteer Army and the Draft shows that the supply curve of labor to any one occupation (here the military) is undoubtedly upward sloping and possibly quite elastic.

Market Supply Curve for Labor

We can construct a market supply of labor curve from individual supply curves by "adding" them up. At each possible wage rate, we add together the quantity of labor offered by each person in order to arrive at a market total. One particularly interesting aspect of this procedure is that as the wage rate rises, more people may be induced to enter the labor force. That is, rising wages may induce some people who were not previously employed to take jobs. Figure 19.4 illustrates this possibility for a simple case of two individuals. For a real wage below w_1, neither person chooses to work in the market. Consequently, the market supply curve of labor (Panel c) shows that no labor is supplied at real wages below w_1. A wage in excess of w_1 causes person 1 to enter the labor market. However, as long as wages fall short of w_2, person 2 will not work. Only at a wage rate above w_2 will both people choose to take a job. As Panel c in Figure 19.4 shows, the possibility of the entry of these new workers makes the market supply of labor somewhat more responsive to wage rate increases than would be the case if we assumed that the number of workers were fixed. Changing wage rates may not only induce current workers to alter their hours of work, but perhaps more important, they may change the composition of the work force. As Application 19.3: Changing Labor Force Participation for Married Women and Older Males shows, such effects have been especially pronounced for older men and married women in the United States over the past 25 years.

APPLICATION 19.2

The Volunteer Army and the Draft

The question of the elasticity of the supply of labor played an important role in the mid-1960s debate over the costs of establishing an all-volunteer army in the United States. If the supply of labor to the military were elastic, volunteers could be attracted with relatively small increases in existing pay schedules. An inelastic supply, on the other hand, would require sharp increases in defense costs as a result of the elimination of military conscription.

Labor Supply and the Costs of the Draft

To study this issue, W. Y. Oi in 1967 calculated a supply curve for military personnel.[1] His basic results are presented in Table 1. There is clear evidence that increases in military pay encouraged enlistments. For example, Oi showed that an increase in the first-term pay of enlistees from the then-present level of $2,500 to a level more nearly approximating civilian wages (about $3,600 for unskilled 18-year-olds in 1965) would have increased enlistments by 40 percent. Notice, however, that the supply curve tended to become more inelastic as potential wages were raised still further. Raising wages from $4,700 to $5,900 would attract only 13 percent more enlistments. This may indicate that the military draft may involve very high implicit costs for some draftees who would be willing to pay quite a lot to avoid service.

Table 1
Supply Curve of Voluntary Enlistments in the Armed Forces in 1965

Annual First-Term Pay	Enlistments
$2,500	260,000
3,600	365,000
4,700	415,000
5,900	470,000

Source: W. Y. Oi, "The Economic Cost of the Draft," *American Economic Review* (May 1967): 39–62.

The Volunteer Force

Following the cessation of hostilities in Vietnam in the early 1970s, the U.S. military moved rapidly toward the establishment of an all-volunteer force. Experiences since that time have been quite consistent with what had been predicted by Oi and others; that is, enlistments proved to be rather responsive to military pay. One study of the years 1967 to 1979, for example, found that the supply elasticities for enlistments in the Army and Navy exceed 1 and are especially high for later years in which the threat of a draft had largely disappeared.[2] Interestingly, these authors also found that supply elasticities to the Marines and Air Force were much lower than for the other armed services. For the case of the Marine Corps, they attributed this finding to the special nature of that branch of the armed forces: it appears that a segment of the population wants to join almost regardless of wages. The Air Force is also a special case because of the specialized training it provides. The allure of high-wage civilian jobs following service in the Air Force appears to outweigh the effects of current wages on enlistments.

To Think About

1. The "costs" of hiring soldiers are usually taken to be the wages they are paid. With a military draft, is that a correct way to account costs? How would you measure the costs of military service to a draftee?
2. Some people say that a draft is the only fair way to raise an army since only with a draft will the burden of military service be "equally shared." Do you agree? Ideally, how would the costs of military service be shared under a draft relative to the costs under a volunteer force? How did the draft of the 1960s actually work in practice?

[1]W. Y. Oi, "The Economic Cost of the Draft," *American Economic Review* (May 1967): 39–62. Oi's calculations have been simplified in this example, and they do not correspond exactly to those in the original article. The cost figures do not include forgone rents that would be earned by "true" volunteers in moving to a volunteer army (because they would be paid more under the new pay scales than was necessary to attract them into the army).

[2]See Colin Ash, Bernard Udis, and R. F. McNowan, "Enlistments in the All-Volunteer Force: A Military Personnel Supply Model and Its Forecasts," *American Economic Review* (March 1983): 145–155.

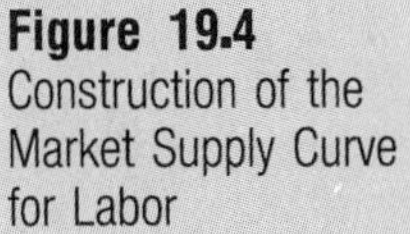

Figure 19.4
Construction of the Market Supply Curve for Labor

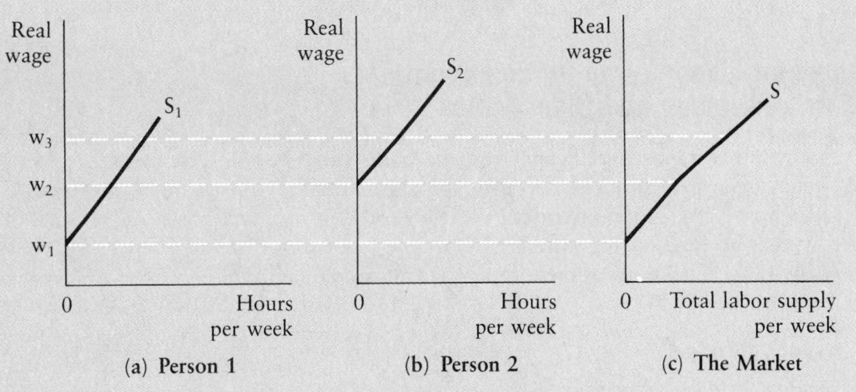

As the real wage rises, the supply of labor may increase for two reasons. First, higher real wages may cause each person to work more hours. Second, higher wages may induce more people (for example, person 2) to enter the labor market.

Occupational Choice and Compensating Wage Differentials

So far this chapter has primarily treated the labor market as a single market. All labor was assumed to be of the same quality and all jobs were assumed to be equally attractive so we could speak of the wage as being set by supply and demand in one market. In reality, of course, wages differ greatly among individuals and among jobs.

There are three reasons for these differentials. First, workers have different levels of skills. These differences in skills may cause some workers to be more productive than others; in a competitive market for labor, those with greater skills will earn higher wages. Second, some workers may receive wages that are essentially monopoly rents. If workers can successfully limit access to certain jobs, they may succeed in improving their own wages. Finally, wage rates may differ among jobs because some jobs are more pleasant than others. More enjoyable jobs will attract a large supply of applicants, and this may cause the wage rates to be lower than in less desirable ones. In this section we restrict our attention to this third reason for wage differentials.

The notion that differing characteristics of jobs may lead to differential wages has long been noted by economists. In *The Wealth of Nations*, for example, Adam Smith observed that

> ...the whole of the advantages and disadvantages of the different employments of labour...must, in the same neighbourhood, be either equal or continually tending to equality. If in the same neighbourhood there is any employment either more or less advantageous than the rest, so many people would crowd into it in the one case, and so many would desert it in the other, that its advantages would soon return to the level of other employments....

APPLICATION 19.3

Changing Labor Force Participation for Married Women and Older Males

Probably the two most significant trends in labor market behavior in the United States during the past three decades have been (1) the increasing tendency for married women to hold paying jobs and (2) the decline in work by older men. Both of these trends are illustrated in Table 1.

Expanding Female Labor Force Participation

For women in the prime age category 25–34, the increase in labor force participation has been spectacular. The fraction of married women aged 25–34 who are in the work force more than doubled between 1960 and 1987. Many reasons have been proposed to explain this major social phenomenon. Economists have tended to focus on expanding job opportunities and real wages for women as a principal explanation. Because married women have good alternative uses for their time (work in the home rather than work in the market), substitution effects from higher real wages would be expected to be large, so labor supply will increase in response to higher wages. Sociologists, on the other hand, tend to attribute the increasing work by married women to political and cultural factors. That is, they attribute the change to a shift in the supply curve rather than a move along it in response to higher wages. Whatever the cause, these labor force statistics show greater responsiveness in labor supply behavior of a large segment of the population than was believed likely in earlier times.

Table 1
Labor Force Participation Rates, 1960–1987

Year	Married Females Age 25–34	Married Males Age 65 and Over
1960	27.7%	37.1%
1965	32.1	31.1
1970	39.3	30.2
1975	48.3	23.7
1980	59.3	20.4
1987	67.5	17.4

Source: Statistical Abstract of the United States, 1988, (Washington D.C.: U.S. Government Printing Office, 1988), Table 622.

The Case of Older Men

Interestingly, the labor force trend for older married men has been precisely opposite to that for younger married women. As Table 1 shows, between 1960 and 1987 the labor force participation rate for married men over 65 fell to less than half its initial level. The pattern is all the more puzzling given the improvement in the health of older men that occurred over this period. Such improvements should have resulted in more rather than less work activity by this group.

Although it is possible that the figures simply reflect a backward-bending supply of labor in response to higher wages, most economists have instead focused on issues of retirement as being the primary cause. Most important, the rapid growth in Social Security coverage of the elderly coupled with rising real benefit amounts may have encouraged increasingly large numbers of workers to retire in recent years. Other provisions of the program (such as the reduction in benefits that results when the elderly do take jobs) have had a similar effect of discouraging work. Policymakers have been especially concerned about these trends (most importantly because they threaten the financial integrity of Social Security) and have taken some steps to try to reverse them.[1]

To Think About

1. How does income taxation affect the labor supply decisions of married women? Can you predict the effect of taxes on their wages? Would special tax treatment of the earnings of married couples increase or decrease labor supply by married women?
2. Would the availability of Social Security benefits at retirement cause people to work more or less during their prime working years? Might your answer depend on whether Social Security encourages people to retire earlier than they would in the absence of the program?

[1]For a more complete discussion of these issues in the theory of labor supply, see R. G. Ehrenberg and R. G. Smith, *Modern Labor Economics,* 2d ed. (Glenview, Ill: Scott, Foresman, 1985), Chapters 6 and 7.

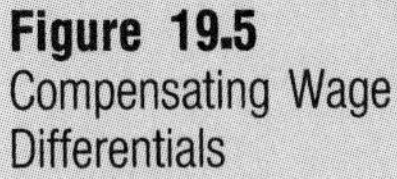

Figure 19.5
Compensating Wage Differentials

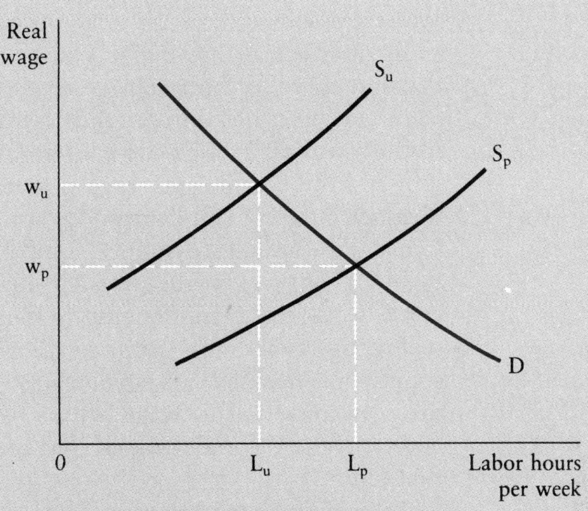

The demand curve for labor is assumed to be the same for both a "pleasant" job and an "unpleasant" one. However, the supply curves (S_p and S_u, respectively) differ for the two types of jobs. This causes wages to differ between the jobs. The higher wage rate for the unpleasant job (w_u) is said to "compensate" for the nature of the job.

> [But] pecuniary wages . . . are everywhere in Europe extremely different according to the different employments of labour . . . this difference arises partly from certain circumstances in the employments themselves, which, either really, or at least in the imaginations of men, make up for a small pecuniary gain in some and counter-balance a great one in others. . . .[2]

Smith then stresses the difference between the "whole advantages and disadvantages" of a particular job and the wages paid for the job. Even with perfect freedom of access to jobs and no skill differentials, wage rate differences can persist because of differences in the attractiveness of certain jobs. The market operates to equate the total attractiveness of jobs, not just the pecuniary rewards of these jobs. To capture such effects economists use the term **compensating wage differentials** to describe differences in wages that arise solely because of differing characteristics of jobs. The wage rate differences "compensate" for the differing job characteristics.

Compensating wage differentials
Differences in wages caused by differing job characteristics.

A Graphical Demonstration

Figure 19.5 illustrates a simple example of the way in which compensating differentials might arise. It assumes that there are two jobs: one "pleasant,"

[2]Adam Smith, *The Wealth of Nations,* Cannan ed. (New York: Modern Library, 1937), Chapter 10, p. 1.

the other "unpleasant." The demand curves of firms for workers to fill those jobs are assumed to be the same for both jobs. There are no differences in the skills of workers that might lead to differing marginal value products. The demand curve for both jobs is represented by the curve D.

Because the jobs differ in their attractiveness, however, the supply of labor to them will differ. The curve S_u represents the supply curve to the unpleasant job, and the equilibrium wage is given by w_u. At this wage firms in the unpleasant industry will demand L_u hours of labor input, and this is what individuals are willing to supply. Similarly, the curve S_p represents the supply curve of workers to the pleasant job. This curve lies to the right of the S_u curve because of the differences in the jobs. At any given wage individuals are willing to supply more labor to the pleasant job. Through the interaction of supply and demand, an equilibrium wage rate of w_p will be established for the pleasant job. This wage will be below w_u, and the difference between w_u and w_p is the wage differential that compensates for the unpleasantness of the first job.

The equilibrium shown in Figure 19.5 is stable: there is no incentive for a worker to transfer from one job to the other. As Smith predicted, the "net advantages" of the two jobs have been equalized. Measuring these differentials is not only interesting in itself, but the information may be useful for a variety of other purposes, as Application 19.4: Compensating Wage Differentials shows.

Labor Unions

Workers may at times find it useful to join a labor union in order to pursue goals that can more effectively be achieved through group action. Sometimes joining a union is completely voluntary. In many cases, however, compulsory membership (the closed shop) is required in order to maintain an effective union and prevent other workers from getting a free ride without paying union dues. This section examines the goals that an effective union might pursue, and how this pursuit will affect the wage rate.

Unions' Goals and the Monopoly Supply Decision

As in our discussion of the theory of the firm, we start our analysis of union behavior by describing the goals a union might seek. A first assumption we might make is that the goals of a union represent what its members want. This assumption avoids the problem of modeling the personal aspirations of union leaders, which may be in conflict with rank-and-file goals. Union leaders are therefore assumed to be conduits for expressing the desires of the membership.

Strong unions can be treated in the same way as monopoly firms. The union faces a demand curve for labor; because it is the sole source of supply, it can choose the point on this curve at which it will operate. The point that is actually chosen by the union will obviously depend on the particular goals

APPLICATION 19.4

Compensating Wage Differentials

Tables 1 and 2 provide some very tentative estimates of compensation wage differentials. Table 1 shows that jobs that have high mortality rates also have higher annual wages (other things being the same). In 1967 individuals chose among jobs as if they were putting an implicit value of about $176,000 on their own lives.[1] In other words, employees seemed willing to accept an increase in the annual probability of dying on a job of one-tenth of 1 percent in exchange for $176 extra in annual salary. Although that conclusion is controversial and may, for a variety of reasons, be too low (for instance, it disregards the costs that a person's death may impose on his or her family), there are many situations in which assigning some estimated value for a life is essential. Workplace health and safety legislation, for example, must reach some compromise between the benefits of safer methods of production and the costs of such safety.

Table 1
Compensating Wage Differentials for Differential Death Rates, by Occupations, 1967

Occupation	Additional Annual Deaths per 100,000	Estimated Increment to Annual Salary
Bartenders	179	$315
Boilermakers	230	405
Fire fighters	44	77
Lumberjacks	256	451
Mine operatives	176	310
Police and detectives	78	137
Taxicab drivers	182	320
Teamsters	114	201

Source: R. Thaler and S. Rosen, "The Value of Saving a Life: Evidence from the Labor Market" in *Household Production and Consumption*, N. E. Terleckyj, ed. (New York: National Bureau of Economic Research, 1975), pp. 265–298. Data computed from Tables 1 and 3.

Table 2
Compensating Wage Differentials for Unpleasant Working Conditions, 1967

	Addition to Wage Provided by Job Attribute			
	White Males	Black Males	White Females	Black Females
Repetitive jobs	10.3%	7.7%	22.3%	25.6%
Jobs in a poor work environment	6.8	−7.7	3.3	19.5

Source: R. E. B. Lucas, "Hedonic Wage Equations and Psychic Wages in the Returns to Schooling," *American Economic Review* (September 1977): Table 1, p. 554.

Valuing Working Conditions

Because it is very difficult to define "working conditions" of jobs in objective and quantifiable ways, measuring compensating differentials for "unpleasant" jobs is even more difficult than measuring differentials associated with risks of loss of life. The results of R. E. B. Lucas's attempt at measurement are reported in Table 2. These results show that, on the whole, people do seem to receive somewhat higher wages for jobs that are repetitive in nature or that require working in an unpleasant environment (that is, one characterized by heat, cold, noise, or some other unpleasant feature).

To Think About

1. Why bother to put a value on life at all? Isn't all life essentially beyond valuation?
2. How can the idea of compensating wage differentials be reconciled with the everyday observation that some very unpleasant jobs (such as those of trash collectors or day laborers) are not paid very well whereas executives in fancy, comfortable offices may be paid a great deal?

[1]For an up-to-date summary of studies of the value of a life, see A. Fisher, L. G. Chestnut, and D. M. Violette, "The Value of Reducing Risks from Death," *Journal of Policy Analysis and Management* (Winter 1989): 88–100.

Figure 19.6
Three Possible Points on the Labor Demand Curve That a Monopoly Union Might Choose

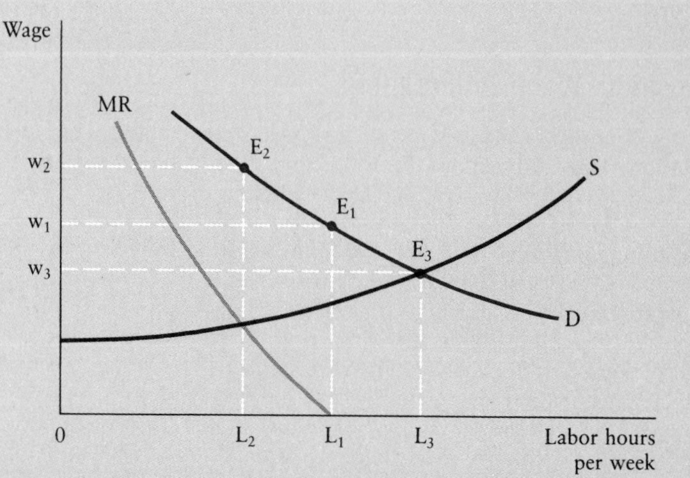

A union that has a monopoly in the supply of labor may choose any point on the demand curve for labor that it prefers. Three such points are shown in the figure. At point E_1 total labor payments $(w \cdot L)$ are maximized; at E_2 the economic rent that workers receive is maximized; and at E_3 the total amount of labor hired is maximized.

it has decided to pursue. Three possible choices are illustrated in Figure 19.6. The union may, for example, choose to offer that quantity of labor that maximizes the total wage bill $(w \cdot L)$. If this is the case, it will offer that quantity for which the marginal revenue from labor demand is equal to zero. This quantity is given by L_1 in Figure 19.6, and the wage rate associated with this quantity is w_1. The point E_1 is therefore this union's preferred wage-quantity combination. Notice that at wage rate w_1 there may be an excess supply of labor, and the union must somehow allocate those jobs that are available among the workers who want them. It may, for example, adopt a seniority or apprenticeship scheme that preserves high-wage jobs for its most senior workers.

Another possible goal that the union may pursue would be to choose to supply the quantity of labor that maximizes the total economic rent obtained by its members. In this way the union would be acting in a way similar to a monopoly firm by maximizing the "profits" (that is, wages in excess of opportunity costs) of its members. To do so would require the union to choose that quantity of labor for which the additional total wages obtained by having one more employed union member (the marginal revenue) are equal to the extra cost of luring that member into the market. The union should therefore choose that quantity, L_2, at which the marginal revenue curve crosses the supply curve. The wage rate associated with this quantity is w_2, and the desired wage-quantity combination is labeled E_2 in the diagram. Again, under this combination, some workers who desire to work at the prevailing wage

APPLICATION 19.5

Unionization of Fire Fighters

Our analysis so far has suggested that unions may be able to exert some influence on the terms of labor contracts. Here we examine such effects as a result of the unionization of fire fighters by the International Association of Fire Fighters (IAFF). The market for fire fighters is one in which union influences could be particularly pronounced. Because there is no effective private competition for the services provided by municipal fire departments, once the IAFF gains recognition as the bargaining agent with a city, it does not have to be concerned about the erosion of that position through competition. Similarly, a city's demand for fire fighters is likely to be inelastic with respect to wage changes since there are few possibilities for substituting capital for labor.

Empirical Evidence

A 1971 study by Orley Ashenfelter tended to support the presumption that unionization of fire fighters can have significant labor market effects.[1] Table 1 summarizes Ashenfelter's findings for small (population 25,000 to 50,000) and moderate-size (population 50,000 to 100,000) cities for 1966. Three bargaining goals of the IAFF were examined: hourly wage rates, annual salaries, and weekly hours of work. The hours-of-work goal was included because fire fighters typically spend long hours on duty waiting for calls (the typical workweek is about 56 hours) and there is some public sympathy for reductions in those hours. Of course, a reduction in hours not accompanied by a proportionate reduction in annual salary implies an increase in the hourly wage. Bargaining over hours is one way in which the IAFF may have been able to achieve higher wages.

Table 1
Effects of Unionization of Fire Fighters, All U.S. Cities, 1966 (Percentage Difference between Union and Nonunion Cities)

	Small Cities	Moderate-Size Cities
Percentage difference in weekly hours	−5.8%	−8.5%
Percentage difference in annual salary	+10.1	+1.0
Percentage difference in hourly wage	+16.0	+9.4

Source: O. Ashenfelter, "The Effect of Unionization on Public Sector Wages: The Case of Fire Fighters," *Industrial and Labor Relations Review* (January 1971): 191–202. Abstracted from Tables 2 and 3.

Table 1 shows that fire fighters represented by the IAFF tended to work 6 to 8 percent fewer hours than did nonunionized fire fighters. Those reductions in hours were not matched by reductions in annual salaries in unionized cities—indeed, annual salaries tended to be slightly higher in such cities. Consequently, hourly wages paid to fire fighters represented by the IAFF were 9 to 16 percent higher than those paid to nonunion workers. The unique nature of fire fighting may result in these data overstating the economic impact of unions in the economy as a whole. But, most studies of other industries have also concluded that the effects of unions on relative wage rates are in the 10 to 20 percent range.[2] It appears that unions do have a substantial influence on wage determination.

To Think About

1. Fire fighters are not usually hired by private firms. Rather, they work for municipal governments. How would you develop a theory of these governments' demands for workers? Would their demand curves be negatively sloped? How, for example, might a town respond to an increase in the wages of fire fighters?
2. Might fire fighters' unions have a positive effect on productivity that largely offsets the higher wages they obtain? Or might the union, through various restrictive work rules, actually reduce productivity?

[1]O. Ashenfelter, "The Effect of Unionization on Public Sector Wages: The Case of Fire Fighters," *Industrial and Labor Relations Review* (January 1971): 191–202.

[2]Some authors have suggested that the effects of unions on costs of production may not be this great since unionized workers may also be more productive than nonunionized workers. For a discussion of the issues, see R. B. Freeman and J. L. Medoff, *What Do Unions Do?* (New York: Basic Books, 1984).

are left unemployed. Perhaps the union may "tax" (by charging dues) the large economic rent earned by those who do work in order to transfer income in the form of layoff benefits to those who don't.

A third possibility would be for the union to aim for maximum employment of its members. This would involve choosing the point w_3, L_3, which is precisely the point that would result if the market were organized in a perfectly competitive way. No employment greater than L_3 could be achieved, since the quantity of labor that union members supply would be reduced for wages less than w_3.

Other Union Goals: Job Security and Fringe Benefits

Although the union goals illustrated in Figure 19.6 are those that are easiest to diagram, that list is by no means exhaustive. Two other important goals that unions may seek, for example, are job security and a variety of nonwage fringe benefits. Job security is particularly important in industries such as durable goods manufacturing or construction in which there are major cyclical influences on product demand and on the demand for labor. Unions may seek to reduce the risks of such fluctuations for their members by establishing contractual rights to jobs. In that way the variability in workers' wage incomes will be reduced, and (as we showed in Chapter 7) this reduction raises workers' utility.

Fringe benefits such as pensions, vacations, insurance coverage, and generally better working conditions are also of considerable value to workers. Because such benefits are frequently of low public visibility in negotiating sessions and are often nontaxable to workers, they have come to constitute an increasingly important part of firms' total labor costs.

Such additional union goals can be taken into account in two ways. First, the price of labor should be generalized to include indirect forms of compensation in addition to the usual hourly wage rate. Obviously, firms and workers bargain over the total package of compensation, not just one part of it. Related to this is a second observation: Unions may be willing to forgo wage rate increases to obtain other types of benefits. They may, as Application 19.5 shows for the case of fire fighters, opt for more leisure time instead of higher wages. Although diagramming such other goals may be difficult, these goals do play a major role in many labor negotiations.

Summary

In this chapter we have examined several questions about the supply of labor and how supply decisions may affect wage rates. Our primary conclusions are:

- The market wage rate represents the opportunity cost of leisure for individuals. It shows how nonwork time can be traded for income (and consumption) in the marketplace.

- A utility-maximizing individual will choose to work that number of hours for which the MRS of leisure for consumption is equal to the market wage. That is, the individual will equate the rate at which he or she is willing to trade leisure for consumption to the market opportunity cost of that leisure.
- A change in the wage rate has both substitution and income effects on people's choices. The effects work in opposite directions. A higher real wage, for example, will have a substitution effect that encourages people to work more, but an income effect that encourages them to work less.
- If jobs differ in their attractiveness, this will show up in the supply of labor for those jobs. Differentials in wage rates will arise that compensate people for differing job characteristics.
- If workers join together to form a union, they may exert some monopoly power in the labor market. The supply decisions made by the monopoly union will depend on the goals it chooses to pursue. It is likely that unions can raise market wages for those who get jobs.

Review Questions

1. Economists tend to approach the study of labor supply in a relatively backward way by looking at the demand for "leisure." What do economists mean by "leisure"? Why does an individual's demand for leisure also constitute a supply of labor? If leisure is viewed as a consumption good, what is its price?
2. Use the concept of the opportunity cost of time to discuss the following:

   a. Who might be expected to pay the higher fares to fly the faster Concorde to Europe.
   b. Who would be likely to stand in long lines and even camp out overnight to purchase tickets to a sporting event.
   c. For whom greens fees are a larger fraction of the total cost of a golf game—a prospering physician or an unemployed laborer.
   d. How the degree of traffic congestion affects who drives to work and who takes mass transit.

3. In Chapter 4 we showed that, for a normal good, income and substitution effects tend to work in the same direction causing price rises to result in a decline in quantity demanded. Can a similar argument be made for the relationship between the price and quantity of leisure consumed? What is different about these two situations?
4. Use the time allocation model to discuss the effects on an individual's hours of work of

   a. The receipt of a substantial amount of outside income.
   b. The imposition of a tax on wages.
   c. An increase in the general price level with no concomitant increase in wages.
   d. National legislation establishing a maximum workweek of 35 hours.

5. Why might a person choose not to work? How would Figure 19.2 look in this case? What changes in such a person's budget constraint might lure him or her into the labor market?

6. The illustration of compensating wage differentials in Figure 19.5 shows two supply curves together with a single demand curve. Why is only the demand curve shown even though the figure shows the wages for two occupations? What does the use of the single demand curve implicitly assume about the workers who might take either job? Why is that an appropriate assumption for measuring compensating differentials?
7. Explain how information on compensating wage differentials might be used to find the value that workers implicitly place on their lives. What would such an estimate assume about workers' knowledge of the risks of various jobs? Can you think of reasons why such labor market information might understate the true value of a life?
8. Why do workers join a union? What do they expect to gain? What do they have to give up? Why is a union more effective than a single worker in bargaining with employers?
9. If a union can be analyzed as a monopoly supplier of labor, why is that analysis so much more complicated than our analysis of the monopoly supplier of a good? Why is the profit-maximization assumption not applicable to a union?
10. Suppose a monopoly union represented all of the employees of a firm that was a monopsony hirer of these workers. Why might the goals of these two market participants be in conflict? How might such a conflict be resolved? (See also problem 19.6.)

Problems

19.1 Suppose there are 8,000 hours in a year (actually there are 8,760) and that an individual has a potential market wage of \$5 per hour.

a. What is the individual's full potential income if he or she could work 8,000 hours? If he or she chooses to devote 75 percent of this income to leisure, how many hours will be worked?
b. Suppose a rich uncle dies and leaves the individual an annual income of \$4,000 per year. If he or she continues to devote 75 percent of full income to leisure, how many hours will be worked?
c. How would your answer to part b change if the market wage were \$10 per hour instead of \$5 per hour?
d. Graph the individual's supply of labor curve implied by parts b and c.

19.2 Mrs. Smith has a guaranteed income of \$10 per day from an inheritance. Her preferences require her always to spend half her potential income on leisure (H) and consumption (C).

a. What is Mrs. Smith's budget constraint in this situation?
b. How many hours will Mrs. Smith devote to work and to leisure in order to maximize her utility given that her market wage is \$1.25? \$2.50? \$5.00? \$10.00?
c. Graph the four different budget constraints and sketch in Mrs. Smith's utility-maximizing choices. (Hint: when graphing budget constraints, remember that when $H = 24$, $C = 10$, not 0.)
d. Graph Mrs. Smith's supply of labor curve.

19.3 Mr. Peabody has a utility function of $U = \sqrt{C \cdot H}$ and is maximizing his utility at $U = 20$ when he works 14 hours a day. Would he be willing to give up an hour of his leisure to drive Mrs. Atterboy to the wrestling match if she offered him \$5?

*19.4 An individual receives utility from daily income (Y), given by

$$U(Y) = 100Y - \tfrac{1}{2}Y^2.$$

The only source of income is earnings. Hence Y = wL, where w is the hourly wage and L is hours worked per day. The individual knows of a job that pays \$5 per hour for a certain 8-hour day. What wage must be offered for a construction job where hours of work are random with a mean of 8 hours and a variance of 36 hours to get the individual to accept this more "risky" job? *Hint:* This problem makes use of the statistical identity

$$E(X^2) = \text{Var } X + E(X)^2,$$

where E means "expected value."

19.5 Suppose a union has a fixed supply of labor to sell. If the union desires to maximize the total wage bill, what wage rate will it demand? How would your answer change if unemployed workers were paid unemployment insurance at the rate u per worker and the union now desired to maximize the sum of the wage bill and the total amount of unemployment compensation?

*19.6 Suppose the supply curve for labor to a firm has the form

$$L = 100w$$

where w is the market wage. Suppose that the marginal expense of hiring workers is

$$ME_L = L/50.$$

Suppose also that the firm's demand (marginal value product) curve has the form

$$L = -50MVP_L + 450.$$

a. If the firm is a monopsonist, how many workers will it hire in order to maximize profits? What wage will it pay?
b. If the supply of labor is monopolized, how many workers should be provided to the firm in order to maximize the total wage bill (wL)? What will the wage rate be?
c. If the market has both a monopsony on the demand side and a monopoly on the supply side, what can you say about the "equilibrium" outcome? How will this compare to the competitive solution?

*19.7 A welfare program for low-income people offers a family a basic grant of \$6,000 per year. This grant is reduced by \$.75 for each \$1 of other income the family has.

a. How much in welfare benefits does the family receive if it has no other income? If the head of the family earns \$2,000 per year? How about \$4,000 per year?

---

* Denotes a problem that is rather difficult.

b. At what level of earnings does the welfare grant become zero?
c. Assume that the head of this family can earn $4 per hour and that the family has no other income. What is the annual budget constraint for this family if it does not participate in the welfare program? That is, how are consumption (C) and hours of leisure (H) related?
d. What is the budget constraint if the family opts to participate in the welfare program? (Remember, the welfare grant can only be positive.)
e. Graph your results from parts c and d.
f. Suppose the government changes the rules of the welfare program to permit families to keep 50 percent of what they earn. How would this change your answer to parts d and e above?
g. Using your results from part f, can you predict whether the head of this family will work more or less under the new rules described in part f?

CHAPTER 20

Pricing of Capital

The study of capital as a factor of production is extremely important in economics. For example, economists have traditionally assigned an important role to capital accumulation as a source of economic growth. One of the major reasons for income increasing over time is the increasing amount of productive equipment workers have at their disposal. To understand where this equipment comes from and the incentives that lead to its accumulation requires that we study capital. Similarly, Keynesian economic theory assigns an important role to investment as one component of aggregate demand. Since net investment comes about because firms want to add to the amount of capital they have available, it is again important to understand the factors that go into the firms' decisions. For this reason, capital theory is central to modern macroeconomics. The purpose of Chapter 20 is to provide a simple analysis of capital pricing that is relevant to these and many other issues.

Definition of Capital

Capital stock
The total amount of machines, buildings, and all other manmade, nonlabor resources in an economy.

When we speak of the **capital stock** of an economy, we mean the total amount of machines, buildings, and other nonlabor resources that are in existence at some point in time. These assets represent some portion of an economy's past output that was not consumed then. This past output was instead invested to be used for production in the future. All societies, from the most primitive to the most advanced, engage in this sort of capital accumulation. A bushman's taking time off from hunting to make arrows, people in a modern society using part of their incomes to buy houses, or governments taxing citizens in order to purchase dams and post office buildings are all pursuing the same sort of activity—some portion of the economy's current output is being invested for use in producing additional goods in future periods. Present sacrifice for future gain is the essential aspect of all capital accumulation.

Rate of Return

Rate of return
The increase in future output made possible by investing one unit of current output in capital accumulation.

The process of capital accumulation is pictured schematically in Figure 20.1. In both panels of the figure, society is initially consuming level C_0 and has been doing so for some time. At time 1 a decision is made to withhold some current output (amount s) rather than consuming it. Starting in time 2 this investment is put to use producing additional consumption goods. An important concept connected with this process is the **rate of return** earned on this investment. In Panel a, all of the investment is used to produce additional output only in time 2. Consumption is increased by amount x in time 2 and then returns to its prior level, C_0. Society has saved for one period in order to have an orgy of consumption in the next one. A measure of the one-period rate of return from this activity would be

$$r_1 = \frac{x}{s} - 1. \tag{20.1}$$

If $x > s$ (if more consumption comes out of this process than went into it), we would say that the one-period rate of return to capital accumulation is positive. For example, if investing 100 units of current output permitted society to consume an extra 110 units next year, the one-period rate of return would be .10 (= 110/100 − 1) or 10 percent.

In Panel b of Figure 20.1 society is assumed to take a more long-term view in its consumption activities. Again, an amount s is invested at time 1. Now, however, this investment is used to raise the consumption level for all periods in the future. If the permanent level of consumption is raised to $C_0 + y$, we define the perpetual rate of return to be

$$r_\infty = \frac{y}{s}. \tag{20.2}$$

If capital accumulation succeeds in raising C_0 permanently, r will be positive. For example, suppose society invested 100 units of output in time 1 to be devoted to capital accumulation. If this capital would permit output to be raised by 10 units for every period in the future (starting at time 2), the perpetual rate of return would be 10 percent.

When economists speak of the rate of return on capital, they have in mind something between these two extremes. Somewhat loosely they define the rate of return in an economy to be the terms at which current output that is invested can be turned into goods consumed at some future date. The next section shows how market forces operate to determine this rate.

Figure 20.1
Two Views of Capital Accumulation

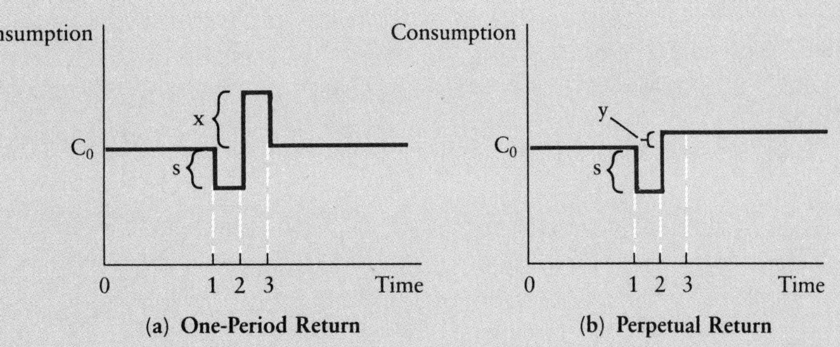

In Panel a, society withdraws some current consumption (s) in order to gorge itself (with x extra consumption) in the next period. The one-period rate of return would be measured by $x/s - 1$. The society in Panel b takes a more long-term view and uses s to increase its consumption perpetually by y. The perpetual rate of return would be given by y/s.

Determination of the Rate of Return

In a market economy the actual rate of return on capital will depend on the technical possibilities for investing present goods to make future goods, and on the preferences of people for present versus future goods. An equilibrium rate of return will reflect both the return to capital accumulation that is technically feasible and the return that individuals are willing to accept.

A Supply-Demand Analysis

Future goods
Goods that are purchased today by investing some present output as capital whose output is then consumed in the future.

Determination of this equilibrium rate of return can be illustrated by considering the supply and demand for what we might call **future goods.** Such goods are "purchased" today by setting aside some capital investment. When the output from that capital is consumed, it is called a future good. Simple examples of future goods include those yielded by growing grapes for wine or trees for lumber. Once an investment in these goods has been made, they increase in value over time—wine and timber offer a rate of return. Although purchasing machinery in the U.S. economy is much more complicated than planting trees, the activities are similar in that they represent investing present goods for use in producing goods to be consumed in the future. It is the market equilibrium that arises in this process that we wish to study.

A simple market for future goods is pictured in Figure 20.2. The horizontal axis shows the quantity of future goods traded (F). This is the quantity of actual consumption that will occur in the future. On the vertical axis we have recorded the relative price of these future goods (P_F). This price records the number of current goods (for example, pounds of seedlings) that must be sacrificed to get one future good (for example, one pound of lumber). The de-

Figure 20.2
The Market for Future Goods

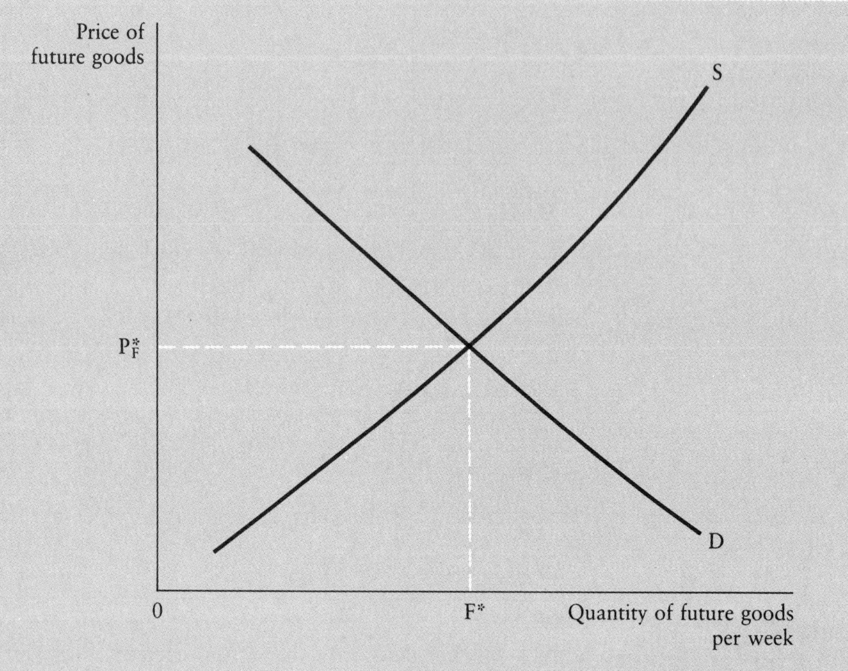

The terms at which present goods trade for future goods (P_F) through capital accumulation is set by demand and supply conditions. It is likely that P_F^* will be less than one. We define the rate of return (r) by the formula $1/1 + r = P_F^*$. Since $P_F^* < 1$, r will be positive.

mand curve for future goods is drawn sloping downward on the assumption that the lower their price, the greater the quantity people will demand. In other words, the smaller the required sacrifice of present goods, the greater will be people's demands for goods in the future. The supply curve for future goods slopes upward because of the assumption that the process of investing capital for the production of future goods may run into diminishing returns. As the amount of future goods produced increases, the marginal cost (in terms of the present investment required) of producing them rises. Expanding the production from a wood lot of a fixed size requires progressively more in the way of initial investment of workers' time, soil improvements, and care in spacing seedlings.

Equilibrium Price of Future Goods

Equilibrium in the market shown in Figure 20.2 is at P_F^*, F^*. At that point the supply and demand for future goods are in balance, and the required amount of current goods will be invested in order to produce F* in the future.[1]

There are a number of reasons to expect that P_F^* will be less than one: that is, it will cost less than the sacrifice of one current good to "buy" one good in the future. On the demand side it might be argued that people require some reward for waiting. Everyday slogans ("a bird in the hand is worth two in the bush," "live for today") and more substantial realities such as the uncertainty of the future and the finiteness of life suggest that people are generally impatient in their consumptive decisions. Capital accumulation such as that shown in Figure 20.1 will take place only if the current sacrifice is in some way worthwhile.

There are also supply reasons for believing P_F^* will be less than one. All of these involve the idea that capital accumulation is "productive": investing one good currently will ultimately yield more than one good in the future. Tree farmers, vineyard operators, and cheesemakers "abstain" from selling their wares currently in the belief that time will make them more valuable in the future.[2] Similarly, building steel mills or power stations may ultimately yield more in the future value of output than was used to produce these capital goods. Application 20.1: The Rate of Return to Storing Wine illustrates a particularly rewarding example of this productivity from investing.

The Equilibrium Rate of Return

We can now show the relationship of the rate of return (r) to what we have called the price of future goods by the formula

$$P_F^* = \frac{1}{1 + r}. \qquad [20.3]$$

Since we believe that P_F^* will be less than one, r will be positive. For example, if $P_F^* = .9$, r will equal approximately .1, and we would say that the rate of return to capital accumulation is 10 percent.[3] By investing one unit of current output, the consumption of future goods can be increased by 1.1. The

[1]This is a much simplified form of an analysis originally presented by Irving Fisher in *The Rate of Interest* (New York: Macmillan, 1907).

[2]For a discussion of these examples in the context of "Austrian" capital theory, see Marc Blaug, *Economic Theory in Retrospect* (Homewood, Ill.: Irwin, 1962), Chapter 12.

[3]More precisely, if $P_F^* = .9$, r will be .11111 . . . since

$$.9 = \frac{1}{1 + .1111\ldots}.$$

APPLICATION 20.1

The Rate of Return to Storing Wine

Laying down rare wine to age is a particularly simple yet rewarding example of capital accumulation—present consumption of wine is forgone in the hope of obtaining more enjoyable consumption in the future. Although there are no objective standards to measure how much a wine's taste improves each year, prices for bottles of wine of various ages provide a good estimate of the returns obtained by oenophiles. In a 1981 study, Elizabeth Jaeger examined results for the Hueblein Wine Auction for red Bordeaux wines and California cabernet sauvignons over the period 1969–1977.[1] Overall, she calculated that wines being auctioned yielded average annual rates of return of over 20 percent, a figure well in excess of returns available on financial investments (such as Treasury bills) during the period. At least for these particular years, it appears that aging of wine offered a substantial incentive to delay consumption.

Is Wine a Good Investment?

One question immediately suggested by these results is why returns to storing wine are so high. Jaeger suggests the principal explanation is that storing wine is a risky enterprise. Besides the problem of protecting wine against breakage and temperature changes, there is major uncertainty as to whether a particular vintage will age properly. The chemistry involved in the changing properties of wine over time is very delicate. Undetectable differences among rare wines when they are first bottled may lead to major discrepancies in their quality as they age. Discovering that a particular red vintage is aging poorly can lead to sharp price drops, reflecting the wine's lowered quality.

Jaeger finds some evidence to support this explanation for wine's high rates of return by comparing older and younger vintages. She calculates a much higher rate of return on the younger vintages since these are subject to great risks and potential disappointments. Older vintages, on the other hand, have shown that they age well, and purchasing them involves a lesser risk. For these older vintages, rates of return were not significantly higher than those obtainable on relatively safe financial investments.

To Think About

1. When is the right time to sell wine that is rising in value? Should a winery hold onto its product until it has ceased to appreciate further? Or should the product be sold while it is still rising in value? What is the opportunity cost of keeping wine in the barrel?
2. How does the rate of return on other investments affect the behavior of winery owners with respect to aging their product? Would an increase in alternative returns result in fine wines being aged for longer or shorter periods? Do you think wine fanciers really make such calculations?

[1]Elizabeth Jaeger, "To Save or Savor: The Rate of Return to Storing Wine," *Journal of Political Economy* (June 1981): 584–592.

rate of return and P_F are equivalent ways of measuring the terms on which present goods can be turned into future goods.[4]

[4]It is important to make a distinction between the rate of return (r) and interest rates (R) actually observed in real-world markets (say, on savings accounts or on bonds). Since we live in a world of inflation, market interest rates will reflect both the rate of return on capital accumulation and the expected change in prices (since lenders will want to be compensated for the fact that they will be repaid in devalued dollars). If the expected proportional change in the price level is given by P_e, R and r are related by

$$R = r + P_e.$$

For example, if r = .05 (5 percent) and P_e = .04 (4 percent), the market interest rate will be R = .09 (9 percent).

In the remainder of this chapter we assume that the equilibrium rate of return, r, has been established by the process shown in Figure 20.2. That rate provides a measure of the benefits of capital accumulation to all people who are considering it. We will show how they take account of r in all of the decisions they make that concern the allocation of resources over time.

Rental Rate on Machines and the Theory of Investment

Any firm will rent machines in accordance with the principles of profit maximization derived in Chapter 18. Specifically, a profit-maximizing firm will hire that number of machines for which the marginal value product (MVP) from hiring one more is equal to the machine's market rental rate (v). This section first investigates the determinants of machines' market rental rates by assuming that firms rent all the equipment they use. Later, we examine the particular problems raised because most firms own the machines they use rather than renting them.

Determinants of Market Rental Rates

Consider a firm in the business of leasing machines to other firms. Hertz and Avis lease automobiles, banks lease computers and aircraft to other operators, and Taylor Rental rents everything from punch bowls to chain saws. Suppose that such a rental firm owns a machine that has a current market value of P. If it sold the machine outright, the firm could get P for it. How much will the firm charge its clients for the use of the machine?

The firm owning this machine faces two kinds of costs: physical depreciation on the machine and the opportunity cost of having its funds tied up in the machine rather than in an investment earning the prevailing rate of return. If depreciation costs per period (say, each year) are a constant percentage (d) of the machine's market value (P) and if the market rate of return on other investments is given by r, then the total costs to the machine owner for one year are given by

$$dP + rP = P(r + d). \tag{20.4}$$

If we assume that the machine rental market is perfectly competitive, the workings of the market will ensure that the rental rate per year for the machine (v) is exactly equal to these long-run costs of the machine owner. Hence we have the basic result that

$$v = P(r + d). \tag{20.5}$$

The annual rental rate is the sum of interest and depreciation costs that the rental company incurs. For example, suppose that the rate of return on alternative investments is 5 percent per year (that is, .05) and that the physical depreciation rate is 4 percent per year (.04). Suppose also that the current market price of a particular machine is $100. In this simple example, the machine would have a rental rate of $9 [$100 × (.05 + .04)] per year. The opportunity cost of the funds invested in the machine is $5, and the remaining $4 reflects the costs of physical deterioration over the year.

A Nondepreciating Machine

In the case of a machine that does not depreciate (d = 0), Equation 20.5 can be written in a simpler way:

$$\frac{v}{P} = r. \qquad [20.6]$$

This says that in equilibrium an infinitely long-lived (nondepreciating) machine is equivalent to a perpetual bond and must yield the prevailing rate of return. The rental rate as a percentage of the machine's price must be equal to r. If v/P exceeds r, everyone would rush out to buy machines, since they yield more than the prevailing interest rate. For example, if v = $10 per year and a machine sells for $100, a firm in the machine rental business will earn 10 percent on the funds it invests in machines. If alternative investments yield only 8 percent, the rental business is a very profitable one and new firms would enter it. Alternatively, if v/P is below r, no one would be in the business of leasing out machines, since more could be made on alternative investments. Hertz would do better putting its funds in a bank (at 8 percent interest) rather than investing in cars if each $20,000 car rented for only $1,000 per year (5 percent).

Ownership of Equipment

To this point we have assumed that firms rent all of the machines they use. Although such rental does take place in the real world, more commonly firms own the machines they use. A firm will buy a machine and use its services, in combination with the labor the firm hires, to produce output. Ownership of machines makes the analysis of the demand for capital slightly more complicated than analyzing the demand for labor. By recognizing the important distinction between a stock and a flow, we can show that these two demands are quite similar.

A firm uses capital services to produce output. These services are a flow magnitude. It is the number of machine-hours that is relevant to the productive process (just as it is labor-hours), not the number of machines per se. Frequently, the assumption is made that the flow of capital services is proportional to the stock of machines (100 machines can, if fully employed for one hour, deliver 100 machine-hours of service). In this case, these two different concepts can be used synonymously. If during a period a firm desires a certain number of machine-hours, this is usually taken to mean that the firm needs a certain number of machines to provide them. The firm's demand for capital services is also a demand for capital ownership.

A profit-maximizing firm in perfect competition will choose its level of inputs so that the marginal value product from an extra unit of any input is equal to its cost. This result also holds for the demand for machine hours. The cost of capital services is given by the rental rate (v) in Equation 20.5. This cost is borne by the firm whether it rents the machine in the open market or owns the machine itself. In the former case, machine rental is an explicit cost; in the latter case, it is an implicit cost since the firm could lease its equipment to another user if it chose to do so. In either case the opportunity cost of machine use is given by the market rental rate v. The fact of ownership is, to a first approximation, irrelevant to the determination of cost, and we can treat all firms as if they rent capital equipment. Firms that own machines can be viewed as renting those machines from themselves. In the process, they incur an opportunity cost of v.

Theory of Investment

If a firm finds that it desires more capital services than can be provided by its currently existing stock of machinery, it has two choices. First, it may hire the additional machines that are needed in the rental market. This would be formally identical to its decision to hire additional labor. Second, the firm can buy new machinery to meet its needs. We call this purchase of new equipment by the firm (net) **investment**.

Investment
The purchase of new capital.

Investment demand is an important component of aggregate demand in macroeconomic theory. Usually it is assumed that investment demand (that is, the demand for machines) is inversely related to the rate of return on alternative investments. It is easy now to demonstrate the links in this argument. A fall in the prevailing rate of return, r, will, *ceteris paribus,* decrease the rental rate on capital (Equation 20.5). Because forgone investment returns represent an implicit cost for the owner of a machine, a fall in r in effect reduces the cost of capital inputs. This fall in v implies that capital has become a relatively less expensive input and, as we showed in Chapter 18, this will prompt firms to increase their capital use. Firms may then either rent additional machines from others or buy new equipment for their own use.

It is this latter effect (the buying of new equipment) that is termed investment. The relationship between changes in r and investment demand is therefore just one aspect of the theory of firms' demand for inputs. Because the rate of return is an important determinant of the rental rate on capital, a fall in r has an effect on investment by causing the quantity of capital demanded by firms to increase. If the firm's current stock of machinery cannot deliver the desired number of machine-hours, investment in new machinery will take place.

Tax Policy and Investment

Until now we have assumed that a potential user of capital faces only two types of costs: (1) implicit costs arising from forgone returns on alternative investments and (2) explicit costs of the machine's physical deterioration. Taxes represent a third type of cost that can also influence decisions on capital use. In the United States and many other countries, the corporate profits tax is not only an important source of government revenue, it is also a major policy tool that has been used to influence investment decisions.[5]

A Graphical Demonstration

When taxes are imposed on capital equipment, Equation 20.5 must be modified to take them into account. Now there are three costs that a machine owner must pay: interest, physical depreciation, and taxes. Consequently, the rental rate on a machine will now be

$$v = P(r + d) + T, \qquad [20.7]$$

where T represents the taxes on a machine that must be paid by the owner each period. A higher T implies a higher rental cost, and a lower T implies a lower cost. Figure 20.3 shows the effect that a reduction in T (and v) will have on the firm's desired level of capital inputs. Initially, the rental rate on capital is given by v_1; the firm produces q_1 by using K_1 units of capital input per period.

Now suppose T declines. Using Equation 20.7, this will cause a machine's rental rate to fall to v_2. As was the case for labor, this fall in the rental rate will create both substitution and output effects, which cause more capital to be hired. In Panel a in Figure 20.3 the substitution effect causes the optimal input combination to move to point B on the q_1 isoquant. The fall in v also causes the firm's marginal cost curve to shift downward to MC′. Output is increased to q_2; at this output level, the firm now wishes to hire K_2 units of capital input. Since the firm may not have a sufficient stock of capital equipment on hand to provide this level of services, it may have to buy additional equipment. In other words, it may engage in investment. This is the sequence of events by which changes in governmental tax policy are related to the generation of investment incentives. In Application 20.2: Effects of Tax Policies on Investment, we examine the success of some specific tax measures that were intended to spur investment in this way.

[5]Although this tax is termed a profits tax, as we showed in Chapter 10, it is not a tax on economic profits, but rather on both economic profits and on the net output (marginal value product) of machines. It is this taxation of machines' net incomes that affects investment decisions. A tax only on economic profits would have no such effect since it would not affect profit-maximizing or cost-minimizing input choices.

Figure 20.3
Effects of a Reduction in Taxes on the Demand for Capital Services

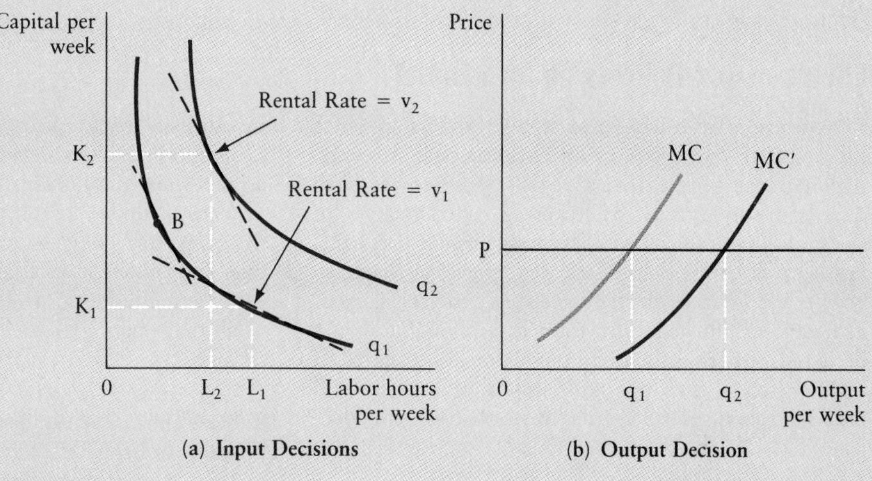

(a) **Input Decisions** (b) **Output Decision**

If tax policies change the rental rate on capital, this will change the demand for capital services. For example, a reduction in taxes will cause the rental rate to fall from v_1 to v_2. This will create both substitution (from K_1, L_1 to B) and output (from B to K_2, L_2) effects, which cause the quantity of capital services demanded to increase (from K_1 to K_2). This increased demand for services may prompt firms to buy new machines.

Present Discounted Value and Investment

Present discounted value
The present value of funds payable in the future after taking account of the opportunity cost of interest forgone.

The theory of firms' demand for capital is often presented in a form different from the one we have used. This alternative form is termed the **present discounted value** theory of investment demand. Rather than treating the renting of machines similarly to the hiring of labor and centering attention on the rental rate (as we have done), this other approach looks directly at the firm's decision to purchase a machine. The theory concerns the demand for machines rather than the demand for the services of machines. This distinction between the two approaches is, however, not very important. Here we will show that this alternative approach predicts the same behavior as does the rental rate approach we have been using.

Present Discounted Value

In order to describe the present discounted value criterion for investment, we must first discuss the procedure that should be used to add up sums of money that are to be received in different time periods. Since the purchaser of a machine will collect net income (or, more properly, the marginal value product) from the machine over several periods into the future, we need to know how to add up these amounts. Although some formal aspects of this question are

APPLICATION 20.2

Effects of Tax Policies on Investment

Federal tax policies have been widely used to influence the overall level of investment over the past 35 years. Although the general thrust of these policies has been to increase investment by lowering taxes, changes in the profits tax rate have not been the primary way this has been accomplished. Rather, complex changes have been made in accounting procedures, and special credits have been allowed for investment. Although it would be inappropriate to describe these changes in detail, a brief sketch of the three most important policies will indicate how investment incentives have been provided.

Accelerated Depreciation

In 1954, federal tax policy was changed to allow firms to write off the costs of their investments in plant and equipment more rapidly than previously. That policy allowed firms to postpone the taxes owed on the income generated by newly purchased machinery. In essence, firms received an interest-free loan of their tax liability from the government. By one estimate this relatively subtle change in accounting principles reduced the rental rate on capital by as much as 20 percent.[1]

Useful Lifetime Guidelines

Another provision for accelerated depreciation was instituted in 1962. Under this provision what were defined as the "useful lifetimes" of various types of equipment for tax purposes were shortened. For example, the statutory minimum useful life of a car was reduced from four to three years. This made it possible for firms to gain further benefits from accelerated depreciation, and effective rental rates on capital were reduced another 2 or 3 percent.

[1]R. E. Hall and D. W. Jorgenson, "Tax Policy and Investment Behavior," *American Economic Review* 57 (June 1967): 391–414. All of the other numbers for the 1960s in this example are also taken from this source.

Investment Tax Credit

An additional tax change in 1962 was the institution of an investment tax credit for machinery and equipment purchases. Under that policy, 7 percent of the amount firms invested could be taken as a credit against taxes due. That policy reduced effective rental rates by 7 percent—essentially the U.S. Treasury paid for 7 percent of all machinery and equipment purchases.

Effects of the Tax Policies in the Early 1960s

Table 1 shows the estimated effect of each of these tax policies on firms' total gross investment in equipment in 1963. As our theoretical discussion suggested, the reduction in rental rates had a substantial effect on the demand for capital equipment, increasing total pur-

Table 1

Change in Gross Investment in Equipment as a Result of Federal Tax Policy, 1963 (Billions of 1954 Dollars)

	Manufacturing Equipment	Non-manufacturing Equipment
Total gross investment	$8.461	$17.982
Change due to:		
Accelerated depreciation	0.549	1.141
Useful lifetime guidelines	0.315	0.656
Investment tax credit	0.867	1.808
Total effect of federal tax policy	1.731	3.605
Tax effect as a percentage of total gross investment	20.5%	20.0%

Source: R. E. Hall and D. W. Jorgenson, "Tax Policy and Investment Behavior," *American Economic Review* 57 (June 1967): 391–414, Tables 3, 4, and 5.

chases by about 20 percent over what they would have been under older, less generous tax laws. Clearly, tax policy provides a powerful lever with which the federal government can affect investment and, through investment, the overall pace of economic activity. The relatively high levels of employment experienced during the mid-1960s in the United States may have been in part the result of such policies.

Tax Policies of the Reagan Administration

In the first year of the Reagan administration, a similar set of investment-oriented tax policies was enacted as part of the Economic Recovery Tax Act (ERTA) of 1981. Changes introduced under this act included a new form of accelerated depreciation (Accelerated Cost Recovery System—ACRS) and an increased investment tax credit. Adoption of the ACRS was a particularly important innovation. It eliminated the prior concept of "useful lifetime guidelines" for determining depreciation allowances and substituted a simplified scheme in which any asset fell into one of four classes with tax lives of 3, 5, 10, or 15 years. For most capital assets these lives were considerably shorter than had been the case previously. Most notably, the depreciation period for all equipment used to conduct research and development activities was reduced to a short 3 years where the previous guidelines had required much longer periods. Adoption of the ACRS also brought much greater uniformity into the tax treatment of various industries' investments. For example, under prior laws, depreciation periods for producers' equipment ranged from over 14 years for ships and boats to over 12 years for turbines to 5 years for trucks and tractors. Similarly, depreciation periods for buildings ranged from 17 to more than 40 years. Under the ACRS, depreciation periods were set at a uniform 5 years for most equipment and 10 or 15 years for buildings. It was hoped that such changes would result in a more uniform tax treatment of investment decisions across industries, thereby mitigating some of the anomalies that had developed under the prior system.

The overall effect of the ERTA changes was to reduce taxes substantially (reducing effective rental rates) on firms' capital investments. Indeed, some analysts even suggested that the tax rates under ERTA on many types of equipment were negative; that is, the government was effectively subsidizing this type of investment.[2] Possibilities for this subsidy having a major effect on firms' investment behavior were rather limited, however. The tax law was changed again in 1982 (under the pompously titled Tax Equity and Fiscal Responsibility Act), and the prior subsidy was largely eliminated. Indeed, this latter law raised the tax rates on some types of investment to above their pre-1981 levels. The likely overall effect of the Reagan changes on actual investment incentives was therefore unclear. Actual investment performance since 1982 has been similarly erratic.

To Think About

1. Why does the government adopt policies to encourage investment? Won't private markets do enough investment without government subsidies? What goals is the government trying to achieve with such tax policies? Are there better ways to accomplish these goals?
2. Depreciation policies are usually based on the actual purchase price of a machine. Is this definition of depreciation consistent with economists' notions of production costs? What are the actual costs involved in using a machine? Are these necessarily related to the machine's price perhaps many years ago? How does the failure to use accurate cost measures for firms' depreciation affect their investment decisions?

[2]See Donald Fullerton and Y. K. Henderson, "Long Run Effects of the Accelerated Recovery System," *National Bureau of Economic Research Working Paper*, No. 828 (revised, February 1983).

Table 20.1
Present Value of $1 Payable at Various Dates

Interest Rate (r)	1 Year	2 Years	3 Years	10 Years	20 Years
3%	$.970	$.943	$.915	$.744	$.544
4	.962	.925	.889	.676	.456
5	.952	.907	.864	.614	.377
6	.943	.890	.840	.558	.312
7	.935	.873	.816	.508	.258

presented in the appendix to this chapter, it is possible here to provide an intuitive explanation of the logic that economists employ.

One dollar today is worth more than a dollar that will not be received until a later date. If a dollar is available today, it can be invested and earn interest at the prevailing rate, r. Conversely, if a dollar is not received until next year, some interest must be forgone. The current dollar is more valuable. Specifically, a dollar today will grow to 1 + r dollars next year. We might therefore define the present value of $1 to be paid next year as $1/(1 + r). This is the amount that, if invested today at an annual interest rate r, will yield $1 in one year. If you invest $.95 today at 5 percent, you will have $1 next year. The present value of $1 to be received one year from now is $.95.

It is easy to generalize the idea of present value to any number of periods. If $1 is invested for two years, for example, it will grow to $\$1 \cdot (1 + r) \cdot (1 + r) = \$1 \cdot (1 + r)^2$. The present value of $1 payable in two years would be $\$1/(1 + r)^2$. This is the amount that would have to be invested today in order to obtain $1 in two years. These results can be summarized by

$$\text{Present value of \$1 payable in one year} = \frac{\$1}{(1 + r)};$$

$$\text{Present value of \$1 payable in two years} = \frac{\$1}{(1 + r)^2};$$

$$\text{Present value of \$1 payable in three years} = \frac{\$1}{(1 + r)^3};$$

$$\text{Present value of \$1 payable in n years} = \frac{\$1}{(1 + r)^n}. \qquad [20.8]$$

In order to illustrate the implications of the present value concept, Table 20.1 shows the present value of $1 payable in 1, 2, 3, 10, and 20 years in the future for five possible interest rates. For example, if r is 4 percent, the present value of $1 payable in one year is $.962. If about $.96 is invested today at 4 percent, it will grow to $1 by the end of one year. If the interest rate is 7 percent, an investment of only $.26 will grow to $1 in 20 years. In general, the present value of a dollar to be paid at some date in the future declines as the interest rate increases. The higher r is, the more heavily future payments are discounted since the opportunity costs of lost interest are greater. Similarly, for any particular interest rate, dollars payable in the distant future are worth less than those payable in the near term. Again, such distant payments are discounted more heavily because of the greater opportunity costs involved. Published tables and calculators are available for calculating present values, and these can be most helpful for economic analyses that involve sums of money payable over time.

Present Discounted Value Approach to Investment Decisions

When a firm buys a machine, it is in effect buying a stream of net revenues in future periods. In order to decide whether or not to purchase the machine, the firm must assign some value to this stream. Since the revenues will accrue to the firm in many future periods, the logic of the preceding argument suggests that the firm should compute the present discounted value of this stream. Only by doing so will the firm have taken adequate account of the opportunity costs associated with alternative assets it might have bought.

Consider a firm in the process of deciding whether to buy a particular machine. The machine is expected to last n years and will give its owner a stream of monetary returns (that is, marginal value products) in each of the n years. Let the return in year i be represented by R_i. If r is the interest rate, and if this rate is expected to prevail for the next n years, the present discounted value (PDV) of the machine to its owner is given by

$$\text{PDV} = \frac{R_1}{1 + r} + \frac{R_2}{(1 + r)^2} + \cdots + \frac{R_n}{(1 + r)^n}. \qquad [20.9]$$

This represents the total value of the stream of payments that is provided by the machine, once adequate account is taken of the fact that these payments occur in different years. If the PDV of this stream of payments exceeds the price (P) of the machine, the firm should make the purchase. Even when the opportunity costs of the interest payments that the firm could have earned on its funds had it not purchased the machine are taken into account, the machine promises to return more than it will cost to buy, and firms would rush out to buy machines. On the other hand, if P exceeds the machine's PDV, the firm would be better-off investing its funds in some alternative that promises a rate of return of r. When account is taken of forgone interest, the machine does not pay for itself. No profit-maximizing firm would buy such a machine.

In a competitive market the only equilibrium that can persist is one where the price of a machine is exactly equal to the present discounted value of the net revenues it provides. Only in this situation will there be neither an excess demand for machines nor an excess supply of machines. Hence, market equilibrium requires that

$$P = PDV = \frac{R_1}{1 + r} + \frac{R_2}{(1 + r)^2} + \cdots + \frac{R_n}{(1 + r)^n}. \qquad [20.10]$$

Present Discounted Value and the Rental Rate

For simplicity, assume now that machines do not depreciate and that the marginal value product is the same in every year. This uniform return will then also equal the rental rate for machines (v), since that is what another firm would be willing to pay for the machine's use during each period. With these simplifying assumptions we may write the present discounted value from machine ownership as

$$PDV = \frac{v}{1 + r} + \frac{v}{(1 + r)^2} + \cdots + \frac{v}{(1 + r)^n} + \cdots, \qquad [20.11]$$

where the dots (...) indicate that payments go on forever. But since in equilibrium P = PDV, the appendix to this chapter shows how we can solve Equation 20.11 as

$$P = \frac{v}{r} \qquad [20.12]$$

or

$$r = \frac{v}{P}, \qquad [20.13]$$

which is the same as Equation 20.6 ($v/P = r$). For this case the present discounted value criterion gives results identical to those outlined earlier using the rental rate approach. In equilibrium a machine must promise owners the prevailing rate of return.

We have again demonstrated the algebraic relationship between a machine's current price, the rental rate on the machine, and the market rate of return. In particular, an increase in r will decrease the machine's PDV, and firms will be less willing to buy machines for the same reasons that we discussed before—opportunity costs are too high. This result is quite general. The present discounted value approach to investment and the rental rate approach are alternative ways of phrasing the same idea. However, as Application 20.3: The Economist and the Car Dealer illustrates, PDV calculations can be useful in a wide variety of other contexts. Many of these are encountered every day.

APPLICATION 20.3

The Economist and the Car Dealer

In 1985 an economist well known to this author ventured into an automobile showroom to buy a new car. He quickly settled on a no-frills family car with a final price tag of $10,000 (in round numbers). Before reaching a final agreement with the salesman, the nervous economist was introduced to the manager of the firm who was supposed to close the deal.

A Common Sales Pitch

The manager's pitch was a smooth one. "You look like a sensible and frugal buyer," he said. "Do I have a deal for you! We have just signed a great financing package with a local bank to make car loans. I can let you have this car now and all you have to do is pay back $3,100 per year for the next four years. You will pay back $12,400—$10,000 for the car and $2,400 in finance charges. If instead you pay for the car with $10,000 in cash, you'll lose, say, 7 percent each year by taking your money out of the bank. This amounts to $2,800 over four years. By financing with us you save $400."

The Economist Smells a Rat

This final appeal to opportunity cost sounded good to the economist, but he smelled a rat. How could the car dealer (or dealer's bank) offer more favorable financing than the economist made on his account at that same bank? Something was wrong. As the startled car dealer looked on, the economist pulled out his calculator to evaluate the present value of the repayment scheme being proposed. He used 7 percent as his opportunity cost:

$$\text{PDV of auto loan} = \frac{\$3{,}100}{1.07} + \frac{\$3{,}100}{(1.07)^2} + \frac{\$3{,}100}{(1.07)^3} + \frac{\$3{,}100}{(1.07)^4} = 500 \quad .$$

So this loan was actually more costly than paying for the car with cash even after accounting for opportunity costs. To cinch the analysis, the economist pressed the dealer to reveal the true interest rate in his offer (which by law he was required to do). After some grumbling about how such figures "distort the real picture," he announced the true cost as 9.2 percent—considerably more than the economist made in his paltry savings account. The "deal" being offered was no deal at all. After a bit more verbal sparring, the economist was handed back to the salesman (who seemed embarrassed by the whole episode) and proceeded to buy the car with cash. He has not taken the car back to this dealer for service since then, however.

An Explanation

The trick in the car dealer's offer is obvious. He was not offering to lend the purchase price of the car for four years. Instead, the scheme he proposed (similar to all consumer credit purchase schemes) required repayment of some of the loan's principal each year. Effectively, the economist would have been borrowing an average of much less than $10,000 for the entire period. The car dealer's opportunity cost calculations were misleading, and the economist was (at least on this occasion) saved from a costly mistake by a simple application of the present value concept.

To Think About

1. Suppose the car dealer had allowed his entire $12,400 charge to be paid at the end of four years. Then, would his argument be correct? How much would the economist save by taking such a deal?
2. How would you compute the "true" interest charge on the car dealer's offer? Does this figure actually "distort the true picture"? In general, do laws requiring disclosure of true interest charges seem desirable?

Human Capital

One important application of the theory of capital concerns a rather different kind of investment from what we have been discussing so far—the investment people can make in themselves. They can do this in a variety of ways. Individuals can acquire a formal education, they may accept apprenticeships and learn skills on the job, they can spend considerable efforts in looking for better jobs, or they can purchase various kinds of medical services that maintain them in good health. All of those activities can be looked upon as "investments" since both time and resources are sacrificed currently in the hope that this will somehow pay off in the future.

Human capital
Capital in the form of learned abilities acquired through training, education, or experience.

By acquiring skills or buying good health, people are adding to their stock of **human capital** in much the same way that the purchase of machines by firms adds to the firms' stock of physical capital. There is substantial evidence that most additions to human capital are quite productive—they help people to increase their earnings in future years. In fact, it has been found that individuals make many investments in themselves that yield returns substantially in excess of the prevailing rate of return on other investments.[6] In this section we discuss how such calculations are made and look at some of the ways in which human capital differs from physical capital.

Calculating the Yield on an Investment

Yield
The interest rate at which the present discounted value of the returns from an investment are exactly equal to the investment's current cost.

Conceptually, it is an easy matter to compute the **yield** that an individual receives from an investment in human capital (or on any other kind of capital investment, for that matter). Suppose that the cost of an investment that someone is intending to make is given by C. Suppose also that the investment is expected to raise this person's earnings in each year in the future and that these additions to earnings are given by $I_1, I_2, \ldots, I_n$. We wish to know what interest rate, i, will discount these earnings increments to make them exactly equal to C. Mathematically, we know C and I, and we wish to find that value of i that solves the equation

$$C = \frac{I_1}{1 + i} + \frac{I_2}{(1 + i)^2} + \cdots + \frac{I_n}{(1 + i)^n}. \qquad [20.14]$$

The value of i that solves Equation 20.14 would be called yield (or, sometimes, rate of return) on this particular investment (see the appendix to this chapter for a discussion of this calculation). Application 20.4: Yields on In-

[6]For a thorough analysis of the educational aspects of human capital formation, see G. S. Becker, *Human Capital,* National Bureau of Economic Research (New York: Columbia University Press, 1964). For a treatment of the human capital approach to the study of medical expenditures, see Michael Grossman, *The Demand for Health,* National Bureau of Economic Research Occasional Paper 119 (New York: Columbia University Press, 1972).

APPLICATION 20.4

Yields on Investments in Schooling and On-the-Job Training

The two most important human capital investments people make are in formal schooling and in on-the-job training. Costs of investment in schooling are of two types. First are explicit costs such as tuitions and fees, transportation costs, and other incidental expenses. A second, and probably larger, component of schooling costs is the implicit opportunity costs of forgone earnings while in school. Since most skills that are specific to a particular occupation are probably learned on the job, wages will be lower during this learning period. The costs of on-the-job training are composed primarily of these temporarily forgone wages.

Costs of Human Capital Investments

A 1970 study by Thomas Johnson attempted to estimate the dollar costs of these two types of human capital investments.[1] A few of the author's results for males in 1959 are presented in Table 1. Most workers require about the same degree of initial preparation when starting out on a job. As would be expected, the costs of formal schooling rise rapidly for individuals with higher educational levels. Workers with less than a high school education have invested relatively little in formal schooling (less than $4,000—composed primarily of forgone earnings). More than three-quarters of such workers' total human capital investments are in on-the-job training. For more highly educated people, formal schooling costs constitute about two-thirds of their total investment.

Table 1
Investments in Human Capital and the Yield of Those Investments for White Males in the Northern United States, 1959

Years of Education Completed	Total Investment in Human Capital	Total Lifetime Income	Yield on Investment in Human Capital
9–11	$19,076	$220,025	24.6%
12	24,112	245,433	21.5
13–15	28,463	278,323	17.5
16	46,016	341,856	15.5
17+	63,771	380,626	13.5

Source: Thomas Johnson, "Returns from Investment in Human Capital," *American Economic Review* (September 1970): 546–560, Table 3.

Yields on These Investments

The investments in human capital shown in Table 1 seem to pay off in increasing total lifetime incomes. For example, on average, individuals with a college education earned nearly $100,000 more over their lifetimes than did those with only a high school education. The final column of Table 1 presents the percentage yields on total human capital investments. The yields diminish for higher levels of formal education. This suggests some kind of diminishing return to human capital investments may exist. As for any other economic activity, it appears to be possible to push investments in human capital too far. Indeed, more recent data tend to indicate that the returns to college education have fallen below those in Table 1, primarily because of the rapid increase in the number of college graduates over the past 20 years. Current yields are, however, still above yields on alternative investments that people might make (savings accounts, bonds, and so forth), and this may reflect the unique nature of human capital investments.

To Think About

1. If education offers such a high return, why should it be subsidized by the government? Doesn't the high return give people an adequate incentive to purchase their own education? Can you think of reasons why one might want to subsidize, say, elementary and secondary education? Do these reasons also apply to professional training such as medical or law school?
2. If workers obtain higher wages as a result of on-the-job training, who pays for that training? Do firms have an incentive to provide the training or do workers in effect pay for it by accepting low wages when they are new on the job?

[1] Thomas Johnson, "Returns from Investment in Human Capital," *American Economic Review* (September 1970): 546–560.

vestments in Schooling and On-the-Job Training illustrates some results that are typically obtained from this kind of calculation in the study of the returns to schooling or on-the-job training. These studies tend to confirm that human capital investment is very important and often yields surprisingly high returns.

Special Features of Human Capital

Although the analogy between human and physical capital provides many insights into the nature of people's decisions about gaining skills and education, it should not be pushed too far. Human capital has a number of special properties that make it unique among the assets an individual can buy. Contrary to other assets, human capital cannot (in the absence of slavery) be sold. The owner of human capital is inextricably tied to his or her past investments. Although a person may "rent" out this investment to employers for a wage, he or she may not sell it in the way a firm might sell a machine it no longer needed.

Human capital also depreciates in a rather unusual way. It is totally lost upon the death of its owner. This makes the investment rather risky. Finally, the acquisition of human capital may take substantial time. Whereas a firm seeking to buy a drill press may only have to spend five minutes to make a phone call, people who wish to improve their skills must usually invest considerable time, perhaps years, in doing so. The irreversibility of time makes this process of human capital investment all the more risky. It is not surprising, therefore, that these investments frequently offer high returns.

Pricing of Exhaustible Natural Resources

As a final application of capital theory, we consider how markets will price finite natural resources over time. Much concern has been expressed about the possible exhaustion of some finite resources. In the mid-1970s, for example, considerable attention was focused on the adequacy of known petroleum reserves. More recently, concern has been expressed about the supply of a wide variety of exhaustible resources ranging from stocks of various fish and wildlife species to the amount of farmland. Our principal focus here is on the implications for the pricing of such resources that stem from the fact that these resources can be used up. In Chapter 21 we look at some other questions about the allocation of both exhaustible and renewable natural resources.

Scarcity Costs

What makes the production of exhaustible resources different from the production of any other economic good is that current production from a finite resource stock reduces the amount of the resource available for the future.

Figure 20.4
Scarcity Costs Associated with Exhaustible Resources

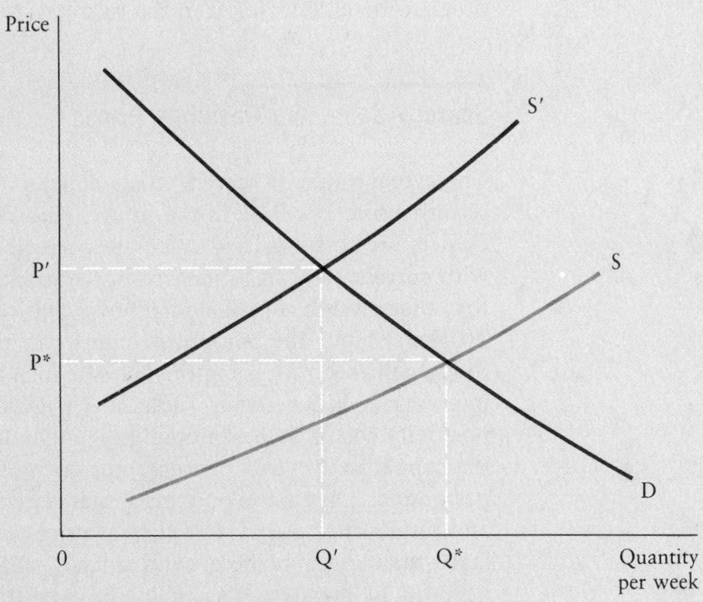

Firms that produce exhaustible resources will take into account both current marginal production costs and the opportunity costs of forgone future production. The market supply curve for such firms (S′) will be above their marginal cost curves to the extent of those scarcity costs.

This might be contrasted to the usual case of production in which firms' activities during one year have no effect on their production activities the next year. Producers of an exhaustible resource must therefore take an additional cost into account in their current production decisions: the opportunity cost of forgone sales in the future. Economists define the **scarcity costs** associated with current production of an exhaustible resource as the value of forgone future sales that cannot be made because of this current production. Recognition of such costs does not imply that profit-maximizing firms will produce no output and constantly hoard their resources for some future time. But they will be careful to incorporate the full opportunity costs of current sales in their decisions.

Scarcity costs
The opportunity costs of forgone future production that cannot be made because of current production that uses exhaustible resources.

The implications of scarcity costs for pricing are illustrated in Figure 20.4. In the absence of those costs, the industry supply curve for the resource would be given by S, and that curve would, as usual, reflect the marginal costs of actually producing (that is, drilling, mining, or refining) the resource. Scarcity costs (related to the finiteness of the ultimately available resource supply) shift firms' marginal cost curves upward. The new market supply curve is S′. The gap between S′ and S reflects the opportunity costs associated with forgone future sales. Current output is reduced (from Q* to Q′) when firms recognize the finiteness of the resource supply. This reduction reflects firms' preference for withholding some of the resource from current supply in order to be able to sell it in the future.

Scarcity Costs and Resource Prices

The actual value of scarcity costs depends on firms' perceptions about what resource prices will be in the future. Knowledge of those prices is required if owners are to be able to calculate correctly the opportunity costs associated with current sales from their resource stocks. As a simple example, suppose a firm that owns a copper mine knows that copper will sell for $1 per pound in 20 years. Since the amount of copper in the mine is fixed, selling a pound today will mean forgoing this $1 sale in 20 years. If we assume that the real interest rate is 5 percent, Table 20.1 shows that the present value of this opportunity cost is $.38. Assuming the mine owner is indifferent between selling the copper in 20 years or today, the current market price should also be $.38 per pound. That is the only price that reflects an equilibrium between present and future sales. Any lower current price would encourage the mine owner to leave the copper in the ground since it will be worth more later even taking account of forgone interest in the meantime. A current price above $.38 would, on the other hand, cause the owner to sell as much copper as possible today and not wait for 20 years.

Our calculation of scarcity costs proceeds by comparing the price of copper to its actual production costs. If the marginal cost of producing a pound of copper is $.20, then scarcity costs would be $.18 per pound—the amount by which the current equilibrium price exceeds marginal production cost. In this case, the fact that price exceeds marginal cost is not a sign of inefficiency. Instead, it shows that all costs are fully reflected in the price.

The Time Pattern of Resource Prices

An important implication of this discussion is that in the absence of any changes in production costs or in expectations about future prices, the market price of copper would be expected to increase over time at the rate of return on alternative investments. If r is 5 percent, for example, real copper prices would be expected to rise at 5 percent a year.[7] Only by following that path would prices always equal the present value of $1 in year 20.

This result can be shown intuitively from another perspective. Any firm will evaluate its resource holdings in the same way as it evaluates any other investment. Investments in resources should yield the same return (r) as those

[7]Since r is a "real" rate of return (that is, corrected for inflation), the prediction here is that the price of the resource relative to the price of all other goods should rise at the rate r. This result was first rigorously shown by Harold Hotelling in "The Economics of Exhaustible Resources," *Journal of Political Economy* (April 1931): 137–175.

APPLICATION 20.5

What Should the Price of Oil Be?

Did the 1982 market price of crude oil (about $34 per barrel) reflect scarcity costs arising from the finite nature of oil reserves, or did it more properly reflect (perhaps temporary) monopoly rents? The possibility that the price represented actual marginal costs of production can be readily dismissed since there was general agreement that the marginal costs of the lowest cost producer (Saudi Arabia) were around $2 to $3 per barrel.

An Assumed Price Pattern

In order to assess scarcity costs in 1982, we have to assume something about the future price of oil. Although there is considerable disagreement on that subject, there is some consensus that by the year 2020 (38 years from 1982) energy will be generally available from new technologies (solar, fusion, tidal, geothermal, and so forth) at the equivalent of $50 to $70 per barrel of oil (in 1982 prices).[1] Taking the upper range of these numbers and assuming that r is 4 percent gives

$$\text{PDV of a barrel of oil} = \frac{\$70}{(1.04)^{38}} = \$15.77 \qquad [20.15]$$

as the equilibrium present value. The 1982 market price was more than twice what appeared to be dictated by the scarcity value of oil.

[1]See, for example, W. D. Nordhaus, "The Allocation of Energy Resources," *Brookings Papers on Economic Activity*, No. 3 (1973): 529–570.

The Decline of OPEC Power

The Organization of Petroleum Exporting Countries (OPEC) cartel may have exercised quite a bit of monopoly influence in setting the market price during the late 1970s and early 1980s. Experiences since 1982 are consistent with this interpretation The worldwide recession of 1982–1983 put severe pressure on the OPEC pricing structure. By 1985 there was serious bickering within the cartel over how to allocate production among its members, and this resulted in further price weakness. By early 1986 the market price for oil had fallen into the $14 to $15 range, suggesting that most of OPEC's power to determine prices had been eroded and that the price of oil now closely reflected both production and scarcity costs.

To Think About

1. The notion that OPEC acted as a monopoly cartel and raised the price of crude oil is based on a simple, single-period model of monopoly behavior. How does the recognition that oil is a finite resource affect that model? If OPEC sharply raises oil prices currently, won't it find that it has too much oil left to sell at some date in the future? What restraints on current behavior of the cartel are provided by the need to sell oil profitably in the future?
2. The model of finite resource pricing that we present assumes the amount of resources is known. How would the analysis change if the quantities of resource reserves were not known accurately and could only be discovered through exploration? How would unexpected new finds affect resource prices?

alternatives. Only if the real prices of finite resources increase at the rate r will they provide such a return to their owners. If resource prices were rising slower than this rate, natural resources would be an inferior investment, and owners should put their funds elsewhere. A rate of price rise above r per year is also unsustainable in the long run because investors would bid up the current price of resources to reflect their investment desirability. This bidding up of prices would continue until the possibility for further increases in excess of the prevailing rate was eliminated. This principle of the pricing of scarce finite resources can be used to study a variety of economic issues, as Application 20.5: What Should the Price of Oil Be? illustrates for the case of crude oil.

Summary

The fundamental concept introduced in this chapter is the rate of return (or real interest rate), which shows the terms at which present goods can be exchanged for future goods. It is this "price" that ties together economic decisions made in different time periods. The rate of return is a primary influence on the allocation of resources over time. We show these effects in several contexts:

- The rate of return, because it represents an important opportunity cost incurred by firms that own machines, directly affects firms' input choices. A higher rate of return raises the rental costs of capital and thereby discourages investment.
- The real interest rate is also important for calculating the present value of payments to be made in different time periods. Such payments can only be compared once the opportunity costs of interest forgone are taken into account.
- Human capital represents a particular type of investment that people may make in themselves. Rates of return on such investments may be rather high, possibly because of the risky features of these investments.
- Exhaustible resources pose important allocational problems because using some quantity of them in one year precludes the use of those resources in later years. The logic of interest rate computations suggests that the relative price of finite resources should increase over time at a rate equal to the real rate of interest.

Review Questions

1. What is capital? How does an economy "accumulate" capital? Could an economy ever experience a decline in its stock of capital? How is the abstract view of capital accumulation pictured in Figure 20.1 related to the actual process of firms increasing the capital stock by purchasing new machines? Can you explain these ideas using a production possibility frontier for present and future goods?
2. Suppose that the economy produced only one, all-purpose good called jelly. How would capital accumulation occur in such an economy? How would you measure the rate of return as described in Figure 20.1? Would the jelly rate of return (that is, the ratio of final jelly output to jelly investment) be a real or a nominal rate of return?
3. A simple formula for the rental rate on a piece of capital equipment is $v = P(r + d)$. Explain why the price (P) used here is the current price of the machine. Why wouldn't it be correct to use the machine's original purchase price? How might the analysis be expanded to allow for the possibility that the machine's price might change over time? (See Application 9.1 for some additional insights.)
4. Explain the sequence of events through which a change in the interest rate affects a firm's demand for capital input. Why is this sequence essentially the same regardless of whether the firm owns its capital or rents it from someone else?
5. Why does a tax on capital affect a firm's profit-maximization input choice but a tax on pure economic profits does not? How might the U.S. corporate profits

tax (see Application 10.1) be changed so that it more closely resembles a tax on pure corporate profits?

6. In our discussion of present discounted value we usually only examined the value of "one dollar" payable at various times. How is the case of any number of dollars a trivial generalization of this? More importantly, explain why the PDV of any given number of dollars is lower the higher the interest rate is or the longer the time until the dollars are to be paid.
7. Suppose the general level of prices was increasing and that capital rental rates were rising in line with all other prices. Can a firm use these nominal rental rates in making a PDV calculation for an intended investment? If so, should the firm use a nominal or a real interest rate to make its calculation? Alternatively, if the firm decides to adjust future rental rates for inflation, which interest rate should it use?
8. Why does the analysis of Chapter 19 suggest that the opportunity cost of time may be a major cost of human capital accumulation? Give some examples of this opportunity cost. For example, what fraction of the total cost of your education would you estimate is represented by such costs?
9. Why are scarcity costs relevant for the pricing of finite natural resources but not for the production of standard manufactured goods? Doesn't the sale of, say, one more automobile reduce the stock of potentially available new cars in exactly the same way that the sale of a barrel of oil reduces the stock of oil? What is the economic difference?
10. In Application 20.5 we had to make some assumption about the price of oil in the year 2020 in order to be able to calculate current scarcity costs. Why was such an assumption necessary? Should the price in 2020 be the nominal price of oil then or should it be adjusted to the current price level to control for inflation?

Problems

20.1 Mr. Moneybags is thinking of buying a bond issued by the ABC Corporation. Mr. Moneybags' economist friend tells him that a fair price for the bond is the bond's present discounted value. The face value of the bond is \$10,000, which will be given to Mr. Moneybags at the end of five years. In addition, the bond promises to pay five "coupons" of \$1,000 at the end of each year. Assuming the market interest rate (i) is 12 percent annually, what is a fair price for the bond? What if i = 8 percent instead? What is the relationship between bond prices and interest rates?

20.2 The president of the Acme Landfill Company has estimated that the purchase of 10 more deluxe dump trucks can bring in added revenues of \$100,000 a year for the life of the trucks. The trucks have a life span of seven years and cost \$50,000 each. If the company can earn a 10 percent rate of return on investments in alternative ventures, should it go ahead and purchase the trucks? What if the company found that it could only earn a 9 percent return on its alternative investments? Should it go ahead with the purchase?

20.3 A high pressure life insurance salesman was heard to make the following argument: "At your age a \$100,000 whole life policy is a much better buy than a similar term policy. Under a whole life policy you'll have to pay \$2,000 per year for the first four years, but nothing more for the rest of your life. A term policy will cost you \$400 per year, essentially forever. If you live 35 years, you'll pay only \$8,000 for the whole life policy, but \$14,000 for the term policy. Surely the whole life is a better deal."

Assuming the salesman's life expectancy assumption is correct, how would you evaluate this argument? Specifically, calculate the present discounted value of the premium costs of the two policies assuming that the interest rate is 10 percent.

20.4 Suppose J. P. Miser obtains utility from present and future consumption (C_1 and C_2) and that she has a certain amount of dollars (Y) to allocate between these goods.

a. If the interest rate is r, what will the budget constraint in this problem be?
b. Using the budget constraint from part a, show graphically how Y will be allocated between C_1 and C_2 to maximize utility. What will the tangency condition for a utility maximum be in this situation?
c. Suppose r were to increase. What will happen to the utility-maximizing choices for C_1 and C_2?

*20.5 Assume that an individual expects to work for 40 years, then retire with a life expectancy of an additional 20 years. Suppose also that the individual's earnings rise at a rate of 3 percent per year and that the interest rate is also 3 percent (the overall price level is constant in this problem). What (constant) fraction of income must the individual save in each working year to be able to finance a level of retirement income equal to 60 percent of earnings in the year just prior to retirement?

20.6 The No-Flite Golfball Company manufactures cut-proof golfballs and is thinking of investing in a new name. Its media personnel have come up with two suggestions: "Astro-Flite" and "Jack Nickless." It is cheaper to switch to Astro-Flite since the second name will involve legal fees for dealing with a well-known golfer who is likely to get upset by the whole thing. The second name, however, is expected to bring in more business than the first. If the costs and payoffs are as given below, and the firm expects to go out of business in five years, is it worth it to make a name switch, and if so, to which name?

	Cost	Yearly Return	Interest Rate
Astro-Flite	$3,800	$1,000	10%
Jack Nickless	5,000	1,400	10

Would your answer change if the interest rate were 15 percent?

20.7 Some foresters suggest that timber plots be managed so as to achieve "maximum sustainable yield." Would an economist agree that a single tree should be grown to maturity before it is cut down and sold as lumber (since trees begin to grow more slowly as they get older)? How would an economist manage a whole forest of trees? How might the problem be complicated by a forest of trees of widely different ages (and growth rates)?

*20.8 Suppose Scotch increases in value as it ages. In particular, the value of Scotch at any time t is given by $V = 100t - 6t^2$ and the proportional growth rate in that value is $(100 - 12t)/V$. Graph this Scotch function. At what value of t is V as large as possible? Is that when the Scotch should be bottled? If the interest rate is 5 percent, when should the Scotch be bottled?

*Denotes a problem that is rather difficult.

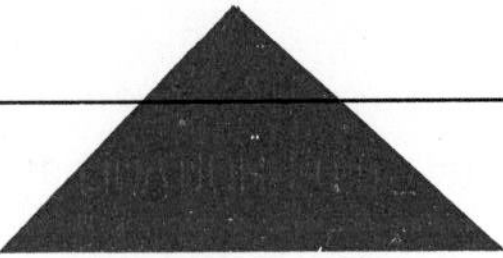

APPENDIX TO CHAPTER 20
COMPOUND INTEREST

People encounter compound interest concepts almost every day. Calculating returns on bank accounts, deciding on the true cost of an automobile loan, and buying a home with a mortgage all involve the use of interest rate computations. This appendix shows how some of those computations are made. The methods introduced are useful not only in economics classes, but in many personal economic decisions too.

Interest

Interest
Payment for the current use of funds.

Interest is payment for the time value of money. A borrower gets to use funds for his or her own purposes for a time and in return pays the lender some compensation. Interest rates are usually stated as some percentage of the amount borrowed (the principal). For example, an annual interest rate of 5 percent would require someone who borrowed $100 to pay $5 per year in interest.

Throughout this appendix we assume that the market has established an annual interest rate, i, and that this interest rate will persist from one year to the next. It is a relatively simple matter to deal with interest rates that change from one period to another, but we do not consider them here. We are also not particularly interested in whether i is a "nominal" interest rate (such as a rate quoted by a bank) or a "real" interest rate that has been adjusted for any inflation that may occur over time.[1] The mathematics of compound interest is the same for both nominal and real interest rates.

Compound Interest

Compound interest
Interest paid on prior interest earned.

If you hold funds in a bank for more than one period, you will receive **compound interest**—that is, you will receive interest not only on your original principal but also on the interest that you earned in prior periods and left in the bank. Compounding is relatively complicated and results in rather dramatic growth over long periods.

[1]Nominal and real interest rates can be related by the formula $i = r + P_e$, where i is the nominal interest rate per year, r is the real interest rate, and P_e is the expected annual rate of inflation. Often the real interest rate, r, is assumed to equal the rate of return on capital accumulation.

Interest for One Year

If you invest \$1 at the interest rate of i, at the end of one year you will have

$$\$1 + \$1 \cdot i = \$1 \cdot (1 + i). \qquad [20A.1]$$

For example, if i is 5 percent, at the end of one year, you will have

$$\$1 + \$1 \cdot (.05) = \$1 \cdot (1.05) = \$1.05. \qquad [20A.2]$$

Interest for Two Years

If at the end of the first year you leave your money in the bank, you will now earn interest on both the original \$1 and on your first year's interest. At the end of two years you will therefore have

$$\begin{aligned} \$1(1 + i) + \$1 \cdot (1 + i) \cdot i &= \$1 \cdot (1 + i)(1 + i) \\ &= \$1 \cdot (1 + i)^2. \end{aligned} \qquad [20A.3]$$

To understand Equation 20A.3 it is helpful to expand the term $(1 + i)^2$. Remember from algebra that

$$(1 + i)^2 = 1 + 2i + i^2. \qquad [20A.4]$$

At the end of two years, \$1 will grow to

$$\begin{aligned} \$1 \cdot (1 + i)^2 &= \$1 \cdot (1 + 2i + i^2) \\ &= \$1 + \$1 \cdot (2i) + \$1 \cdot i^2. \end{aligned} \qquad [20A.5]$$

At the end of two years you will have the sum of three amounts:

1. Your original \$1.
2. Two years' interest on your original \$1—$\$1 \cdot 2i$.
3. Interest on your first year's interest—$[(\$1 \cdot i) \cdot i] = \$1 \cdot i^2$.

If, again, the interest rate is 5 percent, at the end of two years you will have

$$\$1 \cdot (1.05)^2 = \$1 \cdot (1.1025) = \$1.1025. \qquad [20A.6]$$

This represents the sum of your original \$1, two years' interest on the \$1 (that is, \$.10), and interest on the first year's interest (5 percent of \$.05, which is \$.0025). The fact that you will have more than \$1.10 is a reflection of compounding. As we look at longer and longer periods of time, the effects of this compounding become much more pronounced.

Interest for Three Years

If you now leave these funds, which after two years amount to $\$1 \cdot (1 + i)^2$, in the bank for another year, at the end of this third year you will have

$$\begin{aligned} \$1 \cdot (1 + i)^2 + \$1 \cdot (1 + i)^2 \cdot i &= \$1 \cdot (1 + i)^2(1 + i) \\ &= \$1 \cdot (1 + i)^3. \end{aligned} \quad [20A.7]$$

For an interest rate of 5 percent, this amounts to

$$\$1 \cdot (1 + .05)^3 = \$1 \cdot 1.157625 = \$1.157625. \quad [20A.8]$$

The fact that you get more than simply your original \$1 and three years' simple interest (\$.15) again reflects the effects of compounding.[2]

A General Formula

By now the pattern should be clear. If you leave your \$1 in the bank for any number of years, n, you will have, at the end of that period,

$$\text{Value of \$1 compounded for n years} = \$1 \cdot (1 + i)^n. \quad [20A.9]$$

With a 5 percent interest rate and a period of 10 years, you would have

$$\$1 \cdot (1.05)^{10} = \$1 \cdot 1.62889\ldots = \$1.62889. \quad [20A.10]$$

Without compounding you would have had \$1.50—your original \$1 plus 10 years' interest at \$.05 per year. The extra \$.12889 comes about through compounding.

To illustrate the effects of compounding further, Table 20A.1 shows the value of \$1 compounded for various time periods and interest rates.[3] Notice how compounding becomes very important for long periods. For instance, Table 20A.1 shows that, at a 5 percent interest rate, \$1 grows to be \$131.50 over 100 years. This represents the original \$1, simple interest of \$5 (\$.05 per year for 100 years), and a massive \$125.50 in interest earned on prior interest. At higher interest rates the effect of compounding is even more pronounced since there is even more prior interest on which to earn interest. At a

---

[2]As an exercise, you may wish to expand $(1 + i)^3$ and see whether you can explain the meaning of each of the four terms in the expression.

[3]Because these computations are burdensome, they are often made using either a calculator or interest rate tables. Calculators capable of doing fairly sophisticated interest calculations can be purchased for about \$10 in 1990.

Table 20A.1
Effects of Compound Interest for Various Interest Rates and Time Periods with an Initial Investment of $1

Years	Interest Rate: 1 Percent	3 Percent	5 Percent	10 Percent
1	$1.01	$ 1.03	$ 1.05	$ 1.10
2	1.0201	1.0609	1.1025	1.2100
3	1.0303	1.0927	1.1576	1.3310
5	1.051	1.159	1.2763	1.6105
10	1.1046	1.344	1.6289	2.5937
25	1.282	2.094	3.3863	10.8347
50	1.645	4.384	11.4674	117.3909
100	2.705	19.219	131.5013	13,780.6123

1 percent interest rate, only about 26 percent of the funds accumulated over 100 years represent the effects of compounding. At a 10 percent interest rate more than 99.9 percent of the huge amount accumulated represents the effects of compounding.

Compounding with Any Dollar Amount

The use of $1 in all of the computations we have made so far was for convenience only. Any other amount of money grows in exactly the same way. Investing $1,000 is just the same as investing a thousand one-dollar bills—at an interest rate of 5 percent this amount would grow to $1,050 at the end of 1 year [$1,000 · (1.05)]; it would grow to $1,629 at the end of 10 years [$1,000 · (1.629)]; and to $131,501 at the end of 100 years [$1,000 · 131.501].

Algebraically, D dollars invested for n years at an interest rate of i will grow to

$$\text{Value of \$D invested for n years} = \$D \cdot (1 + i)^n. \qquad [20A.11]$$

Application 20A.1: Compound Interest Gone Berserk illustrates some particularly extreme examples of using this formula.

Present Discounted Value

Because interest is paid on invested dollars, a dollar you get today is more valuable than one you won't receive until next year. You could put a dollar you receive today in a bank and have more than a dollar in one year. If you wait a year for the dollar, you will do without this interest that you could have earned.

Economists use the concept of **present discounted value** (sometimes called *present value*) to reflect this opportunity cost notion. The present discounted

APPLICATION 20A.1

Compound Interest Gone Berserk

The effects of compounding can be gigantic if a sufficiently long period is used. Consider the author's two favorite examples

Manhattan Island
Legend has it that in 1623 Dutch settlers purchased Manhattan Island from the native Americans living there for trinkets worth about \$24. Suppose these native Americans had invested this \$24 at 5 percent interest for the 367 years between 1623 and 1990. Using Equation 20A.11, in 1990 they would have

$$\$24 \cdot (1.05)^{367} = \$24 \cdot 69{,}189{,}574 = \$1{,}660{,}549{,}773.$$

Over 367 years, their \$24 would have grown to more than \$1.6 billion. With a higher interest rate (say, 10 percent) the figure would be much larger—probably exceeding by far the entire actual value of Manhattan Island in 1990.

Horse Manure
In the 1840s the horse population of Philadelphia was growing at nearly 10 percent per year. Projecting this growth into the future, the city fathers began to worry about excessive crowding and potential pollution of the streets from manure. So they passed restrictions on the number of horses allowed in the city. It's a good thing! If the 1840 horse population of 50,000 had continued to grow at 10 percent per year into the 1980s, there would have been quite a few:

$$\begin{aligned}\text{Number of horses} &= 50{,}000 \cdot (1 + i)^{140} \\ &= 50{,}000 \cdot (1.10)^{140} \\ &= 31{,}185{,}000{,}000.\end{aligned}$$

With these 31 billion horses the manure problem would have been severe—amounting to perhaps 200 feet per year over the entire city. The City of Brotherly Love (the author's hometown) was spared this fate through timely governmental action.

To Think About

1. The tongue-in-cheek nature of these examples suggests there is probably something wrong with such simplistic applications of compound interest. Explain carefully why the calculations for each of the examples are pure nonsense.
2. At high interest rates, compounding can produce spectacular results even for relatively short time periods. In the late 1970s for example, it was possible to invest in bonds that yielded 15 percent per year. How much would you have to invest now at 15 percent to have \$1 million in, say, 45 years when you retire? Do you think this calculation is "reasonable"? What does it overlook?

Present discounted value
The current value of funds payable in the future after taking account of the opportunity cost of interest forgone.

value of the dollar you will not get for one year is simply the amount you would have to put in a bank now to have \$1 at the end of one year. If the interest rate is 5 percent, for example, the present value of \$1 to be obtained in one year is about \$.95—if you invest \$.95 today, you will have \$1 in one year, so \$.95 accurately reflects the present value of \$1 in one year.

An Algebraic Definition

More formally, if the interest rate is i, the present discounted value of \$1 in one year is \$1/(1 + i) since

$$\frac{\$1}{1+i} \cdot (1 + i) = \$1. \qquad [20A.12]$$

If i = 5 percent, the present discounted value (PDV) of \$1 in one year is

$$\text{PDV} = \frac{\$1}{1.05} = \$.9524 \qquad [20A.13]$$

and

$$\$.9524 \cdot 1.05 = \$1. \qquad [20A.14]$$

A similar computation would result for any other interest rate. For example the PDV of \$1 payable in one year is \$.971 if the interest rate is 3 percent, but \$.909 when the interest rate is 10 percent. With a higher interest rate, the PDV is lower because the opportunity costs involved in waiting to get the dollar are greater.

Waiting two years to get paid involves even greater opportunity costs than waiting one year since now you forgo two years' interest. At an interest rate of 5 percent, \$.907 will grow to be \$1 in two years—that is, $\$1 = \$.907 \cdot (1.05)^2$. Consequently, the present value of \$1 payable in two years is only \$.907. More generally, for any interest rate, i, the present value of \$1 payable in two years is

$$\text{PDV of \$1 payable in two years} = \$1/(1 + i)^2 \qquad [20A.15]$$

and for the case of a 5 percent interest rate

$$\begin{aligned}\text{PDV of \$1 payable in two years} &= \$1/(1.05)^2 \\ &= \$1/1.1025 \\ &= \$.907 \qquad [20A.16]\end{aligned}$$

General PDV Formulas

The pattern again should be obvious. With an interest rate of i, the present value of \$1 payable after any number of years, n, is simply

$$\text{PDV of \$1 payable in n years} = \$1/(1 + i)^n. \qquad [20A.17]$$

Calculating present values is the reverse of computing compound interest. In the compound interest case (Equation 20A.9) the calculation requires multiplying by the interest factor $(1 + i)^n$ whereas in the present discounted value case (Equation 20A.17) the calculation proceeds by dividing by that factor. Similarly, the present value of any number of dollars (\$D) payable in n years is given by:

$$\text{PDV of \$D payable in n years} = \$D/(1 + i)^n. \qquad [20A.18]$$

Again, by comparing Equations 20A.11 and 20A.18 you can see the different ways that the interest factor $(1 + i)^n$ enters into the calculations.

Table 20A.2
Present Discounted Value of $1 for Various Time Periods and Interest Rates

Year until Payment Is Received	Interest Rate			
	1 Percent	3 Percent	5 Percent	10 Percent
1	$.99010	$.97087	$.95238	$.90909
2	.98030	.94260	.90703	.82645
3	.97059	.91516	.86386	.75131
5	.95147	.86281	.78351	.62093
10	.90531	.74405	.61391	.38555
25	.78003	.47755	.29531	.09230
50	.60790	.22810	.08720	.00852
100	.36969	.05203	.00760	.00007

Note: These amounts are the reciprocals of those in Table 20A.1

In Table 20A.2 the author has again put his calculator to work to compute the present discounted value of $1 payable at various times and for various interest rates. The entries in this table are the reciprocals of the entries in Table 20A.1 since compounding and taking present values are different ways of looking at the same process. In Table 20A.2 the PDV of $1 payable in some particular year is smaller, the higher the interest rate. Similarly, for a given interest rate, the PDV of $1 is smaller the longer it is until the $1 will be paid. With a 10 percent interest rate, for example, a dollar that will not be paid for 50 years is worth less than one cent ($.00852) today. Application 20A.2: Zero-Coupon Bonds shows how such PDV calculations apply to a rapidly growing type of financial asset.

Discounting Payment Streams

Dollars payable at different points of time have different present values. One must be careful in calculating the true worth of streams of payments that occur at various times into the future—simply adding them up is not appropriate. Consider a situation that has irritated the author for some time. Many state lotteries promise grand prizes of $1 million (or, sometimes, much more) that they pay to the winners over 25 years. But $40,000 per year for 25 years is not "worth" $1 million. Indeed, at a 10 percent interest rate the present value of such a stream is only $363,200—much less than half the amount falsely advertised by the state. This section describes how such a calculation can be made. There is really nothing new to learn about discounting streams of payments—performing the calculations always involves making careful use of the general discounting formula in Equation 20A.18. However, repeated use of that formula may be very time consuming (if a stream of income is paid, say, at one hundred different times in the future), and our main purpose here is to present a few shortcuts.

APPLICATION 20A.2

Zero-Coupon Bonds

Federal Treasury bonds sometimes include coupons that promise the owner of the bond a certain semiannual interest payment. For example, a 30-year $1 million bond issued in 1990 with a 10 percent interest rate would include 60 semiannual coupons that represent the government's promise to pay $50,000 (that is, half of 10 percent of $1 million) on January 1 and July 1 of each year. The image of a Scrooge-like "coupon clipper" collecting regular interest payments in this way is a popular figure for financial cartoonists.

The Invention of Zero-Coupon Bonds

Unfortunately, this form of bond is not particularly convenient for investors. Bonds (and their attached coupons) may be lost, cashing the coupon necessitates a trip to the bank, and there is no easy way to reinvest interest payments to obtain the benefits of compounding. As a remedy for some of these problems, in the late 1970s some financial firms began to introduce *zero-coupon* bonds based on the Treasury obligations. These worked as follows: A brokerage firm would buy a bond (say, the $1 million bond described above). Then it would "strip" the coupons from the bond and sell these as separate investments. For example, it would sell a coupon representing a $50,000 interest payment on January 1, 2013, to an investor who wished to invest his or her funds until then.

Use of the PDV Formula

How much would such a stripped coupon be worth? The present discounted value formula gives the answer. If the interest rate is 10 percent, the present value of $50,000 payable in 2013 (23 years from January 1, 1990) is

$$\frac{\$50{,}000}{(1+i)^{23}} = \frac{\$50{,}000}{(1.10)^{23}} = \frac{\$50{,}000}{8.954} = \$5{,}583.$$

So the coupon would sell for $5,583 and would grow to nearly nine times this amount by 2013 when it was redeemed. Such a financial investment offers considerable advantages to an investor who does not want to be bothered with semiannual coupons, and zero-coupon bonds have proven to be quite popular.

To Think About

1. Does an investor who buys a zero-coupon bond have to leave his or her funds in that investment until the payment is due? Would someone who sells before this due date lose all interest earned? Are zero-coupon investments more risky than ordinary bonds?
2. Do the financial institutions offering zero-coupon bonds have to use Treasury coupons for their promises of future payments? Couldn't they just make the promises themselves and sell them in the market? What advantages are offered by using Treasury bond coupons as the basis for zero-coupon investments?

An Algebraic Presentation

Consider a stream of payments that promises $1 per year starting next year and continuing for three years. By applying Equation 20A.18 it is easy to see that the present value of this stream is

$$\text{PDV} = \frac{\$1}{1+i} + \frac{\$1}{(1+i)^2} + \frac{\$1}{(1+i)^3}. \qquad [20A.19]$$

If the interest rate is 5 percent, this value would be

$$\frac{\$1}{1.05} + \frac{\$1}{(1.05)^2} + \frac{\$1}{(1.05)^3} = \$.9523 + \$.9070 + \$.8639$$
$$= \$2.7232. \qquad [20A.20]$$

Consequently, just as for the lottery, $1 a year for three years is not worth $3, but quite a bit less because of the need to take forgone interest into account in making present value calculations.

If the promised stream of payments extends for longer than three years, additional terms should be added to Equation 20A.19. The present value of $1 per year for five years is

$$\text{PDV} = \frac{\$1}{1 + i} + \frac{\$1}{(1 + i)^2} + \frac{\$1}{(1 + i)^3} + \frac{\$1}{(1 + i)^4} + \frac{\$1}{(1 + i)^5}, \qquad [20A.21]$$

which amounts to about $4.33 at a 5 percent interest rate. Again, $1 per year for five years is not worth $5.

Equation 20A.21 can be generalized to any number of years (n) by just adding the correct number of terms:

$$\text{PDV} = \frac{\$1}{1 + i} + \frac{\$1}{(1 + i)^2} + \cdots + \frac{\$1}{(1 + i)^n}. \qquad [20A.22]$$

Table 20A.3 uses this formula to compute the value of $1 per year for various numbers of years and interest rates. Several features of the numbers in this table are important to keep in mind when discussing present values. As noted previously, none of the streams is worth in present value terms the actual number of dollars paid. The figures are always less than the number of years for which $1 will be paid. Even for low interest rates the difference is substantial. With a 3 percent interest rate, $1 per year for 100 years is worth only $31 in present value. At higher interest rates, the effect of discounting is even more pronounced. A dollar each year for 100 years is worth less than $10 in present value terms with an interest rate of 10 percent.

Perpetual Payments

The value of a stream of payments that goes on "forever" at $1 per year is reported as the final entry in each column of Table 20A.3. To understand how this is calculated, we can pose the question in a slightly different way. How much ($X) would you have to invest at an interest rate of i to yield $1 a year forever? That is, we wish to find $X that satisfies the equation

$$\$1 = i \cdot \$X. \qquad [20A.23]$$

But this just means that

$$\$X = \$1/i, \qquad [20A.24]$$

Table 20A.3
Present Value of $1 per Year for Various Time Periods and Interest Rates

Years of Payment	Interest Rate: 1 Percent	3 Percent	5 Percent	10 Percent
1	$ .99	$ .97	$ .95	$ .91
2	1.97	1.91	1.86	1.74
3	2.94	2.83	2.72	2.49
5	4.85	4.58	4.33	3.79
10	9.47	8.53	7.72	6.14
25	22.02	17.41	14.09	9.08
50	39.20	25.73	18.26	9.91
100	63.02	31.60	19.85	9.99
Forever	100.00	33.33	20.00	10.00

Perpetuity
A promise of a certain number of dollars each year, forever.

which is the way the entries in the table were computed. For example, the present value of $1 per year forever with an interest rate of 5 percent is $20 (= $1/.05). With an interest rate of 10 percent the figure would be $10 (= $1/.10). Such a permanent payment stream is called a **perpetuity**. Although these are technically illegal in the United States (although many people set up "permanent" endowments for cemetery plots, scholarships, and prize funds) other countries do permit such limitless contracts to be written. In the United Kingdom, for example, perpetuities originally written in the 1600s are still bought and sold. Equation 20A.24 shows that even though such perpetuities in effect promise an infinite number of dollars (since the payments never cease), in present value terms they have quite modest values. Indeed, for relatively high interest rates, there isn't much difference between getting $1 a year for 25 or 50 years and getting it forever. At an interest rate of 10 percent, for example, the present value of a perpetuity (which promises an infinite number of dollars) is only $.92 greater than a promise of a dollar a year for only 25 years. The infinite number of dollars to be received after year 25 are only worth $.92 today![4]

[4]Using the formula for perpetuities provides a simple way of computing streams that run for only a certain number of years. Suppose we wished to evaluate a stream of $1 per year for 25 years at a 10 percent interest rate. If we used Equation 20A.22, we would need to evaluate 25 terms. Instead, we could note that a 25-year stream is an infinite stream less all payments for year 26 and beyond. The present value of a perpetual stream is

$$\frac{\$1}{i} = \frac{\$1}{.10} = \$10$$

whereas the present value of a perpetual stream that starts in year 25 is

$$\frac{\$10}{(1 + i)^{25}} = \frac{\$10}{(1 + .10)^{25}} = \frac{\$10}{10.83} = \$.92.$$

The value of a 25-year stream is

$$\$10 - \$.92 = \$9.08,$$

which is the figure given in Table 20A.3.

More generally, a stream of $1 per year for n years at the interest rate i has a present value of

$$\text{PDV} = \frac{\$1}{i} - \frac{\$1/i}{(1 + i)^n}.$$

Varying Payment Streams

The present value of a payment stream that consists of a fixed number of dollars each year can be calculated by multiplying the value of \$1 per year by that amount. In the lottery illustration with which we began this section, for example, we calculated the present value of \$40,000 per year for 25 years. This is 40,000 times the entry for \$1 per year for 25 years at 10 percent from Table 20A.3—40,000 · \$9.08 = \$363,200. The present value of any other constant stream of dollar payments can be calculated in a similar fashion.

When payments vary from year to year, the computation can become more cumbersome. Each payment must be discounted separately using the formula given in Equation 20A.18. We can show this computation in its most general form by letting D_i represent the amount to be paid in any year i. Then the present value of this stream would be

$$PDV = \frac{D_1}{1 + i} + \frac{D_2}{(1 + i)^2} + \frac{D_3}{(1 + i)^3} + \cdots + \frac{D_n}{(1 + i)^n}. \quad [20A.25]$$

Here each D could be either positive or negative depending on whether funds are to be received or paid out. In some cases the computations may be rather complicated (as Application 20A.3: Mortgage Market Innovations illustrates) so it may be a good idea to get a calculator that does the drudgery for you.

Frequency of Compounding

So far we have talked only about interest payments that are compounded once a year. That is, interest is paid at the end of each year and does not itself start to earn interest until the next year begins. In the past that was how banks worked. Every January 1 depositors were expected to bring in their bank books so that the past year's interest could be added to them. People who withdrew money from the bank prior to January 1 often lost all the interest they had earned so far in the year.

Since the 1960s, however, banks and all other financial institutions have started to use more frequent, usually daily, compounding. This has provided some extra interest to investors, because more frequent compounding means that prior interest earned will begin itself to earn interest more quickly. In this section we use the tools we have developed so far to explore this issue.

As before, assume the annual interest rate is given by i (or in some of our examples 5 percent). But now suppose the bank agrees to pay interest two times a year—on January 1 and on July 1. If you deposit \$1 on January 1, by July 1 it will have grown to be \$1 · (1 + i/2) since you will have earned half a year's interest. With an interest rate of 5 percent, you will have \$1.025 on July 1. For the second half of the year you will earn interest on \$1.025, not just on \$1. At the end of the year you will have \$1.025 · 1.025 = \$1.05063, which is slightly larger than the \$1.05 you would have with an-

APPLICATION 20A.3

Mortgage Market Innovations

High interest rates since the late 1970s have made it very difficult for young people to afford to buy a house using an ordinary mortgage. With an ordinary mortgage, the borrower agrees to pay a fixed amount each month for the duration of the mortgage (usually 30 years). For example, with an interest rate of 10 percent a would-be buyer of a $100,000 home would have to pay $10,600 in annual mortgage payments ($883 per month) because the present value of $10,600 per year for 30 years is precisely the $100,000 needed to buy the house. Since such high mortgage payments may not be affordable by many young people—especially in the early years of trying to establish a family when their incomes are fairly low—they may seek alternative payment schedules that more closely meet their economic circumstances. It is important to understand the nature of the problem young people face. They are not "too poor" to afford a $100,000 house in any absolute sense. But, they are at an early stage in their careers when their earnings are low and are expected to grow. They also can reasonably expect the values of their homes to increase, if only they can get into the market in the first place.

In response to these needs, banks have devised mortgages with payment streams that more closely meet people's life patterns. There are, of course, an infinite number of possible payment streams that have a present value of $100,000 so there is plenty of room for innovations. Here we illustrate two of them.

Balloon Payments

With a balloon payment mortgage, some interest charges are pushed to the end of the mortgage in order to reduce monthly costs early in the mortgage. For example, a borrower can reduce his or her annual payments to about $8,800 ($733 per month) by agreeing to make a single balloon payment of $300,000 at the end of 30 years (presumably when the house will have appreciated substantially).

Graduated Payments

With a graduated payments scheme, mortgage payments will increase over time to reflect the borrower's increased earnings. For example, the borrower might agree to pay $7,000 per year for the first 10 years, $15,000 for the next 10 years, and $23,000 for the final 10 years and still get $100,000 currently to buy the house.

Numerous other schemes were devised during the early 1980s to further cushion the initial shock of mortgage payments. As interest rates fell in the middle of the decade, the attractiveness of these innovations declined as people seemed to prefer a fixed payment scheme. By the end of the decade, however, mortgage rates were again rising and various mortgage innovations began to reappear.

To Think About

1. Doesn't paying $300,000 at the end of 30 years seem like a huge amount to save only $2,000 per year in mortgage payments? Explain why the balloon payment has to be so large to obtain a sizable reduction in payments.
2. Why don't people always opt for graduated payment schemes (assuming their incomes will grow)? Why might people want to spend a higher fraction of their income on housing when they are young than when they are old? Does the desire for fixed payments come more from lenders than borrowers?

nual compounding. More generally, with an interest rate of i, semiannual compounding would yield

$$\$1(i + 1/2)(1 + i/2) = \$1(1 + i/2)^2 \quad [20A.26]$$

at the end of one year. That this is superior to annual compounding can be shown with simple algebra:

$$\begin{aligned} \$1 \cdot (1 + i/2)^2 &= \$1(1 + i + i^2/4) \\ &= \$1 \cdot (1 + i) + \$1 \cdot i^2/4, \end{aligned} \quad [20A.27]$$

Table 20A.4
Value of $1 at a 5 Percent Annual Interest Rate Compounded with Different Frequencies and Terms

Years on Deposit	Frequency			
	Annual	Semiannual	Monthly	Daily
1	$ 1.0500	$ 1.0506	$ 1.0512	$ 1.0513
2	1.1025	1.1038	1.1049	1.1052
3	1.1576	1.1596	1.1615	1.1618
5	1.2763	1.2801	1.2834	1.2840
10	1.6289	1.6386	1.6471	1.6487
25	3.3863	3.4371	3.4816	3.4900
50	11.4674	11.8137	12.1218	12.1803
100	131.5013	139.5639	146.9380	148.3607

which is clearly greater than $1 · (1 + i). The final term in Equation 20A.27 simply reflects the interest earned in the first half of the year $1 · (i/2) times the interest rate in the second half of the year (i/2). This is the bonus earned by semiannual compounding.

We could extend this algebraic discussion to more frequent compounding—quarterly, monthly, or daily—but little new information would be added. More frequent compounding would continue to increase the effective yield that the 5 percent annual interest rate actually provides. Table 20A.4 shows how the frequency of compounding has this effect over time periods of various durations. The gains of using monthly rather than annual compounding are relatively large, especially over long periods of time when small differences in effective yields can make a big difference. Gains in going from monthly to daily compounding are fairly small, however. The extra yield from compounding even more frequently (every second?) are even smaller.[5] Most banks currently utilize daily compounding both because they have been forced to do so by competitive pressures and because they find it fairly easy to adapt computer programs to make such payments.

Calculating Yields

The compound interest formulas we have introduced so far can be easily reversed to solve for the interest return promised on an investment if the payments and the investment's present value are known. As a very simple example, suppose someone promises to give you $105 in one year if you give them $100 today. Obviously, the interest rate promised here (what is more

[5]An approximation to daily compounding is provided by the instantaneous compounding formula

$$\text{Value of \$1 in year } n = e^{in},$$

where i is the annual interest rate and e is the base of natural logarithms (= 2.71828...). For an explanation, see Walter Nicholson, *Microeconomic Theory: Basic Principles and Extensions,* 4th ed. (Hinsdale, Ill.: Dryden Press, 1989), pp. 700–703.

Yield
The interest rate at which the present discounted value of the returns from an investment are exactly equal to the investment's current cost.

formally called the **yield**) is 5 percent. By comparing this yield to the yield on other investment options available, you can decide whether to give your \$100 to this person.

In general, if an investment promises to pay D dollars n years from now and will charge you P dollars for this promise, we can use Equation 20A.18 to write

$$P = D/(1 + i)^n, \qquad [20A.28]$$

but now we wish to solve this equation for the yield, i. To find the yield on a promise of, say, \$1,000 in 10 years that costs \$400 today, we would write

$$\$400 = \$1{,}000/(1 + i)^{10} \qquad [20A.29]$$

and manipulate this expression to solve for i:

$$(1 + i)^{10} = \$1{,}000/\$400 = 2.5$$

or

$$1 + i = (2.5)^{1/10}. \qquad [20A.30]$$

At this stage you will need either a calculator or a set of yield tables since raising numbers to strange exponential powers is not easy to do by hand. Performing such a calculation gives

$$1 + i = (2.5)^{1/10} = 1.096 \qquad [20A.31]$$

or

$$i = .096. \qquad [20A.32]$$

So this investment has a yield of 9.6 percent.

More Complex Cases

In more complex cases investments will often promise different payments in various future periods, and the rights to these payments can be purchased for some present cost. For example, when a firm buys a machine, it is really purchasing the right to the stream of future profits that the machine generates. Calculating the yield (or what is sometimes called the *internal rate of return*) on such an investment again requires use of the present value formulas introduced earlier. Suppose that an automobile repair shop is thinking of buying an electronic engine tester that costs \$10,000. The shop will earn \$2,000 each year on this tester and will be able to sell it for \$5,000 in five years when a new model becomes available. What is the yield from buying the tester? Using the present value formula from Equation 20A.25 gives

$$\$10{,}000 = \frac{\$2{,}000}{1+i} + \frac{\$2{,}000}{(1+i)^2} + \frac{\$2{,}000}{(1+i)^3} + \frac{\$2{,}000}{(1+i)^4} + \frac{\$2{,}000}{(1+i)^5} + \frac{\$5{,}000}{(1+i)^5} \quad [20A.33]$$

—that is, the present cost of the tester (\$10,000) should be equated to the present value of \$2,000 per year for five years plus the present value of the price the machine will bring when it is sold.

Solving Equation 20A.33 by hand for the yield, i, is no simple task, but it can easily be done by modern calculators. The author's calculator provides a solution of $i = 12.15$ percent as the yield on this testing machine. The repair shop can compare this yield to that available on other equipment it might buy or to the return banks are offering to decide whether to purchase the tester. Making such yield calculations therefore offers a convenient way of comparing the returns available from alternative investments that may provide very different payment streams. Our example in Chapter 20 about the economist and the car dealer shows how these kinds of calculations can provide valuable information to would-be users of credit.

Summary

This appendix surveys the mathematical calculations that surround compound interest concepts. Dollars payable at different points in time are not equally valuable (since those payable in the distant future require the sacrifice of some potential interest), and it is important to be careful in making comparisons among alternative payment schedules. In discussing this issue we show that:

- In making compound interest calculations, it is necessary to take account of interest that is paid on prior interest earned. The interest factor $(1 + i)^n$—where n is the number of years over which interest is compounded—reflects this compounding.
- Dollars payable in the future are worth less than dollars payable currently. To compare dollars that are payable at different dates requires using present discounted value computations to allow for the opportunity costs associated with forgone interest.
- Evaluating payment streams requires that each individual payment be discounted by the appropriate interest factor. It is incorrect simply to add together dollars payable at different times.
- More frequent compounding leads to higher effective returns since prior interest paid begins to earn interest more quickly. There is an upper limit to the increased yield provided, however.
- The present discounted value formula can also be used to calculate yields on investments. The availability of such yields provides a convenient way to compare alternative investments in which the actual payment streams may be quite different.

PART 7

LIMITS OF THE MARKET

Prior sections of this book have focused at length on the ways in which markets allocate resources. Although the equilibria described were not always efficient, they were arrived at through some type of interaction of the forces of supply and demand. Only on a few occasions (for example, in our discussion of the regulation of natural monopolies) have we analyzed how nonmarket actors (for example, government regulators) might affect observed outcomes. In this final part, we will move away somewhat from our examination of market forces and explore some situations where nonmarket influences may be quite important. We will show that, for some allocational questions, markets will perform relatively poorly and other economic institutions (most importantly, the government) may play decisive, though not necessarily better, allocational roles.

Chapter 21 addresses problems raised by goods that have externality or spillover effects. For these goods simple market transactions may not accurately reflect all of the economic consequences of consumption and production—some misallocations of resources may occur. In Chapter 21 we first look at externalities between two specific economic actors such as a manufacturing firm that harms nearby residents because it pollutes the air. We show how this situation can be viewed as a failure to define property rights fully and how full specification of such rights may improve the resulting allocation of resources. In some cases, however, such a full specification of property rights may be very costly and, as we show, some form of regulation may be preferable.

Chapter 22, the final chapter in this book, focuses on goods that benefit a large number of individuals who cannot be prevented from receiving such benefits. These goods are called "public goods." Besides examining in detail the attributes of such goods, we also investigate some of the problems involved in achieving an efficient level of output for them. In particular, we look at public choice theory which is in part concerned with modeling the operation of voting for governmental decisions when many other allocational decisions are made using market mechanisms. We show that the Pareto optimality of voting procedures is open to question in many important cases. ▲

CHAPTER 21

Externalities and Property Rights

Externalities are effects of the actions of one economic actor on other actors that are not adequately reflected in the market. A manufacturing plant that pollutes the air causing serious health problems for people nearby is creating such an externality. Our goal in this chapter is to analyze why markets may fail to allocate resources efficiently in this situation. We also show various ways in which the problems posed by externalities can be controlled. More generally, our study of externalities provides insights into the nature and problems of private property; the issue of property rights and how they influence the allocation of resources is an underlying theme of this chapter.

Defining Externalities

Externality
The effect of one party's economic activities on another party that is not taken into account by the price system.

Before launching into a detailed analysis, we should be precise in defining exactly what an externality is, since there has been substantial confusion over this point in economics. An **externality** is an effect of one economic actor's activities on another actor's well-being that is not taken into account by the normal operations of the price system. This definition stresses the direct, nonmarket effect of one actor on another such as soot falling out of the air or toxic chemicals appearing in drinking water. The definition does not include effects that take place through the market. If I buy an item that is on sale before you do, I may keep you from getting it and thereby affect your well-being. That is not an externality in our sense because the effect took place in a market setting.[1] Its occurrence does not necessarily affect the ability of markets to allocate resources efficiently. Before examining why true externalities may distort the allocation of resources, our definition may be made more concrete by giving a few examples.

Examples of Externalities

Externalities can occur between any two economic actors. Here we first illustrate negative (harmful) and positive (beneficial) externalities between firms. We then examine externalities between people and firms and conclude by considering a few externalities between people.

Externalities between Firms

Consider two firms—one producing eyeglasses, another producing charcoal (this is an actual example from nineteenth-century English law). The production of charcoal is said to have an external effect on the production of eyeglasses if the output of eyeglasses depends not only on the amount of inputs chosen by the eyeglass firm but also on the level at which the production of charcoal is carried on. Suppose these two firms are located near each other, and the eyeglass firm is downwind from the charcoal firm. In this case, the output of eyeglasses may depend not only on the level of inputs the eyeglass firm uses itself but also on the amount of charcoal in the air, which affects its precision grinding wheels. The level of pollutants, in turn, is determined by the output of the charcoal firm. Increases in charcoal output would cause fewer high-quality eyeglasses to be produced even though the eyeglass firm has no control over this negative effect.[2]

The relationship between two firms may also be beneficial. Most examples of positive externalities are rather bucolic in nature. Perhaps the most famous, proposed by James Meade, involves two firms, one producing honey by raising bees and the other producing apples.[3] Because the bees feed on apple blossoms, an increase in apple production will improve productivity in the honey industry. The beneficial effects of having well-fed bees is a positive externality to the beekeeper. Similarly, bees pollinate apple crops and the beekeeper provides an external benefit to the orchard owner. Later in this chapter we examine this situation in greater detail since, surprisingly enough, the beekeeper–apple grower relationship has played an important role in economic research on the significance of externalities.

---

[1]Sometimes such effects are called "pecuniary" externalities to distinguish them from the "technological" externalities we will be discussing.

[2]We will find it necessary to redefine the assumption of "no control" considerably as the analysis of this chapter proceeds.

[3]James Meade, "External Economies and Diseconomies in a Competitive Situation," *Economic Journal* (March 1952): 54–67.

Externalities between Firms and People

Firms' productive activities may impact directly on individuals' well-being. A firm that produces air pollution imposes costs on people living near the firm in the form of ill health and increased dust and grime. Similar effects arise from firms' pollution of water (for example, mining firms that dump their waste into Lake Superior, reducing the lake's recreational value to people who wish to fish there), misuse of land (strip mining that is an eyesore and may interfere with water supplies), and production of noise (airports that are located near major cities). In all of these cases, at least on first inspection, it seems that firms will not take any of these external costs into consideration when making decisions on how much to produce.

Of course, people may also have external effects on firms. Drivers' auto pollution harms the productivity of citrus growers, cleaning up litter and graffiti is a major expense for shopping centers, and the noise of Saturday night rock concerts on college campuses probably affects motel rentals. In each of these cases, as for the cases of externalities produced by firms, there may be no simple way for the affected parties to force the people who generate the externalities to take the full costs of their actions into account.

Externalities between People

Finally, the activity of one person may affect the well-being of someone else. Playing a radio too loud, smoking cigars, or driving during peak hours are all consumption activities that may negatively affect the utility of others. Planting an attractive garden or shoveling the snow off one's sidewalk may, on the other hand, provide beneficial externalities. Often, however, these activities will not be reflected in market transactions among the people involved.

Reciprocal Nature of Externalities

Although these examples of externalities picture one actor as the cause of the problem and some other actor as the helpless victim (or beneficiary), that is not in fact the case. By definition, externalities require (at least) two parties and in a sense each should be regarded as the "cause." If the producer of eyeglasses had not located its factory near the charcoal furnace, it would not have suffered any negative effects on its grinding wheels; if individuals didn't live below airport flight paths, noise would only be a minor problem; and if you were out of earshot, it wouldn't matter that someone else had the radio's volume turned up. Recognizing these reciprocal relationships is not intended to exonerate polluters, only to clarify the nature of the problem. In all of these cases two economic actors are seeking to use the same resource, and (as we illustrate in Application 21.1) there are no unambiguous economic principles for deciding whose claim is stronger. Rather, as we shall see, in studying

APPLICATION 21.1

Reciprocal Effects of Externalities, Past and Present

Sometimes the reciprocal effects of externalities are made explicit in the law. Legal doctrine is constantly evolving as such interrelationships become more apparent. This is illustrated by two important concerns occurring nearly one hundred years apart.

Steam Engines and Crops

As railroads spread throughout the English countryside in the latter part of the nineteenth century, they began to have a variety of effects on the environment. Cultivation moved toward rail lines since they promised reduced transportation costs for crops. At the same time, however, the steam engines of the day tended to spew sparks and cinders over the landscape, thereby posing the threat of fire. As such interactions along rail lines became more frequent, a body of common law developed to sort out legal liability in various instances.

A. C. Pigou was one of the first economists to explore the train-crops relationship in detail. In his view, the operators of steam engines were at fault and should be held liable for any damage done. R. M. Coase attacked this conclusion in his famous article on social cost by pointing out that as early as 1860 railroads had been granted exemption from such liability, possibly because Parliament recognized the reciprocal nature of the externality and found it preferable to encourage the growth of railroads.[1] One side effect of such a stance was to discourage cultivation along rail right-of-ways, thereby minimizing the number of accidental fires. By not getting embroiled in a fruitless pursuit of who was "at fault" in this situation, Parliament may have improved the allocation of resources.

[1]For a complete discussion, see R. M. Coase, "The Problem of Social Cost," *Journal of Law and Economics* (October 1960): 1–44.

Anti-Smoking Laws

A modern-day equivalent of the railroad sparks question is the debate over cigarette smoke. Again, the situation is a reciprocal one—both smokers and nonsmokers wish to use the air around them. Although it may be difficult for nonsmokers to admit, their demand for fresh air has no more intrinsic worth than does the smoker's demand for the right to enjoy his or her habit unencumbered.

Despite this symmetry, government at all levels has been adopting increasingly more stringent rules about smoking. In many localities, smoking is banned in public places, federal law bans smoking on all flights shorter than two hours, and laws are starting to appear that guarantee a "smoke-free" workplace. Through all of this, smokers have been relatively docile in yielding their rights. Perhaps the anti-smoking laws represent a relatively efficient way of defining matters since those who can most easily change their behavior are being asked to do so (it is, for example, easier for a smoker not to smoke on a plane flight than it is for a nonsmoker to exit the plane). In establishing such laws, the government is not necessarily adopting a position about whose rights are more "worthy." Rather, it is deciding how the air can be used best.

To Think About

1. Isn't the idea of reciprocal externalities fairly farfetched in some situations? How can the victims of toxic waste disposal (such as homeowners at Love Canal) in a chemical dumpsite, for example, be assigned blame for what is happening to them?
2. Should colleges and universities impose a no smoking rule in classrooms and dormitories? How are objections to smoking handled without such a ban? Would matters be improved with administrative action?

externalities it is important to understand their reciprocal nature and how this affects the allocation of resources. In this way we can explore how various ways of coping with externalities may affect the behavior of all of the parties involved.

Externalities, Markets, and Allocational Efficiency

It has traditionally been argued that the presence of externalities such as those we have just described can cause a market to operate inefficiently. We discussed the reasons for this briefly in Chapter 13, and will repeat these reasons here using the example of eyeglass and charcoal producers. Production of eyeglasses is assumed to produce no externalities, but is assumed to be negatively affected by the level of charcoal output. We now show that resources may be allocated inefficiently in this situation. Remember that for an allocation of resources to be efficient it is required that price be equal to social marginal cost in each market (see Chapter 13 for a discussion of this point). If the market for eyeglasses is perfectly competitive (as we assume both markets to be), their price will indeed be equal to this good's private marginal cost. Since there are no externalities in eyeglass production, there is no need to make a distinction between private and social marginal cost in this case.

Social costs
Costs of production that include both input costs and costs of the externalities that production may cause.

For charcoal production, the story is more complex. The producer of charcoal will still produce that output for which price is equal to private marginal cost. This is a direct result of the profit-maximization assumption. However, because of the negative effect that production of charcoal has on eyeglass production, it will not be true that private and social marginal costs of charcoal production are equal. Rather, the true **social cost** of charcoal production is equal to the private cost *plus* the cost that charcoal production imposes on eyeglass firms in terms of reduced or inferior output. The charcoal-producing firm does not recognize this effect and produces where price is equal to private marginal cost (which in this case is lower than social marginal cost). Since now the social marginal cost of charcoal production exceeds charcoal's price, this is a clear sign that too much charcoal is being produced. Society would be made better-off by reallocating resources away from charcoal production and toward the production of other goods (including eyeglasses). In this case, at least as we have described it so far, relying on the operation of competitive markets (and the self-interest of the charcoal firm) has not produced an efficient allocation of resources. Because of the externality in charcoal production, prices no longer carry the correct information about marginal costs that is necessary to achieve efficiency.

A Graphic Demonstration

Figure 21.1 illustrates the possible misallocation of resources that results from the externality in charcoal production. Assuming that the charcoal producer is a price taker, the demand curve for its output is simply a horizontal

Figure 21.1
An Externality in Charcoal Production Causes an Inefficient Allocation of Resources

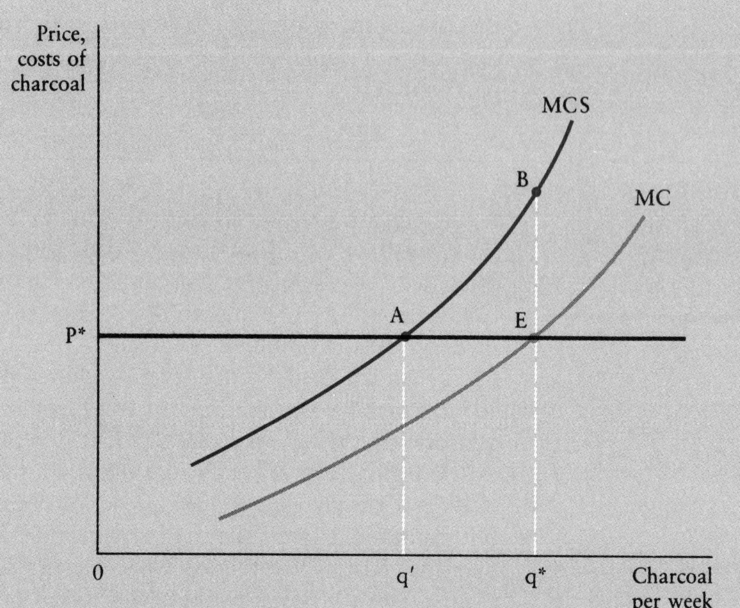

Because production of charcoal imposes external costs on eyeglass makers, social marginal costs (MCS) exceed private marginal costs (MC). In a competitive market the firm would produce q* at a price of P*. At q*, however, MCS > P* and resource allocation could be improved by reducing output to q′.

line at the prevailing market price (say, P*). Profits are maximized at q* where price is equal to the private marginal cost of producing charcoal (MC). Because of the externality that charcoal production imposes on eyeglass makers, however, the social marginal cost of this production (MCS) exceeds MC as shown in Figure 21.1. The vertical gap between the MCS and the MC curves is a measure of the harm that producing an extra unit of charcoal imposes on eyeglass makers. At q*, the social marginal cost of producing charcoal exceeds the price people are willing to pay for this output (P*). Resources are misallocated, and production should be reduced to q′ where social marginal cost and price are equal. In making this reduction, total social costs (area ABq*q′) are reduced to a greater extent than is total spending on charcoal (given by area AEq*q′). This comparison shows how the allocation of resources is improved by a reduction in charcoal output since costs are reduced to a greater extent than are consumers' expenditures on charcoal. Consumers can reallocate their spending toward something else that involves lower social costs than charcoal does. Now we examine various ways in which this desirable reduction in charcoal output might be brought about.

Traditional Solutions to the Externality Problem

To study possible solutions to the problems that externalities pose for the allocation of resources, we will first assume that production techniques are fixed.[4] Under this assumption, prescriptions such as "force charcoal producers to use alternative production techniques that yield less soot" are outside the frame of analysis. Later in this chapter we will look at such other ways of coping with externalities, but to do so here would obscure the issue of how the charcoal producer can be prompted to reduce output. Even in this limited case, there are still three approaches that may bring about reduced output—taxation, merger, and bargaining.

Taxation

By imposing a suitable excise tax on the firm generating an externality, the government can cause the output of this firm to be reduced—thereby shifting resources into other uses. This classic remedy to the externality problem was first lucidly put forward in the 1920s by A. C. Pigou.[5] Although it has been somewhat modified, it remains one of the "standard" answers given by economists. The central problem for regulators becomes one of obtaining sufficient empirical information so that the correct tax structure can be enacted.

The taxation solution is illustrated in Figure 21.2. Again, MC and MCS represent the private and social marginal costs of charcoal production, and the market price of charcoal is given by P^*. An excise tax of amount t (see Chapter 11) would reduce the net price received by the firm to $P^* - t$, and at that price the firm would choose to produce q'. The tax causes the firm to reduce its output to the socially optimal amount. At q' the firm incurs private marginal costs of $P^* - t$ and imposes external costs on eyeglass makers of t per unit. The per-unit tax is therefore exactly equal to the extra costs that charcoal producers impose on eyeglass producers.[6] Application 21.2 shows

---

[4]It is also assumed that the detrimental effects of the production of charcoal do not affect anyone else in the economy other than eyeglass producers. Similarly, our discussion of externalities takes place within a partial equilibrium framework in which the rest of the economy is assumed to be perfectly competitive.

[5]A. C. Pigou, *The Economics of Welfare,* 4th ed. (London: Macmillan, 1946). Pigou also stressed the desirability of providing subsidies to firms that produce beneficial externalities. More recent literature has stressed that such taxes and subsidies must be based directly on the costs (or benefits) of the externalities (rather than on the total costs of the goods themselves) if efficiency is to be achieved. Later in this chapter we show this result.

[6]If the charcoal firm here represents an entire industry, then the tax would, as in Chapter 11, raise the market price of charcoal. If the industry exhibited constant costs, in the long run price would rise by the exact amount of the tax and demand would be reduced to the socially optimal level by that price rise. In this case the tax would be fully paid by charcoal consumers in the long run. If charcoal production exhibited increasing costs, some portion of the Pigovian tax would be paid by suppliers of inputs to the charcoal industry.

APPLICATION 21.2

Power Plant Emissions and Acid Rain

Electric power plants that burn coal emit a variety of unhealthy by-products, most importantly sulfur. Existing environmental regulations require such power plants to achieve certain emission standards, mainly by "scrubbing" the coal fumes in their exhaust stacks. Since that process is very costly, a number of economists and other observers have suggested that taxing sulfur emissions might obtain the same results at much lower resource costs. For example, an early proposal by Wisconsin senator William Proxmire would have taxed sulfur emissions at an initial rate of 5 cents per pound, with the rate rising to 20 cents over a period of years. By providing utilities with an incentive to shift to lower sulfur coal, this plan would have substantially mitigated the need for scrubbing.

Effects of an Emissions Tax

A. Schlottmann and L. Abrams attempted to estimate the effects of the tax proposed by Proxmire on both coal production and sulfur emissions in the United States.[1] A summary of their results is presented in Table 1. Overall, the authors estimated that a 5 cent per pound tax would reduce annual sulfur emissions by about 1 million tons (a 12 percent reduction), with the 20 cent tax leading to nearly a 5 million ton reduction (a greater than 40 percent reduction). These reductions came partly from a reduced level of coal use and partly from a shift in coal supplies from regions with high sulfur content coal (parts of Appalachia and the Midwest) to regions with low sulfur content coal (the West). These changes would have imposed additional costs on utilities both because of the need to switch to imported oil as a fuel and because of the increased costs involved in transporting coal. Such costs may be rather small compared to alternative ways of dealing with sulfur or to the health hazards involved in continuing high levels of sulfur emissions.

Table 1
Estimated Effects of a Tax on Sulfur Emissions and Coal Production

	Tax per Pound				
	0¢	5¢	10¢	15¢	20¢
Emissions (millions of tons)	11.4	10.0	8.5	7.5	6.7
Coal production (millions of tons)					
Appalachia	308	301	292	277	259
Midwest	150	135	93	89	78
West	49	56	74	84	90
U.S. total	507	492	459	450	427

Source: A. Schlottmann and L. Abrams, "Sulfur Emissions Taxes and Coal Resources," *Review of Economics and Statistics* (February 1977): 50–55; Tables 2 and 3.

[1]A. Schlottmann and L. Abrams, "Sulfur Emissions Taxes and Coal Resources," *Review of Economics and Statistics* (February 1977): 50–55.

Pigovian tax
A tax or subsidy on an externality that brings about an equality of private and social marginal costs.

how such a **Pigovian tax** might work in practice as a partial solution to the problem of electric power plant emissions.

Merger and Internalization

A second traditional cure for the allocational problems caused by externalities between two firms would be for these firms to merge. If there were a

The Acid Rain Debate

During the 1980s the debate over power plant emissions came to focus more explicitly on the problem of "acid rain." Evidence of increasing levels of acidity in lakes in the northeastern United States and Canada suggested (though by no means proved) that sulfur emissions from midwestern power plants were having greater effects than had previously been believed. Environmentalists were quick to adopt the image of "acid" falling from the sky to argue for much stricter controls on electric power generation.

Unfortunately, the debate over what to do about acid rain quickly became mired in both scientific and political controversy. On the scientific level, there is relatively little long-term data with which to test the acid rain hypothesis. Comparisons among various areas of the country also pose problems since it is very difficult to identify two areas that are similar in every respect except this exposure to power plant emissions. One major government assessment concludes that "about half" of all the lakes in sensitive areas might acidify if subjected to enough pollutants, but that conclusion is at best only a guess based on very imperfect extrapolations.[2]

Because the benefits and costs of policies to reduce sulfur emissions would be unevenly distributed among regions of the country, the politics of acid rain is even more complex than the scientific issues. The basic problem is that power plants in the midwestern states of Illinois, Indiana, Michigan, and Ohio are the major source of sulfur dioxide emissions, but the northeastern states would be the major beneficiaries of a program to reduce those emissions. Most proposed plans for dealing with acid rain take no account of such differences, but instead stress the adoption of national emission standards or national taxes on coal. Because such approaches do not focus on areas where emissions pose the greatest danger, they may not be economically efficient.[3] But they probably reflect the only political consensus that is possible. Once legislators' reelection needs come into play, economic considerations usually take a back seat.

To Think About

1. Would an excise tax on coal have the same effect as a tax on sulfur emissions? How would such a tax affect utilities' choices of inputs? Relative to the emissions tax, how would an excise tax affect utility firms' willingness to invest in antipollution equipment?
2. Suppose the sole goal of an anti-acid rain policy were to reduce the danger to rivers and lakes in the northeastern United States. How should an emissions tax be structured to achieve that goal? Why wouldn't a uniform tax do as well?

[2]U.S. Congress, Office of Technology Assessment, *Acid Rain and Transported Air Pollutants: Implications for Public Policy* (Washington, D.C.: U.S. Government Printing Office, 1984).

[3]See R. W. Crandall, *Controlling Industrial Pollution: The Economics and Politics of Clean Air* (Washington, D.C.: The Brookings Institution, 1983).

single firm producing both charcoal and eyeglasses, this firm would recognize the detrimental effect that charcoal production has on its glass-grinding equipment. In effect, the combined firm would now pay the full social marginal costs of charcoal production because it now incurs these costs directly. In other words, the firm's manager would now take the marginal cost curve for charcoal production to be MCS and would produce q', where price equals this marginal cost. This is exactly what is required for efficiency.

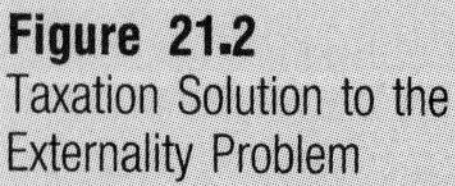

Figure 21.2
Taxation Solution to the Externality Problem

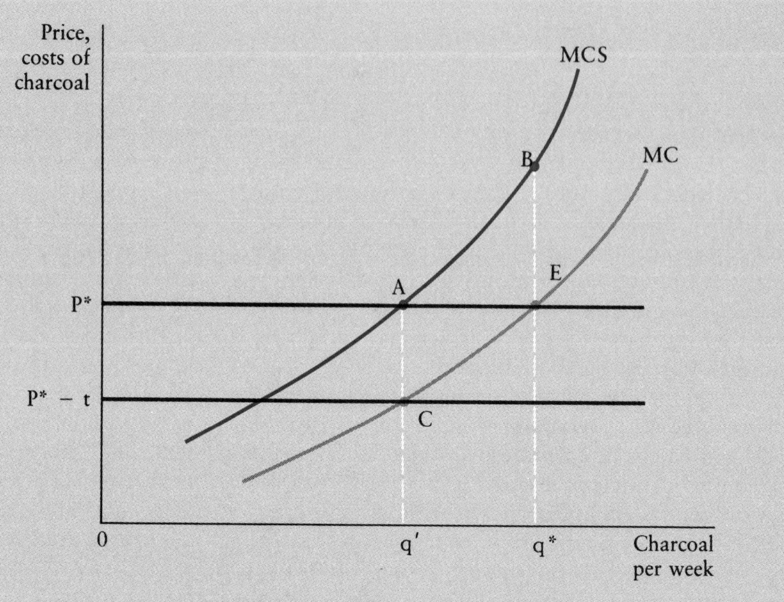

An excise tax of amount t would reduce the net price of charcoal to P* − t. At that price the firm would choose to produce the socially optimal level of charcoal output (q′).

Internalization of an externality Incorporation of the social marginal costs of an externality into an economic actor's decisions (as through taxation or merger).

Economists would say that the externality in production has been **internalized** as a result of the merger.

Bargaining

One important question we might still ask about this analysis is if the charcoal producer's actions impose a cost on the eyeglass maker, why doesn't the eyeglass maker "bribe" the charcoal firm to cut back on its output? Presumably the gain of a cutback to the eyeglass firm (the reduction in eyeglass costs is given by area ABEC in Figure 21.2) would exceed the loss of profits to charcoal makers (area AEC in the figure), and some bargaining arrangement might be worked out that would monetarily benefit both parties. Both firms would be irrational not to recognize such a possibility, and it would seem that the benefits of internalization could be obtained without actually going through a merger. After all, people do bargain with their neighbors about loud music or maintaining the yard. Such bargaining between economic actors might therefore be a third way to attain efficiency. Because this possibility suggests that the externality problem may, in some cases, "cure itself," we will examine it in a bit more detail.

Property Rights, Bargaining, and the Coase Theorem

To explore the bargaining issue further, we need to introduce the concept of property rights to show how these rights might be traded voluntarily between the two firms. Simply put, **property rights** are the legal specification of who owns a good and of the types of trades that the current owner is allowed to make. Some goods may be defined as **common property** that is owned by society at large and may be used by anyone; others may be defined as **private property** that is owned by specific people. Private property may either be *exchangeable* or *nonexchangeable,* depending on whether the good in question may or may not be traded to someone else. In this book we have been primarily concerned with exchangeable private property, and we will consider these types of property rights here.[7]

Property rights
The legal specification of who owns a good and the trades the owner is allowed to make with it.

Common property
Property that may be used by anyone without cost.

Private property
Property that is owned by specific people who may prevent others from using it.

Costless Bargaining and the Free Market

For the purposes of the charcoal-eyeglass externality, it is interesting to consider the nature of the property right that might be attached to the air shared by the charcoal and eyeglass firms. Suppose property rights were defined so as to give sole rights to use of the air to one of the firms, but that the firms were free to bargain over exactly how the air might be used. At first, you might think that if rights to the air were given to the charcoal producer, pollution would result, whereas if rights were given to the eyeglass firm, the air would remain pure and grinding machines would work properly. This might not be the case since your snap conclusion disregards the bargains that might be reached by the two parties. Indeed, several authors have argued that if *bargaining is costless,* the two parties left on their own will arrive at the efficient output (q'), and this result will be true regardless of who "owns" the rights to use the air.

Ownership by the Polluting Firm

Suppose the charcoal firm owns the right to use the air as it wishes. It must then add the costs (if any) related to this ownership into its total costs. What are the costs associated with air ownership? Again the opportunity cost notion provides the answer. For the charcoal firm, the costs of using the air as a dumping place for its dust are what someone else is willing to pay for this resource in its best alternative use. In our example, only the eyeglass maker has some alternative uses for the air (to keep it clean), and the amount that this

[7]Two important examples of privately owned goods that are not exchangeable are a person's human capital (this could be sold only in a society that permitted slavery) and a person's vote (a private good that is provided by the state).

firm would be willing to pay for clean air is precisely equal to the external damage done by charcoal pollution. If the charcoal firm calculates its costs correctly, its marginal cost curve (including the implicit cost of air use rights) becomes MCS in Figure 21.2. The firm will therefore produce q' and sell the remaining air use rights to the eyeglass maker for a fee of some amount between AEC (the lost profits from producing q' rather than q^* tons of charcoal) and ABEC (the maximum amount the eyeglass maker would pay to avoid having charcoal output increased from q' to q^*).

Ownership by the Injured Firm

A similar result would occur if eyeglass makers owned the rights to use the air as they pleased. In this case the charcoal producer would be willing to pay up to its total profits for the right to pollute the air (assuming, as we have all along, that there is no less damaging way to make charcoal). The eyeglass maker will accept these payments as long as they exceed the costs imposed on it by the charcoal firm's pollution. The ultimate result of bargaining will be for the charcoal firm to offer a payment for the right to "use" the air to dispose of the amount of soot and ash associated with output level q'. The eyeglass maker will not sell the rights to undertake any further pollution into "its" air because what the charcoal firm would be willing to pay (P − MC) falls short of the cost of this additional pollution (MCS − MC). Again, as when the charcoal firm had the property rights for air usage, an efficient allocation can be reached by relying on voluntary bargaining between the two firms. In both situations some production of charcoal takes place, and there will therefore be some air pollution. Having no charcoal output (and no pollution) would be inefficient in the same sense that producing q^* is—scarce resources would not be efficiently allocated. In this case there is some "optimal level" of air pollution that may be achieved through bargains between the firms involved.

The Coase Theorem

We have shown that the two firms left on their own can arrive at the efficient output level (q'). Assuming that bargaining is costless, both parties will recognize the advantages of striking a deal. Each will be led by the "invisible hand" to the same output level that would be achieved through an ideal merger. That solution will be reached no matter how the property rights associated with air use are assigned. The pollution-producing firm has exactly the same incentives to choose an efficient output level as does the injured firm. The ability of the two firms to bargain freely causes the true social costs

Coase theorem
If bargaining is costless, the social cost of an externality will be taken into account by the parties, and the allocation of resources will be the same no matter how property rights are assigned.

of the externality to be recognized by each in its decisions. This result is sometimes referred to as the **Coase theorem** after the economist Ronald Coase, who first proposed it in this form.[8]

Distributional Effects

There are distributional effects that do depend on who is assigned the property rights to use the air. If the charcoal firm is given the air rights, it will get the fee paid by the eyeglass maker, which will make the charcoal producer at least as well off as it was producing q^*. If the eyeglass firm gets the rights, it will receive a fee for air use that at least covers the damage the air pollution does. Because, according to the Coase result, the final allocation of resources will be unaffected by the way in which property rights are assigned,[9] any assessment of the desirability of the various possibilities might be made on equity grounds. For example, if the owners of the charcoal firm were very wealthy and those who make eyeglasses were poor, we might argue that ownership of the air use rights should be given to eyeglass makers on the basis of distributional equity. If the situation were reversed, one could argue for giving the charcoal firm the rights. The price system may often be capable of solving problems in the allocation of resources caused by externalities, but, as always, it will not necessarily achieve equitable solutions.[10] Such issues of equity in the assignment of property rights arise in every allocational decision, not only in the study of externalities, however.

The Role of Bargaining Costs

The result of the Coase theorem depends crucially on the assumption of zero bargaining costs. If the costs (real or psychological) of striking bargains were high, the workings of this voluntary exchange system might not be capable of achieving an efficient result. In the next section we examine an important type of externality for which bargaining costs are indeed quite high—

---

[8]See Ronald Coase, "The Problem of Social Cost," *Journal of Law and Economics* (October 1960): 1–44.

[9]Assuming that the wealth effects of how property rights are assigned do not affect demand and cost relationships in the charcoal market.

[10]Matters of equity cannot easily be established here on *a priori* grounds. It would be inappropriate to argue that the charcoal firm has an inalienable right to the use of the air, or that eyeglass makers have a basic right to clean air. The desires of the two firms are strictly competitive and, as we saw in our discussion of the reciprocal nature of externalities, any arguments about the intrinsic rights of one party can symmetrically be applied to the other.

APPLICATION 21.3

Bargains in the Orchard—Bees and Apples

Earlier in this chapter we described James Meade's example of the beneficial externalities between beekeepers and apple growers—bees pollinate apples, and apples provide nectar for honey. Since the costs of bargaining between these two producers are probably low, the Coase theorem suggests that there may be incentives to internalize these externalities through private contracts.

Bee Contracting in Washington

S. N. S. Cheung's fascinating investigation of beekeeping in Washington State shows that such contracts are very well developed.[1] Terms of contracts between beekeepers and farmers typically take into account both the benefits that various crops provide to beekeepers (in the form of honey) and the benefits that farmers get from having bees pollinate their crops. For crops such as clover and alfalfa, which have high honey yields, beekeepers usually pay rent to farmers for the right to have their bees use the farmers' land. On the other hand, apple and cherry growers must "rent" bees to provide pollination because the honey yield from those crops is low. Although Meade's classic example has a certain bucolic appeal, economic incentives seem to have limited its importance in the real world.

Lessons from the Bees

This episode clearly illustrates the importance of the interplay between theory and empirical evidence in developing economic models. To an economic theorist, Meade's example was compelling—generations of students (including your author) were taught it as gospel. But, despite the theory, beekeepers and orchard owners continued to develop their elaborate set of contracts. Indeed, a quick look in the Yellow Pages in many cities confirms the importance of these contracts—by all appearances bee rental is a thriving business. Other examples of hypothetical market imperfections that have been undermined by real-world evidence include a purported absence of markets for recyclable material (these markets are, in many cases, flourishing), the presumed undesirable properties of markets for human blood or human organs (which seem to operate rather well where they are permitted), and (as we shall see in the next chapter) the presumption that public-type goods (such as lighthouses or roads) must be provided by the government. In all of these cases the benefits from voluntary transactions that are predicted by the Coase theorem keep occurring despite the most dire predictions based on incomplete theories.

To Think About

1. Not every beekeeper enters into contracts with growers for nectar. Instead, many allow their bees to forage (and pollinate) anywhere the bees choose to go. What sort of factors would determine whether there were formal contracts between beekeepers and growers?
2. Can you think of other examples of beneficial externalities in which some kind of payment is made by the beneficiary? For example, how do apartment and condominium complexes pay for landscaping services? Or, how do mall owners pay for indoor plants, fountains, and parking lot maintenance?

[1] S. N. S. Cheung, "The Fable of the Bees: An Economic Investigation," *Journal of Law and Economics* (April 1973): 11–33.

environmental externalities. We show that for such externalities it is unlikely that the competitive market will attain an efficient outcome and then proceed to look at other remedies. Still, as Application 21.3: Bargains in the Orchard—Bees and Apples shows, the price system often has a surprising power to handle certain types of externalities.

Bargaining Costs, Environmental Externalities, and Environmental Regulation

It is commonly believed that markets seem to have failed to cope with many externalities related to the environment. Firms and individuals routinely pollute the air and water through their disposal activities; noise levels in urban areas are often so high as to be harmful to residents' health; and the array of signs and posters along most major highways creates what some people regard as "visual pollution." In view of the Coase theorem, a natural first question to ask about these externalities is why they have not been internalized through bargaining. It would seem that those who are harmed by the externalities could bargain with those who create them and thereby improve the allocation of resources.

The principal reason that Coase-type agreements do not occur in these cases is that *high bargaining costs* are often associated with most environmental externalities. It is frequently difficult to organize people harmed by these externalities into an effective bargaining unit and to calculate the monetary value of the losses each has suffered.[11] Similarly, most legal systems have been set up primarily to adjudicate disputes between two specific plaintiffs rather than to represent the rights of large, diffuse groups such as those who may be affected by environmental damage. These factors make bargaining costs extremely high in many cases. It is possible that these costs exceed the possible efficiency gains that can be obtained by successful bargaining.

Bargaining Costs and Allocation

In cases characterized by high transactions or bargaining costs, the assignment of ownership rights can have significant allocational effects. If, as is normally the case, disposal of refuse into air and water is treated as use of common property, this in effect assigns use rights to each firm. The firm may use the air and water around it in any way it chooses, and high bargaining costs will prevent it from internalizing any external costs into its decisions. For this reason, pollution-producing activities may be operated at a higher

[11] Many of the problems that arise in the provision of public goods are important impediments to group environmental action. Once pollution is abated, it is abated for everyone. The benefits are nonexclusive. Consequently, it may be to the advantage of each person to adopt the position of a free rider. See Chapter 22 for a further discussion of this free rider issue.

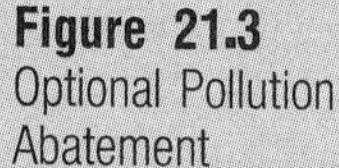

Figure 21.3
Optional Pollution Abatement

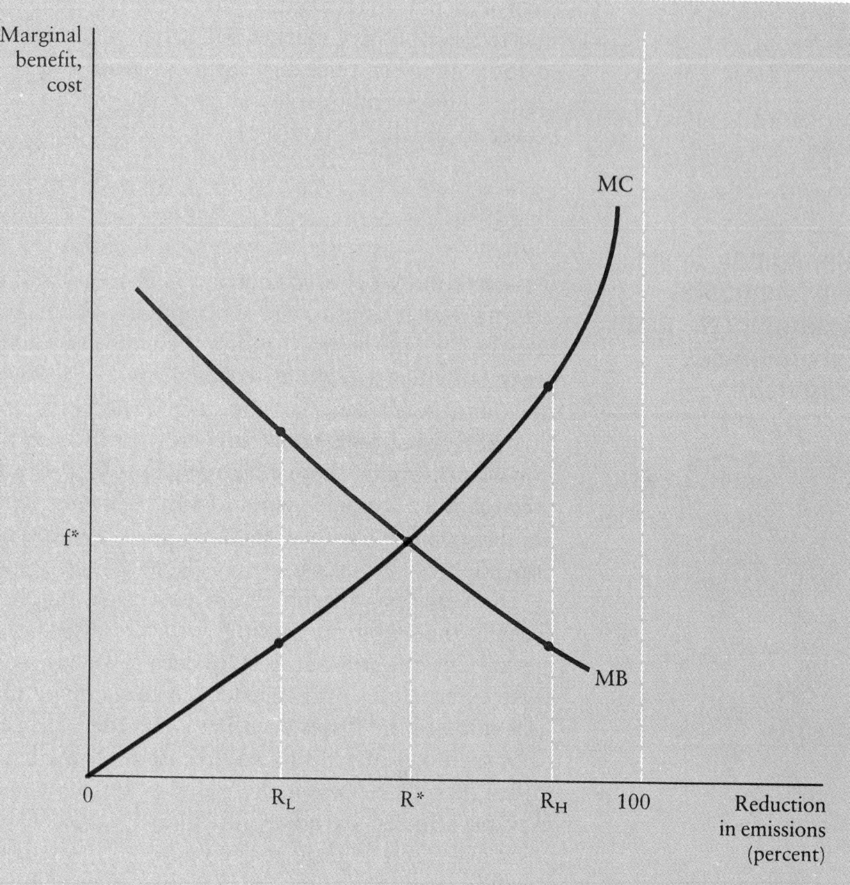

The MB and MC curves show the marginal benefits and marginal costs, respectively, of pollution abatement. R* represents an optimal allocation of resources to this purpose. Such an outcome may be attained through the imposition of an effluent fee of f*, through the sale of marketable pollution permits, or through direct controls.

level than would be optimal unless specific types of control mechanisms (such as Pigou-type taxes) are employed.

Environmental Regulation

In order to examine a few of the issues that arise in designing environmental controls, we shall adopt a very simple model of this regulatory process.[12] The

[12]For a more complete discussion, see W. J. Baumol and W. E. Oates, *The Theory of Environmental Policy,* 2d ed. (Cambridge, England: Cambridge University Press, 1988).

horizontal axis in Figure 21.3 shows percentage reductions in environmental pollution from some source below what would occur in the absence of any regulation. The curve MB in the figure shows the additional social benefits obtained by reducing such pollution by one more unit. These benefits consist of possibly improved health, the availability of additional recreational or aesthetic benefits, and improved production opportunities for other firms. The curve is intended to reflect all of the potentially valuable outcomes that anti-pollution efforts might have. As for most economic activities, this provision of benefits is assumed to exhibit diminishing returns—the curve MB slopes downward to reflect the fact that the marginal benefits from additional reductions in pollution decline as stricter controls are implemented. The health gains from removing the final .001 percent of pollutants are therefore assumed to be rather small, perhaps because the natural environment can easily handle some amount of pollutants on its own.

The curve MC in Figure 21.3 represents the marginal costs incurred in reducing environmental emissions. These costs include both forgone profits from a lower output and actual costs associated with using anti-pollution equipment. The positive slope of this curve reflects our usual assumptions of increasing marginal costs. Controlling the first 50 or 60 percent of pollutants is assumed to be a relatively low-cost activity, but controlling the last few percentage points is assumed to be rather costly. As reductions in emissions approach 100 percent, marginal costs associated with further reductions rise very rapidly.

Given this configuration, it is clear that R^* is the optimal level of pollution reduction. For reductions less than R^* (say, R_L), the marginal benefits associated with further tightening of environmental controls exceed the marginal cost of achieving lower pollution levels, so emissions should be reduced further. Reductions in excess of R^* are also inefficient, however—environmental control can be pushed too far. At R_H the marginal cost of emissions control exceeds the marginal benefits obtained so less strict regulation may be desirable. To noneconomists the notion that there is an optimal level of pollution (that R^* is less than 100 percent) may sound strange, but this result simply reflects the general principles of resource allocation we have been studying throughout this book. As Application 21.4: The Phosphate Ban and Clean Clothes shows, excessive environmental control can be as costly to society as inadequate control.

Fees, Benefits, and Direct Controls

There are three general ways that emissions reductions of R^* might be attained through environmental policy.[13] First, as in our previous discussion,

[13]In our discussion we will assume that government regulators face no adverse incentives of their own—they only seek to achieve R^*. Some of the discussion in Chapter 22 may suggest the possible shortcomings of this assumption.

APPLICATION 21.4

The Phosphate Ban and Clean Clothes

Most modern laundry detergents contain phosphates. These are added to provide greater cleaning power and to impart a longer useful life to fabrics. Phosphates also encourage the growth of algae and other water-based plants (phosphates are a major ingredient in fertilizer), which may be potentially harmful to the environment. Increased organic matter in lakes and streams leads to a reduced oxygen content of the water, and this may kill fish.

Regulating Phosphates

Legislators and regulators have been quite concerned about phosphates from detergents making their way into streams and rivers. In the late 1970s several localities banned the sale of laundry detergents containing phosphates, and some states have followed suit. Because these bans are easy to impose and seem to represent only trivial inconvenience for consumers (there are other types of detergents available), they have not involved the extensive debate that many other environmental regulations have.

Inefficiency of a Complete Ban

Although phosphate bans may be politically expedient, our analysis in this chapter suggests that such dramatic measures seldom produce efficient results. Alternative, more carefully targeted actions may result in resources being used more wisely. For example, a 1984 study of phosphate bans in Wisconsin and North Carolina estimates that these imposed costs of about $50 to $70 per household per year in the form of extra laundry additives needed, increased fabric wear, and decreased wash quality.[1] Gains in terms of improved water quality were generally not detectable. Even if there were gains in water quality, the study shows that these could be obtained more cheaply (for about one-fourth to one-third the cost) by adopting waste water treatment methods than by banning phosphate detergents. In this case, the politics of the regulatory process seems to have resulted in at least as much inefficiency in the allocation of resources as did the initial externality it was intended to cure.

To Think About

1. What other regulatory strategies (instead of an outright ban) might be used to address the phosphate problem? How would a Pigovian tax operate in this case? Would it be preferable to a ban? Why didn't government officials follow such an approach?
2. Some people argue that economists' proposals of pollution taxes (or similar licensing arrangements) are wrong since they "let people with the money simply pay for doing wrong." Do you agree? Aren't strict regulatory controls (or, better yet, outright bans on pollution) a better approach to preserving the environment?

[1]The report is summarized in W. Kip Viscusi, "Phosphates and the Environmental Free Lunch," *Regulation* (September/December 1984): 53–55.

the government may adopt a Pigovian or "effluent fee" of f^* for each percent that pollution is not reduced. Faced with such a charge, the polluting firm will choose the optimal emissions reduction level, R^*. For reductions less than R^*, the fee exceeds the marginal cost of pollution abatement so a profit-maximizing firm will opt for abatement. Reductions in emissions of more than R^* would be unprofitable, however, so the firm will opt to pay the fee on $100 - R^*$ percent. One important feature of the fee approach is that the firm itself is free to choose what combination of output reduction and adoption of pollution control technology achieves R^* at minimal cost.

A very similar allocational result would be attained if governmental regulators issued permits that permitted firms to "produce" 100 − R* percent of their unregulated emissions levels. In this case, Figure 21.3 implies that if such permits were freely tradable, they would sell for a price of f*. In this case, the market for pollution permits ensures that the optimal level of emissions reductions will be attained at minimal social cost.

A third regulatory strategy would be simply to implement reductions of R* through direct controls. In this case, which tends to be the one most often followed in the United States, firms would be told the level of emissions they would be allowed. Such a direct approach can, in principle, duplicate the allocational solutions provided by Pigovian taxation and marketable permits. If, as is often the case, direct control is also accompanied by specification of the precise mechanism by which R* is to be achieved (for example, through the installation of a special kind of pollution control equipment) the cost-minimization incentives incorporated in the other two approaches may be lost.

Uncertainty in Environmental Regulation

Of course, the approach to environmental regulation illustrated in Figure 21.3 is extremely simplistic. For many actual environmental problems (such as the "greenhouse effect," which is discussed in Application 21.5), both the benefits and costs associated with various abatement strategies may be very poorly understood. Simply calculating the optimal level of pollution abatement may be subject to considerable uncertainty. In such cases, the three control mechanisms discussed in the previous section may no longer be equivalent—some approaches may be more likely to achieve an efficient outcome than others. Actual outcomes will depend on the incentives the various control strategies offer and on the degree to which property rights are fully defined and whether some limited Coase-type bargaining is able to occur.

The Evolution of Property Rights—Economics and the Law

Legal definitions of property rights change over time. Some goods that were at one time commonly owned (most land, for example) have in more recent times become primarily private property. Similarly, some goods that were at one time private (such as roads, bridges, lighthouses, and fire companies) have increasingly become publicly owned. Traditionally, such changes have been regarded as primarily legal or political in origin. Although economic analysis could illustrate the implications of various property rights assignments, it was believed to have little to say about how assignments were in fact made.

More recently, several economists have argued that the way societies choose to define property rights is strongly motivated by economic consider-

APPLICATION 21.5

The Greenhouse Effect and What to Do about It

In recent years considerable concern has been voiced that the continued burning of fossil fuels combined with increasing deforestation throughout the world will lead to a buildup of carbon dioxide in the atmosphere. This buildup will, it is feared, result in a gradual warming of the earth prompting vast climatic changes. This possibility has come to be known as the "greenhouse effect."

Scientific Evidence

Most evidence suggests that the earth has been gradually warming over the past 100 years. A best guess puts the increase in mean temperature at about 0.5°C from 1880 to 1980. During the same period concentrations of carbon dioxide and other gases from combustions in the atmosphere have also increased—primarily as a result of increasing industrialization. One estimate puts the increase at about 20 percent over the past 100 years.[1] There is currently considerable uncertainty about whether these two facts are connected. Attempts at modeling carbon dioxide buildup in the atmosphere have encountered numerous theoretical difficulties, and the actual data continue to pose unanswered puzzles (such as the fact that there appears to have been little buildup during the period 1945–1970—a period of rapid economic growth throughout the world).

The Policy Dilemma

The uncertainties in the scientific basis for the greenhouse effect pose a major dilemma for policymakers. This dilemma is illustrated in Figure 1. The marginal costs associated with combating the greenhouse effect (say, by imposing major restrictions on electricity production and automobile use) are shown by the MC curve. The increasingly steep slope of this curve illustrates the sharply increasing costs associated with heroic efforts to combat the effect. The curve MB in Figure 1 reflects the best scientific estimate of the bene fits from restricting carbon dioxide emissions. Uncertainty about these benefits is reflected by the curves MB′ and MB″—the benefits may be either greater or smaller than those based on the best guess Notice that although emissions reductions of R* are optimal if the best scientific estimates prove correct, the possible losses from such a policy are not symmetric. If the true benefits are given by MB′, losses given by area ABE will be encountered because of underregulation. On the other hand, if true benefits are given by MB″, much greater losses, given by area EDC, will be encountered from overregulation. The effect of sharply increasing marginal costs combined with scientific uncertainty is to suggest caution in the adoption of heroic control efforts.

Figure 1

Optimal Abatement and Scientific Uncertainty

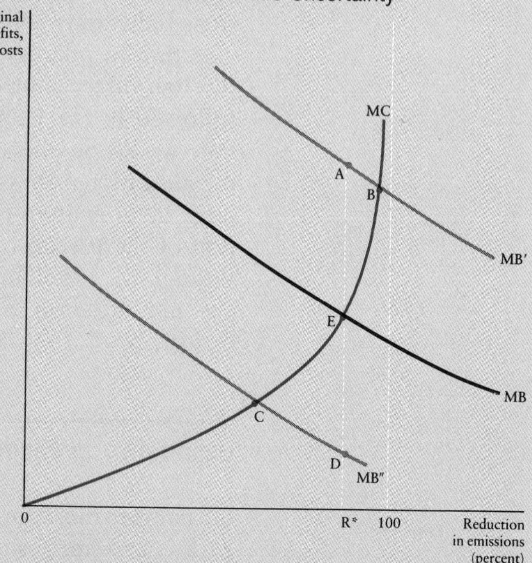

Losses from a policy of R* are given by area ABE if benefits prove to be larger than expected, but they are given by area EDC if benefits prove to be smaller than expected.

To Think About

1. The notion that the greenhouse effect should be approached cautiously seems directly contrary to the dramatic approach advocated by many environmentalists. Under what conditions would a more restrictive policy approach be favored?
2. Can you think of other current or past environmental externalities for which scientific evidence about their effects was highly uncertain? Are these situations accurately reflected by Figure 1?

[1]G. J. MacDonald, "Scientific Evidence for the Greenhouse Effect," *Journal of Policy Analysis and Management* (Spring 1988): 425–444.

ations. In particular, it has been suggested that private property rights come into existence when it becomes efficient for those affected by externalities to internalize them through transactions in private property; that is, when the benefits of coping with the externalities exceed the costs of enforcing private property rights.[14] In broad terms, the hypothesis is that legal institutions (notably the way in which property rights are defined) evolve over time toward economically efficient outcomes. For example, Application 21.6: Land Contracts in the California Gold Rush shows how one type of land contract changed very rapidly in response to market pressures. Other cases that have been examined include product liability law, land zoning law, and even criminal law.[15] As a more extensive illustration of the issues, we look briefly at how economic incentives may encourage the conversion of common property to private property.

The Common Property Problem

Resources are termed *common property* if they can be used by anyone without a direct charge. As our discussion of air and water pollution showed, this is frequently the case for the natural environment—enforcement of private property rights is simply too costly. Other examples of common property include the radio and television spectrum (although rights to particular wavelengths have been created by the government), fishing and mining in the oceans or Antarctica, and the use of outer space for satellites or other purposes. As a specific example we examine the case of ocean fishing, but similar issues arise in all cases of common ownership.

Ocean Fisheries and Common Property

Ocean fisheries are, in most cases, common property.[16] Anyone wishing to catch fish need only rent or buy a boat and proceed to a desirable location. Because most fishing grounds are treated as common property, there may be a tendency for the areas to be overfished from a long-run viewpoint. Each fisherman will adopt a policy of increasing his or her catch up to the point at which the marginal cost of catching additional fish is equal to the price

---

[14]See Harold Demsetz, "Toward a Theory of Property Rights," *American Economic Review, Papers and Proceedings* (May 1967): 347–359.

[15]R. A. Posner, *Economic Analysis of Law,* 2d ed. (Boston: Little, Brown and Company, 1977).

[16]This section is based on H. S. Gordon, "The Economic Theory of a Common-Property Resource: The Fishery," *Journal of Political Economy* (April 1954): 124–142; and on Anthony Scott, "The Fishery: The Objectives of Sole Ownership," *Journal of Political Economy* (April 1955): 116–124.

APPLICATION 21.6

Land Contracts in the California Gold Rush

The degree to which externalities affect the allocation of resources can have an impact on how property rights are defined in legal contracts. Since legal agreements among people can take a wide variety of forms, it is likely that contractual provisions will be chosen that prove mutually beneficial. Changes in the general economic environment would be likely to change the provisions that are regarded as optimal.

Gold Claims

An interesting example is provided by land contracts in California gold fields during the period 1848–1860.[1] Because California had only recently become independent from Mexico when gold was discovered in 1848, few explicit statutes governed the enforcement of miners' claims to land. Rather, a group of miners would stake out a claim and rely primarily on their own devices to prevent "claim-jumping." Usually a group of 6–10 miners would band together to enforce and protect their claim to an area. Among the miners on a given claim, sharing contracts initially predominated. That is, the miners would work together in panning for gold and would share equally the output that resulted from the process. This type of contract offered two advantages over a more individualistic approach to mining. First, risk was reduced since every miner would obtain the same share of output rather than facing the probability of choosing the wrong mining location. Second, miners could achieve some economies of scale in building the equipment necessary for efficiency in searching stream banks and beds and in policing their claims against others.

Development of Formal Land Contracts

By late 1849, population in the California gold fields had expanded rapidly, producing pressures to change the form of mining contracts. Greater population necessitated larger numbers of miners on each claim (mainly in order to protect the claim). That resulted in greater problems of shirking the work by some miners involved in sharing contracts. Also the risk reduction benefits of sharing contracts declined as claim characteristics became better understood and secondary markets in mine property developed. Hence, the form of mining contracts began to change toward a simple land contract. Under that contract, each miner on a claim was given property rights to a specific land parcel. By mid-1850 the land contract was incorporated into the U.S. mining laws. Sharing contracts in California proved to be a short-lived contractual response to the special conditions of 1848.

To Think About

1. Why were sharing contracts more efficient for small mining claims than for large ones? More generally, are output-sharing arrangements more difficult to develop in large organizations than small ones? How might your observations apply to communal farms or similar types of arrangements?
2. Suppose an investor provided the funding to find and develop a gold mine. What kind of contract would you expect to be developed between this owner and the miners? How might the miners be paid—with a direct salary, with a share of the gold, or with a share of the mine's profits?

---

[1]This example is based on J. Umbeck, "A Theory of Contract Choice and the California Gold Rush," *Journal of Law and Economics* (October 1977): 421–437.

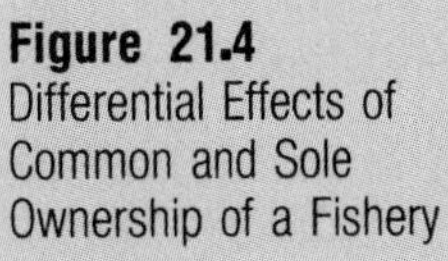

Figure 21.4
Differential Effects of Common and Sole Ownership of a Fishery

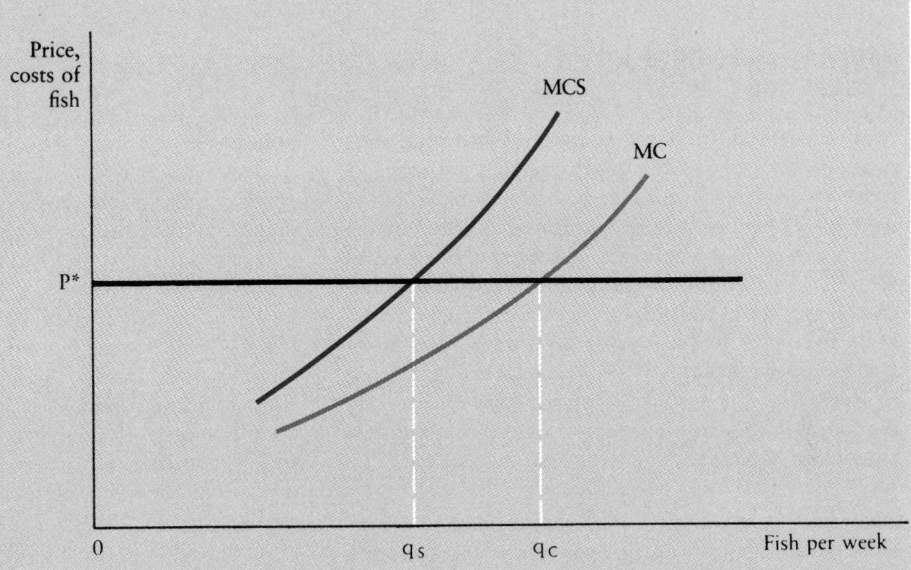

Under common ownership, fishermen will recognize only current operating costs as reflected by MC and will produce output level q_C. If the fishery is owned by a single firm, this firm would produce at a point (q_S) where price is equal to a comprehensive measure of marginal costs (MCS). The efficiency gains associated with such private ownership may encourage the evolution of legal specifications of property rights.

of fish. Although such a policy may lead to short-run profit maximization, it also runs the risk of so depleting the stock of fish that the future catch may be endangered. Because the fisheries are "owned" in common, individual fishermen will not take these additional costs of resource depletion into account.

This argument is illustrated in Figure 21.4. Suppose that the price of fish is given by P* and the marginal cost curve for the current year's output is given by MC. Under common ownership, each fishing firm will produce output level q_C since this output level maximizes current profits. If the fishery were solely owned by one firm, that firm would consider both the present and future operating costs of its actions. Since increasing the current year's catch tends to reduce the catch (and the profits) in future years, the firm will regard its marginal cost curve as being MCS. This curve reflects both current operating costs and the future costs of reduced harvests. The sole owner would choose to produce output level q_s since this provides maximum profits when full costs are taken into account.

APPLICATION 21.7

Applying Economics to Oysters and Lobsters

Because shellfish are found along the continental shelf in relatively isolated beds, enforcement of property rights in such resources is less costly than for ocean fisheries. These property rights may be enforced by the state like any other legal right, or they may be enforced informally by custom, heredity, and a shotgun. Whatever the source of the property rights, our analysis suggests that shellfish producers who operate under a system of private property will recognize the divergence between private and social marginal costs and will, in the long run, be more productive than those who fish on common property.

Oysters

Some direct evidence on this possibility was provided in a 1975 study of oyster production by R. J. Agnello and L. P. Donnelley.[1] The authors noted that states differ widely in the proportion of privately owned oyster grounds. In Virginia, for example, about 74 percent of oysters produced are from privately owned grounds, whereas in neighboring Maryland the figure is less than 17 percent. The authors found clear evidence that oyster producers were more productive in states with a high level of private property. In Virginia, for example, the average physical productivity of oyster fishermen was nearly 60 percent higher than in Maryland. More generally, the authors found that a 10 percent increase in the proportion of oyster grounds that were privately owned led to an increase of 338 pounds in the annual oyster catch of each producer. They attribute this result to the greater efficiency with which private oyster beds can be managed.

[1]R. J. Agnello and L. P. Donnelley, "Property Rights and Efficiency in the Oyster Industry," *Journal of Law and Economics* (October 1975): 521–533.

Lobsters

A similar result was obtained by F. W. Bell in a study of lobstering.[2] In this case, however, the author found that property rights were only weakly enforced (by custom rather than by law) and that the common property nature of most production decisions led to overproducing. In 1966, by Bell's calculations there may have been twice as many lobster traps in use as efficiency considerations would dictate. A reduction in the number of traps to the optimal level would have increased the catch by nearly 10 pounds per trap. Bell suggested that such a reduction might be brought about through state regulation, but our analysis indicates that it might better be achieved through a more complete definition of property rights in the industry.

To Think About

1. Many New England towns used to have "commons." This was land owned by the town that anyone could use—primarily as a place for livestock to graze. What would you expect might happen to such common land? Do New England towns still have commons? How do they regulate the use of this land?
2. How does the common property problem arise in the case of hunting? Can you think of any animals that were severely threatened by this problem? How do you explain cases where overhunting does not seem to be a serious problem?

[2]F. W. Bell, "Technological Externalities and Common Property Resources: An Empirical Study of the U.S. Northern Lobster Industry," *Journal of Political Economy* (January/February 1972): 148–158.

Private Property and Internalization

This analysis shows that when resources are commonly owned they may be overused. Under common ownership, each fishing firm imposes an external cost on others by not recognizing the effect its fishing has on future harvests. A firm that could enforce sole ownership of the fishery would internalize this externality and would operate the fishery on a sustained yield basis. Moves in recent years by several countries such as the United States, Canada, and Chile to define 200-mile "economic zones" beyond the traditional 12-mile territorial limit can be viewed as a partial application of this principle. By expanding their limits, these countries are attempting to create a property right to surrounding fisheries and thereby to internalize the negative externalities of overfishing. In cases where property rights are more easily enforced (along the shore or in rivers and lakes), this process has gone even further, leading to potentially large efficiency gains. Application 21.7: Applying Economics to Oysters and Lobsters illustrates some of these gains for the case of shellfish.

Summary

We began this chapter with a demonstration of the misallocation of resources that may be created by an externality. That misallocation occurs because of a divergence between private and social marginal costs that leads economic actors, acting in their own self-interest, to make choices that may not be efficient. Using this concept we show:

- The traditional method for correcting the allocational bias of an externality, first proposed by A. C. Pigou, is to impose an optimal tax on the firm creating the externality.
- When bargaining costs are low and property rights are fully specified, no governmental intervention may be required to cope with an externality. Private negotiations between the parties may result in an efficient allocation regardless of how the property rights are actually assigned (the Coase theorem).
- Some externalities, such as those associated with environmental pollution, involve high bargaining costs. In this case, governmental regulation may be required to achieve an efficient allocation (although regulation does not guarantee such a result).
- Environmental regulation can proceed through the use of fees, pollution permits, or direct control. In the simplest case, these can have identical outcomes. In actuality, however, the incentives incorporated under each may result in quite different results.
- In some cases, legal specification of private property rights will evolve as a way of solving various allocational problems. Common property may become private as a way of controlling overuse externalities.

Review Questions

1. If one firm raises the costs of another firm by bidding against it for its inputs, that is not an externality by our definition. But, if a firm raises the costs of another firm by polluting the environment, that is an externality. Explain the distinction between these two situations. Why does the second lead to an inefficient allocation of resources but the first does not?
2. Explain why externalities usually arise from two parties trying to use the same resource. Why does this demonstrate that externalities are reciprocal in nature? Why is it important to recognize this reciprocal nature in designing policies to address externalities?
3. Our general definition of economic efficiency focuses on mutually beneficial transactions. Explain why the presence of externalities may result in some mutually beneficial transactions being forgone. Illustrate these using Figure 21.1.
4. The taxation and merger solutions to the externality problem both succeed by transforming a social cost into an explicit cost. For each solution explain why this is so and how recognition of social costs prompts firms to behave efficiently.
5. The proof of the Coase theorem requires that firms recognize both the explicit and implicit costs of their decisions. Explain a situation where a firm's failure to curtail pollution may cause it to incur implicit costs. Why is the assumption of zero bargaining costs crucial if the firm is to recognize these costs?
6. Why are bargaining costs in two-person externalities likely to be low? Why are these costs likely to be quite high when many economic actors are involved? Provide examples of each type of situation.
7. Explain why the level of emissions control R^* in Figure 21.3 is economically efficient. Why would the levels of abatement given by R_L and R_H result in inefficiency? What kinds of inefficient trades would be occurring at these levels of abatement?
8. Figure 21.3 shows that an emissions fee can be chosen that attains the same level of pollution reduction as does direct control. Explain why firms would make the same choices under either control method. Would this equivalence necessarily hold if government regulators did not know the true marginal costs of emissions control?
9. If the conditions of the Coase theorem hold, the allocation of resources will be the same no matter which party is assigned the property rights. Why, if bargaining is costly, does it matter how property rights are defined? Provide an example of how property rights might be defined efficiently or inefficiently in such a situation.
10. Suppose certain legal contracts were defined in an inefficient manner. Why would this generate pressures to change the law? What forces might prevent such changes?

Problems

21.1 A firm in a perfectly competitive industry has patented a new process for making widgets. The new process lowers the firm's average cost curve, meaning this firm alone (although still a price taker) can earn real economic profits in the long run.

a. If the market price is \$20 per widget and the firm's marginal cost curve is given by $MC = .4q$ where q is the daily widget production for the firm, how many widgets will the firm produce?
b. Suppose a government study has found that the firm's new process is polluting the air and estimates the social marginal cost of widget production by this firm to be $MCS = .5q$. If the market price is still \$20, what is the socially optimal level of production for the firm? What should the amount of a government-imposed excise tax be in order to bring about this optimal level of production?
c. Graph your results.

21.2 On the island of Pago-Pago there are two lakes and 20 fishermen. Each fisherman gets to fish on either lake and gets to keep the average catch on that lake. On Lake X the total number of fish caught is given by:

$$F^X = 10L_X - 1/2\ L_X^2,$$

where L_X is the number of fishermen on the lake. The amount an additional fisherman will catch is $MP_X = 10 - L_X$.
For Lake Y the relationship is

$$F^Y = 5L_Y$$

a. Under this organization of society, what will the total number of fish caught be?
b. The chief of Pago-Pago, having once read an economics book, believes that she can raise the total number of fish caught by restricting the number of fishermen allowed on Lake X. What is the correct number of fishermen on Lake X to allow in order to maximize the total catch of fish? What is the number of fish caught in this situation?
c. Being basically opposed to coercion, the chief decides to require a fishing license for Lake X. If the licensing procedure is to bring about the optimal allocation of labor, what should the cost of a license be (in terms of fish)?
d. Does this problem prove that a "competitive" allocation of resources may not be optimal?

*21.3 Suppose that the oil industry in Utopia is perfectly competitive and that all firms draw oil from a single (and practically inexhaustible) pool. Each competitor believes that he or she can sell all the oil he or she can produce at a stable world price of \$10 per barrel, and that the cost of operating a well for one year is \$1,000.

Total output per year (Q) of the oil field is a function of the number of wells (N) operating in the field. In particular,

$$Q = 500N - N^2,$$

*Denotes a problem that is rather difficult.

and the amount of oil produced by each well (q) is given by

$$q = \frac{Q}{N} = 500 - N.$$

The output from the Nth well is given by

$$MP_N = 500 - 2N.$$

a. Describe the equilibrium output and the equilibrium number of wells in this perfectly competitive case. Is there a divergence between private and social marginal cost in the industry?
b. Suppose that the government nationalizes the oil field. How many oil wells should it operate? What will total output be? What will the output per well be?
c. As an alternative to nationalization, the Utopian government is considering an annual license fee per well to discourage overdrilling. How large should this license fee be to prompt the industry to drill the optimal number of wells?

*21.4 Three types of contracts are used to specify how tenants of a plot of agricultural land may pay rent to the landlord. Rent may be paid (1) in money (or a fixed amount of agricultural produce); (2) as a fixed proportionate share of the crop; or (3) in "labor dues," by working on other plots owned by the landlord. How might these alternative contract specifications affect tenants' production decisions? What sorts of transaction costs might occur in the enforcement of each type of contract? What economic factors might affect the type of contract specified in different places or during various historical periods?

21.5 There is currently considerable controversy concerning product safety. Two extreme positions might be termed *caveat emptor* (let the buyer beware) and *caveat vendor* (let the seller beware). Under the former scheme, producers would have no responsibility for the safety of their products: buyers would absorb all losses. Under the latter scheme this liability assignment would be reversed; firms would be completely responsible under law for losses incurred from unsafe products. Using simple supply and demand analysis, discuss how the assignment of such liability might affect the allocation of resources. Would safer products be produced if firms were strictly liable under law?

21.6 Inventors are not usually able to capture all the profits arising from their inventions. Inventions tend to become public property that can be freely used without paying royalties to the inventor. Develop a supply-demand diagram that demonstrates how this externality may cause too few inventions to be produced. How might the adoption of patent laws mitigate this problem by granting property rights to inventions? What inefficiencies might be created by patents?

---

*Denotes a problem that is rather difficult.

21.7 Develop an example of interpersonal externalities similar to the one that illustrates interfirm externalities in Chapter 21. Show how the assumption of zero bargaining costs permits exchanges between the two persons to bring about an optimal allocation of resources even in the presence of this type of externality.

21.8 Suppose a monopoly produces a harmful externality. Use the concept of consumer surplus to analyze whether an optimal tax on the polluter would necessarily be a welfare improvement.

CHAPTER 22

Public Goods and Public Choice

In Chapter 13 we showed that some goods are not necessarily suited to production through private markets since they have zero marginal costs of serving another person and benefit everyone. A national defense policy, for example, can protect one more person at zero marginal cost, and no one can be excluded from this protection even if he or she doesn't want it. Such goods tend to be produced by the government and are paid for through compulsory taxation. Our goal in this chapter is to study some of the issues that arise in this process. We begin by defining public goods and examining the problems that such goods pose for the allocation of resources. We then show why these goods will often be produced by governments and show that, at least in theory, such actions could result in an efficient allocation of resources. In the final sections of the chapter, we examine the ways governments actually work and raise some doubts about whether they will ultimately choose efficient solutions. Our general purpose in this final chapter then is to investigate the behavior of the government as an important economic actor.

Public Goods

What does a government do? Economists might define governmental activities with one general statement: A government produces public goods. The general term *public goods* in this definition could refer to all those effects a government has on the members of society. These effects include all the tangible goods and services provided by the government (for example, national defense, postal services, education, and so forth) and are also intended to include the various intangible benefits (or costs) of citizenship, such as providing justice or building national character. In a sense, governments are not very different from other organizations (such as labor unions, professional associations, fraternities and sororities, or the American Legion) that provide benefits to, and impose obligations on, their members. The distinguishing characteristic of government is its ability to produce public goods on a very large scale and to finance these goods with compulsory taxes.

Attributes of Public Goods

The above discussion of public goods is circular—governments are defined as producers of public goods, and public goods are defined as the stuff government produces. Many economists (most notably, Paul Samuelson) have tried to attach a more specific, technical definition to the term *public good.*[1] The purpose of such a definition is to differentiate those goods that are public by nature from those that are suitable for private markets.[2] The most common definitions of public goods stress two attributes that seem to characterize many of the goods governments produce: nonexclusivity and nonrivalry.

Nonexclusivity

One property that distinguishes public goods is whether people may be excluded from the benefits the goods provide. For most private goods, such exclusion is indeed possible. I can easily be excluded from consuming a hamburger if I don't pay for it. In some cases, exclusion is either very costly or impossible. National defense is the standard example. Once an army or navy is set up, everyone in a country benefits from its protection whether they pay for it or not. Similar comments apply on a local level to such goods as mosquito control or inoculation programs against disease. In these cases, once the programs are implemented, all of the residents of a community benefit from them and no one can be excluded from those benefits, regardless of whether he or she pays for them. These **nonexclusive goods** can be contrasted with exclusive private consumption goods (such as automobiles or motion pictures) for which exclusion is a simple matter. Those who do not pay for such private goods do not receive the services these goods promise.

Nonexclusive goods Goods that provide benefits that no one can be excluded from enjoying.

[1]See Paul A. Samuelson, "The Pure Theory of Public Expenditure," *Review of Economics and Statistics* (November 1954): 387–389.

[2]Usually the implication is that governments should not produce private goods since the competitive market will do a better job of this.

Nonrivalry

Nonrival goods
Goods that additional consumers may use at zero marginal costs.

A second property that characterizes many public goods is nonrivalry. A **nonrival good** is one for which benefits can be provided to additional users at a zero marginal social cost. For most goods, consumption of additional amounts involves some marginal costs of production. Consumption of one more hot dog, for example, requires that various resources be devoted to its production. For some goods, however, this is not the case. Consider one more automobile crossing a highway bridge during an off-peak period. Since the bridge is already there anyway, one more vehicle crossing it requires no additional resources and does not reduce consumption of anything else. One more viewer tuning into a television channel involves no additional cost even though this action would result in additional consumption taking place. Consumption by additional users of such a good is nonrival in that this additional consumption involves zero marginal social costs of production; such consumption does not reduce other people's ability to consume.

Categories of Public Goods

The concepts of nonexclusivity and nonrivalry are in some ways related. Many goods that are nonexclusive are also nonrival. National defense and mosquito control are two examples of goods for which exclusion is not possible and for which additional consumption takes place at zero marginal cost. Many other instances might be suggested.

These concepts are not identical. Some goods may possess one property, but not the other. It is, as shown in Chapter 21, impossible (or at least very costly) to exclude some fishing boats from ocean fisheries, yet one more boat imposes social costs in the form of a reduced catch for all concerned. Similarly, use of a bridge during off-peak hours may be nonrival, but it is possible to exclude potential users by erecting toll booths. Table 22.1 presents a cross-classification of goods by their possibilities for exclusion and their rivalry. Several examples of goods that fit into each of the categories are provided. Many of the examples (in boxes other than the upper left corner in the table—exclusive, rival private goods) are often produced by the government. Nonrival goods are sometimes privately produced—there are private bridges, swimming pools, and highways that consumers must pay to use even though this use involves zero marginal cost. Nonpayers can be excluded from consuming these goods, so a private firm may be able to cover its costs.[3] Still,

[3]Nonrival goods that permit imposition of an exclusion mechanism are sometimes referred to as *club goods* since provision of such goods might be organized along the lines of private clubs. Such clubs might then charge a "membership" fee and permit unlimited use by members. The optimal size of a club is determined by the economies of scale present in the production process for the club good. For an analysis, see R. Cornes and T. Sandler, *The Theory of Externalities, Public Goods, and Club Goods* (Cambridge, England: Cambridge University Press, 1986).

Table 22.1
Types of Public and Private Goods

		Exclusive: Yes	Exclusive: No
Rival	Yes	Hot dogs, automobiles, houses	Fishing grounds, public grazing land, clean air
	No	Bridges, swimming pools, scrambled satellite television signals	National defense, mosquito control, justice

Public goods
Goods that provide nonexclusive benefits to everyone in a group and that can be provided to one more user at zero marginal cost.

even in this case the resulting allocation of resources will be inefficient because price will exceed marginal cost.

For simplicity we will define **public goods** as having both of the properties listed in Table 22.1. That is, such goods provide nonexclusive benefits and can be provided to one more user at zero marginal cost. Public goods are both nonexclusive and nonrival.

Public Goods and Market Failure

Our definition of public goods suggests why private markets may not produce them in adequate amounts. For exclusive private goods, the purchaser of that good can appropriate the entire benefits of the good. If Smith eats a pork chop, for example, that means the chop yields no benefits to Jones. The resources used to produce the pork chop can be seen as contributing only to Smith's welfare, and he or she is willing to pay whatever this is worth. The resource cost of a private good can be "attributed" to a single person.

For a public good, this will not be the case. In buying a public good, any one person would not be able to appropriate all the benefits the good offers. Since others cannot be excluded from benefiting from the good and since others can use the good at no cost, society's potential benefits from the public good will exceed the benefits that accrue to any single buyer. The resource cost should not be attributed solely to one purchaser. However, the potential purchaser will not take the potential benefits of this purchase to others into account in his or her expenditure decisions. Consequently, private markets will tend to underallocate resources to public goods.

An Example of Public Goods Externalities

As an example of the allocational problems raised by the nature of public goods, suppose a consumer is deciding to purchase either an automobile or an elaborate mosquito sprayer. The automobile and the mosquito sprayer have the same price, but the automobile yields more direct utility to the consumer. The automobile will be bought since that is the utility-maximizing decision for this person to make. From a social point of view, that may not be the best allocation of resources. The automobile increases social welfare only to the extent that this one person derives benefits from its use. Mosquito control can provide external benefits to many people in addition to its benefits to the purchaser. The purchaser will not take those extra benefits into account in his or her decision (even though they can be provided to others at zero cost). From a social point of view, resources may be underallocated to mosquito control (and to public goods in general).

A Graphical Demonstration

Problems raised by the nature of public goods can be demonstrated with partial equilibrium analysis by examining the demand curve associated with such goods. In the case of a private good, we found the market demand curve (see Chapter 5) by summing people's demands horizontally. At any price, the quantities demanded by each person are summed up to calculate the total quantity demanded in the market. The market demand curve shows the marginal evaluation that people place on an additional unit of output. For a public good (which is provided in about the same quantity to everyone) we must add individual demand curves vertically. To find out how society values some level of public good production, we must ask how each person values this level of output and then add up these valuations.

This idea is represented in Figure 22.1 for a situation with two people. The total demand curve for the public good is the vertical sum of each person's demand curve. Each point on the curve represents what person 1 and person 2 together are willing to pay for the particular level of public good production. Producing one more unit of the public good would benefit both people; so, to evaluate this benefit, we must sum each person's evaluation of the good. This is shown in Figure 22.1 by adding what person 1 is willing to pay to what person 2 is willing to pay. In private markets, on the other hand, the production of one more unit benefits only the person who ultimately consumes it.[4] Because each person's demand curve in Figure 22.1 is below the total demand for the public good, no buyer is willing to pay what the good is worth to society as a whole. Therefore, although Application 22.1: Are Lighthouses Public Goods? offers a warning about jumping to conclusions, in

[4]If MC_P and MC_G represent the marginal costs of a public and a private good, respectively, then (somewhat loosely) the conditions for optimality in the production of a private good are given by

$$MC_G = MV_G^1 = MV_G^2 = \cdots = MV_G^n$$

and for the public good by

$$MC_P = MV_P^1 + MV_P^2 + \cdots + MV_P^n,$$

where MV_G and MV_P are the marginal valuations (that is, the amount each individual is willing to pay for one more unit) of the two goods. For a more extensive discussion, see Paul A. Samuelson, "The Pure Theory of Public Expenditure," *Review of Economics and Statistics* (November 1954): 387–389.

Figure 22.1
Derivation of the Demand for a Public Good

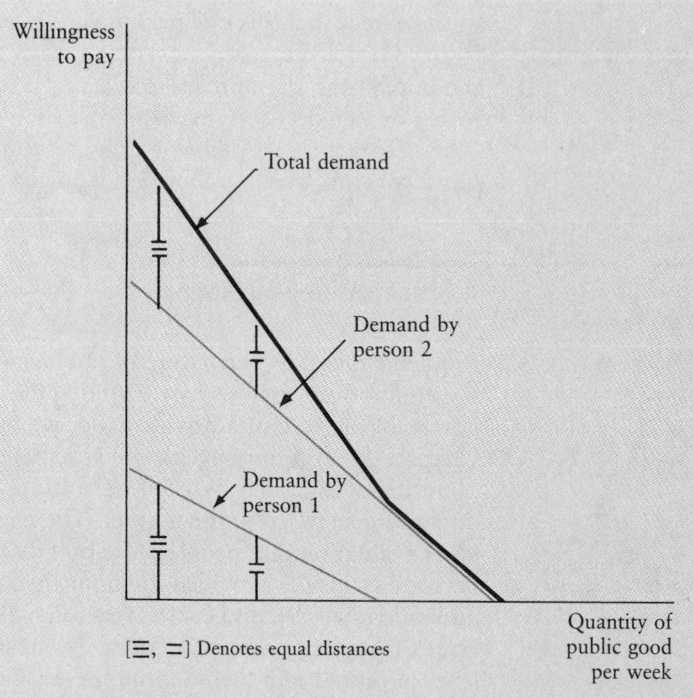

Since a public good is nonexclusive, the price that people are willing to pay for one more unit (their marginal valuations) is equal to the sum of what each individual would pay. Here person 1's willingness to pay is added vertically to person 2's to get the total demand for the public good.

many cases private markets seem to undervalue the benefits of public goods and underallocate resources to them.

Voluntary Solutions to the Problem

Since public goods cannot be traded efficiently in competitive markets, a number of economists have examined how such goods might be provided by the government and financed through taxation. One approach investigates whether an efficient allocation of resources to public goods might come about voluntarily; that is, people would agree to be taxed in exchange for the benefits that the public good provides. Perhaps the earliest statement of how such an equilibrium might arise was provided by the German economist Erik Lindahl in 1919.[5] Lindahl's argument can be illustrated graphically for a so-

[5]Most of Lindahl's writings are in German. Excerpts from them are reprinted in translation in R. A. Musgrave and A. T. Peacock, eds., *Classics in the Theory of Public Finance* (London: Macmillan, 1958).

APPLICATION 22.1

Are Lighthouses Public Goods?

Lighthouses have played an important role in the development of the theory of public goods. Our categories in Table 22.1 suggest that lighthouses have both properties that tend to be associated with public goods: (1) the light provided is a nonexclusive good, offering guidance to everyone who sees it; and (2) the light is nonrival since an additional ship can make use of it at zero marginal cost. It is not surprising that lighthouses are often used as textbook examples of public goods.

Private Lighthouses

Just because lighthouses have the characteristics of public goods does not mean that they must be owned and operated by the government. Private ownership is still possible, provided the owners have some way to collect from those who use the lighthouse. In a fascinating history of lighthouses in England, Ronald Coase shows that during the seventeenth and eighteenth centuries most were indeed privately owned.[1] Owners were then provided with the legal right to collect "light dues" from shipowners who visited British ports. Apparently, the business of operating lighthouses was a thriving one during this period, and many enterprising entrepreneurs entered the market in response to profit opportunities.

The Government Takeover

In 1836 the British Parliament granted an exclusive franchise to operate all lighthouses to Trinity House, a quasi-governmental body. The era of private ownership came to an end. Reasons for Parliament's decision are somewhat unclear. Some members argued that monopoly provision of lighthouse services through the government would be more efficient (though, as for many cases of multiplant monopolies, the source of such efficiencies is not obvious since each productive unit remains small). Others adopted a more political stance, arguing that lighthouses simply should be government-owned as a source of national pride (or, indeed, of political patronage). Regardless of which of these arguments was finally persuasive, the debate shows that in some cases whether the government decides to produce a particular good may be less a matter of the good's technical properties than of prevailing political institutions and attitudes.

To Think About

1. Lighthouses may not provide nonexclusive benefits—conceivably a lighthouse keeper could turn off the light for ships that haven't paid their dues. With modern communications equipment, especially radar for ship sightings, this is even more feasible today than in eighteenth-century England. Would adoption of a system of communications that resulted in lighthouses' output becoming an exclusive good improve the efficiency of resource allocation?
2. In the case of lighthouses and other public goods that might be "privatized" (for example, elementary education through a system of government-financed vouchers), is it necessary for the government to set prices for these goods? How would light dues be determined if they were not set by the government?

[1] Ronald Coase, "The Lighthouse in Economics," *Journal of Law and Economics* (October 1974): 357–376.

ciety with only two individuals (again the ever-popular Smith and Jones). In Figure 22.2 the curve labeled SS shows Smith's demand for a particular public good. Rather than using the price of the public good on the vertical axis, we instead assume that the share of the public good's cost that Smith must pay varies from 0 percent to 100 percent. The negative slope of SS indicates that at a higher tax "price" for the public good, Smith will demand a smaller quantity of it.

Jones's demand for the public good is derived in much the same way. Now, however, we record the proportion paid by Jones on the right-hand

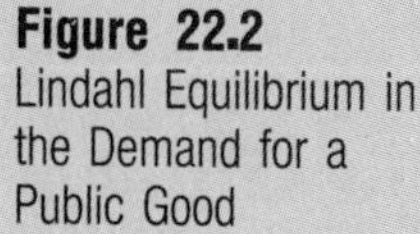

Figure 22.2
Lindahl Equilibrium in the Demand for a Public Good

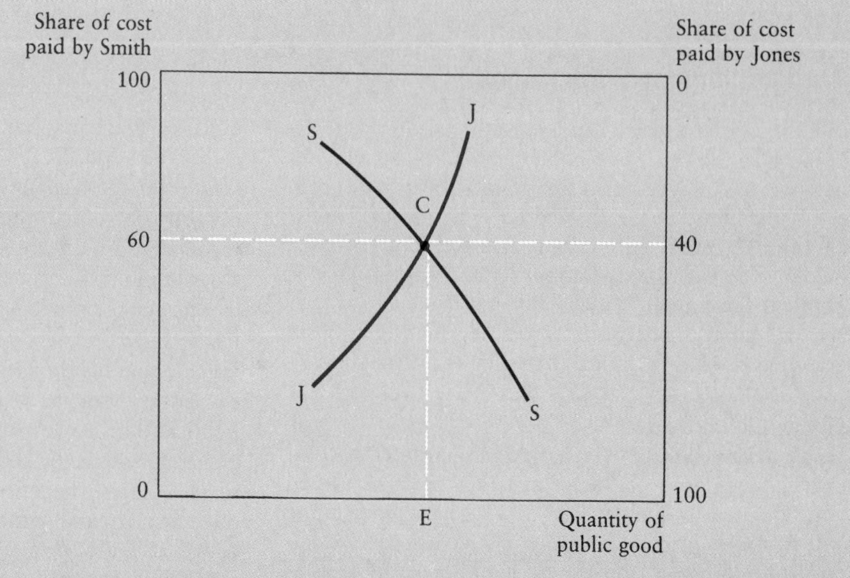

The curve SS shows that Smith's demand for a public good increases as the tax share that Smith must pay falls. Jones's demand curve for the public good (JJ) is constructed in a similar way. The point C represents a Lindahl equilibrium at which OE of the public good is supplied with Smith paying 60 percent of the cost. Any other quantity of the public good is not an equilibrium since either too much or too little funding would be available.

vertical axis of Figure 22.2 and reverse the scale so that moving up the axis results in a lower tax price paid. Given this convention, Jones's demand for the public good (JJ) has a positive slope.

The Lindahl Equilibrium

The two demand curves in Figure 22.2 intersect at C, with an output level of OE for the public good. At this output level Smith is willing to pay, say, 60 percent of the good's cost whereas Jones pays 40 percent. That point C is an equilibrium is suggested by the following argument. For output levels less than OE, the two people combined are willing to pay more than 100 percent of the public good's cost. They will vote to increase its level of production (but see the warnings about this statement in the next section). For output levels greater than OE, the people are not willing to pay the total cost of the public good being produced and may vote for reductions in the amount being provided. Only for output level OE is there a **Lindahl equilibrium** where the tax shares precisely pay for the level of public good production undertaken by the government.

Lindahl equilibrium
Balance between people's demand for public goods and the tax shares that each must pay for them.

Not only does this allocation of tax responsibilities result in an equilibrium in people's demands for public goods, but it is also possible to show that this equilibrium is efficient.[6] The tax shares introduced in Lindahl's solution to the public goods problem play the role of "pseudo" prices that mimic the functioning of a competitive price system in achieving efficiency. Unfortunately, for reasons we now examine, this solution is at best only a conceptual one.

Discovering the Demand for Public Goods: The Free Rider Problem

Deriving the Lindahl solution requires knowledge of the optimal tax share for each person. A major problem arises in how such data might be collected. Although, through their voting patterns, people may provide some information about their preferences for public goods (a topic we take up later in this chapter), that information is usually too sketchy to permit Lindahl's tax shares to be computed. Most voting methods do not record the intensity of people's desires for various public goods. As an alternative, a government might ask people how much they are willing to pay for particular packages of public goods, but the results of this poll might be extremely inaccurate. In answering the question, people may feel that they should understate their true preferences for fear they will ultimately have to pay what the good is worth to them in the form of taxes. From each person's point of view, the proper strategy is to understate true preferences in the hope that others will bear the burden of paying taxes. Since no one can be excluded from enjoying the benefits of a public good, the best position to occupy is that of a **free rider.** Each person, by acting in his or her own self-interest, may ensure that society underestimates the demand for public goods and underallocates resources to their production.

Free rider
A consumer of a nonexclusive good who does not pay for it in the hope that other consumers will.

The free rider problem arises in all organizations that provide collective goods to their members. For example, as we saw in Chapter 19, labor unions generally are able to obtain better wages and working conditions in unionized plants. Workers in such plants have an incentive to enjoy the benefits of unionization while at the same time refusing to join the union. They thereby avoid the payment of dues. In order to combat such free rider problems, unions quite often insist on a "closed," or "union," shop. Similar problems arise in collecting blood on a voluntary basis. Since people know that they will get all the blood they need if they have to be hospitalized, the tendency is to be a free rider and refrain from donating. Even in your own home, you may understate your interest in a clean room in the hope someone else will clean it.

[6]For a derivation, see Walter Nicholson, *Microeconomic Theory: Basic Principles and Extensions,* 4th ed. (Hinsdale, Ill.: The Dryden Press, 1989), pp. 733–734.

Compulsory Taxation

As these examples illustrate, the free rider problem can be solved only by some sort of compulsion. This compulsion may arise out of a sense of group solidarity or civic pride (people do give blood in America, and far more do in England), or it may require legal or quasi-legal force (as in the union case). For governments the necessity to tax people to force them to pay for public services is inescapable, and some voting schemes have been proposed that gather the sort of information required for a Lindahl equilibrium. None of these offers a particularly effective solution to the free rider problem, however. As Application 22.2: Searching for Free Riders illustrates, this type of behavior is relatively common, and a variety of social mechanisms are used to control it.

Local Public Goods

Some economists have suggested that the public goods problem may be more tractable on a local than on a national level.[7] Because individuals are relatively free to move from one locality to another, they may indicate their preferences for local public goods by choosing to live in communities that offer them utility-maximizing public goods taxation packages. "Voting with one's feet" provides a mechanism for revealing public goods demand in much the same way that "dollar voting" reveals private goods demand. People who want high-quality schools or a high level of police protection can "pay" for them by choosing to live in highly taxed communities. Those who prefer not to receive such benefits can choose to live elsewhere. Similar arguments apply to other types of organizations that offer packages of public goods for their members—people can choose which package of goods they prefer by choosing which clubs to join. Whether such actions can completely reveal the demand for public goods (even on a local level) remains an unsettled question, however. We now examine more common ways in which people express their demands for public goods—through the political process.

Direct Voting and Resource Allocation

Voting is used to decide on allocational questions in many institutions. In some instances, people vote directly on policy questions. That is the case in New England town meetings and many statewide referenda (such as those discussed later in Application 22.5) and for many of the public policies

[7]See C. M. Tiebout, "A Pure Theory of Local Expenditures," *Journal of Political Economy* (October 1956): 416–424.

APPLICATION 22.2

Searching for Free Riders

The notion that people will behave as free riders when making decisions about public goods seems intuitively reasonable. It draws directly on the model of rational decision making that we developed in Part II. Finding actual examples of free rider behavior in the real world is difficult, however. Of course, everyone has had experiences of people shirking group responsibilities (the author's children tend to disappear when it's time to do yard work). A major problem arises in deciding whether this represents free riding or simply indicates that the good being provided is of little value to a person (perhaps the children don't care what the yard looks like). Since preferences are difficult if not impossible to measure, the search for free riders has turned in other directions.

A Free Rider Experiment

Some researchers have tried to demonstrate free rider behavior in experiments. The subjects (usually college students) are given some money that they may either keep or contribute to some public good (often a pot of money) that they will share equally. For example, five students might each be given $10 and told that they can keep the $10 or put some of it into a common fund that will be doubled and split evenly. If every student contributes $10, each will receive $20 in return. Each person has an incentive to cheat on this deal. If one student doesn't contribute and the four others do, the one who doesn't contribute will get to keep the original $10 and will receive $16 more ($40 contributed and then doubled, then split five ways) for a total of $26. Each person has an incentive to be a free rider. What is individually rational is collectively irrational if everyone is a free rider, since everyone then ends up with only $10.

Experimental Results

Results of such simple experiments do indicate that free ridership exists and may become more significant as an experiment is repeated.[1] Sometimes as many as half or more of the students involved take the free rider position. In many cases, cooperative behavior also tends to appear. Especially if the students can talk together, they may choose cooperative solutions that outwit the game and the professor who is conducting it. Some students, however, will usually continue to cheat on such cooperative strategies to their own advantage.

To Think About

1. How do you solve the free rider problems that arise in your own living arrangements? Who (if anyone) cleans the room, buys essential provisions, or plans the parties? By what methods do you control free riding?
2. Charities also face a free rider problem in getting people to contribute. What are some of the methods used by charities such as United Way, the Red Cross, or the local public television station to coerce would-be free riders into contributing?

[1]For a summary of some of these experiments, see T. S. McCaleb and R. E. Wagner, "The Experimental Search for Free Riders," *Public Choice* (September 1985): 479–490.

adopted in Switzerland. Direct voting also characterizes the social decision procedure used for many smaller groups and clubs such as farmers' cooperatives, university faculties, or the local Rotary Club. In other cases, societies have found it more convenient to utilize a representative form of government in which people directly vote only for political representatives, who are then charged with making decisions on policy questions.

To study how public choices are made, we begin with an analysis of direct voting. Direct voting is important not only because such a procedure may apply to some cases but also because elected representatives often engage in direct voting (such as in the U.S. Congress), and the theory we illustrate applies to those instances also. Later in the chapter we take up special problems of representative government.

Majority Rule

Because so many elections are conducted on a majority rule basis, we often tend to regard that procedure as a natural and, perhaps, optimal one for making social choices. But a quick examination suggests that there is nothing particularly sacred about a rule requiring that a policy obtain 50 percent of the vote to be adopted. In the U.S. Constitution, for example, two-thirds of the states must adopt an amendment before it becomes law. And 60 percent of the U.S. Congress must vote to limit debate on controversial issues. Indeed, in some institutions (Quaker meetings, for example), unanimity may be required for social decisions. Our discussion of the Lindahl equilibrium concept suggests that there does indeed exist a distribution of tax shares that would obtain unanimous support in voting for public goods. But arriving at such unanimous agreements poses difficult information problems and may be subject to strategic ploys and free rider behavior by the voters involved. To examine in detail the forces that lead societies to move away from unanimity and to choose some other determining fraction would take us too far afield here. We instead assume throughout our discussion of voting that decisions are made by majority rule. You may be able to think of some situations that might call for a decisive proportion of other than 50 percent.

The Paradox of Voting

In the 1780s the French social theorist M. de Condorcet observed an important peculiarity of majority rule voting systems—they may not arrive at an equilibrium but instead may cycle among alternative options. Condorcet's paradox is illustrated for a simple case in Table 22.2. Suppose there are three voters (Smith, Jones, and Fudd) choosing among three policy options. These policy options represent three levels of spending on a particular public good (A = low, B = medium, and C = high), but Condorcet's paradox would arise even if the options being considered do not have this type of ordering associated with them. Preferences of Smith, Jones, and Fudd among the three policy options are indicated by the order listed in the table. For example, Smith prefers option A to option B and option B to option C, but Jones prefers option B to option C, and option C to option A. The preferences described in Table 22.2 give rise to Condorcet's paradox.

Consider a vote between options A and B. Option A would win, since it is favored by Smith and Fudd and opposed only by Jones. In a vote between options A and C, option C would win, again by two votes to one. But in a vote of option C versus option B, the previously defeated option B would win, and consequently social choices would cycle. In subsequent elections, any choice

Table 22.2
Preferences That Produce the Paradox of Voting

Voter	Order of Preferences		
Smith	A	B	C
Jones	B	C	A
Fudd	C	A	B

A=Low-spending policy.
B=Medium-spending policy.
C=High-spending policy.

that was initially decided upon could later be defeated by an alternative, and no decision would ever be reached. In this situation, the option finally chosen will depend on such seemingly unrelated issues as when the balloting stops or how items are ordered on an agenda rather than being derived in some rational way from the preferences of voters.

Single-Peaked Preferences and the Median Voter Theorem

Condorcet's voting paradox arises because of the degree of irreconcilability in the preferences of voters. We might ask whether restrictions on the types of preferences allowed might yield situations where equilibrium voting outcomes are more likely. A fundamental result about this probability was discovered by Duncan Black in 1948.[8] Black showed that equilibrium voting outcomes can always occur in cases where the issue being voted upon is one-dimensional (such as how much to spend on public goods) and where voters' preferences are "single-peaked."

To understand what *single-peaked* means, consider again Condorcet's paradox. In Figure 22.3 we illustrate the preferences that gave rise to the paradox by assigning hypothetical utility levels to options A, B, and C that are consistent with the preferences recorded in Table 22.2. For Smith and Jones, preferences are single-peaked—as levels of public goods' expenditures rise, there is only one local utility-maximizing choice (A for Smith, B for Jones). Fudd's preferences, on the other hand, have two local peaks (A and C). It is these preferences that produced the cyclical voting pattern. If, instead, Fudd had preferences represented by the dashed line in Figure 22.3 (where C is now the only local peak), there would be no paradox. In that case, option B would be chosen since that option would defeat both A and C by votes of two to one. Here B is the preferred choice of the *median voter* (Jones) whose preferences are "between" the skewed preferences of Smith and the revised preferences of Fudd.

[8]Duncan Black, "On the Rationale of Group Decision Making," *Journal of Political Economy* (February 1948): 23–24.

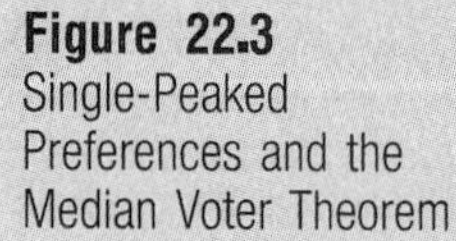

Figure 22.3
Single-Peaked Preferences and the Median Voter Theorem

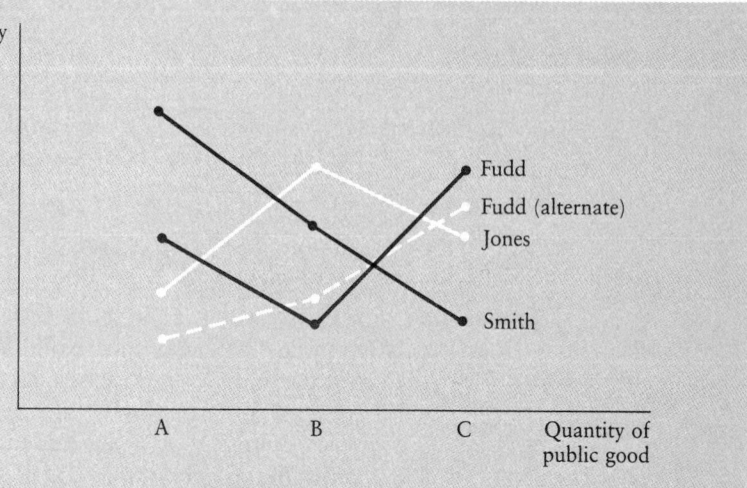

This figure illustrates the preferences in Table 22.2. Smith's and Jones's preferences are single-peaked, but Fudd's have two peaks, and these yield the voting paradox. If Fudd's instead had been single-peaked (the dashed lines), option B would be chosen as the preferred choice of the median voter (Jones).

Median voter
A voter whose preferences for a public good represent the middle point of all voters' preferences for the good.

Black's result is quite general and applies to any number of voters. If choices are one-dimensional and preferences are single-peaked, majority rule will result in selection of that project that is most favored by the **median voter.** Therefore, that voter's preference will determine what social choices are made. Application 22.3: Voting for School Budgets shows that in some cases this theory can explain observed decisions on public spending fairly well.

Unfortunately, the median voter theorem may be of only limited general importance, since many issues of public choice, unlike voting for school budgets, are not one-dimensional. Consider, for example, choosing among alternative environmental policies. These may involve varying levels of spending, choices of locations for polluting firms, and types of pollution permitted. In such a case, people's preferences are likely to be both varied and quite complex. In describing how people vote on these issues, the single-peaked notion loses much of its intuitive appeal, and there are no simple median voter theorems.

Intensity of Preferences, Logrolling, and Efficient Resource Allocation

So far, we have discussed voting schemes in which voters can choose which of two options they prefer but have no opportunity to express the intensity of their feelings. In these situations majority rule can result in adoption of policies that are only mildly favored by the majority but are despised by a minority. To prevent that, minority voters may adopt logrolling (or vote-trading) techniques.

APPLICATION 22.3

Voting for School Budgets

Decisions about spending for public schools provide examples of public choice theory in which the median voter theorem may be applicable. Voters have rather definite preferences about the proper level for such spending, and, on the whole, those preferences are probably single-peaked. For this reason, voting patterns in elections related to school financing questions have been more intensively studied by economists than any other public issue.

Voting on Long Island

For example, Robert Inman examined voting patterns in 58 Long Island (New York) school districts that determine their annual funding for schools through a budget referendum.[1] He found that levels of per-pupil spending in these towns were heavily influenced by the income of the median voter and by the share of taxes this voter would be expected to bear. Although higher income voters can expect to pay higher taxes (principally because they own more expensive houses upon which school property taxes are levied), the author still found that high median income districts will choose to spend more on education than low-income districts—that is, a high-income elasticity of demand for education tends to dominate voters' decisions.

[1]Robert Inman, "Testing Political Economy's 'As If' Proposition: Is the Median Income Voter Really Decisive?" *Public Choice* (1978): 45–65.

Influence of Small Groups

Although Inman's results suggested that the median voters (in his case, moderate-income, middle-aged homeowners with children) tend to dominate the voting patterns, he also found that some smaller segments of the population may affect the voting results. Most important of these groups are older voters whose children have already passed through the public schools. These voters tend to favor smaller school budgets and have the effect of reducing public school spending somewhat. Other groups, such as renters and Catholic parents (who may not send their children to public schools) also tend to have some influence in Inman's results. In most cases, however, preferences of the median voter prove to be decisive in setting school budgets.

To Think About

1. In many localities, school budgets are determined by elected school boards, not by direct referenda. How do you think such indirect budget-setting procedures would affect the results of the median voter theorem? What pressures might bring about systematic departures of actual spending from what might be chosen by the median voter?
2. Are there ways in which median voter groups could encourage other groups to vote with them on school budget issues? How, for example, might median voters blunt the low spending preferences of older voters, renters, or people who send their children to private schools?

Table 22.3 provides an example of logrolling. In it the preferences about three projects (in terms of utility gains or losses) for five voters are recorded. If all the projects are voted on individually, all will pass—always by a vote of three to two. That these outcomes may not be desirable can be seen by summing the utility levels (assuming that can be done) for each project; by this criterion, only project C is "worthwhile." Both A and B yield a net negative utility level to society as a whole. These examples clearly show why majority rule may not result in an efficient allocation of revenues.

Perhaps the inefficient projects in Table 22.3 might be stopped through logrolling. Suppose voters 1 and 5 agree to "trade" votes; that is, voter 1 agrees to oppose project B, providing voter 5 will oppose project A. Such a trade makes both people better-off than they would be should both projects

Table 22.3
Intensity of Preferences and Logrolling

Voter	Utility Gain or Loss: Project A	Project B	Project C
1	−5	2	2
2	−5	6	6
3	3	2	10
4	3	−5	−5
5	3	−7	−7

be adopted. With the trading of votes, both projects fail by three to two votes.[9]

Unlike voluntary trading in competitive markets, however, all vote trading does not promise Pareto optimality. Not all projects that are beneficial will be accepted, and not all of those that are harmful will be turned down. Consider a two-way choice between projects A and C. In that case, voters 1 and 5 can still profitably trade votes, ensuring that both project A (undesirable) and project C (desirable) are defeated.

As this example suggests, there is no very close connection between the concept of free trading in votes and choosing efficient resource allocations. There are no general efficiency theorems about vote trading and resource allocation. Nevertheless, the prevalence of "back-scratching" and "pork barrel" politics in legislative bodies is a prevalent phenomenon that clearly does affect which public goods are produced.

Analysis of Representative Government

In a representative government, voters vote for candidates, not policies. Successful candidates represent their constituencies in making policy choices. Here we examine a few of the issues that have been raised about this kind of indirect representation of individual preferences.

As in the theory of the firm, we start our analysis by examining the motives of government leaders. It might, for instance, be proposed that government leaders act for the "social good." At least two realities argue against assuming such benevolent motivations. First, the notion of "social good" is extremely ill-defined. It is simply not true that everyone in society has the same view of the way things should be. Second, the assumption of selfless political leadership is in marked contrast to the self-interest assumption that underlies both the theory of the individual and the theory of the firm we de-

[9]This trade imposes a negative externality on voters 2 and 3 (who are worse-off without both projects than with both) and a positive externality on voter 4.

veloped earlier. There seems no very persuasive reason why people should change their basic motivations upon elevation to political office.

The Majority Principle

One theory of political motivation has been put forward by Anthony Downs. In *An Economic Theory of Democracy,* he hypothesizes that

> parties in democratic politics are analogous to entrepreneurs in a profit-seeking economy. So as to attain their private ends, they formulate whatever policies they believe will gain the most votes, just as entrepreneurs produce whatever products will gain the most profits....[10]

In other words, parties act to *maximize political support.* In order to pursue this goal, parties must contend with uncertainty in many respects. A party is uncertain how any particular policy choice will affect political support. This is true not only because it may be hard to find out who benefits from government action, but also because policies must be adopted before the policies of the party (or parties) out of power are known. This strategic advantage of those out of power is significantly modified, however, by the control that the party in power has over the public's access to information.

Perhaps the most interesting general conclusion that Downs draws from his model is that the party in power will generally adopt a *majority principle* in its policy decisions. It will pursue only those policies for which more votes are gained than are lost, and it will pursue such policies up to the point at which the marginal gain in votes from those benefiting from the policy equals the marginal loss in votes from those being hurt by the policy. The analogy between party motivation and profit maximization is quite close.

Pluralism

Downs's view of the nature of the political process can be contrasted with another, more commonly held view. This alternative conception examines the *pluralistic* nature of democratic government. Social decisions are assumed to be made by the interaction of many powerful special interest groups. Presumably these groups wield some influence over political leaders by virtue of campaign contributions, friendship, superior knowledge of special issues, or perhaps by direct measures of corruption. Whatever the avenues of control, it is assumed that interest groups are the primary molders of the legal system.

Two assessments of pluralism have been put forward. The first optimistically predicts that the interaction of numerous pressure groups will, in some

[10]Anthony Downs, *An Economic Theory of Democracy* (New York: Harper & Row, 1957), p. 295.

sense, produce a socially desirable outcome. Laws that are ultimately passed represent an equilibrium among numerous groups. Because no one group has significant power (at least not on all issues), the resulting equilibrium will generally be representative of the society as a whole.

Interest Groups and Rent-Seeking Behavior

This beneficial assessment of pluralism has been questioned by many authors. One of the most interesting objections was put forward by Mansur Olson.[11] He pointed out that there is a systematic bias in a pluralistic society that causes only certain kinds of interest groups to exercise political power. In particular, Olson argues that only groups that represent narrow special interests will arise; groups representing the broad "public" interest will be weak or nonexistent. The reason for this tendency, Olson explains, lies in the nature of the public good a special interest group provides to its members. In a close-knit group, each member can recognize the benefits of group action, and there may be strong sanctions against being a free rider. Groups such as the National Rifle Association or the United Automobile Workers may be quite effective in pursuing their goals through government action. In some cases the gains will be largely psychological—for example, members of the Sierra Club enjoy knowing that national parks will be protected and enlarged. In other cases the gains will be monetary. In the early 1980s, for example, some U.S. automobile companies pressed for and won "voluntary" export restraints with the Japanese, presumably with the goal of increasing their profits. Similarly, specialized groups of agricultural producers may find it in their economic interest to enlist the government's help in restricting supply, as shown in Application 22.4. Economists call these activities examples of **rent-seeking behavior.** Special interest groups who feel they may have success in obtaining profits by seeking government favors will probably do so. Such behavior is simply another application of the profit-maximization hypothesis.

Rent-seeking behavior
Firms or individuals influencing government policy to increase their own welfare.

For representing broad questions of public interest, Olson sees a problem. In such cases the direct gains to the people who participate in the political process may be small even though social gains from the policies they advocate may be large. People will have a tendency to refrain from such political activities—they will be susceptible to the free rider problem. Consider, for example, the benefits of free trade. Economists have expounded on these benefits at least since Ricardo's time, but any single person would probably gain little direct benefit from petitioning the government for free trade. Although the total social benefits of a free trade policy may be quite large, the gains are spread so broadly over the population that no one person (unless he or she happens to be a Toyota dealer) would be interested in spending the time and

[11] See Mansur Olson, *Logic and Collective Action* (Cambridge, Mass.: Harvard University Press, 1965), especially Chapters 5 and 6.

APPLICATION 22.4

Rent Seeking through Agricultural Marketing Orders

The agricultural marketing order program operated by the U.S. Department of Agriculture provides a clear example of how the rent-seeking activities of narrow special interest groups can affect legislation. Under the program, the government imposes supply restrictions on 47 relatively minor agricultural commodities, including almonds, cranberries, navel oranges, lemons, spearmint oil, raisins, and, to take an extremely odd case, kiwi fruit. These supply restrictions take a variety of forms including limiting what planters may grow, prorationing orders on how much may be sold during any given week, and restricting the kinds of technology that can be used for production in the industry. The reasons given for such constraints on supply vary. Most often, these are claimed to be needed in order to "assure stable prices" or to "guarantee" that the produce supplied is of sufficient quality.

Economic Effects of the Orders

Most economists who have examined the programs carefully, however, conclude that their primary result is to increase both overall costs to consumers and growers' profits. Even seemingly minor restrictions can be quite effective in this regard. For example, it is estimated that restrictions on the number of lemons that may be harvested cost consumers about $45 million per year and that the overall impact of the program for lemons is probably much higher because of the limits placed on new production techniques such as "shrink-wrap" packaging. For navel oranges, costs as high as $72 million per year arise from the use of quality grading systems that restrict the supply of fresh oranges sold and require that many navel oranges be crushed for concentrate—a use for which they are ill-suited.[1]

Why the Special Interests Succeed

Of course, none of these costs constitutes a very large part of the typical person's spending for food. Overall, it is doubtful that the programs add a few tenths of 1 percent to such costs. Kiwi fruits and cranberries are simply not important enough in people's budgets for them to get very excited about the restrictions. For the growers involved, however, the supply restrictions may be extremely important. It is not surprising, therefore, that grower organizations tend to dominate congressional lobbying about the market order program.

To Think About

1. A purported benefit of the market order program is to stabilize prices for the goods involved. How might the program have this effect? Would a stabilized high price be preferable to fluctuating prices for consumers?
2. Why are market order programs accepted by Congress? After all, cranberries or almonds are only grown in a few congressional districts. Why don't the vast majority of members (who have no growers in their districts) vote to stop the programs since at least some of their constituents would be made better-off by such a move?

[1]See, for example, T. M. Lenard and M. P. Mazur, "Harvest of Waste: The Marketing Order Program," *Regulation* (May/June 1985): 19–26.

effort necessary for a successful lobbying effort. According to Olson, broad issues of public interest will be underrepresented and special interests will be overrepresented in the political process.

Reelection Constraint

By combining Downs's and Olson's theories of government action, we can construct a realistic third alternative. It is undoubtedly true that interest

APPLICATION 22.5

Economics and the Tax Revolt

In recent years a number of states have passed tax limitation statutes, and a constitutional amendment has been proposed to serve the same purpose at the federal level. In this example we summarize some of the empirical research that has tried to explain the nature of this "tax revolt." The tax limitation idea largely originated in California with the passage of "Proposition 13" in 1977. That ballot initiative required that property in California be taxed at a maximum rate of 1 percent of the 1975 fair market value and imposed sharp limits on tax increases in future years. It resulted in a decline in local property tax revenues of nearly 60 percent between fiscal 1978 and fiscal 1979.

Two hypotheses have been proposed to explain why voters demanded such a drastic change in policy. The first views Proposition 13 as a demand for changing the sources of local tax revenues without reducing local expenditures significantly. Under this view citizens were largely content with the existing levels of local services but wanted state tax sources (primarily income and sales taxes) to take over a larger share of the burden. A second hypothesis views Proposition 13 as a statement by voters that local government had grown too large and that voters wished to see a cutback in both taxes and expenditures.

Results from Proposition 13

In a 1979 paper, Attiyeh and Engle examined voting patterns on Proposition 13 in an attempt to differentiate between these hypotheses.[1] They found such patterns tended to contradict the notion that voters simply wished to change the sources of local government financing. For example, communities in which property tax levies had been rising most dramatically did not appear to favor Proposition 13 disproportionately. On the other hand, the authors found clear evidence that voters wished a reduction in both tax rates and expenditures, although their results suggested that a somewhat less dramatic reduction might have received even more voter support. In all then, Attiyeh and Engle's results imply that local government in California had expanded beyond the bounds that voters believed to be optimal. The success of Proposition 13 clearly showed, however, that there were limits to that expansion.

Tax Limitation in Massachusetts and Michigan

Evidence from studies of other tax limitation initiatives tends to be somewhat contradictory as to voters' motivation. For example, Ladd and Wilson used personal survey data to examine voter patterns in Massachusetts in connection with the 1980 passage of "Proposition $2\frac{1}{2}$"—a proposal very similar to Proposition 13.[2] Consistent with the California study, they also found evidence to contradict the notion that voters simply wanted to shift the source of local revenues (say, from the property tax to the income tax). But voters feared the loss of "vital" services and did not seem to want large cutbacks. Instead they preferred "greater efficiency" in government but seemed to be quite vague as to what actual policies that might require. Similar conclusions have been obtained by studying voters' opinions in connection with a 1978 vote in Michigan on the "Headler amendment" to limit state taxes. Again voters clearly wanted a reduction in taxes, but the evidence on what public services they might willingly forgo was quite mixed. Hence, whether such proposals represent a rather confused quest for a nonexistent "free lunch" or whether voters have in mind some more systematic alteration in existing tax expenditure patterns is difficult to determine given the data currently available.

To Think About

1. Since World War II the fraction of GNP devoted to government has risen in virtually every Western country. How do you explain this rise? Would a law that limited government spending to a set fraction of GNP be a good idea?
2. Many American politicians favor a balanced-budget amendment to the U.S. Constitution. Does the analysis of this chapter provide any reasons for thinking this amendment is a good idea? What kinds of economic arguments might you use to support the amendment? What arguments might be used to oppose it?

---

[1] Richard Attiyeh and Robert F. Engle, "Testing Some Propositions about Proposition 13," *National Tax Journal* (June 1979): 131–146.

[2] H. Ladd and J. B. Wilson, "Why Voters Support Tax Limitations—Proposition $2\frac{1}{2}$," *National Tax Journal* (June 1982): 127–148.

groups exercise considerable influence over legislation, and Olson is probably right when he theorizes that the public interest will be underrepresented. However, Olson's model does not take sufficient account of the motives of political leaders. Lobby groups probably do give utility (and money!) to political leaders, and these leaders may follow the dictates of the lobbyists. But a legislator does not have an unconstrained utility-maximization problem. Rather, he or she must operate subject to the *constraint of reelection*. The legislator must pay some attention to Downs's majority principle, although this attention will by no means be absolute.

Bureaucracies

Although governmental policies in a representative democracy are enacted by elected officials, they are usually implemented by and operated through bureaucratic agencies. Because those agencies typically possess monopoly power in the production of the services with which they are charged, it is possible that they exercise an independent influence on the direction of policy. For example, Niskanen hypothesizes that government agencies seek to maximize their budgets (perhaps because high budgets yield utility to bureaucrats).[12] A major implication of that hypothesis is that in the interchange between elected officials and bureaucracies, decisions will be reached that tend to overallocate resources to the public sector (relative to what would be preferred by the median voter).

Several authors have attempted to estimate such allocational effects empirically.[13] They generally conclude that the data are consistent with the budget-maximization hypothesis. However, this empirical work is, of necessity, quite simple. More sophisticated modeling awaits the development of better data sources and more precise analytic models of the bureaucratic process. Application 22.5: Economics and the Tax Revolt illustrates some of the problems in analyzing how voters feel about whether actual levels of resources allocated to the government are too high.

Summary

In this chapter we examine the economic theory of public goods and of the public choices that lead to the government providing such goods. Studying such subjects is a fairly recent activity for economists, and the theory described here is far from complete. We simply do not understand how resources are allocated through political "markets" as well as we understand

[12]W. A. Niskanen, *Bureaucracy and Representative Government* (Chicago: Aldine, 1971).

[13]See, for example, T. E. Borcherding, *Budgets and Bureaucrats: The Sources of Government Growth* (Durham, N.C.: Duke University Press, 1975).

how they are allocated in private markets. Still, applying economic logic to what are basically political issues leads to a number of important conclusions:

- Pure public goods have the property of nonexclusivity and nonrivalry—once the good is produced, no one can be excluded from receiving the benefits it provides, but additional people may benefit from the good at zero cost.
- These properties pose a problem for private markets since people will not freely choose to purchase such goods in economically efficient amounts. Resources may be underallocated to public goods.
- In theory, compulsory taxation can be used to provide public goods in efficient quantities by charging taxpayers what the goods are worth to each of them. However, measuring this demand may be very difficult because each person has an incentive to act as a free rider by understating his or her preferences.
- Direct voting may produce paradoxical results. However, in some cases, majority rule will result in the adoption of policies favored by the median voter.
- Analysis of representative government is made complicated by the need to consider the actual motives of elected political leaders. In some cases, such leaders will make choices in ways that maximize political appeal (that is, maximize votes). Narrow special interests and bureaucracies may often result in other choices being made, however.

Review Questions

1. For each of the following goods, explain whether it possesses the nonexclusive property, the nonrival property, or both. If the good does not have the characteristics of a public good but is, nevertheless, produced by the government, can you explain why?

   a. Television receivers
   b. Over-the-air television transmissions
   c. Cable TV transmissions
   d. Elementary education
   e. College education
   f. Electric power
   g. Delivery of first-class mail
   h. Low-income housing

2. Explain why private production of nonexclusive or nonrival goods may be inefficient. Is the nature of the inefficiency the same for both types of goods? What principles of economic efficiency are violated in each case?
3. The Lindahl solution to the public goods problem promises economic efficiency on a voluntary basis. Why would each person voluntarily agree to the tax assessments determined under the Lindahl solution? What choice is he or she being asked to make?
4. What information would a government need if it wished to institute a Lindahl scheme for public goods provision? Why is it unlikely to be able to obtain that information accurately?
5. Why is the "paradox of voting" a paradox? What, if anything, is undesirable about a voting scheme that cycles?

6. The median voter theorem predicts that majority rule voting will result in selecting that level of expenditure that is favored by the median voter. To what types of public questions might this theorem be applicable? For what cases would it probably not apply? What role does the "single-peaked" assumption play in the theorem?
7. "Under perfect competition voting with dollars achieves economic efficiency, but democratic voting (one person–one vote) offers no such promise." Do you agree? Why does the specification of one vote per person interfere with the ability to achieve economic efficiency?
8. Why would elected representatives not vote in the way favored by the median voter? What types of information problems arise in representatives judging voters' preferences? What problems arise in voters assessing representatives' performance?
9. Why would individuals or firms engage in rent-seeking behavior? How much will they spend on such behavior? What are the externalities associated with rent seeking?
10. Why might bureaucracies have special information about certain public goods? In what ways might such access to information affect the process of providing such goods?

Problems

22.1 Suppose there are only two people in society. The demand curve for person A for mosquito control is given by

$$q_A = 100 - P.$$

For person B the demand curve for mosquito control is given by

$$q_B = 200 - P.$$

a. Suppose mosquito control is a nonexclusive good—that is, once it is produced everyone benefits from it. What would be the optimal level of this activity if it could be produced at a constant marginal cost of $50 per unit?

b. If mosquito control were left to the private market, how much might be produced? Does your answer depend on what each person assumes the other will do?

c. If the government were to produce the optimal amount of mosquito control, how much will this cost? How should the tax bill for this amount be allocated between the individuals if they are to share it in proportion to benefits received from mosquito control?

22.2 Suppose there are three people in society who vote on whether the government should undertake specific projects. Let the net benefits of a particular project be $150, $140, and $50 for persons A, B, and C, respectively.

a. If the project costs $300 and these costs are to be shared equally, would a majority vote to undertake the project? What would be the net benefits to each person under such a scheme? Would total net benefits be positive?

b. Suppose the project cost $375 and again costs were to be shared equally. Now would a majority vote for the project and total net benefits be positive?

c. Suppose (presumably contrary to fact) votes can be bought and sold in a free market. Describe what kinds of results you might expect in parts a and b.

22.3 Suppose that education provides both private benefits and nonexclusive public benefits to individuals. Any particular level of educational output provides equal amounts of these types of benefits. How should resources be allocated in order to attain efficient production of this semipublic good? How might production of the good be financed?

*22.4 Suppose that there are N individuals in an economy with three goods. Two of the goods are pure nonexclusive public goods, whereas the third is an ordinary private good.

a. What conditions must hold for resources to be allocated efficiently between either of the public goods and the private good?
b. What conditions must hold for resources to be allocated efficiently between the two public goods?

22.5 In an economy characterized by a hierarchy of government units (for example, federal, state, and local governments), what criteria might be used to determine which public goods are produced by which level of government? How would economies of scale in production affect your answer?

---

*Denotes a problem that is rather difficult.

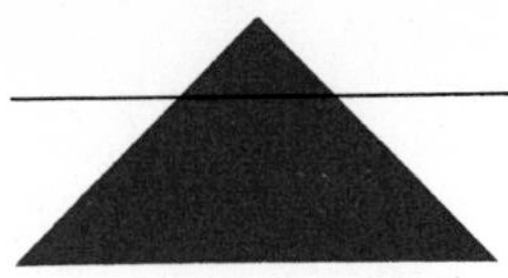

SOLUTIONS TO ODD-NUMBERED PROBLEMS

This section contains brief solutions to the odd-numbered problems in this book. These solutions should be helpful both for students trying to solve the specific problems and as a general review for many of the concepts presented.

Chapter 2

2.1 a. If $x = 0$, then $y = 15$.

b. $y = 0, 0 = 15 + 3x$
$-3x = 15$
$x = -5.$

c. $x = 3, y = 15 + 3(3) = 15 + 9 = 24.$
$x = 4, y = 15 + 3(4) = 15 + 12 = 27.$
If x increases by 1, y increases by 3.

d., e., f. (graph)

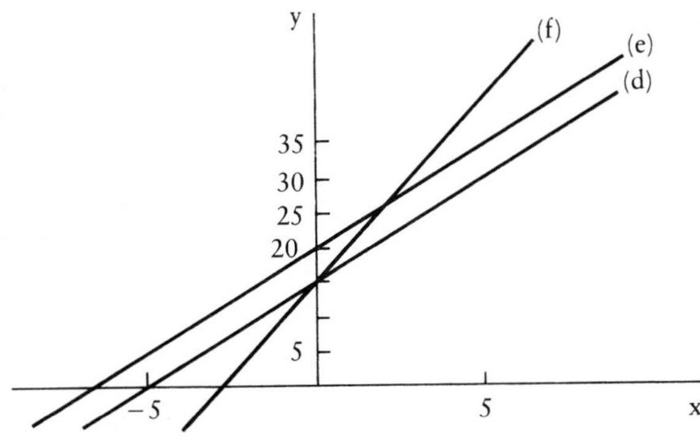

e. (graph)

i. If $x = 0$, then $y = 20$.

ii. $y = 0, 0 = 20 + 3x$
$-3x = 20$
$x = -20/3 = -6\ 2/3.$

iii. $x = 3, y = 20 + 3(3) = 20 + 9$
$= 29.$
$x = 4, y = 30 + 3(4) = 20 + 12$
$= 32.$
If x increases by 1, y increases by 3.

f. (graph)

i. If $x = 0, y = 15.$

ii. $y = 0, 0 = 15 + 5x$
$-5x = 15$
$x = -3.$

iii. $x = 3, y = 15 + 5(3) = 15 + 15$
$= 30.$
$x = 4, y = 15 + 5(4) = 15 + 20$
$= 35.$
If x increases by 1, y increases by 5.

2.3

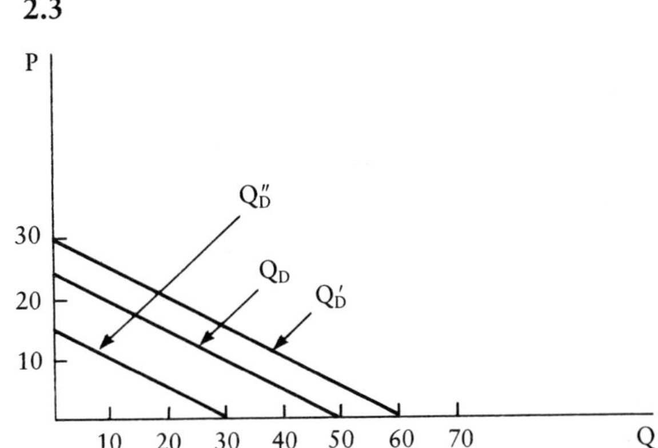

The algebraic solution proceeds as follows:

a. $Q_D = 40 - 2P + .001\ I, I = 10{,}000,$
so $Q_D = 50 - 2P.$
If $P = 0$, then $Q_D = 50.$
If $P = 10$, then $Q_D = 50 - 2(10) = 30.$
If Q_D equals 0, then $0 = 50 - 2P$
$2P = 50$
$P = 25.$

b. $I = 20{,}000$ changes Q_D to $Q_{D'} = 60 - 2P$.
If $P = 0$, then $Q_D = 60$.
If $P = 10$, then $Q_D = 40$.
If Q_D equals 0, then $0 = 60 - 2P$
$$2P = 60$$
$$P = 30.$$

c. $Q_D = 40 - 2P + .001\ I$, $P = P_p + 10$.
Substituting:
$$Q_{D''} = 40 - 2(P_p + 10) + .001\ I$$
$$= 40 - 2P_p - 20 + .001\ I$$
$$= 20 - 2P_p + .001\ I.$$
If $I = 10{,}000$, then $Q_{D''} = 30 - 2P_p$.
If $P_p = 10$, then $Q_D = 10$.
If $P_p = 0$, then $Q_D = 30$.
If Q_D equals 0, then $0 = 30 - 2P_p$
$$2P_p = 30$$
$$P_p = 15.$$

2.5

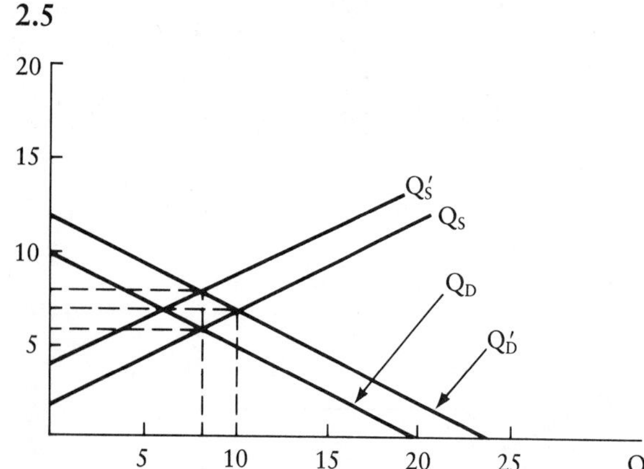

The algebraic solution proceeds as follows:

a. $Q_D = -2P + 20.$
$Q_S = 2P - 4.$
Set $Q_D = Q_S$: $-2P + 20 = 2P - 4$
$$24 = 4P$$
$$P = 6.$$
Substituting for P gives: $Q_D = Q_S = 8$.

b. Now $Q_{D'} = -2P + 24$.
Set $Q_D = Q_S$: $-2P + 24 = 2P - 4$
$$28 = 4P$$
$$P = 7.$$
Substituting gives: $Q_{D'} = Q_S = 10$.

c. $P = 8$, $Q = 8$ (see graph)

2.7 a. $T = .01\ I^2$.
$I = 10$, $T = .01(10)^2 = 1$.
Taxes = \$1,000.
$I = 30$, $T = .01(30)^2 = 9$.
Taxes = \$9,000.
$I = 50$, $T = .01(50)^2 = 25$.
Taxes = \$25,000.

b.

	Average Rate	Marginal Rate
I = 10,000	10%	20%
I = 30,000	30%	60%
I = 50,000	50%	100%

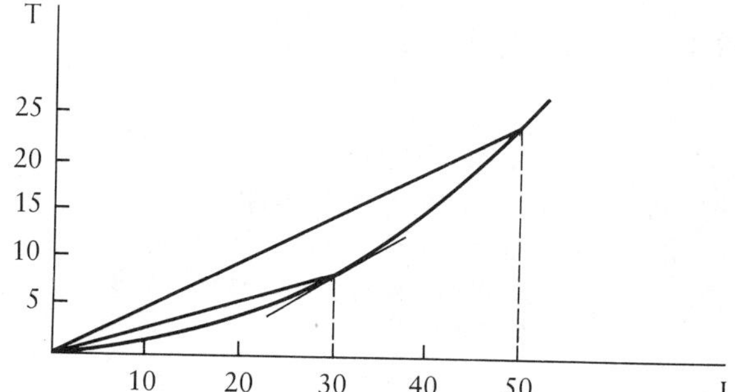

2.9

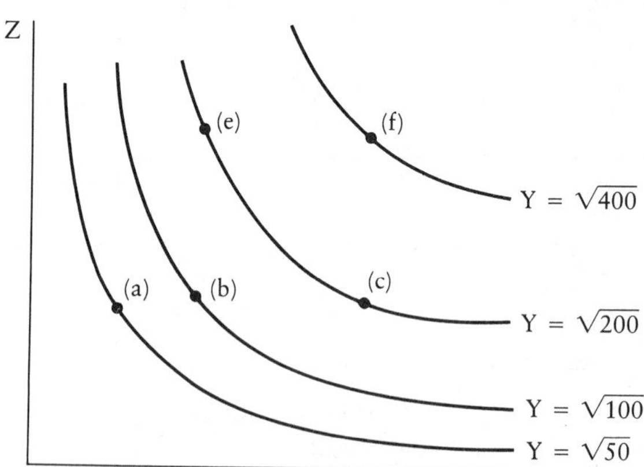

a. $2X + Z = 20$, $Z = -2X + 20$,
$-Z/X = -2$, $Z = 2X$, $X = 5$, $Z = 10$.

b. $X + Z = 20$, $Z = -X + 20$,
$-Z/X = -1$, $Z = X = 10$.

c. $X + 27 = 40$, $Z = -1/2X + 20$,
$-Z/X = -1/2$, $X = 20$, $Z = 10$.

d. $X + 5Z = 100$, $Z = -1/5X + 20$,
$-Z/X = -1/5$, $X = 50$, $Z = 10$.

e. $2X + Z = 40$, $Z = -2X + 40$, $-Z/X = -2$, $X = 10$, $Z = 20$.
f. $X + Z = 40$, $Z = -X + 40$, $-Z/X = -1$, $Z = 20 = X$.

Chapter 3

3.1 a. $\frac{\$8.00}{\$.40/\text{apple}} = 20$ apples can be bought.
b. $\frac{\$8.00}{\$.10/\text{orange}} = 80$ oranges can be bought.
c. 10 apples cost:
10 apples × \$.40/apple = \$4.00, so there is \$8.00 − \$4.00 = \$4.00 left to spend on oranges which means
$\frac{\$4.00}{\$.10/\text{an orange}} = 40$ oranges can be bought.
d. One less apple frees \$.40 to be spent on oranges, so $\frac{\$.40}{\$.10/\text{orange}} = 4$ more oranges can be bought.
e. \$8.00 = \$.40 × number of apples + \$.10 × number of oranges = $.40A + .10 \cdot 0$.

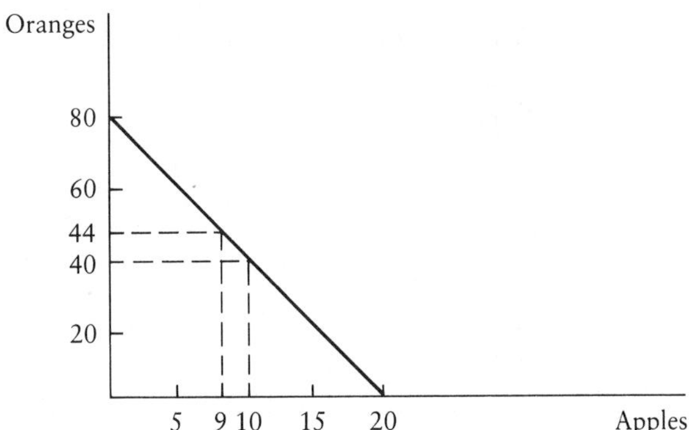

3.3 To graph the indifference curves, use U^2 instead of U. U = 10 means $U^2 = 100 = D \cdot C$. Hence, indifference curves are rectangular hyperbolas.

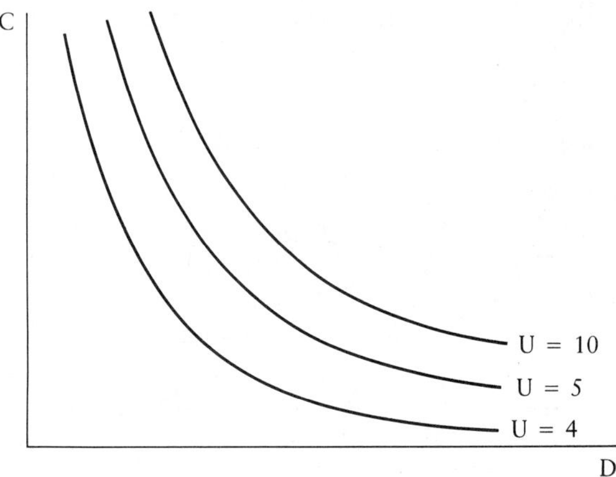

3.5
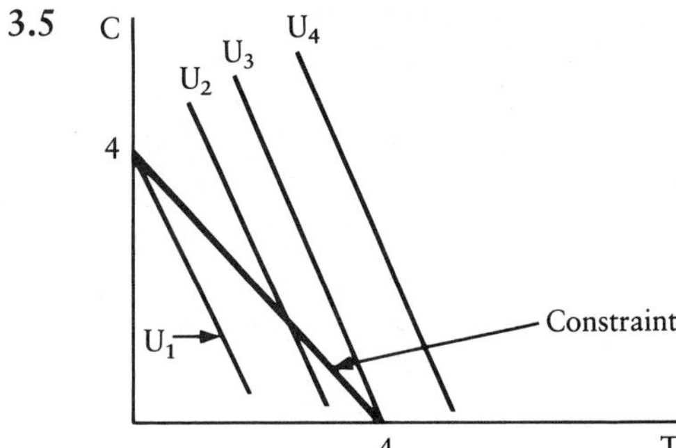

Indifference curves are straight lines: The slope of these lines is −4/3. Therefore, MRS = 4/3—this person is willing to give up 4/3 units of C to get one more T. She would buy where her budget constraint intersects her indifference curve (maximizing U), which is at T = 4, C = 0. If she had more income, she would not buy more coffee (she would maximize utility by buying more tea). If the price of coffee fell to \$2, she would buy all coffee maximizing her utility at $U = 3C + 4T = 3(6) + 4(0) = 18$.

3.7

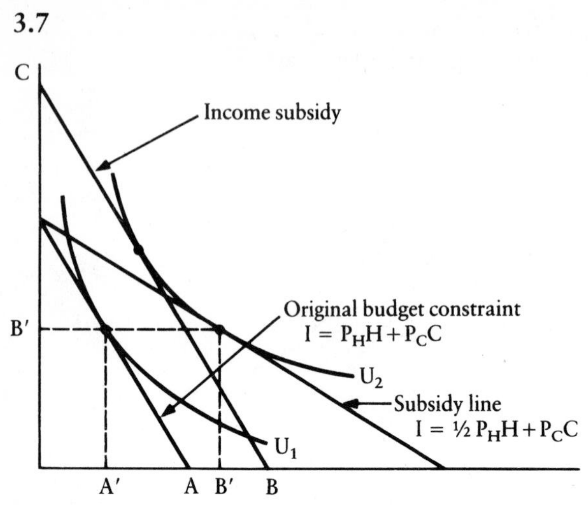

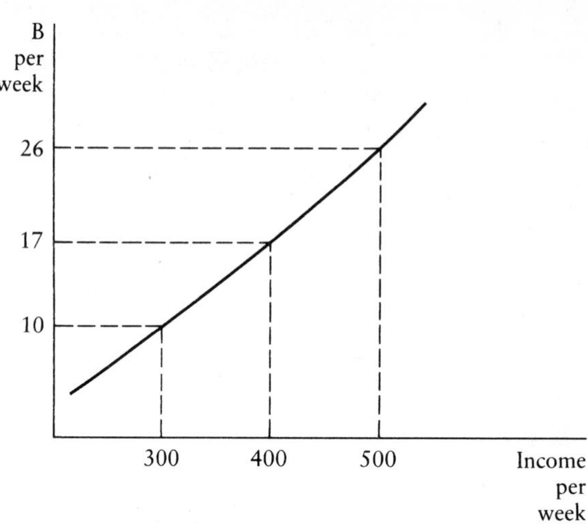

Income subsidy is cheaper since AB < A′B′.

3.9 Such a policy would be more likely to reduce utility of low-income people. High-income people would probably buy the required housing quality anyway.

Chapter 4

4.1

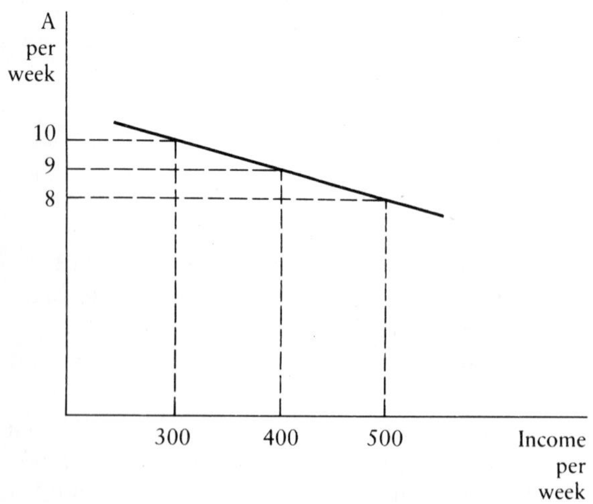

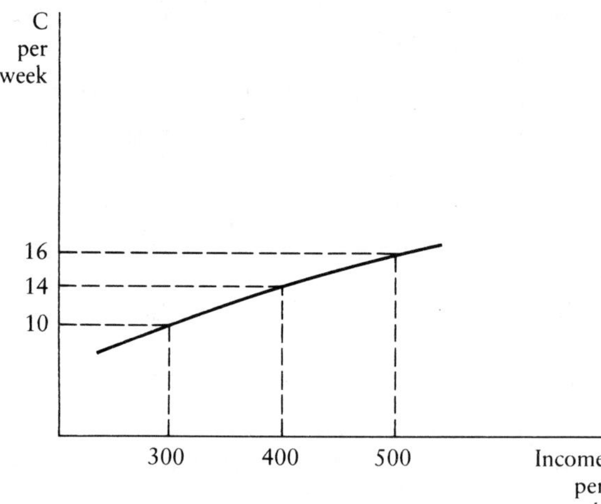

Note: A is inferior
B is a luxury
C is a necessity

4.3 In the figure, Mr. Wright is required to buy \$50 worth of clothing. Given this constraint, he can only attain utility level U_0. With an unconstrained choice, U_1 can be attained.

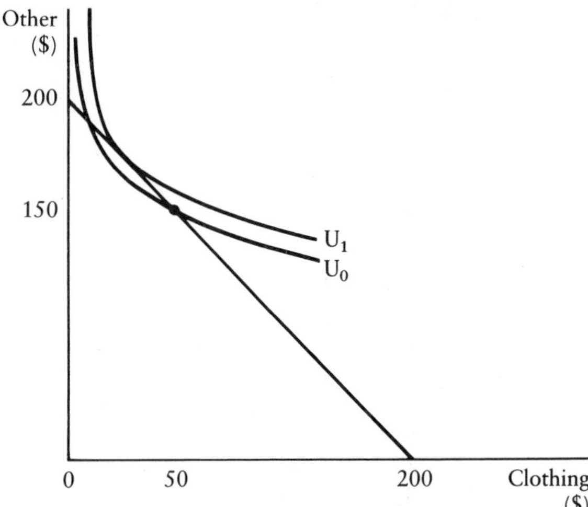

4.5 If the price of potatoes rises, the quantity purchased will also rise. Hence the amount available to spend on automobiles falls. Since the price of automobiles is unchanged, the quantity bought must fall.

4.7 a. $PB = 2J$ and $.05PB + .1J = 3$

$$5PB + 10J = 300$$
$$PB + 2J = 60$$
$$\therefore 4J = 60 \quad J = 15, \quad PB = 30$$

b. $P_J = \$.15 \quad PB = 2J \quad .05PB + .15J = 3$

$$5PB + 15J = 300 \qquad 25J = 300$$
$$J = 12, PB = 24$$

c. To continue buying J = 15, PB = 30, David would need to buy 3 more ounces of jelly and 6 more ounces of peanut butter.

Increase by: $3(.15) + 6(.05) = \$.75$.

d.

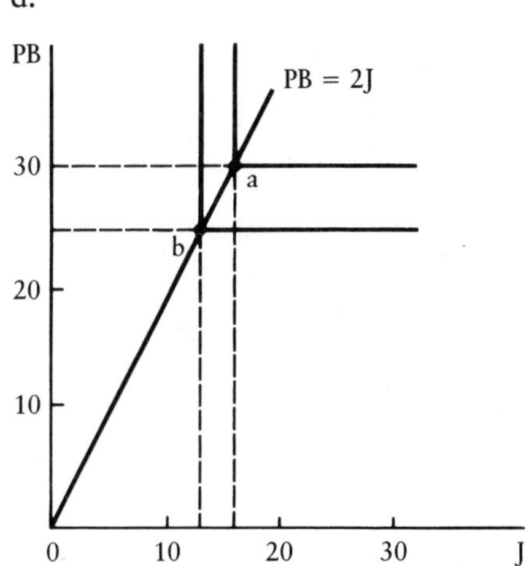

e. Since David uses only PB + J to make sandwiches (in fixed proportions), and because bread is free, it is just as though he buys sandwiches where $P_{sandwich} = 2P_{PB} + P_J$.

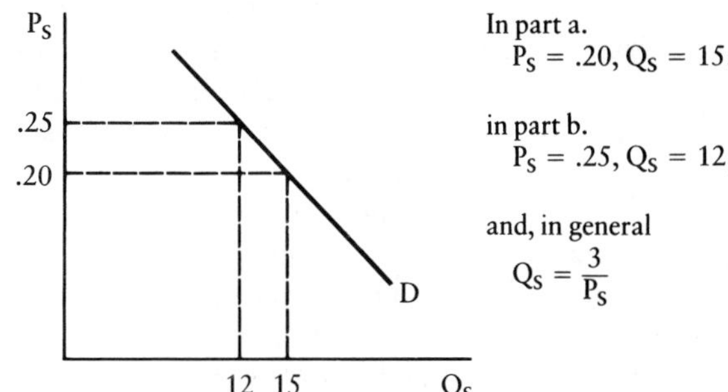

In part a.
$P_S = .20, Q_S = 15$;

in part b.
$P_S = .25, Q_S = 12$;

and, in general
$Q_S = \frac{3}{P_S}$

f. There is no substitution effect due to the fixed proportion. A change in price results in only an income effect.

4.9

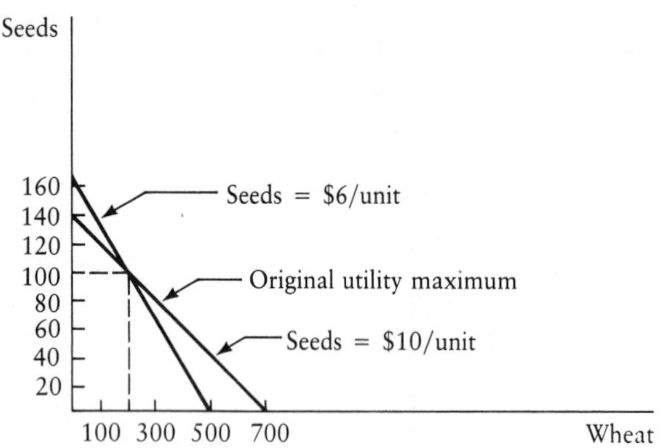

a. Started with 200 wheat, 100 sunflower seeds. Since he sells 20 units of sunflower seeds, he can buy 100 more units of wheat (will consume 300 in all).
b. If he continues to sell 20 units of sunflower seeds, he will only be able to get an additional \$120/\$2 = 60 units of wheat, so he'd be worse off. It is clear from the graph that the new constraint is northeast (Sam can be better off) of the old one only where Sam consumes more sunflower seeds than he produces, so he must sell wheat and buy sunflower seeds with the new prices.
c. In this case, the income effect is not the usual one since the lower sunflower seed price does not imply a higher real income, as in the usual case, since Sam's income is a function of the price of sunflower seeds.
(Graphically, the lower price causes a rotation around the point 200 wheat, 100 sunflower seeds rather than around the wheat intercept.)

Chapter 5

5.1 Q = 500 − 50P.

a. If P = 2, Q = 400.
P = 3, Q = 350.
P = 4, Q = 300.
P = 0, Q = 500.

b.

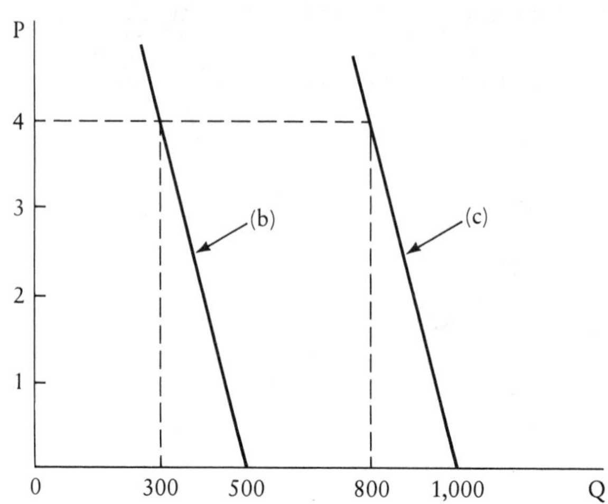

c. Q = 1000 − 50P.
If P = 2, Q = 900.
P = 3, Q = 850.
P = 4, Q = 800.
P = 0, Q = 1000.
(See previous graph.)

5.3 a.

	Tom	Dick	Harry	Total
P = 50	0	0	0	0
= 35	30	20	0	50
= 25	50	60	25	135
= 10	80	120	100	300
= 0	100	160	150	410

b. "Total" column in part a.
c.

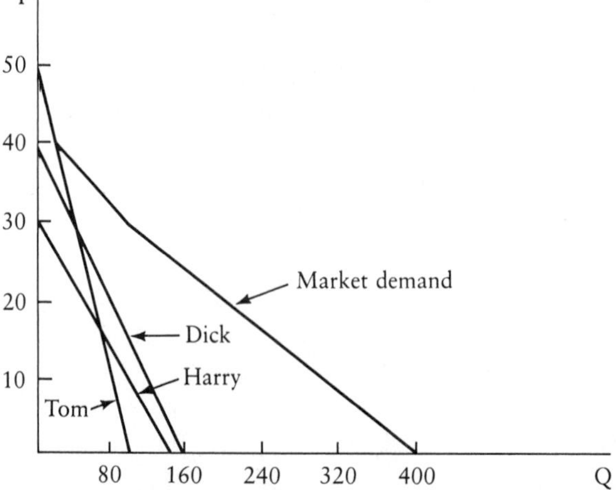

d. Above graph.

5.5 a. If price of X rises by 1 percent, quantity will fall by 2 percent since $e_{x,P_x} = -2$. Therefore X will be 980.
b. If the price of Y rises by 1 percent, quantity of X will rise by 0.5 percent since $e_{x,P_y} = 0.5$. Therefore, X will be 1005.
c. If income rises by 1 percent, quantity of X demanded will increase by 0.8 percent since $e_{x,I} = 0.8$. Therefore, quantity of X demanded will increase to 1008.

5.7 A numerical example will be sufficient here. Since ham and cheese are used in a fixed relationship, there is really only one good—ham and cheese sandwiches. Since this is the only good, the price elasticity of demand for it must be −1—that is, P · Q is constant.

a. If $P_H = P_C$, then ham constitutes 1/2 the price of a sandwich. If P_H rises by, say, 10 percent, cost of a sandwich rises by 5 percent so quantity purchased falls by 5 percent. Elasticity is, therefore, 5%/10% = −1/2.
b. For similar reasons, using the same numerical example, cross price elasticity is −1/2.
c. If $P_H = 2P_C$, ham now constitutes 2/3 the cost of a sandwich. If P_H rises by 10 percent, the cost of a sandwich rises by 6.6 percent and quantity must fall by 6.6 percent. Elasticity is 6.6%/10% = −2/3. Similar logic shows that cross price elasticity is −1/3.

5.9 $e_{X,PX} = -.6 \quad e_{X,PY} = -.8 \quad e_{X,I} = ?$
A 1 percent rise in income is the same as 1 percent drop in P_X, P_Y. With such a drop, X would increase by 0.6 + 0.8 = 1.4%. Hence, $e_{X,I} = 1.4$.

Chapter 6

6.1 a. Pizza = 40 Chianti = 20 Cost = $100
b. Pizza = 50 Chianti = 25 Cost = $100
c. -f.

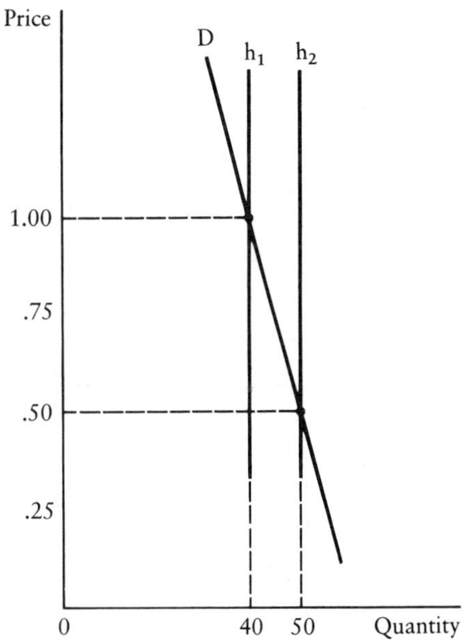

The compensated curves, h_1 and h_2, are vertical because there are no substitution effects in Irene's demand for pizza.

6.3

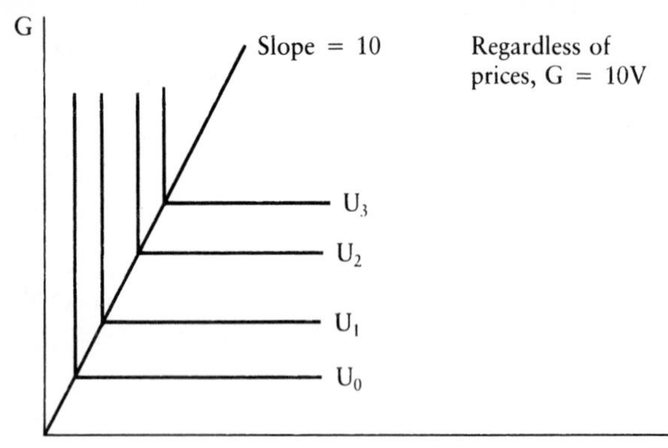

Base year index:

$$\frac{I_2}{I_1} = \frac{P_{G1}G_2 + P_{V1}V_2}{P_{G1}G_1 + P_{V1}V_1} = \frac{P_{G1}G_2 + P_{V1}(10G_2)}{P_{G1}G_1 + P_{V1}(10G_1)}$$

$$= \frac{G_2(P_{G1} + 10P_{V1})}{G_1(P_{G1} + 10P_{V1})} = \frac{G_2}{G_1}.$$

Current year index:

$$\frac{I_2}{I_1} = \frac{P_{G2}G_2 + P_{V2}V_2}{P_{G2}G_1 + P_{V2}V_1} = \frac{P_{G2}G_2 + P_{V2}(10G_2)}{P_{G2}G_1 + P_{V2}(10G_1)}$$

$$= \frac{G_2(P_{G2} + 10P_{V2})}{G_1(P_{G2} + 10P_{V2})} = \frac{G_2}{G_1}.$$

6.5 a. $U_{1986} = \sqrt{40 \cdot 40} = 40$

$U_{1987} = \sqrt{20 \cdot 80} = 40$

b. $I^{86} = P_X^{86} \cdot X^{86} + P_Y^{86}Y^{86}$

$= \$1 \cdot 40 + \$1 \cdot 40 = \$80$

$I^{87} = P_X^{86} \cdot X^{87} + P_y^{86}Y^{87}$

$= \$1 \cdot 20 + \$1 \cdot 80 = \$100$

$\frac{I^{87}}{I^{86}} = \frac{5}{4} > 1$, so real income in 86 prices is higher in 1987.

c. $I^{86} = P_X^{87}X^{86} + P_Y^{87}Y^{86}$

$= \$4 \cdot 40 + \$1 \cdot 40 = \$200$

$I^{87} = P_X^{87}X^{87} + P_Y^{87}Y^{87}$

$= \$4 \cdot 20 + \$1 \cdot 80 = \$160$

$\frac{I^{87}}{I^{86}} = \frac{4}{5} < 1$, so real income in 87 prices is lower in 1987.

d. Results of calculations depend on which prices are used. It may be necessary to use some combination of the two indices to get a true picture.

6.7

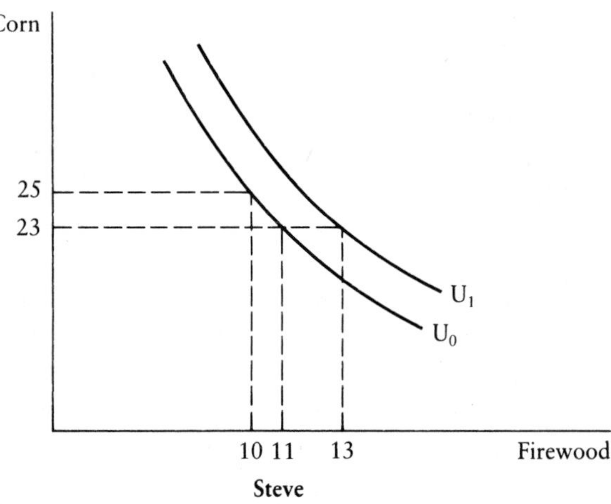

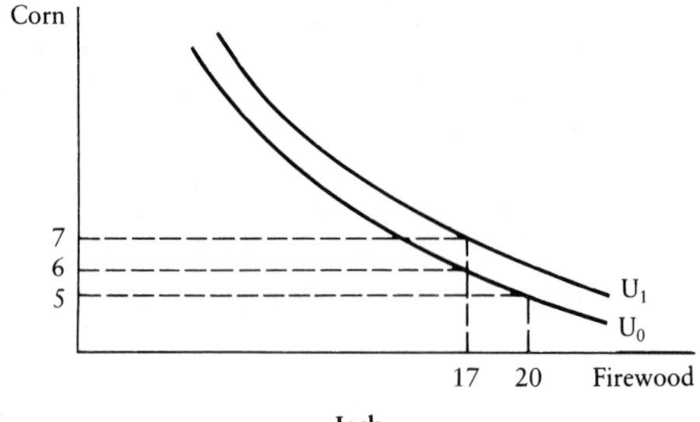

6.9 a.

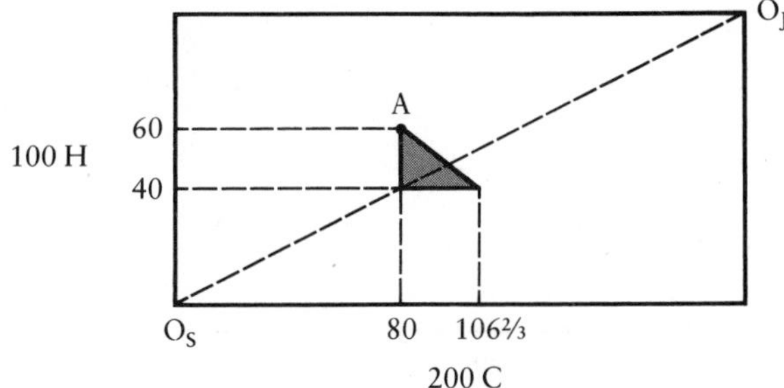

Mutually beneficial trades fall in the shaded triangular region.

b. Since Smith requires fixed proportions, anything else gives him an extra amount of one of the goods that could be given away with no loss of utility.

c. Contract curve is entire diagonal of box in part a; only shaded portion is attainable.

Chapter 7

7.1 a. $E(1) = .50(100) + .50(-100) = 0.$
$E(2) = .75(100) + .25(-300) = 0.$
$E(3) = .90(100) + .10(-900) = 0.$

b.

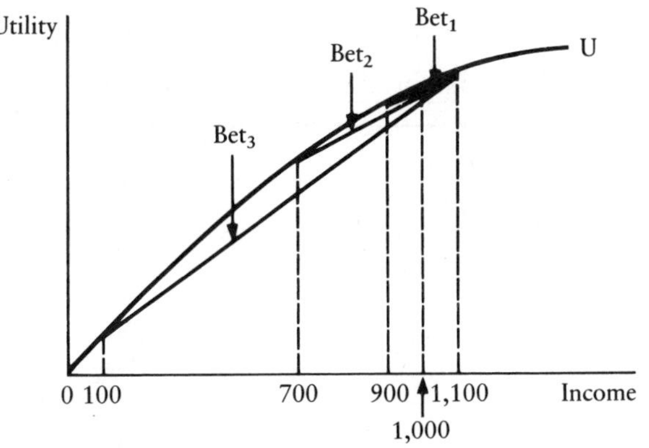

Assume, for simplicity, current income is $1,000.

c. Bet 1 will be preferred since it has smaller variability.

7.3

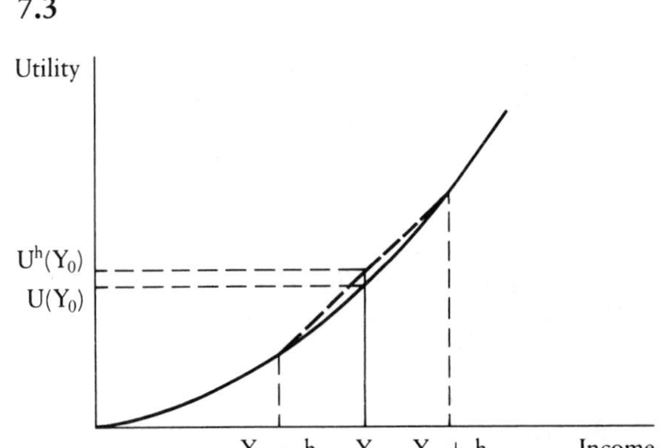

Since $U^h > U$, the individual will gamble, even on unfair bets. This would be limited by the individual's resources; he or she could eventually run out of money by taking unfair bets.

7.5 P must be large enough so that expected utility with bet is greater than or equal to that without bet:

$$P \ln(1{,}100{,}000) + (1 - P) \ln(900{,}000) \geq \ln(1{,}000{,}000)$$

$$13.9108P + 13.7102(1 - P) \geq 13.8155$$

$$.2006P \geq .1053$$

$$P \geq .525.$$

7.7

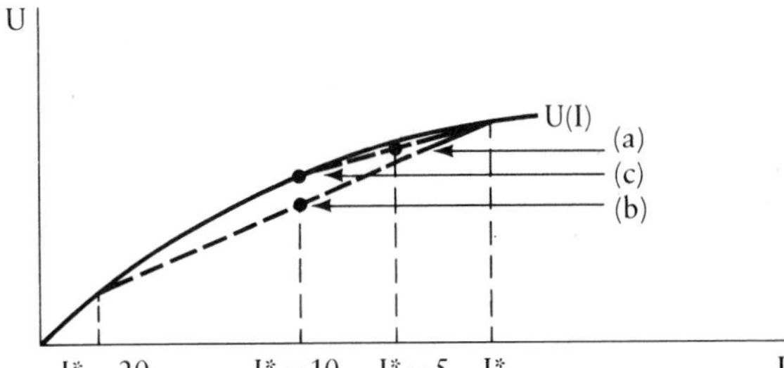

Note $U_c > U_b$. Hence, increasing fine is more effective.

7.9 a. Premium = (.8)(.5)(1,000) + (.2)(.5)(1,000) = 500.

b. For *blue* without insurance
$E(U) = .8 \ln 9{,}000 + .2 \ln 10{,}000$
$= 9.1261$
with insurance
$E(U) = \ln(9{,}500) = 9.1590$
Will buy insurance.
For *brown* without insurance
$E(U) = .2 \ln(9{,}000) + .8 \ln(10{,}000)$
$= 9.1893.$
Better off without insurance.

c. Since only blue buy insurance, fair premium is 800. Still pays this group to buy insurance.
$(E(U) = 9.1269)$
Brown will still opt for no insurance.

d. Blue premium = 800 $E(U) = 9.1269$
Brown premium = 200 $E(U) = 9.1901.$
So brown is better off under a policy that allows separate rate setting.

Chapter 8

8.1 a. $K = 6$ $Q = 6K + 4L = 6(6) + 4L$
$= 36 + 4L.$
If $Q = 60$, $4L = 60 - 36 = 24$, $L = 6.$
If $Q = 100$, $4L = 100 - 36 = 64$, $L = 16.$

b. $K = 8$ $Q = 6K + 4L = 6(8) + 4L$
$= 48 + 4L.$
If $Q = 60$, $4L = 60 - 48 = 12$, $L = 3.$
If $Q = 100$, $4L = 100 - 48 = 52$,
$L = 13.$

c. $RTS = 2/3$: If L increases by 1 unit, can keep Q constant by decreasing K by 2/3 units.

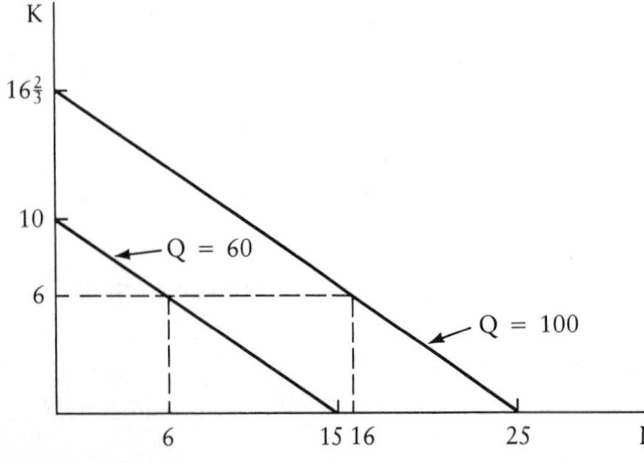

8.3 a.

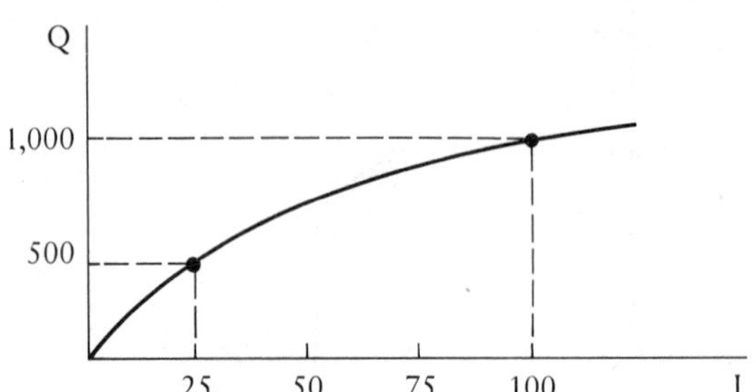

b. $AP_L = \dfrac{Q}{L} = \dfrac{100}{\sqrt{L}}$

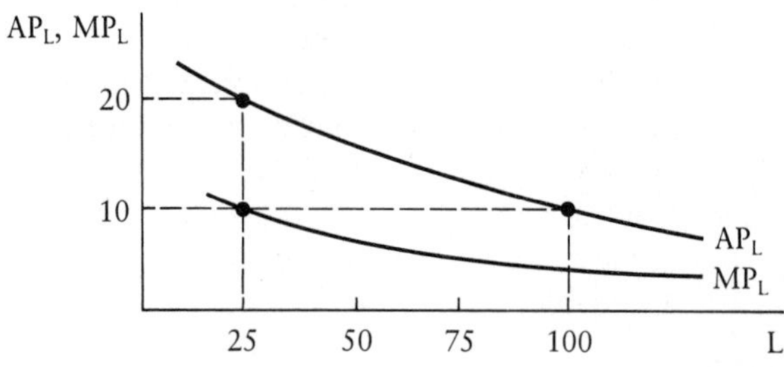

c. Graph above. Since the AP_L is everywhere decreasing, then each additional worker must be contributing less than the average of the existing workers, bringing the average down. Therefore, the marginal productivity must be lower than the average.

8.5 $Q = KL - .8K^2 - .2L^2$
Average productivity

$$\frac{Q}{L} = K - .8\frac{K^2}{L} - .2L = 10 - \frac{80}{L} - .2L$$

a. Average productivity reaches maximum at $L = 20$, $Q = 40$. $MP_L = 0$ at $L = 25$.

b.

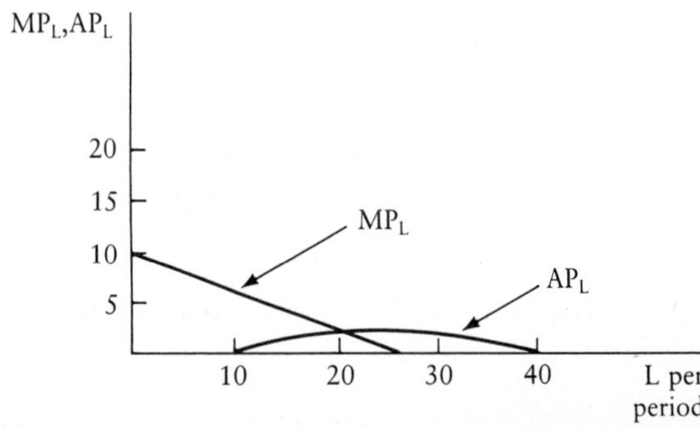

c. $K = 20.\ Q = 20L - 320 - .2L^2$

$Q/L = 20 - \frac{320}{L} - .2L$

Average productivity reaches maximum at $L = 40$, $Q = 472$. $MP_L = 0$ at $L = 50$.

8.7 a. In 8.4 $a = b = \frac{1}{2}$.

b. If we use 2K, 2L have $Q = (2K)^a(2L)^b = 2^{a+b}K^aL^b$ and if $a + b = 1$, this is twice K^aL^b

c. d. From b it follows that output will less than double or more than double if $a + b < 1$ or $a + b > 1$.

e. Function can exhibit any returns to scale desired depending on the values of a and b.

Chapter 9

9.1 a.

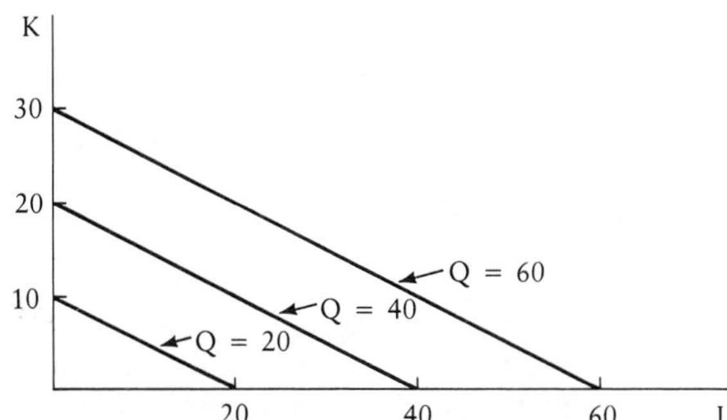

RTS = 1/2 since if L is increased by one, K can be reduced by 1/2 while holding Q constant.

b. Since $RTS = \frac{1}{2} < \frac{w}{v} = 1$, the manufacturer will use only K. For $Q = 20$, $K = 10$; $Q = 40$, $K = 20$; $Q = 60$, $K = 30$. The manufacturer's expansion path is simply the K axis.

c. If $v = \$3$, say $RTS = 1/2 > w/v = 1/3$, the manufacturer will use only L. For $Q = 20$, $L = 20$; $Q = 40$, $L = 40$; $Q = 60$, $L = 60$. Now the manufacturer's expansion path is the L axis.

9.3 a. This is a cubic cost curve. It resembles Figure 9.4d.

b. $AC = TC/Q = Q^2 - 40Q + 430$

This is a parabola. It reaches a minimum at the axis of symmetry:

$Q = -(-40)/2 = 20$

At $Q = 20$ $\quad AC = 400 - 800 + 430 = 30.$

c. At $Q = 20$ $\quad MC = 3(400) - 1600 + 430 = 30.$

d.

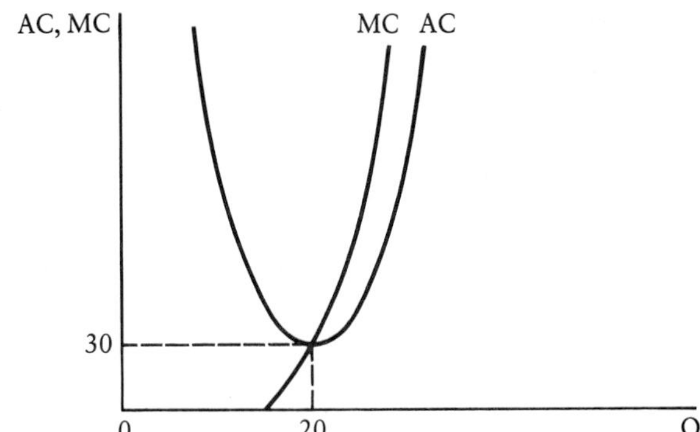

9.5 a. $Q = 2\sqrt{K \cdot L}$. $\quad K = 100$,

$Q = 2\sqrt{100 \cdot L}$. $\quad Q = 20\sqrt{L}$.

$\sqrt{L} = \frac{Q}{20}$. $\quad L = \frac{Q^2}{400}$.

$STC = vK + wL = 1(100) + 4\frac{(Q^2)}{400}$

$= 100 + \frac{Q^2}{100}$.

$SAC = \frac{STC}{Q} = \frac{100}{Q} + \frac{Q}{100}$.

b. $SMC = \frac{Q}{50}$. If $Q = 25$,

$STC = 100 + \frac{(25)^2}{100} = 106.25.$

$SAC = \frac{100}{25} + \frac{25}{100} = 4.25.$

$SMC = \frac{25}{50} = .50.$

If $Q = 50$, $STC = 100 + \frac{(50)^2}{100} = 125.$

$SAC = \frac{100}{50} + \frac{50}{100} = 2.50.$

$SMC = \frac{50}{50} = 1.$

If $Q = 100$, $STC = 100 + \frac{(100)^2}{100} = 200.$

$SAC = \frac{100}{100} + \frac{100}{100} = 2$

$SMC = \frac{100}{50} = 2.$

If $Q = 200$, $STC = 100 + \frac{(200^2)}{100} = 500.$

$SAC = \frac{100}{200} + \frac{200}{100} = 2.50.$

$SMC = \frac{200}{50} = 4.$

c.

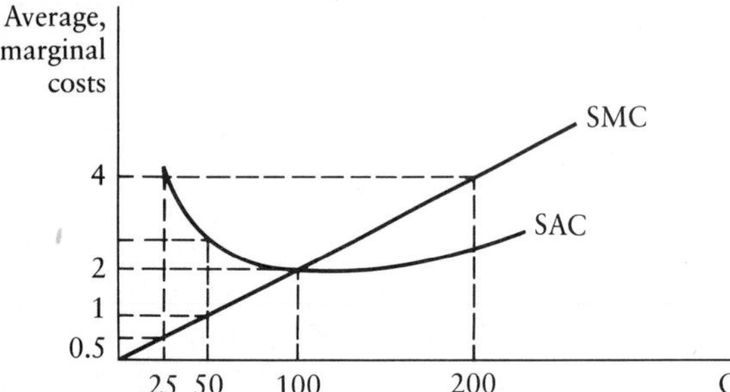

d. As long as the marginal cost of producing one more unit is below the average cost curve, average costs will be falling. Similarly, if the marginal cost of producing one more unit is higher than the average cost, then average costs will be rising. Therefore, the SMC curve must intersect the SAC curve at its lowest point.

9.7 To minimize, costs should equate the marginal productivities of labor in each plant. If labor were more productive in one plant than another, costs could be lowered by moving workers.

a. $MP_{L1} = MP_{L2}$. $5/2\sqrt{L_1} = 5/\sqrt{L_2}$.
$2\sqrt{L_1} = \sqrt{L_2}$. $L_2 = 4L_1$.
$Q_1 = 5\sqrt{L_1}$; $Q_2 = 10\sqrt{L_2} = 10\sqrt{4L_1} = 20\sqrt{L_1}$
Hence $Q_2 = 4Q_1$.

b. $4Q_1 = Q_2$ so, $Q_1 = 1/5Q$. $Q_2 = 4/5Q$ where Q is total output.

$STC \text{ (Plant 1)} = 25 + wL_1 = 25 + \frac{Q_1^2}{25}$

$STC \text{ (Plant 2)} = 100 + wL_2 = 100 + \frac{Q_2^2}{100}$

$$STC = STC \text{ (Plant 1)} + STC \text{ (Plant 2)}$$
$$= 25 + \frac{Q_1^2}{25} + 100 + \frac{Q_2^2}{100}$$
$$= 125 + \frac{(1/5Q)^2}{25} + \frac{(4/5Q)^2}{100}$$
$$= 125 + \frac{1/25Q^2}{25} + \frac{16/25Q^2}{100}$$
$$= 125 + \frac{20/25Q^2}{100}$$
$$= 125 + \frac{Q^2}{125}.$$

$MC = \frac{2Q}{125}$. $AC = \frac{125}{Q} + \frac{Q}{125}$.

$MC(100) = \frac{200}{125} = \$1.60.$

$MC(125) = \$2.00.$ $MC(200) = \$3.20.$

c. In the long run, because of constant returns to scale, can change K so doesn't really matter where production occurs. Could split evenly or produce all output in one plant.
$TC = K + L = 2Q$. $AC = 2 = MC$.

d. If there were decreasing returns to scale, then should let each firm have equal share of production. AC and MC, not constant anymore, are increasing functions of Q so do not want either plant to be too large.

9.9 Each average cost curve reaches a minimum when its slope is 0. This occurs at only one point on the AC curve. Consequently, other tangencies cannot also be minima. The draftsman was correct.

Chapter 10

10.1 a. Set P = MC. 20 = .2q + 10.
10 = .2q. q = 50.

b. Maximum Profits = TR − TC =
$(50 - 20) - [.1(50)^2 + 10(50) + 50] =$
1000 − 800 = 200.

c.

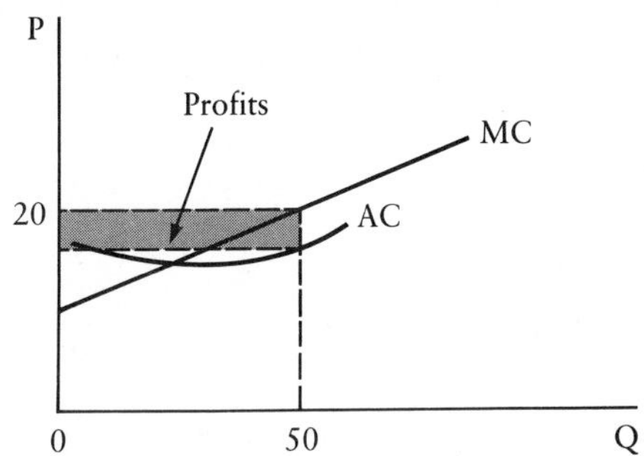

10.3 If P is constant, the TR = P · q is simply a straight line through the origin. Profits will be maximized where the slope of the TR curve (which is the price) is equal to the slope of the TC curve (that is to marginal cost).

10.5 Here the demand curve has a constant elasticity of −2. Hence,

$$MR = P\left(1 + \frac{1}{e}\right) = \frac{1}{2}P$$

but $P^2 = \frac{256}{q}$, so $P = \frac{16}{\sqrt{q}}$ so $MR = \frac{8}{\sqrt{q}}$.

For profit maximization, MR = MC,

$$\frac{8}{\sqrt{q}} = .001q,$$

$$8000 = q^{3/2}$$

Hence, q = 400. $P = \frac{16}{20} = .80.$

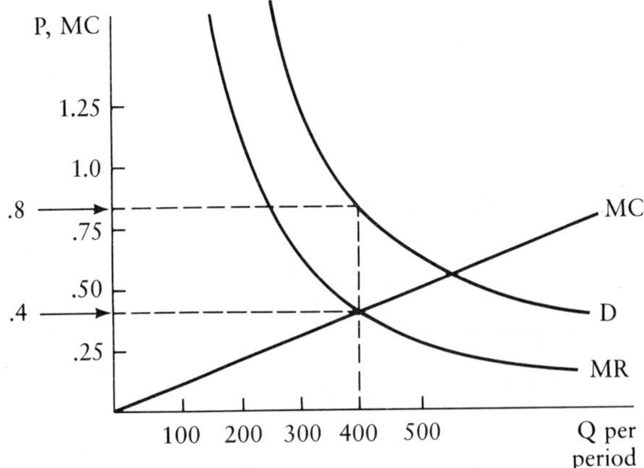

10.7 a. $TR = P \cdot q = \frac{(100 - q) \cdot q}{2}$

$$= 50q - \frac{1}{2}q^2.$$

MR = 50 − q.
Noncalculus proofs can be done graphically or with a table.

b. Max. π: MR = MC.
MR = 50 − q.
MR = MC: 50 − q = 10. q = 40,
P = 30, π = P · q − 10q
= 1200 − 400 = 800.

c. Max. Revenue: MR = 0. 50 − q = 0.
q = 50, P = 25,
π = P · q − 10q
= 1250 − 500 = 750.

d. Constraint π = 768. $50/q - q^2/2 - 10q = 768$. Use quadratic formula or factor: q = (32, 48), but trying to max revenue so choose q = 48, P = 26.

e.

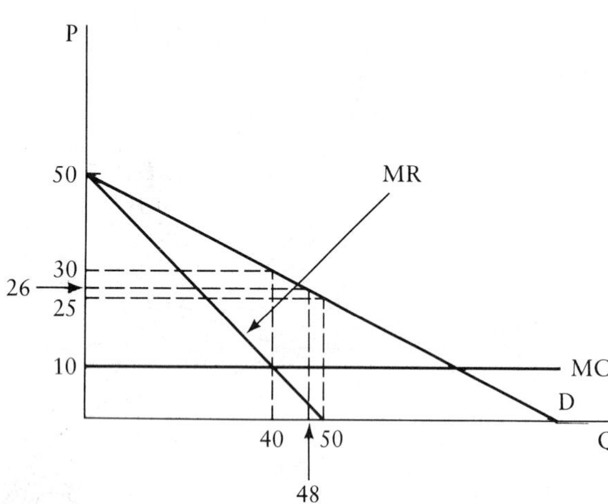

e. If the firm continues to hire 400 workers it will have no severance costs and profits of

$$\begin{aligned} TR - TC &= 15(200) \\ &\quad - (1{,}000 + .05(200^2)) \\ &= 3{,}000 - (1{,}000 + 2{,}000) \\ &= 0, \end{aligned}$$

which is better than in part d. An output level of 180 ($L = 324$) would yield an overall profit for the firm.

Chapter 11

11.1 For temporary price changes, hiring and severance costs might be regarded as marginal costs since they arise in connection with short-term changes in input use. For permanent price changes, however, these are more like fixed costs since they do not affect hourly wage rates.

11.3 a. $STC = vK + wL$
$= 10 \cdot 100 + wL$
$= 1{,}000 + 5L,$

but $q = 10\sqrt{L}$ so $L = \dfrac{q^2}{100}$.

Hence, $STC = 1{,}000 + q^2/20$.

b. Use $P = MC$.
$20 = .1q$, so $q = 200$.
$L = q^2/100$, so $L = 400$.

c. If $P = 15$, $P = MC$ implies $15 = .1q$ or $q = 150$, $L = 225$.

d. Cost will be 175 to reduce L from 400 to 225. With $q = 150$, Profits $= TR - TC = 15(150) - (1{,}000 + .05q^2) = 2{,}250 - (1{,}000 + 1{,}125) = 125$. After paying severance cost of 175 the firm will incur a loss of 50.

11.5

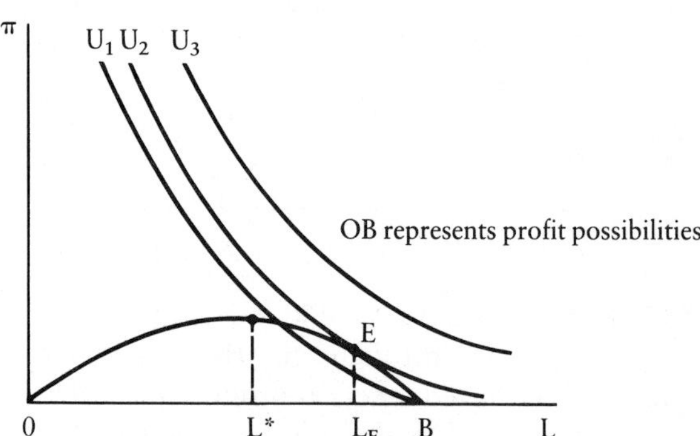

a. Draw π, L indifference curves – optimum point of E. If optimum is to be at L^*, slope of indifference curve must be 0 there, i.e.:
$MRS = MU_L/MU_H = 0 \quad \therefore MU_L = 0.$

b. Draw indifference curve through B, $0(U_1)$. This shows levels of π, L indifferent to $L = B$, $\pi = 0$. π' (Marshallian profits) equals distance between curve 0B and U_1. If that is to be maximized at E, slope of U_1 at L_E must equal slope of 0B at E = slope U_2 at E. QED.

11.7 a. Again we use $P = MC$.
$30 = .02q$, so $q = 1{,}500$.

$$\begin{aligned} \text{Profits} &= TR - TC \\ &= 30(1500) - (.01q^2 + 10{,}000) \\ &= 45{,}000 - (22{,}500 + 10{,}000) \\ &= 12{,}500. \end{aligned}$$

b. Now costs $= .75 \cdot STC$
$= .0075q^2 + 7{,}500.$
$SMC = .75(.02q) = .015q.$

$P = MC$ implies $30 = .015q$ or $q = 2{,}000$.
In this case
$$\begin{aligned}\text{Profits} &= TR - TC\\ &= 30(2{,}000) - (.0075q^2 + 7{,}500)\\ &= 60{,}000 - (30{,}000 + 7{,}500)\\ &= 22{,}500.\end{aligned}$$

c. Ted would pay up to 22,500 − 12,500 = 10,000 per week for the company.

Chapter 12

12.1 a. Set supply equal to demand to find equilibrium price:
$$\begin{aligned}Q_S = 1{,}000 &= Q_D = 1{,}600 - 600P.\\ 1{,}000 &= 1{,}600 - 600P.\\ 600 &= 600P\\ P &= 1/\text{lb}.\end{aligned}$$

b. $$\begin{aligned}Q_S = 400 &= 1{,}600 - 600P.\\ 600P &= 1{,}200.\\ P &= 2/\text{lb}.\end{aligned}$$

c. $$\begin{aligned}Q_S = 1{,}000 &= 2{,}200 - 600P.\\ 1{,}200 &= 600P.\\ P &= 2/\text{lb}.\end{aligned}$$
$$\begin{aligned}Q_S = 400 &= 2{,}200 - 600P.\\ 600P &= 1800.\\ P &= 3/\text{lb}.\end{aligned}$$

d.

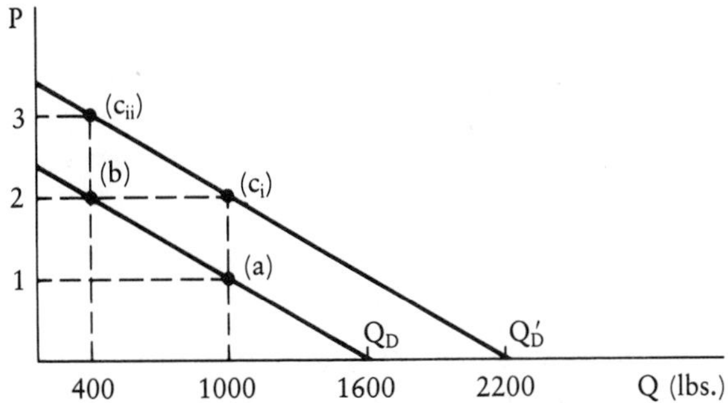

12.3 a. Supply = 100,000. In equilibrium, $100{,}000 = Q_S = Q_D = 160{,}000 - 10{,}000P$ or $P = 6$.

b. For any one firm, quantity supplied by other firms is fixed at 99,900. Demand curve is
$$\begin{aligned}Q_{D'} &= 160{,}000 - 10{,}000P - 99{,}900\\ &= 60{,}100 - 10{,}000P.\end{aligned}$$
If quantity supplied is 0, $Q_{S'} = 0 = Q_{D'} = 60{,}100 - 10{,}000P$, or $P = 6.01$.
If quantity supplied is 200, $Q_{S'} = 200 = Q_{D'} = 60{,}100 - 10{,}000P$, or $P = 5.99$.
Elasticity − Slope of demand × P/Q for market.
$$e_{Q,P} = -10{,}000 \cdot \frac{6}{100{,}000} = -.6.$$
For a single firm, demand is much more elastic:
$$e_{Q,P} = -10{,}000 \cdot \frac{6}{100} = -600.$$
A change in quantity supplied does not affect price very much.

12.5 a. Short Run: MR = P so P = MC.
$$\begin{aligned}P &= q^2 + 20q + 100.\\ P &= (q + 10)^2.\\ \sqrt{P} &= q + 10.\\ q &= \sqrt{P} - 10.\end{aligned}$$

b. $P = 121$. $q = \sqrt{121} - 10 = 1$.
$P = 169$. $q = \sqrt{169} - 10 = 3$.
$P = 256$. $q = \sqrt{256} - 10 = 6$.

c. $\pi = TR - TC$. $P = 121$.
$$\begin{aligned}\pi &= 1 \cdot (121) - [.33(1)^3 + 10(1)^2 + 100(1) + 48].\\ &= 121 - 158.33 = -37.33.\end{aligned}$$
$P = 169$.
$$\begin{aligned}\pi &= 3(169) - [.33(3)^3 + 10(3)^2 + 100(3) + 48].\\ &= 507 - 446.91 = 60.09.\end{aligned}$$
$P = 256$.
$$\begin{aligned}\pi &= 6(256) - [.33(6)^3 + 10(6)^2 + 100(6) + 48].\\ &= 1536 - 1079.28 = 456.72.\end{aligned}$$

12.7 $C = q^2 + wq = q^2 + .002Qq$

a. If $w = 10$, $C = q^2 + 10q$.
$MC = 2q + 10 = P$. Hence,
$q = P/2 - 5$.

Industry Supply: $Q = \sum_{1}^{1,000} q$
$= 500P - 5,000.$
At P = 20, Q = 5,000; at P = 21, Q = 5,500.

b. Here MC = 2q + .002Q. Set = P.
q = P/2 − .001Q.
Total $Q = \sum_{i}^{1,000} q = 500P - Q.$
Therefore, Q = 250P.
P = 20, Q = 5,000.
P = 21, Q = 5,250.
Supply is more steeply sloped in this case of interactions—increasing production bids up the wages of diamond cutters.

12.9 a. In long-run equilibrium, AC = P and MC = P, so AC = MC.

$$.01q - 1 + \frac{100}{q} = .02q - 1.$$

$$\frac{100}{q} = .01q.$$

$$\frac{10,000}{q} = q.\ q^2 = 10,000.$$

q = 100 gallons.

$$AC = .01(100) - 1 + \frac{100}{100}$$
$$= 1 - 1 + 1 = 1.$$

MC = .02(100) − 1 = 2 − 1 = 1.

b. In the long run, P = MC P = \$1.
Q_D = 2,500,000 − 500,000(1) = 2,000,000 gallons. The market supplies 2,000,000 gallons so

$$\frac{2,000,000 \text{ gallons}}{100 \text{ gallons/station}} = 20,000 \text{ gas stations.}$$

c. In the long run, P = \$1 still since the AC curve has not changed.
Q_D = 2,000,000 − 1,000,000(1) = 1,000,000 gallons

$$\frac{1,000,000 \text{ gallons}}{100 \text{ gallons/station}} = 10,000 \text{ gas stations.}$$

Chapter 13

13.1 a. Production possibility frontier:

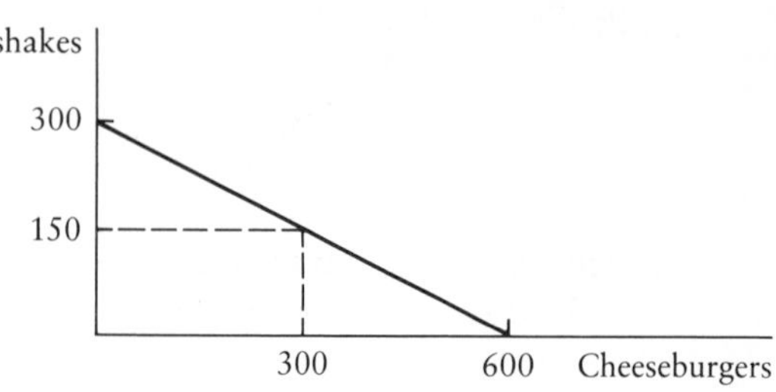

b. M = 1/2C. C + 2M = 600.
C + 2(1/2C) = 600. 2C = 600.
C = 300. M = 150.

c. −slope = RPT = 1/2. Under efficient economy, RPT = MRS = $\frac{P_C}{P_M}$ so $\frac{P_C}{P_M} = \frac{1}{2}$.

13.3 a. Production possibility frontier:

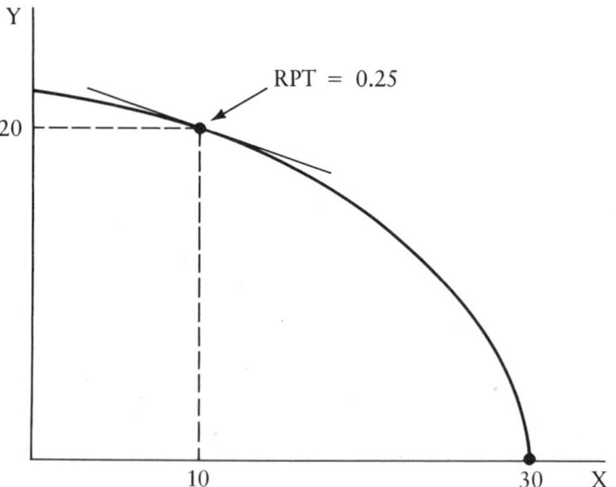

b. If Y = 2X, $X^2 + 2(2X)^2 = 900$.
$9X^2 = 900$; X = 10, Y = 20.

c. If $X = 9$ on the production possibility frontier,

$$Y = \sqrt{\frac{819}{2}} = 20.24.$$

If $X = 11$ on the frontier,

$$Y = \sqrt{\frac{779}{2}} = 19.74.$$

Hence, RPT is about 0.25.

13.5 $H = 16$, $L_F + L_C = 8$ $F^2 + C^2 = 8$.
$U = 4F^{1/4}C^{1/4}$.
$C = F$ since the goods enter utility symmetrically.
$C = F = 2$, $H = 16$, $U = 4\sqrt{2} = 5.66$.

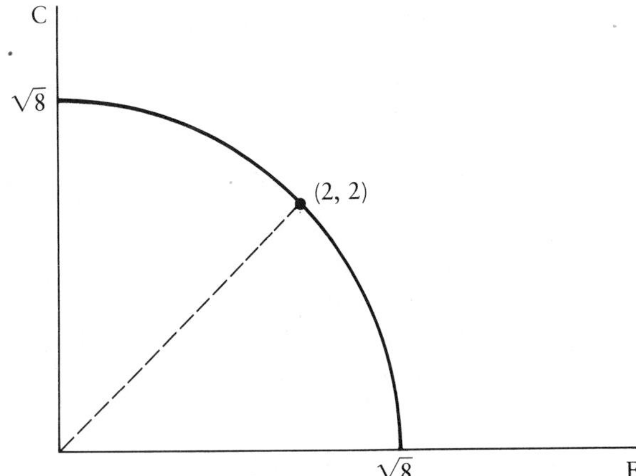

13.7 a. $X_A^2 = L_X$, $Y_A^2 = L_Y$, $X_A^2 + Y_A^2 = L_X + L_Y = 100$. Same for region B $\therefore 4X_B^2 + 4Y_B^2 = 100$.

b. RPT's should be equal.

c. $RPT_A = -\dfrac{dY}{dX} = X_A/Y_A$.

$RPT_B = -\dfrac{dY}{dX} = X_B/Y_B$.

But $X_A^2 + Y_A^2 = 4(X_B^2 + Y_B^2)$.
Some algebra shows that
$X_A = 2X_B$; also $Y_A = 2Y_B$.
$X_T = X_A + X_B = 3X_B$. $X_T^2 = 9X_B^2$.
$Y_T = Y_A + Y_B = 3Y_B$. $Y_T^2 = 9Y_B^2$.
$X_T^2 + Y_T^2 = 9(X_B^2 + Y_B^2) = 9/4 \times 100$
$= 225$.
If $X_T = 12$ $X_T^2 = 144$
$Y_T = \sqrt{225 - 144} = 9$.
Note: If labor could move, would set marginal physical products equal.
In this case, can show that
$X_T^2 + Y_T^2 = 250$
If $X_T = 12$ $Y_T = \sqrt{250 - 144}$
$= 10.3$.
Note improvement over part c.

13.9 a. D

b. E

c. $E(U) = .6(L) + .4(H)$.
$EU_A = 50$, $EU_B = 52$, $EU_C = 48.6$,
$EU_D = 51.5$, $EU_E = 50$,... Choose B.

d. Max $E(U) - |U_1 - U_2|$
Values:
A: $50 - 0 = 50$.
B: $55 - 30 = 25$.
C: $49.5 - 9 = 40.5$
D: $51.75 - 2.5 = 49.25$.
E: $57 - 54 = 3$.

Choose A.

e. It shows that a variety of different social choices might be made depending on the criteria being used.

Chapter 14

14.1

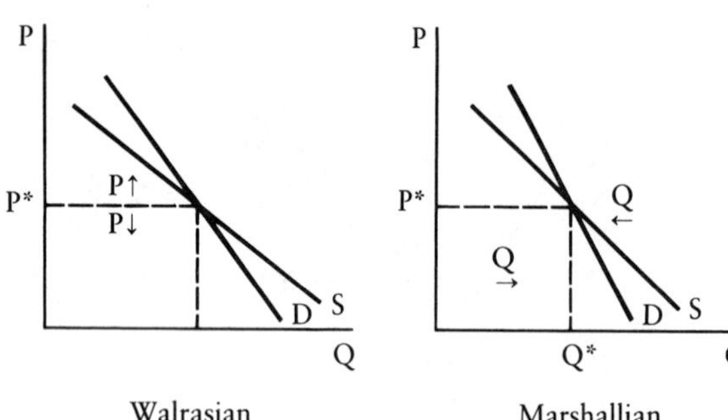

14.3

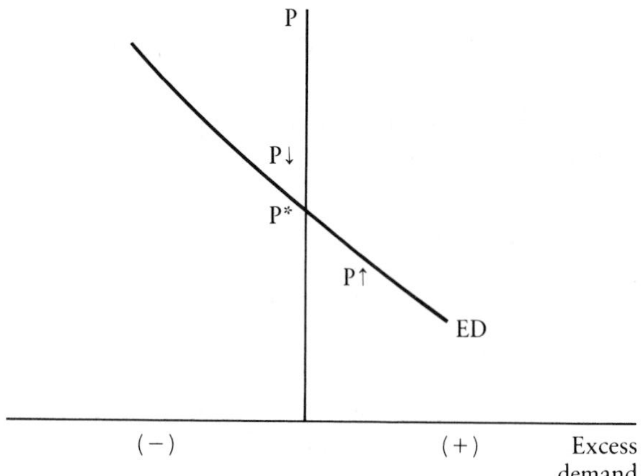

a. ED is negatively sloped since usually D is negatively sloped, S is positively sloped.
b. ED = 0 when D = S.
c. ED > 0; P rises; ED < 0; P falls—see graph.
d. ED could be positively sloped if S were negatively sloped and the absolute value of its slope exceeded that of the demand curve.

e. Process described in (c) would be reversed.

14.5 a. $Q_t = 100 - 2P_t \quad Q_t = 70 + E(P_t)$
In equilibrium, $E(P_t) = P_t$
$100 - 2P_t = 70 + P_t$, $3P_t = 30$
$P^* = \$10$, $Q^* = 80$.

b. If suppliers use last year's price to predict this year's price yields: $E(P_t) = P_{t-1}$, thus $Q_t = 70 + P_{t-1}$, $Q_t = 100 - 2P_t$. Equating Q^D and Q^S gives $70 + P_{t-1} = 100 - 2P_t$ or

$$P_t = -\frac{1}{2}P_{t-1} + 15.$$

If initial $P_0 = \$8$, then next period's price will be

$$P_1 = -\frac{1}{2}(8) + 15 = \$11$$

$$P_2 = -\frac{1}{2}(11) + 15 = \$9.5$$

$$P_3 = -\frac{1}{2}(9.5) + 15 = \$10.25$$

Therefore, it will take three periods for the price to get within \$.25 of equilibrium price of \$10.

c. The farmers would notice the oscillating price and make some more "rational" prediction. Perhaps, $E(P_t) = P^* = 10$.

14.7 a. $\overline{P} = 10{,}000$ so demand is
$Q_D = 15{,}000 - P$.
Supply assumption implies
$Q_S = P - 5{,}000$.
$Q_D = Q_S$ implies $P^* = 10{,}000$.

b. With $P^* = 10{,}000$ $\overline{P}$ of cars traded is 7,500.

c. Now $Q_D = 11{,}250 - P$
$Q_D = Q_S$ implies $P^* = 8{,}125$
$\overline{P} = 6{,}562$.

d. As these cases suggest, there is no equilibrium price at which $\overline{P} = P^*$.

14.9 a. Assuming new information arrives in unpredictable random ways, the two theories are equivalent.

b. They can't outguess the market, but they may provide diversification or "prudence" for those who demand it.

Chapter 15

15.1 a. P = 53 − Q.
For maximum profits, set MR = MC:
MR = 53 − 2Q = MC = 5.
Q = 24, P = 29.
π = TR − TC = 24 · 29 − 24 · 5 = 696 − 120 = 576.
Consumer surplus = $\frac{1}{2}(53 - 29) \cdot 24 = 288$.

b. MC = P = 5, P = 5, Q = 48.

c. Consumer surplus = $\frac{1}{2}(48)^2 = 1152$.
1152 > Profits + consumer surplus = 576 + 288 = 864
Deadweight loss = 1152 − 864 = 288
Also ½ Δ Q · Δ P = ½(24) (24)

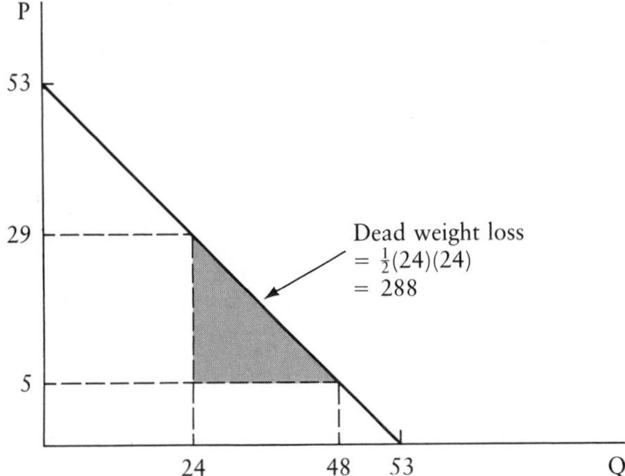

15.3 a. AC = MC = 10, Q = 60 − P,
MR = 60 − 2Q. For profit max.,
MC = MR. 10 = 60 − 2Q, 2Q = 50,
Q = 25, P = 35.
π = TR − TC = (25) (35) − (25) (10) = 625

b. AC = MC = 10, Q = 45 − .5P.
MR = 90 − 4Q. For profit max.,
MC = MR, 10 = 90 − 4Q, 80 = 4Q,
Q = 20, P = 50.
π = (20) (50) − (20) (10) = 800.

c. AC = MC = 10, Q = 100 − 2P,
MR = 50 − Q. For profit max.,
MC = MR, 10 = 50 − Q, Q = 40,
P = 30.
π = (40) (30) − (40) (10) = 800.

d.

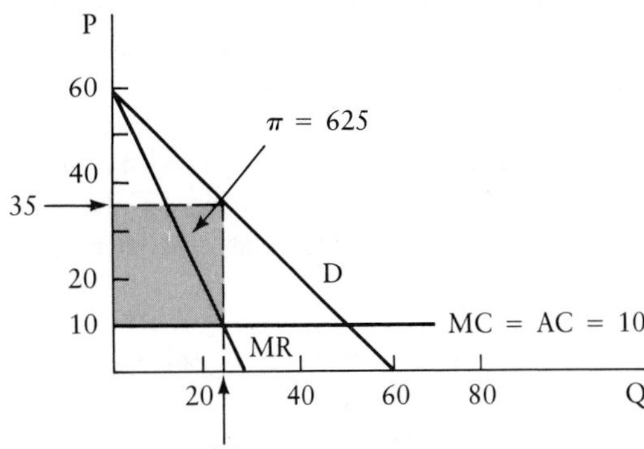

Part a

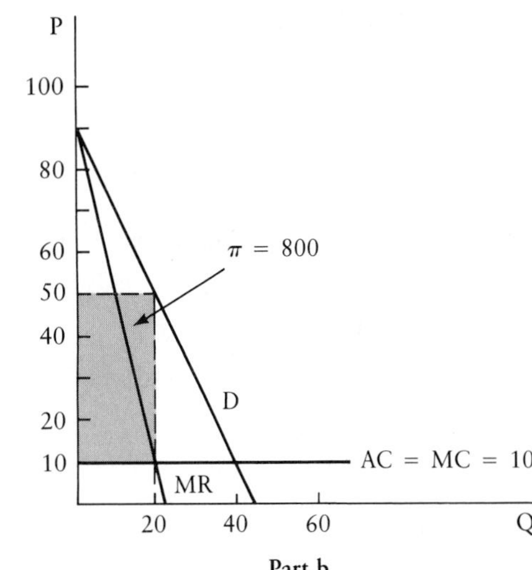

Part b

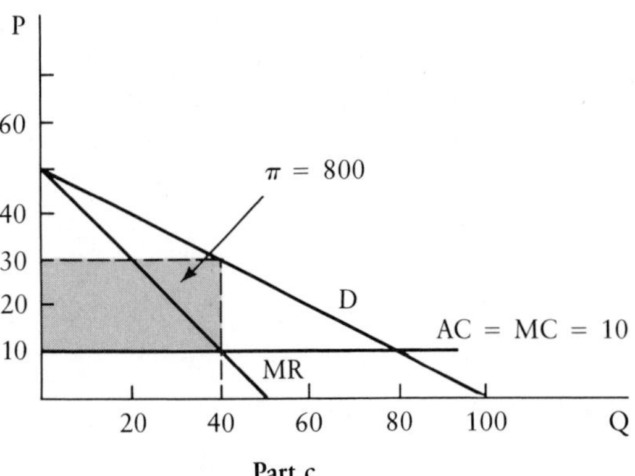

Part c

The supply curve for a monopoly is a single point, namely, that quantity for which MC = MR. Any attempt to connect equilibrium points (price-quantity points) on the market demand curves has little meaning and brings about a strange shape. One reason for this is that as the demand curve shifts, its elasticity (and its MR curve) often changes, bringing about widely varying price and quantity changes.

c.

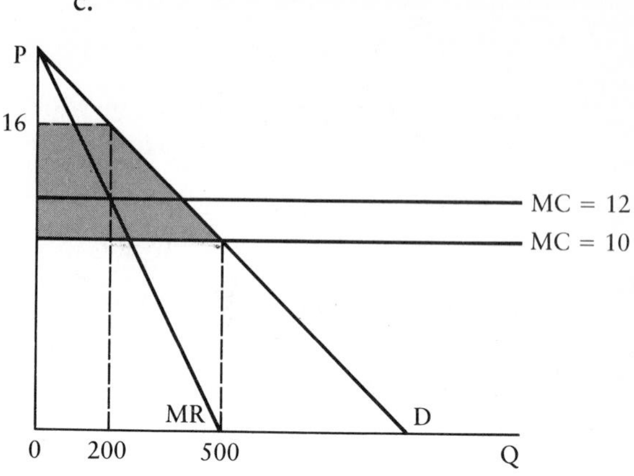

15.5 A multiplant monopolist will still produce where MR = MC and will equalize MC among factories.
$MR = 100 - 2(q_1 + q_2)$ and $MC_1 = MC_2$.
$q_1 - 5 = .5q_2 - 5$. $q_1 = .5q_2$.
$MR = 100 - 2(.5q_2 + q_2)$.
$MR = MC_2$. $100 - 2(1.5q_2) = .5q_2 - 5$.
$3.5q_2 = 105$.
$q_2 = 30$ and $q_1 = 15$, so $Q_T = 45$.

15.7 $Q_D = 1000 - 50P$ $\quad MR = 20 - Q/25$
MC = 10 under PC
MC = 12 under monopoly

a. *Perfect competition:*
P = MC = 10.
$Q_D = 1000 - 50(10) = 500 = Q_S$.
Monopoly:
MC = MR
$12 = 20 - Q/25$
$300 = 500 - Q$
$Q = 200 \quad 200 = 1000 - 50P$
$50P = 800 \quad P = 16$

b. Loss of consumer surplus due to monopolization can easily be obtained from the graph (shaded portion). Area shaded portion = (16 − 10) (200) + ½(16 − 10) (500 − 200) = 1200 + 900 = 2100.

Chapter 16

16.1 a. $q_1 = 9 \quad q_2 = 9$
Profits of each = 0.

b. $q_1 = 11 - P_1$. Set P = ½(11+2) = 6.5.
Now $q_1 = 4.5$
$\pi = 4.5(6.5 - 2) = 20.25$.

c. Same as (b) $\quad P_2 = 6.5 \quad q_2 = 4.5$.

d. (b) and (c) are inconsistent. Need to use Cournot reaction functions (See Chapter 17).

e. $q_1 = 10 - ½P$
$q_2 = 10 - ½P$
Set P = ½(20 + 2) = 11
$q_1 = q_2 = 4.5$
Profits of each = 4.5(11 − 2) = 40.5

16.3 Most literature suggests that "planned obsolescence" is a profitable strategy for a monopoly, but not so under perfect competition since entrants would produce more durable commodities. The difficult part of the theory of durability is how to treat the market for used goods and the degree of substitutability between new and used goods.

16.5 Might still produce different goods depending on nature of demand and cost conditions.

16.7 Might compare low point of AC curve to what price would be if firm producing that output were to enter.

16.9

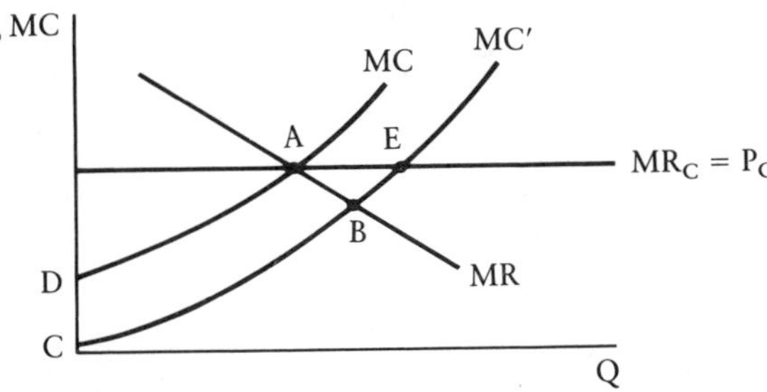

Fellner gives the following analysis:
$MR_C = P_C$ is demand facing competitive firm.
MR is the marginal revenue curve for the monopolist.
Innovation shifts MC to MC′.
Potential profits for competitive firms are CDAE.
For monopoly CDAB.
Hence innovation is more profitable for the competitive firm. It is more likely to adopt the innovation.

Chapter 17

17.1 $Q = 150 - P$. $MC = 0$.

a. A zero cost monopolist would produce that output for which MR is equal to 0 (MR = MC = 0). MR = 0 at one half of the demand curve's horizontal intercept (1/2(150) = 75). Q = 75, P = 75.
$\pi = (75)(75) = \$5625$.

b. $q_1 + q_2 = 150 - P$.
Demand curve for firm 1:
$q_1 = (150 - q_2) - P$.
Profit maximizing output level:
$$q_1 = \frac{150 - q_2}{2}.$$
Demand curve for firm 2:
$q_2 = (150 - q_1) - P$.
Profit maximizing output level:
$$q_2 = \frac{150 - q_1}{2}.$$
Market equilibrium:
$$q_1 = \frac{150 - (150 - q_2)}{2}.$$
$$q_1 = \frac{150 - (75 - q_1/2)}{2} = 37.5 + \frac{q_1}{4}.$$
$4q_1 = 150 + q_1$.
$3q_1 = 150$.
$q_1 = 50$, $q_2 = 50$, $P = 50$.
$\pi_1 = \pi_2 = \$2{,}500$. $\pi_{total} = 5{,}000$.

c. Under perfect competition P = MC = 0. Q = 150, P = 0, $\pi = 0$.

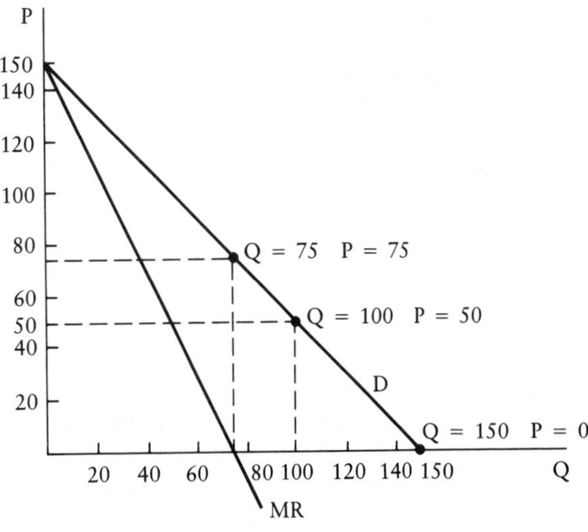

17.3 $P = 53 - q_1 - q_2 - \cdots - q_n$

$$\pi_1 = 53q_1 - q_1^2 - q_1 \sum_{i=2}^{n} q_i - 5q_1$$

Argue by symmetry: $q_1 = q_2 = \cdots = q_n$.

$$\pi_1 = 53q_1 - q_1^2 - q_1(n-1)q_i - 5q_1.$$

$$\frac{\partial \pi_1}{\partial q_1} = 48 - 2q_1 - (n-1)q_i = 0.$$

$q_1 = 24 - (n-1)q_i$ Let

$q_i = q_1 \qquad q_1 = \dfrac{48}{n+1}$

$$P = 53 - \frac{48n}{n+1}$$

As n gets larger, P approaches 5.0, profits approach 0.

17.5 a. Payoffs from Smith's perspective are +3, −1.

		Jones' Strategies		
		1	2	3
Smith's Strategy	1	+3	−1	−1
	2	−1	+3	−1
	3	−1	−1	+3

This game is similar to the one in Figure 17.4 in that it has no equilibrium pair.

b. Expected payoff to mixed strategy is for Smith

$$\frac{1}{3}(3) + \frac{1}{3}(-1) + \frac{1}{3}(-1) = \frac{1}{3}$$

for Jones it is

$$\frac{1}{3}(-3) + \frac{1}{3}(1) + \frac{1}{3}(1) = -\frac{1}{3}$$

This mixed strategy is an equilibrium since neither player has an incentive to depart from it even if he or she knows what the other is doing (assuming the strategy choices are truly random).

17.7 See *Instructor's Manual.*

17.9 See *Instructor's Manual.*

Chapter 18

18.1 Demand: $L = -50w + 450$.
Supply: $L = 100w$.

a. $S = D$. $100w = -50w + 450$. $w = 3$, $L = 300$.

b. D: $L = -50(w - s) + 450$.
s = subsidy
$w = \$4$. $L_s = 400 = -50(4 - s) + 450$.
$s = 3$.
Total subsidy is $400 \times 3 = \$1{,}200$.

c. $w = \$4$. $D = 250$. $S = 400$. $U = 150$.

d.

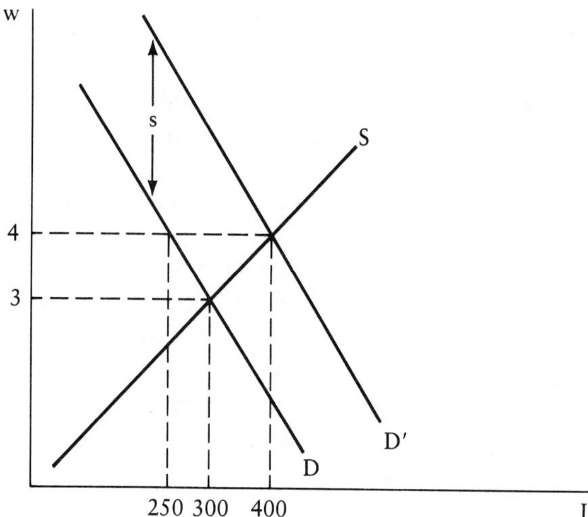

18.3 a. Five laborers: Put them where MP_L is greatest. First laborer goes to A, second goes to B, third goes to A, fourth goes to C, fifth goes to A. Output = 21 + 8 + 5 = 34.
MP of last worker is 4.

b. $P \cdot MP_L = \$1.00 \times 4 = \$4.00 = w$.
Five laborers, $wL = \$20$.
$\pi = TR - TC = PQ - wL$
$= \$34 - \$20 = \$14$.

18.5 a. $w = v = \$1$, so K and L will be used in a one-to-one ratio.

$TC = w \cdot L + v \cdot K = L + K = 2L$,

so $AC = \frac{2L}{q} = \frac{2L}{\sqrt{KL}} = \frac{2L}{\sqrt{LL}} = 2$ and

$MC = 2$.

b. $P = 2$, so $Q = 400{,}000 - 100{,}000(2)$ $= 200{,}000$ pipe.

$q = \frac{200{,}000 \text{ pipe}}{1{,}000 \text{ firms}} = 200$ pipe/firm.

$q = 200 = \sqrt{L \cdot K} = L$, so 200 workers are hired per firm, 200,000 by the industry.

c. $w = \$2$, $v = \$1$, so $K/L = 2$

$TC = wL + vK$

$= 2L + K = 4L = 2\sqrt{2}\,q$.

so $AC = MC = 2\sqrt{2}$.

d. $P = 2\sqrt{2}$. $Q = 400{,}000 - 100{,}000(2\sqrt{2}) = 117{,}157$.

$L = \frac{117{,}157}{\sqrt{2}} = 83{,}000$ workers hired by the industry.

e. If $Q = 200{,}000$ at the new wage,

$L = \frac{200{,}000}{\sqrt{2}} = 141{,}000$ workers

would have been hired by the industry. So if Q was unchanged, 59,000 fewer workers would have been hired = substitution effect. The remaining 58,000 fewer workers are the result of the lower output = output effect.

18.7 Supply: $L = 80w$. $ME_L = \frac{L}{40}$.

Demand: $L = 400 - 40MVP_L$

a. For monopsonist $ME_L = MVP_L$

$L = 400 - 40MVP_L$.

$40MVP_L = 400 - L$.

$MVP_L = 10 - \frac{L}{40} \cdot \frac{L}{40} = 10 - \frac{L}{40}$.

$\frac{2L}{40} = 10$. $L = 200$.

Get w from supply curve:

$w = \frac{L}{80} = \frac{200}{80} = \$2.50$.

b. For Carl, the marginal expense of labor now equals the minimum wage and in equilibrium the marginal expense of labor will equal the marginal revenue product of labor.

$W_m = ME_L = MVP_L$

$W_m = \$3.00$.

Carl's Demand	Supply
$L = 400 - 40MVP_L$	$L = 80w$
$L = 400 - 40(3)$	$L = 80(3)$
$L = 280$.	$L = 240$.

Demand > supply. Carl will hire 240 workers, with no unemployment.

To study effects of minimum, try \$3.33 and \$4.00

$W_m = \$3.33$

$L = 400 - 40(3.33) = 267$. $\quad L = 80(3.33) = 267$.

Demand = supply, Carl will hire 267 workers, with no unemployment.

$W_m = \$4.00$

$L = 400 - 40(4.00) = 240$. $\quad L = 80(4.00) = 320$.

Supply > demand, Carl will hire 240 workers, unemployment = 80.

c.

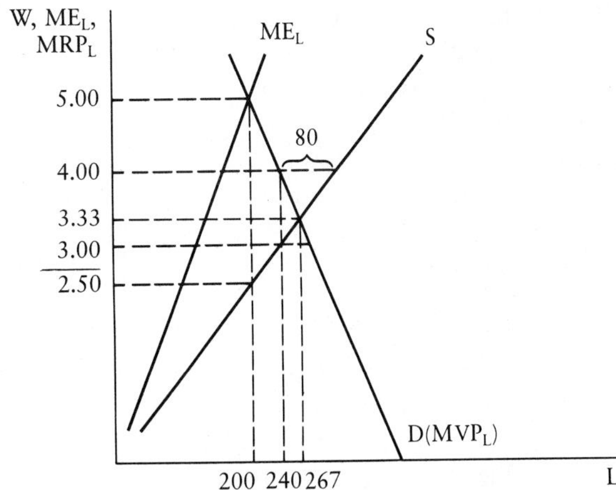

d. Under perfect competition, a minimum wage means higher wages but fewer workers employed. Under monopsony, a minimum wage may result in higher wages and more workers employed as shown by cases studied in part b.

18.9 Here marginal value product is \$10 per hour:

$$ME_{Lm} = \frac{\sqrt{L_m}}{2} = 10, \text{ so } L_m = 400,$$

$$w_m = \frac{20}{3} = 6.67.$$

$$ME_{Lf} = \frac{L_f}{50} = 10, \text{ so } L_f = 500, w_f = 5.$$

$L_T = 900.$

Profits on machinery = 9,000 − 5(500) − 6.67(400) = 3,833. If same wage w = MVP_L = 10, L = 1,000 + 900 = 1,900. Profits = 19,000 − 1900 · w = 19,000 − 19,000 = 0.

Chapter 19

19.1 a. 8,000 hrs/year × \$5/hr = \$40,000/year. 3/4 × \$40,000/yr = \$30,000/yr at leisure.

$$\frac{\$30,000}{5} = 6,000 \text{ hours of leisure.}$$

Work = 2,000 hours.

b. 3/4 × \$44,000/yr = \$33,000/yr at leisure.

$$\frac{\$33,000}{5} = 6,600 \text{ hours of leisure.}$$

Work = 1,400 hours.

c. Now full income = \$84,000.
3/4 × \$84,000 = \$63,000.
Leisure = 6,300 hours.
Work = 1,700 hours.
Hence, higher wage leads to more labor supply. Note that in part a, labor supply is perfectly inelastic at 2,000 hours.

d.

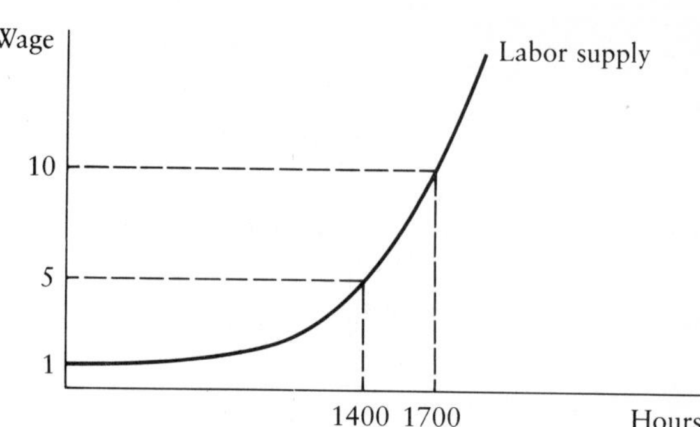

19.3 $U = 20 \qquad \sqrt{C \cdot H} = 20 = \sqrt{10C}$

$$10C = 400$$
$$C = 40.$$

If he gives up 1 hour of leisure H = 9, but 5 more dollars, C = 45.
$\sqrt{45 \cdot 9} = 20.13 > 20$, ∴ yes, he will.

19.5 This can be most easily solved using a graph.

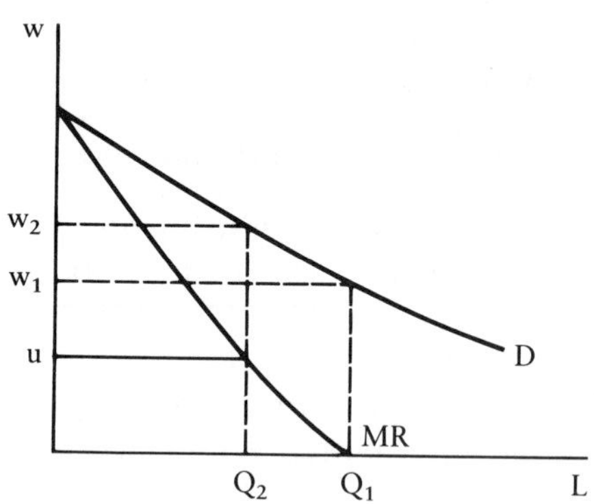

To maximize wage bill, set wage at w_1. Here marginal revenue is 0. With unemployment compensation at u, set wage at w_2. Beyond Q_2 additional revenue brought in by offering one more worker on the market falls short of what that worker could get from unemployment insurance.

19.7 a. Grant = 6,000 − .75(I)

If I = 0	Grant = 6,000.
I = 2,000	Grant = 4,500.
I = 4,000	Grant = 3,000.

b. Grant = 0 when 6,000 − .75I = 0.
I = 6,000/.75 = 8,000.

c. Assume there are 8,000 hours in the year.
Full income $= 4 \cdot 8{,}000 = 32{,}000 = C + 4H$.

d. Full income $= 32{,}000 + \text{grant}$
$= 32{,}000 + 6{,}000 - .75 \cdot 4(8{,}000 - H)$
$= 38{,}000 - 24{,}000 + 3H$
$= C + 4H$
or $14{,}000 = C + H$.

e.

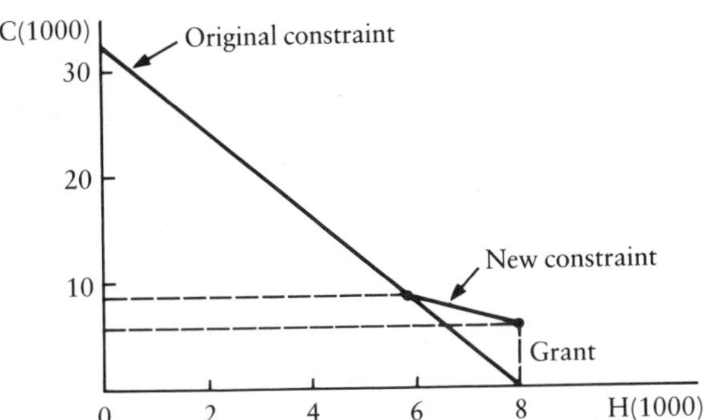

f. New budget constraint is $22{,}000 = C + 2H$.

g. Income and substitution effects of change work in opposite directions (see graph).

Chapter 20

20.1 If i = 12%,

$$\text{price} = \text{PDV} = \frac{1{,}000}{(1+.12)} + \frac{1{,}000}{(1+.12)^2} + \frac{1{,}000}{(1+.12)^3} + \frac{1{,}000}{(1+.12)^4} + \frac{1{,}000}{(1+.12)^5} + \frac{10{,}000}{(1+.12)^5}$$

PDV = \$9,279.

If i = 8%,

$$\text{price} = \text{PDV} = \frac{1{,}000}{(1+.08)} + \frac{1{,}000}{(1+.08)^2} + \frac{1{,}000}{(1+.08)^3} + \frac{1{,}000}{(1+.08)^4} + \frac{1{,}000}{(1+.08)^5} + \frac{10{,}000}{(1+.08)^5}$$

PDV = \$10,799.

When interest rates go down, bond prices go up. It is an inverse relationship.

20.3 Assuming premiums paid at end of year, $\text{PDV}_{\text{whole life}} = \$6{,}340$. $\text{PDV}_{\text{term}} = \$3{,}858$. The salesman is wrong, the term policy represents a better value to this consumer.

20.5 Let Y_t = Income in year t $= Y_0(1.03)^t$
S_t = Savings in year t $= sY_t = sY_0(1.03)^t$.
Accumulated savings

$$= \sum_{t-0}^{40} s_t(1.03)^{40-t}$$
$$= \sum_{t=0}^{40} sY_0(1.03)^t(1.03)^{40-t}$$
$$= 40sY_0(1.03)^{40}$$

PDV of dissavings:

$$\text{PDV} = \sum_{t=0}^{20} .6Y_0(1.03)^{40} \cdot (1.03)^{t-20}$$

Equate the two streams to solve for s:

$$s = \frac{\text{PDV}}{40Y_0(1.03)^{40}} = \frac{6Y_0(1.03)^{40}(15.9)}{40Y_0(1.03)^{40}} = \frac{.6(15.9)}{40} = .24,$$

which is much higher than the average savings rate in the United States (about 5%).

20.7 Each tree should be cut down when the rate of interest (opportunity cost) is equal to the tree's rate of growth. Maximum sustainable yield proceeds to point where growth becomes zero. It neglects opportunity cost of interest.

Chapter 21

21.1 a. $MC = .4q$. $P = \$20$. Set $P = MC$.
$20 = .4q$. $q = 50$.

b. $SMC = .5q$. Set $P = SMC$. $20 = .5q$. $q = 40$.
At optimal production level of $q = 40$, the marginal cost of production is $MC = .4q = .4(40) = 16$, so the excise tax $t = 20 - 16 = \$4$.

c.

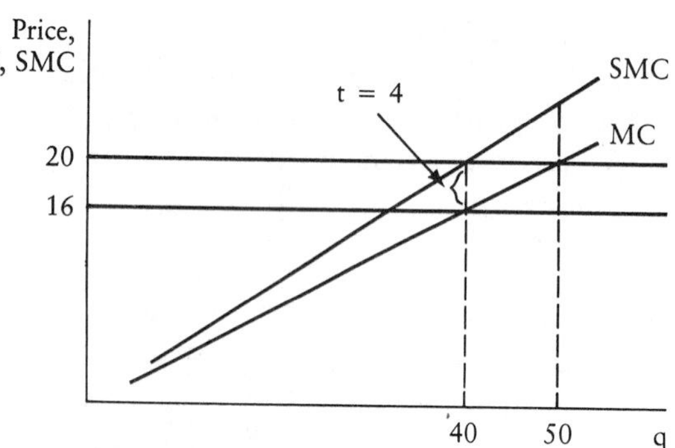

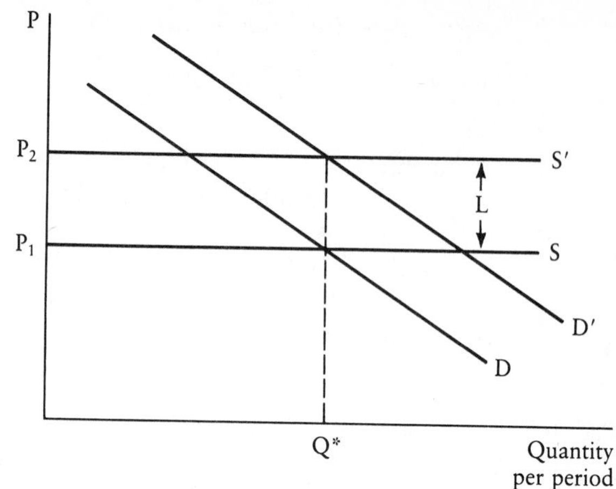

21.3 AC = MC = 1000/well.

a. Produce where revenue/well = 1,000 = 10q = 5,000 − 10N. N = 400. There is an externality here because drilling another well reduces output in *all* wells.
b. Produce where MVP = MC of well.
Total value = $5{,}000N - 10N^2$.
MVP = 5,000 − 20N = 1,000.
N = 200.
Let Tax = X. Want revenue/well − X = 1,000 when N = 200. At N = 200, average revenue/well = 3,000. Charge X = 2,000.

21.5 Under *caveat emptor,* buyers would assume all losses. The demand curve under such a situation might be given by D. Firms (that assume no liability) might have a horizontal long-run supply curve of S. A change in liability assignment would shift both supply and demand curves. Under *caveat vendor,* losses (of amount L) would now be incurred by firms, thereby shifting the long-run supply curve to S′.

Individuals now no longer have to pay these losses and their demand curve will shift upward by L to D′. In this example then, market price rises from P_1 to P_2 (although the real cost of owning the good has not changed) and the level of production stays constant at Q*. Only if there were major information costs associated with either the *caveat emptor* or *caveat vendor* positions might the two give different allocations. It is possible also that L may be a function of liability assignment (the moral hazard problem) and this would also cause the equilibria to differ.

21.7 One example of this type of externality would be an individual who refused to trim a hedge that bordered a neighbor's property. The neighbor might, if he or she valued a trimmed hedge, offer to trim it (at least one side of it) thereby internalizing the externality. In general, one might expect that such agreements are common since bargaining costs are low when only two individuals are involved.

Chapter 22

22.1 a. Marginal valuation for a = P = 100 − q_a; for b, marginal valuation = P = 200 − q_b. Because of the public good nature of mosquito control there should be added "vertically."
Marginal value = 300 − 2q (since $q_a = q_b$).
Set this = 50, gives q = 125.
b. Free rider problem could result in having no production.
c. Total cost = 50 × 125 = $6,250.
Area under demand curve for a = $4,688; for b = $17,188.
May want to share costs in proportion to these values.

22.3 Resources should be allocated so that the sum of people's marginal valuations of education's public benefits plus the private benefit for the marginal buyer equals the marginal cost of producing one more unit. It might be financed through a combination of compulsory taxes and user fees. For example, elementary and secondary education might be publicly financed (if it provided all public goods), whereas university education might be funded privately if its benefits were private.

22.5 If different localities have different tastes for a certain public good, then it should be produced by local governments. But if the good can be supplied uniformly over the whole state (example, state police), then it should be produced by the state. Diseconomies of scale may make it more efficient to produce countrywide or statewide services on a statewide or local basis.

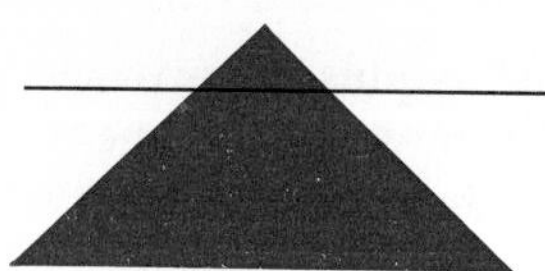

GLOSSARY

Accounting cost The concept that goods or services cost what was paid for them. (p. 218)
Adverse selection When buyers and sellers have different information, market outcomes may exhibit adverse selection—the quality of goods or services traded will be biased toward market participants with better information. (p. 174, 409)
Agent The role of making economic decisions for another party, such as the manager of a firm being hired to act for the owner. (p. 299)
Asymmetric information A situation in which buyers and sellers have different amounts of information about a market transaction. (p. 409)
Average cost Total costs divided by output—a common measure of cost per unit. (p. 227)
Average productivity The ratio of total output produced to the quantity of a particular input employed. (p. 197)

Backward bending labor supply curve Labor supply curve in which higher real wages cause less labor to be supplied because the income effect outweighs the substitution effect. (p. 552)
Barriers to entry Factors that prevent new firms from entering a market or industry. (p. 421)
Bayesian decision theory Definition of subjective probabilities for outcomes of a game and use of those probabilities in making strategic decisions. (p. 498)
Binding constraint The presence of one or more resources that effectively limits the amount that can be produced. If a particular input is not fully utilized, it does not pose a binding constraint in production. (p. 392).
Budget constraint The limit that income places on the combinations of goods and services that an individual can buy. (p. 71)

Capital stock The total amount of machines, buildings, and all other manmade, nonlabor resources in an economy. (p. 567)
Cartel model A model of oligopoly pricing in which firms coordinate their decisions to act as a multiplant monopoly. (p. 451)
***Ceteris paribus* assumption** In economic analysis, holding all other factors constant so that only the factor being studied is allowed to change. (p. 56)
Coase theorem If bargaining is costless, the social cost of an externality will be taken into account by the parties, and the allocation of resources will be the same no matter how property rights are assigned. (p. 623)
Cobweb model A model of price adjustment in which some trading takes place at non-equilibrium prices. (p. 405)
Common property Property that may be used by anyone without cost. (p. 621)
Comparative statics The investigation of new choices people make when conditions change, as compared to the choices they made under the former conditions. (p. 89)
Compensated demand curve A demand curve drawn on the assumption that other prices and utility are held constant. Income effects of price changes are compensated for along the curve and it reflects only substitution effects. (p. 145)
Compensating wage differentials Differences in wages caused by differing job characteristics. (p. 557)
Competitive fringe Group of firms that act as price takers in a market dominated by a price leader. (p. 454)
Complements Two goods such that when the price of one increases, the quantity demanded of the other falls. (p. 106)
Complete preferences The assumption that an individual is able to state which of any two options is preferred. (p. 59)
Composite good Combining expenditures on several different goods whose relative prices do not change into a single good for convenience in analysis. (p. 83)
Constant cost industry An industry in which the entry or exit of firms has no effect on the cost curves of the firms in the industry. (p. 331)
Consumer price index (CPI) The current value of the market basket of goods and services purchased by a typical household compared to a base year value of the same market basket. (p. 148)
Consumer surplus The extra value individuals receive from consuming a good over what they pay for it. What people would be willing to pay for the right to consume a good at its current price. (p. 148)
Contestable market Market in which entry and exit are costless. (p. 463)
Contour lines Lines in two dimensions that show the sets of values of the independent variables that yield the same value for the dependent variable. (p. 40)
Contract curve The set of all efficient allocations of the existing goods in an exchange situation. Points off that curve are necessarily inefficient, since individuals can be made unambiguously better off by moving to the curve. (p. 161)

Cournot equilibrium A solution to the Cournot model in which each firm makes the correct assumption about what the other firm will produce. (p. 482)
Cournot model A model of duopoly in which each firm assumes the other firm's output will not change if it changes its own output level. (p. 481)
Cross-price elasticity of demand The percentage change in the quantity demanded of a good in response to a 1 percent change in the price of another good. (p. 132)

Deadweight loss A loss of consumer surplus that is not transferred to another economic actor. (p. 431)
Decreasing cost industry An industry in which the entry of firms decreases the costs of the firms in the industry. (p. 339)
Demand function A representation of how quantity demanded depends on prices, income, and preferences. (p. 90)
Dependent variable In algebra, a variable whose value is determined by another variable or set of variables. (p. 28)
Derived demand Demand for a factor of production that is determined by the demand for the good it produces. (p. 510)
Direct approach To verify economic models, the direct approach examines the validity of the assumptions on which the model is based. (p. 18)
Diversification The spreading of risk among several options rather than choosing only one. (p. 178)
Dual linear programming problem A minimization problem related to a primal linear programming maximization problem; often involves computation of appropriate resource prices. (p. 394)

Economically efficient allocation of resources A technically efficient allocation of resources in which the output combination also reflects people's preferences. (p. 365)
Economic cost The cost concept that goods or services cost the amount required to keep them in their present use; the amount that they would be worth in their next best alternative use. (p. 218)
Economic profits The difference between a firm's total revenues and its total economic costs. (p. 221)
Economic rent The amount by which payments to a factor exceed the minimal amount required to retain it in its present use. (p. 511)
Edgeworth box diagram A graphic device for illustrating all of the possible allocations of two goods (or two inputs) which are in fixed supply. (p. 358)
Efficient markets hypothesis The hypothesis that all information is reflected in prevailing market prices. (p. 183)
Efficient wage A wage above the market wage paid to encourage a worker to remain with a firm. (p. 298)
Elasticity The measure of the percentage change in one variable brought about by a 1 percent change in some other variable. (p. 122)
Equilibrium price The price at which the quantity demanded by buyers of a good is equal to the quantity supplied of the good by sellers. (p. 12, 316)
Equity The fairness of the distribution of goods or utility. (p. 375)
Excess demand The extent to which quantity demanded exceeds quantity supplied at a particular price. (p. 400)
Expansion path The locus of cost-minimizing input combinations a firm will choose to produce various levels of output (when the prices of inputs are held constant). (p. 225)
Expected value The average outcome from an uncertain gamble. (p. 168)
External price effects Effects that changes in the level of production of an industry have on the prices of inputs to that industry. (p. 320)
Externality The effect of one party's economic activities on another party that is not taken into account by the price system. (p. 372, 611)

Fair games Games that cost their expected value. (p. 168)
Fair insurance Insurance for which the premium is equal to the expected value of the loss. (p. 174)
Firm Any organization that turns inputs into outputs. (p. 191)
Fixed costs Costs associated with inputs that are fixed in the short run. (p. 234)
Fixed-proportions production function A production function in which the inputs must be used in a fixed ratio to one another. (p. 206)
Free rider A consumer of a nonexclusive good who does not pay for it in the hope that other consumers will. (p. 649)
Functional notation A way of denoting the fact that the value taken on by one variable (Y) depends on the value taken on by some other variable (X) or set of variables. (p. 28)
Future goods Goods that are purchased today by investing some present output as capital whose output is then consumed in the future. (p. 569)

Game theory The study of the strategies used by the players in a game and the payoffs they receive. (p. 488)
General equilibrium model An economic model of a complete system of markets. (p. 16)
Giffen's paradox A situation in which the increase in a good's price leads people to consume more of the good. (p. 103)

Homogeneous demand function Demand does not change when prices and income increase in the same proportion. (p. 91)
Human capital Capital in the form of learned abilities acquired through training, education, or experience. (p. 584)

Imperfect competition A market situation in which buyers or sellers have some influence on the prices of goods or services. (p. 372)
Income effect The part of the change in quantity demanded of a good whose price has changed that is caused by the change in real in-

come that results from the price change. (p. 94)
Income effect of a change in w Movement to a higher indifference curve in response to a rise in the real wage rate. If leisure is a normal good, a rise in w causes an individual to work less. (p. 550)
Income elasticity of demand The percentage change in the quantity demanded of a good in response to a 1 percent change in income. (p. 131)
Increase or decrease in demand The change in demand for a good caused by changes in the price of another good, income, or preferences. Graphically represented by a shift of the entire demand curve. (p. 111)
Increase or decrease in quantity demanded The increase or decrease in quantity demanded caused by a change in the good's price. Graphically represented by the movement along a demand curve. (p. 111)
Increasing cost industry An industry in which the entry of firms increases the costs of the firms in the industry. (p. 335)
Independent variable In an algebraic equation, a variable that is unaffected by the action of another variable and may be assigned any value. (p. 28)
Index number An average of many different trends into one number. (p. 148)
Indifference curve A curve that shows all the combinations of goods or services that provide the same level of utility. (p. 62)
Indifference curve map A contour map that shows the utility an individual obtains from all possible consumption options. (p. 66)
Indirect approach To verify economic models, the indirect approach asks if the model can accurately predict real-world events. (p. 18)
Individual demand curve A graphic representation of the relationship between the price of a good and the quantity of it demanded by a person, holding all other factors constant. (p. 106)
Inferior good A good that is bought in smaller quantities as income increases. (p. 92)
Initial endowments The initial holdings of goods from which trading begins. (p. 376)
Intercept The value of Y when X equals zero. (p. 30)
Internalization of an externality Incorporation of the social marginal costs of an externality into an economic actor's decisions (as through taxation or merger). (p. 620)
Investment The purchase of new capital. (p. 575)
Isoquant A curve that shows the various combinations of inputs that will produce the same amount of output. (p. 200)
Isoquant map A contour map of a firm's production function. (p. 198)

Job-specific skills Skills learned on a job about how to do that specific job better. (p. 295)
Joint products The inseparable combination of two goods in production or consumption. (p. 460)

Kinked demand curve model A model in which firms believe that price increases result in a very elastic demand, while price decreases result in an inelastic demand for their products. (p. 452)

Law of diminishing returns Hypothesis that the cost associated with producing one more unit of a good rises as more of that good is produced. (p. 11)
Leisure Time spent in any activity other than market work. (p. 546)
Lindahl equilibrium Balance between people's demand for public goods and the tax shares that each must pay for them. (p. 648)
Linear function An equation that is represented by a straight-line graph. (p. 30)
Linear programming A mathematical technique for finding the maximum (or minimum) value for a linear function whose variables are subject to linear constraints. (p. 390)
Long run The period of time in which a firm may consider all of its inputs to be variable in making its decisions. (p. 231)
Long-run elasticity of supply The percentage change in quantity supplied in the long run in response to a 1 percent change in price. (p. 337)

Marginal cost The additional cost of producing one more unit of output. (p. 228)
Marginal expense The cost of hiring one more unit of an input. Will exceed the price of the input if the firm faces an upward-sloping supply curve for the input. (p. 528)
Marginal physical productivity The additional output that can be produced by one more unit of a particular input while holding all other inputs constant. (p. 193)
Marginal rate of substitution (MRS) The rate at which an individual is willing to reduce consumption of one good when he or she gets one more unit of another good while remaining equally well off. The negative of the slope of an indifference curve. (p. 63)
Marginal rate of technical substitution (RTS) This shows the amount by which one input can be reduced while holding output constant when one more unit of another input is added. The negative of the slope of an isoquant. (p. 200)
Marginal revenue The extra revenue a firm receives when it sells one more unit of output. (p. 267)
Marginal revenue product The extra revenue obtained from selling the output produced by hiring an extra worker or machine. (p. 518)
Marginal value product A special case of marginal revenue product in which the firm is a price taker for its output. (p. 519)
Market demand The total quantity of a good or service demanded by all potential buyers. (p. 118)
Market demand curve The relationship between the total quantity demanded of a good or service and its price holding all other factors constant. (p. 118)
Market period A short period of time during which quantity supplied is fixed. (p. 316)
Markup pricing Determining the selling price of a good by adding a

percentage to the average cost of producing it. (p. 278)
Median voter A voter whose preferences for a public good represent the middle point of all voters' preferences for the good. (p. 654)
Microeconomics The study of the economic choices individuals and firms make and how those choices create markets. (p. 6)
Models Simple theoretical descriptions that capture the essentials of how the economy works. (p. 8)
Monopolistic competition Market in which each firm faces a negatively sloped demand curve and there are no barriers to entry. (p. 462)
Monopoly rents The profits that a monopoly earns in the long run. (p. 426)
Monopsony A firm that is the only hirer in a particular input market. (p. 528)
Moral hazard The effect that having insurance has on the behavior of the insured. (p. 175)

Nash equilibrium A choice of strategies by the players of a game such that once all the strategies are known, no player has an incentive to choose a different strategy. (p. 490)
Natural monopoly A firm that exhibits diminishing average cost over a broad range of output levels. (p. 422)
Nonexclusive goods Goods that provide benefits that no one can be excluded from enjoying. (p. 642)
Nonrival goods Goods for which additional consumers may use them at zero marginal costs. (p. 643)
Normal good A good that is bought in greater quantities as income increases. (p. 91)
Normative analysis Theories that make judgments about how the economy's resources should be used. (p. 21)

Opportunity cost The cost of a good or service as measured by the alternative uses that are forgone by producing the good or service. (p. 16, 217)
Output effect The effect of an input price change on the amount of the input that the firm hires that results from a change in the firm's output level. (p. 525)

Pareto efficient allocation An allocation of available resources in which no mutually beneficial trading opportunities are unexploited. That is, an allocation in which no one person can be made better off without someone else being made worse off. (p. 159)
Partial equilibrium model An economic model of a single market. (p. 14)
Payoffs The outcomes of a game for each player. Payoffs depend on what strategies have been chosen. (p. 489)
Perfectly competitive price system An economic model in which individuals maximize utility, firms maximize profits, there is perfect information about prices, and every economic actor is a price taker. (p. 350)
Pigovian tax A tax or subsidy on an externality that brings about an equality of private and social marginal costs. (p. 618)
Player A participant in a game. May be an individual, a firm, or groups of individuals and firms. (p. 488)
Positive economic analysis Theories that explain how resources actually are used in an economy. (p. 21)
Present discounted value The present value of funds payable in the future after taking account of the opportunity cost of interest forgone. (p. 577, 597)
Price discrimination The practice of charging different prices for a good in different markets. (p. 435)
Price elasticity of demand The percentage change in the quantity demanded of a good in response to a 1 percent change in its price. (p. 122)
Price leadership model Model in which one dominant firm takes reactions of all other firms into account in its output and pricing decisions. (p. 454)
Price taker A firm or individual whose decisions regarding buying or selling have no effect on the prevailing market price of a good or service. (p. 269)
Prisoner's dilemma A game in which the players' most desirable joint outcome is unstable because each player has an incentive to cheat in the strategy actually chosen. (p. 494)
Private property Property that is owned by specific people who may prevent others from using it. (p. 621)
Probability The relative frequency with which an event occurs. (p. 167)
Product group Set of differentiated products that are highly substitutable for one another. (p. 457)
Production function The mathematical relationship between inputs and outputs. (p. 191)
Production possibility frontier A graph showing all possible combinations of goods that can be produced with a fixed amount of resources. (p. 16, 360)
Property rights The legal specification of who owns a good and the trades the owner is allowed to make with it. (p. 621)
Public goods Goods that provide nonexclusive benefits to everyone in a group and that can be provided to one more user at zero marginal cost. (p. 374)

Quadratic function An equation that includes terms in X^2 and (possibly) X. (p. 34)
Quasi-competitive model A model of oligopoly pricing in which each firm acts as a price taker. (p. 450)

Rate of product transformation The negative of the slope of the production possibility frontier which shows the opportunity costs involved in producing more of one good and less of some other good. (p. 361)
Rate of return The increase in future output made possible by investing one unit of current output in capital accumulation. (p. 568)

Rational expectations Basing price expectations on complete information about the equilibrium price determined by the interaction of supply and demand in a market. (p. 408)
Reaction function In the Cournot model a function or graph that shows how much one firm will produce given what the other firm produces. (p. 481)
Rental rate (v) The cost of hiring one machine for one hour. (p. 218)
Rent-seeking behavior Firms or individuals influencing government policy to increase their own welfare. (p. 658)
Returns to scale The rate at which output increases in response to proportional increases in all inputs. (p. 202)
Revenue maximization A goal for firms in which they work to maximize their total revenue rather than profits. (p. 277)
Risk aversion The tendency of people to refuse to accept fair games. (p. 170)

Scarcity costs The opportunity costs of forgone future production that cannot be made because of current production that uses exhaustible resources. (p. 587)
Shadow prices Prices for resources in a dual linear programming problem. For resources that represent binding constraints on production, shadow prices will be positive. For resources that do not represent binding constraints, shadow prices are zero. (p. 395)
Short run The period of time in which a firm must consider some inputs absolutely fixed in making its decisions. (p. 231)
Short-run elasticity of supply The percentage change in quantity supplied in the short run in response to a 1 percent change in price. (p. 323)
Short-run supply curve The relationship between market price and quantity supplied of a good in the short run. (p. 319)
Shutdown price The price below which the firm will choose to produce no output in the short run. Equal to minimum average variable cost. (p. 255)
Simultaneous equations A set of equations with more than one variable that must be solved together for a particular solution. (p. 42)
Slope The direction of a line on a graph. Shows the change in Y that results from a unit change in X. (p. 30)
Social costs Costs of production that include both input costs and costs of the externalities that production may cause. (p. 615)
Stable equilibrium A situation in which market forces cause price to move to its equilibrium level. (p. 405)
Stackelberg model A generalization of the Cournot model in which at least one firm knows the other's reaction function. (p. 485)
Strategies The various courses of action open to players of a game. (p. 489)
Subscripts The use of small numbers at the bottom of variables to identify them as separate variables. (p. 46)
Substitutes Two goods such that if the price of one increases, the quantity demanded of the other rises. (p. 106)
Substitution effect of a change in w Movement along an indifference curve in response to a change in the real wage. A rise in w causes an individual to work more. (p. 550)
Substitution effect The part of the change in quantity demanded of a good whose price has changed that is caused by substitution of the good that is now relatively cheaper for the other that is now relatively more costly. A movement along an indifference curve. (p. 94)
Supply-demand model A model describing how a good's price is determined by the behavior of the individuals who buy the good and the firms that sell it. (p. 8)
Supply response The change in quantity of output in response to a change in demand conditions. (p. 315)
Survivorship principle The idea that in competitive markets, only profit-maximizing firms are likely to survive. (p. 277)

Tax incidence theory The study of the final burden of a tax after considering all market reactions to it. (p. 334)
Technical progress A shift in the production function that allows a given output level to be produced using less inputs. (p. 212)
Technically efficient allocation of resources An allocation of the available resources such that producing more of one good requires producing less of some other good. (p. 357)
Theory of choice The interaction of preferences and income that causes people to make the choices they do. (p. 56)
Transactions costs Costs involved in making market transactions and in gathering information with which to make those transactions. (p. 403)
Transitivity of preferences The property that if A is preferred to B, and B is preferred to C, then A must be preferred to C. (p. 61)

Unstable equilibrium A situation in which market forces cause price to move away from its equilibrium level. (p. 406)
Utility The pleasure, satisfaction, or need fulfillment that people get from their economic activity. (p. 56)

Variable costs Costs associated with inputs that can be varied in the short run. (p. 234)
Variables The basic elements of algebra, usually called X, Y, and so on, that may be given any numerical value in an equation. (p. 28)

Wage rate (w) The cost of hiring one worker for one hour. (p. 218)

Yield The interest rate at which the present discounted value of the returns from an investment are exactly equal to the investments' current cost. (p. 584)

Zero-sum game A game in which the amount which one player loses the other player wins. (p. 490)

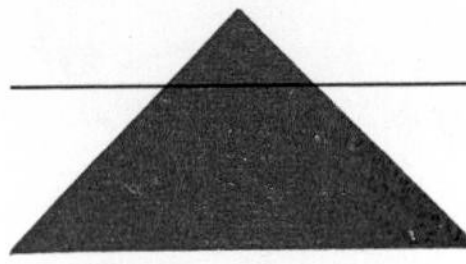

Name Index

Aaron, Henry J., 101n
Abrams, L., 618
Agnello, R. J., 634
Akerlof, George, 409
Allen, R. G. D., 152n
Andersen, R., 134n
Anderson, W., 135n
Aristotle, 9n
Arrow, K. J., 206n, 375n
Ash, Colin, 554n
Ashenfelter, Orley, 561
Attiyeh, Richard, 660

Bailey, E. E., 442n
Baily, M. N., 211n
Bain, J. S., 471n
Barzel, Yoram, 334n
Baumol, William J., 277, 463n, 626n
Bayes, Thomas, 498
Becker, Gary S., 96, 537n, 546n, 548n, 584n
Bell, F. W., 110, 232n, 634
Benham, L., 134n, 182n
Berger, T., 407n
Berndt, E. R., 209
Bernoulli, Daniel, 170
Bhagat, Sanjai, 304n
Black, Duncan, 653, 654
Blaug, Marc, 571n
Blinder, A. S., 120n
Bolton, Roger E., 364n
Bond, E. W., 413n
Borcherding, T. E., 661
Borts, George, 233
Boudreau, B., 412n
Braithwait, S. D., 151
Brickley, James A., 304n, 307n
Browning, E. K., 147n
Burke, Edmund, 5
Burkhauser, R. V., 529n
Bush, George, 15, 211

Carlin, A., 243n
Carnegie, Andrew, 486
Carter, Jimmy, 15, 486
Caves, D. W., 233n
Cavin, Edward, 297n
Chamberlin, E. H., 462n
Cheung, S. N. S., 624
Chewtnut, L. G., 559n
Chow, Gregory C., 134n
Christensen, L. R., 232n, 233n
Clark, J. C., 232n
Cline, W. R., 160n
Coase, Ronald, 291, 614, 623, 647
Cohen, H. A., 232n
Cookenboo, L., 43
Cornes, R., 643n
Corson, Walter, 371n
Cournot, Augustin, 481
Cowling, K., 434
Crandall, R. W., 619n
Cyert, R. M., 281

Daly, A., 356n
Darwin, Charles, 7
David, Paul A., 58n
Davis, J. M., 60n
Deaton, A., 120n
De Condorcet, M., 652
De Leeuw, F., 134n
Demsetz, Harold, 463, 631n
Dirlam, J. B., 281
Domencich, T. A., 548n

Donnelley, L. P., 634
Dorfman, Robert, 388n
Downs, Anthony, 657
Dukakis, Michael, 15
Dwyer, G. P., 103n

Eckaus, R. S., 208n
Edgeworth, F. Y., 157
Ehrenberg, R. G., 371n, 556n
Elsinger, K. G., 134n
Engel, Ernst, 93
Engle, Robert F., 660
Epple, D. N., 340n
Erlich, Isaac, 70

Fechner, 58
Ferguson, E. C., 526n
Finegan, T. A., 529n
Fisher, A., 559n
Fisher, Irving, 571n
Fleming, M. C., 232n
Flood, Curt, 535
Fog, B., 281
Ford, Gerald, 120
Freeman, R. B., 561n
Freidman, Milton, 18–19, 120, 276
Fuchs, Victor, 302
Fuller, J. G., 484n
Fullerton, Donald, 579n

Gale, David, 396n
Gapinski, J. H., 520
Garber, P. M., 407n
Garr, Elbert, 486
Geehan, R., 232n
George, Henry, 513, 514
Giffen, Robert, 102–104
Gordon, H. S., 631n
Greene, W. H., 232n
Grossman, Michael, 584n

Hall, R. E., 281, 578n
Halvorsen, R. F., 134n
Hamermesch, Daniel, 548
Hamilton, J. L., 461
Harberger, Arnold, 434
Hashimoto, Masanori, 299n
Hausman, Jerry A., 101
Haverkamp, George, 60n
Heien, Dale M., 135n
Henderson, Y. K., 579n
Hendricks, K., 412n
Hershey, Alan, 297n
Hicks, J. R., 106n
Hogarty, T. F., 134n
Holderness, Clifford, 306
Hotelling, Harold, 588
Houthakker, H. S., 134n
Huang, J., 134n, 135n
Hume, David, 379, 380, 381n

Icahn, Carl, 306
Inman, Robert, 655
Intriligator, M. D., 375n

Jaeger, Elizabeth, 572
Jansson, J. O., 205
Jarrell, G. A., 307n
Jefferson, Thomas, 422
Jensen, Michael C., 179n, 300n
Johnson, H. G., 342n
Johnson, Lyndon B., 470
Johnson, Thomas, 585

Jorgenson, D. W., 578n
Jureen, L., 134n

Kahn, Alfred, 275
Kaplan, A. D. H., 281
Katz, H. C., 199n
Kawanaabe, N., 160n
Keefe, J. H., 199n
Keeler, T. E., 233, 243n
Kefauver, Estes, 484
Kemper, Peter, 233n
Kennedy, John F., 486
Kerachsky, Stuart, 297n
Khazzoom, J. D., 340n
Kirp, David, 424n
Klarman, Herbert, 134n, 232n
Kochan, T. A., 199n
Koenka, R., 232n
Koo, A. Y. C., 60n
Kravis, I. B., 153n
Krebs, John R., 7n
Kronsjo, T. O. M., 160n

Lanzillotti, R. F., 281
Lapan, H. E., 499n
Lave, Lester, 180
Lease, Ronald C., 304n
Lehn, K., 413n
Lenard, T. M., 659n
Lester, R. A., 276n
Lindahl, Erik, 646, 649
Lindsey, C. M., 103n
Lowell, Francis Cabot, 244
Lucas, R. E. B., 559
Luce, R. Duncan, 492n, 498n
Luttrell, C. B., 15

McAfee, R. P., 318n
MacAvoy, P. W., 441n
McCaleb, T. S., 651n
McClure, C. E., 265n
MacDonald, G. J., 630n
McDougall, I. A., 342n
McFadden, Daniel, 548n
McGee, J. S., 467
Machina, M. J., 500n
Machlup, Fritz, 276n
McMillan, J., 318n
McNowan, R. F., 554n
Malthus, Thomas, 12, 195, 340
Manning, W. G., 136n
March, J. G., 281
Markusen, J. R., 493
Marshall, Alfred, 12, 13, 14, 16, 17, 18, 23, 24, 27, 53, 93n, 103n, 315, 325, 401, 403, 460, 461
Marvel, H., 183
Mayer, T., 356n
Mazur, M. P., 659
Meade, James, 612, 624
Meadows, Donnella H., 20
Meckling, William, H., 300n
Medoff, J. L., 561n
Meyer, J. R., 275n
Misket, T. C., 134n
Morgan, W. D., 128
Morgenstern, O., 488n
Morrison, S., 275n, 466
Mueller, D. C., 434
Murdock, David, 306
Murphy, N. B., 232n
Musgrave, R. A., 646n
Muth, John, 408

Nash, John, 490
Nelson, J. P., 517
Nerlove, M., 340n
Netter, J. M., 407n
Newhouse, J. P., 136, 520n
Nicholson, Walter, 82n, 106n, 146n, 272n, 297n, 352n, 371n, 605n, 649n
Niskanen, W. A., 661
Nixon, Richard M., 120
Nordhaus, W. D., 589n

Oates, W. E., 626n
Oi, W. Y., 438n, 554
Olson, Mansur, 658, 661

Panzar, J. C., 463n
Pareto, Vilfredo, 159
Parks, R. F., 243n
Pauly, M., 176n
Peacock, A. T., 485n, 646n
Pechman, Joseph H., 101n
Perlman, M., 136n
Phelps, C. E., 136
Pickens, T. Boone, 306
Pigou, A. C., 614, 617, 635
Porter, R. H., 412n
Posner, R. A., 433n, 632n
Posner, Victor, 306
Pratt, J. W., 304n
Proxmire, William, 618

Quandt, R. E., 410n
Quigley, J. M., 233n

Radford, R. A., 380
Raiffa, Howard, 492n, 498n
Reagan, Ronald, 15, 120, 139, 579
Reder, Melvin, W., 58n
Ricardo, David, 10–12, 17, 508, 514, 516, 517
Robinson, K., 441n
Rockefeller, 467
Rosen, H. S., 410n
Rosen, Sherwin, 559
Rosenthal, G., 134n
Rubin, P. H., 302n
Rydenfelt, S., 338n

Samuelson, Paul A., 82n, 388n, 642, 645n
Sandler, T., 499n, 643n
Scherer, F. M., 486n
Schlottman, A., 618
Schmalensee, Richard, 458n, 459n
Schneerson, D., 205
Schultz, T. W., 96n
Schumpeter, J. A., 9n, 442n, 473
Scott, Anthony, 631n
Scully, G. W., 535
Sen, Amartya, 375n
Sheehan, Dennis, 306
Shefrin, H. M., 70n
Shepherd, W. G., 472
Shoven, John B., 353n
Siegfried, J. J., 134n, 135n
Simon, H. A., 18
Small, K. A., 243n
Smeeding, Timothy M., 101n
Smith, Adam, 9, 11, 20, 23, 69, 202, 232, 299, 300, 349, 354, 369, 381, 396, 408, 555, 557
Smith, B. A., 340n
Smith, J. K., 424n
Smith, R. G., 556n
Smith, V., 404n
Snape, R. M., 342n
Soffer, Eileen, 424n
Solow, R. M., 388n
Spence, Michael, 468n
Stephens, David W., 7n
Sternlieb, George, 338n
Stigler, George J., 132n
Stiglitz, Joseph E., 298n, 414n
Suits, D. B., 128, 134n
Sumner, M. T., 334
Swanson, J. A., 233n
Sweezy, P. M., 452, 453

Thach, Nguyen Co, 338
Thaler, Richard H., 70n, 559
Thorpe, E. O., 169n
Tiebout, C. M., 650n
Tinic, S. M., 427n
Tucker, A. W., 494

Udis, Bernard, 554n
Umbeck, J., 632n

Violette, D. M., 559n
Viscusi, W. Kip, 628n
Von Neumann, John, 488n
Von Stackelberg, Heinrich, 485

Wagner, R. E., 651n
Walley, John, 353n
Walras, Leon, 400, 401
Ward, R., 334
Weber, 58
Weinstein, A. A., 60
Welch, Finis, 529n
West, R. R., 427n
Westhoff, Frank, 60n
Wigle, R. W., 493
Williams, T., 160n
Willig, R. D., 463n
Wilson, E. O., 7n
Wilson, J. B., 660
Winston, C., 275n, 466
Wold, H., 134n
Wood, D. O., 209

Zardoshty, F., 134n, 135n
Zeckhauser, R. J., 304n
Zevin, R. B., 244n
Zimmerman, M. B., 340n

Subject Index

Accelerated Cost Recovery System (ACRS), 579
Accounting cost, 218
Acid rain, 618
Adverse selection, 174–175, 409
  and group health insurance, 176
Advertising, 458–461
  cigarette, 461
  as information, 460–461
  joint products and, 460
  price, 182
Agent, 299. *See also* Managers
  conflicts in relationship with, 299–303
  in franchising and medicine, 302
Agricultural production, and long-run price elasticities, 340
Agriculture, paradox of, 127
Airline deregulation, 466
  profit maximization and, 275
Allocation
  bargaining costs and, 625
  and externalities, 615–616
  of public goods, 644–645
  of resources, 631, 656–657
  of time, 548–549
Allocational efficiency, 472–473
Antitrust action
  and IBM, 470
  and Standard Oil, 467
Assumptions, and economic models, 18–19
Asymmetric information, 409
Asymmetries, and auctions, 412
AT&T, breakup of, 441
Auctioneer, and recontracting, 400
Auctions
  common value, 412
  and very short-run pricing, 318
Automobiles, substitution effects among, 125
Average cost, 227–228
  short-run, 259–261
Average productivity, 195–**197**
  of labor, 250–251
  in steel production, 196
Average revenue curve, 273

Backward bending labor supply curve, 552–553
Bads
  economic, 67
  theory of, 61n
Balance in consumption, 64–65
Balloon mortgage payments, 604
Bargaining
  costless, and free market, 621
  and environmental regulation, 626–627
  and externalities, 620
  and property rights, 621–624
  role of, 623–624
Barriers to entry, 421, 464–468
  and breakfast cereal producers, 459
  legal, 422–423
  licensing as, 423, 424
  technical, 422
Barter, and money, in POW camp, 380
Baseball, free agents in, 413
Baseball players, and monopsony in market for, 535
Bayesian decision rules, 497–500
Bayesian decision theory, 498
  and information theory, 500
Behavior, economic models of, 22–23
Benefits
  labor unions and, 562
  and long-term implicit contractors, 298, 299

Bid rigging, 484
Binding constraint, 392
Biology, foraging behavior and economic scarcity and, 7
Black markets, 76–77
Bonds, zero-coupon, 600
Box diagram, Edgeworth, 358–359
Brand proliferation, in breakfast cereals, 459
Breakfast cereals, entry barriers and, 459
Budget constraint, 71–72
  algebraic approach to, 72–73
  and comsumption/leisure utility-maximizing choices, 547
  price increase and shift in, 98
Bureaucracies, 661

Calculator costs, declines in, 244
Calculus
  elementary, 37n
  and slope of function, 31n
Canada, and U.S. trade policy, 493
Capital
  accumulation of, 568, 569
  marginal revenue product of, 518
  pricing of, 567–607
  rate of return on, 568
Capital costs, 218–219
Capital/energy production relationship, 209
Capital stock, 567–568
Cartel
  and baseball hiring, 535
  and dairy price supports, 326
  and electrical equipment conspiracy, 484
  monopsonistic, 534
Cartel model, 451–452
  OPEC and, 456
***Ceteris paribus* assumption, 56,** 57, 59
  and comparative statistics, 89
  and empirical studies of demand, 132–134
  and individual demand curve, 106
  and physical productivity curves, 197–198
Change in demand, 121
Change in quantity demanded, 121
Chicken, game of, 496
Childbearing, economics of, 548
Children, as inferior goods, 96
Choice
  applications of theory of, 143–165
  and demand, 53–54
  theory of, 56
Cigarette
  advertising of, 461
  taxes on, 334
Closed shop, 649
Coase theorem, 622–**623**
Cobb-Douglass production function, 250n
Cobweb model, 405, 406
Collusion, 483, 484
Commodity money, 379
Common property, 621, 632–633
Common value auctions, 412
Comparative statistics, 89
Compensated demand curve, 109n, 144–148, **145**
Compensating wage differentials, 555–558, **557**
  for differential death rates, 559
Competition, monopolistic, 462. *See also* Imperfectly competitive markets; Perfect competition
Competitive equilibrium, and information, 399–417
Competitve fringe, 454
Complements, 67–69, 105–**106**

Complete preferences, 59–61
Composite good, 83
Compounding, frequency of, 603–605
Compound interest, 593–607
  effects of, 597
Compulsory taxation, 650
Computer
  IBM in market for, 470
  modeling with, 353
Concave total cost curve, 227, 228–229
Conglomerate mergers, 471
Constant cost industry, 331
  long-run equilibrium for, 331–332
  specific tax on perfectly competitive, 333
Constant return, and RTS, 253–254
Constant returns to scale, 202
Constrained choices, 69
Constraints
  binding, 392
  budget, 71–73
Consumer Price Index (CPI), 148–152
  problems of, 152
  substitution bias of, 150, 151
Consumer Reports, 178
Consumer surplus, 148, 354n–355n
Consumption
  balance in, 64–65
  fish, and religious practices, 110
  income and, 93
  and income taxes, 120
  transivity in, 60
Contestable market, 463
  and industry structure, 462–464, 465
Contestability, of airlines, 466
Contour lines, 40–42
  and oil pipelines, 43
Contract curve, 161
Contracts
  explicit and implicit, 294, 296, 298
  in firm, 294
  and Japanese *Nenko* system, 299
  and job-specific skills, 295
  and long-term employment, 295–296
  management, 303
  with managers, 298–303
  with workers, 294–298
Convex total cost curve, 227, 228–229
Corn Laws debate, and production possibilityy frontier, 370
Corporate income (profits) tax, 265
Corporate raiders, 306
Cost curves, 226–231. *See also* Long-run cost curves
  average, 229, 230–231
  long-run, 257
  marginal, 228–229
  and monopoly profits, 428, 429
  shifts in, 242–245
  short-run, 239–240
  short-run fixed and variable, 235–236
  short-run total, 236
  total, 227, 228–229
Costless bargaining, and free market, 621
Cost minimization, 221–222, 254–257
  and expansion path, 256–257
  and input choice, 222–224
  input flexibility and, 237–238
Costs. *See also* Social costs
  accounting, 218
  average, 227–228
  bargaining, 623–624

basic concepts of, 217–222
capital, 218–219
declines in, and technical progress, 244
economic, 218, 219, 220
entrepreneurial, 219
fixed short-run, 234–235
implicit, 218
inefficient, and takeovers, 305
labor, 218
long-run, findings on, 232
marginal, 228, 267–268
minimization of, 221–222
opportunity, 16–17, 217–218
and output effect, 527–528
in railroad and refuse collection industries, 233
short-run average variable, 240–241
short-run total, 234–235
variable short-run, 234–235
Cournot equilibrium, 482–483
Cournot model, 481–488
CPI. *See* Consumer Price Index
Cross-price elasticity of demand, 132
estimates of, 135–137
Curves. *See* Cost curves; Demand curves; Individual demand curve; Long-run supply curve
average revenue, 273
compensated demand, 144–148
contract, 161
cost, 226–231
indifference, 62–65
marginal revenue, 273–274
market demand, 117
shifts in supply and demand, 322–328
short-run supply, 319–320

Dairy price supports, and short-run supply and demand, 326
Deadweight loss, 431
numerical illustration of 433–435
Decision rule, Bayesian, 497–500
Decrease in demand, 111
Decrease in quantity demanded, 111
Decreasing cost industry, 339
long-run supply curve of, 341
Decreasing returns to scale, 203
Defense spending, and production possibility frontier, 364
Delta notation, 31
Demand
change in, 121
and choice, 53–54
cross-price elasticity of, 132
derived, 510
effect of increase in the short run, 322
empirical studies of, 132–137
excess, 400
income elasticity of, 131
marginal productivity theory of factor, 516–522
market, 117–141
price elasticity of, 122–131
for public good, 646
shifts in, 316
shift in, and long-run equilibrium, 332
Demand curves
compensated, 144–148
and derived demand, 510
elasticity of, 273n
estimating, 132–134
individual, 106–111
marginal revenue curve and, 274
marginal revenue for downward-sloping, 269
price elasticity and shape of, 123
shape of, 323–324
shift in vs. movement along stationary, 111
shifts in, 324–325
Demand function, 90–91
homogeneous, 91
Dependent variable, 28
Deregulation
of airlines, 466
and stock exchange seats, 427
Derivative, 31n
Derived demand, 510–511
for inputs, 223–224
Diminishing returns, 10–12
Direct approach, 18
Discounting payment streams, 599–603
algebraic presentation of, 600
and perpetual payments, 601–603
Discrimination, in hiring, 534–536, 537
Disequilibrium, and unemployment, 410–411
Disequilibrium pricing, models of, 403–408
Disneyland, pricing at, 438
Distributional effects
and externalities, 623
of monopoly, 431, 432
Diversification, 178
and mutual funds, 179
and risk reduction, 175–178
Draft (army), costs of, 554
Duality, and pricing of inputs, 394–397
Dual linear programming problem, 394–397
Duopoly models, 479–480
Cournot model, 481–488
as non-zero sum game, 495–497
Stackelberg leadership model, 483–485, 487
Durable goods, 317–319
Dynamic efficiency, 473

Economically efficient allocation of resources, 365
Economic analysis, positive and normative, 19–21
Economic cost, 218
of home owning, 220
using, 219–220
Economic efficiency, 357–360
failure of markets to achieve, 369–375
and information, 408–414
Economic growth, and monopoly, 442–443
Economic man, 55
Economic models, 5–25, *See also* Models
of behavior, 22–23
empirical examples of, 19
Economic profits, 221
and cost minimization, 222
Economic Recovery Act of 1981, 39
Economic Recovery Tax Act (ERTA), 579
Economic rent, 511–514. *See also* Ricardian rent
and opportunity cost, 512–513
Economics
defining, 6
mathematics in, 27–46
microeconomics and, 6
and U.S.-Soviet wheat trade, 15
Economic Theory of Democracy, An, 657
Economists, 5–6
and car dealer, 583
early, 8–9
Marshall, Alfred, and, 12
Smith, Adam, 9–10
verification of theoretical models by, 18–19
Economy
general equilibrium view of, 351–352
two-good, 367–369
Edgeworth box diagram, 158, 159, **358**
and efficient input use, 357–359
and Pareto efficient allocation, 159
for exchange, 376
Education, yield on investment in, 585
Efficiency
allocational, 472–473
demonstration of, 354–355
economic, 357–360, 408–414
equilibrium and, 349–397
and equity, 375–377
in exchange, 158–159
and long-run equilibrium, 330n
and Pareto efficient allocations, 159
of perfect competition, 365–369
perfectly competitive prices and, 368
Efficiency of output mix, 366, 367
Efficient allocations, 359–360
Efficient markets hypothesis, 183
Efficient wage, 298
Elasticity, 121–**122.** *See also* Cross-price elasticity of demand; Income elasticity of demand; Price elasticity of demand
of agricultural demand, 127
of demand, 273n
long run, of supply, 337–339
market demand and, 117–141
short-run supply, 322–323
of short-run supply curve, 325
Elasticity of substitution, 206n
Electrical equipment, conspiracy and, 484
Electricity demand, model for predicting, 20
Employment
and Japanese *Nenko* system, 299
long-term contracts, 295–296
and monopsony, 533–534
short-time compensation, 297
Energy/capital production relationship, 209
Engel's studies, 93
Entrepreneurial costs, 219
Entry. *See also* Barriers to entry
and long-run equilibrium, 329–330
by new firms, 461, 462–468
Envelope, 239n
Environmental regulation
and externalities, 625–629
and greenhouse effect, 630
and phosphate ban, 628
Equilibrium
competitive, 399–403
Cournot, 482
and economic efficiency, 349–397
experiments with, 404
general, 350–352
and information, 411–414
Lindahl, 648–649
long run, 329, 330
long run, for constant cost industry, 331–332
Nash, 490, 491–492, 493, 496
and Pareto efficiency, 414
stable, 405
strategic, and games, 489–490
supply and demand, in cassette tape market, 328
unemployment and, 410–411
zero-profit, 462
zero-sum game, 491
Equilibrium price, 316
in short run, 320–322
and speculation, 407
Equity, 375
inefficiency and, 375–377
and voluntary exchange, 375–376
Excess burden of tax, 147
Excess demand, 400
Exchange
efficiency in, 158–159
money and, in POW camp, 380
and Pareto, Vilfredo, 159
and voluntary trade, 154–156
Expansion path, 225
and cost minimization, 256–257
of firm, 224–226
Expected value, 168
probability and, 167–168
Expenditures
and income, 93
and price elasticity, 124–126
Explicit contracts, 294
Externality, 372–373, 611
acid rain as, 618
and allocational efficiencies, 615–616
bees/apples example of beneficial, 624
and eyeglass/charcoal production, 615–616
between firms, 612
between firms and people, 614
and greenhouse effect, 630
between people, 613
and property rights, 611–639
of public goods, 644–645
reciprocal nature of, 613–615
and resource allocation in California gold rush, 632

solutions to problem of, 617–620
External price effects, 320

Factor of production
capital as, 567
demand for, 509–543
and marginal productivity theory of factor demand, 516–522
and monopsony, 528–533
pricing, 507–508
Fair games, 168
Fair insurance, 174
Fair rate of return, 442
Fair resource allocation, 375
Fiat money, 377–378
and monetary veil, 379–381
Fire fighters, labor unions and, 561
Firm, 189, **191.** *See also* Nonprofit firms
contracts within, 294
expansion path of, 224–226
goals of, 264
inputs of, and costs, 221
and managers' contracts, 298–330
market for, 303–307
nature of, 263–264
as price taker, 269
and profit maximization, 18
size and scope of, 293–294
theory of the, 291–311
and workers' contracts, 294–298
Fishery, property rights and, 631–633
Fixed costs, 234–235
Fixed-proportions production function, 206–**207**
Forecasting, of weather, 180
Franchise, as monopoly, 423
Franchising, principals and agents in, 302
Free rider, 649–650
experiment with, 651
Free trade, 370–371
Functional notation, 28
Functions
linear, 29
of one variable, 27–37
quadratic, 28, 29, 34–37
of two or more variables, 37–42
Future goods, 569–570
equilibrium price of, 570–571
market for, 570

Gains from trade, 155
distribution of, 156, 157
and nations, 160
Gambling, and risk, 169
Game, 488
of chicken, 496
fair, 168
theory of, 488–490
zero-sum, 490–497
Games against nature, 497–500
Game theory, 479–505. *See also* Game
and terrorism, 499
Gasoline prices, 182
and substitution effects among automobiles, 125
General equilibrium, 349–397
General equilibrium model, 16
and computers, 353
Giffen's paradox, 102–104, **103**
GNP, growth rates in per capita, 211
Goods. *See also* Public goods
durable, 317–319
homogeneous, 450–455
inferior, 92
market for, 457
nonexclusive, 642
nonrival, 643
normal, 91
price changes of, 92–106
price decreases and, 104–105
public, 641–664
relationships between, 105–106
useless, 67

Government
analysis of, 656–661
and public goods, 641–642
and steel production, 486
Graduated mortgage payments, 604
Grain policy, 15
Graphing
functions of one variable, 29–37
functions of two variables, 40–42
Greenhouse effect, 630
Group health insurance, 176

Happiness, pursuit of, and money, 58
Headler amendment, 660
Health insurance
group, 176
national, 136
Hiring
discrimination in, 534–536, 537
profit-maximizing decision and, 524
Home economics, 55
Home ownership, economic costs of, 220
Homogeneity, and demand function, 90–91
Homogeneous demand function, 91
Homogeneous goods, pricing of, 450–455
Horizontal mergers, 471
Housing
and long-run supply elasticities, 340
rent control and, 338
and rents, in Washington, D.C., 517
Human capital, 584–586

IBM, antitrust action against, 470
Imperfect competition, 372, 419, 420
Imperfectly competitive markets, pricing in, 449–477
Implicit contracts, 294, 296
and efficient wage, 298
Implicit cost, 218
Income
changes in, 91–92
and consumption, 93
effects of increasing, 92
international comparisons of real, 153
and utility, relationship between, 70
Income changes, effect on market demand, 121
Income effect, 94
and Giffen's paradox, 102–104
for inferior good, 99–102
from price decrease, 94–97
and price increase, 97–99
Income effect of a change in w, 550
Income elasticity of demand, 131
estimates of, 134–135
representative, 134
Income subsidies, 101
Income tax, 101
and consumption, 120
Income tax structure, changing, 38–39
Increase in demand, 111
Increase in quantity demanded, 111
Increasing cost industry, 335–336
Increasing returns to scale, 203
Independent variable, 28
Index number, 148–154
problems with, 152–154
Indifference curve, 62–63
and marginal rate of substitution (MRS), 63–64
Indifference curve map, 65–69, **66,** 78
and Edgeworth box, 158
and inferiority, 94
and particular preferences, 67–69
Indifference curves, and price changes, 104–105
Indirect approach, 18
Individual demand curve, 106–111
factors causing shifts in, 110
shape of, 108–109
shifts in, 109–111
Industrial organization, field of, 449–450
Industrial organization theory, 468–473
and firm conduct, 471–472

and industry performance, 472–473
market structure and, 468–471
U.S., 469
Industry structure
contestable markets and, 462–464, 465
determination of, 464
mergers and, 471
Inelasticity. *See* Elasticity
Infant industries, 339–342
and tariff protection, 342
Inferior good, 92
children as, 96
substitution and income effects for, 99–102
Inferior inputs, 225–226
Inflation, 91, 149–152
Information
advertising as, 460–461
asymmetric, 181, 409
and competitive equilibrium, 399–417
and economic efficiency, 408–414
and equilibrium, 411–414
imperfect, 374
prices and, 182
special properties of, 181–183
and uncertainty, 167–188
value of, to raisin growers, 180
Information theory, and Bayesian decision theory, 500
Initial endowments, 376
Input choice, cost minimizing, 222–224
Input demand
by nonprofit firms, 520
price changes and, 526–528
Input prices
changes in, 242–245
responses to changes in, 522–526
Inputs
derived demand for, 223–224
duality, and pricing of, 394–397
efficient use of, 357–359
of firm, 221
inferior, 225–226
inflexibility and cost minimization, 237–238
and monopsony, 528–531
profit-maximizing choice, 521
Input substitution
in less developed countries, 208
and production function, 203–209
and technical progress, 212
Insider trading, 304
Insurance
fair, 174
group health, and adverse selection, 176
and moral hazard, 175, 176
national health, 136
and risk reduction, 172–173
unfair, 174
Integration, and firm, 293
Intercept, 30–31, 32–34
changes in, 32–34
Interest, 593–596
compound, 593–607
Interest groups, and rent-seeking behavior, 658–659
Interest rates, and rate of return, 572
Internalization of an externality, 620, 635
Internal rate of return, 606
Investors, 423n
Investment, 575
present discounted value and, 577–582
tax policy and, 576–579
theory of, 575
yield on, 584–586
Investment tax credit, 578, 579
Investment theory, rental rate and, 573–575
Invisible hand, 9, 23, 349, 396
Irrational economic behavior, 70
Isoquant, 200
Isoquant map, 198
with constant, decreasing, and increasing returns to scale, 204
and efficient allocation, 359

with fixed proportions, 207
of simple production function, 251–253

Japan
automobile production by, 199
Nenko system in, 299
Job search, and opportunity cost of time, 549
Job security, labor unions and, 562
Job-specific skills, 295
Joint products, 460

Kinked demand curve model, 452–454

Labor
and allocation of time, 545–549
average and marginal product curves for, 193–197
as average productivity, 195–197
contracts with, 294–298
costs of, 218, 530
demand for, 526
diminishing marginal physical productivity of, 193–195
marginal and average productivities of, 250–251
marginal revenue product of, 518
as market pressure, 303–305
market supply curve for, 553
and monopsony, 531–532
pricing of, 545–566
supplier of, 550–552
and volunteer army, 554
Labor force, changing participation in, 556
Labor supply curve, backward-bending, 552–553
Labor unions, 558–562
and closed or union shop, 649
and fire fighters, 561
monopoly supply decision of, 558–562
Laissez-faire, 369
Land rent, 513–514
Law, and economics, 629–635
Law of diminishing returns, 11
Layoffs, 297
Leisure, 546
opportunity cost of, 546–547
Lemons model, and assymmetric information, 413
Leveraged buyouts, (LBOs), 265
License
entry restriction by, 424
and monopoly, 423
Lighthouses, as public goods, 647
Limits to Growth, The, 20
Lindahl equilibrium, 648–649
Linear demand curve, 480n
and price elasticity, 129–131
Linear function, 29–30
graph of, 30
intercepts, 30–31, 32–34
and property tax assessment model, 36
slope, 30–32
Linear programming, 388–397, **390**
and dual problem, 394–397
Logrolling, 654–656
Long run, 231, 329–342
findings on costs, 232
monopoly behavior in, 425n
Long-run cost curves, 257
and short-run cost curves, 261–262
Long-run elasticity of supply, 337–339
Long-run per unit cost curves, 241–242
Long-run pricing model, 332–334
Long run supply, 330–334
Long-run supply curve, 332, 335–342
for cigarettes, 334
shape of, 335–342
Long-run supply elasticities, 340
Long-run total costs, short-run total costs and, 238–239
Long-term contracts, 298, 299
Lump-sum principle, 100–101

Machine, rental rates, ownership, and, 573–575
Majority principle, 657
Majority rule, and voting, 652
Managers, contracts with, 298–303. *See also* Agent
Many-good cases, 82–83
Marginal cost, 228, 267–268
and rate of product transformation, 362
and shape of production possibility frontier, 363
short-run, 259–261
Marginal cost pricing, and natural monopoly, 437–439
Marginal expense, 528
Marginalism, 12
in input choices, 268–269
and profit maximization, 266
and slope, 38
Marginal physical productivity, 193–198
diminishing, 193–195
Marginal physical productivity curve, 194, 195
Marginal productivity of labor, 250–251
Marginal productivity theory of factor demand, 516–522
Marginal rate of substitution (MRS), 63–64
diminishing, 64–65, 75–76
Marginal rate of technical substitution (RTS), 200
diminishing, 201–202
Marginal revenue, 267–273
and airline deregulation, 275
curve, 273–274
for downward-sloping demand curve, 269
and price elasticity, 271–273
and textbook royalties, 279
Marginal revenue product, 518
Marginal utility, diminishing, and risk aversion, 171
Marginal utility of a good, 64n
Marginal value product, 519
labor curve, 521
Market
advantage of, 292
contestable, 462–464
limits of, 609
and short-run supply curve, 320
Market adjustments, and transactions costs, 402–403
Market basket, and CPI, 152
Market compensated demand curve, 145
Market for corporate control, 303–307
Market definition, 457
Market demand, 118
and elasticity, 117–141
income changes and, 121
Market demand curves, 118
Market equilibrium, 12–13. *See also* Equilibrium
changes in, 13–14
describing, 23
and differentiated products, 457–458
under imperfect competition, 451
Market experiments, 403
Market failure, public goods and, 644–649
Market period, 316
Market prices, information and, 183
Market restrictions, legal, 356
Markets
economic efficiency in, 357–360
and failure to achieve economic efficiency, 369–375
imperfectly competitive, 449–477
missing, 356
models of many, 14–16
Market separation, and price discrimination, 435–437
Market structure, 468–473
Market supply curve, for labor, 553, 555
Markup pricing, 278–280
by major corporations, 281
Marriage, transitivity in, 60
Marshallian economics, and Giffen's paradox, 103n
Marshallian quantity adjustment, 401–402
Marshall supply-demand cross, 13–14
Marxist economists, and value of goods, 9n
Maximin decision rule, 491n
Median voter, 653–**654**

Medicine, principals and agents in, 302
Mergers, 471
of airlines, 406
and externalities, 618–620
and takeovers, 307
Microeconomics, 6
Minimax decision rule, 491n
Minimum wage, 529
Models, 8. *See also* Theoretical models
economic, 5–25
general equilibrium, 16
limits to growth, 20
of many markets, 14–16
partial equilibrium, 14–16
for predicting electricity demand, 20
Monetary veil, 379–381
Money, 8
as accounting standard, 378–379
commodity, 379
exchange and, in POW camp, 380
and happiness, 58
and perfect competition, 377–381
Monopolistic competition, 462
Monopoly
AT&T as, 441
benefits of, 442–443
causes of, 421–423
costs of, 432–433
distortions caused by, 430–433
and IBM, 470
and labor unions, 558–562
natural, 422, 437–439
and output choice, 480
and perfect competition in market, 430
and predatory pricing by Standard Oil, 467
and price discrimination, 435–437
problems with, 428–430
profit maximization of, 423–428
regulation of, 437–442
social costs of, 434
stock exchange seats and, 427
Monopoly markets, pricing in, 421–448
Monopoly rents, 426–428
Monopoly supply curve, 426
Monopsony, 528–533
in baseball player market, 535
as cartel, 534
causes of, 533–534
exploitation and, 532–533
and hiring discrimination, 534–536
and input choice, 530–531
labor choice of, 531–532
Moral hazard, 175, 176
Mortgage market, payment streams in, 604
MRS. *See* Marginal rate of substitution
Multiple regression analysis, 133
Mutual funds, and risk reduction, 179

Nash equilibrium, 490, 491–492, 496
tariff/policy, 493
National health insurance, 136
Natural monopoly, 422. *See also* Monopoly
Natural resources
pricing of exhaustible, 586–589
and supply elasticity, 340
Nature, games against, 497–500
Nenko system, 299
Nonequilibrium zero-sum games, 492
Nonexclusive goods, 642
Nonlinear functions, 34–37
and quadratic functions, 34–37
slope of, 37
Nonprofit firms, input demand by, 520
Nonrival goods, 643
Nonwage compensation, 298
Non-zero-sum games, 492–494
Normal good, 91
Normative analysis, 21

Occupational choice, and wages, 555–558
Ocean fisheries, and property rights, 631–633
Ocean shipping, and returns to scale, 205

Oil, pricing of, 589
Oil pipelines, and contour lines, 43
Oil prices, decline in, 284
Older workers, labor force participation of, 556
Oligopoly
  entry and, 463
  and kinked demand curve pricing model, 453
Oligopoly markets. *See* Game
Oligopoly models, and differentiated products, 457–458
Oligopoly pricing, quasi-competitive model of, 450
On-the-job training, yield on investment in, 585
OPEC, 589
  and limits to growth model, 20
  price decline and, 284
  pricing strategy of, 456
Opportunity cost, 16–17, 217–218
  economic rent and, 512–513
  of leisure, 546–547
  and present discounted value, 596–597
  and production possibility frontier, 363
  of time, 548
Output
  and profit maximization, 266
  and value added, 192n
Output choices, 268–269
Output effect, 525–526, 527–528
Outputs, efficient mix of, 363–365

Paradox of agriculture, 127
Paradox of voting, 652–654
Pareto efficiency, equilibrium and, 414
Pareto efficient allocation, 15
Partial equilibrium model, 14–16
Payments, discounting, 599–602
Payoffs, 489
Pecuniary externality, 612n
Per capita GNP, growth rates in, 211
Perfect competition
  conditions interfering with, 372–375
  efficiency of, 365–369
  equity, efficiency, and, 377
  and money, 377–381
  monopoly and, 430
Perfect complements, 67–69
Perfectly competitive market
  and long run, 329–342
  pricing in, 315–347
  and short run, 319–328
  and very short run, 315–319
Perfectly competitive model, 313
Perfectly competitive prices, and efficiency, 368
Perfectly competitive price system, 349–350
Perfect substitutes, 67
Permanent income hypothesis, 120
Perpetual payments, 601–603
Perpetuity, 602
Pigovian tax, 618
Player, 488–489
Pluralism, 657–658
Political motivation, 657–661
Politics, and U.S.-Soviet trade, 15
Pollution. *See also* Environmental regulation
  abatement of, 626
  abatement of, and scientific uncertainty, 630
  and eyeglass/charcoal problem of externalities, 621–624
  and phosphate regulation, 628
Pork barrel politics, 656
Positive economic analysis, 19–**21**
Poverty
  and happiness, 58
  minimum wage and, 529
Power plant emissions, and acid rain, 618
Predatory pricing, 467
Preferences
  and choices, 80
  complete, 59–61
  and paradox of voting, 653–654
  voter, and resource allocation, 654–656
Present discounted value, 577, 596–599
  algebraic definition of, 597–598
  formulas for, 598–599
  and investment, 577–582
  and rental rate, 582
Present value, 596
  and automobile financing, 583
Price
  equilibrium, 316
  equilibrium level of, 400
  of goods, changes in, 92–106
  as rationing device, 316
  short-run determination of, 320–322
Price changes
  input demand and, 526–528
  welfare effects of, 145–146, 147
Price controls
  rent controls as, 308
  and shortages, 336–337
Price determination
  cobweb model of, 406
  early views of, 11
  supply-demand model of, 8
  theory of, 12
Price discrimination, 435
  at Disneyland, 438
  and monopoly, 435–437
Price elasticity of demand, 122–131
  constancy of, 126–129
  and demand curve shape, 123
  estimates of, 134–135
  and legal gambling, 128
  linear demand curves and, 129–131
  and marginal revenue, 271–273
  and national health insurance, 136
  representative, 134
  substitution effect and, 123–124
  and time, 124
  and total expenditures, 124–126
  values of, 122–123
Price leadership, 485–487
Price leadership model, 454–55
  OPEC and, 456
Prices
  and information, 182
  input, 522–526
  relative, and perfectly competitive market, 350
  and Smith, Adam, 9–10
  and unreliable models, 20
Price system, perfectly competitive, 349–350
Price taker, 269
  and marginal productivity, 518
  short-run supply decisions by, 280–285
  short-term supply curve for, 282
Pricing
  of capital, 567–607
  cartel model of, 451–452
  of exhaustible natural resources, 586–589
  of homogeneous goods, 450–455
  in imperfectly competitive markets, 449–477
  kinked demand curve model of, 452–545
  of labor, 545–566
  in monopoly markets, 421–448
  in monopsonistic labor market, 532
  of oil resources, 589
  in perfectly competitive market, 315–347
  predatory, 467
  price leadership model of, 454–455
  quasi-competitive model of, 450
  in time periods, 315–316
  two-tier, 439–440
  in very short run, 316–319
Primal maximization problem, 394
Principal-agent relationships, 299–303
Principles of Economics, 12, 27, 401
Prisoner's dilemma, 494–495
Private goods, types of, 644
Private property, 621
  and internalization, 635
Probability, 167
  and expected value, 167–168
Producer surplus, 354n–355n
Product curve for labor, average and marginal productivity and, 194
Product differentiation, 455–458
Product group, 457
Production, pricing factors of, 507–508. *See also* Factor of production
Production function, 191–192
  Cobb-Douglas, 250n
  fixed-proportions, 206–207
  input substitution and, 203–208
  numerical example of, and cost curves, 250–262
  and returns to scale, 202–203
  short-run, 231–234
  simplified, 192–193
Production possiblity frontier, 16, 17, **360**–361
  construction of, 391–392
  and Corn Laws, 370
  for "guns and butter," 364
  and opportunity cost, 363
  shape of, 362–363
  for two-good economy, 367–369
Productivity
  energy and capital and, 209
  and Japanese automobile production, 199
  marginal physical, 193–198
  worldwide decline in, 211
Profit, and market for firms, 305–307
Profitability, of monopoly, 428
Profit center, 276, 396
Profit maximization, 18
  and airline deregulation, 275
  alternatives to, 277–280
  assumption, 22–23
  criticisms of hypothesis, 274–277
  labor input and, 521–522
  and long run, 329
  and marginalism, 266
  and marginal productivity theory of factor demand, 516
  and markup pricing, 278–280
  of monopoly, 423–428
  output and, 266
  and price determination in monopoly market, 425
  and short-run supply decisions by price-taking firm, 280–285
  and supply, 263–289
Profits
  corporate tax on, 265, 576n
  economic, 221–222
  economic definition of, 330n
  monopoly, 426–428, 442–443
Progressive income taxation, 38–39
Property
  common, 621, 632
  private, 621, 635
Property rights, 621
  evolution of, 629–635
  externalities and, 611–639
  and ocean fisheries, 631–633
Property tax assessment, linear model for, 36
Proposition 2½ 660
Proposition 13, 660
Public goods, 373–374, **644**
  allocations of, 644–645, 646–648
  attributes of, 642–643
  categories of, 643–644
  externalities of, 644–645
  and free rider problem, 649–650
  lighthouses as, 647
  and Lindahl equilibrium, 648–649
  local, 650
  and market failure, 644–649
  and public choice, 641–664
  types of, 644

Quadratic function, 28, 29, **34**–37
  graph of, 35
  roots of, 35n
Quality and quantity, and children, 96
Quasi-competitive model, 450
Quasi rent, 512n

Railroad industry, costs in, 233
Raisin industry, and weather forecast information, 180

Rate of product transformation (RPT), 361
as ratio of marginal costs, 362–363
Rate regulation, 442
Rate of return, 568
determination of, 569–573
equilibrium, 571–573
to storing wine, 572
Rate of technical substitution (RTS), 200–202
Rational economic behavior, 70
Rational expectations, 406–**408**
Rationing, 76–77
Reaction function, 481
Cournot, 482
Real income, international comparisons of, 153
Realistic and unrealistic assumptions, 18–19
Real-world events, and economic theories, 19
Recontracting, 400
Reelection constraint, 659–661
Refuse collection industry, costs in, 233
Regression analysis, multiple, 133
Regulation
environmental, 625–629
of monopoly, 437–442
rate, 442
Relative prices, 350n
Religious practices, and fish consumption, 110
Rent
and commuting time, in Washington, D.C., 517
economic, 511–514
land, 513–514
quasi, 512n
Ricardian, 514–516
short-run and long-run, 512n
Rental rate (v), 218
and investment theory, 573–575
present discounted value and, 582
Rent controls, 338
Rents, monopoly, 426–428
Rent-seeking behavior, 658
and agricultural marketing orders, 659
Resource prices
scarcity costs and, 588
time pattern of, 588
Resources
allocations of, 159, 458–459
pricing of exhaustible, 586–589
productivities of, and Ricardian rent, 516
scarcity of, 6
technically efficient allocation of, 357
voting for allocation of, 650–656
Retailing, and markup pricing, 281
Returns to scale, 202–203
and ocean shipping, 205
Revenue, marginal, 267–273
Revenue curve
average, 273
marginal, 273–274
Revenue maximization, 274–278
Ricardian rent, 514–516
Risk
aversion to, 168–172
and blackjack systems, 169
uninsurable, 174–175
Risk aversion, 170
graphic analysis of, 171–172
Risk reduction
methods of, 172–178
mutual funds and, 179
RTS, constant returns and, 253. *See also* Marginal rate of technical substitution; Rate of technical substitution

Scarcity, 6
in natural world, 7
and opportunity cost, 16–17
Scarcity costs, 586–588, **587**
and resource prices, 588
School budgets, voting for, 655
Schooling, yield on investment in, 585
Sex discrimination, 537
Shadow prices, 395
Shortages
in housing, 338
price controls and, 336–337
Short run, 231, 320–328
equilibrium prices in, 320–322
monopoly behavior in, 425n
price determination in, 320–322
production function, 231–234
Short-run average and marginal costs, 259–261
Short-run average variable costs (SAVC), 240–241
Short-run cost curves, 257–262
and long-run cost curves, 261–262
per-unit, 239–242
total, average, and marginal, 258
Short-run costs, and traffic congestion, 243
Short-run elasticity of supply, 323
Short-run price determination, 320–322
Short-run supply, 319–320
elasticity of, 322–323
Short-run supply and demand, and dairy price supports, 326
Short-run supply curve, 319–320
Short-run supply decisions, by price-taking firm, 280–285
Short-run total costs, 234–235
curve for, 236
and long-run total costs, 238–239
Short-time compensation, and layoffs, 297
Shutdown price, 285
decision about, 283–285
Simultaneous equations, 42–45
changing solutions for, 44
grouping, 44–45
solving, 45
Single-input prices, 522–524
Single-peaked preferences, 653–654
Slope, 30–32
changes in, 32, 33
and marginalism, 38
of short-run supply curve, 319–320
Smoking laws, and externalities, 614
Social costs, 217, **615**
and externalities, 615–616
of monopoly, 434
Soviet wheat trade, 15
Specific tax, 332, 333
Speculation, 407
Sports, transitivity in, 60
Stable equilibrium, 405–406
Stackelberg leadership model, 483
Stackelberg model, 485
Standard Oil, and predatory pricing, 467
States
elastic demand and gambling in, 128
short-time compensation in, 297
Static efficiency, 472
Steel, price leadership in, 486
Steel production, average productivity in, 196
Stock exchange seats, deregulation and, 427
Stock ownership, and managers, 303, 304
Stock purchase plans, 304
Straight-line (linear) demand curve. *See* Linear demand curve
Strategic equilibrium, and games, 489–490
Strategies, 489
Subscripts, 46
Subsistence, Ricardo and, 11
Substitutes, 105–**106**
Substitution, elasticity of, 206n. *See also* Input substitution
Substitution bias, of Consumer Price Index, 150, 151
Substitution effect, 94, 524–**525,** 527
among automobiles, 125
and demand curves, 109n
for inferior good, 99–102
from price decrease, 94–97
and price elasticity, 123–124
and price increase, 97–99
Substitution effect of a change in w, 550
Supply
assumptions about, 509–510
long-run elasticity of, 337–339
profit maximization and, 263–289
short-run, 319–320
Supply curve
backward-bending labor, 552–553
individual's, for labor, 552
long-run, 332
market, for labor, 553, 555
monopoly, 426
and production possibility frontier, 17
shape of, 324–325
shape of long-run, 335, 342
shifts in, 323–324
short-run, 319–320
short-run for price-taking firm, 282, 283
Supply and demand, 8–14
pricing factors, 509, 510
Supply and demand curves, 12, 13–14
and Marshall cross, 13–14
shifts in, 322–328
Supply-demand model of price determination, 8
Supply response, 315
timing of, 315–316
Survivorship principle, 277
and market for firms, 276–277

Takeovers
candidates for, 305
mergers and, 307
Tangency rule
and diminishing MRS, 75–76
and indifference curve map, 78
Tariffs
and free trade, 370
and gains from trade, 160
and infant industry protection, 342
Nash equilibrium, 493
Taxation
compulsory, 650
and externalities, 617–618
as externality solution, 620
and tax revolt, 660–661
Taxes
cigarette, 334
corporate income (profits), 265
excess burden of, 147
income, 120
and lump-sum principle, 100–101
modeling impact of, 353
Pigovian, 618
on power-plant emissions, 618
Tax incidence theory, 332–**334**
Tax income and tax liability, 38
Tax policy
and investment, 576, 578–579
Tax Reform Act of 1986, 39
Technical change, and input substitution, 210
Technically efficient allocation of resources, 357
Technical progress, 212
Technological innovation, and costs, 244, 245
Technology, changes in, 210–212
Terrorism, game theory and, 499
Textbook royalties, and marginal revenue, 279
Textile costs, declines in, 244
Theoretical models, verification of, 18–19
Theory of "bads," 61n
Theory of choice, 56
application of, 143–165
and compensated demand curves, 144–148
and index numbers, 148–154
and voluntary trade gains, 154–161
Theory of exchange, and Pareto, Vilfredo, 159
Theory of the firm, 291–311
Time
allocation of, 545–549
opportunity cost of, 548
and price elasticity, 124
Tools, mathematical, 27–51
Total cost curves, 227, 228–229
Total factor productivity, decline in, 211
Trade
both parties gain from, 155, 156

and Edgeworth box, 156–158
mutually beneficial, 157–158
among nations, 160
resistance to 370–371
voluntary, 154–161
Trade adjustment policy, 371
Trading, insider, 304
Traffic congestion, and short-run costs, 243
Transactions costs, 402–**403**
market adjustments and, 402
and missing markets, 356
Transitive, 61
Transportation costs, and opportunity cost of time, 548
Two-input prices, 524
Two-tier pricing, 439–440

Uncertainty
and auctions, 412
and information, 167–187
Underdeveloped countries, input substitution and, 208
Unemployment
and equilibrium, 410–411
teenage, 529
Unions. *See* Labor unions
Union shop, 649
United States-Canada, tariff policies and, 493
Unit elastic demand, 124
Unstable equilibrium, 406
Useless good, 67
Util, 57
Utility, 56
assumptions about, 59–62
from consuming two goods, 56–57
diminishing marginal, 171
and income, relationship between, 170
maximization of, 55–87
measurability of, 57–59
rationing and, 76–77
Utility maximization
choices, for special types of goods, 81
graphic analysis of, 71–75
and leisure/work hours, 547–549
model of, 79–82
numerical example of, 76–79
Utility-maximization hypothesis, 69–71

Value, Aristotle's definition of, 9n
Value added, 192n
Value maximization, 389
linear programming solution for, 392–394
Values, of price elasticity of demand, 122–123
Variable
dependent, 28
independent, 28
Variable costs, 234–235
Variables, 27–**28**
functions of two or more, 37–42
Vertical mergers, 471
Very short run
applicability of model, 317–319
pricing in, 316–319
Voluntary exchange, and equity, 375–376
Voluntary trade
gains from, 154–161
indifference curves, 62–65
Volunteer army, 554
Vote-trading techniques. *See* Logrolling
Voting
paradox of, 652–654
and resource allocation, 650–656
for school budgets, 655–656

Wage rate (w), 218
income and substitution effects of change in real, 550–553
Wages, occupational choice and, 555–558
Walrasian price adjustment, 400–401
Washington, D.C., housing costs and commuting time in, 517
Washington Water Power System, default of, 20
Wealth of Nations, The, 9, 10, 555
Welfare effects, 145–146, 147
Wheat trade, U.S.-Soviet, 15
Wine, storage of, and rate of return, 572
Winner's curse, 412
Women
and hiring discrimination, 536n, 537
labor force participation of, 556
Work, flexibility of, 549
Workers, contracts with, 294–298
World Dynamics, 20

Yield, 584, 606
calculating, 605–607
on investment, 584–586
on investment in schooling, 585

Zero-coupon bonds, 600
Zero-profit equilibrium, 462
Zero-sum game, 490–497
duopoly model as, 495
non-, 492–494
non-equilibrium, 492
and Prisoner's dilemma, 494–495